7. Include a *SASE* that is large enough and contains sufficient postage to return all items.

8. Address your package to the proper contact person.

9. Mail first class. Do not send your package via certified or registered mail unless requested.

10. Keep a record of the date, the song titles, and the companies to which you submit material.

D1396900

For more information on submitting demos by mail, see Getting Started on page 7.

1994

Songwriter's Market

Where & How to Market Your Songs

Edited by
Cindy Laufenberg

WRITER'S DIGEST BOOKS
CINCINNATI, OHIO

Distributed in Canada by McGraw-Hill,
300 Water Street,
Whitby Ontario L1N 9B6.
Also distributed in Australia by Kirby Books,
Private Bag No. 19, P.O. Alexandria NSW
2015.

Managing Editor, Market Books Department:
Constance J. Achabal; Supervising
Editor: Mark Garvey

*International Standard Serial Number
0161-5971
International Standard Book Number
0-89879-610-5*

Contents

Resources

From the Editor

Most of you have probably heard a hit song on the radio and thought, "Hey, I could write a better song than that!" And perhaps you could. But it takes more than just writing great songs to be a successful songwriter. In order to get your songs heard, you have to get them into the hands of industry professionals who can make them into hits. More than any other business, the music industry relies heavily on contacts. In order for your songs to be heard, you need to make contact with the right people.

That's where the 1994 *Songwriter's Market* comes in. It contains over 2,000 listings of music publishers, record companies and producers, managers and performing groups seeking new music. 700 of those listed are new to this edition. Whether you're a country songwriter, a performer in a punk band, a jingle writer or a musical playwright, you'll find an abundance of contacts within these pages. All of the markets listed here are actively seeking new music and are interested in hearing what you have to offer.

Along with the market listings, the 1994 *Songwriter's Market* features articles that provide basic yet vital information for both the beginning songwriter and the songwriter/performer. Getting Started discusses just that: how to get your music career off the ground. It provides an overview of the music industry, with a discussion of the structure of the business and how to go about getting your songs heard by industry professionals.

Many beginning songwriters are interested in finding a partner to write with but have no idea how to locate one. How to Find and Work with a Co-writer provides basic information on how and where to find other writers to work with, along with guidelines on how to make your collaboration a successful one.

The Business of Songwriting discusses in further detail the workings of the music industry. It covers topics that all songwriters need to know about, such as copyright information, what to look for when signing a contract and the ripoffs that songwriters should avoid.

For those of you who are not only songwriters but performers as well, The Road to a Record Deal de-mystifies the process of signing with a record label. It explores the best ways for you to get noticed by industry executives, and what to do once you've gotten their attention.

And finally there's Trends and Advances in the Music Industry, which explains some of the new technologies and trends that are influencing the music industry, and how they will affect you as a songwriter.

This year's Insider Reports (called Close-ups in previous editions) focus more on those working within the industry rather than on artists and songwriters. The professionals profiled in this edition are all from independent companies listed in *Songwriter's Market*. Independent companies are usually more open to hearing new music than most major companies. Independents have smaller overhead costs and don't rely on number one hits to stay in business, so they are more willing to work with unknown artists. Pay attention to what those profiled have to say; I think you'll find their advice helpful and insightful.

Being a successful songwriter in today's music industry takes more than just talent and ambition. You need to be as educated as you can about your craft and the music business, and *Songwriter's Market* is here to help. We're offering you some contacts and good advice to get you started—it's up to you to take it from there. Good luck!

How to Get the Most Out of Songwriter's Market

The hardest task for you, the aspiring songwriter, is deciding where and to whom to submit your music. You're reading this book in the hope of finding information on good potential markets for your work. You may be seeking a publisher who will pitch your music, a record company that will offer you a recording contract, or a chamber music group or theater company to produce and perform your music live. *Songwriter's Market* is designed to be a tool to help you make those submission decisions. Read the informational articles, Insider Report interviews and section introductions for an overview of the industry. With careful research you can target your submissions and move toward achieving your goals.

Where do you start?

It's easiest to move from the very general to the very specific. The book is divided into Markets and Resources. The Resources section contains listings and information on organizations, workshops, contests and publications to help you learn more about the music industry and the craft of songwriting. The Markets section contains all the markets seeking new material and is the part of the book you will need to concentrate on for submissions.

Markets is further divided into sections corresponding to specific segments of the industry. This is of particular help to composers of music for the theater and concert hall, who can find prospective markets in the Play Producers & Publishers and Fine Arts sections, respectively. Composers of audiovisual (film and TV) and commercial music will also find a section of the book, Advertising, AV and Commercial Music Firms, devoted to these possibilities.

The general markets

If you don't fall into these specific areas, you will need a little more work to target markets. Questions you need to ask are: Who am I writing this music for? Are these songs that I have written for an act I now belong to? Am I a songwriter sending my music to someone hoping to have it accepted and recorded by an artist?

If you fall into the first category, writing songs for an existing group or for yourself as a solo artist, you're probably trying to advance the career of your act. Your demo is a promotional tool for your act as well as your songs. Because you're seeking to further your act's career, recordings are a goal. They represent a documentation of your act's abilities, as well as an opportunity to make money and build an audience. If you're seeking a recording contract, the Record Companies section may be the place to start (for more information, see The Road to a Record Deal on page 27). Look also at the Record Producers section. Independent record producers are constantly on the lookout for up-and-coming groups. They may also have strong connections with record companies looking for acts, and will pass your demo on or recommend the act to a record company. And if your act doesn't yet have representation, your demo submission may be included as part of a promotional kit sent to a prospective manager listed in the Managers and Booking Agents section.

If you are a songwriter seeking to have your songs recorded by other artists, you may submit to some of these same markets, but for different reasons. The Record Producers section contains mostly independent producers who work regularly with particular artists, rather than working full-time for one record company. Because they work closely with a limited number of clients, they may be the place to send songs written with a specific act in mind. The independent producer may be responsible for picking cuts for a recording project. The Managers and Booking Agents section may be useful for the same reason. Many personal managers are constantly seeking new song material for the acts they represent, and a good song sent at the right time can mean a valuable cut for the songwriter.

The primary market for songwriters not writing with particular artists in mind will be found in the Music Publishers section. Music publishers are the jacks-of-all-trades in the industry, having knowledge about and keeping abreast of developments in all other segments of the music business. They act as the first line of contact between the songwriter and the music industry.

If you're uncertain about which markets will have the most interest in your material, review the introductory explanations at the beginning of each section. It will aid in explaining the various functions of each segment of the music industry, and will help you narrow your list of possible submissions.

Now what?

You've identified the market categories you're thinking about sending demos to. The next step is to research within each section to find the individual markets that will be the most interested in your work.

Most users of *Songwriter's Market* should check three items in the listings: location of the firm, the type of music the firm is interested in hearing, and their submission policy. Depending on your personal concerns, any of these items could be considered a point of departure for you as you determine which markets to send your music to.

If it's important to send your work to a company close to your home for more opportunities for face-to-face contact, location should be checked first. Each section contains listings from all over the U.S. as well as the rest of the world. You may be interested in submitting to firms in the music hub cities (Nashville, Los Angeles and New York). If you're looking in the Music Publisher or Record Company sections, go first to the back of the sections for geographical listings of music publishers and record companies in or near the music hubs.

Your music isn't going to be appropriate for submission to all companies. Most music industry firms have specific music interests and needs, and you also need to do your homework in this area in order to be sure that your submissions are actually being seen and heard by companies who have a genuine interest in them. To find this information turn to the Category Index located at the back of the book. There are 18 general categories of music listed for the Music Publishers, Music Print Publishers, Record Companies, Record Producers and Managers and Booking Agents sections. Locate the category of music that best describes the material you write, and refer to the companies listed under those categories. (Keep in mind that these are general categories; some companies may not be listed in the Category Index because they either accept all types of music or the music they are looking for doesn't fit into any of the general categories.) When you've located a listing, go to the Music subheading. It will contain, in **bold** type, a more detailed list of the styles of music a company is seeking. Pay close attention to the types of music described. For instance, if the music you write fits the category of "Rock," there can be many variations on that style. One listing under the "Rock" category may be interested in hard rock, another in country rock, and another in soft rock. These are three very different styles of music, but they all fall under the same general category. The Category Index is there to help you narrow down the listings within a certain music genre; it is up to you to narrow them down even further to fit the type of music you write. The music styles are listed in descending order of importance; so if your particular specialty is country music, you may want to search out those listings that list country as their first priority as your primary targets for submissions.

Finally, when you've placed the listings geographically and identified their music preferences, read the How to Contact subheading. This will give you pertinent information about what to send as part of a demo submission and how to go about sending it. Not all of the markets listed in *Songwriter's Market* accept unsolicited submissions, so it's important to read this information carefully. Most companies have carefully considered their submission policy, and packages that do not follow their directions are returned or discarded without evaluation. Follow the instructions: it will impress upon the market your seriousness about getting your work heard and purchased.

You've now identified markets you feel will have the most interest in your work. Read the complete listing carefully before proceeding. Many of the listings have individualized information important for the submitting songwriter. Then, it's time for you to begin preparing your demo submission package to get your work before the people in the industry. For further information on that process, turn to Getting Started.

Important information on market listings

● *Although every listing in* Songwriter's Market *is updated, verified or researched prior to publication, some changes are bound to occur between publication and the time you contact any listing.*
● *Listings are based on interviews and questionnaires. They are not advertisements, nor are markets reported here necessarily endorsed by the editor.*
● *A word about style: This book is edited (except for quoted material) in the masculine gender because we think "he/she," "she/he," "he or she," "him or her" or "they" in copy is distracting. We bow to tradition for the sake of readability.*
● *Looking for a particular market? Check the Index. If you don't find it there, it is because 1) It's not interested in receiving material at this time. 2) It's no longer in business or has merged with another company. 3) It charges (counter to our criteria for inclusion) for services a songwriter should receive free. 4) It has failed to verify or update its listing annually. 5) It has requested that it not be listed. 6) We have received reports from songwriters about unresolved problems they've had with the company. Check the '93-94 Changes list at the end of each section to find why markets appearing in the 1993 edition do not appear in this edition.*
● *A word of warning. Don't pay to have your song published and/or recorded or to have your lyrics—or a poem—set to music. Read "Ripoffs" in The Business of Songwriting section to learn how to recognize and protect yourself from the "song shark."*
● Songwriter's Market *reserves the right to exclude any listing which does not meet its requirements.*

Key to Symbols and Abbreviations

* *new listing in all sections*
SASE — *self-addressed, stamped envelope*
SAE — *self-addressed envelope*
IRC — *International Reply Coupon, for use in countries other than your own.*

(For definitions of terms and abbreviations relating specifically to the music industry, see the Glossary in the back of the book.)

Getting Started

The music industry can be a strange, foreign place to someone who is not familiar with it. There's a major label market and an independent market. The music "hub" cities, New York, Los Angeles and Nashville, all have different ways of operating and different expectations. To exist and thrive in this marketplace without being overwhelmed is one of the major challenges to the aspiring songwriter. Songwriters who not only survive but succeed are those who have taken time before entering the market to learn as much as they can about the music industry and how it works.

Educating yourself can be done through experience, study or a combination of the two. Experience is an effective teacher, but it can also be a very cruel and costly one. Study can be just as effective and a little less painful. Many sources exist to help you educate yourself about the intricacies of the music industry *before* you jump in. Local and national songwriter groups and performing rights societies can be a great source of information. Reading, studying and learning to use the information contained in source books like *Songwriter's Market* expand your understanding of the marketplace and make you a better business person. Through study, you will be able to more effectively market yourself and your work in a highly competitive business, and do it in a professional manner.

Improving your craft

The music industry wouldn't exist without music—your songs. Your artistic vision and output are what appears on recordings, radio and in concerts. There are no patterns, forms, or paths that will guarantee success in songwriting. It's important to develop a personal vision and stick with it. Finding your personal way of working and allowing it to stand on its own will display your individuality and make your work interesting to those listening.

When working on songs, look for feedback everywhere. Collaborators, song critique sessions with your local songwriting group and submissions to publishers will help you identify strengths and weaknesses in your music and give you guidance in how to improve your craft. Improving your songwriting technique is important; it will free you to write songs you'll be happy with. Feedback will also create connections within the industry and continue your education, not only in the craft of songwriting, but in the business as well. You must never stop being a student when working in the music industry.

The structure of the music business

The music industry in the United States traditionally revolves around three hub cities: New York, Los Angeles and Nashville. Power is concentrated in those areas because that is where most of the record companies, publishers, songwriters and performers are. Many people who are trying to break into the music business—in whatever capacity—move to one of those three cities in order to be close to the people and companies they want to contact. From time to time a regional music scene will heat up in a non-hub city such as Austin, Seattle or Atlanta. When this happens, songwriters and performers in that city experience a kind of musical Renaissance complete with better paying gigs, a creatively charged atmosphere in which to work and active interest from the major labels. All this is not to say that a successful career cannot be nurtured from any city in the country. It can be, particularly if you are a songwriter. The disadvantages one faces by not being in a major music center can be offset somewhat by phone and mail contact with industry people and, if possible, occasional trips to the music hub nearest you. For the serious songwriter, a well-planned, once-a-year trip to New York, Los Angeles or Nashville to attend a seminar or to call on record companies and music publishers can be of immense value in expanding music industry contacts and learning how the business operates. There are, of course, many smaller, independent companies located in cities across the country. A career of international scope can be started on the local level, and some may find a local career more satisfying, in its own way, than the constant striving to gain the attention of a major label.

The perspective of any company, big or small, must begin with the buying public. Their support, in the form of money spent on records and other kinds of musical entertainment, keeps the record companies in business. Because of that, record companies are anxious to give the public what they want. In an attempt to stay one step ahead of public tastes, record companies hire people who have a facility for spotting musical talent and anticipating trends and put them in charge of finding and developing new recording acts. These talent scouts are called "A&R representatives." "A&R" stands for artist and repertoire, which simply means they are responsible for finding new artists and matching songs to artists. The person responsible for the recording artist's finished product—the record—is called the producer. It is the producer's job to bring the recording artist out of the studio with a good-sounding, saleable product. His duties often involve choosing the songs to be included on the album, so record producers are great contacts for songwriters. Some A&R reps produce the bands they discover.

The A&R reps and the producers are helped in their search for songs (and sometimes artists) by the music publisher. A publisher is really a songwriter's representative who, for a percentage of the profits (typically 50% of all publisher/songwriter earnings), tries to find commercially profitable uses for the songs in his catalog. A good publisher stays in close contact with several A&R reps, trying to find out what kinds of projects are coming up at the record companies and whether any songs in his catalog might be of use.

When a song is recorded and commercially released, the record company, the recording artist, the producer, the publisher and the songwriter all stand to profit. Recording artists earn a negotiated royalty from their record company based on the number of records sold. Publishers and songwriters earn mechanical royalties (based on records sold) and performance royalties (based on radio air play). Producers are usually paid either a negotiated royalty based on sales or a flat fee.

Until you establish relationships with specific professionals in the industry who appreciate your music and are willing to work with you on a regular basis, you should submit your material to as many appropriate contacts as you can find. Based on what we've just discussed, you can see that appropriate contacts would include A&R reps, producers and publishers. You can add managers to that list. Depending on how "big" the artist is, he may have a personal and/or road manager. These people have direct access to the artists they manage, and they're always on the lookout for hit songs for them.

Any method of getting your songs heard, published, recorded and released is the best way if it works for you. In this book music publishers, record companies, record producers and managers are listed with specifications on how to submit your material to each. If you can't find the person or company you're looking for, there are other sources of information you can try. Check trade publications such as *Billboard* or *Cash Box*, available at most local libraries. These periodicals list new companies as well as the artists, labels, producers and publishers for each song on the charts. There are several tipsheets available that name producers, managers and artists currently looking for new material. Album covers and cassette j-cards can be excellent sources of information. They give the name of the record company, producer, and usually the manager of the artist or group, and reveal who publishes the songs on the album. Liner notes can be revealing as well, telling how a song came to someone's attention, how a musical style evolved or what changes or new projects lie ahead for the artist. Be creative in your research—any clue you uncover may give you an edge over your competition.

Submitting your songs

When it comes to showing people what you have to offer, the tool of the music industry is a demonstration recording—a demo. Most people prefer cassettes because they're so convenient. Songwriters make demos showcasing their songs and musicians make demos of their performances. These demos are then submitted to various professionals in the industry. It's acceptable to submit your songs to more than one person at a time (this is called simultaneous submission). Most people try their best to return tapes if a self-addressed, stamped envelope is included in the submission, but even with the best intentions in the world sometimes it just doesn't happen. (A person screening tapes might open dozens of packages, take the tapes out and put them all in a bag or box, and listen to them in the car on his way to and from the office, thus separating the tapes from their SASEs. *Always* put your name, address and phone number on every item in your submission package, including the tape itself.)

The one exception to simultaneous submissions is when a publisher, artist or other industry professional asks if he may put a song of yours on "hold." This means he intends to record it, and he doesn't want you to give the song to anyone else. Sometimes he'll give a song back to you without recording it, even if it's been on hold for months. Sometimes he'll record your song but decide that it's not as strong as his other material and so he won't include your song on his album. If either of these things happens, you're free to pitch that song to other people again. (You can protect yourself from having a song on hold indefinitely. Either establish a deadline for the person who asks for the hold, i.e., "You can put my song on hold for x number of months." Or modify the hold to specify that you will pitch the song to other people, but you will not sign a deal without allowing the person who has the song "on hold" to make you an offer.) When someone publishes your song, you grant that publisher exclusive rights to your song and you may not pitch it to other publishers (though you *may* pitch it to artists or producers who are interested in recording the song without publishing it themselves).

Demo quality

The production quality of demos can vary widely, but even simple demos with just piano/vocal or guitar/vocal need to sound clean, with the instrument in tune and the lyrics sung clearly with no background noise. Many songwriters are investing in equipment such as four- or eight-track recorders, keyboards and drum machines—for recording demos at home. Other writers like to book studio time, use live musicians, and get professional input from an engineer and/or producer. It's also possible to hire a demo service to do it all for you. Ultimately, you'll have to go with what you can afford and what you feel best represents your song. Once you have a master recording of your song, you're ready to make cassette copies and pitch your song to the contacts you've researched.

Some markets indicate that you may send for evaluation a video of your act in performance or a group doing your songs, in lieu of a standard cassette or reel-to-reel demo. Most of our listers have indicated that a videocassette is not required, but told us the format of their VCR should a songwriter or artist want to send one. It's always a good idea to check with the company first for appropriate video format and television system, especially if it's an international market. Be aware that the television systems vary from country to country. For example, a Beta or VHS format tape recorded using the U.S. system (called NTSC) will not play back on a standard English VCR (using the PAL system) even if the recorder formats are identical. It is possible to transfer a video demo from one system to another, but the expense in both time and money may outweigh its usefulness as opposed to a standard audio demo. Systems for some countries include: NTSC—U.S., Canada and Japan; PAL— United Kingdom, Australia and West Germany; and SECAM—France.

Submitting by mail

Here are guidelines to follow when submitting material to companies listed in this book:

• Read the listing and submit exactly what a company asks for and exactly how it asks that it be submitted.

• Listen to each of your demos before submitting them to make sure the quality is satisfactory.

• Enclose a brief, neat cover letter of introduction. Indicate the types of songs you're submitting and recording artists you think they might suit. If you are a writer/artist looking for a record deal yourself, or pitching your demo for some reason other than for another artist to record your songs, you should say so in your letter. Have specific goals.

• Include typed or legibly printed lyric sheets. If requested, include a lead sheet. Place your name, address and phone number on each lead or lyric sheet.

• Neatly label each tape and tape box with your name, address, phone number and the names of the songs on the tape in the sequence in which they are recorded.

• Keep records of the dates, songs and companies you submit to.

• Include a SASE for the return of your material. Your return envelope to companies based in countries other than your own should contain a self-addressed envelope (SAE) and International Reply Coupons (IRC). Be certain the return envelope is large enough to accommodate your material, and include sufficient postage for the weight of the package.

• Wrap the package neatly and write (or type on a shipping label) the company's address and your return address so they are clearly visible. Your package is the first impression a company has of you and your songs, so neatness is very important.

• Mail first class. Stamp or write "First Class Mail" on the package and on the SASE you enclose. Don't send by registered mail unless the listing specifically requests it. The recipient must interrupt his day to sign for it and many companies refuse all registered mail.

If you are writing to inquire about a company's current needs or to request permission to submit, your query letter should be neat (preferably typed), brief and pleasant. Explain the type of material you have and ask for their needs and current submission policy.

To expedite a reply, you should enclose a self-addressed, stamped postcard asking the information you need to know. Your typed questions (see the Sample Reply Form) should be direct and easy to answer. Also remember to place the company's name and address in the upper lefthand space on the front of the postcard so you'll know which company you queried. Keep a record of queries, like tape submissions, for future reference.

Sample Reply Form

I would like to hear:
(   ) "Name of Song" (   ) "Name of Song" (   ) "Name of Song"
I prefer:
(   ) reel-to-reel (   ) cassette (   ) videocassette
*   (   ) Beta (   ) VHS*
 With:
(   ) lyric sheet (   ) lead sheet (   ) either (   ) both
(   ) I am not looking for material at this time, try me later.
(   ) I am not interested.

Name   *Title*

If a market doesn't respond within several weeks after sending your demo, don't despair. As long as your submission is in the possession of a market there is a chance someone is reviewing it. That opportunity ends when your demo is returned to you. If after a reasonable length of time you still haven't received word on your submission, follow up with a friendly letter giving detailed information about your demo package.

Submitting in person

A trip to Los Angeles, Nashville or New York will give you insight as to how the music industry functions. You should plan ahead and schedule appointments to make the most of your time while you're there. It will be difficult to get in to see some people, as many professionals are extremely busy and may not feel meeting out-of-town writers is their highest priority. Other people are more open to, and even encourage, face-to-face meetings. They may feel that if you take the time to travel to where they are, and you're organized and persistent enough to schedule meetings, you're more advanced and more professional than many aspiring songwriters who blindly submit inappropriate songs through the mail.

You should take several cassette copies and lyric sheets of each of your songs. More than one of the companies you visit may ask that you leave a copy. If the person who's reviewing material likes a song, he may want to play it for someone else. There's also a good chance the person you have the appointment with will have to cancel (expect that occasionally), but wants you to leave a copy of your songs so he can listen and contact you later. *Never* give someone the last or only copy of your material—if it is not returned to you, all the effort and money that went into your demo will be lost.

Many good songs have been rejected simply because they weren't deemed appropriate by one listener at one particular time, so don't take rejection personally. Realize that if one or two people didn't like your songs, they just could have been having a bad day. However, if there seems to be a consensus about your work, like the feel of the song isn't quite right or a lyric needs work, you should probably give the advice some serious thought. Listen attentively to what the reviewers say and summarize their comments when you return home. That information will be invaluable as you continue to submit material to those people who now know you personally.

"Talent and persistence will help you make it."

If there is one songwriter who knows about talent and persistence, it's Jon Ims. Ims came into national success in 1991 as writer of the number one country hits "She's In Love With the Boy," recorded by Trisha Yearwood and "Falling Out of Love," recorded by Reba McEntire. Named BMI's Country Songwriter of the Year in 1992, Jon Ims has been working diligently at his craft for most of his life to reach the level of success he now enjoys.

photo by Alan L. Mayor

Jon Ims

Beginning his musical career at age 16 in various rock bands and hitting the coffee house folk circuit soon after, Ims led the romantic life of a road musician for almost 10 years. After relocating to Denver in the late 70s, he felt confident enough about his material to start entering songwriting contests.

"I entered the American Song Festival, local ones," he says. "And I ended up winning every one I entered. Over the years when I wasn't getting any recognition, that really kept me going." Throughout those lean years, Ims began pitching his songs on a regional level to people he opened shows for. "Rita Coolidge, Dr. John, all the bluesmen from Chicago, it didn't matter who they were. As time passed, a lot of regional bands started cutting my songs. I began to get a regional reputation."

Ims was beginning to live a comfortable life doing what he loved to do. "Then out of the blue, this girl in Albuquerque did an artist demo (which included one of his songs) and sent it all over Nashville. As a result, 'She's In Love With the Boy' was noticed by a number of people, and eventually by Trisha Yearwood." Yearwood's version went to number one on the country charts, followed almost immediately by Reba McEntire's rendition of "Falling Out of Love."

A move to Nashville in 1991 came *after* his national success. The biggest difference between living in a music hub and any other city, Ims says, is the sense of community. "You walk out the door and Chet Atkins is walking in . . . that's access to people. You can go out to the clubs and see talent all around town. It's inspirational, and also lets you know the level of talent. And the wonderful support . . . when you're trying to get your career going, it's important to meet people."

Aside from meeting as many people in the industry as you can, what other advice would Ims give to aspiring songwriters? "Establish your reputation," he advises. "It's best to perform your own material, but if you can't, get the best session musicians and singer to do your demo. Then see whoever you can see in record company and music publisher offices. If you're talented, you'll get a shot."

And the most important thing a songwriter can do to improve his craft? "Be ruthlessly honest about your talent and about each song you write," says Ims. "The music business is difficult. Talent and persistence will help you make it."

How to Find and Work with a Co-writer

Throughout the history of popular music, many hit songs have been written by songwriting teams. Think about it for a minute and you could probably come up with dozens of them: Lennon and McCartney, Rodgers and Hammerstein, Jagger and Richards, Bacharach and David . . . the list goes on. Check out any recent *Billboard* Hot 100 Singles chart and you'll find that a majority of those successful hit songs are collaborative efforts. With so many people doing it and being very successful at it, working with a co-writer (or writers) sounds like it could be a recipe for success for a songwriter who just can't seem to do it alone. If you're finding yourself at a roadblock when it comes to writing successful songs, a co-writer may be just what you need.

Why work with a co-writer?

There are many reasons why you might consider working with a co-writer. Perhaps you've written some killer lyrics, but melodies give you trouble. Or, you've got a lot of great melodies floating around your head but no words to go with them. Maybe you think the songs you write are pretty good, but you'd really like to bounce your ideas off someone else. A co-writer can help you find that elusive melody and those insightful lyrics, as well as hand out some helpful advice. With a co-writer, you're likely to come up with twice as many ideas as you could on your own—many you probably would have never thought of. Writing with a partner can provide you with the incentive to do the absolute best work you can do, since the success of the song is important not only to you but to another person. And even if collaborating with another writer doesn't drive your songs to the top of the charts, it's a great way to get instant feedback and constructive criticism of your work, which can only make you a better and more professional songwriter.

Finding a co-writer

Where do you go about finding other songwriters interested in writing with someone else? You're going to have to do some digging, but you'll discover they're out there. Probably the best place to start is with your local songwriting organization. To find out if there are any songwriting organizations in your area, consult the listings in the Organizations section of this book. If there aren't any near where you live, see if there are any local branches of the larger, national groups. Organizations such as Nashville Songwriters Association International (NSAI) have regional groups operating in different parts of the United States, and the National Academy of Songwriters offers information on how to begin your own songwriting group. Contact these and other national organizations for further information.

Many songwriting organizations sponsor workshops, critique sessions and seminars, which are ideal places to find a co-writer. Meet and talk with the other writers at these functions. Get to know performers in local clubs, or check out the local musician's union. Run ads in songwriting magazines or the newsletters of your local songwriting organizations. If you run an ad, be specific. State what type of music you write, whether you're interested in a lyricist or a melody writer (or both), and where you can be reached. Writer's nights and open mike nights, sponsored by local clubs, are another excellent place to meet and talk with other writers. If none of these works try posting an ad in local music stores or college music departments. Be aggressive in your networking. The more people you meet, the better your chances of finding a perfect writing partner.

Compatibility

Once you've located someone you'd like to write with, the most important thing to remember is that you both must have the same philosophies and goals regarding the songs you're writing. If you're looking to write a hit song and you meet a writer who is only interested in writing avant-garde compositions, you may want to keep looking for a more compatible writing partner.

Your partner's work habits should also be taken into consideration. If you're the type of person who gets out of bed at the crack of dawn and writes until noon, and your prospective partner likes to sleep until noon and does his best writing after watching David Letterman, perhaps you should look for someone who's more of a morning person. It's also a good idea to find a writer who will agree in advance on your scheduled writing sessions and hours. You may decide to work every day from 10 in the morning to 3 in the afternoon in your home office, with an hour break for lunch. Or you may decide to work from 6 to 10 at night in your living room every other day.

The important thing to remember is that you should respect and treat each other as professionals. When you make an appointment to get together, show up on time and be ready to work. Set times and meeting places for your songwriting sessions, and stick to them. The best thing to do is to have a specific place for writing, not just "Meet me down at Joe's Cafe for coffee and we'll throw some ideas around." That's not to say you won't get any great ideas while hanging out at Joe's, but you'll probably be more productive in a somewhat more private setting. Whether it's an actual office in your home, your kitchen or your partner's living room, your working space should be free from all distractions (phones, children, television sets) so you can concentrate on one thing—writing. Having an actual "office" for writing may sound too structured for real creativity, but it will encourage you to treat your songwriting seriously. If you treat it as a hobby, that's all it will ever be.

Discipline

Collaboration is an excellent way to discipline yourself in your craft. How many times have you said, "Tomorrow I'm going to sit down after my morning cup of coffee and work on my songs until lunch," only to find yourself taking out the garbage, running errands, and otherwise making any excuse NOT to write? If you've got an appointment to keep with someone, you're much less likely to get sidetracked. And when that person is a key player in your success or failure as a songwriter, most likely (if you're serious about being successful) you're going to do all you can to make sure you're there.

The responsibilities of collaboration

So you've found a partner with whom you've discussed all of the above, and it looks like you might make a great team. Your working habits mesh perfectly; you've got a place to write; your schedules are set; and you're both ready to get down to some serious songwriting. But wait. There are a few responsibilities that you and your partner must discuss as you begin working together.

Collaborator agreements

Since this is a business (you're both in the business of writing songs), the legal, monetary and ethical responsibilities of both partners must be considered as you begin to work together. It's important to remember that songs are actual property that can be sold, willed and assigned. When entering into a collaboration, it's a good idea to have a written agreement between you and your partner. You probably think it's too early to even consider these things, but further down the road, if your songs become hits and artistic or personal differences break you and your partner apart, it's in everyone's best interest to have the legal aspects of your partnership down on paper. The National Academy of Songwriters has a Collaborator's Agreement Contract you may want to look over and consider signing with your partner, or you may decide to draft your own. Either way, a collaborator's agreement should be considered sometime during the writing of a song or, at the latest, immediately after a song is completed. For specific information on what a collaborator's agreement should include, see the sidebar.

Guidelines for a collaborator's agreement

To avoid any future problems, it's a good idea for you and your co-writer to draft a Collaborator's Agreement as you begin working together. Here are some points to consider:

1. On the agreement, be sure to identify all parties involved. Include their name, address and Social Security number.

2. Include the names of the songs you are collaborating on.

3. Identify who writes the lyrics and who writes the music. (Lyric writers and melody writers are both entitled to an equal share of the composition). If there is no distinction, clearly state that in the agreement.

4. State the exact percentages to each writer for royalties collected and expenses incurred (such as having demos made, etc.). This should, in most cases, be an equal split.

5. Provide for the possibility of an additional co-writer being brought in later. This will cover things like foreign language lyrics or a different musical arrangement. Be sure to include a change in percentage of royalties to reflect an additional writer.

6. State that all writers will have the power of attorney. This way, if one of the writers is out of town or cannot be tracked down, the other writers can act on an opportunity regarding the song. The agreement must be notarized in order for this clause to hold any legal authority.

7. State whether or not any writer can make future changes to the composition, and whether changes need to be agreed upon by all of the writers.

8. Provide for arbitration in case of any disputes, either through an organization such as the National Academy of Songwriters (NAS) or another group or individual. State that the decision of the arbitrator is binding for all parties.

9. Date and sign the agreement, have it notarized if power of attorney is given, and make sure each writer gets a copy.

Keep in mind that these are only general guidelines to consider when entering into a Collaborator's Agreement. They are not meant as a substitute for having an entertainment attorney draft an agreement.

Royalty allocations

Before you copyright a song, you must be clear as to exactly who the writers are and the amount they will share in any royalties the song may generate. Legally, co-writers of a song each own undivided, equal interests in a song. If two people wrote it, each gets 50%. If four people wrote the song, each gets 25%. This is true even without a written agreement. Let's say that you and your partner worked on a song together, but he did very little work and you came up with most of the ideas. You feel you have a bigger interest in the song, but without a written agreement stating so, if both your names are on that song, you each own 50%. If, however, you both signed an agreement stating that you would get 70% of any royalties and your partner 30%, that arrangement would be reflected in the division of any future earnings. You and your partner can agree to any kind of unequal royalty split. Just remember that the agreement must be IN WRITING.

When should you equally divide the song royalties, and when should you ask for an uneven split? That's up to you and your writing partner, and should be discussed as you begin to write together. If the two of you start from scratch on a song and you're both working on it together, a 50/50 split would be fair. If you write the lyrics and your partner the melody, splitting royalties in half would be appropriate. However, if a writer comes to you and has a melody and chorus lyrics already written, and asks you to write just the lyrics for the verses, an adjustment in royalty allocation will have to be made, since one writer has already done more than half the work. The best thing to do in a situation like this is to discuss with your partner the value of each other's contributions, and make it part of your written agreement.

Sharing ownership

You and your co-writer have other responsibilities to each other. You shouldn't do anything to a song, whether it's finished or not, without the consent of your co-writer. You can't "take out" your partner's contribution and get someone else to replace it. Legally, your original partner still owns half of the song. If you decide you would like to take the song to a third writer, don't do it without the consent of your co-writer. If you are offered a publishing agreement, you cannot sign it without the consent of all the writers involved. A writer cannot grant any exclusive rights to a song without the permission of the co-writers. Each co-writer should give credit to the other writers when visual credit for the song appears. Also, make sure all writers agree before entering a song in any sort of contest. That way, if you win a prize, all writers will share in the winnings.

Keep in mind that you and your co-writer are in a business partnership. The general rule of thumb when you've written a joint work is not to do ANYTHING with that song without the consent of your co-writer. Not only is that the legal thing to do, but it will also prevent any misunderstandings between you. Never hesitate to consult an entertainment attorney if you have ANY qualms about anything you and your partner decide on. Be honest with your partner from the beginning—you'll avoid a lot of headaches down the line.

For a more detailed discussion of the legal responsibilities of collaborators, refer to *Protecting Your Songs and Yourself* by Kent Klavens, and Pat and Pete Luboff's *88 Songwriting Wrongs and How to Right Them*, both published by Writer's Digest Books.

Working with a co-writer

Two integral components of a successful songwriting partnership are trust and respect. Each partner must be able to say exactly what he feels without fear of hurting the other's feelings. Speak up if something's bothering you; your partner will respect your honesty. But be diplomatic about it. If your partner comes to you with an idea you absolutely hate, don't shriek, "Oh, that's horrible, that's the worst idea I've ever heard, are you crazy?" It's best to use simple common courtesy, and say something like, "I'm not sure if that will work; let's try something different." Treat your partner the way you would want to be treated. Accept criticism gracefully, and remember that you're both working toward the same goal—to write a killer song. Take a positive attitude toward his criticism; analyze it and learn from it. Demand the best from your partner, and don't give him anything less than your absolute best.

When it comes to the actual writing process and you're throwing around ideas, don't hold back. Don't be surprised (or insulted) if they're not accepted by your partner; just keep throwing out more ideas until you agree on something. Working with a partner gives you the opportunity to think out loud—verbalize your ideas, no matter how silly or weird they may sound to you. The free flow of ideas is the cornerstone of an effective collaboration.

Remember that there are no "rules" to collaboration, no proven method of success that works for everyone. Some co-writing teams prefer to work together face to face while writing songs, while others may prefer to work separately and then put their ideas together. Others may prefer working over the phone, especially when the two writers live far apart. The key is to find the techniques that work for you and your partner—and for the songs.

Working with a co-writer can be a tricky balancing act, and it may or may not work for you. You may find that working with a partner brings out a creative side you never knew you had, and the songs you write together are the best work you've ever done. Or you may discover that working with another writer just doesn't work. Whether it's rewarding and profitable or frustrating and unproductive, collaboration is, most importantly, a learning experience. Keep your mind focused on the fact that, whether you've discovered your perfect writing companion or found that you prefer to work alone, you've gained an important insight into what makes YOU tick as a songwriter. In the music business, any experience, good or bad, is valuable experience. Learn from the advantages and disadvantages collaboration can bring, and it will only help make you more professional and educated in your craft.

For a comprehensive look at collaboration, read Walter Carter's *The Songwriter's Guide to Collaboration*, published by Writer's Digest Books.

The Business of Songwriting

The music industry is a confusing and constantly changing place, with its own language, contracts and technology. It can be quite impersonal, despite the sometimes very personal output it produces. It is important to remember that music publishers, record companies and all others involved are in it for one reason: to make money. Companies are interested in minimizing their expenses while maximizing profit, usually at the expense of the artist. That is why it is imperative for you to be as educated about the technical aspects of the business as you are about your craft. Signing a contract without knowing exactly what you are getting into can ruin your career. If you want to succeed in the fiercely competitive music business, you must be aware of all the aspects of the industry to avoid being taken advantage of. You must do all you can to educate yourself in the business of songwriting in order to function on the same professional level as those working in the industry.

Copyright

When you create a song and put it down in some fixed or tangible form, it is a property you own and is automatically protected by copyright. This protection lasts for your lifetime (or the lifetime of the last surviving author, if you co-wrote the song) plus 50 years. When you prepare demos, lyric sheets and lead sheets of your songs, you should put notification of copyright on all the copies of your song (on the lyric or lead sheet and on the label of a cassette). The notice is simply the word "copyright" or the symbol © followed by the year the song was created (or published) and your name: © 1993 by John L. Public.

For the best protection, you can register your copyright with the Library of Congress. Although a song is copyrighted whether or not it is registered, such registration establishes a public record of your claim to copyright that could prove useful in any future litigation involving the song. Registration also entitles you to a potentially greater settlement in a copyright infringement suit. To register your song, request a government form PA, available on request from the Copyright Office. Call (202)707-9100 to order forms. It is possible to register groups of songs for one fee, but you cannot add future songs to that particular collection.

Once you receive the PA form, you will be required to return it, along with a registration fee and a tape or lead sheet of your song, to the Register of Copyrights, Library of Congress, Washington DC 20559.

It may take as long as four months to receive your certificate of registration from the Copyright Office, but your songs are protected from the date of creation, and the date of registration will reflect the date you applied for registration.

If you ever feel that one of your songs has been stolen—that someone has unlawfully infringed on your copyright—you will need to have proof that you were the original creator of the work. Copyright registration is the best method of creating proof of a date of creation. You *must* have your copyright registered in order to file a copyright infringement lawsuit. One important way people prove a work is original is to keep their rough drafts and revisions of songs, either on paper or on tape, if they record different versions of the song as they go along.

True copyright infringement is rarer than many people think. For one thing, a title cannot be copyrighted, nor can an idea, nor can a chord progression. Only specific, fixed melodies and lyrics can be copyrighted. Second, a successful infringement suit would have to prove that another songwriter had access to your completed song and that he deliberately copied it, which is difficult to do and not really worthwhile unless the song is a smash hit. Song theft sometimes happens, but not often enough to allow yourself to become paranoid. Don't be afraid to play your songs for people or worry about creating a song that might sound similar to someone else's. Better to spend your time creating original songs, register the copyrights you intend to actively pitch to music professionals, and go ahead and make contacts to get your material heard.

Contracts

The Songwriter's Guide of America (SGA) has drawn up a Popular Songwriter's Contract which it believes to be the best minimum songwriter contract available. The Guild will send a copy of the contract at no charge to any interested songwriter upon request (they do ask that you include a self-addressed stamped envelope with your request). SGA will also review free of charge any contract offered to its members, checking it for fairness and completeness. (See the Guild's listings in the Organizations section.)

The following list, taken from a Songwriter's Guild of America publication entitled "10 Basic Points Your Contract Should Include" enumerates the basic features of an acceptable songwriting contract:

1. Work for Hire. When you receive a contract covering just one composition you should make sure that the phrases "employment for hire" and "exclusive writer agreement" are not included. Also, there should be no options for future songs.

2. Performing Rights Affiliation. If you previously signed publishing contracts, you should be affiliated with either ASCAP, BMI or SESAC. All performance royalties must be received directly by you from your performing rights organization and this should be written into your song contract. (The same goes for any third party licensing organization mutually agreed upon.)

3. Reversion Clause. The contract should include a provision that if the publisher does not secure a release of a commercial sound recording within a specified time (one year, two years, etc.), the contract can be terminated by you.

4. Changes in the Composition. If the contract includes a provision that the publisher can change the title, lyrics or music, this should be amended so that only with your previous consent can such changes be made.

5. Royalty Provisions. Basically, you should receive fifty percent (50%) of all publisher's income on all licenses issued. If the publisher prints and sells his own sheet music and folios, your royalty should be ten percent (10%) of the wholesale selling price. The royalty should not be stated in the contract as a flat rate ($.05, $.07, etc.).

6. Negotiable Deductions. Ideally, demos and all other expenses of publication should be paid 100% by the publisher. The only allowable fee is for the Harry Fox Agency collection fee, whereby the writer pays one half of the amount charged to the publisher. Today's rate charged by the Harry Fox Agency is 4.5%.

7. Royalty Statements and Audit Provision. Once the song is recorded and printed, you are entitled to receive royalty statements at least once every six months. In addition, an audit provision with no time restriction should be included in every contract.

8. Writer's Credit. The publisher should make sure that you receive proper credit on all uses of the composition.

9. Arbitration. In order to avoid large legal fees in case of a dispute with your publisher, the contract should include an arbitration clause.

10. Future Uses. Any use not specifically covered by the contract should be retained by the writer to be negotiated as it comes up.

For a more thorough discussion of the somewhat complicated subject of contracts, see these two books published by Writer's Digest Books: *The Craft and Business of Songwriting*, by John Braheny and *Music Publishing: A Songwriter's Guide*, by Randy Poe.

The ripoffs

As in any other business, the music industry has its share of dishonest, greedy people who try to unfairly exploit the talents and aspirations of others. Most of them employ similar methods of attack which you can learn to recognize and avoid. These "song sharks" prey on beginners—those writers who are unfamiliar with ethical industry standards. Song sharks will take any song—quality doesn't count. They don't care about future royalties, because they get their money upfront from songwriters who don't know better.

Here are some guidelines to help you recognize such a person or company:
• Never pay to have your songs published. A reputable company interested in your songs assumes the responsibility and cost of promoting your material. That company invests in your song because it expects a profit once the song is recorded and released.
• Never pay a fee to have a publisher make a demo of your songs. Some publishers may take the demo expense out of your future royalties, but you should never have to pay upfront for demo costs for a song that is signed to a publisher.
• Never pay to have your music "reviewed" by a company that may be interested in publishing, producing or recording it. Reviewing material—free of charge—is the practice of reputable companies looking for hits for their artists or recording projects.
• Never pay to have your lyrics or poems set to music. "Music mills"—for a price—may use the same melody for hundreds of lyrics and poems, whether it sounds good or not. Publishers recognize one of these melodies as soon as they hear it.
• Read all contracts carefully before signing and don't sign any contract you're unsure about or that you don't fully understand. Don't assume any contract is better than no contract at all. Remember that it is well worth paying an attorney for the time it takes him to review a contract if you can avoid a bad situation that may cost you thousands of dollars in royalties if your song becomes a hit.
• Don't pay a company to pair you with a collaborator. Better ways include contacting organizations which offer collaboration services to their members (for more information, see the article How to Find and Work with a Co-writer on page 15).
• Don't sell your songs outright. It's unethical for anyone to offer you such a proposition.
• If you are asked by a record company or some other type of company to pay expenses upfront, beware. Many expenses incurred by the record company on your behalf may be recoupable, but you should not be paying cash out of your pocket to a company that either employs you as an artist or owns your master recording. If someone offers you a "deal" that asks for cash upfront, it's a good idea to ask to speak with other artists who have signed similar contracts with them before signing one yourself. Weigh the expenses and what you have to gain by financing the project yourself, then make your decision. Read the stipulations of the contract carefully, however, and go over them with a music business attorney. Research the company and its track record, and beware of any company that won't answer your questions or let you know what it has done in the past. If it has had successes and good working relationships with other writers and artists, it should be happy to brag about them.

● Before participating in a songwriting contest, read all of the rules closely. Be sure that what you're giving up (in the way of entry fees, publishing rights, etc.) is not greater than what you stand to gain by winning the contest. See the introduction to the Contests and Awards section for more advice on this.

● There is a version of the age-old chain letter scheme with a special twist just for songwriters and musicians. The letter names five songwriters whose tapes you are supposed to order. You then add your name to the letter and mail it to five more songwriters who, in turn, send you $7 each for your tape. Besides the fact that such chain letters or "pyramid" schemes generally fail, the five "amateur" songwriters named in the letter are known song sharks. Don't fall for it.

● Verify any situation about an individual or a company if you have doubts. Contact the performing rights society with which it is affiliated. Check with the Better Business Bureau in the town where it is located or the state's attorney general's office. Contact professional organizations you're a member of (and the national ones listed in the Organizations section of this book) and inquire about the reputation of the company.

Record keeping

It is a good idea to keep a ledger or notebook containing all financial transactions related to your songwriting. Your record keeping should include a list of income from royalty checks as well as expenses incurred as a result of your songwriting business: cost of tapes, demo sessions, office supplies, postage, traveling expenses, dues to songwriting organizations, class and workshop fees and publications of interest. It's also advisable to open a checking account exclusively for your songwriting activities, not only to make record keeping easier, but to establish your identity as a business for tax purposes.

Your royalties will not reflect tax or other mandatory deductions. It is the songwriter's responsibility to keep track of income and file appropriate tax forms. Contact the IRS or an accountant who serves music industry clients, for specific information.

International markets

Everyone talks about the world getting smaller, and it's true. Modern communication technology has brought us to the point at which media events and information can be transmitted around the globe instantly. No business has enjoyed the fruits of this progress more than the music industry. The music business of the 1990s is truly an international industry. American music is heard in virtually every country in the world, and music from all over the world has taken a firm hold on America's imagination over the past few years.

Those of you who have been buying *Songwriter's Market* over the years may have noticed a steady increase in the number of international companies listed. We believe these listings, though they may be a bit more challenging to deal with than domestic companies, provide additional opportunities for songwriters to achieve success with their music, and it is obvious from the response we get to our listing questionnaires that companies all over the world are very interested in music.

If you consider signing a contract with an enthusiastic publisher from a country outside the United States, use the same criteria that we referred to earlier when making a decision as to the acceptability of the contract.

The Road to a Record Deal

If you're a songwriter who not only writes songs but performs them as part of a group or as a solo act, you're probably looking for more than just a publishing deal. Most likely you're interested in not only getting your songs heard but showcasing your musical talent as well. Whether you're a solo folk singer or member of a five piece heavy metal band, you want your music to be heard and appreciated by the buying public. The best way to go about getting your songs heard by as many people as possible is to release a recording of your music. And in order to do that effectively, you're looking for what every performer seems to be after these days: a record deal.

The elusive, mysterious record deal. On the surface, it seems deceptively simple: Someone at a record company hears your music; they love it; you sign a contract; and stardom follows. If only it were that easy! In the music business there are no hard and fast rules. At times, it seems like the exception is the rule. For every band who struggled for years and worked their way tirelessly to the top there's the guy who was noticed in a subway station and was signed to a major label deal within a week. Unfortunately, there is no surefire way to guarantee that you'll get a record deal, no magic combination of steps that will assure you success. Many books have been written about it and it's been discussed extensively at various music conventions, yet no one can come up with a single, this-is-the-way-you-do-it formula for getting a record deal. It has a lot to do with talent, perseverance, and being in the right place at the right time, but you need a lot more than just luck and talent. If you do a little research you'll find that most performers who have lasted, who were not just another flash in the pan, have painstakingly and carefully built their careers step by step to get where they are. While there is nothing you can do to guarantee instant success, there are steps you can take to help increase your chances of getting noticed by a record label and signing a successful deal.

Major label deals vs. independent label deals

Before you think about trying to get a record deal, you have to decide exactly what you want out of your career. Are you looking to take your performing career as far as you can, to be as famous as, say, Michael Jackson, Garth Brooks, or Guns 'n' Roses? If so, you're going to need the backing of a major record label to help you get there. Major labels have the money, influence and distribution needed to propel your act to the top of the charts. While independent and major labels are the same in that they both release records, distribute them to retail and promote them, independent labels can only go so far with the limited resources they have. They just don't have the ability to distribute records in massive quantities like the major labels do, nor do they have the money to promote their releases nationwide like the majors can. That is why, if you're interested in getting your music heard on the widest scale possible, a major label deal is desirable.

How independent labels can help you

Before you start knocking on the doors of Columbia and Warner Bros. Records, however, realize that a successful career in the music business is a long term investment, not something that's going to happen overnight. It is extremely rare these days for any major label to sign an unknown, new act. Sure, it happens once in a while (obviously the New Kids on the Block didn't have to struggle for years before being noticed), but those are the exceptions. Most performers who have reached some level of success were not overnight discoveries, although it may seem like they were.

One example is the success of Nirvana. Few people had heard of the band before their number one album *Nevermind* hit the charts in 1992. But look a little closer and you'll find out that years before Nirvana signed a deal with Geffen Records, they had a full length album and some singles released on Sub Pop Records, an independent label out of Seattle. Nirvana spent years gathering a loyal following with their indie releases and by touring all over the country. Sub Pop believed in the band, signed them to a deal, and helped them gain an underground following. When their fan base started reaching beyond the underground, major labels became interested and the band decided to sign with Geffen. With the added distribution and promotion that a major label provides, Nirvana saw their first major label release go to number one. Without the groundwork laid by Sub Pop, however, and the efforts of the band in touring and promoting themselves, Geffen wouldn't have even known the band existed, and the major label deal would never have happened.

If you're interested in getting a major label deal, it makes sense to look to independent record labels to get your start. Independent labels have always been a vital part of the music industry (many major labels, such as A&M, started out as indies), and their influence on the majors is increasing. Many major record companies use independent labels as a testing ground for future acts. If a performer can be successful on an indie, it's likely he could be successful on a major. In the current economic atmosphere at major labels — with extremely high overhead costs for developing new bands and the fact that only 10% of acts on major labels actually make any profit — they're not willing to risk everything on an unknown act. Most major labels won't even consider signing a new act that hasn't had some indie success.

But don't think of independent labels as simply farming grounds for the majors. Many independent record companies have acts signed with them that have been with them for years, building a steady and loyal audience. This is especially true of labels that cater to a narrowly defined type of music that isn't chart driven, such as blues and folk. Indie labels are more willing than the majors to take a chance on new and innovative forms of music. While they may not be able to provide the extensive distribution and promotion that a major label can, indie labels can help make an artist a regional success, and may even be able to help the performer see a profit as well. With the lower overhead and smaller production costs that an independent label operates on, it's much easier to be a "success" on an indie label than on a major.

Let's go back to the indie label Sub Pop for an example. Sebadoh, an alternative rock act that gained a national underground following over the past few years, had many major labels — including Columbia and Polygram — offering the band large advances and major label deals. Sebadoh, however, decided to sign with Sub Pop instead. Why? The record industry is unique in the entertainment business in that the creative artist is responsible for the entire cost of producing the work. A general industry rule holds that a band has to sell one album for every dollar spent on production and marketing. Because of the high costs of running a major record label, most of their acts have to sell at least 500,000 records in order to start making money, and that's an awful lot of records for a new, unknown band to sell. At an indie like Sub Pop, however, operating costs are much lower and one of their acts can start making money after selling only 10,000 copies of a new release. Sebadoh, doubting that they would be able to sell hundreds of thousands of their first record, felt they would rather make money now than perhaps never make any signed to a major. Signing with an indie label can help an act further its career and make money at the same time.

Attracting A&R

Before you get any kind of record deal, independent or major, you have to get out there and establish yourself as an artist. Remember that the A&R people at major labels are interested in acts that are already established, that are able to attract an audience. They just don't have the time or money to waste on a totally unknown, unproven act. By starting your career on a local level and building from there, you can start to cultivate a following and prove to the major labels that you can be a success. A&R people figure that if an act can be successful locally, there's a good chance they could be successful nationally, too.

Cultivating a regional following

One of the most important things you as a performer can do to start getting noticed is to play gigs wherever you can. Start playing the cool clubs in your hometown and expand from there. Once you start getting booked at local clubs in your hometown, start a mailing list. Have the fans who come to your shows sign up and send them a postcard to let them know where and when you'll be playing next. Also include on your mailing list the names of writers at local newspapers, and make sure they know when and where you're going to be playing so they can check out your shows. Each review you get in the local press will catch the attention of more people who might come out and see your act, and you'll start attracting a following.

Many performers wonder if it's necessary to move to a music hub city such as Los Angeles, New York or Nashville to increase their chances of getting noticed. Most industry professionals think it isn't. Speaking at the 1993 South by Southwest Music Conference in Austin, Geffen A&R guru Tom Zutaut (who signed Guns 'n' Roses) said, "People don't move to LA or New York City anymore to get signed. We go to where they are." By moving to a music hub you may be closer physically to most of the major companies, but you'll also encounter much more competition than you would back home. Stay where you're comfortable; it's probably easier (and more cost effective) to conquer the music scene in Gainesville, Florida, than it is in Los Angeles or New York.

As you begin booking shows locally, it's important for you to have a recording of your act. Whether it's a single, an EP or a full length cassette or CD, you need something people can listen to when they're not at your shows. Make the recording the best you possibly can within your means. Remember, this recording is going to represent you to the public. Make sure you get this recording into the hands of local press (send it to the attention of the music or entertainment editor) and to the music directors of college radio stations, who are usually quite open to playing music by new artists. Sell copies to the people who are most interested in them—the fans at your shows. This recording will also be a tool for you to use when trying to book shows out of town, and for submitting to independent record companies in the hope of getting a deal.

Creating a "Buzz"

Once you've covered the clubs in your home town and are attracting a fairly good following, branch out. Book gigs in cities around your hometown, and widen the circle as you begin to get more popular. Once this starts to happen, you'll find that a "buzz" is developing. What this means is that people are talking about you; your act is getting favorable reviews, you're being written about in local and regional music papers and more and more people are coming to see you play. Word of mouth about your powerful performance, your incredible stage presence or your emotional, touching songs is traveling to places outside of your hometown, perhaps even outside of your home state. All of this attention, this "buzz" you're generating, is not only getting to your fans but to influential people in the music industry as well. A&R people, at the independent labels and at the majors, will start to pay attention.

What are A&R people looking for?

All this talk about A&R people makes them sound like elusive, all-powerful gods with the fate of your career in their hands. A&R representatives, especially those at the major labels, can be very influential, but basically they're just talent scouts. Working as key decisionmakers in the signing of acts to labels, most of them look for the same things in the acts they sign: a distinctive sound, charisma, powerful songs, a powerful voice and a drive to succeed. But it may also depend on the particular A&R person and the type of music you perform. Some A&R people are merely trend chasers, while others look for truly innovative acts to sign. A&R people in the R&B and country fields look for artists with definite radio appeal; hit songs are vital for success in this arena. Pop artists must rely heavily on a look, or an image, along with their music to get their songs heard on the radio. Rock music, however, is a little less concerned with hit songs and more with the excitement and following a band generates. A rock band can be a success without ever having a hit single. Nine Inch Nails, an industrial rock band on Interscope Records, saw one of their recent releases go platinum with very little radio airplay. Word of mouth, based mainly on the band's live performance, sold those millions of records, not chart topping singles. Nine Inch Nails even went on to win a Grammy in 1993, their popularity based almost solely on word of mouth.

As you're busy cultivating your career base and watching it expand, you should be sending your demos and press kits to independent labels in the hope of landing a deal. Independent labels are interested in signing new bands that are creating interest on a local level, or bands they think have some potential. A&R people at independent labels are much easier to get in touch with than those at the majors. In many cases, the A&R executive at an indie is the owner of the label itself! While it's nearly impossible to get an unsolicited demo heard at a major label, independent labels are open to hearing new acts. They're interested in the same things that the majors are, things such as a distinctive sound and powerful songs. But the independents are more willing to take a chance on new sounds than the majors are.

Your first record deal

You can build a regional following and create a buzz about your act, but there is only so much you can do on your own. Independent labels can provide the distribution, promotion and contacts you couldn't get by yourself, along with the financial backing to make it all happen. Once you find an independent label that's interested in signing your act, there are several things you must consider before signing any contract.

Independent label contracts are usually not as long and complicated as major label ones, but they are still binding, legal contracts. As in any contract, make sure the terms are in the best interest of both you *and* the record company. Avoid anything in your contract that you feel is too restrictive. Try to work out something with the label that you feel comfortable with, so you don't feel like you're obligated to that indie label for the next ten years.

The label will most likely have a clause in its contract stating that they will retain all rights to the masters of any recordings you do while under contract with them. In other words, they will actually own the masters. If you leave the indie label to sign with someone else, you can't take them with you. Indie labels do this so they can re-issue the material, or sell it to a major, and make a profit if you go on to make a name for yourself. Don't panic if you're asked to sign away your rights to your masters. Most indie labels will ask for this, and it's not unreasonable. After the initial support they gave you as an aspiring artist, they feel they should reap some of the profits if you make it big in the future. You should not, however, give away your publishing rights. If you give all your publishing rights away to the record company, they will always be entitled to receiving income on songs that may be re-recorded by another label, or by another artist, down the road. It's in your own best interest to retain your publishing rights.

Another provision usually found in indie contracts is a "buy-out clause." Not all contracts have them, but many do to serve the interests of both the artist and the label. Let's say that after your first indie release, some major labels are interested in signing you, but you're still under contract to the indie label. If the indie is protected by a buy-out clause, they can release you from your contract but be entitled to a percentage of your royalties on any future major label releases. If we go back to our Nirvana/Sub Pop example, Nirvana was signed to Sub Pop, but wanted to be released from their contract so they could sign with a major. Sub Pop agreed to release Nirvana from their contract—in exchange for a royalty of over 2% on the band's future record sales. For Nirvana, it meant getting a major label deal. For Sub Pop, it meant over $1 million in revenue for their label from the sales of an album they didn't even release.

On to the majors

Once you've released some independent product and you're gaining more and more attention, it's important to get some legal representation if you haven't already. A competent entertainment lawyer is crucial at this point in your career. Be sure whoever you get to represent you is an actual entertainment lawyer, not a real estate lawyer or a divorce lawyer. With their extensive contacts within the industry, entertainment lawyers can get your music into the hands of influential A&R representatives at major labels. They are also essential when it comes to actually signing a contract with a major label. A basic recording contract can run from 40-100 pages, and you need a lawyer to help you understand it. A lawyer is also essential in helping you negotiate a deal that is in your best interest.

Contracts

Record company contracts are weighted heavily in the favor of the record company, not the artist, which is why it is important to have legal representation. If you are not well versed in the art of negotiating contracts, you will most likely be giving away more than you have to and not getting as much as you could. A recording contract is made up of many elements, and every contract is different from another. Among the things you will be asked to consider:

● How many records will the company commit to? Most major label deals are for several albums, but some companies give themselves the option of releasing you from your contract if your first album doesn't sell well.

● Will they offer tour support? For many bands, tour expenses are their own responsibility.

● Will they provide a budget for a video? Some record companies don't make videos for all their acts; it's an expensive promotional tool.

● What royalty rate are they willing to pay you, and will that royalty be calculated on 100% of record sales, or will they have an allowance for breakage and returns? Most companies pay royalties on only 90% of sales, to offset the cost of albums that are damaged or returned.

● What kind of advance are they offering? Remember that an advance is really only a loan that you have to pay back with your royalties. Bands should ask for an amount based on what they sold on an independent level, and what they think they can sell. Managers and lawyers tend to want as much as they can get, but you should make sure it's a reasonable amount so you won't be indebted to the company for years.

● What sort of a recording budget are they offering? The amount of money you spend on your recording will also have to be paid back through royalties, so an excessive budget isn't just a license to spend a lot of time in the studio. You should try to get the best product you can for the lowest budget, so you can start making money from your royalties sooner.

● Are they asking you to give up any publishing rights? And are they offering you a publishing advance? A publishing advance is the same as a recording contract advance; you have to pay it back through publishing royalties. If you sign with the label's publishing arm, make sure the deal is competitive and that the advance cannot be cross-collateralized against your royalties. Otherwise, you don't get any record royalties until your publishing advance is repaid.

Those are only some of the elements that make up a recording contract at a major label. The things you need to consider when offered a deal with a major record label are complicated, and at this stage in your career you can't afford to try to figure it out on your own. With a good lawyer to help you examine and question all aspects of your contract, you can work out a deal that will benefit both you and the company. Don't feel you have to sell your soul just to get a deal; keep in mind that everything is negotiable. If the record company wants you badly enough, they will consider all kinds of proposals.

Gaining the attention of the major players in the music industry is hardly an easy task, but with some persistence and hard work it can be done. The music industry is an extremely competitive field, and if you want your talent to stand out from the rest you must do your homework and learn to work within the system. The best way for you, the aspiring performer, to get recognized is through hard work and perseverance. The executives at major record companies are looking for self starters who are creating excitement on their own—not sitting around waiting for a record company to do it for them.

Perhaps one of the biggest mistakes a performer can make is playing only to get a record deal. If the only reason you're in this business is because you want to be a millionaire, you may as well pack it in right now and pick another career. If you're performing your music because it's what you love to do, and you're doing all you can to get noticed because you believe in your music and want others to hear it, you just may have the drive necessary to succeed. Even if, after all your hard work, that major label deal still eludes you, at least you have the satisfaction of knowing you tried and you were able to spend most of your time doing what you love to do—creating music.

Trends and Advances
in the Music Industry

The music industry is constantly changing and evolving. New technologies emerge to replace old ones, and the kind of music that's "hot" one year may be gone by the next. Some of the biggest changes that will affect songwriters in 1994 are in the areas of new digital technology and the acceptance of a wider range of music by consumers.

Music trends

If you take a look at the *Billboard* Hot 100 Singles and Top 200 charts, you'll see quite a cross section of music dominating the top positions. Country music has really come into its own in the past few years, with many country artists having hits not only on the country charts but crossing over to the pop charts as well. Artists like Garth Brooks and Billy Ray Cyrus are selling like multiplatinum rock artists, something the country music industry probably would have never imagined.

"Alternative rock" — or "college rock" or "modern rock" — has jumped from the college radio charts onto the pop charts also, mainly due to the fact that major labels are signing up many alternative acts. It's much more viable these days for an act that was considered to be an "alternative" act to have a hit record — Nirvana proved that with their number one album. Before, alternative acts were considered unsalable to mainstream audiences — the music was, literally, an "alternative" to what was being heard on the radio. But now that it's being heard on Top 40 radio, can it really be considered "alternative" anymore?

Another growing trend on the charts is the continued rise of rap music. Albums by artists like NWA and Ice Cube are debuting at number one on the *Billboard* charts, proving rap to be a viable source of popular music that has risen far above the underground where it began.

How will these trends affect you?

The fact that NWA, Garth Brooks, Metallica, Michael Bolton and Nirvana can share the number one album spot on the *Billboard* 200 shows that what was considered "popular" years ago no longer holds true. Country, metal or rap artists are no longer relegated to being hits in regional areas. They now sell hundreds of thousands of records on a national level. Record companies seem to be more open to experimenting with new music and taking chances on new artists. This is great news for you as a songwriter, because it makes it that much easier to get your work heard and accepted, no matter what kind of music you write. Record companies no longer look to pop stars to supply them with hits. A country singer can become an international superstar, as can a rapper from the streets.

Advances in technology

The never-ending format wars in the music industry continue to escalate. After the demise of the 8-track tape, the analog cassette became the format of choice for consumers seeking a portable, inexpensive way to listen to their favorite music. When the CD, which offered digital sound quality and durability, came along, LPs found themselves on the way out. Even though consumers have embraced the CD as their format of choice, two new formats have been introduced to consumers in the past year.

Sony's MiniDisc, a 3.5 inch disc that resembles a computer disk, is being touted as a digital counterpart of cassettes. Like the analog cassette, the Mini-Disc can record music—with the added advantage that you can record over a MiniDisc many times without losing fidelity.

Matsushita and Philips have entered the format wars as co-developers of the digital compact cassette, or DCC. DCCs can record digitally encoded music and are the same size as analog cassettes. The hardware needed to play DCCs also accommodates analog tapes, making it easier for consumers to transfer their already-existing cassette library to the new DCC format.

Even though DCC and MD are new, the CD still has many advantages. CDs are cheaper than either DCCs or MDs (a blank, 60 minute MD costs around $14; a prerecorded DCC runs around $24). They're more durable than either of the new formats and, perhaps most importantly, the sound quality of the DCC and the MiniDisc are inferior to that of the CD.

Perhaps the biggest appeal of DCC and MD is their ability to record, which is something you can't do with a standard CD. They're also more portable than CDs, with their smaller size and the introduction of portable DCC and MD players just hitting the market. It's hard to say if consumers will look at these new formats as replacements for CDs, or as a companion to them. They can record their favorite CDs onto DCC or MiniDisc for use in a portable player. As with any introduction of a new format, only time will tell if consumers are willing to embrace yet another brand-new technology. With the CD revolution just barely behind us, who's to say another new format won't come along in five years and make DCCs and MDs obsolete?

Also on the horizon is the concept of digital transmission. Basically, this is the transmission of digital quality music via cable, telephone wire or satellite. It revolutionizes the way music is brought into the home, providing the consumer with unlimited access to prerecorded music. Digital cable audio networks, like a pay-per-view cable TV network, will offer subscribers various channels of prerecorded, CD-quality music for a monthly fee. Want to hear the new Garth Brooks album? No need to go out and buy it; just punch it up on the audio network. Digital transmission is already being prepared for consumer use — two networks have already begun recruiting subscribers, offering more than 30 channels of 24-hour, commercial-free, CD-quality prerecorded music for $10 a month. They hope to be serving up to 3 million customers by the end of 1993.

How will these advances affect you?

Along with the new capabilities to record digitally comes the problem of increased home taping. If you can tape your friend's copy of the new Prince album, with digital sound quality, why should you go out and buy it yourself? Songwriters, musicians, publishers and record companies have been aware of this for a while, and lobbied the government to make some provisions for the loss of sales they encounter from the practice of home taping. The Audio Home Recording Act, which was signed into law at the end of 1992, imposes a royalty on the sale of digital blank tape and recording devices. It's likely to generate over $100 million per year, and the funds will be disbursed into two funds, one for owners of the copyrights on sound recordings (the record companies) and another for owners of the musical copyrights (publishers and writers). The disbursement of these funds is still being worked out, but it's clearly a victory for songwriters, who for years were losing hard earned royalties through home taping, and feared losing even more with the advent of new digital formats.

The development of new technology not only affects record companies and songwriters but artists as well. Whenever the industry introduces a new format, the cost of developing it is passed on, unfortunately, to the artist. When the DCC and MD were introduced in the fall of 1992, most major record labels asked their artists to take as much as a 50% reduction from their usual royalty rate on the new formats. Already, artists are asked to take a 25% packaging deduction on CD packaging, because, at the time of their introduction, manufacturing costs to produce CDs were much higher than those of LPs and cassettes. Even though CDs are now being mass produced, and the cost of manufacturing has gone down considerably, artists are still being asked to take the 25% reduction. Now, with the new DCC and MD formats, artists will be asked to take a reduction on those formats also. Many artists are starting to speak out about this, stating it's unfair that they should be asked to subsidize the research and development costs of new formats. Hopefully within the next year a more reasonable arrangement can be worked out to benefit both the record companies and the artists.

The advent of digital transmission poses a problem regarding the publishing and mechanical rights of artists. The introduction of this new technology will change the face of the music industry as we know it. At this time, the principal source of revenue for everyone in the music business is record sales. With digital transmission, there is no need to leave your home to buy tapes or CDs — the music is automatically broadcast into your home. What will happen to the music industry at the retail level? Will the market for prerecorded music be eliminated? And, if records aren't "sold," how will artists, producers and writers generate income? These are questions that many in the industry are asking. The passage of a performance rights bill is now being considered to cover the interests of artists and writers who would lose mechanical income if record sales decline as a result of digital transmission. This is an area that will be changing rapidly in the next year, and hopefully the legislation needed to protect the rights of artists will keep up with the technology.

With new advances in technology and the acceptance of all types of music by consumers, 1994 will be a year of great changes for the music industry. The introduction of new formats and technologies such as digital transmission will affect not only the way we listen to music but how artists and writers are compensated for their talent.

But even with all these changes, there is one thing that hasn't been affected: the need for quality songs. No matter what new technologies come and go and what type of music seems to be popular at the moment, the need for songs, good songs, is always a constant. Keeping on top of the changing trends in the music business is just another way for you, as a songwriter, to figure out where you fit in, and where you're most likely to be a success.

The Markets

Music Publishers

Contrary to what the name may imply, a music publisher doesn't actually "publish" a song. The printing of sheet music is handled by music print publishers, and companies that provide those services can be found in the next section of this book.

Basically, a music publisher is a person in the business of finding songs and trying to get them recorded by artists. The music publisher works as an advocate for you and your songs, representing you as a song plugger, administrator, networking resource, collaborator contact and more. The knowledge and personal contacts a music publisher can provide may be one of the most valuable resources available for an aspiring songwriter just beginning to learn about the music industry.

Music publishers are responsible for taking songs and attempting to maximize their potential income through recordings, use in the media and other areas. While this is his primary task, the music publisher may also handle administrative matters such as copyrighting songs, collecting royalties for the songwriter, arranging and administering foreign rights and producing new demos of the music submitted to him. To be successful, a music publisher must be able to deal with the other segments of the music industry, including A&R personnel, producers, distributors, managers and lawyers. The music publisher must have extensive knowledge not only of his own segment of the industry, but of all the others as well.

Locating a music publisher

How do you go about finding a music publisher that will work well for you? First, you need to find out what kind of music a publisher actually handles. If a particular publisher works mostly with country music and you write jazz, the contacts he has within the industry will hardly be of any use to you. You need to find a publisher more suited to the type of music you write. Each listing in this section will provide information about the type of music that publisher is most interested in; the music types are in boldface to make them easier to locate. You will also want to refer to the Category Index at the back of the book, which lists companies by the type of music they work with. This is a very important area to consider as you do research to identify which companies to submit to. "Shotgunning" (sending out many packages without regard for music preference or submission policy) your demo packages is rarely a successful route to take. Not only is it a waste of time and money, but it may also damage your reputation, labeling you as an unprofessional songwriter with no regard for the workings and policies of the music business. Be very selective when deciding who to send your demos to.

After you've found some companies you think may be interested in your work, find out what songs have been successfully handled by those publishers. Most music publishers are happy to provide you with this information in order to attract quality material. Use this information; contact the songwriters already working with the company and ask them their opinion of how the publisher works. An important question to keep in mind as you're researching music publishers is: Would you work with them if they weren't in the position they're in? If you can't work with a publisher on a personal level, chances are your material won't be represented as you would like it to be.

Another issue to consider is the size of the publisher. The publishing affiliates of the major music conglomerates are huge, handling catalogs of thousands of songs by hundreds of songwriters. Unless you are an established songwriter, your songs probably won't receive enough attention. Smaller, independent publishers offer several advantages. First, independent music publishers are located all over the country, making it easier for you to work face-to-face rather than by mail or phone. Smaller companies usually aren't affiliated with a particular record company, and are therefore able to pitch your songs to many different labels and acts. Independent music publishers are usually interested in a smaller range of music, allowing you to target your submissions more accurately. The most obvious advantage to working with a smaller publisher is the personal attention they can bring to you and your songs. The independent publisher is more likely to work harder to maximize the income your songs can generate, not only for you but for himself.

Publishing contracts

Once you've located a publisher you like and he's interested in shopping your work, the next thing to check is the publishing contract. It would be a good idea to have this (or any music business contract) reviewed by a competent entertainment lawyer. It's important to ask questions about anything you don't understand, especially if you're new in the business. Songwriter organizations such as the Songwriter's Guild of America also provide contract review services. Use these resources to help you learn about music business language and what constitutes a fair music publishing contract.

The knowledge you gain from contract review may help you to identify the music industry's unethical practitioners. The "song shark," as he's called,

Networking and contacts are vital to aspiring songwriters

As one of the most successful independent publishers in the industry, family-owned Bug Music represents an extensive and eclectic group of writers. Handling the material of artists as diverse as Roseanne Cash, Iggy Pop, the Lemonheads, the Guess Who and the late Muddy Waters, Bug works with a wide variety of musical styles. Along with this comes a wide variety of submissions from hopeful new songwriters. As Director of Administrative/Creative Services at Bug, Connie Ambrosch sees many of these packages come across her desk.

Connie Ambrosch

"I've tried in the past to listen to everything that I get," she says, "but we're swamped. I feel badly about it, but unsolicited tapes get a form letter response. If a writer has a referral from one of our writers, a manager or someone at a label, we listen to them. Those are considered forms of solicitation."

While that may sound disheartening to most aspiring songwriters, Ambrosch sees an alternative to mailing out unsolicited submissions on your own. "The best thing to do, if you're going to spend hundreds of dollars doing mailings, is to go to an attorney who has contacts," she offers. "They may charge a couple of hundred dollars to send out your tapes, but at least you know, being solicited by a lawyer, you've got a better chance of getting your songs heard." To send a demo to a publisher completely unsolicited, she continues, "You've got a 10% chance of getting heard, tops, and even that's getting more restricted."

Since networking is such a vital part of succeeding in the music business, Ambrosch feels that songwriters would do well to look to songwriting organizations for help and guidance. "I think it's a good idea to join [organizations such as] the National Academy of Songwriters," she suggests. "They, along with ASCAP and BMI, regularly offer different workshops, showcases and demo listening sessions. They'll bring publishers from around the area to come in and listen to and critique the material."

Along with the chance to meet industry contacts and get songs critiqued by professionals, these organizations offer a necessary commodity to songwriters—support. "I think one of the most valuable exercises is to be involved in some sort of songwriters group," Ambrosch adds. "Look for support. Don't isolate yourself somewhere just writing. Don't do all the work on your own; look for feedback from anywhere you can get it."

makes his living by asking a songwriter to pay to have a song published, will ask for more than the statutory royalties and may even ask you to give up all rights to a song in order to have it published. If you're asked about these so-called "options" by a potential publisher, don't do it. Although none of these practices is illegal, it's certainly not ethical, and no successful publisher uses these methods. *Songwriter's Market*, to the best of our knowledge, contains only honest companies interested in hearing new material. (For more on "song sharks," see The Business of Songwriting.)

Submitting material to a publisher

When submitting material to a company, always keep in mind that a professional, courteous manner goes a long way in making a good impression. When you submit through the mail, make sure your package is neat and meets the particular needs of the publisher. Review their submission policy carefully, and follow it to the letter. Disregarding this information will only make you look like an amateur in the eyes of the company you're submitting to. This section is filled with helpful information and reflects the need for every conceivable style of music, from alternative rock to country to rap to gospel. The information is all here—remember to be selective.

Listings of companies in countries other than the U.S. will have the name of the country in **bold** type. You will find an alphabetical list of these companies at the end of this section. Also at the end of this section is an index of publishers in the New York, Los Angeles and Nashville metropolitan areas, which will prove helpful when planning a trip to one of these major music centers.

*a HI-TEK PUBLISHING COMPANY, Opera Plaza 601, VanNess Ave., E3-141, San Francisco CA 94102. (510)455-6652. Fax: (510)455-6651. Owner: Thomas L. Wallis. Music publisher. Estab. 1989. Publishes 10-25 songs/year; publishes 5 new songwriters/year. Works with composers and lyricists; teams collaborators. Pays standard royalty.
How to Contact: Submit demo tape by mail. Unsolicited submissions are OK. Prefers cassette (or VHS videocassette) with 3-5 songs and lyric sheet. SASE. Reports in 1 month.
Music: Mostly **country**; also **MOR**. Published "Earthquake" (by Boots Tafolca/Denny Hemingson), recorded by Ray Sanders on Pacific Coast Records; "I Want To Cheat Tonight (Pay Later On)" (by T.L. Wallis), recorded by Ray Sanders on a Hi-Tek Pub. Records; and "The Fall"(by T.L. Wallis), recorded by Ray Sanders on Hi-Tek Pub. Records.
Tips: "Be original and creative. Write something that has never been written before."

A STREET MUSIC, Dept. SM, 445 W. 45th St., New York NY 10036. (212)903-4773. Fax: (513)531-4744. A&R Director: K. Hall. Music publisher and record producer (A Street Music). ASCAP. Estab. 1986. Publishes 25-30 songs/year; publishes 5 new songwriters/year. Works with composers. Pays standard royalty.
How to Contact: Submit demo tape—unsolicited submissions are OK. Prefers cassette or DAT with 3 songs. Lyric sheets optional. "SASE *only* will receive reply; for tape return include adequate postage."
Music: Mostly **rock (heavy to pop/radio oriented)**; will listen to **R&B (dance-oriented, radio/pop oriented)**. Published "Feeding Time at the Zoo" (by Nicarry/Strauss), recorded by Ripper Jack (heavy rock); "Zeudus" (by Weikle), recorded by Zeudus (heavy instrumental rock); and "When My

Thoughts Return to You" (by Brad Mason), recorded by Debbie O. (pop/blues), all on A Street Records.

Tips: "Don't send sloppy, first-draft, off-the-cuff demos. Put your best foot forward. If you cannot sell it to us, then how can we hope to place it with an artist?"

*ABIDING LOVE MUSIC PUBLISHING, 1209 N. 45th, Milwaukee WI 53208. President: L.L. Russell. Music publisher and record company (Creation Records and Kei Records). BMI. Estab. 1986. Publishes 1-7 songs/year; publishes 1-2 new songwriters/year. Works with composers and lyricists; teams collaborators. Pays standard royalty.
Affiliate(s): AR-Jess Music, Gospel Music Association, and American Music Network Inc.
How to Contact: Submit a demo tape by mail—unsolicited submissions are OK. Prefers cassette with 1-4 songs and lyric sheet. "Send a good tape, and make your first impression count." SASE. Reports in 1-2 months.
Music: Mostly **gospel, MOR, R&B,** pop and **country/western.** Published "There's Only One Way" written and recorded by Laf'eet' Russell on Creation Records (gospel).
Tips: "Send commercial songs. Listen to the radio to learn whats commercially current."

ABINGDON PRESS, Dept. SM, 201 8th Avenue, South, Nashville TN 37203. (615)749-6158. Music Editor: Gary Alan Smith. Music publisher. ASCAP. Publishes approximately 100 songs/year; publishes as many new songwriters as possible.
How to Contact: Submit a manuscript and/or a demo tape by mail—unsolicited submissions are OK. "Unsolicited material must be addressed with Gary Alan Smith's name on the first line." Prefers cassette with no more than 4 songs and lyric sheet. "Please assure name and address are on tapes and/ or manuscripts, lyric sheets, etc." SASE. Reports in 1 month.
Music: Mostly **"sacred choral and instrumental;** we do not publish separate octavos currently."
Tips: "Focus material on mid-size, volunteer church choirs and musicians."

ACCENT PUBLISHING CO., Dept. SM, 3955 Folk-Ream Rd., Springfield OH 45502. (513)325-5767. President/Owner: Dave Jordan. Music publisher, record company (Dove Song Records). Estab. 1989. Publishes 4-6 songs/year; publishes 3 new songwriters/year. Works with composers and lyricists; teams collaborators. Pays negotiable royalty.
How to Contact: Submit demo tape—unsolicited submissions are OK. Prefers cassette (or VHS videocassette) with 2 songs and lyric or lead sheet. SASE. Reports in 8-10 weeks.
Music: Mostly **country, gospel** and **R&B;** also **pop, soft rock** and **rap.** Published "Am I The One" written and recorded by David Reeves; "The Only Thing Missing Is You" (by Johnson/Jordan), recorded by Chris Baldwin; and "Missing You" (by Justin Slusher), recorded by Orderly Revolution, all on Dove Song Records.
Tips: "Write with feeling, catchy title and hook. Be willing to re-write until the song is good! Send a well-recorded demo."

AIM HIGH MUSIC COMPANY (ASCAP), 1300 Division St., Nashville TN 37203. (615)242-4722. (800)797-4984. Fax: (615)242-1177. Producer: Robert Metzgar. Music publisher and record company (Stop Hunger Records International). Estab. 1971. Publishes 250 songs/year; publishes 5-6 new songwriters/year. Hires staff writers. Works with composers and lyricists; teams collaborators. "Our company pays 100% to all songwriters."
Affiliate(s): Aim High Music (ASCAP), Bobby & Billy Music (BMI), Billy Ray Music (BMI).
How to Contact: Submit a demo tape by mail—unsolicited submissions are OK. Prefers cassette or VHS videocassette with 5-10 songs and lyric sheet. "I like to get to know songwriters personally prior to recording their songs." Does not return unsolicited material. Reports in 6 weeks to 2 months.
Music: Mostly **country, traditional country** and **pop country;** also **gospel, southern gospel** and **contemporary Christian.** Published "Big Old Heartache" written and recorded by Carl Butler on Columbia Records; *Those Crying Times,* written and recorded by Tommy Overstreet on MCA Records; and *Solid Ground,* written and recorded by B. Enriquez on Sony Records.
Tips: "Never write songs that have already been written a thousand times. Come to us with fresh, new and different material."

 The asterisk before a listing indicates that the listing is new in this edition. New markets are often the most receptive to unsolicited submissions.

ALEXIS, P.O. Box 532, Malibu CA 90265. (213)463-5998. President: Lee Magid. Music publisher, record company, personal management firm, and record and video producer. ASCAP. Member AIMP. Estab. 1950. Publishes 50 songs/year; publishes 20-50 new songwriters/year. Works with composers. Pays standard royalty.
Affiliate(s): Marvelle (BMI), Lou-Lee (BMI), D.R. Music (ASCAP) and Gabal (SESAC).
How to Contact: Submit a demo tape—unsolicited submissions are OK. Prefers cassette (or VHS videocassette of writer/artist if available) with 1-3 songs and lyric sheet. "Try to make demo as clear as possible—guitar or piano should be sufficient. A full rhythm and vocal demo is always better." SASE. Reports in 1 month "if interested."
Music: Mostly **R&B, jazz, MOR, pop** and **gospel;** also **blues, church/religious, country, dance-oriented, folk** and **Latin.** Published "I Still Want You" (by T. Carpenter) and "Cheer Up" (by J. Hawkins), recorded by Tramaine Hawkins on Sparrow Records (gospel); and "Dog Eat Dog World" (by T. Turner), recorded by Julie Miller on LMI Records (blues).
Tips: "Create a good melody-lyric and a good clean demo tape. A home recording will do."

ALHART MUSIC PUBLISHING, P.O. Box 1593, Lakeside CA 92040. (619)443-2170. President: Richard Phipps. Music publisher. BMI. Estab. 1981. Releases 4 singles/year. Works with songwriters on contract. Pays standard royalty.
How to Contact: Write or call first and obtain permission to submit. Prefers cassette with 2 songs and lyric or lead sheets. SASE.
Music: Mostly **country;** also **R&B.** Released "Party For One," "Don't Turn My Gold To Blue," and "Blue Lady" (by Dan Michaels), on Alhart Records (country).

ALJONI MUSIC CO., 8010 International Village Dr., Jacksonville FL 32211. (904)745-0897. Creative Manager: Ronnie Hall. Director/Producer: Al Hall, Jr. Music publisher, record producer (Hallways to Fame Productions). BMI. Estab. 1971. Publishes 4-8 songs/year; publishes 1-2 new songwriters/year. Teams collaborators. Pays standard royalty.
Affiliate(s): Hallmarque Musical Works Ltd. (ASCAP).
How to Contact: Submit demo tape—unsolicited submissions are OK. Prefers cassette (or VHS videocassette) with no more than 3 songs and lead sheet. SASE. Reports in 6-8 weeks.
Music: Mostly **rap, dance/R&B** and **jazz.** Published *U Ain't Know* (by Don Hall), recorded by H IIO on 1st Coast Posse Records (rap); *Night Thang* (by J. Hall/A. Hall), recorded by Cosmos Dwellers on Hallway Int'l Records; and *You Bop 2* written and recorded by Al Hall, Jr. on Hallway Int'l Records.
Tips: "Rap—rise above the rest! Dance/R&B—songs should have a good hook and a meaningful story line. Jazz—send solid straight ahead stuff as well as electronically oriented material."

ALL ROCK MUSIC, P.O. Box 2296, Rotterdam 3000 CG **Holland.** Phone: (31) 1862-4266. Fax: (32) 1862-4366. President: Cees Klop. Music publisher, record company (Collector Records) and record producer. Estab. 1967. Publishes 50-60 songs/year; publishes several new songwriters/year. Pays standard royalty.
Affiliate(s): All Rock Music (England) and All Rock Music (Belgium).
How to Contact: Submit demo tape by mail. Prefers cassette. SAE and IRC. Reports in 4 weeks.
Music: Mostly **50s rock, rockabilly** and **country rock;** also **piano boogie woogie.** Published "Loving Wanting You," by R. Scott (country rock) and "Ditch Digger" by D. Mote (rock), both recorded by Cees Klop on White Label Records; "Bumper Boogie" (by R. Hoeke), recorded by Cees Klop on Downsouth Records (boogie); and "Spring In April" by H. Pepping (rock).

ALLEGED IGUANA MUSIC, 44 Archdekin Dr., Brampton ON L6V 1Y4 **Canada.** President: Randall Cousins. Music publisher and record producer (Randall Cousins Productions). SOCAN. Estab. 1984. Publishes 80 songs/year. Works with composers and lyricists; teams collaborators.
Affiliate(s): Alleged Iguana (SOCAN), Secret Agency (SOCAN) and AAA Aardvark Music (SOCAN).
How to Contact: Write first and obtain permission to submit a tape. Prefers cassette or VHS videocassette with 3 songs and lyric sheet. Does not return unsolicited material. Reports in 8 weeks.
Music: Mostly **country, country-rock** and **A/C;** also **pop** and **rock.** Published *Some Rivers Run Dry* (by David Weltman), recorded by Diane Raeside; *Easy For You To Say*, written and recorded by Mark LaForme; and *Corners* (by Di Fronzo-Nollette), recorded by Ericka all on Roto Noto Records.

Listings of companies in countries other than the U.S. have the name of the country in boldface type.

*ALLEGHENY MUSIC WORKS, 306 Cypress Ave,. Johnstown PA 16602. (814)535-3373. Fax: (814)266-1912. Managing Director: Al Rita. Music publisher, record company (Allegheny Records). Estab. 1991. Works with composers and lyricists; teams collaborators. Pays standard 50% royalty.
Affiliate(s): Allegheny Music Works Publishing (ASCAP), Tuned on Music (BMI).
How to Contact: Submit demo tape by mail. Unsolicited submissions are OK. Prefers cassette with 3 songs and lyric/lead sheet (eiher one or the other—both not necessary). SASE. Reports in 2-4 weeks.
Music: Mostly **country, pop, adult contemporary;** also **gospel, R&B** and **contemporary Christian.** Published "Lonesome Doesn't Live Here Anymore" (by Mark McLelland and Joey Katsos), recorded by Mark McLelland; "When You Entered My Life," (by J. Aleshevich and A. Rita), recorded by Dale Davis; and "The Best Thing 'Bout Today Is It's Over" (by J. Listock and R.B. Fox, Jr.), recorded by "Country" Joe Liptock, all on Allegheny Records.
Tips: "Investing in cheap demos is more often than not a costly mistake. Make sure the material is well crafted and that the demo sparkles and shines."

ALLISONGS INC., 1603 Horton Ave., Nashville TN 37212. (615)292-9899. President: Jim Allison. Music publisher, record company (ARIA Records), record producer (Jim Allison, AlliSongs Inc.) BMI, ASCAP. Estab. 1985. Publishes more than 50 songs/year. Works with composers and lyricists. 5 staff writers.
Affiliate(s): Jims' Allisongs (BMI), d.c. Radio-Active Music (ASCAP) and Annie Green Eyes Music (BMI).
How to Contact: Send chrome cassette and lyric sheet. Does not return material. *Will call you* if interested.
Music: Mostly **country.** Published "What Am I Gonna Do About You" (by Allison/Simon/Gilmore), recorded by Reba McEntire on MCA Records (country); "Preservation of the Wild Life" (by Allison/Young), recorded by Earl Thomas Conley on RCA Records (country); and "Against My Will" (by Hogan), recorded by Brenda Lee on Warner Bros. Records (pop).
Tips: "Send your best—we will contact you if interested."

ALTERNATIVE DIRECTION MUSIC PUBLISHERS, Dept. SM, 101 Pine Trail Crescent, Ottawa, Ontario K2G 5B9 **Canada.** (613)225-6100. President and Director of Publishing: David Stein. Music publisher, record company (Parade Records), record producer and management firm (Alternative Direction Management). SOCAN. Estab. 1980. Publishes 5-10 songs/year; publishes 2-3 new songwriters/year. Works with composers; teams collaborators. Pays standard royalty.
How to Contact: Submit demo tape—unsolicited submissions are OK. Prefers cassette (or VHS videocassette) with 2-4 songs. SASE if sent from within Canada; American songwriters send SAE and $2 for postage and handling. Reports in 1 month.
Music: Uptempo **rock, uptempo R&B** and **uptempo pop.** Published "Big Kiss" (by David Ray), recorded by Theresa Bazaar on MCA Records (pop/dance) and Cindy Valentine on CBS Records (rock), Kyana on Parade Records (R&B); The edge on Parade Records (rock) and "Paris in Red" on Parade Records.
Tips: "Make certain your vocals are up front in the mix in the demos you submit. I am looking only for uptempo R&B and pop songs with a strong chorus and killer hooks. Don't send me any MOR, country, blues or folk music. I don't publish that kind of material."

AMALGAMATED TULIP CORP., Dept. SM, 117 W. Rockland Rd., Box 615, Libertyville IL 60048. (708)362-4060. President: Perry Johnson. Music publisher, record company and record producer. BMI. Estab. 1968. Publishes 12 songs/year; publishes 3-6 new songwriters/year. Pays standard royalty.
Affiliate(s): Mo Fo Music.
How to Contact: Submit a demo tape—unsolicited submissions are OK. Prefers cassette with 3-5 songs and lyric sheet. SASE. Prefers studio produced demos. Reports in 6 months.
Music: Mostly **rock, top 40/pop, dance** and **R&B;** also **country, MOR, blues** and **easy listening progressive.** Published "This Feels Like Love to Me" (by Charles Sermay), recorded by Sacha Distel (pop); "Stop Wastin' Time" (by Tom Gallagher), recorded by Orjan (country); and "In the Middle of the Night," recorded by Oh Boy (pop).
Tips: "Send commercial material."

AMERICATONE INTERNATIONAL, 1817 Loch Lomond Way, Las Vegas NV 89102-4437. (702)384-0030. Fax: (702) 382-1926. President: Joe Jan Jaros. Estab. 1975. Publishes 50 songs/year. Pays standard royalty.
Affiliate(s): Americatone Records International, Christy Records International USA., Rambolt Music International.
How to Contact: Submit demo tape—unsolicited submissions OK. Prefers cassettes, "studio production with top sound recordings." SASE. Reports in 2 months.
Music: Mostly **country, jazz, R&R, Spanish, classic ballads.** Published *The Ice Princess,* recorded by Sunset; *The Best of Penelope,* recorded by Penelope; *Santa Ana Winds,* recorded by Johnny Bytheway; and *Dick Shearer and His Stan Kenton Spirits,* recorded by Dick Shearer.

*AMICOS II MUSIC, LTD., P.O. Box #320-158, Brooklyn NY 11232-0003. (718)332-7427. President: Ziggy Gonzalez. Music publisher, record producer. Estab. 1989. Publishes 10-20 songs/year; publishes up to six (6) new songwriters/year. Hires staff songwriters. Works with lyricists. Pays standard 50% royalty.

Affiliate(s): Christian II Music (ASCAP), Millenium Music (ASCAP), Amicos II Music (BMI).

How to Contact: Submit demo tape by mail. Unsolicited submissions are OK. Prefers cassette (or VHS videocassette) with 1-5 songs, lyric and lead sheet (if available). "Quality is stressed, submit songs on good cassettes (CRD2/high bias or metal)." SASE. Reports in 1 month.

Music: Mostly **R&B/pop, dance/house, Latin freestyle**; also **hip hop/rap, adult contemporary** and **Christian contemporary**. Published "In Your Eyes" (by J. Ortiz/E. Garcia), recorded by Visage on On A Roll Records; "Love You, Love You" (by H. Gonzales/L. Love) and "Alone" (by J. Ortiz/H. Gonzalez), recorded by Jaidie on Cutting Records.

Tips: "Submit 'pretty' melodic songs."

AMIRON MUSIC, Dept. SM, 20531 Plummer St., Chatsworth CA 91311. (818)998-0443. Manager: A. Sullivan. Music publisher, record company, record producer and manager. ASCAP. Estab. 1970. Publishes 2-4 songs/year; publishes 1-2 new songwriters/year. Pays standard royalty.

Affiliate(s): Aztex Productions, and Copan Music (BMI).

How to Contact: Prefers cassette (or Beta or VHS videocassette) with any number songs and lyric sheet. SASE. Reports in 10 weeks.

Music: **Easy listening, MOR, progressive, R&B, rock** and **top 40/pop**. Published "Lies in Disguise," "Rapid," and "Let's Work It Out" (by F. Cruz), recorded by Gangs Back; and "Try Me," written and recorded by Sana Christian; all on AKO Records (all pop). Also "Boys Take Your Mind Off Things" (by G. Litvak), recorded by Staunton on Les Disques Records (pop).

Tips: Send songs with "good story-lyrics."

ANGELSONG PUBLISHING CO., 2723 Westwood Dr., Nashville TN 37204. (615)298-2826 (615)833-9678. President: Mabel Birdsong. BMI, ASCAP. Music publisher and record company (Birdsong Records). Publishes 2 albums/year; publishes 2 new songwriters/year.

Affiliate(s): Prosperous (ASCAP).

How to Contact: Write or call first and obtain permission to submit. Prefers cassette with maximum 4 songs and lyric sheet. Does not return unsolicited material. Reports in 2-3 weeks, "if requested."

Music: Mostly **gospel, country** and **MOR**; also **pop**. Published All CD's by Petra; "If You Died Tonight" (by G. Ashworth/D. Sigmon), recorded by Don; and "Revelation" (by Chris Fox), recorded by Abby Gail on Angelsong Records.

ANOTHER AMETHYST SONG, 273 Chippewa Dr., Columbia SC 29210-6508. (803)750-5391. Contact: Manager. Music publisher, record company (Amethyst Group). BMI. Estab. 1985. Publishes 70 songs/year; publishes 20 new songwriters/year. Works with composers. Pays standard royalty.

How to Contact: Prefers cassette (or VHS videocassette) with 3-7 songs and lyric sheet; include any photos, biographical information. SASE. Reports in 5 weeks.

Music: Mostly **alternative rock, pop, new wave, techno, R&B, industrial** and **eclectic** styles. Recently published "Complicated Love" and "Back in the Race" (by C. Sargent and C. Hamblin), recorded by True Identity; "If You Had Your Mind Made Up," written and recorded by Kourtesy; "Surrender To The Order" (by U.S. Steel); and "Get to the Point" (by Synthetic Meat), all on Antithesis Records. Other artists include The Sages, Ted Neiland and New Fire Ceremony.

Tips: "Simplicity is the key. A hit is a hit regardless of the production. Don't 'overkill' the song! We mainly sign artist/writers. Get ready to cooperate and sign what's necessary. Send as close to an album as possible. We move fast to gain airplay, press and bookings. We also have our artists/writers do showcases."

*ANOTHER APPROACH MUSIC PUBLISHING COMPANY (BMI), 1022 Miss Annies Dr. SW, Jacksonville AL 36265. (205)435-9339. President/Owner: Thomas C. Van Dyke. Music publisher and record company. Estab. 1992. Publishes approx. 10 songs/year; publishes approx. 2 new songwriters/year. Works with composers and lyricists; teams collaborators. Pay negotiable.

How to Contact: Write or call first and obtain permission to submit. Prefers cassette with any number of songs and lyric or lead sheet. "If we like it we'll contact you." SASE. Reports in 2 weeks or 1-2 months.

Music: Mostly **R&B, soul** and **gospel**; also **jazz, rock** and **easy listening**. Published "Saturday Night" (by Thomas C. Van Dyke) and "Situations" (by Keith Rowe, Thom Van Dyke), both recorded by Van Dyke; and "Images," written and recorded by Thomas Van Dyke and M. Brown, all on Another Approach Records.

*ANTELOPE PUBLISHING INC., 23 Lover's Lane, Wilton CT 06897. (203)384-9884. President: Tony LaVorgna. Music publisher. Estab. 1982. Publishes 15-20 new songs/year; publishes 3-5 new songwriters/year. Works with composers and lyricists. Pays standard 50% royalty.
How to Contact: Submit demo tape by mail. Prefers cassette with lead sheet. Does not return material. Reports in 2 weeks.
Music: Mostly **acoustic jazz, MOR vocal.** Published "Clevelandtown" on North Country Records and "Somewhere Near" both written and recorded by LaVorgna on Just N Time Records; and "Night Crawler" (by T. Dean), recorded by LaVorgna on Antelope Records.

*APON PUBLISHING CO., Box 3082, Steinway Station, Long Island City, NY 11103. Manager: Don Zemann. Music publisher, record company (Apon, Supraphon, Panton and Love Records) and record producer. ASCAP. Estab. 1957. Publishes 250 songs/year; publishes 50 new songwriters/year. Teams collaborators. Pays standard royalty or according to special agreements made with individual songwriters.
How to Contact: Write or call first and obtain permission to submit. Prefers cassette (or VHS Videocassette) with 1-6 songs and lyric sheet. SASE. Reports in 3 weeks to one month.
Music: New Age, classical, background music, dance-oriented, easy listening, folk and international. Published "Who Knows" (by B. Sedlacek), recorded by BRNO Radio Orchestra on Panton Records (background music); "Operatic Arias" (by Peter Dvorsky), recorded by Slovak Symphony Orchestra; "You Are Everywhere" (by Karel Gott), recorded by J. Staidl Orchestra.
Tips: "We are sub-publishers for pop music from overseas. We publish and record background music for the major background systems operational all over the world. Need only top quality, no synthesizer recordings."

ART AUDIO PUBLISHING COMPANY/TIGHT HI-FI SOUL MUSIC, 9706 Cameron Ave., Detroit MI 48211. (313)893-3406. President: Albert M. Leigh. Professional Manager: Dolores M. Leigh. Music publisher and record company. BMI, ASCAP. Pays standard royalty.
Affiliate(s): Leopard Music (London), Pierre Jaubert, Topomic Music (France), ALPHABET (West Germany), KMW Publishing (South Africa).
How to Contact: Submit demo tape — unsolicited submissions are OK. Prefers cassette with 1-3 songs and lyric or lead sheets. "Keep lyrics up front on your demo." SASE. Reports in 2 weeks.
Music: **House, dance, movie sound tracks** and **songs for TV specials for the younger generation, uptempo pop rock, mellow R&B dance, uptempo country, uptempo gospel, rap, soul, hip hop.** Published "Jesus Showed Us the Way" (by Willie Ayers), recorded by The Morning Echoes of Detroit on Nashboro Records; "I'm Singing Lord," written and recorded by Willie Ayers on X-Tone Records; and "Twon Special" (by Jesse Taylor), recorded by Rock and Roll Sextet on Echoic High Fidelity Records.
Tips: "Basically we are interested only in a new product with a strong sexual uptempo title with a (hook) story. Base it on the good part of your life — no sad songs; we want hot dance and rap. Arrange your songs to match the professional recording artist."

ART OF CONCEPT MUSIC, 3603-23rd St., San Francisco CA 94110. General Manager: Trevor Levine. Music publisher, record company (Fountainhead Records). BMI. Estab. 1989. Publishes 6 songs/year; publishes 1 new songwriter/year. Works with composers and lyricists. Pays standard royalty.
How to Contact: Does not accept unsolicited material. To submit a tape, first send a self-addressed stamped #10 envelope (not a postcard). Guidelines will be returned to you. Reports back on tapes in 3 months — *only* if interested in using the material submitted.
Music: Mostly **pop/rock ballads**, "**moderate-paced meaningful rock** (not 'good time rock and roll' or dance music)." Published "My Silent Daughter," "Fortress" and "If This Is Goodbye," all written and recorded by Trevor Levine on Fountainhead Records.
Tips: "We are interested in songs with powerful melodic and lyrical hooks — songs that are beautiful, expressive and meaningful, with uniquely dissonant or dramatic qualities that really *move* the listener. Our songs deal with serious topics, from inner conflicts and troubled relationships to anthems, story songs and message songs which address social and political issues, government corruption, women's and minority issues and human and animal rights. Keep the song's vocal range within an octave, if possible, and no more than 1½ octaves. The music should convey the meaning of the words. Please only contact us if you are interested in having your songs recorded by an artist other than yourself. We listen to the tapes we receive as time permits; however, if the first 20 seconds don't grab us, we move on to the next tape. So always put your best, most emotional, expressive song first, and avoid long introductions."

ASSOCIATED ARTISTS MUSIC INTERNATIONAL (AAMI), Maarschalklaan 47, 3417 SE Montfoort, **The Netherlands.** Phone: (0)3484-2860. Fax: (31)3484-2860. General Manager: Joop Gerrits. Music publisher, record company (Associated Artists Records), record producer (Associated Artists Productions) and radio and TV promoters. BUMA. Estab. 1975. Publishes 200 songs/year; publishes 50 new

songwriters/year. Works with composers; teams collaborators. Pays by agreement.
Affiliate(s): BMC Publishing Holland (BUMA); Hilversum Happy Music (BUMA); Intermelodie and Holland Glorie Productions.
How to Contact: Submit demo tape by mail—unsolicited submissions are OK. Prefers compact cassette (or VHS videocassette). SAE and IRC. Reports in 6 weeks.
Music: Mostly **disco, pop** and **Italian disco**; also **rock, gospel (evangelical), musicals, MOR** and **country**. Works with Electra Salsa, who "reached the top 40 in the Benelux countries, and the disco dance top 50." Published "Words" (by Fitoussi), recorded by F.R. David on Ariola Records.
Tips: "In a competive and hard market as Europe we need very good products written-composed and produced by talented people and artists."

ASTRODISQUE PUBLISHING, 6453 Conroy Rd, #1001, Orlando FL 32811. (407)295-6311. President: Richard Tiegen. Music publisher, record company (Plum Records) and record producer (Richard Tiegen/Magic Sound Productions). BMI. Estab. 1980. Publishes 15 songs/year; publishes 10 new songwriters/year. Works with composers and lyricists; teams collaborators. Pays standard royalty. "Charges recording and production fees."
How to Contact: Write first to obtain permission to submit. Prefers cassette (or VHS videocassette). Does not return unsolicited material. Reports in 2 weeks.
Music: **Rock, R&B** and **country**; also **New Age** and **acoustic**. Published "Star Train Express," "Too Hot to Handle" and "I Need Your Love," (all by Letourneau), recorded by Dixie Train on Plum Records.
Tips: "Ask what we are currently looking for stylistically."

ASTRON MUSIC PUBLISHING, 4746 Bowes Ave., P.O. Box 22174, Pittsburgh PA 15122. Director, A&R Manager: Renee Asher. Music publisher, record company. Estab. 1991. Publishes 20 songs/year. Works with composers and lyricists. Pays standard royalty.
How to Contact: Submit demo tape by mail—unsolicited submissions are OK. Prefers cassette (or VHS videocassette if available) with 3-5 songs and lyric sheet. "Include promotional packages for artists and list of any credits." SASE. Reports in 2 months.
Music: Mostly **rock, pop, heavy metal**; also **alternative, reggae** and **country**. Published *Little Mistress* and *Northern Skies* (by D. Glatz), recorded by Peacefield on Green Sun Records (folk-rock).
Tips: "Be as professional as possible. We are looking for the same things record labels are looking for. Prefer groups with established base and strong independent release status. NO PHONE CALLS."

AUDIO MUSIC PUBLISHERS, 449 N. Vista St., Los Angeles CA 90036. (213)653-0693. Contact: Ben Weisman. Music publisher, record company and record producer. ASCAP. Estab. 1962. Publishes 25 songs/year; publishes 10-15 new songwriters/year. Works with composers and lyricists; teams collaborators. Pays standard royalty.
How to Contact: Submit a demo tape—unsolicited submissions are OK. "No permission needed." Prefers cassette with 3-10 songs and lyric sheet. "We do not return unsolicited material without SASE. Don't query first; just send tape." Reports in 2 weeks.
Music: Mostly **pop, R&B, rap, dance, funk, soul** and **rock (all types).**

*AUGUST NIGHT MUSIC, P.O. Box 676 Station U, Etobicoke, (Toronto) Ontario M8Z 5P7 **Canada**. (416)233-0547. Catalog Manager: Margo Clarke. Music publisher, record company (Whippet Records), record producer. Estab. 1988. Publishes 6-10 songs/year. Publishes 2 new songwriters/year. Works with composers and lyricists. Pays standard royalty.
How to Contact: Submit demo tape by mail. Unsolicited submissions are OK. Prefers cassette with 3-4 songs and lyric sheet. "Label everything in your package: name, address, phone #; use exact time loaded cassettes if possible." SASE (usually sent back including a critique of the material). Reports in 3 weeks.
Music: Mostly **pop/rock, ballads, country; R&B, New Age**. Published *Don't Let Your Heart Break* (by Dan Alksnis), recorded by Denny Doe; "Solitary Blue" (by Dan Hartland), recorded by Kathryn Eve; *If We Could Start Again* (by D'Aoust/Courville), recorded by Denny Doe, all on Whippet Records.
Tips: "Although we can 'hear' a song, make the best demo you can afford; write, write, copyright, make your presentation 'professional.' You are competing with Don Henley, Billy Joel, Diane Warren, Lyle Lovett."

*AUNTIE ARGON MUSIC, Box 4125, West Hills CA 91308. Director: Steve Hobson. Music publisher. BMI. Estab. 1988. Publishes 2-4 songs/year; 1 new songwriter/year. Works with composers and lyricists. Pays standard royalty.
Affiliate(s): Mama Freon Music (ASCAP).
How to Contact: Write first and obtain permission to submit a tape. Prefers cassette with 1-3 songs with lyric sheets. Does not return unsolicited material. "Unsolicited material goes directly into the trash!!" Reports in 2 weeks.

Music: Mostly **mainstream pop/top 40, country** and **novelty**. Published "Goodness Will Come" and "In the Shadow of Your Wings" (by Steve Hobson and Jill Heller), recorded by Jill Heller on Pops Neon Records.

AVC MUSIC, Dept. SM, #200, 6201 Sunset Blvd., Los Angeles CA 90028. (213)461-9001. Fax: (213)962-0352. President: James Warsinske. Music publisher. ASCAP. Estab. 1988. Publishes 30-60 songs/year; publishes 10-20 new songwriters/year. Works with composers and lyricists; teams collaborators. Pays standard royalty.
Affiliate(s): AVC Music (ASCAP) and Harmonious Music (BMI).
How to Contact: Submit demo tape—unsolicited submissions OK. Prefers cassette or VHS videocassette with 2-5 songs and lyric sheet. "Clearly labelled tapes with phone numbers." SASE. Reports in 1 month.
Music: Mostly **R&B/soul, pop and rock;** also **rap, metal** and **dance**. Published "Let It Be Right," written and recorded by Duncan Faure on AVC Records (pop/rock); "Melissa Mainframe" (by Hohl/Rocca), recorded by Rocca on Life Records (pop/rap) and "In Service" (by Michael Williams), recorded by Madrok on AVC Records (rap).
Tips: "Be yourself, let your talents shine regardless of radio trends."

*AXBAR PRODUCTIONS, Box 12353, San Antonio TX 78212. (512)829-1909. Business Manager: Joe Scates. Music publisher, record company, record producer and record distributors. BMI. Member CMA. Estab. 1978. Publishes 30 songs/year; publishes 10-12 new songwriters/year. Works with composers. Pays standard royalty.
Affiliate(s): Axe Handle Music (ASCAP), Scates and Blanton (ASCAP).
How to Contact: Submit a demo tape—unsolicited submissions are OK. Arrange personal interview. Prefers cassette (or VHS videocassette) with 1-5 songs and lyric sheet. SASE. Reports as soon as possible, but "we hold the better songs for more detailed study."
Music: Mostly **country;** also **country crossover, comedy, blues, MOR** and **rock (soft)**. Published "Daylight," written and recorded by Kenny Dale on EMI-NZ (country); "Like Smoke In The Wind," recorded by Billy D. Hunter on Axbar (country); "Since My Woman Set Me Free," written and recorded by Jackson Boone on Trophy Records (country); and "Heartache County" recorded by Mark Chesnutt on Axbar (country).
Tips: "Send only your best efforts. We have plenty of album cuts and flip sides. We need hit songs."

B. SHARP MUSIC, 24 rue Gachard, 1050 Brussels **Belgium**. Phone: (02)649-28-47. Fax: (02)648-79-31. Music publisher, record company (B. Sharp, Selection Records) and record producer (Pletinckx). Estab. 1950. Works with composers. Pays standard royalty.
Affiliate(s): Prestation Music and Multi Sound.
How to Contact: Submit demo tape—unsolicited submissions are OK. Prefers cassette. SASE. Reports in 1 month.
Music: **Jazz** and **instrumental music**. Published *Soty*, written and recorded by Jacques Pirotton; *Early Spring*, written and recorded by Etienne Verschueren, and *My Impression*, written and recorded by Gino Lattuca, all on B. Sharp Records.

BABY HUEY MUSIC, P.O. Box 121616, Nashville TN 37212. (615)269-9958. President: Mark Stephan Hughes. Music publisher, record company. BMI. Estab. 1969. Publishes 50-100 songs/year; publishes 4-5 new songwriters/year. Hires staff writers. Pays standard royalty.
Affiliate(s): Krimson Hues Music (BMI).
How to Contact: Submit demo tape—unsolicited submissions are OK. Prefers cassette with 3 songs and lyric sheet. SASE. Reports in 3 months.
Music: **Christian;** focusing on praise worship and scripture songs. Published "Jesus Says," written and recorded by Lanier Ferguson; "He'll Make a Way," written and recorded by Kathy Davis; and "You Are Exalted," written and recorded by Mark Stephan Hughes, all on Fresh Start Records.
Tips: "Make a demo worthy of your song. Your presentation reflects your confidence in your material. Always give it the best consideration you can afford. Be led by the Spirit."

*BABY RAQUEL MUSIC, #1235, 1204 Ave. U, Brooklyn NY 11239. (718)376-3399. President: Mark S. Berry. Music publisher. ASCAP, BMI. Estab. 1984. Publishes 5-10 songs/year; publishes 1-2 new songwriters/year. Teams collaborators. Pays standard royalty.
Affiliate(s): Raquels Songs (BMI), administered by All Nations Music.
How to Contact: Submit a demo tape by mail—unsolicited submissions are OK. Prefers cassette with 1-3 songs and lyric sheet. SASE. Reports in 2-3 weeks.
Music: Mostly **alternative, pop/dance** and **pop/rock**. Published "Say Goodbye" (by M. Berry, M. Sukowski), recorded by Indecent Obsession on MCA Records (rock); "I Feel Love" (by M. Smith, M. Berry), recorded by Fan Club on Epic Records (pop/dance); and "Crazy for You" (by M. Berry), recorded by White Heat on CBS/Carras Records (rock).

BAD GRAMMAR MUSIC, Suite 320, 825 Sierra Vista, Las Vegas NV 89109. Music Director: Joe Trupiano. Music publisher, record company (Rockit Records), record producer (Rockit Enterprises) and management company. Estab. 1982. BMI. Publishes 10-20 songs/year; publishes 10-20 new songwriters/year. Receives 250 submissions/year. Works with composers and lyricists; teams collaborators. Pays standard royalty.
How to Contact: Submit a demo tape—unsolicited submissions are OK if submitting according to listing. Prefers cassette (or VHS videocassette) with 3-4 songs and lyric sheet. SASE. Reports in 2 months.
Music: Mostly **dance-oriented, pop/rock** and **rock**; also **A/C, top 40/ballads** and **country**. Published "Passion's Fire" (by W. Bradley), recorded by Hot Rod Hearts (country/pop); "Main Emotion" (by R. Mitchell), recorded by Oscar Charles; and "Ace of Spades" (by L. Phelps), recorded by Laya Phelps, all on Rockit Records.
Tips: "Tell a definite story using plenty of nouns and verbs to add color and paint a distinct picture in the listener's mind. Write from the heart, but don't be afraid to be commercial. Listen to the radio. Notice how distinct the hooks must be."

BAGATELLE MUSIC PUBLISHING CO., 400 San Jacinto St., Houston TX 77002. (713)225-6654. President: Byron Benton. BMI. Music publisher, record company and record producer. Publishes 40 songs/year; publishes 2 new songwriters/year. Pays standard royalty.
Affiliate(s): Floyd Tillman Publishing Co.
How to Contact: Submit demo tape by mail—unsolicited submissions are OK. Prefers cassette (or videocassette) with any number of songs and lyric sheet. SASE.
Music: Mostly **country**; also **gospel** and **blues**. Published "Everything You Touch," written and recorded by Johnny Nelms; "This Is Real" and "Mona from Daytona," written and recorded by Floyd Tillman; all on Bagatelle Records (country).

BAL & BAL MUSIC PUBLISHING CO., P.O. Box 369, LaCanada CA 91012-0369. (818)548-1116. President: Adrian P. Bal. Music publisher, record company (Bal Records) and record producer. ASCAP. Member AGAC and AIMP. Estab. 1965. Publishes 2-6 songs/year; publishes 2-4 new songwriters/year. Works with composers; teams collaborators. Pays standard royalty.
Affiliate(s): Bal West Music Publishing Co. (BMI).
How to Contact: Submit a demo tape—unsolicited submissions are OK. Prefers cassette with 3 songs and lyric sheet. SASE. Reports in 6 weeks.
Music: Mostly **MOR, country, rock** and **gospel**; also **blues, church/religious, easy listening, jazz, R&B, soul** and **top 40/pop**. Published "Right To Know" and "Fragile" (by James Jackson), recorded by Kathy Simmons; "You're a Part of Me," "Can't We Have Some Time Together," "You and Me" and "Circles of Time," all written and recorded by Paul Richards (A/C); "Dance to the Beat of My Heart" (by Dan Gertz) recorded by Ace Baker (medium rock); all on Bal Records.

BALANCE OF POWER MUSIC, Dept. SM, #F402, 132 N. El Camino Real, Encinitas CA 92024. (619)436-1193. President: Mark Allyn. Music publisher. BMI. Estab. 1988. Publishes 10-20 songs/year; publishes 2-3 new songwriters/year. Works with composers and lyricists. Pays standard royalty.
How to Contact: Submit demo tape by mail—unsolicited submissions are OK. Prefers cassette (or VHS videocassette if available) with 1 song only per tape, lyric or lead sheets (if possible). "Name and address on cassette tape. Tapes will not be returned to songwriter. Send SASE for response." Does not return unsolicited material. Reports in 2 months minimum.
Music: Mostly **rock, pop and alternative**; also **country-rock, R&B** and **A/C**. Published "Alone," written and recorded by The Cry on B.O.P. Records (alternative); "Tomorrows Child" (by Gregory Page), recorded by Baba Yaga (rock); and "Geneva" (by Steve Saint), recorded by Club of Rome (rock alternative), both on 4th Wave Records.
Tips: "Please have a master quality tape. Balance of Power very rarely accepts low quality demos. No correspondence without SASE. We are very interested in BMI writers."

BARKING FOE THE MASTER'S BONE, #520, 1111 Elm St., Cincinnati OH 45210-2271. Office Manager: Kevin Curtis. Music publisher. BMI. Estab. 1989. Publishes 16 songs/year; publishes 2 new songwriters—year. Works with composers and lyricists; teams collaborators. Pays negotiable royalty.
Affiliate(s): Beat Box Music (ASCAP), Feltstar (BMI)
How to Contact: Submit demo tape—unsolicited submissions are OK. Prefers cassette (or VHS videocassette) with 3 songs. Does not return unsolicited material. Reports in 2 weeks.
Music: Mostly **country, soft rock** and **pop**; also **soul, gospel** and **rap**. Published "Queen of R-and-B"; "Playboy's Paradise"; and "Thrill Me Easy" (by Kevin Curtis/Dave Arps), recorded by Santar.
Tips: "Take a lesson from seasoned performers such as Bette Midler, Ray Charles and Chaka Khan, the noted 'Queen of R-and-B,' all of whom continue to allow their own brand of musical style to affect generations to come."

BARTOW MUSIC, 324 N. Bartow St., Cartersville GA 30120. (404)382-1442. Publishing Administrator: Jack C. Hill. Producer: Tirus McClendon. Music publisher and record producer (HomeBoy, Ragtime Productions). BMI. Estab. 1988. Publishes 5 songs/year; 5 new songwriters/year. Works with composers and lyricists; teams collaborators. Pays standard royalty.
How to Contact: Submit a demo tape by mail—unsolicited submissions are OK. Prefers cassette (or VHS videocassette) with 3 songs and lyric sheets. Does not return unsolicited material. Reports in 1 month.
Music: R&B, pop, dance and **house.** Published "Emerson Girl" (by D. Maxwell), recorded by D.G.I. Posse (rap); "Give You All My Love" (by A. Hall), recorded by Daybreak (R&B); and "Dreaming" (by T. McClendon), recorded by The Girls, all on Bartow Music.

BEARSONGS, Box 944, Birmingham, B16 8UT **England.** Phone: 44-021-454-7020. Managing Director: Jim Simpson. Music publisher and record company (Big Bear Records). Member PRS, MCPS. Publishes 25 songs/year; publishes 15-20 new songwriters/year.
How to Contact: Prefers reel-to-reel or cassette. SAE and IRC. Reports in 2-3 weeks.
Music: Blues and **jazz.**

EARL BEECHER PUBLISHING, P.O. Box 2111, Huntington Beach CA 92647. (714)842-8635. Owner: Earl Beecher. Music publisher, record company (Outstanding and Morrhythm Records) and record producer (Earl Beecher). BMI, ASCAP. Estab. 1968. Publishes varying number of songs/year. Works with composers. Pays standard royalty.
How to Contact: Submit a demo tape—unsolicited submissions are OK. "Please do not call in advance." Cassettes only. SASE. Reports in 2-8 weeks.
Music: Pop, ballads, rock, gospel and **country.** Published "No Easy Answers," written and recorded by Tom Adelstein (pop/rock); "A Love Inside," written and recorded by Patti O'Hara (pop/rock); and "El Negro Gato II," written and recorded by Alix St. Felix (jazz), all on Morrhythm Records.
Tips: "I am interested mainly in people who want to perform their songs and release albums on one of my labels rather than to submit material to my existing artists."

BENYARD MUSIC CO., 8624 Van Wyck Expressway, Jamaica NY 11418-1959. (718)657-5432. President: Kevin Benyard. Music publisher and record producer (Stone Cold Productions). BMI, Harry Fox Agency. Estab. 1987. Publishes 5 songs/year; publishes 3 new songwriters/year. Works with composers and lyricists. Pays standard royalty.
How to Contact: Write first and obtain permission to submit. Prefers cassette with 2-5 songs and lyric sheet. Does not return unsolicited material. Reports in 1 month. "No unsolicited material accepted ever."
Music: Mostly **R&B, jazz fusion, rock, top 40.** Published "Pretend the Love Away" (by K. Benyard and D. Watkins) and "Saturday" (by K. Benyard), both recorded by Debra Watkins on Jeanae Records.
Tips: "Always be different."

BERANDOL MUSIC LTD., Unit 220, 2600 John St., Markham ON L3R 3W3 **Canada.** (416)475-1848. A&R Director: Ralph Cruickshank. Music publisher, record company (Berandol Records), record producer and distributor. BMI. Member CMPA, CIRPA, CRIA. Estab. 1969. Publishes 20-30 songs/year; publishes 5-10 new songwriters/year. Works with composers. Pays standard royalty.
How to Contact: Submit demo tape with 2-5 songs—unsolicited submissions OK. Does not return unsolicited material. Reports in 1 week.
Music: Mostly **instrumental, children's** and **top 40.**
Tips: "Strong melodic choruses and original sounding music receive top consideration."

HAL BERNARD ENTERPRISES, INC., P.O. Box 8385, 2612 Erie Ave., Cincinnati OH 45208. (513)871-1500. Fax: (513)871-1510. President: Stan Hertzman. Professional Manager: Pepper Bonar. Music publisher, record company and management firm. Publishes 12-24 songs/year; 1-2 new songwriters/year. Works with composers. Pays standard royalty.
Affiliate(s): Sunnyslope Music (ASCAP), Bumpershoot Music (BMI), Apple Butter Music (ASCAP), Carb Music (ASCAP), Saiko Music (ASCAP), Smorgaschord Music (ASCAP) and Clifton Rayburn Music (ASCAP).
How to Contact: Submit a demo tape—unsolicited submissions are OK. Prefers cassette with 3 songs and lyric sheet. SASE. Reports in 6 weeks.
Music: Rock, R&B and **top 40/pop.** Published "Young Lions," "Men in Helicopters," "Phone Call From the Moon," "Standing In the Shadow," "Inner Revolution" and "This Is What I Believe In" all written and recorded by Adrian Belew on Atlantic Records (progressive pop), and "Exaggeration," "Master of Disaster" and "Stella," all recorded by psychodots on Strugglebaby Records.

Tips: "Best material should appear first on demo. Cast your demos. If you as the songwriter can't sing it—don't. Get someone who can present your song properly, use a straight rhythm track and keep it as naked as possible. If you think it still needs something else, have a string arranger, etc. help you, but still keep the *voice up* and the *lyrics clear*."

BEST BUDDIES, INC., Dept. SM, 2100 8th Ave. South, Nashville TN 37204. (615)383-7664. Contact: Review Committee. Music publisher, record company (X-cuse Me) and record producer (Best Buddies Productions). BMI. Estab. 1981. Publishes 18 songs/year. Publishes 1-2 new songwriters/year. Works with composers and lyricists. Pays standard royalty.
Affiliate(s): Swing Set Music (ASCAP), Best Buddies Music (BMI).
How to Contact: Write first and obtain permission to submit. Must include SASE with permission letter. Prefers cassette (or VHS videocassette) with maximum 3 songs. SASE. Reports in 8 weeks. Do not call to see if tape received.
Music: Mostly **country, rock and roll** and **pop**; also **gospel** and **R&B**. Published "Somebody Wrong is Looking Right" (by King/Burkholder), recorded by Bobby Helms; "Give Her Back Her Faith in Me" (by Ray Dean James), recorded by David Speegle on Bitter Creek Records (country); and "I Can't Get Over You Not Loving Me" (by Misty Efron and Bobbie Sallee), recorded by Sandy Garwood on Bitter Creek Records (country).
Tips: "Make a professional presentation. There are no second chances on first impressions."

*BETHLEHEM MUSIC PUBLICATIONS, P.O. Box 201, Tecumseh OK 74873. (405)598-6379. President/Manager: Darrell V. Archer. Music publisher, record company, and record producer. Estab. 1970. Publishes 50 songs/year; publishes 8-10 new songwriters/year. Works with composers or lyricists; teams collaborators. Pays standard royalty. Print publications pay a different royalty (normally 10% of retail) that is divided between the writers.
Affiliate(s): Archer Music, Rapture Music Publications, Courier Records, Conarch Publications, Rapture Records.
How to Contact: Write or call first and obtain permission to submit or to arrange personal interview. Prefers cassette with 3 songs and lyric or lead sheet. Make sure all lyrics are either typewritten or neatly printed and that your submissions are accompanied by a SASE. Reports in 2 months.
Music: Mostly **MOR sacred, Southern gospel** and **easy listening contemporary**; also **spirituals, choir material** and **youth/children's material**. Published *There's Not a Doubt* (by Archer), recorded by Morning Chapel Hour on Courier Records (gospel); *Lord, Wrap Me Up In You* (by Walker), recorded by Archer on Courier Records (contemporary); and *Just As I Am* (by Lehmann), recorded by Bethlehem Choir on Bethlehem Records (traditional).
Tips: "Make sure your song has good form and focus. Try to approach your subject matter in a fresh way or from a new perspective."

BETH-RIDGE MUSIC PUBLISHING CO., Dept. SM, Suite 204, 1508 Harlem, Memphis TN 38114. (901)274-2726. Professional Manager: Janelle Rachal. Music publisher, record company, record producer and recording studio. BMI. Estab. 1978. Publishes 40 songs/year; publishes 10 new songwriters/year. Pays standard royalty.
Affiliate(s): Chartbound Music Ltd. (ASCAP).
How to Contact: "Write to see what our needs are." Prefers 15 or 7½ ips reel-to-reel or cassette (or VHS videocassette) with 3-5 songs and lyric sheet. SASE. Reports in 1 month.
Music: Mostly **R&B, top 40, dance** and **blues**; also **soul** and **gospel**. Published "Hooked on Love," written and recorded by Eddie Mayberry on Blue Town Records (blues/R&B); "Love Song" (by Steve-A), recorded by First Class Crew on GCS Records; and "Call on Jesus" (by various artists), recorded by Voices of Hope on GCS Records (gospel).

BETTER TIMES PUBLISHING/DORIS LINDSAY PUBLISHING, Dept. SM, 1203 Biltmore Ave., High Point NC 27260. (910)882-9990. President: Doris Lindsay. Music publisher, record company (Fountain Records) and record producer (Successful Productions). BMI, ASCAP. Estab. 1979. Publishes 40 songs/year; publishes 6 new songwriters/year. Works with composers and lyricists; teams collaborators. Pays standard royalty.
Affiliate(s): Doris Lindsay Publishing (ASCAP), Better Times Publishing (BMI).
How to Contact: Submit a demo tape by mail—unsolicited submissions are OK. Prefers cassette with 2 songs and lyric sheet. SASE. Reports in 2 months.
Music: Mostly **country, pop, contemporary gospel**. Also **wedding songs, blues, Southern gospel** and **novelty**. Published "Share Your Love," written and recorded by Mitch Snow on Fountain Records (country); "What Did You Do With Your Old 45's" (by Hanna/Pickard), recorded by Bobby Vinton on Curb Records (country/pop); "Back In Time," written and recorded by Mitch Snow on Fountain Records (country); and "Another Notch on My Guitar," written and recorded by Larry La Vey on Fountain Records (blues).
Tips: "Have a professional demo made."

BETTY JANE/JOSIE JANE MUSIC PUBLISHERS, 7400 N. Adams Rd., North Adams MI 49262. (517)287-4421. Professional Manager: Claude E. Reed. Music publisher and record company (C.E.R. Records). BMI, ASCAP. Estab. 1980. Publishes 20+ songs/year; 10 new songwriters/year. Works with composers and lyricists; teams collaborators. Pays standard royalty.
Affiliate(s): Betty Jane Music Publishing Co. (BMI) and Josie Jane Music Publishing Co. (ASCAP).
How to Contact: Submit a demo tape by mail—unsolicited submissions are OK. Prefers cassette or 7½ ips reel-to-reel with up to 5 songs and lyric or lead sheets. "We prefer typewritten and numbered lyric sheets and good professional quality demo tapes." SASE. Reports in 2-3 weeks.
Music: Mostly **gospel** and **country western**; also **R&B**. Published "Resurrection City" (by C. Cravey), recorded by Jimmie Davis; "Let's All Get Ready" (by C. Reed) and "Keys to the Kingdom" (by Lynn Morris), recorded by the Great Day Singers, all on C.E.R. Records.
Tips: "Try to be original, present your music in a professional way, with accurate lyric sheets and well made demo tape. Send SASE with a sufficient amount of postage if you wish material returned."

BIG SNOW MUSIC, P.O. Box 279, Hopkins MN 55343. (612)942-6119. President: Mitch Viegut. Vice President and General Manager: Mark Alan. Music publisher. BMI. Estab. 1989. Publishes 30 new songs/year; publishes 4 new songwriters/year. Works with composers and lyricists; teams collaborators. Pays standard royalty.
How to Contact: Write first and obtain permission to submit. Prefers cassette with 3 songs and lyric sheet. SASE. Reports in 2-3 months.
Music: Mostly **rock**, **metal** and **pop/rock**. Published "Somewhere" (by Mitch Viegut) (pop) and "85 mph" (by Mitch Viegut, Dave Saindon, Roger Prubert) (rock) both on Curb Records and "Thief in the Night" (by Doug Dixon and Mitch Viegut) on Premiére Records (rock), all recorded by Airkraft.

BLACK STALLION COUNTRY PUBLISHING, Box 368, Tujunga CA 91043. (818)352-8142. Fax: (718)352-2122. President: Kenn Kingsbury. Music publisher and book publisher (*Who's Who in Country & Western Music*). BMI. Member CMA, CMF. Publishes 2 songs/year; publishes 1 new songwriter/year. Pays standard royalty.
How to Contact: Prefers 7½ ips reel-to-reel or cassette with 2-4 songs and lyric sheet. SASE. Reports in 1 month.
Music: Bluegrass, country and R&B.
Tips: "Be professional in attitude and presentation. Submit only the material you think is better than anything being played on the radio."

*BLENHEIM MUSIC, 14 Brickendon Green, Hertford S91 38PB **England**. (09)92-86404. Proprietor: John Dye. Music publisher. PRS, MCPS. Estab. 1982. Teams collaborators. Pays standard royalty.
How to Contact: Submit a demo tape by mail—unsolicited submissions are OK. Prefers cassette with any number of songs and lyric sheet. SASE. Reports in 2 months.
Music: Mostly **pop**, **country** and **reggae**; also **comedy songs**. Published *The Minstrel*, *Fire and Water* and *Fire in the Desert*, all written and recorded by Nemo James on Rosie Records (folk/MOR).

BLUE HILL MUSIC/TUTCH MUSIC, 308 Munger Lane, Bethlehem CT 06751. Contact: Paul Hotchkiss. Music publisher, record company (Target Records, Kastle Records) and record producer (Red Kastle Records). BMI. Estab. 1975. Published 20 songs/year; publishes 1-5 new songwriters/year. Pays standard royalty.
Affiliate(s): Blue Hill Music (BMI) and Tutch Music (BMI).
How to Contact: Write first and obtain permission to submit a tape. Prefers cassette with 2 songs and lyric sheet. "Demos should be clear with vocals out in front." SASE. Reports in 3 weeks.
Music: Mostly **country** and **country/pop**; also **MOR** and **blues**. Published "Everyday Man" (by M. Terry), recorded by M. Terry on Roto Noto Records (country/pop); "Thinking 'Bout You" (by P. Hotchkiss), recorded by Susan Manning on Target Records (country); and "Stop Look Listen" (by P. Hotchkiss), recorded by Beverly's Hillbilly Band on Trophy Records (country).

*BLUE SPUR MUSIC GROUP, INC. (ASCAP), 358 W. Hackamore, Gilbert AZ 85234. (602)892-4451. Director of A&R: Esther Burch. President: Terry Olson. A&R: Beve Rhyan Cole. Music publisher, artist development/management, promotion. Estab. 1990. Royalty varies.
How to Contact: Write or call first and obtain permission to submit. Prefers cassette with 3-5 songs and lyric sheet. "Please send only songs protected by copyright. Please be sure submissions are cassette form and call for coded submission number to insure your material will be given our full attention." Does not return unsolicited material. Reports back in 6-12 weeks.
Music: Mostly **contemporary country** and **gospel**.
Tips: "Study the market carefully, listen to the trends, attend a local songwriter's association; be committed to your craft and be persistent. Write, write and re-write!"

*BOAM (ASCAP), P.O. Box 201, Smyrna GA 30081. (404)432-2454. A&R: Tom Hodges. Music publisher. Estab. 1965. Publishes 20 songs/year; publishes 4 new songwriters/year. Teams collaborators. Pays standard royalty of 50%.
Affiliate(s): Mimic Music, Stepping Stone, Skip Jack (BMI).
How to Contact: Submit demo tape by mail. Unsolicited submissions are OK. Prefers cassette (or VHS videocassette) with 6 songs and lyric or lead sheet. SASE. Reports in 3 weeks.
Music: Mostly **country, R&B** and **MOR**; also **rock, gospel** and **folk**. Published *Sons of The South*, written and recorded by Spencer; *Thank You For Roses*, written and recorded by Clayton; and *Heartbreak Rd.* (by Corey), recorded by C&N Cole, all on Trend Records.

BoDe MUSIC (ASCAP), Suite 228, 18016 S. Western Ave., Gardena CA 90248. President: Tory Gullett. Music publisher. Estab. 1990. Publishes 12-15 songs/year; publishes 6-10 new songwriters/year. Pays standard royalty.
Affiliate(s): Gullett Music (BMI).
How to Contact: Submit demo tape by mail — unsolicited submissions are OK. Prefers cassette with 3 songs and lyric sheet. SASE. Reports in 1 month.
Music: Country. Published "How Many Times" (by Nathan Kory); "The Other Side" (by Kheri Han); and "The Best Heartache a Cheater Ever Had" (by Paul Austin and Sarah Summers).
Tips: "Clint Black, Garth Brooks and Travis Tritt are your competition. Strive to make your songs as good as or better than theirs."

*BOK MUSIC, P.O. Box 17838, Encino CA 91416. Fax: (818)705-5346. President: Monica Benson. Music publisher. Estab. 1989. Publishes 30 songs/year; 20 new songwriters/year. Works with composers and lyricists; teams collaborators. Pays standard 50% royalty.
Affiliate(s): Wild Pink Music (ASCAP).
How to Contact: Submit demo tape by mail. "Do not call!!" Prefers cassette with 4 songs and lyric sheet. SASE. Reports in 3 weeks.
Music: Mostly **pop/A/C, R&B** and **rock**. Published "So Intense" (by Essra Mohawk), recorded by Lisa Fischer on Elektra Records; "Hoops of Fire" (by Nina Ossoff/Jeff Franzel/Porter Carroll), recorded by Temptations on Motown Records; "Remember Who You Are" (by Lynn DeFino/Roxanna Ward), recorded by Phyllis Hyman on MoJazz Records (all R&B).
Tips: "I look for great lyrics."

BONNFIRE PUBLISHING, P.O. Box 6429, Huntington Beach CA 92615-6429. (714)962-5618. Contact: Eva and Stan Bonn. Music publisher, record company (ESB Records) and record producer. ASCAP, BMI. Estab. 1987. Pays standard royalty.
Affiliate(s): Bonnfire Publishing (ASCAP) and Gather 'Round Music (BMI).
How to Contact: Submit demo cassette with lyric sheet. Unsolicited submissions OK. SASE. Reports in 1 week.
Music: Country (all forms). Published "I Miss You" (by Ken Francisco), recorded by Richard Freed on Kansa Records (country); "Freeway Cowboy" (by Joey Katsos/Mark McLelland), recorded by Joe Terry on Fanfare Records; "I'm in Love With A Married Man" (by Marda Philpott/Eva Bonn/Gene Rabbai), recorded by Freida Hurst on Broadland International Records (country); and "All I Need" and "Two Faced" (by Jack Schroeder), recorded by John P. Swissholm on ESB Records (country).

BRENTWOOD MUSIC, INC., 316 Southgate Ct., Brentwood TN 37027. (615)373-3950. Fax: (615)373-0386. A&R Director: Jack Jezioro. Music publisher, record company. Estab. 1980. Publishes 35-50 songs/year; publishes 1-2 new songwriters/year. Works with lyricists; teams collaborators. Pays standard royalty on publishing; 10% print publishing royalty.
Affiliate(s): New Spring Publishing (ASCAP), Bridge Building Music (BMI) and Designer Music (SESAC).
How to Contact: Submit demo tape — unsolicited submissions are OK. Prefers cassette with 2-3 songs and lyric or lead sheet. Does not return unsolicited material. Reports in 6-9 months.
Music: Mostly **choral anthems, children's** and **praise/worship**; also **country, jazz** and **comedy**. Published *When the Time Comes* (by David Kavich), recorded by Sandi Patti on Benson Records (LP); *Seed of Love* (by Daryl Mosley), recorded by The New Tradition; and *Love Knows* (by Mark Baldwin), recorded by the Brentwood Jazz Quartet, both on Brentwood Records (both LP's).

How to Get the Most Out of Songwriter's Market (at the front of this book) contains comments and suggestions to help you understand and use the information in these listings.

Tips: "Study our product line (available at any Christian bookstore), analyze the type of material we use and submit music in the same overall style."

BRONX FLASH MUSIC, INC., 3151 Cahuenga Blvd. W., Los Angeles CA 90068. (213)882-6127. Fax: (213)882-8414. Professional Manager: Michael Schneider. Music publisher. BMI, ASCAP. Estab. 1990. Publishes 50 songs/per year; publishes 1-2 new songwriter per year. Hires staff writers. Works with composers and lyricists; teams collaborators. Royalty varies depending on particular songwriter (never less than 50%).
Affiliate(s): Eagles Dare Music (ASCAP) and Kenwon Music (BMI).
How to Contact: Write or call first for permission to submit. Prefers cassette with maximum of 3 songs. Does not return unsolicited material. Reports in 1 month.
Music: Mostly **pop, R&B** and **rock**. Published "You are My Home" (by F. Wildhorn), recorded by Peabo Bryson/Linda Eder; and *The Scarlet Pimpernel* (by F. Wildhorn) (cast album), both on EMI.
Tips: "Keep it clever. Keep it short."

BUG MUSIC, INC., Dept. SM, 9th Floor, 6777 Hollywood, Los Angeles CA 90028. (213)466-4352. Contact: Fred Bourgoise. Music publisher. BMI, ASCAP. Estab. 1975. Other offices: Nashville and London. We handle administration.
Affiliate(s): Bughouse (ASCAP).
How to Contact: Prefers cassette. Does not return unsolicited material.
Music: All genres. Published "Joey," by Concrete Blonde; "Angel Eyes" (by John Hiatt), recorded by Jeff Healy on Arista Records; "Full Moon Full of Love" (by Leroy Preston), recorded by K.D. Lang; and "Thing Called Love" (by John Hiatt), recorded by Bonnie Raitt.

BURIED TREASURE MUSIC, 524 Doral Country Dr., Nashville TN 37221. Executive Producer: Scott Turner. Music publisher and record producer (Aberdeen Productions). ASCAP. Estab. 1972. Publishes 30-50 songs/year; publishes 3-10 new songwriters/year. Works with composers and lyricists. Pays standard royalty.
Affiliate(s): Captain Kidd Music (BMI).
How to Contact: Submit a demo tape—unsolicited submissions are OK. Prefers cassette (or VHS videocassette) with 1-4 songs and lyric sheet. Reports in 2 weeks. "Always enclose SASE if answer is expected."
Music: Country and **country/pop**; also **rock, MOR** and **contemporary**. Published "I Will" (by S. Rose), recorded by B. Bare, Mel Tillis, Roy Clark on Hallmark Records; *You Did It All* (by Turner/Baumgartner), recorded by Shelby Lynne on Sony CBS Records; "The Angels' Song" (by T. Graham), recorded by Lynn Anderson and B. Baker on Polygram Records; and "I Still Can't Say Goodbye," written and recorded by Chet Atkins on Sony Records (all country).
Tips: "*Don't* send songs in envelopes that are 15″x 20″, or by registered mail. It doesn't help a bit. Say something that's been said a thousand times before . . . only say it differently. A great song doesn't care who sings it. Songs that paint pictures have a better chance of ending up as videos. With artists only recording 10 songs every 18-24 months, the advice is . . . Patience!"

*BILL BUTLER MUSIC (BMI), P.O. Box 20, Hondo TX 78861. (210)426-2112. President: Bill Butler. Music publisher and record producer. Estab. 1979. Publishes 75 songs/year; publishes 3-6 new songwriters/year. Works with composers or lyricists; teams collaborators. Pays standard royalty of 50%.
Affiliate(s): Republic of Texas Publishing (ASCAP) and Hill Country Publishing (BMI).
How to Contact: Submit demo tape by mail. Unsolicited submissions are OK. Prefers cassette with 3-5 songs and lyric sheet. "Must be quality demos with lyrics clearly understandable." Does not return unsolicited material. Reports in 6 weeks.
Music: Mostly **country, country rock** and **soul**; also **R&B** and **Tejano**. Published "Love Without End, Amen" and "Baby Blue" (by Aaron Barker), recorded by George Strait on MCA Records (country); and "Taste of Freedom," written and recorded by Aaron Barker on Atlantic Records (country).
Tips: "We look for lyrics that are different from most songs. They must say the same thing as other songs, but from a fresh perspective."

C.A.B. INDEPENDENT PUBLISHING CO., P.O. Box 26852, Oklahoma City OK 73126. Artist Relations: Christopher Stanley. Music publisher and record company (Ms'Que Records, Inc.). BMI. Estab. 1988. Publishes 30 songs/year; publishes 15 new songwriters/year. Works with composers. Pays standard royalty.
Affiliate(s): (C.A.B.) Creative Artistic Broadening Industries, Publishing (BMI).
How to Contact: Write first and obtain permission to submit. Prefers cassette or VHS videocassette with 3 songs. SASE. Reports in 2 months.
Music: Mostly **R&B, rock, pop**; also **jazz** and **New Age**. Published *Always*, written and recorded by Leisure; *Heart Felt* (by D.C. Cooper), recorded by Heart; and *Coming Home* (by Cathy Fleming), recorded by Magnolia, all on Ms'Que Records.

Tips: "Make sure you submit your best songs. Look at what you do and what's going on around you and the world and write about it."

CALIFORNIA COUNTRY MUSIC, 112 Widmar Pl., Clayton CA 94517. (510)672-8201. Owner: Edgar J. Brincat. Music publisher, record company (Roll On Records). BMI. Estab. 1985. Publishes 30 songs/ year; publishes 2-4 new songwriters/year. Works with composers and lyricists; teams collaborators. Pays standard royalty.
Affiliate(s): Sweet Inspirations Music (ASCAP).
How to Contact: Submit a demo tape by mail—unsolicited submissions are OK. Prefers cassette with 3 songs and lyric sheet. Any calls will be returned collect to caller. SASE. Reports in 2-4 weeks.
Music: Mostly **MOR, contemporary country** and **pop**; also **R&B, gospel** and **light rock**. Published "Broken Record" (by Dianne Baumgartner/Horace Linsley), "Outskirts of Phoenix" (by Petrella Pollefeyt), "Write to P.O. Box 33" (by Michael Gooch/Susan Branding) and "Never Thought Of Losing You" (by Jeanne Dickey-Boyter/Gina Dempsey), all recorded by Edee Gordon and the Flash Band.
Tips: "Listen to what we have to say about your product. Be as professional as possible."

***CALINOH MUSIC GROUP**, Suite #8, 1208 16th Ave. S., Nashville TN 37212. (615)320-9222. Contact: Ann Hofer or Tom Cornett. Music publisher. Estab. 1992. Publishes 50 songs/year; publishes 10 new songwriters/year. Teams collaborators. Pays standard royalty.
Affiliate(s): Little Liberty Town (ASCAP) and West Manchester Publishing (BMI).
How to Contact: Submit demo tape by mail. Unsolicited submissions are OK. Prefers cassette with 3 songs and lyric sheet. "Include SASE." Does not return unsolicited material.
Music: Mostly **country, gospel** and **pop**.

CALVARY MUSIC GROUP, INC., Dept. SM, 142 8th Ave. N., Nashville TN 37203. (615)244-8800. President: Dr. Nelson S. Parkerson. Music publisher and record company ASCAP, BMI, SESAC. Publishes 30-40 songs/year; publishes 2-3 new songwriters/year. Pays standard royalty.
Affiliate(s): Songs of Calvary, Music of Calvary and LifeStream Music, Soldier of the Light, Torch-bearer Music.
How to Contact: Accepting material at this time.
Music: **Church/religious, contemporary Christian, gospel** and **wedding music**.

***CAMEX MUSIC**, 535 5th Ave., New York NY 10017. (212)682-8400. APR: Alex. Music publisher, record company, record producer. Camerica Music, Camex Productions. Estab. 1976. Publishes 100 songs/year; publishes 10 new songwriters/year. Hires staff songwriters. Works with composers and lyricists. Query for royalty terms.
How to Contact: Submit demo tape by mail. Unsolicited submissions are OK. Prefers cassettes with 5-10 songs and lyric sheet. Send press kit. SASE. Reports in 3 months.
Music: Mostly **alternate, rock, pop, A/C**.
Tips: "Keep the market in mind."

CARAVELL MAIN SAIL MUSIC, P.O. Box 1646, Branson MO 65616. (417)334-7040. President: Keith O'Neil. Music publisher, record producer (Caravell Recording Studio). ASCAP. Estab. 1989. Publishes 5 new songwriters/year. Works with composers and lyricists. Pays standard royalty of 50%.
Affiliate(s): White River Valley Music (BMI).
How to Contact: Submit demo tape by mail—unsolicited submissions are OK. Prefers cassette with 3 songs and lyric sheet. SASE. Reports in 6 weeks.
Music: Mostly **country, pop** and **gospel**. Published "Outlaws Get the Ladies" and "5th Generation," by Lanee Griffith on White River Valley Records; "The Darlin' Boys" and "The Wizard of Song," by Rodney Dillard on Vanguard Records; and "In the Meadow" by Jackie Pope on Caravell Records.

DON CASALE MUSIC, INC., 377 Plainfield St., Westbury NY 11590. (516)333-7898. President: Don Casale. Record producer, music publisher, artist management; affiliated recording studio. Estab. 1979. Deals with artists, songwriters, managers and agents. Fee derived from sales royalty.
Affiliate(s): Elasac Music (ASCAP), Don Casale Music (BMI).
How to Contact: "I will accept unsolicited cassettes (except during August and September) with ONE or TWO songs and legible, typed lyric sheets (no registered mail). No "lyrics-only" submissions. Please include address and phone number and letter stating exact purpose (publishing deal? record deal? etc.); anything else you'd like to say is welcome, too (I frown on 'form' letters). Press kit, bio and photo(s) or VHS videocassette are helpful, if available. For return of your material, always include SASE (envelope *must* be large enough to handle contents). If you don't need your material returned, include a *signed* note stating so and only include SASE for my response letter. Sorry, but I will not listen or correspond without SASE. A call first is very welcome (between 12 noon and 12 midnight EST), but not necessary, or you may inquire first by mail (with SASE). I'll listen to every note of your

music and respond to you as soon as possible, usually between two weeks and two months, depending on volume of submissions. A maximum of two submissions per year, unless I request more (and sometimes I do)."

Music: Everything but jazz and classical.

Tips: "Submitted songs should have a 'special' nature about them; a different quality and lyric. Melodies should be particularly 'catchy' and memorable. Songs should be *in tune with the current radio market*. I want only 'career-starting,' top 10 singles; not B sides or album fillers. Please try to be SELECTIVE and send me that ONE SONG you think is a KILLER; that ONE SONG that JUMPS OFF THE TAPE! Don't include a second song just because there's room on the cassette; if I hear something I like, I'll ask for more. REALLY! Songwriters seeking a publishing contract need only a simple, in-tune, clear version of the song(s); a big production and recording, although welcome, is not necessary. Artists seeking a recording contract should submit a 'quality' performance (musically and vocally), incorporating their very best effort and their own, preferably unique, style. Your recording needn't be master quality, but your performance should be. I give extra points for following my instructions to the letter."

ERNIE CASH MUSIC, INC., 744 Joppa Farm Rd., Joppa MD 21085. (301)679-2262. President: Ernest W. Cash. Music publisher, record company (Continental Records, Inc.), record producer (Vision Music Group, Inc.) and Vision Video Production, Inc. BMI. Estab. 1987. Publishes 30-60 songs/year; publishes 10-15 new songwriters/year. Works with composers and lyricists; teams collaborators. Pays standard royalty.

Affiliate(s): Big K Music, Inc. (BMI), Guerriero Music (BMI) and Deb Music (BMI).

How to Contact: Call first and obtain permission to submit and/or to arrange personal interview. Prefers cassette (VHS videocassette if available) with 3 songs and lyric sheet. SASE. Reports in 2 weeks.

Music: Mostly **country, gospel** and **pop**; also **R&B** and **rock**. Published *Another Birthday* (by Carl F. Becker); *Send it To Heaven* (by Mack Vickory); and *Doctor of Love* (by Ernie Cash); all recorded by Ernie Cash on Continental Records.

Tips: "Give me a call, I will review your material."

CASTLE MUSIC CORP., Dept. SM, Suite 201, 50 Music Square W., Nashville TN 37203. (615)320-7003. Fax: (615)320-7006. Publishing Director: Eddie Russell. Music publisher, record company, record producer. Estab. 1969. Pays standard royalty.

Affiliate(s): Alley Roads Music (BMI), Eddie Ray Music (ASCAP), Cats Alley Music (ASCAP) and Flattop Music (SESAC).

How to Contact: Submit demo tape by mail–unsolicited submissions are OK. Prefers cassette with 3 songs and lyric sheet. SASE. Reports as soon as possible.

Music: Mostly **country, pop** and **gospel**. Published "You Him or Me," written and recorded by Carl Butler and "Think Like a Man, Work Like a Dog" (by Ruthie Steele and Bethany Reynolds), recorded by Tammie Sue and *Women Like You*, written and recorded by Doug Cotton, all on Castle Records.

CATHARINE COURAGE MUSIC LTD., 48 De Lisle Rd., Bournemouth Dorset BH3 7NG **England**. (202)529755. Director: Mike Shepstone. Music publisher. PRS/MCPS. Estab. 1981. Publishes 7 songs/year. Works with composers. Pays standard royalty.

How to Contact: Submit a demo tape by mail—unsolicited submissions OK. Prefers cassette with two songs and lyric sheet. SASE. "Don't forget we are answering from the U.K., so no USA stamps." Reports in 6 weeks.

Music: Mostly **pop, rock/pop** and **R&B**.

Tips: "We are looking for songs for female artists."

*CEDAR CREEK MUSIC (BMI), Suite 503, 44 Music Square E., Nashville TN 37203. (615)252-6916. Fax: (615)329-1071. President: Larry Duncan. Music publisher, record company (Cedar Creek Records), record producer and artist management. Estab. 1981. Publishes 100 songs/year; publishes 30 new songwriters/year. Works with composers and/or lyricists; teams collaborators. Pays standard royalty.

How to Contact: Submit demo tape by mail. Unsolicited submissions are OK. Prefers cassette (VHS videocassette) with 4-6 songs and lyric sheet (typed). Does not return unsolicited material. Reports in 1 month.

Music: Mostly **country, country/pop** and **country/R&B**; also **pop, R&B** and **light rock**. Published "Rough Road to Fame" and "Lifetime Affair," written and recorded by Larry Duncan on Cedar Creek Records; and *One of the Good Ol' Boys* (by Debra McClure, Danny Neal and Tony Glenn Rast), recorded by Kym Wortham on ADD Records.

Tips: "Submit your best songs and a good full demo with vocal upfront and 5 instruments on tracks backing the singer. Use a great demo singer."

*CENTURY CITY MUSIC PUBLISHING, 2207 Halifax Cres., Calgary T2M 4E2 **Canada.** (403)282-2555. Producer/Manager: Warren Anderson. Music publisher, record company (Century City Records) and record producer (Warren Anderson). SOCAN. Estab. 1983. Publishes 1-6 songs and 1-6 new songwriters/year. Works with composers and lyricists; teams collaborators. Pays standard royalty.
How to Contact: Write first and obtain permission to submit a tape. Prefers cassette or VHS videocassette with 4 songs and lyric and lead sheets. Reports in 1 month.
Music: Mostly **country rock, rock** and **folk rock;** also **alternative.** Published "Hand Me Down Clown" (by W.R. Hutchinson), recorded by W. Anderson (folk rock); "1000 Miles Away," written and recorded by Damian Follett (folk rock); and "Hot From The Streets," written and recorded by Warren Anderson (rock); all on Century City Records.
Tips: "Keep trying! To impress me you will have to send me more than one 4-song demo tape submission per year. I'm looking for consistency and quality. A small independent publisher can be much more effective in promoting a few good songwriters compared to a large multinational organization where the focus is diffused over a much broader market."

CHAPIE MUSIC (BMI), Dept. SM, 228 W. 5th, Kansas City MO 64105. (816)842-6854. Owner: Chuck Chapman. Music publisher, record company (Fifth Street Records), record producer (Chapman Recording Studios). BMI. Estab. 1977. Publishes 6 songs/year. Works with composers; teams collaborators. Pays standard royalty.
How to Contact: Call to get permission to submit tape. Prefers cassette with 1-3 songs and lyric sheet. SASE. Reports in weeks.
Music: Mostly **country, pop, gospel;** also **jazz, R&B** and **New Age.** Published "Lonely Country Road" and "Talkin 'Bout," both written and recorded by Mike Eisel; and "Sometimes Takes A Woman" (by Greg Camp), recorded by Rick Loveall, all recorded on Fifth Street Records (country).
Tips: "Make it commercial—with a twist on the lyrics."

*CHARIS MUSIC, P.O. Box 997, Florida, Transvaal **South Africa** 1710. 2711-674-2030 or 2711-674-2031. Fax: 2711-472-1660. Publishing Department: Jenny Crickmore-Thompson. Music publisher and record producer (Grace Music Pty Ltd). SAMRO/SARRAL. Estab. 1981. Publishes 10-20 songs/year; publishes 10-20 new songwriters/year. Works with composers and lyricists; teams collaborators. "The publisher shall pay to the composer a royalty of 10% of the retail selling price of all printed copies of work sold by or on behalf of the publisher and paid for in all countries, provided that if the publisher arranges any agency for the sale of his edition of the work in any country outside the territory, the royalty payable to the composer in respect of sales in such country shall be 5%."
Affiliate(s): "We are sub-publishers in South Africa for Word Inc., Tempo, Fairhill, Jubilee, Sandy Music, Word Music (UK), Benson, Meadowgreen, Bud John."
How to Contact: Submit a demo tape by mail—unsolicited submissions are OK. Prefers cassette with 1 or more songs, lyric sheets and lead sheets. SAE and IRC for return.
Music: Interested in **gospel only.** Published "Let the Nations Praise the Lord" (by Anamarie Pringle), "I Thank You" (by Nicola Smart) and "Child Be a Song" (by Billy Joubert), all recorded by SABC on Grace Music (all gospel).

CHEAVORIA MUSIC CO. (BMI), 1219 Kerlin Ave., Brewton AL 36426. (205)867-2228. President: Roy Edwards. Music publisher, record company and record producer. Estab. 1972. Publishes 20 new songwriters/year. Works with composers and lyricists; teams collaborators. Pays standard royalty.
Affiliate(s): Baitstring Music (ASCAP).
How to Contact: Write first to get permission to submit. Prefers cassette with 3 songs and lyric sheet. Does not return unsolicited material. Reports in 1 month.
Music: Mostly **R&B, pop** and **country;** also **good ballads.** Published "Forever and Always" written and recorded by James Rootwood on Bolivia Records (country).

*CHESTLER PUBLISHING CO. (BMI), 1376 Ready Ave., Burton MI 48529-2052. (313)742-0770. Owner: Harry F. Chestler. Music publisher, record company and record producer. Estab. 1967. Publishes 2 songs/year; publishes 1 new songwriter/year. Works with composers and/or lyricists. Pays standard royalty.
How to Contact: Write first and obtain permission to submit or to arrange personal interview. Prefers cassette. Does not return unsolicited material. Reports in 1 month.
Music: Mostly **country, rock** and **gospel;** also **rap.**
Tips: "Don't spend a lot of money on demos."

CHINA GROOVE, 404 St. Henri, Montreal, Quebec H3C 2P5 **Canada.** (514)871-8481. Publisher: Mario Rubnikowich. Music publisher. SDE, SOCAN. Estab. 1987. Publishes 6-10 songs/year; publishes 3 new songwriters/year. Hires staff songwriters. Works with team collaborators. Pays standard royalty.

Affiliate(s): Foxtrot (SOCAN).
How to Contact: Submit a demo tape by mail—unsolicited submissions are OK. Prefers cassette or 15 ips reel-to-reel with 3 songs and lyric sheet and lead sheet. SASE. Reports in 3-5 weeks.

*SONNY CHRISTOPHER PUBLISHING (BMI), P.O. Box 9144, Ft. Worth TX 76147-2144. (817)595-4655. Owner: Sonny Christopher. Music publisher, record company and record producer. Estab. 1974. Publishes 20-25 new songs/year; publishes 3-5 new songwriters/year. Pays standard royalty.
How to Contact: Write first and obtain permission to submit. Prefers cassette with lyric sheet. SASE. Reports in 3 months.
Music: Mostly **country, rock** and **blues.** Published "Texas Shines Like A Diamond," written and recorded by Sonny, on Sabre Records; *I'm Learning Not To Love You* written and recorded by Ronny Collins and "Sourmash Whiskey And Red Texas Wine" written and recorded by Howard Crockette on Texas International Records.
Tips: "Stay with it. A winner *never* quits and a quitter never *wins.*"

*CIMIRRON MUSIC (BMI), (formerly Hot Knobs Music), 607 Piney Point Rd., Yorktown VA 23692. (804)898-8133. President: Lana Puckett. Music publisher, record company and record producer. Estab. 1986. Publishes 10-20 songs/year. "Royalty depends on song and writer."
How to Contact: Write first and obtain permission to submit. Prefers cassette and lyric sheet. SASE. Reports in 3 months.
Music: Mostly **country, acoustic, folk** and **bluegrass.** Published *Cornstalk Pony* written and recorded by L. Puckett; *Some Things Never Change* (written and recorded by K. Penson), and *Farmer of Love* (by K. Penson/Lana Puckett), recorded by K. Penson, all on Cimirron Records.
Tips: "It needs to be a great song *musically* and *lyrically.*"

CISUM, Box 192, Pittsburg KS 66762. (316)231-6443. Partner: Kevin Shawn. Music publisher, record company (Cisum), record producer (Cisum). BMI, SESAC and ASCAP. Estab. 1985. Publishes 100 songs/year. Works with composers and lyricists; teams collaborators. Pays standard royalty.
How to Contact: Write first and obtain permission to submit a tape. Prefers cassette (or VHS videocassette if available) and lyric sheet. "Unpublished, copyrighted, cassette with lyrics. Submit as many as you wish. We listen to everything, allow 3 months. When over 3 weeks please call."
Music: Mostly **novelty, country** and **rock;** also **pop, gospel** and **R&B.** Published "Angry Gun" (by R. Durst), recorded by Gene Straser on Antique Records (country); "Smooth Talk" (by Rhuems), recorded by Rich Rhuems on Antique Records (country); "Mailman Mailman" (by Strasser), recorded by Willie & Shawn on Cisum Records (novelty).
Tips: "Good demo, great song; always put your best effort on the tape first."

*CITY PUBLISHING CO., 840 Windham Ave., Cincinnati OH 45229. (513)559-1210. President: Roosevelt Lee. Music publisher, record company and record producer. BMI. Publishes 8 songs/year. Pays standard royalty.
Affiliate(s): Carriage Publishing Co. (BMI).
How to Contact: Submit demo tape by mail—unsolicited submissions are OK. Prefers cassette with maximum of 4 songs and lyric sheet. SASE. Reports in 1 month.
Music: Mostly **rap, gospel, pop, reggae.** Published "Instantpart," written and recorded by Gradual Taylor; "Fat Rat," written and recorded by Albert Washington; and "Hey Little Girl" (by Robert Hill), recorded by Roosevelt Lee, all on Westworld Records.
Tips: "I am looking for finished masters."

*CLEAR POND MUSIC (BMI), Suite 114, 128 Grant Ave., Santa Fe NM 87501. (505)983-3245. Fax: (505)982-9168. Publisher: Susan Pond. Music publisher and record producer (Crystal Clear Productions). Estab. 1992. Publishes 10-20 songs/year; publishes 1-5 new songwriters/year. Works with composers and/or lyricists; teams collaborators. Pays standard royalty. "We use the Songwriter's Guild Contract."
How to Contact: Write and obtain permission to submit. Prefers cassette with 1-3 songs and lyric sheet. SASE. Reports in 1 month.
Music: Mostly **pop, pop/rock** and **country/contemporary;** also A/C. Published "Her Heart's On Fire," on Paylode Records and "There's Only You" and "Falling Star" on Maxim Records, all written and recorded by David Anthony, and "Runaway Heart," written and recorded by Michael Sierra on Comstock Records.
Tips: "Write very strong hook melodies with tight lyrics; know the business, do your homework. Have good studio demos. Study lyric writing and music; be realistic about your goals."

*CLEARWIND PUBLISHING, P.O. Box 42381, Detroit MI 48242-0381. (313)336-9522. "A Contemporary Christian Publishing and Management Company." Contact: A&R Department Director. Music publisher and personal management company (Clearwind Management). Estab. 1983. Publishes 12-

15 songs/year; publishes 2-4 new songwriters/year. Pays standard royalty.

How to Contact: Write. "Do NOT call! Unsolicited submissions will be returned unopened." Prefers cassette (or VHS videocassette) with 2 songs and lyric sheet. (NO more than TWO songs!) Does not return unsolicited material. Reports in 1-3 months.

Music: Mostly **pop, highly commercial country** and **R&B;** also **highly commercial rock.** Published *Champion* and "What A Friend" written and recorded by Ron Moore, on Morada Records.

Tips: "Write what the market wants because that is who will buy your music. Always try to be commercial and strive to write a hit. Most importantly, don't give up!"

R.D. CLEVÈRE MUSIKVERLAG, Postfach 2145, D-63243 Neu-Isenburg, **Germany.** Phone: (6102)51065. Fax: (6102)52696. Professional Manager: Tony Hermonez. GEMA. Music publisher. Estab. 1967. Publishes 700-900 songs/year; publishes 40 new songwriters/year. Works with composers and lyricists; teams collaborators. Pays standard royalty.

Affiliate(s): Big Sound Music, Hot Night Music, Lizzy's Blues Music, Max Banana Music, R.D. Clevère-Cocabana-Music, R.D. Clevère-Far East & Orient-Music, R.D. Clevère-America-Today-Music.

How to Contact: "Do not send advance letter(s) asking for permission to submit your song material, just send it." Prefers cassette with "no limit" on songs and lyric sheet. SAE and a minimum of two IRCs. Reports in 3 weeks.

Music: Mostly **pop, disco, rock, R&B, country** and **folk;** also **musicals** and **classic/opera.**

Tips: "If the song submitted is already produced/recorded professionally on 16/24-multitrack-tape and available, we can use this for synchronization with artists of the various record companies/record producers."

CLIENTELE MUSIC, 252 Bayshore Dr., Hendersonville TN 37075. (615)822-2364. Fax: (615)824-3400. Director: Thornton Cline. Music publisher. Estab. 1989. Publishes 15 songs/year; publishes 10 new songwriters/year. Works with composers and lyricists. Pays standard 50% royalty.

Affiliate(s): Clientele Music (ASCAP) and Incline Music (BMI).

How to Contact: Submit demo tape by mail—unsolicited submissions are OK. Prefers cassette with 1 song and lyric sheet. "Send only radio ready demos—your No. 1 songs." SASE. Reports in 3-4 weeks.

Music: Mostly **R&B/dance, pop/dance** and **pop/ballads;** also **soul, country** and **contemporary Christian.** Published "One Dance Away From Love" (by T. Cline/R. Ryan), recorded by Teena M. on Atlantic Records; "She Doesn't Know What She's Missing" (by Swiegoda/Cline), recorded by The Manhattans on Cardiac Records; and "Love Saved The Best for Last" (by Wilson/Cline), recorded by Billy and Sarah Gaines on ABC Productions Movie of the Week-TV movie "Notorious."

Tips: "Need killer, conversational lyrics (not trite) and killer, catchy strong melodies. Keep current. Be very professional when submitting! Submit typewritten lyrics and typed cover letters only!! Also, submit your bio or tell me what you've had recorded."

*CLING MUSIC PUBLISHING, P.O. Box 7731, Beverly Hills CA 90212-7731. (310)338-9976. President: Tina Thompson. Music publisher and record producer. Hires staff songwriters. Works with composers and lyricists; teams collaborators. Pays standard royalty.

How to Contact: Write and obtain permission to submit. Prefers cassette with lyric sheet. SASE. Reports in 6 weeks.

Music: Mostly **blues, rock** and **country;** also **jazz** and **rap.** Published "Love Must Go On" (by T. Thompson), recorded by King S. Miller (R&B); "Only A Fool" (by Kent Harris), recorded by Ty Karim (R&B); and "Movin & Groovin," written and recorded by J.D. Nichelson, all on Roach Records.

*CLOTILLE PUBLISHING (SOCAN), 9 Hector Ave., Toronto, Ontario M6G3G2 **Canada.** (416)533-3707. Manager: Al Kussin. Music publisher, record company (Slak Records) and record producer (Slak Productions). Estab. 1988. Publishes 5 songs/year; publishes 1 new songwriter/year. Teams collaborators. Pays standard royalty.

How to Contact: Submit a demo tape by mail—unsolicited submissions are OK. Prefers cassette with 3 songs and lyric sheet. "Recording quality must be sufficient to convey the total impact of song." SASE. Reports in 6 weeks.

Music: Mostly **pop, R&B** and **dance.** Published *Total Recall* (by A. Coelho/A. Kussin), recorded by A&A Groove Co. on Quality Records; and "Duck" (by M. Monroe), recorded by Mystah Monroe on Slak Records.

Tips: "Submit good commercial material with strong hooks and interesting form. On most submissions, lyrics are usually cliched and substandard. Production quality must be adequate to get the song across."

*COD OIL PRODUCTIONS LIMITED, Box 8568, St. John's, Newfoundland A1B 3P2 **Canada.** (709)579-2133. General Manager: Wilson Temple. Music publisher. Works with composers and lyricists. Pays standard 50% royalty.

How to Contact: Submit demo tape by mail. Unsolicited submissions OK. Prefers cassette and lyric sheet. SASE. Reports in 1 month.
Music: Mostly **country.**

COFFEE AND CREAM PUBLISHING COMPANY, Dept. SM, 1138 E. Price St., Philadelphia PA 19138. (215)842-3450. President: Bolden Abrams, Jr. Music publisher and record producer (Bolden Productions). ASCAP. Publishes 20 songs/year; publishes 4 new songwriters/year. Works with composers and lyricists; teams collaborators. Pays standard royalty.
How to Contact: Prefers cassette (or VHS videocassette) with 1-4 songs and lyric or lead sheets. Does not return unsolicited material. Reports in 2 weeks "if we're interested."
Music: Mostly **dance, pop, R&B, gospel** and **country.** Published "No Time for Tears" (by Bolden Abrams/Keith Batts), recorded by Gabrielle (R&B ballad); "Sly Like a Fox" (by Regine Urbach), recorded by Joy Duncan on Ultimate Records (pop/dance); "If I Let Myself Go" (by Jose Gomez/Sheree Sando), recorded by Evelyn "Champagne" King on RCA Records (pop/ballad).

*JERRY CONNELL PUBLISHING CO. (BMI), 130 Pilgrim Dr., San Antonio TX 78213. (210)344-5033. Partner: Jerry Connell. Music publisher and record producer. Publishes 75 songs/year; publishes 50 new songwriters/year. Works with composers and lyricists; teams collaborators. Pays standard royalty.
Affiliate(s): Old Bob Music. (ASCAP).
How to Contact: Submit demo tape by mail. Unsolicited submissions are OK. Prefers cassette with lyric or lead sheet (if possible). Does not return unsolicited material. Reports in 1 month.
Music: Mostly **country, gospel/religious** and **tejano;** also **jazz, easy listening** and **rock.** Published "Dos Tacos de Chorito Por Favor" (by Steve Mallett), recorded by Tom Frost on Indian Grass Records; "Ride Cowboy Ride" written and recorded by Richard Wolfe and *Chester Field Blues* written and recorded by Jimmy Jack, on Cherokee Records.
Tips: "A song should have a melody that is a grabber, a lyric that expresses familiar ideas in a new and unusual way and, most important, have a beginning, middle and end."

CONTINENTAL COMMUNICATIONS CORP., Dept. SM, 523 Route 303, Orangeburg NY 10962. (914)365-9093. President: Robert Schwartz. ASCAP, BMI. Estab. 1952. Music publisher and record company (Laurie Records and 3C Records). Publishes 50 songs/year; publishes 5-10 new songwriters/year. Works with composers and lyricists; teams collaborators. Pays standard royalty.
Affiliate(s): 3 Seas Music (ASCAP) and Northvale Music (BMI).
How to Contact: Submit demo tape—unsolicited submissions OK. Prefers cassette. SASE. "Submit only a few of the most commercial songs with lead sheets and demo." Reports in 3 weeks.
Music: Mostly **rock.** Published "Because of You," written and recorded by B. Sunkel on Laurie Records (pop); "Complicated," written and recorded by Allen Bros. on 3C Records (urban); and "Lament 62" (by D. Groom and P. Renari), recorded by D. Groom on Laurie Records (pop).

THE CORNELIUS COMPANIES, Dept. SM, Suite #1, 1017 17th Ave. S., Nashville TN 37212. (615)321-5333. Owner/Manager: Ron Cornelius. Music publisher and record producer (The Cornelius Companies, Ron Cornelius). BMI, ASCAP. Estab. 1987. Publishes 60-80 songs/year; publishes 2-3 new songwriters/year. Occasionally hires staff writers. Works with composers and lyricists; teams collaborators. Pays standard royalty.
Affiliate(s): RobinSparrow Music (BMI).
How to Contact: Write or call first and obtain permission to submit a tape. Prefers cassette with 2-3 songs. SASE. Reports in 2 months.
Music: Mostly **country** and **pop.** Published "Time Off for Bad Behavior" (by Lorry Latimer), recorded by Confederate Railroad on Atlantic Records; and "You're Slowly Going Out of My Mind" (by Gordon Dee), recorded by Southern Tracks; both on CBS Records; "These Colors Never Run" (by Gordon Dee).

COSGROVE MUSIC INC., P.O. Box 2234, Amagansett NY 11930. (516)329-0753. Fax: Same. President: Lance Cosgrove. Estab. 1989. Publishes 15 songs/year; publishes 4-8 new songwriters/year. Works with composers and lyricists. Pays standard royalty.
How to Contact: Submit demo tape—unsolicited submissions are OK. Prefers cassette with 1-2 songs and lyric sheet. "Send only the amount of songs requested." SASE. Reports in 1-2 months.
Music: Mostly **pop/rock, R&B** and **contemporary country;** also **heavy metal.** Published *Everything You Do (You're Sexing Me)* (by Beau Hill, Fiona and Lance Cosgrove), recorded by Fiona on Atlantic Records (LP); "Primetime Love" and "Red Lightning" (by Lance Cosgrove), recorded by Lance on Cosgrove Records.
Tips: "Send hit singles only. Don't waste time on album cuts."

COSMOTONE MUSIC, Suite 412, 3350 Highway 6, Houston TX 77478. Music publisher, record company (Cosmotone Records, Cosmotone Studios) and record producer. ASCAP. Estab. 1984. Publishes 10 songs/year; publishes 2 new songwriters/year. Works with lyricists; teams collaborators. Pays standard royalty.
How to Contact: Write first and obtain permission to submit a tape. Include SASE. "Will respond only if interested."
Music: All types. Published "Padre Pio," "Sonnet XVIII" and "O Let Me Be," all written and recorded by Lord Hamilton on Cosmotone Records (Christian/rock pop); and "Dance For Padre Pio" and "The True Measure of Love" by Rafael Brom (Christian progressive).

COTTAGE BLUE MUSIC, P.O. Box 121626, Nashville TN 37212. (615)726-3556. Contact: Neal James. Music publisher, record company (Kottage Records) and record producer (Neal James Productions). BMI. Estab. 1971. Publishes 30 songs/year; publishes 3 new songwriters/year. Receives 200 submissions/month. Works with composers only. Pays standard royalty of 50%.
Affiliate(s): James & Lee (BMI), Neal James Music (BMI) and Hidden Cove Music (ASCAP).
How to Contact: Submit demo tape—unsolicited submissions OK. Prefers cassette with 2 songs and lyric sheet. SASE. Reports in 4-6 weeks.
Music: Mostly country, gospel and rock/pop; also R&B. Published "Are You Sure?" (by P.J. Hawk/ Neal James), recorded by P.J. Hawk; "Room by Room" (by Hank Cochran/Neal James/Billy Don Burns) recorded by PJ Hawk (country); and "Thunder In Carolina" (by Jesse James), recorded by Doc Lee, all on Kottage Records.
Tips: "Screen material carefully before submitting."

COUNTRY BREEZE MUSIC, 1715 Marty, Kansas City KS 66103. (913)384-7336. President: Ed Morgan. Music publisher and record company (Country Breeze Records and Walkin' Hat Records). BMI, ASCAP. Estab. 1984. Publishes 100 songs/year; publishes 25-30 new songwriters/year. Receives 130 submissions/month. Teams collaborators. Pays standard royalty.
Affiliate(s): Walkin' Hat Music (ASCAP).
How to Contact: Submit a demo tape—unsolicited submissions are OK. Prefers cassette (or VHS videocassette) with 4-5 songs and lyric sheet. SASE. "The songwriter/artist should perform on the video as though on stage giving a sold-out performance. In other words put heart and soul into the project. Submit in strong mailing envelopes." Reports in 2 weeks.
Music: Mostly country (rock/pop/traditional), gospel (Southern/bluegrass and black) and rock. Published "Hangover Blues" (by J. Amburgey), recorded by Johnny Amburgey on Country Breeze Records; "Country Preacher" (by J. Amburgey), recorded by Montgomery Creek and *His Love* (by E. Morgan), recorded by Jackie Doss, both on Angel Star Records.
Tips: "Make sure your voice is clear and out front."

COUNTRY STAR MUSIC, 439 Wiley Ave., Franklin PA 16323. (814)432-4633. President: Norman Kelly. Music publisher, record company (Country Star, Process, Mersey and CSI) and record producer (Country Star Productions). ASCAP. Estab. 1970. Publishes 20-30 songs/year; publishes 2-3 new songwriters/year. Works with composers and lyricists; teams collaborators. Pays standard royalty.
Affiliate(s): Kelly Music Publications (BMI) and Process Music Publications (BMI).
How to Contact: Submit demo tape—unsolicited submissions are OK. Prefers cassette with 1-4 songs and lyric or lead sheet. SASE. Reports in 2 weeks.
Music: Mostly country (80%); also rock, gospel, MOR and R&B (5% each). Published "Lightning," written and recorded by George Medina on Mersey Records (rock); "Missing in Action" (by Len Marshall), recorded by Tom Booker (country); and "He Doesn't Love Here Anymore," written and recorded by Linn Roll (country), both on Country Star Records.
Tips: "Send only your best songs—ones you feel are equal to or better than current hits."

LOMAN CRAIG MUSIC, P.O. Box 111480, Nashville TN 37222-1480. (615)331-1219. President: Loman Craig. Engineer/Producer: Tommy Hendrick. Music publisher, record company (Bandit Records— HIS Records), record producer (Loman Craig Productions). BMI, ASCAP, SESAC. Estab. 1979. Publishes 15 songs/year; publishes 5 new songwriters/year. Works with composers and lyricists. Pays standard royalty.
Affiliate(s): Outlaw Music of Memphis (BMI), We Can Make It Music (BMI), Doulikit Music (SESAC), HIS Records (gospel) and Bandit Records (country).
How to Contact: Submit a demo tape by mail—unsolicited submissions are OK. Prefers cassette with 2-3 songs and lyric sheet. "Does not have to be a full production demo." SASE. Reports in 4-6 weeks.
Music: Mostly country and pop; also bluegrass and gospel. Published "I Can't See Me Gone" (Craig-Craig), recorded by James Bryan on Bandit Records; and "Between The Whiskey And The Beer," written and recorded by James Bryan on Bandit Records.

CREEKSIDE MUSIC, Dept. SM, 100 Labon St., Tabor City NC 28463. (919)653-2546. Owner: Elson H. Stevens. Music publisher, record company (Seaside Records) and record producer (Southern Sound Productions). BMI. Estab. 1978. Publishes 30 songs/year; publishes 5 new songwriters/year. Works with composers, lyricists; teams collaborators. Pays 25-50% royalty from record sales.
How to Contact: Submit demo tape—unsolicited submissions OK. Prefers cassette with 3 songs and lead sheets. SASE. Reports in 1 month.
Music: Mostly country, rock and gospel; also "**beach music.**" Published "I'll Never Say Never Again" (by G. Todd and S. Hart) and "Long Country Road" (by G. Taylor), both recorded by Sherry Collins (country); and "Heaven's Ready" (by E. Watson), recorded by The Watson Family (gospel), all on Seaside Records.
Tips: "Be original—search for 'the hook'."

CREOLE MUSIC LTD., The Chilterns, France Hill Dr., Camberley, Surrey GU15 3QA **England.** Director: Bruce White. Music publisher. PRS/MCPS. Estab. 1966. Publishes 20-30 songs/year; publishes 2-3 new songwriters/year. Teams collaborators. Pays standard royalty of 50% ("sometimes higher, 60-40%").
How to Contact: Submit a demo tape by mail—unsolicited submissions OK. Prefers cassette with 3-4 songs. SASE. Reports in 6 weeks.
Music: Mostly pop, dance and rock. Published "Sweet Cherrie," recorded by UB40 on Dep/Virgin Records (reggae); and "Up Town Sharon" (by E. Auld), recorded by In Crowd on Silver Edge Records (pop).
Tips: "We are seeking to acquire or sub publish 'active' publishing catalogs or single titles."

CSB KAMINSKY GMBH, Wilhelmstrasse 10, 2407 Bad Schwartau, **Germany.** Phone: (0451)21530. General Manager: Pia Kaminsky. GEMA, PRS. Music publisher and collecting agency. Estab. 1978. Publishes 2-4 songs/year; 1 new songwriter/year. Teams collaborators. Pays 50% if releasing a record; 85% if only collecting royalties.
Affiliate(s): Leosong Copyright Management, Ltd. (London, United Kingdom and Sydney, Australia).
How to Contact: Write and submit material. Prefers cassette or VHS videocassette. Does not return unsolicited material. Reports in 4 weeks.
Music: Mostly pop; also rock, country and reggae.

***CUDE & PICKENS PUBLISHING,** 519 N. Halifax Ave., Daytona Beach FL 32118. (904)252-0381. A&R Director: Bobby Lee Cude. Music publisher, record company and record producer. BMI. Estab. 1978. Publishes 12 songs/year. Pays standard royalty.
Affiliate(s): Blaster Boxx Hits (BMI).
How to Contact: Write first and obtain permission to submit. Does not return unsolicited material.
Music: Mostly country; also easy listening, gospel, MOR, top 40/pop and Broadway show. Published "Tony the Tenor," "Queenie" and "Star of the Show" (by Cude & Pickens), recorded by Fred Bogert on Hard Hat Records.

CUMBERLAND MUSIC GROUP, INC., Suite 175, 42 Music Square West, Nashville TN 37203. (615)865-7685. C.E.O.: Michael E. Lawson. Music publisher and record company (Psychotronic). Works with musicians/artists and songwriters on contract. Royalty varies per contract; statutory rate to publishers per song on records.
Affiliate(s): Obfuscated Music (ASCAP), Cucumberland Music (SESAC), Perspicacious Music (BMI), Psychotronic Publishing (BMI), S.U.Y.T. Publishing (BMI), zzi music (ASCAP).
How to Contact: Submit demo tape—unsolicited submissions OK. Prefers cassette, DAT or VHS videocassette (if available) with 3-5 songs and lyric sheet. SASE. Reports in 2 months.
Music: Mostly folk, bluegrass, rock, pop, jazz, blues and college alternative. "No gospel." Published "Throwing Stones" (by Tommy Thompson); "Maria" (by John Keane) and "Rose on Fire" (by J. Thomas Griffith), all recorded by The Dillards on Vanguard Records (folk rock).
Tips: "Have patience, we will contact you if we can use material."

CUNNINGHAM MUSIC, Dept. SM, 23494 Lahser, Southfield MI 48034. (313)948-9787. President: Jerome Cunningham. Music publisher. BMI. Estab. 1988. Publishes 8-9 songs/year; publishes 2 new songwriters/year. Teams collaborators. Pays standard royalty.
How to Contact: Submit a demo tape by mail—unsolicited submissions are OK. Prefers cassette (or VHS videocassette if available) with 3 songs and lyric sheet. SASE. Reports in 3 weeks.
Music: Mostly R&B, gospel and jazz; also pop and rock. Published "Can't Teach Old Dog Tricks" written and recorded by Vernon B. on 2-Hot Records (R&B).
Tips: Main reason for rejection of submitted material includes: "Incomplete songs, no melody involved. Overall, just poorly prepared presentations."

CUPIT MUSIC (BMI), P.O. Box 121904, Nashville TN 37212. (615)731-0100. President: Jerry Cupit. Music publisher and record producer (Jerry Cupit Productions). Publishes 30 songs/year; publishes 6 new songwriters/year. Hires staff songwriters. Works with composers and lyricists; teams collaborators. Pays standard 50% royalty.
Affiliate(s): Cupit Memaries (ASCAP).
How to Contact: Not accepting unsolicited material at this time.
Music: Mostly **country, Southern rock** and **gospel/contemporary Christian**. Published *I Know What You Got Up Your Sleeve* recorded by Hank Williams Jr. on Warner Bros. Records; "Jukebox Junkie," recorded by Ken Mellons on Epic Records; and "For Crying Out Loud," recorded by Clinton Gregory on Step One Records.
Tips: "Keep vocals up front on demos, study correct structure, always tie all lines to hook!"

D.S.M. PRODUCERS INC., 161 W. 54th, New York NY 10019. (212)245-0006. Producer: Suzan Bader. Music publisher, record producer and management firm (American Steel Management Co.). ASCAP. Estab. 1979. Publishes 25 songs/year; publishes 10 new songwriters/year. "Publishes and releases 10 CDs a year for TV, feature films and radio." Works with composers and lyricists. Pays standard royalty.
Affiliate(s): Decidedly Superior Music (BMI).
How to Contact: Write or call first and obtain permission to submit. Prefers cassette (or VHS videocassette) and lyric or lead sheet. SASE. "Include SASE or we do not review nor respond to material." Reports in 3 months.
Music: Mostly **top 40, R&B/dance, CHR** and **rock**; also **jazz, country** and **instrumental tracks for background music**. Published "I've Been Hurt," written and recorded by H. Lacy (R&B, rock); "Little Thing in Life," written and recorded by Peter Halperin (R&B, jazz); and "Saloon Goonies," written and recorded by Ron Mendelsohn, both on AACL Records (comedy).
Tips: "Get your demo to sound like a master. Now looking for instrumental master."

DAGENE MUSIC, P.O. Box 410851, San Francisco CA 94141. (415)822-1530. President: David Alston. Music publisher, record company (Cabletown Corp.) and record producer (Classic Disc Production). ASCAP. Estab. 1986. Hires staff songwriters. Works with composers; teams collaborators. Pays standard royalty.
Affiliate(s): Dagene Music, 1956 Music.
How to Contact: Write or call first and obtain permission to submit a tape. Prefers cassette with 2 songs and lyric sheet. "Be sure to obtain permission before sending any material." Does not return unsolicited material. Reports in 1 month.
Music: Mostly **R&B/rap, dance** and **pop**. Published "Mind Ya Own" (by Bernard Henderson/Marcus Justice), recorded by 2wo-Dominatorz on Dagene Records; "Started Life" (by David/M. Campbell), recorded by Star Child on Dagene Records; and "Lies," written and recorded by David on Cabletown Records (all rap).
Tips: "It's what's in the groove that makes people move."

DAN THE MAN MUSIC, Suite 12, 19465 Lorain Rd., Cleveland OH 44126-1957. President: Daniel L. Bischoff. Music publisher, record company (Dan The Man Records) and management firm (Daniel Bischoff Management). ASCAP, BMI. "We have some major label connections. Always looking for top country hit material. Also interested in strong pop-rock material." Pays standard royalty.
Affiliate(s): Bischoff Music Publishing Co. (BMI). Long Island Music (ASCAP).
How to Contact: Submit a demo tape—unsolicited submissions OK. Please send cassette or VHS tape and lyrics. Does not return unsolicited material. Reports in 1 month.
Music: Country, pop/rock. Published "Gently Break A Heart" (by C. Brumfield) and "Just a Heartache Ago" (by A. Glenn Duke), both recorded by Tommy Becker on Dan The Man Records (country).

DARBONNE PUBLISHING CO., Dept. SM, Route 3, Box 172, Haynesville LA 71038. (318)927-5253. President: Edward N. Dettenheim. Music publisher and record company (Wings Record Co.). BMI. Estab. 1987. Publishes 50 songs/year; publishes 8-10 new songwriters/year. Works with composers and lyricists; teams collaborators. Pays standard royalty.
How to Contact: Submit a demo tape—unsolicited submissions are OK. Prefers cassette or 7½ ips reel-to-reel with up to 12 songs and lyric sheet. SASE. Reports in 6 weeks.
Music: Mostly **country** and **gospel**. Published "Bitter Taste of Leaving," written and recorded by T.J. Lynn on Wings Records (country); "Mama" (by E. Dettenheim), recorded by Donna Ray on Wings Records (country); and "Turner Hotel" (by E. Dettenheim), recorded by T.J. Lynn on Wings Records (country).
Tips: "The better the demo—the better your chances of interesting your listener."

DE DAN MUSIC, Dept. SM, 200 Regent Dr., Winston-Salem NC 27103. (919)768-1298. Contact: Dave Passerallo. Music publisher, record company (Boom/Power Play Records) and record producer (Boom Productions Inc.). BMI. Estab. 1989. Publishes 24 songs/year; publishes 2 new songwriters/year. Teams collaborators. Pays standard royalty.

How to Contact: Write first and obtain permission to submit a tape. Prefers cassette or VHS video-cassette with 2 songs and lead sheet. SASE. Reports in 3 weeks.
Music: Mostly **pop** and **rock**; also **rap**. Published "I Wanna Know," by Rodney Ballad and John Cody; "Ripped Jeans" and "The Good Ones," both written by John Cody; all produced by D. Passerallo for Boom Productions on Boom/Powerplay Records.
Tips: "Submissions must be worthy of national release and have mass appeal."

THE EDWARD DE MILES MUSIC COMPANY, 8th Floor, 4475 Allisonville Rd., Indianapolis IN 46205. (317)546-2912 or 549-9006. Attn: Professional Manager. Music publisher, record company (Sahara Records), management, bookings and promotions. BMI. Estab. 1984. Publishes 50-75 songs/year; publishes 5 new songwriters/year. Hires staff songwriters. Works with composers and lyricists; teams collaborators. Pays standard royalty of 50%.
How to Contact: Submit demo tape — unsolicited submissions OK. Prefers cassette with 1-3 songs and a lyric sheet. SASE. Reports in 1 month.
Music: Mostly **top 40 pop/rock, R&B/dance** and **C&W**; also **musical scores for TV, radio, films and jingles.** Published "Dance Wit Me" and "Moments," written and recorded by Steve Lynn (R&B); and "No Mercy" (by D. Evans and A. Mitchell), recorded by Multiple Choice (rap), all on Sahara Records.
Tips: "Copyright all songs before submitting to us."

DEAN ENTERPRISES MUSIC GROUP, Dept. SM, P.O. Box 620, Redwood Estates CA 95044-0620. (408)353-1006. Attn: Executive Director. Music publisher, record producer, record company (Centaur Records); Member: NAS, TSA, CMRRA, NARAS, Harry Fox Agency. Estab. 1989. Publishes 4-6 songs/year; publishes 3-5 new songwriters/year. Pays standard royalty to writers.
Affiliate(s): Whispering Echoes Music (ASCAP), Mikezel Music Co. (ASCAP), Teenie Deanie Music Co. (BMI) and Minotaur Records.
How to Contact: "Unsolicited submissions are OK. Prefers maximum of 6 songs with typed lyric sheets and brief letter of introduction. Material must be copyrighted and unassigned. Prefers to keep tapes on file, but will return if fully paid SASE is included. A free evaluation is given with first class SASE, even if tape not returned. Reports in 2-6 weeks. PLEASE, no phone calls. Show name, address, phone number and (c) sign on tape and lyric sheets."
Music: Mostly **country, pop, novelty, MOR/easy listening, soft/easy rock, dance (Hi NRG, house, pop), folk, top 40, R&B.** No instrumentals, rap music, jazz, heavy metal, punk/acid rock. Published The Memory Brothers and Bobby Petersen.
Tips: "Learn to handle rejection. Listen to the feedback you get. Learn your craft. Join songwriting organizations, read songwriting books and network as much as possible. Opportunity, talent and connections are the name of the game in the music industry. Watch out for the sharks. NEVER pay to have your song published or recorded if you're a songwriter."

DELEV MUSIC COMPANY, 7231 Mansfield Ave., Philadelphia PA 19138-1620. (215)276-8861. President: W. Lloyd Lucas. Music publisher, record company (Surprize Records, Inc.), record producer and management. BMI, ASCAP, SESAC, SGA, and CMRRA. Publishes 6-10 songs/year; publishes 6-10 new songwriters/year. Pays standard royalty.
Affiliate(s): Sign of the Ram Music (ASCAP), Gemini Lady Music (SESAC), and Delev Music (BMI).
How to Contact: Submit demo tape — unsolicited submissions OK. Prefers cassette (or VHS videocassette) with 1-3 songs and lyric sheet. Send all letter size correspondence and cassette submissions to: P.O. Box 6562, Philadelphia, PA 19138-6562. Larger than letter-size to the Mansfield Avenue address. "Video must be in VHS format and as professionally done as possible. It does not necessarily have to be done at a professional video studio, but should be a very good quality production showcasing artist's performance." SASE. "We will not accept certified mail." Reports in 1 month.
Music: **R&B ballad** and **dance-oriented, pop ballads, crossover** and **country/western.** Published "If Love Comes Again" (by Tyrone W. Brown); "Say It Again" (by Richard Hamersma & Gerry Magallan); and "Tomorrow" (by Jerry Dean Lester, Wayne Gamache & lazlo nemeth), all recorded by Jerry Dean on Surprize Records.
Tips: "Songs submitted must be lyrically and melodically strong with good strong hook lines, and tell a story that will appeal to and be related to by the radio-listening and record-buying public. Most important is that the demo be a clear quality product with understandable vocal and lyrics out front."

FRANK DELL MUSIC, Box 7171, Duluth MN 55807. (218)628-3003. President: Frank Dell. Music publisher, record company, record producer and management. Estab. 1980. Publishes 2 songs/year. Works with composers and lyricists; teams collaborators. Pays standard royalty.

Affiliate(s): Albindell Music (BMI).

How to Contact: Submit demo tape by mail. Unsolicited submissions are OK. Prefers cassette. SASE. Reports in 3 weeks.

Music: Mostly **country, gospel** and **pop.** Published "Memories," written and recorded by Frank Dell; "She'll Be There" (by F. Dell and D. Yargling) and *Where Rose Never Fades* (by various), both recorded by Frank Dell all on MSM Records (country).

*DELPHA'S MUSIC PUBLISHERS (BMI), Box 329, Mulberry AR 72947. (501)997-1557. Fax: (501)997-1557. CEO: Delpha J. Rosson. Music publisher. Estab. 1989. Publishes 1 song/year; publishes 2 new songwriters/year. Works with lyricists; teams collaborators. Pays standard royalty.

How to Contact: Submit demo tape by mail. Unsolicited submissions are OK. Prefers cassette with 1 song and lyric sheet. "Prefers copyrighted material." SASE. Reports in 4-6 weeks.

Music: Mostly **country, pop** and **gospel.** Published "The Liberator" (by Gibbs/Ridener), recorded by Charlie Ridener on Bolder Bluff Records.

Tips: "Make sure that your song is protected before you send it to anyone. Do not pay anyone for publishing."

DEMI MONDE RECORDS & PUBLISHING LTD., Foel Studio, Llanfair Caereinion, POWYS, **Wales.** Phone: (0938)810758 and (0952)883962. Managing Director: Dave Anderson. Music publisher, record company (Demi Monde Records & Publishing Ltd.), record producer (Dave Anderson). Member MCPS. Estab. 1983. Publishes 50-70 songs/year; publishes 10-15 new songwriters/year. Works with composers and lyricists; teams collaborators. Pays standard royalty.

How to Contact: Submit a demo tape—unsolicited submissions are OK. Prefers cassette (or VHS videocassette) with 3-4 songs. SAE and IRC. Reports in 1 month.

Music: Mostly **rock, R&B** and **pop.** Published "I Feel So Lazy" (by D. Allen), recorded by Gong (rock); "Phalarn Dawn" (by E. Wynne), recorded by Ozric Tentacles (rock); and "Pioneer" (by D. Anderson), recorded by Amon Dual (rock), all on Demi Monde Records.

DENNY MUSIC GROUP, Dept. SM, 3325 Fairmont Dr., Nashville TN 37203-1004. (615)269-4847. Contact: Pandora Denny. ASCAP, BMI, SESAC. Estab. 1983. Music publisher, record company (Dollie Record Co., Jed Record Production) and record producer. "Also owns Denny's Den, a 24-track recording studio designed for songwriters, which won a Grammy in 1990." Publishes 100 songs/year; 20 new songwriters/year. Works with composer and lyricists; teams collaborators. Pays standard royalty.

How to Contact: Write or call first and obtain permission to submit. Prefers cassette with 3 songs and lyric sheet. Reports in 6 weeks.

Music: Mostly **country, gospel** and **MOR.** Published "Cashmere Cowboy" (by F. Hannaway, country); "Inside Information" (by J. Martin, R&B); and "Closer to You" (by T. Rooney, pop).

DIAMOND WIND MUSIC, P.O. Box 311, Estero FL 33928. (813)267-3957. Fax: (813)267-6000. President: Reenie Diamond. Music publisher, record company (Diamond Wind Records) and record producer (Diamond Wind Productions). BMI. Estab. 1991. Publishes 25-50 songs/year; publishes 10 new songwriters/year. Works with composers and lyricists; teams collaborators. Pays standard royalty.

How to Contact: Write first and obtain permission to submit. Prefers cassette (or VHS videocassette) with 3 songs and lyric sheet. "Photo and bio extremely helpful." Does not return unsolicited material. Reports in 4-6 weeks.

Music: Mostly **country, country blues** and **country pop/rock;** also **pop** and **R&B.** Published "Thunder In My Heart" and "Mama I Love You" (by M.L. Northam), recorded by Bronze Bonneville on Continental Records (country); and "Diamond Den," written and recorded by Reenie Diamond on Diamond Wind Records (country).

Tips: "Prepare your demo thoughtfully with a clean, upfront vocal. If you are a self-contained singer/ songwriter, be willing to invest in your own career."

DINGO MUSIC, 4, Galleria Del Corso, Milan **Italy** 20122. Phone: (02)76021141. Fax: 0039/2/76021141. Managing Director: Guido Palma. Music publisher and record company (Top Records). SIAE. Estab. 1977. Publishes 30-35 songs/year; publishes 5 new songwriters/year. Hires staff writers. Works with composers and lyricists. Pays standard royalty of 50% and 10% on printed copies.

Affiliate(s): Top Records, Kiwi, Sap, Smoking.

How to Contact: Submit demo tape by mail—unsolicited submissions are OK. Prefers cassette with 2 songs. Reports in 1 month with International Reply Coupon enclosed.

Music: Mostly interested in **rock, pop** and **R&B** (pop); also **New Age** and **gospel.** Published "Il Cuore E' Nudo . . . e I Pesci Cantano" (by Ivan Cattaneo) on Top Records; "Per un po" (by Palma) on Dingo Records (pop); "Giovani Leoni" (by Paolo Luciani) on Top Records, "Emozioni Vietate Agli Adulti" (by Gianluca Perrone) on Dingo Records (pop).

DIRECT MANAGEMENT GROUP, #G, 947 N. La Cienega Bl., Los Angeles CA 90069. (310)854-3535. Partners: Martin Kirkup and Steve Jensen. ASCAP, BMI. Estab. 1989. Publishes 10 songs/year; publishes 2-5 new songwriters/year. Works with composers and lyricists; teams collaborators. Pays variable royalty.
Affiliate(s): Direct World Music (ASCAP), Direct Planet Music (BMI).
How to Contact: Write first and obtain permission to submit with reply card enclosed. Prefers cassette with 3 songs and lyric and lead sheet. SASE. Reports in 3 months.
Music: Rock, pop and **alternative.** Published "Our Last Time" (by Hanes), recorded by The Robert Cray Band on Mercury Records.

*DISCAPON PUBLISHING CO., Box 3082, Lic NY 11103. (718)721-5599. Contact: Discapon. Music publisher (Discapon). ASCAP. Estab. 1980. Publishes 100 songs/year. Works with composers. Pays standard royalty.
How to Contact: Write or call first and obtain permission to submit. Does not return unsolicited material. Prefers cassette with 2-6 songs. SASE. Reports in 2 months.
Music: Mostly **background music without words;** also **classical.**

*DISCOVERING MUSIC LTD., Room A, Haven Commercial Bldg. 24/F, Tsing Fung St., **Hong Kong.** Phone: (852)8071297. General Manager: Keith Yip. Music publisher. C.A.S.H. Estab. 1986. Publishes 20-30 songs/year; publishes 2-3 new songwriters/year. Pays standard royalty.
How to Contact: Submit a demo tape by mail—unsolicited submissions are OK. Prefers cassette. Does not return unsolicited material. Reports in 1 week.
Music: Mostly **pop, R&B** and **rock.**

*D'NICO INTERNATIONAL, 1627 N. Laurel Ave., Los Angeles CA 90046. (213)650-1334. Manager: Dino Nicolosi. Music publisher. Estab. 1983. Works with composers. Pays standard royalty.
Affiliate(s): Tillandsia Music, Unche Chico Music, EP2, DYCA Music, Ana Hi Music (ASCAP), D'Nico Music, Amanza Music, Ben Conga Music, Axel Music, L.B. Wilde Music, Diam Music (BMI).
How to Contact: Submit demo tape by mail. Unsolicited submissions are OK. Prefers cassette and lyric sheet. Does not return unsolicited material. Reports in 2 months.
Music: Mostly **pop-dance, pop rock** and **Latin;** also **R&B, ballads** and **70's music.** Published *It's A Latin Thing* (by A. Rubalcava/D. Snyder), recorded by Gerardo on Interscope Records; "Vanidosa" (by Bibi Cross-Nicolosi), recorded by Timberiche on Tonovsa Records; "Sueno Contigo" (by Ana Hi), recorded by Jose Alberto on Sony Records; and *No Se Tu*, recorded by Armando Manzanero on WEA Latina.

DOC PUBLISHING, 2514 Build America Drive, Hampton VA 23666. (804)827-8733. A&R: Judith Guthro. Music publisher. SESAC, BMI, ASCAP, SOCAN. Estab. 1975. Publishes 30-40 songs/year; 20 new songwriters/year. Works with composers and lyricists; teams collaborators. Pays standard royalty.
Affiliate(s): Dream Machine (SESAC), Doc Holiday Music (ASCAP).
How to Contact: Submit a demo tape—unsolicited submissions are OK. Does not return submissions. Reports in 2 weeks.
Music: Mostly **country** and **cajun.** Published "Mr. Jones—The Final Chapter," written and recorded by Big Al Downing; "Cajun Stripper," written and recorded by Doug Kershaw; and "Two Hearts," written and recorded by Jon Washington of the Fortunes.

*DON DEL MUSIC (BMI), 902 N. Webster, Port Washington WI 53074. (414)284-5242. Manager: Joseph C. DeLucia. Music publisher, record company (Cha Cha Records) and music promoter—"Wisconsin Singer/Songwriter Series." Estab. 1955. Works with composers and lyricists. Pays standard royalty (negotiable).
How to Contact: Write and obtain permission to submit. Prefers cassette with 4-6 songs and lyric sheet. "A simple arrangement is much better than a major production—make sure the lyrics can be heard." SASE. Reports in 2 months.
Music: Mostly **acoustic folk, country** and **R&B.**

*DORÉ RECORDS (ASCAP), 1608 Argyle, Hollywood CA 90028. (213)462-6614. Fax: (213)462-6197. President: Lew Bedell. Music publisher and record company. Estab. 1960. Publishes 15 songs/year; publishes 15 new songwriters/year. Pays standard royalty. Artist royalties vary.
How to Contact: Submit demo tape by mail. Unsolicited submissions are OK. Prefers cassette and lyric sheet. Does not return unsolicited material. Reports in 2 weeks.
Music: Mostly **all kinds;** also **novelty** and **comedy.** Published *Percolator* (by Biden & Freeman), recorded by the Ventures on EMI Records; and *Ten-Uh-See*, written and recorded by Steve Rumph on Dore Records.
Tips: "Currently seeking an R&B group with male lead vocals. No rap."

BUSTER DOSS MUSIC, Box 13, Estill Springs TN 37330. (615)649-2577. President: Buster Doss. Music publisher and record company (Stardust). BMI. Estab. 1959. Publishes 500 songs/year; publishes 50 new songwriters/year. Teams collaborators. Pays standard royalty.
How to Contact: Write or call first and obtain permission to submit a tape. Prefers cassette with 2 songs and lyric sheets. SASE. Reports in 1 week.
Music: Mostly **country;** also **rock.** Published "Blue Monday" (by Buster Doss), recorded by Tommy D on Doss Records; "High As A Kite," written and recorded by Mick O'Reilly on Thunderhawk Records; and "Knocks Me to My Knees" (by Steve Ledford), recorded by Linda Wunder on Stardust Records.

*DREAM SEQUENCE MUSIC, LTD. (BMI), P.O. Box 2194, Charlottesville VA 22902. (804)295-1877. President: Kevin McNoidy. Music publisher. Estab. 1987. Publishes 12-15 songs/year; publishes 2-3 new songwriters/year. Works with composers and lyricists; teams collaborators. Usually pays standard royalty, "but everything is negotiable."
How to Contact: Submit demo tape by mail. Unsolicited submissions are OK. Prefers cassette with 3-5 songs and lyric sheet. Does not return unsolicited material. Reports in 3-4 weeks.
Music: Mostly **rock, pop** and **R&B.** Published *The Next Room,* written and recorded by Modern Logic (pop); *Silent Eyes,* written and recorded by Melissa McGinty (ballad); and *Fire* (by Michael Levine), recorded by Watertown (rock), all on DSM, Ltd.

DUANE MUSIC, INC., 382 Clarence Ave., Sunnyvale CA 94086. (408)739-6133. President: Garrie Thompson. Music publisher. BMI. Publishes 10-20 songs/year; publishes 1 new songwriter/year. Pays standard royalty.
Affiliate(s): Morhits Publishing (BMI).
How to Contact: Prefers cassette with 1-2 songs. SASE. Reports in 1 month.
Music: Blues, country, disco, easy listening, rock, soul and **top 40/pop.** Published "Little Girl," recorded by The Syndicate of Sound & Ban (rock); "Warm Tender Love," recorded by Percy Sledge (soul); and "My Adorable One," recorded by Joe Simon (blues).

DUPUY RECORDS/PRODUCTIONS/PUBLISHING, INC., 2505 North Verdugo Rd., Glendale CA 91208. (818)241-6732. President: Pedro Dupuy. Music publisher, record company and record producer. ASCAP. Songwriters Guild. Estab. 1980. Publishes 50 songs/year; publishes 4 new songwriters/year. Works with composers and lyricists; teams collaborators. Hires staff writers. Pays standard royalty.
How to Contact: Write or call first about your interest or arrange a personal interview. Prefers cassette with 2-4 songs and lyric sheet. SASE. Reports in 1 month.
Music: Mostly **R&B** and **pop;** also **easy listening, jazz, MOR, soul** and **top 40.** Published "Find a Way," "I Don't Wanna Know," "Precious Love," "Livin for Your Love" and "Show Me The Way," all written and recorded by Gordon Gilman. Other artists include Robert Feeney, John Anthony and Kimo Kane.
Tips: "Songs should have very definitive lyrics with hook."

*EARITATING MUSIC PUBLISHING (BMI), P.O. Box 1101, Gresham OR 97030. Owner: Steve Montague. Music publisher. Estab. 1979. Publishes 0-40 songs/year; publishes 0-5 new songwriters/year. Works with composers or lyricists; teams collaborators. Pays individual per song contract, usually greater than 50% to writer.
How to Contact: Submit demo tape by mail. Unsolicited submissions are OK. Prefers cassette with lyric sheet. "Submissions should be copyrighted by the author. We will deal for rights if interested." Does not return unsolicited material. No reply unless interested.
Music: Mostly **rock, contemporary Christian** and **country;** also **folk.**
Tips: "Melody is most important, lyrics second. Style and performance take a back seat to these. A good song will stand with just one voice and one instrument."

*EARTH DANCE MUSIC, P.O. Box 241, Newbury Park CA 91320. (805)499-9912. Fax: (805)499-9047. President: Gil Yslas. Music publisher. Estab. 1990. Publishes 90-120 songs/year; publishes 6-10 new songwriters/year. Hires staff writers. Works with composers. Pays standard royalty.
How to Contact: Write first and obtain permission to submit. Prefers cassette. "Interested in master quality catalogs." Does not return unsolicited material. Reports in 1 month.
Music: Mostly **instrumental, TV-background** and **world music;** also **adult contemporary** and **new acoustic.** *The Unicorn,* written and recorded by R. Searles; and *Winter Air,* written and recorded by Aerial Logic, both on Sundown Records.

EARTHSCREAM MUSIC PUBLISHING CO., 8377 Westview Dr., Houston TX 77055. (713)464-GOLD. Contact: Jeff Johnson. Music publisher, record company and record producer. Estab. 1975. BMI. Publishes 12 songs/year; publishes 4 new songwriters/year. Pays standard royalty.

Affiliate(s): Village Sky Music (ASCAP).
How to Contact: Prefers cassette (or videocassette) with 2-5 songs and lyric sheet. SASE. Reports in 6 weeks.
Music: New rock, country and **top 40/pop.** Published "Ride of a Lifetime" (by Greg New), recorded by Billy Rutherford on Earth Records; "Goodbye Sexy Carol" written and recorded by Terry Mitchell (new age) and "Do You Remember" (by Pennington/Wells), recorded by Perfect Strangers (pop rock), on Weeny Dog Records.

ECCENTRAX MUSIC CO., 80855 Coon Creek Rd., Armada MI 48005. (517)348-1136. President: Debbie Coulon. Music publisher (Multi-Music Management). ASCAP. Estab. 1990. Publishes 3 songs/year; publishes 2 new songwriters/year. Works with composers and lyricists; teams collaborators. Pays standard royalty.
How to Contact: Write first and obtain permission to submit. Prefers cassette with 3 songs and lyric sheet. "Please make sure lyrics are understandable." SASE. Reports in 6-8 weeks.
Music: Mostly **pop, country** and **rock;** also **children's** and **R&B.** Published "Until That Day" and "It Happens," written and recorded by Allen Bondar; and "When I'm With You" (by A. Bondar/V. Ripp), recorded by G. Worth, all on Eccentrax Records.
Tips: "Include your name and address on demo tape and typed lyrics."

*EDITION MUSICA, Webgasse 43, Vienna A-1060 **Austria.** Phone: (1)597-56-46. Publishing Manager: Michael Hufnagl. Music publisher and record company (OK-Musica). AKM. Estab. 1982. Works with composers and lyricists; teams collaborators.
How to Contact: Submit a demo tape by mail—unsolicited submissions are OK or call first and obtain permission to submit. Prefers cassette with 4-6 songs. Does not return unsolicited material. Reports in 2 weeks.
Music: Mostly **rock, pop** and **dance.**
Tips: "Send us a demo. If we have an artist for it we will release it."

ELECT MUSIC PUBLISHING, P.O. Box 22, Underhill VT 05489. (802)899-3787. Founder: Bobby Hackney. Music publisher and record company (LBI Records). BMI. Estab. 1980. Publishes 24 songs/year; publishes 3 new songwriters/year. Works with composers and/or lyricists; teams collaborators. Pays standard royalty.
How to Contact: Submit a demo tape by mail—unsolicited submissions are OK. Prefers cassette and VHS videocassette with 3-4 songs and lyric sheet. SASE. Reports in 4-6 weeks.
Music: Mostly **reggae, R&B** and **rap;** also **New Age, rock** and some **country.** Published "Serious," recorded by The Hackneys; "Keeping My Eye On You," recorded by Lambsbread; and "Like An Ocean," recorded by Karrie Taylor; all written by Bobby Hackney and recorded on LBI Records.
Tips: "Be patient, always send proper SASE for your tape and bio."

*ELEMENT MOVIE AND MUSIC, Box 30260, Bakersfield CA 93385. Producer: Jar the Superstar. Music publisher, record company and record producer. BMI. Publishes 2 songs/year; publishes 2 new songwriters/year. Hires staff writers. Pays standard royalty.
How to Contact: Write first about your interest or arrange personal interview. "Query with resume of credits. Do not mail songs without permission! We are taking interviews only." Prefers 15 ips reel-to-reel or cassette with 1-3 songs. Does not return unsolicited material. Reports in 3 months.
Music: Mostly **R&B, rock, soul, gospel, jazz, progressive, easy listening** and **top 40/pop;** also **blues, children's, choral, church/religious, classical, country, dance-oriented, MOR, Spanish** and **music for feature films.** Published "The Enegy Conspiracy" from the soundtrack album on Element Records; "She's Sweet to Me" (by Jar the Superstar); "God Will Post Your Bail" (by Judge A. Robertson) (Christian pop); "What Could I'll Done Without Jesus Around" (by Jar the Superstar); and "Put Nothing Over God" (by Jar the Superstar) on Element Records (church rock).

EMANDELL TUNES, 10220 Glade Ave., Chatsworth CA 91311. (818)341-2264. President/Administrator: Leroy C. Lovett, Jr. Estab. 1979. Publishes 6-12 songs/year; 3-4 new songwriters. Receives 10-15 submissions/month. Pays standard royalty.
Affiliate(s): Ben-Lee Music (BMI), Birthright Music (ASCAP), Northworth Songs, Chinwah Songs, Gertrude Music (all SESAC); LMS Print/Publishings Co. and Nadine LTD, Music/Artist Management Company, Stein am Rhien, Switzerland.
How to Contact: Write first to get permission to submit tape. Prefers cassette (or videocassette) with 4-5 songs and lead or lyric sheet. Include bio of writer, singer or group. SASE. Reports in 4-6 weeks.
Music: Inspirational, contemporary gospels and **chorals.** Published "Surely Goodness and Mercy" (by Kevin Allen & Peppy Smith) on WFL Records; "Blessed Assurance" (new adaptation/arrangement by Alisa Caston), on K-Tel Records (Gospel Compilation); and "Everlasting Love" (by Phil Stewart), recorded by Mississippi Mass Choir on Savoy Records. Licensed "How I Got Over" (Clara Ward)

Gertrude Music on TV mini-series, "Call To Glory" and "Come on Children" (Edwin Hawkins) Birthright Music in Syndication—"Laverne & Shirley."
Tips: "Always submit top quality sounding demo. Keep it simple, and send bio about writer(s)."

*EMF PRODUCTIONS, Suite D, 1000 E. Prien Lake Rd., Lake Charles LA 70601. (318)474-0435. President: Ed Frege. Music publisher, record producer. Estab. 1984. Works with composers and lyricists. Pays standard 50% royalty.
How to Contact: Submit demo tape by mail. Unsolicited submissions are OK. Prefers cassette (or VHS videocassette) with 4 songs and lyric sheet. Does not return material. Reports in 6 weeks.
Music: Mostly **R&B, pop, rock**; also **country, gospel.**

*EMPEROR OF EMPERORS (ASCAP), 16133 Fairview Ave., Fontana CA 92336. (909)355-2372. Producer: Stephen V. Mann. Music publisher, record company, record producer (Emperor Productions) and distributor. Estab. 1979. Publishes 250-1,000 songs/year; publishes 50 new songwriters/year. Hires staff writers. Works with composers and lyricists; teams collaborators. Pays standard royalty in most cases, but negotiable.
How to Contact: Submit demo tape by mail. Unsolicited submissions are OK. Prefers cassette album material with 12-15 songs and lyric or lead sheet. Quality stressed instead of quantity. Material is kept on file.
Music: Mostly **rock & roll, pop** and **country/western**; also **rap, jazz, soul, heavy metal, gospel, traditional Indian, New Age, folk, techno, blues,** and **reggae.** Published *Black Flight* and *Sign of the Times*, written and recorded by Blues Bo Jack; and *Joshey Junume* (by Stephen V. Mann), recorded by Mala Ganguly, all on Emperor of Emperors.
Tips: "Melody should be suitable for motion picture soundtracks. Top-notch quality only."

EMPTY SKY MUSIC COMPANY, 14th St., P.O. Box 626, Verplanck NY 10596. Promotional Manager: Lisa Lancaster. Music publisher, record company (Empty Sky, Yankee, Verplanck) and record producer (Rick Carbone for Empty Sky). ASCAP, BMI. Estab. 1982. Publishes 15-20 songs/year; publishes 10 new songwriters/year. Works with composer and lyricists; teams collaborators. Pays standard royalty.
Affiliate(s): Empty Sky Music (ASCAP) and Rick Carbone Music (BMI).
How to Contact: Submit a demo tape by mail—unsolicited submissions are OK. Prefers cassette with 3-5 songs and lyric sheet. SASE. Reports in 3-4 months.
Music: Mostly **country, gospel** and **pop**; also **rap, rock** and **rap/gospel.** Published "You'll Never Guess" (by William Indelli), recorded by The Dependents; "Made in the Shade," written and recorded by Leo Stephens, both on Empty Sky Records; and "You're a Part of Me," written and recorded by Bob Martinson on RCM Records.
Tips: "Send quality cassette tapes, not cheap 2 for $1.00 cassettes."

EMZEE MUSIC, Box 3213, S. Farmingdale NY 11735. (516)420-9169. President: Maryann Zalesak. Music publisher, record company (Ivory Tower Records, Avenue Records). Estab. 1970. Publishes 30 songs/year; publishes 10 new songwriters/year. Hires staff songwriters. Works with composers and lyricists; teams collaborators. Pays standard royalty.
How to Contact: Submit demo tape by mail. Unsolicited submissions are OK. Prefers cassette with 3 songs and lyric sheet. SASE. Reports in 7-8 weeks. "Press kits are preferred."
Music: Mostly **rock, pop** and **country**; also **R&B** and **rap.** Published *Drawn To You* (by Emma Zale); *Let It Go* and *Mephista* (both written and recorded by Zale), all on Vagabond Records.
Tips: "Be persistent, organized, and dedicated."

ENTERTAINMENT SERVICES MUSIC GROUP, 42 Music Square W., Nashville TN 37203. (615)252-8282. Executive Administrator: Curt Conroy. Music publisher. BMI. Estab. 1990. Publishes 50-60 songs/year. Pays standard royalty.
How to Contact: Submit a demo tape by mail—unsolicited submissions are OK. Prefers "good quality 3-4 song demo" and lyric sheet. "Guitar or piano-vocal OK." Does not return submitted materials. Reports within 2-4 weeks.
Music: Mostly **country (traditional), country rock** and **country pop**; also **country blues.** Published *Live at Joe's* (by Pinto Bennett) on MCM Records; *McAfee's Breeze Vol. III*, written and recorded by Boo Boo McAfee on American Percussion Records; and "In the Wings," written and recorded by David Stewart on ESI Records, TNN video.
Tips: "Listen to and study current records coming out of Nashville and try to develop a "current feel" for the marketplace. Write with specific artists in mind. Company sponsors The Nashville Songwriters Continuing Series. Company periodically selects 12 new original songs by 12 new or unsigned writers, produces a professionally packaged cassette and distributes this cassette to industry decision makers. Selected writers contribute to production costs but enjoy having their material presented in a unique and elite fashion. Request special submission packets by mail."

ERTIS MUSIC COMPANY, Dept. SM, P.O. Box 80691, Baton Rouge LA 70898. (504)924-3327. Fax: (504)766-4112. Publisher: Johnny Palazzotto. ASCAP. Estab. 1977. Publishes 10-15 songs/year. Pays standard royalty.
Affiliate(s): Blue Rouge Music (ASCAP).
How to Contact: Submit a demo tape by mail—unsolicited submissions are OK. Prefers cassette with 3-5 songs. SASE. Reports in 2-4 weeks.
Music: Mostly **country** and **zydeco.** Published "Come on Home" (by Major Handy), recorded by Nathan & Cha-Chas on Rounder Records (zydeco); "Come on Home," written and recorded by Major Handy on Bedrock Records (zydeco); and "Laissez Les Bon" (by Kelly, J. Didier), recorded by Queen Ida on Sonet Records (zydeco).

*EUDAEMONIC MUSIC, P.O. Box 371 Peck Slip Station, New York NY 10272. (212)495-6622. President: Gary Leet. Music publisher. Estab. 1992. Publishes 10 songs/year; publishes 2 new songwriters/year. Pays standard royalty.
How to Contact: Submit demo tape by mail. Unsolicited submissions are OK. Prefers cassette (or VHS videocassette) with as many songs as you feel appropriate. Does not return unsolicited material. Reports in 2 months.
Music: Mostly **progressive/alternative rock, new wave/punk rock** and **progressive folk;** also **off the wall.** Published "Laughing Song" and "Scratch & Claw" (by Mica), recorded by Altered Boys on URATV Records; and "Ice Ages," written and recorded by Chris Grimes on Industrial Records.
Tips: "Music always comes first, a really rockin' tune. Then clever lyrics is a nice bonus. Above all, creativity is most important."

EVER-OPEN-EYE MUSIC, Wern Fawr Farm, Pencoed, MID, Glam CF356NB **United Kingdom.** Phone: (0656)860041. Managing Director: M.R. Blanche. Music publisher and record company (Red-Eye Records). PRS. Member PPL and MCPS. Estab. 1980. Publishes 6 songs/year. Works with composers and lyricists; teams collaborators. Pays negotiable amount.
How to Contact: Submit demo tape by mail—unsolicited submissions are OK. Prefers cassette (or VHS videocassette). Does not return unsolicited material.
Music: Mostly **R&B, gospel** and **pop;** also **swing.** Published "Breakdown Song," "Shadow of the Sun" and "Outside Looking In," written by Finn/Jones on Red Eye Records.

EVOPOETICS PUBLISHING, P.O. Box 71231, Milwaukee WI 53211-7331. (414)332-7474. President: Dr. Martin Jack Rosenblum. Music publisher and record company (Roar Records). ASCAP. Estab. 1969. Receives 20 submissions/month. Works with composers.
Affiliate(s): Roar Recording, American Ranger Incorporated and Lion Publishing.
How to Contact: Submit demo tape by mail—unsolicited submissions are OK. SASE. Reports in 1 week.
Music: **Progressive rock and roll with a serious poetic lyric intent.** Published *Free Hand* (by Rosenblum), recorded by Blues Riders on Flying Fish Records.

EXCURSION MUSIC GROUP, P.O. Box 9248, San Jose CA 95157. (408)252-3392. President: Frank T. Prins. Music publisher, record company (Excursion Records) and record producer. BMI, ASCAP. Estab. 1976. Publishes 25 songs/year; publishes 5 new songwriters/year. Hires staff writers. Works with composers and lyricists; teams collaborators. Pays standard royalty.
Affiliate(s): Echappee Music (BMI), Excursion Music (ASCAP).
How to Contact: Write or call first and obtain permission to submit. Prefers cassette or VHS videocassette with 3 songs and lyric sheet. SASE. Reports in 2-3 weeks.
Music: Mostly **pop, country** and **gospel;** also **rock** and **R&B.** Published "Red Roses in My Hand" and *Always,* written and recorded by Ian Ballard; and *Time Clock Livin'* (by Wayne and Homer Osborne), recorded by Ian Ballard, all on Excursion Records.
Tips: "Keep writing and honing your craft!"

EYE KILL MUSIC, Dept. SM, P.O. Box 242, Woodland PA 16881. A&R: John Wesley. Music publisher. ASCAP. Estab. 1987. Publishes 10 songs/year; publishes 6 new songwriters/year. Works with composers and lyricists. Pays standard royalty.

How to Contact: Submit a demo tape by mail—unsolicited submissions are OK. Prefers cassette with 3 songs and lyric sheet. SASE. Reports in 1 month.

Music: Mostly **country** and **rock**. Published "All Over For You" (by Cindy Stone) and "Here Again" (by Guy Stone), both recorded by Paul White; "Two Lonely Hearts," written and recorded by John Maine, Jr., all on Eye Kill Records (all country).

DOUG FAIELLA PUBLISHING, 16591 County Home Rd., Marysville OH 43040. (513)644-8295. President: Doug Faiella. Music publisher, record company (Studio 7 Records) and recording studio. BMI. Estab. 1984. Publishes 25 songs/year; publishes 5 new songwriters/year. Works with composers and teams collaborators. Pays standard royalty.

How to Contact: Write to obtain permission to submit a tape. SASE. Prefers cassette with 3 songs and lyric sheets. Does not return unsolicited material. Reports in 4 weeks.

Music: Mostly **country, gospel** and **rock**.

FAMOUS MUSIC PUBLISHING COMPANIES, Suite 1000, 3500 W. Olive Ave., Burbank CA 91505. (818)566-7000, FAX (818)566-6680. Creative Dept. Lisa Wells-Cronin, Roanna Gillespie, Robyn Roseman, Ellie Schwimmer. Estab. 1929. Publishes 500+ songs/year; 5+ new songwriters/year. Hires staff songwriters. Works with composers and lyricists; teams collaborators. Pays standard royalty.

Affiliate(s): Famous Music (ASCAP) and Ensign Music (BMI).

How to Contact: Write or call first and obtain permission to submit. Prefers cassette with 3 songs and lyric sheet. Does not return unsolicited material. Reports in 2-3 months.

Music: Mostly **rock, R&B** and **pop**. Published "End of the Road" (by Babyface/Reid/Simmons), recorded by Boyz II Men on LaFace/Arista Records; "Faithful" (by Martin Page), recorded by Go West and "Leave It Alone," written and recorded by Living Colour, both on Epic Records.

F&J MUSIC. 23, Thrayle House, Stockwell Road, London SW9 0XU **United Kingdom.** (071)737-6681/(081)672-6158. Fax: (071)737-7881. Managing Director: Errol Jones. Music publisher and record company (Leopard Music/Jet Set International Records). PRS, BMI. Estab. 1978. Publishes 75 songs/year. Publishes 35 new songwriters/year. Works with composers and lyricists; teams collaborators. Pays standard royalty.

Affiliate(s): EURUSA Worldwide Publishing Affiliate (BMI) and F&J Music Publishing (PRS).

How to Contact: Write first and obtain permission to submit. Prefers cassette (or VHS PAL videocassette) with 3 songs, lyric sheet and lead sheet. Include biography, resume and picture. SASE. Reports in 2 weeks.

Music: Mostly **dance, soul** and **pop**; also **ballads, reggae** and **gospel**. Published "Time After Time," (by Guy Spell), recorded by Rico J. on Leopard Music/Jet Set International Records (disco/soul); "I Need You" (by F. Campbell/E. North Jr.), recorded by Big Africa (soul/reggae); and "God is Beauty," written and recorded by Evelyn Ladimeji (gospel); both on Leopard Music.

*FAT CITY PUBLISHING, #2, 1226 17th Ave. S., Nashville TN 37212. (615)320-7678. Fax: (615)321-5382. Vice President: Edward Michael. Music publisher, record company (Fat City Artists), record producer and booking agency (Fat City Artists). Estab. 1972. Publishes 25+ songs/year; publishes 10+ new songwriters/year. Hires staff writers. Works with composers and lyricists; teams collaborators. Pays standard royalty.

Affiliate(s): Fort Forever (BMI).

How to Contact: Submit demo tape by mail. Unsolicited submissions are OK. Prefers cassette (or VHS videocassette) with 4-6 songs and lyric sheet. SASE. Reports in 2 weeks.

Music: Mostly **rock, country** and **blues**; also **alternative, rockabilly** and **jazz**.

Tips: "Provide as much information and material as possible."

FEZSONGS, Dept. SM, 429 S. Lewis Rd., Royersford PA 19468. (215)948-8228. Fax: (215)948-4175. President: Jim Femino. Music publisher, record company (Road Records) and record producer (independent). ASCAP. Estab. 1970. Publishes 12-15 songs/year; publishes 1-2 new songwriters/year. Works with composers and lyricists; teams collaborators. Pays standard royalty. "Charges in advance for demo recording services, only if needed."

How to Contact: Submit a demo tape by mail with permission only. Prefers cassette (or VHS videocassette) with 3-4 songs and lyric sheet. SASE. Reports in 4-6 weeks.

Music: Mostly **country**. Published "Where Do You Go" (by J. Femino and J. Douglas) and "Maybe" (by J. Femino); and "Next Stop Ecstasy" (by J. Femino and H. Linsley), all recorded by Jim Femino on Road Records.

Tips: "Write, write, re-write then write some more."

FIRST MILLION MUSIC, INC., Dept. SM, P.O. Box 292164, Nashville TN 37229-2164. (615)872-7967. Vice President: Peggy Bradley. Music publisher. ASCAP. Estab. 1983. Publishes 4 songs/year; 2 new songwriters/year. Pays standard royalty.

Affiliate(s): Old Guide Music (BMI).

How to Contact: Submit a demo tape by mail—unsolicited submissions are OK. Prefers cassette with 3 songs and lyric sheet. SASE. Reports in 2 weeks.

Music: Mostly **country, pop** and **R&B**. Published "Love" (by Ruddy), recorded by Jill Jordan on Maxx Records (country/uptempo); and "Jewel of the Mississippi" (by Lips Prat), recorded by Don Juan on Maxx Records (country/ballad).

FIRST RELEASE MUSIC PUBLISHING, 6124 Selma Ave., Hollywood CA 90028. (213)469-2296. President: Danny Howell. Music publisher. BMI, ASCAP, SACEM, GEMA, PRS, MCPS. Publishes 30-50 songs/year. Hires staff songwriters. Pays standard royalty; co-publishing negotiable. "Very active in obtaining cover records and film and TV uses, i.e., *Arsenio Hall, Lethal Weapon III,* many others."

Affiliate(s): Fully Conscious Music, Criterion Music, Cadillac Pink, Atlantic Music, Illegeal Songs, I.R.S. Songs, Reggatta Music, Magnetic Publishing Ltd., Animal Logic Publishing and Blue Turtle Music.

How to Contact: "We *never* accept unsolicited tapes or phone calls—you must have referral or be requested." Returns all unsolicited material. Reports only if interested, but "retain personally written critique for every song I agree to accept."

Music: "We are interested in great songs and great writers. We are currently successful in all areas." Published "Maybe It Was Memphis" (by Mike Anderson), recorded by Pam Tillis on Arista Records (country); and "This Girl" (by C. Converse and M. Mahan), recorded by Tina Bellison on Impact Records (R&B).

Tips: "Show up at one of my guest workshops and play me the last song you would ever play for a publisher; not the worst, the last! Educate yourself as to what writers we represent before pitching me (i.e., Sting, Lyle Lovett, Concrete Blonde)."

FIRST TIME MUSIC (PUBLISHING) U.K. LTD., Sovereign House, 12 Trewartha Road, Praa Sands, Penzance, Cornwall TR20 9ST **United Kingdom.** Phone: (0736)762826. Fax: (0736)763328. Managing Director: Roderick G. Jones. Music publisher, record company (First Time Records, licensed and subsidiary labels), record producer and management firm (First Time Management and Production Co.). PRS. Member of MCPS. Estab. 1986. Publishes 500-750 songs/year; 20-50 new songwriters/year. Hires staff writers. Works with composers and lyricists; teams collaborators. Pays standard royalty; "50-60% to established and up-and-coming writers with the right attitude."

Affiliate(s): Subsidiary and administered catalogues. Sub-publishing worldwide (new associations welcome).

How to Contact: Submit a demo tape—unsolicited submissions are OK. Prefers cassette, 1⅞ ips cassette (or VHS videocassette "of professional quality") with unlimited number of songs and lyric or lead sheets, but not necessary. Reports in 4-10 weeks. SASE in U.K.—SAE and IRC if outside U.K. "Postal costs in the U.K. are much higher than the U.S.—one IRC doesn't even cover the cost of a letter to the U.S., let alone the return of cassettes. Enclose the correct amount for return and contact as stated." Reports in 4-10 weeks.

Music: Mostly **country** and **folk, pop/soul/top 20/rock, country with an Irish/Scottish crossover;** also **gospel/Christian.** Published "The Robinsons Ball" (by Pete Arnold), recorded by Brendan Shine on Play Records (MOR/country); "Sentimental Over You" (by Rod Jones/Colin Eade), recorded by PJ Proby on J'ace Records (pop); "I Wouldn't Have It Any Other Way" (by Bill Allen), recorded by Kenny Paul on Luvinikind Records (country).

Tips: "Have a professional approach—present well produced demos. First impressions are important and may be the only chance you get. Remember that you as a writer/artist are in a competitive market. As an active independent -international publisher we require good writers/artists and product. As a company we seek to work with writers. If the product is good then we generally come up with something in the way of covers. Writers are advised to join the Guild of International Songwriters and Composers in the United Kingdom."

FIVE ROSES MUSIC GROUP, (formerly Five Roses Publishing Company), P.O. Box 417, White Sulpher Springs NY 12787. (914)292-4042. President: Sammie Lee Marler. Music publisher, record company, management. BMI. Estab. 1989. Publishes 50-75 songs/year. Works with composers and lyricists. Pays standard royalty.

How to Contact: Submit a demo tape by mail—unsolicited submissions are OK. Prefers cassette with 3 songs. SASE. Reports in 3 weeks.

Music: Mostly **country and western, bluegrass, country rock, country gospel, gospel, light rock, R&B, children's.** Published "Little One," recorded by Dawn L. & The Dads, on Angelstar Records.

Tips: "We care about the songwriter and keep in personal contact with them. We are one happy family at Five Roses. Always include a SASE for material return. If you are new at songwriting and are looking for a publisher to further your career you should contact us first. We have opened doors for many new songwriters."

FLAMING STAR WEST, Box 2400, Gardnerville NY 89410. (702)265-6825. Owner: Ted Snyder. Music publisher, record company (Flaming Star Records) and record producer (Flaming Star Records). BMI. Estab. 1988. Works with composers and lyricists; teams collaborators. Pays standard royalty.
How to Contact: Submit a demo tape by mail—unsolicited submissions are OK. Prefers cassette or VHS videocassette with up to 5 songs and lyric sheets. "If you are sure of your music, you may send more than 5 songs. No heavy metal. All other types." SASE. Reports in 3 weeks.
Music: Mostly **country, pop** and **rock** and **country rock**; also **gospel, R&B, New Age** and **calypso.** Published "Jezabel" (country) and "For the Sake of My Children" (ballad), both written and recorded by Ted Snyder on Flaming Star Records.
Tips: "Listen to what is on the radio, but be original. Put feeling into your songs. We're looking for songs and artists to promote overseas. Flaming Star Records is a launching pad for the new recording artist. We try to help where we can."

FOCAL POINT MUSIC PUBLISHERS (BMI), Dept. SM, 920 McArthur Blvd., Warner Robins GA 31093. (912)923-6533. Manager: Ray Melton. Music publisher and record company. BMI. Estab. 1964. Publishes 4 songs/year; publishes 1 new songwriter/year. Works with composers. Pays standard royalty. "Songwriters must have BMI affiliation."
How to Contact: Write first to get permission to send a tape. Prefers cassette with 2-4 songs and lead sheet. Prefers studio produced demos. SASE. Reports in 3 months.
Music: Mostly **country** and **gospel**; also **"old-style pop and humor."** Published "Everything Turned Out Good" (by Helen Thomas), recorded by Barbara Richardson on Club 45 Records (country).
Tips: "Try it out on your friends. Go to workshops. Belong to a songwriters group."

*MARK FOSTER MUSIC COMPANY, Box 4012, Champaign IL 61824-4012. (217)398-2760. Fax: (217)398-2791. President: Jane C. Menkhaus. Music publisher. Estab. 1962. Publishes 20-30 songs/year; publishes 4-5 new songwriters/year. Works with composers. Pays 5-10% over first 3,000 copies choral music sold.
Affiliate(s): Marko Press (BMI) and Fostco Press (ASCAP).
How to Contact: Submit demo tape by mail. Unsolicited submissions are OK. Prefers cassette and 1 copy choral manuscript (must be legible). Include brief bio of composer/arranger if new. SASE. Reports in 4-6 months.
Music: Mostly **sacred SATB, secular SATB** and **sacred and secular treble & male choir**; also **conducting books** and **Kodaly materials.** Published "Before Your Throne" (by Bradley Ellingboe); "City on the Hill" (by Marvin V. Curtis); and "Jubilant Song" (by René Clausen).
Tips: "Must be well-constructed piece to begin with, manuscript should be in decent format preferable with keyboard reduction."

FOUR NEWTON PUBLISHING (BMI), Rt. 1, Box 187-A, Whitney TX 76692. (817)694-4047. President: Allen Newton. Music publisher, record company (Pristine Records, Pleasure Records, Cactus Flats, MFN). BMI, ASCAP. Estab. 1980. Publishes 20 songs/year; publishes about 10 new songwriters/year. Receives hundreds of submissions/year. Works with composers and lyricists; teams collaborators. Pays standard royalty.
Affiliate(s): Stephash Publishing (ASCAP).
How to Contact: Submit a demo tape by mail—unsolicited submissions are OK. Prefers cassette with 3-6 songs and lyric sheets. SASE. Reports in 4-6 weeks.
Music: Mostly **country, rock** and **R&B**; also **pop, gospel** and **New Age.** Published "Texas Mile," written and recorded by D. Nowell on Pleasure Records; "Don't Want No Strangers" (by D. Van Horne), recorded by Marcel Evans; and "Medicine Man" (by A. Martin/J. Willoughby), recorded by Jet Black Machine, both on Pristine Records.
Tips: "Study the material charting. Learn from the pros."

FOX FARM RECORDING, 2731 Saundersville Ferry Rd., Mt. Juliet TN 37122. (615)754-2444. President: Kent Fox. Music publisher, record producer and demo production recording studio. BMI, AS-CAP. Publishes 20 songs/year; publishes 5 new songwriters/year. Works with composers and lyricists; teams collaborators. Pays standard royalty.
Affiliate(s): Blueford Music (ASCAP) and Mercantile Music (BMI).
How to Contact: SASE. Prefers cassette with 4 songs and lyric sheet. Reports in 1 month.
Music: Country, bluegrass and **contemporary Christian.**
Tips: "If your song is good enough to become a hit, it's worth investing money for a good demo: drums, bass, guitar, keyboard, fiddle, sax, vocals etc."

FOXWORTHY MUSIC INC., Dept. SM, 4002 Liggett Dr., San Diego CA 92106. (619)226-4152. President: Douglas Foxworthy. Music publisher, record company (Foxworthy Records) and record producer (Foxworthy Productions). BMI. Estab. 1982. Publishes 5 songs/year; publishes 1 new songwriter/year. Teams collaborators. Pays standard royalty.

Affiliate(s): Foxworthy Music (BMI), Expanding Universe Music (BMI).
How to Contact: Submit a demo tape by mail—unsolicited submissions are O.K. Prefers cassette with 3 songs and lyric sheets. Does not return unsolicited material. Reports in 6 weeks.
Music: Mostly **pop, rock** and **R&B**; also **rap** and **New Age.** Published "Time Out" (by Gary Hyde), recorded by CinCinT (R&B); "Warp Drive" (by Mike Redmond), recorded by Rag Band (rap); and "Avatar," written and recorded by Foxworthy (New Age), all on Foxworthy Records.

FRICK MUSIC PUBLISHING CO., 404 Bluegrass Ave., Madison TN 37115. (615)865-6380. Contact: Bob Frick. Music publisher, record company and record producer. BMI. Publishes 50 songs/year; publishes 2 new songwriters/year. Works with lyricists. Pays standard royalty.
Affiliate(s): Sugarbakers Music (ASCAP).
How to Contact: Write or call first to get permission to submit. Prefers 7½ ips reel-to-reel or cassette (or videocassette) with 2-10 songs and lyric sheet. SASE. Reports in 2 weeks.
Music: Mostly **gospel**; also **country, rock** and **top 40/pop.** Published "I Found Jesus in Nashville" (by Lin Butler), recorded by Bob Scott Frick; "Good Lovin'," written and recorded by Teresa Ford, all on R.E.F. Records.

*THE FRICON ENTERTAINMENT CO., INC., 1048 S. Ogden Dr., Los Angeles CA 90019. (213)931-7323. Attn: Publishing Department. Music publisher. Music supervision (Fricon Music/BMI; Fricout Music/ASCAP). Pays standard royalty.
How to Contact: Write first and obtain permission to submit. Include SASE. Prefers cassette with 1 song and lyric sheet. Does not return unsolicited material without SASE. Reports in 6 weeks.
Music: Mostly **TV** and **film.** Also **gospel, R&B, rock, pop, dance** and **country.**

*FROG AND MOOSE MUSIC, Box 40784, Nashville TN 37204. (615)331-1469. Publisher: Steven R. Pinkston. Music publisher and record producer (Third Floor Productions). BMI. Estab. 1988. Publishes 10 new songwriters/year. Teams collaborators. Pays standard royalty.
How to Contact: Submit a demo tape by mail—unsolicited submissions are OK. Prefers cassette or DAT (or VHS videocassette) with 3 songs and lyric or lead sheets. SASE. Reports in 2 months.
Music: Mostly **pop, gospel** and **rock**; also **R&B** and **blues.**

*FRONTLINE MUSIC GROUP, P.O. Box 28450, Santa Ana CA 92799-8450. Director of Music Publishing: Kenneth Hicks. Music publisher and record company (Frontline Records). Estab. 1987. Works with composers and lyricists; teams collaborators. Pays standard royalty.
Affiliate(s): Broken Songs (ASCAP) and Carlotta Publishing (BMI).
How to Contact: Submit demo tape by mail. Unsolicited submissions are OK. Prefers cassette with 3 songs and lyric sheet. "Address to Broken Songs." Does not return unsolicited material. Reports in 1-2 months.
Music: Mostly **pop, rock** and **R&B.**
Tips: "Frontline is a Christian Record Company. The songs we would publish should have lyrics that are wholesome and/or point to a relationship with Jesus."

FROZEN INCA MUSIC, Suite 333, 1800 Peachtree St., Atlanta GA 30309. (404)355-5580. Fax: (404)351-2786. President: Michael Rothschild. Music publisher, record company and record producer. Estab. 1981. Publishes 12 songs/year; publishes 3 new songwriters/year. Works with composers and lyricists; teams collaborators. Pays negotiated percentage.
Affiliate(s): Landslide Records.
How to Contact: Submit demo tape by mail. Unsolicited submissions are OK. Prefers cassette with 6-12 songs and lyric sheet. SASE. Reports in 1 month.
Music: Mostly **R&B, blues** and **rap**; also **gospel, country** and **rock.** Published "Highway Man" (by T. Ellis and Eddie Cleaveland); "Sign of the Blues" (by T. Ellis and K. Simmons); and "My Restless Heart" (by T. Ellis), all recorded by Landslide on Alligator Records (LP).
Tips: "We look for strong rhythmic hooks."

*G FINE SOUNDS, Suite 13G, 2 Washington Square Village, New York NY 10012-1701. (212)995-1608. Fax: (212)995-4043. President: Jonathan P. Fine. Music publisher, record producer, artist management. Estab. 1986. Publishes 25+ songs/year. Publishes 4+ new songwriters. Works with composers and lyricists; teams collaborators.
How to Contact: Submit demo tape by mail. Unsolicited submissions are OK. Prefers high bias cassette (or VHS videocassette if available); 3 songs and lyric sheet. "Prefers DAT or metal cassette. SASE. Reports in 2 months.
Music: Mostly **rap, alternative rock, dance music/R&B**; also **rock, reggae.** Published "Ring the Alarm," "Be Bo" and "Back Off" (by Lyvio G/Fu-Schnickens), recorded by Fu-Schnickens, on Jive Records.
Tips: "Send innovative material of superior quality."

GALAXIA MUSICAL S.A. De C.V., Leibnitz 130, D.F. 11590 **Mexico**. (525)250-0378. Fax: (525)254-5790. Managing Director: Arq. Jose G. Cruz. Music publisher. SACM. Publishes 100-150 songs/year. Works with composers and lyricists; teams collaborators. Pays standard royalty.
How to Contact: Write first and obtain permission to submit. "Will only accept submissions from writers who are very familiar with type of music currently being produced in Mexico and Spanish speaking territories." Prefers cassette (or VHS videocassette) with 1-5 songs. Does not return unsolicited material. Reports in 2 weeks.
Music: Latin pop ballads and rock. *"We only place songs with local Latin artists."*
Tips: "A well-prepared demo signals good craftmanship. Please do not contact us if you are not very familiar with the Latin market."

ALAN GARY MUSIC, P.O. Box 179, Palisades Park NJ 07650. President: Alan Gary. Music publisher. ASCAP, BMI. Estab. 1987. Publishes a varying number of songs/year. Works with composers and lyricists. Pays standard royalty.
How to Contact: Submit demo tape—unsolicited submissions are OK. Prefers cassette (or VHS videocassette) with lyric sheet. SASE.
Music: Mostly **pop, R&B** and **dance**; also **rock**, **A/C** and **country**. Published "Liberation" (by Gary/Julian), recorded by Les Julian on Music Tree Records (A/C); "Love Your Way Out of This One" (by Gary/Rosen), recorded by Deborah Steel on Bad Cat Records (contemporary country); and "Dueling Rappers" (by Gary/Free), recorded by Prophets of Boom on You Dirty Rap! Records (rap/R&B).

GENERAL JONES MUSIC, Dept. SM, 3252 Grenoble Lane, Memphis TN 38115. (901)365-1429. Owner: Danny Jones. Music publisher, record producer and recording engineer. Estab. 1980. BMI. Publishes 3-4 songs/year; publishes 1-2 new songwriters/year. Works with composers and lyricists; teams collaborators. Pays standard royalty.
Affiliate(s): General Jones Music (BMI) and Danny Jones Productions.
How to Contact: Write or call first and obtain permission to submit. Prefers cassette (or VHS videocassette) with 3 songs and lyric or lead sheet. SASE. Reports in 1 month.
Music: **Rock, country** and **R&B**. Published "King of the Cowboys" (by Larry Carney/Roy Rogers, Jr.), recorded by Roy Rogers, Jr. on RCA Records (country); "I Eat Roadkill" (by Dan Hyer), recorded by 50 FT (rock); and "Don't Cheat on Me," written and recorded by Keith Swinton and Steve Rarick (rock), all on RCA Records.

GENETIC MUSIC PUBLISHING, 10 Church Rd., Merchantville NJ 08109. (609)662-4428. Contact: Whey Cooler or Jade Starling. Music publisher, record company (Svengali) and record producer (Whey Cooler Production). ASCAP. Estab. 1982. Publishes 1-5 songs/year. Pays standard royalty.
Affiliate(s): Cooler By A Mile (ASCAP), BC Music (ASCAP) and Baggy Music (BMI).
How to Contact: Write first and obtain permission to submit a tape. Prefers cassette. Does not return unsolicited material. Reports in 3 weeks.
Music: Mostly **dance, R&B** and **pop**; also **rock** and **jazz**. Published "Better Better Be Good to Me" (by Starling/Cooler), "Techno Xtar" (by Cooler/Wink) and "Hard Core Poison" (by Wink), all recorded by Pretty Poison on Svengali/Warlock Records.
Tips: "Submissions are reviewed and put on file for one year before being reviewed again. During that time they are regularly submitted to various projects for consideration. If they are accepted then a publishing deal between ourselves and the songwriter will result."

***GIFT OF GRACE MUSIC (BMI)**, P.O. Box 25, Albertlea MN 56007. (507)526-5678. Music publisher and record producer. Primarily publishes songs co-written with artist or performer. Estab. 1988. Publishes 10 songs/year. Works with composers and lyricists. Pays standard royalty.
How to Contact: Write first and obtain permission to submit. Prefers cassette and lyric sheet. Does not return unsolicited material. Reports in 1 month.
Music: Mostly **gospel** and **country**. Published "Jesus", *Jesus Won't You Walk With Me* and *You Ain't Gonna Be-Bop Into Heaven* (by J. Hager/D. McHan), recorded by Don McHan on Power of Truth Records.
Tips: "Submit a decent demo and lyric sheet."

GIFTNESS ENTERPRISE, Dept. SM, Suite #5, 1315 Simpson Rd. NW, Atlanta GA 30314. (404)642-2645. Contact: New Song Department. Music publisher. BMI, ASCAP. Publishes 30 songs/year; publishes 15 new songwriters/year. Employs songwriters on a salary basis. Works with composers and lyricsts; teams collaborators. Pays standard royalty.
Affiliate(s): Blair Vizzion Music (BMI) and Fresh Entertainment (ASCAP).
How to Contact: Submit demo tape—unsolicited submissions are OK. Prefers cassette with 4 songs and lyric or lead sheet. SASE. Reports in 1 month.
Music: Mostly **R&B, pop** and **rock**; also **country, gospel** and **jazz**. Published "This Time" (dance) and "Always Girl" (ballad) (by Cirocco), recorded by Georgio on RCA Records; "Broken Promises" (by J. Calhoun), recorded by S.O.S. Band on Tabu/A&M Records (dance).

GLOBEART PUBLISHING, A Division of GlobeArt Inc., P.O. Box 520, New York NY 10028-0005. (212)249-9220. Fax: (212)861-8130. President: Jane Peterer. Music publisher. BMI, ASCAP. Estab. 1989. Publishes 50 songs/year; publishes 2 new songwriters/year. Works with composers/lyricists. Pays standard royalty.
Affiliate(s): GlobeSound Publishing (ASCAP).
How to Contact: Submit a demo tape by mail—unsolicited submissions are OK. Prefers cassette (or videocassette) with 3-5 songs and lyric or lead sheet. SASE. Reports in 6 weeks.
Music: Mostly **pop/R&B, jazz** and **gospel;** also **New Age** and **country.** Published *One Kingdom* (by Coley/Roebuck), recorded by Burning Core on MBI Records; *Urban Primitive* (by Richard Applegate), recorded by Applegate on Media Orphan Records; and *Beautiful Morning,* written and recorded by Rebbein on Pice Records.
Tips: "Be professional."

GO STAR MUSIC, Dept. SM, Suite #20, 4700 Belle Grove Rd., Baltimore MD 21225. (410)789-1005. Fax: (410)789-1006. Owner: William E. Baker. Music publisher, record company (Go Records) and record producer (International Music). Estab. 1988. Publishes 50-100 songs/year; 50 new songwriters/year. Pays standard royalty.
Affiliate(s): Billy Baker and Associates, Go Records, Infinity Productions and Independent International Music Associates.
How to Contact: Submit a demo tape. Unsolicited submissions are OK. "Limit 4 songs with lyric sheets, bio and photo. SASE with phone number. List what you would like to achieve." Prefers cassette and lyric or lead sheet. SASE. Reports in 3 weeks.
Music: Mostly **rock, pop, country, R&B, New Age** and **gospel.** Published "If You're Not Here" (by Paula Anderson/Pam Bailey), recorded by Closin' Time On Go Records (country); "Numbered Door" (by Roger Ware), recorded by Doug Beacham on Go Records (country); and "Carolina Blue (by Jim Hession), recorded by John Anthony on Go/Silver Dollar Records (country).

JAY GOLD MUSIC PUBLISHING, P.O. Box 409, East Meadow NY 11554-0409. (516)486-8699. President: Jay Gold. Music publisher. BMI. Estab. 1981. Publishes 25 songs/year; 6 new songwriters/year. Works with composers and lyricists; teams collaborators. Pays standard royalty.
How to Contact: Submit a demo tape by mail—unsolicited submissions are OK. Prefers cassette with 2 songs and lyric sheets. SASE. Reports in 6 weeks. "Use only high quality chrome cassettes for submissions."
Music: Mostly **pop, rock** and **country.** Published "Tough Guy" (by Jay Gold), recorded by Jail Bait on *Star Search* TV show (pop); "All the Wrong Reasons," written and recorded by Jay Gold on Turbo Records (pop); and "Long Time" (by Jay Gold), recorded by Joe-Joe Bentry on Cardinal Records.
Tips: "Make the best demo you can afford. It's better to have a small publisher pushing your songs than a large one keeping them on the shelf."

S.M. GOLD MUSIC, % Compositions, Inc., 36 E. 22nd St., 2nd Floor, New York NY 10010. President: Steven M. Gold. Music publisher and jingle/TV/film score producer. ASCAP. Publishes 5 songs/year. "We employ freelance and staff songwriters/composers who are well-versed in all styles of popular music." Pays standard royalty or cash advance (buy-out).
How to Contact: Submit a demo tape—unsolicited submissions are OK. Prefers cassette with 2 songs. Does not return unsolicited material. No calls please.
Music: All types of popular music (top 40).
Tips: "We're not looking for 'album tracks' or 'B sides.' Hits only!"

GORDON MUSIC CO., INC., Dept. SM, P.O. Box 2250, Canoga Park CA 91306. (818)883-8224. Owner: Jeff Gordon. Music publisher, record company (Paris Records). ASCAP, BMI. Estab. 1950. Publishes 10-20 songs/year. Works with composers and lyricists; teams collaborators. Pays standard royalty or arrangements of many kinds can be made between author and publisher.
Affiliate(s): Marlen Music (ASCAP), Sunshine Music (BMI) and Gordon Music (ASCAP).
How to Contact: Submit demo tape—unsolicited submissions are OK. Prefers cassette (or VHS videocassette) with 3-4 songs and lyric or lead sheets. Does not return unsolicited material. Reports in 1 month.
Music: Mostly **pop, children's** and **rock;** also **jazz.** Published "Izzy, Post of West" and "The Corsican Cat," both written and recorded by Champie (childrens); and "Alfred Hitchcock" (by D. Kahn and M. Lenard), recorded by Failsafe (TV theme); all on Paris Records.

*JON GORR CUSTOM MUSIC, (formerly MassMedia), 828 Vista St., Pittsburgh PA 15212. (412)323-9331. President: Jon Gorr. Music publisher (MassMedia Records), record producer (Jon Gorr), advertising/jingle agency and planetarium soundtracks and film scoring. BMI. Estab. 1983. Publishes 10 songs/year; publishes 1-2 new songwriters/year. Works with composers and lyricists. Pays standard royalty.

How to Contact: Submit a demo tape by mail—unsolicited submissions are OK. Prefers cassette with 3 songs. Does not return unsolicited material. Reports in 1 month.

Music: Mostly **rock, New Age** and **reggae**. Published *Gifts From The Heart*, written and recorded by Kim Bobrowski; *Home For The Holidays* written and recorded by WWSW; and *Star Of Bethlehem*, written and recorded by Jon Gorr. Also published "Beat of My Heart" and "If You Must Leave," from the Fox TV show "The Heights."

RICHARD E. GOWELL MUSIC, Dept. SM, 45 7th St., Auburn ME 04210. (207)784-7975. Professional Manager: Rich Gowell. Music publisher and record company (Allagash Country Records, Allagash R&B Records, Gowell Records). BMI. Estab. 1978. Publishes 10-30 songs/year; 5-10 new songwriters/year. Works with composers and lyricists. Pays standard royalty.
Affiliate(s): Global Allagash Music Co. (ASCAP).
How to Contact: Submit a demo tape by mail—unsolicited submissions are OK. Prefers cassette with 2-4 songs and lyric sheets. SASE. Reports in 2-6 weeks.
Music: Mostly **country, pop** and **R&B**. Published "Back Home" (by J. Main), recorded by Larry Main (pop/country); "Straight Country Songs" (by J. Gillespie), recorded by Larry Beaird (country); and "Is It My Body You Want," written and recorded by Rich Gowell (50s rock) all on Allagash Country Records.
Tips: "Have a great song with a professional demo and keep plugging to the right people."

*GRADUATE MUSIC LTD., St. Swithun's Institute, The Trinity, Worcester WR1 2PN **United Kingdom**. Phone: (0905)20882. Fax: (0905)726677. Managing Director: David Virr. Music publisher and record company (Graduate Records Ltd.). PRS and MCPS. Estab. 1980. Publishes 25 songs/year; 2 new songwriters/year. Works with composers and lyricists. Pays negotiable royalty.
How to Contact: Write first and obtain permission to submit. Does not return unsolicited material.
Music: Mostly **rock, pop** and **anything original**. Published "Heartache Avenue" (by Tibenham/Mason), recorded by The Maisonettes on Ready, Steady, Go! Records (60's pop); "Who Is Innocent" (by George Borowski), recorded by Guitar George on Graduate Records (rock); and "The Earth Dies Screaming," by UB40 on Graduate Records (reggae).

*GREEN DOG PRODUCTIONS, 1311 Candlelight Ave., Dallas TX 75116. (214)298-9576. President: Paul S. Ketter. Music publisher, record company (Sagittar Records) and record producer. Estab. 1958. Publishes 12-15 songs/year; publishes 1-3 new songwriters/year. Works with composers and lyricists; teams collaborators. Pays standard royalty.
Affiliate(s): Pineapple Music Publishing Co. (ASCAP) and Big State Music Publishing Co. (BMI).
How to Contact: Submit demo tape by mail. Unsolicited submissions are OK. Prefers cassette with 6 songs and lyric sheet. SASE. Reports in 1 week to 3 months.
Music: Mostly **country, folk** and **novelty**. Published "Lovin' Bound" (by Benettau), recorded by PJ Kamel; "Theodore" (by Gregory-Pul), recorded by Dave Gregory; and *Only A Woman* (by Baumgardner), recorded by Bunnie Mills, all on Sagittar Records.
Tips: "Study the top ten hits of today's charts—write for that market. There is always a market for a solid hit song."

GREEN MEADOWS PUBLISHING (BMI), Rt #4 Box 92, Charlotte Dr., Beaver Dam KY 42320. (502)274-3169. Executive Director: Robert Bailey. Music publisher, record company. Estab. 1991. Publishes 10 songs/year; publishes 2-3 new songwriters/year. Works with composers and lyricists. Pays standard royalty.
How to Contact: Write or call first to obtain permission to submit. Prefers cassette with 5 songs and lyric sheet. Does not return unsolicited material. Reports in 2 months.
Music: Mostly **rock, folk, country**; also **gospel, blues** and **R&B**. Published "Where Did Our Lovin' Go," "Land up High," and "Oh Kentucky," all written and recorded by Robert Bailey on Beatle Records.

*GROOVELAND MUSIC, 1324 Oakton, Evanston IL 60202. (708)328-4203. Fax: (708)328-4236. Creative Director: Alan J. Goldberg. Music publisher. Estab. 1990. Publishes 6-12 songs/year; publishes 1-2 new songwriters/year. Teams collaborators. Pays standard royalty.
Affiliate(s): Hitsource Publishing (BMI).
How to Contact: Write or call first and obtain permission to submit. Prefers cassette with 3 songs and lyric sheet. Does not return unsolicited material. Reports in 1-4 months.
Music: Mostly **pop, dance** and **rap**; also **country** and **R&B**. Published *Come On Home*, written and recorded by Dallas Wayne on Morgan Records.

*FRANK GUBALA MUSIC, Hillside Rd., Cumberland RI 02864. (401)333-6097. Contact: Frank Gubala. Music publisher and booking agency.
How to Contact: Prefers cassette and lead sheet. Does not return unsolicited material. Reports in 3 months.
Music: Blues, disco, easy listening, MOR, top 40/pop, rock and **country.**

HALO INTERNATIONAL P.O. Box 101, Sutton MA 01590. Professional Manager: John Gagne. Music publisher, record company (MSM Records, Halo Records, Bronco Records), record producer; artists signed to labels only. BMI. Estab. 1979. Publishes 1-4 songs/year. Receives up to 300 submissions/year. Works with composers and lyricists; teams collaborators. Pays standard royalty.
Affiliate(s): Pick the Hits Music (ASCAP), Mount Scott Music (BMI).
How to Contact: Write first and obtain permission to submit a tape. Prefers cassette with 2 songs and lyric sheets. Does not return unsolicited material. Reports in 2-3 weeks.
Music: Mostly **contemporary country, traditional country, pop-rock** and **folk.** Also working with playwrights and composers for musical and theater works with incidental music. Published "Here Comes the Rain Again" (by M. Lewis/M. Brush), recorded by Gwen Newton on Halo Records (country); *The Windows* (by J.S. Gagne), recorded by Terry Michaels on Allagash Records (country); and Sound Score: "Hamlet" (written and recorded by J.S. Gagne), on MSM Records (theater).
Tips: "Keep writing. Like any other craft you will improve only through practice."

HAMMER MUSIK GMBH, Christophstr. 38, 7000 Stuttgart 1, **Germany.** Phone: (0711)6487620-27; Fax: (0711)6487629. Manager: Ingo Kleinhammer. GEMA. Estab. 1982. Music publisher and record company (Avenue and Boulevard). Publishes 100 songs/year; publishes 5 new songwriters/year. Works with composers and lyricists; teams collaborators. Pays standard royalty.
Affiliate(s): Belmont, Music Avenue, Platz Musikverlage, Edition Niteline, MMC Garden Of Music Publ., CMK, Modulation, Cross Town, Mediaphon, Musicolor, Hörvergnügen, Fun Freaks (GEMA); Edel Songs, Edition Cuppamore, TGM (SESAC).
How to Contact: Submit a demo tape—unsolicited submissions are OK. Prefers cassette or VHS videocassette. SAE and IRC. Reports in 6 weeks.
Music: Mostly **dance** and **disco;** also **jazz, rock** and **pop.** Published *Alice In Fashionland* (by Snyder, Florian), on Edelton Records; *Peer Gynt* (by Barber, Volker), on Edel Records; and "A Man Like You" (by Lopicic, Zeljko), on RoughTrade Records.

HAMSTEIN PUBLISHING COMPANY, INC., P.O. Box 163870, Austin TX 78716. Contact: Director, Creative Services. Music publisher and record producer (Lone Wolf Productions). ASCAP, BMI, SESAC. Estab. 1968. Publishes 600 songs/year. Works with composers and lyricists; teams collaborators. Pays standard royalty.
Affiliate(s): Hamstein Music Company (ASCAP), Howlin' Hits Music, Inc. (ASCAP), Red Brazos Music, Inc. (BMI), Great Cumberland Music (BMI), Edge O'Woods Music (ASCAP), Risin' River Music (SESAC), Stroudacaster Music (BMI), Stroudavarious Music (ASCAP), Stroudosphere Music (SESAC), Hamstein Music Limited (PRS), Hamstein Music Publishing France SARL (SACEM).
How to Contact: Write first and obtain permission to submit a tape. Prefers cassette or VHS videocassette with 3 songs and lyric sheet. SASE. Reports in 1 month.
Music: Mostly **pop/dance, rock** and **country;** also **R&B, gospel** and **instrumental.** Published *Recycler* (by Gibbons, Hill, Beard), recorded by ZZ Top on Warner Bros. Records (rock); and *Killin' Time*, written and recorded by Clint Black on RCA/BMG Records (country).

HAPPY HOUR MUSIC, Dept. SM, 5206 Benito St., Montclair CA 91763. (714)621-9903. Fax: (714)621-2412. President: Judith M. Wahnon. Music publisher and record company (Happy Hour Music). BMI. Estab. 1985. Publishes 5 songs/year; publishes 3 new songwriters/year. Works with composers.
How to Contact: Write first and obtain permission to submit a tape. Prefers cassette. SASE. Reports in 3 weeks.
Music: Mostly **jazz** and **Brazilian contemporary.** Published "The New Lambadas" (by Loão Parahyba); "Alemão Bem Brasileiro" (by Olmir Stocker); "Hermeto Pascoal Egrupo" (by Hermeto Pascoal); and Antonio Adolfo, all on Happy Hour Records (Brazilian).

Remember: Don't "shotgun" your demo tapes. Submit only to companies interested in the type of music you write. For more submission hints, refer to Getting Started on page 7.

HARMONY STREET MUSIC, Box 4107, Kansas City KS 66104. (913)299-2881. President: Charlie Beth. ASCAP. Estab. 1985. Music publisher, record company (Harmony Street Records), and record producer (Harmony Street Productions). Publishes 30-50 songs/year; publishes 15 new songwriters/year. Pays standard royalty.
Affiliate(s): Harmony Lane Music (BMI).
How to Contact: Prefers cassette (or VHS videocassette) with 1-3 songs and lyric sheet or lead sheet. SASE. "Due to the large amount of submissions that we receive we are no longer able to return unsolicited material. We will report within 6 weeks if we are interested."
Music: Country, gospel, rockabilly, pop, R&B, bluegrass and **rock.** Published "Count Me Present" (by Paulette Howard and Bob Warren), recorded by Cindi Crowley on T&M Records; "I Keep Comin' Back To You" (by Terry Allen and Sue Mahurin), recorded by Terry Allen on Harmony Street Records (country); "So Many Women, So Little Time" (by Edna Mae Foy and Virgil Hooks), recorded by Don Malena on Starquest Records; and "Don't Tell My Heart" (by Scott Hansgen), recorded by Tony Mantor on Harmony Street Records (country).
Tips: "Start with a good strong hook and build your song around it. A song is only as good as the hook or idea. Make each line and verse say something. Keep your lyrics and melody fairly simple but interesting. Your chorus should stand out musically (usually up-lifting). Demos should be clear and clean with voice out front. Try to keep your songs three minutes or less. Songs must be original both musically and lyrically. Send only your best."

***JOHANN HARTEL MUSIKVERLAG**, Nibelungenring 1, A-3423 St. Andrä–Wörden, Austria 0043-2242/33-519. Contact: Hans Hartel. Music Publisher. AKM. Estab. 1985. Publishes 100 songs/year. Publishes 5 new songwriters/year. Hires staff writers. Works with composers and lyricists; teams collaborators. Pays "usual standard royalties per AKM/Austro Mechana."
Affiliate(s): Elisabeth Lindl, Edition Dum Dum, Edition Magnum, Edition Cactus.
How to Contact: Submit a demo tape by mail—unsolicited submissions O.K. Prefers cassette with 3 songs and lyric sheet. SASE. Reports in 1 month "only if interested."
Music: Mostly **pop, German pop** and **instrumental**; also **ethno** and **New Age.** Published "Ciao Amore" (by Jonny Blue), recorded by Hans Hartel (German pop single).

***HAWK'S BILL MUSIC**, P.O. Box 910, Orange VA 22960. (703)672-9120. President: Parke Stanley. Music publisher. Estab. 1991. Works with composers and/or lyricists; teams collaborators. Pays standard royalty.
How to Contact: Submit demo tape by mail. Unsolicited submissions are OK. Prefers cassette with lyric sheet. SASE. Reports in 2 weeks.
Music: Mostly **country rock, country** and **R&B;** also **crossover** and **pop.**
Tips: "Learn the song techniques that artists are looking for, particularly hooks featuring plays-on-words and antonyms (two words with opposite meanings). Use vivid imagery. Constantly write down hit songs from the radio and observe their rhyming patterns. Express everyday situations in a new way. Positive, up-tempo songs have a better chance of being cut. Write us and ask for our free tip sheets to make your songs more competitive. We have Music Row connections."

***HEARTBEAT MUSIC**, 282 Bruce Ct., Westerville OH 43081. (614)882-5919. Vice President: Stephen Bashaw. Music publisher and record company. Estab. 1987. Publishes 25-30 songs/year; publishes 5-10 new songwriters/year. Works with composers or lyricists; teams collaborators. Pays standard royalty.
Affiliate(s): RGK Heartbeat Music (ASCAP), RGK Heartlight Music (BMI).
How to Contact: Call first to arrange personal interview. Submit demo tape by mail. Unsolicited submissions are OK. Prefers cassette and lyric sheet. SASE. Reports in 3-4 weeks.
Music: Mostly **adult contemporary Christian, black gospel** and **inspirational;** also **Christian rock/pop.** Published *The Word Is* (by Matt Huesmann); *Church, Do You Have It* (by James Mitchell); and *Forgive Me* (by Matt Huesman), all recorded by Heartlight Studios on Heartbeat Music Records.

HEAVEN SONGS, C-300, 16776 Lakeshore Dr., Lake Elsinore CA 92330. Contact: Dave Paton. Music publisher, record company and record producer. BMI. Publishes 30-50 songs/year; publishes 10 new songwriters/year. Pays standard royalty.
How to Contact: Prefers 7½ ips reel-to-reel or cassette with 3-6 songs and lyric sheet. SASE. Reports in 2 weeks.
Music: Country, dance-oriented, easy listening, folk, jazz, MOR, progressive, R&B, rock, soul and **top 40/pop.** Published "Daddy's Blue Eyes" and "Hurry Home Soldier," both by Linda Rae and Breakheart Pass.
Tips: Looking for "better quality demos."

HEAVY JAMIN' MUSIC, P.O. Box 1622, Hendersonville TN 37077. (615)822-1044. Manager: S.D. Neal. Music publisher. BMI, ASCAP. Estab. 1970. Publishes 10 songs/year; publishes 4-10 new songwriters/year. Works with composers. Pays standard royalty.

Affiliate(s): Sus-Den (ASCAP), Valynn (BMI) and Dr. Canada (ASCAP).
How to Contact: Submit a demo tape—unsolicited submissions are OK. Prefers 7½ ips reel-to-reel or cassette (or VHS videocassette) with 2-6 songs and lyric sheet. SASE. Reports in 3-4 weeks.
Music: Mostly **rock** and **country**; also **bluegrass, blues, easy listening, folk, gospel, jazz, MOR, progressive, Spanish, R&B, soul, top 40/pop** and **rock-a-billy.** Published "Hold Me," written and recorded by Richie Derwald on Terrock Records (rock); "That's It," written and recorded by Dixie Dee on Rock-A-Billy Records (rock); and *Baby, You're Gone* (by D. Daniels), recorded by Susan Sterling on Toronto Records (C&W).

*HENDERSON GROUP MUSIC, 125 Powell Mill Rd., Spartanburg SC 29301. (803)576-5832. Owner/President: Dr. Barry Henderson. Music publisher and Artist Management. Estab. 1990. Publishes 10-20 songs/year; publishes 2-3 new songwriters/year. Works with composers; teams collaborators. Pays standard royalty.
Affiliate: HPL Communications (BMI).
How to Contact: Submit demo tape by mail. Unsolicited submissions are OK. Prefers cassette with 3-4 songs. Does not return material. Reports in 2-3 months.
Music: Mostly **country, pop** and **rock.** Published *Gone To The Country,* written and recorded by Joe Bennett on HGM Records.
Tips: "The song has to be commercial."

HENLY MUSIC ASSOCIATES, 45 Perham St., W. Roxbury MA 02132. (617)325-4594. President: Bill Nelson. Music publisher, record company (Woodpecker Records) and record producer. ASCAP. Estab. 1987. Publishes 5 songs/year; publishes 5 new songwriters/year. Works with composers and lyricists; teams collaborators. Pays standard royalty.
How to Contact: Submit a demo tape by mail—unsolicited submissions are OK. Prefers cassette with 4 songs and lyric sheet. SASE. Reports in 1 month.
Music: Mostly **country, pop** and **gospel.** Published "Big Bad Bruce" (by J. Dean), recorded by B.N.O. (pop); "Do You Believe in Miracles" (by B. Nelson), recorded by Parttime Singers (country); and "Don't Hurry with Love" (by B. Nelson and B. Bergeron), recorded by Bill Nelson (country); all on Woodpecker Records.

HEUPFERD MUSIK VERLAG GmbH, Box 30 11 28, Ringwaldstr. 18, Dreieich 63303 **Germany.** Phone and fax: (06103)86970. General Manager: Christian Winkelmann. Music publisher. GEMA. Publishes 60-100 songs/year; publishes 2-3 new songwriters/year. Works with composers and lyricists. Pays "royalties after GEMA distribution plan."
Affiliate(s): Edition Payador (GEMA) and Song Bücherei (book series).
How to Contact: Write first and obtain permission to submit. Prefers cassette and lead sheet. SAE and IRC. Reports in 1 month.
Music: Mostly **folk, jazz, fusion;** also **New Age, rock** and **ethnic music.** Published "Valse Mélancolique," written and recorded by Rüdiger Oppermann on Wuntertüte Records (new age); and "Rainy Sundays" (by Andy Irvine), recorded by Andy Irvine and others on Wundertüte Records.

*HICKORY LANE PUBLISHING AND RECORDING (SOCAN, ASCAP), P.O. Box 2275, Vancouver, British Columbia V6B 3W5 **Canada.** President: Chris Michaels. A&R Manager: Dave Rogers. Music publisher, record company and record producer. Estab. 1988. Publishes 3 songs/year; publishes 3 new songwriters/year. Hires staff writers. Works with composers and lyricists; teams collaborators. Pays standard royalty.
How to Contact: Submit demo tape by mail. Unsolicited submissions are OK. Prefers cassette (or VHS videocassette) with 1-5 songs. SASE. Reports in 4-6 weeks.
Music: Mostly **country, MOR** and **gospel;** also **soft rock, musical compositions** and **children's music.** Published "Yesterdays Fool"; "Country Drives Me Wild"; and "Without You And Me", all written and recorded by Chris Michaels on Hickory Lane Records.
Tips: "Keep the vocals up front, have feeling in your song with a strong melody, easy lyrics. Be original."

HICKORY VALLEY MUSIC, 10303 Hickory Valley, Ft. Wayne IN 46835. President: Allan Straten. Music publisher, record company (Yellow-Jacket Records) and record producer (Al Straten Productions). ASCAP, BMI. Estab. 1988. Publishes 10 songs/year; publishes 5 new songwriters/year. Works with composers. Pays standard royalty.
Affiliate(s): Hickory Valley Music (ASCAP), Straten's Song (BMI).
How to Contact: Submit a demo tape by mail—unsolicited submissions are OK. Prefers cassette with 3-4 songs and lyric sheets. SASE. Reports in 3-4 weeks.
Music: Mostly **country** and **MOR.** Published "I'd Love To See You Again," and "Call Me" (by Grogg/Staten), recorded by April; both on Yellow-Jacket Records (country).
Tips: "Keep it simple—write about one single moment in time and be prepared to re-write."

HICKY'S MUSIC BMI, Dept. SM, 2540 Woodburn Ave., Cincinnati OH 45206. (513)681-5436. A&R Director: Smiley Hicks. Music publisher. BMI. Estab. 1985. Publishes 8 songs/year; publishes 4 new songwriters/year. Works with composers and lyricists; teams collaborators. Pays royalty.
How to Contact: Write first to get permission to submit a tape. Prefers cassette with 4 songs and lyric sheets. No porno or dirty lyrics, please. SASE. Reports in 4 weeks.
Music: Mostly **R&B, gospel** and **danceable pop**; also **rap**. Published "Stingy" (by Wavier, Hickland), recorded on Vibe Records (dance); and "Heartbeat" (by Barber, Hickland), recorded on Vibe Records (dance).

HIGH DESERT MUSIC CO., 29526 Peoria Rd., Halsey OR 97348-9742. (503)491-3524. A/R: Karl V. Black. Music publisher. BMI. Estab. 1976. Publishes 20 songs/year. Works with composers and lyricists; teams collaborators. Pays standard royalty.
How to Contact: Submit a demo tape by mail—unsolicited submissions are OK. Demos do not have to be professional. Cassette only. "Be sure name is on everything submitted." Does not return material. No SASE required.
Music: Holiday, country, MOR, pop, R&B, gospel. Recording artists include Higginbothem, Larry LaVey and Don McHan.
Tips: "Make sure lyrics make sense. After listening to a song you should not have to ask 'What's the name of that song?' "

HIGH-MINDED MOMA PUBLISHING & PRODUCTIONS, 10330 Cape Arago, Coos Bay OR 97420. (503)888-9276. Contact: Kai Moore Snyder. Music publisher and production company. BMI. Pays standard royalty.
How to Contact: Prefers 7½ ips reel-to-reel, CD or cassette with 4-8 songs and lyric sheet. SASE. Reports in 1 month.
Music: Country, MOR, rock (country) and top 40/pop.
Tips: "We have just started to accept outside material."

HISTORY PUBLISHING CO., Dept. SM, Box 7-11, Macks Creek MO 65786. (314)363-5432. President: B.J. Carnahan. Music publisher, record company (BOC, History) and record producer (AudioLoft Recording Studios). BMI. Estab. 1977. Publishes 10-15 songs/year; 2 new songwriters/year. Works with composer and lyricists. Pays standard royalty.
How to Contact: Write first and obtain permission to submit a tape. Prefers cassette with 2 songs and lyric sheets. "We prefer not to keep songs on file. Send a good, clean demo with vocal up front." SASE. Reports in 1 month.
Music: Mostly **country** and **gospel**. Published "Big Texas Waltz" (by G. Terry), recorded by Merle Haggard on Curb Records (country); "Remember the Alimony" (by J.B. Haynes), recorded by Bill and Roy on Gallery II Records (country); and "Grovespring Swing" (by F. Stowe), recorded by F. Stowe on History Records (country).

HIT & RUN MUSIC PUBLISHING INC., Dept. SM, 1841 Broadway, Suite 411, New York NY 10023. (212)956-2882. Creative Director: Joey Gmerek. Assistant: Jennifer Chin. Music publisher. ASCAP. Publishes 20-30 songs/year; publishes 2 new songwriters/year. Hires staff writers. Works with composers and lyricists; teams collaborators. Pays standard royalty.
Affiliate(s): Charisma Music Publishing USA Inc. (ASCAP), Hidden Pun Music Publishing Inc. (BMI).
How to Contact: Write or call first and obtain permission to submit a tape. Prefers cassette (or VHS videocassette) with lyric sheet. Does not return unsolicited material.
Music: Mostly **pop, rock** and **R&B**; also **dance**. Published "The Living Years" (by Mike Rutherford & B.A. Robertson), recorded by Mike & The Mechanics on Atlantic (pop); "Saltwater" written and recorded by Julian Lennon on Atlantic Records (pop); "I Can't Dance" (by Phil Collins/Mike Rutherford/Tony Banks) recorded by Genesis on Atlantic Records (pop) and "It's not a Love Thing," written and recorded by Geoffrey Williams on Gian Records (pop/R&B).

HITSBURGH MUSIC CO., P.O. Box 1431, 233 N. Electra, Gallatin TN 37066. (615)452-0324. President/General Manager: Harold Gilbert. Music publisher. BMI. Estab. 1964. Publishes 12 songs/year. Receives 30 submissions/month. Pays standard royalty.
Affiliate(s): 7th Day Music (BMI).
How to Contact: Submit demo tape by mail—unsolicited submissions are OK. Prefers cassette (or quality videocassette) with 2-4 songs and lead sheet. Prefers studio produced demos. Reports in 6 weeks. Does not return unsolicited material.
Music: Country and MOR. Published "Make Me Yours" (by K'leetha Gilbert), recorded by Kim Gilbert; and "The Last Kiss" (by Hal Gilbert), recorded by Jean; and "The Depth of His Love" (by H. Gilbert), recorded by Kim Gilbert, all on Southern City Records (pop).

HITSOURCE PUBLISHING, 1324 Oakton, Evanston IL 60202. (708)328-4203. President: Alan J. Goldberg. Music publisher. BMI. Estab. 1986. Publishes 12 songs/year; publishes 3-6 new songwriters/year. Receives 150 submissions/year. Works with composers. Pays standard royalty.
Affiliate(s): Grooveland Music (ASCAP).
How to Contact: Write or call first and obtain permission to submit. Prefers cassette with 2 songs and lyric sheet. SASE. Reports in 1 to 6 months. "No reply if we are very busy." Does not return unsolicited material.
Music: Country, pop, rock 'n' roll, R&B and **dance.** Published "Hostage," written and recorded by TS Henry Webb; "Love Without End" (by H. Berkman) and "Be A Good Girl" (by Juan Lopez), recorded by Organic Theatre, all on Webb Records.
Tips: "Come up with an original idea and develop that idea with original and memorable melody and lyrics. Send me a great song, not a good song, that an established artist would want to risk their career on."

HOLY GRAIL PUBLISHING, 13313 Perthshire St., Austin TX 78729. (512)219-1355. Vice President/A&R: Gary A. Coll. Music publisher and record company (Pendragon Records). BMI. Estab. 1987. Publishes 50 songs/year; publishes 5-10 new songwriters/year. Works with composers. Pays standard royalty.
How to Contact: Write or call first and obtain permission to submit a tape. Prefers cassette with 3 songs and lyric sheet. "Include a self-addressed stamped envelope." Does not return unsolicited material. Reports in 3 months. "We now (freelance) produce for artists in the Texas area. Please write for terms and prices."
Music: Mostly **jazz, rock** and **pop;** also **gospel.** Published "Theft," written and recorded by C.A. Collier; *Charlie Chaplin's Factory* (by J. Cook), recorded by J. Cook and others; and "Lion's Creed" (by Tom Kross and S. Wilcox), recorded by Young Thunder, all on Pendragon Records (metal).
Tips: "Pray . . . real real hard!"

HOLY SPIRIT MUSIC, Box 31, Edmonton KY 42129. (502)432-3183. President: W. Junior Lawson. Music publisher and record company. BMI. Member GMA, International Association of Gospel Music Publishers. Estab. 1973. Publishes 4 songs/year; publishes 2 new songwriters/year. Pays standard royalty. Works with composers.
How to Contact: Submit demo tape—unsolicited submissions OK. Prefers cassette with 2 songs and lyric sheet. SASE. Reports in 3 weeks.
Music: Mostly **Southern gospel;** also **MOR, progressive** and **top 40/pop.** Published "Excuses," "More Excuses" and "My God Knows What I Need," recorded by The Kingsmen on River Song Records.
Tips: Send "good clear cut tape with typed or printed copy of lyrics."

*HOLYROOD PRODUCTIONS, 40 Sciennes, Edinburgh EK9 1NH **Scotland**. Contact: Neil Ross. PRS. Estab. 1973. Publishes 10-20 songs/year; publishes 1-2 new songwriters/year. Works with composers.
Affiliate(s): Ad-Chorel Music (PRS).
How to Contact: Submit a demo tape by mail—unsolicited submissions are OK. Prefers cassette with 2-3 songs. Does not return unsolicited material. Reports in 3 weeks.
Music: Mostly **pop, dance, MOR;** also **traditional.** Published "Your Wish," written and recorded by Santos on Holyrood Records (dance); "Come Together," written and recorded by Howie J & Co. on REL Records (pop); and "Radio" (by Gordon Campbell), recorded by Shakin' Stevens on Epic Records.

HUMANFORM PUBLISHING COMPANY, Box 158486, Nashville TN 37215. (615)373-9312. Publisher: Kevin Nairon. BMI. Music publisher. Pays standard royalty.
How to Contact: Submit demo tape by mail—unsolicited submissions are OK. Prefers cassette with 4 songs and lyric and lead sheets. SASE. Reports in 4 weeks.
Music: Mostly **blues (traditional).** Publishes "The Rain Is Falling" and "I Need Your Love" (by Kevin Nairon), recorded by Sleepy Joe on CS Records.
Tips: "Please strive for maximum quality when making your demo. Write about your own experiences in a standard blues format."

HUMONGOUS MUSIC PUBLISHING, INC., (formerly Broozbee Music, Inc.), Suite 308, 38 East 28th St., New York NY 10016. (212)447-6000. Fax: (212)447-6003. Executive Vice President: Bruce B. Fisher. Music publisher, record company (Big Productions Records), record producer and management company. ASCAP. Estab. 1992. Publishes 12 songs/year; publishes 6 new songwriters/year. Teams collaborators. Pays standard royalty. "If co-publishing with major publisher, pays less than the statutory rate."
Affiliate: XXL Music Publishing (BMI).
How to Contact: Submit a demo tape by mail—unsolicited submissions are OK. Prefers cassette or VHS videocassette with 3 songs and lyric sheet. "Send the best possible representation of the material." SASE. Reports in 2 months.

Music: Mostly **R&B/dance, pop/dance** and **alternative rock**. Published "Butt Naked" (by P. Punzone and P. Falcone); "I Love Music" (by G. Sicard and B.B. Fisher), recorded by Charm on Turnstyle/ Atlantic Records. (hip/house)
Tips: "The song has to fit in the musical styles we listed. Be professional. Listen before you submit. Does your song compare to the quality of songwriting on the radio? Be realistic. The music industry does not pat you on the back. Competition is fierce. Expect rejection. The flavor of the week makes it, not always the best song."

*INTERNATIONAL MUSIC NETWORK (BMI), #300, 3151 Cahuenga Blvd. W., Los Angeles CA 90068. (213)882-6127. Fax: (213)874-4602. Professional Manager: Michael Carey Schneider. Music publisher. Estab. 1985. Publishes 30-50 songs/year; publishes 1 or 2 new songwriters/year. Works with composers and lyricists; teams collaborators. Pays depending on individual situations.
How to Contact: Call first and obtain permission to submit. Prefers cassette with 3 songs and lyric sheet. SASE. Reports in 6 weeks.
Music: Mostly **R&B/dance, pop** and **rock**. Published "Fallen," written and recorded by Lauren Wood on EMI Records (*Pretty Woman* soundtrack); and *More Than Just The Two Of Us* (by Michael Carey Schneider), recorded by Sneaker.

*INTERPLANETARY MUSIC, 584 Roosevelt, Gary IN 46404. (219)886-2003. President: James R. Hall III. Music publisher, record company (Interplanetary Records), record producer and booking agency. Estab. 1972. BMI. Publishes 10 songs/year; publishes 4 new songwriters/year. Works with composers and teams collaborators. Pays standard royalty.
How to Contact: Call first and obtain permission to submit, or to arrange personal interview. Prefers cassette. SASE. Reports in 5 weeks.
Music: R&B, top 40/urban contemporary. Published "Make It Last" (by James R. Hall/Lamont Robin) and "No Love" (by James R. Hall/K. Henry), both recorded by Carolyn Hall on Interplanetary Records (pop/R&B).

*IRON SKILLET MUSIC, B-105, Richard Jones Rd., Nashville TN 37215. (615)297-8595. Fax: (615)292-7178. Executive Vice President: Claude G. Southall. Music publisher, record company (Rustic Records Inc.), record producer. Estab. 1984. Publishes 20 songs/year. Pays standard 50% royalty.
Affiliate(s): Covered Bridge Music (BMI), Town Square Music (SESAC). Submit demo tape by mail. Unsolicited submissions are OK. Prefers cassette with 3 songs and lyric sheet. SASE. Reports in 3 months.
Music: Mostly **country**. Published "Turn off the Lights," "You Make Me Feel Like Dancin," "Maybe This Time" all written and recorded by Holt Wilson, all recorded by Rustic Records.
Tips: "Material should be attention grabbing from start to finish with good hook."

IVORY PALACES MUSIC, 3141 Spottswood Ave., Memphis TN 38111. (901)323-3509. President: Jack Abell. Music publisher, record producer and sheet music publisher. ASCAP. Estab. 1978. Publishes 5 songs/year; publishes 1 new songwriter/year. Works with composers and lyricists; teams collaborators. Pays standard royalty; sheet music: 10% of retail. "Computerized music typesetting services require a 50% deposit."
How to Contact: Write first and obtain permission to submit. Prefers cassette with 2-5 songs and lyric sheet. "Submit simple demo with clear vocal." SASE. Reports in 2 months.
Music: Mostly **religious, educational** and **classical**; also **children's** and **folk**. Published "Little One," written and recorded by T. Starr (Christian); "Larkin's Dulcimer Book," written and recorded by Larkin Bryant (folk); and "Sonatina Concertata" (by J.M. Spadden), recorded by L. Jackson (classical), all on Ivory Palaces.

JACLYN MUSIC, 306 Millwood Dr., Nashville TN 37217-1604. (615)366-9999. President: Jack Lynch. Music publisher, producer, recording company (Jalyn, Nashville Bluegrass and Nashville Country, Recording Companies) and distributor (Nashville Music Sales). BMI, ASCAP. Estab. 1967. Publishes 50-100 songs/year; 25-50 new songwriters/year. Works with composers and lyricists. Pays standard royalties.
Affiliate(s): Jaclyn Music (BMI), JLMG (ASCAP), Jack Lynch Music Group (parent company) and Nashville Country Productions.
How to Contact: Submit a demo tape—unsolicited submissions are OK. Send good quality cassette recording, neat lyric sheets and SASE. Prefers 1-4 selections per tape. Reports in 1 month.
Music: Country, bluegrass, gospel and **MOR**. Published "He Isn't You" (by Sara Hull), recorded by Elaine George on Jalyn Records; "Somewhere Along The Line" (by Vicki Watts), recorded by Elaine George on Jalyn Records; and "The Nashville Blues" (by Lynch/Urich), recorded by Paul Woods on NCP Records.

JANA JAE MUSIC, P.O. Box 35726, Tulsa OK 74153. (918)749-1647. Secretary: Sue Teaff. Music publisher, record company (Lark Records) and record producer. BMI. Estab. 1977. Publishes 5-10 songs/year; publishes 1-2 new songwriters/year. Pays standard royalty.
How to Contact: Submit demo tape by mail—unsolicted submissions OK. Prefers cassette (or VHS videocassette) with 4-5 songs and lyric and lead sheet if possible. Does not return unsolicited material.
Music: Country, pop and instrumentals (classical or country). Published "Fiddlesticks," "Mayonnaise," "Bus 'n' Ditty" (by Steven Upfold), and "Let the Bible Be Your Roadmap" (by Irene Elliot), all recorded by Jana Jae on Lark Records.

JAELIUS ENTERPRISES, Route 2, Box 94B, Royse City TX 75189. (818)899-4446. Owner: James Cornelius. Music publisher. ASCAP, BMI. Publishes 3-5 songs/year; publishes 3 new songwriters/year. Pays standard royalty.
Affiliate(s): Jaelius Music (ASCAP), Hitzgalore Music (BMI), Air Rifle Music (ASCAP) and Bee Bee Gun Music (BMI).
How to Contact: Write first and obtain permission to submit. Prefers cassette. SASE. Reports in 3 weeks.
Music: Mostly pop, country and gospel; also R&B. Published "So It Shall Be" (by G. Penny/Lang), recorded by K.D. Lang on Sire Records; "Feeling in Love" (by John Cale), recorded by J.J. Cale on Silvertone Records; and "I Didn't Wanna Boogie" (by Jerry Allison), recorded by Sylvie on Playback Records.
Tips: "Today's market requires good demos. Strong lyrics are a must."

*JAMMY MUSIC PUBLISHERS LTD., The Beeches, 244 Anniesland Rd., Glasgow G13 1XA, **Scotland**. Phone: (041)954-1873. Managing Director: John D. R. MacCalman. Music publisher and record company. PRS. Estab. 1977. Publishes 45 songs/year; publishes 2 new songwriters/year. Works with composers and lyricists. Pays royalty "in excess of 50%."
How to Contact: Write first and obtain permission to submit. Does not return unsolicited material. Reports in 2 months.
Music: Mostly rock, pop, country and instrumental; also Scottish. Published "The Wedding Song," (by Bill Padley/Grant Mitchell), recorded by True Love Orchestra on BBC Records (pop); *The Old Button Box* (by D.McCrone), recorded by Foster & Allen on Stylus Records; and "Absent Friends" (by D. McCrone), recorded by Dominic Kirwan on Ritz Records.
Tips: "We are now working with a small writers' roster and it's unlikely we would be able to take new writers in the future."

JA/NEIN MUSIKVERLAG GMBH, Hallerstr. 72, D-20146 Hamburg **Germany**. Phone: (40)4102161. Fax: (040)448850. General Manager: Mary Dostal. Music publisher, record company and record producer. GEMA. Publishes 100 songs/year; publishes 20 new songwriters/year. Works with composers and lyricists; teams collaborators. Pays 50-60% royalty.
Affiliate(s): Pinorrekk Mv., Star-Club Mv., and Wunderbar Mv. (GEMA).
How to Contact: Submit a demo tape—unsolicited submissions are OK. Prefers cassette (or VHS videocassette) and lyric sheet. SAE and IRC. Reports in 2 months.
Music: Mostly rock, pop, MOR and blues. Published "Die Nordseeküste" (by K. Büchner), recorded by Klaus & Klaus on Polydor Records (MOR); "Heat It Up" (by A. Zwingenberger), recorded by Axel Zwingenberger on Vagabond Records (blues); and "Ficken" (by Hengst), recorded by Die Braut on Lux Records (rock).
Tips: "Send single-A-side material only, plus photos (if artist). Leave 2-3 seconds space between the songs. Enclose lyrics. We only give negative reply if SAE and IRC is enclosed. And good isn't good enough!"

JASPER STONE MUSIC (ASCAP)/JSM SONGS (BMI), P.O. Box 24, Armonk NY 10504. President: Chris Jasper. Vice President/General Counsel: Margie Jasper. Music publisher. ASCAP, BMI. Estab. 1986. Publishes 20-25 songs/year. Works with composers; teams collaborators. "Each contract is worked out individually and negotiated depending on terms."
How to Contact: Submit a demo tape by mail—unsolicited submissions are OK. Prefers cassette with maximum of 3 songs and lyric sheets. SASE. Reports in 2-3 weeks.
Music: Mostly R&B/pop, rap and rock. Published "Make It Last," recorded by Chaka Khan on Warner Bros. Records; *Praise The Eternal* (written and recorded by Chris Jasper) and *Out Front* (written and recorded by Out Front), both on Gold City Records.
Tips: "Keep writing. Keep submitting tapes. Be persistent. Don't give it up. Send your best songs in the best form (best production possible.)"

JAY JAY PUBLISHING, 35 NE 62nd St., Miami FL 33138. (305)758-0000. Contact: Walter Jagiello. Music publisher, record company (Jay Jay Record and Tape Co.) and record producer. BMI. Estab. 1958. One of the founders of NARAS. Publishes 30 songs/year. Pays standard royalty.

How to Contact: Submit a demo tape—unsolicited submissions are OK. Prefers reel-to-reel or cassette (or VHS videocassette) with 2-6 songs and lyric sheet. Does not return unsolicited material. Reports in 2 months.

Music: Mostly **pop, country, polkas, waltzes** and **comedy.** "The type of songs that were made in the 50's and 60's. No rock and roll." Published *How I Love You Darlin'* (by Walter Jagiello) and *Lillian Polka* (by C. Siewierski/W. Jagiello), both recorded by Li'l Wally on Jay Jay Records.

Tips: "Make songs simple lyrics, simple melody, true to life! Send audio demo, sheet music with lyrics."

*JEDO INC., 5062 Calatrana Dr., Los Angeles CA 91364-1807. (818)703-0083. Fax: (818)784-5842. Vice President-Creative: Jon Devirian. Music publisher and record producer. Estab. 1978. Publishes 20 songs/year; publishes 2 new songwriters/year. Hires staff writers. Works with composers and lyricists; teams collaborators. Pays standard royalty.

Affiliate(s): J.E.D.O. Music, Worthless Music (ASCAP), SUKI Music, Pointless Music (BMI).

How to Contact: Write or submit demo tape by mail. Unsolicited submissions are OK. Prefers cassette (or VHS videocassette) with 5 songs and lyric sheet. SASE. Reports in 2 weeks.

Music: Mostly **pop/rock, country** and **R&B ballads;** also **alternative music.** Published "I Handle Snakes," written and recorded by Tonio K. on A&M Records (alternative rock); and "San Antonio Stroll" (by P. Noah), recorded by Tanya Tucker on MCA Records (country).

Tips: "We are partial to intriguing lyrics with strong melodies and hook chorus. Alternative writing styles are encouraged as well. Arrangement ideas and hook riffs are desired, feel free to submit more than one arrangement but keep it simple."

JELLEE WORKS MUSIC, P.O. Box 16572, Kansas City MO 64133. Phone: (800)283-SONG. President: Jimmy Lee. Music publisher, record company (Heart Land Records), record producer (Jellee Works Productions) and songwriter recording services. ASCAP, BMI. Estab. 1983. Publishes 24-36 songs/year; publishes 12-15 new songwriters/year. "Will work one on one with select songwriters to help them get started." Works with composers and lyricists; teams collaborators. Pays standard royalty.

Affiliate(s): Jellee Works Music (BMI) and Jellee Music Works (ASCAP).

How to Contact: Write first to obtain permission to submit, or write to arrange personal interview. Prefers cassette with no more than 2 songs per tape (or VHS videocassette) and lyric sheet. SASE. Reports in 4-6 weeks.

Music: Mostly **country, gospel** and **MOR;** also **country crossover, rock-a-billy** and **pop.** Published *We'll Meet Again* (by Bess Schuler), recorded by Berry & West; *Number One Song* (by Marilyn Townsend), recorded by Barb Sinor; and *Your Letter Came Today* (by Goy Renfroe), recorded by David Zeller, all on Heart Land Records.

Tips: "Learn to be professional. We put out a monthly newsletter dedicated to teaching the grassroots songwriter how to achieve success in this business by not only learning the craft but by opening the right doors."

JENNACO-ALEXAS PUBLISHING CO. (BMI), 3365 W. Millerberg Way, W. Jordan UT 84084. (801)566-9542. A&R: Patrick Melfi. Music publisher and record company (Alexas Records). BMI. Estab. 1976. Publishes 6-10 songs/year; publishes 2-3 new songwriters/year. Hires staff writers. Works with composers and lyricists. Pays standard royalty.

Affiliate(s): The Music Group (ASCAP), Alexas Music Productions (ASCAP).

How to Contact: Write first and obtain permission to submit. Prefers cassette or VHS videocassette with 1-3 songs and lyric sheet. SASE. Reports in 2 months.

Music: Mostly **country, pop** and **gospel.** Published *She's On Her Own* (by Melfi/Masters) recorded by Leroy Parnell on Arista Records (country), "Between Your Heart & Mine" (by Melfi) recorded by Prophesy on Atlantic Records (MOR) and *Child of God* (by Melfi/Kone) recorded by Sheri Sampson on Godley Music (gospel).

Tips: "Write from the heart! Write a good story and compliment it with a strong melody. We look for story songs like "Where Have You Been," recorded by Kathy Mattea or "Change My Mind," recorded by Oak Ridge Boys, written by AJ Masters and Jason Bloome."

JERJOY MUSIC, P.O. Box 1264, Peoria IL 61654-1264. (309)673-5755. Professional Manager: Jerry Hanlon. Music publisher. BMI. Estab. 1978. Publishes 4 songs/year; publishes 2 new songwriters/year. Pays standard royalty.

How to Contact: Submit a demo tape—unsolicited submissions are OK. Prefers cassette with 4-8 songs and lyric sheet. SASE. Reports in 2 weeks.

Music: Country (modern or traditional), **gospel/Christian, Irish music.** Published *If The Good Lord Is Willing* (by Sammie Marler/BobbyRoyce); *Jesus In the Picture* (by Rob Hull); and "The Calling" (by Jerry Hanlon), all recorded by Jerry Hanlon on UAR Records.

Tips: "Be 'real' in what you write. Don't submit any song that you don't honestly feel is strong in commercial value."

JOEY BOY PUBLISHING CO., 3081 NW 24th St., Miami FL 33142. (305)633-7469. Director: Allen Johnston. Music publisher. BMI. Estab. 1985. Publishes 100-150 songs/year; publishes 12-15 new songwriters/year. Works with composers and lyricists; teams collaborators. Pays standard royalty.
Affiliate(s): Joey Boy Publishing Co. (BMI), Beam of Light (ASCAP) and To Soon To Tell (SESAC).
How to Contact: Submit demo tape by mail—unsolicited submissions are OK. Prefers cassette with no more than 3 songs and lyric sheets. "Type or print lyric sheet legibly please!" SASE. Reports in 6-8 weeks.
Music: Mostly **R&B, rap**; also **dance, jazz** and **comedy**. Published "30's and Low's" and *Kings of Bass* by Bass Patrol, on Joey Boy Records (bass); "La Passola" (by A. Santos), recorded by Wilfrido Vargas on T.H. Ralven Records (Spanish); and *Gangsta Bass* (by A. Cuff), recorded by Miami Boyz (bass) on On Top Records.
Tips: "Be true to your trade and write about the things you know."

JOF-DAVE MUSIC, 1055 Kimball Ave., Kansas City KS 66104. (913)342-8456. Owner: David E. Johnson. Music publisher, record company (Cymbal Records). ASCAP. Estab. 1984. Publishes 60 songs/year; 4 new songwriters/year. Works with composers. Pays standard royalty.
How to Contact: Write or call first and obtain permission to submit a tape. Prefers cassette with 3-4 songs and lyric or lead sheets. SASE. Reports in 1 month.
Music: Mostly **rock, pop** and **rap**; also **serious music, country, R&B**. Published "Frozen Roses," and "The Gumdrops Symphony" (by Don Grace), recorded by Ken Garrett; and "I Have A Dream," written and recorded by Reed Greenfield, all on Cymbal Records.

LITTLE RICHIE JOHNSON MUSIC, 318 Horizon Vista Blvd., Belen NM 87002. (505)864-7441. Manager: Tony Palmer. Music publisher, record company (LRJ Records) and record producer. BMI. Estab. 1959. Publishes 50 songs/year; publishes 10 new songwriters/year. Works with composers. Pays standard royalty.
Affiliate(s): Little Cowboy Music (ASCAP).
How to Contact: Submit a demo tape—unsolicited submissions are OK. SASE. Reports in 6 weeks.
Music: Country and **Spanish**. Published "Where Did She Go New Mexico" (by Jerry Jaramillo) and "Jumpin Joe's" (by Bruce Cooper), recorded by Little Richie Johnson on LRJ Records (C&W).

*AL JOLSON BLACK & WHITE MUSIC, 114 175th Ave. S., Nashville TN 37203. (615)244-5656. President: Albert Jolson. Music Publisher. BMI. Estab. 1981. Publishes 65 songs/year; 50 new songwriters/year. Works with composers and lyricists; teams collaborators. Pays standard royalty.
Affiliate(s): Jolie House Music (ASCAP).
How to Contact: Submit a demo tape—unsolicited submissions are OK. Prefers cassette with 3 songs and lyric sheet. Send: Attn. Johnny Drake. SASE. Reports in 6 weeks.
Music: Mostly **country crossover, light rock** and **pop**. Published "Come Home To West Virginia" (by Scott Phelps), recorded by Kathy Mattea; "Ten Tiny Fingers Ten Tiny Toes" (by David John Hanley), recorded by Kelly Dawn on ASA Jolson Records (country); and "Indiana Highway" recorded by Staggerlee on ASA Jolson Records (country).
Tips: "Make sure it has a strong hook. Ask yourself if it is something you would hear on the radio 5 times a day. Have good audible vocals on demo tape."

JOSENA MUSIC, P.O. Box 566, Los Altos CA 94022. President: Joe Nardone. Music publisher and producer. SESAC. Estab. 1983. Publishes 30 songs/year; publishes 1-2 new songwriters/year. Hires staff songwriters. Works with composers and lyricists. Pays standard royalty.
Affiliate(s): Reigninme Music (SESAC).
How to Contact: Write first and obtain permission to submit a tape. Prefers cassette with 3 songs and lyric sheet. Does not return unsolicited material. Reports in 2 months if interested.
Music: Mostly **Christian rock/pop, pop** and **gospel**; also **modern rock** and **Latin Music** as well—**flamenco, rumba style** (Spanish) and **Spanish ballads**. Published "Coming Home," (by Dino Veloz/Joe Nardone), recorded by Joe Nardone (modern Christian rock); "Make Us One" (by Lee Kalem/Joe Nardone); recorded by Lillie Knauls (gospel); and "Go God's Way" and "In A World," written and recorded by Joe Nardone (jazz).
Tips: "Be persistent, send your best material. Get other opinions before submission."

JUMP MUSIC, Langemunt 71, 9420 AAIGEM, **Belgium**. Phone: (053)62-73-77. General Manager: Eddy Van Mouffaert. Music publisher, record company (Jump Records) and record producer. Member of SABAM S.V., Brussels. Publishes 100 songs/year; publishes 8 new songwriters/year. Works with composers and lyricists. Pays royalty via SABAM S.V.

How to Contact: Submit demo tape by mail. Prefers cassette. Does not return unsolicited material. Reports in 2 weeks.
Music: Mostly **easy listening, disco** and **light pop**; also **instrumentals**. Published "Ach Eddy" (by Eddy Govert), recorded by Samantha and Eddy Govert (light pop); "Vanavond" (by Eddy Govert), recorded by Danny Brendo (light pop), both on Scorpion Records; and "Wien Bleist Wien" (by Eddy Govert) recorded by Le Grand Julot (light pop) on B.M.P. Records.
Tips: "Music wanted with easy, catchy melodies (very commercial songs)."

*JUNGLE BOY MUSIC (BMI), 1230 Hill St., Santa Monica CA 90405-4708. (310)452-7004. Fax: (310)452-7035. President: Robert Anderson. Music publisher. Estab. 1982. Publishes 30 songs/year. Publishes 4 new songwriters/year. Hires staff songwriters. Works with composers and lyricists; teams collaborators. Pays standard 50% royalty.
How to Contact: Submit demo tape by mail. Unsolicited submissions are OK. Prefers cassette (or DAT) with up to 5 songs. SASE. Reports in 3 weeks.
Music: Mostly **rock, pop, R&B**; also **country** and **rap**. Published "Can't Stand This Heat" (by Paul Sabu), recorded by Lee Aaron, "Dream Burnin' Down" and "In My Blood," written and recorded by Paul Sabu on Now & Then Records.
Tips: "Believe in your song and don't be afraid to send it in, you never know."

JUST A NOTE, 1058 E. Saint Catherine, Louisville KY 40204. (503)637-2877. General Partner: John V. Heath. Music publisher, record companies (Hillview, Estate) and record producer (MVT Productions). ASCAP and BMI. Estab. 1979. Publishes 35 songs/year; publishes 10-15 new songwriters/year. Works with composers and lyricists. Pays standard royalty.
Affiliate(s): Two John's Music (ASCAP).
How to Contact: Submit a demo tape by mail—unsolicited submissions are OK. Prefers cassette, 7½ ips reel-to-reel or VHS videocassette with 3 songs and lead sheet. SASE. Reports in 3 weeks.
Music: Mostly **pop, country, R&B** and **MOR**; also **gospel**. Published *Old Age* and *Rose*, written and recorded by Mark Gibbs on Hillview Records; and *Area Code 502*, written and recorded by Adonis, on Estate Records.

*KANSA RECORDS CORPORATION, P.O. Box 1014, Lebanon TN 37088. (615)444-3865. Secretary and Treasurer/General Manager: Kit Johnson. Music publisher, record company and record producer. Estab. 1972. Publishes 30 to 40 songs/year; publishes 20 to 30 new songwriters/year. Works with composers and lyricists. Pays standard royalty. "Charges for demo services."
Affiliate(s): Great Leawood Music, Inc. (ASCAP) and Twinsong Music (BMI).
How to Contact: Submit demo tape by mail. Unsolicited submissions are OK. Prefers cassette and lyric sheet. SASE. Reports in 1 month.
Music: Mostly **country, MOR** and **Christian**. Published *Where Would She Be Without Me* (by Max Berry), recorded by John Daly; *New York Times* (by Richard Freed) and *Eternally Broke* (by Max Berry), both recorded by Lucky Lee, all on Kansa Records.

KAUPPS & ROBERT PUBLISHING CO. (BMI), P.O. Box 5474, Stockton CA 95205. (209)948-8186. Fax: (209)942-2163. President: Nancy L. Merrihew. Music publisher, record company (Kaupp Records), and manager and booking agent (Merri-Webb Prod. and Most Wanted Bookings). Estab. 1990. Publishes 15-20 songs/year; publishes 5+ new songwriters/year. Works with composers and lyricists; teams collaborators. Pays standard royalty.
How to Contact: Write or call first and obtain permission to submit. Prefers cassette (or VHS videocassette if available) with 3 songs maximum and lyric sheet. "If artist send PR package." SASE. Reports in 1 month.
Music: Mostly **country, R&B, A/C rock**; also **pop, rock** and **gospel**. Published *Love Isn't Blind At All*, written and recorded by Dan Alice; "Why Do You Do Me This Way" (by Nancy Merrihew/Rick Webb), recorded by Nanci Lynn; and *Made In Texas*, written and recorded by Stephen Bruce, all on Kaupp Records.
Tips: "Know what you want, set a goal, focus in on your goals, be open to constructive criticism, polish tunes and keep polishing."

KAREN KAYLEE MUSIC GROUP, R.O. #11 Box 360, Greensburg PA 15601. (412)836-0966. President: Karen Kaylee. Music publisher. BMI. Estab. 1989. Publishes 15-20 songs/year; publishes 3 new songwriters/year. Works with composers and lyricists; teams collaborators. Pays standard royalty.
Affiliate(s): Den-Hawk Music Group (ASCAP).
How to Contact: Submit demo tape—unsolicited submissions are OK. Prefers cassette (or VHS videocassette) with 3-5 songs and lyric sheet. "No phone calls please." Does not return unsolicited material. Reports in 1 month.

Music: Mostly **country, gospel** and **traditional country.** Published "Gone Again" (by Carlene Haggerty), and "Only God" (by Matt Furin), recorded by Karen Kaylee; and "There's a Reason," written and recorded by Lisa Amadio, all on Ka-De Records.

Tips: "Send only your best material—clean demos. Be professional. Your song must be better than the ones on the radio. Don't get discouraged. There are hits that haven't been written yet. I listen to every tape."

*KEEP CALM MUSIC LIMITED, Falcon Mews, London SW12 9SJ **England.** (081)675-5584. Fax: (081)675-6313. Professional Manager: Joanna Underwood. Music publisher, record company and record producer (Don't Panic Productions Ltd.). PRS. Member MCPS. Publishes approximately 50-75 songs/year. Works with composers. Pays varying royalty.

Affiliate(s): Yo Bro, Low Spirit (UK office), The Brothers Organisation.

How to Contact: Submit demo tape by mail—unsolicited submissions are OK. Prefers cassette with maximum 5 songs and lyric sheet. Does not return unsolicited material. Reports in 1 month.

Music: Mostly **R&B,** also **black/dance** and **pop;** also **high energy** and **rock.** Published "Asi Me Gusta," written and recorded by Chimo Bayo (house) and"Wee Are The Girls" (by Peter/Ward), recorded by Wee Papa Girls (pop/dance), both on Brothers Organisation Records. Sub-publishers for Technotronic, Westbam and D.J. Dick.

KEL-CRES PUBLISHING (ASCAP), 2525 East 12th St., Cheyenne WY 82001. (307)638-9894. A&R Manager: Gary J. Kelley. Music publisher, record company (Rough Cut Records) and record producer. Estab. 1989. Publishes 2 songs/year. Receives 100 submissions/year. Works with team collaborators. Pays standard royalty.

Affiliate(s): Kelley-Kool Music (BMI).

How to Contact: Submit a demo tape by mail—unsolicited submissions are OK. Prefers cassette, CD's or DAT (or VHS videocassette) with 3 songs and lyric sheets. Guitar/piano demo with "words up front" is sufficient. SASE. Reports in 1 month.

Music: Mostly **country, country rock, rock-a-billy.** Published "Serena," "Shoobie-Nah," and "Jailhouse Blues" (by Tim Anderson); and "Heart Mender" (by Bob Man) on Rough Cut Records.

Tips: "Keep songs simple, very few lyrics with strong repeated "hook-line.""

GENE KENNEDY ENTERPRISES, INC., 3950 N. Mt. Juliet Rd., Mt. Juliet TN 37122. (615)754-0417. President: Gene Kennedy. Vice President: Karen Jeglum Kennedy. Music publisher, record company (Door Knob Records), record producer, distributor and promoter. ASCAP, BMI, SESAC. Estab. 1975. Publishes 30-40 songs/year; publishes 15-20 new songwriters/year. Works with composers and lyricists. Pays standard royalty.

Affiliate(s): Chip 'n Dale Music Publishers (ASCAP), Door Knob Music Publishing (BMI) and Lodestar Music (SESAC).

How to Contact: Prefers cassette or 7½ ips reel-to-reel with 1-3 songs and lyric sheet. "We will not accept anything we have to sign for." SASE. Reports in 3 weeks.

Music: **Country** and **gospel.** Published "Praise Ye The Lord" (by Linda Almond), recorded by Dave Jeglum (gospel); "Open For Suggestions" (by Wyndi Harp), recorded by Perry La Pointe (country); and "I've Had Enough of You" (by Johnette Burton), recorded by Debbie Rich (country); all on Door Knob Records.

KENNING PRODUCTIONS, Box 1084, Newark DE 19715. (302)737-4278. President: Kenneth Mullins. Music publisher and record company (Kenning Records). BMI. Publishes 30-40 songs/year.

How to Contact: Prefers cassette. Does not return unsolicited material.

Music: Mostly **rock, new wave** and **country;** also **blues, jazz** and **bluegrass.** Published "Crazy Mama," written and recorded by K. Mullins; "Work Me Over," (by J. Lehane/K. Mullins), recorded by K. Mullins, both on Kenning Records (both rock); and "This Time," (by K. Mullins).

KENO PUBLISHING, P.O. Box 4429, Austin TX 78765-4429. (512)441-2422. Owner: Keith A. Ayres. Music publisher and record company (Glitch Records). BMI. Estab. 1984. Publishes 12 songs/year; publishes 10 new songwriters/year. Works with composers and lyricists; teams collaborators. Pays standard royalty.

How to Contact: Write first and obtain permission to submit a tape. Prefers cassette (and/or VHS videocassette if available) with 2-3 songs and lyric or lead sheets. Does not return unsolicited material.

Music: Rock, rap, reggae and **pop;** also **metal, R&B alternative** (all types). Published "I Wrote the Note" (by George Alistair Sanger), recorded by European Sex Machine (computerized); "Here It Is" (by John Patterson), recorded by Cooly Girls (rap); and "Kick'em in the Ass" (by Los Deflectors/Keith Ayres), recorded by Ron Rogers (rock); all on Glitch Records.

*KEYSTONE MUSIC GROUP INC., #B412, 6986 El Camino Real, Carlsbad CA 92009. (619)931-9256. Creative Director: Charls Senter. Estab. 1972. Publishes 5-10 songs/year. Publishes 0-3 new songwriters/year. Hires staff songwriters. Works with composers and lyricists; teams collaborators.
How to Contact: Submit demo tape by mail. Unsolicited submissions are OK. Prefers cassette (or VHS videocassette if available) with 3 songs. Mark submissions "unsolicited." SASE. Reports in 1 month.
Music: Mostly **country, pop/rock, R&B.** Published "Love at First Sight" (by Glen Burtmk and Dennis De Young), recorded by Styx on A&M Records; "America" (by Sammy Johns), recorded by Waylon Jennings on RCA Records; "All You Get from Love is a Love Song" (by S. Eaton), recorded by The Carpenters on A&M Records.
Tips: "Keep submitting if feedback is positive. A good song transcends all trends."

KINGSPORT CREEK MUSIC PUBLISHING, P.O. Box 6085, Burbank CA 91510. Contact: Vice President. BMI. Music publisher and record company (Cowgirl Records). Estab. 1980. Works with composers, lyricists; teams collaborators. Pays standard royalty.
How to Contact: Submit a demo tape—unsolicited submissions are OK. Prefers cassette (or VHS videocassette) with any number of songs and lyric sheet. Does not return unsolicited material. "Include photos and bio if possible."
Music: Mostly **country** and **gospel;** also **R&B** and **MOR.** Published "Who Am I," "Golden Wedding Ring" and "Let's Give Love," all written and recorded by Melvena Kaye on Cowgirl Records.
Tips: "Videocassettes are advantageous."

KOKE, MOKE & NOKE MUSIC, Dept. SM, Box 724677, Atlanta GA 30339. (404)355-0909. General Manager: Bryan Cole. Music publisher, record company (Ichiban). BMI. Estab. 1986. Publishes 30-40 songs/year. Works with composers and lyricists; teams collaborators. Pays standard royalty.
How to Contact: Submit a demo tape by mail—unsolicited submissions are OK. Prefers cassette with 4-5 songs and lyric sheets. "Put contact name and number on the tape." Does not return unsolicited material. Reports back in 2 weeks.
Music: Mostly **blues, old R&B style, urban contemporary (dance, rap)** and **pop.** Published "I'd Rather Be Alone" (by Buzz Amato), recorded by Billy Paul on Ichiban Records (R&B); "Straight From Heaven" (by Mark Ford, Joey Johnson), recorded by Rev. Charles McLean on Miracle Records (gospel); "What's the Name of That Thing?" (by Gary "B.B." Coleman), recorded on Ichiban Records (blues).
Tips: "Write from the heart and soul, not the head. Listen to some of our records for direction."

KOMMUNICATION KONCEPTS, Dept. SM, Box 2095, Philadelphia PA 19103. (215)848-7475. President: S. Deane Henderson. Music publisher and management firm. Publishes 10-15 songs/year; publishes 6 new songwriters/year. Pays standard royalty.
How to Contact: Prefers cassette (or VHS videocassette) with 4-8 songs and lyric sheets. Does not return unsolicited material. Reports in 2 weeks.
Music: **Dance-oriented, easy listening, gospel, MOR, R&B, rock, soul, top 40/pop, funk** and **heavy metal.** Published "Fantasy" and "Monica, Brenda and Lisa," recorded by Helen McCormick; "Hot Number" (by John Fitch), recorded by The Racers (heavy rock); "Save and Cleanse Me Jesus" and "In God's Hand" (by Verdelle C. Bryant), recorded by Verdelle & Off Spring Gospel Singers (gospel); "Free the Godfather" and "Illusion of Love" (by Hall Sound Lab in collaborations with Future Step Sirkle).

KOZKEEOZKO MUSIC, Suite 602, 928 Broadway, New York NY 10010. (212)505-7332. Professional Managers: Ted Lehrman and Libby Bush. Music publisher, record producer and management firm (Landslide Management). ASCAP. Estab. 1978. Publishes 5 songs/year; publishes 3 new songwriters/year.
How to Contact: Write first and obtain permission to submit. Cassettes (or VHS ½" videocassettes) with 2 songs maximum and typewritten lyric sheet for each song. SASE. Reports in 2-3 weeks.
Music: Mostly **soul/pop, dance, pop/rock** (no heavy metal), **A/C** and **country.** Published "Ain't No Cure For You" (by Ed Chalfin and Tedd Lawson), recorded by Dan Kramer on Thunder Records (pop), "We Are Now, We Are Forever" (by Ed Chalfin and Tedd Lawson) recorded by the Platters; and "This Heart's Gonna Heal," recorded by Deborah Dotson/Doug Parkinson on Rich River Records.
Tips: "Keep abreast of what's happening in pop music today but don't copy. Be unique."

KREN MUSIC PUBLISHING, P.O. Box 5804, Hacienda Heights CA 91745. (818)855-1692. Co-owner: Kris Clark. Music publisher, record producer (Kren Music Productions). BMI. Estab. 1985. Publishes 10-20 songs/year; publishes 5-10 new songwriters/year. Works with composers and lyricists; teams collaborators. Pays standard royalty.

How to Contact: Submit a demo tape by mail—unsolicited submissions OK. Prefers cassette with 3 songs and lyric sheet. SASE. Reports in 4-6 weeks.
Music: Mostly **country, pop** and **rock**; also **gospel** and **New Age.** Published "Where Fools are Kings" (by Jeffrey Steele), recorded by Steve Wariner on MCA Records (country).
Tips: "Make your song the best you possibly can and present a demo tape that reflects such."

KRUDE TOONZ MUSIC, P.O. Box 308, Lansdale PA 19446. (215)855-8628. President: G. Malack. Music publisher. ASCAP. Estab. 1988.
Affiliate(s): Teeze Me Pleeze Me Music (ASCAP).
How to Contact: Write first and obtain permission to submit a tape. Prefers cassette (or VHS videocassette if available) with 3 songs. SASE.
Music: Mostly **rock** and **pop.** Published "Tonight," "Fantasy" and "Love Or Lust" (by G. Malack), recorded by Roughhouse on CBS Records (rock).

LACKEY PUBLISHING CO., Dept. SM, Box 269, Caddo OK 74729. (405)367-2798. President: Robert F. Lackey. Music publisher and record producer. BMI. Publishes 6-8 songs/year; publishes 3-4 new songwriters/year. Pays standard royalty.
How to Contact: Submit demo tape—unsolicited submissions are OK. Prefers cassette with 1-10 songs. SASE. Reports in 2 months.
Music: Mostly **country** and **MOR;** also **bluegrass, blues, church/religious, easy listening, folk, gospel, progressive, R&B** and **top 40/pop.** Published "The Devil In Tight Blue Jeans," written and recorded by Franklin Lackey (country); "Teenager in Love," written and recorded by Sherry Kenae (pop/country); and "The Rose of Goodbye" (by Franklin Lackey), recorded by Sherry Kenae (progressive country), all on Uptown Records.
Tips: "Make every word count on the lyrics."

LANSDOWNE AND WINSTON MUSIC PUBLISHERS, Dept. SM, #318, 1680 Vine St., Hollywood CA 90028. (213)462-2848. President: Lynne Robin Green. Music publisher. ASCAP, BMI. Estab. 1958. Publishes 20 songs/year; publishes 20 new songwriters/year. Works with composers and lyricists. Pays standard royalty.
Affiliate(s): Bloor Music Publishers (BMI); Ben Ross Music (ASCAP); Hoffman House Music Publisher (BMI); Clemitco Publishers (BMI).
How to Contact: Submit a demo tape by mail—unsolicited submissions are OK. Prefers cassette with 1-3 songs and lyric sheets. "Must enclose SASE or no reply." SASE. Reports back in 3 weeks. "No calls."
Music: Mostly **R&B (ballads), hip-hop, pop-rock, mainstream jazz vocal songs;** also **alternative.** Published "Streetdance," written and recorded by King Errisson on Ichiban Records (R&B worldbeat); "Old Home Place" recorded by The Dillards on Vanguard Records (bluegrass); and "After the Quake," recorded by Hammer Easternway.
Tips: "You must strive for great story in lyric, memorable melody and great chorus hooks with an original approach to each song's creative aspect."

LARI-JON PUBLISHING (BMI), 325 W. Walnut, Rising City NE 68658. (402)542-2336. Owner: Larry Good. Music publisher, record company (Lari-Jon Records) and record producer (Lari Jon Productions). Estab. 1967. Publishes 20 songs/year; publishes 2-3 new songwriters/year. Teams collaborators. Pays standard royalty.
How to Contact: Submit a demo tape by mail—unsolicited submissions are O.K. Prefers cassette with 5 songs and lyric sheet. "Be professional." SASE. Reports in 2 months.
Music: Mostly **country, gospel—Southern** and **50's rock.** Published *Happy Valley June* and *Glory Bound Train* (written and recorded by Tom Campbell); and *Hanging From the Bottom* (written and recorded by Johnny Nace), all on Lari-Jon Records.

LATIN AMERICAN MUSIC CO., INC., P.O. Box 1844, Cathedral Station, New York NY 10025. (212)993-5557. Fax: (212)993-5551. Contact: D. Vera. Music Publisher. Estab. 1970. Publishes 20 songs/year; publishes 5 new songwriters/year. Works with composers and lyricists; teams collaborators. Pays standard royalty.
Affiliate(s): The International Music Co.
How to Contact: Write or call first and obtain permission to submit. Prefers cassette. Does not return unsolicited material. Reports in 2 months.
Music: Mostly **Latin American;** also **reggae.** Published "La Finquita" (G. Rosario), recorded by the Believers; "Se Me Van" (by T. Sanchez), recorded by Pupy on CBS Records (LP); and "Te Siento," written and recorded by Lan Franco on Audio Records (LP).

LCS MUSIC GROUP, INC., 6301 N. O'Connor Blvd., The Studios of Las Colinas, Building One, Irving TX 75039. (214)869-0700. Contact: Publishing Assistant. Music publisher. BMI, ASCAP, SESAC. Works with composers. Pays standard royalty.
Affiliate(s): Bug and Bear Music (ASCAP), Chris Christian Music (BMI), Court and Case Music (ASCAP), Home Sweet Home Music (ASCAP) and Monk and Tid Music (SESAC), Preston Christian Music (BMI).
How to Contact: Submit a demo tape by mail—unsolicited submissions are OK. Prefers cassette with lyric sheet (only necessary if the words are difficult to understand). "Put all pertinent information on the tape itself, such as how to contact the writer. Do not send Express!" Does not return unsolicited material. Reports in 2 months.
Music: Mostly **contemporary Christian** and **inspirational**. Published "The Me Nobody Knows" (by Vincent Grimes), recorded by Marilyn McCoo on Warner Alliance (contemporary Christian); "Calling You," written and recorded by Eric Champion on Word Records (contemporary Christian); "Warrior for the Lord" (by Brent Tallent), recorded by Marilyn McCoo on Warner Alliance Records (inspirational).
Tips: "Listen to the cutting edge of whatever style you write—don't get caught in a rut stylistically."

*LE GRANDE FROMAGE/CHEDDAR CHEESE MUSIC, 8739 Sunset Blvd., Los Angeles CA 90069. (310)659-9820. Fax: (310)652-0907. President: Jan Rhees. Estab. 1988. Publishes 30 songs/year. Publishes 5 new songwriters/year. Works with composers and lyricists; teams collaborators.
How to Contact: Call first and obtain permission to submit. Prefers cassette (or VHS videocassette if available) with 3 songs and lyric sheet. SASE. Reports in 3-4 weeks.
Music: R&B, pop/alternative, jazz; all forms of music. Published *A Woman Knows* (by Chris McCarty), recorded by Martina McBride on CA Records (country); "Touch" (by S. Lane), recorded by Diane Schuur on GRP Records (jazz); and "Love In the Making" (by S. Lane/D. Winzeler), recorded by Barry White and Mona Lisa on Quality Records.
Tips: "Write the best song you can—demo it to enhance the SONG—be tenacious and patient."

*LIGHTHOUSE MUSIC COMPANY, INC., 2 Cielo Ctr., 1250 Loop 360 S., Austin TX 78746. (512)327-7964. Fax: (512)327-3262. Creative Manager: Bitsy Rice. Music publisher. Estab. 1990. Publishes 40 songs/year. Hires staff writers. Works with composers; teams collaborators. Pays standard royalty.
Affiliate(s): Son Of A Bits Music (ASCAP) and Son Of A Bill Music (BMI).
How to Contact: Call first and obtain permission to submit. Prefers cassette with 2 songs and lyric sheet. "Please only two songs per tape. The quality of the tapes is very important—clean vocals a must." SASE. Reports in 3-4 weeks.
Music: Mostly **country**, **pop/rock** and **R&B**; also **fabulous songs in any genre**. Published "A Heart That Can" (by Patti Dixon), recorded by Dixie Chicks on CCR Records (country); "Spurs" (by Vance Sorrells), recorded by California on Sugar Hill Records (country/rock); and "Vintage Love" (by Holland Young), recorded for movie: Black Magic Woman.
Tips: "We don't want you to spend a lot of money on a demo, just make sure that it is clear and clean. Simple is good—but make sure the vocalist is in tune and is better than average. Poor vocals are very distracting—they draw our attention away from the song, and make it hard for us to listen objectively."

DORIS LINDSAY PUBLISHING (ASCAP), 1203 Biltmore Ave., High Point NC 27260. (919)882-9990. President: Doris Lindsay. Music publisher and record company (Fountain Records). Estab. 1979. Publishes 20 songs/year; publishes 4 songwriters/year. Works with composers and lyricists; teams collaborators. Pays standard royalty.
Affiliate(s): Better Times Publishing (BMI) and Doris Lindsay Publishing (ASCAP).
How to Contact: Submit demo tape by mail—unsolicited submissions are OK. Prefers cassette with 2 songs. "Submit good quality demos." SASE. Reports in 2 months.
Music: Mostly **country**, **pop** and **contemporary gospel**. Published *Service Station Cowboy* (by Hess Ryder), recorded by Ace Diamond; "Share Your Love," written and recorded by Mitch Snow; and "America's Song" (by Cathy Roeder), recorded by Terry Michaels, all on Fountain Records.
Tips: "Present a good quality demo (recorded in a studio). Positive clean lyrics and up-tempo music are easiest to place."

LINEAGE PUBLISHING CO., Box 211, East Prairie MO 63845. (314)649-2211. (Nashville branch: 7205 Nashboro Blvd., Apt. D, Nashville TN 37217. (615)366-4975.) Professional Manager: Tommy Loomas. Staff: Alan Carter and Joe Silver. Music publisher, record producer and record company. BMI. Pays standard royalty.
How to Contact: Query first. Prefers cassette with 2-4 songs and lyric sheet; include bio and photo if possible. SASE. Reports in 1 month.
Music: **Country**, **easy listening**, **MOR**, **country rock**, and **top 40/pop**. Published "Yesterday's Teardrops," and "Round & Round," (by Phil and Larry Burchett), recorded by The Burchetts on Capstan Records (country).

LIN'S LINES, #434, 156 5th Ave., New York NY 10010. (212)691-5631. President: Linda K. Jacobson. Music publisher. ASCAP. Estab. 1978. Publishes 4 songs/year; publishes 4 new songwriters/year. Works with composers and lyricists; teams collaborators. Pays standard royalty.
How to Contact: Submit a demo tape by mail—unsolicited submissions are OK. Prefers cassette or VHS or ¾" videocassette with 3-5 songs and lyric or lead sheet.; SASE. Reports in 6 weeks.
Music: Mostly **rock, pop** and **rap**; also **world music, R&B** and **gospel**.

LION HILL MUSIC PUBLISHING CO. (BMI), P.O. Box 110983, Nashville TN 37222-0983. (615)731-6640. Publisher: Wayne G. Leinsz. Music publisher, record company (Richway Records). BMI, ASCAP. Estab. 1988. Publishes 40-50 songs/year; publishes a few new songwriters/year. Receives 1,000 submissions/year. Works with composers and lyricists; teams collaborators. Pays standard royalty.
Affiliate(s): Mollies Pride Music Publishing Co. (ASCAP).
How to Contact: Submit a demo tape by mail—unsolicited submissions are OK. Prefers cassette with 3 songs and lead sheets. Does not return unsolicited material. Reports back in 4 weeks.
Music: Mostly **country, pop, humorous**; also **gospel** and **bluegrass**. Published "You & Me & Her Memory" (by Michaels), recorded by Jill Michaels; "Ghost of Simon Dill" (by Madison), recorded by Bobby Adkins; and "Love Is All It Takes" (by Harrelson), recorded by Michael Harrelson, all on Richway Records.

THE LITHICS GROUP, P.O. Box 272, Garden City AL 35070. (205)352-4873. President: Dennis N. Kahler. "We are always on the lookout for new material. We have links now with major publishers and good contacts to some top artists. Whenever time permits, we offer comments and critique on material we receive to help new writers develop their skills." Publishes 12 songs/year. Pays standard royalty.
Affiliate(s): Terra Lithic (ASCAP), Pyra Lithic (BMI).
How to Contact: Submit demo tape—unsolicited submissions welcomed. "Send cassette tape with no more than 4 songs, including lyric sheets, along with SASE mailer if you wish your tape returned (or $1.50 money order to cover cost of mailer and postage) to our letterhead address. We will reply as soon as possible, with comments on your material. If you wish a reply, but don't need the tape returned, a long SASE with first class postage will be sufficient."
Music: Primarily interested in **country/western** and **gospel music**. We look for songs emotionally charged, unique and with good word pictures." Published "Don't Toy With My Emotions", which has been re-assigned to a major publisher for further pitching. Presently we have several songs being pitched in the Nashville Market.
Tips: "As an 'outside', unknown writer, you must write material as good as or better than established writers to get noticed. Work on your craft to *become competitive!* We aways recommend the 'How-to' books offered by Writer's Digest as a shortcut to learning."

*LITTLE POND PRODUCTIONS, P.O. Box 20594, Portland OR 97220. (503)254-5776. Fax: (503)254-1239. Vice President: JoAnna Burns-Miller. Music publisher, record company and record producer. Estab. 1985. Publishes 10-15-20 songs/year; publishes 1 or 2 new songwriters/year. Hires staff writers. Works with composers and lyricists; teams collaborators. Pays standard royalty or flat fee.
How to Contact: Submit demo tape by mail. Unsolicited submissions are OK. Prefers cassette with 2 songs and lyric or lead sheet. "Send clear recordings." SASE. Reports in 2-3 months.
Music: Mostly **New Age, spiritual** and **MOR**; also **contemporary soft pop**. Published "Making Changes," "Remember Me," and "You Held My Hand," all written and recorded by JoAnna Burns-Miller on Little Pond Productions.
Tips: "Keep it clean, simple, obvious "hook," good story with a lesson, moral. Need good strong lyrics sung by a great singer."

*LONNY TUNES (BMI), P.O. Box 460086, Garland TX 75046. President: Lonny Schonfeld. Music publisher. BMI. Estab. 1988. Publishes 6-8 songs/year; publishes 2-3 new songwriters/year. Works with composers. Also works with comedians in securing recordings for comedy material. Pays standard royalty.
How to Contact: Submit a demo tape by mail—unsolicited submissions are OK. Prefers cassette with 3-5 songs and lyric sheets. Make sure lyric and melody stand out. Does not return unsolicited submissions. Reports in 6-8 weeks.
Music: Mostly **pop, rock, children's** and **country**. Published "One Word Question" (by L. Schonfeld, used on the Jerry Lewis Telethon); "The Little Bitty Chicken" (by Charles Goodman—children's) and "Alice" (by Robert Styx—Larry Stones).
Tips: "Be careful not to use clichés in your lyrics. Stay away from songs that talk about "drinking away your troubles.""

THE LORENZ CORPORATION, Dept. SM, 501 E. Third St., Dayton OH 45401-0802. (513)228-6118. Contact: Editorial Department. Music Publisher. ASCAP, BMI. Estab. 1890. Publishes 500 songs/year; 10 new songwriters/year. Hires staff writers. Works with composers and lyricists; teams collaborators. Pays standard royalty.
How to Contact: Submit manuscript (completely arranged); tape not necessary. SASE. Reports in 4 months.
Music: Interested in **religious/Christian, high school choral** and **organ/piano music;** also **band music.**

*LOVEFORCE INTERNATIONAL, P.O. Box 241648, Los Angeles CA 90024. Submissions Manager: T. Wilkins. Music publishers, record company and international record promotion company. BMI. Estab. 1979. Publishes 5-10 songs/year; publishes 2 new songwriters/year. Pays standard royalty.
How to Contact: Write first and obtain permission to submit. Prefers cassette (or VHS videocassette) with 2 songs maximum and lyric sheet. "SASE a must." Reports in 1 month.
Music: Mostly **pop, rock** and **R&B;** also **ballads, country** and **gospel.** Published "I Wanna Be Good To You," written and recorded by Bandit on LoveForce International; "Betweeen Two People," written and recorded by Spiderworks on Sinbad Records; also an instrumental LP by Bandit released in the People's Republic of China on a Chinese record label.

LOVEY MUSIC, INC., P.O. Box 630755, Miami FL 33163. (305)935-4880. President: Jack Gale. Music publisher. BMI, ASCAP. Estab. 1981. Publishes 25 songs/year; publishes 10 new songwriters/year. Pays standard royalty.
Affiliate(s): Cowabonga Music, Inc. (ASCAP).
How to Contact: Submit a demo tape by mail—unsolicited submissions are OK. Prefers cassette or VHS videocassette with 1-2 songs and lyric sheets. Does not return unsolicited material. Reports in 2 weeks if interested."
Music: Mostly **country crossover** and **country.** Published *Louisiana Legs* (by Rocky Priola), recorded by Del Reeves; *If You Want My Love* (by Hayne Davis), recorded by Robin Right; and *Why Do You Use Me* (by Larry Agovino), recorded by Susan Smith, all on Playback Records (country).

*JERE LOWE PUBLISHING (BMI), 603 E. Broadway, Denver City TX 79323-3311. (806)592-8020. Fax: (806)592-9486. Owner: Jeré Lowe. Music publisher, record company (FAB 5 Records) and record producer (Loco Sounds). Estab. 1990. Publishes 10 songs/year; publishes 3 new songwriters/year. Works with composers and lyricists. Pays standard royalty.
How to Contact: Submit demo tape by mail. Unsolicited submissions are OK. Prefers cassette (or any videocassette) with 3 songs and lyric sheet. "Best demos help sell songs." SASE. Reports in 1 month.
Music: Mostly **new** or **young country, R&B** and **Spanish;** also **pop-top 40, children's** and **adult contemporary.** Published "Far Away" (by Tim Teikert); "Fall Always Brings the Leaves" (by Chuck Melugin); and "Miss You Everyday" (by Jim Mack).
Tips: "I screen 300 songs a month for 6 major publishing firms—in the U.S.A. Please send your best songs and best quality demo. I cannot do anything with a poor demo."

THE LOWERY GROUP of Music Publishing Companies, 3051 Clairmont Rd. NE, Atlanta GA 30329. (404)325-0832. General Professional Manager: Cotton Carrier. Music publisher. ASCAP, BMI. Estab. 1952. Publishes 100 songs/year; publishes varying number of new songwriters/year. Works with composers and lyricists. Pays standard royalty.
Affiliate(s): Lowery Music Co., Inc. (BMI); Low-Sal, Inc. (BMI); Low-Twi, Inc. (BMI); Low-Ab Music (BMI); Low-Bam Music (BMI); Low-Ja Music (BMI); Low-Rico Music (BMI); Low-Thom Music (BMI); Eufaula Music (BMI); Steel City Music (BMI); Wonder Music (BMI); Eternal Gold Music (BMI); New Testament Music (BMI); Songs of Faith (BMI); Brother Bill's Music (ASCAP); Miss Delta Music (ASCAP); Terri Music (ASCAP); and Holy Ground Music (ASCAP).
How to Contact: Prefers cassette with 3 songs and lyric sheet. Does not return unsolicited material. "No response unless we wish to publish the song."
Music: Country, MOR and pop; also gospel, rock and comedy. Published "Homesick" by Travis Tritt on Warner Brothers Records; "A Christmas Card," by Doug Stone on Epic Records; "I've Been Lonely For So Long," by Mick Jagger on Atlantic Records; and "Santa Claus Is Watching You," by Ray Stevens on Clyde Records.

*LUCRECIA MUSIC (ASCAP), Box 39A16, Los Angeles CA 91402. (213)668-2213. Owner: L. Spry. Music publisher. Works with composers and lyricists; teams collaborators. Pays standard royalty. "We also consider administration of publishing."

Affiliate(s): Aicercul Music (BMI).
How to Contact: Submit demo tape by mail. Unsolicited submissions are OK. Prefers cassette with 3-4 songs and lyric sheet. Does not return unsolicited material. Reports in 2-3 weeks.
Music: Mostly **rock, pop** and **alternative;** also **R&B.** Published "Up On Solid Ground" (written and recorded by Kim Allen) and *All I Want Is You* (by Lucy Russo), recorded by Lucrecia on Zylon Records; and *Aladdins Lamp* (by Kenan/Russo/Waters), recorded by Betty Boop & Beat Boop Tunes).
Tips: "Write for female vocals or neutral gender lyrics. Write hits for both mainstream and alternative markets."

HAROLD LUICK & ASSOCIATES MUSIC PUBLISHER (BMI), P.O. Box B, Carlisle IA 50047. (515)989-3748. President: Harold L. Luick. Music publisher, record company, record producer and music industry consultant. BMI. Publishes 25-30 songs/year; publishes 5-10 new songwriters/year. Pays standard royalty.
How to Contact: Write or call first about your interest. Prefers cassette with 3-5 songs and lyric sheet. SASE. Reports in 1 month.
Music: **Traditional country** and **hard core country.** Published "Mrs. Used To Be," written and recorded by Joe E. Harris, on River City Music Records (country); and "Ballad of Deadwood S.P.," written and recorded by Don Laughlin on Kajac Records (historical country).
Tips: "Ask yourself these questions: Does my song have simplicity of lyric and melody? Good flow and feeling? A strong story line? Natural dialogue? Hook chorus, lyric hooks, melody hooks? If it doesn't, then why should a publisher or A&R person take the time to listen to it? Most material that is sent to us is also sent simultaneously to several other publishers. If we are going to publish a song, the writer must assure us that the same music submission isn't floating around out there somewhere."

JIM McCOY MUSIC, Rt. 2, Box 114 H, Berkeley Springs WV 25411. Owners: Bertha and Jim McCoy. Music publisher, record company (Winchester Records) and record producer (Jim McCoy Productions). BMI. Estab. 1973. Publishes 20 songs/year; publishes 3-5 new songwriters/year. Pays standard royalty.
Affiliate(s): New Edition Music (BMI).
How to Contact: Write first and obtain permission to submit. Prefers cassette, 7½ or 15 ips reel-to-reel (or VHS or Beta videocassette) with 6 songs. Does not return unsolicited material. Reports in 1 month.
Music: Mostly **country, country/rock** and **rock;** also **bluegrass** and **gospel.** Published "I'm Getting Nowhere" (written and recorded by J.B. Miller) on Hilton Records; "One More Time" (by S. Howard), recorded by Carl Howard and *Touching Your Heart* (written and recorded by Jim McCoy), both on Winchester Records.

DANNY MACK MUSIC, 3484 Nicolette Dr., Crete IL 60417. (708)672-6457. General Manager: Daniel H. Mackiewicz. Music publisher and independent record producer. Estab. 1984. Publishes 1-8 songs/year. Pays standard royalty.
Affiliate(s): Syntony Publishing (BMI), Briar Hill Records (1992 Label of the Year Award, CMAA).
How to Contact: Submit demo tape—unsolicited submissions OK. Prefers cassette or phono records with no more than 4 songs and typed lyric sheets. SASE. Reports in 2 weeks.
Music: Mostly **country, gospel, (southern/country)** and **polka.** Published "The New Anniversary Waltz" and "Da Bulls, Da Bears, Da Beer," written and recorded by Danny Mack; and "In The Doghouse with Daisy" (by G. Skupien), recorded by Danny Mack (novelty polka), all on Briar Hill Records.
Tips: "Send me your best, don't explain to me why you think your song is commercial. This business is speculation. Most of all, get to the point, be honest and send me songs not egos. I can tell which is which."

MACMAN MUSIC, INC. (ASCAP), Dept. SM, Suite 200, 3903 SW Kelly, Portland OR 97201. (503)221-0288. Fax: (503)227-4418. Secretary: David Leiken. Music publisher and record producer. ASCAP, BMI. Estab. 1980. Publishes 8-10 songs/year; publishes 1-2 new songwriters/year. Works with composers and lyricists; teams collaborators. Pays "deal by deal."
Affiliate(s): Fresh Force Music, Inc.
How to Contact: Submit a demo tape by mail—unsolicited submissions are OK. Prefers cassette with lyric sheet. Does not return unsolicited material. Reports "only if we are interested."
Music: Mostly **R&B, blues/rock** and **rock.** Published *If You Were Mine* (by Larry Bell), recorded by U-Krew on Enigma/Capitol Records (rap/funk); *Corbin's Place,* written and recorded by Dennis Springer on Nastymix Records, and *I Shouted Your Name* (by Marlon McClain), recorded by Curtis Salgado on BFE/JRS Records.

MAJESTIC CONTROL MUSIC, Box 330-568, Brooklyn NY 11233. (718)919-2013 and (718)486-6419. A&R Department: Alemo and Hank Love. Music publisher, record company (Majestic Control Records) and record producer (Alemo and Hank Love). BMI. Estab. 1983. Hires staff writers. Works with lyricists. Pays standard royalty.
How to Contact: Write or call first and obtain permission to submit. Prefers cassette with 3 songs. SASE. Reports in 3 weeks.
Music: Mostly **rap, R&B** and **reggae**; also **house.** Published "Cold Sweat" (by Curtis, Moye, Davis), recorded by Majestic Productions (rap 12″); *Lovely, Lovely* (by M. Lowe), recorded by M.C. Lovely (rap LP); and "Front Line" (by Curtis, Moye, Davis), recorded by Majestic Productions (rap 12″); all on Majestic Control Records.
Tips: "Send me something funky."

*MAKERS MARK GOLD (ASCAP), 3033 W. Redner St., Philadelphia PA 19121. (215)236-4817. Record Producer: Paul Hopkins. Music publisher and record producer. Estab. 1991. Pays standard royalty.
How to Contact: Submit demo tape by mail. Unsolicited submissions are OK. Prefers cassette with 2-4 songs. Does not return material. Reports in 4-6 weeks.
Music: Mostly **R&B, hip hop** and **rap;** also **pop.** Published "Silent Love," "Something for Nothing," and "One & Only," (by E. Monk/P. Hopkins/G. Reed), recorded by Elaine Monk; and "Get Funky" (by P. Hopkins/G. Reed/C. Caruttor), recorded by Larry Larr on Ruffhouse/Columbia Records.

MANAPRO (MANAGEMENT ARTIST PRODUCTIONS), 82 Sherman St., Passaic NJ 07055. (201)777-6109. Executive Producer: Tomasito Bobadilla. Music publisher and production company. ASCAP, BMI. Estab. 1987. Publishes 2 songs/year; publishes 3-4 songwriters/year. Hires staff songwriters. Works with lyricists; teams collaborators. Pays standard royalty.
Affiliate(s): No Mas (BMI), In Che (ASCAP).
How to Contact: Submit a demo tape by mail—unsolicited submissions are OK. Prefers cassette with 2 songs and lyric sheet. SASE. Reports in 2 months.
Music: Mostly **pop, dance** and **rock;** also **R&B** and **New Age.** Published "Fascination" and "Consistence" (by Andy Pimen), by Karizma on Metropolitan Records (dance/pop); "One Way" (by Chene Garcia), by Mellow Dee on Halogram (hip house); and "2 Hearts" (by Pacheso), recorded by Time Chambers on Requeslime Records (dance/pop).
Tips: "Songs should have very catchy hooks, must also be very instrumental."

*MANBEN MUSIC (ASCAP), 3117 SW 17 St., Miami FL 33145. (305)443-5674. President: Manny Benito. Music publisher. Estab. 1988. Publishes 20 songs/year; publishes 1-2 new songwriters/year. Teams collaborators (very seldom). Pays standard royalty.
How to Contact: Write first and obtain permission to submit. Prefers cassette with lyric sheet. SASE. Reports in 4-6 weeks.
Music: Mostly **rap, country** and **pop;** also **Latin music.** Published *Quiero Volver Contigo* (by Manny Benito), recorded by La Mafia on Sony Records; *Yo Soy Tu* (by Manny Benito), recorded by Jessica Cristina on Sony Records; and *Cuanto Vale Tu Amor* (by Manny Benito), recorded by La Luz Orchestra on RMM Records.
Tips: "Send songs with a very strong and catchy chorus."

THE MARCO MUSIC GROUP INC., P.O. Box 24454, Nashville TN 37202. (615)269-7074. Professional Manager: Jeff Hollandsworth. Music publisher. Estab. 1988. Publishes approximately 50-75 songs/year; 5-10 new songwriters/year. Pays standard royalty.
Affiliate(s): Goodland Publishing Company (ASCAP), Marc Isle Music (BMI) and Gulf Bay Publishing (SESAC).
How to Contact: Submit demo tape—unsolicited submissions OK. Prefers cassette with 2 songs maximum and lyric sheet. SASE. Reports in 3 weeks.
Music: **Country, Christian.** Published "My Way Or The Highway" (by Reynolds/Fritz); "Mama's Rocking Chair" (by S. Clark); and "I'm Runnin' Out of Memories" (by F. Powers), all recorded by Debra Dudley on Concorde Records.
Tips: "Prefer songs with 'radio-friendly' universal appeal."

*ANDY MARVEL MUSIC, P.O. Box 133, Farmingville NY 11738. President: Andy Marvel. Music publisher, record company (Alyssa Records) and record producer (Marvel Productions and Ricochet Records). ASCAP. Estab. 1981. Publishes 30 songs/year; publishes 10 new songwriters/year. Works with composers and lyricists; teams collaborators. Pays standard royalty.
Affiliate(s): Andysongs (BMI) and Bing, Bing, Bing Music (ASCAP).
How to Contact: Write first and obtain permission to submit. Prefers cassette (or VHS videocassette) with 3 songs and lyric sheet. Returns only with SASE. "Do not call." Not accepting mail until Dec. 1993. Collaborators write "Collaborate" on envelope.

Music: Mostly **pop, R&B** and **top 40**; also **country**. Published "Learning to Live with a Heartache" (by Andy Marvel/Sheree Sano), recorded by Andy Marvel on Alyssa Records (pop); and "Love Will Never Be the Same Without You" (by Andy Marvel/Don Levy), recorded by John Wesley Shipp on Jamie Records (pop).

Tips: "Be patient. Your tape will be listened to. It helps if your song is produced, but it's not necessary."

*THE MATHES COMPANY, P.O. Box 22653, Nashville TN 37202. (615)252-6912. Owner: David W. Mathes. Music publisher, record company (Star Image, Heirborn, Kingdom), record producer (The Mathes Company) and music industry consultant. BMI, ASCAP, SESAC. Estab. 1962. Records 30-50 sessions/year; publishes 10-30 new songwriters/year. Pays standard royalty. Also offers home study course: "The Business Side of the Music Business" through Institute of Recording Arts & Sciences. Produces custom sessions on artists. (Union and non-union labels available) for upfront fee for production and manufacturing. Also produces quality demos for writers for fee."

Affiliate(s): Sweet Singer Music (BMI), Sing Sweeter Music (ASCAP) and Star of David (SESAC).

How to Contact: Submit a demo tape by mail—unsolicited submissions are OK. "Registered or certified mail refused." Prefers cassette (VHS videocassette) with maximum of 3 songs and lyric sheet. "Only positive country songs (not controversial, political, demeaning or sex oriented). Only gospel songs that are not rock contemporary, and no new age music." SASE. Reports in 1 month.

Music: Mostly **gospel (country), country** and **instrumental**; also **jingle ideas**. Published "I'm in Ohio Now (with Georgia on My Mind)" (by C. Donald Frost), recorded by Johnny Newman on Star Image Records; and "My Love For You" (by David Mathes/DeAnna Mathes), recorded by Warner Mack on Sapphire Records (both country).

Tips: "Submit only your best songs and follow submission requirements."

MEDIA PRODUCTIONS/RESISTOR MUSIC, 1001½ Elizabeth St., Oak Hill WV 25901. (304)465-1298. Producer: Doug Gent. Music publisher, record company (Resistor Records) and record producer (Media Productions). ASCAP. Estab. 1985. Publishes 20 songs/year; publishes 3 new songwriters/year. Receives 100-120 submissions/year. Works with composers and lyricists; teams collaborators. Pays standard royalty.

Affiliate(s): Capacitor Music (BMI).

How to Contact: Submit a demo tape by mail—unsolicited submissions are OK. Prefers cassette with 3 songs and lyric sheet. Does not return unsolicited material. Reports in 1 month.

Music: Mostly **country, gospel** and **R&B**; also **top 40** and **rock**. Published *Mailbox 24* (by Lee/Lee), recorded by Preston Lee; *Rockin' Away* (by Huffman/Godsey) and *Baby I'll Try* (by Reed/Godsey), recorded by Delnora Reed, all on Resistor Records.

Tips: "Know your craft and learn the business—be professional."

MEGA-STAR MUSIC, 248 W. 5th St., Deer Park NY 11729. (212)713-5229. General Manager: Barry Yearwood. Music publisher, record producer (Barry Yearwood) and management firm (Power Brokerage Management). Estab. 1984. Publishes 4 songs/year; publishes 4 new songwriters/year. Pays standard royalty.

How to Contact: Submit demo tape—unsolicited submissions OK. Prefers cassette with 4 songs. SASE. Reports in 1 month.

Music: Mostly **dance** and **R&B**; also **pop**. Published "Dancing to the Beat," written and recorded by Henderson and Whitfield on Park Place Records; "Solar Flight," written and recorded by Richard Bush on Island Records; and "Mind Your Own Business," written and recorded by R. Bush on Laser-7 Records.

MERRY MARILYN MUSIC PUBLISHING, 33717 View Crest Dr., Lake Elsinore CA 92532. (909)245-2763. Owner: Marilyn Hendricks. Music publisher. BMI. Estab. 1980. Publishes 10-15 songs/year; publishes 3-4 new songwriters/year. Pays standard royalty.

How to Contact: Submit a demo tape—unsolicited submissions are OK. No more than 3 songs per submission, one song per cassette. "Submit complete songs only. No lyrics without music." SASE. Reports in 3 weeks (depending on volume of submissions).

Music: Mostly **country** and **MOR**. Published "Betting On Love," "This Old Dog" and "Goodbye In Your Eyes," by J. Hendricks.

Tips: "Submit a GREAT song. 'Good' is no longer good enough. The song must be great to get attention!"

*MIRACLE MILE MUSIC/BLACK SATIN (BMI), P.O. Box 35449, Los Angeles CA 90035. (310)281-8599. A&R: Robert Riley. Music publisher, record company (Miles Ahead) and record producer. Estab. 1968. Publishes 75 songs/year. Hires staff writers. Works with composers and lyricists; teams collaborators. Pays standard royalty.

Affiliate(s): Family Affair (ASCAP) and Respect Music (BMI).
How to Contact: Submit demo tape by mail. Unsolicited submissions are OK. Prefers cassette with 4 songs and lyric sheet. SASE. Reports in 2 weeks, "sometimes minutes."
Music: Mostly **R&B, R&B/pop** and **country**; also **pop**. Published "I'm Glad We Found Love" (by Jim Stewell), recorded by Whitney Houston on Arista Records (R&B/pop); "In The Hands Of Love" (by Craig Haynes), recorded by Patti LaBelle on M.C.A. Records (pop/R&B); and "Couldn't We Forget" (by Milton Gunsberg), recorded by Anne Murray on Capitol Records (pop).
Tips: "Don't be predictable. Have a fresh approach at a lyric, melody and concepts."

MONEYTIME PUBLISHING CO. (BMI), 742 Rowley St., Owosso MI 48867. (517)723-1796. Director: Jon Harris. Music publisher and record company (Moneytime Records). BMI. Estab. 1990. Publishes 15 songs/year; publishes 3-5 new songwriters/year. Works with lyricists. Pays standard royalty.
How to Contact: Submit a demo tape by mail—unsolicited submissions are OK. Prefers cassette with 4-6 songs. Does not return unsolicited material. Reports in 4-6 weeks.
Music: Mostly **rap, R&B** and **dance**; also **house, funk** and **soul**. Published "I'll Trip" and "No Parole" (by Jon H. Harris), recorded by The Mad Rapper; and "Different Directions," written and recorded by Joe Stasa, all on Moneytime Records (rap).

***MONTINA MUSIC**, Box 702, Snowdon Station, Montreal, Quebec H3X 3X8 **Canada**. Professional Manager: David P. Leonard. Music publisher. SOCAN. Estab. 1963. Pays standard royalty. Works with composers, lyricists; teams collaborators.
Affiliate(s): Sabre Music (SOCAN).
How to Contact: Submit a demo tape—unsolicited submissions are OK. Prefers cassette, phonograph record (or VHS videocassette) and lyric sheet. Does not return unsolicited material.
Music: Mostly **top 40**; also **bluegrass, blues, country, dance-oriented, easy listening, folk, gospel, jazz, MOR, progressive, R&B, rock** and **soul**.
Tips: "Maintain awareness of styles and trends of your peers who have succeeded professionally. Understand the markets to which you are pitching your material. Persevere at marketing your talents. Develop a network of industry contacts, first locally, then regionally and nationally."

MOON JUNE MUSIC, 4233 SW Marigold, Portland OR 97219. President: Bob Stoutenburg. Music publisher. BMI. Estab. 1971. Pays standard royalty.
How to Contact: Submit demo tape—unsolicited submissions OK. Prefers cassette (or VHS videocassette) with 2-10 songs. SASE. Reports in 2 months.
Music: **Country**.

***MUD CAT MUSIC (BMI)**, P.O. Box 971, Haleyville AL 35565. (205)486-5412. President: Max B. Clarkson. Music publisher. Estab. 1991. Publishes 4-5 songs/year. Publishes 2 new songwriters/year. Works with composers and lyricists. Pays standard 50% royalty.
How to Contact: Submit demo tape by mail. Unsolicited submissions are OK. Prefers cassette with 1 song and lyric sheet. SASE. Reports in 1 month.
Music: Mostly **country**, also songs with **Native American themes**. Published *All The Lips (I've Ever Kissed)*, (by M. Clarkson/S. Marler), *Long Time Burning* (by M. Clarkson/F. Long); and *Why Can't Young Love Last Forever* (by M. Clarkson), all recorded by Max B. Clarkson on B-Tone Records.
Tips: "I like songs that tell a story—don't leave me hanging."

MUSIC FACTORY ENTERPRISES, INC., Suite 300, Ford & Washington, Norristown PA 19401. (215)277-9550. President: Jeffrey Calhoon. Music publisher, record company (MFE Records). BMI. Estab. 1984. Publishes 8 songs/year. Receives 4 submissions/month. Works with composers and lyricists; teams collaborators. Pays standard royalty.
Affiliate(s): Robin Nicole Music (BMI).
How to Contact: Write or call first and obtain permission to submit a tape. Prefers cassette with 3-4 songs, lyric sheet and lead sheet. "Make sure notations are clear and legible." SASE. Reports in 3 weeks.
Music: Mostly **20th Century Minimalism, world beat, alternative rock/pop** and **New Age**. Published "Stillwater," "River Run" and "Shamont," all written and recorded by Gregory Darvis on MFE Records (New Age).
Tips: "Develop every song fully, be different, submit best quality product you can."

The types of music each listing is interested in are printed in boldface.

MUSIC IN THE RIGHT KEYS PUBLISHING COMPANY (BMI), 3716 W. 87th St., Chicago IL 60652. (312)735-3297. President: Bert Swanson. Music publisher. Estab. 1985. Member CMA. "A noted publisher." Publishes 200-500 songs/year; publishes 15-25 new songwriters/year. Works with composers. Pays standard royalty.
Affiliate(s): High 'n Low Notes (ASCAP).
How to Contact: Submit a demo tape by mail—unsolicited submissions are OK. Prefers cassette with 3-8 songs and lyric and lead sheets. SASE. Reports in 5 weeks.
Music: Mostly **country, gospel** and **pop**; also **R&B** and **MOR**. Published "Loving the Night Away" and "Drinking Out of Hand," (by B. Swanson), recorded by C. Fisher on Write Way Records; and "She Sure Is Something," (by B. Swanson), recorded by R. Spinnato on Low Notes Records.
Tips: "Always submit a good demo for presentation of a good quality production."

*THE MUSIC ROOM PUBLISHING GROUP, P.O. Box 219, Redondo Beach CA 90277. (310)316-4551. President/Owner: John Reed. Music publisher and record producer. Estab. 1982. Works with composers. Pays standard royalty.
Affiliate(s): Black House Music (BMI), Music Room Productions.
How to Contact: Submit demo tape by mail. Unsolicited submissions are OK. Prefers cassette with 3 songs and lyric sheet. SASE. Reports in 2 weeks.
Music: Mostly **pop/rock/R&B** and **crossover**. Published *My Delite* (by G. Swan), recorded by New Cowboys on Midnight Records (soundtrack); "Tropical Fantasy" (by C. Ace/J. Reed), recorded by Cassandra on MRP Records; and *Martial Arts* (written and recorded by G. Swan), on Weston Records (soundtrack).

*MUSIC SALES CORPORATION (ASCAP), 225 Park Ave. S., New York NY 10003. (212)254-2100. Fax: (212)254-2013. Professional/Creative Manager: Philip "Flip" Black. Music publisher. Estab. 1935. Publishes 100 songs/year; publishes 5 new songwriters/year. Works with composers and lyricists; teams collaborators. Pays standard royalty.
Affiliate(s): Embassy Music Corporation (BMI).
How to Contact: Write first and obtain permission to submit. Prefers cassette with lyric sheet. Does not return unsolicited material. Reports in 2 months.
Music: Mostly **rock, easy listening** and **country**; also **R&B**. Published "Hot Cherie" (by Bishop, etc.), recorded by Hardline on MCA Records; "What A Little Moonlight Can Do" (by Woods), recorded by Robert Palmer on EMI Records; and "Kid Gloves" (by Carlton), recorded by Larry Carlton Palmer on GRP Records.
Tips: "Submit hits, hits, hits!"

MUSICA ARROZ PUBLISHING, 5626 Brock St., Houston TX 77023. (713)926-4432. Administrator of Publishing: David Lummis. Music publisher. ASCAP, BMI. Estab. 1986. Publishes 50 songs/year; publishes 10 new songwriters/year. Works with composers; teams collaborators. Pays standard 50% royalty.
Affiliate(s): Musica Arroz (ASCAP), Defiance Music (ASCAP), Musica Elena (BMI).
How to Contact: Write first and obtain permission to submit a tape. Prefers cassette with 5-6 songs and lyric sheet. SASE. Reports in 6 weeks.
Music: Mostly **Latin (in Spanish), rap (in Spanish), jazz**; also **country** and **rock (in Spanish)**. Published *Somos Dos Gatos* (by Joe Martinez), recorded by the Hometown Boys and *C'est La Vie* (by Jerry Rodriguez), recorded by Mercedez, both on Discos MM; also *Como Quiriera* (by Jose Quintanilla), recorded by Los Monarchas on Double H Records.
Tips: "Do *not* send music other than that in which we are most interested."

MYKO MUSIC, #D203, 1324 S. Avenida, Tucson AZ 85710. (602)885-5931. President: James M. Gasper. Music publisher, record company (Ariana Records) and record producer (Future 1 Productions). BMI. Estab. 1980. Publishes 4 songs/year; publishes 2 new songwriters/year. Works with composers. Pays standard royalty.
How to Contact: Submit a demo tape—unsolicited submissions are OK. Prefers cassette (or ½" VHS videocassette) with 3 songs and lyric sheet. SASE Reports in 1 month.
Music: **Top 40, dance rock, AOR, R&B, country rock** or **Tex-Mex**. Published "Love's A Mess" (by J. Gasper/T. Privett); "On It All" and "Holding On" (by T. Privett), all recorded by The Doll House on Ariana Records.
Tips: "Listen to the radio, be true to yourself."

CHUCK MYMIT MUSIC PRODUCTIONS, 9840 64th Ave., Flushing NY 11374. A&R: Chuck Mymit. Music publisher and record producer (Chuck Mymit Music Productions). BMI. Estab. 1978. Publishes 3-5 songs/year; publishes 2-4 new songwriters/year. Works with composers and lyricists; teams collaborators. Pays standard royalty.

Affiliate(s): Viz Music (BMI) and Tore Music (BMI).
How to Contact: Submit a demo tape by mail—unsolicited submissions are OK. Prefers cassette or VHS videocassette with 3-5 songs and lyric and lead sheets. "Bio and picture would be helpful." SASE. Reports in 3-6 weeks.
Music: Mostly **pop, rock** and **R&B**. Published "Giving You My Love" (by Nata and Schal), recorded by Laura Dees on VIN Records (pop/ballad); "Tu Eras Mi Corazon" (by C. Mymit), recorded by Maria Calbrera on Amigo Records (latin rock); and "Have A Heart" (written and recorded by Caroline Asaje) on PMI Records.
Tips: "Have strong confidence in your work but please follow our policy. Don't be afraid to write complex things."

NADINE MUSIC, P.O. Box 2, Fronhof 100, CH-8260 Stein am Rhein **Switzerland**. Phone: (054)415415. Fax: (054)415420. Professional Manager: Freddy J. Angstmann. Music publisher, record producer, management firm and booking agency. SUISA, SESAC, BMI, ASCAP. Publishes 50-100 songs/year. Works with composers. Pays standard royalty.
Affiliate(s): Nadine Music (SESAC), Joecliff Music (BMI) and Lauren Music (ASCAP).
How to Contact: Submit demo tape—unsolicited submissions are OK. Prefers cassette (or VHS videocassette [PAL]) with lyric and lead sheets. "Clearly label each item you send; include photo and bio if possible." Does not return unsolicited material. Reports in 3 weeks.
Music: **Gospel, blues** and **jazz**; also **R&B** and **classical**. Published "How Long Will My Journey Be," written and recorded by Rev. Thompson on Koch Records (gospel); "True Blues," written and recorded by Jerry Ricks on Bayer Records (blues); and "Medley" (by Gershwin/Baker), recorded by Baker on K Records (jazz).

NAMAX MUSIC PUBLISHING, P.O. Box 24162, Richmond VA 23224. President: Nanette Brown. Music publisher. BMI. Estab. 1989. Publishes 2-4 songs/year; publishes 2 new songwriters/year. Works with composers; teams collaborators. Pays standard royalty.
How to Contact: Write first and obtain permission to submit. Prefers cassette with 2 songs and lyric sheet. "No phone calls please." SASE. Reports in 6 weeks.
Music: Mostly **R&B, urban contemporary** and **pop/top 40**; also **contemporary gospel**. Published "Cynthia" (by Richard Williams), recorded by SoRich on Peak Records (R&B dance).
Tips: "Namax is looking for well constructed songs that deliver a positive message. Material should be as polished as possible."

NASETAN PUBLISHING, Box 1485, Lake Charles LA 70602. (318)439-8839. Contact: Eddie Shuler. Music publisher. BMI. Estab. 1964. Publishes 35 songs/year; 9 new songwriters/year. Pays standard royalty.
Affiliate(s): Tek Publishing.
How to Contact: Submit demo tape—unsolicited submissions are OK. Prefers cassette with 4 songs maximum and lyric or lead sheet. Reports in 8 weeks.
Music: **Novelty songs** and **story songs**. Published "Doctor Oh Doctor," "Call The Cops Have a Family Reunion," and "Slow Horse Trail Ride," all recorded by Bob Brown the Barnyard Troubadour on Goldband Records.
Tips: "Song must have strong storyline with broad appeal for us to be interested."

*NASHVILLE MUSIC GROUP, P.O. Box 111416, Nashville TN 37211-1416. (615)834-4124. Manager: Cindy Brooks. Music publisher and production company. Estab. 1993. Publishes 12 songs/year; publishes 1-2 new songwriters/year. Works with composers and lyricists; teams collaborators. Pays standard royalty.
Affiliate(s): Four Flags Music (ASCAP), Brooks Bros. Publishers (BMI), Enchantment Music (BMI).
How to Contact: Submit demo tape by mail. Unsolicited submissions are OK. Prefers cassette with 3 songs and lyric sheet. SASE. Reports in 2 weeks.
Music: Mostly **country, rock** and **gospel**; also **alternative** and **blues**. Published *100 Years Too Late*, written and recorded by Ted Scanlon on Goldust Records; *Cowboy Icon* (by E. Johnson) and "This Cowboy's Hat" (by Jake Brooks), recorded by Chris Le Doux on Liberty Records.

NASHVILLE SOUND MUSIC PUBLISHING CO., P.O. Box 728, Peterborough, Ontario K9J 6Z8 **Canada**. (705)742-2381. President: Andrew Wilson Jr. Music publisher. SOCAN. Estab. 1985. Publishes 10 songs/year; publishes 5 new songwriters/year. Pays standard royalty.
Affiliate(s): Northern Sound Music Publishing Co. (SOCAN).
How to Contact: Submit demo tape—unsolicited submissions are OK. Prefers cassette or 7½ ips reel-to-reel with 2-4 songs and lyric sheet. "Please send only material you do not want returned. We have an open door policy." Reports in 2 weeks.

Music: Mostly **country, country/pop** and **crossover country**. Published "Just Beyond the Pain" and "Feelin' In My Bones" (by Carol Wakeford), recorded by Charlie Louvin and Crystal Gale on Playback Records. Also published "Let An Old Race Horse Run" (by Ron Simons), recorded by Tommy Cash on Playback Records (country).
Tips: "Send me a well crafted song, both lyrically and musically! You need great hooks!"

*NATIONAL TALENT, P.O. Box 14, Whitehall MI 49461. (616)894-9208. 1-800-530-9255. President: Sharon Leigh. Vice President: Jay Ronn. Music publisher and record company (United Country). BMI. Estab. 1985. Publishes 7-8 songs/year. Teams collaborators. Pays standard royalty.
Affiliate(s): House of Shar (BMI).
How to Contact: Submit a demo tape by mail—unsolicited submissions are OK. Prefers cassette with 1-10 songs and lyric sheet. SASE. Reports in 1 month.
Music: Country and gospel. Published "Mistletoe" (by Prohaska), recorded by Jay Ronn; "Blue Days" (by Duncan), recorded by Lexi Hamilton; and "I Believe In Country" (by Koone), recorded by Bobbie G. Rice, all on United Records.

NAUTICAL MUSIC CO., Box 120675, Nashville TN 37212. (615)255-1068. Owner: Ray McGinnis. Music publisher and record company (Orbit Records, Ray McGinnis). BMI. Estab. 1965. Publishes 25 songs/year; 10 new songwriters/year. Works with composers. Pays standard royalty.
How to Contact: Submit demo tape—unsolicited submissions are OK. Prefers cassette with 4 songs and lyric sheets. SASE. Reports in 6-8 weeks.
Music: Mostly **country ballads** and **country rock**. Published "No More Tears" (by D. Connor), "I Never Stopped Loving You" and "Hometown Rodeo" (by M. Deryer), all recorded by Debra Lee on Orbit Records.
Tips: "The trend is back to traditional country music with songs that tell a story."

NEBO RIDGE PUBLISHING COMPANY, P.O. Box 194 or 457, New Hope AL 35760. President: Walker Ikard. Manager: Jim Lewis. Music publisher, promotions firm, record producer, record company (Nebo Record Company), management firm (Nebo Management) and booking agency (Nebo Booking Agency). ASCAP. Estab. 1985. Pays standard royalty.
How to Contact: Submit demo tape—unsolicited submissions are OK. Prefers cassette demo tape (or VHS videocassette) with 1 song and lyric sheet. "A VHS video of a song would be helpful but not absolutely necessary." Does not return unsolicited material. Reports as soon as possible.
Music: Mostly **modern** and **traditional country, modern** and **traditional gospel, country/rock, rock and roll, pop, MOR** and **bluegrass**. Published "Heartache," written and recorded by Robyn Lane; "Love Memories," written and recorded by Anita Taft; and "Down The Road," written and recorded by Linda Pearl, all on Nebo Records.
Tips: "We like to get to know songwriters and singers who contact our company, so it would be a good idea if a songwriter or singer sends a personal bio and 1 or 2 full-length photos for our files. Also, we will be signing several female singers to our Nebo Record label, so all female singers should contact us soon for a review."

*NERVOUS PUBLISHING, 4/36 Dabbs Hill Lane, Northolt, Middlesex, London, **England**. Phone: (4481)963-0352. Managing Director: Roy Williams. Music publisher, record company and record producer. MCPS, PRS and Phonographic Performance Ltd. Estab. 1979. Publishes 100 songs/year; publishes 25 new songwriters/year. Works with composers and lyricists. Pays standard royalty; royalties paid directly to US songwriters.
How to Contact: Submit a demo tape—unsolicited submissions are OK. Prefers cassette with 3-10 songs and lyric sheet. "Include letter giving your age and mentioning any previously published material." SAE and IRC. Reports in 3 weeks.
Music: Mostly **psychobilly, rockabilly** and **rock** (impossibly fast music—ex.: Stray Cats but twice as fast); also **blues, country, R&B** and **rock** (50s style). Published *Hot Rod Satellite* (by Whitehouse), recorded by Frenzy on Rage Records; "Balls Balls" (by Koinuma), recorded by The Falcons; and *BC Stomp* (by Rasmussen), recorded by The Taggy Tones, both on Nervous Records.
Tips: "Submit *no* rap, soul, funk—we want *rockabilly*."

NETWORK SOUND MUSIC PUBLISHING INC., 345 Sprucewood Rd., Lake Mary FL 32746-5917. (407)321-3702. Fax: (407)321-2361. President, A&R: Vito Fera. Office Manager, A&R: Rhonda Fera. Music publisher, record company (S.P.I.N. Records), record producer (Network Sound Productions Inc.). ASCAP. Estab. 1980. Publishes 10 songs/year; publishes 3 new songwriters/year. Hires staff writers "on agreement terms." Pays standard royalty.
Affiliate(s): Fera Music Publishing (BMI).
How to Contact: Submit a demo tape by mail or UPS with 3 songs maximum and lyric sheet. Unsolicited submissions are OK. Prefers cassette (or VHS videocassette). "Package song material carefully. Always label (name, address and phone) both cassette and lyric sheet. Copyright songs. If you need

assistance or advice on submission procedures or packaging, please contact us." SASE. Reports in 4 weeks.

Music: Mostly **dance/pop, R&B, rock/light, soundtracks** and **children's music.** Published "Only Lover" (by Ron Beverly & Levi McDaniel), recorded by Jerry Dean; co-published with Delev Music "Tomorrow" (by Wayne Gamache, Jerry Lester & Lazlo Nemeth); "Say It Again" (by Richard Hamersma & Gerry Magallan) and "If Love Comes Again" (by Tyrone W. Brown), recorded by Jerry Dean on SPIN and Surprize Records (R&B).

Tips: "Carefully follow each music publisher's review instructions. Always include lyrics and a SASE for reply. A professional package and music production will help your songs stand out amongst the crowd. Always deliver exciting new music to the music industry. Use short intros and 'quality' vocalists to record your demo. Supply us with your best songs, commercial styling and catchy lyrics but not too personal. As you write, try to imagine a manor artist singing your song. If you can't, rewrite it! Finally, read every available songwriting book and publication."

A NEW RAP JAM PUBLISHING, P.O. Box 683, Lima OH 45802. (219)424-5766 or (419)228-8562. President: James Milligan. Music publisher, record company. New Experience Records/Party House Publishing (BMI), Grand Slam Records/A New Rap Jam Publishing (ASCAP). Estab. 1989. Publishes 30 songs/year; publishes 2-3 new songwriters/year. Hires staff songwriters. Works with composers and lyricists; teams collaborators. Pays standard royalty.

How to Contact: Submit demo tape by mail. Unsolicited submissions are OK. Prefers cassette with 3-5 songs and lyric sheet or lead sheet. SASE. Reports in 1 month.

Music: Mostly **R&B, pop, rock/rap;** also **contemporary, gospel, country, soul.** Published "Tell Me If You Still Care," recorded by T.M.C.; "Gigolos Get Lonely Too" (by Morris Day and the Time), recorded by T.M.C. and James Junior.

Tips: "Believe in yourself. Work hard. Keep submitting songs and updates on new songs you have written. Most of all be somewhat patient. If there is interest you will be contacted."

NEWCREATURE MUSIC, Box 148296, Nashville TN 37214-8296. President: Bill Anderson, Jr. Professional Manager: G.L. Score. Music publisher, record company, record producer and radio and TV syndicator. BMI. Publishes 25 songs/year; publishes 2 new songwriters/year. Pays standard royalty.

Affiliate(s): Mary Megan Music (ASCAP).

How to Contact: Submit demo tape by mail—unsolicited submissions are OK. Prefers 7½ ips reel-to-reel or cassette (or videocassette) with 4-10 songs and lyric sheet. SASE. Reports in 1 month.

Music: Country, gospel, jazz, R&B, rock and top 40/pop. Published *When A Good Love Comes Along*, *The Storm Is Gone* and *I've Come Home to You*, all written and recorded by Gail Score on Landmark Records.

*THE JOSEPH NICOLETTI MUSIC CO. (ASCAP), P.O. Box 2818, Newport Beach CA 92659. (714)494-0181. Fax: (714)494-0982. President A&R: Joseph Nicoletti. Music publisher. Estab. 1976. Publishes 30-60 songs/year; publishes approx. 40 songwriters/year. Works with composers and lyricists; teams collaborators. Pays standard royalty.

Affiliate(s): Global Village Music Co. (ASCAP).

How to Contact: Submit demo tape by mail. Unsolicited submissions are OK. Prefers cassette with up to 5 songs and lyric sheet. "You may want to type a cover letter about yourself." SASE. Reports in 2-3 weeks.

Music: Mostly **country, pop** and **rock;** also **R&B, gospel** and **adult contemporary.** Published "Let's Put the Fun Back In Rock 'n Roll" (by B. Feldman/J. Nicoletti), recorded by Fabian, Frankie Avalon/Bobby Rydell on A&M Records (pop); "Step Into The Light" and "Soldiers Eyes" (written and recorded by J. Nicoletti), on California Int. Records.

Tips: "Send only what you think is your best material!"

*NO MAS MUSIC (BMI), 23 Market St., Passaic NJ 07055. (201)777-6109. Fax: (201)458-8303. President: Tomasito Bobadilla. Music publisher. Estab. 1989. Publishes 4 songs/year; publishes 3-5 new songwriters/year. Hires staff writers. Teams collaborators. Pays standard royalty.

Affiliate(s): Ito Dito Music (ASCAP).

How to Contact: Submit demo tape by mail. Unsolicited submissions OK. Prefers cassette with 3 songs and lyric sheet. SASE. Reports in 3 months.

Music: Mostly **dance, alternative rock** and **pop/ballads;** also **R&B.** Published *Consistence* (by Andy Pimen), recorded by Karizma on Metropolitan Records (dance).

*NON-STOP MUSIC PUBLISHING, 915 W. 100 South, Salt Lake City UT 84104. (801)531-0060. Fax: (801)531-0346. Vice President: Michael L. Dowdle. Music publisher. Estab. 1990. Publishes 50-100 songs/year; publishes 3-4 new songwriters/year. Works with composers and lyricists; teams collaborators. Pays negotiable royalty.

Affiliate(s): Non-Stop Outrageous Publishing, Inc. (ASCAP), Non-Stop International Publishing, Inc. (BMI) and Airus International Publishing.
How to Contact: Submit demo tape by mail. Unsolicited submissions are OK. Prefers cassette with lyric or lead sheet, where possible. Does not return unsolicited material. Reports in 4-6 weeks.
Music: Mostly **pop, R&B** and **country**; also **jazz** and **new age**. Published *Emerald Mist* and *Wishing Well* (written and recorded by Sam Cardon); and *A Brighter Day* (written and recorded by Mike Dondle), all on Airus Records.

*N-THE WATER PUBLISHING, INC. (ASCAP), L221, 11902 Jones Rd., Houston TX 77070. (713)890-8486. Publishing Administrator: De Andrea Y. Canada. Music publisher, record company (Rap-A-Lot Records) and record producer. Estab. 1985.
How to Contact: Write first and obtain permission to submit. Prefers cassette with 4 songs. SASE. Reports in 2-3 months.
Music: Mostly **rap** and **R&B**. Current artists include The Geto Boys, Dana Dane, Scarface, Bushwick Bill.

OBH MUSIKVERLAG OTTO B. HARTMANN, Box 2691, Ch-6901 Lugano **Switzerland**. Fax and phone: 0041(91)685586. President: Otto B. Hartmann. Music publisher, record company (OKAY/EXPO, Kick/OBH) and record producer. Estab. 1968. Publishes 100 songs/year; publishes 2 new songwriters/year. Hires staff writers. Works with composers and lyricists. Pays standard royalty.
Affiliate(s): Edition Plural (classical).
Music: Mostly **rock, jazz, folk, pop** and **R&B**; also **classical**.

*OH MY GOSH MUSIC, 5146 Hill Dr., Memphis TN 38109. (901)789-5296. Owner: Gerald McDade. Music publisher and record producer (Home Town Productions). BMI. Estab. 1985. Publishes 1-6 songs/year; publishes 1-6 new songwriters/year. Works with composers and lyricists; teams collaborators. Pays standard royalty.
How to Contact: Submit a demo tape by mail—unsolicited submissions are OK. Prefers cassette (or VHS videocassette if available) with 2-4 songs and lyric sheet. SASE. Reports in 6 weeks.
Music: Mostly **traditional country, country rock** and **rock-a-billy**; also **gospel**. Published "Matilda Bay" (written and recorded by Eddie Ruth), on Hometown Records.
Tips: "Be positive, be current, be different, be committed."

OKISHER MUSIC, P.O. Box 20814, Oklahoma City OK 73156. (405)755-0315. President: Mickey Sherman. Music publisher, record company (Seeds Records, Okart Records, Homa Records and Okie Dokie Records), record producer and management firm (Mickey Sherman's Talent Management). BMI. Estab. 1973. Member OCMA. Publishes 10-15 songs/year; publishes 2-3 new songwriters/year. Works with composers and lyricists. Pays standard royalty.
How to Contact: Submit demo tape—unsolicited submissions OK. Prefers 7½ ips reel-to-reel or cassette (or VHS videocassette) with 1-3 songs and lyric sheet. "Don't let the song get buried in the videocassette productions; a bio in front of performance helps. Enclose press kit or other background information." Does not return unsolicited material. Reports in 3 months.
Music: Mostly **blues, country** and **ballads**; also **easy listening, jazz, MOR, R&B** and **soul**. Published "Leave Your Number" written and recorded by Dale Langley; "Cookin' and Jukin'," written and recorded by Jana Jarvis; and "Make My Pain Walk Away," written and recorded by Jan Jo, all on Seeds Records.
Tips: "Have a 'hook' in the lyrics. Use good quality tape/lyric sheet and clean recording on demos."

OLD SLOWPOKE MUSIC, P.O. Box 52681, Tulsa OK 74152. (918)742-8087. President: Rodney Young. Music publisher, record producer. BMI. Estab. 1977. Publishes 24-36 songs/year; publishes 2-3 new songwriters/year. Works with composers and lyricists; teams collaborators. Pays standard royalty.
How to Contact: Write or call first and obtain permission to submit. Prefers cassette with 4 songs and lyric sheet. SASE. Reports in 12 weeks to 6 months.
Music: Mostly **rock, country** and **R&B**; also **jazz**. Published *Blue Dancer*, written and recorded by Chris Blevins on CSR Records; *She Can't Do Anything Wrong* (by Davis/Richmond), recorded by Bob Seger on Capitol Records; and *Hardtimes* (by Brad Absher), on CSR Records.

*RONNIE OLDHAM MUSIC PUBLISHING (BMI), 202 Auburn St., Florence AL 35630. (205)767-7667. President: Ronnie Oldham. Music publisher, record company (Gazebo Records) and record producer. Estab. 1990. Publishes 20-30 songs/year; publishes 3-6 new songwriters/year. Works with composers and lyricists; teams collaborators. Pays standard royalty.
How to Contact: Submit demo tape by mail. Unsolicited submissions are OK. Prefers cassette with 2-4 songs and lyric sheet. "Send as good a demo as possible." Does not return unsolicited material. Reports in 2 months. "No response unless we wish to publish your song."

Music: Mostly **country, R&B** and **pop**; also **gospel, MOR** and **rock.** Published *Rollin' Stone* (by Ronnie and Bobby Oldham), recorded by Dick Allen on THZ Records (R&B/pop); and *Men of The Bible* (written and recorded by Barbara Staggs), on Gazebo Records (gospel).
Tips: "Be original, keep it simple and keep on trying."

O'LYRIC MUSIC, Suite 1, 1837 Eleventh St., Santa Monica CA 90404. (213)452-0815. President: J. O'Loughlin. Creative Director: Kathryn Haddock. Music publisher, manager (O'Lyric Music Management) and production company. BMI, ASCAP. Member California Copyright Conference. Estab. 1980. Publishes 50-75 songs/year; publishes 10-15 new songwriters/year. Hires staff writers; pays $20,000/year—"only duty expected is songwriting. Writers paid by royalties earned and by advances." Pays standard royalty to outside writers.
Affiliate(s): O'Lyrical Music (ASCAP).
How to Contact: Submit demo tape—unsolicited submissions OK. Prefers cassette with 1-3 songs and lyric sheet. Does not return materials. "Contact on acceptance only." Please no phone calls.
Music: Mostly **R&B, rock, top 40, dance** and **country**; also **contemporary jazz** and **soul.** Published "I Live for Your Love" (by P. Reswick/S. Werfil/A. Rich), recorded by Natalie Cole on Manhattan Records (R&B/crossover); "Mr. Right" (by T. Shapiro/M. Garvin), recorded by Smokey Robinson on Motown Records (R&B/crossover); and "I've Still Got the Love We Made" (by Shapiro/Garvin/Waters), recorded by Reba McEntire (country/crossover). Production company works with Double T (Next Plateau Records), Cactus Choir (Atlantic Records) and Yosefa (International artist, Departure Records).
Tips: "Please follow our policy without exception."

ONE FOR THE MONEY MUSIC PUBLISHING CO. (BMI), P.O. Box 18751, Milwaukee WI 53218. (414)527-4477. President: Michael W. White. Music publisher, record company (World Class Record Co.) and record producer (MW Communications). BMI. Estab. 1989. Publishes 4-6 songs/year. Works with composers and lyricists; teams collaborators. Pays standard royalty.
How to Contact: Submit demo tape—unsolicited submissions are OK. Prefers cassette or VHS videocassette with 6-8 songs and lyric sheet (if possible). SASE. Reports in 2-3 months.
Music: Mostly **country-rock, country-pop** and **country**; also **rock** and **R&B.** Published "Whoops I'm in Love Again" (by White, Kowalski, Barker, Goetzke); "Twenty Three Days" (by M.W. White); and "Just Remember I'm Still Lovin' You" (by Kowalski, White, Barker); all recorded by Sky Harbor Band on World Class Records (country rock).

*ONE HOT NOTE MUSIC INC., P.O. Box, 454 Main St., Cold Spring Harbor NY 11724. (516)367-8544. Fax: (516)367-8507. A&R: Greg MacMillan. Music publisher, record company (Reiter Records Ltd.). Estab. 1989. Publishes 200 songs/year. Publishes 10 new songwriters/year. Works with composers and lyricists; teams collaborators. We take 100% of publishing but can be negotiated based upon trace history of composer.
How to Contact: Submit demo tape by mail. Unsolicited submissions are OK. Prefers cassette. Does not return material.
Music: Mostly **pop, rock, jazz**; also **dance, country** and **rap.** Published "Be My Baby" written and recorded by T.C. Kross on Reiter Records; "Ready or Not" (by Lange/Bastianelli), recorded by Yolanda Yan on Cinepoly Records and by Camille Nivens on BMG Records.
Tips: "Make the song as well produced and recorded as you can."

OPERATION PERFECTION, Suite 206, 6245 Bristol Pkwy., Culver City CA 90230. Contact: Larry McGee. Vice-President: Darryl McCorkle. Music publisher. BMI. Estab. 1976. Publishes 15 songs/year; publishes 1-2 new songwriters/year. Works with composers and lyricists. Pays standard royalty.
How to Contact: Submit a demo tape—unsolicited submissions OK. Prefers cassette (or VHS videocassette) with 1-4 songs and lyric sheet. "Please only send professional quality material!" SASE. Reports in 2 months.
Music: **Rock, rap, pop, MOR/adult contemporary** and **R&B.** Published "We're Number One" (by Liz Davis), recorded by The Saxon Sisters on Boogie Band (rock); "Captain Freedom" and "Got It Going On" (by Alan Walker), recorded by Executives on Crossover Records.
Tips: "Study past, present and future trends in the music industry."

ORCHID PUBLISHING, Bouquet-Orchid Enterprises, 204 Crestview St., Minden LA 71055. (318)377-2538. President: Bill Bohannon. Music publisher, record company, record producer (Bouquet-Orchid Enterprises) and artist management. BMI. Member CMA, AFM. Publishes 10-12 songs/year; publishes 3 new songwriters/year. Works with composers and lyricists; teams collaborators. Pays standard royalty.
How to Contact: Submit demo tape—unsolicited submissions OK. Prefers cassette with 3-5 songs and lyric sheet. "Send biographical information if possible—even a photo helps." SASE. Reports in 1 month.

Music: Religious ("Amy Grant, etc., contemporary gospel"); **country** ("Garth Brooks, Trisha Year-wood type material"); and **top 100/pop** ("Bryan Adams, Whitney Houston type material"). Published *Make Me Believe* (written and recorded by Adam Day); "Spare My Feelings" (by Clayton Russ), recorded by Terri Palmer; and "Trying to Get By" (by Tom Sparks), recorded by Bandoleers, all on Bouquet Records.

ORDERLOTTSA MUSIC, 6503 York Rd., Baltimore MD 21212. (410)377-2270. President: Jeff Order. Music publisher and record producer (Jeff Order/Order Productions). BMI. Estab. 1986. Publishes 20 songs/year; publishes 3-4 new songwriters/year. Works with composers and lyricists. Pays standard royalty.
How to Contact: Write first to submit a tape. Prefers cassette with 3 songs. SASE. Reports in 1 month.
Music: Prefers **contemporary instrumental music,** but will listen to **all types.** Published "Won't You Dance With Me," recorded by Tiny Tim (dance); "Sea of Tranquility," "Isis Unveiled," and "Keepers of the Light," written and recorded by Jeff Order on Order Records (instrumental new age).
Tips: "Submit high-quality, well-recorded and produced material. Original styles and sounds. Don't waste our time or yours on copying the music of mainstream artists."

OTTO PUBLISHING CO., P.O. Box 16540, Plantation FL 33318. (305)741-7766. President: Frank X. Loconto. Music publisher, record company (FXL Records) and record producer (Loconto Productions). ASCAP. Estab. 1978. Publishes 25 songs/year; publishes 1-5 new songwriters/year. Pays standard royalty.
Affiliate(s): Betty Brown Music Co. (BMI), and Clara Church Music Co. (SESAC), True Friends Music (BMI).
How to Contact: Prefers cassette with 1-4 songs and lyric sheet. SASE. Reports in 1 month.
Music: Mostly **country, MOR, religious** and **gospel.** Published "Sewing Without Pins" (TV theme) and "Safety Sam" (novelty), both by Frank X. Loconto, recorded by Loconto Productions. Theme Song for "Nightly Business Reports," nationally syndicated TV show, written and recorded by Frank X. Loconto. Also published "Seminole Man" (by Loconto), recorded by James Billie on FXL Records (country).

*PADRINO MUSIC PUBLISHING (BMI,SESAC), 1001 Highway 77, Bishop TX 78343. (512)584-3735. Fax: (512)584-3803. Proprietor: Jesus Gonzales Solis. Music publisher. Estab. 1993. Publishes 4 songs/year. Pays standard royalty. "Padrino Music is owned by Jesus Gonzales Solis, who is at this time the sole composer, publishing his own music."
How to Contact: Submit demo tape by mail. Unsolicited submissions are OK. Prefers cassette with lead sheet. SASE. Reports in 2 weeks.
Music: Mostly **Spanish rancheras, Latin ballads** and **cumbias.** Published *Quiero Saber Lo Sabes De Mi* (by Solis), recorded by La Sombra on Fonovisa Records.
Tips: "Write what you feel; no matter how outrageous, there is a purpose to everything that is written. Never give up if you believe in yourself, your time will come. Be persistent."

*PALMETTO PRODUCTIONS, P.O. Box 1376, Pickens SC 29671. President: Brian E. Raines. Music publisher, record company and record producer. Estab. 1985. Publishes 5 songs/year. Publishes 3 new songwriters/year. Works with composers and lyricists; teams collaborators. Pays standard royalty.
Affiliate(s): Brian Raines Music Co. (ASCAP) and Brian Song Music Co. (BMI).
How to Contact: Submit demo tape by mail. Unsolicited submissions are OK. Prefers cassette (or VHS videocassette) with 1 song. Does not return unsolicited material. Reports in 3 months.
Music: Mostly **gospel, contemporary Christian** and **country.** Published *Take It To Jesus* (by Dale Cassell), recorded by Triniti on Mark V Records; "Since I Met You" (written and recorded by Brian Raines), on Palmetto Records; and *From The Heart* (written and recorded by Jim Hubbard), on Hubbit Records.
Tips: "Send only one song."

J. S. PALUCH COMPANY, INC./WORLD LIBRARY PUBLICATIONS, INC., 3825 N. Willow Rd., P.O. Box 2703, Schiller Park IL 60176-0703. Music Editors: Nicholas T. Freund, Betty Z. Reiber, Ron Rendek, Laura Denkler. Music publisher. SESAC. Estab. 1913. Publishes 50 or more songs/year; publishes varying number of new songwriters/year; recordings. Works with composers and lyricists; teams collaborators. "Pays pro-rated 5% for text or music alone; 10% for both."

Refer to the Category Index (at the back of this book) to find exactly which companies are interested in the type of music you write.

How to Contact: Submit demo tape and/or manuscript by mail—unsolicited submissions are OK. Prefers cassette with any number of songs, lyric sheet and lead sheet. SASE. Reports in 3 months.
Music: Sacred music, hymns, choral settings, descants, psalm settings, masses; also children's sacred music. Published "Music for the Banquet" (by William Ferris); "Christ Is the Image" (by Paul French); and "Just a Closer Walk With Thee" (arr. by James Marchionda/Mark Rachelski) (all sacred).
Tips: "Make your manuscript as legible as possible, with clear ideas regarding tempo, etc. Base the text upon scripture."

*PANCHO'S MUSIC CO., 3121 29th Ave., Sacramento CA 95820. (916)455-5278. Contact: Frank Lizarraga. Music publisher. BMI. Estab. 1980. Publishes 3 songs/year; publishes 1 new songwriter/year. Works with lyricists. Pays standard royalty.
How to Contact: Write or call first and obtain permission to submit. Prefers cassette (or VHS videocassette) with 3 songs, lyric sheet and brief resume/fact sheet. SASE. Reports in 2 months.
Music: Mostly **Latin, pop** and **rock**; also **country**. Published "100 Miles of Bad Road" and "You Belong With Me" (by F. Lizarraga), recorded by Andre and Pancho; and "I Wonder. . . Why" (by Adam Lizarraga), recorded by Adam D, all on A.D. Records.
Tips: "We specialize in Latin music and prefer bilingual songwriters."

PANDISC RECORDS, 38 NE 167 St., Miami FL 33162. (305)948-6466. President: Bo Crane. Music publisher and record company (Pandisc, Jamarc). ASCAP, BMI. Estab. 1979. Publishes 50 songs/year; publishes 3-6 new songwriters/year. Works with composers and lyricists; teams collaborators. Pays standard royalty.
Affiliate(s): Whooping Crane Music (BMI) and Hombre Del Mundo (ASCAP).
How to Contact: Submit a demo tape by mail—unsolicited submissions are OK. Prefers cassette with 3 songs and lyric sheet. Does not return unsolicited material.
Music: Mostly **rap** and **R&B**. Published "B Girls" (by C. Trahan/L. Johnson), recorded by Young & Restless (rap); and "I Can't Let Go" (by Y. Israel), recorded by Joey Gilmore (blues), both on Pandisc Records; and "I Seen Your Boyfriend," (by Baily/Daniels), recorded by Get Fresh Girls on Breakaway Records (rap).

PARCHMENT HARBOR MUSIC, P.O. Box 10895, Pleasanton CA 94588. (510)828-9430. CEO: P.A. Hanna. Music publisher, record company (Wingate Records). BMI. Estab. 1989. Publishes 12 songs/year; publishes 4 new songwriters/year. Teams collaborators. Pays standard royalty.
Affiliate(s): Hugo First Publishing (ASCAP).
How to Contact: Write and obtain permission to submit a tape or write to arrange personal interview. Prefers cassette with 3 songs and lyric sheet. SASE or no returns. Reports in 2 months.
Music: Mostly **pop, country** and **contemporary Christian**; also **country rock** and **blues.** Published *Different Roads* (by R. Davidson, J. Crofton, W. Muncy and C. Peterson), recorded by Cross Street; "Nevada Nights" (by D. Hanna), recorded by Neon Nites; and *Family Man* (by M. Ross), recorded by Marty Ross, all on Wingate Records.
Tips: "Tight lyrics with a message. Professional demo and presentation."

*PARRAVANO MUSIC, 17 Woodbine St., Cranston RI 02910. (401)785-2677. Owner: Amy Parravano. Music publisher, record company (Peridot Records), record producer (Peridot Productions). Estab. 1986. Publishes 5 songs/year. Works with composers and lyricists. Pays standard 50% royalty.
How to Contact: Submit demo tape by mail. Unsolicited submissions are OK. Prefers cassette with 3-4 songs and lyric sheet. Lead sheets are optional. Reports in 1 month.
Music: Mostly **country, gospel, folk**; also **MOR, children's,** and **novelty.** Published "America" (by Stamm/Parravano), recorded by Amy Parravano on Stop Hunger Records; "His Light Shines Down on Me" and "Trust in Him" both by Amy Parravano, recorded by Amy Beth on Peridot Records.
Tips: "Be sure that it is something that you would want to listen to. Not only is there a wealth of song ideas in the world around us; but within us too."

PDS MUSIC PUBLISHING, P.O. Box 412477, Kansas City MO 64141-2477. Contact: Submissions Department. Music publisher and record company (PDS Records, Universal Jazz, PDS Associated labels). ASCAP, BMI. Estab. 1988. Publishes 30 songs/year; publishes 3-4 new songwriters/year. Works with composers and lyricists. Pays standard royalty.
Affiliate(s): PDS Universal (ASCAP), PDS Worldwide (BMI).
How to Contact: Write first and obtain permission to submit a tape. Prefers cassette with 5-10 songs and lyric sheet. Does not return unsolicited material. Reports in 2 months.
Music: Mostly **rap** and **R&B**. Published "I Like the Things You Do" (by Derrick Peters/Kevin Griffin), recorded by Kevin Griffin on PDS Records (R&B); "The Way You Make Me Feel" (by D. Peters), recorded by Legacy on PDS Records (R&B).
Tips: "Follow directions and be patient."

PECOS VALLEY MUSIC, 2709 West Pine Lodge, Roswell NM 88201. (505)622-0244. President: Ray Willmon. Music publisher. BMI. Estab. 1989. Publishes 15-20 songs/year; publishes 3-4 new songwriters/year. Works with composers and lyricists; teams collaborators. Pays standard royalty.
How to Contact: Submit a demo tape by mail—unsolicited submissions are OK. Prefers cassette (or VHS cassette if available) with 2-4 songs and lyric sheet. SASE. Reports in 1 month.
Music: Mostly **country-western** and **soft rock**. Published "Sunrise" by Ruben Wells; "Wait Till Tomorrow" by J.A. Swartz; "You Will Do" by Jason Marks; and "No Where To Go" by Ray Willmon, all on Sun Country Records (country).
Tips: "Write original lyrics with an understandable story line with correct song form (i.e., AAAA, AABA, ABAB)."

PEERMUSIC, 8159 Hollywood Blvd., Los Angeles CA 90069. (213)656-0364. Fax: (213)656-3298. Assistant to the head of Talent Acquisitions: Nicole Bahuchet. Music publisher and artist development promotional label. ASCAP, BMI. Estab. 1928. Publishes 600 songs/year (worldwide); publishes 1-2 new songwriters/year. Hires staff songwriters. Works with composers and lyricists; teams collaborators. Royalty standard, but negotiable.
Affiliate(s): Peer Southern Organization (ASCAP) and Peer International Corporation (BMI).
How to Contact: Write first and obtain permission to submit. "We do NOT accept unsolicited submissions." Prefers cassette and lyric sheet. Does not return unsolicited material. Reports in 6 weeks.
Music: Mostly **pop, rock** and **R&B**. Published "Run to You" (by Jud Friedman/Allan Rich), recorded by Whitney Houston on Arista Records (pop); "Can't Cry Hard Enough" (by Williams/Williams/Etzioni), recorded by The Williams Brothers on Warner Bros. Records (rock); and "I'm Gonna Get You" (by A. Scott/Bizarre, Inc./Toni C.), recorded by Bizarre, Inc. on Columbia Records (pop).

PEGASUS MUSIC, 27 Bayside Ave., Te Atatu, Auckland 8, **New Zealand**. Professional Manager: Errol Peters. Music publisher and record company. APRA. Estab. 1981. Publishes 20-30 songs/year; publishes 5 new songwriters/year. Works with composers and lyricists; teams collaborators. Pays 3-5% to artists on contract and standard royalty to songwriters; royalties paid directly to US songwriters.
How to Contact: Submit a demo tape—unsolicited submissions are OK. Prefers cassette with 3-5 songs and lyric sheet. SAE and IRC. Reports in 1 month.
Music: Mostly **country**; also **bluegrass, easy listening** and **top 40/pop**. Published *He's Left the Building* (by Ginny Peters and C. Stone), recorded by Dennis Marsh on Ode Records (country); *Butterfly Wings*, written and recorded by Ginny Peters on Pegasus Records (country); and *Morning Love Song*, written and recorded by Tina Whall on Ode Records (country).
Tips: "Be very direct and do not use too many words. Less is better."

PERFECTION MUSIC PUBLICATION (BMI), P.O. Box 4094, Pittsburgh PA 15201. (412)782-4477. President: Edward J. Moschetti. Music publisher and record company (Century Records). Estab. 1953. Works with composers.
Affiliate(s): Regal Music Publications (ASCAP).
How to Contact: Write first and obtain permission to submit. Prefers cassette. SASE. Reports in 1 month.
Music: **Ballads, country** and **pop**.

*JUSTIN PETERS MUSIC (BMI), 3609 Donna Kay Dr., Nashville TN 37211. (615)331-6056. Fax: (615)831-0991. President: Justin Peters. Music publisher. Estab. 1981. Publishes 5-10 new songwriters/year. Pays standard royalty.
Affiliate(s): Lita Music (ASCAP) and Tourmaline Music, Inc. (BMI).
How to Contact: Call first and obtain permission to submit. Prefers cassette with 3 songs and lyric sheet. Does not return unsolicited materials. Reports in 1 month.
Music: Mostly **gospel, country** and **R&B**. Published "Chisel Meets the Stone," recorded by 4 Him on Benson Records; "Love Still Changing Hearts," recorded by Imperials on Starsong Records; and "Wipe a Tear," recorded by Russ Taff and Olanda Daper on Word Records, all written by Justin Peters.
Tips: "Learn your craft and submit quality work."

PHILIPPOPOLIS MUSIC, 12027 Califa St., North Hollywood CA 91607. President: Milcho Leviev. Music publisher. BMI. Member GEMA, NARAS. Estab. 1975. Publishes 3-5 songs/year; publishes 1-2 new songwriters/year. Works with lyricists. Pays standard royalty.
How to Contact: Submit demo tape—unsolicited submissions are OK. Prefers cassette with 1-3 songs. Prefers studio produced demos. Does not return material. Reports in 1 month.
Music: **Jazz** and **classical fusion**. Published *Monday Morning* and *California Winter* (by Leviev); and *Manipulation* (by Spassov), all recorded by Katoomi Quartet on Balicantor Records.

PLACER PUBLISHING, Box 11301, Kansas City KS 66111. (913)287-3495 (night). Owner: Steve Vail. Music publisher, record company (System Records) and record producer. ASCAP. Estab. 1980. Publishes 2 songs/year; publishes 1 new songwriter/year. Works with composers and lyricists. Pays standard royalty.
How to Contact: Submit a demo tape—unsolicited submissions are OK. Prefers cassette (or VHS or Beta ½" videocassette) with 10-12 songs. Does not return unsolicited material. Reports in 4-8 weeks.
Music: Only **progressive/alternative.** Published "Echo Lake," "Mother Earth, Father Sky" and "The Path" (all by Vail and Studna), recorded by Realm on System Records (progressive rock).

PLANET DALLAS RECORDING STUDIOS, P.O. Box 191447, Dallas TX 75219. (214)521-2216. Producer, Music publisher, record producer (Rick Rooney) and recording studio (Planet Dallas). BMI, ASCAP. Estab. 1985. Publishes 20 songs/year; 2-3 new songwriters/year. Works with composers and lyricists; teams collaborators. Pays standard royalty; also depends on deal/studio involvement.
Affiliate(s): Stoli Music (BMI) and Planet Mothership Music (ASCAP).
How to Contact: Submit demo tape. Prefers cassette with 1-3 songs and lyric sheet. SASE for reply. Reports in 8 weeks.
Music: Mostly **modern rock.** Published "This Property is Condemned" (by P. Sugg), recorded by Maria McKee on Geffen Records (pop); "Tickle" (by U Know Who), recorded by U Know Who on WE—Mix Records (rap); and "Hydrogen City" (by Hydrogen City), recorded by Hydrogen City on H1 Records (rock).

PLATINUM PRODUCTIONS PUBLISHING, 406 Centre St., Boston MA 02130. (617)983-9999. A&R Rep.: Akhil Garland. Music publisher, record company. Estab. 1989. Publishes 2 new songs/year; 2 new songwriters/year. Works with composers and lyricists; teams collaborators. Pays standard royalty.
How to Contact: Submit demo tape—unsolicited submissions are OK. Prefers CD or cassette with 4 songs and lyric sheet. SASE. Reports in 2 months.
Music: Mostly **reggae, folk** and **world beat;** also **rap/R&B** and **rock.** Published *4 O'Clock* (by J. Nicholson), recorded by Tiny Pupils; "Fair Weather" (by Dan Rogers), recorded by Irations; and "Changes" (by D. Garfield), recorded by The Bulbous Ones, all on Monarch Records.

POLLYBYRD PUBLICATIONS LIMITED, P.O. Box 8442, Universal CA 91608. (818)508-8990. Fax: (818)505-0420. Professional Manager: Maxx Diamond. Music publisher (Kelli Jai, Pollyann, Ja Nikki, Lonnvaness, Branmar and PPL Music). ASCAP, BMI, SESAC. Estab. 1979. Publishes 100 songs/year; publishes 25-40 new songwriters/year. Hires staff writers. Works with composers and lyricists; teams collaborators. Pays standard royalty.
Affiliate(s): Kellijai Music (ASCAP), Pollyann Music (ASCAP), Ja'Nikki Songs (BMI), Branmar Songs International (BMI), Lonnvanness Songs (SESAC) and PPL Music (ASCAP).
How to Contact: Submit demo tape—unsolicited submissions are OK. Prefers cassette or VHS videocassette with 4 songs and lyric and lead sheet. SASE. Reports in 6 weeks.
Music: Published "Hero" (by J. Jarrett), recorded by The Band AKA (dance-R&B); "Anything" (by D. Mitchell), recorded by D.M. Groove (dance-R&B); and "Cool Fire" (by J. Jarrett), recorded by Katrina Gibson, all on Bouvier/Sony Records (dance/pop).

PORTAGE MUSIC, 16634 Gannon W., Rosemont MN 55068. (612)432-5737. President: Larry LaPole. Music publisher. BMI. Publishes 5-20 songs/year. Pays standard royalty.
How to Contact: Submit demo tape by mail—unsolicited submissions are OK. Prefers cassette with 3 songs and lyric sheet. Does not return unsolicited material. Reports in 2 months.
Music: Mostly **country** and **country rock.** Published "King of the Surf," "My Woodie" and "A-Bone" (by L. Lapole), recorded by Trashmen.
Tips: "Keep songs short, simple and upbeat with positive theme."

PPI/PETER PAN INDUSTRIES, 88 St. Francis St., Newark NJ 07105. (201)344-4214. Senior Vice President (and songwriter): Joseph M. Porrello. Product Manager: Marianne Eggleston. Music publisher, record company (Compose Records, Current Records, Parade Video, Ironbound Publishing, record producer (Dunn Pearson, Jr.); also outside producers. ASCAP, BMI. Estab. 1928. Publishes over 100 songs/year. Hires staff songwriters. Works with composers and lyricists; teams collaborators. Pays standard royalty "based on negotiation."
Affiliate(s): Ironbound Publishing (ASCAP), Ina Kustik, Sweet Basil, Benco/World Music.
How to Contact: Submit a demo tape by mail—unsolicited submissions are OK. Prefers cassette (or VHS videocassette if available) with 5-7 songs. "Please include name, address and phone numbers on all materials, along with picture, bio and contact information." SASE. Reports in 2-3 months.
Music: Mostly **children's**—audio, **R&B** and **jazzy;** also **exercise**—video, **rock** and **classical.** Published "Where Do Trolls Come From" (by Barry Hirschberg), recorded by various artists on Peter Pan Records; "Frankie Paul," written and recorded by Frankie Paul on Tassa/Compose Records (reggae);

and "Manhattan Jazz Reunion," written and recorded by Manhattan Jazz Reunion on Compose/Sweet Basil Records (jazz).
Tips: "Submit materials professionally packaged with typewritten correspondence."

PREJIPPIE MUSIC GROUP, Box 2849, Trolley Station, Detroit MI 48231. (313)581-1267. Partner: Bruce Henderson. Music publisher, record company (PMG Records) and record producer (PMG Productions). BMI. Estab. 1990. Publishes 50-75 songs/year; publishes 2-3 new songwriters/year. Hires staff writers. Teams collaborators. Pays standard royalty.
How to Contact: Submit a demo tape by mail—unsolicited submissions are OK. Prefers cassette with 3-4 songs and lyric sheet. "No phone calls please." SASE. Reports in 6 weeks.
Music: Mostly **techno/house, funk/rock, dance**; also **alternative rock, experimental** and **jingle-oriented** music. Published "Evangeline" (by Bourgeoisie Paper Jam), recorded by Bourgeoisie Paper Jam on PMG Records (alternative rock); and "We're on The Move Now" (by the Prejippies), recorded by the Prejippies on Black Toxic Records (techno/alternative).
Tips: "Think your arrangements through carefully. Always have a strong hook (whether vocal-oriented or instrumental)."

PRESCRIPTION COMPANY, 70 Murray Ave., Port Washington NY 11050. (516)767-1929. President: David F. Gasman. Music publisher and record producer. BMI. Pays standard royalty.
How to Contact: Call or write first about your interest. Prefers cassette with any number of songs and lyric sheet. "Send all submissions with SASE (or no returns)." Reports in 1 month.
Music: Bluegrass, blues, children's, country, dance-oriented, easy listening, folk, jazz, MOR, progressive, R&B, rock, soul and top 40/pop. Published "You Came In," "Rock 'n' Roll Blues" and "Seasons" (by D.F. Gasman), all recorded by Medicine Mike on Prescription Records.
Tips: "Songs should be good and written to last. Forget fads—we want songs that'll sound as good in 10 years as they do today. Organization, communication and exploration of form are as essential as message (and sincerity matters, too)."

JIMMY PRICE MUSIC PUBLISHER, Sun-Ray Production Company, 1662 Wyatt Parkway, Lexington KY 40505. (606)254-7474. Owner: Jimmy Price. Music publisher, record company (Sun-Ray, Sky-Vue) and record producer (Jimmy Price Music Publisher). BMI. Estab. 1950. Works with composers and lyricists. Pays standard royalty.
Affiliate(s): Jimmy Price Productions (BMI).
How to Contact: Submit a demo tape by mail—unsolicited submissions are OK. Prefers cassette or track ½ or Full 7½ ips reel-to-reel with 3-7 songs and lyric sheet. SASE. Reports in 5-6 weeks.
Music: Mostly **country, gospel** and **bluegrass**. Published "Close to You" (by S. Drouin); "Texas Little Cutie" (by J.T. Price), both recorded by Carry Vice on Sun-Ray Records (country); and "That's OK I Love You" (by R.E. Johnson), recorded by R.E. Johnson on Sky-Vue Records (country).
Tips: "I must have the lyrics to meter. If a person does not know what I mean about bringing lyrics to meter, please check a gospel hymn song book. You will see in each and every staff there is a music note for each and every word or syllable. This way, should I want to add a composition in print I can do so."

PRITCHETT PUBLICATION (Branch), P.O. Box 725, Daytona Beach FL 32114-0725. (904)252-4848. Vice President: Charles Vickers. Music publisher and record company. (Main office in California.) BMI. Estab. 1975. Publishes 21 songs/year; publishes 12 new songwriters/year. Works with composers and lyricists. Pays standard royalty.
Affiliate(s): Alison Music (ASCAP), Charles H. Vickers (BMI).
How to Contact: Write first and obtain permission to submit. Prefers cassette with 6 songs and lyric or lead sheet. SASE.
Music: **Gospel, rock-disco** and **country**. Published *Walkin On The Water* (by Charles Vickers), recorded by Charles Vickers on King of Kings Records (gospel); and "It'll Be A Cold Day" (by Leroy Pritchett), recorded by Ray Sanders on Allagash Country Records (country).

PROPHECY PUBLISHING, INC., P.O. Box 4945, Austin TX 78765. (512)459-6036. President: T. White. Music publisher. ASCAP. Pays standard royalty, less expenses; "expenses such as tape duplicating, photocopying and long distance phone calls are recouped from the writer's earnings."
Affiliate(s): Black Coffee Music (BMI).
How to Contact: Write first and obtain permission to submit. Does not return unsolicited material. "No reply can be expected unless we're interested."
Music: Published "The Sun and Moon and Stars" and "Woman of the Phoenix," (by Vince Bell), performed by Nancy Griffith on MCA Records and Elektra Records; *King of Dixie*, written and recorded by Tom Elskes on Amazing Records; and *Just Outside, Upside Down*, written and recorded by Bill Colbert on Dolittle Records.
Tips: "Get an album track on a major label."

PUBLISHING CENTRAL, 7251 Lowell Dr., Overland Park KS 66204. (913)384-6688. Director of Publishing: David Jackson. Music publisher. "We are also a theatrical agency." SAG, ITAA. Estab. 1961. Publishes 5 songs/year; publishes 3 new songwriter/year. Teams collaborators. Pays standard royalty.
Affiliate(s): Jac-Zang (ASCAP), Bunion (BMI), Very Cherry (ASCAP), All Told (BMI).
How to Contact: Submit a demo tape—unsolicited submissions are OK. Prefers cassette with 1-3 songs and lead sheets. Does not return unsolicited material. Reports in 3 months.
Music: Mostly **country rock, pop** and **rock**; also **gospel, reggae, alternative** and **soul (Southern)**.
Tips: "Know your trade. Be able to write (manuscript) music. Learn basic music skills—theory etc. Become more sophisticated."

PURPLE HAZE MUSIC, P.O. Box 1243, Beckley WV 25802. President: Richard L. Petry. (304)252-4836. A & R: Carol Lee. Music publisher. BMI. Estab. 1968. Publishes 3-5 songs/year; publishes 3-4 new songwriters/year. Pays standard royalty.
How to Contact: Submit demo tape—unsolicited submissions are OK. Prefers cassette with 3-5 songs and lyric sheet. SASE. Reports in 1-2 months.
Music: Country, pop/top 40 and **R&B/crossover.** Published "My Old Friend," written and recorded by Chuck Paul on Rising Sun Records; and "Home Sweet W.V.," written and recorded by Dave Runyon on Country Bridge Records.
Tips: "Make sure your song is well written. Submit professional demo by professionals. You are competing with Nashville's best. Type up your lyrics in capital letters, block style and double space between your verses and chorus. Be sure your songs are well structured, for our Nashville program."

PUSTAKA MUZIK EMI (Malaysia) SDN. BHD., Suite 10.01, 10th Floor, Exchange Square, off Jalan Semantan, Damansara Heights, 50490 Kuala Lumpur, **Malaysia**. Phone: 03-6277511. Contact: Publishing Manager. Music publisher and record company. Publishes 50 songs/year; publishes 15 new songwriters/year. Works with composers and lyricists; teams collaborators. Pays standard royalty.
How to Contact: Submit demo tape—unsolicited submissions are OK. Prefers cassette and lyric or lead sheet. Does not return unsolicited material. Reports in 1 month.
Music: Mostly **MOR, country** and **commercial jazz**; also **blues** and **rock.** Published *Di Alam Fana Cinta* (by Fauzi Marzuki), recorded by Photograph on Sinar Records; *Kekasih Awaf Dan Akhir* (by Fauzi Marzuki), recorded by Jamal, and *Pada Syurga Diwajahmu* (by Fauzi Marzuki), recorded by Nash, both on Warner Records.
Tips: "Please send us properly recorded demo tape containing commercial pop, rock musical material."

QUAN-YAA RECORDS, P.O. Box 16606, Philadelphia PA 19139-0606. (215)747-2256. Fax: (215)471-0415. Vice President of Marketing/Sales: Jackie Campbell. Music publisher, record company. Estab. 1990. Publishes 15 songs/year; publishes 5 new songwriters/year. Works with composers and lyricists; teams collaborators. Pays standard royalty.
Affiliate(s): Quan-Ya Music Publishing and Quan-Tree Music Publishing (BMI).
How to Contact: Call first and obtain permission to submit. Prefers cassette (or VHS videocassette) with 3 songs. "Put name, address and phone number on cassette." SASE. Reports in 4-6 weeks.
Music: Mostly **R&B, rap** and **reggae**; also **pop, country** and **salsa.** Published "Juiced Me" (by Curry/Burch/Virtue), recorded by Ho-Tip and Lambchops (R&B); "Trapped in the Middle" (by Curry/Virtue/Bailey/Bush/Campbell), recorded by Barbara Walker; and "I'm Out to Getcha" (by Bush/Campbell/Jefferson), recorded by Francesco.
Tips: "If the first songs are not accepted do not hesitate to submit again and again."

*QUARK, INC., P.O. Box 7320, New York NY 10150-7320. (212)838-6775. Manager: Curtis Urbina. Music publisher, record company (Quark Records and Q-Rap Records), record producer (Curtis Urbina). Estab. 1986. Publishes 12 songs/year; 2 new songwriters/year. Teams collaborators. Pays standard royalty of 50%.
Affiliate(s): Quarkette Music (BMI) and Freedurb Music (ASCAP).
How to Contact: Submit demo tape by mail. Prefers cassette with 4 songs. Does not return unsolicited material. Reports in 4-6 weeks.
Music: New Age *only*! (Looking for instrumentals only!)

*QUEEN ESTHER MUSIC PUBLISHING (ASCAP), 449 N. Vista St., Los Angeles CA 90036. Owner: Len Weisman. Music publisher. Pays standard royalty.
Affiliate(s): House of Sound Music (BMI).
How to Contact: Submit demo tape by mail. Unsolicited submissions are OK. Prefers cassette. SASE. Reports in 2 months.
Tips: "If I send back your tape with no response, it's a reject, but please keep sending."

R. J. MUSIC, 10A Margaret Rd., Barnet, Herts. EN4 9NP **United Kingdom.** Phone: (01)440-9788. Managing Directors: Roger James and Laura Skuce. Music publisher and management firm (Roger James Management). PRS. Pays negotiable royalty (up to 50%).
How to Contact: Prefers cassette with 1 song and lyric or lead sheet. "Will return cassettes, but only with correct *full* postage!"
Music: Mostly MOR, **blues, country** and **rock;** also **chart material.** "No disco or rap!"

R.T.L. MUSIC, (formerly Le Matt Music, Ltd.), %Stewart House, Hillbottom Rd., Highwycombe, Buckinghamshire **United Kingdom** HP124HJ. Phone: (0630)647374. Fax: (0630)647612. Art Director: Ron Lee. Music publisher, record company and record producer. MCPS, PRS. Member MPA, PPL. Estab. 1971. Publishes 30 songs/year; publishes 10 new songwriters/year. Works with composers, lyricists; teams collaborators. Pays standard royalty.
Affiliate(s): Lee Music, Ltd., Swoop Records, Grenoville Records, Check Records, Zarg Records, Pogo Records, Ltd., R.T.F.M., Value for Money Productions, Lee Sound Productions, Le Matt Distributors, Hoppy Productions.
How to Contact: Submit demo tape—unsolicited submissions OK. Prefers 7½ or 15 ips reel-to-reel or cassette (or VHS 625/PAL system videocassette) with 1-3 songs and lyric and lead sheets. "Make sure name and address are on reel or cassette." SAE and IRC. Reports in 6 weeks.
Music: All types. Published *Witch Woman, Monster In A Movie* and *Spooky Sue* (by Ron Dickson), recorded by Nightmare on Zarg Records.

*RAHSAAN PUBLISHING, 335 Merrimac St., Newburyport MA 01950-0764. (508)463-3028. Fax: (508)465-7441. Owners: Tom and Rosemarie Reeves. Music publisher, record company (Cat's Voice) and record producer. Estab. 1982. Publishes 4 songs/year; publishes 4 new songwriters/year. Hires staff writers. Works with composers and lyricists; teams collaborators. "Royalty depends on project, but standard usually applies."
Affiliate(s): Cat's Voice (ASCAP) and Black Gold (BMI).
How to Contact: Submit demo tape by mail. Unsolicited submissions are OK. Prefers cassette (or VHS videocassette) with 3 songs and lyric or lead sheet. "Songwriters must be copyrighted; send copy of form." Does not return unsolicited material. Reports in 2 weeks.
Music: Mostly **rock, New Age** and **reggae;** also **country, light rock** and **R&B.** Published *Zig Zag* (by Joey Zark), recorded by Andy Henry, and *Carry On* (written and recorded by Andy Henry), on Black Gold Records; and *Nadene* (by Lucian Parken), recorded by Boiler Rm. 6 on Cat's Voice Records.
Tips: "Lead sheet, copyright register form, clear cassette with guitar and voice or piano and voice."

*RANA INTERNATIONAL MUSIC GROUP, INC., P.O. Box 106, Valhalla NY 10595. (914)741-2576. President: Raffaele A. Nudo. Vice President: Wesley C. Kranitz. Music publisher and record company (CHRISMARIE Records). Estab. 1990. Publishes 3-5 songs/year; publishes 2-4 new songwriters/year. Works with composers and lyricists. Pays standard royalty.
Affiliate(s): Big Z Productions (ASCAP), President: Ted Zuccarelli, and CHRISMARIE Records (BMI) A&R Director: Peggy Cooney.
How to Contact: Submit demo tape by mail. Unsolicited submissions are OK. Prefers cassette (or VHS videocassette with 3-4 songs and lyric sheet. "Include SASE." Does not return material. Reports in 6 weeks.
Music: Mostly **pop, rock** and **ballads;** also **country, R&B** and **new music.** Published "Tears of Hurt," written and recorded by Niko; "Glorious Victory," written and recorded by Tom Hughes and "Just A Matter of Time," written and recorded by DECLARATION, all on CHRISMARIE Records.
Tips: "Music should never overshadow the lyrics. Stay positive and have faith in your talent. All submissions must include name, phone number, etc. on all items."

*RAVING CLERIC MUSIC PUBLISHING/EUROEXPORT ENTERTAINMENT, P.O. Box 4735, Austin TX 78765-4735. (512)452-2701. Fax: (512)452-0815. President: L.A. Evans. Music publisher, record company (RCM Productions), record producer, artist management and development. Estab. 1985. Publishes 15-20 songs/year. Publishes 7-10 new songwriters/year. Works with composers and lyricists; teams collaborators. Pays standard 50% royalty.
How to Contact: Write or call first and obtain permission to submit. Prefers cassette (or VHS videocassette if available) with 3 songs maximum and lyric sheet. "Submissions of more than 3 songs will not be listened to." Does not return material. "Does not accept unsolicited material." Reports in 3-4 weeks.
Music: Prefers **alternative rock, pop, R&B;** also **country, blues, rap/urban.** Published "True Revelation" and "Latin Showdown" (by Mattos-Engle), recorded by Unknown Soul on RCM Productions; and "All My Friends" (by Abbott-Kirk), recorded by Argument Clinic on ERG Records.
Tips: "Write hooks that get stuck in the brain, playing over and over til it drives the listener out of his mind. Infectious hooks make hits."

RED BOOTS TUNES, 5503 Roosevelt Way NE, Seattle WA 98105. (206)524-1020. Fax: (206)524-1102. Music publisher. ASCAP. Estab. 1991. Publishes 25 songs/year; publishes 2-3 new songwriters/year. Teams collaborators. Pays standard royalty.
How to Contact: Submit a demo tape by mail. Prefers cassette with 2-3 songs and lyric sheet. SASE. Reports in 6-8 weeks.
Music: Mostly **country**; also **R&B/rock**. Published "Cowboy Rap" and "Some Day," written and recorded by Holt and Walker on Black Boot Records.
Tips: "Have professional looking lyric sheets and good quality tapes."

REN MAUR MUSIC CORP., 521 5th Ave., New York NY 10175. (212)757-3638. President: Rena L. Feeney. Music publisher and record company. BMI. Member AGAC and NARAS. Publishes 6-8 songs/year. Pays 4-8% royalty.
Affiliate(s): R.R. Music (ASCAP).
How to Contact: Prefers cassette with 2-4 songs and lead sheet. SASE. Reports in 1 month.
Music: R&B, rock, soul and **top 40/pop**. Published "Same Language," "Do It to Me and I'll Do It to You," and "Once You Fall in Love" (by Billy Nichols), recorded by Rena; and "Lead Me to Love" (by Brad Smiley), recorded by Carmen John (ballad/dance), all on Factory Beat Records.
Tips: "Send lead sheets and a good, almost finished cassette ready for producing or remixing."

RHYTHMS PRODUCTIONS, Whitney Bldg., P.O. Box 34485, Los Angeles CA 90034. President: Ruth White. Music publisher and record company (Tom Thumb Records). ASCAP. Member NARAS. Publishes 4-6 cassettes/year. Receives 10-12 submissions/month. Pays negotiable royalty.
Affiliate(s): Tom Thumb Music.
How to Contact: Submit tape with letter outlining background in educational children's music. SASE. Reports in 2 months.
Music: "We're only interested in **children's songs** that have educational value. Our materials are sold in schools and homes, so artists/writers with a teaching background would be most likely to understand our requirements." Published "Professor Whatzit®," series including "Adventures of Professor Whatzit & Carmine Cat,"(cassette series for children) and "First Reader's Kit. We buy completed master tapes."

RIDGE MUSIC CORP., 38 Laurel Ledge Ct., Stamford CT 06903. President/General Manager: Paul Tannen. Music publisher and manager. Estab. 1961. BMI, ASCAP. Member CMA. Publishes 12 songs/ year. Pays standard royalty.
Affiliate(s): Tannen Music Inc. and Deshufflin, Inc.
How to Contact: Submit demo tape—unsolicited submissions OK. Prefers cassette with 3 songs and lyric sheet. SASE. Reports in 2 months.
Music: Country, rock, top 40/pop and **jazz.**

*RISING STAR MUSIC PUBLISHERS, 710 Lakeview Ave. NE, Atlanta GA 30308. (404)872-1431. Fax: (404)872-3104. President: Barbara Taylor. Music publisher and record company (Rising Star Records). Estab. 1987. Publishes 5-6 songs/year; publishes 3 new songwriters/year. Works with composers. Pays standard royalty.
How to Contact: Write or call first and obtain permission to submit. Prefers cassette with 3 songs and lyric or lead sheet. "Make them as professional looking as possible." SASE. Reports in 3 months.
Music: Mostly **New Age, jazz-instrumental** and **classical**; also **new world, children's** and **other forms of instrumental music**. Published *Dreamrunner* (by Brad Rudisail); *Two English Dances* (by Kent Pendleton); and *Oh Watch The Stars* (by John Krumich), all on Rising Star Records.
Tips: "To be treated professionally, one must act and look professional. We take professionals seriously, and others do too. We don't follow trends. New trends are created by those who break the old ones."

FREDDIE ROBERTS MUSIC, P.O. Box 203, Rougemont NC 27572. (919)477-4077. Manager: Freddie Roberts. Music publisher, record company, record producer (Carolina Pride Productions), and management firm and booking agency. Estab. 1967. BMI. Publishes 45 songs/year; publishes 15 new songwriters/year. Works with composers, lyricists; teams collaborators. Pays standard royalty.
How to Contact: Write first about your interest or to arrange personal interview. Prefers 7½ ips reel-to-reel or cassette with 1-5 songs and lyric sheet. SASE. Reports in 5 weeks.
Music: Mostly **country, MOR** and **top 40/pop**; also **bluegrass, church/religious, gospel** and **Southern rock**. Published "Any Way You Want It" (by B. Fann), recorded by Sleepy Creek (southern rock) on Bull City Records; "Just A Little" (by C. Justis), recorded by Dean Phillips (country) on Ardon Records; and "He Knows What I Need" (by J. Dobbs), recorded by the Roberts Family (gospel) on Bull City Records.
Tips: "Write songs, whatever type, to fit today's market. Send good, clear demos, no matter how simple."

ROB-LEE MUSIC, P.O. Box 37612, Sarasota FL 34237. Vice Presidents: Rodney Russen, Eric Russen, Bob Francis. Music publisher, record company (Castle Records, Rock Island Records and Jade Records), record producer and manager. ASCAP. Estab. 1965. Publishes 18-36 songs/year; publishes 6 new songwriters/year. Teams collaborators. Pays standard royalty.

Affiliate(s): Heavy Weather Music (ASCAP).

How to Contact: Submit a demo tape—unsolicited submissions OK. Prefers cassette (or VHS videocassette) with 4-8 songs and lyric sheet. Does not return unsolicited material. Reports in 2 weeks.

Music: Dance-oriented, easy listening, MOR, **R&B, rock, soul, top 40/pop** and **funk.** Published "The Ultimate Male" (by Preston Steele), recorded by Noelle on TCB Records; "Ryan's Express," written and recorded by Ryan Shayne on Castle Records; and *Slams, Jams and Body Slams* (by various), recorded by IWA Westlero on Rock Island Records.

ROCKER MUSIC/HAPPY MAN MUSIC, P.O. Box 73, 4501 Spring Creek Rd., Bonita Springs, FL 33923-6637. (813)947-6978. Executive Producer: Dick O'Bitts. BMI, ASCAP. Estab. 1960. Music publisher, record company (Happy Man Records, Condor Records and Air Corp Records), record producer (Rainbow Collections Ltd.) and management firm (Gemini Complex). Publishes 25-30 songs/year; publishes 8-10 new songwriters/year. Works with composers; teams collaborators. Pays standard royalty.

How to Contact: Submit a demo tape—unsolicited submissions are OK. Prefers cassette (or VHS videocassette if possible) with 4 songs and lyric or lead sheet. SASE. Do not call. "You don't need consent to send material." Reports in 1 month.

Music: Country, rock, pop, gospel, Christian and **off-the-wall.** Published "Hang Tough" and "Girls of Yesterday" (by Lou Cate), recorded by Holly Ronick; and "When You Get Your Woman" (by Ri Hamilton), recorded by Colt Cipson, all on Happy Man Records (country).

ROCKFORD MUSIC CO., Suite 6-D, 150 West End Ave., New York NY 10023. Manager: Danny Darrow. Music publisher, record company (Mighty Records), record and video tape producer. BMI, ASCAP. Publishes 1-3 songs/year; publishes 1-3 new songwriters/year. Teams collaborators. Pays standard royalty.

Affiliate(s): Corporate Music Publishing Company (ASCAP) and Stateside Music Company (BMI).

How to Contact: Submit a demo tape—unsolicited submissions are OK. Prefers cassette with 3 songs and lyric sheet. "SASE a must!" Reports in 1-2 weeks. *"Positively no phone calls."*

Music: Mostly **MOR** and **top 40/pop;** also **adult pop, country, adult rock, dance-oriented, easy listening, folk** and **jazz.** Published "Look To The Wind" (by Peggy Stewart/ D. Darrow) (MOR); "Telephones," (by Robert Lee Lowery and Danny Darrow) (rock); and "Better Than You Know" (by Michael Greer), all recorded by Danny Darrow on Mighty Records.

Tips: "Listen to top 40 and write current lyrics and music."

*RONDOR INTERNATIONAL MUSIC PUBLISHING, 360 N. La Cienega, Los Angeles CA 90048. (310)289-3500. Fax: (310)289-4000. Senior Vice President Creative: Brenda Andrews. Music publisher. Estab. 1965. Hires staff writers. Works with composers and lyricists; teams collaborators. Pays standard royalty.

Affiliate(s): Almo Music Corp. (ASCAP) and Irving Music, Inc. (BMI).

How to Contact: Write or call first and obtain permission to submit. Prefers cassette (or VHS videocassette) with 3 songs and lyric sheet. "Send DATs if possible, discography if applicable." SASE.

Music: All types. Published songs by En Vogue, Dire Straits and Melissa Etheridge.

Tips: "Give only your best, be original."

ROOTS MUSIC, Box 111, Sea Bright NJ 07760. President: Robert Bowden. Music publisher, record company (Nucleus Records) and record producer (Robert Bowden). BMI. Estab. 1979. Publishes 2 songs/year; publishes 1 new songwriter/year. Works with composers and lyricists; teams collaborators. Pays standard royalty.

How to Contact: Submit a demo tape—unsolicited submissions are OK. Prefers cassette (or VHS videocassette) with 3 songs and lyric sheet; include photo and bio. "I only want inspired songs written by talented writers." SASE. Reports in 3 weeks.

Music: Mostly **country** and **pop;** also **church/religious, classical, folk, MOR, progressive, rock (soft, mellow)** and **top 40.** Published "Always", "Selfish Heart" and "Hurtin'" (by Bowden), all recorded by Marco Sission on Nucleus Records (country).

ROSE HILL GROUP, 1326 Midland Ave., Syracuse NY 13205. (315)475-2936. A&R Director: V. Taft. Music publisher. Estab. 1979. Publishes 1-15 songs/year; publishes 1-5 new songwriters/year. Works with composers and lyricists; teams collaborators. Pays standard royalty.

Affiliate(s): Katch Nazar Music (ASCAP) and Bleecker Street Music (BMI).
How to Contact: Submit demo tape—unsolicited submissions are OK. Prefers cassette. SASE. Reports in 2-4 weeks.
Music: Mostly **pop/rock, pop/dance** and **contemporary country.** Published "True Love Never Dies" (by D. Jacobson), recorded by Z Team; and "Win Some, Lose Some" (by Jr. Carlsen), recorded by Fox, both on Sunday Records (pop ballad); and "Noah Jones" (by G. Davidian), recorded by IO on Cherry Records (pop/dance).
Tips: "Write simple, memorable melody lines; strong, real story lines."

STEVE ROSE MUSIC, #6K, 115 E. 34th St., New York NY 10016. (212)213-6100. Manager: Steve Rose. Uses Nashville contacts to pitch to majors and indies.
How to Contact: "If you have had an indie cut, send 3 of your best with publishing open on a quality cassette with typed lyric sheets. Enclose 29¢ SASE. Replies as soon as possible. No SASE, no response. Put your phone number on everything as I will call if interested. Comments, but not cassettes, are returned on songs I pass. Don't box cassettes and don't staple anything."
Music: **Country** mainly, "although I may be able to pitch ultra-professionally demoed, killer power ballads in NYC. Nothing seasonal or novelty or clever. Nothing with a title that's been a hit (or even close)."
Tips: "Nashville, for the out-of-town writer, makes Japan look good, free trade-wise. My only tip is not to pour any money into any portion of the music business where there's no return. Also, don't let independents rip you off by implying they can get your songs cut by majors. Ultimately, no matter how good the song, it comes down to connections and money."

*ROSEMARK PUBLISHING, P.O. Box 295, Atco NJ 08004. (609)753-2653. Manager: Robert Fitzpatrick. Music publisher, record producer (Studio B) and copyright consultant for artists. BMI. Estab. 1988. Publishes 12 songs/year; publishes 3 new songwriters/year. Hires new staff writers. Works with composers and lyricists. Pays standard royalty.
Affiliate(s): Studio B Records.
How to Contact: Submit a demo tape, unsolicited submissions are OK. Prefers cassette with 3 songs and lyric or lead sheets. "Demo can be 2 or more tracks. But it must be clean." SASE. Reports in 6-8 weeks.
Music: Mostly **top 40/pop, easy listening** and **country;** also **MOR, gospel** and **R&B.** Published "Relax and See," written and recorded by Roscoe Tee (MOR); "Why?" (by Bobby David), recorded by Bob Thomas (top 40); and "Sharing All the Joys of Life" (by Mark Daniel), recorded by Katie Rose (pop), all on Studio B Records.
Tips: "Be professional and have patience. Music has become too "programmed" and over-produced. We need to get back to honest simplicity."

ROYAL FLAIR PUBLISHING, Box 438, Walnut IA 51577. (712)366-1136. President: Bob Everhart. Music publisher and record producer. BMI. Estab. 1967. Publishes 5-10 songs/year; publishes 1-2 new songwriters/year. Works with composers and lyricists. Pays standard royalty.
How to Contact: Submit a demo tape—unsolicited submissions are OK. Prefers cassette with 2-6 songs. SASE. Reports in 9 weeks.
Music: Traditional country, bluegrass and **folk.** Published "Hero of Gringo Trail," "Time After Time" and "None Come Near," written and recorded by R. Everhart on Folkways Records; and "Smoky Mountain Heartbreak," written and recorded by Bonnie Sanford (all country).
Tips: "Song definitely has to have old-time country flavor with all the traditional values of country music. No sex, outlandish swearing, or drugs-booze type songs accepted. We have an annual Hank Williams Songwriting Contest over Labor Day weekend and winners are granted publishing."

SABTECA MUSIC CO., Box 10286, Oakland CA 94610. (415)465-2805. A&R: Sean Herring. President: Duane Herring. Music publisher and record company (Sabteca Record Co.). ASCAP, BMI. Estab. 1980. Publishes 8-10 songs/year; 1-2 new songwriters/year. Works with composers and lyricists; teams collaborators. Pays standard royalty.
Affiliate(s): Sabteca Publishing (ASCAP), Toyiabe Publishing (BMI).
How to Contact: Write or call first and obtain permission to submit a tape. Prefers cassette with 2 songs and lyric sheet. SASE. Reports in 1-2 weeks.
Music: Mostly **R&B, pop** and **country.** Published "Route 49," "Heartache" and "Just In the Nick of Time" (by Duane Herring), all recorded by Johnny B. on Sabteca Records (country).

SADDLESTONE PUBLISHING, 264 "H" St., Box 8110-21, Blaine WA 98230. Canada Address: 8821 Delwood Dr., Delta B.C., V4C 4A1 **Canada.** (604)582-7117. Fax: (604)582-8610. President: Rex Howard. Music publisher, record company (Saddlestone) and record producer (Silver Bow Productions). SOCAN, BMI. Estab. 1988. Publishes 100 songs/year; publishes 12-30 new songwriters/year. Hires staff writers. Works with composers and lyricists; teams collaborators. Pays standard royalty.

Affiliate(s): Silver Bow Publishing (SOCAN, ASCAP).
How to Contact: Submit a demo tape by mail—unsolicited submissions are OK. Prefers cassette with 5-7 songs and lyric sheet. "Make sure vocal is clear." SASE. Reports in 6 weeks.
Music: Mostly **country, rock** and **pop**; also **gospel** and **R&B**. Published *She's Something* (by J.E.Wilson), recorded by Razzy Bailey on Slammin Records; *Nothin Better To Do* (by Marsh Gardner), recorded by Bill Lowden on ESU Records; and "Where Does Wind Go" (by C. Wayne Lammers), recorded by Bill Benson on Kansa Records.
Tips: "Submit clear demos, good hooks and avoid long intros or instrumentals. Have a good singer do vocals."

*SAMUEL THREE PRODUCTIONS (BMI), 4056 Shady Valley Dr., Arlington TX 76013. (817)274-5530. President: Samuel Egnot. Music publisher and record company (Alpha Recording Co.). Estab. 1992. Publishes 12 songs/year; publishes 7 new songwriters/year. Works with composers and lyricists. Pays standard royalty.
How to Contact: Write or call first to arrange personal interview. Submit demo tape by mail. Unsolicited submissions are OK. Prefers cassette with lead sheet. SASE. Reports in 1 month.
Music: Mostly **country, country-gospel** and **gospel**; also **southern gospel**. Published "One-Minus-One Equals Me"(by Robert "G.L." Fogle); "Never Stop Loving You" (by Robert Fogle/Sam Egnot); and "Jesus Is My Power" (by Sam & Bea Egnot) (gospel); all recorded by Alpha Recording on Samuel III Records.
Tips: "Be aggressive in getting your demos out. Don't stop at one turndown, send to another and another till you feel it's going to receive recognition. If it's good to you, ask for perhaps another musical group to consider redoing your material."

*TRACY SANDS MUSIC, Suite 119, 2166 W. Broadway, Anaheim CA 92804-2446. (714)992-2652. Vice President, A&R: Harold Shmoduquet. Music publisher, record company (Orange Records, Beet Records), record producer (Orange Productions). BMI. Estab. 1977. Publishes 12 songs/year; publishes 4 new songwriters/year. Pays standard royalty.
Affiliate(s): Fat Cat Music (BMI), Lipstick Traces Music (BMI) and Bastion Music (BMI).
How to Contact: Submit a demo tape by mail—unsolicited submissions are OK. Prefers cassette with 2-3 songs and lyric sheet. SASE. Reports in 2 months.
Music: All types. Published "My Pants Are Way Too Tight" (by Benjamin Antin), recorded by Benny Grunch; *Euradice,* written and recorded by Greg James, both on Beet Records; *Woman's World* (by Robert Wahlsteen), recorded by Jubal's Children on Swak Records.
Tips: "We are mostly interested in "sixties" themes: Psychedelia, anti-establishment, etc., unsigned material from the era."

SARISER MUSIC, Box 211, Westfield MA 01086. (413)967-5395. Operations Manager: Alexis Steele. Music publisher and record company (Sweet Talk Records). BMI. Publishes 6-12 songs/year; publishes 1-2 new songwriters/year. Works with composers and lyricists; teams collaborators. Pays standard royalty.
How to Contact: Write first and obtain permission to submit. No calls. Prefers cassette or 7½ ips reel-to-reel with 3-4 songs and lyric or lead sheet. "Lyrics should be typed; clear vocal on demo." SASE. Reports in 6 weeks.
Music: Mostly **country/pop, country/rock** and **educational material**; also **soft rock** and **rockabilly.** "We're interested in 50s/60s style 4-part harmony." Published "One Last Kiss" (by Sparkie Allison), recorded by Moore Twinz on MMT Records (country); "Sweet Talk" and "Ride a Rainbow," written and recorded by Sparkie Allison and Ginny Cooper on Sweet Talk Records (country/pop).
Tips: "Lyrics must have positive message. No cheatin' songs. Be unique. Try something different."

WILLIAM A. SAULSBY MUSIC COMPANY, 311 W. Monroe St. #4872, Jacksonville FL 32202. Producer: Aubrey Saulsby. Estab. 1985. Publishes 8-10 songs/year. Pays standard royalty.
How to Contact: Write first and obtain permission to submit. Prefers cassette or 7½" reel and lyric sheet. Does not return unsolicited material.
Music: Mostly **R&B, rap** and **jazz**; also **blues, pop** and **top 40**. Published "Because You're Mine" and "Free" (by Willie A. Saulsby), recorded by William Icey; and "The Way That I Am" (by Willie A. Saulsby), recorded by Willie Bones, all on Hibi Dei Hipp Records.

How to Get the Most Out of Songwriter's Market (at the front of this book) contains comments and suggestions to help you understand and use the information in these listings.

SCI-FI MUSIC, P.O. Box 941, N.D.G., Montreal, Quebec H4A 3S3 **Canada**. (514)487-4551. President: Gary Moffet (formerly guitarist/composer with April Wine). Music publisher. SOCAN. Estab. 1984. Publishes 10 songs/year; publishes 2 new songwriters/year. Works with composers; teams collaborators. Pays standard royalty.
How to Contact: Submit demo tape—unsolicited submissions OK. Submit cassette with 3-10 songs and lyric sheet. Does not return material. Reports in 1 month.
Music: Mostly **rock** and **pop**. Published *Make Ends Meet*; *Babylon*; and *Back to Reality* (written and recorded by Mindstorm), all on Aquarius/Capitol Records.

***TIM SCOTT MUSIC GROUP**, 96 St. James Ave., Springfield MA 01109. (413)746-8302. Fax: (413)746-6262. President: Timothy Scott. Music publisher. Estab. 1993. Publishes 20-50 songs/year; publishes 10 songwriters/year. Hires staff writers. Works with composers and lyricists; teams collaborators. Pays standard royalty.
Affiliate(s): Tim Scott Music (ASCAP) and Tim Scott Songs (BMI).
How to Contact: Submit demo tape by mail. Unsolicited submissions are OK. Prefers cassette with 3-5 songs and lyric sheet. SASE. Reports in 4-6 weeks.
Music: Mostly **rap, R&B** and **pop**; also **country, rock** and **gospel**. Published "Faithful" and "Holding On" (by Johnnie Hatchett), recorded by Physical Attraction; and "Cable TV Is Just A Joke" (written and recorded by Tim Scott), all on Nightowl Records.

SCRUTCHINGS MUSIC, 429 Homestead St., Akron OH 44306. (216)773-8529. Owner/President: Walter E.L. Scrutchings. Music publisher. BMI. Estab. 1980. Publishes 35 songs/year; publishes 10-20 new songwriters/year. Hires staff songwriters. Works with composers and lyricists; teams collaborators. Pays standard royalty of 50%. "Songwriters pay production costs of songs."
How to Contact: Submit a demo tape—unsolicited submissions are OK. Prefers cassette (or videocassette if available) with 2 songs, lyric and lead sheet. Does not return unsolicited material. Reports in 3-4 weeks.
Music: Mostly **gospel, contemporary** and **traditional**. Published "The Joy He Brings" (by R. Hinton), recorded by Akron City Mass; "God Has the Power" (by W. Scrutchings), recorded by Gospel Music Workshop Mass on Savoy Records (gospel); and "My Testimony" (by A. Cobb), recorded by Akron City Family Mass Choir on Scrutchings Music (gospel).
Tips: "Music must be clear and uplifting in message and music."

SEGAL'S PUBLICATIONS, Box 507, Newton MA 02159. (617)969-6196. Contact: Charles Segal. Music publisher and record producer (Segal's Productions). BMI, SAMRO. Estab. 1963. Publishes 80 songs/year; publishes 6 new songwriters/year. Works with composers and lyricists. Pays standard royalty.
Affiliate(s): Charles Segal's Publications (BMI). Charles Segal's Music (SESAC).
How to Contact: Submit demo tape—unsolicited submissions OK. Prefers cassette (or VHS videocassette) with 3 songs and lyric or lead sheet. Does not return unsolicited material. Reports in 4 months.
Music: Mostly **rock, pop** and **country**; also **R&B, MOR** and **children's songs**. Published "Thauda Mina" (by Segal/Hay), recorded by Afro Bach on Spin Records (African); "Change" (by Hay) and "Friends" (by Segal/Hay).
Tips: "Try and come up with some gimmick. Think of a good hook."

***WILLIAM SEIP MUSIC INCORPORATED**, Box 515, Waterloo, Ontario N2J 4A9 **Canada**. (519)741-1252. President: William Seip. Music publisher, record company (H&S Records) and management firm (William Seip Management Inc.). CAPAC. Estab. 1987. Publishes 10-30 songs/year; publishes 1-3 new songwriters/year. Works with composers; teams collaborators. Pays per negotiated contract.
Affiliate(s): Lyell Communications.
How to Contact: Submit a demo tape—unsolicited submissions are OK. Prefers cassette with 3 songs. Does not return unsolicited material. Reports in 1 month.
Music: Mostly **rock** and **pop**. Published "Gypsy Wind," written and recorded by Ray Lyell on Aim/Spy Records.

SELLWOOD PUBLISHING, 170 N. Maple, Fresno CA 93702. (209)255-1717. Owner: Stan Anderson. Music publisher, record company (TRAC Record Co.) and record producer. BMI. Estab. 1972. Publishes 10 songs/year; publishes 3 new songwriters/year. Pays standard royalty.
How to Contact: Submit a demo tape—unsolicited submissions are OK. Prefers cassette (or VHS videocassette) with 2 songs and lyric sheet. SASE. Reports in 2 weeks.
Music: Mostly **traditional country** and **country rock**. Published "Whiskey Blues"; "Dan"; and "Night Time Places," all written by Jimmy Walker on TRAC Records.

***SHADOWLAND PRODUCTIONS**, 3 Lancet Court, Shawnee OK 74873. Music Editor: Russell Walker. Music publisher, record company and record producer. Estab. 1991. Publishes 48-60 songs/year; publishes 15-20 new songwriters/year. Works with composers and lyricists; teams collaborators. Pays "50%

on material that is recorded. Much of publishing thrust is in the area of printed music, which normally has standard royalty of 10% of cover price. Much of our work is done with new writers under a cooperative publishing program in which some of production costs are shared with writer. Such an arrangement gives their material a fair chance in the highly competitive market place."
Affiliate(s): Calvary's Shadow Publications, Morning Dew Publications, Shadowland Records, Shadowland Productions.
How to Contact: Submit demo tape by mail. Unsolicited submissions are OK. Prefers cassette with 3 songs and lyric or lead sheet. If lyrics are handwritten, make sure printed and legible with SASE on all submissions. SASE. Reports in 6-8 weeks.
Music: Mostly **Southern gospel/spiritual, MOR, sacred, contemporary Christian**; also **choral anthems, children's songs** and **seasonal.** *The Man Called Jesus* (by Richards) (gospel); *I Heard the Voice of Jesus Say* (by Stephens) (sacred); and *I Can't Even Call My Soul My Own* (by Walker) (gospel jazz), all recorded by Shadowland Singers on Shadowland Records.
Tips: "We are a publisher of gospel and sacred music. We need material that specifically addresses a personal relationship with Christ, a born-again experience, the reality of God's presence, the depth of His love, a Christian's role in the world, etc. Almost any subject matter is appropriate if it is approached from a Christian perspective."

SHA-LA MUSIC, INC., 137 Legion Place, Hillsdale NJ 07642. (201)664-1995. Fax: (201)664-1955. President: Robert Allen. Music publisher. Estab. 1987. Publishes 20-30 songs/year; publishes 1-4 new songwriters/year. Works with composers and lyricists. Pays standard royalty.
Affiliate(s): Sha-La Music (BMI) and By The Numbers Music (ASCAP).
How to Contact: Submit demo tape by mail—unsolicited submissions are OK. Prefers cassette with 3 songs and lyric sheet. "Keep package neat to make a good impression." SASE. Reports in 1-2 weeks.
Music: Mostly **R&B, pop, dance**; also **rock** and **a/c.** Published *Catch Me If You Can*, written and recorded by Jr. C on Tassa Records; "All My Love," (by Jr. C/D. Bond), recorded by Jr. C on Tassa Records; and "Brotherman" (by Basil Gamson), recorded by Bass Dance on Celluloid Records.
Tips: "Keep it simple and clean. Concentrate on quality."

SHANKMAN DE BLASIO MELINA, INC., 2434 Main St. #202, Santa Monica CA 90405. (310)399-7744. Fax: (310)399-2027. Contact: Laurent Besencon. Music publisher, personal management. Playhard Music (ASCAP), Playfull Music (BMI). Estab. 1979. Hires staff songwriters. Works with composers and lyricists; teams collaborators.
How to Contact: Write and call first and obtain permission to submit. Prefers cassette (or VHS or Beta videocassette if available) with 3 songs and lyric sheet. SASE. Reports in 2 months.
Music: Mostly **contemporary hit songs: pop, R&B, dance, rock, ballads.** Published *Roll the Dice* (by Gina Gomez), recorded by Color Me Badd on Giant Records; *A Little Bit Of Love* (by Claude Gaudette), recorded by Celine Dion on Columbia Records; and *Waiting For The Day* (by Gina Gomez) recorded by Shai on Gasoline Alley/MCA Records.
Tips: "Write hits!"

*SHAOLIN MUSIC, P.O. Box 387, Hollywood CA 90078. (818)506-8660. President: Richard O'Connor. Vice President, A&R: Michelle McCarty. Music publisher, record company (Shaolin Film and Records) and record producer (The Coyote). ASCAP. Estab. 1984. Works with groups that have own material. Pays standard royalty.
How to Contact: Prefers cassette with 3-4 songs and lyric sheet. Include bio and press kit. Does not return unsolicited material. Reports in 2 months.
Music: Mostly **rock, hard rock** and **pop**; also **soundtracks.** Published "Christ Killer"; *Wishwood Bridge*; and "Great Salt Lake," all written and recorded by The Coyote, on Shaolin Film and Records.
Tips: "No matter how clever, cute, or pretty a song is: if it doesn't *mean something* or *create an emotion* it's just exercises."

SHU'BABY MONTEZ MUSIC, 1447 North 55th St., Philadelphia PA 19131. (215)473-5527. President: Leroy Schuler. Music publisher. BMI. Estab. 1986. Publishes 25 songs/year; publishes 15 new songwriters/year. Pays standard royalty.
How to Contact: Write or call first and obtain permission to submit. Prefers cassette with 3 songs and lyric sheet. SASE. Reports in 5 weeks.
Music: Mostly **R&B, pop** and **hip-hop.** Published "I'd Rather Be By Myself," written and recorded by EBO; "War In Philadelphia," written and recorded by Tom White; and "In Love Again" (by Leroy Schuler), recorded by Barbara St. Lee, all on Logic Records.
Tips: "Write a song with strong drum beats and lyrics."

SIEGEL MUSIC COMPANIES, 2 Hochlstr, 80 Munich 8000 **Germany.** Phone: 089-984926. Managing Director: Joachim Neubauer. Music publisher, record company, (Jupiter Records and 69-Records) and record producer. Estab. 1948. GEMA. Publishes 1,500 songs/year; publishes 50 new songwriters/

year. Hires staff songwriters. Works with composers and lyricists. Pays 60% according to the rules of GEMA.
Affiliate(s): Ed. Meridian, Sound of Jupiter Ltd. (England), Sounds of Jupiter, Inc. (USA), Step Two (Austria), Step One (Holland), Step Four (France), Step Five (Brazil), Step Six (Scandinavia), Step Seven (Australia), Step Eight (Belgium) and Yellowbird (Switzerland). Gobian Music (ASCAP), Symphonie House Music (ASCAP).
How to Contact: Submit demo tape—unsolicited submissions are OK. Prefers cassette (or VHS videocassette, but not necessary). SAE and IRC. Reports in 6 weeks.
Music: Mostly **pop, disco** and **MOR**; also **country** and **soul.** Published *Neon Cowboy* (by Siegel), recorded by the Bellamy Brothers on Jupiter Records (country); *Sadeness* (by Curly MC), recorded by Enigma on Virgin Records (dance pop); and "Nana" (by T. Stenzel), recorded by Nuke on LMV Records.

SILICON MUSIC PUBLISHING CO., Ridgewood Park Estates, 222 Tulane St., Garland TX 75043. President: Gene Summers. Vice President: Deanna L. Summers. Public Relations: Steve Summers. Music publisher and record company (Domino Records, Ltd. and Front Row Records). BMI. Estab. 1965. Publishes 10-20 songs/year; publishes 2-3 new songwriters/year. Pays standard royalty.
How to Contact: Prefers cassette with 1-2 songs. Does not return unsolicited material. "We are usually slow in answering due to overseas tours."
Music: Mostly **rockabilly** and **50s' material;** also **old-time blues/country** and **MOR.** Published "Black on Saturday Night" and "Ballad of Jerry Lee" (by Joe Hardin Brown), both unreleased; and "Domino" (by James McClung & Dea Summers), recorded by Gene Summers on Domino Records.
Tips: "We are very interested in 50s rock and rockabilly *original masters* for release through overseas affiliates. If you are the owner of any 50s masters, contact us first! We have releases in Holland, Switzerland, England, Belgium, France, Sweden, Norway and Australia. We have the market if you have the tapes! Sample recordings available! Send SASE for catalogue."

*SILVER THUNDER MUSIC GROUP, P.O. Box 41335, Nashville TN 37204. (615)254-5566. President: Rusty Budde. Music publisher, Record producer (Larry Butler Productions). Estab. 1985. Publishes 500 songs/year. Publishes 5-20 new songwriters/year. Hires staff songwriters. Works with composers and lyricists. Pays standard royalty.
How to Contact: Write to obtain permission to submit. Prefers cassette (or VHS videocassette if available). Does not return material.
Music: Mostly **country, pop, R&B.** Published *Rock N Cowboys,* written and recorded by Jeff Chunn on NA Records; *This Ain't the Real Thing* (by Rusty Budde), recorded by Les Taylor on CBS Records; and "Feel Again" (by Rusty Budde), recorded by Keli Derring on S.T.R. Records.
Tips: "Send clear clean recording on cassette with lyric sheets."

SILVERFOOT PUBLISHING, 4225 Palm St., Baton Rouge LA 70808. (504)383-7885. President: Barrie Edgar. BMI. Music publisher, record company (Gulfstream Records) and record producer (Hogar Musical Productions). Estab. 1977. Publishes 20-30 songs/year; publishes 8-20 new songwriters/year. Pays standard royalty.
How to Contact: Submit a demo tape—unsolicited submissions are OK. Prefers cassette with maximum 4 songs and lyric sheet. "Patience required on reporting time." SASE. Reports in 6 months or sooner.
Music: Mostly **rock, pop, blues** ("not soul") and **country.** Published "Come Home" (by B. Meade/V. Trippe), "Hopeless Romantic" (by David Ellis) and "Rico & Lila" (by Dennis Ferado).

SIMPLY GRAND MUSIC, INC., P.O. Box 41981, Memphis TN 38174-1981. (901)272-7039. President: Linda Lucchesi. Music publisher. ASCAP, BMI. Estab. 1965. Works with composers and lyricists; teams collaborators. Pays standard royalty.
Affiliate(s): Memphis Town Music, Inc. (ASCAP) and Beckie Publishing Co. (BMI).
How to Contact: Write or call first to get permission to submit a tape. Prefers cassette with 1-3 songs and lyric sheet. SASE. Reports in 6 weeks.
Music: Mostly **pop** and **soul;** also **country** and **soft rock.**
Tips: "We are the publishing home of 'Wooly Bully'."

*SINGING ROADIE MUSIC GROUP, 1050 Leatherwood Rd., White Bluff TN 37187-5300. (615)952-5190 General Manager: Garth Shaw. Music publisher, member CMA. BMI, ASCAP. Estab. 1984. Publishes 3-10 songs/year; publishes 1-3 new songwriters/year. Pays standard royalty.

Listings of companies in countries other than the U.S. have the name of the country in boldface type.

Affiliate(s): Singing Roadie Music (ASCAP), Helioplane Music (BMI).
How to Contact: Submit a demo tape by mail—unsolicited submissions are OK. No calls, please. Prefers cassette with 1-3 songs and lyric sheets. SASE. Reports in 1 month.
Music: Country, all styles, from traditional to contemporary. Co-published "Just Married" (by Rod Stone/Terri Lynn Weaver), recorded by Terri Lynn on Intersound Records; "She Wins" (by Cubey Pitcher/Al Goll), recorded by Ronna Reeves on Mercury Records; and "Bed of Roses" (by Rex Benson, Steve Gillette), recorded by Kenny Rogers on Reprise Records.
Tips: "If you're a great writer and a terrible singer, find a great demo singer!"

*SINGLE MINDED MUSIC, 32 Queensdale Rd., London W11 4SB **England**. Phone: (071)602-5200. Fax: (071)602-0704. Director: Tony Byrne. Estab. 1985. Publishes 20+ songs/year. Publishes 2-5+ new songwriters/year. Works with composers and lyricists; teams collaborators. Query for royalty terms.
How to Contact: Submit demo tape by mail. Unsolicited submissions are OK. Prefers cassette (or VHS videocassette if available) with 3 songs. SASE. Reports in 1 month.
Music: Mostly **rock, dance, pop.**

SINUS MUSIK PRODUKTION, ULLI WEIGEL, Teplitzer Str. 28/30, 1 Berlin 33 West Berlin **Germany**. (030)825-5056. Fax: (030)825-4082. Owner: Ulli Weigel. Music publisher, record producer and producer of radio advertising spots. GEMA, GVL. Estab. 1976. Publishes 20 songs/year; publishes 6 new songwriters/year. Works with composers and lyricists; teams collaborators. Pays according to GEMA conditions.
Affiliate(s): Sinus Musikverlag H.U. Weigel GmbH.
How to Contact: Submit a demo tape by mail—unsolicited submissions are O.K. Prefer cassette (or VHS videocassette) with up to 10 songs and lyric sheets. SASE. Reports in 6 weeks.
Music: Mostly **rock, pop** and **New Age;** also **background music for movies/advertising.** Published "Simple Story" recorded by MAANAM on RCA (Polish rock Group); and "Terra-X-Melody" (by Franz Bartzsch), on Hansa (TV background music); *Die Musik Maschine* (by Klaus Lage), recorded by CWN Productions on Hansa Records (pop/German); and "Maanam" (by Jakowskyl/Jakowska), recorded by CWN Productions on RCA Records (pop/English).
Tips: "Take more time working on the melody than on the instrumentation."

SISKATUNE MUSIC PUBLISHING CO., 285 Chestnut St., West Hempstead NY 11552. (516)489-0738. Fax: (516)565-9425. President: Mike Siskind. Vice President Creative Affairs: Rick Olarsch. Music publisher. Estab. 1981. Publishes 20 songs/year; 10 new songwriters/year. Works with composers and lyricists. Pays standard royalty.
How to Contact: Submit demo tape—unsolicited submissions are OK. Prefers cassette with up to 3 songs and lyric sheet. "Send any and all pertinent information." SASE. Reports in 6-8 weeks.
Music: Mostly **rock, country;** **dance** and **ballads.** Co-published "When I Was Young" by In Fear of Roses and "If I Had Wings" by Georgi Smith. "We have a catalog of more than 200 songs."
Tips: "I'm more concerned with the song."

SIZEMORE MUSIC, P.O. Box 23275, Nashville TN 37202. (615)385-1662. Fax: (615)383-3731. Contact: Gary Sizemore. Music publisher, record company (The Gas Co.) and record producer (Gary Sizemore). BMI. Estab. 1960. Publishes 5 songs/year; 1 new songwriter/year. Works with composers and lyricists; teams collaborators. Pays standard royalty.
How to Contact: Submit a demo tape by mail—unsolicited submissions are OK. Prefers cassette (or VHS videocassette) with lyric sheets. SASE.
Music: Mostly **soul** and **R&B;** also **blues, pop** and **country.** Published "Liquor and Wine" and "The Wind," written and recorded by K. Shackleford on Heart Records (country); and "She's Tuff" (by Jerry McCain), recorded by The Fabulous Thunderbirds on Chrysalis Records (blues).

*SNEAK TIP MUSIC, Suite 3A, 9805 67th Ave., Flushing NY 11375. (718)271-5149. President: Gerald Famolari. Music publisher, record company (Sneak Tip Records). BMI. Estab. 1990. Publishes 10 songs/year. Works with composers and lyricists.
Affiliate(s): Uncle J. Music (BMI).
How to Contact: Submit demo tape by mail—unsolicited submissions are OK. Prefers cassette. SASE. Reports in 2-4 weeks.
Music: Mostly **house, club** and **freestyle;** also **rap** and **R&B.** Published *2 The Break A Dawn*, recorded by Norty Cotto; *Urban Coalition* and *Groove Legion*, recorded by Norty Cotto/B.B. Keys, all by 2 Bad Bros. on Sneak Tip Records.

*SOCIETE D'EDITIONS MUSICALES ET ARTISTIQUES "ESPERANCE", 85 Rue Fondary, Paris 75015 **France**. Phone: (1) 45 77 30 34. Manager: Michel David. Music publisher and record company (Societe Sonodisc). SACEM/SDRM. Estab. 1972. Publishes 50 songs/year; 20 new songwriters/year. Pays negotiable rates.

How to Contact: Submit a demo tape, unsolicited submissions are OK. Prefers cassette (or VHS videocassette). SAE and IRC. Reports in 2 weeks.
Music: **African, West Indian, Arabian** and **salsa music**. Published "Exile" (by Ina Cesaire), recorded by Ralph Tamar on GD Production (West India); "Les Années Folles" (by Roland Brival), recorded by Ralph Tamar on GD Production (West India); "Wakaele" (by Sekou Diabate), recorded by Bambeya Jazz Esperance (African); and "Diniya," written and recorded by Kante Manfila on Esperance (African).
Tips: "See that the style of your songs fits in with the music we distribute."

*SONG CELLAR, 1024 16th Ave. South, Nashville TN 37212. (615)256-7507. Owner: Jack Cook. Music publisher, record producer. Estab. 1984. Works with lyricists; teams collaborators. Pays standard 50% royalty.
Affiliate(s): Song Cellar Music (ASCAP), Juke Music (BMI), Cook In Music (SESAC).
How to Contact: Submit demo tape by mail. Unsolicited submissions are OK. Prefers casette (or VHS videocassette if available) with 3-5 songs and lyric sheet. "If we like it — we'll contact you." Does not return material.
Music: Mostly **rock/country, R&B/country, pop/country;** also **gospel/country, gospel/rock, gospel/pop.**
Tips: "Send a good, well arranged, well performed song on a good, clean cassette."

SONG FARM MUSIC, P.O. Box 24561, Nashville TN 37202. (615)742-1557. President: Tom Pallardy. Music publisher and record producer (T.P. Productions). BMI. Member NSAI. Estab. 1980. Publishes 2-5 songs/year; publishes 1-2 new songwriters/year. Teams collaborators. Pays standard royalty.
How to Contact: Submit a demo tape — unsolicited submissions are OK. Prefers cassette with maximum 2 songs and lyric or lead sheet. SASE required with enough postage for return of all materials. Reports in 4-6 weeks.
Music: Mostly **country, R&B** and **pop;** also **crossover** and **top 40**. Published "Mississippi River Rat" (by J. Hall, R. Hall, E. Dickey), recorded by Tom Powers on Fountain Records (Cajun country); "Today's Just Not the Day" (by J. Bell, E. Bobbitt), recorded by Liz Draper (country); and "In Mama's Time" (by T. Crone), recorded by Pat Tucker on Radioactive Records (country/pop).
Tips: "Material should be submitted neatly and professionally with as good quality demo as possible. Songs need not be elaborately produced (voice and guitar/piano are fine) but they should be clear. Songs must be well constructed, lyrically tight, good strong hook, interesting melody, easily remembered; i.e., commercial!"

*SONG WIZARD MUSIC (ASCAP), P.O. Box 931029, Los Angeles CA 90093. (213)461-8848. Fax: (213)461-0936. Owner: Dave Kinnoin. Music publisher, record company and record producer. Estab. 1987. Publishes 12 songs/year; publishes 2 new songwriters/year. Works with composers and lyricists; teams collaborators. "We give Songwriters Guild of America contracts."
How to Contact: Submit demo tape by mail. Unsolicited submissions are OK. Prefers cassette with 3 songs and lyric sheet. SASE. Reports in 2 month.
Music: Mostly **children's**. Published *Good Friends Like Mine* (by Kinnoin/Hammer); *Children of the World* and *Dunce Cap Kelly*, (by Kinnoin), all recorded by Dave Kinnoin on Song Wizard Records.
Tips: "We like fresh, pure rhymes that tell a funny or touching story."

*SONGFINDER MUSIC, 4 Reina Lane, Valley Cottage NY 10989. (914)268-7711. Owner: Frank Longo. Music publisher. ASCAP. Estab. 1987. Publishes 20 songs/year; publishes 5-10 new songwriters/year. Works with composers; teams collaborators. Pays standard royalty.
Affiliate(s): Spring Rose Music (BMI).
How to Contact: Submit a demo tape by mail — unsolicited submissions are OK. Prefers cassette with 2 songs and lyric sheets. SASE. "No SASE — no returns." Reports in 4 weeks.
Music: Mostly **MOR, top 40, soft rock, country/pop** and **uptempo country**. Published "There's Nothing Between Us" (by F. Longo/Billy Ready), recorded by "Lauralee" on Gold Wax Records; "I'll Be There For You" (by J. Kaplan), recorded by J. Capplan on Hit City Records; and "Little White Slippers" (by F. Longo/Jay Gorney), recorded by Tony Sands on Lost Gold Records.
Tips: "Listen to what's being played on the radio. Be professional. Good demos get good results. Up tempo positive lyrics are always wanted. Success needs no apology — failure provides no alibi."

*SONGRITE CREATIONS PRODUCTIONS (BMI), 692 S.E. Port St. Lucie Blvd., Port St. Lucie FL 34984. President: J.A. Blecha. Music publisher, record company and recording artist. Estab. 1990. Publishes 50 songs/year; publishes 20 new songwriters/year. Works with composers and lyricists; teams collaborators. Pays standard royalty.
Affiliate(s): Sine Qua Non Music (ASCAP).
How to Contact: Submit demo tape by mail. Unsolicited submissions are OK. "Send only your best one or two unpublished songs (with bio, press, number of songs written, releases, awards, etc.)." Prefers cassette (or videocassette) with 2-3 songs (2 each style) and lyric sheet. SASE. Reports in 4-6 weeks.

Music: Mostly **contemporary country, pop (AC)** and **gospel**; also **R&B, blues** and **novelty**. Published *Shades Of Blue* (by J.A. Blecha), recorded by Judy Welden on Treasure Coast Records; "What Happens Now" (by J.A. Blecha), recorded by Judy Welden on Sabre Records; and "Movin' " (by L.J. Kolander), recorded by Lisa Joy on Sabre Records.

Tips: "Demo tapes must be well-produced and current sounding. Be prepared for a re-write if lyrics are not conversational and in the best possible meter. Believe in yourself and your talent and you will not get discouraged easily!"

SONGWRITERS' NETWORK MUSIC PUBLISHING, P.O. Box 190446, Dallas TX 75219. President: Phil Ayliffe. Music publisher and record company (Songwriters' Network Records). ASCAP. Estab. 1983. Publishes 3 songs/year. Works with composers and lyricists. Pays standard royalty.

How to Contact: Submit demo tape—unsolicited submissions OK. Prefers cassette with 3 songs and lyric sheets. Does not return unsolicited material. Reports in 6 months.

Music: Mostly **pop, MOR** and **adult contemporary country**. Published "Dark & Dirty Days," "The Easter Basket Song" and "Bears," all written and recorded by Phil Ayliffe on Songwriters' Network Records.

SOUL STREET MUSIC PUBLISHING INC., 265 Main St., East Rutherford NJ 07073. (201)933-0676. President: Glenn La Russo. Music publisher. ASCAP. Estab. 1988. Publishes 20 songs/year; publishes 5 new songwriters/year. Works with composers. Pays standard royalty.

How to Contact: Submit a demo tape—unsolicited submissions are OK. Prefers cassette with 3 songs and lyric sheet. SASE. Reports in 2 months.

Music: Only **R&B, dance** and **rap**. Published "Touch Me" (by Carmichael), recorded by Cathy Dennis on Polydor Records (dance); "Symptoms of True Love" (by Harman/Weber), recorded by Tracey Spencer on Capitol Records (R&B); and "Thinking About Your Love," written and recorded by Skipworth and Turner on Island Records (R&B).

SOUND ACHIEVEMENT GROUP, P.O. Box 24625, Nashville TN 37202. (615)883-2600. President: Royce B. Gray. Music publisher. BMI, ASCAP. Estab. 1985. Publishes 120 songs/year; publishes 4 new songwriters/year. Works with composers and lyricists; teams collaborators. Pays standard royalty.

Affiliate(s): Song Palace Music (ASCAP) and Emerald Stream Music (BMI).

How to Contact: Submit a demo tape—unsolicited submissions are OK. Prefers cassette (or VHS videocassette if available) with 3 songs and lyric sheet. SASE. Reports in 3 months.

Music: **Gospel.** Published "You Are" (by Penny Strandberg Miller), recorded by Revelations on New Wind Records (gospel); "I Want My Life To Count" (by Sammy Lee Johnson), recorded by Sammy Lee Johnson on Image Records (gospel); and "The Wonder of Christmas" (by Giorgio Longdo/John Ganes), recorded by Giorgio Longdo on Candle Records (gospel).

*SOUND CELLAR MUSIC, 706 E. Morgan, Dixon IL 61021. (815)288-7029. Music publisher, record company, record producer, recording studio. Estab. 1987. Publishes 15-25 songs/year. Publishes 5 or 6 new songwriters/year. Works with composers. Pays standard 50% royalty. "No charge obviously for publishing, but if we record the artist there is a small reduced fee for rental of our studio.

How to Contact: Submit demo tape by mail. Unsolicited submissions are OK. Prefers cassette with 3 or 4 songs and lyric sheet. Does not return material. Reports in 3-4 weeks.

Music: Mostly **metal, country, rock;** also **pop, rap, blues.** Published *Plague* written and recorded by Blind Witness; *Death Become Us* written and recorded by Lefwitch; *Supply and Demand* written and recorded by Todd Jones all on Cellar Records.

Tips: "Don't worry about the style of your music. We want people who write songs from the heart. We are not concerned with music styles, just good music."

SOUND COLUMN PUBLICATIONS, (formerly Sound Column Companies), Country Manor, 812 S. 890 East, Orem UT 84058. (801)225-9975. President/General Manager: Ron Simpson. Music publisher, record company (SCP Records) and record producer (Sound Column Productions). BMI, ASCAP, SESAC. Member CMA, AFM. Estab. 1968. Publishes 20 songs/year; publishes 2-3 new songwriters/year. Hires staff writers. Listens to complete songs only. Pays standard royalty.

Affiliate(s): Ronarte Publications (ASCAP), Mountain Green Music (BMI), Macanudo Music (SESAC).

How to Contact: Submit demo tape (3 songs max) with lyric sheet. "We listen to everything. No phone calls, please." SASE. Reports as time permits.

Music: Mostly **pop, country** and **A/C.** "We seem to have had a hot hand in country and contemporary folk this year: 'Norma Jean Riley' (#1 country record by Diamond Rio, Arista Records), was written by Rob Honey, our writer. We also helped writers Gary and Robin Earl ('Grandma's Garden'), and Kim Simpson ('Goodbye I Love You') derive some royalty income."

Tips: "We maintain a very small catalog, accepting just a few songs a year, but work hard for our writers. Song submissions seem to be getting better and better. Thanks, writers, for making 1993 our best year ever."

*SOUND RESOURCES (BMI), P.O. Box 16046, Chattanooga TN 37416-0046: Owner: Steve Babb. Music publisher, record company (Arion Records) and record producer. Estab. 1992. Publishes 30-40 songs/year; publishes 4-5 new songwriters/year. Works with composers and lyricists. Pays standard royalty.
Affiliate(s): Lazeria Music (BMI).
How to Contact: Submit demo tape by mail—unsolicited submissions are OK. Prefers cassette with lyric sheet. "DAT (digital audio tape) submissions or metal tape preferred." SASE. Reports in 2 months.
Music: Mostly **art rock, New Age** and **progressive rock;** also **electronic music, cyber-punk** and **avant-garde.** Published "The River Song"(by Stephen De'arque) and "Song of the Dunadan"(by De'arque/Schendel), both recorded by Glass Hammer; and "Cruisin'"(by De'arque/Schendel), recorded by The Wild, all on Arion Records.
Tips: "I'm not looking for music which reflects current trends. I'm looking for songs that will create the next trend! Your demos need to be energetic and well produced."

*SOUNDS-VISION MUSIC, P.O. Box 3691, La Mesa CA 91944-3691. (619)447-1146. Fax: (800)447-1132. Owner: Rod Hollman. Music publisher, record company, record producer and distributor. Estab. 1986. Publishes 30 songs/year. Publishes 3-4 new songwriters/year. Works with composers and lyricists. "Royalty amount varies per contract."
Affiliate(s): Xpresh'N Series Music (BMI).
How to Contact: Submit demo tape by mail. Unsolicited submissions are OK. Prefers cassette with 1-5 songs. Does not return material. Reports in 3-4 weeks.
Music: Mostly **flamenco, gypsy music, international;** also **classical guitar.** Published *Este Gitano* (by Remedios Flores); *Seguidillas* (by Rodrigo); and *Rumba del Viento* (by Raquel Flores), all on Sounds-Vision Records.

SOUTHERN MOST PUBLISHING COMPANY, P.O. Box 97, Climax Springs MO 65324. (314)374-1111. President/Owner: Dann E. Haworth. Music publisher, record producer (Haworth Productions), engineer. BMI. Estab. 1985. Publishes 10 songs/year; 3 new songwriters/year. Hires staff songwriters. Works with composers and lyricists; teams collaborators. Pays standard royalty.
Affiliate(s): Boca Chi Key Publishing (ASCAP).
How to Contact: Submit demo tape—unsolicited submissions are OK. Prefers cassette with 3 songs and lyric sheet. SASE. Reports in 6-8 weeks.
Music: Mostly **rock, R&B** and **country;** also **gospel** and **New Age.**
Tips: "Keep it simple and from the heart."

*SPHEMUSATIONS, 12 Northfield Rd., Onehouse, Stowmarket Suffolk 1P14 3HR **England.** Phone: 0449-613388. General Manager: James Butt. Music publisher. Estab. 1963. Publishes 200 songs/year; publishes 6 new songwriters/year. Works with lyricists; teams collaborators. Pays standard royalty.
How to Contact: Submit demo tape—unsolicited submissions are OK. Prefers cassette (or VHS or Beta videocassette). SAE and IRC. Reports in 3 months.
Music: Mostly **country, blues** and **jazz,** also **"serious modern music."** Published "Satyr's Song" (by J. Playford, J. Butt), "The Weeper" (by J. Playford, J. Butt); and "O. Moon" (by J. Keats, J. Butt), all on Sphemusations Records.

*SPINWILLY MUSIC PUBLISHING, 214 State Rd., Media PA 19063. (215)565-5099. Director A&R: Rick Smith. Music publisher, record company (Radio Records, Stardiner Records). Estab. 1987. Publishes 5 songs/year. Works with composers and lyricists. Pays standard 50% royalty.
How to Contact: Call first to arrange personal interview. Prefers cassette with 3 songs and lyric sheet. Does not return material. Reports in 2 months.
Music: Published *Slip It In* and "Politician" (by R.D. Anjolell), recorded by Almighty Shuhorn on Radio/August Records; and *The Bensons,* written and recorded by The Bensons on Radio Records.
Tips: "Believe in your work, keep writing and be open to criticism."

SPRADLIN/GLEICH PUBLISHING, P.O. Box 80083, Phoenix AZ 85060. (602)840-8466. Manager: Lee Gleich. Music publisher. BMI. Estab. 1988. Publishes 4-10 songs/year; 2-4 new songwriters. Works with composers and lyricists. Pays standard 50% royalty.
Affiliate(s): Spradlin/Gleich Publishing (BMI), Paul Lee Publishing (ASCAP).
How to Contact: Write first for permission to submit. Prefers cassette with 3 songs and lyric or lead sheet. "It must be very good material, as I only have time for promoting songwriters who really care." SASE. Reports in 3 weeks.

Music: Mostly **country** geared to the US and European country markets. Published "Stranger in Your Heart," written and recorded by Travis Allen on Courage Records; "Sounds of Home" (by Smith, Waymen), recorded by Parrish Wayne Horshburgh; and "Dancin Shoes," written and recorded by Kurt McFarland on Comstock Records (country).
Tips: "Send me a request letter, then send me your best song. If it is a quality song that will create interest by us for more material. We are now publishing mostly all country and rock-a-billy!"

STANG MUSIC INC., 753 Capitol Ave., Hartford CT 06106. (203)951-8175. Producer: Jack Stang. Music publisher, record company (Nickel Records) and record producer (Jack Stang). BMI. Estab. 1970. Publishes 20 songs/year; publishes 2 new songwriters/year. Hires staff writers. Works with composers; teams collaborators. Pays standard royalty.
How to Contact: Submit a demo tape—unsolicited submissions are OK. Prefers cassette with 3 songs and lyric sheets. SASE. Reports in 3 weeks.
Music: Mostly **rock, pop, top 40** and **R&B**; also **country**. Published "One Heart" (by Finns Field), recorded by Ray Alaire on Nickel Records (pop/rock).

STAR INTERNATIONAL, INC., P.O. Box 470346, Tulsa OK 74147. President: MaryNell Jetton. Music publisher. ASCAP. Estab. 1989. Pays standard royalty. Publishing varies.
How to Contact: Interested in both new and established songwriters. Do not submit demo tape; write first. Enclose SASE for reply. Reports in 4-6 weeks. Does not accept unsolicited certified mail.
Music: "We prefer songwriters who are professional, who have narrowed their concentration to no more than 2 styles of music, who welcome professional advice, and who are serious about a career in music. The information we are interested in seeing in a query letter is that which pertains to your experience as a songwriter, musician, or performer only. Most importantly, if we request some of your material, please follow our submission guidelines."

STARBOUND PUBLISHING CO., Dept. SM, 207 Winding Rd., Friendswood TX 77546. (713)482-2346. President: Buz Hart. Music publisher, record company (Juke Box Records, Quasar Records and Eden Records) and record producer (Lonnie Wright and Buz Hart). BMI. Estab. 1970. Publishes 35-100 songs/year; publishes 5-10 new songwriters/year. Works with composers and lyricists; teams collaborators. Pays standard royalty.
How to Contact: Obtain permission before submitting a demo tape. Prefers cassette with 3 songs and lyric sheet. SASE. Reports in 5-6 weeks.
Music: Mostly **country, R&B** and **gospel**. Published "Maybe I Won't Love You Anymore" (by Barbara Hart, Buz Hart), recorded by Johnny Lee on Curb Records; "Let it Slide" (by James Watson/Buz Hart), recorded by Stan Steel on Gallary II Records; and "Country Boy's Dream," recorded by Charlie Louvin, Waylon Jennings, and George Jones on Playback Records.

*STELLAR MUSIC INDUSTRIES, P.O. Box 30166, Memphis TN 38130-0166. (901)458-2472. Fax: (901)458-2476. Vice President: S.D. Burks. Music publisher. Estab. 1977. Publishes 100 songs/year; publishes 3-5 new songwriters/year. Hires staff writers. Pays standard royalty.
Affiliate(s): Rodanca Music (ASCAP) and Bianca Music (BMI).
How to Contact: Submit demo tape by mail. Unsolicited submissions are OK. Prefers cassette (or VHS videocassette) with 4-6 songs and lyric sheet. SASE. Reports in 6 weeks.
Music: Mostly **R&B, country** and **blues**; also **rap** and **rock**. Published *Walk Away* (by O. Hoskins), recorded by Percy Milem on Goldwax Records (soul); "Nothing Between Us" (by F. Longo), recorded by Lauralea on Goldwax Records (country); "Bad By Myself" (by Total Package), recorded by Total Package on Rap-N-Wax Records (rap).

JEB STUART MUSIC CO., Box 6032, Station B, Miami FL 33123. (305)547-1424. President: Jeb Stuart. Music publisher, record producer and management firm. BMI. Estab. 1975. Publishes 4-6 songs/year. Teams collaborators. Pays standard royalty.
How to Contact: Submit a demo tape—unsolicited submissions are OK. Prefers cassette or disc with 2-4 songs and lead sheet. SASE. Reports in 1 month.
Music: Mostly **gospel, jazz/rock, pop, R&B** and **rap**; also **blues, church/religious, country, disco** and **soul**. Published "I Want to Make Love To You on Christmas Baby," written and recorded by Jeb Stuart on Esquire Int'l Records (blues/ballad); "Showdown" (by Chuck Jones), recorded by Priorty Impact on Esquire Int'l Records (R&B); "No One Should Be Alone On Christmas" (by C. Jones), recorded by Jeb Stuart on Esquire Int'l Records (reggae) and "Got Me Burnin' Up" (by Cafidia), recorded by Jeboria Stuart on Great American Records (pop rock).

SUEÑO PUBLISHING CO., Box 175 (Port City), Mooresville NC 28115. (704)663-3249. President: Don Edison Moose. Music publisher, record company. Estab. 1973. Publishes 6-12 songs/year. Publishes 6-12 new songwriters/year. Works with composers and lyricists; teams collaborators. "We pay 100% songwriter royalties. (*SM note: 100% of songwriter royalties represents 50% of a songs total earnings.*)

How to Contact: Submit demo tape by mail. Unsolicited submissions are OK. Prefers cassette (video-cassette if available). SASE.
Music: Mostly **country, rock, gospel, soul, Latin;** also **pop.** Published "Cathy" and "Rebel the Rain Deer" written and recorded by D. Moore on Moose Records; "All I can Offer You Is This Rose" (by R. Parham) and "Rebel the Reindeer—A Second Version" (by D. Moose) both on Sueño Records.
Tips: "Send typed lyrics and cassette demo."

SUGAR MAMA MUSIC, #805, 4545 Connecticut Ave. NW, Washington DC 20008. (202)362-2286. President: Jonathan Strong. Music publisher, record company (Ripsaw Records) and record producer (Ripsaw Productions). BMI. Estab. 1983. Publishes 3-5 songs/year; publishes 2 new songwriters/year. Works with composers and lyricists. Pays standard royalty.
Affiliate(s): Neck Bone Music (BMI) and Southern Crescent Publishing (BMI).
How to Contact: Submit demo tape—unsolicited submissions OK. Prefers cassette and lyric sheet. SASE. Reports in 1-3 months.
Music: Mostly **country, blues, rockabilly** and **traditional rock.** Published "It's Not the Presents Under My Tree" (by Billy Poore and Tex Rubinowitz), recorded by Narvel Felts on Renegade Records (country).
Tips: "Send no more than 3-4 songs on cassette with lyric sheet and SASE with sufficient postage. Only authentic country, blues, rockabilly or roots rock and roll.

SUGARFOOT PRODUCTIONS, P.O. Box 1065, Joshua Tree CA 92252. A&R Director: Sheila Dobson. Music publisher, record company (Sugarfoot, Babydoll, Durban), record producer (Sugarfoot Records). ASCAP. Estab. 1987. Publishes 10-15 songs/year; publishes 4 new songwriters/year. Works with composers and lyricists; teams collaborators. Pays negotiable royalty; statutory rate per song on records.
How to Contact: Submit a demo tape—unsolicited submissions are OK. Prefers cassette with 3 songs and lyric sheet. "Make sure tape and vocal are clear." Does not return material. Reports in 1-2 months.
Music: Mostly **jazz, blues, swing, country, R&B, salsa, dance;** also **bassas, conga; Cuban, easy listening.** Published "Not for Love" (by Elijah), recorded by Sugarfoot on Westways Records (R&B); "You're Blue" (by Deke), recorded by Jam'n Jo on Durban Records (jazz); and "2 Me An Yu" (by Dobby), recorded by Aleets on Breton Records (jazz).
Tips: "Listen to Irving Berlin, Cole Porter, Gershwin, Carmichael for professional music and lyrics."

SULTAN MUSIC PUBLISHING, P.O. Box 461892, Garland TX 75046. (214)271-8098. President: Don Ferguson. Music publisher, record company (Puzzle Records), record producer and booking agency (Don Ferguson Agency). BMI. Publishes 15 songs/year, including some new songwriters. Works with composers and lyricists; teams collaborators. Pays standard royalty.
Affiliate(s): Illustrions Sultan (ASCAP).
How to Contact: Prefers cassette with 3 songs and lyric sheet. SASE. Reports in 3 weeks.
Music: Mostly **country;** also **MOR.** Published "What Does It Take," written and recorded by Derek Hartis on Puzzle Records (C&W); "After Burn," written and recorded by Phil Rodgers (jazz); and "Ain't No Way" (by G. Duke), recorded by Flash Point (rock), all on Puzzle Records.
Tips: "The best quality demo makes the listener more receptive."

*SUN STAR SONGS, P.O. Box 787, Gatlinburg TN 37738. (615)436-4121. Fax: (615)436-4017. President: Tony Glenn Rast. Music publisher. Estab. 1965, reactivated 1992. Works with composers and lyricists; teams collaborators. Pays standard royalty.
How to Contact: Submit demo tape by mail. Unsolicited submissions OK. Prefers cassette with 3 songs and lyric sheets. SASE. Reports in 2 weeks.
Music: Mostly **country, Christian country-gospel, bluegrass;** also **pop-rock.**

*SUNFROST MUSIC, P.O. Box 231, Cedarhurst NY 11516-0231. (516)791-4795. Publisher: Steve Goldmintz. Estab. 1985. Publishes 36 songs/year. Publishes 1-2 new songwriters/year (usually by collaboration). Works with composers and lyricists; teams collaborators. Pays standard 50% royalty.
Affiliate(s): Anglo American Music, Manchester, England.
How to Contact: Write first to arrange personal interview or communication. Prefers cassette. SASE. Reports in 5-6 weeks.
Music: Mostly **pop, rock, folk;** also **children's, country, R&B.** Published *Brain Dead* (by S. Goldmintz), recorded by T.J. Gunn; *Song Of The Sea* (by B. Shaw), recorded by Del Ahanti on Angl/Am Records; *Mahalo Mahalo* (by S. Goldmintz), recorded by Cousin Steve (deal pending).
Tips: "After the song is done, the work begins and your local contacts may be just as important as the unknown publisher that you are trying to reach. Build your own network of writers. Let's put the 'R' back into 'A&R.'"

SUNSONGS MUSIC/HOLLYWOOD EAST ENTERTAINMENT, 52 N. Evarts Ave., Elmsford NY 10523. (914)592-2563. Professional Manager: Michael Berman. Music publisher, record producer and talent agency. Estab. 1981. BMI, ASCAP, SESAC. Publishes 20 songs/year; publishes 10 new songwriters/year. Pays standard royalty; co-publishing deals available for established writers.
Affiliate(s): Media Concepts Music and Dark Sun Music (SESAC).
How to Contact: Submit demo tape—unsolicited submissions OK. Prefers cassette with 3-4 songs and lyric sheet. SASE. Reports in 1 month.
Music: Dance-oriented, techno-pop, R&B, rock (all styles) and **top 40/pop.** Published "Paradise (Take Me Home)" (by Henderson/Riccitelli), recorded by Lisa Jarrett on Ro-Hit Records (dance); "Come Back to Me" (by Henderson/Riccitelli), recorded by The Joneses on Warner Bros. Records (R&B), and "Christmas Rappin' " by Grand Rapmasters on Essex Records.
Tips: "Submit material with strong hook, good demo, and know the market being targeted by your song."

SUPER RAPP PUBLISHING, Demo mailing: Suite 128, 3260 Keith Bridge Rd., Cumming GA 30131. Main office: #204, 23 Music Sq. East, Nashville TN 37203; (615)742-7408. President: Ron Dennis Wheeler. Music publisher. BMI. Estab. 1964. Publishes 100 songs/year; 20-25 new songwriters/year. "Sometimes hires staff writers for special projects." Pays standard royalty.
Affiliate(s): Do It Now Publishing (ASCAP), RR&R Music (BMI), Aicram Music (BMI).
How to Contact: "Send a demo tape/professionally recorded—if not, response time may be delayed. If you need a tape produced or song developed, contact RR&R Music Inc. first before submitting a badly produced tape. Unsolicited submissions are OK. Send music trax with and without lead vocals. Lyric sheet and chords. Also send music score if possible. Prefers 15 ips and a cassette copy. Clarity is most important. SASE is a must if you want submission returned. Responds only if interested."
Music: Gospel, rock and **pop;** also **country** and **R&B.** "No New Age." Published "She's Half the Man I Am" (by R. Wheeler/L. Brown) and "Take Me Down Lover's Lane" (by R.D. Wheeler), recorded by Ron Dennis Wheeler on RR&R Records; and "Two Shades of Blue" (by R. McGibony/R.D. Wheeler), recorded by Bill Scarbrough on Legends Records.

*SUPREME ENTERPRISES INT'L CORP., 3rd Floor, 12304 Santa Monica Blvd., Los Angeles CA 90025. (818)707-3481. Fax: (818)707-3482. G.M. Copyrights: Lisa Lew. Music publisher, record company and record producer. Estab. 1979. Publishes 20-30 songs/year; publishes 2-6 new songwriters/year. Works with composers and lyricists. Pays standard royalty.
Affiliate(s): Fuerte Suerte Music (BMI).
How to Contact: Write or call first and obtain permission to submit. Prefers cassette. SASE. Reports in 2 weeks.
Music: Mostly **Latin pop, reggae in Spanish and English** and **Cumbias ballads in Spanish.** Published *Meneaito* (written and recorded by Gary); *America* (written and recorded by Renato); and *Reggae Sam* (written and recorded by Reggae Sam), all on BMG Records.
Tips: "A good melody is a hit in any language."

*SWEET GLENN MUSIC (BMI), P.O. Box 1067, Santa Monica CA 90406. (310)452-0116. Fax: (310)465-4287. Vice President Talent: Mr. Friedwin. Music publisher and management company. Estab. 1980. Publishes 3-5 songs/year; publishes 1 new songwriter/year. Hires staff writers. Works with composers. Royalty rate varies.
Affiliate(s): Sweet Karol Music (ASCAP).
How to Contact: Write first and obtain permission to submit. "You must write before submitting." Reports in 2 months.
Music: Mostly **hip hop/funk, retro R&B** and **country.** Published "Rhythm of Romance" (by Scott), recorded by Randy Crawford.
Tips: "Must be part of a performing act or established producer/arranger-writer only!"

DALE TEDESCO MUSIC CO., 16020 Lahey St., Granada Hills CA 91344. (818)360-7329. Fax: (818)886-1338. President: Dale T. Tedesco. General Manager: Betty Lou Tedesco. Music publisher. BMI, ASCAP. Estab. 1981. Publishes 20-40 songs/year; publishes 20-30 new songwriters/year. Works with composers and lyricists; teams collaborators. Pays standard royalty.
Affiliate(s): Dale Tedesco Music (BMI) and Tedesco Tunes (ASCAP).
How to Contact: Submit a demo tape—unsolicited submissions are OK. Prefers cassette with 1-2 songs and lyric sheet. SASE or postcard for critique. "Dale Tedesco Music hand-critiques all material submitted. Free evaluation." Reports in 2 weeks.
Music: Mostly **pop, R&B** and **A/C;** also **dance-oriented, R&B, instrumentals** (for television & film), **jazz, MOR, rock, soul** and **ethnic instrumentals.**
Tips: "Listen to current trends and touch base with the publisher."

TEK PUBLISHING, P.O. Box 1485, Lake Charles LA 70602. (318)439-8839. Administrator: Eddie Shuler. Music publisher, freelance producer. ASCAP, BMI. Estab. 1956. Publishes 50 songs/year; publishes 35 new songwriters/year. Teams collaborators. Pays standard royalty.
Affiliate(s): TEK Publishing (BMI), Nassetan (BMI) and EMFS Music (ASCAP).
How to Contact: Submit a demo tape—unsolicited submissions are OK. Prefers cassette with 3 songs and lyric sheet. "Return postage is required for return of material." SASE. Reports in 2 months.
Music: Mostly **country** and **R&B**; also **cajun, humorist** and **zydeco**. Published "Yesterday's News," recorded by Cari Gregory (contemporary pop); "No Lowdown Boogie" (blues) and "Breaking Down the Door" (Cajun), recorded by Mickey Newman.
Tips: "KEEP WRITING. If you write a thousand songs, and even one is a hit it was all worthwhile. Concentrate on what's going on by listening to broadcasts and see what others are doing. Then try to determine where your story fits."

*TEN OF DIAMONDS MUSIC PUBLISHING (BMI), Suite 661, 880 Front St., Lahaina, Maui HI 96761. (808)661-5151. A&R Director: Diane Christopher. Music publisher, record company (Survivor Records/Dream Makers Records/H.I.T. Records) and record producer (Maui). BMI, ASCAP. Estab. 1974. Publishes 1-15 songs/year; publishes 1-15 new songwriters/year. Works with composers and lyricists; teams collaborators. Pays standard royalty.
Affiliate(s): Maui No Ka Oi Publishing (ASCAP), Ten of Diamonds Music (BMI).
How to Contact: Submit a demo tape by mail—unsolicited submissions are OK. Prefers cassette and VHS videocassette with 3-4 songs and lyric or lead sheet. SASE. Reports in 1 month.
Music: Mostly **pop, country** and **R&B**; also **classical, Hawaiian** and **jazz/fusion**. Published "Diane," written and recorded by Jason (country rock); *Carry On* (by Jason and Bonnie Frederics), recorded by Jason; and "Back to the Streets," written and recorded by Kieli Hookipa, all on Survivor Records.

*TENDER TENDER MUSIC (BMI), #105, 158 W. 81st St. SE, New York NY 10024. (212)724-5624. Publisher: Christopher Berg. Music publisher. Estab. 1990. Publishes 5-10 songs/year; publishes 1 new songwriter/year. Works with composers and lyricists; teams collaborators. Pay negotiable.
How to Contact: Submit demo tape by mail. Unsolicited submissions are OK. Prefers cassette (or VHS videocassette) with 3 songs and lyric, score or lead sheet. SASE. Reports in 1 month.
Music: Mostly **concert songs, concert instrumental, opera**; also **musical theater, ballads** and **rock**. Published *Steps, St. Paul and All That* and *Poem* (by Christopher Berg), recorded by Paul Sperry on Albany Records (classical).
Tips: "Write something which tickles the mind, not only the body."

*THIS BEATS WORKIN' MUSIC INC. (ASCAP), 235 West End Ave., New York NY 10023. (212)799-7170. Fax: (212)799-7236. Assistant to the President: Kristin Lovgren. Music publisher, producer/songwriter management. Estab. 1989. Publishes 15-20 songs/year; publishes 3 or 4 new songwriters/year. Works with composers and lyricists. Pays various amount.
How to Contact: Submit demo tape by mail. Unsolicited submissions are OK. Prefers cassette with lyric sheet. SASE. Reports in 1 month.
Music: Mostly **pop, house/hip-hop** and **dance**; also **anything different/unique**. Published "Deeper and Deeper" (by Pettibone/Ciccone/Shimkin) and "Vogue" (by Pettibone/Ciccone), both recorded by Madonna on Warner Bros. Records; also "Broken Glass" (by Vasquez/Lauper/De Peyer), recorded by Cyndi Lauper on Epic Records.
Tips: "Great hook, great track, different ideas—be creative! If it "sounds just like" don't bother to send. Make sure demo vocal is good."

TIKI ENTERPRISES, INC., 195 S. 26th St., San Jose CA 95116. (408)286-9840. President: Gradie O'Neal. Music publisher, record company (Rowena Records) and record producer (Jeannine O'Neal and Gradie O'Neal). BMI, ASCAP. Estab. 1967. Publishes 40 songs/year; publishes 12 new songwriters/year. Works with composers; teams collaborators. Pays standard royalty.
Affiliate(s): Tooter Scooter Music (BMI), Janell Music (BMI) and O'Neal & Friend (ASCAP).
How to Contact: Submit a demo tape—unsolicited submissions are OK. Prefers cassette with 3 songs and lyric or lead sheets. SASE. Reports in 3 weeks.
Music: Mostly **country, Mexican, rock/pop gospel, R&B, New Age**. Published "Uptown Underground Mix" (by Marcus Bernard), recorded by True Colors (rap); "Teach Me To Dance Real Slow" (by Terry Heban), recorded by Jaque Lynn (country); and "Boogie All Night" (by Jeannine O'Neal), recorded by Jaque Lynn (Mexican), all on Rowena Records.

*TKO MUSIC, INC., P.O. Box 130, Hove, East Sussex BN3 6QU **England**. (71)736-5520. Fax: (0273)540969. President—Music Publishing: Arthur Braun. Music publisher, record company and major European concert promoter. Estab. 1952. Publishes 15-20 songs/year; publishes 4 new songwriters/year. Hires staff writers. Works with composers and lyricists; teams collaborators. Negotiable rate.

Affiliate(s): Whole Armor Music (ASCAP) and Full Armor Music (BMI).
How to Contact: Submit demo tape by mail. Unsolicited submissions are OK. Prefers cassette with lyric sheet. "Be sure to include SASE for return." Reports in 1 month.
Music: Mostly **dance, R&B** and **rock**; also **country, gospel** and **ballads**.
Tips: "Never give up and always work on developing your craft."

TOMPAUL MUSIC CO., 628 South St., Mount Airy NC 27030. (919)786-2865. Owner: Paul E. Johnson. Music publisher, record company, record producer and record and tape distributor. BMI. Estab. 1960. Publishes 25 songs/year. Works with composers. Pays standard royalty.
How to Contact: Submit a demo tape—unsolicited submissions are OK. Prefers cassette tapes with 4-6 songs and lyric or lead sheet. SASE. Reports in 2 months.
Music: Mostly **country, bluegrass** and **gospel**; also **church/religious, easy listening, folk, MOR, rock, soul** and **top 40**. Published "Paul's Ministry" (by Early Upchurch), recorded by "The Isaacs" on Morning Star Records (gospel); "Long Journey Home" (by Paul Edgar Johnson), recorded by Bobby Lee Atkins on Rural Records (country); and "D.J.S. Theme (written and recorded by Bobby Lee Atkins) on Rural Records (bluegrass).
Tips: "Try to write good commercial type songs, use new ideas, listen to the songs that are played on radio stations today; you could get some ideas. Don't try to make alterations in a song already established."

TORO'NA MUSIC, Box 88022, Indianapolis IN 46208. Contact: A&R Director. Music publisher (Toro'na Music) and record producer (I. McDaniel). BMI. Estab. 1987. Publishes 3 songs/year; publishes 1 new songwriter/year. Hires independent staff writers. Pays standard royalty.
How to Contact: Write first and obtain permission to submit a tape. Direct all correspondence to A&R department. Prefers cassette with 3 songs and lyric sheets. Does not return unsolicited material. Reports in 8 weeks.
Music: Mostly **top 40, R&B** and **gospel**; also **rap**. Published "Second Chance" (ballad-LP) and "Free-style" (jazz) (by I. McDaniel), recorded by I. McDaniel on Toro'na Records; and "Don't Say No" (by I. McDaniel), recorded by Payage on Brendo Kent Pub (ballad LP).
Tips: "Write first about your interests. No phone calls please."

*TOULOUSE MUSIC PUBLISHING CO., INC., Box 96, El Cerrito CA 94530. Executive Vice President: James Bronson, Jr. Music publisher, record company and record producer. BMI. Member AIMP. Publishes 1 new songwriter/year. Hires staff writers. Pays standard royalty.
How to Contact: Prefers cassette with 2-4 songs and lyric sheet. SASE. Reports in 1 month.
Music: **Bluegrass, gospel, jazz, R&B** and **soul**.

TRANSITION MUSIC CORP., Suite 700, 6290 Sunset Blvd., Los Angeles CA 90028. Professional Manager: Kim Frascarelli. Music publisher and management firm. BMI, ASCAP. Member NMPA. Estab. 1982. Publishes 35 songs/year; publishes 10 new songwriters/year. Teams collaborators.
Affiliate(s): Creative Entertainment Music (BMI), Pushy Publishing (ASCAP).
How to Contact: Write or call first and obtain permission to submit. Prefers cassette with 1-3 songs and lyric sheet. SASE. Reports in 6 weeks.
Music: **R&B** and **dance**. Published *I Wish They Could Have Stayed*, written and recorded by Steve Santoro for New Line Cinema; "Rock Me All Night" (by Frank Maddalone/Marco Mariangeli) recorded by Marco Mariangeli; and "The Yeah Song," (by Murphy/Jones/Gumbs), recorded by Eddie Murphy on Motown Records.
Tips: "Please submit top quality radio-ready demos."

*TRANSWORLD WEST MUSIC GROUP, Suite #83, 1102 North Brand Blvd., Glendale CA 91202. (818)543-7538. Fax: (818)241-2494. Managing Director: Timothy M. Burleson. Music publisher and commercial music firm/scoring service. Estab. 1991. Publishes 20-50 songs/year; publishes 20-25 new songwriters/year. Hires staff writers. Works with composers and lyricists; teams collaborators. Pays standard royalty. At times a "flat fee" is negotiated.
Affiliate(s): Bowie Enterprises, Vance Bowie Music (BMI) and TransWorld West Music Publishing (BMI).
How to Contact: Submit demo tape by mail. Unsolicited submissions are OK. No cold calls! No phone calls until tapes have been accepted, and contracts are being negotiated! Prefers cassette (or ½" videocassette) with 4 songs or instrumentals and lyric or lead sheet. Does not return unsolicited material, prefers to keep on file for future consideration. Reports in 1 month.
Music: **All styles.** Published "I Deserve It" (written and recorded by Reuben B. Mayo); "Chillin' Round Midnight" and "Love Exchange" (written and recorded by Vance Bowie), all on Bowie Productions Records.

Tips: "Send well produced, quality demos that represent your best material. Innovative and progressive individuals will get top priority and consideration. Stay focused on current market trends worldwide. And most important, keep the faith! The world will always need good music, and the special people that create it!"

TROPICAL BEAT RECORDS/POLYGRAM, Dept. SM, P.O. Box 917, Bala Cynwyd PA 19004. (215)828-7030. President: Steven Bernstein. Music publisher and record company. Estab. 1973. BMI. Publishes 50 songs/year; publishes 3-4 new songwriters/year. Employs songwriters on a salary basis. Teams collaborators.
How to Contact: Prefers cassette. Does not return unsolicited material.
Music: R&B and **dance** ONLY. Published "Closer than Close" (by Terri Price), recorded by Jean Carne; and "Lonely Road" (by Bryan Williams), recorded by Rose Royce, both on Omni Records (both R&B); and "Love Won't Let Me Wait," by Luther Vandross.

TRUSTY PUBLICATIONS, 8771 Rose Creek Rd., Nebo KY 42441. (502)249-3194. President: Elsie Childers. Music publisher, record company (Trusty Records) and record producer. BMI. Member CMA. Estab. 1960. Publishes 2-3 songs/year; publishes 2 new songwriters/year. Pays standard royalty.
Affiliate(s): Sub-publishers: Sunset Music (Italy) and White Label (Holland).
How to Contact: Submit a demo tape—unsolicited submissions are OK. Prefers cassette (or VHS videocassette) with 2-4 songs and lead sheet. SASE. Reports in 1 month.
Music: Mostly **country, R&B, rock, contemporary Christian, Southern gospel, hip hop, club** and **dance;** some **rap.** Published "I Wanna Dance," "My Charms Just Ain't Enough," and "If You Ain't Got It," all by Childers and Williams, recorded by Noah Williams on Trusty Records.
Tips: "Harmony is in! So put lots of it in your songs."

*TUFFIN MUSIC ENTERPRISES, P.O. Box 566, Naperville IL 60566. (708)416-6606. Fax: (708)416-3313. President: Paul Kurth. Music publisher. Estab. 1990. Publishes 2 songs/year. Publishes 1-2 new songwriters. Hires staff songwriters. Works with composers and lyricists; teams collaborators. Pays standard royalty.
Affiliate(s): Tuffin Music (BMI).
How to Contact: Submit demo tape by mail. Unsolicited submissions are OK. Prefers cassette (or VHS videocassette) with 1-5 songs and lyric or lead sheet (if available). "We prefer copyrighted material." SASE. Reports in 3 weeks.
Music: Mostly **country, rock, adult contemporary;** also **novelty, educational, instructional.** Published "From the Heart" (by Paul and Joan Kurth), recorded by Jean Dunnon on Muffaletta Records.
Tips: "Demo should be of high quality and as close to finished commercial concept as possible."

TWIN TOWERS PUBLISHING CO., Dept. SM, 8833 Sunset Blvd., Penthouse, Los Angeles CA 90069. (310)659-9644. President: Michael Dixon. Director of Publishing: Chris Kinsman. Music publisher and booking agency (Harmony Artists, Inc.). Works with composers and lyricists. Publishes 24 songs/year. Pays standard royalty.
How to Contact: Call first to get permission to submit a tape. Prefers cassette with 3 songs and lyric sheet. SASE. Will respond only if interested.
Music: Mostly **pop, rock** and **R&B.** Published "Magic," from *Ghostbusters* soundtrack on Arista Records; and "Kiss Me Deadly" (by Lita Ford), on RCA Records.

*TWO FOLD MUSIC, P.O. Box 388, Goodlettsville TN 37072. (615)831-6242. Manager: Roland Pope. Music publisher. BMI. Estab. 1978. Publishes 50 songs/year. Pays standard royalty.
How to Contact: Submit a demo tape by mail—unsolicited submissions are OK. Prefers cassette with 4 songs and lyric sheet. "Include return address and phone number." SASE. Reports in 1 month.
Music: Mostly **country, gospel** and **rock.** Published *Uncle Troy's* (by Ralph Naimon), *That's Another Thing* (by Chuck Melvsin), and *That Lovin' You Feelin'* (by Roland Pope), all recorded by Wayne Nelson on Spec Records.

*TWO/POLYGRAM MUSIC PUBLISHING, 122 McEvoy St., Alexandria NSW 2015 **Australia.** Phone: (02)581-1234. Professional Manager: Kim Green. Music publisher. Estab. 1988. Works with composers and lyricists.
How to Contact: Submit demo tape by mail. Unsolicited submissions are OK. Prefers cassette with 3 songs and lyric sheet. Does not return unsolicited material. Reports in 4-6 weeks.
Music: Mostly **top 40, pop** and **rock.**

UBM, Mommsenst. 61, 5000 Koln 41 **Germany.** Phone: 43 13 13. President: Uwe Buschkotter. Music publisher, record company and record producer. GEMA (Germany), BMI (USA). Estab. 1968. Publishes 100 songs/year; publishes 10 new songwriters/year. Works with composers. Pays standard royalty.

How to Contact: Submit a demo tape. Prefers cassette (or VHS videocassette) and lead sheets. Does not return unsolicited material. Reports in 4 weeks.
Music: Mostly **jazz, pop, MOR, funk** and **easy listening**; also **classical**.

UNIVERSAL STARS MUSIC, INC., HC-80, Box 5B, Leesville LA 71446. National Representative: Sherree Stephens. Music publisher and record company (Robbins Records). BMI. Publishes 12-24 songs/year; publishes 1 new songwriter/year. Pays standard royalty.
Affiliate(s): Headliner Stars Music Inc.
How to Contact: Prefers cassette with 1-6 songs and lyric or lead sheets. Does not return unsolicited material. Reports in 1 month, if interested.
Music: Mostly **religious**; also **bluegrass, church, country, folk, gospel** and **top 40/pop**. Published "Jesus, You're Everywhere," "I Can Depend On You," and "I Just Came to Thank You Lord" (by Sherree Stephens), recorded by J.J. and S. Stephens on Robbins Records (religious).

VAAM MUSIC GROUP, P.O. Box 29688, Hollywood CA 90029-0688. (213)664-7765. President: Pete Martin. Music publisher and record producer. ASCAP, BMI. Estab. 1967. Publishes 9-24 new songs/year; varying number of new songwriters per year. Pays standard royalty.
Affiliate(s): Pete Martin Music.
How to Contact: Prefers cassette with 2 songs maximum and lyric sheet. SASE. Reports in 1 month. "Small packages only."
Music: **Top 40/pop, country** and **R&B**. "Submitted material must have potential of reaching top 5 on charts." Published "Good Girls" (by Kevin Bird), recorded by Valerie Canon on Carrere/CBS Records (R&B dance); "The Greener Years," recorded by Frank Loren on Blue Gem Records (country/MOR); "Bar Stool Rider" (by Peggy Hackworth); and "I Love a Cowboy," written and performed by Sherry Weston in the feature film "Far Out Man," with Tommy Chong (of Cheech & Chong comedy team) and also co-starring Martin Mull.
Tips: "Study the top 10 in charts in the style that you write. Stay current and up to date to today's market."

VALET PUBLISHING CO., #273, 2442 NW Market, Seattle WA 98107. (206)524-1020. Fax: (206)524-1102. Publishing Director: Buck Ormsby. Music publisher and record company (Etiquette/Suspicious Records). BMI. Estab. 1961. Publishes 5-10 songs/year. Hires staff songwriters. Pays standard royalty.
How to Contact: Submit a demo tape—unsolicited submissions OK. Prefers cassette with 3-4 songs and lyric sheets. SASE. Reports in 6-8 weeks.
Music: Mostly **R&B, rock, pop**; also **dance** and **country**. Published "Black Lace" (by Roger Rogers), recorded by Kinetics on Etiquette Records (rock); "Hunger and Emotion" (by Rogers/Caldwell), recorded by Kinetics on Etiquette Records (pop); and "One More Time" (by Morrill/French), recorded by Kent Morrill on Suspicious Records (R&B).
Tips: "Production of tape must be top quality; or lyric sheets professional."

VICTORY MUSIC, P.O. Box 6132, Elberton GA 30635. Professional Manager: Dianna Kirk. Music publisher. Estab. 1991. Works with composers and lyricists. Pays standard royalty.
Affiliate(s): Wild Katt Music.
How to Contact: Write first and obtain permission to submit. Prefers cassette with 3 songs and lyric sheet. SASE. Reports in 2-3 weeks.
Music: Mostly **heavy metal, rock, dance**. Published "Big Fat Women," "You Dropped a Bomb," "Living in Sin" (by Greg Timms).
Tips: "Always include a SASE if you want a response."

*VOICE NOTES PUBLISHING, 7526 Standifer Gap Rd., Chattanooga TN 37421. (615)624-0815. Music publisher, record company (GO-ROC-CO-POP Records). ASCAP. Estab. 1984. Publishes 20 songs/year; publishes 1-5 new songwriters/year. Works with composers and lyricists; teams collaborators. Pays standard royalty.
Affiliate(s): Voice Score Publishing (BMI).
How to Contact: Submit a demo tape by mail—unsolicited submissions are OK. Prefers cassette with 3-5 songs and lyric or lead sheets. "Have melody out front, words and diction clear." SASE. Reports in 3 months.
Music: Mostly **gospel, rock, country, pop** and **R&B**. Published "Silent River" (by John Reilly) and "Come On And Cry" (by Bruce Newman), recorded in album and video by Keith Hartline (rock ballad); "Get Your Own Money" (by Sharon Lewis), and "Ghost Of Music Row" (by Horace Hatcher

---

The types of music each listing is interested in are printed in boldface.

and Ed Smith), recorded by RENĀ (country); all recorded on GO-ROC-CO-POP Records.

VOKES MUSIC PUBLISHING (BMI), Box 12, New Kensington PA 15068-0012. (412)335-2775. President: Howard Vokes. Music publisher, record company, booking agency and promotion company.
How to Contact: Submit cassette (3 songs only), lyric or lead sheet. SASE. Reports within a week.
Music: Traditional country-bluegrass and **gospel.** Published "A Million Tears" (by Duke & Null), recorded by Johnny Eagle Feather on Vokes Records; "I Won't Be Your Honky Tonk Queen" (by Vokes-Wallace), recorded by Bunnie Mills on Pot-Of Gold Records; and "Break The News" (by Vokes-Webb), recorded by Bill Beere on Oakhill Records.
Tips: "We're always looking for country songs that tell a story, and only interested in hard-traditional-bluegrass, country and country gospel songs. Please no "copy-cat-song writers.""

M & T WALDOCH PUBLISHING, INC. (BMI), 4803 S. 7th St., Milwaukee WI 53221. (414)482-2194. VP, Creative Management: Timothy J. Waldoch. Music publisher. Estab. 1990. Publishes 2-3 songs/year; publishes 2-3 new songwriters/year. Works with composers and lyricists; teams collaborators. Pays standard royalty.
How to Contact: Submit demo tape—unsolicited submissions are OK. Prefers cassette with 3-6 songs and lyric sheet or lead sheet. "We prefer a studio produced demo tape." SASE. Reports in 2-3 months.
Music: Mostly **country/pop, rock, top 40 pop**; also **melodic metal, dance, R&B.** Published "It's Only Me" and "Let Peace Rule the World" (by Kenny LePrix), recorded by Brigade on SBD Records (rock LP).
Tips: "We want songs with strong melodies and well crafted lyrics. Read *The Craft of Lyric Writing* by Sheila Davis and other books on songwriting to help you develop your craft."

WARNER/CHAPPELL MUSIC, INC., Dept. SM, 1290 6th Ave., New York NY 10019. (212)399-6910. V.P. Creative Services: Kenny McPhearson. Music publisher. ASCAP, BMI, SESAC. Estab. 1811. Publishes hundreds of songs/year; publishes hundreds of new songwriters/year. Hires staff songwriters. Works with composers and lyricists; teams collaborators.
Affiliate(s): WB Music Corp. (ASCAP), Warner Tamerlane Publishing Corp. (BMI), W.B.M. Music Corp. (SESAC), Warner/Elektra/Asylum Music Inc. (BMI), Warner/Refuge Music Inc. (ASCAP), Warner/Noreale Music Inc. (SESAC), Chappell & Co. (ASCAP), Intersong U.S.A. Inc. (ASCAP), Rightsong Music Inc. (BMI), Unichappell Music Inc. (BMI), Tri-Chappell Music, Inc. (SESAC), Lorimar Music A Corp (ASCAP), Lorimar Music B Corp (BMI), Roliram Lorimar Music (BMI), Marilor Music (ASCAP), Goldline Music (ASCAP) Silverline Music (BMI) and Oakline Music (SESAC).
How to Contact: "Must be solicited by an attorney or management firm." Company policy prohibits unsolicited submissions.
Music: Mostly **pop, rock, R&B** and **country**; also **rap, jazz** and **new music.**
Tips: "Submit your best song because sometimes you only get to make a first impression. Submit a song you feel most comfortable writing regardless of style."

WATCHESGRO MUSIC, #106, 900 9th Ave., S., Nashville TN 37212. (615)329-3991. President: Eddie Carr. Music publisher. BMI. Estab. 1987. Publishes 100 songs/year; publishes 5 new songwriters/year. Teams collaborators. Pays standard royalty.
Affiliate(s): Watch Us Climb Music (ASCAP).
How to Contact: Write first and obtain permission to submit. Prefers cassette. SASE. Reports in 1 week.
Music: Published "7th & Sundance" (by Aileen/Dempsey), recorded by Rita Aileen (country); "Eatin' My Words" (by M. Jones), recorded by Michael Jones; and "Precious Memories" (by D. Horn), recorded by Cindy Jane, all on Interstate 40 Records (country singles). "Get Me Just As Close," by Marion Hammers; "The Winter," by Frank Pilgrim; "If I Had My Way," by Melisa Michaels; "Life Time Love Affair," by Stacy Johnson, all on Interstate 40 Records.

*WAZURI MUSIC (BMI), P.O. Box 374, Fairview NJ 07022. (201)313-9112. Fax: (201)941-3987. President: Linwood M. Simon. Music publisher. Estab. 1981. Publishes 23 songs/year. Publishes 6 new songwriters/year. Pays standard 50% royalty.
Affiliate(s): Linwood Maxwell Music (BMI), Gloria Gaynor Music (ASCAP).
How to Contact: Prefers cassette with 2 songs and lyric sheet.
Music: Mostly **pop, R&B, jazz**; also **gospel.** Published "Guess Who" (by G. Gaynor); "Top Shelf" and "Love Affaire" (by L. Simon), all recorded by Gloria Gaynor on New Music Records.

WEAVER WORDS OF MUSIC, P.O. Box 803, Tazewell VA 24651. (703)988-6267. President: H. R. Cook. Music publisher and record company (Fireball Records). BMI. Estab. 1978. Publishes 12 songs/year; varying number of new songwriters/year. Works with composers and lyricists; teams collaborators. Pays standard royalty.

How to Contact: Submit a demo tape—unsolicited submissions are OK. Prefers cassette with 3 songs and lyric or lead sheets. SASE. Reports in 2 weeks.
Music: Mostly **country**. Published "Winds of Change," written and recorded by Cecil Surrett; "Texas Saturday Night" and "Old Flame Burning," written and recorded by H.R. Cook; all on Fireball Records (country).

WEEDHOPPER MUSIC, 1916 28th Ave. S., Birmingham AL 35209-2605. (205)942-3222. President: Michael Panepento. BMI. Estab. 1985. Music publisher (Chapel Lane) and Chapel Lane Productions (an Artist Development firm); management firm (Airwave Production Group, Ltd.). Publishes 4-6 songs/year; publishes 3 new songwriters/year. Works with composers and lyricists. Pays standard royalty.
Affiliate(s): Panepentunes (ASCAP); Panelips (BMI).
How to Contact: Write first and obtain permission to submit. Prefers cassette or 15 ips reel-to-reel with 3 songs. SASE. Reports in 10 weeks.
Music: Mostly **pop/rock, AOR, R&B/jazz** and **rock**; also all others. Published "Home" and "Land of Kings" (by Hammrick), recorded by The Skeptics on Pandem Records (modern rock). Works with new artists Vallejo, Parousia.
Tips: "Send us the best possible demo/example of your work."

BERTHOLD WENGERT (MUSIKVERLAG), Hauptstrasse 100, D-7507 Pfinztal-Soellingen, **Germany**. Contact: Berthold Wengert. Music publisher. Teams collaborators. Pays standard GEMA royalty.
How to Contact: Prefers cassette and complete score for piano. International Reply Coupon. Reports in 4 weeks. "No cassette returns!"
Music: Mostly **light music** and **pop**.

BOBE WES MUSIC, P.O. Box 28609, Dallas TX 75228. (214)681-0345. President: Bobe Wes. Music publisher. BMI. Publishes 20 songs/year. Pays standard royalty.
How to Contact: Submit a demo tape—unsolicited submissions are OK. Prefers cassette. "State if songs have been copyrighted and if you have previously assigned songs to someone else. Include titles, readable lyrics and your full name and address. Give the same information for your co-writer(s) if you have one. State if you are a member of BMI, ASCAP or SESAC. Lead sheets are not required. Comments will follow only if interested." SASE. No certified mail accepted.
Music: Blues, country, disco, gospel, MOR, **progressive**, rock (hard or soft), soul, top 40/pop, polka, Latin dance and instrumentals. "Special interest in **Christmas songs**."

WEST BROADWAY MUSIC, Dept. SM, Suite 401, 68 Water St., Vancouver, British Columbia V6B 1A4 **Canada**. (604)669-7270. Professional Manager: Michael Goodin. Music publisher and management company. SOCAN. Estab. 1989. Publishes 12-15 songs/year; publishes 1-3 new songwriters/year. Works with composers; teams collaborators. Pays standard royalty.
How to Contact: Write or call first and obtain permission to submit a tape. Prefers cassette with 3-5 songs and lyric sheet. SASE. Reports in 4-6 weeks.
Music: Mostly **pop, dance** and **rock**; also **R&B**. Published "Might as Well Party," written and recorded by Al Rodger on Criminal Records (pop); and "Your Place or Mine" (by Al Rodger), recorded by Sharon Lee Williams on Virgin Records (R&B/dance).
Tips: "Looking for more active songwriters instead of new talent."

WESTUNES MUSIC PUBLISHING CO., 167 Main St., Metuchen NJ 08840. (908)548-6700. Fax: (908)548-6748. A&R Director: Kevin McCabe. Music publisher and management firm (Westwood Entertainment Group). ASCAP. Publishes 15 songs/year; publishes 2 new songwriters/year. Works with composers and lyricists. Pays standard royalty.
How to Contact: Write first and obtain permission to submit. Prefers cassette with 3 songs and lyric sheet. SASE. Reports in 6 weeks.
Music: Mostly **rock**; also **pop**. Published "Life Goes On" (by K. Munson), recorded by Frontier on Westwood Records; "Uncertain" (written and recorded by Kurbjaw), on Changing Records; and "Save Me" (by Jim Forest), recorded by Kidd Scruff on Azra Records.
Tips: Submit a "neat promotional package; attach biography of the songwriter."

WHITE CAR MUSIC (BMI), 11724 Industriplex, Baton Rouge LA 70809. (504)755-1400. Contact: Nelson Blanchard. Music publisher, record company (White Car Records/Techno Sound Records), record producer. BMI, ASCAP. Estab. 1988. Publishes 15 songs/year; publishes 2 new songwriters/year. Works with composers and lyricists; teams collaborators. Pays standard royalty.

Affiliate(s): Char Blanche Music (ASCAP).
How to Contact: Submit a demo tape by mail—unsolicited submissions are OK. Prefers cassette with 4 songs. Does not return unsolicited material. Reports in 2 weeks.
Music: Mostly **country, rock** and **pop**; also **R&B**. Published "Leading Man" (by Butch Reine), recorded by Atchafalaya on White Car Records (country); "Sail On" (by Blanchard, Watts, Bullion), recorded by Johnsteve on Stebu Records (rock); and "Crazy Bound" (by Blanchard), recorded by Tareva on White Car Records (country).

WHITEWING MUSIC (BMI), 413 N Parkerson Ave., Crowley LA 70526. (318)788-0773. Fax: (318)788-0776. Engineer: Eddie Bonin. Music publisher and record company (Master-Trak, Showtime, Par T, MTE, Blues Unlimited, Kajun, Cajun Classics). Estab. 1946. Publishes 12-15 songs/year. Publishes 6 new songwriters/year. Pays standard royalty.
Affiliate(s): Jamil Music (BMI), Whitewing Music (BMI).
How to Contact: Submit demo tape by mail—unsolicited submissions are OK. Prefers cassette (or VHS videocassette) with 6 songs and lyric or lead sheets. SASE. Reports in 5-6 weeks.
Music: Mostly **C/W, rock, MOR**; also **cajun**. Published *Down Home Alive* (by various), recorded by Wayne Toups on MTE Records.

WILCOM PUBLISHING, Box 4456, West Hills CA 91308. (818)348-0940. Owner: William Clark. Music publisher. ASCAP. Estab. 1989. Publishes 10-15 songs/year; publishes 1-2 new songwriters/year. Works with composers and lyricists. Pays standard royalty.
How to Contact: Write first and obtain permission to submit a tape. Prefers cassette with 1-2 songs and lyric sheet. SASE. Reports in 3 weeks.
Music: Mostly **R&B, pop** and **rock**; also **country**. Published "Girl Can't Help It" (by W. Clark, D. Walsh and P. Oland), recorded by Stage 1 on Rockit Records (top 40).

SHANE WILDER MUSIC, P.O. Box 3503, Hollywood CA 90078. (818)508-1433. President: Shane Wilder. Music publisher (BMI), record producer (Shane Wilder Productions) and management firm (Shane Wilder Artists Management). Estab. 1960. Publishes 25-50 songs/year; publishes 15-20 new songwriters/year. Works with composers. Pays standard royalty.
How to Contact: Submit demo tape—unsolicited submissions OK. Prefers cassette (or VHS videocassette) with 3 songs and lyric sheet. "Include SASE if you wish tape returned. Photo and resume should be sent if you're looking for a producer." Reports in 2-4 weeks.
Music: Mostly **traditional country** and **crossover**. Published "No Vacancy" by (Glenda Sue Foster) on Texas Music Masters; "Don't Touch My Life" (by Adrianne) on Rambo Star Records; and "Bring Back Your Love" (by Melanie Kay), recorded by Anne Murray on Capitol Records (country).
Tips: "We no longer accept songs with a reversion clause due to so many artists writing their own songs."

WIL-TOO/WIL-SO MUSIC, P.O. Box 120694, Nashville TN 37212. President: Tom Wilkerson. Music publisher, record producer. ASCAP, BMI. Estab. 1969. Publishes 10 songs/year; 2-3 new songwriters/year. Works with composers and lyricists; teams collaborators. Pays standard royalty.
How to Contact: Submit a demo tape—unsolicited submissions OK. Prefers cassette with 3 songs. SASE. Reports in 2 weeks.
Music: Mostly **country, gospel** and **contemporary Christian** and **pop**. Published *Lady of Light*; "If There's a Miracle" and "Bridge of Peace" (by Wilkerson-Fielder), recorded by Joyful Pilgrim on Lightstone Records (Christian).

WIND HAVEN PUBLISHING, 6477 Emerson Ave. S., St. Petersburg FL 33707. (813)343-5456. Contact: Joe Terry. Music publisher, record company, record producer. Estab. 1982. Publishes around 50 songs/year. Works with composers and lyricists; teams collaborators. Standard contract.
How to Contact: Submit demo tape—unsolicited submissions are OK. Prefers cassette with 6 songs and lyric sheet. SASE. Reports in 3-6 weeks.
Music: Mostly **country, gospel, easy listening**; also **pop-country, bluegrass, rock-a-billy**. Published "Time For One More Tear" and "Why Waste Tears," written and recorded by Joe Terry on Fanfare Records; and "City Life" (by Donna McComb and Joe Terry), recorded by Joe Terry, all on Wind Haven Records.

*WINDSWEPT PACIFIC ENTERTAINMENT, Suite 200, 9320 Wilshire Blvd., Beverly Hills CA 90212. (310)550-1500. Fax: (310)247-0195. Senior Director, Creative Services: John Anderson. Estab. 1988. Works with composers and lyricists.

Affiliate(s): Full Keel Music Co. (ASCAP), Longitude Music Co. (BMI).
How to Contact: Write first and obtain permission to submit. Prefers cassette (or DAT) with 3-5 songs and lyric sheet. Does not return material. Reports in 4-6 weeks.
Music: Interested in any hit material, all genres. Published "Save the Best for Last" (by Wendy Waldman), recorded by Vanessa Williams (pop/R&B) and "Get A Leg Up," written and recorded by John Mellencamp on Mercury Records (rock); "Please Don't Go" (by H. Casey/R. Finch), recorded by KWS on Nettwerk/Next Plateau Records (dance). Artist roster includes: Quincy Jones III, The Cramps, Rick Vincent, Bang Tango, Sky Cries Mary, Dramarama, Final Cut, Skatenigs and Kitaro.

*WINSTON & HOFFMAN HOUSE MUSIC PUBLISHERS (ASCAP/BMI), #318, 1680 N. Vine St., Hollywood CA 90028. President: Lynne Robin Green. Music publisher. Estab. 1958. Publishes 20 songs/year; publishes 10-15 new songwriters/year. Works with composers and lyricists. Pays standard royalty.
Affiliate(s): Landsdowne Music Publishers (ASCAP), Bloor Music (BMI), Clemitco Publishing (BMI) and Ben Ross Music (ASCAP).
How to Contact: Submit demo tape by mail. Unsolicited submissions are OK. "No calls." Prefers cassette with 3 songs maximum and lyric sheet. "*Must* SASE, or *no* reply! No calls." Reports in 3 weeks.
Music: Mostly **R&B dance, ballads, hip hop, vocal jazz, alternative/R&B**; also **pop ballads**. Published *After the Quake* (by Harvey Scales), recorded by Hammer on Eastern Way Records; *Old Home Place* (by Jayne-Webb), recorded by Travis Tritt on Warner Bros. Records; and *IRAZU* (by Bonilla), recorded by Luis Bonilla Latin Jazz All Stars on DA Records.
Tips: "If artist, send bio and picture; if songwriter, send only your *very* best. Don't call unless solicited! I listen to everything, reply with SASE *only*. Write from the head and the heart, strong hooks, great melodies!"

*WITHOUT PAPERS MUSIC PUBLISHING INC., 2366 Woodhill Rd., Cleveland OH 44106. (216)791-2100. Fax: (216)791-7117. President: Michele Norton. Music publisher. Estab. 1992. Publishes 4 songs/year. Publishes 2 new songwriters/year. Hires staff songwriters. Works with composers and lyricists; teams collaborators. "Royalties are negotiated—songwriters currently at 50%."
How to Contact: Call first and obtain permission to submit. Prefers cassette with lyric sheet. Does not return material. Reports in 2 weeks.
Music: Mostly **rock-n-roll, R&B, country** (with R&B or rock base); also **children's, classical, different, commercial.** Published *Guitar For You, Make It Burn, Too High A Price* and *Had Another Girl* (all by Stutz Bearcat), recorded by Armstrong/Bearcat, on Strange Attractor Records.
Tips: "Be patient and be willing to work with us and the song."

WONDERWAX PUBLISHING, P.O. Box 4641, Estes Park CO 80517. President: James Haber. Music publisher, record company (DG Records; Wonderwax Records). BMI. Estab. 1983. Publishes 25 songs/year; publishes 10 new songwriters/year. Pays standard royalty.
How to Contact: Submit a demo tape—unsolicited submissions are OK. Prefers cassette with your best 2 songs and lyric sheets. Send clear demos, please. SASE. Reports in 1 week to 3 months.
Music: Mostly **pop, alternative, grunge**, will listen to **R&B** and **country**. Rock submissions only in the alternative genre. Published "Instant Satisfaction" (by M. Cunningham), slated '93 release; "Vain" (by J. Upham); "Boxer" (by Scott Roberts) on Wonderwax Records; and "Some Guy Named Paul" (by Slash N.F.), recorded by Degeneration on Wonderwax Records (psychodance 45).
Tips: "We prefer full demos, please keep this in mind when submitting. We are a "writer friendly" organization, our contracts for publishing are the standard Songwriters Guild variety. Protect yourself! Have all contracts reviewed by a lawyer or by the guild itself, do not be taken advantage of! We are especially interested in alternative rock. Submit your best efforts, bio-pictures, press kit. Show us how professional you really are, if I'm "taken away" by your demo, I'll help you one step at a time, right through this monster called the music business, is anyone out there?"

WOODRICH PUBLISHING CO., P.O. Box 38, Lexington AL 35648. (205)247-3983. President: Woody Richardson. Music publisher and record company (Woodrich Records) and record producer. BMI. Estab. 1959. Publishes 25 songs/year; publishes 12 new songwriters/year. Works with composers; teams collaborators. Pays 50% royalty less expenses.
Affiliate(s): Mernee Music (ASCAP), Melstep Music (BMI) and Tennesse Valley Music (SESAC).
How to Contact: Submit a demo tape—unsolicited submissions are OK. Prefers cassette with 2-4 songs. Prefers studio produced demos. SASE. Reports in 2 weeks.
Music: Mostly **country** and **gospel**; also **bluegrass, blues, choral, church/religious, easy listening, folk, jazz, MOR, progressive, rock, soul** and **top 40/pop**. Published *I've Got Love In My Genes* (by Richardson, Earley and Cozine), recorded by Sammy Long; *The Rodney King Ordeal* (by E. Cornell), recorded by Phil Coley; and *Don't You Buy No Ugly Truck* (by Rocky Johnson), recorded by Ron Earley, all on Woodrich Records.

Tips: "Use a studio demo if possible. If not, be sure the lyrics are extremely clear. Be sure to include a SASE with *sufficient* return postage."

WORD MUSIC, Division of Word, Inc., Dept. SM, Suite 1000, 5221 N.O'Connor Blvd., Irving TX 75039. (214)556-1900. Creative Director: Debbie Atkins, Word Records: Suite 200, 3319 West End Ave., Nashville TN 37203. (615)385-9673. Music publisher and record company. ASCAP. Member GMA. Publishes 200 songs/year; publishes 1-2 new songwriters/year. Teams collaborators. Pays standard royalty.
Affiliate(s): Rodeheaver (ASCAP), Dayspring (BMI), The Norman Clayton Publishing Co. (SESAC), Word Music (ASCAP), and 1st Monday (ASCAP).
How to Contact: Write or call first to get permission to submit a tape. Prefers cassette (or VHS videocassette) with 1-3 songs and lead sheet. SASE. "Please send a demonstration tape of a choir singing your anthem to Ken Barker, Print Director." Reports in 10 weeks.
Music: Mostly **contemporary Christian, Southern gospel, Black gospel, inspiration.** Published "Make His Praise Glorious," recorded by Sandi Patti on Word Records (inspirational) and "Watercoloured Ponies," written and recorded by Wayne Watson on Dayspring Records.
Tips: "Lead sheets, or final form—anything submitted—should be legible and understandable. The care that a writer extends in the works he submits reflects the work he'll submit if a working relationship is started. First impressions are important."

WORLD FAMOUS MUSIC CO., Dept. SM, 1830 Spruce Ave., Highland Park IL 60035. (708)831-4162. President: Chip Altholz. Music publisher, record producer. ASCAP. Estab. 1986. Publishes 25 songs/year; 3-4 new songwriters/year. Works with composers and lyricists. Pays standard royalty.
How to Contact: Submit a demo tape—unsolicited submissions are OK. Prefers cassette with 3 songs and lyric sheet. SASE. Reports in 1 month.
Music: Mostly **pop, R&B** and **rock.** Published "Jungleman," "Automatic" and "All the Stars" (by N. Bak) recorded by Ten-28 on Pink Street Records (pop/dance).
Tips: "Have a great melody, a lyric that is visual and tells a story and a commercial arrangement."

*XMAS MUSIC (ASCAP), P.O. Box 5149, Sherman Oaks CA 91413. (818)995-6230. President: Randall Paul. Music publisher. Works with composers and lyricists. Pays standard royalty.
Affiliate: Xmas Songs (BMI).
How to Contact: Submit demo tape by mail. Unsolicited submissions are OK. Prefers cassette with 2 songs and lyric sheet. SASE.
Music: **Seasonal songs** only.

YORGO MUSIC, 615 Valley Rd., Upper Montclair NJ 07043. (201)746-2359. President: George Louvis. Music publisher. BMI. Estab. 1987. Publishes 5-10 songs/year; publishes 3-5 new songwriters/year. Works with composers and lyricists; teams collaborators. Pays standard royalty.
How to Contact: Submit demo tape—unsolicited submissions OK. Prefers cassette with 1-3 songs and lyric or lead sheets. "Specify if you are a writer/artist or just a writer." Does not return unsolicited material. Reports in 1-3 months.
Music: Mostly **R&B, dance** and **pop;** also **ballads** and **pop metal.** Published "To the Maximum" (by S. Stone, S. McGhee, G. Louvis), recorded by Steve D the Destroyer on Q-Rap Records (rap); "Love Me True" (by G. Louvis), recorded by Kimiesha Holmes on Quark Records (dance).
Tips: "We also own two production companies and have access to quite a few artists and labels. Be honest about your material; if you wouldn't buy it, don't send it. We are looking for songs and artists."

*YOUNG BOB PUBLISHING CO., 410 Harvard Rd. N., Babylon NY 11703. (516)669-1872. President: Steve Young. Music publisher. ASCAP. Estab. 1988. Publishes 20 songs/year; publishes 2-3 new songwriters/year. Hires staff writers. Works with composers; teams collaborators. Pays standard royalty.
How to Contact: Write first and obtain permission to submit. Prefers cassette, 15 ips reel-to-reel or ¾-VHS videocassette with 4 songs and lyric or lead sheets. Does not return unsolicited material. Reports in 4 weeks.
Music: Mostly **dance, R&B** and **rock-pop.** Published "I Burn" (by Jones), recorded by M. Jones on Profile (dance); "Lust 4 U" (by Jones/London), on MCA Records; and "Time is Right" (by Padova), recorded by Sassa on Profile (dance).

YOUNG GRAHAM MUSIC (BMI), 19 Music Square W., Nashville TN 27203. (615)255-5740. Vice President: Valerie Graham. Music publisher, record company (Bear Records) and record producer (Bear Records). BMI. Estab. 1989. Publishes 10 songs/year; publishes 4-5 new songwriters/year. Works with composers and lyricists; teams collaborators. Pays standard royalty.

How to Contact: Submit a demo tape—unsolicited submissions are OK. Prefers cassette with 3 songs and lyric sheet. SASE. Reports in 2 weeks.
Music: Mostly **country** and **traditional**. "Red Neck" (by Sanger Shafer), recorded by J. Wright; "Eyes As Big As Dallas" (by Gary McCray), recorded by Autumn Day; and "Girls Like Her" (by Wimberly-Hart), recorded by J. Wright; on Bear Records (all country).

*YOUR BEST SONGS PUBLISHING, P.O. Box 2893, Ventura CA 93002. (805)641-3105. Fax: (800)247-1088. General Manager: Craig Markovich. Music publisher. Estab. 1988. Publishes 10-30 songs/year. Publishes 1-4 new songwriters/year. Works with composers and lyricists. Query for royalty terms.
How to Contact: Submit demo tape by mail. Unsolicited submissions are OK. Prefers cassette with 1-3 songs and lyric sheet. "Submit your 1-3 best songs per type of music. Use separate cassettes per music type and indicate music type on each cassette." SASE. Reports in 1-2 months.
Music: Mostly **alternative, rock/blues, pop/rock**; also **progressive, adult contemporary**, some **heavy metal**. Published "Only Love Remains" (by J.P. Jones), "Circus of Love" (by J.C. Mark) and "Whilpool of Space" (by Z. Qull), recorded by J.C. Mark on Cybervoc, Inc.
Tips: "Not necessary to have a full blown production; just require good lyrics, good melodies and good rhythm in a song."

ZATCO MUSIC, (formerly Greenaway), 38 Evelyn St., Boston MA 02126. (617)296-3327. Artist Relations: Janice Tritto. Music publisher. ASCAP, BMI. Estab. 1985. Publishes 5-7 songs/year; 3-4 new songwriters/year. Works with composers and lyricists; teams collaborators. Pays standard royalty.
Affiliate(s): Stargard Publishing (BMI).
How to Contact: Submit a demo tape by mail—unsolicited submissions are O.K. Prefers cassette or VHS videocassette with 5 or less songs and lyric or lead sheets. SASE. Reports in 6 weeks.
Music: Mostly **R&B, dance** and **pop**; also **rap** and **reggae**. Published "Don't Ring My Phone" and "Sexy" (by Floyd Wilcox), recorded by Unquik Approach; and "What I Did For Love" (by Addison Martin), recorded by Mixed Emotions, all on Stargard Records.

*ZAUBER MUSIC PUBLISHING, P.O. Box 5087, V.M.8.O., Vancouver, British Columbia V6B 4A9 Canada. (604)528-9194. Professional Manager: Martin E. Hamann. Music publisher and record producer. Estab. 1981. Publishes 3-5 songs/year; publishes 1-2 new songwriters/year. Hires staff writers. Works with composers and lyricists; teams collaborators. Pays minimum 50% to writer.
Affiliate(s): Merlin Productions and Zauberer Music (SOCAN).
How to Contact: Submit demo tape by mail. Unsolicited submissions are OK. Prefers cassette with lyric or lead sheet. SASE. Reports in 2-3 weeks.
Music: Mostly **dance, pop/R&B** and **rock**; also **techno** and **Euro-pop**. Published "Stranded" (by Airey/MacRuder), recorded by D-Tango on Phonogram Records; "Dancing" (by B. Moulan), recorded by Brian Cairn on Merlin Records; and "All The Right Moves", written and recorded by Wolfgang/Wolfgang on Merlin Records.
Tips: "Send 3 songs only, the most commercial first. Hire the best singer available. Uptempo songs work best."

Geographic Index
Music Publishers

The U.S. section of this handy geographic index will quickly give you the names of music publishers located in or near the music centers of Los Angeles, New York and Nashville. Of course, there are many valuable contacts to be made in other cities, but you will probably want to plan a trip to one of these established music centers at some point in your career and try to visit as many of these companies as you think appropriate. The International section lists, geographically, markets for your songs in countries other than the U.S.

Find the names of companies in this index, and then check listings within the Music Publishers section for addresses, phone numbers and submission details.

Los Angeles
Alexis
Audio Music Publishers
AVC Music
Bronx Flash Music, Inc.
Bug Music, Inc.
Cling Music Publishing
Direct Management Group
D'Nico International
Doré Records
Dupuy Records/Productions/Publishing, Inc.
Famous Music Publishing Companies
First Release Music Publishing
The Fricon Entertainment Co., Inc.
International Music Network
Jedo Inc.
Jungle Boy Music
Kingsport Creek Music Publishing
Lansdowne and Winston Music Publishers
Le Grande Fromage/Cheddar Cheese Music
Loveforce International
Lucrecia Music
Miracle Mile Music/Black Satin
O'Lyric Music
Operation Perfection
Peermusic

Philippopolis Music
Pollybyrd Publications Limited
Queen Esther Music Publishing
Rhythms Productions
Rondor International Music Publishing
Shankman De Blasio Melina, Inc.
Shaolin Music
Song Wizard Music
Supreme Enterprises Int'l Corp.
Sweet Glenn Music
Transition Music Corp.
Twin Towers Publishing Co.
Vaam Music Group
Shane Wilder Music
Windswept Pacific Entertainment
Winston & Hoffman House Music Publishers

Nashville
Abingdon Press
Aim High Music Company
Al Jolson Black & White Music
Allisongs Inc.
Angelsong Publishing Co.
Baby Huey Music
Best Buddies, Inc.
Brentwood Music, Inc.
Buried Treasure Music

Calinoh Music Group
Calvary Music Group, Inc.
Castle Music Corp.
Cedar Creek Music
Clientele Music
Continental Communications Corp.
Cosgroove Music Inc.
The Cornelius Companies
Cottage Blue Music
Loman Craig Music
Cumberland Music Group, Inc.
Cupit Music
Denny Music Group
Entertainment Services Music Group
Fat City Publishing
First Million Music, Inc.
Fox Farm Recording
Frog and Moose Music
Heavy Jamin' Music
Humanform Publishing Company
Iron Skillet Music
Jaclyn Music
Gene Kennedy Enterprises
Lion Hill Music Publishing Co.
The Marco Music Group Inc.
The Mathes Company
Nashville Music Group
Nautical Music Co.
Newcreature Music

Justin Peters Music
Silver Thunder Music
  Group
Sizemore Music
Song Cellar
Song Farm Music
Sound Achievement Group
Watchesgro Music
Wil-Too/Wil-So Music
Young Graham Music

New York
A Street Music
Amicos II Music, Ltd.
Apon Publishing Co.
Baby Raquel Music
Camex Music
D.S.M. Producers Inc.
Emzee Music
Eudaemonic Music
G Fine Sounds
Alan Gary Music
Globeart Publishing
S.M. Gold Music
Hit & Run Music Publish-
  ing Inc.
Humongous Music Publish-
  ing, Inc.
Jasper Stone Music/JSM
  SongsKozkeeozko Music
Latin American Music Co.,
  Inc.
Lin's Lines
Majestic Control Music
Manapro (Management
  Artist Productions)
Mega-Star Music
Music Sales Corporation
Chuck Mymit Music Pro-
  ductions
No Mas Music
PPI/Peter Pan Industries
Prescription Company
Quark, Inc.
Ren Maur Music Corp.
Rockford Music Co.
Steve Rose Music
Sha-La Music, Inc.
Siskatune Music Publishing
  Co.
Sunsongs Music/Hollywood
  East Entertainment
Tender Tender Music
This Beats Workin' Music
  Inc.

Warner/Chappell Music,
  Inc.

International

Australia
Two/Polygram Music Pub-
  lishing

Austria
Edition Musica
Johann Hartel Musikverlag

Belgium
B. Sharp Music
Jump Music

Canada
Alleged Iguana Music
Alternative Direction Mu-
  sic Publishers
August Night Music
Berandol Music Ltd.
Century City Music Publish-
  ing
China Groove
Clotille Publishing
Cod Oil Productions Lim-
  ited
Hickory Lane Publishing
  and Recording
Montina Music
Nashville Sound Music Pub-
  lishing Co.
Sci-Fi Music
William Seip Music Incor-
  porated
West Broadway Music
Zauber Music Publishing

France
Societe d'Editions Musi-
  cales et Artistiques "Esperance"

Germany
R.D. Clevere Musikverlag
CSB Kaminsky GmbH
Hammer Musik GmbH
Heupferd Musik Verlag
  GmbH
Ja/Nein Musikverlag GmbH
Siegel Music Companies
Sinus Musik Production,
  Ulli Weigel
UBM

Berthold Wengert (Musikv-
  erlag)

Holland
All Rock Music
Associated Artists Music
  International
Hong Kong
Discovering Music Ltd.

Italy
Dingo Music

Malaysia
Pustaka Muzik EMI (Ma-
  laysia) SDN. BHD.

Mexico
Galaxia Musical S.A. De
  C.V.

New Zealand
Pegasus Music

South Africa
Charis Music

Switzerland
Nadine Music
OBH Musikverlag Otto B.
  Hartmann

United Kingdom
Bearsongs
Blenheim Music
Catharine Courage Music
  Ltd.
Creole Music Ltd.
Demi Monde Records &
  Publishing Ltd.
Ever-Open-Eye Music
F&J Music
First Time Music (Publish-
  ing) U.K. Ltd.
Graduate Music Ltd.
Holyrood Productions
Jammy Music Publishers
Keep Calm Music Limited
Nervous Publishing
R.J. Music
R.T.L. Music
Single Minded Music
Sphemusations
TKO Music, Inc.

Music Publishers/'93-'94 Changes

The following markets appeared in the 1993 edition of *Songwriter's Market* but are absent from the 1994 edition. Most of these companies failed to respond to our request for an update of their listing for a variety of reasons. For example, they may have gone out of business or they may have requested deletion from the 1994 edition because they are backlogged with material. If we know the specific reason, it appears within parentheses.

Aeroscore Music Co.
Akrana Music (requested deletion)
Bekool Music (not accepting submissions)
M. Bernstein Publishing Co. (charges to review)
Big City Music, Inc. (unable to contact)
Blade to the Rhythm Music
Blue Umbrella Music Publishing Co./Parasol Music Publishing Co. (requested deletion)
BMG Ariola Belgium N.V. Publishing
BMG Music Publishing, Inc. (not accepting submissions)
Bob-A-Lew Music (not accepting submissions)
Johnny Bond Publications
Boogietunes Musikproduktion GmbH
Branch Group Music
Cactus Music and Gidget Publishing
Canvirg Music
Capitol Star Artist Ents., Inc.
Center for the Queen of Peace (affiliate of Cosmotone Music)
Centerfield Productions (unable to contact)
Chip 'N' Dale Music Publishers, Inc. (affiliate of Gene Kennedy Enterprises, Inc.)
Chris Music Publishing (requested deletion)
Chrysalis Music Group
Cowabonga Music, Inc. (affiliate of Lovey Music, Inc.)
Cowboy Junction Flea Market and Publishing Co. (not accepting submissions)
Jeff Dayton Music (not accepting submissions)
Don't Call Me (D.C.M.) Music
Door Knob Music Publishing, Inc. (affiliate of Gene Kennedy Enterprises, Inc.)
Drezdon Blaque Music
Educational Circus Company
Fairwood Music Limited
Fradale Songs (backlog of submissions)
Freko Records
Fretboard Publishing
Fulltilt Music (unable to contact)

Gallo Music Publishers
GFI West Music Publishing
Gil-Gad Music (no longer in business)
GMG Music
Gold Sound Music Inc. (charges to review)
Gotown Publishing (requested deletion)
Green Dolphin Music (requested deletion)
Mitch Greene Music
Guerrilla Music
Mark Hannah Music Group (requested deletion)
Happy Day Music Co. (requested deletion)
Hello Tomorrow Music Group
High Pockets Publishing (charges to review)
How the West Was Sung
Hybner Music
I.B.D. Concepts Inc.
In the Studio Publishing (not accepting submissions)
Intermedia Musik Service GmbH
It's Really Rob Music
Janell Music
Jaylo-Bellsar Music Co.
Joe Keene Music Co. (requested deletion)
Keeny-York Publishing
Butch Kelly Productions and Publishing (charges to review)
Keristene Music, Ltd.
Ralph Krueger Musikverlag
L Train Publishers (unable to contact)
The Langford Cove Music Group (no longer in business)
Lantana
Larrikin Music
Laymond Publishing Co., Inc.
Lemon Square Music
Leo-Vincent Music/Omni-Praise Music
Lexington Alabama Music Publishing Co.
Light Force Music
Linwood Maxwell Music (affiliate of Wazuri Music)
Live Note Publishing (BMI)
Lodestar Music (affiliate of Gene Kennedy Enterprises, Inc.)
Looking Good Music

Lynclay Publications Inc.
Mac-Attack Publishing
Magnemar
Major Bob/Rio Bravo Music (requested deletion)
Makin Tracks Music
Marullo Music Publishers
Microstar Music
Mighty Twinns Music
Mimic Music
Mini Max Publishing
Miramare Music UK Ltd.
Mofo Music (affiliate of Amalgamated Tulip Corp.)
Doug Moody Music
The Fred Morris Music Group
Mountain Heritage Music Co.
MSM Musikverlag Wien
Music City Music (Australia)
Neon Notes (requested deletion)
Nettwork Productions
Nise Productions Inc.
Now & Then Music
NRP Music Group
Old Empress Music/Doghouse Productions
One Hundred Grand Music
Osprey Entertainment Group Inc.
Pady Music Publishing Co.
R.A. Painter Music Publishing (charges to review)
Park J. Tunes
Passing Parade Music
Penny Thoughts Music
Pin Publishing (charges to review)
Pine Island Music
Platinum Boulevard Publishing
Pratt and McClain Music (ASCAP)
Prince/SF Publications (no longer publishing)
Puddletown Music Publishing (does not use outside songwriters)
QMark Music
Ragland Publications
Record Company of the South (RCS) & Vetter Music Pub. (requested deletion)
Red Bus Music International, Ltd.
Jack Redick Music
G. Ricordi & C. Spa
RLB Music Publishing
Rockland Music
Rustron Music Publishers

Sawmills Music
Schmerdley Music (temporarily
out of business)
Scotti Brothers Music Publish-
ing
Sea Dream Music
Seychelles Music
Siebenpunkt Verlags GmbH
Silver Chord Music
Soprano Music Co.
Sotex Music
Sound Image Publishing
Sound Spectra Music
Speedster Music
Star Song Communications
Stonebess Music Co.
Stonehand Publishing
Strawberry Soda Publishing
(charges to review)

Street Singer Music
Stylecraft Music Co.
Sugarbakers Music
Sultry Lady Music
Sunflare Songs/Records
Sweet Inspiration Music (affili-
ate of California Country
Music)
Sweet Tooth Music Pub. Co.
Synchro Sound Music AB
Tabitha Music, Ltd.
Tanger-Music Publishing Co.,
Inc.
Thema-Verlag
Time Minstrel Music
Tooter Scooter Music (BMI)
Topomic Music
Treasure Trove Music

Tri-She Kieta Publishers, Inc.
TWL Publishing Group
Udder Publishing/Golden Gelt
Publishing
United Entertainment Music
Utter Nonsense Publishers (re-
quested deletion)
Valentine Musikverlag
Vin-Joy Music
Virgin Boy Publishing
Warner/Chappell Musikverlag
Gesellschaft m.b.H.
Wayne and Lacey
Whimsong Publishing ASCAP
White Cat Music
Wild Angel
Maurice Wilson's Music Co.
(charges to review)

Music Print Publishers

The music print publisher's function is much more specific than that of the music publisher. Music publishers try to exploit a song in many different ways: on records, videos, movies and radio/TV commercials, to name a few. But, as the name implies, music print publishers deal in only one publishing medium: print.

Although the role of the music print publisher has virtually stayed the same over the years, demand for sheet music has declined substantially. Today there are only a few major sheet music publishers in operation, along with many minor ones.

Most songs and compositions fall into one of two general categories: popular or educational music. Popular songs are pop, rock, adult contemporary, country and other hits heard on the radio. They are printed as sheet music (for single songs) and folios (collections of songs). Educational material includes pieces for chorus, band, orchestra, instrumental solos and instructional books. In addition to publishing original compositions, print publishers will sometimes print arrangements of popular songs.

Most major publishers of pop music won't print sheet music for a song until a popular recording of the song has become a hit single, or at least is on the *Billboard* Hot 100 chart. Most of the companies listed here indicate the lowest chart position of a song they've published, to give you a better idea of the market.

Chart action is obviously not a factor for original educational material. What the print publishers look for is quality work that fits into their publishing program and is appropriate for the people who use their music, such as school and church choirs, school bands or orchestras.

When dealing with music print publishers, it is generally unacceptable to send out simultaneous submissions; that is, sending identical material to different publishers at the same time. Since most of the submissions they receive involve written music, whether single lead sheets or entire orchestrations, the time they invest in evaluating each submission is considerable — much greater than the few minutes it takes to listen to a tape. It would be discourteous and unprofessional to ask a music print publisher to invest a lot of time in evaluating your work and then possibly pull the deal out from under him before he has given you an answer.

Writers' royalties range from 10-15% of the retail selling price of music in print. For educational material that would be a percentage of the price of the whole set (score and parts). For a book of songs (called a folio), the 10-15% royalty would be pro-rated by the number of songs by that writer in the book. Royalties for sheet music are paid on a flat rate per sheet, which is usually about one-fifth of the retail price. If a music publisher licenses print publishing to a music print publisher, print royalties are usually split evenly between the music publisher and songwriter, but it may vary. You should read any publishing contract carefully to see how print deals fit in, and consult your attorney if you have any questions.

BOSTON MUSIC CO. (ASCAP), 172 Tremont St., Boston MA 02111. (617)426-5100. Contact: Editorial Department. Prints 100 pieces/year, both individual pieces and music books. Pays 10% royalty.
How to Contact: Write or call first and obtain permission to submit. SASE. Reports in 5 months.
Music: Choral pieces, educational material, instrumental solo pieces, method books and **"piano instructional materials that piano teachers would be interested in."** Published "Gavotte and Musette" (by Frederick Werlé) (piano solo); "Concord Hymn" (by Linda Grom) (choral piece); and "Chuckles" (by Rémi Bouchard) (piano collection).
Tips: "We are *not* interested in today's 'pop' music or in vocal music. We are essentially an educational publishing house specializing in keyboard teaching material."

BOURNE COMPANY, 5 W. 37th St., New York NY 10018. (212)391-4300. Contact: Editorial Department. Estab. 1917. Publishes education material and popular music.
Affiliate(s): ABC Music, Ben Bloom, Better Half, Bogat, Burke & Van Heusen, Goldmine, Harborn, Lady Mac, Murbo Music.
How to Contact: Write first and obtain permission to submit. Write first to arrange personal interview. Does not return unsolicited material. Reports in 3-6 months.
Music: Band pieces, choral pieces and **handbell pieces.** Published "You Can Count on Me" (by S. Cahn/N. Monath) (2 part choral); "Unforgettable" (by Gordon) recorded by Natalie Cole on Elektra Records (vocal duet);and "The Songs of Charlie Chaplin."

DAVIKE MUSIC CO., Dept. SM, P.O. Box 8842, Los Angeles CA 90008. (310)318-5289. Owner: Isaiah Jones, Jr. Estab. 1965. Prints 4 songs/year, mostly individual songs. Publishes 3 new songwriters/year. Pays 50% royalty. Works with composers and lyricists; teams collaborators.
How to Contact: Submit demo tape—unsolicited submissions are OK. Prefers cassette and lead and lyric sheets or complete score. SASE. Reports in 2 months.
Music: Mostly **gospel, pop, R&B** and **inspirational;** also **folk** and **country.** Published "The Miracle God" by I. Jones and G. Cowart (contemporary gospel) and "God Never Fails" (by Isaiah Jones and J. Hailey), recorded by Inez Andrews on Word Records (gospel).

EMANDELL TUNES, 10220 Glade Ave., Chatsworth CA 91311. (818)341-2264. SESAC affiliate. Administrator: Leroy C. Lovett Jr. Prints 15-20 songs/year, both individual songs and folios. Lowest chart position held by song published in sheet form is 36. Pays statutory royalty or 15¢/song to songwriter for each sheet sold or parts thereof for folios.
Affiliate(s): Birthright Music (ASCAP), Northworth Songs (SESAC), Ben-Lee Music (BMI) and Adarom Music (ASCAP), Chinwah Songs (SESAC), and Gertrude Music (SESAC).
How to Contact: Write and obtain permission to submit. Prefers cassette (or videocassette showing performance—will return) and lyric and lead sheets. SASE. Reports in 4-6 weeks.
Music: Inspirational, contemporary gospels, and **chorals.** Published "Surely Goodness and Mercy" (by Kevin Allen & Peppy Smith), on WFL Records; "Blessed Assurance" (new adapt/arr. by Alisa Canton), on K-Tel Records; and "Everlasting Love" (by Phil Stewart), recorded by Mississippi Mass Choir on Savoy Records.
Tips: "Always submit top quality sounding demo. Keep it simple."

*MARK FOSTER MUSIC COMPANY, Box 4012, Champaign IL 61824-4012. (217)398-2760. Fax: (217)398-2791. President: Jane C. Menkhaus. Music print publisher, music publisher and retail music division. Estab. 1962. Publishes 20-30 pieces/year; mostly choral music and books. Publishes 3-4 new songwriters/year. Pays 5-10% over first 3,000 copies sold.

Affiliate(s): Fostco (ASCAP) and Marko (BMI).
How to Contact: Submit demo tape by mail. Unsolicited submissions are OK. Prefers cassette with 1 song and choral manuscript. If new composer/arranger, submit bio. Does not return material.
Music: Mostly **sacred SATB, secular SATB** and **sacred and secular treble and male choir music;** also **conducting books** and **Kodaly materials.** Published "Before Your Throne" (by Bradley Ellingboe); "City on the Hill" (by Marvin V. Curtis); and "Jubilant Song" (by René Clausen).
Tips: "Must be well-constructed piece to begin with, manuscript should be in decent format, preferably with keyboard reduction."

GENEVOX MUSIC GROUP, 127 9th Ave. N., Nashville TN 37234. (615)251-3770. SESAC, ASCAP and BMI affiliate. Estab. 1986. Music Production Manager: Mark Blankenship. Prints 75-100 songs/year; publishes 10 new songwriters/year. Pays 10% royalty.
How to Contact: Submit demo tape and choral arrangement, lead sheet or complete score. Unsolicited submissions are OK. Prefers cassette with 1-5 songs. SASE. Reports in 2 months.
Music: Choral, orchestral, instrumental solo and **instrumental ensemble pieces.** "We publish all forms of **sacred music** including solo/choral for all ages, and instrumental for handbell, organ, piano and orchestra." Published "Worthy of Worship" by Terry York and Mark Blankenship, arranged by Tom Fettke; "Piano For All Times" by Mark Hayes; "And the Show Goes On" by Dennis and Nan Allen; "Mastering Musicianship in Handbells" by Donald E. Allured.
Tips: "Most of what we publish is designed for use by church choirs and instrumentalists. Middle-of-the-road, traditional anthems or hymn arrangements in an SATB/keyboard choral format stand the best chance for serious consideration."

HAMMER MUSIK GMBH, Christophstr. 38, 7000 Stuttgart 1, **Germany.** Phone: (0711)648-7620-7. Fax: (0711)648-7625. Contact: Ingo Kleinhammer. Prints mostly individual songs. Interested in receiving band pieces, choral pieces and orchestral pieces. Pays 10% royalty/song to songwriter for each sheet sold. Publishes 100 original songs/year.
How to Contact: Prefers cassette. SAE and IRC. Reports in 2 weeks.
Music: Mostly **dance, disco** and **pop;** also **rock** and **jazz.** Published "Hit You" (by Volker Barber), "Stop The World" (by Jerome Des Arts and Deborah Sasson), and "I'll Be Forever Your Man" (by Jerome Des Arts and Maria Monrose), all recorded by Oh Well, all dance music.

HINSHAW MUSIC, INC., Box 470, Chapel Hill NC 27514-0470. (919)933-1691. ASCAP affiliate. Editor: Don Hinshaw. Estab. 1975. Prints 100 pieces/year, both individual pieces and music books. Publishes educational material. Pays 10% royalty.
Affiliate(s): Hindon Publications (BMI) and Chapel Hill Music (SESAC).
How to Contact: "Send the complete score. Lyric sheets and/or tapes alone are not acceptable. We do not review lyrics alone. Cassette tapes may be sent in addition to the written ms. Send clear, legible photocopies, *not* the original. Submit only 2 or 3 mss at a time that are representative of your work. An arrangement of a copyrighted work will not be considered unless copy of written permission from copyright owner(s) is attached. Accepts unsolicited submissions. Once an ms has been submitted, do not telephone or write for a 'progress report.' Be patient." Returns unsolicited material with SASE. Reports in 3 months.
Music: Choral pieces, organ and **instrumental music.** Published "Music to Hear" (by G. Shearing); and *Magnificat* (by J. Rutter), recorded by Collegium.
Tips: "Submit your ms to only one publisher at a time. It requires considerable time and expense for us to thoroughly review a work, so we want the assurance that if accepted, the ms is available for publication. We are unable to 'critique' rejected works. A pamphlet, 'Submitting Music for Publication' is available with SASE."

IVORY PALACES MUSIC, 3141 Spottswood Ave., Memphis TN 38111. (901)323-3509. Estab. 1978. President: Jack Abell. Publishes educational material. Prints 5 songs/year, mostly book/tape combinations. Pays 10% retail price or 50% license income.
How to Contact: Write first and obtain permission to submit. Prefers cassette and lyric sheet. Does not return material. Reports in 6-8 months.
Music: Orchestral pieces, instrumental solo pieces, instrumental ensemble pieces, methods books and **religious songs.** Published "Sonatina Concertata" (by Joe McSpadden), recorded by Linda Jackson and Strings by Archive (classical); "Chamber Music Primer" (by Taylor), recorded by Abell/Jackson/

The asterisk before a listing indicates that the listing is new in this edition. New markets are often the most receptive to unsolicited submissions.

Long (classical); and "Sonatina Concertata 2" (by McSpadden), recorded by Jackson (classical).
Tips: "There should be a demand for the music to be published through established performances."

JUMP MUSIC, Langemunt 71, 9420 Aaigem, **Belgium**. Phone: (053)62-73-77. Estab. 1976. General Manager: Eddy Van Mouffaert. Publishes educational material and popular music. Prints 150 songs/year, mostly individual songs. Pays 5% royalty.
How to Contact: Prefers cassette and lead sheet or complete score. Does not return unsolicited material. Reports in 2 weeks.
Music: Pop, ballads, band pieces and **instrumentals**. Published "Wien Bleibt Wien" (by Eddy Govert), recorded by Le Grand Julot (accordion); and "Leven Als Een Cowboy" (by Eddy Govert), recorded by Evelien.

LILLENAS PUBLISHING CO., Dept. SM, P.O. Box 419527, Kansas City MO 64141. (816)931-1900. Fax: (816)753-4071. Contact: Music Editor. Music print publisher. ASCAP, BMI, SESAC. Estab. 1930. Publishes 30-40 songs/year; publishes 3-5 new songwriters/year. Works with composers and lyricists; teams collaborators. Pays standard royalty.
Affiliate(s): Pilot Point Music (ASCAP), PsalmSinger Music (BMI) and Lillenas Publishing Co. (SESAC).
How to Contact: Submit demo tape and/or sheet music—unsolicited submissions are OK. Prefers cassette with 1-3 songs and lead sheet. Does not return unsolicited submissions. Reports in 2-3 months.
Music: Mostly **contemporary Christian, traditional gospel** and **sacred anthems**; also **patriotic** and **sacred instrumental**. Published "We Shall All Be Changed" (by Tom Fettke); "He is the Amen" (by David Ritter); and "It's Alright Now" (by Mosie Lister) (all choral).
Tips: "We're looking for music that fits the needs of the evangelical church market. Choral music is our forte, but artist-oriented songs are acceptable."

HAROLD LUICK & ASSOCIATES, Box B, Carlisle IA 50047. (515)989-3748 and 989-3676. BMI affiliate. President: Harold Luick. Prints 4-5 songs/year, mostly individual songs. Lowest chart position held by a song published in sheet form is 98. Pays 4% royalty.
How to Contact: Write and obtain permission to submit or submit through publisher or attorney. Prefers cassette or reel-to-reel and lyric sheet. SASE. Reports in 3 weeks.
Music: Mostly **traditional country;** also **novelty songs**. Published "Mrs. Used To Be," written and recorded by Joe Harris on River City Records (country).
Tips: "Send us song material that is conducive to type of market today. Good commercial songs."

*PLYMOUTH MUSIC CO., INC., 170 NE 33rd St., Ft. Lauderdale FL 33334. (305)563-1844. General Manager: Bernard Fisher. Music publisher. Estab. 1953. Prints 50 pieces/year: individual pieces, individual songs, music books and folios. Pays 10% of retail selling price.
Affiliate(s): Aberdeen Music, (ASCAP), Galleria Press (ASCAP), Walton Music (ASCAP), and Music for Percussion (BMI).
How to Contact: Write first and obtain permission to submit. Prefers cassette and lead sheet or complete score. SASE. Reports in 6-8 weeks.
Music: Choral pieces and **percussion music.**
Tips: "Send choral music for church and school with cassette tape if available. Manuscripts should be legible."

THEODORE PRESSER CO., Dept. SM, One Presser Place, Bryn Mawr PA 19010. (215)525-3636. Fax: (215)527-7841. ASCAP, BMI and SESAC affiliate. Contact: Editorial Committee. Member MPA. Publishes 90 works/year. Works with composers. Pays varying royalty.
Affiliate(s): Merion Music (BMI); Elkan Vogel, Inc. (ASCAP); and Mercury Music Corp. (SESAC).
How to Contact: Unsolicited submissions are OK. Prefers cassette with 1-2 works and score. "Include return label and postage." Reports in 2 weeks.
Music: Serious, educational and **choral music.** "We primarily publish serious music by emerging and established composers, and vocal/choral music which is likely to be accepted in the church and educational markets, as well as gospel chorals of high musical quality. We are *not* primarily a publisher of song sheets or pop songs."

R.T.F.M., % Stewart House, Hillbottom Rd., Highwycombe, Buckinghamshire HP124HJ **United Kingdom**. Phone: (0630)647374. Fax: (0630)647612. A&R: Ron Lee. Publishes educational material and popular music. Prints 40 songs/year, mostly individual songs. Lowest chart position held by a song published in sheet form is 140. Pays 50% royalty.
Affiliate(s): Lee Music Ltd., Pogo Records Ltd. and R.T.L. Music.
How to Contact: Submit demo tape—unsolicited submissions are OK. Prefers cassette or 7½ or 15 ips reel-to-reel and lyric and lead sheets or complete score. Include photo and bio. SAE and IRC. Reports in 6 weeks.

Music: All types: **band, orchestral, instrumental solo** and **instrumental ensemble** pieces; also **radio, TV** and **film music** (specializes in jingles/background music). Published "Judy's Not Judy in the Bath," "Phobias" and "Time Bombs" (by Phil Dunn), recorded by Orphan, all on Swoop Records.

E.C. SCHIRMER ● BOSTON, Dept. SM, 138 Ipswich St., Boston MA 02215. (617)236-1935. President: Robert Schuneman. Prints 200 pieces/year, mostly individual pieces and music books. Pays 10% royalty on sales and 50% on performance/license.
Affiliate(s): Galaxy Music Corporation (ASCAP), E.C. Schirmer Music Co. Inc. (ASCAP), Ione Press, Inc. (BMI), Highgate Press (BMI).
How to Contact: Query with complete score and tape of piece. Prefers cassette. "Submit a clean, readable score." SASE. Reports in 6-8 months.
Music: Choral pieces, orchestral pieces, instrumental solo pieces, instrumental ensemble pieces, methods books, books on music, keyboard pieces.

SHELLEY MUSIC, 177 Balmoral Dr., Bolingbrook IL 60440. President: Guy Shelley. Music publisher. Guy Smilo Music (BMI). Estab. 1992. Publishes 20-50 songs/year; publishes 4 new songwriters/year. Works with composers and lyricists. Pays 10% standard sheet music royalty.
How to Contact: Write first and obtain permission to submit. Prefers cassette with 1-3 songs and lyric sheet. SASE. Reports in 6 months. "No phone calls!"
Music: Mostly **classical (educational).** Published "Progress," "Summer Afternoon" and "Time Shifter," all piano pieces written by Donna Shelley.
Tips: "Have a finished score and a clean demo. Only submit your best material."

WILLIAM GRANT STILL MUSIC, Suite 422, 4 S. San Francisco St., Flagstaff AZ 86001-5737. (602)526-9355. ASCAP affiliate. Estab. 1983. Manager: Judith Anne Still. Publishes educational material and classical and popular music. Prints 2-3 arrangements/year; 2-3 new arrangers/year. Works with arrangers only. Pays 10% royalty for arrangements sold. "We publish arrangements of works by William Grant Still. This year we are especially interested in developing a catalog of clarinet arrangements, though other sorts of arrangements may be considered."
How to Contact: Query. Does not return unsolicited material. Reports in 1 month.
Music: Mostly **instrumental solo pieces.** Published "Mother and Child" by Timothy Holley (classical); "Memphis Man" by Bert Coleman, for organ (popular); and "Coquette," by Anthony Griggs (classical).
Tips: "We suggest that the prospective arranger familiarize himself with the music of William Grant Still, prepare a sample arrangement and submit it after having been given permission to do so."

3 SEAS MUSIC/NORTHVALE MUSIC, 450 Livingston St., Norwood NJ 07648. (201)767-5551. Vice President: Gene Schwartz. Prints mostly individual songs. Lowest chart position held by a song published in sheet form is 20. Pays 14¢/song to songwriter for each sheet sold.
How to Contact: Unsolicited submissions are OK. Prefers cassette and lyric sheet or complete score. SASE.
Music: **Rock** and **Top 40.** Published "Stay With Me" (by James Denton) and "Take Me" (by Peter Mechtinal) recorded by Maurice Williams; "Someday Again," written and recorded by Bill Senkel, all on Laurie Records (pop).
Tips: "Write something fresh and different."

TRANSCONTINENTAL MUSIC PUBLICATIONS, Dept. SM, 838 Fifth Ave., New York NY 10021. (212)249-0100. Senior Editor: Dr. Judith B. Tischler. Music publisher. ASCAP. Estab. 1941/1977. Publishes 2 new songwriters/year. Works with composers. Pays 10% royalty. "We publish serious solo and choral music. The standard royalty is 10% except for rentals—there is no cost to the songwriter."
How to Contact: Call first and obtain permission to submit a tape. Prefers cassette. "We usually do not accept lead sheets. Most all of our music is accompanied. Full and complete arrangements should accompany the melody." SASE. Reports in 10-12 months.
Music: Only **Jewish vocal** and **Jewish choral.** Published "Numi Numi" by Stern (classical); "Biti" (by Isaacson) (Bat Mitzvah Solo) and "Shalom Aleidliean" (by Kaluraweff), recorded by Milnes on Ross Records (choral).
Tips: "Submit clean manuscript or computer typographer with accompaniment. Suitable material of sacred or secular Jewish relevance."

VIVACE PRESS, NW 310 Wawawai Rd., Pullman WA 99163. (509)334-4660. Fax: (509)334-3551. Contact: Jonathan Yordy. Publishes mostly classical pieces. Estab. 1990. Publishes 25 pieces of music/year; publishes several new composers/year. Works with composers. Pays 10% royalty for sheet music sales.

How to Contact: Submit demo tape and sheet music—unsolicited submissions OK. Prefers cassette. SASE. Reports in 1 month.
Music: Mostly **specialty historical classical, contemporary classical keyboard** and **sacred choral**; also **youth musicals.** Published *18th Century Women Composers*, by Mary Hester Park; *Quantum Quirks of a Quick Quaint Quark*, by Marga Richter; and *Sonatine d'Amour*, by Arnold Rosner.
Tips: "Know our catalog to determine our intended market. If you haven't heard any compositions we carry, don't submit."

THE WILLIS MUSIC COMPANY, 7380 Industrial Rd., Florence KY 41042. (606)283-2050. SESAC affiliate. Estab. 1899. Editor: David B. Engle. Publishes educational material. Prints 100 publications/year; "no charted songs in our catalog." Pays 5-10% of retail price or outright purchase.
How to Contact: Prefers fully notated score. SASE. Reports in 3 months.
Music: Mostly **early level piano teaching material**; also **instrumental solo pieces, methods books** and **"supplementary materials-educational material only."**

Music Print Publishers/'93-'94 Changes

The following markets appeared in the 1993 edition of *Songwriter's Market* but are absent from the 1994 edition. Most of these companies failed to respond to our request for an update of their listing or requested deletion.

A & C Black (Publishers) Ltd.
Lantana Music (unable to contact)
Phoebus Apollo Music Publishers
Sea Dream Music

Record Companies

The role of the record company is to record and release records, cassettes and CDs—the mechanical products of the music industry. They sign artists to recording contracts, decide what songs those artists will record, and finally determine which songs to release. They are also responsible for providing recording facilities, securing producers and musicians, and overseeing the manufacture, distribution and promotion of new releases.

The costs incurred by a record company, especially the major labels, are substantially larger than those of other segments of the music industry. The music publisher, for instance, considers only items such as salaries and the costs of making quality demos. Record companies, at great financial risk, pay for all those services discussed above. It's estimated that 8% of acts on the major labels are paying for the losses incurred by the remaining 92%.

This profit/loss ratio and the continuing economic crunch have caused changes in the record industry. The major labels are signing fewer new acts and are dropping unprofitable ones. This means a shrinking market among the majors for new songs for their acts. Also, the continuing fear of copyright infringement suits has closed avenues to getting new material heard by the majors. They don't listen to unsolicited submissions . . . period. Only songs recommended by attorneys, managers and producers major label employees trust and respect are being heard by A&R people, who have much of the input on what songs should be performed and recorded by a particular act.

Recommendations by key music industry people may be hard to come by, but they're not impossible. Songwriters must remember that talent alone does not guarantee success in the music business. You must be recognized through contacts, and the only way to make contacts is through networking. Networking is the process of building an interconnecting web of acquaintances within the music business. The more industry people you meet, the larger your contact base becomes, and the more your chances of meeting someone with the clout to get your demo into the hands of the right people increase. If you want to get ahead in this business, and you want to get your music heard by key A&R representatives, networking is imperative.

Networking opportunities are also available at regional and national music conferences and workshops. You should try to attend at least one or two of these events each year. It's a great way to increase the number and quality of your music industry contacts.

Because of the continuing changes and shrinking market the majors represent, the independent labels take on a new significance for your work. Since they're located all over the country, they're much easier to contact and can be important in building a local base of support for your music. Independent labels usually concentrate more on a specific type of music, which will help you target those companies your submissions should be sent to. And since the staff at an indie label is smaller, there are fewer channels to go through to get your music heard by the top personnel of the company.

Independent labels are seen by many as a stepping stone to a major recording contract. Very few artists are signed to a major label at the start of their careers; usually, they've had a few independent releases that helped build their reputation in the industry. Major labels watch the independent record labels closely to locate up-and-coming bands and new trends. But independents aren't just farming grounds for future major label acts; many bands have long-term relationships with indies, and prefer it that way. Independent labels continue to define a new role for themselves as they pick up the slack caused by the cutbacks and rising overhead of the majors. (For more information on working with indie labels, see "The Road to a Record Deal" on page 27)

Most of the following listings are independent labels. They are the most receptive to new material. Just because the companies are small doesn't mean you should forget professionalism. When submitting material to a record company, be very specific about what you are submitting and what your goals are. If you are strictly a songwriter and the label carries a band you believe would properly present your song, state that in your cover letter. If you are an artist looking for a contract, make sure you showcase your strong points as a performer in the demo package. Whatever your goals are, follow submission guidelines closely, be as neat as possible and include a top-notch demo. If you need more information concerning a company's requirements, write or call for more details.

At the end of this section, you will find a Geographic Index listing alphabetically the record companies in the major music centers—New York, Los Angeles and Nashville—in order to help you plan a future trip to one or more of these cities. There is also an alphabetical list of international listings appearing in this section.

You will want to refer to the Category Index at the back of the book. It lists companies by the type of music they're interested in hearing and will help you in researching what companies to submit to.

INSIDER REPORT

Chicago indie helps bands generate interest

"In the bands that I sign," says Mike Potential, president/head of A&R at Limited Potential Records in Chicago, "I look for two things: music that I personally enjoy, and music and an image that can be properly marketed. The main skill of an A&R person is insight. The bands I've had the most success with are the ones I've simply had a special feeling about."

Some of the bands that Potential had a 'special feeling' about include the Smashing Pumpkins, who had their first single released on Limited Potential and recently signed with Virgin Records; and the Poster Children, who signed with Sire Records after putting their first album out on Limited Potential. As the main decision maker at the small indie label, Potential is more interested in what a band has to offer rather than the type of music they play.

Mike Potential

"I'm not looking for any one type of music," he says. "My roster ranges from pop to garage rock to metal. It's the quality of the package, not the genre. I would define 'package' as musical quality, dedication, and occasionally 'looks'—but I would say that the willingness of an act to play every night, to tour, or to do whatever it takes to promote themselves, combined with the right songs, is most important."

Once Potential signs a band, he plays an active role in trying to get them signed to a major label. "My role in getting my acts signed to majors," he explains, "has been primarily to promote the band as much as possible, thereby bringing more attention from the majors. The Smashing Pumpkins did very well with the product they released on Limited Potential, well enough to attract the attention of Sub Pop chief Jon Poneman—their Sub Pop single, combined with the efforts of myself and other local luminaries, attracted the management team of Raymond Coffer Management. This in turn led to the interest of Virgin Records.

"There's a lot involved with getting an act a 'hot' reputation," he continues, "but throughout all of this the Pumpkins were playing every show they could get. Playing live is the key here. No matter how much you promote an album, there's nothing to promote the record and the band like a live appearance."

Putting out successful indie product and performing whenever you can may be deciding factors in getting signed to a major label. "Majors are looking strictly for marketability," Potential says. "The thing that has drawn major label attention to my acts has been a 'good street buzz.' If an A&R person sees a band generating interest on its own, it will be even easier with the resources of a big label. Many times, an A&R person will contact me because of a review they've read in *CMJ* or *Gavin*. If they see that a band is 'hot,' they don't want to be left out."

*A COMPANY CALLED W, P.O. Box 618 Church St. Station, New York NY 10008. (212)409-1272. President: Walt Goodridge. Record company. Estab. 1990. Releases 2-3 singles, 1-2 LPs, 2-3 EPs, 1-2 CDs/year. Works with musicians/artists. Pays 5-8% royalty to artists on contract; statutory rate to publisher per song on record.
How to Contact: Submit demo tape by mail. Unsolicited submissions are OK. Prefers cassette (or VHS videocassette) with 3-4 songs. SASE. Reports in 4-6 weeks.
Music: Mostly **rap**; also **reggae, R&B** and **dance.** Released "Food For Thought" (by Glen Brooks), recorded by The God Squad; "Canufeelit?" written and recorded by Antoine; "Cold Chill" (by Homer Hill), recorded by Tru 2 Do; and "2-B-Positive" written and recorded by N-Controle, all on A Company Called W Records.
Tips: "Buy *RAP: This Game of Exposure* and *This Business of Music* and familiarize yourself with as much of the industry as possible!"

*AARSON RECORDS %Entertainment Management Enterprises, 454 Alps Rd., Wayne NJ 07470. (201)694-3333. President: Richard Zielinski. Labels include Aarson Records and Unicorn Records. Record company and manager. Estab. 1983. Works with musicians/artists on contract.
How to Contact: Submit demo tape by mail. Unsolicited submissions are OK. Prefers cassette (or VHS videocassette) with 4 songs and lyric sheet. SASE. Reports in 1 month.
Music: Mostly **rock, metal** and **urban.** Artists include Mirror's Image and Sinful.

*ACOUSTIC DISC, 7957 Nita, Canoga Park CA 91304. (818)704-7800. Senior Vice President, Business Affairs: Craig R. Miller. Record company, music publisher (Dawg Music, BMI), record producer (David Grisman, Dawg Productions). Estab. 1989. Releases 4 cassettes, 4 CDs/year. Works with musicians on record contract.
How to Contact: Call first and obtain permission to submit. Prefers cassette with at least 3 songs. Does not return material. Reports in 1 month.
Music: Acoustic and **instrumental.** Previous releases have included Jerry Garcia, David Grisman, Enrigue Coria, Jacob do Bandolin and others.

ADOBE RECORDS, Dept. SM, Box W, Shallowater TX 79363. (806)873-3537. President: Tom Woodruff. Record company. Estab. 1989. Releases 5 LPs/year. Works with musicians/artists, storytellers and poets on contract. Pays statutory rate.
How to Contact: Write (attn: Sue Swinson) or call first and obtain permission to submit. Prefers cassette or VHS videocassette with 3 songs and lyric or lead sheet. Does not return unsolicited material. Reports in 3 months.
Music: Cowboy Western, folk, bluegrass, C&W, jazz and **blues.** Released *Texas When Texas Was Free* and *Deep in the Heart* written and recorded by A. Wilkinson; and *Moon Light on the Colorado*, arranged and recorded by J. Stephenson; all on Adobe Records.

AIR CENTRAL RECORDINGS, 3700 S. Hawthorne, Sioux Falls SD 57105. Owners: William Prines III or Vesta Wells-Prines. Labels include Omnigram Records. Record company. Estab. 1983. Releases 2 singles, 4-6 LPs and 2-3 CDs/year. Works with musicians/artists on contract. Pays statutory rate to publisher per song on record.
How to Contact: Write to obtain permission to submit. Prefers cassette with 3 songs. SASE. Reports in 3 months.
Music: Mostly **country, pop** and **gospel**; also **rock** and **R&B.** Released "I Am A Star" written and recorded by Carol Kiefer on Air Central Records (pop); and "Love Made Manifest" written and recorded by Tom Bierer on Air Central Records (gospel).

AIRWAVE PRODUCTION GROUP, INC., 1916 28th Ave. S., Birmingham AL 35209. (205)870-3239. President: Michael Panepento. Artist development and production company and artist management company. Estab. 1985. Releases 5 CDs/year. Works with musicians/artists on contract and hires musicians for in-house studio work. Pays 50% royalty to artists on contract; varying rate to publishers per song on record.
How to Contact: Submit demo tape—unsolicited submissions are OK. Prefers cassette with 3 songs and lyric sheets. SASE. Reports in 10 weeks.
Music: Mostly **pop/top 40, rock** and **R&B**; also **country** and **jazz.** Released albums by Brother Cane (Virgin Records), Slick Lilly (Zeal Records), Vallejo (Pandem Records), Rick Carter and the Loveland Orchestra (Prairie Eden Records) and Kelly Black (T.B.A.).

The asterisk before a listing indicates that the listing is new in this edition. New markets are often the most receptive to unsolicited submissions.

ALCAZAR RECORDS, Box 429, Waterbury VT 05676. (802)244-7845. Manager: Mitch Cantor. Labels include Fogarty's Cove, Fretless, Alacazam!, Tara Records, Round River Records, Dunkeld Records, Audio Outings, Gadfly Records, Keltia Musique, Mark Rubin Productions, Mineral River, NSO Records, Outer Green, Well-N-Tune Productions and Record Rak Records. Estab. 1977. Releases numerous cassettes and CDs/year. Works with musicians/artists on record contract, songwriters on royalty contract and musicians on salary for in-house studio work. Pays statutory rate to publishers per song on records.
How to Contact: Write or call first and obtain permission to submit. Prefers cassette (or VHS videocassette) with 3 songs and lyric sheet. Does not return material. Reports in 6 weeks.
Music: Children's, folk and **blues;** also **pop/soft rock** and **avant-garde.** Artists include Doc Watson, Odetta, George Gritzbach, Priscilla Herdman, Rory Block, Utah Phillips, Eric Bogle, Fred Koller, Dave Van Ronk, Sara Banham, Radhika Miller and Mike and Carleen McCornack.
Tips: "Study our releases; are you/your songs appropriate for us? If someone knows everything we've put out and insists they're right for the label, that person/artist will get a serious listen."

ALEAR RECORDS, % McCoy, Route 2, Box 114, Berkeley Springs WV 25411. (304)258-9381. Labels include Master Records, Winchester Records and Real McCoy Records. Record company, music publisher (Jim McCoy Music, Clear Music, New Edition Music/BMI), record producer and recording studio. Releases 20 singles and 10 LPs/year. Works with artists and songwriters on contract; musicians on salary. Pays 2% minimum royalty to artists; statutory rate to publishers for each record sold.
How to Contact: Write first and obtain permission to submit. Prefers 7½ ips reel-to-reel or cassette with 5-10 songs and lead sheet. Does not return unsolicited material. Reports in 1 month.
Music: Bluegrass, church/religious, country, folk, gospel, progressive and **rock.** Released *Touch Your Heart*, written and recorded by Jim McCoy; "Leavin'," written and recorded by Red Steed, both on Winchester Records; and "The Taking Kind" (by Tommy Hill), recorded by J.B. Miller on Hilton Records. Other artists include Carroll County Ramblers, Bud Arnel, Nitelifers, Jubilee Travelers and Middleburg Harmonizers.

ALISO CREEK PRODUCTIONS INCORPORATED, Box 8174, Van Nuys CA 91409. (818)787-3203. President: William Williams. Labels include Aliso Creek Records. Record company. Estab. 1987. Releases 4 LPs and 4 CDs/year. Works with musicians/artists and songwriters on contract. Pays negotiable royalty to artists on contract. Pays statutory rate to publisher per song on record.
How to Contact: Write and obtain permission to submit. Prefers cassette with 3 songs and lyric sheet. SASE. Reports in 3-4 weeks.
Music: Mostly **New Age, new acoustic, children's music;** also **rock, pop** and **country.** Released *Change* written and recorded by Steve Kenyata (new world) and *Take a Trip* (by Bob Menn), recorded by various artists (children's), both on Aliso Creek Records.
Tips: "We are looking for career singer/songwriters with well-developed material and performance skills and the desire to tour."

ALLAGASH COUNTRY RECORDS, 45 7th St., Auburn ME 04210. (207)784-7975. President/A&R Director: Richard E. Gowell. Labels include Allagash Country Records, Gowell Records and Allagash R&B Records. Record company, music publisher (Richard E. Gowell Music/BMI) and record producer. Estab. 1986. Releases 3-5 singles and 1-3 LPs/year. Works with musicians/artists and songwriters on contract. Pays 3-25% royalty to artists on contract; statutory rate to publisher per song on record.
How to Contact: Submit demo tape—unsolicited submissions OK. Prefers cassette with 2-12 songs and lyric or lead sheet. SASE. Reports in 2-6 weeks.
Music: Mostly **country, pop/country** and **country rock;** also **R&B/pop.** Released "Don't Wake Me" and "I Want to See Her Again" written and recorded by Kevin Cronin (country); "Back Home" (by J. Main) recorded by Larry Main (pop/country) and "Is It My Body You Want?" (by R.E. Gowell) recorded by Rich Gowell (50s rock), all on Allagash Records.
Tips: "We release compact discs worldwide and lease out album projects on singer/songwriters that have original unpublished masters available. 10-12 songs/masters in above styles that we accept, are contracted for this promotion. We work with many new acts with commercial material."

*ALLEGHENY MUSIC WORKS, 306 Cypress Ave,. Johnstown PA 15902. (814)535-3373. Managing Director: Al Rita. Labels include Allegheny Records. Record company, music publisher (Allegheny Music Works Publishing/ASCAP and Tuned on Music/BMI). Estab. 1991. Works with musicians/ artists or songwriters on royalty contract. Pays 8-12% royalty to artists on contract; statutory rate to publisher per song on record.
How to Contact: Submit demo tape by mail. Unsolicited submissions are OK. Prefers cassette with

3 songs and lyric sheet or lead sheet. SASE. Reports in 2-4 weeks.

Music: Mostly **country, pop, adult contemporary**; also **church/religious, all other kinds except hard rock, metal** and **rap.** "We are interested in leasing masters for overseas sub-licensing." Released "Twenty Seven Inches Tall" (by Catesby Jones and Hank Sable), recorded by "Country" Joe Liptock; "The Best Is Yet To Come" (by Mark McLelland and Marie Vosgerau), recorded by Mark McLelland; and "The Macy's Thanksgiving Day Parade" (by Alberta Hoffman, Dan Rita and A. Rita), recorded by "Country" Joe Liptock all on Allegheny Records.

Tips: "First, be talented, professional and committed. Second, have sufficient financial backing in place to do your project(s) right. Understand that it's wise to economize; it's extravagant to spend either more or less than it takes to get the job done!"

ALPHABEAT, Box 12 01, D-6980 Wertheim/Main, **Germany.** Phone: (09342)841 55. Owner/A&R Manager: Stephan Dehn. A&R National Manager: Marga Zimmermann. Press & Promotion: Alexander Burger. Disco Promotion: Matthias Marth. Music Service: Wolfgang Weinmann. Creative Services: Heiko Köferl. Record company and record producer. Releases vary "depending on material available." Works with musicians/artists on contract; hires musicians for in-house studio work. Also works through "license contract with foreign labels." Payment to artists on contract "depends on product." Payment: conditional on German market.

How to Contact: Submit demo tape—unsolicited submissions are OK. Prefers cassette (or PAL videocassette) with maximum of 3 songs and lyric sheet. "When sending us your demo tapes, please advise us of your ideas and conditions." SAE and IRC. Reports in 2 weeks.

Music: Mostly **dance/disco/pop, synth/pop** and **electronic**; also **R&B, hip hop/rap** and **ballads**. Artists include Martin King, Red Sky, Fabian Harloff, Silent Degree, Mode Control, Mike M.C. & Master J., Skyline, Lost in the Dessert, Oriental Bazar, Voice In Your Head, Love Game, Alpha W. Synthoxx.

Tips: "We are a distributor of foreign labels. If foreign labels have interest in distribution of their productions in Germany (also Switzerland and Austria) they can contact us. We distribute all styles of music of foreign labels. Please contact our department "Distribution Service.""

*ALTERNATIVE RECORD CO. LTD., 12 Cherry Place, Staten Island NY 10314-6912. President/Chief Executive: Vinny DeGeorge. Record company and producer. Estab. 1976. Releases 5 singles/year, 2 12" singles, 3 LPs and 1 EP/year. Works with musicians/artists and songwriters on contract and hires musicians for in-house studio work and promotion for live acts. Royalty is negotiable; statutory rate to publishers per song on records.

How to Contact: Submit demo tape by mail—unsolicited submissions are OK. Prefers cassette (or videocassette if available) with 3 songs. Does not return unsolicited material. Reports in 3 months.

Music: All types. Released "Man Overboard," recorded by TD2; "This Is The Way," recorded by Strokes; and "Night of the Living Dean," recorded by Nevin Broome, all on Alternative Records.

ALTERNATIVE RECORDS, P.O. Box 46, Eugene OR 97440-0046. (503)344-3616. A&R: KC Layton. Labels include Gravity, Alternative Archive. Record company. Estab. 1979. Releases 3-4 singles, 5 LPs, 1 EP and 5 CDs/year. Works with musicians/artists on record contract. Pays 17% royalty to artists on contract; statutory rate to publisher per song on record.

How to Contact: Write first and obtain permission to submit. Be sure to include SASE! Prefers cassette (or VHS videocassette if available) with 5 songs and lyric sheet. SASE. Reports in 4 weeks.

Music: Mostly **rock (alternative), pop (again, alternative in nature), country/rock**; also **experimental** and **industrial.** Released "Burn It Low," written and recorded by John Nay; *Trust*, written and recorded by Two Pound Planet, both on Alternative Records; and *Wes Montgomery Blues*, written and recorded by Sheep Theatre on Alternative Archives Records. Also released *Songs from the Hydrogen Jukebox* by Two Pound Planet, produced by Mitch Easter. Other artists include Robert Vaughn, 77's and Zoo People.

Tips: "Every release we've done has consistently been praised by fans and critics alike so we seek to make every album something that will hold up over the years, not just attempting to mimic trend of the day. It's important that your vision of your art be as focused as possible."

*ALYSSA RECORDS, Box 133, Farmingville NY 11738. President: Andy Marvel. Labels include Ricochet Records and Alyssa Records. Record company, music publisher (Andy Marvel Music/ASCAP, Bing Bing Bing Music/ASCAP, and Andysongs/BMI), and record producer (Marvel Productions). Estab. 1981. Releases 12-15 singles, 1 12" single and 4 LPs/year. Works with musicians/artists and songwriters.

Listings of companies in countries other than the U.S. have the name of the country in boldface type.

How to Contact: Write first and obtain permission to submit. Prefers cassette (or VHS videocassette) with 3 songs and lyric sheet. Return only with SASE. "Do not call." Not accepting mail until Dec. 1993.

Music: Mostly **pop, R&B,** and **Top 40**; also **country**. Released "You Can't Hide Your Fantasies," by Andy Marvel, Steve Perri and Tom Siegel; "Express (10 Items Or Less)," by Andy Marvel; and "Meant To Be," by Andy Marvel and Don Levy, all recorded by Andy Marvel on Alyssa Records.

AMERICATONE RECORDS INTERNATIONAL USA, 1817 Loch Lomond Way, Las Vegas NV 89102-4437. (702)384-0030. Fax: (702)382-1926. Estab. 1975. Record company, producer and music publisher. Publishes 50 songs/year. Releases 5 12″ singles, 5 EPs and 8 CDs/year. Pays standard royalty. **Affiliates:** The Rambolt Music International (ASCAP), Christy Records International.

How to Contact: Submit demo tape by mail. Prefers cassettes and studio production with top sound recordings and lyric sheets. SASE. Reports in 4 weeks.

Music: Mostly **country, jazz, R&R, Spanish, classic ballads.** Published *The Ice Princess,* recorded by Sunset; *The Best of Penelope,* recorded by Penelope; and *Santa Ana Winds,* by Johnny Bytheway, all on Americatone International Records.

THE AMETHYST GROUP LTD./ANTITHESIS RECORDS, 273 Chippewa Dr., Columbia SC 29210-6508. No phone calls please. Contact: A&R. Labels include Amethyst Records and Antithesis Records, Amaryllis Records, Analysis Records, Gizmo Records. Record company, music publisher (Another Amethyst Song/BMI) and management firm. Estab. 1979. Releases 10 CD's. Works with musicians/artists on contract. Pays 5-15% royalty to artists on contract. Pays statutory rate to publishers per song on record. International distribution, management, marketing firm. "Our forte is management, with overseas marketing."

How to Contact: Submit demo tape—unsolicited submissions are OK. Prefers cassette (or VHS videocassette) with 3-7 songs and lyric sheet. SASE. Reports within 3-5 weeks only if interested. "Always include return postage for any reply."

Music: Mostly **alternative, rock** and **R&B**; also **techno, industrial, space, rock, new music, jazz/rap** and **heavy metal.** Released "Surrender to the Order" recorded by US Steel; "Media" recorded by Political Asylum on Antithesis Records (rock). Other artists include J. Blues, Carnage and Silhouette.

Tips: "Try to be realistic about someone investing in your material."

*AMI RECORDS, 394 W. Main St., Hendersonville TN 37075. (615)822-7595. Vice President: Kevin Waugh. Record company, music publisher (Silver Heart Music, BMI; Silver Dust Music, ASCAP), record producer. Estab. 1981. Works with musicians/artists on record contract or songwriters on royalty contract. Pays statutory rate rate to publisher per song on record. No advance for services.

How to Contact: Write or call first and obtain permission to submit. Prefers cassette (or VHS videocassette if available) with 5 songs and lyric sheets. Does not return material. Reports in 2 months.

Music: Mostly **country, pop, light rock.**

AMIRON MUSIC/AZTEC PRODUCTIONS, 20531 Plummer St., Chatsworth CA 91311. (818)998-0443. General Manager: A. Sullivan. Labels include Dorn Records and Aztec Records. Record company, booking agency and music publisher (Amiron Music). Releases 2 singles/year. Works with artists and songwriters on contract. Pays 10% maximum royalty to artists on contract; standard royalty to songwriters on contract. Pays statutory rate to publishers.

How to Contact: Prefers cassette and lead sheet. SASE. Reports in 3 weeks.

Music: **Dance, easy listening, folk, jazz, MOR, rock** ("no heavy metal") and **top 40/pop.** Released "Look In Your Eyes," by Newstreet; and "Midnight Flight," recorded by Papillon.

Tips: "Be sure the material has a hook; it should make people want to make love or fight. Write something that will give a talented new artist that edge on current competition."

*ANGRY NEIGHBOR RECORDS, P.O. Box 66462, Houston TX 77266. (713)645-6995. Music Submissions: John. Labels include Boot Lick Records (a specialty label). Record company, record producer (Angry Neighbor). Estab. 1991. Releases 5 singles, 2 EPs and 2 CDs/year. Works with musicians/artists on record contract. Pays 5% of product, up to 50% of profits. "All artists keep their own publishing!!!"

How to Contact: Submit demo tape by mail. Unsolicited submissions are OK. Prefers cassette (or VHS videocassette if available) with at least 2 or 3 songs and lyric sheet and press kit! Does not return material. Reports in 2 months.

Music: Mostly **punk rock,** and **garage bands**; also **experimental, unusual, no metal.** Released *B.L.&T.,* written and recorded by Peglegasus (space pop); *Really Red,* written and recorded by Really Red (early punk); *Bad America* (by Dashboard Mary), recorded by Angry Neighbor (next big thing), all on Angry Neighbor Records. Other artists include Stinkerbell, Happy Fingers Institute, Blunt, Butt Trumpet, Three Day Stubble, Pony Time, Stoole Sample, The Obsessed, Squat Thrust.

Tips: "Send tapes, flyers, bio, info, press, etc., the more outlandish and over the top, the better chance we have of doing something."

*ANOTHER APPROACH RECORDING COMPANY, 1022 Miss Annies Dr., Jacksonville AL 36265. (205)435-9339. President/Owner: Thomas C. Van Dyke. Record company and music publisher (Another Approach Music Publishing Co./BMI and Avesta Entertainment Enterprise/Entertainment Organization). Estab. 1992. Releases 10 singles or 1 LP/cassette/year. Works with musicians/artists on record contract or songwriters on royalty contract. Pays standard royalty to artists on contract; pays statutory rate to publishers per song on records.
How to Contact: Write or call first and obtain permission to submit. Prefers cassette with any number of songs and lyric or lead sheet. SASE. Reports in 2 weeks—2 months.
Music: Mostly **R&B, soul** and **gospel;** also **jazz, rock** and **easy listening.** Released "Saturday Night" (by Thomas C. Van Dyke), recorded by Van Dyke; "Situations" (by Keith Rowe and Thomas Van Dyke), recorded by Van Dyke; and "Images" (by Thomas Van Dyke and Michael Brown), recorded by Van Dyke and Brown, all on Another Approach Records.
Tips: "Be professional in thoughts, words, actions, desires, have good material, pleasant attitude, and be honest."

*ANTELOPE RECORDS INC., 23 Lovers Lane, Wilton CT 06897. (203)384-9884. President: Tony Lavorgna. Record company. Estab. 1982. Releases 2 CDs/year. Works with songwriters on royalty contract. Payment negotiable; statutory rate to publisher per song on record.
How to Contact: Submit demo tape by mail. Unsolicited submissions are OK. Prefers cassette with lead sheet. Does not return material.
Music: Mostly **jazz** (acoustic), **MOR** (vocal). Released *Swing Fever* (by Alice Schweitzer), recorded by Swing Fever (MOR vocal); *Atlanta Allstar* and *Quartet Plays* (by Bill Evans), recorded by Atlanta Allstar Quartet on Antelope Records. Other artists include Jeri Brown.

*ARION RECORDS, P.O. Box 16046, Chattanooga TN 37416-0046. President/Owner: Steve Babb. Record company, music publisher (Sound Resources/BMI). Estab. 1992. Releases 7-10 cassettes, 3 CDs/year. Works with musicians/artists on record contract. Pays 10% royalty to artists on contract; statutory rate to publishers per song on record.
How to Contact: Submit demo tape by mail. Unsolicited submissions are OK. Prefers DAT or cassette (metal if possible) with 3-4 songs and lyric sheet. SASE. Reports in 2 months.
Music: Mostly **progressive rock, art rock** and **New Age;** also **electronic music.** Released *Journey of the Dunadan*, written and recorded by Glass Hammer; *Endless* and *Poems and Music of Stephen DéArque*, both written and recorded by Stephen DéArque, all on Arion Records. Other artists include Perrin Davis, Fred Schendel, Buddy Matherly and The Wild.
Tips: "We are looking for unique music, nothing trendy. Music which deals with a Sci-Fi or fantasy theme is a plus but not necessary. Don't worry about radio airplay, just send your best."

*ARTIFEX RECORDS, 604 Overview, Franklin TN 37064. (615)791-0297. President: Peter Miller. Record company. Estab. 1989. Works with musicians/artists on record contract. Pays 10% royalty to artists on contract; 75% of statutory rate.
How to Contact: Submit demo tape by mail. Unsolicited submissions are OK. Prefers cassette (or VHS videocassette if available). Does not return material. Reports in 10 weeks.
Music: Mostly **contemporary jazz fusion.** Released *3rd Coast Jazz* (by various); *Walk With Me* (by Angella Christie) and *Sound of Brazil* (by Jesse Passoa) all on Artifex Records.

ASSOCIATED ARTISTS MUSIC INTERNATIONAL, Maarschalklaan 47, 3417 SE Montfoort, **The Netherlands.** Phone: (0)3484-2860. Fax: 31-3484-2860. Release Manager: Joop Gerrits. Labels include Associated Artists, Disco-Dance Records and Italo. Record company, music publisher (Associated Artists International/BUMA-STEMRA, Hilversum Happy Music/BUMA-STEMRA, Intermedlodie/BUMA-STEMRA and Hollands Glorie Productions), record producer (Associated Artists Productions) and TV promotions. Estab. 1975. Releases 10 singles, 25 12″ singles, 6 LPs and 6 CDs/year. Works with musicians/artists and songwriters on contract.
How to Contact: Submit demo tape—unsolicited submissions OK. Prefers compact cassette or 19 cm/sec reel-to-reel (or VHS videocassette) with any number of songs and lyric or lead sheets. Records also accepted. SAE and IRC. Reports in 2 months.
Music: Mostly **dance, pop, house, hip hop,** and **rock.** Released "Bailar Pegados" (by Anjurez), recorded by Sergio Dalma on Armada Records (ballad); "2V231" (by Picotto) recorded by Anticappella on Live Records (house/techno); and "Extrasyn" (by Bortolotti), recorded by RFTR on Media Records (house/techno).
Tips: "We invite producers and independent record labels to send us their material for their entry on the European market. Mark all parcels as 'no commercial value—for demonstration only.' We license productions to record companies in all countries of Europe and South Africa."

ATLANTIC RECORDING CORP., 9229 Sunset Blvd., Los Angeles CA 90069. (310)205-7460. A&R Director: Kevin Williamson. Contact: Paul Cooper. Labels include Atco, Cotillion, East-West and Atlantic. "We distribute Island, Virgin, Interscope, Mammoth and Third Stone Records." Record company, music publisher. Estab. 1948. Works with artists on contract, songwriters on royalty contract and musicians on salary for in-house studio work.

How to Contact: Prefers cassette with 3 songs (or VHS videocassette). SASE. Reports in 2 weeks. Does not return material.

Music: Blues, disco, easy listening, folk, jazz, MOR, progressive, R&B, rock, soul and **top 40/pop.** Artists include Debbie Gibson, Mike & the Mechanics, INXS, Yes, AC/DC, Pete Townsend, Bette Midler, Ratt, Skid Row, Crosby, Stills, Nash & Young, Genesis, Phil Collins and Robert Plant.

ATTACK RECORDS, Box 3161, Atlanta GA 30302. Producer: C.E. Scott. Labels include Ambush Records. Record company and music publisher (BMI). Estab. 1965. Releases 12 singles, 4 12″ singles, 3 LPs, 4 EPs and 3 CDs/year. Works with musicians/artists and songwriters on contract. Pays 3% royalty to artists on contract; statutory rate to publisher per song on record.

How to Contact: Submit demo tape—unsolicited submissions are OK. Prefers cassette or VHS videocassette with 3 songs and lead sheets. SASE. Reports in 6 weeks.

Music: Mostly **pop** and **R&B.** Released "I Wanna Dance With You," "Wild Flower" and "Slow Dance," (all recorded by Sybyo) on Attack Records (pop). Other artists include Sheila Davis, Barbara Rush, The CD's and Cy Boy.

Tips: "Please be patient and write according to the current music trends. We will contact you if we like your material. We're most open to female-oriented, and pop hard-hitting R&B roster."

AUBURN RECORDS AND TAPES, Box 96, Glendale AZ 85311. (602)435-0314. Owner: Frank E. Koehl. Record company and music publisher (Speedster Music/BMI). Estab. 1962. Releases 1-4 singles/year. Works with musicians/artists and songwriters on contract. Pays statutory rate.

How to Contact: Submit a demo tape—unsolicited submissions are OK. SASE. Reports in 3 weeks.

Music: Mostly **country, folk** and **bluegrass.** Released "Mr. Woolworth" recorded by Al Ferguson; "Lottery Fever" recorded by Troy McCourt; and "Burglar Man" recorded by Al Ferguson, all on Auburn Records (country/comical).

Tips: "I am looking for songs that are country and comical or the traditional country sound."

AUTOGRAM RECORDS, Burgstr. 9, 48301 Nottuln 1, **Germany.** (02502) 6151. Fax: 1825. Contact: A&R Department. Labels include Autonom, Folk-Record, costbar, Basilikum and Roots. Record company. Releases 20-25 CDs, 10 CD singles and 2 LPs/year. Works with musicians/artists and song-writers on contract. Pays 5% of retail price to artists on contract.

How to Contact: Submit demo tape—unsolicited submissions are OK. Prefers cassette with minimum 3 songs and lyric sheet. Does not return material. Reports in 1-2 months. "No stylistic imitations, (no cover versions)."

Music: New country, country/folk-rock, singer-songwriter (languages mainly German, English, Dutch), **ethnic folk music, blues** and **contemporary guitar music;** also **classical, contemporary, bluegrass** and **historical** (reissues). Released "Inchtomanie"/"White Sheep," written and recorded by The Inchtabokatables; "Wieder Luft Zum Atem" and "Playing For Keeps," written and recorded by Till Kahrs; and "Down Under," written and recorded by Eric Bogle.

AVANT-GARDE RECORDS CORP., 12224 Avila Dr., Kansas City MO 64145. (816)942-8861. Director A&R/President: Scott Smith. Record company, music publisher and record producer. Estab. 1983. Releases 3 LPs and 3 CDs/year. Pays statutory rate.

How to Contact: Write first and obtain permission to submit. Prefers cassette (or VHS videocassette if available) with 4 songs. SASE. Reports in 8 weeks.

Music: Mostly **themes, new standards** and **pop classical,** (no New Age) on piano only. Released *Take A Bow, Concerto Themes Nocturne in E Flat,* and *40th Anniversary Collector's Edition,* recorded by Ferrante & Teicher on Avant-Garde Records.

Tips: "Only send instrumentals—no lyrics. Piano recordings get top priority. Prefer semi-established concert-pianist caliber."

AVC ENTERTAINMENT INC., Suite 200, 6201 Sunset Blvd., Hollywood CA 90028. (213)461-9001. President: James Warsinske. Labels include AVC Records. Record company and music publisher (AVC Music/ASCAP, Harmonious Music/BMI). Estab. 1988. Releases 6-12 singles, 6-12 12″ singles, 3-6 LPs and 3-6 CDs/year. Works with musicians/artists and songwriters on contract. Pays rate of 75% to publishers.

How to Contact: Submit demo tape—unsolicited submissions OK. Prefers cassette and VHS videocassette with 2-4 songs and lyric sheet. SASE. Reports in 1 month.

Music: Mostly **R&B/rap, pop** and **rock;** also **funk/soul, dance** and **metal.** Released "In Service" (by Michael Williams) recorded by Madrok on AVC Records (rap); "There's a New Today" written and recorded by Duncan Faure on AVC Records (pop/rock) and "Melissa Mainframe" (by Hohl/Rocca) recorded by Rocca on AVC Records (pop/rock). Other artists include 7th Stranger and Biscuit.

Tips: "Be original and contemporary, we take our time selecting our artists, but stay committed to them."

AZRA INTERNATIONAL, Box 459, Maywood CA 90270. (213)560-4223. A&R: Jeff Simins. Labels include World Metal, Metal Storm, Azra, Iron Works, Not So Famous David's Records and Masque Records. Record company. Estab. 1978. Releases 10 singles, 5 LPs, 5 EPs and 5 CDs/year. Works with artists on contract. "Artists usually carry their own publishing." Pays 10% royalty to artists on contract; statutory rate to publishers for each record sold.
How to Contact: Submit demo tape—unsolicited submissions are OK. Prefers cassette (or VHS videocassette) with 3-5 songs and lyric sheet. Include bio and photo. SASE. Reports in 3 weeks.
Music: Mostly **rock, heavy metal, Christian** and **New Age**; also **novelty**. Released "Unity Fields" (by Chris Fogelsong), recorded by Subjugator on World Metal Records; *Pull*, written and recorded by Alan Ichyasu on Condor Records; and *Medusa* (by Joe Famulare), recorded by Terminal Reign on Azra Records. Other artists include Toe Suck and Omicron.
Tips: "Submit songs that are memorable."

AZTLAN RECORDS, P.O. Box 5672, Buena Park CA 90622. (714)822-7151. Manager: Carmen Ortiz. Record company, record distributor, music publisher. Estab. 1986. Releases 1 LP and 1 CD/year. Works with musicians/artists on record contract. Royalty paid to artist on contract varies.
How to Contact: Submit demo tape—unsolicited submissions are OK. SASE.
Music: Mostly **alternative, industrial, experimental**; also **gothic, performance poetry** and **ethnic**. Released *Nirvana* written and recorded by 12 artists (compilation LP); *Awaken*, written and recorded by 7 artists (compilation LP); and *Der Kirshewasser*, written and recorded by Angel of the Odd (alternative), all on Aztlan Records. Other artists include Cecilia, Stereotaxic Device, Black Tape for A Blue Girl, Dichroic Mirror, Pleasure Center and Spiderbaby.
Tips: "Die rather than compromise what you are doing. Music is your life."

BAGATELLE RECORD COMPANY, 400 San Jacinto St., Houston TX 77002. (713)225-6654. President: Byron Benton. Record company, record producer and music publisher (Floyd Tillman Music Co.). Releases 20 singles and 10 LPs/year. Works with songwriters on contract; musicians on salary for in-house studio work. Pays negotiable royalty to artists on contract.
How to Contact: Prefers cassette and lyric sheet. SASE. Reports in 2 weeks.
Music: Mostly **country**; also **gospel**. Released "This is Real," by Floyd Tillman (country single); "Lucille," by Sherri Jerrico (country single); and "Everything You Touch," by Johnny Nelms (country single). Other artists include Jerry Irby, Bobby Beason, Bobby Burton, Donna Hazard, Danny Brown, Sonny Hall, Ben Gabus, Jimmy Copeland and Johnny B. Goode.

BAL RECORDS, Box 369, La Canada CA 91012-0369. (818)548-1116. President: Adrian Bal. Record company, record producer and music publisher (Bal & Bal Music Publishing Co./ASCAP, Bal West Music Publishing Company/BMI). Estab. 1965. Releases 2-6 singles/year. Works with artists and songwriters on contract; musicians on salary for in-house studio work. Works with composers and lyricists; teams collaborators. Pays standard royalty to artists on contract; statutory rate to publishers for each record sold.
How to Contact: Submit demo tape by mail-unsolicited submissions are OK. Prefers cassette (or videocassette) with 1-3 songs and lyric or lead sheet. SASE. Reports in 6+ weeks.
Music: **Rock, MOR, country/western, gospel** and **jazz**. Released "Fragile" (by James Jackson), recorded by Kathy Simmons (med. rock); "Right to Know" (by James Jackson), recorded by Kathy Simmons (med. rock); "Dance to the Beat of My Heart" (by Dan Gertz), recorded by Ace Baker (med. rock) and "You're A Part of Me," "Can't We Have Some Time Together," "You and Me" and "Circles of Time" by Paul Richards (A/C).
Tips: "Consider: Will young people who receive an allowance go out and purchase the record?"

*BANDIT RECORDS, P.O. Box 111480, Nashville TN 37222. (615)331-1219. President: Loman Craig. Labels include HIS Records (gospel). Record company, record producer (Loman Craig Productions). Estab. 1979. Releases 5 singles, 2 LPs/year. Works with custom sessions. Pays statutory rate to publisher per song on record. "There is a charge for demo and custom sessions."
How to Contact: Submit demo tape by mail. Unsolicited submissions are OK. Prefers cassette with 2-3 songs and lyric sheet. SASE. Reports in 4-6 weeks.
Music: Mostly **country, ballads, gospel**. Released "Can't See Me Gone" (by Craig-Craig) and "Whiskey and Beer" (by J. Bryan), both recorded by James Bryan (country); and "Daddy" (by P. Pentell), recorded by Patty Pentell (ballad) all on Bandit Records. Other artists include Chadd D. Allen, Pat Riley, Allen Gray, Wally Jemmings.
Tips: "Send a clear sounding demo and readable lyric sheets. Since we are a small independent record label, we do have to charge for services rendered."

*BEACON RECORDS, P.O. Box 3129, Peabody MA 01961. (603)893-2200. Principal: Tony Ritchie. Labels include Beacon Records and VISTA Records. Record company, music publisher. Releases 12 LPs and 12 CDs/year. Works with musicians/artists on record contract, songwriters on royalty contract or musicians on salary for in-house studio work.
How to Contact: Submit demo tape by mail. Unsolicited submissions are OK. Does not return unsolicited material. Reports in 1-2 months.
Music: Mostly **folk, Celtic, folk-rock;** also **country, New Age, blues.** Recorded *Emmeline* (by M.L. Drouin), recorded by Pendragon; *Shoes That Fit Like Sand*, written and recorded by Diane Taraz; and *Beth* (by Fowler/Shulman), recorded by Aztec Two-Step on Beacon Records. Other artists include Tempest, Jeff Wilkinson, David Rea.

*BEAU-JIM RECORDS INC., Box 2401, Sarasota FL 34230-2401. President: Buddy Hooper. Record company, music publisher (Beau-Jim Music, Inc./ASCAP and Beau-Di Music, Inc./BMI), record producer and management firm. Estab. 1972. Member CMA, NSAI, NMA, AGAC. Releases 4 singles and 2 LPs/year. Works with artists and songwriters on contract.
How to Contact: Prefers cassette with lyrics (or videocassette) with 3-5 songs on demo. SASE. Reports in 3 weeks.
Music: Country.

BELMONT RECORDS, 484 Lexington St., Waltham MA 02154. (617)891-7800. President: John Penny. Labels include Belmont Records and Waverly Records. Record company and record producer. Works with musicians on salary for in-house studio work. Pays standard royalty to artists on contract; statutory rate to publisher per song on record.
How to Contact: Write first and obtain permission to submit. Prefers cassette with 3 songs and lyric sheet. SASE. Reports in 3 weeks.
Music: Mostly **country.** Released *One Step At a Time*, recorded by Cheri Ann on Belmont Records (C&W); and *Tudo Bens Sabe*, recorded by Familia Penha (gospel). Other artists include Stan Jr., Tim Barrett, Jackie Lee Williams, Robin Right, Mike Walker and Dwain Hathaway.

*BERANDOL MUSIC, Unit 220, 2600 John St., Markham, Ontario L3R 3W3 **Canada.** (416)475-1848. A&R: Ralph Cruickshank. Record company, music publisher (Berandol Music/SOCAN). Estab. 1947. Works with musicians/artists on record contract or songwriters on royalty contract. Pays 10-15% royalty to artists on contract; statutory rate to publisher per song on record.
How to Contact: Submit demo tape by mail. Unsolicited submissions are OK. Prefers cassette with 4 songs. Does not return material. Reports in 2 weeks.
Music: Mostly **instrumental, children's, CHR (top 40).**

*BEYOND RECORDS CORP., 569 Countyline Rd., Ontario NY 14519. (716)265-0260. Contact: A&R. Labels include VIBE (alternative). Record company and music publisher (Great Beyond Music/ASCAP). Estab. 1992. Releases 12 CDs/year. Works with musicians/artists on record contract, songwriters on royalty contract. Pays statutory rate to publishers per song on records.
How to Contact: Submit demo tape by mail. Unsolicited submissions are OK. Prefers cassette (or VHS videocassette). SASE. Reports in 3-4 weeks.
Music: Mostly **modern rock, pop** and **alternative/punk;** also **country.** Released *New Generation*, recorded by Exploding Boy (rock); *Bug Jar Compilation*, by various (alternative); and *Heart in a Rock Place*, recorded by Bill Crosby (rock), all on Beyond Records. Other artists include Nod and In One.
Tips: "Besides great songs, we're looking for strong live performers. It's important for the artist to be able to showcase their material in a live setting. The songwriter should have a strong sense of his or her direction and not just mimic current trends."

BGM RECORDS, Dept. SM, 8806 Lockway, San Antonio TX 78217-3824. (210)654-8773. Contact: Bill Green. Labels include Casa Verde (ASCAP), BGM and Rainforest Records. Record company, music publisher (Bill Green Music) and record producer. Estab. 1979. Releases 10 singles and 2-3 LPs/year. Works with songwriters on contract.
How to Contact: Prefers cassette. SASE. Reports in 2 months.
Music: Mostly **contemporary country** and **traditional country.** Released "Cajun Baby" (by H. Williams, H. Williams Jr.), recorded by Doug Kershaw (country cajun); "Photographic Memory" (by B. Boyd), recorded by Billy Mata (country); and "Boogie Queen" (by Jenkins, Green), recorded by Doug Kershaw (country cajun); all on BGM Records. Other artists include David Price.

BIG PRODUCTIONS RECORDS, Suite 308, 37 E. 28th St., New York NY 10016. (212)447-6000. President: Paul Punzone. Record company, music publisher (Humongous Music/ASCAP) and record producer (Big Productions and Publishing Co., Inc.). Estab. 1989. Releases 10 12″ singles/year. Works with musicians/artists and songwriters on contract and hires musicians for in-house studio work. Pays 10% royalty to artists on contract; ¾ of statutory rate to publisher per song on record.

How to Contact: Submit demo tape—unsolicited submissions are OK. Prefers cassette or VHS videocassette with 3 songs and lyric sheet. SASE. Reports in 2 months.
Music: Mostly 12" **house tracks, vocal house** and **hip hop**; also **rap, R&B** and **pop**. Released "Mission Accomplished," recorded by Big Baby; "Loose Flutes," recorded by Picture Perfect; and "Get Up," recorded by Big Baby; all written by P. Punzone, G. Sicard and B.B. Fisher on Big Productions Records (house track 12"). Other artists include Charm on Atlantic Records.
Tips: "We are seeking completed house/sample for immediate release. Send best representation of your work for song or artist submissions."

*BIG ROCK PTY. LTD., P.O. Box, Dulwich Hill, NSW 2203 **Australia.** Phone (02)5692152. A&R Manager: Chris Turner. Labels include Big Rock Records, Sound Energy. Record company, music publisher (A.P.R.A.), record producer (Big Rock P/L). Estab. 1979. Releases 5 singles, 10 LPs and 10 CDs/year. Works with musicians/artists on record contract. Pays 5% royalty to artists on contract.
How to Contact: Submit demo tape by mail. Unsolicited submissions are OK. Prefers cassette with 6 songs and lyric sheet. SASE. Reports in 6 weeks.
Music: Mostly **rock, R&B,** and **pop**.

BLACK & BLUE, Suite 152, 400D Putnam Pike, Smithfield RI 02917. (401)949-4887. New Talent Manager: Larry Evilelf. Record company. Releases 5-20 LPs, 3-8 EPs, 5-20 CDs/year. Works with musicians/artists on record contract. Pays statutory rate to publisher per song on record. Royalty rate varies.
How to Contact: Write and obtain permission to submit. Prefers cassette (or VHS videocassette) with 3 songs and lyric sheet or lead sheet. Does not return material. Reports in 3 weeks. Replies only if interested.
Music: Mostly **eclectic, alternative rock, hardcore;** also **speed metal, C&W** and **grind core**. Released *Empty* (by Don McCloud), recorded by Bloody Mess and The Skabs; *Geffen* (by Lyndon Cox), recorded by Boorish Boot; and *Inside You Forever* (by John Radcliffe), recorded by Northwinds, all on Black & Blue Records. Other artists include Rick Rebel.
Tips: "Be truly original. Sound alikes and trend followers are really not given serious consideration regardless of how good they are."

*BLACK DIAMOND RECORDS INC., P.O. Box 8023, Pittsburg CA 94565. (510)427-1314. President: Jerry "J". Labels include "In The House" Records and Jairus Records. Record company, music publisher (BMI), record producer (Bo/Joe Productions, In The House Productions). Estab. 1988-89. Releases 300 singles, 300 12" singles, 300 LPs, 300 EPs and 300 CDs/year. Works with musicians/artists on record contracts, songwriters on royalty contract or musicians on salary for in-house studio work. Pays 5½-16½% royalty to artists on contract; ½ statutory rate to publisher per song on record.
How to Contact: Submit demo tape by mail. Unsolicited submissions are OK. Prefers cassette with 2-4 songs and lyric sheet. Does not return material. Reports in 4-6 weeks to 3 months.
Music: Mostly **R&B, hip hop, MO Country/Mo Jazz, hip hop rap;** also **jazz, blues, rock/roll**. Released " Glad It Was U" (R&B hip hop) and "Can't Do Without" (R&B ballad) both (by Jerry J., Joe Brown), recorded by Deanna Dixon; and *Gramm* (by Will King, O. Jotojo Cleveland), recorded by Gramm (rap) all on Black Diamond Records. Other artists include Hony & Cynamon, Selec, Shejlia/ Dela, Acytezc, Lady's of Color, T.K.T.

BLACK DOG RECORDS, Rt. 2 Box 38, Summerland Key FL 33042. (305)745-3164. Executive Director: Marian Joy Ring. A&R Contact: Rusty Gordon, (Rustron Music Productions), 1156 Park Lane, West Palm Beach, FL 33417. (407)686-1354. Record company. Estab. 1989. Releases 2-6 singles and 3 LPs/ year. Pays standard royalty to artists on contract; statutory rate to publishers per song on record.
How to Contact: Submit demo tape by mail to W. Palm Beach address or write or call first at (407)686-1354 and obtain permission to submit. Prefers cassette with 3-6 songs and lyric or lead sheet. SASE required for all correspondence. Reports in 4-6 weeks.
Music: Mostly **pop, R&B** and **folk-rock;** also **New Age** and **cabaret**. Released *Rising Cost of Love*, "Song for Pedro," "Reflections" and "Same Moon," all written and recorded by Marian Joy Ring on Black Dog Records.

BLUE GEM RECORDS, Box 29688, Hollywood CA 90029. (213)664-7765. Contact: Pete Martin. Record company and record producer (Pete Martin Productions). Estab. 1981. Works with musicians/artists on contract. Pays 6-15% royalty to artists on contract; statutory rate to publisher per song on record.
How to Contact: Submit demo tape—unsolicited submissions are OK. Prefers cassette with 2 songs. SASE. Reports in 3 weeks.
Music: Mostly **country** and **R&B;** also **pop/top 40** and **rock**. Released "The Greener Years," written and recorded by Frank Loren (country); "It's a Matter of Loving You" (by Brian Smith), recorded by Brian Smith & The Renegades (country); and "Two Different Women" (by Frank Loren and Greg

Connor), recorded by Frank Loren (country); all on Blue Gem Records. Other artists include Sherry Weston (country).

Tips: "Study top 10 on charts in your style of writing and be current!"

BLUE WAVE, 3221 Perryville Rd., Baldwinsville NY 13027. (315)638-4286. President/Producer: Greg Spencer. Labels include Blue Wave and Blue Wave/Horizon. Record company, music publisher (G.W. Spencer Music/ASCAP) and record producer (Blue Wave Productions). Estab. 1985. Releases 3 LPs and 3 CDs/year. Works with musicians/artists on contract. Royalty varies; statutory rate to publishers per song on records.

How to Contact: Submit demo tape—unsolicited submissions are OK. Prefers cassette (or VHS or Beta videocassette—live performance only) if available and as many songs as you like. SASE. "We contact only if we are interested." Allow 6 weeks.

Music: Mostly **blues/blues rock, roots rock** and **roots R&B/soul**; also **roots country/rockabilly** or **anything with "soul."** Released "Dangerous Man" (by Pete McMahon), recorded by Kingsnakes; "Big Talk" (by Joe Whiting/Mark Doyle), recorded by Backbone Slip; and "Cold Hearted Woman," written and recorded by Built for Comfort, all on Blue Wave Records (blues/rock).

Tips: "Send it only if it's great, what you send must come from the soul. Not interested in top 40, so-called "hits" or commercial music. I'm looking for real, original artists or those who can make someone else's music their own. The singer must be convincing and be able to deliver the message. Please don't call, I listen to everything sent and I will call if you're what I'm looking for. Please, no lyric sheets or photos, I like to listen without any preconceived notions."

BOGART RECORDS, Box 63302, Phoenix AZ 85082. Owner: Robert L. Bogart Sr. Record company. Estab. 1991. Works with musicians/artists and songwriters on contract and hires musicians for in-house studio work. Pays standard but negotiable royalty to artists on contract; statutory rate to publisher per song on record.

How to Contact: Submit demo tape—unsolicited submissions are OK. Prefers cassette with 4 songs and lyric sheet. SASE. Reports in 1 month.

Music: Mostly **country, R&B** and **rock**; also **pop, New Age** and **gospel.** Released "I'd Be Ly, In" written and recorded by James Beckwith on Bogart Records (country single). Other artists include Tim Tesch and Earl Eric Brown.

BOLIVIA RECORDS, 1219 Kerlin Ave., Brewton AL 36426. (205)867-2228. President: Roy Edwards. Labels include Known Artist Records. Record company, record producer and music publisher (Cheavoria Music Co.). Estab. 1972. Releases 10 singles and 3 LPs/year. Works with artists and songwriters on contract; musicians on salary for in-house studio work. Pays 4-5% royalty to artists on contract; statutory rate to publishers for each record sold.

How to Contact: Write first. Prefers cassette with 3 songs and lyric sheet. All tapes will be kept on file. Reports in 1 month.

Music: Mostly **R&B, country** and **pop**; also **easy listening, MOR** and **soul.** Released "You Are My Sunshine" and "If You Only Knew" written and recorded by Roy Edwards on Bolivia Records (R&B). Other artists include Bobbie Roberson and Jim Portwood.

*BONAIRE MANAGEMENT INC., 7774 Torreyson Dr., Los Angeles CA 90046. (213)876-0367. President: Clive Corcoran. Labels include Bo and AVA. Record company, music publisher (ASCAP and SOCAN), record producer. Estab. 1977. Releases 2 singles, 5 LPs, 5 CDs. Works with musicians/artists on record contract or songwriters on royalty contract.

How to Contact: Call first and obtain permission to submit. Prefers cassette (or VHS videocassette if available) with 3 songs and 3 lyric sheets. SASE. Reports in 2 weeks.

Music: Mostly **rock, pop.** Other artists include SAGA.

BOOGIE BAND RECORDS, Suite 206, 6245 Bristol Pkwy., Culver City CA 90230. Contact: Larry McGee. Labels include Classic Records and Mega Star Records. Record company, music publisher (Operation Perfection Publishing), record producer (Intrigue Productions) and management firm (LMP Management). Estab. 1976. Releases 6 singles, 3 12" singles, 1 LP, 4 EPs and 2 CDs/year. Works with musicians/artists and songwriters on contract; musicians on salary for in-house studio work. Pays 10% royalty to artists on contract; statutory rate to publishers per song on record.

How to Contact: Submit demo tape by mail—unsolicited submissions are OK. Prefers cassette with 1-4 songs and lyric sheet. SASE. Reports in 2 months. "Please only send professional quality material."

Music: **Urban contemporary, dance, rock, MOR/A/C, pop, rap** and **R&B.** Released *Starflower* (by Joe Cacamisse), recorded by Star Flower (A/C); *Too Tough* (by Terrence Jones), recorded by En-Tux (pop); and *Got It Going On* (by Alan Walker), recorded by Executives, all on Mega Star Records. Other artists include Love Child and Heavy Luv.

Tips: "Make your song as commercial, crossover and as current as possible."

BOUQUET RECORDS, Bouquet-Orchid Enterprises, 204 Crestview St., Minden LA 71055. (318)377-2538. President: Bill Bohannon. Record company, music publisher (Orchid Publishing/BMI), record producer (Bouquet-Orchid Enterprises) and management firm. Releases 3-4 singles and 2 LPs/year. Works with artists and songwriters on contract. Pays 5-8% maximum royalty to artists on contract; pays statutory rate to publishers for each record sold.
How to Contact: Submit demo tape—unsolicited submissions are OK. Prefers cassette with 3-5 songs and lyric sheet. SASE. Reports in 1 month.
Music: Mostly **religious** (contemporary or country-gospel, Amy Grant, etc.), **country** ("the type suitable for Clint Black, George Strait, Patty Loveless, etc.") and **top 100** ("the type suitable for Billy Joel, Whitney Houston, R.E.M., etc."); also **rock** and **MOR**. Released "A Brighter Day" (by Bill Bohannon), recorded by Adam Day (country); "Tear Talk" (by John Harris), recorded by Susan Spencer (country); and "Justify My Love" (by Bob Freeman), recorded by Bandoleers (top 40) all on Bouquet Records.
Tips: "Submit 3-5 songs on a cassette tape with lyric sheets. Include a short biography and perhaps a photo. Enclose SASE."

BOVINE INTERNATIONAL RECORD COMPANY, 593 Kildare Rd., London, Ontario N6H 3H8 **Canada.** A&R Director: J.A. Moorhouse. Labels include Bovine and Solid Ivory Records. Record company. Estab. 1977. Releases 1-10 singles and 1-5 LPs/year. Works with musicians/artists on contract and musicians on salary for in-house studio work. Pays 30-40% royalty to artists on contract; statutory rate to publisher per song on record.
How to Contact: Write first and obtain permission to submit. Do not phone. Prefers cassette with 2-3 songs and lyric and lead sheets. SAE and IRC. Reports in 1 to 3 months.
Music: Mostly **country, pop** and **R&B**; also **children's, blues** and **jazz.** Released "I Left Her Behind," written and recorded by J. Moorhouse on Sabre Records; and *John Moorhouse Favorites* and "Just Because" (by various), recorded by John Moorhouse on Bovine International Records.
Tips: "Forward a demo of 2-3 of your best songs. Keep lyrics up front. Enclose typed lyric sheet."

***BRIARHILL RECORDS**, 3484 Nicolette Dr., Crete IL 60417. (708)672-6457. A&R Director: Danny Mack. Record company, music publisher (Syntony Publishing/BMI), record producer (The Danny Mack Music Group). Estab. 1983. Releases 3-4 singles, 1 LP, 2 EPS, 1 CD/year. Works with musicians/artists on record contract or songwriters on royalty contract. Pays 5% royalty to artists on contract; statutory rate to publisher per song on record.Charges songwriters in advance for custom demo services only.
How to Contact: Submit demo tape by mail. Unsolicited submissions are OK. Prefers cassette with 3 songs and lyric sheet. SASE. Reports in 3 weeks.
Music: Mostly **country, novelty, polka**; also **Southern gospel, Christmas.** Released "Heaven Bound" (by D. O'Connor/S. Fowler), recorded by Danny Mack (country); "The New Anniversary Waltz" (by D. Mack/G. Skupien), recorded by Danny Mack (MOR); "Da Bulls Da Bears Da Beer" (by Danny Mack), recorded by Danny Mack and George Skupien (novelty polka) all on Briarhill Records. Other artists include The Polka Naturals, Mike Surratt and The Continentals of Washington D.C.
Tips: "We are a small but very aggressive independent company. If we are interested in your material for recording by one of our artists we pay the costs. We will do custom recording projects and production fees are charged to client. We insist the artist/writer be specific in his query or submission. Briarhill was a 1992 recipient of Indie Label of the Year from the CMAA. Always mention the *Songwriter's Market* when contacting us."

BROKEN RECORDS INTERNATIONAL, 305 S. Westmore Ave., Lombard IL 60148. (708)916-6874. International A&R: Roy Bocchieri. Labels include Broken Records International. Record company. Estab. 1984. Works with musicians/artists on contract. Payment negotiable.
How to Contact: Submit demo tape—unsolicited submissions are OK. Prefers cassette or CDs (or VHS videocassette) with at least 2 songs and lyric sheet. Does not return material. Reports in 8 weeks.
Music: Mostly **rock, pop** and **dance**; also **acoustic** and **industrial.** Released *Electric*, written and recorded by LeRoy on Broken Records (pop).

***BSW RECORDS**, P.O. Box 2297, Universal City TX 78148. (210)653-3987. President: Frank Wilson. Record company, music publisher (BSW Records/BMI) and record producer. Estab. 1987. Releases 12 singles, 4 LPS and 6 CDs/year. Works with musicians/artists on record contract or songwriters on royalty contract. Pays statutory rate to publisher per song on record.
How to Contact: Submit demo tape by mail. Unsolicited submissions are OK. Prefers cassette (or ¾" videocassette) with 3 songs and lyric sheet. SASE. Reports in 3-5 weeks.
Music: Mostly **country, rock** and **blues.** Released *Erma*, "Out The Window on a Breeze"; and "Art of The Heart" (by D. Fleming), all recorded by Paradise Canyon on BSW Records (country). Other artists include Candee Land, Bobby Lloyd, Jess DeMaine and Stan Crawford.

BULL CITY RECORDS, Box 6, Rougemont NC 27572. (919)477-4077. Manager: Freddie Roberts. Record company, record producer and music publisher (Freddie Roberts Music). Releases 20 singles and 6 LPs/year. Works with songwriters on contract. Pays standard royalty to artists on contract; statutory rate to publishers for each record sold.
How to Contact: Write or call first about your interest or to arrange personal interview. Prefers 7½ ips reel-to-reel or cassette (or videocassette) with 1-5 songs and lyric sheet. "Submit a clear, up-to-date demo." SASE. Reports in 3 weeks.
Music: Mostly **country, MOR, Southern rock** and **top 40/pop**; also **bluegrass, church/religious, gospel** and **rock/country**. Released "Redeemed" (by Jane Durham), recorded by Roberts Family (southern gospel); "Almost" (by Rodney Hutchins), recorded by Billy McKellar (country) and "Not This Time" (by D. Tyler), recorded by Sleepy Creek (southern rock), all on Bull City Records.

*CACTUS RECORDS, Nibelungenring 1, A-3423 St. Andrä-Wördern, **Austria** 0043-2242/33-519. Contact: Hans Hartel. Labels include Ha Ha Soundwave. Record company, music publisher and record producer (Hans Hartel). Estab. 1985. Releases 10 singles, 2 12″ singles, 4 LPs and 2 CDs/year. Works with musicians/artists on contract, songwriters on contract and musicians on salary for in-house work.
How to Contact: Submit demo tape by mail. Prefers cassette with 3 songs and lyric sheet. Does not return unsolicited material. Reports in 1 month "only if interested."
Music: Mostly **pop, German pop** and **instrumentals**; also **ethno** and **new age**. Released *Mengiani* (by Cheikh M'Boup), recorded by Edwin Pfanzagl on Soundwave Records; "Bella Maria" (by Chris White), recorded by Hans Hartel on Cactus Records; and "In mein Herz" (by Jonny Blue), recorded by Hans Hartel on Cactus Records. Other artists include Duncan Mlango, Chris White, Kids Can't Wait, Tam Tam des Damels d'Afrique, Weekend, Foxey, Johnny and the Credit Cards and Jonny Blue.
Tips: "You should have enough material for at least one album."

*CAFFEINE DISK, P.O. Box 3451, New Haven CT 06515. (203)562-0793. A&R Director: John Notsure. Record company. Estab. 1992. Releases 3 singles, 3 LPs, 4 EPs and 1 CD/year. Works with musicians/artists on record contract. "Special arrangements are often made."
How to Contact: Submit demo tape by mail. Unsolicited submissions are OK. Prefers cassette with 3-4+ songs, bio and press. Does not return material. Reports in 3-6 weeks.
Music: Alternative, rock, punk/pop; also **noise, avant-garde**. Released *Blood From the Streets of New Haven*, by various artists; "Trinity," by VMJ; and *The Sharklong Player*, by The Gravel Pit all on Caffeine Disk Records, all alternative rock. Other artists include Quest of the Moonbreed, Shiv, Flowerland, Blind Justice, The Streams, The Philistines Jr., Mighty Purple.
Tips: "If your demo percolates our ears it may be what we're looking for. Nothing is too loud or messy. Anything propelled by caffeine!"

CAMBRIA RECORDS & PUBLISHING, Box 374, Lomita CA 90717. (310)831-1322. Fax: (310)833-7442. Director of Recording Operations: Lance Bowling. Labels include Charade Records. Record company and music publisher. Estab. 1979. Releases 5 cassettes and 6 CDs/year. Works with artists on contract; musicians on salary for in-house studio work. Pays 5-8% royalty to artists on contract; statutory rate to publisher for each record sold.
How to Contact: Write first. Prefers cassette. SASE. Reports in 2 months.
Music: Mostly **classical**. Released *Songs of Elinor Remick Warren* on Cambria Records. Other artists include Marie Gibson (soprano), Mischa Leftkowitz (violin), Leigh Kaplan (piano), North Wind Quintet, Sierra Wind Quintet and many others.

CAPSTAN RECORD PRODUCTION, Box 211, East Prairie MO 63845. (314)649-2211. Nashville Branch: Nashville TN 37217. (615)649-2211. Contact: Joe Silver or Tommy Loomas. Labels include Octagon and Capstan Records. Record company, music publisher (Lineage Publishing Co.) and record producer (Silver-Loomas Productions). Works with artists on contract. Pays 3-5% royalty to artists on contract.
How to Contact: Write first about your interest. Prefers cassette (or VHS videocassette) with 2-4 songs and lyric sheet. "Send photo and bio." SASE. Reports in 1 month.
Music: Country, easy listening, MOR, country rock and **top 40/pop**. Released "Dry Away the Pain," by Julia Brown (easy listening); "Country Boy," by Alden Lambert (country); "Yesterday's Teardrops," by The Burchetts (country); and "Round & Round," by The Burchetts. Other artists include Bobby Lee Morgan, Skidrow Joe and Fleming.

*CARLYLE RECORDS, INC., 1217 16th Ave. S., Nashville TN 37212. (615)327-8129. President: Laura Fraser. Record company. Estab. 1986. Releases 3 12″ singles, 6 LPs/year, 4 EPs and 6 CDs. Works with musicians and artists on contract. Pays compulsory rate to publisher per song on record.

How to Contact: Submit demo tape by mail—unsolicited submissions are OK. Prefers cassette (or VHS videocassette). Does not return unsolicited material. Reports in 1 month.
Music: Mostly rock. Released "Orange Room" (by Michael Ake), recorded by the Grinning Plowmen; *All Because of You*, written and recorded by Dorcha; and *Sun* (by John Elliot), recorded by Dessau, all on Carlyle Records.

*CARMEL RECORDS, 2331 Carmel Dr., Palo Alto CA 94303. (415)856-3650. Contact: Jeanette Avenida. Label includes Edgetone, Accoustic Moods, Rainin' Records Fountain. Record company, record producer. Estab. 1987. Releases 4 singles, 4 LPs/year. Payment as negotiated, statutory rate to publisher per song on record.
How to Contact: Write first and obtain permission to submit. Prefers cassette (or VHS videocassette if available) and lyric sheet. SASE. Reports in 6 months.
Music: Mostly AC, **folk/rock, classical**; also **instrumental, rock.** Released *Rain* written and recorded by JOTL on Edgetone Records; *Lover Come Back* (by various), recorded by Marjorie-Jean on Carmel Records; *Classical Moods* (by various), recorded by Carmen Dragon on Acoustic Moods Records. Other artists include Fred Clarke, Imges From The Sky, Rainin' Records.
Tips: "Send a complete demo with lyric sheet. Call to follow up. Be very nice—do something to make your submission different."

CAROLINE RECORDS, INC., 11th Floor, 114 W. 26th St., New York NY 10001. (212)989-2929. Director Creative Operations: Lyle Preslar. Labels include Caroline Records, exclusive manufacturing and distribution of Plan 9 Records, EG, Editions EG, Sub-Pop, Realworld, Earthworks and Antler Subway Records. Record company and independent record distributor (Caroline Records Inc.). Estab. 1985. Releases 3-4 12″ singles, 10 LPs, 1-2 EPs and 10 CDs/year. Works with musicians/artists on record contract. Pays varying royalty to artists on contract; statutory rate to publisher per song.
How to Contact: Submit demo tape—unsolicited submissions are OK. Prefers cassette with lead sheets and press clippings. SASE. Reports in 1 month.
Music: Mostly **alternative/indie rock.** Released *My Aquarium*, written and recorded by Drop Nineteens; *New Wave*, written and recorded by The Auteurs; and *Oreo Dust*, written and recorded by Fudge, all on Caroline Records. Other artists include Idaho, Action Swingers, Paula Kelley, Revolver.
Tips: "When submitting a demo keep in mind that we have never signed an artist who does not have a strong underground buzz and live track record. We listen to all types of 'alternative' rock, metal, funk and rap but do not sign mainstream hard rock or dance. We send out rejection letters so do not call to find out what's happening with your demo."

CAROUSEL RECORDS, INC., 1273½ N. Crescent Hts. Blvd., Los Angeles CA 90046. (213)650-6500. A&R: Stuart Lanis. Record company, music publisher and record producer. Estab. 1963. Releases 3-6 12″ singles and 1-3 LPs/year. Works with musicians and songwriters on contract. Pays statutory rate.
How to Contact: Prefers cassette with 3-6 songs and lyric sheet. SASE. Reports in 3-4 weeks.
Music: **Top 40, MOR, country, gospel** and **children's.**

CASARO RECORDS, 932 Nord Ave., Chico CA 95926. (916)345-3027. Contact: Hugh Santos. Record company, record producer (RSA Productions). Estab. 1988. Releases 5-8 LPs/year. Works with musicians/artists and songwriters on contract; session players. Pays 7% royalty to artists on contract; statutory rate to publisher per song on record.
How to Contact: Write first and obtain permission to submit. Prefers cassette with full project demo and lyric sheet. Does not return unsolicited material. Reports in 4-6 weeks.
Music: **Jazz** and **country**; also **R&B** and **pop.** Released "If It Wasn't For Time" written and recorded by Borthwick (country); "Take One" written and recorded by Robinson (jazz) and *Sound of Christmas* (by various), recorded by Lory Dobbs (big band/LP), all on Casaro Records. Other artists include Marcia Dekorte, Pam Dacus, John Peters and Charlie Robinson.
Tips: "Produce your song well (in tune—good singer). It doesn't need to be highly produced—just clear vocals. Include lyric sheet."

*CAT'S VOICE PRODUCTIONS, P.O. Box 564, Newburyport MA 01950. (508)463-3028. Owner: Tom Reeves. Record company, music publisher (Rahsaan Publishing/ASCAP), record producer (Boston Tom) and recording studio (Reel Adventures II). Estab. 1982. Releases 8 singles, 4 12″ singles, 20 LPs, 6 EPs and 50 CDs/year. Works with musicians/artists on record contract, songwriters on royalty contract or musicians on salary for in-house studio work. Pays 15-25% royalty to artists on contract.
How to Contact: Submit demo tape by mail. Unsolicited submissions are OK. Prefers cassette (or VHS videocassette) with 3 songs and lyric sheet. Does not return material. Reports in 2 weeks.
Music: Mostly **rock, R&B** and **country**; also **reggae, new age** and **alternative.** Released *Cleanshot* (by Cleanshot) recorded by Asmega on Cat's Voice Records; *Andy Henry* and "Lucian Parken" (by Cleanshot), recorded by Asmega on Black Gold Records; and "Hot, Wet, Pink and Stinky," recorded

by the Mangled Ducklings on Cat's Voice Records. Other artists include Buddy Sullivan, Billy DeNuzzio, CoCo, Ned Claffin, Carl Armano, Myzz, and Barrio Productions.

*CEDAR CREEK RECORDS™, Suite 503, 44 Music Square E., Nashville TN 37203. (615)252-6916. Fax: (615)329-1071. President: Larry Duncan. Record company, music publisher (Cedar Creek Music/BMI), record producer (Cedar Creek Productions). Estab. 1992. Releases 20 singles, 5 LPs and 5 CDs/year. Works with musicians/artists on record contract or songwriters on royalty contract. Pays 10% royalty to artists on contract; statutory rate to publisher per song on record.
How to Contact: Submit demo tape by mail. Unsolicited submissions are OK. Prefers cassette (or VHS videocassette). Does not return material. Reports in 1 month.
Music: Mostly **country, country/pop** and **country/R&B**; also **pop, R&B** and **light rock**. Released "Rough Road to Fame" and "Lifetime Affair," recorded by Larry Duncan on Cedar Creek Records; and *One of the Good Ol' Boys* (by Debra McClure/Danny Neal/Tony Glenn Rast), written and recorded by Kym Wortham on ADD Records.
Tips: "Submit your best songs on a good fully produced demo or master."

*CELLAR RECORDS, 706 E. Morgan, Dixon IL 61021. (815)288-7029. Owners: Todd Joos or Bob Brady. Record company, music publisher (Sound Cellar Music, BMI), record producer (Todd Joos), recording studio (Cellar Studios). Estab. 1987. Releases 4-6 singles, 12 cassettes, 6 EPs, 2-3 CDs/year. Works with musicians/artists on record contract on songwriters on royalty contract. Pays 30% royalty to artists on contract; statutory rate to publisher per song on record. Charges in advance "if they use our studio to record."
How to Contact: Submit demo tape by mail. Prefers cassette (or VHS videocassette if available) with 3-4 songs and lyric sheet. Does not return material. Reports in 3-4 weeks.
Music: Mostly **metal, country, rock**; also **pop, rap, blues**. Released *Plague*, written and recorded by Blind Witness (thrash metal); *Death Becomes Us* written and recorded by Lefwitch (metal); *Walk with Anger*, written and recorded by Decadenza (speed metal), all on Cellar Records. Other artists include Manic Oppression, The Hyltons and James Miller.
Tips: "Make sure your live act is well put together. Send a clear sounding cassette with lyrics."

*CEREBRAL RECORDS, 1236 Laguna Dr., Carlsbad CA 92008. (619)434-2497. Vice President: Laura Maher. Record company, music publisher (Cerebral Records/BMI), record producer (Cerebral Records), recording studio. Estab. 1991. Releases 1-3 LPs and 1-3 CD/year. Pays negotiable royalty.
How to Contact: Write or call first and obtain permission to submit. Prefers cassette. SASE. Reports within 2 months.
Music: Mostly **progressive rock**. Released *You Fool You* and *I'll Be Back* written and recorded by State of Mind on Cerebral Records.
Tips: "Have fun. Write songs you like. Cover 'em with hooks and fill 'em with intelligence. Keep on growing as an artist."

CHA CHA RECORDS, 902 N. Webster St., Port Washington WI 53074. (414)284-5242. President: Joseph C. De Lucia. Labels include Cap and Debby. Record company, record producer, and music publisher (Don Del Music/BMI). Estab. 1955. Releases 1 single and 1 LP/year. Works with artists/musicians and songwriters on contract. Pays negotiable royalty to artists on contract and publishers per song on record.
How to Contact: Write first and obtain permission to submit. Prefers cassette with 4-6 songs and lyric sheet. SASE. Reports in 3 months.
Music: **Country, folk, acoustic jazz, rock**, and **religious**.

*CHALLEDON RECORDS, 5th Floor, Pembroke One Bldg., Virginia Beach VA 23462. General Counsel: Richard N. Shapiro. Record company, music publisher (Challedon Publishing Co./BMI) and record producer (Challedon Productions). Member NAIRD. Estab. 1990. Releases 1-2 LPs/year. Works with musicians/artists and songwriters on contract.
How to Contact: Write first and obtain permission to submit. Prefers cassette with 3 songs and lyric sheet. Does not return unsolicited material. Reports in 4 weeks.
Music: Mostly **rock/pop, college radio rock**. Released *Hired Gun* (featuring J. Sullivan), recorded by Hired Gun at Master Sound for Challedon Records. Other artists include Richard Neal.
Tips: "Want acts with existing live show; prefer acts proximate to Virginia area, but not mandatory. Looking for rock acts with very unique sound and no ordinary, routine lyrics. Want players, not poseurs."

CHATTAHOOCHEE RECORDS, 15230 Weddington St., Van Nuys CA 91411. (818)788-6863. Contact: Chris Yardum. Record company and music publisher (Etnoc/Conte). Member NARAS. Releases 4 singles/year. Works with artists and songwriters on contract. Pays negotiable royalty to artists on contract.

How to Contact: Submit demo tape—unsolicited submissions are OK. Prefers cassette with 2-6 songs and lyric sheet. SASE. Reports in 6 weeks "if interested."
Music: Rock.

CHERRY RECORDS, 9717 Jensen Dr., Houston TX 77093. (713)695-3648. Vice President: A.V. Mittel-stedt. Labels include AV Records, Music Creek. Record company, music publisher (Pen House Music/BMI) and record producer (AV Mittelstedt Productions). Estab. 1970. Releases 10 singles and 5 LPs/year. Works with musicians/artists and songwriters on contract and hires musicians for in-house studio work. Pays varying royalty to artists on contract; statutory rate to publishers per song on record.
How to Contact: Submit demo tape—unsolicited submissions are OK. Prefers cassette with 2 songs. SASE. Reports in 3 weeks.
Music: Mostly **country** and **pop.** Released "Too Cold at Home" (by B. Hardin), and "Girls Like Her" (by Wimberly-Hart), recorded by Mark Chesnutt on Cherry Records (country); and "Half of Me" (by Wimberly/Trevino), recorded by Geronimo Trevino on AV Records (country crossover). Other artists include Randy Cornor, Roy Hilad, Georgie Dearborne, Kenny Dale, Karla Taylor and Borderline.

CHERRY STREET RECORDS, Box 52681, Tulsa OK 74152. (918)742-8087. President: Rodney Young. Record company, music publisher. Estab. 1990. Releases 2 CD/year. Works with musicians/artists and songwriters on contract. Pays 5-15% royalty to artists on contract; statutory rate to publisher per song on record.
How to Contact: Write first and obtain permission to submit. Prefers cassette (or Beta or VHS videocassette) with 4 songs and lyric sheet. SASE. Reports in 4-6 months.
Music: **Rock, country, R&B; jazz.** Released *Blue Dancer* (by Chris Blevins) and *Hardtimes* (by Brad Absher) on CSR Records (country rock); also *She Can't Do Anything Wrong* (by Davis/Richmond), recorded by Bob Seger on Capitol Records. Other artists include Larry Robkoff.
Tips: "We are a songwriter label—the song is more important to us than the artist. Send only your best 4 songs."

CIMIRRON/RAINBIRD RECORDS, 607 Piney Point Rd., Yorktown VA 23692. (804)898-8155. President: Lana Puckett. Vice President: Kim Person. Record company. Releases at least 3 CDs and cassettes/year. Works with musicians/artists on contract. Pays variable royalty to artists on contract. Pays statutory rate.
How to Contact: Write. Prefers cassette with 1-3 songs and lyric sheet. SASE. Reports in 3 months.
Music: Mostly **country-bluegrass, New Age** and **pop.** Released *Nutcracker Suite* and *Solos and Duets* written and reacorded by Steve Bennett (guitar); *Forever and Always* and *Memories from Home* (by Lana Puckett and Kim Person), recorded by Lana & Kim (country); all on Cimirron/Rainbird Records.

*CIRCLE "M" RECORDS, 289 Fergus St. S, Mount Forest, Ontario N0G 2L2 **Canada.** (519)323-2810. Contact: Clare Adlam. Label include C.B.A. Records. Record company, music publisher (Clar-Don Publishing, Amalda Publishing), record producer (Clare Adlam Enterprises).
How to Contact: Submit demo tape by mail. Unsolicited submissions are OK. Write first to arrange personal interview. Prefers cassette and lyric sheet or lead sheet.
Music: Mostly **country, gospel, R&B.** Released *Lost in the Wilderness*, written and recorded by C. Adlam; *Saving To-day For To-morrow* (by C. Adlam), recorded by Bonnie Brigant; *Country Music I Tip My Hat to You*, written and recorded by Ted Morris, all on C.M. Records.

CITA COMMUNICATIONS INC., Dept. SM, 676 Pittsburgh Rd., Butler PA 16001. (412)586-6552. A&R/Producer: Mickii Taimuty. Labels include Phunn! Records and Tropē Records. Record company. Estab. 1989. Releases 6 singles, 3 12″ singles, 3 LPs, 2 EPs and 5 CDs/year. Works with musicians/artists on record contract. Pays artists 10% royalty on contract. Pays statutory rate to publishers per song on records.
How to Contact: Call first and obtain permission to submit. Prefers cassette (or VHS, Beta or ¾″ videocassette) with a maximum of 6 songs and lyric sheets. SASE. Reports in 8 weeks.
Music: Interested in **rock/dance music** and **contemporary gospel;** also **rap, jazz** and **progressive country.** Released "Forged by Fire", written and recorded by Sanxtion on Tropē Records; "I Cross My Heart" (by Taimuty/Nelson), recorded by Melissa Anne on Phunn! Records; and "Fight the Fight," written and recorded by M.J. Nelson on Tropē Records. Other artists include Most High, Sister Golden Hair and Countdown.

Refer to the Category Index (at the back of this book) to find exactly which companies are interested in the type of music you write.

*CLR LABEL GROUP, 1400 Aliceanna, Baltimore MD 21231. (410)675-7300. A&R Director: Stephen Janis. Labels include Ultra-Ethereal Records, Calvert Street CLR Records. Record company, music publisher (ASCAP). Estab. 1989. Releases 5-10 12″ singles, 10 LPs, 2 EPs and 12 CDs/year. Works with musicians/artists on contract or songwriters on royalty contract. Pays 10-12% royalty to artists on contract; ¾ statutory rate to publisher per song on record.
How to Contact: Write or call first and obtain permission to submit. Prefers cassette. Does not return material.

COLLECTOR RECORDS, Box 2296, Rotterdam 3000 CG **Holland**. Phone: (1862)4266. Fax: (1862)4366. Research: Cees Klop. Labels include All Rock, Downsouth, Unknown, Pro Forma and White Label Records. Record company, music publisher (All Rock Music Pub.) and record producer (Cees Klop). Estab. 1967. Releases 10 singles and 30 LPs/year. Works with musicians/artists and songwriters on contract. Pays standard royalty to artist on contract.
How to Contact: Prefers cassette. SAE and IRC. Reports in 1 month.
Music: Mostly **50's rock, rockabilly, hillbilly boogie** and **country/rock**; also **piano boogie woogie**. Released "Spring in April" (by Pepping/Jellema), recorded by Henk Pepping on Down South Records (50's rock); "Go Cat Go" (by Myers), recorded by Jimmy Myers on White Label Records (50's rock) and "Knocking On the Backside" (by T. Redell), recorded by T. Redell on White Label Records (50's rock).

COMMA RECORDS & TAPES, Postbox 2148, 63243 Neu-Isenburg, **Germany**. Phone: (6102)52696. General Manager: Roland Bauer. Labels include Big Sound, Comma International and Max-Banana-Tunes. Record company. Estab. 1969. Releases 50-70 singles and 20 LPs/year. Works with musicians/artists and songwriters on contract. Pays 7-10% royalty to artists on contract.
How to Contact: Prefers cassette and lyric sheet. Reports in 3 weeks. "Do not send advance letter asking permission to submit, just send your material, SAE and minimum two IRCs."
Music: Mostly **pop, disco, rock, R&B** and **country**; also **musicals**.

*COMMUNITY 3, 7 Dunham Place, Brooklyn NY 11211. (718)599-2205. Label Manager: Albert Garzon. Labels include Community 3 Russia, VERB. Record company. Estab. 1985. Releases 5-10 singles, 10 CDs/year. Works with musicians/artists on record contract or songwriters on royalty contract. Pays various royalties to artists on contract.
How to Contact: Submit demo tape by mail. Unsolicited submissions are OK. Prefers cassette (or VHS videocassette if available) with 5-7 songs. Does not return material. "We only respond if we like material."
Music: Mostly **rock, grunge, post-punk**; also **ethnic, jazz**. Released *Manres of Behavior* (by various), recorded by Kolibri on Community 3 Records (Russian pop); *Viva la Vulva* (by various), recorded by Astro Zombies on VERB Records (punk rock); *In the Va Bank Kitchen*, written and recorded by Va Bank on Community 3 Russia.
Tips: "Be original and have some talent. Be willing and ready to work hard touring, promoting, etc."

COMSTOCK RECORDS LTD., Suite 114, 10603 N. Hayden Rd., Scottsdale AZ 85260. (602)951-3115. Fax: (602)951-3074. Canadian, United States and European distribution on Paylode & Comstock Records. Production Manager/Producer: Patty Parker. President: Frank Fara. Record company, music publisher (White Cat Music/ASCAP, Rocky Bell Music/BMI, How the West Was Sung Music/BMI), Nashville Record Production and International Record Promotions. Member CMA, BBB, CCMA, BCCMA, British & French C&W Associations and CARAS. "Comstock Records, Ltd. has three primary divisions: Production, Promotion and Publishing. We distribute and promote both our self-produced recordings and outside master product." Releases 24-30 singles and 5-6 CDs/year. Works with artists and songwriters on contract; musicians on salary. Pays 10% royalty to artists on contract; statutory rate to publishers for each record sold. "Artists pay distribution and promotion fee to press and release their masters."
How to Contact: Submit demo tape—unsolicited submissions OK. Prefers cassette (or VHS videocassette) with 1-4 songs "plus word sheet. Enclose stamped return envelope if cassette is to be returned." Reports in 2 weeks.
Music: **Western music, A/C** and **country**. Released "Boogie Woogie Man" (by Charles Ingram), recorded by Rick Dean; "The Cost of Loving You," written and recorded by Sherry Holly; and "Soul Shakin' Man," written and recorded by Cari Schauer, all on Comstock Records. Other artists include The Roberts Sisters, Colin Clark, Carl Freberg, Jess Owen, Patti Mayo, Steve Cooley, Rydin' High and Mesquite Country.
Tips: "We have an immediate need for country material for our European division. Our international division consists of master distribution and promotion to the following nations: England, France, Germany, Belgium, Ireland, Luxembourg, The Netherlands, Scotland, Switzerland, Norway and Canada. Also Denmark and Austria. We do video promotion with air play promotions to C&W networks across North America."

*CONTINENTAL RECORDS, 744 Joppa Farm Rd., Joppatowne MD 21085. (410)679-2262. General Manager: Ernest W. Cash. Record company and music publisher (Ernie Cash Music/BMI). Estab. 1986. "We cover all musical services." Pays 8% royalty to artists on contract.
How to Contact: Call first and obtain permission to submit. Prefers cassette (or VHS videocassette) with 3 songs and lyric sheet. SASE. Reports in 2 weeks.
Music: Mostly **country** and **gospel.** Published *Just-Us-Three* (written and recorded by Just Us Bros.); *Another Birthday* (by Carl Becker), recorded by Ernie C. Penn; and *The Dream* (written and recorded by Bill Michael), all on Continental Records. Other artists include Johnny Ray Anthony, Ernie Cash, Bobby Helms, Eddie Baker, Clay Price and Jimmy Buckley.

COSMOTONE RECORDS, Suite 412, 3350 Hwy. 6, Houston TX 77478-4406. Labels include Cosmotone Music and Center for the Queen of Peace. Record company and music publisher. Estab. 1984. Releases 1 single, 1 12″ single and 1 LP/year. Works with songwriters on contract and hires musicians on salary for in-house studio work. Pays statutory rate to publishers per song on record.
How to Contact: Write first and obtain permission to submit. Prefers cassette (or VHS videocassette). "Will contact only if interested."
Music: All types. Released "Padre Pio," written and recorded by Lord Hamilton on Cosmotone Records (Christian/pop/rock); and "The Sounds of Heaven," "Peace of Heart," and "The True Measure of Love," by Rafael Brom (Christian progressive).

COUNTRY BREEZE RECORDS, 1715 Marty, Kansas City KS 66103. (913)384-7336. President: Ed Morgan. Labels include Country Breeze Records, Angel Star Records and Midnight Shadow Records. Record company, music publisher (Country Breeze Music/BMI and Walkin' Hat Music/ASCAP). Releases 15 7″ singles and 20 cassettes/year. Works with musicians/artists and songwriters on contract. Pays 25% royalty to artists on contract; statutory rate to publisher per song on record.
How to Contact: Submit demo tape—unsolicited submissions are OK. Prefers studio-produced demo with 3 songs and lyric sheet. SASE. Reports in 2 weeks.
Music: All types **country.** Released "Memories," written and recorded by Johnny Amburgey; "Stranded Betweeen Dallas and a Heartache" (by E. Morgan/E. Livermore), recorded by Billy Poe; and "Caution, Heartache Ahead" (by Mary Morgan), recorded by Eric Anderson all on Country Breeze Records (country). Other artists include Edging West, Buckshot, Jill Rogers, April Sloane.
Tips: "When submitting an artist package we require 3 of your best songs, a short bio and recent photo. Make sure your voice is out front and the songs are strong, both in lyrics and melody."

COUNTRY SHOWCASE AMERICA, 385 Main St., Laurel MD 20707. (301)854-2917. President: Francis Gosman. Record company. Estab. 1971. Releases 5 singles/year. Works with musicians/artists and songwriters on contract. Pays 3% royalty to artists on contract; statutory rate to publishers for each record sold.
How to Contact: Submit demo tape—unsolicited submissions are OK. Prefers cassette and lyric sheet. SASE. Replies in 1 month.
Music: Country. Released "More Than Once In A While" and "Almost In Love" (by Fisher/Weller); and "Tent Meeting Blues" (by Gosman/Vague) all recorded by Johnny Anthony on CSA Records (country).
Tips: "Keep it simple, with words understandable."

COUNTRY STAR INTERNATIONAL, 439 Wiley Ave., Franklin PA 16323. (814)432-4633. President: Norman Kelly. Labels include CSI, Country Star, Process and Mersey Records. Record company, music publisher (Country Star/ASCAP, Process and Kelly/BMI) and record producer (Country Star Productions). Member AFM and AFTRA. Estab. 1970. Releases 10-15 singles and 8-10 LPs/year. Works with musician/artists and songwriters on contract. Works with lyricists and composers. Pays 8% royalty to artists on contract; statutory rate to publishers for each record sold. "Charges artists in advance only when they buy records to sell on personal appearances and show dates."
How to Contact: Prefers cassette with 2-4 songs and lyric or lead sheet. Unsolicited submission OK. SASE. Reports in 2 weeks.
Music: Mostly **C&W** and **bluegrass.** Released "Screaming Demons," written and recorded by Randy Miles; "Missing In Action" (by Len Marshall), recorded by Tom Booker, both on Country Star Records; and "Tell Me What Shall I Do" (by Dave Martin), recorded by Mere Image on CSI Records. Other artists include Ron Lauer, Junie Lou, Linn Roll, Brenda Mae, Tammi McClean and George Mesina.
Tips: "Send only your best efforts."

*COURIER RECORDS, P.O. Box 201, Tecumseh OK 74873. (405)598-6379. President-Manager: Darrell V. Archer. Labels include Rapture Records, Conarch Recordings. Record company, music publisher (Bethlehem Music Publications, Archer Music, Rapture Music Publications) and record producer (Conarch Productions). Estab. 1985. Releases 8-10 singles, 12-15 LPs/year. Works with musicians/artists on record contract, songwriters on royalty contract, musicians on salary for in-house studio work and lyricists. Pays .80-1.00 per unit; statutory rate to publisher per song on record.

How to Contact: Submit demo tape by mail. Unsolicited submissions are OK. Prefers cassette (or VHS videocassette) with 3 songs and lyric or lead sheet. SASE. Reports in 2-3 months.

Music: Mostly **MOR sacred, Southern gospel** and **easy listening contemporary;** also **spirituals, choir material** and **youth/children's material.** Released *Children of the Lord* (by Archer) and *Teach the Children* (by Richards) (MOR); and *Handful of Dust* (by Meade) (traditional), all recorded by Archer on Courier Records. Other artists include The Chosen Few, Brush Arbor Voices, Legacy Orchestra and Vocal Bouquet Acappella Singers.

Tips: "We are especially interested in material that can be adapted to choral use. This can be songs of almost any type except heavy rock or rap. Keep this in mind when submitting your material for review."

COWBOY JUNCTION FLEA MARKET AND PUBLISHING CO., Highway 44 W., Lecanto FL 32661. (904)746-4754. Contact: Elizabeth Thompson. Record company, record producer (Cowboy Junction Publishing Co.) and music publisher (Cowboy Junction Flea Market and Publishing Co.). Estab. 1957. Releases 3 or more singles, 1-2 12″ singles and 1-2 LPs/year. Works with musicians/artists and songwriters on contract. Pays 50% royalty.

How to Contact: Not accepting submissions at this time.

Music: Country, gospel, bluegrass and **C&W.** Released "Desert Storm," "You Are the One" and "It Really Doesn't Matter Now" all by Boris Max Pastuch and recorded by Buddy Max on Cowboy Junction Records (C&W). Other artists include Izzy Miller, Wally Jones, Leo Vargason, Johnny Pastuck, Troy Holliday and Pappy Dunham.

Tips: "Come to one of our shows and present your song (Flea Market on Tuesdays and Fridays, country/bluegrass show every Saturday), closed July and August."

*CREATIVE LIFE ENTERTAINMENT, INC., 196 Tuxedo Ave., Highland Park MI 48203. (313)537-0590. Contact: A&R Department. Record company, music publisher (BMI) and record producer (Juan "JAS" Shannon). Estab. 1990. Releases 4 singles, 2 12″ singles, 5 LPs, 5 EPs and 5 CDs/year. Works with musicians/artists on record contract, songwriters on royalty contract, musicians on salary for in-house studio work and transcribers/music copyist/computer programmers. Pays 3-15% royalty to artists on contract; statutory rate to publisher per song on record. "Charges for copying, postage, faxes unless represented exclusively."

How to Contact: Submit demo tape by mail. Unsolicited submissions are OK. Prefers cassette (or VHS videocassette) with 3-4 songs, lyric sheet and photo. SASE. Reports in 3 weeks.

Music: Mostly **pop, rock** and **R&B;** also **hip hop (rap), alternative, gospel** and **country.** Released "All Banged Up" and *Sex, Party, Rock & Roll* (written and recorded by EZ Bang); and "If You Want A Man" (by Juan Shannon), recorded by Calvin May, all on C.L.E. Records. Other artists include Troy Jackson, Peace, Brigade and For Bad Girls Only.

Tips: "Know enough about the business to be comfortable with being flexible or know enough to listen. Be professional and work hard. Believe in yourself until you cannot believe in anything. (Hint: This never happens!)"

*CROWN MUSIC COMPANY, P.O. Box 2363, Brentwood TN 37024. Vice President: E. Burton. Music publisher (BMI). Estab. 1990. Releases 15-20 singles, 5-15 CDs/year. Works with musicians/artists on record contract or songwriters on royalty contract. Pays 15% royalty to artists on contract; statutory rate to publisher per song on record.

How to Contact: Submit demo tape by mail. Write first to arrange personal interview. Prefers cassette (or VHS videocassette if available) and lyric sheet or lead. SASE. Reports in 5-8 weeks.

Music: Mostly **country, pop, rock.** Other artists include Jeff Chance, David Frizzell, Ed Bruce, Buck Owens and Doug Stone.

Tips: "Please send a bio/picture and any other history of yourself as a performer/songwriter. What are your goals?"

*CUCA RECORD CO. (Division of American Music Co.), 3830 Hwy. 78, Mt. Horeb WI 53572. (608)695-1794. President: Jim Kirchstein. Labels include Night Owl, Top Gun, Jolly Dutchman, Sound Odessy, Age of Aquarius, Sara, Make Mine Old Time. Record company, music publisher (BMI). Estab. 1959. Releases 12 LPs and 2 CDs/year. Works with musicians/artists on record contract or songwriters on royalty contract. Pays 8-12% royalty to artists on contract; statutory rate to publisher per song on record.

How to Contact: Submit demo tape by mail. Unsolicited submissions are OK. Prefers cassette. SASE. Reports in 1 month.

Music: Mostly **Chicago style blues** and **old time.** Released "Mule Skinner Blues" (by Rogers), recorded by Fendermen; *Genius of Earl Hooker* (written and recored by Earl Hooker); and *Birdlegs* (by Banks), recorded by Birdlegs Pauline, all on Cuca Records. Other artists include Seven Sounds, Jimmy Dawkins, Billy Duncans, Harvey Scales, H.C. Reed and Comic Books.

Tips: "Submit material only after artist or songwriter has recorded the best."

*CYMBAL RECORDS, 1055 Kimball Ave., Kansas City KS 66104. (913)342-8456. CEO/President: David E. Johnson. Record company, music publisher (JOF-Dave Music/ASCAP). Estab. 1984. Releases 2 singles, 2 LPs and 2 CDs/year. Works with musicians/artists on record contract or songwriters on royalty contract. Pays 10-20% royalty to artists on contract; 50% to publisher per song on record.

How to Contact: Write or call first and obtain permission to submit. Prefers cassette with 4 songs and lyric sheet. SASE. Reports in 1 month.

Music: Mostly **pop, rock** and **jazz;** also **country, rap** and **classical.** Released "I Have a Dream," written and recorded by Reed Greenfield (pop) and "Frozen Roses" (by Don Grace), recorded by Ken Garrett (classical), both on Cymbal Records. Other artists include Ben Sher and David Wilkerson.

DAGENE RECORDS, Box 410851, San Francisco CA 94141. (415)822-1530. President: David Alston. Labels include Cabletown Corp. Record company, music publisher (Dagene Music) and record producer (David-Classic Disc Productions). Estab. 1990. Works with musicians/artists and songwriters on contract and hires musicians on salary for in-house studio work. Pays statutory rate to publishers per song on record.

How to Contact: Write or call first and obtain permission to submit. Prefers cassette (or VHS videocassette) with 2 songs and lyric sheet. Does not return unsolicited material.

Music: Mostly **R&B/rap, dance** and **pop;** also **gospel.** Released "Mind Ya Own" (by Bernard Henderson/Marcus Justice) recorded by 2WO Dominatorz on Dagene Records; "Started Life" (by David/M. Campbell) recorded by Star Child on Dagene Records and "Lies" written and recorded by David on Cabletown Records (all rap 12"). Other artists include Taxi.

*ALAN DALE PRODUCTIONS, 1630 Judith Lane, Indianapolis IN 46227. (317)786-1630. President: Alan D. Heshelman. Labels include ALTO Records. Record company. Estab. 1990. Works with musicians/artists on record contract or songwriters on royalty contract.

How to Contact: Submit demo tape by mail. Unsolicited submissions are OK. Prefers cassette with 3 songs. SASE. Reports in 4-6 weeks.

Music: Mostly **adult contemporary, country, jazz, gospel,** New Age. Released "Better Than Before" (by Johnna Maze); "Haunting Love" (adult) and "In Love With Me" (contemporary) both by Alan Dale, all recorded by Trinia on A.D.P. Records. Other artists include Still Water.

Tips: "Create a writing style with good paraphrasing and excellent vocals."

DAT BEAT RECORDS, INC., Suite 4303, 333 E. Ontario, Chicago IL 60611. (312)751-0906. Contact: Robert Shelist. Labels include UBAD Records. Record company. Estab. 1989. Works with musicians/artists and songwriters on contract and hires musicians for in-house studio work. Pays 5-15% royalty to artists on contract; rate to publisher per song on record varies.

How to Contact: Submit demo tape—unsolicited submissions are OK. Prefers cassette with 4 songs and lyric sheet or lead sheet. Does not return unsolicited material. Reports in 2-3 weeks.

Music: Mostly **rap, pop, dance;** also **R&B, rock** and **New Age.** Released *Fever for the Flavor* written and recorded by O.Z. on UBAD Records; *Strictly Soul* recorded by 2 Damn on Dat Beat Records.

DEMI MONDE RECORDS AND PUBLISHING, LTD., Foel Studio, Llanfair Caereinion, Powys, Wales, **United Kingdom.** Phone: (0938)810758. Managing Director: Dave Anderson. Record company and music publisher (Demi Monde Records & Publishing, Lts.) and record producer (Dave Anderson). Estab. 1983. Releases 5 12" singles, 10 LPs and 6 CDs/year. Works with musicians/artists and songwriters on contract; hires musicians for in-house studio work. Pays 10-12% royalty to artists on contract; statutory rate to publisher per song on record.

How to Contact: Prefers cassette with 3-4 songs. SAE and IRC. Reports in 1 month.

Music: Rock, R&B and pop. Released *Hawkwind* and *Amon Duul II & Gong* (by Band), and *Groundhogs* (by T.S. McPhee), all on Demi Monde Records.

*DETROIT MUNICIPAL RECORDINGS, P.O. Box 20879, Detroit MI 48220. (313)547-2722. Fax: (313)547-5477. Label Director: Jameson MacBeth. Director A&R: Brice Rivers. Record company (BMI). Estab. 1992. Released 2 LPs and 2 CDs in '92. Works with musicians/artists on record contract, band and tour management. Pays 30-49% royalty to artists on contract; statutory rate to publisher per song on record.

How to Contact: Submit demo tape by mail. Unsolicited submissions are OK. Prefers cassette or CD with minimum of 4 songs. Does not return materials. Reports in 1-2 months.
Music: Mostly **alternative college** or **guitar type non-dance** or **non-industrial**. Released "The Complete Works of . . ." and "Christmas Eve Get Together With . . . ," recorded by Goober and the Peas on DMR Records. Other artists include PRIM U.K.

*DIAMOND WIND RECORDS, P.O. Box 311, Estero FL 33928. President: Reenie Diamond. Record company and music publisher (BMI). Estab. 1991. Pays standard royalty to artists on contract; statutory rate to publisher per song on record.
How to Contact: Write first and obtain permission to submit. Prefers cassette (or VHS videocassette) with 3 songs and lyric sheet. Does not return material. Reports in 4-6 weeks.
Music: Mostly **country, country blues** and **country pop/rock**; also **pop** and **R&B**. Released "Thunder In My Heart" and "Mama I Love You" (by M.L. Northam), recorded by Bronze Bonneville on Continental Records; and "Diamond Den" (written and recorded by Reenie Diamond) on Diamond Wind Records.

*DIGITALIA RECORDS, 234 Columbus Dr., Jersey City NJ 07302. (201)963-1621. Vice President/A&R: Charles Farley. Record company and record producer. Estab. 1992. Releases 10 12" singles/year. Works with musicians/artists on record contract. Pays 10-13% royalty to artists on contract; statutory rate to publisher per song on record.
How to Contact: Submit demo tape by mail. Unsolicited submissions are OK. Prefers cassette (or VHS videocassette) with 2-3 songs and lyric sheet. Does not return material. Reports in 3 weeks.
Music: Rap and **dance**. Released "Hey Jude" (by Lennon/McCartney), recorded by Wedgie & Veronica on Cohort Records (dance); "Brick House" (by Commodores), recorded by Loose Bruce on Arista Records (rap); and "I'm the Man" (by Brad Turk/Mitch Moses), recorded by M.C. Sneak on Digitalia Records (rap). Other artists include KXXK, Infamous Down & Out and EXXE.
Tips: "Send only your best material—no filler."

*DISC-TINCT MUSIC, INC., 111 Cedar Lane, Englewood NJ 07631. (201)568-7066. President: Jeffrey Collins. Labels include Echo USA, Dancefloor, Soul Creation and Soul Vibes. Record company, music publisher (Distinct Music, Inc./BMI, Distinct Echo Music/ASCAP), record producer (Echo USA Productions). Estab. 1985. Releases 50 12" singles, 10 LPs, 4 EPs and 15 CDs/year. Works with musicians/artists on record contract or songwriters on royalty contract. Pays 5-8% royalty to artists on contract; two-thirds of statutory rate to publisher per song on record.
How to Contact: Submit demo tape by mail. Unsolicited submissions are OK. Prefers cassette (or VHS videocassette) with up to 5 songs. SASE. Reports in 1 month.
Music: Mostly **R&B, dance, house/techno**. Released "Count on Me" (by W. Robinson), recorded by Eboneé on Echo USA/Soul Creation Records; "Hands on You" (by Coley/Collins), recorded by The Escorts on Soul Vibes Records; "Girl Ya Slammin" (by D. Nails), recorded by Danny B. Smooth on Echo USA Records. Other artists include Debbie Blackwell/Cook, Eleanor Grant, Black Rebels, George Kerr, Quincy Patrick.
Tips: "Submit good promo-tapes. List songs clearly."

DOMINO RECORDS, LTD., Ridgewood Park Estates, 222 Tulane St., Garland TX 75043. Contact: Gene or Dea Summers. Public Relations/Artist and Fan Club Coordinator: Steve Summers. Labels include Front Row Records. Record company and music publisher (Silicon Music/BMI). Estab. 1968. Releases 5-6 singles and 2-3 LPs/year. Works with artists and songwriters on contract. Pays negotiable royalties to artists on contract; standard royalty to songwriters on contract.
How to Contact: Prefers cassette (or VHS videocassette) with 1-3 songs. Does not return material. SASE. Reports ASAP.
Music: Mostly **50's rock/rockabilly**; also **country, bluegrass, old-time blues** and **R&B**. Released "The Music of Jerry Lee," by Joe Hardin Brown (country single); "Ready to Ride" (from the HBO Presentation *Backlot*), by Pat Minter (country single); and *Les Rois Du Rockabilly* and *Juke Box Rock and Roll*, by Gene Summers (50s LPs), *School of Rock 'N Roll* by Gene Summers (50s EP) and "Cactus In The Snow" by Pat Minter (C&W).
Tips: "If you own masters of 1950s rock and rock-a-billy, contact us first! We will work with you on a percentage basis for overseas release. We have active releases in Holland, Switzerland, Belgium, Australia, England, France, Sweden, Norway and the US at the present. We need original masters. You must be able to prove ownership of tapes before we can accept a deal. We're looking for little-known, obscure recordings. We have the market if you have the tapes! Sample records available. Send SASE for catalogue. We are also interested in C&W and rockabilly *artists* who have not recorded for awhile but still have the voice and appeal to sell overseas. *We request a photo and bio with material submission.*"

*DUKE STREET RECORDS, 121 Logan Ave., Toronto, Ontario M4M 2M9 **Canada**. President: Andrew S. Hermant. Record company, music publisher (Red Sky Music & Top Side Charlie/SOCAN), record producer (Horsefeathers Music Company) and studio recording. Estab. 1980. Releases 4 LPs/year. Works with musicians/artists on record contract, songwriters on royalty contract or musicians on salary for in-house studio work.
How to Contact: Submit demo tape by mail. Unsolicited submissions are OK. Prefers cassette (or VHS videocassette) with 3-4 songs and lyric sheet. SASE. Reports in 1-2 months.
Music: Mostly **rock, pop** and **jazz**. Released *Ipsofacto* (by Rik Emmett) and *Three Hands* (by Don Ross) both on Duke Street Records. Other artists include Danny Brooks, John Cody and Moe Koffman.

DUPUY RECORDS/PRODUCTIONS/PUBLISHING, INC., 2505 N. Verdugo Rd., Glendale CA 91208. (818)241-6732. President: Pedro Dupuy. Record company, record producer and music publisher (Dupuy Publishing, Inc./ASCAP). Releases 5 singles and 3 LPs/year. Works with artists and songwriters on contract; musicians on salary for in-house studio work. Pays negotiable rate to publishers for each record sold.
How to Contact: Write or call first or arrange personal interview. Prefers cassette with 2-4 songs and lyric sheet. SASE. Reports in 1 month.
Music: **Easy listening, jazz, MOR, R&B, soul** and **top 40/pop**. Artists include John Anthony, Robert Feeney and Kimo Kane.
Tips: Needs "very definite lyrics with hook."

*E.A.R.S. INC., Box 8132, Philadelphia PA 19101. (215)328-1619. President/General Manager: Jim Miller. Labels include Encounter Records and Electro Jazz Music. Record company (BMI) and record producer (E.A.R.S. Inc.). Estab. 1986. Releases 3 cassettes and 3 CDs/year. Works with musicians/artists on record contract, musicians on salary for in-house studio work. Pays 10-20% royalty to artists on contract; statutory rate to publisher per song on record.
How to Contact: Submit demo tape by mail. Unsolicited submissions are OK. Prefers cassette (or VHS or BETA videocassette). SASE. Reports within 6 months.
Music: Jazz. Released *Tunnel Vision*, recorded by Reverie; *Blue Nite*, recorded by Andy Lalasis/John Mulhern; and *Street Blues*, recorded by "Father John" D'Amico, all on E.A.R.S. Inc. Records. Other artists include Evelyn Simms, Leslie Savoy Burrs, Suzanne Cloud, Richard Drueding, Don Glanden and KMQ.
Tips: "Shop your stuff around. Consider us the last resort of record labels. Only contact us if you *have* to get your stuff out because you *know* it's so good it's been rejected by everyone else."

E.S.R. RECORDS, 61 Burnthouse Lane, Exeter, Devon EX2 6AZ **United Kingdom**. Phone: (0392)57880. M.D: John Greenslade. Record company (P.R.S.) and record producer (E.S.R. Productions). Estab. 1965. Releases 4 singles and 10 LPs/year. Works with musicians on salary for in-house studio work. Pays standard royalty; statutory rate to publisher per song on records.
How to Contact: Submit demo tape by mail—unsolicited submissions are OK. Prefers cassette with 4 songs and lyric sheet. SASE. Reports in 1 month.
Music: Mostly **country** and **MOR**. Released "The Best Is Yet To Come" (by John Greenslade), recorded by Marty Henry (country); "Tomorrow" (by John Greenslade), recorded by Mascarade (MOR); and "A Kind Of Loving" (by T. Jennings), recorded by Mike Scott (MOR), all on E.S.R. Records. Other artists include Kar Barron, Johnny Solo, Barracuda, Johnny Ramone, Sunset Haze and Tony Royale.

*EARACHE RECORDS/EARACHE SONGS, 70A Greenwich Ave. #457, New York NY 10011. Label Director: Jim Welch. Labels include SubBass Records. Record company and music publisher (PRS/BMI). Estab. 1986. Releases 6 singles, 6 12″ singles, 12 LPs, 6 EPs and 12 CDs/year. Works with musicians/artists on record contract. Pays various royalty; various rate to publisher per song on record.
How to Contact: Submit demo tape by mail. Unsolicited submissions are OK. Prefers cassette (or ½″ VHS videocassette) with 3-4 songs. Does not return material. Reports in 3 weeks.
Music: Mostly **alternative, metal** and **rock**; also **techno/rave** and **industrial/experimental**. Released *Pure* (by Justin Brodrick), recorded by Godflesh on Earache Records (alternative); *Soul Sacrifice*, written and recorded by Cathedral, on Earache/Columbia Records (rock/metal); and *Utopia Banished*, written and recorded by Napalm Death, on Earache Records (alternative/metal). Other artists include Fudge Tunnel, Morbid Angel, Carcass, Entombed, Brutal Truth and Bolt Thrower.
Tips: "Be original!"

*ELEMENT RECORDS, Box 30260, Bakersfield CA 93385-1260. President: Judge A. Robertson. Record company. Estab. 1978. Releases 5 singles and 5 EPs/year. Works with musicians/artists on contract. Pays standard royalty.

How to Contact: Write first to arrange personal interview. Prefers cassette with 1 or more songs and lyric sheet.
Music: All types. Released "I Like You The Way You Are" written and recorded by Jar The Superstar (funk); "God They May Not Love You" and "Let the Beauty Of The Lord Come Down On Us" by Judge A. Robertson (gospel); and "Spirits of Truth," by Jar The Superstar (Christian pop).

*EMPTY SKY RECORDS, P.O. Box 626, Verplanck NY 10596. Producer/Manager: Rick Carbone. Labels include Verplanck, Yankee Records. Record company, music publisher and record producer (Rick Carbone-Empty Sky). Estab. 1982. Releases 15-20 singles, 2 12″ singles, 2 LPs, 1 EP and 1 CD/ year. Works with musicians/artists and songwriters on contract. Pays 8-10% royalty to artists on contract; statutory rate to publisher per song on record.
How to Contact: Submit demo tape by mail. Unsolicited submissions are OK. Prefers cassette with 3-5 songs and lyric sheet. SASE. Reports in 2-3 months.
Music: Mostly **country, gospel** and **pop**; also **rap, rock** and **rap/gospel.** Released "The Bowling Ball" (by Carl Becker), recorded by GutterBall Band on Empty Sky Records (pop); "I Wanna Be In NY City" (by M. LaJiness/R. Sanders), recorded by Ray Sanders on Yankee Records (rock); and "White Water" (by Eleanor Aldridge), recorded by Phil Coley on Verplanck Records (country). Other artists include The Dependents, The Sweetarts, Bosco, The Sack Dance Band, True Blue, Wylie Justice, Leo Stephens and Denny and Ray.

EMZEE RECORDS, Box 3213, S. Farmingdale NY 11735. (212)724-2800, (516)420-9169. President: Dawn Kendall. Labels include Avenue A Records, Ivory Tower Records. Record company, music publisher (Emzee Music/BMI). Estab. 1970. Releases 35 singles, 20 12″ singles, 15 LPs, 15 EPs, 20 CDs/year. Works with musicians/artists and songwriters on contract and hires musicians for in-house studio work. Royalty to artists on contract varies; statutory rate to publisher per song on record.
How to Contact: Submit demo tape—unsolicited submissions are OK. Prefers cassette with 3 songs and lyric sheet. SASE. Press kit needed.
Music: Mostly **pop, rock, country**; also **R&B** and **gospel.** Released *Cryin'* and *Mephista*, written and recorded by Emma Zale (rock) on Vagabond Records; and *Prelude In A* (by John Sanders), recorded by Clave on Avenue A Records. Other artists include Bonnie Bowers and Ingnd Mayi.
Tips: "Don't be influenced by what people think. Write what you *feel*."

ESB RECORDS, Box 6429, Huntington Beach CA 92615-6429. (714)962-5618. Executive Producers: Eva and Stan Bonn. Record company, music publisher (Bonnfire Publishing/ASCAP, Gather' Round/ BMI), record producer (ESB Records). Estab. 1987. Releases one 1 single, 1 LP and 1 CD/year. Works with musicians/artists and songwriters on contract. Pays negotiable royalty to artists; pays statutory rate to publisher per song on record.
How to Contact: Submit demo tape by mail—unsolicited submissions are OK. SASE. Reports in one week.
Music: Country, all formats. Released "Toe Tappin Country Man," "All I Need" and "Two Faced." (by Schroeder) recorded by John P. Swisshelm, all on ESB Records (country).

ETIQUETTE/SUSPICIOUS RECORDS, 2442 N.W. Market #273, Seattle WA 98107. (206)524-1020; Fax: (206)524-1102. President: Buck Ormsby. Labels include Etiquette Records, Black Boot Records and Suspicious Records. Record company and music publisher (Valet Publishing). Estab. 1962. Releases 2-3 CDs/year. Works with musicians/artists and songwriters on contract. Pays varying royalty to artists on contract. Pays statutory rate to publisher per song on record.
How to Contact: Submit demo tape—unsolicited submissions are OK. Prefers cassette with 3-4 songs and lyric sheets. SASE. Reports in 6-8 weeks.
Music: Mostly **R&B, rock** and **pop**; also **country.** Released "Witch," "Psycho" and "Don't Believe In Christmas" (by J. Roslie), recorded by Sonics on Etiquette Records (rock).
Tips: "Tapes submitted should be top quality—lyric sheets professional."

*EVOLVING RECORDING PRODUCTIONS, #379, 2269 Chestnut, San Francisco CA 94123. (707)277-7211. Owner/President: Christopher Grihstead. Labels include Evolving Records. Record company. Estab. 1985. Releases 1-3 LPs and 1-3 CDs. Works with musicians/artists on record contract; songwriters on royalty contract; or developing artists. Pays negotiable royalty to artists on contract and negotiable rate to publishers per song on record. Charges in advance for some studio costs.
How to Contact: Submit demo tape by mail. Unsolicited submissions are OK. Prefers cassette with 1-4 songs and lyric sheet or lead sheet if possible. SASE. Reports in 2 weeks.
Music: Mostly **adult contemporary, pop, pop/jazz**; also **MOR, country.** Relesed *Formations* (by Christo Grihstead), recorded by C. Grihstead (adult contemporary); *Break Away*, recorded by Roy-Sharon Break (adult jazz) both on Evolving Records. "I'm currently looking for new artists, developing writers."

Tips: "Please type lyrics. Be sure to include SASE. Do not send material that is not in our genre. I'm willing to work with artists that have potential. We have a 16 track digital facility and produce inexpensively."

EXCLUSIVE RECORDING CO., (formerly In-House Publishing, Inc.), 146-05 130th Ave., South Ozone Park NY 11436. President: Barry Jones. Record company. Estab. 1985. Pays negotiated royalty.
How to Contact: Submit demo tape by mail—unsolicited submissions are OK. Prefers cassette with 4 songs and lyric sheet. "Include a music career resume and indicate *Songwriter's Market* referral." Does not return material. Reports in 1 month.
Music: Mostly **popular** and **dance**.
Tips: "Submit a quality recording that's easy to listen to."

EXCURSION RECORDS, Box 9248, San Jose CA 95157. President: Frank T. Prins. Labels include Echappee Records. Record company, music publisher (ASCAP/BMI), record producer (Frank T. Prins). Estab. 1982. Releases 2-5 singles, 1 LP and 1 EP/year. Works with musicians/artists and songwriters on contract. Pays 5-6% royalty to artists on contract; statutory rate to publisher per song on record.
How to Contact: Write or call first and obtain permission to submit. Prefers cassette (or VHS videocassette if available) with 3 songs and lyric sheet and lead sheet. SASE. Reports in 2-3 weeks.
Music: Mostly **pop**, **rock** and **country**; also **gospel** and **R&B**. Released "Red Roses In My Hand" and *Always*, both written and recorded by Ian Ballard; also *Time Clock Livin'* (by Wayne and Homer Osborne), recorded by Ian Ballard, all on Excursion Records. Other artists include Bittersweet.
Tips: "Keep writing and develop craft!"

EYE KILL RECORDS, Box 242, Woodland PA 16881. A&R: John Wesley. Record company, music publisher (Eye Kill/ASCAP). Estab. 1987. Releases 6 singles, 10 12" singles, 10 LPs, 10 EPs and 10 CDs/year. Works with songwriters on contract. Pays statutory rate to publisher per song on record.
How to Contact: Submit demo tape—unsolicited submissions are OK. Prefers cassette with 3 songs and lyric sheets. SASE. Reports in 4 weeks.
Music: Mostly **country** and **rock**; also **southern rock**. Released "JC Carr," written and recorded by Lori Gator (country); "So Far Away," written and recorded by Lori Gator (country); "Helpless," written and recorded by RJ Walli (country); and "Hearts Afire," written and recorded by Brad Peters, all on Eyekill Records.
Tips: "Send good clean cassettes of your best 3 songs."

FAME AND FORTUNE ENTERPRISES, P.O. Box 121679, Nashville TN 37212. (615)244-4898. Producers: Jim Cartwright and Scott Turner. Labels include Fame and Fortune Records and National Foundation Records. Record company, music publisher (Boff Board Music/BMI) and record producer. Estab. 1976. Releases 6 singles, 6 LPs and 6 CDs/year. Works with musicians/artists and songwriters on contract. Pays statutory rate to publishers per song on records. Charges for "production services on recording sessions."
How to Contact: Submit demo tape—unsolicited submissions are OK. Prefers cassette (or VHS videocassette) with 4 songs and lyric sheet. SASE. Reports in 6-10 weeks.
Music: Mostly **country**, **MOR**, **med. rock**, and **pop**. Released "Streets of Truth," written and recorded by Scott Stallard on CSA Records. Other artists include Angel Connell, Marty James, Don Deiser, Gret Stewart, Greg Cole and Scott Dixon Baker.
Tips: "We have expanded our company and now have Fame & Fortune Management (artist development and management). Potential artists *must* have financial backers in place. Contact Jim Cartwright or Susan Roach."

*FARR RECORDS, P.O. Box 1098, Somerville NJ 08876. Vice President: Candace Campbell. Record company. Estab. 1973. Releases 150 singles, 12 LPs and 12 CDs/year. Works with musicians/artists on record contract, songwriters on royalty contract. Pays various royalty; statutory rate to publisher per song on record.
How to Contact: Submit demo tape by mail. Unsolicited submissions are OK. Prefers cassette (or VHS videocassette) with 4+ songs and lyric sheet. SASE. Reports in 1 month.
Music: Mostly **rock**, **pop** and **country**; also **R&B**.

*FAT CITY ARTISTS, Suite 2, 1226 17th Ave. S., Nashville TN 37212. (615)320-7678. President: Rusty Michael. Record company, music publisher (Fort Forever/BMI), record producer (Creative Communications Workshop) and booking agency (Fat City Artists). Estab. 1972. Releases 4-6 singles, 4-6 LPs, 4-6 EPs and 4-6 CDs/year. Works with musicians/artists on record contract, songwriters on royalty contract and producers for demo work. Pays 12-15% royalty to artist on contract for demo work; statutory rate to publisher per song on record.

How to Contact: Submit demo tape by mail. Unsolicited submissions are OK. Prefers cassette (or VHS videocassette) with 4-6 songs and lyric sheet. SASE. Reports in 2 weeks.

Music: Mostly **rock, country** and **blues**; also **alternative, rockabilly** and **jazz**.

Tips: "Provide us with as much information as you can with regard to your material and act and we will provide you with an evaluation as soon as possible. Our advertising/promotion division specializes in developing effective artist promotional packages, including demos, videos, video presskits, photography and copy. We will evaluate your present promotional material at no cost."

*FEARLESS RECORDS, P.O. Box 2324, Whittier CA 90610. (310)946-9766. A&R Director: Steve James. Record company, music publisher (Shelf Music, BMI), record producer. Estab. 1990. Releases 5 LPs and 2 CDs/year. Works with musicians/artists on record contract, songwriters on royalty contract or musicians on salary for in-house studio work. Pays 12% royalty to artists on contract; statutory rate to publisher per song on record.

How to Contact: Submit demo tape by mail. Unsolicited submissions are OK. Prefers cassette (or VHS videocassette) with 4 songs and lyric sheet. SASE. Reports in 3 weeks.

Music: Mostly **country, pop, R&B**; also **rock, rap**. Released "Dance With Me" and "Moment of Truth" (by Tisbert/Mrock); and "Think it Over" (by Buddy Holly), all recorded by Steve James on Fearless Records. Other artists include Latin Side of Soul, Hot Rod Hearts, Crossover, Rod Coleman, Carol Martini and Ryan Flynn.

Tips: "Be ready to work with Steve James, who has been very consistent producing hit records for the last 10 years."

*FIFTH STREET RECORDS, 228 W. 5th St., Kansas City MO 64105. (816)842-6854. Office Manager: Gary Sutton. Record company, music publisher (Chapie Music Publishing, BMI). Estab. 1980. Releases 24 LPs and 12 CDs/year. Works with musicians/artists/artists on record contact or songwriters on royalty contract. Pays various royalties to artists on contract; statutory rate to publisher per song on record.

How to Contact: Call first and obtain permission to submit. Prefers cassette with 3 songs and lyric sheet. Does not return material. Reports in 1 month.

Music: Mostly **black gospel, country, rock/pop**; also **jazz, southern gospel, urban**. Released *Statement of Direction* (by Vic Jones), recorded by Joy Unlimited; *Don't Want 2 Be Left* (by D. Horne), recorded by John McConnell (black gospel); *Poet & Wealthy Man* written and recorded by Land-Hildebrand (pop gospel), all on Fifth Street Records. Other artists include Bob McCarthy, Deliverence Temple and DayStar.

Tips: "Write in the style of our artists. Write meaningful lyrics with a wide range of appeal."

*FINK-PINEWOOD RECORDS, P.O. Box 5241, Chesapeake VA 23324. (804)627-0957. Labels include Bay Port Records. Record company. Estab. 1954.

How to Contact: Submit demo tape by mail. Unsolicited submissions are OK. Prefers cassette with 2 songs. SASE. Reports in 3 weeks.

Music: Mostly **soul-blues, soul-gospel**.

Tips: "Try to work with a growing small label, one that is unknown with commercial broadcasting media!"

FIRST TIME RECORDS, Sovereign House, 12 Trewartha Rd., Praa Sands, Penzance, Cornwall TR20 9ST **England**. Phone (0736)762826. Fax: (0736)763328. Managing Director A&R: Roderick G. Jones. Labels include Pure Gold Records, Rainy Day Records, Mohock Records. Registered members of Phonographic Performance Ltd. (PPL). Record company, music publisher (First Time Music Publishing U.K. Ltd./MCPS/PRS), and record producer (First Time Management & Production Co.). Estab. 1986. Works with musicians/artists and songwriters on contract; hires musicians for in-house studio work and as commissioned. Royalty to artists on contract varies; pays statutory rate to publishers per song on record subject to deal.

How to Contact: Prefers cassette with unlimited number of songs and lyric or lead sheets, but not necessary. SAE and IRC. Reports in 1-3 months.

Music: Mostly **country/folk, pop/soul/top 20, country with an Irish/Scottish crossover**; also **gospel/ Christian** and **HI NRG/dance**. Released *Songwriters and Artistes Compilation Volume III*, on Rainy Day Records; "The Drums of Childhood Dreams," (by Pete Arnold), recorded by Pete Arnold on Mohock Records (folk) and *The Light and Shade of Eddie Blackstone* (by Eddie Blackstone), recorded by Eddie Blackstone on T.W. Records (country).

Tips: "Writers should learn patience, tolerance and understanding of how the music industry works, and should present themselves and their product in a professional manner and always be polite. Listen always to constructive criticism and learn from the advice of people who have a track record in the music business. Your first impression may be the only chance you get, so it is advisable to get it right from the start."

FLAMING STAR WEST, Box 2400, Gardnerville NV 89410. (702)265-6825. Owner: Ted Snyder. Record company (Flaming Star Records) and record producer. BMI. Estab. 1988. Works with composers and lyricists; teams collaborators. Pays standard royalty.
How to Contact: Submit a demo tape—unsolicited submissions are OK. Prefers cassette or VHS videocassette with up to 5 songs and lyric sheets. "If you are sure of your music, you may send more than 5 songs. No heavy metal. All other types." SASE. Reports in 3-4 weeks.
Music: Mostly **country, pop** and **rock** and **country rock;** also **gospel, R&B,** and **calypso.** Published "Scene of the Crime" and "Little Things" (by Bobby Goldsboro) and "One More Night" (by Jay Lacy), all recorded by Ted Snyder on Flaming Star Records (country).
Tips: "Listen to what is on the radio, but be original. Put feeling into your songs. We're looking for LPs and artists to promote overseas. If you have LP masters we may be interested. If you need you record produced we may be able to help. Flaming Star Records is a launching pad for the new recording artist. We try to help where we can. We are submitting songs to artists such as Glen Campbell, Kenny Rogers and Bill "Crash" Craddock among many others."

FLYING HEART RECORDS, Dept. SM, 4026 NE 12th Ave., Portland OR 97212. (503)287-8045. Owner: Jan Celt. Record company. Estab. 1982. Releases 2 LPs and 1 EP/year. Works with musicians/artists and songwriters on contract and hires musicians for in-house studio work. Pays 2-10% royalty to artists on contract; negotiable rate to publisher per song on record.
How to Contact: Submit a demo tape by mail. Unsolicited submissions are okay. Prefers cassette with 1-10 songs and lyric sheets. Does not return material. "SASE required for *any* response." Reports in 3 months.
Music: Mostly **R&B, blues** and **jazz;** also **rock.** Released "Get Movin" (by Chris Newman), recorded by Napalm Beach (rock); "Down Mexico Way" (by Chris Newman), recorded by Napalm Beach (rock); and "Which One Of You People" (by Jan Celt), recorded by The Esquires (R&B); all on Flying Heart Records. Other artists include Janice Scroggins, Tom McFarland and Obo Addy.
Tips: "Express your true feelings with creative originality and show some imagination. Use high quality cassette for best sound."

*FOLK ERA RECORDS, 705 S. Washington St., Naperville IL 60540. (708)305-0770. Vice President: Mike Fleischer. Record company. Estab. 1989. Released 6-12 LPs and 6-12 CDs/year. Works with musicians/artists on record contract. Pays negotiable rate to artist and publisher.
How to Contact: Write first and obtain permission to submit. Prefers cassette (or VHS videocassette) with 3-5 songs. Does not return material.
Music: Mostly **folk, bluegrass** and **acoustic country;** also **Celtic folk, traditional gospel** and **acoustic blues.** Released *Martin Greigh,* written and recorded by Taylor Whiteside; *World Class Folk,* written and recorded by Brandywine Singers; and *Arranmore Live,* written and recorded by Arranmore, all on Folk Era Records.

*FOREFRONT RECORDS, P.O. Box 1964, Hoboken NJ 07030-1308. (201)653-1990. Owner: Michael O. Young. Labels include Radcore Records. Record company. Estab. 1985. Works with musicians/artists on record contract. Pays 5-10% royalty to artist on contract; statutory rate to publisher per song on record.
How to Contact: Submit demo tape by mail. Unsolicited submissions are OK. Prefers cassette. Does not return material. Reports in 1-2 month.
Music: Mostly **punk, hardcore** and **heavy metal;** also **alternative.** Released *Cirkus Berzerkus,* recorded by the AG's; *WACT,* recorded by the Fiendz; and "Seersucker," recorded by Soda Can, all on Forefront Records.
Tips: "Have good, original material, patience and money."

*FOUNTAIN RECORDS, 1203 Biltmore Ave., High Point NC 27260. (919)882-9990. President: Doris W. Lindsay. Record company, music publisher (Better Times Publishing/BMI, Doris Lindsay Publishing/ASCAP) and record producer. Estab. 1979. Releases 3 singles and 1 LP/year. Works with musicians/artists and songwriters on contract. Pays 5% royalty to artists on contract; statutory rate to publishers per song on record.
How to Contact: Submit demo tape by mail—unsolicited submissions are OK. Prefers cassette with 2 songs and lyric sheets. SASE. Reports in 2 months.
Music: Mostly **country, pop** and **gospel.** Released "American Song" (by Roedy/Michaels), recorded by Terry Michaels; "Share Your Love" and "Back In Time," written and recorded by Mitch Snow, all on Fountain Records.
Tips: "Have a professional type demo and include phone and address on cassette."

FOUNTAINHEAD RECORDS, 3603-23rd St., San Francisco CA 94110. General Manager: Trevor Levine. Record company, music publisher (Art of Concept Music/BMI). Estab. 1989. Releases 1 single and 1 cassette/year. Works with musicians/artists and songwriters on contract. Pays 10% royalty to artists on contract; statutory royalty to publisher for each record sold.

How to Contact: Does not accept unsolicited material. To submit a tape, first send a self-addressed stamped #10 envelope (not a postcard). Guidelines will be returned to you. Reports back on tapes in 3 months—*only* if interested in using the material submitted.

Music: Mostly **pop/rock ballads**, "**moderate-paced meaningful rock** (not 'good time rock and roll' or dance music)." Released "My Silent Daughter," "Fortress" and "If This Is Goodbye," written and recorded by Trevor Levine on Fountainhead Records.

Tips: "We are interested in songs with powerful melodic and lyrical hooks—songs that are beautiful, expressive and meaningful, with uniquely dissonant or dramatic qualities that really *move* the listener. Our songs deal with serious topics, from inner conflicts and troubled relationships to anthems, story songs and "message songs" which address social and political issues—government corruption, women's and minority issues, human and animal rights. Keep the song's vocal range within an octave, if possible, and no more than 1½ octaves. The music should convey the meaning of the words. Please only contact us if you are interested in having your songs recorded by an artist other than yourself. We listen to tapes we receive as time permits; however, if the first 20 seconds don't grab us, we move on to the next tape. So always put your best, most emotional, expressive song first, and avoid long introductions."

FRESH ENTERTAINMENT, Suite 5, 1315 Simpson Rd. NW, Atlanta GA 30314. (404)642-2645. Vice President, Marketing/A&R: Willie Hunter. Record company and music publisher (Hserf Music/ASCAP, Blair Vizzion Music/BMI). Releases 5 singles and 2 LPs/year. Works with musicians/artists and songwriters on contract. Pays 7-10% royalty to artists on contract.

How to Contact: Prefers cassette (or VHS videocassette) with at least 3 songs and lyric sheet. Unsolicited submissions accepted. SASE. Reports in 2 months.

Music: Mostly **R&B, rock** and **pop**; also **jazz, gospel** and **rap**. Released "This Time (by Cirocco) recorded by Georgio on RCA (R&B/dance); "Broken Promises" (by J. Calhoun) recorded by SOS Band on A&M Records (R&B/dance) and "Sticking to You" (by Cirocco) recorded by Andrew Logan on Motown Records (dance/R&B). Other artists include Sir Anthony with Rare Quality, and Larion.

Tips: "Be creative in packaging material."

FRESH START MUSIC MINISTRIES, Box 121616, Nashville TN 37212. (615)269-9984. President: Mark Stephan Hughes. Record company, record producer (Mark Stephan Hughes). Estab. 1989. Releases 4 LPs/year. Works with musicians/artists and songwriters on contract. Pays 3-10% royalty to artists on contract; pays statutory rate to publishers per song on record.

How to Contact: Submit demo tape—unsolicited submissions are OK. Prefers cassette (or VHS videocassette) with 3 songs and lyric sheet. SASE.

Music: **Christian**; also **praise/worship, pop/rock** and **R&B**. Released *Hallowed Be Thy Name*, written and recorded by Lanier Ferguson; and *Lost Without Your Love* (by Mark Stephan Hughes), recorded by Kathy Davis, all on Fresh Start Records.

*FRETBOARD PUBLISHING, P.O. Box 40855, Nashville TN 37204. (615)269-5638. Contact: A&R Dept. Labels include Mosrite Records, Gospel Encounters Records. Record company, music publisher (BMI). Estab. 1962. Releases 1-4 singles, 3 LPs and 3 CDs/year. Works with songwriters on royalty contract. Pays statutory rate to publisher per song on record.

How to Contact: Write first and obtain permission to submit. Prefers cassette with 3 songs and lyric sheet. Does not return material.

Music: Mostly **country** and **gospel**.

FRONTLINE MUSIC GROUP, Box 28450, Santa CA 92799-8450. Contact: Kenny Hicks. Labels include Frontline Records, MYX Records, Intense Records, Joyful Heart Music. Record company, music publisher (Broken Songs Publishing/ASCAP, Carlotta Music/BMI). Estab. 1985. Releases 50 CDs/year. Works with musicians/artists and songwriters on contract. Pays 75-100% rate to publishers per song on record.

How to Contact: Prefers cassette (or VHS videocassette) with 3-4 songs and typed lyric sheet. Does not return unsolicited material. Must include SASE for return of product. "We only reply on those of interest—but if you've not heard from us within 4 weeks we're not interested."

Music: Mostly **gospel/contemporary/Christian, rock/pop** and **R&B**; also **worship** and **praise** and **children's product**. Released *We Can Heal the Pain* (by Tim and Lary Melby), recorded by Liason; *Can't Live Without Jesus*, written and recorded by Jon Gibson; and *Show Me* (by Nicole Coleman, Dave Mullen and David Cox), recorded by Nicole, all on Frontline Records.

Tips: "Put your best songs at the top of the tape. Submit a *brief* background/history. Listen to product on the label and try writing for a specific artist. Be professional; please don't hound the label with calls."

*FULLMOON ENTERTAINMENT/MOONSTONE RECORDS, 6930 Sunset Blvd., Los Angeles CA 91604. (213)957-0091. Contact: A&R Dept. Record company, music publisher (Taley Music/BMI, Terror Tunes/ASCAP). Estab. 1991. Releases 8 CDs/year. Works with musicians/artists on record contract, songwriters on royalty contract, musicians on salary for in-house studio work. Pays negotiable royalty to artists on contract.

How to Contact: Submit demo tape by mail. Unsolicited submissions are OK. Prefers cassette (or VHS-NTSC videocassette) with 3-5 songs and lyric sheet. SASE. Reports in 1 month.

Music: Mostly **hard rock, rock, alternative/dance**; also **pop** and **blues**. Released *Bad Channels* (by Blue Oyster) and *Dr. Mordrid* (by Richard Band), both recorded by Blue Oyster Cult; and *Netherworld* written and recorded by David Bryan, all on Moonstone Records (sound track). Other artists include David Arkenstone and Pino Donnagio.

Tips: "Your songs must be competitive (in content and presentation) with the best writers out there. We are a film and record company and work with only the best—the best old pros and the best new comers."

G FINE RECORDS/PRODUCTIONS, Box 180 Cooper Station, New York NY 10276. (212)995-1608. President: P. Fine. Record company, music publisher (Rap Alliance) and record producer (Lyvio G.). Estab. 1986. Works with musicians/artists on contract. Pays 7-12% royalty to artists on contract; statutory rate to publisher per song on record.

How to Contact: Submit demo tape—unsolicited submissions are OK. Prefers cassette. Include SASE for return of tape. Reports in 2-3 months.

Music: Mostly **"Undercore," college/alternative rock, rap, dance** and **R&B**. Released "Ring the Alarm" (by Lyvio G/Fu-Schnickens) recorded by Fu-Schnickens on Jive Records (rap). Other artists include 8 Ball, Peter Righteous and 148th St. Black.

*GANVO RECORDS, P.O. Box 36152, Oklahoma City OK 73136. (405)424-8612. A&R Director: Kathy James. Record company, music publisher (Wink Two Music, BMI), record producer (LaMarr & Ria). Estab. 1988. Releases 3 singles, 5 12″ singles, 3 LPs, 3 EPs/year. Works with musicians/artists on record contract or songwriters on royalty contract. Pays 20-25% royalty to artists on contract; statutory rate to publisher per song on record.

How to Contact: Submit demo tape by mail. Unsolicited submissions are OK. Prefers cassette with 3-5 songs and lyric sheet. Does not return material. Reports in 4-6 weeks.

Music: Mostly **soul/R&B, hip hop, contemporary jazz**; also **gospel, soft rock**. Released *Definitely Slammin'* (by Bob Jackson), recorded by Tune N 2 (hip hop); *Techs N Effect* (by Darion Haggin and Paul Cheadle), recorded by Undecided UND (rap); and *Church of Triumphant* (by Vilot Alberty), recorded by Church of Triumphant (gospel), all on Ganvo Records. Other artists include The L&M Progect.

Tips: "Demo should be the best quality possible-it does matter. We are not looking for potential, be professional."

GATEWAY, 4960 Timbercrest, Canfield OH 44406. (216)533-9024. President: A. Conti. Labels include Endive. Record company, music publisher (Ashleycon/BMI), and record producer. Estab. 1987. Works with musicians/artists and songwriters on contract. Pays 1-7% royalty to artists on contract.

How to Contact: Submit demo tape—unsolicited submissions are OK. SASE. Reports in 6-8 weeks.

Music: Video game market. *Algorithmic music* only. **Incidental** music. Released "Channel 2" (by A. Conti); "Livin On 20", recorded by Artboys; and "Zsa Zsa its" (by Sandle), all on Endive.

Tips: "Include explanation of algorithm used. Make it excellent music."

*GENERIC RECORDS, INC., 433 Limestone Rd., Ridgefield CT 06877. (203)438-9811. President: Gary Lefkowith. Labels include Outback, GLYN. Record company, music publisher (Generic/BMI), record producer. Estab. 1976. Releases 1-2 singles, 1-2 12″ singles, 1 LP and 1 CD/year. Works with musicians/artists on record contract, songwriters on royalty contract or musicians on salary for in-house studio work. Pays 5% royalty to artists on contract; statutory rate to publisher per song on record.

How to Contact: Submit demo tape by mail. Unsolicited submissions are OK. Prefers cassette with 2-3 songs. SASE. Reports in 4 weeks.

Music: Mostly **alternative rock, rock, pop**; also **country** and **rap**. Released "Bad Attitude" (by A.B. Merrill) and "I'd Rather Be Dancing" (by G. Lefkowith), both recorded by HiFi on Generic Records; and "Be My Girl" (by G. Lefkowith), recorded by John Fantasia on Outback Records. Other artists include Loose Change, Kenny Christian and JNB.

Tips: "Send only the best 2 or 3 tunes. Doesn't have to be master quality but don't send a poor dub that's almost inaudible. Also, don't send a lot of promo material, let the music do the talking."

GENESEE RECORDS, INC., 100 N. Chicago, Litchfield MI 49252. (517)542-2400. President: Junior A. Cole. Record company, music publisher (J.A. Cole Publishing) and record producer. Releases 3 singles/year. Works with musicians/artists on contract. Pays standard royalty.

How to Contact: Submit demo tape—unsolicited submissions OK. Prefers cassette. Does not return material. Reports in 3 months.
Music: Country. Released "Rollin' Road," "Love Lines" and "Nature Child" (by Junior A. Cole), recorded by Country Express on Genesse Records.

GLOBAL PACIFIC RECORDS, 270 Perkins St., Sonoma CA 95476. (707)996-2748. A&R: Howard Sapper. Record company and music publisher (Global Pacific Publishing). Releases 10 singles, 12 LPs and 12 CDs/year. Works with musicians/artists and songwriters on contract; hires musicians for in-house studio work. Pays 9% royalty to artists on contract; statutory rate to publishers per song on record.
How to Contact: Call first and obtain permission to submit. Prefers cassette with 3 songs. "Note style of music on envelope." Does not return material. Reports in 3 months.
Music: Mostly New Age, pop, jazz, "pop/quiet storm"; also rock, blues and classical. Released "Mystic Fire," written and recorded by S. Kindler (jazz); "Seasons," written and recorded by M. Johnathon and "Mango Cooler," written and recorded by C.M. Brothman, all on Global Pacific Records. Other artists include Bob Kindler, David Friesen, Georgia Kelly, Ben Tavera King, Paul Greaver and Morgan Fisher.
Tips: "Write us a hit! Know your label and market you are targeting."

GOLD CITY RECORDS, INC., Box 24, Armonk NY 10504. (914)273-6457. President: Chris Jasper. Vice President/General Counsel: Margie Jasper. Labels include Gold City Label (independent distribution and distribution through majors, including CBS). Record company. Estab. 1986. Releases 5-10 singles, 5-10 12″ singles, 3-5 LPs and 3-5 CDs/year. Works with musicians/artists and songwriters on contract and hires musicians for in-house studio work. Pays statutory rate to publisher per song on record.
How to Contact: Submit demo tape—unsolicited submissions are OK. Prefers cassette with 3 songs and lyric sheets. SASE. Reports in 3-4 weeks.
Music: Mostly R&B/gospel. Released *Praise The Eternal*, written and recorded by Chris Jasper; and *Outfront*, written and recorded by Outfront, both on Gold City Records.

GOLDBAND RECORDS, Box 1485, Lake Charles LA 70602. (318)439-8839. President: Eddie Shuler. Labels include Folk-Star, Tek, Tic-Toc, Anla, Jador and Luffcin Records. Record company and record producer. Works with artists and songwriters on contract; musicians on salary for in-house studio work. Pays 3-5% royalty to artists on contract; standard royalty to songwriters on contract.
How to Contact: Prefers cassette with 2-6 songs and lyric sheet. SASE. Reports in 2 months.
Music: Blues, country, easy listening, folk, R&B, rock and top 40/pop. Released *Katie Webster Has the Blues* (blues) and "Things I Used to Do" (blues), by Katie Webster; "Waiting For My Child," by Milford Scott (spiritual); "Gabriel and Madaline," by Johnny Jano (cajun country); and "Cajun Disco," by the La Salle Sisters (disco). Other artists incude Jimmy House, John Henry III, Gary Paul Jackson, Junior Booth, Rockin Sidney, Ralph Young, Tedd Dupin, R. Sims, Mike Young and Everett Brady.

GOLDEN TRIANGLE RECORDS, 1051 Saxonburg Blvd., Glenshaw PA 15116. Producer: Sunny James. Labels include Rocken Robin and Shell-B. Music publisher (Golden Triangle/BMI) and record producer (Sunny James). Estab. 1987. Releases 8 singles, 6 12″ singles, 10 LPs and 19 CDs/year. Receives 5 submissions/year. Works with musicians/artists and songwriters on contract and hires musicians for in-house studio work. Pays 10% royalty to artists on contract; statutory rate to publishers per song on record.
How to Contact: Submit demo tape—unsolicited submissions are OK. Prefers cassette, 15 IPS reel-to-reel (or ½″ VHS videocassette) with 3 songs and lyric or lead sheets. SASE. Reports in 1 month.
Music: Mostly progressive R&B, rock and A/C; also jazz and country. Released "Astor" (by S. Bittner) recorded by P. Bittner on Shell-B Records (rock); "Those No's" (by R. Cvetnick) recorded by J. Morello on Rocken Robin Records (R&B); and "Most of All" (by F. Johnson) recorded by The Marcels on Golden Triangle Records (A/C). Other artists include The original Mr. Bassman Fred Johnson of the Marcels (Blue Moon).

*GOLDWAX RECORD CO., INC., Suite 325, 3181 Poplar Ave., Memphis TN 38130-0166. (901)458-2285. A&R: Jimmy Willis. Labels include Bandstand, Beale Street, Abec and Rap-N-Wax. Record company, music publisher (Bianca Music/BMI, Rodanca Music/ASCAP). Estab. 1964. Releases 50

How to Get the Most Out of Songwriter's Market (at the front of this book) contains comments and suggestions to help you understand and use the information in these listings.

singles, 20 12" singles, 50 LPs, 30 CDs/year. Works with musicians/artists on record contract or songwriters on royalty contract. Pays standard royalty to artists on contract; statutory rate to publisher per song on record.

How to Contact: Submit demo tape by mail. Unsolicited submissions are OK. Prefers cassette (or VHS videocassette if available) with 3-4 songs and lyric sheet. SASE. Reports in 6 weeks.

Music: Mostly **R&B, country, rock;** also **blues, gospel.** Released "Nothing Between Us" (by Frank Longo), recorded by Lauralea; and "Walk A Way" (by Ollie Hoskins), recorded by Percy Milem, both on Goldwax Records; and "Burn, Make It" (by Darrell Coats), recorded by Total Package, on Rap-N-Wax Records. Other artists include Black Oak Arkansas, Ruby Andrews, Santana Milem, Black Is Black, B.C.D.

*GOPACO LIMITED, P.O. Box 664, Lombard IL 60148. Managing Director: Neale Parker. Labels include Griffin Music. Record company. Estab. 1988. Releases 15 LPs, 15 CDs/year. Works with musicians/artists on records contract. Pays 10-15% royalty to artists on contract; statutory rate to publisher per song on record.

How to Contact: Submit demo tape by mail. Unsolicited submissions are OK. Prefers cassette with 4-6 songs. SASE. Reports in 4-6 weeks.

Music: Mostly **classic rock, pop, heavy metal.** Released *Hawklords Live*, recorded by Hawkwind (heavy metal); *No Jive*, recorded by Nazareth (rock); *S/T*, recorded by Deliverance (heavy metal), all on Griffin Records. Other artists include Pendragon.

Tips: "We are looking mainly for groups with a good press repertoire."

*GORDON MUSIC CO. INC., P.O. Box 2250, Canoga Park CA 91306. (818)883-8224. A&R: Barney Gordon. Labels include Paris Records. Record company, music publisher. Estab. 1981. Releases 4 singles, 2 LPs, 2 CDs/year. Works with musicians/artists on record contract or songwriters on royalty contract.

How to Contact: Call first and obtain permission to submit. Prefers cassette (or VHS videocassette if available) with 3-4 songs and lyric sheet or lead sheet. Does not return material. Reports in 4-6 weeks.

Music: Mostly **children's, country-western, pop;** also **jazz.** Released *Izzy: Pest of West* written and recorded by Champ; *I'm a Gooslee* (by Champ), and "Armor Woman" (by J.G. Elliot), recorded by The Googles, all on Paris Records (children's).

GO-ROC-CO-POP RECORDS, % Voice Notes Publishing Co., 7526 Standifer Gap Rd., Chattanooga TN 37421. (615)624-0815. President: B.J. Keener. Record company. Estab. 1984. Works with musicians/artists and songwriters on contract. Pays standard royalty to artists on contract.

How to Contact: Submit demo tape—unsolicited submissions are OK. Prefers cassette (or VHS videocassette) with 1-5 songs and lyric sheets. SASE. Reports in 3 months.

Music: Mostly **gospel, rock, R&B, country** and **pop.** Released *Get Your Own Money* (by Sharon Lewis), recorded by RENA; *Ghost of Music Row* (by Hatcher & Smith), recorded by RENA; and *Come On & Cry* (by Bruce Newman), recorded by Keith Hartline, all on GO-ROC-CO-POP Records. Other artists include LaWanda and Billy Joe.

Tips: "Be sincere, hard working and flexible, with a desire to succeed."

GRASS ROOTS RECORD & TAPE/LMI RECORDS, Box 532, Malibu CA 90265. (213)463-5998. President: Lee Magid. Record company, record producer, music publisher (Alexis/ASCAP, Marvelle/BMI, Lou-Lee/BMI) and management firm (Lee Magid Management Co.). Also SESAC. Member AIMP, NARAC. Estab. 1967. Releases 4 LPs and 4 CDs/year. Works with musicians/artists and songwriters on contract. Pays 3-5% royalty to artists on contract; pays statutory rate to publishers per song on record.

How to Contact: Submit demo tape—unsolicited submissions are OK. Prefers cassette with 3 songs and lyric sheet. "Please, no 45s." SASE. Reports in 4-6 weeks.

Music: Mostly **pop/rock, R&B, country, gospel, jazz/rock** and **blues;** also **bluegrass, children's** and **Latin.** Released "Jesus Is Just Alright" (by A. Reynolds), recorded by D.C.Tack on Forefront Records; "Praise the Name of Jesus" (by C. Rhone), recorded by Tramaine Hawkins on Sparrow Records; and "Dog Eat Dog World" (by Twist Turner), recorded by Julie Miller on Grassroots Records. Other artists include Gloria Lynne, Co Co, and Killer Miller Blues Band.

*GREENLEE RECORDS, Suite 321, 2459 SE TV Hwy, Hillsboro OR 97123. (503)293-3409. Fax: (503)648-2261. President: Venise Rivera. Labels include Gold Touch Productions. Member: NACB, NARAS, BMI, FCC licensed. Record company and music publisher (publishing by Penny's Enterprises/BMI). Estab. 1990. Releases 2-6 singles, 1-4 LPs and 2-4 EPs/year. Negotiates agreements. Royalty paid to artist, publishers and writers vary.

How to Contact: Submit demo tape by mail. Unsolicited submissions are OK. Prefers cassette (or VHS or 8mm videocassette) with 2-6 songs and lyric sheet. Does not return material. Reports in 2-8 weeks.

Music: Mostly **acoustical music, jazz,** and **pop/adult contemporary**; also **world music, R&B/pop/dance** and **classical/jazz instrumental**. Released "Love Is Still", written and recorded by Sunny Hilden (A/C); "Say Things That You Don't Mean," written and recorded by Jackie Carlyle (MOR); and "Just A Picture on The Wall" (by E. Davis/J. Davis), recorded by Elo Davis (country), all on Greenlee Records.

Tips: "Send your best material, don't give up the dream, be patient . . ."

*FRANK GUBALA MUSIC, 41 Hillside Rd., Cumberland RI 02864. (401)333-6097. Contact: Frank Gubala. Music publisher and record producer. Estab. 1962. Works with musicians/artists on record contract, songwriters on royalty contract.

How to Contact: Submit demo tape by mail. Unsolicited submissions are OK. Prefers cassette with 1 song and lyric or lead sheet. Does not return material. Reports in 2 months.

Music: Mostly **pop** and **contemporary**; also **C&W.**

*GULFSTREAM RECORDS, 4225 Palm St., Baton Rouge LA 70808. (504)383-7885. President: Barrie Edgar. Record company, music publisher (Silverfoot) and record producer (Hogar). Estab. 1980.Works with musicians/artists and songwriters on contract; musicians on salary for in-house studio work. Pays 3-6% royalty to artists on contract. Pays statutory rate to publishers per song on records.

How to Contact: Submit demo tape by mail—unsolicited submissions are OK. Prefers cassette with 4 songs and lyric sheet. SASE. Reports in 1-6 months.

Music: Mostly **rock** and **country**. Released "Louisiana's Basin Child," by Top Secret on Gulfstream Records (rock single). Other artists include Joe Costa.

*HALLWAY INTERNATIONAL RECORDS/1ST COAST POSSE, 8010 International Village Dr., Jacksonville FL 32211. Record company, music publisher (Aljoni Music Co./BMI), Hallmarque Musical Works, Ltd./ASCAP), record producer (Hallways to Fame Productions) and video makers (Cosmic Eye). Estab. 1971. Releases 4-6 singles, 8 12″ singles and 6 LPs/year. Works with musicians/artists on record contract, songwriters on royalty contract. Pay negotiated; statutory rate to publisher per song on record.

How to Contact: Submit demo tape by mail. Unsolicited submissions are OK. Prefers cassette (or VHS videocassette) with 2-4 songs and lyric or lead sheet. SASE. Reports in 6-8 weeks.

Music: Mostly **rap, R&B** and **jazz**; also **world,** (others will be considered). Released *Night Thang* (by J. Hall/A. Hall, Jr.), recorded by Hall Bros./Cosmos Dwellers on Hallway International Records (world/jazz); *Secret Dreams* (by Cosmos/A. Hall Jr.), recorded by Ronnie Is Cosmos (R&B); *U Ain't Know* (by Don Hall), recorded by H II O on 1st Coast Posse Records (rap). Other artists include Akshun Jaxon, Da Hood and Al Money.

Tips: "Rap, R&B-dance, jazz-world is what we do best—so, send your best and we'll do the rest!!"

*HALOGRAM, 23 Market St., Passaic NJ 07055. (201)777-6109. President: Tomasito Bobadilla. Record company. Estab. 1989. Releases 6 singles, 6 12″ singles, 3 LPs and 1 EP/year. Works with musicians/artists on record contract, musicians on salary for in-house studio work. Pays 6-8% royalty to artist on contract; statutory rate to publisher per song on record.

How to Contact: Submit demo tape by mail. Unsolicited submissions are OK. Prefers cassette with 3 songs and lyric or lead sheet. SASE.

Music: Mostly **dance, alternative rock** and **pop**; also **R&B** and **New Age.** Released "Invasion" (by Cool Say), recorded by Say Cees (dance); and "Dirty Laundry" (by Concept One), recorded by Dirty Laundry (dance), both on Halogram Records. Other artists include Lori Adams, Bettye Jordan and 3 Men on Moon Trip.

H&S RECORDS, Box 515, Waterloo, Ontario N2J 4A9 **Canada.** (519)741-1252. President: William Seip. Record company and music publisher (William Seip Music, Inc.). Estab. 1978. Releases 1-2 LPs and 1-2 CDs/year. Works with musicians/artists on contract. Pays negotiable royalty to artists on contract.

How to Contact: Submit demo tape—unsolicited submissions are OK. Prefers cassette with 3 songs and lyric sheet. Does not return material. Reports in 1 month.

Music: Mostly **commercial rock, top 40** and **hard rock**. Released *Breaking Loose*, written and recorded by Helix on H&S Records; and *Ray Lyell*, written and recorded by Ray Lyell on A&M Records.

HAPPY MAN RECORDS, Box 73, 4501 Spring Creek Dr., Bonita Springs FL 33923. (813)947-6978. Executive Producer: Dick O'Bitts. Labels include Happy Man, Condor, Con Air. Record company, music publisher (Rocker Music/BMI, Happy Man Music/ASCAP) and record producer (Rainbow Collection Ltd.). Estab. 1972. Releases 4-6 singles, 4-6 12″ singles, 4-6 LPs and 4 EPs/year. Works with

musicians/artists and songwriters on contract. Pays statutory rate to publishers per song on records.
How to Contact: Submit demo tape—unsolicited submissions are OK. Prefers cassette (or VHS videocassette) with 3-4 songs and lyric sheet. SASE. Reports in 4 weeks.
Music: All types. Released "Old Kentucky Home" (by Roger Wade), recorded by Colt Gipson; "Diamonds & Chills" (by Don Goodwin), recorded by Mary Ann Kennedy and *4 For the Road*, written and recorded by Overdue Band, all on Happy Man Records (country). Other artists include Ray Pack, Challengers, Bengter Sisters, and Scott Emerick.

HARMONY STREET RECORDS, Box 4107, Kansas City, KS 66104. (913)299-2881. President: Charlie Beth. Record company, music publisher (Harmony Street Music/ASCAP and Harmony Lane Music/BMI), and record producer (Harmony Street Productions). Estab. 1985. Releases 15-30 singles, 4-6 LPs and 3-5CDs/year. Works with musicians/artists and songwriters on contract; musicians on salary for in-house studio work. Pays 10% royalty (retail) to artists on contract; pays statutory rate to publishers per song on record.
How to Contact: Prefers cassette (or VHS videocassette) with no more than 3 songs and lyric or lead sheet. OK for artists to submit album projects, etc., on cassette. Also photo and bio if possible. "Due to the large amount of submissions that we receive we are no longer able to return unsolicited material. We will report within 6 weeks if interested. Please include a full address and telephone number in all submitted packages."
Music: Mostly **country, gospel, rockabilly, pop, R&B, bluegrass** and **rock**. Released "Smooth Talkin' Man" (by Terry Allen & Sue Mahurin), recorded by Terry Allen (country), "If She Leaves My Heart When She Goes" (by Edna Mae Foy and Val Zudell), recorded by Tony Mantor (country); "Like the Flip of a Coin" (by Woody Waldroup), recorded by Woody Wills (country), all on Harmony Street Records; and "What a Little Love Can Do" (by Paulette Howard), recorded by Wendy Bagwell and the Sunliteres, on Cannon Records. Other artists include Scott Hansgen, The Dusters, Terry Diebold and Georgia Carr.
Tips: "Songs submitted to us must be original, commercial and have a good strong hook. Submit only your best songs. Demos should be clear and clean with voice out front. We are interested in working with commercial artists with a commercial style and sound, professional attitude and career goals. Our records are released world wide and also available for sales world wide. Our standards are high and so are our goals."

HEATH & ASSOCIATES, #1058, E. Saint Catherine, Louisville KY 40204. (502)637-2877. General Partner: John V. Heath. Labels include Hillview Records and Estate Records. Record company, music publisher (Two John's Music/ASCAP), record producer (MVT Productions and Just a Note/BMI). Estab. 1979. Releases 8-10 singles, 3 12" singles, 4-5 LPs, 3 EPs and 3 CDs/year. Works with musicians/artists and songwriters on contract. Pays 5-10% royalty to artists on contract; statutory rate to publisher per song on record.
How to Contact: Submit demo tape—unsolicited submissions are OK. Prefers cassette, 7½ ips reel-to-reel or VHS videocassette with 3 songs and lead sheets. SASE. Reports in 2 weeks.
Music: Mostly **pop, country, R&B** and **MOR**; also **gospel**. Released "Dry Those Tears," written and recorded by Donald Dodd on Hillview Records (MOR); "Hot," written and recorded by The Word on Estate Records (gospel); and "Crazy Trucker," written and recorded by Michael Palko on Hillview Records (country).
Tips: "Be professional in submissions."

HELION RECORDS, Suite 216, 8306 Wilshire Blvd., Beverly Hills CA 90211. (818)352-9174. A&R: Dunia Abbushi. Record company and record producer (Greg Knowles). Estab. 1984. Releases 4 CDs/year. Works with musicians/artists on contract; hires musicians for in-house studio work. Pays 5-15% royalty to artists on contract; statutory rate to publisher for each record sold.
How to Contact: Call first and obtain permission to submit. Prefers cassette with 3-4 songs and lyric or lead sheet. Does not return material. "SASE for reply." Reports in 3 weeks.
Music: Mostly **R&B** and **pop**; also **country** and **comedy**. Released "Car Phone," by Sheeler and Sheeler; "Swingstreet," by Miriam Cutler; "Santa's Flight Test," by Barry Friedman and Greg Knowles; and *Angel* and "Telephone Blues," by Diana Blair.
Tips: "Treat your work as a business first and an art form second. You need the business head to get you into the door—then we can see how good your music is."

HERITAGE MUSIC, #311, 41 Antrim Cr., Scarborough Ontario M1P4T1 **Canada**. (416)292-4724. President: Jack Boswell. Record producer and record company (Condor-Oak). Estab. 1967. Deals with artists and songwriters. Produces 10-15 cassettes/CDs/year. Fee derived from sales royalty, lease or purchase masters.
How to Contact: Submit demo tape by mail—unsolicited submissions are OK.
Music: Interested in **instrumental** fiddle, steel guitar, Dobro, piano, etc. Also **country gospel, yodel, square dance, bluegrass**.

HIBI DEI HIPP RECORDS, #4872, 311 W. Monroe St., Jacksonville FL 32202. (904)448-3534. Producer: Aubrey Saulsby. Record company, music publisher (WASMC/BMI). Estab. 1986. Releases 4-6 singles, 2 12″ singles, 1 LP, 1 EP, 1 CD/year. Works with musicians/artists and songwriters on contract and hires musicians for in-house studio work. Pays standard royalty.
How to Contact: Write and obtain permission to submit. Prefers cassette 9 or 7½″ reel with 3 songs and lyric sheets. Does not return unsolicited material.
Music: Mostly **R&B, rap, jazz**; also **blues, pop** and **top/40**. Released "Because You're Mine" and "Free," both recorded by William Icey and "The Way That I Am" recorded by Willie Bones, all written by Willie A. Saulsby (R&B). Other artists include Hob Slob, King William.

*HICKORY LANE PUBLISHING AND RECORDING, P.O. Box 2275, Vancouver, British Columbia V6B 3W5 **Canada.** (614)465-1408. President: Chris Michaels. A&R Manager: David Rogers. Labels include Hickory Lane Records. Record company, music publisher and record producer. Estab. 1985. Releases 3 singles, 3 LPs and 3 CDs/year. Works with musicians/artists on record contract. Pays standard rate royalty to artists on contract; statutory rate to publisher per song on record.
How to Contact: Submit demo tape by mail. Unsolicited submissions are OK. Prefers cassette (or VHS videocassette if available) with 1-5 songs and lyric sheet or lead sheet (if available). SASE. Reports in 6 weeks.
Music: Mostly **country, MOR, gospel**; also **soft rock, musical compositions** and **children's music.** Released "Yesterday's Fool," "Country Drives Me Wild," and "Without You and Me," all written and recorded by Chris Michaels on Hickory Lane Records.
Tips: "Keep vocals up front. Have feeling in your song with a strong melody. Easy lyrics. Be original."

HOLLYROCK RECORDS, Suite C-300, 16776 Lakeshore Dr., Lake Elisnore CA 92330. A&R Director: Dave Paton. Record company, record producer and music publisher (Heaven Songs/BMI). Releases 4 singles and 6 LPs/year. Works with artists and songwriters on contract; musicians on salary for in-house studio work. Pays negotiable royalty to artists on contract; statutory rate to publishers for each record sold.
How to Contact: Prefers 7½ ips reel-to-reel or cassette with 3-6 songs and lyric sheet. SASE. Reports in 2 weeks.
Music: **Progressive, top 40/pop, country, easy listening, folk, jazz, MOR** and **rock**. Released *Everything* (movie soundtrack) and *Get Outta Town* (double cassette package).

*HOMEBASED ENTERTAINMENT CO., 96 St. James Ave., Springfield MA 01109. (413)746-8302. President: Timothy Scott. Labels include Night Owl Records, Second Time Around Records, Southend-Essex Records. Record company and music publisher (Tim Scott Music/ASCAP, Tim Scott Songs BMI). Estab. 1993. Releases 3 singles, 2 LPs and 2 CDs/year. Works with musicians/artists on record contract, songwriters on royalty contract, musicians on salary for in-house studio work. Pays 10-15% royalty to artists on contract; statutory rate to publisher per song on record.
How to Contact: Submit demo tape by mail. Unsolicited submissions are OK. Prefers cassete (or VHS videocassette) with 3-5 songs and lyric sheet. SASE. Reports in 4-6 weeks.
Music: Mostly **pop, R&B,** and **rap**; also **country, rock** and **gospel**. Released "Faithful" and "Holding On" (by Johnnie Hatchett), recorded by Physical Attraction; and "Cable TV is Just a Joke," written and recorded by Tim Scott, all on Nightowl Records. Other artists include TC, Lethal.

HOMESTEAD RECORDS, Box 800, Rockville Centre NY 11570. (516)764-6200. A&R Director: Alan Mann. Labels include Rockville Records. Record company. Estab. 1983. Releases 12 singles, 12 LPs, 2 EPs and 12 CDs/year. Works with musicians/artists on contract. Pays 10-13% royalty to artists on contract; ¾ of statutory rate to publisher per song on record.
How to Contact: Submit demo tape—unsolicited submissions are OK. Prefers cassette with 4 songs. Does not return material. Reports in 2-3 months.
Music: Mostly **punk rock** and **rock**. Other artists include Love Child, Cake Kitchen, Trumans Water, Babe the Blue Ox and Table.

*HORIZON RECORDING STUDIO, Rt. 1 Box 306, Seguin TX 78155. (512)372-2923. Studio Manager: Mark Rubenstein. Labels include Route One Records. Record company, music publisher (BMI). Estab. 1989. Works with songwriters on royalty contract or musicians on salary for in-house studio work. Pays 5% royalty to artists on contract.
How to Contact: Submit demo tape by mail. Unsolicited submissions are OK, write first to arrange personal interview. Prefers cassette (or VHS videocassette if available) with 6 songs and lyric sheet. Does not return material. Reports in 2 months.
Music: Mostly **pop, country, gospel**; also **R&B,** and **jazz**. Other artists include Mike Lord and Tom Gruning.
Tips: "Be persistent but patient."

*HOT RECORDS, P.O. Box 326, Spit Junction, NSW 2088 **Australia**. Phone (02)5502634. Fax: (02)5161103. Vice President: Lynlea McIntyre. Record company. Estab. 1983. Releases 2 singles and 6 CDs/year. Works with musicians/artists on record contract. Pays 50/50 or net profit to artists on contract; statutory rate to publisher per song on record.
How to Contact: Submit demo tape by mail. Unsolicited submissions are OK. Prefers cassette with 4 songs and lead sheet. Does not return material. Reports in 1 month.
Music: Mostly **rock, pop, jazz**; also **country, R&B** and **gospel**. Released *Black Ticket Day*, written and recorded by Ed Kuepper (rock); *Autocannibalism* (by Ed Kuepper), recorded by Aints (trash); and *Heaven on a Stick* (by Lovelock/Stedman/Leonie), recorded by Celibate Rifles (rock), all on Hot Records.
Tips: "Write original but well-structured songs."

HOTTRAX RECORDS, 1957 Kilburn Dr., Atlanta GA 30324. (404)662-6661. Vice President, A&R: Oliver Cooper. Labels include Dance-A-Thon, Hardkor. Record company and music publisher (Starfox Publishing). Releases 12 singles and 3-4 CDs/year. Works with musicians/artists and songwriters on contract. Pays 5-7% royalty to artists on contract.
How to Contact: Prefers cassette with 3 songs and lyric sheet. SASE. "We will not return tapes without adequate postage." Reports in 3 months. "When submissions get extremely heavy, we do not have the time to respond/return material we pass on. We do notify those sending the most promising work we review, however."
Music: Mostly **top 40/pop, rock** and **country**; also **hardcore punk** and **jazz-fusion**. Released *P Is For Pig*, written and recorded by The Pigs (top 40/pop); "The World May Not Like Me" (by Mike Fitzgerald), recorded by Mike Angelo (rock); and *Introducing The Feel*, written and recorded by The Feel (new rock), all on Hottrax Records; also "The Condom Man," recorded by Big Al Jano and "Ms. Perfection," by Larry Yates (urban contemporary). Other artists include Burl Compton (country), Michael Rozakis & Yorgos (pop), Starfoxx (rock), The Night Shadows (rock), The Bop (new wave), Secret Lover, The Bob Page Project (blues/jazz) and Roger "Hurricane" Wilson (blues rock).

*ICHIBAN RECORDS, Suite D, 2310 Marietta Blvd., Atlanta GA 30318. (404)355-0909. General Manager Publishing: Bryan Cole. Labels include Wrap, Wild Dog. Record company, music publisher (Koke, Moke and Noke Music, BMI), record producer. Estab. 1982. Releases 50 LPs, 50 CDs/year. Work with musicians/artists on record contract, songwriters on royalty contract. Pays various royalties to artists on contract; statutory rate to publisher per song on record.
How to Contact: Submit demo tape by mail. Unsolicited submissions are OK. Prefers cassette with 4 songs and lyric sheet. SASE. Reports in 2 months.
Music: Mostly **R&B, 60's style soul, blues**; also **alternative rock, rock**. Released *Something Mighty Wrong*, recorded by Tyrone Davis on Ichiban Records (soul/R&B); *Party Tuff or Stay Home*, recorded by The Shadows on Wild Dog Records (blues); *Power Stance*, recorded by Fleshtones on Naked Language (alternative).
Tips: "Research the people you are sending songs to, to know what they do—for example, don't send a country song to M.C. Hammer."

*I'LL CALL YOU RECORDS, P.O. Box 94, London SW1V 4PH **England**. Phone: (071)834-8337. Fax: (071)834-8331. Managing Director: E. Richard Bickersteth. Labels include G.N.M.C. Records. Record company. Estab. 1986. Releases 3 albums, 4 CDs/year. Works with musicians/artists on contract. Pays negotiable royalty to artists on contract; statutory rate to publisher per song on record.
How to Contact: Submit demo tape by mail. Unsolicited submissions are not returned. Prefers cassette (or VHS videocassette) with 3 songs and lyric or lead sheets.
Music: Mostly **rock** and **pop**; also **blends of music**. Released *Aggressive Sunbathing* and "Quirk," written and recorded by Fat and Frantic (rock skiffle); *The Mystery of The Universe*, written and recorded by Andy McCullough and The Clarinet Connection (classical rock); "Today is Heaven" (by Stephen Petit); and "The Music of the Orient Express" (by Andy McCullough & Barrie Guard), all on I'll Call You Records. Other artists include John Peters and Mind the Gap.
Tips: "A commitment to live performance is vital as well as an interesting fusion of musical styles."

INTERSTATE 40 RECORDS, Apt. 106, 900 19th Ave. S., Nashville TN 37212-2125. (615)329-3991. President: Eddie Lee Carr. Labels include Tracker Records. Record company and music publisher (Watchesgro Music/BMI and Watch Us Climb/ASCAP). Estab. 1979. Releases 12 singles, 1 LP and 2 CDs/year. Works with musicians/artists on contract. Pays 50% royalty to artists on contract; statutory rate to publisher per song on record.
How to Contact: Submit demo tape—unsolicited submissions are OK. Prefers cassette with 3 songs. SASE. Reports in 2 weeks.
Music: Mostly **country**. Movie and TV credits include "Young Guns of Texas," "Story of Evil Knievel," "Alias Smith & Jones," "The Christopher Columbus Story" and "Cochise."

JALYN RECORDING CO., 306 Millwood Dr., Nashville TN 37217. (615)366-9999. President: Jack Lynch. Labels include Nashville Bluegrass and Nashville Country Recording Company. Record company, music publisher (Jaclyn Music/BMI), record producer, film company (Nashville Country Productions) and distributor (Nashville Music Sales). Estab. 1963. Releases 1-12 LPs/year. Works with musicians/artists and songwriters on contract; hires musicians for in-house studio work; also produces custom sessions. Pays 5-10% royalty to artists on contract; statutory rate to publisher per song on record.
How to Contact: Submit demo tape—unsolicited submissions are OK. Prefers cassette with 1-4 songs and lyric sheets. SASE. Reports in 2 weeks.
Music: Country, bluegrass, gospel and **MOR**. Released *Life's Rugged Path* (by Otis Johnson), recorded by Glenda Ryder on NCP-301 Records; *Too Much to Dream Last Night*, written and recorded by Lonnie Pierce on NCP-303 Records; and *Somewhere Along The Line* (by Vicki Watts), recorded by Elaine George on Jalyn Records.
Tips: "Send good performance on cassette, bio, picture and SASE."

JAMAKA RECORD CO., 3621 Heath Lane, Mesquite TX 75150. (214)279-5858. Contact: Jimmy Fields. Labels include Felco and Kick Records. Record company, record producer and music publisher (Cherie Music/BMI). Estab. 1955. Releases 2 singles/year. Works with artists and songwriters on contract; hires musicians for in-house studio work. Works with in-house studio musicians on salary. Pays .05% royalty to artists on contract; statutory rate to publishers for each record sold.
How to Contact: Prefers cassette with songs and lyric sheet. "A new singer should send a good tape with at least 4 strong songs, presumably recorded in a professional studio." Does not return without return postage and proper mailing package.
Music: Country and **progressive country**. Released "Cajun Baby Blues" and "If You Call This Loving," recorded by Steve Pride.
Tips: "Songs should have strong lyrics with a good story, whether country or pop."

J&J MUSICAL ENTERPRISES LTD., Box 575, Kings Park NY 11754. (516)265-5584. Contact: Jeneane Claps. Labels include JAJ Records. Record company and record production. Estab. 1983. Releases 2-3 singles, 1-2 12″ singles, 1-2 LPs, 1-2 EPs and 1-2 CDs/year. Works with musicians/artists on contract and hires musicians for in-house studio work. Pays variable royalty to artists on contract; variable rate to publisher per song on record.
How to Contact: Write first and obtain permission to submit. Prefers cassette with 4 songs and lyric sheet. SASE. Reports in 3-4 weeks. "Typed letters preferred."
Music: Mostly **progressive** and **jazz**. Released "Picnic," "Sightseeing" and "Tang," all written and recorded by J. Claps on JAJ Records (jazz/pop).
Tips: "Be neat, short and present 2-4 songs."

*JIMMY JANGLE RECORDS, 42 Music Square W., Nashville TN 37203. (615)255-3078. President: Jim Kimball. Record company. Estab. 1992. Releases 2 LPs and 2 CDs/year. Works with musicians/artists on record contract, songwriters on royalty contract. Pay negotiable—9% up; statutory rate to publisher per song on record.
How to Contact: Write first and obtain permission to submit. Prefers cassette with 1-4 songs and lyric sheet. Does not return material. Reports in 4-6 weeks.
Music: Only **children's music**. Released *Calling All Kids!* and *Miles of Smiles* (by various), recorded by Scooter on Jimmy Jangle Records (children's).
Tips: "Only interested in children's music. Prefer songs with a strong story line, message or theme."

JOEY BOY RECORDS INC., 3081 NW 24th St., Miami FL 33142. (305)635-5588. Contact: Chavela Frazier. Labels include J.R. Records, American Faith Records. Record company. Estab. 1985. Releases 50 singles, 50 12″ singles, 15-20 EPs and 15-20 CDs/year. Works with musicians/artists on contract. Pays 6% royalty to artists on contract; statutory rate to publisher per song on record.
How to Contact: Write first and obtain permission to submit. Prefers cassette with 3 songs and lyric sheets. SASE. Reports in 6-8 weeks.
Music: Mostly **bass, rap** and **dance**; also **jazz** and **comedy**. Released "I Am Bass Man" (by Brian Graham), recorded by D.J. Fury; "Dogga Mix II" (by Keith Bell/Labrant Dennis), recorded by The Dogs; and "Bang Them Thighs" (by Edward Lopez), recorded by Creepdog, all on Joey Boy Records. Other artists include Mega JON Bass, Ant D & The Puppies and Two Trick Daddys.
Tips: "Be creative in your writing and exercise patience in your business dealings. Go through the proper channels of submission, be creative and persistent."

JOYFUL SOUND RECORDS, 130 87th Ave. N., St. Petersburg FL 33702. A&R: Mike Douglas. Record company and music publisher (Nite Lite Music/BMI). Releases various number of compilations/year. Pays statutory royalty to writers and publishers.

How to Contact: "When submitting, send a cassette with 4 songs and lyric or lead sheets. Do not write asking permission to submit. Clearly label each item you send with your name and address." Does not return material. Reports in 6-8 weeks.
Music: **Children's music** and **contemporary children's Christian** songs. Releases compilations of children's music produced by Jodo Productions.
Tips: "I'm looking for unpublished works—also am not really interested in promoting someone else's finished LP or single. Don't send me material because you like it. Send me songs that others will like."

JUMP RECORDS & MUSIC, Langemunt 71, 9420 Aaigem **Belgium.** Phone: (053)62-73-77. General Manager: Eddy Van Mouffaert. Labels include Yeah Songs and Flower. Record company, music publisher (Jump Music) and record producer. Estab. 1976. Releases 40 singles, 3 LPs and 3 CDs/year. Works with musicians/artists and songwriters on contract. Pays 5% royalty to artists on contract; statutory rate to publisher per song on record.
How to Contact: Submit demo tape—unsolicited submissions are OK. Prefers cassette. Does not return material. Reports in 2 weeks.
Music: Mostly **easy listening, disco** and **light pop;** also **instrumentals.** Released "Ach Eddy," recorded by Eddy & Samantha on Style Records; "Wien Bleibt Wien," recorded by Le Grand Julot on BMP Records; and "Vanavond," recorded by Danny Brendo on Scorpion Records, all by Eddy Govert (popular). Other artists include Rocky, Eigentijdse Jeugd, Marijn Van Duin, Connie-Linda, Guy Lovely, Tom Davys, Laurie, Cindy, Patrik, Allan David, Peggy Christy, Aswin, Little Cindy, Sandra More, Dolly, Danny Brendo, Christle Love, Sandra Tempsy, Dick Benson, Angie Halloway and Ricky Morgan.

KAUPP RECORDS, Box 5474, Stockton CA 95205. (209)948-8186. President: Nancy L. Merrihew. Record company, music publisher (Kaupp's and Robert Publishing Co./BMI), record producer (Merri-Webb Productions). Estab. 1990. Releases 1 single and 4 LPs/year. Works with musicians/artists and songwriters on contract and hires musicians for in-house studio work. Pays standard royalty; statutory rate to publisher per song on record.
How to Contact: Write or call first and obtain permission to submit. Prefers cassette (or VHS videocassette if available) with 3 songs. SASE. Reports in 1 month.
Music: Mostly **country, R&B** and **A/C rock;** also **pop, rock** and **gospel.** Released *Love Isn't Blind At All,* written and recorded by Dan Alice; "Why Do You Do Me This Way" (by Nancy Merrihew/Rick Webb), recorded by Nanci Lynn; and *Made In Texas,* written and recorded by Stephen Bruce, all on Kaupp Records. Other artists include David "Dude" Westmoreland, California Gold, Mike Glover, Steve Boutte, Shane "Rockin' Round Boy" Burnett and Gary Epps.
Tips: "Know what you want, set a goal, focus in on your goals, be open to constructive criticism, polish tunes and keep polishing."

KICKING MULE RECORDS, INC., Box 158, Alderpoint CA 95511. (707)926-5312. Head of A&R: Ed Denson. Record company and music publisher (Kicking Mule Publishing/BMI and Desk Drawer Publishing/ASCAP). Member NAIRD. Releases 12 LPs/year. Works with artists on contract. Pays 10-16% royalty to artists on contract; standard royalty to songwriters on contract.
How to Contact: Submit demo tape—unsolicited submissions are OK. Prefers reel-to-reel or cassette with 3-5 songs. SASE. Reports in 1 month.
Music: **Bluegrass, blues** and **folk.** Released *Solo Guitar* by Tom Ball (folk); *Christmas Come Anew* by Maddie MacNeil (folk); and *Cats Like Angels* by Bob Griffin (piano folk). Other artists include Michael Rugg, Neal Hellman, Bert Jansch, John Renbourn, Stefan Grossman, John James, Happy Traum, Fred Sokolow, Bob Stanton, Bob Hadley, Leo Wijnkamp, Jr., Mark Nelson, Lea Nicholson and Hank Sapoznik.
Tips: "We are a label mostly for instrumentalists. The songs are brought to us by the artists but we contract the artists because of their playing, not their songs. First, listen to what we have released and don't send material that is outside our interests. Secondly, learn to play your instrument well. We have little interest in songs or songwriters, but we are quite interested in people who play guitar, banjo or dulcimer well."

*KING KLASSIC RECORDS, P.O. Box 460173, San Antonio TX 78246. (210)822-6174. Contact: Dennis Bergeron or Phil Baker. Labels include Super God and Zoinks! Record company. Estab. 1985. Releases 5 LPs and 5 CDs/year. Works with musicians/artists on contract. Pays various royalty to artists on contract.
How to Contact: Submit demo tape by mail. Unsolicited submissions are OK. Prefers cassette or CD. SASE. Reports in 2 weeks.
Music: "**Anything good and heavy!**" Released *Mirror of Sorrow* (by John Perez), recorded by Solitude; *Day In Day Out* (by Pete Toomey), recorded by Bitches' Sin; and *Landscape of Life,* written and recorded by Genocide, all on King Klassic Records.

Tips: "Please no more crappy tapes of some loser and his lame songs! Out of 1,000 tapes sent in response to last year's *Songwriter's Market* listing only maybe 20 had any business leaving the "artist's" home. If it's not good – throw it away and save me the trouble!"

KING OF KINGS RECORD CO., 38603 Sage Tree St., Palmdale CA 93551-4311. (Branch office: P.O. Box 725, Daytona Beach FL 32015-0725. (904)252-4849.) President: Leroy Pritchett. A&R Director: Charles Vickers. Labels include L.A. International. Record company and music publisher (Pritchett Publications/BMI). Estab. 1978. Releases 1 single and 1 LP/year. Works with musicians/artists and songwriters on contract. Pays 5-10% royalty to artists on contract; statutory rate to publishers per song on record.
How to Contact: Write first for permission to submit. Prefers cassette and lyric sheet. SASE. Reports in 1 month.
Music: Mostly **gospel**; also **country**. Released "Walkin' On the Water," "If God Be For You" and "Let Your Light Shine," all written and recorded by Charles Vickers on King of Kings Records.

KINGSTON RECORDS, 15 Exeter Rd., Kingston NH 03848. (603)642-8493. Coordinator: Harry Mann. Record company, music publisher (Strawberry Soda Publishing/ASCAP). Estab. 1988. Releases 3-4 singles, 2-3 12″ singles, 3 LPs and 2 CDs/year. Works with musicians/artists and songwriters on contract. Pays 3-5% royalty to artists on contract; statutory rate to publisher per song.
How to Contact: Submit demo tape – unsolicited submissions are OK. Prefers cassette, 15 ips reel-to-reel or VCR videocassette with 3 songs and lyric sheet. SASE. Reports in 6-8 weeks.
Music: Mostly **rock**, **country** and **pop**; "no heavy metal." Released *Two Lane Highway*, written and recorded by Doug Mitchell Band on Kingston Records (folk/rock).

KOTTAGE RECORDS, Box 121626, Nashville TN 37212. (615)726-3556. President: Neal James. Record company, music publisher (Cottage Blue Music/BMI) and record producer (Neal James). Estab. 1979. Releases 4 singles, 2 LPs and 3 CDs/year. Works with musicians/artists on contract. Pays standard royalty to artists on contract; statutory rate to publisher per song on record.
How to Contact: Write or call first and obtain permission to submit. Prefers cassette with 2 songs and lyric sheet. SASE. Reports in 4 weeks.
Music: Mostly **country**, **rock/pop** and **gospel**; also **R&B**. Released "Are You Sure" (by P.J. Hawk/ Neal James), "It's Been One Of Those Days" (by Hank Cochran/Troy Martin/Tony Stampley), both recorded by P.J. Hawk (country); "Don't Walk Down My Street" and "I Close My Eyes," both written and recorded by Judie Bell (contemporary country), all on Kottage Records.

KRYSDAHLARK MUSIC, Box 26160, Cincinnati OH 45226. President: Jeff Krys. Artist Management/ production company and publisher designed to produce and shop music to record labels and produc-ers. Estab 1986.
How to Contact: Not accepting unsolicited submissions at this time.
Music: Released *Elinor Revisited* (by Chris Dahlgren), recorded by Ekimi (jazz); *Breathe Me* (by Hamrick/Larkin), recorded by Sleep Theatre (mod. rock); and *Gaudete* (trad. English), recorded by The Village Waytes (classical), all on Krysdahlark Records.

LAMAR MUSIC GROUP, Box 412, New York NY 10462. Associate Director: Darlene Barkley. Labels include Lamar, MelVern, Wilson, We-Us and Co. Pub. Record company, music publisher (BMI), and workshop organization. Estab. 1984. Releases 10-12 12″ singles and 2-4 LPs/year. Works with musi-cians/artists and songwriters on contract and hires musicians for in-house studio work. Pays standard royalty to artists on contract; statutory rate to publisher per song. "We charge only if we are hired to do 'work-for-hire' projects."
How to Contact: Write first and obtain permission to submit. Prefers cassette with 2 songs. Does not return material. Reports in 1 month.
Music: Mostly **R&B**, **rap** and **pop**. Released "So In Love" (by R. Robinson), recorded by L. Williams on Macola Records (R&B/dance); "Lose You Love" (by R. Robinson), recorded by Vern Wilson on Lamar Records (R&B/dance); and "Feel Like a Woman" (by Wilson/Johnson), recorded by S. Taylor on MelVern Records (R&B/ballad). Other artists include Barry Manderson and Co/Vern.
Tips: "Members of our company function as singers, songwriters, musicians, producers, executive producers. We basically have all graduated from college in areas related to music or the music business. We either teach about music and the music business or we perform in the business. If you sincerely want to be in this industry this is the type of work you will need to do in order to succeed. It is not as easy as you think."

The types of music each listing is interested in are printed in boldface.

LANDMARK COMMUNICATIONS GROUP, Box 148296, Nashville TN 37214. Producer: Bill Anderson, Jr. Labels include Jana and Landmark Records. Record company, record producer and music publisher (Newcreature Music/BMI and Mary Megan Music/ASCAP) and management firm (Landmark Entertainment). Releases 10 singles, 8 LPs, and 8 CDs/year. Works with musicians/artists and songwriters on contract; hires musicians for in-house studio work. Teams collaborators. Pays 5-7% royalty to artists on contract; statutory rate to publishers for each record sold.
How to Contact: Prefers 7½ ips reel-to-reel or cassette with 4-10 songs and lyric sheet. SASE. Reports in 1 month.
Music: Country/crossover, gospel, jazz, R&B, rock and **top 40/pop**. Released *Joanne Cash Yates Live ... w/Johnny Cash*, on Jana Records (gospel); *Play It Again Sam*, recorded by Michael L. Pickern on Landmark Records (country); *Millions of Miles*, recorded by Teddy Nelson/Skeeter Davis (Norway release) (country); *Always*, recorded by Debi Chasteen on Landmark Records (country); "You Were Made For Me" by Skeeter Davis and Teddy Nelson on Elli Records/Norway; and *Someday Soon*, recorded by Pam Fenelon on Bil-Mar Records (country).

LANDSLIDE RECORDS, Suite 333, 1800 Peachtree St., Atlanta GA 30309. (404)355-5580. President: Michael Rothschild. Record company, music publisher (Frozen Inca Music/BMI) and record producer. Estab. 1981. Releases 2 12″ singles, 6 LPs, 6 CDs/year. Works with musicians/artists and songwriters on contract. Pays negotiable rate to artists on contract and publishers per song on record.
How to Contact: Submit demo tape—unsolicited submissions are OK. Prefers cassette with 6-12 songs and lyric sheet. SASE. Reports in 1 month.
Music: Mostly **R&B, blues, rap**; also **gospel, country** and **techno-pop**. Released *Cool On It* and *Fanning The Flames*, both written and recorded by Tinsley Ellis; and *Tore Up*, written and recorded by Nappy Brown, on Alligator Records (blues). Other artists include Alvin Antonio Youngblood and Gerald Jackson.

LANOR RECORDS, Box 233, 329 N. Main St., Church Point LA 70525. (318)684-2176. Contact: Lee Lavergne. Labels include Lanor Records. Record company and music publisher (Jon Music/BMI). Releases 8-10 cassettes a year. Works with artists and songwriters on contract. Pays 3-5% royalty to artists on contract; statutory rate to writers for each record sold.
How to Contact: Prefers cassette with 2-6 songs. SASE. Reports in 2 weeks.
Music: Mostly **country**; also **rock, soul, zydeco, cajun** and **blues**. Released "*Cajun Pickin'*," recorded by L.A. Band (cajun); *Rockin' with Roy*, recorded by Roy Currier and *Zydeco All Night*, recorded by Joe Walker (zydeco), all on Lanor Records.
Tips: Submit "good material with potential in today's market. Use good quality cassettes—I don't listen to poor quality demos that I can't understand."

LARI-JON RECORDS, 325 W. Walnut, Rising City NE 68658. (402)542-2336. Owner: Larry Good. Record company, music publisher (Lari-Jon Publishing/BMI) and record producer (Lari-Jon Productions). Estab. 1967. Releases 15 singles and 5 LPs/year. Works with songwriters on royalty contract.
How to Contact: Submit demo tape—unsolicited submissions are OK. Prefers cassette with 5 songs and lyric sheet. SASE. Reports in 2 months.
Music: Mostly **country, gospel-Southern** and **50s' rock**. Released *Glory Bound Train*, written and recorded by Tom Campbell; "Pick Me Up On Your Way Down" (by Harlan Howard), recorded by Larry Good; and *Hanging From The Bottom*, written and recorded by Johnny Nace, all on Lari-Jon Records (country). Other artists include Kent Thompson and Brenda Allen.

LARK RECORD PRODUCTIONS, INC., Suite 520, 4815 S. Harvard, Tulsa OK 74135. (918)749-1648. Vice-President: Sue Teaff. Record company, music publisher (Jana Jae Music/BMI) and record producer (Lark Talent and Advertising). Estab. 1980. Works with musicians/artists on contract. Payment to artists on contract negotiable; statutory rate to publishers per song on record.
How to Contact: Submit demo tape—unsolicited submissions are OK. Prefers cassette or VHS videocassette with 3 songs and lead sheets. Does not return material.
Music: Mostly **country, bluegrass** and **classical**; also **instrumentals**. Released "Fiddlestix" (by Jana Jae); "Mayonnaise" (by Steve Upfold); and "Flyin' South" (by Cindy Walker); all recorded by Jana Jae on Lark Records (country). Other artists include Syndi, Hotwire and Matt Greif.

***LBJ PRODUCTIONS**, 8608 W. College St., French Lick IN 47432. (812)936-7318. Director A&R: Janet S. Jones. Owner/Producer: Larry Jones. Labels include Stone Country Records, SCR Gospel, SCR Rock. Record company, music publisher (Plain Country Publishing/ASCAP, Riff-Line Publishing/BMI), record producer (LBJ Productions) and produce radio-spot ads and jingles. Releases 2-4 singles, 3-6 LPs, 2-3 EPs and 1-2 CDs/year. Works with musicians/artists on record contract, songwriters on royalty contract, musicians on salary for in-house studio work. Pays 10-14% royalty to artists on contract; statutory rate to publisher per song on record.

How to Contact: Write first and obtain permission to submit or arrange personal interview. Prefers cassette (or VHS videocassette) with 4-6 songs and lyric sheet. SASE. Reports in 3-6 weeks.

Music: Mostly **country, gospel, rock**; also **R&B, MOR** and **pop**. Released *Sounds Of A Hillbilly Song* (by G. Dixon), recorded by Gordon Ray; *Goodtime Song* (by D. Sargent), recorded by Tammy Easterday; and *Do You Feel The Same?* (by Purkhiser/Nicholson), recorded by Desert Reign, all on SCR Records. Other artists include Rosalee Bateman, Change Of Heart and The Guitar Gang.

Tips: "Make a good first impression. Put the song on your demo tape that you think is strongest first. If you catch our ear we'll listen to more music. We are not looking for someone that does imitations, we need new and exciting people with styles that cry out for attention. But remember make your submissions to the point and professional—we'll decide if you've got what we want."

LE MATT MUSIC LTD., % Stewart House, Hill Bottom Rd., Highwycombe, Buckinghamshire, HP12 4HJ **England.** Phone: (0630)647374. Fax: (0630)647612. Contact: Ron or Cathrine Lee. Labels include Swoop, Zarg Records, Genouille, Pogo and Check Records. Record company, record producer and music publisher (Le Matt Music, Ltd., Lee Music, Ltd., R.T.F.M. and Pogo Records, Ltd.). Member MPA, PPL, PRS, MCPS. Estab. 1972. Releases 30 12″ singles, 20 LPs and 20 CDs/year. Pays negotiable royalty to artists on contract; statutory rate to publishers for each record sold. Royalties paid to US songwriters and artists through US publishing or recording affiliate.

How to Contact: Submit demo tape—unsolicited submissions are OK. Prefers 7½ or 15 ips reel-to-reel or cassette (or VHS or PAL standard videocassette) with 1-3 songs and lyric sheet. Include bio and photo. SAE and IRC. Reports in 6 weeks.

Music: Mostly interested in **pop/top 40**; also interested in **bluegrass, blues, country, dance-oriented, easy listening, MOR, progressive, R&B, 50s' rock, disco, new wave, rock** and **soul**. Released *I'm A Rep, Eat 'Em Up* and *99* (by R.C. Bowman), recorded by Chromatics on Swoop Records. Other artists include Amazing Dark Horse, Nightmare and Daniel Boone.

LEGS RECORDS, 825 5th St., Menasha WI 54952. (414)725-4467. Executive President: Lori Lee Woods. Labels include Sand Dollar Records. Record company, music publisher (Lori Lee Woods Music/BMI) and record producer. Works with musicians/artists and songwriters on contract.

How to Contact: Write first and obtain permission to submit. Prefers cassette (or VHS videocassette) with 3 songs and lyric or lead sheet. SASE. Reports in 1 month.

Music: Mostly **country, rock** and **gospel.**

JOHN HEADLEY LENNON MUSIC LTD., (formerly John Lennon Records), Suite 104D, 720 Spadina Ave., Toronto, Ontario M5S 2T9 **Canada.** (416)962-5000. Fax: (416)962-5000. Contact: Oliver Moore. Record company, music publisher (SOCAN) and record producer. Estab. 1979. Releases 3 singles, 2 12″ singles, 1 LP and 2 CDs/year. Works with musicians/artists and songwriters on contract. Pays 5% royalty to artists on contract. Charges advance production fee.

How to Contact: Submit demo tape by mail. Unsolicited submissions OK. Prefers cassette (or VHS videocassette) with 4 songs and lyric sheets. Does not return material. Reports in 1 month.

Music: Mostly **top 40 pop, R&B, dance, rap** and **gospel/country.** Released *Alone In the Dark* (by Gerry Tymstra), recorded by Kim Crystal; "Broken Hearts," written and recorded by Milton Price; and "Let Your Feelings Show" (by Roger Cook), recorded by Yvonne Moore, all on 0692 Records.

Tips: "Be professional with recording projects and your presentations."

LEOPARD MUSIC, 23 Thrayle House, Stockwell Rd., London, SW9 0XU **England.** Phone: (071)737-6681/081672-6158. Fax: (071)737-7881. Executive Producer: Errol Jones. Vice President: Terri Schiavo. Labels include Jet Set Records International (US). Record company (PRS, BMI) and record producer. Releases 15 singles and 2 LPs/year. Works with musicians/artists and songwriters on contract and hires musicians for in-house studio work. Pays 4-12% royalty to artists on contract, statutory rate to publishers per song on record.

How to Contact: Write first and obtain permission to submit. Prefers cassette (or VHS/PAL videocassette) with 3 songs. SASE. Reports in 2 weeks.

Music: Mostly **dance music, soul** and **pop**; also **ballad, reggae** and **gospel.** Released "Time After Time" (by Guy Spell), recorded by Rico J; "I Need You" (by E. Campbell and E. North Jr.), recorded by Big Africa; and *God is Beauty*, written and recorded by Evelyn Ladimeji; all on Leopard Music Records. Other artists include Zoil Foundations and Michael Eytle.

Tips: "Create strong original songs, and artists must have good image."

*LIMITED POTENTIAL RECORDS, P.O. Box 268586, Chicago IL 60626. (312)764-9636. A&R: Mike Potential. Record company. Estab. 1988. Releases 5 singles, 1 12″ single, 6 LPs, 2 EPs and 6 CDs/year. Works with musicians/artists on record contract, musicians on salary for in-house studio work. Pays 8-12% royalty to artists on contract; ¾ statutory rate to publisher per song on record.

How to Contact: Submit demo tape by mail. Unsolicited submissions are OK. Prefers cassette (or VHS videocassette if available) with 3-5 songs. SASE. Reports in 1-2 weeks.

Music: Mostly **alternative rock, pop**. Released "Godliness" (by Eddy/Callahan), recorded by OO OO WA (pop); "Pure Evil" (by Freedberg), recorded by The Satanics (rock); and "Ride" (by T. Taylor) recorded by Brainiac (new wave), all on Limited Potential Records. Other artists include Throw, Godspeaks, Catherine, The Luck of Eden Hall and Chickenboy.

Tips: "Don't send a tape with excuses like 'Oh, we're not happy with the recording but we're really good live,' send the best possible representation of your music. We're not impressed with pages of press from local papers, your music stands or dies on its own."

LION HUNTER MUSIC, Box 110678, Anchorage AK 99511. Vice President: Clive Lock. Record company (BMI). Estab. 1989. Releases 1 single and 1 CD/year. Works with musicians/artists on contract. Pays negotiable royalty to artists on contract; statutory rate to publisher per song on record.

How to Contact: Write first and obtain permission to submit. Prefers cassette with 3 songs and lyric sheet. Does not return material. Reports in 3 weeks.

Music: Mostly **rock, pop** and **R&B**. Released "Hide Away" (by Connett/Lock), recorded by Abandon on Lion Hunter Music (pop/rock).

LOADING BAY RECORDS, 586 Bristol Road, Selly Oak, Birmingham B29 6BQ **England**. Phone (21)472-2463. Fax: (21)414-1540. M.D.: Duncan Finlayson. Labels include Loading Bay Records, Two Bears Music, Time Records (Italy) and Made Up Records. Record company and record producer (Loading Bay Productions). Estab. 1988. Releases 35 12″ singles, 3 LPs and 3 CDs/year. Works with musicians/artists on contract and "negotiates one-off licensing deals." Pays 10% royalty; statutory rate to publishers per song on record.

How to Contact: Submit demo tape—unsolicited submissions are OK. Prefers cassette (or D.A.T.) with several songs. Does not return material. Reports in 2 months.

Music: Mostly **Hi-NRG-dance** and **disco dance**. Released "Save Your Love" (by T. Hendrik), recorded by Bad Boys Blue on Loading Bay Records; "Diamond Eyes" (by G. Maiolini), recorded by Vanessa on Time Records; and "When You Tell Me," written and recorded by Kelly on Loading Bay Records. Other artists include Rofo, Samantha Gilles, Sheila Steward, Claudia T., Baccara, Shot In The Dark and Kelly Marie.

*LOCONTO PRODUCTIONS/SUNRISE STUDIO, 10244 NW 47 St., Sunrise FL 33351. (305)741-7766. President: Frank X. Loconto. Labels include FXL Records. Record company, music publisher (Otto Music Publishing, ASCAP), recording studio. Estab. 1978. Releases 10 singles, 10 LPs and 5 CD/year. Works with musicians/artists on record contract, songwriters on royalty contract and musicians on salary for in-house studio work. Pays standard royalty to artists on contract; statutory rate to publisher per song on record.

How to Contact: Write first and obtain permission to submit. Prefers cassette with lyric sheet or lead sheet. SASE.

Music: "We are a full service professional recording studio. Released "La Horida" and "Barry U," written and recorded by Frank Locanto; and "Believe In America" (by Frank Locanto), recorded by The Lane Brothers, all on FXL Records. Other artists include Connie Francis, Kenny Martin, Michael Moog and Donna Shaleff.

Tips: "Be sure to prepare a professional demo of your work and don't hesitate to seek 'professional' advice."

LRJ, Box 3, Belen NM 87002. (505)864-7441. Manager: Tony Palmer. Labels include Little Richie, Chuckie. Record company. Estab. 1959. Releases 5 singles and 2 LPs/year. Works with musicians/artists on contract.

How to Contact: Submit demo tape—unsolicited submissions are OK. Prefers cassette. SASE. Reports in 1 month.

Music: Mostly **country**. Released "If Teardrops Were Pennies" (by Carl Butler), recorded by Myrna Lorrie; "Sing Me a Love Song," written and recorded by Myrna Lorrie; "Auction of My Life" written and recorded by Joe King; "Where Was I When You Stopped Loving Me" and "Helpless' recorded by Alan Godge, all on LRJ Records.

LUCIFER RECORDS, INC., Box 263, Brigantine NJ 08203-0263. (609)266-2623. President: Ron Luciano. Labels include TVA Records. Record company, music publisher (Ciano Publishing and Legz Music), record producer (Pete Fragale and Tony Vallo) and management firm and booking agency (Ron Luciano Music Co. and TVA Productions). Works with artists and songwriters on salary and contract. "Lucifer Records has offices in South Jersey; Palm Beach, Florida; Sherman Oaks, California; and Las Vegas, Nevada."

How to Contact: Arrange personal interview. Prefers cassette with 4-8 songs. SASE. Reports in 3 weeks.
Music: Dance, easy listening, MOR, rock, soul and top 40/pop. Released "I Who Have Nothing," by Spit-N-Image (rock); "Lucky," and "Smoke Ya," by Legz (rock); and "Love's a Crazy Game," by Voyage (disco/ballad). Other artists include Bobby Fisher, Jerry Denton, FM, Zeke's Choice and Al Caz.

*M.R.E. RECORDING PRODUCTIONS, 433 S. Hobson, Mesa AZ 85204. Owner: A. Wesley Millet III. Labels include M.R.E. Records. Record company, record producer. Estab. 1979. Musicians/artists on record contract, musicians on salary for in-house studio work. Pays statutory rate to publisher per song on record. Charges songwriter in advance for publicity/public relations.
How to Contact: Submit demo tape by mail. Unsolicited submissions are OK. Prefers cassette with 1 or more (prefer 3) songs and lead sheet. SASE. Reports in up to 1 year.
Music: Mostly country, gospel/religious, patriotic (pro-USA, constitution and liberty); also light rock'n roll, Christian holiday and cheery and funky music. Released "Petite Sweet Cute Carolyntime" (by A.W. Millet III and L.R. Mumford), recorded by Larry R. Mumford on M.R.E. Records.

MAJESTIC CONTROL RECORDS, Box 330-568, Brooklyn NY 11233. (718)398-0244. A&R Department: Alemo. Record company, music publisher (Majestic Control Music/BMI) and record producer (Alemo, Half Pint and Hank Love). Estab. 1983. Works with musicians/artists on contract.
How to Contact: Submit demo tape—unsolicited submissions are OK. Prefers cassette with 3 songs. SASE. Reports in 4 weeks.
Music: Mostly rap, dance and reggae; also house. Released "Don't Let The Sweet Name Fool Ya" and "Gash Your Whole Head Up" (by M. Lowe), recorded by M.C. Lovely (rap) on Majestic Control Records. Other artists include King Shahid, MC Tatiana, Lil Cuba, P-King.

*MAKESHIFT MUSIC, P.O. Box 557, Blacktown, NSW 2148 **Australia**. Phone: (612)626-8991. Manager: Peter Bales. Record company, music publisher (Aria and Apra). Estab. 1980. Releases 10 singles and 5 CDs/year. Works with musicians/artists on record contract, songwriters on royalty contract or musicians on salary for in-house studio work. Pays statutory rate to publisher per song on record.
How to Contact: Submit demo tape by mail. Unsolicited submissions are OK. Prefers cassette (or PAL/VHS videocassette if available) with 4-6 songs and lyric sheet. Does not return material. Reports in 1month.
Music: Mostly rock/pop. Released *The Sessions* (by various), recorded by Sessions; *Nujar*, written and recorded by Scott Johnson; *The Big House*, written and recorded by Pavla, all on Makeshift Records (rock/pop). Other artists include Chimps from Chump and Generation.
Tips: "Provide bio, lyrics, 4-6 songs, no schmulz."

*MARCH RECORDS, P.O. Box 578396, Chicago IL 60657. (312)296-4321. Label Director: John McFadden. Record company. Estab. 1991. Releases 6 singles, 8 LPs, 2 EPs and 8 CDs/year. Works with musicians/artists on record contract. Pays 10-20% royalty to artists on contract; statutory rate to publisher per song on record.
How to Contact: Submit demo tape by mail. Unsolicited submissions are OK. Prefers cassette. Does not return material. Reports in 2 months.
Music: Mostly indie rock, indie pop. Released "It's No Lie" (by M. Rew), recorded by Catherine; "Flowerbox" (by P. Klik/Y. Bruner), recorded by Big Hat; and "Sox on Spot" (by D. Deibler), recorded by House of Large Sizes, all on March Records. Other artists include Star Children, Sometime Sweet Susan, Crossed Wire, Melting Hopefuls.

MARIAH RECORDS, Box 310, Carmichael CA 95609-310. President: Mari Minice. Record company. Estab. 1986. Releases 1 single/year. Works with musicians/artists on contract. Pays varying royalty to artists on contract; negotiable rate to publishers per song on record.
How to Contact: Submit demo tape—unsolicited submissions are OK. Prefers cassette with any number of songs and lyric sheets. Does not return material. Reports in 4 months.
Music: Mostly country/contemporary, pop and rock. Released "Closer to Heaven" (by Jill Wood), recorded by Rachel Minke on Mariah Records (country).
Tips: "Keep it country—female, contemporary or traditional."

MASTER-TRAK ENTERPRISES, Dept. SM, 413 N. Parkerson, Crowley LA 70526. (318)788-0773. General Manager and Chief Engineer: Mark Miller. Labels include Master-Trak, Showtime, Kajun, Blues Unlimited, Par T and MTE Records. Recording studio and record companies. Releases 20 singles and 6-8 LPs/year. Works with musicians/artists on contract. Pays 7% artist royalty. (No studio charges to contract artists.) Studio available on an hourly basis to the public. Charges for some services: "We charge for making audition tapes of any material that we do not publish."

How to Contact: Submit demo tape by mail—unsolicited submissions are OK. Prefers cassette and lead sheet. Does not return material.

Music: Mostly **country, rock, R&B, cajun, blues** and **zydeco**. Released "That's When I Miss You" (by J. Runyo), recorded by Sammy Kershaw; "Please Explain," written and recorded by Wade Richards, both on MTE Records; and "My Heart Is Hurting," written and recorded by Becky Richard on Kajun Records. Other artists include Al Ferrier, Fernest & The Thunders, River Road Band, Clement Bros. and Lee Benoit.

Tips: "The song is the key. If we judge it to be a good song, we record it and it sells, we are happy. If we misjudge the song and/or the artist and it does not sell, we must go back to the drawing board."

*THE MATHES COMPANY, P.O. Box 22653, Nashville TN 37202. (615)252-6912. Owner: David Mathes. Labels include Rising Star (custom)/Star Image (country), Heirborn (country gospel)/Kingdom (Christian). Record company, record producer and Institute of Recording Arts & Sciences (home study course). Estab. 1962. Releases 12-15 LPs and 10 CDs/year. Works with songwriters on royalty contract and artists for custom productions. Pays statutory rate to publisher per song on record. "Charges for demo services not connected with publishing."

How to Contact: Submit demo tape by mail. Unsolicited submissions are OK. Prefers cassette (or VHS videocassette) with 2-3 songs and lyric sheet. SASE. Reports in 1 month.

Music: Mostly **gospel** and **country**; also **spoken word, MOR** and **instrumental**. Released *My Love For You* (by David & Deanna Mathes), recorded by Warner Mack on Sapphire Records (country); *I'm In Ohio Now With Georgia On My Mind* (by Don Frost), recorded by Johnny Newman on Star Image (country) and *Hello Jesus Hello* (by Craig Anderson), recorded by De Anna on Heirborn Records (country/gospel). Other artists include The Ballards and Harry Greenberg.

Tips: "Songs must be positive country or gospel, with strong messages, not out of date and not political or controversial. Artists must have unique vocal style, good stage presence, have past performances and long term commitment."

MCA RECORDS, 8th Floor, 1755 Broadway, New York NY 10019. (212)841-8000. East Coast A&R Director: Susan Dodes. East Coast Vice President: Bruce Dickinson. Labels include Costellation, Cranberry, Curb, IRS, Motown, London, Zebra and Philly World. Record company and music publisher (MCA Music). Works with musicians/artists on contract.

How to Contact: Call first and obtain permission to submit. Prefers cassete (or VHS videocassette) and lyric or lead sheet. SASE.

MCI ENTERTAINMENT GROUP, P.O. Box 8442, Universal City CA 91608. (818)505-0488. Fax: (818)505-0420. Vice President A&R: Jaeson Effantic. Labels include Bouvier, Credence, PPL. Record company. Estab. 1979. Releases 50-60 singles, 12 12″ singles, 6 LPs and 6 CDs/year. Works with musicians/artists and songwriters on contract and hires musicians for in-house studio work. Pays 8-15% royalty to artists on contract; statutory rate to publisher per song on record.

How to Contact: Write first and obtain permission to submit. Prefers cassette or videocassette with 2 songs. SASE. Reports in 4-6 weeks.

Music: Released *Night Song* (by Gip Noble), recorded by Phuntaine on Bouvier Records (jazz); *Fynne as I can B* (by Santiono), recorded by I.B. Phyne on Credence Records (pop); and *Love Song* (by DM Groove), recorded by Dale Mitchell on Bouvier Records (R&B). Other artists include Big Daddy and Blazers, Lejenz and Condottiere.

Tips: "Don't limit yourself to just one style of music. Diversify and write other styles of songs."

*MEGA RECORDS APS., Linnesgade 14A-DK 1361, Copenhagen K **Denmark**. Phone: (4533)11 77 11. Fax: (4533)13 40 10. A&R Director: Damian Wilson. Labels include C.O.M.A. Records, Funky Buddha Records. Record company and music publisher. Estab. 1982. Releases 150-200 singles, 75-100 12″ singles, 50-75 LPs and 50-75 CDs/year. Works with musicians/artists and songwriters on contract; hires musicians for in-house studio work.

How to Contact: Call first and obtain permission to submit. Prefers cassette with 1 song and lyric sheet. Does not return material. Reports in 3 weeks.

Music: Mostly **crossover dance, pop/rock** and **hard rock**; also **strong ballads**. Released "All That She Was," written and recorded by Ace of Base, and "Open Sesame," written and recorded by Leila K, both on Mega Records. Other artists include Disneyland After Dark, The Overlords, The Colours Turn Red, Laban, Seventy'Leven, Sky High, Technotronic, Jive Bunny, Sybil, Eric & The Good Good Feeling, De La Soul, Information Society, Digital Underground, Fancy, Camouflage, Al Agani, Captain Hollywood, Bizzare Inc., The Chippendales and Bass Bumpers.

*MEGAFORCE WORLDWIDE ENTERTAINMENT, 210 Bridge Plaza Dr., Manalapan NJ 07726. (908)972-3456. Director A&R: Maria Ferrero. Labels include Megaforce Records Inc. Record company. Estab. 1983. Releases 5 LPs, 2 EPs and 5 CDs/year. Works with musicians/artists on record contract. Pays various royalties to artists on contract; ¾ statutory rate to publisher per song on record.

How to Contact: Submit demo tape by mail. Unsolicited submissions are OK. Prefers cassette (or ¾" videocassette if available) with 4 songs. Does not return unsolicited material. Reports in 3 months.
Music: Mostly **rock**. Released *Chemical Imbalance*, written and recorded by Skatenigs; *F Sharp*, written and recorded by Nudeswirl and *Fire in the Kitchen*, written and recorded by Warren Haynes, all on Megaforce Records.
Tips: "Don't compromise—do what you want to do creatively."

*MERKIN RECORDS INC., 310 E. Biddle St., Baltimore MD 21202. (410)234-0048. President: Joe Goldsborough. Labels include Protocool Records. Record company. Estab. 1988. Releases 5-6 singles, 5-10 LPs, 3-5 EPs, 5-10 CDs/year. Works with musicians/artists on record contract. Pays 9-16% royalty to artists on contract; statutory rate to publisher per song on record. "Nothing if we don't get part of publishing."
How to Contact: Submit demo tape by mail. Unsolicited submissions are OK. Prefers cassette with 3 songs. "If we don't like, you might not hear from us. If you can't say something nice don't say anything at all."
Music: Mostly **eclectic alternative rock**. Released *Strange Loop*, written and recorded by Edsel; *Gnaw*, written and recorded by Stranger Than Fiction; *Shit Cool It's the Honeycomb Generation*, written and recorded by Buttsteak, all on Merkin Records. Other artists include Monkey Spank, Antic Hay, Lambs Eat Ivy, Liquor Bike, Berserk and One Spot Fringe Head.
Tips: "We want to hear from driven musicians doing something new. All our artists write their own songs. We are interested in unique, visionary people playing songs that mean something to them. Standard pop or metal will do better somewhere else."

*METRO RECORDS, 216 3rd Ave. N., Minneapolis MN 55401. (612)338-3833. A&R Director/Staff Producer: James Walsh. Labels include Mars and Black Pearl. Record company, record producer, artist management and development/talent agency. Estab. 1991. Releases 3-4 singles, 1-2 EPs and 5-10 CDs/year. Works with musicians/artists on record contract. Pays 5-20% royalty to artists on contract; statutory rate to publishers per song on record.
How to Contact: Call first and obtain permission to submit. Prefers cassette (or VHS videocassette if available) with 3-4 songs and lyric sheet or lead sheet. SASE. Reports in 2-3 weeks.
Music: Mostly **pop, rock, country**; also **jazz**. Released *Suite Sorrow* (by Arthur/Mackin), recorded by Northcoast on Black Pearl Records (contemporary jazz); "Teach Your Children" (by Graham Nash), recorded by Nielsen White (country) and *Feel the Fire* (by Seaman/Halgrimson), recorded by Mata Hari (rock), both on Metro Records. Other artists include Chainsaw, Icebreaker, Billy Zack, One Horse, Mark Allen, Trouble Shooter.
Tips: "Be prepared to make a commitment to the label and your career. The level of your commitment will be mirrored by our company. As an artist, be prepared to back up your recorded product live."

*MFE RECORDS, 500 E. Washington St., Norristown PA 19401. (215)277-9550. President: Jeffrey Calhoon. Record company, music publisher (BMI). Estab. 1984. Releases 5 LPs. Works with musicians/artists on record contract, musicians and producers on a per project basis. Pays 5-50% royalty to artists on contract; statutory rate to publishers per song on record.
How to Contact: Write or call first and obtain permission to submit. Prefers cassette with 3 songs and lyric sheet. SASE. Reports in 3 weeks.
Music: Mostly **alternative rock, hard rock, pop rock**; **20th century, New Age**. Released *Bulkhead*, recorded by Naked Twister and *Rusts, Snats & Heart Rot*, recorded by Monkey 101, both on MFE Records. Other artists include Amy Carr, Krunch and Robert Moran.
Tips: "Be different, have something new or clever to say."

MIGHTY RECORDS, Suite 6-D, 150 West End, New York NY 10023. (212)873-5968. Manager: Danny Darrow. Labels include Mighty Sounds & Filmworks. Record company, music publisher, record producer (Danny Darrow). Estab. 1958. Releases 1-2 singles, 1-2 12" singles and 1-2 LPs/year. Works with songwriters on royalty contract and hires musicians for in-house studio work. Pays standard royalty to artists on contract; statutory rate to publishers per song on record.
How to Contact: Submit demo tape—unsolicited submissions are OK. "No phone calls." Prefers cassette with 3 songs and lyric sheet. SASE. Reports in 1-2 weeks.
Music: Mostly **pop, country** and **dance**; also **jazz**. Released "Wonderland of Dreams" and "Let There Be Peace" (by Phil Zinn), and "Doomsday" (by R.L. Lowery and Phil Zinn), all recorded by Danny Darrow all on Mighty Records.
Tips: "Listen to the hits of Richie, Manilow, Houston and Rogers and write better songs."

*MILES AHEAD RECORDS, P.O. Box 35449, Los Angeles CA 90035. (310)281-8599. A&R: Robert Riley. Record company, music publisher (BMI/ASCAP), record producer. Estab. 1968. Releases 10 singles, 2 12" singles, 10 LPs and 10 CDs/year. Works with musicians/artists on record contract, songwriters on royalty contract, musicians on salary for in-house studio work. Pay negotiated; statutory rate to publisher per song on record.

How to Contact: Submit demo tape by mail. Unsolicited submissions are OK. Prefers cassette with 4 songs and lyric sheet. SASE. Reports in 2 weeks.

Music: Mostly **R&B, pop** and **country;** also **gospel/pop.** Released "Love Is Gone" (by Murlin McGar), recorded by Jessica Taylor (R&B/pop); "Ugly Woman" (by Miles Grayson), recorded by Sterling Harrison (R&B); and "Forgive & Forget" (by Joan Sturgis), recorded by Kim Brown (pop), all on Miles Ahead Records. Other artists include Brenda Sorrenson and Paul Bryant.

Tips: "Be yourself, but above all be in touch with the heartbeat of what is true to be a commercial product."

MINDFIELD RECORDS, 4B, 500 ½ E. 84th St., New York NY 10028. (212)861-8745. A&R: Ashley Catob. Record company, music publisher (Mia Mind Music/ASCAP) and record producer (I.Y.F. Productions). Estab. 1985. Releases 10 singles, 6 12″ singles, 4 LPs and 4 CDs/year. Works with musicians/artists and songwriters on contract. Payment to artists on contract varies; statutory rate to publisher per song on record.

How to Contact: Call first and obtain permission to submit. Prefers cassette (or VHS videocassette) with 3 songs. SASE. Reports in 2 months.

Music: Mostly **rap, house** and **hip hop;** also **dance, top 40** and **AOR.** Released "Cosmic Climb" and "Gods" (by Werner/Sargent), recorded by Madonna (dance); and "So Phony" and "Shelter" written and recorded by Jade, all on Mindfield Records. Other artists include P.O.A., Metal L and Papa HaHa.

Tips: "Submit demos on DAT cassettes for best sound quality."

MIRROR RECORDS, INC., 645 Titus Ave., Rochester NY 14617. (716)544-3500. Vice President: Armand Schaubroeck. Labels include House of Guitars Records. Record company and music publisher. Works with artists and songwriters on contract and hires musicians for in-house studio work. Royalty paid to artists varies; negotiable royalty to songwriters on contract.

How to Contact: Prefers cassette or record (or videocassette). Include photo with submission. SASE. Reports in 2 months.

Music: **Folk, progressive, rock, punk** and **heavy metal.** Released "Don't Open Til Doomsday" and "Drunk on Muddy Water" by Chesterfield Kings; and "Through The Eyes of Youth" by Immaculate Mary.

MISSILE RECORDS, Box 5537 Kreole Station, Moss Point MS 39563. (601)475-2098. "No collect calls." President/Owner: Joe F. Mitchell. Record company, music publisher (Bay Ridge Publishing/BMI) and record producer (Missile Records; have also produced for Happy Hollow Records, Myra Records, JB Records, RCI and Wake Up Records). Estab. 1974. Releases 20 singles and 6 LPs/year. Works with artists on contract. Pays 8-10% royalty to artists on contract; statutory rate to publishers for each record sold.

How to Contact: Write first and obtain permission to submit. Include #10 SASE. "All songs sent for review must include sufficient return postage." Prefers cassette with 3-6 songs and lyric sheets. Does not return material. Reports in 6 weeks.

Music: Mostly **country, gospel, rap** and **R&B;** also **soul, MOR, blues, rock, pop,** and **bluegrass.** Released "You Owe Some Back to Me" and "Hello Heartbreak" by Ann Black; "I'll Always Miss You" and "Another Lonely Christmas" by T.C. Bullock; all on Missile Records (country). Other artists include Herbert Lacey, Rich Wilson, Lori Mark, Jerry Wright, Danny Keebler and Jerry Ann. "Also considering songs on master tape for release in the US and abroad."

Tips: "If a recording artist has exceptional talent and some backing then Missile Records will give you our immediate attention. A bio and cassette tape and picture of the artist should be submitted along with sufficient return postage."

MODERN BLUES RECORDINGS, Box 248, Pearl River NY 10965. (914)735-3944. Owner: Daniel Jacoubovitch. Record company. Estab. 1985. Releases 1-2 LPs and 1-2 CDs/year. Works with musicians/artists and songwriters on contract.

How to Contact: Write or call first and obtain permission to submit. Does not return material. Reports in 2-4 weeks.

Music: **Blues, R&B, soul, rock.** Released "Poison Kisses," written and recorded by Jerry Portnoy; "Ida's Song," written and recorded by J. Vaughn; and "Frances," written and recorded by Johnson/Maloney, all on Modern Blues Recordings. Other artists include Clayton Love.

MODERN MUSIC VENTURES, INC., 5626 Brock St., Houston TX 77023. (713)926-4436. Chief Operations Officer: David Lummis. Labels include Discos MM, Double H Records. Record company. Estab. 1986. Releases 12 singles, 2 12″ singles, 6 LPs, 2 EPs and 6 CDs/year. Works with musicians/artists on record contract. Pays statutory rate to publisher per song on record. Distributed by Capitol/EMI.

How to Contact: Write first and obtain permission to submit. Prefers cassette with 5 songs and lyric sheets. SASE. Reports in 6 weeks.

Music: Mostly **Latin (in Spanish)**, **country** and **jazz**; also **rap (in Spanish)**. Released *El Poderde Una Mujer* (by Joe Martinez), recorded by The Hometown Boys; *Por Ti* (by Albert Gonzalez), recorded by The Choice; and *Todo es Gris* (by Lupe Olivares), recorded by The Basics, all on Discos MM. Other artists include Mercedez, Los Pekadores, Los Monarcas, Los Dos Gilbertos, Ellos and Dallazz.

*MODERN VOICES PRODUCTIONS, 289 Little Neck Rd., Centerport NY 11721. (516)754-6800. President: Glenn Deveau. Vice President: Chris Pati. Record producer. Estab. 1991. Releases 10 singles, 5 12" singles, 2-3 LPs, 2-3 EPs and 10 CDs/year. Pays 7% royalty to artists on contract; statutory rate to publisher per song on record.

How to Contact: Submit demo tape by mail. Unsolicited submissions are OK. Prefers cassette (or videocassette) with 2-3 songs and lyric sheet. Does not return material. Reports in 1 month.

Music: Mostly **dance, pop** and **R&B**; also **pop/rock, rap** and **alternative**. Released "Move It," "I Want Love" and "I Got A Notion," all written and recorded by Chris Pati on Modern Voices Records. Other artists include Iyona, Bobby G, (Brian) "Deva B", Tracy Robins, Judy Busch and Jeannie.

Tips: "If you are looking to get a fair shot in this industry we offer a program called "Artist Development Program"—for a very low fee we write, produce, release, shop test press, and promote first single so new artist have a head start instead of just having a finished demo. Great exposure."

MONARCH RECORDINGS, (formerly Platinum Productions), 406 Centre St., Boston MA 02130. (617)983-9999. A&R Rep: Akhil Garland. Record company. Estab. 1989. Releases 4 singles, 2 LPs, 6 EPs, 2 CDs/year. Works with musicians/artists and songwriters on contract and hires musicians for in-house studio work. Pays 8% royalty to artists on contract; statutory rate to publisher per song on record.

How to Contact: Submit demo tape by mail—unsolicited submissions are OK. Prefers cassette or CD with lyric sheet. SASE. Reports in 6 weeks.

Music: Mostly **reggae, folk** and **world beat**; also **rap/R&B** and **rock**. Recorded "Change Your Mind" and "Goin' Nowhere" (by R. Mills), recorded by Jonathan Wells; also "Mr. Morning" (by S. Augustine), recorded by M. Bryant, all on Monarch Recordings.

MONEYTIME RECORDS, 742 Rowley St., Owosso MI 48867. (517)723-1796. Director: Jon Harris. Record company and music publisher (Moneytime Publishing Co./BMI). Estab. 1990. Releases 6 singles, 2 12" singles, 3 LPs, 2 EPs and 3 CDs/year. Works with musicians/artists on record contract. Pays 10% royalty to artists on contract; statutory rate to publisher per song on record.

How to Contact: Submit demo tape—unsolicited submissions are OK. Prefers cassette with 4-6 songs and lyric sheets (picture and bio if possible). Does not return material. Reports in 4 weeks.

Music: Mostly **rap, R&B** and **dance**; also **house, funk** and **soul**. Released *I'll Trip* and "Rednecks" (by Jon Harris), recorded by The Mad Rapper; and *Different Directions*, recorded by Joe Stasa, all on Moneytime Records.

Tips: "Put the best you have on the front of the tape, and have copyrights secured."

*MONTICANA RECORDS, P.O. Box 702, Snowdon Station, Montreal, Quebec H3X 3X8 **Canada**. General Manager: David P. Leonard. Labels include Dynacom and Monticana Records. Record company, record producer and music publisher (Montina Music/SOCAN). Estab. 1963. Works with artists and songwriters on contract. Pays negotiable royalty to artists on contract; statutory rate to publishers for each record sold.

How to Contact: Submit demo tape by mail—unsolicited submissions are OK. Prefers phonograph record (or VHS videocassette) and lyric sheet. Does not return material.

Music: Mostly **top 40, blues, country, dance-oriented, easy listening, folk, gospel, jazz, MOR, progressive, R&B, rock** and **soul**.

MOR RECORDS, 17596 Corbel Court, San Diego CA 92128. (619)485-1550. President: Stuart L. Glassman. Record company and record producer. Estab. 1980. Releases 3 singles/year. Works with musicians on salary for in-house studio work. Pays 4% royalty to artists.

Market conditions are constantly changing! If you're still using this book and it is 1995 or later, buy the newest edition of Songwriter's Market at your favorite bookstore or order directly from Writer's Digest Books.

Affiliate: MOR Jazztime.

How to Contact: Submit demo tape—unsolicited submissions are OK. Prefers cassette (or VHS videocassette). SASE. Reports in 1 month.

Music: Mostly **pop instrumental/vocal MOR**; also **novelty** songs. Released "The Maltese Falcon ... A Simple Solution" by Wally Flaherty (comedy); "Symphony" (public domain) by Piano Man (instrumental pop) and "Fall Softly Snow" (by Jean Surrey), recorded by Al Rosa; all on MOR Records. Other artists include Frank Sinatra Jr., Dave Racan, Dave Austin.

Tips: "Send original work. Do not send 'copy' work. Write lyrics with 'hook.' "

*MORGAN CREEK MUSIC GROUP, #600, 1875 Century Park E., Los Angeles CA 90067. (310)284-8282. Contact: A&R. Labels include Morgan Creek Records. Record company. Estab. 1991. Releases 12 singles, 4 12″ singles, 12 LPs, 3 EPs and 12 CDs/year. Works with musicians/artists on record contract.

How to Contact: Submit demo tape by mail. Unsolicited submissions are OK. Prefers cassette (or VHS videocassette if available). SASE.

Music: Mostly **rock/pop/alternative**, **R&B**, **country**; also **soundtrack** songs. Artists include Mary's Danish, Miracle Legion, Auto & Cherokee, Little Feat, Chris Kowarko and Shelby Lynne.

*MOUNTAIN RAILROAD RECORDS, INC., 36-24th Ave., Venice CA 90291. Fax: (310)822-5404. Director of A&R: Irie Wright. Record company, music publisher (Mountain Railroad Music/ASCAP, 2nd Chance/BMI). Estab. 1973. Releases 2-5 LPs and 2-5 CDs/year. Works with musicians/artists on record contract, songwriters on royalty contract. Pays negotiated royalty to artists on contract; negotiated rate to publishers per song on records.

How to Contact: Submit demo tape by mail. Unsolicited submissions are OK. Prefers cassette (or VHS videocassette if available) with 3 songs and lyric sheet. Does not return material. Reports in 1-2 months.

Music: Mostly **rock, pop, folk**; also **country** and **blues**. Released *Living Ain't Easy*, written and recorded by Jerry Giddens (folk/pop); *Fast Folk* (by Rod MacDonald Odetta, Peter Yarrow and more), recorded by various artists; and *Reheated*, written and recorded by Canned Heat (blues/rock), all on Mountain Railroad Records.

Tips: "Concentrate on writing great songs. Develop an audience by performing live regularly. Record demos to spotlight vocals and songs."

MS'QUE RECORDS INC., P.O. Box 26852, Oklahoma City OK 73126. A&R Representative: Christopher Stanley. Record company and music publisher (CAB Publishing Co./BMI). Estab. 1988. Releases 10 singles, 20 LPs and 20 CDs/year. Works with musicians/artists and songwriters on contract and hires musicians for in-house studio work. Pays statutory rate to publisher per song on record.

How to Contact: Write first and obtain permission to submit. Prefers cassette or VHS videocassette with 3 songs and lead sheet. SASE. Reports in 1-2 months.

Music: Mostly **R&B**, **pop** and **rock**; also **gospel** and **jazz**. Released "Together" (by C. Freeman), recorded by Cash & Co.; "We've Just Begun" (by C. Freeman), recorded by Cash & Co.; and "Everybody Sing" (by S. DeBrown), recorded by Emotions, all on Ms'Que Records.

Tips: "Be yourself first. Work hard, because that's what it takes. Don't be afraid to say what you want, but be careful because you just may get what you asked for."

MULE KICK RECORDS, 5341 Silverlode Dr., Placerville CA 95667. (916)626-4536. Owner: Doug McGinnis, Sr. Record company and music publisher (Freewheeler Publishing/BMI). Estab. 1949. Works with musicians/artists and songwriters on contract and hires musicians for in-house studio work. Pays artists 6¢ per album; statutory rate to publishers.

How to Contact: Submit demo tape—unsolicited submissions are OK. Prefers cassette with 6-10 songs and lyric and lead sheet. SASE. Reports in 1 month.

Music: Mostly **C&W, jazz-AB**, and **c-rock**; also **pop**. Released "One Man Job" and "Please Play Me A Song" (by Mary Voigt), recorded by Coye Wilcox; and "Mighty Big Man" (by Helen Faye), recorded by Ray Jones, all on Lu-Tex Records (country). Other artists include Don McGinnis, Dub Taylor.

Tips: "Keep country country."

MUSCLE SHOALS SOUND GOSPEL, Box 915, Sheffield AL 35660. (205)381-2060. Executive Director: Jerry Mannery. Estab. 1986. Releases 6 LPs/year. Works with musicians/artists and songwriters on contract and hires musicians for in-house studio work. Pays 8% royalty to artists on contract; statutory rate to publisher per song.

How to Contact: Write first and obtain permission to submit. Prefers cassette (or VHS videocassette) with 4 songs. Does not return material. Reports in 8 weeks.

Music: Mostly **gospel, inspirational**. Released "Magnify Him," by Keith Pringle; and "The Promise," by Ricky Dillard (new generation chorale).

MUSIC OF THE WORLD, Box 3620, Chapel Hill NC 27515-3620. President: Bob Haddad. Record company and music publisher (Owl's Head Music/BMI). Estab. 1982. Releases 10 CDs/year. Works with musicians/artists on contract and hires musicians for in-house studio work. Royalty paid to artists on contract varies; statutory rate to publisher per song on record.
How to Contact: "Do *not* submit unsolicited demos; they will be disregarded.Write first, and request permission. The label is only interested in gigging bands, *not* individual song writers."
Music: Only world music. Released "I Remember" and "Fieso Jaiye," written and recorded by I.K. Dairo (Afro pop); and "Grodlaten," written and recorded by Anders Rosén (jazz), all on M.O.W. Records.
Tips: "Submit only traditional world music, or ethnic-influenced modern music."

*MUSIC SERVICE MANAGEMENT, P.O. Box 7171, Duluth MN 55807. (218)628-3003. President: Frank Dell. Record company, music publisher (Frank Dell Music/BMI) and record producer (MSM). Estab. 1970. Releases 2 singles, 1 LP and 1 CD/year. Works with musicians/artists on record contract, songwriters on royalty contract, musicians on salary for in-house studio work. Pays 10% royalty to artists on contract; statutory rate to publisher per song on record.
How to Contact: Submit demo tape by mail. Unsolicited submissions are OK. Write first to arrange personal interview. Prefers cassette with 2 songs. Reports in 1 week.
Music: Mostly country and gospel. Released "Memories," written and recorded by Frank Dell on MSM. Other artists include Luna Axle and Betty Lee.

*MUSICA SCHALLPLATTEN VERTRIEB GES.M.B.H., Webgasse 43, Vienna A-1060 **Austria**. Phone: (1)597 56 46. A&R National: Michael Hufnagl. Labels include OK-Records. Record company, music publisher, record producer (OK-Musica) and publishing company (Ed. Musica). Estab. 1949. Works with musicians/artists and songwriters on contract. Pays 7% royalty to artists on contract.
How to Contact: Submit demo tape by mail—unsolicited submissions are OK—or call first and obtain permission to submit. Prefers cassette with 4-6 songs. Does not return material. Reports in 2 weeks.
Music: Mostly rock, pop and dance. Released *Big Trouble in Paradise* (by Gung-Ho), recorded by Mr. Moder; "Touch by Touch," written and recorded by Joy; and "I'm In It For Love" (by Goldmark-Henderson), recorded by Andy Baum, all on OK Records.
Tips: "If we are interested in singer or song we will contact you. For overseas-artists we are more interested in songs."

NARADA PRODUCTIONS, 1845 N. Farwell Ave., Milwaukee WI 53202. (414)272-6700. Contact: Michele Frane. Record company. Estab. 1983. Releases 30 recordings/year.
How to Contact: Submit demo tape by mail. Unsolicited submissions are OK. Prefers cassette, DAT or CD. Does not return material. Reports in 2 months.
Music: Instrumental music, especially with world beat or adult contemporary jazz influences; also film and television soundtracks.

NEPHELIM RECORD (STUDIO WORKS), 404 ST-Henri, Montreal Quebec H3C 2P5 **Canada**. (514)871-8481. Producer: Mario Rubnikowich. Music publisher (SDE, CAPAC) and record producer. Estab. 1986. Releases 10 singles, 2 12″ singles, 6 LPs and 2 CDs/year. Works with musicians/artists and songwriters on contract and hires musicians for in-house studio work.
How to Contact: Submit demo tape—unsolicited submissions are OK. Prefers cassette with 3 songs and lyric or lead sheets. SASE. Reports in 5 weeks.
Music: Mostly New Age, pop and R&B; also rock, metal and relaxation. Released "Young/Donato" (by Young/Donato), on Just In Times Records (jazz); "Paul Lauzon" (by Paul Lauzon) on Blue Wing Records (therapy); and "Just for Laughs" (by Serge Fiori), on Radio Quebec (radio comedy). Other artists include Michel Laverdiere, Robert LaFond, Oréalis, John Oakley, Marc Chapleau and John Bodine.

*NEP-TUNE RECORDS, INC., Box 3011, Country Club IL 60478. (708)798-9408. A&R Department: Mark Surrucci or Tony Shayne. Record company and 32 track all digital recording studio.
How to Contact: Prefers cassette, DAT (or VHS or Beta videocassette) with maximum of 3 songs; lyric sheet optional. SASE. Reports in 1 month.
Music: Mostly dance, top-40, R&B, hip-hop and new metal rock. Released "What U-Gonna Do About My Love", written and recorded by Vernon Badie; "Kiss Off" (by Tony Shayne), recorded by Ami Stewart; and *Cool Contempo* written and recorded by Dean Davis, all on Nep-Tune Records. Other artists include Rustin' Jammin Harris, Katie-K, Nate Harris, Linda Clifford, Cool Posse, Double Trouble, Mirror Image, The The.
Tips: "Submit a legible, thoughtful presentation short and to the point. We prefer lyrics *without* 4 letter words."

NERVOUS RECORDS, 7-11 Minerva Rd., London NW10 6HJ, **England**. Phone: 4481-963-0352. Managing Director: R. Williams. Record company (Rage Records), record producer and music publisher (Nervous Publishing and Zorch Music). Member MCPS, PRS, PPL, ASCAP, NCB. Releases 10 CDs/year. Works with songwriters on royalty contract. Pays 5-12% royalty to artists on contract; statutory rate to publishers per song on records. Royalties paid directly to US songwriters and artists or through US publishing or recording affiliate.
How to Contact: Submit demo tape—unsolicited submissions OK. Prefers cassette with 4-15 songs and lyric sheet. SAE and IRC. Reports in 2 weeks.
Music: Psychobilly and **rockabilly**. "No heavy rock, AOR, stadium rock, disco, soul, pop—only wild rockabilly and psychobilly." Released "Balls Balls" (by Koinuma), recorded by the Falcons on Nervous Records (psychobilly); "Hot Rod Satellite" (by Whitehouse), recorded by Frenzy on Rage Records (rockabilly); and "B.C. Stomp" (by Rasmussen), recorded by Toggy Tones on Nervous Records (rockabilly). Other artists include Restless, Long Tall Texans, Psycho Bunnies, Sonny West and The Blue Cats.
Tips: "Send only rockabilly or psychobilly."

NETTWERK PRODUCTIONS, 1250 W. 6th Ave., Vancouver, British Columbia V6H 1A5 **Canada**. (604)654-2929. A&R Assistant: Simon Hussey. Record company, music publisher (Nettwerk Productions/SOCAN). Estab. 1984. Releases 12-15 singles, 6 LPs, 2 EPs, 6 CDs/year. Works with musicians/artists and songwriters on contract.
How to Contact: Submit demo tape—unsolicited submissions are OK. Prefers cassette. Does not return material. Reports in 2-3 months.
Music: Mostly **rock, punk-funk, dance**; also **rap** and **urban-dance, folk-rock**. Released *Solace* by Sarah McLachlan; *Welcome To My Dream* by MC900 Ft. Jesus; and *Like Stars in My Hands* by Single Gun Theory. Other artists include Brothers & Systems, Consolidated, Skinny Puppy, Hilt, Itch and Lava Hay.
Tips: "The music should stand out; try not to copy what you have heard five other bands do before. Try to make it sound interesting to the listeners."

NEW EXPERIENCE REC/GRAND SLAM RECORDS, Box 683, Lima OH 45802. (219)424-5766 (Indiana); (419)228-8562 (Ohio). Contact: Tanya Milligan. Grand Slam Records. Record company, music publisher (A New Rap Jam Publishing/ASCAP and Party House Publishing/BMI) and record producer (James Milligan). Estab. 1989. Releases 5-10 singles, 5 12″ singles, 3 LPs, 2 EPs, 2 CDs/year. Works with musicians/artists and songwriters on contract and hire musicians for in-house studio work. Pays standard royalty; statutory rate to publisher per song on record.
How to Contact: Submit demo tape—unsolicited submissions are OK. Address material to A&R Dept. or Carl Milligan, Talent Coordinator. Prefers cassette (or VHS videocassette) with 3-5 songs and lyric sheet. SASE. Reports in 1 month.
Music: Mostly **R&B, pop** and **rock/rap**; also **country, contemporary gospel** and **soul/top 40**. Released "Tell Me If You Still Care" (by SOS Band), recorded by T.M.C. and James Junior; "Playful Jane," written and recorded by Lavel Jackson; and "Jerome Black" (by D. Bacon/M.Day), recorded by Volume 10, all on New Experience Records. Other artists include Anthony Milligan (soul gospel singer), UK Fresh Crew (rap group), Carl Milligan (gospel singer) and Tammy Oats.

NICKEL RECORDS, 753 Capitol Ave., Hartford CT 06106. (203)951-8175. Producer: Jack Stang. Record company, record producer (Jack Stang) and music publisher (Stang Music Publishing/BMI). Estab. 1975. Releases 5 singles, 2 12″ singles and 5 CDs/year. Works with musicians/artists and songwriters on contract. Pays 6-10% royalty to artists on contract for each record sold. Pays statutory rate to publishers per song on record.
How to Contact: Submit demo tape by mail. Unsolicited submissions are OK. Prefers cassette with 1-3 songs and lyric sheet. SASE. Reports in 6 weeks.
Music: Mostly **rock, pop** and **R&B**; also **gospel**. Released *Girls Like You*, written and recorded by Bill Chapin; *Smokin*, by Joe Frazier, "It's So Easy to Fall in Love," by Ray Alaire and Sky, all on Nickel Records. Other artists include Kenny Hamber, Michael Kelly, Perfect Tommy, Alpha Sonas, Damon Sky and Dagmar.

NICKLE PLATE RECORDS, Box 140821, Chicago IL 60614-0821. President: Frederick S. Koger. Record company and music publisher ("L" Train Publishers/ASCAP). Estab. 1987. Releases 3 singles and 3 12″ singles/year. Works with musicians/artists and songwriters on contract. Pays 10% royalty to artist on contract.
How to Contact: Submit demo tape—unsolicited submissions are OK. Prefers cassette with 3-5 songs and lyric or lead sheets. SASE. Reports in 3 weeks.
Music: Mostly **R&B, rap** and **pop**; also **rock** and **gospel**. Released "Throw Down," written and recorded by David Johnson; "The Girl Next Door," written and recorded by Sara Lynn; and "Two On Top" (by Big Mike), recorded by Tony, all on Nickle Plate Records.

Tips: "Stay with one format. Be serious. Make sure tape is clear, not muffled. Be patient. Things take time and money. Make sure the music is the best that you can do."

*NIGHTFLITE RECORDS INC., 4091 Pheasant Run, Mississanga, Ontario L5L 2C2 **Canada**. (416)820-6400. A&R: Joey Cee. Labels include JCO Records. Record company and music publisher. Estab. 1981. Works with songwriters on royalty contract. Pays 4% royalty to artists on contract; statutory rate to publisher per song on record.
How to Contact: Write or call first and obtain permission to submit. Prefers cassette (or VHS videocassette) with 2-3 songs and lyric sheet. Does not return material. Reports in 1-3 month.
Music: Mostly **contemporary pop, country** and **rock**; also **new age**. Released "Nature's Eyes" (by Joey Cee), recorded by Voices of Hope (pop); *Stars On Steel* (by various), recorded by Stars on Steel (A/C); and *Playboy Street Rock* (by various), recorded by various artists (rock), all on Nightflite Records. Other artists include Joey Paul, Power Patrol, Camilleri and Elay Orchestra.
Tips: "Spell out exactly the type of arrangement (business) you are looking for and be realistic in your expectations."

NORTH STAR RECORDS, 95 Hathaway St., Providence RI 02907. (401)785-8400. Executive Vice President: Richard Waterman. Record company and music publisher (Publishing Name: Blue Gate Music/ASCAP). Estab. 1985. Releases 10-15 LPs/year. Works with musicians/artists and songwriters on contract. Pays statutory royalty to artists on contract; statutory rate to publisher per song on record.
How to Contact: Write first and obtain permission to submit. Prefers cassette with 4-5 songs and lyric sheets. Does not return material. Reports in 1 month.
Music: Mostly **country, R&B** and **rock/folk**; also **acoustic traditional, classical** and **children's music.** Released *Cheryl Wheeler* on North Star Records and *Half-A-Book* on Cypress Records, written and recorded by Cheryl Wheeler (rock/country); and *Time Can Be So Magic*, written and recorded by Bill Thomas on North Star Records (children's). Other artists include Chili Brothers, Arturo Delmoni, New England Music Collection, Mair-Davis Duo and Hubbards.
Tips: "A professional, well thought-out presentation of your best material is necessary to attract the attention of record label personnel."

NOW & THEN RECORDS, Dept. SM, #3, 501 78th St., North Bergen NJ 07047. (201)854-6266. Contact: Shane Faber. Record company, music publisher (Now & Then Music/BMI) and record producer (Shane "the Dr." Faber). Estab. 1980. Works with musicians/artists and songwriters on contract. Pays 10% royalty to artists on contract; statutory rate to publisher per song on record.
How to Contact: Submit demo tape—unsolicited submissions are OK. Prefers cassette with 4 songs and lyric sheet. SASE.
Music: Mostly **pop, dance** and **R&B**; also **rap** and **New Age**. Released *Sneak Attack, Beat the Meter* and *Big Ducks*, all recorded by Bad Sneakers. Other artists include Tenita Jordon (R&B), T.T. (dance), Blackhearts (rap), Shane Faber (pop) and Audrey Smith-Bey (pop).

*NUCLEUS RECORDS, P.O. Box 111, Sea Bright NJ 07760. President: Robert Bowden. Record company and music publisher (Roots Music/BMI). Member AFM (US and Canada). Estab. 1979. Releases 2 singles and 1 LP/year. Works with musicians/artists on contract and hires musicians for in-house studio work. Pays up to 25% royalty for each record sold; statutory rate to publisher per song on record.
How to Contact: Prefers cassette (or videocassette) with any number songs and lyric sheet. Prefers studio produced demos. SASE. Reports in 3 weeks.
Music: Mostly **country** and **pop**; also **church/religious, classical, folk, MOR, progressive, rock (soft, mellow)** and **top 40**. Released "4 O'clock Rock," "Henrey C" and "Will You Miss Me Tonight" (by Bowden), recorded by Marco Sison, all on Nucleus Records.

OCEAN RECORDS INC., P.O. Box 190944, Roxbury MA 02119. Producer: Jackie Whitehead. Record company, music publisher (Mighty Fine Music/ASCAP) and record producer (O.R. Productions). Estab. 1977. Releases 5 singles, 5 12" singles and 4 LPs/year. Works with musicians/artists, songwriters and producers on contract. Pays statutory rate to publisher per song on record.
How to Contact: Submit demo tape—unsolicited submissions are OK. Prefers cassette. Does not return material. Reports in 4-6 weeks.
Music: Mostly **R&B, pop** and **funk**; also **rap** and **gospel**.
Tips: "Make good quality demo tapes with good highs & lows. Do not use a cassette that has been used 20 times or more. Use a new cassette at all times."

*OLD SCHOOL RECORDS, 179 Prospect Ave., Wood Dale IL 60191-2727. Owner/President: Peter J. Gianakopulos. Record company, music publisher (Old School Records/Goosongs, ASCAP). Estab. 1992. Releases 1-2 singles, 1-2 LPs, 1-2 EPs, and 1-2 CDs. Works with musicians/artists on record contract. Pays 10% to artists on contract; statutory rate to publishers per song on record.

How to Contact: Submit demo tape by mail. Unsolicited submissions are OK. Prefers cassette with 3-5 songs and lyric sheet. SASE. Reports in 1 month.
Music: Mostly **alternative rock, blues, pop**; also **funk, punk** and **tribute albums**. Released *Muse*, recorded by The Now on Old School Records (eclectic rock).
Tips: "Be true to your craft. No matter how different the feel of music—take it to the style you feel like writing. Most artists may find their best writing style is different from their listening tastes."

*ON TOP RECORDS, 3081 NW 24th St., Miami FL 33167. (305)635-5588. Contact: Chavela Frazier. Record company. Estab. 1985. Releases 40-50 singles, 10 LPs and 10 CDs/year. Pays 3-6% royalty to artists on contract; standard rate to publisher per song on record.
How to Contact: Write first and obtain permission to submit. Prefers cassette. Does not return material. Reports in 6-8 weeks.
Music: Mostly **bass, rap, dance**; also **R&B, gospel** and **jazz**. Released *Gangsta Bass* (by Andy Cuff, Benton Dennis), recorded by Miami Boyz; *Watch Me Grow* (by Dion Hamilton), recorded by Half-Pint; and *Fury's Bass* (by Brian Graham), recorded by D.J. Fury, all on On Top Records.
Tips: "Copyright all material before submitting to anyone. Be creative and persistence politely."

ONE-EYED DUCK RECORDING AND PUBLISHING, 22 Rainsford Rd., Toronto, Ontario M4L3N4 Canada. (416)694-6900. General Manager: Patricia Erlendson. Record company, music publisher (PROCAN) and record producer. Estab. 1983. Releases 1 LP/year. Works with musicians/artists and songwriters on contract. Pays negotiable rate to artists on contract; statutory rate to publisher per song on record.
How to Contact: Write first and obtain permission to submit. Prefers cassette. SASE. Reports in 1 month.
Music: Mostly **children's**. Released "I Can Do Anything," "Sharing" and "Kidstuff," recorded by Sphere Clown Band on One-Eyed Duck Records (children's).

ORBIT RECORDS, P.O. Box 120675, Nashville TN 37212. (615)255-1068. Owner: Ray McGinnis. Record company, music publisher (Nautical Music Co.) and record producer (Ray Mack Productions). Estab. 1965. Releases 6-10 singles, 6 12" singles and 4 LPs/year. Receives 15-20 submissions/month. Works with musicians/artists on contract. Pays 8-12% royalty to artists on contract; statutory rate to publisher per song on record.
How to Contact: Prefers cassette with 4 songs and lead sheet. Does not return material. Reports in 6-8 weeks.
Music: **Country (ballads), country rock** and **R&B**. Released "Burning Love," written and recorded by Alan Warren (hard rock); "No More Tears" (by D. Cannon), recorded by Debra Lee, both on Orbit Records. Other artists include Steve Wyles.
Tips: "We like artists with individual styles, not 'copy cats'; be original and unique."

*ORINDA RECORDS, P.O. Box 838, Orinda CA 94563. (510)833-7000. A&R Director: Harry Balk. Record company. Works with musicians/artists on record contract, songwriters on royalty contract. Pays negotiable rate to publishers per song on record.
How to Contact: Submit demo tape by mail. Unsolicited submissions are OK. Prefers cassette and lead sheet. Does not return material. Reports in 3 months.
Music: Mostly **pop, rock, jazz**.

*OUTSTANDING & MORRHYTHM RECORDS, P.O. Box 2111, Huntington Beach CA 92647. (714)842-8635. Owner: Earl Beecher. Record company, music publisher (Earl Beecher Publishing/BMI). Estab. 1968. Released 11 LPs and 2 CDs in 1992. Works with musicians/artists, songwriters on royalty contract. Pays $2 royalty/CD sold and 75¢ royalty/cassette sold; statutory rate to publishers per song on record.
How to Contact: Submit demo tape by mail. Unsolicited submissions are OK. "Do not write or call first." Prefers cassette with 3 songs. SASE. Reporting time varies.
Music: Mostly **jazz, rock, pop, country, gospel, R&B, rap**. Released *(Put the) Soul Back in Rock*, written and recorded by Tom Adelstein; *In Your Eyes*, written and recorded by Patti O'Hara, both on Morrhythm Records; and *Huntington Beach* (by Earl Beecher), recorded by Paul Smith on Outstanding Records. Other artists include Shades of Mystery, Joe Valente, The Memory Bros., and Alex St. Felix.
Tips: "Be professional. I'm looking for seasoned performers who wish to release their original material on my labels. Please do not send amateur material."

*P.I.R.A.T.E. RECORDS/H.E.G. MUSIC PUBLISHING, 6381 Hollywood BD #250, Hollywood CA 90028. General Manager: Jefflyn Dangerfield. Record company, music publisher, record producer (The Groove Asylum). Estab. 1989. Releases 30 singles, 10 12" singles, 10 LPs, 10 EPs and 10 CDs/year. Works with musicians/artists in recording contract, songwriters on royalty contract, musicians on salary for in-house studio work. Pays 9-13% royalty to artists on contract; statutory rate to publishers per song on record.

How to Contact: Write first and obtain permission to submit. Prefers cassette (or VHS videocassette if available) with 1-4 songs and lyric sheet. SASE. Reports in 2-3 weeks.

Music: Mostly **R&B (alternative), pop, gospel.** Released "Get Away," recorded by B. Brown on MCA Records; *Precious*, recorded by C. Moore on Silas Records; *Ritual of Love*, recorded by K. White on Warner Records, all by T. Haynes (R&B). Other artists include Freddie Jackson, Boyz of Paradize, Leslie, Cyndie Mysel, Bon Ton, Renee Diggs, Sista Style, A-1 Swift and John Lucian.

Tips: "Just do it!!! Give us a call or have your representative contact us for availability and material."

*PACIFIC ARTISTS RECORDS, 246 Esperanza, Tiburon CA 94920. (415)435-2772. President: Alexandra Morriss. Record company, music publisher and record producer. Estab. 1980. Pay negotiable.

How to Contact: Submit demo tape by mail. Unsolicited submissions are OK. Prefers cassette (or VHS videocassette) with 3 songs and lyric or lead sheet. SASE.

Music: Mostly **jazz/New Age, world** and **children's**; also **country** and **orchestral.** Artists include The Alexandra Quartet, Peggy Monaghan, Doug Gittens, Alexandra Randolph and Randi Morriss.

*PAJER RECORDS, 23 Forest Lane, Black Mountain NC 28711. (704)669-7290. Owner: Jerry Caldwell. Record company, music publisher (Hazewell Music Pub/BMI), record producer (Pajer Music Production). Estab. 1973. Releases 3 singles and 3 EPs/year. Works with musicians/artists on record contract, songwriters on royalty contract. Pays 15% royalty to artists on contract; statutory rate to publishers per song on record.

How to Contact: Submit demo tape by mail. Unsolicited submissions are OK, but not more than 4 at a time on cassette. SASE a must, otherwise tapes not returned. Prefers cassette with 4 songs and lyric sheet. SASE. Reports in 2 weeks.

Music: Mostly **contemporary country, pop/crossover, MOR.** Released "Ode to Elvis," recorded by Phil Coley on Pajer Records (rock); "Where in the World," recorded by So. Passion on Eagle Int. (country); and "Rhythm of the Night," recorded by Jean Shey on Puzzle Records (country). Other artists include Ann Beaman, C.B. Ryan, Max Berry, J. Thomas, Johnny House, Wayne Dorlan, Norman Mays, Sue Stover.

Tips: "Listen to what's being played and sung on radio and TV. Pattern your songs accordingly. Always be professional. Write song lyrics, not poetry (there's a difference). Write the way people talk today. Select a HOOK (clever title) and build your song around that. A song is like a short story—beginning, middle and ending. Seek controversy and resolve it in your lyric structure. Compose interesting melodies."

*PALMETTO PRODUCTIONS, P.O. Box 1376, Pickens SC 29671. (803)859-9614. Fax: (803)859-3814. Owner/Partner: Brian E. Raines. Labels include Palmetto Records (country) and Rosada Records (gospel). Record company, music publisher (Brian Raines Music Co./ASCAP and Brian Song Music Co./BMI) and record producer. Estab. 1985. Releases 3 singles, 2-5 LPs and 3 CDs/year. Works with songwriters on contract and musicians on salary for in-house studio work. Pays standard royalty to artists on contract; statutory rate to publishers per song on record.

How to Contact: Write first and obtain permission to submit. Prefers VHS videocassette with 2-3 songs and lyric sheet. Does not return material. Reports in 3 months.

Music: Mostly **gospel, contemporary Christian** and **country.** Released "Since I Met You," written and recorded by Brian Raines, on Palmetto Records (country); *Jim & Brian*, written and recorded by Raines/Hubbard; and *From the Heart*, written and recorded by Jim Hubbard, both on Hubbit Records (country).

Tips: "Send VHS tape of artist or group *only*! No unsolicited cassettes (audio) accepted. Also, a photo must be included with bio sheet."

*PARADIGM DISTRIBUTION, 3343 Adams Ave., San Diego CA 92116. (619)563-1981. Owner: Karen Merry. Alternative music distributor. Estab. 1984.

How to Contact: Submit demo tape by mail. Unsolicited submissions are OK. Prefers cassette or CD and bio and promo material. SASE. Reports in 3-6 months.

Music: Mostly **New Age, Native American, children's**; also **women's, international.**

Tips: "When submitting to distributor have good promotion in place."

PARAGOLD RECORDS & TAPES, Box 292101, Nashville TN 37229-2101. (615)859-4890. Director: Teresa Parks Bernard. Record company, music publisher (Rainbarrel Music Co./BMI) and record producer. Estab. 1972. Releases 3 singles and 3 LPs/year. Works with musicians/artists and songwriters on contract. Pays statutory rate to publishers.

How to Contact: Write first and obtain permission to submit. Prefers cassette (or VHS videocassette) with 2 songs and lyric or lead sheets. SASE. "Unpublished songs are welcome. Send only outstanding material." Reports in 2 months.

Music: Country and **top 40.** Released "Rose & Bittercreek" and "Bottle of Happiness," written and recorded by Johnny Bernard; and "Daddy's Last Letter" (by J. Bernard), recorded by JLyne, all on Paragold Records (country). Other artists include Sunset Cowboys.
Tips: "Must have high quality demo. Must use SASE if you want answer."

PARC RECORDS INC., Suite 205, 5104 N. Orange Blossom Trail, Orlando FL 32810. (407)292-0021. Executive Assistant: Leslie A. Schipper. Record company (Mister Sunshine Music/BMI). Estab. 1985. Releases 4+ singles, 2 12″ singles, 2 LPs and 2 CDs/year. Works with musicians/artists and songwriters on contract.
How to Contact: Prefers cassette (or VHS videocassette) with 3-5 songs and lyric sheet. SASE. Reports in 6-8 weeks.
Music: Mostly **rock/metal, dance** and **jazz/new wave;** also **A/C** and **R&B.** Released *Lighting Strikes*, recorded by Molly Hatchet on Parc/Capitol Records (rock); *China Sky*, recorded by China Sky on Parc/CBS Records (rock); and *Ana*, recorded by Ana on Parc/CBS Records (dance), (all by various). Other artists include Glen Kelly and Deryle Hughes.
Tips: "Quality songs with good hooks are more important than great production. If it's good, we can hear it."

***PARSIFAL PVBA,** Gulden Vlieslaan, 67, Brugge 8000 **Belgium.** Phone: (050)339516. Contact: Nico Mertens. Labels include Parsifal, Sundown, Double Trouble, Vision, Moonshine, Blue Sting and Discus. Record company, music publisher and record producer. Estab. 1977. Releases 2 singles and 10 CDs/year. Works with musicians/artists on contract; musicians on salary for in-house studio work.
How to Contact: Submit demo tape by mail—unsolicited submissions are OK. Prefers cassette. Does not return material. Reports in 1 month.
Music: R&B and **blues.** Released *Born to Win*, written and recorded by Studebaker John on Double Trouble Records; *Come Inside* (by Bonte/Pierins), recorded by Hideway on Blue Sting Records; and *D for Drive*, written and recorded by Stuffed Babies On Wheels, on Vision Records. Other artists include Steve Samuels (US), Paris Slim (US), Mark Hummel (US), Dave Weld (US), Larry Wise (US), Wailin' Walker (Canada), and Give Buzze (Belgium).

PAULA RECORDS/JEWEL RECORDS/RONN RECORDS, Box 1125, Shreveport LA 71163-1125. (318)227-2228. Owner: Stanley J. Lewis. Record company and music publisher. Works with musicians/artists and songwriters on contract.
How to Contact: Submit demo tape by mail. Unsolicited submissions are OK. Prefers cassette with 3 songs and lyric sheet. SASE.
Music: Mostly **R&B, gospel** and **country.**

PDS RECORDS, Box 412477, Kansas City MO 64141. (800)473-7550. (816)523-5100. Contact: A&R, Dept. 100. Labels include Universal Jazz, PDS Associated labels. Record company, music publisher (PDS Music Publishing/ASCAP/BMI) and record producer (PDS Productions). Estab. 1988. Releases 8-10 singles, 8-10 12″ singles, 3-5 LPs, 8-10 EPs and 3-5 CDs/year. Works with musicians/artists on contract.
How to Contact: Write first and obtain permission to submit. Prefers cassette (or VHS videocassette) with 4-5 songs and lyric sheet. Does not return material. Reports in 2 months.

PENGUIN RECORDS, INC., #2, Box 3031, SW 27th Ave., Miami FL 33133. Product Manager: Michael J. McNamee. Operation Manager: Gregory J. Winters. Labels include Straitgate Records and Kinetic Records. Record company, music publisher. Estab. 1990. Releases 6 singles, 6 12″ singles, 3 LPs and 3 CDs/year. Works with varying number of musicians/artists and songwriters/year. Pays varying royalty.
How to Contact: Obtain permission to submit before sending submissions. Prefers cassette (or VHS videocassette) with 3 songs and lyric sheets. SASE. Reports in 2 months.
Music: Mostly **dance, pop, rock, R&B/rap** and **alternative/dance;** also **industrial** and **Christian.** Released "Give Me a Sign" and "The Face of Fear," recorded on Kinetic Records.
Tips: "Be patient! There's a lot of music out there. Everyone will get a chance."

***PERIDOT RECORDS,** P.O. Box 8846, Cranston RI 02920. Owner/President: Amy Parravano. Record company, music publisher (Peridot/ASCAP), record producer (Peridot Productions). Estab. 1992. Releases 2 singles, 2 12″ singles, 1 LP/year. Works with musicians/artists on record contract. Pays 10% royalty to artists on contract; statutory rate to publisher per song on record.
How to Contact: Submit demo tape by mail. Unsolicited submissions are OK. Prefers cassette with 3-4 songs and lyric sheet or lead sheet. SASE. Reports in 1 month.
Music: Mostly **country, gospel, folk;** also **MOR, children's, novelty.** Released "Grandma's Attic" (by Amy Parravano and Ellen Smith); "His Light Shines Down On Me" and "Trust In Him" (by Amy Parravano), all recorded by Amy Beth on Peridot Records.
Tips: "Send finished demo, completed master reel or DAT ready for record release."

PHOENIX RECORDS, INC., Dept. SM, Box 121076, Nashville TN 27212-1076. (615)244-5357. President: Reggie M. Churchwell. Labels include Nashville International Records and Monarch Records. Record company and music publisher (BMI/ASCAP). Estab. 1971. Releases 5-6 CDs/year. Works with musicians/artists and songwriters on contract. Pays standard royalty to artists on contract; statutory rate to publisher per song on record.
How to Contact: Write first and obtain permission to submit. "You must have permission before submitting any material." Prefers cassette with lyric sheets. Does not return material. Reports in 2-3 weeks.
Music: Mostly **country, rock** and pop; also **gospel.** Released "Left of Center Line" (by Howard Lips), recorded by Catfish on Phoenix Records (country/rock); and "Littlest Cowboy," written and recorded by Sonny Shroyer on Hazzard Records (children's). Other artists include Conrad Pierce and Clay Jerrolds.
Tips: "We are looking for songs with strong hooks and strong words. We are not simply looking for songs, we are looking for hits."

PILOT RECORDS AND TAPE COMPANY, 628 S. South St., Mount Airy NC 27030. (919)786-2865. President and Owner: Paul E. Johnson. Labels include Stork, Stark, Pilot, Hello, Kay, Sugarbear, Southcoast, Songcraft, Bell Sounds, Blue Ridge, Joy, Red Bird and Tornado and Blue Jay. Record company, music publisher (Tompaul Music Company/BMI) and record producer. Estab. 1960. Releases 12 singles and 75 LPs/year. Works with songwriters on contract; musicians on salary for in-house studio work. Pays 30% royalty to artists on contract; statutory rate to publishers per song on record.
How to Contact: Submit demo tape by mail—unsolicited submissions are OK. Prefers cassette with 6 songs and lyric sheet. SASE. Reports in 2 months. "The songwriters should give their date of birth with submissions. This information will be used when copyrighting a songwriter's song."
Music: Mostly **country, gospel** and **bluegrass;** also **rock, folk** and **blues.** Released "Devil's Sweetheart" and "Heartache Street" (by Lee Martin), recorded by Clyde Johnson; and "Rebound Love," written and recorded by Thurman Holder, all on Pilot Records. Other artists include Bobby Atkins, Carl Tolbert, Early Upchurch and Sanford Teague.

PLATINUM BOULEVARD RECORDS, 1558 Linda Way, Sparks NV 89431. (702)358-7484. President: Lawrence Davis. Record company. Estab. 1986. Releases 2 singles and 1 LP/year. Works with musicians/artists on contract. Pays negotiable royalty to artists on contract; statutory rate to publisher per song on record.
How to Contact: Submit demo tape by mail—unsolicited submissions are OK. Prefers cassette (or VHS videocassette) with songs and lyric or lead sheets. Does not return unsolicited material. "We report back only if interested."
Music: Mostly **rock, pop** and **R&B;** also **country, jazz** and **New Age.** Released *Davis*, written and recorded by L.R. Davis on Platinum Blvd. Records (rock LP).
Tips: "When presenting material indicate which artists you have in mind to record it. If you desire to be the recording artist please indicate."

PLAY RECORDS, Box 6541, Cleveland OH 44101. (216)467-0300. President: John Latimer. Record company. Estab. 1985. Releases 3 LPs/year. Works with musicians/artists and songwriters on contract.
How to Contact: Submit demo tape by mail—unsolicited submissions are OK. Prefers cassette (or VHS or ¾" videocassettes) with 5 songs and lyric or lead sheets. SASE. Reports in 6 weeks.
Music: Mostly **rock, pop** and **alternative;** also **blues, jazz** and **R&B.** Released "There Was a Time," written and recorded by The Bellows; "Bombs Away," written and recorded by Serious Nature; and "Mr. Sensible," written and recorded by Mr. Sensible, all on Play Records (rock). Other artists include The French Lenards, 15 60 75, The Adults, Cool Down Daddy, The Bomb, Earl Rays, Zero One, Holy Cows and Ronald Koal.
Tips: "Be patient but persistent. Please correspond by mail only."

PLAYBACK RECORDS, Box 630755, Miami FL 33163. (305)935-4880. Producer: Jack Gale. Labels include Gallery II Records, Ridgewood Records. Record company, music publisher (Lovey Music/ BMI and Cowabonga Music/ASCAP) and record producer. Estab. 1983. Releases 20 CDs/year. Works with musicians/artists and songwriters on contract. Pays statutory rate to publisher per song on record.

Remember: Don't "shotgun" your demo tapes. Submit only to companies interested in the type of music you write. For more submission hints, refer to Getting Started on page 7.

How to Contact: Submit demo tape by mail—unsolicited submissions are OK. Prefers cassette (VHS videocassette if available) with 2 songs and lyric sheet. Does not return materials. Reports in 2 weeks if interested.

Music: Mostly **country.** Released "Mem'ryville" (by Larry Lee), recorded by Sammi Smith; "Back In Harmony" (by Don Silverstein), recorded by Tanya Tucker; and "Achy Breaky Heart" (by Don Von Tress), recorded by Del Reeves, all on Playback Records. Other artists include Ernie Ashworth, Michele Bishop, Jimmy C. Newman, Jack Green, Justin Tubb, Charlie Louvin, Sylvie, Melba Montgomery and Johnny Paycheck.

Tips: "Send only your best. Be open to suggestion. Remember . . . this is a business, not an ego trip."

PLEASURE RECORDS, Rt. 1, Box 187-A, Whitney TX 76692. (817)694-4047. Fax: (817)694-5155. President: Allen Newton. Labels include Cactus Flats, Pristine, MFN, Seneca VII. Record company and music publisher (Four Newton Publishing/BMI, Stethash/ASCAP). Estab. 1986. Releases 12 singles, 3 12″ singles and 1 LP/year. Works with musicians/artists and songwriters on contract. Pays up to 50% royalty to artists on contract; statutory rate to publisher per song on record.

How to Contact: Submit demo tape by mail—unsolicited submissions are OK. Prefers cassette with 3 songs and lyric or lead sheets. SASE. Reports in 4-6 weeks.

Music: Mostly **country, gospel** and **rock;** also **rock-a-billy, R&B** and **Spanish.** Released "Partying With My Pop" and "Hard Drugs For Me" (by Baumgartner/Dwyer/Arnold), recorded by Zen Butcher; and "Memories Of Love," written and recorded by Eric Moberly, all on Pristine Records. Other artists include Rhonda Jones, Sissy Padilla, David Dancer, Eric Matthews, Devarne Thomas, James David, Zen Butcher, Chi Louis, James David and Voices of Joy.

Tips: "Don't give up the dream."

PMG RECORDS, Box 2849, Trolley Station, Detroit MI 48231. President: Bruce Henderson. Record company, music publisher (Prejippie Music Group/BMI) and record producer (PMG Productions). Estab. 1990. Releases 6-12 12″ singles, 2 LPs and 2 EPs/year. Works with musicians/artists on contract. Pays statutory rate.

How to Contact: Submit demo tape by mail—unsolicited submissions are OK. Prefers cassette (or VHS videocassette) with 3-4 songs and lyric sheet. Include photo if possible. No calls please. SASE. Reports in 6 weeks.

Music: Mostly **funk/rock, techno/house** and **dance;** also **alternative rock** and **New Age.** Released *Personality Disorder* by the Prejippies (techno/alternative) and *Frankfather* by Bourgeoisie Paper Jam (alternative rock). Other artists include Urban Transit (house) and Deep Six Honey (alternative/experimental).

Tips: "A strong hook and melody line are your best weapons! We also look for originality."

*POLYGRAM RECORDS, 825 8th Ave., New York NY 10019. (212)333-8000. Contact: A&R Assistant. Record company. Works with artists on contract.

How to Contact: "We review songs submitted by established publishers. Not accepting unsolicited material, but welcome queries when accompanied by press and/or chart clippings and SASE. Do *not* send recordings or lyrics until requested." Recommends referral from a reputable industry source.

Music: Rock, top 40/pop, R&B and **dance/urban.** Current roster includes Bon Jovi, John Mellencamp, Cinderella, Robert Cray, Kiss, Scorpions, Def Leppard, Ugly Kid Joe, Vanessa Williams, Black Sheep, Oleta Adams and Soup Dragons.

Tips: "Be patient—you will be contacted if there's interest. Keep in mind that most of the artists write their own material. We're most open to female-oriented and pop acts to balance out heavy-hitting hard rock and R&B roster."

POP RECORD RESEARCH, 17 Piping Rock Dr., Ossining NY 10562. (914)762-8499. Director: Gary Theroux. Labels include Surf City, GTP and Rock's Greatest Hits. Record company, music publisher (Surf City Music/ASCAP), record producer and archive of entertainment-related research materials (files on hits and hitmakers since 1877). Estab. 1962. Works with musicians/artists and songwriters on contract and writers/historians/biographers, radio, TV and film producers requiring research help or materials. Pays statutory rate to publisher per song on record.

How to Contact: Submit demo tape, press kits or review material by mail. Unsolicited submissions are OK. Prefers cassette (or VHS videocassette). Does not return material.

Music: Mostly **pop, country** and **R&B.** Released "The Declaration" (by Theroux-Gilbert), recorded by An American on Bob Records; "Thoughts From a Summer Rain," written and recorded by Bob Gilbert on Bob Records; and "Tiger Paws," written and recorded by Bob Gilbert on BAL Records; all pop singles. Other artists include Gary and Joan, The Nightflight Singers and Ruth Zimmerman.

Tips: "Help us keep our biographical file on you and your career current by sending us updated bios/press kits, etc. They are most helpful to writers/researchers in search of accurate information on your success."

*POWERCOAT RECORDS, P.O. Box 1791, Bensalem PA 19020. (215)639-5823. Fax: Call first. PR/ A&R: Kathy J. Vulgamott. Record company, music publisher (Powercoat Records/BMI). Estab. 1990. Releases 2 singles, 2 LPs, 1 EP/year. Works with musicians/artists on record contract. Pays 50-75% royalty to artists on contract; negotiable rate to publishers per song on record.
How to Contact: Write first and obtain permission to submit. "Also include cover letter, bio, photo, explain demo recording, detail equipment." Prefers cassette with 3-4 songs and lyric sheet. Does not return material. Reports in 4-6 weeks.
Music: Mostly **contemporary New Age pop, contemporary New Age pop instrumental, New Age rock**; also **soft rock, pop rock instrumental, sound track**. Released *Phylogeny*, written and recorded by Phantom Phorty (contemporary New Age pop instrumental); *Distress Sense* and *Peregrination*, written and recorded by Civil Allen. Other artists includ Visionari.
Tips: "Be meticulous, melodic, but not mainstream. You must be truly dedicated to socially conscious and environmental reform. Quality, sincerity and just plain great music is what must accompany this."

PPI/PETER PAN INDUSTRIES, 88 St. Francis St., Newark NJ 07105. (201)344-4214. Product Manager: Marianne Eggleston. Labels include Compose Records, Current Records, Parade Video, Iron Bound Publishing/Guess Star Records. Record company, music publisher, record producer (Dunn Pearson, Jr.) and outside producers are used also. Estab. 1928. Releases more than 200 cassettes and CDs and 75-80 videos/year. Works with musicians/artists and songwriters on contract. Pays royalty per contract; statutory rate per contract to publisher per song on records. "All services are negotiable!"
How to Contact: Write or call first to obtain permission to submit. Prefers cassette (or VHS videocassette if available) with 3-5 songs and lyric sheet. SASE. Reports in 3 months.
Music: **Pop, R&B**; also **jazz** and **New Age**. Released "Go For The Gusto" (R&B); "Programmed For Love" (jazz); and "Color Tapestry" (jazz) all written and recorded by Dunn Pearson, Jr. on Compose Records; "A Different Light," by David Friedman; and "The Trollies," by Dennis Scott, Grammy Award winner.

PRAIRIE MUSIC RECORDS LTD., Box 438, Walnut IA 51577. (712)366-1136. President: Robert Everhart. Record company and record producer (Prairie Music Ltd.). Estab. 1964. Releases 2 singles and 2 LPs/year. Works with musicians/artists and songwriters on contract. Pays 5% royalty to artists on contract; statutory rate to publisher per song on record.
How to Contact: Submit demo tape by mail. Unsolicited submissions are OK. Prefers cassette. SASE. Reports in 4 months.
Music: Mostly **traditional country, bluegrass** and **folk**. Released "Time After Time," "Street Sleepers" and "Rock of Hollywood," all written and recorded by Bob Everhart on Folkways Records (traditional country). Other artists include Gospel Pilgrims, whose latest release "No One Comes Near" was re-released in Czechoslovakia.

*PRAVDA RECORDS, 3823 N. Southport, Chicago IL 60613. (312)549-3776. Director of A&R: Mark Luecke. Labels include Bughouse. Record company. Estab. 1985. Releases 3-6 singles, 1 EP, 5-6 CDs. Works with musicians/artists on record contract. Pays 10-15% royalty to artists on contract; statutory rate to publishers per song on record.
How to Contact: Submit demo tape by mail. Unsolicited submissions are OK. Prefers cassette with 3-4 songs. Does not return material. Reports in 1-3 months.
Music: Mostly **rock, C&W, metal**; also **polka, big band, spoken word**. Released *Tilt A Whirl*, written and recorded by New Duncan Imperials (rock); *Whatever*, written and recorded by The Slugs (pop), both on Pravda Records; and *Live In Chicago* written and recorded by Hasil Adkins on Bughouse Records (country). Other artists include Javelin Boot, Susan Voelz, Mercy Rule.
Tips: "Know who our artists are."

PRESENCE RECORDS, Box 1101, Cromwell CT 06416. (203)721-1049. President: Paul Payton. Record company, music publisher (Paytoons/BMI), record producer (Presence Productions). Estab. 1985. Pays 1-2% royalty to artists on contract; statutory rate to publisher per song on record.
How to Contact: Write and obtain permission to submit. Prefers cassette with 2-3 songs and lyric sheet. Does not return unsolicited material. Reports in 1 month.
Music: Mostly **Doo-wop (50s), rock & roll, new wave rock, new age**. Released "Davilee/Go On" (by Paul Payton/Peter Skolnik), recorded by Fabulous Dudes (doo-wop); and "Boys Like Girls/Relate 2U," written and recorded by Paul Payton (rock), both on Presence Records.

PRESTO RECORDS, Box 1081, Lowell MA 01853. (617)893-2144. President: Christopher Porter. Record company. Affiliated with Chris Porter Productions Inc. (a booking and management company). Estab. 1989. Releases 2-4 LPs and 2-4 CDs/year. Work with musicians/artists on contract. Pays statutory rate to publisher per song on record.

How to Contact: Submit demo tape by mail—unsolicited submissions are OK. Prefers cassette with 3-4 songs. SASE or SAE and IRC. Reports in 1-2 months.

Music: Mostly **guitar-oriented alternative rock**. Released "Missed Opportunities" (by Adam Boc), recorded by Miranda Warning; "Say Goodbye," written and recorded by Evol Twin; and "Ed McMahon Says" (by Alan Grandy), recorded by The Terrible Parade, all on Presto Records (alternative rock). Other artists include Miles Dethmuffen, The Trojan Ponies, and Classic Ruins.

Tips: "We mainly deal with guitar-oriented rock—accessible but not overly commercial. If a songwriter has a band together and they are playing out live regularly, we would be happy to hear their material if it fits in our guidelines."

PRODISC (PRODISC LIMITADA), Tomás Andrews 089, Santiago **Chile.** Phone: (562)634-1733. Fax: (562)634-4064. A&R Director: Marcelo Marambio. Labels include Cabal (Argentina), Leader Music (Argentina), American Recording (Argentina), Fania (US), RMM&V (US), Ferran Productions (US), Barca (Argentina), W.A.C. (US), Radio Tripoli (Argentina), SonoMusic (Columbia), Del Cielito (Argentina). Record company, Prodin Chile: Promoter & Production Company—same address. Distributed by Sony Music. Estab. 1989 (Prodin was in 1969). Releases 20 singles, 120 LPs/year. Works with musicians/artists on contract. Pays 4-18% royalty to artists on contract; statutory rate to publisher per song.

How to Contact: Submit demo tape by mail—unsolicited submissions are OK. Prefers cassette or VHS videocassette with 2 or more songs. Does not return material. Reports in 1 month.

Music: Mostly **rock/pop, Latin/salsa/tex mex** and **R&B**; also **folk/country, jazz/New Age** and **classic.** Released *La Pachanga* (by Risso-Gomez), recorded by Vilma Palma E. on Barca Records (Latin rock); *Salsa Caliente* (by Nora-Ogimi), recorded by Orq. De La Luz on RMM&V (salsa); and *Dame Vida* (by Cherito), recorded by New York Band on RMM&V (Bachata).

Tips: "Try to have a Latin mind on music."

PUZZLE RECORDS, Box 461892, Garland TX 75046. A&R Director: Don Ferguson. Record company, music publisher (Sultan Music Publishing/BMI and Illustrious Sultan/ASCAP), record producer and booking agency (Don Ferguson Agency). Estab. 1972. Releases 7-8 singles and 2-3 CDs/year. Works with artists and songwriters on contract.

How to Contact: Accepts unsolicited material.

Music: Mostly **country**; also **MOR, jazz** and **light rock**. Released "Leave Me Right Now," written and recorded by Bobby Teesdale (MOR); "Ain't No Way" (by Duke/Osborn/Fox), recorded by Flash Point (rock); and "I'm Hurtin" (by Roy Orbison/Joe Melson), recorded by Mary Craig (country); all on Puzzle Records.

R.E.F. RECORDS, 404 Bluegrass Ave., Madison TN 37115. (615)865-6380. Contact: Bob Frick. Record company, record producer and music publisher (Frick Music Publishing Co./BMI). Releases 10 LPs/year. Works with artists and songwriters on contract.

How to Contact: Submit demo tape by mail—unsolicited submissions are OK. Prefers 7½ ips reel-to-reel or cassette with 2 songs and lyric sheet. SASE. Reports in 2 weeks.

Music: Country, gospel, rock and **top 40/pop**. Released "I Love You In Jesus," "Warm Family Feeling" and "Our Favorites," all by Bob Scott Frick. Other artists include Larry Ahlborn, Francisco Morales, Candy Coleman, Peggy Beard, Bob Myers, The Backwoods Quartet, Jim Mattingly, David Barton, Jim Pommert, The Vision Heirs, Eddie Issacs, Tereasa Ford, Scott Frick & The Prairie Playboys, Steven Lee Caves and Craig Steele.

*RAGE-N-RECORDS, 212 N. 12th St., Philadelphia PA 19107. (215)977-9777. Vice President, A&R: Vincent Kershner. Record company, music publisher (Cornea Publishing/ASCAP) and record producer (David Ivory). Estab. 1986. Releases 3 singles, 2 12″ singles and 5 CDs/year. Works with musicians/artists on record contract, songwriters on royalty contract, musicians on salary for in-house studio work. Pays various royalty to artist; statutory rate to publisher per song on record.

How to Contact: Submit demo tape by mail. Unsolicited submissions are OK. Prefers cassette (or VHS videocassette) with 3-5 songs and lyric sheet. SASE. Reports in 6-8 weeks.

Music: Mostly **rock, pop** and **R&B**; also **jazz** and **blues.** Released "Reindeer Games" (by Pat Godwin), recorded by David Ivory (satirical); "Big Magic Blue" (by Peter's Cathedral), recorded by David Ivory (rock); and "It's A Tough Town" (by The Cutaways!), produced and recorded by David Ivory (rock), all on Rage-N-Records.

RAINFOREST RECORDS, Suite 110, 8855 SW Holly Lane, Wilsonville OR 97070. Director, A&R: Ted Hibsman . Record company. Estab. 1990. Releases 3 singles, 1 LP and 3 CDs/year. Works with musicians/artists on contract. Pays 10% royalty to artists on contract; ¾ statutory rate to publisher per song on record.

How to Contact: Write first and obtain permission to submit. Prefers cassette with 3 songs and lyric sheet. "Also photo and bio helpful." SASE. Reports in 2 months.

Music: Mostly **alternative rock**; also **hip hop** and **industrial musique**. Released *Hello Lovers*, written and recorded by Roger Nusic; *Medicine Sunday* (by Med Sun Music), recorded by Medicine Sunday; and *Escape To Nothing*, written and recorded by Affirmative Action, all on Rainforest Records. Other artists include Young Turks, Caustic Soda, W.O.R.M., The Shaven, The Refreshments and New Bad Things.

Tips: "We are looking for original music with focus. Your music should complement the label's existing roster. It's best to develop your music in front of live audiences first."

*RAP-A-LOT RECORDS, INC., #105, 12337 Jones Rd., Houston TX 77070. (713)890-8486. President: James A. Smith. Labels include Face-To-Face Records, Jungle Style Music, Inc. Record company, music publisher (Rap-A-Lot Records/N-The Water Publishing, Inc./ASCAP), Rap-A-Lot. Estab. 1985. Works with musicians/artists on record contract, songwriters on royalty contract, musicians on salary for in-house studio work.

How to Contact: Write first and obtain permissions to submit. Prefers cassette with 4 songs. Does not return materials. Reports in 2-3 months.

Music: Mostly **rap, R&B**.

*RASPBERRY RECORDS, 3472 Cornell Place, Cincinnati OH 45220-1502. (513)281-2945. Founder: Paul Lippert. Record company and music publisher (Sky Ladder Publishing/ASCAP). Estab. 1991. Releases 1-3 LPs/year. Works with musicians/artists on record contract, songwriters on royalty contract. Pays statutory rate to publisher per song on record.

How to Contact: Submit demo tape by mail. Unsolicited submissions are OK. Prefers cassette with 2-4 songs and lyric sheet. SASE. Reports in less than 3 months.

Music: Mostly **family-oriented, children's** and **folk**. Released *Rainbow In The Sky*, written and recorded by Paul Lippert, on Raspberry Records (children's).

Tips: "I will consider recording songs that are fun, intelligent, creative, rhythmic and respectful of the psychological development of children. I'm looking for music to be enjoyed by families together. I'm also interested in finding artists (active performers) who would like to work co-operatively to facilitate production and marketing of recordings via this label. Please write if interested."

RAZOR & TIE MUSIC, #5A, 214 Sullivan St., New York NY 10012. (212)473-9173. President: Cliff Chenfeld. Labels include Razor Edge Records. Record company. Estab. 1990. Releases 15-20 CDs/year. Works with musicians/artists on contract.

How to Contact: Write first and obtain permission to submit. Prefers cassette with 3 songs and lyric sheet. SASE. Reports in 3 weeks.

Music: Mostly **rock, pop/R&B** and **country**. Released "Everything," by the Ghost Poets; "Sicily," by Elliott Murphy; and "She's My Everything," by Joe Grushecky all on Razor and Tie Records (rock).

*RECA MUSIC PRODUCTION, Nykobingvej 18, 4571 Grevinge DK 4571 **Denmark**. Phone: (45)345-9389. Director: Finn Reiner. Labels include Reca and Favorit. Record company and music publisher (Top Music). Releases 10 singles, 10 LPs and 5 CDs/year. Works with musicians/artists and songwriters on contract; hires musicians for in-house studio work. Pays 5% royalty to artists on contract; statutory rate to publishers per song on record.

How to Contact: Write or call first and obtain permission to submit. Prefers cassette (or VHS videocassette) with 2 songs. SAE and IRC. Reports in 2 weeks.

Music: Mostly **pop, country** and **folk**; also **classical**. Released *Don't Blame It On Texas*, by various writers (country); *Fast Train With Van Dango*, by Svend Petersen (shuffle); and *Classic*, by Peter Vesth (folk), all on RECA Records. Other artists include Bent Larsen, Peter Langberg, Jodle Johnny and The Kuhlau Quartet.

RED DOT/PUZZLE RECORDS, 1121 Market, Galveston TX 77550. (409)762-4590. President: A.W. Marullo, Sr. Record company, record producer and music publisher (A.W. Marullo Music/BMI). Estab. 1952. "We also lease masters from artists." Releases 14 12″ singles/year. Works with artists and songwriters on contract; musicians on salary for in-house studio work. Pays 8-10% royalty to artists on contract; statutory rate to publishers for each record sold.

How to Contact: Prefers cassette with 4-7 songs and lyric sheet. "Cassettes will not be returned. Contact will be made by mail or phone." Reports in 2 months.

Music: **Rock/top 40 dance songs**. Released "Do You Feel Sexy," (by T. Pindrock), recorded by Flash Point (Top 40/rock); "You Put the Merry in My Christmas," (by E.Dunn), recorded by Mary Craig (rock/pop country) and "Love Machine," (by T. Pindrock), recorded by Susan Moninger, all on Puzzle/Red Dot Records.

RED SKY RECORDS, Box 7, Stonehouse, Glos. GL10 3PQ **United Kingdom**. Phone: 0453-826200. Producer: Johnny Coppin. Record company (PRS) and record producer (Red Sky Records). Estab. 1985. Releases 2 singles, 3 albums (CD and tape) per year. Works with musicians/artists and songwriters on contract and hires musicians for in-house studio work. Pays 8-10% to artists on contract; statutory rate to publisher per song on record.
How to Contact: Submit demo tape by mail—unsolicited submissions are OK. Prefers cassette with 3 songs and lyric sheet. SASE. Reports in 6 months.
Music: Mostly **rock/singer-songwriters, modern folk** and **roots music**. Released *Green Bushes*, written and recorded by Paul Burgess (folk); *Full Force of the River*, written and recorded by Johnny Coppin (rock); and *Just For You* (by John Broomhall/Mick Dolan/Johnny Coppin), recorded by Johnny Coppin (rock), all on Red Sky Records. Other artists include Phil Beer.

RED-EYE RECORDS, Wern Fawr Farm, Pencoed, Mid-Glam CF35 6NB **United Kingdom**. Phone: (0656)86 00 41. Managing Director: M.R. Blanche. Record company, music publisher (Ever-Open-Eye Music/PRS). Estab. 1979. Releases 4 singles and 2-3 LPs/year. Works with musicians/artists on contract.
How to Contact: Prefers cassette (or VHS videocassette) or 7½ or 15 ips reel-to-reel with 4 songs. SAE and IRC.
Music: Mostly **R&B, rock** and **gospel**; also **swing**. Released "River River" (by D. John), recorded by The Boys; "Billy" (by G. Williams), recorded by The Cadillacs; and "Cadillac Walk" (by Moon Martin), recorded by the Cadillacs, all on Red-Eye Records. Other artists include Cartoon and Tiger Bay.

*****REVEAL**, 4322 Cleroux, Chomedey, Laval H7T 2E3 **Canada**. (514)687-8966. President, A&R: Peter Riden. Record company, music publisher (Riden Stars Music/BMI), record producer (Reveal) and publisher and editor of THE AFFILIATE presenting the deserving talents. Estab. 1976. Works with musicians/artists on record contract, songwriters on royalty contract, musicians on salary for in-house studio work. Pays 5% of net profit to artists on contract; statutory rate to publisher per song on record.
How to Contact: Submit demo tape by mail. Unsolicited submissions are OK. Prefers cassette (or VHS videocassette) with 2-5 songs and lyric sheet. Does not return material. Reports in 3-5 weeks.
Music: Mostly **rock, progressive** and **country/pop**. Released *Being Nude N Attitude* (by Peter Riden), recorded by Concept on Reveal Records; *Sweet Side Of Things* (by H.P.N.), recorded by H.P.N. on Reveal Records. Other artists include Barry Lubotta, Robert C. Schwelb, Pier Heiken, Elsie T. Childers, Alter Ego and Faces Of Emotion.
Tips: "Do not try to impress by being outrageous. We don't go for this on this side. Very cohesive lyrics are also strongly encouraged. When presenting yourself and your work be as complete as you possibly can. You surely want us to know you clearly, who we are about to give a deserved chance, so be open with us."

RHINO RECORDS LTD., The Chilterns, France Hill Dr., Chamberley Surrey GU153QA **England**. Phone: 0276-686077. Director: Bruce White. Record company. Estab. 1970. Releases 12 singles, 12 12″ singles, 10-15 LPs and 10-15 CDs/year. Works with musicians/artists on record contract. Pays 8-16% royalty to artists on contract. Pays 60-75% royalty to publisher per song on record.
How to Contact: Submit demo tape by mail—unsolicited submissions are OK. Prefers cassette with 3-4 songs. SASE. Reports in 6 weeks.
Music: Interested in **"most types of music."** Released "Take Care," written and recorded by Boris Gardiner (reggae); and "This Is" (by D. Dacres), recorded by Desmond Dekker (reggae), both on Rhino Records; and "Carnival 90," written and recorded by Byron Lee on Dynamic Records (reggae).

*****RIGHTEOUS RECORDS**, 429 Richmond Ave., Buffalo NY 14222. (716)884-0248. Manager, A&R: Dale Anderson. Record company, music publisher (Righteous Babe Music/BMI). Estab. 1991. Releases 2 LPs and 2 CDs/year. Works with musicians/artists on record contract, musicians on salary for in-house studio work. Pays 10-80% to artists on contract; statutory rate to publisher per song on record.
How to Contact: Submit demo tape by mail. Unsolicited submissions are OK. Prefers cassette with 3 or more songs. Does not return material. Reports in 3-4 weeks.
Music: Mostly **folk/acoustic, alternative rock, jazz**. Released *Puddle Dive, Imperfectly* and *Not So Soft*, all written and recorded by Ani DiFranco on Righteous Records.
Tips: "Make honest, uncomplicated music with a strong personal point of view."

RIPSAW RECORD CO., Suite 805, 4545 Connecticut Ave. NW, Washington DC 20008. (202)362-2286. President: Jonathan Strong. Record company, record producer and music publisher (Southern Crescent Publishing/BMI and Sugar Mama Music/BMI). Estab. 1976. Releases 1-2 albums/year. Works with musicians/artists and songwriters on contract. Payment negotiable with artists on contract. Pays standard royalty to songwriters on contract; statutory rate to publishers for each record sold.

How to Contact: Submit demo tape by mail—unsolicited submissions are OK. Prefers cassette and lyric sheet. SASE. "Invite us to a club date to listen." Reports as soon as possible, generally in a month or two.
Music: Country, blues, rockabilly and **"traditional"** rock 'n' roll. Released *Oooh-Wow!*, by the Uptown Rhythm Kings (jump blues). Other artists include Bobby Smith, Billy Hancock, Kid Tater & The Cheaters and Tex Rubinowitz.
Tips: "Keep it true roots rock 'n' roll."

*RISING STAR RECORDS INC., 710 Lakeview Ave. NE, Atlanta GA 30308. (404)872-1431. President: Barbara Taylor. Record company, music publisher (Rising Star Music Publishers). Estab. 1987. Releases 3-4 LPs, 3-4 CDs/year. Musicians/artists on record contract, songwriters on royalty contract. Pays negotiated royalty to artists on contract; negotiated rate to publishers per song on record.
How to Contact: Submit demo tape by mail. Unsolicited submissions are OK, write first and obtain permission to submit. Prefers cassette with 3 songs and lyric sheet or lead sheet. SASE. Reports in 1 month.
Music: Mostly **New Age, instrumental jazz, classical**; also **new world, children's, other forms of instrumental music.** Released *Dreamrunner*, *Storm Rising* and *Reflections* (by Brad Rudisail) and *Seashore Solitude* (by B.T. and J.C.) all on Rising Star Records.
Tips: "Spend the time and money needed to make yourself look professional and serious about your work. If you're serious about yourself, we will be too."

ROACH RECORDS CO., P.O. Box 7731, Beverly Hills CA 90121. (310)338-9976. President: Joseph Chryar. Labels include Asset Records Corporation. Record company. Estab. 1969. Releases 3 singles and 2 LP's/year. Works with musicians/artists on contract. Pays 10% royalty to artists on contract; statutory rate to publishers per song on record.
How to Contact: Write first and obtain permission to submit. Prefers cassette with 3 songs and lyric sheet. Does not return material. Reports in 6-8 weeks.
Music: Mostly **country, R&B** and **pop**; also **rock, jazz** and **blues**. Released "Movin'-Groovin'," written and recorded by J.D. Nechlon (R&B); "Love Must Go On" (by T. Thompson), recorded by King Miller (R&B); and "Charging Star" written and recorded by J. Chryar (country), all on Roach Records. Other artists include Ty Kairm, Ruby Martin.

ROAD RECORDS, 429 S. Lewis Rd., Royersford PA 19468. (215)948-8228. Fax: (215)948-4175. President: Jim Femino. Labels include Road Records. Record company and music publisher (Fezsongs/ASCAP). Estab. 1980. Releases 2-5 singles, 1 LP and 1 CD/year. Works with musicians/artists and songwriters on contract. Pays varying royalty to artists on contract; statutory rate to publisher per song on record.
How to Contact: Write first and obtain permission to submit. Prefers cassette (or VHS videocassette) with 1-3 songs and lyric sheets. SASE. Reports in 4 weeks.
Music: Mostly **country.** Released *All Night Party* (by Jim Femino), "Party Tonight" (by Jim Femino), *Just The Good Stuff* and "Nancy's Song" (by Jim Femino); all recorded by Jim Femino on Road Records (rock). Other artists include Certain Flightless Birds.

ROBBINS RECORDS, INC., HC80, Box 5B, Leesville LA 71446. National Representative: Sherree Scott. Labels include Headliner Stars Records. Record company and music publisher (Headliner Stars Music and Universal Stars Music/BMI). Estab. 1973. Releases 12-14 singles and 1-3 LPs/year. Works with artists and songwriters on contract. Pays standard royalty to artists on contract; statutory rate to publishers for each record sold.
How to Contact: Submit demo tape by mail—unsolicited submissions are OK. Prefers cassette with 1-6 songs and lyric sheet. Does not return material. Reports only if interested.
Music: Mostly **church/religious;** also **bluegrass, country, folk, gospel,** and **top 40/pop.** Released "Jesus, You're Everywhere," "I Can Depend on You," and "I Just Came to Thank You Lord," by J.J. and Sherree Stephens (religious singles). Other artists include Renee Wills and Melodee McCanless.

*ROCK DOG RECORDS, P.O. Box 3687, Hollywood CA 90078. (213)661-0259. A&R Director: Gerry North. Record company, record producer. Estab. 1987. Releases 3 singles, 1-3 12″ singles, 3-5 LPs, 1-3 EPs, 3 CDs/year. Works with musicians/artists on record contract, songwriters on royalty contract, musicians on salary for in-house studio work. Pays negotiable royalty to artists on contract. Charges in advance for materials (tapes, disks, travel).
How to Contact: Submit demo tape by mail. Unsolicited submissions are OK. Prefers cassette (or VHS videocassette) with 3-5 songs and lyric sheet. SASE. Reports in 2 weeks.
Music: Mostly **alternative rock, jazz, New Age;** also **R&B** and **rap.** Released *A Separate Reality* and *Break in the Routine*, written and recorded by Brain Storm (New Age); and *Nasty Day*, written and recorded by Souplex Slam, all on Rock Dog Records. Other artists include Kenny Gray, Ian Ashley, Johnathen Hall, Robert Louden and Steve Smith.

Tips: "Be interested in submitting the best music you have."

*ROCK IN RECORDS, Room A, Haven Commercial Bldg. 24/F, Tsing Fung Street, **Hong Kong**. General Manager: Keith Yip. Record company. Estab. 1981. Releases 6 LPs and 6 CDs/year. Works with musicians/artists on contract and hires musicians for in-house studio work. Pays 5-7% royalty to artists on contract; statutory rate to publishers per song on record.
How to Contact: Submit demo tape by mail. Unsolicited submissions are OK. Prefers cassette (or VHS videocassette if available) with 2 or more songs. Does not return material. Reports in 2 weeks.
Music: Mostly **New Age, rock** and **R&B, pop.** Released "Tonight" (by Yvonne Lau), recorded by Paradox; "Feeling" (by Keith Yip and Yvonne Lau), recorded by Paradox; and "Winter Love" (by Keith Yip and Max Wong), recorded by Cass Phang, (all pop) on Rock In Records.

ROCKIT RECORDS, INC., Suite 320, 825 Sierra Vista, Las Vegas NV 89109. Music Director: Joseph Trupiano. Record company and music publisher (Bad Grammar Music, Inc/BMI). Estab. 1985. Releases 200 cassette LPs/year. Works with musicians/artists and songwriters on contract. Pays artists 10% royalty; statutory rate to publisher per song on record.
How to Contact: Submit demo by mail—unsolicited submissions are OK. Prefers cassette (or VHS videocassette) with 3 songs and lyric sheet. SASE. Reports in 6 weeks.
Music: Mostly **pop/dance, pop/rock** and **rock**; also **alternative rock, New Age urban** and **R&B.** Released "Ace Of Spades," written and recorded by Laya Phelps; "With You By My Side," written and recorded by Carol Martini; and "Mad About You," written and recorded by Joey Harlow, all on Rockit Records. Other artists include Noel, Flavour Mouse, Under The Rose, Michael Lachapelle, Neil Benson, The Guild, The Parlophones, Unexpected Guest.
Tips: "We have now diversified into manufacturing all types of product: CDs, cassettes and cassette singles, vinyl EPs, etc. However, our marketing facilities offer a European presentation of the product for possible mechanical licensing in our European retail markets. So for artists who plan on manufacturing their own product, we offer an excellent outlet for mechanical retail licensing through our label. This is an avenue for raising revenue so that artists may experience the luxury of producing future LP projects because their past release is raising revenue for them."

ROCK'N'ROLL RECORDS, 16 Grove Place, Penarth, S. Glam. CF6 2LD South Wales **United Kingdom**. Phone: (0222) 704279. Director: Paul Barrett. Record company, record producer (Paul Barrett, Robert Llewellyn). Estab. 1991. Releases 3 CDs/year. Works with musicians/artists on contract and hires musicians for in-house studio work. Pays various royalty to artists on contract; statutory rate to publisher per song on record.
How to Contact: Submit demo tape by mail—unsolicited submissions are OK. Prefers cassette with lyric sheet. SASE. Reports in 2 weeks.
Music: Only **fifties rock'n'roll.** Released *The Party's Not Over*, written and recorded by various artists on Rock'n'Roll Records (fifties rock'n'roll). Other artists include Southpaw, Tommy Sands and Jean Vincent.

ROLL ON RECORDS®, 112 Widmar Pl., Clayton CA 94517. (510)672-8201. Owner: Edgar J. Brincat. Record company. Estab. 1985. Releases 2-3 LPs/cassettes/year. Works with musicians/artists and songwriters on contract and hires musicians for in-house studio work. Pays 10% royalty to artists on contract; statutory rate to publisher per song on record.
How to Contact: Submit demo tape by mail—unsolicited submissions are OK. Prefers cassette with 3 songs and lyric sheet. SASE. Reports in 2-4 weeks.
Music: Mostly **contemporary/country,** MOR and **R&B;** also **pop, light rock** and **modern gospel.** Released "Broken Record" (by Dianne Baumgartner/Horace Linsley); "Outskirts of Phoenix" (by Pettrella Pollefeyt); "Write to P.O. Box 33" (by Michael Gooch/Susan Branding) and "Never Thought Of Losing You" (by Jeanne Dicky-Boyter/Gina Dempsey), all recorded by Edee Gordon and the Flash Band.
Tips: "Be professional, write clearly and always enclose an SASE (many people don't)."

*ROOART RECORDS, 355 Crown St., Surry Hills, NSW 2010 **Australia**. A&R Manager: Todd Wagstaff. Record company. Estab. 1988. Releases 30 singles, 2, 12″ singles, 10 LPs, 15 EPS, 10 CDs/year. Works with musicians/artists on record contract. Pays 10-16% royalty to artists on contract; statutory rate to publishers per song on record.

The asterisk before a listing indicates that the listing is new in this edition. New markets are often the most receptive to unsolicited submissions.

How to Contact: Submit demo tape by mail. Unsolicited submissions are OK. Prefers cassette (or VHS videocassette if available) with 3 songs. SASE. Reports in 1 month.
Music: Mostly **alternative, pop, rock**; also **country** and **jazz**. Released *Lily*, by Wendy Matthews (A.O.R.); *Inside Out*, by Ratcat (pop); *Tear of Thought*, by Screaming Jets (hard rock), all on Rooart Records. Other artists include You Am I, Cleopatra Wong, Shanley Del, WPA, Tall Tales & True and Jenny Morris.
Tips: "Music must have an edge, the musician must have the attitude."

*ROSIE RECORDS, 14 Brickendon Green, Hertford Herts SG138PB **England.** Phone: 0992-86404. Proprietor: John Dye. Labels include Rosie Records and Musical Time Box. Record company (Performing Rights Society, MCPS and PPL). Estab. 1982. Releases 2 singles, 2 12″ singles, 2 LPs and 1 CD/year. Works with musicians/artists on contract. Pays 8-12% royalty to artists on contract; statutory rate to publisher per song on record.
How to Contact: Submit demo tape by mail. Unsolicited submissions are OK. Prefers cassette with any song and lyric sheet. SASE. Reports in 2 months.
Music: Mostly **country, pop** and **reggae**; also **comedy songs**. Released *The Minstrel, Fire & Water* and "Fire In The Desert," all written and recorded by Nemo James on Rosie Records.
Tips: "Please submit good quality demos and your own material only."

ROTO-NOTO MUSIC, 148 Erin Ave., Hamilton, Ontario L8K 4W3 **Canada.** (416)796-8236. President: R. Cousins. Labels include Roto-Noto, Marmot, Chandler. Record company, music publisher and record producer. Estab. 1979. Releases 20 singles, 2 12″ singles, 5 LPs and 6 CDs/year. Works with musicians/artists and songwriters on contract and hires musicians for in-house studio work.
How to Contact: Write first and obtain permission to submit. Prefers cassette with 2 songs and lyric sheets. SASE. Reports in 4 weeks.
Music: Mostly **country, pop** and **rock**; also **R&B** and **jazz**. Released "Crazy Infatuation" (by E. Domsy/ R. Cousins), recorded by Diane Raeside (country-rock); "Holdin' On" (by R. Peterson), recorded by Jack Diamond (country-A/C); "Makin' It Easy" (by R. Cousins), recorded by Mark LaForme (country); all recorded on Roto Noto Records. Other artists include Bobby McGee, Jack Diamond Band, Eleven Degrees, Harrison Kennedy and Frequency.

RR&R RECORDS, Suite 128, 3260 Keith Bridge Rd., Cumming GA 30130-0128. Also Suite 204, 23 Music Sq. E., Nashville TN 37203. (615)742-7408. A&R and Producer: Ron Dennis Wheeler. Labels include Rapture Records, Ready Records and Y'Shua Records. Record company, music publisher (Super Rapp Publishing/BMI, Do It Now Publishing/ASCAP and Aircram Music/BMI), record producer (Ron Dennis Wheeler). Estab. 1966. Releases 5 singles, 5 12″ singles, 5 LPs, 5 EPs and 5 CDs/ year. Works with musicians/artists and songwriters on contract; hires musicians for in-house studio work. Pays artists 5-15%; statutory rate to publishers per song on record.
How to Contact: Submit demo tape by mail—unsolicited submissions are OK. Prefers cassette (or VHS videocassette) or 15 ips reel-to-reel with lyric or lead sheet. SASE. Reports in 3 months. "Master track demos."
Music: Mostly **gospel, rock, pop, country** and **R&B**. Released "Legends Never Die" by Bill Scarbrough on RR&R Records (country); "Lord Paint My Mind" (by Mike Murdock), recorded by Ron Dennis Wheeler on Rapture Records; and "Almost Home Again" (by Louis Brown), recorded by Ron Dennis Wheeler (country). Other artists include Rita Van and Rob McInnis, Dan Carroll, Taylor Prichard, Peter Burwin, Bobs Nite Off, Voices of Joy, Jammie Bridge, and "Heather."
Tips: "Do not try to copy another artist or style of music. Better production masters (if possible) get more attention quicker."

RUFFCUT RECORDS, 6472 Seven Mile, South Lyon MI 48178. (313)486-0505. Producer: J.D. Dudick. Record company, music publisher (AL-KY Music/ASCAP, Bubba Music/BMI). Estab. 1991. Releases 5 singles and 4 CDs/year. Pays 12% royalty to artists on contract; statutory rate to publisher per song on record.
How to Contact: Submit demo tape by mail—unsolicited submissions are OK. Prefers cassette with 2 songs and lyric sheet. SASE. Reports in 1 month.
Music: Mostly **rock, pop, country**; also **alternative**. Released "Passion's Fire" (by W. Bradley), recorded by Sassy on Fearless Records (country); and "Breakin Down The Wall" (by Chris Pierce), recorded by Flavour Mouse on Rockit Records (rock).
Tips: "Write songs that mean something, and if other people like it (sincerely) let's hear it. Records sell on musical expression, not marketing hype. Remember to keep the vocals above the music."

SABTECA RECORD CO., Box 10286, Oakland CA 94610. (510)465-2805. President: Duane Herring. Creative Manager: Sean Herring. Record company and music publisher (Sabteca Music Co./ASCAP, Toyiabe Music Co./BMI). Estab. 1980. Releases 3 singles and 1 12″ single/year. Works with songwriters

on contract and hires musicians for in-house studio work. Pays statutory rate to publisher per song on record.
Affiliate: Andre Romare Records.
How to Contact: Write or call first and obtain permission to submit. Prefers cassette with lyric sheet. Does not return material. Reports in 3 weeks.
Music: Mostly **R&B, pop** and **country**. Released "Route 49" and *Heartache* (both by Duane Herring), recorded by Johnny B on Andre Romare Records (country); and *Hooray For You, Girl* (by Walt Coleman/Bill Charles), recorded by Lee Coleman on Sabteca Records (pop). Other artists include Shane and Lil Brown.
Tips: "Improve your writing skills. Keep up with music trends."

SADDLESTONE RECORDS, 264 "H" Street Box 8110-21, Blaine WA 98230. Canada address: 8821 Delwood Drive N. Delta, British Columbia V4C 4A1 **Canada.** (604)582-7117. Fax: (604)582-8610. President: Candice James. Labels include Silver Bow Records. Record company, music publisher (PROCAN, SOCAN, Saddlestone/BMI) and record producer (Silver Bow Productions). Estab. 1988. Releases 50 singles, 30 LPs and 6 CDs/year. Works with musicians/artists on contract. Pays 10% royalty to artists on contract; statutory rate to publishers per song on record.
How to Contact: Submit demo tape—unsolicited submissions are OK. Prefers cassette with 3-5 songs and lyric sheet. SASE. Reports in 3 months.
Music: Mostly **country, pop** and **rock;** also **R&B** and **gospel**. Released *Feel Like Jesse James*, written and recorded by Razzy Bailey; *The Vow* (by Clark/Higging), recorded by Gerry King; and *She Loved The Fool Out Of Me* (by Buck Moore), recorded by Billy Jay Legere, all on Saddlestone Records. Other artists include Silver City, Rick Patterson, Gary MacFarlane, Sunny & Houserockers, Randy Friskie, Tracy Tubb, Joe Lonsdale, Blackwater Jack, Robert Rigby, John McCabe and Barb Farrell.
Tips: "Send original material, studio produced, with great hooks."

SAHARA RECORDS AND FILMWORKS ENTERTAINMENT, 8th Floor, 4475 Allisonville Rd., Indianapolis IN 46205. (317)546-2912. President: Edward De Miles. Record company, music publisher (EDM Music/BMI) and record producer. Estab. 1981. Releases 15-20 12″ singles and 5-10 LPs/year. Works with musicians/artists and songwriters on contract and hires musicians for in-house studio work. Pays standard royalty to artists on contract; pays statutory rate to publishers per song on record.
How to Contact: Submit demo tape—unsolicited submissions are OK. Prefers cassette with 3-5 songs and lyric sheet. SASE. Reports in 1 month.
Music: Mostly **R&B/dance, top 40 pop/rock** and **contemporary jazz;** also **TV-film themes, musical scores** and **jingles**. Released "Hooked on U," "Dance Wit Me" and "Moments," written and recorded by Steve Lynn (R&B), all on Sahara Records. Other artists include Lost in Wonder, Dvon Edwards and Multiple Choice.
Tips: "We're looking for strong mainstream material. Lyrics and melodies with good hooks that grab people's attention."

SAN-SUE RECORDING STUDIO, Box 773, Mt. Juliet TN 37122-3336. (615)754-5412. Labels include Basic Records. Owner: Buddy Powell. Record company, music publisher (Hoosier Hills/BMI) and recording studio (16-track). Estab. 1975. Works with artists and songwriters on contract. Releases 7 singles and 3 LPs/year. Pays 8% royalty to artists on contract; statutory rate to publishers for each record sold.
How to Contact: Submit demo tape—unsolicited submissions are OK. Prefers 7½ ips reel-to-reel or cassette with 2-4 songs. "Strong vocal with piano or guitar is suitable for demo, along with lyrics." SASE. Reports in 2 weeks.
Music: **Church/religious, country,** and **MOR**. Released "Which Way You Going Billy" (by Sandy Powell); "Don't Cry Daddy" (by Sue Powell) and "My Way" (by Jerry Baird), all on Basic Records (MOR). Other artists include Camillo Phelps.
Tips: "Do not give up on your writing because we or some other publisher reject your material."

SCENE PRODUCTIONS, Box 1243, Beckley WV 25802. (304)252-4836. President/Producer: Richard L. Petry. A&R: Carol Lee. Labels include Rising Sun and Country Bridge Records. Record company, record producer and music publisher (Purple Haze Music/BMI). Member of AFM. Releases 1-2 singles and 1-2 LPs/year. Works with musicians/artists and songwriters on contract. Pays 4-5% minimum royalty to artists on contract; standard royalty to songwriters on contract; statutory rate to publishers for each record sold. Charges "initial costs, which are conditionally paid back to artist."
How to Contact: Submit demo tape—unsolicited submissions are OK. Prefers cassette with 2-5 songs and lyric sheet. Prefers studio produced demos. SASE. Reports in 4-8 weeks.
Music: Mostly **country, top 40, R&B/crossover** and **pop/rock;** also **MOR, light** and **commercial rock**. Released "My Old Friend," written and recorded by Chuck Paul (pop), on Rising Sun Records; and "Home Sweet W.V.," written and recorded by Dave Runion on Country Bridge Records.

Tips: "Prepare ahead of time with a very good demo tape presenting your talent. Don't spend a lot on a taping and video. You need some kind of initial financial backing to get your career started. Remember you're investing in yourself. You'll need around $10,000 to get the proper exposure you need. Major labels require around 10 times this to sign you. Deal with a company that is reputable and has music with the trade people, Billboard, Cashbox, R&R and Gavin."

SCP RECORDS, Country Manor, 812 S. 890 East, Orem UT 84058. (801)225-9975. President/General Manager: Ron Simpson. Record company, music publisher and record producer (Sound Column Productions). Member CMA, AFM. Estab. 1968. Releases 3 singles and 5 albums/year. Works with artists and songwriters on contract; hires musicians for in-house studio work. Pays negotiable royalty to artists on contract; statutory rate to publishers for each record sold.
How to Contact: All material for SCP Records should be submitted to Sound Colunmn Publications or The Ron Simpson Music Office, same address as above. Please see those listings under "publishers" and "managers" for submissions criteria.
Music: All styles except pure rap. Released *Destination* by touring singer-songwriter Kim Simpson. "Ballad of John Singer" (by Jim Cunningham) recorded by Rich Pugh, featured on *60 Minutes*.
Tips: Sound Column Publications is currently seeking acoustic-style adult contemporary songs for SCP Records artist Gary Voorhees and positive love ballads for Shawn Keliiliki.

SEASIDE RECORDS, 100 Labon St., Tabor City NC 28463. (919)653-2546. Owner: Elson H. Stevens. Labels include JCB. Record company, music publisher and record producer. Estab. 1978. Releases 10 singles and 15 LPs/year. Works with musicians/artists and songwriters on contract; musicians on salary for in-house studio work, and producers. Pays 3-10% royalty to artists on contract; statutory rate to publisher per song on record.
How to Contact: Submit demo tape—unsolicited submissions are OK. Prefers cassette with 3 songs and lyric or lead sheet. SASE. Reports in 1 month.
Music: Mostly **country, gospel** and **rock;** also **"beach music."** Released "I'll Never Say Never Again" (by G. Todd/T. Everson), recorded by Sherry Collins (country); "Faith of a Tiny Seed" (by R. Lynn), recorded by Randa Lynn (contemporary gospel); "Long Lonesome Road" (by G. Taylor), recorded by Sherry Collins (country); all on SeaSide Records.
Tips: "Send only unpublished material. Songs must have strong hook."

SEEDS RECORDS, Box 20814, Oklahoma City OK 73156. (405)755-0315. Labels include Homa and Okart Records. Record company, record producer, music publisher (Okisher Publishing/BMI), and Mickey Sherman Talent Management. Estab. 1973. Releases 6-12 12" singles, 3 LPs and 3 CDs/year. Works with songwriters on contract and hires in-house studio musicians. Pays 10% royalty to artists on contract; statutory rate to publishers for each record sold.
How to Contact: Submit demo tape—unsolicited submissions OK. Prefers cassette (or videocassette) with 1-3 songs and lyric sheet. Does not return unsolicited material. Reports in 3 months.
Music: Mostly **blues, country** and **ballads;** also **easy listening, jazz, MOR, R&B** and **soul.** Released "Cookin' and Jukin'," written and recorded by Jana Jarvis; "Make My Pain Walk Away," written and recorded by Jan Jo, "Leave Your Number," written and recorded by Dale Langley; "A Brighter Day," written and recorded by Dale Langley (gospel); and "Don't Do the Crime," written and recorded by Jan Jo (rock), all on Seeds Records. Other artists include Charley Shaw, Charles and Barbara Burton, Ronnie McClendon and The Langley Family.

*SHAKY RECORDS, Box 71, Station "C", Winnipeg Manitoba R3M 3X3 **Canada.** (204)932-5212. President: Shaky. Record company, music publisher (Shaky Publishing Co./SOCAN). Estab. 1984. Releases 2 LPs, 2 EPs and 1 CD/year. Works with musicians/artists on record contract, songwriters on royalty contract, musicians on salary for in-house studio work.
How to Contact: Submit demo tape by mail. Unsolicited submissions are OK. Prefers cassette (or VHS videocassette if available) with 4-5 songs and lyric sheet. SASE. Reports in 1 month.
Music: Mostly **hard rock, heavy metal** and **rock.** Released *Strictly Business, Three The Hard Way* and *Bad Boys of Rock* (by B. Johnston), recorded by Lawsuit on Shaky Records. Other artists include The Shake.
Tips: "Build up your song catalog, look to other genres of music to expand your ideas in your type of music. Demo quality is important but songs come first. Write lots, choose wisely."

SHAOLIN FILM & RECORDS, Box 387, Hollywood CA 90078. (818)506-8660. President: Richard O'Connor. A&R: Michelle McCarty. Labels include Shaolin Communications. Record company, music publisher (Shaolin Music/ASCAP) and record producer (The Coyote). Estab. 1984. Releases 2 singles, 1 LP, 1CD and 1EP/year. Works with musicians/artists on record contract.
How to Contact: Submit demo tape—unsolicited submissions are OK. Prefers cassette with 3-4 songs and lyric sheet. Include bio and press kit. Does not return material. Reports in 6 weeks.
Music: Mostly **rock, hard rock** and **pop;** also **soundtracks.** Released "Christ Killer," "Great Salt Lake" and *Wishwood Bridge,* all written and recorded by Coyote on Shaolin Film and Records.

*SHORE RECORDS, P.O. Box 161, Hazlet NJ 07730. (908)888-1846. Director of A&R: Paul Bonanni. Record company, music publisher (BMI), record producer (Bobby Monroe). Estab. 1991. Releases 3 singles and 3 12″ singles/year. Works with musicians/artists on record contract, songwriters on royalty contract. Pays standard rate to artists on contract; 6.25% to publishers per song on record.
How to Contact: Submit demo tape by mail. Unsolicited submissions are OK. Prefers cassette (or VHS videocassette if available) with 3-4 songs and lyric sheet or lead sheet. SASE. Reports in 2 to 6 months.
Music: Mostly **rock/techno, alternative, hard rock/metal**; also **country, R&B** and **dance**. Released *Tri-State's* (by 16 different artists); "What Do All the People Know?" (by Monroes), recorded by Bobby Monroe, both on Shore Records (rock). Other artists include Leap of Faith, Fallon, King for a Day, Simon Quiss, Dog.
Tips: "Provide me with good quality music at more of a commercial/mainstream sound."

SILENT RECORDS, Suite 315, 540 Alabama, San Francisco CA 94110. (415)252-5764. Fax: (415)864-7815. President: Kim Cascone. Record company and record producer (Kim Cascone). Estab. 1986. Releases 15 CDs/year. Works with musicians/artists on contract. Accepts LPs and CDs for consideration and distribution. Pays 10-15% of wholesale as royalty to artists on contract; negotiable rate to publishers per song on record.
Affiliates: Pulse Soniq, Furnace, Sulphur.
How to Contact: Write first and obtain permission to submit. Prefers cassette (or VHS videocassette) with press kit (press clips, bio, etc.). Does not return material. Reports in 6 months.
Music: Mostly **experimental** and **industrial**. Released "Exodus," written and recorded by Pelican Daughters (ambient/pop); and "Hymns from the Furnace" (by Kim Cascone), recorded by PGR (industrial), both on Silent Records and "Xpansion" (by Jeremy Wells), recorded by 68000 on Pulse Soniq Records. Other artists include Elliot Sharp, Controlled Bleeding, Psychic TV and Drome.
Tips: "Formulate a career strategy and learn your market."

SIRR RODD RECORD & PUBLISHING CO., 2453 77th Ave., Philadelphia PA 19150-1820. President: Rodney J. Keitt. Record company, music publisher, record producer and management and booking firm. Releases 5 singles, 5 12″ singles and 2 LPs/year. Works with musicians/artists and songwriters on contract. Pays 5-10% royalty to artists on contract; statutory rate to publishers for each record sold.
How to Contact: Prefers cassette (or videocassette) with 3-5 songs and lyric sheet. SASE. Reports in 1 month.
Music: **Top 40, pop, gospel, jazz, dance** and **rap**. Released "All I Want For Christmas," by The Ecstacies; "What Do You See In Her" and "Guess Who I Saw Today," by Starlene; and "Happy Birthday Baby," by Rodney Jerome Keitt.

SKYLYNE RECORDS, Suite 17, 61 Canal St., San Rafael CA 94901. President/Executive Producer: Jeff Britto. Record company. Estab. 1987. Releases 7 singles and 7 LPs/year, depending on roster.
How to Contact: Write first and obtain permission to submit. Prefers cassette with 3 songs and lyric sheet. SASE. Reports in 4-6 weeks.
Music: **Rap, R&B, dance** and **house**. Released "Sticky Pleasure" (by James McCullum), recorded by Big C and *Funky New Jack Nation* (various artists compilation), both on Skyline Records.

SLAK RECORDS, 9 Hector Ave., Toronto, Ontario M6G3G2 **Canada**. (416)533-3707. President: Al Kussin. Record company, music publisher (Clotille Publishing/PROCAN) and record producer (Slak Productions). Estab. 1986. Releases 2 singles, 2 12″ singles and 1 LP/year. Works with musicians/artists on contract. Pays 8-14% per record sold. Pays statutory rate to publisher per song on record.
How to Contact: Submit demo tape by mail. Unsolicited submissions are OK. Prefers cassette with 3 songs and lyric sheets. SASE. Reports in 2 months.
Music: Mostly **pop, R&B** and **dance**. Released "Go Baby" (by F. Fudge and A. Kussin), recorded by Frankie Fudge; "All Talk" and "In Love" (by Lorraine Scott and A. Kussin), recorded by Lorraine Scott; all on Slak Records (R&B).
Tips: "Most of the material on Slak has been written by me. However, I wish to expand. A small label needs commercial, solid songwriting with good hooks and interesting lyrics."

*SONIC GROUP, LTD., (formerly MSB, Ltd.), #1235, 1204 Ave. 4, Brooklyn NY 11229. (718)376-3399. President: Mark S. Berry. Record company, music publisher (Baby Raquel Music/ASCAP) and record producer (Mark S. Berry). Estab. 1984. Releases 1-2 12″ singles and 1-2 LPs/year. Works with musicians/artists on contract. Pays 12% royalty to artists on contract; statutory rate to publishers.
How to Contact: Submit demo tape by mail. Unsolicited submissions are OK. Prefers cassette or VHS videocassette with 3 songs and lyric sheet. Does not return material. Reports in 2-4 weeks.
Music: Mostly **alternative rock/dance**. Current acts include Strait Jacket and Elvis Manson.

*SOUND ACHIEVEMENT GROUP, INC., P.O. Box 24625, Nashville TN 37202. (615)883-2600. President: Royce B. Gray. Labels include New Wind Records, Sugar Mountain Records, Palace Records, Candle Records, Heart Reign Records, Image Records. Record company. Estab. 1985. Releases 15 singles, 15 LPs, 4 CDs/year. Works with musicians/artists on record contract, songwriters on royalty contract. Pays 5-12% royalty to artists on contract; statutory rate to publishers per song on record.
How to Contact: Submit demo tape by mail. Unsolicited submissions are OK. Prefers cassette (or VHS videocassette) with 3 songs and lyric sheet. SASE. Reports in 3 months.
Music: Mostly **Southern gospel, country gospel, MOR/inspirational;** also **contemporary gospel,** and **Christmas songs.** Released *Whatever It Takes* (by Sam Johnson), recorded by Darla McFadden and *Glorious Hymns of Praise,* recorded by Giorgio Longdo, both on Candle Records; and *Sam's Songs III,* written and recorded by Sam Johnson on Image Records. Other artists include New Spirit Singers, Revelations, Paradise, Heather Stemann and Impact Brass & Singers.
Tips: "Submit quality demos with lyric sheets on all works."

*SOUND MASTERS, 9717 Jensen Dr., Houston TX 77093. (713)695-3648. Producer: A.V. Mittelstedt. Labels include Cherry Records and A.V. Records. Record company, music publisher (Publicare) and record producer. Estab. 1970. Releases 100 singles and 10 LPs/year. Works with musicians/artists and songwriters on contract; hires musicians for in-house studio work. Pays varying royalty to artists on contract; statutory rate to publisher per song on record.
How to Contact: Prefers cassette. SASE. Reports in 3 weeks.
Music: Mostly **country, gospel** and **crossover;** also **MOR** and **rock.** Released "Too Cold at Home" (by Bobby Hardin), recorded by Mark Chestnutt on Cherry Records (country); "You Got The Best of Me" (by J. Fuller/J. Hobbs), recorded by Carolyn Stelle on A.V. Records (country); and "Let's Fall In Love Again" (by R. Shaw/S. Shaw), recorded by Ron Shaw on Cherry Records (country). Other artists include Geronimo Trevino, Jerry Calard, Roy Head and Randy Corner.

STARCREST PRODUCTIONS, INC., 1602 Dellwood Court., Grand Forks ND 58201. (701)772-0518. President: George J. Hastings. Labels include Meadowlark and Minn-Dak Records. Record company, management firm and booking agency. Estab. 1970. Releases 2-6 singles and 1-2 LPs/year. Works with artists and songwriters on contract. Payment negotiable to artists on contract; statutory rate to publishers for each record sold.
How to Contact: Submit demo tape – unsolicited submissions are OK. Prefers cassette with 1-6 songs and lead sheet. SASE. Reports in 3 months.
Music: **Country** and **top 40/pop.** Released "You and North Dakota Nights" (by Stewart & Hastings), recorded by Mary Joyce on Meadowlark Records (country).

STARDUST, Box 13, Estill Springs TN 37330. (615)649-2577. President: Buster Doss. Labels include Stardust, Wizard, Doss, Kimbolon, Flaming Star. Record company, music publisher (Buster Doss Music/BMI) and record producer (Colonel Buster Doss). Estab. 1959. Releases 50 singles and 25 LPs/year. Works with musicians/artists and songwriters on contract and hires musicians for in-house studio work. Pays 8% royalty to artists on contract; statutory rate to publisher per song on record.
How to Contact: Submit demo tape – unsolicited submissions are OK. Prefers cassette with 2 songs and lyric sheets. SASE. Reports in 1 week.
Music: Mostly **country;** also **rock.** Released "Rescue Me" (by P. Hotchkiss), recorded by Tommy D. on Doss Records; "King Bee" (by B. Doss), recorded by Rooster Q. on Stardust Records; and "Would You" (by B. Doss), recorded by R.B. Stone on Stardust Records; all country. Other artists include Johnny Buck, Hobson Smith, Cliff Archer, Linda Wunder, Buck Cody and Tony Andrews.

STARGARD RECORDS, Box 138, Boston MA 02101. (617)296-3327. Artist Relations: Janice Tritto. Labels include Oak Groove Records. Record company, music publisher (Zatco Music/ASCAP and Stargard Publishing/BMI) and record producer. Estab. 1985. Releases 9 singles and 1 LP/year. Works with musicians/artists on contract; hires musicians for in-house studio work. Pays 5-6% royalty to artists on contract; statutory rate to publishers per song on record.
How to Contact: Submit demo tape – unsolicited submissions are OK. Prefers cassette and lyric sheet. SASE. Reports in 6-7 weeks. "Sending bio along with picture or glossies is appreciated but not necessary."
Music: Mostly **R&B, dance/hip hop.** Released "What I Did For Love" (by Addison Martin), recorded by Mixed Emotions; "Sexy" and "Don't Ring My Phone" (by Floyd Wilcox, recorded by U-Nik-Aproch, all on Stargard Records.

STARK RECORDS AND TAPE COMPANY, 628 S. South St., Mount Airy NC 27030. (919)786-2865. President and Owner: Paul E. Johnson. Labels include Pilot, Hello, Sugarbear, Kay, Stork, Bell Sounds, Blue Ridge, Joy, Southcoast, Songcraft, Tornado and Red Bird. Record company, music publisher (Tompaul Music Company/BMI) and record producer (Stark Records and Tape Company). Estab. 1960. Releases 8 singles and 3 LPs/year. Works with songwriters on contract. Pays artists 30%

royalty per record sold; statutory rate to publishers per song on record.

How to Contact: Submit demo tape—unsolicited submissions are OK. Prefers cassette with 3-5 songs and lyric or lead sheets. SASE. Reports in 2 months.

Music: Mostly **pop, country** and **country gospel**; also **bluegrass, bluegrass gospel** and **C&W**. Released "My Best Wishes Go With You" and "Memories Of Pearl Harbor," both written and recorded by Thurman Holden; and "Long Journey Home" (by Paul E. Johnson), recorded by Bobby Lee Atkins, all on Stark Records. Other artists include Early Upchurch, Sanford Teague and Don Sawyers.

Tips: "Try to write commercial type songs, and use the best backup musicians possible."

STATUE RECORDS, 2810 McBain St., Redondo Beach CA 90278. President: Jim Monroe. A&R Director: Lisa Raven. Record company. Releases 5-10 singles and 10-20 LPs/year. Works with musicians/artists and songwriters on contract. Pays 5-10% or negotiable royalty to artists on contract.

How to Contact: Submit demo tape by mail—unsolicited submissions are OK. Prefers "high quality" cassette with 3-5 songs and lyric sheet. Reports in 1 month. "Please include glossy photo(s) if you are a group looking for a recording deal."

Music: Mostly **"up-tempo rock,** with *strong* hooks and **new wave."** Artists include Rude Awakening, Cruella D'Ville, LA Riot, Chosin Few, Wolfgang Elvis, The Hollywood Bears, England 402 and Bill Bream.

STOP HUNGER RECORDS INTERNATIONAL, 1300 Division St., Nashville TN 37203. (615)242-4722. (800)797-4984. Fax: (615)242-1177. Producer: Robert Metzgar. Record company and music publisher (Aim High Music/ASCAP, Bobby and Billy Music/BMI). Estab. 1971. Releases 16-17 singles, 25 LPs and 25 CDs/year. Works with musicians/artists and songwriters on contract and hires musicians for in-house studio work. Pays statutory rate to publisher per song on record.

How to Contact: Submit demo tape by mail. Unsolicited submissions are OK. Prefers cassette or VHS videocassette with 5-10 songs and lyric sheet. Does not return material. Reports in 2 weeks.

Music: Mostly **country, traditional country** and **pop country**; also **gospel, Southern gospel** and **contemporary Christian**. Released *George and Merle* (by H. Cornelius), recorded by Alan Jackson on Arista Records; *Return of the Ghost Riders* (by Jack Patton), recorded by J. Cash on Polygram Records; and *Just the Two Of Us* (by Metzgar/Patterson), recorded by C. Twitty on MCA Records. Other artists include Tommy Cash/Mark Allen Cash (CBS-Sony), Carl Butler (CBS-Sony), Tommy Overstreet (CBS-Sony), Mickey Jones (Capitol), Glen Campbell Band and others.

*STUDIO B RECORDS, P.O. Box 295, Atco NJ 08004. (609)753-2653. Manager: Bob Thomas. Music publisher (Rosemark Publishing/BMI). Estab. 1988. Releases 10-20 singles and 30-50 cassettes/year. Works with musicians on salary for in-house studio work. Pays 10-15% royalty to artist on contract; statutory rate to publisher per song on record.

How to Contact: Submit demo tape by mail. Unsolicited submissions are OK. Prefers cassette with 3-5 songs and lyric sheet. SASE. Reports in 6-8 weeks.

Music: Mostly **top 40/pop, easy listening** and **country**; also **MOR, gospel** and **R&B**. Released "Relax and See," written and recorded by Roscoe Tee (MOR); "Why?" (by Bobby David), recorded by Bob Thomas (top 40); and "Sharing All The Joy of Life" (by Mark Daniel), recorded by Katie Rose (pop), all on Studio B Records.

Tips: "Keep it simple, honest, with a personal touch."

*SUN-RAY/SKY-VUE RECORDS, 1662 Wyatt Parkway, Lexington KY 40505. (606)254-7474. Owner: Jimmy Price. Record company, music publisher (Jimmy Price Music Publisher/BMI), record producer. Works with musicians/artists on record contract, songwriters on royalty contract, musicians on salary for in-house studio work. Pays statutory rate to publishers per song on record.

How to Contact: Submit demo tape by mail. Unsolicited submissions are OK. Prefers cassette with 3-4 songs and lyric sheet. SASE a must. Reports in 10-12 days.

Music: Mostly **country, gospel**.

Tips: "The compositions must be lyric wise also music wise to meter! Should a writer not know what I am referring to, he can check a good country song or church hymnal book, and will find each and every word or syllables which are parts of words will have some type of musical note above it."

*SUNSHINE RECORDS LTD., 228 Selkirk Ave., Winnipeg, Manitoba R2W 2L6 **Canada**. (204)586-8057. Manager A&R: Ness Michaels. Other labels include Jamco International, Cherish, Baba's. Record company, music publisher (Rig Publishing/SOCAN), record producer. Estab. 1974. Releases 20 12″ singles, 125-150 cassettes, 10-20 CDs/year. Works with musicians/artists on record contract, songwriters on royalty contract. Pays 5-18% royalty to artists on contract; ¾% to publishers per song on record.

How to Contact: Submit demo tape by mail. Unsolicited submissions are OK. Prefers cassette with 3 songs and lyric sheet. Does not return material. Reports in 1 month.

Music: Mostly **country, pop, gospel**; also **polka music**.

Tips: "Submit good sounding demos."

SURPRIZE RECORDS, INC., 7231 Mansfield Ave., Philadelphia PA 19138-1620. (215)276-8861. President: W. Lloyd Lucas. Director of A&R: Darryl L. Lucas. Labels include SRI. Record company and record producer (Surprize Records, Inc.). Estab. 1981. Releases 4-6 singles, 1-3 12″ singles and 2 LPs/year. Works with musicians/artists and songwriters on contract. Pays 6-10% royalty to artists on contract; statutory rate to publisher per song on record.
How to Contact: Submit demo tape by mail—unsolicited submissions are OK. Prefers cassette or VHS videocassette with 3 songs and lyric or lead sheet. SASE. Reports in 1 month. "We will *not* accept certified mail!"
Music: Mostly **R&B ballads, R&B dance oriented** and **crossover country**. Released "If Love Comes Again" (by T. Brown); "Say It Again" (by R. Hamersma/G. Magahan); "Tomorrow" (by Lester Camache/Nemeth); and "Only Lover" (by L. McDaniel/R. Beverly), all recorded by Jerry Dean (R&B). Other artists include Lamar (R&B ballad and dance), Rosella Clemmons-Washington (jazz).
Tips: "Be dedicated and steadfast in your chosen field whether it be songwriting and/or performing. Be aware of the changing trends. Watch other great performers and try to be as good, if not better. 'Be the best that you can be.' And as Quincy Jones says, 'Leave your egos at the door' and take all criticisms as being positive, not negative. There is always something to learn."

*SURVIVOR RECORDS, Suite 661, 880 Front St., Lahaina, Maui HI 96761. (808)661-5151. A&R Director: Greta Warren. Labels include Rough Diamond, Maui, Revelation. Record company, music publisher (Ten of Diamonds/BMI, Maui No Ka Oi Music/ASCAP), record producer (Maui Music), member Maui Arts & Music Association. Estab. 1974. Releases 1-12 singles, 1-12 12″ singles, 1-12 LPs, 1-12 EPs, 1-12 CDs. Works with musicians/artists on record contract, songwriters on royalty contract. Pays 3-15% royalty to artists on contract; statutory rate to publisher per song on record.
How to Contact: Submit demo tape by mail. Unsolicited submissions are OK. Prefers cassette (or VHS videocassette if available) with 1-5 songs and lyric sheet. SASE. Reports in 1-2 months.
Music: Mostly **pop/rock, country/R&B, reggae;** also **blues, multi-cultural, world beat**. Released "Diane" (by Jason Schwartz), recorded by Maui Cruisers on Rough Diamond Records (country); "Stardust Road" (by Don Gere), recorded by Jason on Survivor Records; *Violet Spiral*, written and recorded by Steve Okerlund on Revelation Records. Other artists include The Missionaries, Johnny Lemo Band, James Collins Blues Band, Axis, String Fever, Huelo Point.
Tips: "We are interested in *great* songs only—simple and dynamic performance and vocal are important for us, being as we promote from Maui and want to attract visitors here to see our artists."

SUSAN RECORDS, Box 1622, Hendersonville TN 37077. (615)822-1044. A&R Director: D. Daniels. Labels include Denco Records. Record company and music publisher. Releases 2-20 singles and 1-5 LPs/year. Works with artists and songwriters on contract. Pays 20¢/record to artists on contract; statutory rate to publishers per song on record. Buys some material outright; payment varies.
How to Contact: Submit demo tape—unsolicited submissions OK. Prefers cassette with 1-6 songs and lead sheet. SASE. Reports in 3 weeks.
Music: **Blues, country, dance, easy listening, folk, gospel, jazz, MOR, rock, soul** and **top 40/pop**.

SWEET TALK RECORDS, Box 211, Westfield MA 01086. (413)967-5395. Operations Manager: Alexis Steele. Labels include Sweet Talk Records. Record company and music publisher (Sariser Music/BMI). Estab. 1987. Releases 2 LPs/year. Works with musicians/artists and songwriters on contract. Pays statutory rate to publisher per song on record.
How to Contact: Write first and obtain permission to submit. No phone calls. Prefers cassette or 7½ ips reel-to-reel (or VHS #¼″ videocassette) with 3-4 songs and lyric or lead sheet. SASE. Reports in 6 weeks.
Music: Mostly **country/pop, country/rock** and **educational material;** also **soft rock** and **rockabilly**. Released "Magic & Music," written and recorded by Sparkie Allison on Sweet Talk Records (jazz); and "One Last Kiss" (by Sparkie Allison) recorded by The Moore Twins on MMT Records (country).
Tips: "Be unique. Try something different. Avoid the typical love songs. We look for material with a universal positive message. No cheatin' songs, no drinkin' songs."

SWOOP RECORDS, Stewart House, Hillbottom Rd., Highwycombe, Bucks, HP124HJ **England**. Phone: (0630)647374. Fax: (0630)647612. A&R Director: Xavier Lee. Labels include Grenoullie, Zarg, RTFM, Pogo and Check. Record company, music publisher (R.T.L. Music) and record producer (Ron Lee). Estab. 1976. Releases 50 singles, 50 12″ singles, 60 LPs and 60 CDs/year. Works with musicians/artists and songwriters on contract. Royalty paid to artists varies; statutory rate to publishers per song on record.
How to Contact: Submit demo tape—unsolicited submissions OK. Prefers cassette, (or PAL videocassette) with 3 songs and lyric or lead sheet. SAE and IRC. Reports in 6 weeks.
Music: Interested in **all types**. Released *Witch Woman, Children of the Night* and *I Wanna Be Shot* (by Ron Dickson), all recorded by Nightmare on Zarg Records. Other artists include Amazing Dark Horse, Daniel Boone and The Cromatics.

*T.O.G. MUSIC ENTERPRISES, 2107 S. Oakland St., Arlington VA 22204. (703)685-0199. President: Teo Graca. Record company, music publisher (Foundation Publishing), record producer. Estab. 1988. Releases 6 singles, 10 LPs, 2 CDs/year. Works with musicians/artists on record contract, songwriters on royalty contract, musicians on salary for in-house studio work. Pays 5-10% royalty to artists on contract; statutory rate to publishers per song on record. Charges in advance for promotion and recording services.

How to Contact: Submit demo tape by mail. Unsolicited submissions are OK. Prefers cassette with 3 songs, lyric sheet and lead sheet are optional. Does not return material. Reports in 2-6 weeks.

Music: All styles. Artists include Fusion Hackers, Michael Davison, Impulse, Chebmorad, Off Ramp, Shatterday.

Tips: "Our promotion and recording programs do not involve publishing. If you're prolific in writing, record as much as you can. It's the best way to show your works to companies that can use your songs."

*TANDEM RECORDS, #191, 1300 Old Bayshore, Burlingame CA 94010. (415)343-1515. Fax: (415)344-3670. A&R Representative: Dave Christian. Record company, music publisher (Atherton Music/ASCAP, Atherton Road Music/BMI). Estab. 1985. Pays statutory rate to publishers per song on record.

Affiliate: Speed Records.

How to Contact: Submit demo tape by mail. Unsolicited submissions are OK. Prefers cassette and lyric sheet. Does not return material. Reports in 1 month.

Music: Mostly **rap, R&B, gospel;** also **modern, techno.** Released *Anyway You Bless Me* (by Steven Roberts), recorded by Rev. Fleetwood Irving; *Faith* (by Dave Sears), recorded by 7 Red 7; and *Marked for Death,* (by Dave Christian), recorded by Chunk, all on Tandem Records. Other artists include Funklab All Stars, Van Damme, Rated X and Tenda Lee.

Tips: "Don't submit until you are sure you are submitting your best work."

TARGET RECORDS, Box 163, West Redding CT 06896. President: Paul Hotchkiss. Labels include Kastle Records. Record company, music publisher (Tutch Music/Blue Hill Music) and record producer (Red Kastle Prod.). Estab. 1975. Releases 6 singles and 4 compilation CDs/year. Works with songwriters on contract. Pays statutory rate to publisher per song on record.

How to Contact: Write first and obtain permission to submit. Prefers cassette with 2 songs and lyric sheet. SASE. Reports in 3 weeks.

Music: **Country** and **crossover.** Released "Dallas to Denver," written and by Michael Terry on Roto Noto Records; "Welcome to the World," (by P. Hotchkiss), recorded by Beverly's Hillbilly Band on Roto Noto Records; and "Stoned to the Bone," written by Paul Hotchkiss on Target Records. Other artists include Susan Rose Manning and Rodeo.

Tips: "Write songs people want to hear over and over. Strong commercial material."

*TAWAS RECORDS, 1376 Ready Ave,. Burton MI 48529. (313)742-0770. President: Harry F. Chestler. Record company, Music publisher (BMI), record producer (Tawas Records). Estab. 1967. Releases 2 singles/year. Works with musicians/artists on record contract, songwriters on royalty contract. Pays standard royalty to artists on contract; statutory rate to publisher per song on record.

How to Contact: Write first to obtain permission to submit. Prefers cassette with 2 songs. Does not return unsolicited material. Reports in 2 weeks.

Music: Mostly **country, rock, gospel;** also **rap.**

Tips: "Don't spend a lot of money on demos."

*TEN SQUARED, INC., P.O. Box 865, N. Hollywood CA 91603. (818)506-3143. President: Michael Wenslow. Record company, music publisher (Ten Squared Music/BMI), record producer (Michael Wenslow). Estab. 1990. Releases 6 singles, 2 12" singles, 4 LPs, 4 CDs/eyar. Works with musicians/artists on record contract, songwriters on royalty contract. Pays 7-10% royalty to artists on contract; negotiable rate to publishers per song on record.

How to Contact: Write first and obtain permission to submit. Prefers cassette and lyric sheet. Does not return material. Reports in 2 weeks.

Music: Mostly **A/C, country, urban contemporary;** also **CHR, NAC.** Released *Crosscountry* (by various), recorded by Branchwater (country); *Wordology 101* (by Dr., Greek/J. Rando, M. Wenslow), recorded by Dr. Greek (Urban C); *Christmas* (by various), recorded by Nancy Rands (AC), all on Ten Squared Records.

Tips: "Letters full of hype go directly to the wastebasket."

Listings of companies in countries other than the U.S. have the name of the country in boldface type.

TEROCK RECORDS, Box 1622, Hendersonville TN 37077. (615)822-1044. Manager: S.D. Neal. Labels include Terock, Susan, Denco, Rock-A-Nash-A-Billy. Record company, record producer, and music publisher (Heavy Jamin' Music/ASCAP). Estab. 1959. "We also lease masters." Member ASCAP, BMI. Releases 8-12 singles and 3-6 12″ singles/year. Works with musicians/artists and songwriters on contract and hires musicians for in-house studio work. Pays artists on contract 25¢ per record sold; standard royalty to publishers per song on record.

How to Contact: Submit demo tape—unsolicited submissions are OK. Prefers cassette with 3-6 songs and lyric sheet. SASE. Reports in 3 weeks.

Music: Mostly **rock'n'roll, country** and **rockabilly;** also **bluegrass, blues, easy listening, folk, gospel, jazz, MOR, progressive, Spanish, R&B, soul** and **top 40/pop.** Released "That's Why I Love You," by Dixie Dee (country); "Born to Bum Around," by Curt Flemons (country); and "Big Heavy," by the Rhythm Rockers (rock).

Tips: "Send your best."

***THIS CHARMING RECORD CO.,** 6 Robin Court, Lupus St., London SWIV 3ED **England.** (+71)834-8337. MDs: Nick Battle, E. Richard Bickersteth. Record company. Releases 1 cassette and 1 CD/year.

How to Contact: Submit demo tape by mail. Unsolicited submissions are OK. Prefers cassette with 3 songs and lyric sheet. Does not return material.

Music: Mostly **pop/rock.** Released *Leather Boots,* recorded by Herbie Armstrong on This Charming Record Co. Records.

***T-JAYE RECORD COMPANY,** 923 Main St., Nashville TN 37206. (615)226-1004. President A&R: Ted Jarrett. Labels include TRJ Records, Signull Records. Record company, music publisher (Ponce-llo Music/ASCAP), record producer. Estab. 1980. Releases 12 singles, 5 12″ singles, 12 LPs/year. Works with musicians/artists on record contract. Pays 7-10% royalty to artists on contract; statutory rate to publishers per song on record.

How to Contact: Write or call first and obtain permission to submit. Prefers cassette with 2 songs and lyric sheet. SASE. Reports in 1 month.

Music: Mostly **R&B, dance, black gospel.** Released "I Want You Back" (by Tim Camp), recorded by Herbert Hunter (R&B); *By and By,* written and recorded by Christain Crusaders (gospel); *On the Road Again* (by Sandis Cooper), recorded by Sons of Glory (gospel) all on T-Jaye Records.

Tips: "Write, rewrite, rewrite and rewrite."

TOP RECORDS, Gall. del Corso, 4 Milano 20122 **Italy.** Phone: (02)76021141. Fax: (0039)276021141. Manager/Director: Guido Palma. Labels include United Colors Productions, Dingo Music, KIWI Record, Smoking Record and Tapes. Estab. 1979. Record company and music publisher. Releases 20 12″ singles, 30 LPs, 15 EPs and 40 CDs/year. Works with musicians/artists and songwriters on contract and hires in-house studio musicians. Pays 8% royalty to artists on contract.

How to Contact: Submit demo tape by mail—unsolicited submissions are OK. Prefers cassette (or videocassette) with 5 songs and lyric sheet. SAE and IRC. Reports in 1 month with IRC.

Music: Mostly **pop** and **dance;** also **soundtracks.** Released *Magica* (by Paolo Luciani) and *Cosi' E'* (by Ivan Cattaneo) on Top Emi Records; and *Una Favola* (by Gianluca Perrone), on Dingo Records. Other artists include Daiano, Morelli, Gianni Dei, Diego D'Aponte, Santarosa.

TOUCHE RECORDS, Box 96, El Cerrito CA 94530. Executive Vice President: James Bronson, Jr. Record company, record producer (Mom and Pop Productions, Inc.) and music publisher (Toulouse Music Co./BMI). Member AIMP. Releases 2 LPs/year. Works with artists and songwriters on contract; musicians on salary for in-house studio work. Pays statutory rate to publishers per song on record.

How to Contact: Prefers cassette with 2-4 songs and lyric sheet. SASE. Reports in 1 month.

Music: Mostly **jazz;** also **bluegrass, gospel, R&B** and **soul.** Released *Bronson Blues* (by James Bronson), *Nigger Music* and *Touché Smiles* (by Smiley Winters), all recorded by Les Oublies du Jazz Ensemble on Touché Records. Other artists include Hi Tide Harris.

TRAC RECORD CO., 170 N. Maple, Fresno CA 93702. (209)255-1717. Owner: Stan Anderson. Record company and music publisher (Sellwood Publishing/BMI). Estab. 1972. Releases 5 singles and 5 LPs and 2 CDs/year. Works with musicians/artists on contract, songwriters on royalty contract and in-house musicians on contract. Pays 13% royalty to artists on contract. Pays statutory rate to publisher per song on record.

How to Contact: Submit demo tape—unsolicited submissions are OK. Prefers cassette (or VHS videocassette) with 2-4 songs and lyric sheet. SASE. Reports in 2 weeks.

Music: Traditional country and **rock.** Released *Whiskey Blues, Dan* and *NightTime Places,* all written and recorded by Jimmy Walker on TRAC Records. Other artists include Gil Thomas, Jessica James, The Rackleys.

*TREASURE COAST RECORDS, 692 SE Port St. Lucie Blvd., Port St. Lucie FL 34984. President: J.A. Blecha. Record company, music publisher (Songrite Creations Productions/BMI, Sine Qua Non Music/ASCAP), record producer and recording artist/songwriter. Estab. 1992. Releases 12-16 singles, 2 LPs, 4 EPs and 2 CDs/year. Works with musicians/artists on record contract, songwriters on royalty contract, songwriters/artists with masters ready for release. Pays 10-15% royalty to artists on contract; statutory rate to publisher per song on record.

How to Contact: Submit demo tape by mail. Unsolicited submissions are OK. "Send only your best unpublished songs (1 or 2 max), send bio, press, number of songs written, releases, awards, etc." Prefers cassette with 1 or 2 songs and lyric sheet. SASE. Reports in 4-6 weeks.

Music: Mostly **contemporary country, pop** (A/C) and **gospel**; also **R&B, blues** and **novelty**. Released *Shades of Blue* (by J.A. Blecha), recorded by Judy Welden on Treasure Coast Records (crossover); "What Happens Now" (by J.A. Blecha), recorded by Judy Welden on Sabre Records (country); and "Movin' " (by Lisa Kolander), recorded by Lisa Joy on Sabre Records (country/swing). Other artists include Alita Marie Davis, Ron Michael Hart, Rich Joyce and Charlotte.

Tips: "Demo must be well-produced and current sounding. Be prepared for a re-write if lyrics are not conversational and in the best possible meter. Believe in yourself and your talent and you will not get discouraged easily!"

TREND RECORDS, P.O. Box 201, Smyrna GA 30081. (404)432-2454. President: Tom Hodges. Labels include Trendsetter, Atlanta's Best, Trend Star, Trend Song, British Overseas Airways Music and Stepping Stone Records. Record company, music publisher (Mimic Music/BMI, Skipjack Music/BMI and British Overseas Airways Music/ASCAP), record producer and management firm. Estab. 1965. Releases 4 singles, 14 LPs and 3 CDs/year. Works with musicians/artists and songwriters on contract, songwriters on royalty contract and musicians on salary for in-house studio work. Pays 15% royalty to artists on contract; standard royalty to songwriters on contract; statutory rate to publisher per song on records.

How to Contact: Submit demo tape—unsolicited submissions are OK. Prefers cassette (or VHS videocassette) with 8-10 songs and lyric lead sheet. SASE. Reports in 3 weeks.

Music: Mostly **R&B, country** and **MOR**; also **gospel, light rock** and **jazz**. Released "Rock Around the Clock" (by De Knight), recorded by Joey Welz; *Heartbreak Road* (by Corey and others), recorded by C&N Cole; and *Sons of the South*, written and recorded by Spencer, all on Trend Records. Other artists include Marlon Frizzell, Phil Coley, Frank Brannon, Ginny Peters, Jim Single and Ray McDonald.

TRUSTY RECORDS, 8771 Rose Creek Rd., Nebo KY 42441. (502)249-3194. President: Elsie Childers. Record company and music publisher (Trusty Publications/BMI). Member NSAI, CMA. Estab. 1950. Releases 2 singles and 2 LPs/year. Receives 8-10 submissions/month. Works with musicians/artists and songwriters on contract. Pays 3% royalty to artists on contract; statutory rate to publishers for each record sold.

How to Contact: Submit demo tape by mail—unsolicited submissions are OK. Prefers cassette with 2-4 songs and lead sheet. SASE. Reports in 1 month.

Music: Mostly **country**; also **blues, church/religious, dance, easy listening, folk, gospel, MOR, soul** and **top 40/pop**. Released "My Charms Just Ain't Enough," "Yes It Do" and "I Wanna Dance" (by E. Childers/N. Williams), recorded by Noah Williams on Trusty Records (country/pop).

TUG BOAT RECORDS, 2514 Build America Drive, Hampton VA 23666. (804)827-8733. A&R: Judith Guthro. Record company, music publisher (Doc Publishing/BMI, Dream Machine/SESAC) and record producer (Doc Holiday Productions). Estab. 1967. Releases 12 singles, 15 12″ singles, 15 LPs, 15 EPs and 8 CDs/year. Works with musicians/artists and songwriters on contract and hires musicians for in-house studio work. Pays varying royalty to artists on contract; statutory rate to publisher per song on record.

How to Contact: Submit demo tape by mail—unsolicited submissions are OK. Prefers cassette with 1 song and lyric sheets. Does not return materials.

Music: Mostly **country, top 40** and **rock**. Released "Mr. Jones," written and recorded by Big Al Downing; "Cajun Baby" (by Hank Williams, Jr. and Sr.), recorded by Doug Kershaw and Hank Jr., and "Don't Mess with My Toot Toot" (by Fats Domino), recorded by Fats Domino and Doug Kershaw, all on Tug Boat Records (country). Other artists include Ronn Craddock, Tracy Wilson, Doc Holiday, Jolene, Eagle Feather, John Lockhart M.D., Marvel Felts, Wyndi Renee, The Showmen, King B & The New Jack Crew.

*TYPETOKEN RECORDS, 1211 Arlington Place, Warrensburg MO 64093 (816)747-5578. Director of Talent Acquisition: Phil Easter. Record company, music publisher (TypeToken Music/BMI). Estab. 1990. Releases 2-3 CDs/year. Works with musicians/artists on record contract. Pays 7-13% royalty to artists on contract; statutory rate to publishers per song on record.

How to Contact: Submit demo tape by mail. Unsolicited submissions are OK. Prefers cassette with 3 or more songs and promo-materials. Including brief bio and personal photo. Does not return unsolicited material. Reports in 1-2 months.

Music: Mostly **industrial/cyber, electronic-experimental, ambient-industrial**; also **acid-house/rave, ambient/space-music, gothic**. Released *Industrial Meditation*, written and recorded by Stone Glass Steel (ambient-industrial); *House of Garbar*, written and recorded by Death in Arcadia (industrial/cyber); and *Night Shades*, written and recorded by Black Beach Moonrise (ambient-space), all on TypeToken Records.

Tips: "Experiment continually. Dare to push the envelope of musical evolution. Embrace the high-tech times in which we live. Blur the line between songwriter and recording artist."

UNIVERSAL-ATHENA RECORDS, Box 1264, Peoria IL 61654-1264. (309)673-5755. A&R Director: Jerry Hanlon. Record company and music publisher (Jerjoy Music/BMI). Estab. 1978. Releases 1-2 singles and 1 LP/year. Works with musicians/artists on contract; hires musicians on salary for in-house studio work. Pays statutory rate to publishers for each record sold.

How to Contact: Submit demo tape—unsolicited submissions are OK. Prefers cassette with 4-8 songs and lyric sheet. SASE. Reports in 2-3 weeks.

Music: Country. Released "The Calling" (by Jerry Hanlon); "Ring Around the Rose" and "Thank You Lord" (by L. Lester), all recorded by Jerry Hanlon on Universal Athena Records (country).

Tips: "Be extremely critical and make realistic comparisons of your work before submission."

*VELVET PRODUCTIONS, 517 W. 57th St., Los Angeles CA 90037. (213)753-7893. Manager: Aaron Johnson. Labels include Velvet, Kenya, Normar and Stoop Down Records. Record company, booking agency and promoter. BMI. Estab. 1965. Releases 5 singles, 2 12″ singles and 3 EPs/year. Works with artists and songwriters on contract. Pays 5% royalty to artists on contract.

How to Contact: Submit demo and/or lead sheet by mail. Arrange personal interview. Prefers cassette with 3-5 songs and lead sheet. SASE. Reports in 2 months.

Music: Blues, gospel, rock, soul and **top 40/pop**. Released "How I Wish You" (by Arlene Bell/Delais Ene), recorded by Arlene Bell on Velvet Records.

*VENTURE BEYOND RECORDS, Box 3662, Santa Rosa CA 95402-3662. (707)528-8695. Record company, music publisher (BMI, ASCAP), record producer, licensed for export and import, sub publisher for NSK, Russia, Estab. 1989. Releases 2 CDs/year. Works with "people we like." Pays all except 2% royalty to artists on contract; all except 2% to publishers per song on record. "Songwriters/artists pay our cost."

How to Contact: Submit demo tape by mail. Unsolicited submissions are OK. Prefers cassette (or VHS videocassette). Does not return material. "We get so many, it's difficult to spend our time returning, but we try." Reports in 1 month.

Music: Only **underground, alternative**. Released *Veer and Tringe* (by Davis Smith), recorded by Prairie Sun; *Just Touching It* (by P. Vampire), recorded by VBR; *Pulsators* (by Campbell), recorded by Prairie Sun, all on Venture Beyond Records.

Tips: "We're looking for good songs and repeatable live performance (as good as the CD). We're not interested in taking the money that's rightfully yours."

VIBE RECORDS, Dept. SM, 2540 Woodburn Ave., Cincinnati OH 45206. (513)961-0602. A&R Director: Smiley Hickland. Record company. Estab. 1985. Releases 2 singles and 3 12″ singles/year. Works with musicians/artists on contract. Pays varying royalty to artists on contract; statutory rate to publisher per song.

How to Contact: Write first and obtain permission to submit. Prefers cassette with 4 songs and lyric sheet. SASE. Reports in 4 weeks.

Music: Mostly **R&B, gospel** and **pop**; also **rap** and **dance**. Released "Heartbeat" (by Hicks) (R&B dance); "All About Town" (by Barber) (pop); and "Stingy" (by Waiver) (R&B dance); all on Vibe Records. Other artists include Kenny Hill, Greg Jackson, Trina Best, Sandy Childress, Tim Napier and Kim Seay.

VOKES MUSIC PUBLISHING & RECORD CO., Box 12, New Kensington PA 15068. (412)335-2775. President: Howard Vokes. Labels include Vokes and Country Boy Records. Record company, booking agency and music publisher. Releases 8 singles and 5 LPs/year. Works with artists and songwriters on contract. Pays 2½-4½¢/song royalty to artists and songwriters on contract.

How to Contact: Submit cassette only and lead sheet. SASE. Reports in 2 weeks.

Music: Country, bluegrass, gospel-old time. Released "Cherokee Trail Of Tears" and "City Of Strangers" by Johnny Eagle Feather and "Portrait Of An Angel" by Lenny Gee, all on Vokes Records.

*WATCH MUSIC COMPANY LTD., 121 Logan Ave., Toronto, Ontario M4M 2M9 **Canada**. President: Ross Munro. Record company, music publisher (Watch Music Company/SOCAN) and record producer. Estab. 1992. Works with musicians/artists on record contract.
How to Contact: Submit demo tape by mail. Unsolicited submissions are OK. Prefers cassette (or VHS videocassette) with 4-6 songs and lyric sheet. Does not return material. Reports in 4-6 weeks.
Music: Mostly **rock, pop** and **country**. Released *The Morganfields* (by Alun Piggins), recorded by The Morganfields on Watch Records (rock).

*WENCE SENSE MUSIC/BILL WENCE PROMOTIONS, P.O. Box 110829, Nashville TN 37222. Contact: Kathy Gaddes. Labels include Six-One-Five Records and Skyway Records. Record company, music publisher (Wence Sense Music/ASCAP), record producer (Bill Wence). Estab. 1984. Releases 4-8 singles, 4 CDs/year. Works with songwriters on royalty contract, musicians on salary for in-house studio work. Pays statutory rate to publishers per song on record.
How to Contact: Call first and obtain permission to submit. Prefers cassette with 1 song. Does not return material. Reports in 3 weeks.
Music: Prefers **country**. Released *Who's Foolin' Who*, written and recorded by Allen Borden on PlayMe Records. *Looking on the Outside* (by Gil Caballero), recorded by Caballero on 615 Records; *You Can Always*, written and recorded by Leon Sieter on Skyway Records. Other artists include Trena and Lanada Cassidy.
Tips: "Send only one song until we request more of you and be patient."

*WHITE CAR RECORDS, 10611 Cal Rd., Baton Rouge LA 70809. (504)755-1400. Owner: Nelson Blanchard. Labels include Techno Sound Records. Record company, music publisher (White Car Music/BMI, Char Blanche/ASCAP) and independent record producer. Estab. 1980. Releases 6 singles, 4 12″ singles, 6 LPs, 1 EP and 2 CDs/year. Works with musicians/artists and songwriters on contract. Pays 7½-20% royalty to artists on contract; statutory rate to publisher per song.
How to Contact: Submit demo tape by mail. Unsolicited submissions are OK. Prefers cassette with 4 songs. Does not return material. Reports in 2 weeks.
Music: Mostly **country, rock** and **pop**; also **R&B**. Released "Time, You're No Friend of Mine" written and recorded by Howard Austin; "Closer to Heaven," written and recorded by Joey Dupuy, both on Techno Sound Records; and "I Read Between the Lines (by Stan Willis), recorded by Nelson Blanchard on White Car Records. Other artists include John Steve, B.J. Morgan and Bayon Country Band.

WHITESTOCKING RECORDS, Box 250013, Atlanta GA 30325. (404)352-2263. A&R Department: Steve C. Hill. Estab. 1990. Releases 4 12″ singles and 4 CDs/year. Works with musicians/artists and songwriters on contract. Pays 5-10% royalty to artists on contract.
Affiliate: Tigersteeth Records.
How to Contact: Submit demo tape—unsolicited submissions are OK. Prefers cassette with 3 songs and lyric sheets. SASE required. Reports in 3 months. Do not call.
Music: **Pop, rock, soul, alternative**—Will listen to all. Elaborate production not necessary—piano/guitar and vocals OK. 2-3-4 part harmonies get special attention. Quality metal will be listened to also.
Tips: "We listen for danceability, musicality and lyrical content. No profanity or worn out rhymes!"

WINDHAM HILL PRODUCTIONS, Box 9388, Palo Alto CA 94305. Contact: A&R Department. Labels include Windham Hill and Windham Hill Jazz. Record company. Estab. 1976. Works with musicians/artists on contract.
How to Contact: Write first and obtain permission to submit. "We are not accepting unsolicited material. Detailed queries are welcome. Do not send recordings until requested. We prefer a referral from a reputable industry person." Prefers cassette with 3 songs. SASE. Reports in 2 months.
Music: Mostly **pop, jazz** and **original instrumental**. Released *Metropolis*, recorded by Turtle Island String Quartet (new acoustic jazz); *Sampler '89*, written and recorded by various artists on Windham Hill Records (instrumental); and *Switchback* (by S. Cossu, Van Manakas), recorded by Scott Cossu on Windham Hill Records (jazz ensemble). Other artists include William Ackerman, George Winston, Philip Aaberg, Michael Hedges, The Nylons and Montreux.

WINGATE RECORDS, Box 10895, Pleasanton CA 94588. (415)846-6194. CEO: P. Hanna. Record company, music publisher (Parchment Harbor Music/BMI and Hugo First Publishing/ASCAP), record producer (Wingate Productions) and artist management. Estab. 1989. Releases 12 singles, 2 LPs and 2 EPs/year. Works with musicians/artists and songwriters on contract. Pays statutory rate to publishers per song on record.
How to Contact: Write and obtain permission to submit. Prefers cassette (or VHS videocassette) with 2 songs and lyric sheet. Does not return material. Reports in 2 months.
Music: Mostly **pop, country** and **rock**; also **contemporary Christian** and A/C. Released *Different Roads* (by J. Crafton/C. Peterson/R. Davidson/W. Muncy), recorded by Cross Street; "Sack the Quarterback" (by P. Hanna/P. Markoch), recorded by Kathy Kennedy; and "Nevada Night" (by P. Hanna), recorded

by Neon Nites, all on Wingate Records. Other artists include Kayla Moore, Robyn Banx, Michael Sea & Island Fever, Kelli Crofton, Marty Ross, Billy Truitt & The Barnstormers.
Tips: "Keep in mind you're pitching your song to artists who are not on a major label. . .yet! Send *the* song that may make their careers soar. . .an attention getter is what the "unknowns" need."

*WIZMAK PRODUCTIONS, P.O. Box 477, Wingdale NY 12594. (914)877-3943. Manager: Geri White. Labels include Wizmak and Eventide. Record company and recording studio (Fulfillment House). Estab. 1986. Releases 4 cassettes/year. Works with musicians/artists on record contract. "Musicians receive a set fee per track for in house studio work." Pays 85¢ to $1.50/record sold to artists on contract; statutory rate to publisher per song on record.
How to Contact: Submit demo tape by mail. Unsolicited submissions are OK. Prefers cassette with 3 songs and lyric sheet. "Also include news article or review of a recent performance." SASE. Reports in 2-4 weeks.
Music: Mostly **dulcimer/folk, traditional (American & Irish)** and **gospel, children's (folk)**; also **contemporary, singer/songwriter** and **pop**. Released *Someone To Watch Over Me*, recorded by Rob Brereton (contemporary and traditional instrumental); *How About You?*, recorded by John Farrell (children's); and *Let's Pretend*, recorded by Thomasina (children's), all on Wizmak Records. Other artists include Jim Pospisil, Jonathan Kruk, Rich Bala and Chris Dentato.
Tips: "Know your direction, establish yourself as a performer on a regional level."

WOODRICH RECORDS, Box 38, Lexington AL 35648. (205)247-3983. President: Woody Richardson. Record company and music publisher (Woodrich Publishing Co./BMI, Mernee Music/ASCAP and Tennessee Valley Music/SESAC) and record producer (Woody Richardson). Estab. 1959. Releases 12 singles and 12 LPs/year. Works with songwriters on contract. Pays 10% royalty to writers on contract; statutory rate to publisher per song on record.
How to Contact: Submit demo tape by mail—unsolicited submissions are OK. Prefers cassette with 4 songs and lyric sheet. "Be sure to send a SASE (not a card) with sufficient return postage." Reports in 2 weeks. "We prefer a good studio demo."
Music: Mostly **country**; also **gospel, comedy, bluegrass, rock** and **jazz**. Released "One Hawaiian Delight" (by R.E. Lee, Jr.), recorded by Mark Ferguson; "You Can't Take That Country Music Out of Me," written and recorded by Al Ward; and "Ugly Truck" (by Rocky Johnson), recorded by Mark Narmore, all on Woodrich Records.
Tips: "Use a good studio with professional musicians. Don't send a huge package. A business envelope will do. It's better to send a cassette *not in a box*."

*WRITE KEY RECORDS, 3716 W. 87th St., Chicago IL 60652. (312)735-3297. President: Bert Swanson. Record company and music publisher (Music In the Right Keys/BMI, High'n Low Notes/ASCAP). Estab. 1985. Releases 15 LPs, 3 EPs and 1 CD/year. Works with songwriters on royalty contract. Pays 50% royalty to artists on contract; statutory rate to publisher per song on record.
How to Contact: Submit demo tape by mail. Unsolicited submissions are OK. Prefers cassette with 3-8 songs and lyric or lead sheet. SASE. Reports in 5 weeks.
Music: Mostly **country, religious** and **pop**; also **R&B** and **MOR**. Released "Loving the Night Away" and "Drinking Out Of Hand" (by B. Swanson), both recorded by C. Fisher on Write Key Records (country).
Tips: "Always submit a good demo for presentation of a good quality production. This would be very impressive to me and other publishers."

*XEMU RECORDS, 300 Main St., Box D1, White Plains NY 10601. A&R Director: Dr. Claw. Record company. Estab. 1992. Releases 1 single and 3 CDs/year. Works with musicians/artists on record contract. Pays negotiable royalty to artists on contract; statutory rate to publishers per song on record.
How to Contact: Submit demo tape by mail. Unsolicited submissions are OK. Prefers cassette with 3 songs and lyric sheet. SASE. Reports in 1 month.
Music: Mostly **alternative** and **progressive rock**. Released "Tapeworm" and "Swamp Gas," written and recorded by Gneanderthal Spongecake on Xemu Records (alternative rock). Other artists include Death Sandwich and The Friends Who Let Their Drunk Friends Drive.
Tips: "Don't do what you should do—do what you deserve to do."

YELLOW JACKET RECORDS, 10303 Hickory Valley, Ft. Wayne IN 46835. President: Allan Straten. Record company. Estab. 1985. Releases 8-10 singles, 1 LP and 1 CD/year. Works with musicians/artists and songwriters on contract; hires musicians for in-house studio work. Pays 7-10% royalty to artists on contract; statutory rate to publisher per song on record.
How to Contact: Submit demo tape by mail—unsolicited submissions are OK. Prefers cassette with 3-4 songs and typed lyric sheet. SASE. Reports in 3-4 weeks.
Music: Country and **MOR**. Released *April In Love* on Yellow Jacket Records. Other artists include Roy Allan.

*YOUNG COUNTRY RECORDS/PLAIN COUNTRY RECORDS, P.O. Box 5412, Buena Park CA 90620. (312)521-9511. Owner: Leo J. Eiffert, Jr. Labels include Eiffert Records and Napoleon Country Records. Record company, music publisher (Young Country Music Publishing Co./BMI, Eb-Tide Music/ BMI), record producer (Leo J. Eiffert, Jr). Releases 10 singles and 5 LPs/year. Works with musicians/ artists on record contract, songwriters on royalty contract, musicians on salary for in-house studio work. Pays negotiable royalty to artists on contract; negotiable rate to publishers per song on record.
How to Contact: Submit demo tape by mail. Unsolicited submissions are OK. "And please make sure your song or songs are copyrighted." Prefers cassette with 2 songs and lyric sheet. Does not return material. Reports in 2 weeks.
Music: Mostly **country, easy rock, gospel** music. Released *Like A Fool*, written and recorded by Pam Bellows on Plain Country Records; *Something About Your Love* (by Leo J. Eiffert, Jr.), recorded by Chance Waite Young (country); *Cajunland*, written and recorded by Leo J. Eiffert, Jr. on Plain Country Records. Other artists include Brandi Holland, Crawfish Band, Larry Settle.

*YOUNG STAR PRODUCTIONS, INC., 5501 N. Broadway, Chicago IL 60640. (312)989-4140. President: Starling Young, Jr. Labels include Gold Karat Records (a wholly owned subsidiary of Young Star Productions, Inc.). Record company, music publisher (Gold Karat Records/ASCAP) and record producer (Young Star Productions, Inc.). Estab. 1991. Releases 70-80 singles, 20-30 12″ singles, 7 LPs, 10 EPs and 9 CDs/year. Works with musicians/artists on record contract, songwriters on royalty contract, musicians on salary for in-house studio work. Pays 6-10% royalty to artists on contract; statutory rate to publisher per song on record or ½ of statutory if we do not own publisher.
How to Contact: Submit demo tape by mail. Unsolicited submissions are OK. Prefers cassette (or VHS videocassette) with 4 songs and lyric or lead sheet. "Insert photo and bio." Does not return material. Reports in 4-6 weeks.
Music: Mostly **R&B, dance** and **blues/jazz**; also **pop/rock, country** and **gospel**. Released "Whatcha Gonna Do" (by Michael Hearn), recorded by Linda Clifford on Gold Karat Records (dance). Other artists include Nanette Frank, Ivan Tutwiler, Robbie Banks, Kenny Davis, Randy Love, Michelle Richard, Diamond Williams and Black Tye.
Tips: "Be established well enough to be accepted as a producer, artist or songwriter seriously. Be patient enough to know that success doesn't happen overnight. But be creative and assertive enough to be ready when it happens. Writing and performing music well is a gift not to be taken likely."

YOUNGHEART MUSIC, Box 6017, Cypress CA 90630. (714)995-7888. President: James Connelly. Record company. Estab. 1975. Releases 1-2 LPs/year. Works with musicians/artists and songwriters on contract. Pays statutory rate.
How to Contact: Submit demo tape—unsolicited submissions are OK. SASE. Reports in 4 weeks.
Music: Mostly children's and educational. Released "Three Little Pig Blues" and "A Man Named King," written and recorded by Greg Scelsa and Steve Millang both on Youngheart Records.
Tips: "We are looking for original, contemporary, motivating music for kids. Songs should be fun, educational, build self-esteem and/or multicultural awareness. New original arrangements of classic songs or nursery rhymes will be considered."

ZANZIBAR RECORDS, 2019 Noble St., Pittsburgh PA 15218. (412)351-6672. A&R Manager: John C. Antimary. Labels include A.W.O.L. Records. Record company and music publisher (RTD Music/ BMI). Estab. 1980. Releases 6-12 singles, 4-8 12″ singles and 6 LPs/year. Works with musicians/artists and songwriters on contract and hires musicians for in-house studio work. Pays 6-8% royalty to artists on contract; statutory rate to publisher per song on record.
Affiliate: Zapple Zone Records.
How to Contact: Submit demo tape by mail. Unsolicited submissions are OK. Prefers cassette (or VHS videocassette) with 4 songs and lyric sheet. SASE. Reports in 2-3 months.
Music: Mostly **rock, progressive** and **R&B**; also **pop, rap** and **metal**. Released "Long Winter" (by T.J. Wilkins), recorded by Affordable Floor (new music); "Going Home" and "Reunion," written and recorded by Lenny Collini (rock), all on Zanzibar Records. Other artists include Bunky Gooch, Necropolis, Post Mortem, Good Earth and Corky Zapple.
Tips: "When sending demos of your songs, please make sure that they are recorded on good cassette tapes."

*ZEROBUDGET RECORDS, P.O. Box 2044, La Crosse WI 54602. (608)783-5818. President/Director A&R: Stephen Harm. "We distribute some titles on the Boat Records label." Record company. Estab. 1982. Works with musicians/artists on record contract. Pays negotiable royalty to artists on contract; negotiable rate to publisher per song on record.

How to Contact: Submit demo tape by mail. Unsolicited submissions are OK. Prefers cassette (or VHS ½" videocassette if available) with 4 songs and lyric sheet. SASE. Reports in 1 month.
Music: Mostly **alternative, modern rock, rockabilly, techno**; also **industrial, rock, pop**. Released *Full Moon, Bad Weather*, written and recorded by Rousers on Boat/Zerobudget Records (rockabilly); *We Play for Beer*, written and recorded by Wizenhiemers (rockabilly) and *Silent Dreams*, written and recorded by Victims, both on Zerobudget Records.
Tips: "Don't follow trends—set 'em. No cliché is ever OK."

*ZONE RECORD CO., 2674 Steele, Memphis TN 38127. (901)357-0064. Owner: Marshall E. Ellis. Releases 4 singles/year. Record company, music publisher and record producer. Works with songwriters on contract; musicians paid by song. Pays 4¢/side royalty to artists on contract.
How to Contact: Call first to arrange personal interview. Submit demo tape by mail—unsolicited submissions are OK. Prefers cassette with 4 songs. "Be sure the words are clear. Don't try to make a master—just a good clean tape." SASE. Reports in 3 weeks.
Music: **Country** and **country/pop**. Released "My Last Hurrah" by Susan Magee and "She Was the Only One" by Al Hansen, both on Zone Records. Other artists include Buddy Fletcher and Larry Manual.

*ZULU RECORDS, 1869 W. 4th Ave., Vancouver, British Columbia V6J 1M4 **Canada**. (604)738-3232. Label Manager: Kevin Smith. Record company. Estab. 1981. Releases 3-4 CDs/year. Deals with musicians/artists on record contract. Pays 10-15% royalty to artists on contract; statutory rate to publishers per song on record.
How to Contact: Submit demo tape by mail. Unsolicited submissions are OK. Prefers cassette. Does not return material.
Music: Mostly **alternative**. Released *Magnum Opiate*, written and recorded by Lung; *S/T*, written and recorded by Coal; *Dust*, written and recorded by Perfume Tree, all on Zulu Records. Other artists include Bob's Your Uncle and Tank Hog.
Tips: "Be creative, do something different and innovative. Don't bother us with mainstream crap."

*ZYLON RECORDS & TAPES, P.O. Box 39A16, Los Angeles CA 90039. (213)668-2213. Director of A&R: K. Slater. Record company. Estab. 1985. Works with musicians/artists on record contract, songwriters on royalty contract, musicians on salary for in-house studio work. Pay varies; pays statutory rate to publisher per song on record.
How to Contact: Submit demo tape by mail. Unsolicited submissions are OK. Prefers casette with 3-12 songs and lyric sheet. Does not return material. Reports in 3-4 weeks.
Music: Mostly **rock, alternative** and **pop**; also **R&B (urban)** and **country**. Released "Cryin' Out Loud," written and recorded by Kim Allen; "The Hunter" (by Lucy Russo), recorded by Lucrecia; and *Lucrecia* (by Russo/Hamel/Kellogg), recorded by Lucrecia, all on Zylon Records. Other artists include Children At Play and Straitjacket (distribution only).
Tips: "Listen to what college radio is doing. Write mainstream hit songs as well as alternative cuts. Write visual songs."

Geographic Index Record Companies

The U.S. section of this handy geographic index will quickly give you the names of record companies located in or near the music centers of Los Angeles, New York and Nashville. Of course, there are many valuable contacts to be made in other cities, but you will probably want to plan a trip to one of these established music centers at some point in your career and try to visit as many of these companies as you think are appropriate. The International section lists, geographically, markets for your songs in countries other than the U.S.

Find the names of companies in this index, and then check listings within the Record Companies section for addresses, phone numbers and submission details.

Los Angeles
Aliso Creek Productions Incorporated
Atlantic Recording Corp.
AVC Entertainment Inc.
Blue Gem Records
Bonaire Management Inc.
Carousel Records, Inc.
Chattahoochee Records
Dupuy Records/Productions/Publishing, Inc.
Fullmoon Entertainment/Moonstone Records
Grass Roots Record & Tape/LMI Records
Helion Records
MCI Entertainment
Miles Ahead Records
Morgan Creek Music Group
Mountain Railroad Records, Inc.
P.I.R.A.T.E. Records/H.E.G. Music Publishing
Roach Records Co.
Rock Dog Records
Shaolin Film & Records
Ten Squared, Inc.
Velvet Productions
Zylon Records & Tapes

Nashville
Bandit Records
Carlyle Records, Inc.
Cedar Creek Records™

Crown Music Company
Fame and Fortune Enterprises
Fat City Artists
Fresh Start Music Ministries
Fretboard Publishing
Interstate 40 Records
Jalyn Recording Co.
Jimmy Jangle Records
Kottage Records
Landmark Communications Group
The Mathes Company
Orbit Records
Paragold Records & Tapes
Phoenix Records, Inc.
San-Sue Recording Studio
Sound Achievement Group, Inc.
Stop Hunger Records International
Susan Records
T-Jaye Record Company
Wence Sense Music/Bill Wence Promotions

New York
A Company Called W
Alternative Record Co. Ltd.
Big Productions Records
Caroline Records, Inc.
Community 3
Digitalia Records

Earache Records/Earache Songs
Emzee Records
G Fine Records/Productions
Gold City Records, Inc.
Halogram
Homestead Records
J&J Musical Enterprises
Lamar Music Group
Majestic Control Records
MCA Records
Mighty Records
Mindfield Records
Modern Blues Recordings
Now & Then Records
Polygram Records
PPI/Peter Pan Industries
Razor & Tie Music
Sonic Group, Ltd.

International

Australia
Big Rock Pty. Ltd.
Hot Records
Makeshift Music
Rooart Records

Austria
Cactus Records
Musica Schallplatten Vertrieb Ges.mbH

Belgium
Jump Records & Music
Parsifal PVBA

Canada
Berandol Music
Bovine International Record Company
Circle "M" Records
Duke Street Records
H&S Records
Heritage Music
Hickory Lane Publishing and Recording
John Headley Lennon Music Ltd.
Monticana Records
Nephelim Record (Studio Works)
Nettwerk Productions
Nightflite Records Inc.
One-Eyed Duck Recording and Publishing
Reveal

Roto-Noto Music
Saddlestone Records
Shaky Records
Slak Records
Sunshine Records
Watch Music Company Ltd.
Zulu Records

Chile
Prodisc (Prodisc Limitada)

Denmark
Mega Records Aps.
Reca Music Production

Germany
Alphabeat
Autogram Records
Comma Records & Tapes

Holland
Associated Artists Music International
Collector Records

Hong Kong
Rock In Records

Italy
Top Records

United Kingdom
Demi Monde Records and Publishing, Ltd.
E.S.R. Records
First Time Records
I'll Call You Records
Le Matt Music Ltd.
Leopard Music
Loading Bay Records
Nervous Records
Red Sky Records
Red-Eye Records
Rhino Records Ltd.
Rock 'N' Roll Records
Rosie Records
Swoop Records
This Charming Record Co.

Record Companies/'93-'94 Changes

The following markets appeared in the 1993 edition of *Songwriter's Market* but are absent from the 1994 edition. Most of these companies failed to respond to our request for an update of their listing for a variety of reasons. For example, they may have gone out of business or they may have requested deletion from the 1994 edition because they are backlogged with material. If we know the specific reason, it appears within parentheses.

Abacus (unable to contact)
AKO Records (affiliate of Amiron Music/Aztec Productions)
Akrana Country (requested deletion)
Amalgamated Tulip Corp. (affiliate of Dharma Records)
Americana Records, Inc. (unable to contact)
Amherst Records
Angel Star Records (affiliate of Country Breeze Records)
A1A Records
Ariana Records
Audem Records
B.P.M. Productions
BCM-USA
Best West Productions
Big Bear Records
Big K Records
Boom/Power Play Records
Brier Patch Music (requested deletion)
The Calvary Music Group
Canyon Creek Records
The CCC Group, Inc.

CDE Records and Tapes
Century City Records and Tapes of Canada
Century Records, Inc. (not accepting submissions)
City Pigeon Records
Clay & Clay, Inc. (requested deletion)
Cloudburst Records
Clown Records
Concorde International Records (requested deletion)
Cowgirl Records
Creole Records, Ltd. (affiliate of Rhino Records Ltd.)
Crystal Ram/April Records
Current Records
Curtiss Records (affiliate of Terock Records)
D.J. International, Inc.
Dark Horse Productions
Dharma Records
Disques Nosferatu Records
Dynamite
East Coast Records Inc.
Executive Records (charges to review)

Factory Beat Records, Inc.
Famous Door Records
Finer Arts Records/Transworld Records (charges to review)
Gallery II Records, Inc. (affiliate of Playback Records)
GCS Records
Global Record Co.
Golden Boy Records
Green Linnet Records
Guerrilla Records
Hacienda Records
Hard Hat Records and Cassettes (does not use outside material)
Hazardous Records
Heart Beat Records
Heart Land Records
Heavy Metal Records
IHS Records
Imaginary Records
Janet Marie Recording
Justin Time Records Inc.
KAM Executive Records (charges to review)
Kilgore Records (requested deletion)

Lana Records/Nugget Records
Liphone Records
Main Tripp Records Inc.
Marz Records (no longer in business)
Maxx Records (not accepting submissions)
MDS Entertainment
Mercury Records
Microstar Records
MSM Records
Musicland Productions (no longer a record company)
Nadine Music
Neon Records (unable to contact)
New Beginning Record Productions
Osprey Entertainment Group, Inc.
Parade
Plankton Records
Playbones Records
Positive Feedback Studios
Premiere Records
Presidential Enterprises Ltd.
Prestation Music
Prime Cut Records
Prince/SF Productions (not accepting submissions)
Pristine Records (affiliate of Pleasure Records)

Rabadash Records Inc.
Radioactive Records (requested deletion)
Razor Records (no longer in business)
Record Company of the South (requested deletion)
Red Bus Records (Int.) Ltd.
Ridgewood Records (affiliate of Playback Records)
Rock City Records
Rodell Records
Rosewood Records (requested deletion)
Round Sound Music (requested deletion)
Rowena Records
RTP International
Saturn Records
Score Productions
Shanachie Records
Signature Records
Silver Jet Records (requested deletion)
Sony Music (not accepting submissions)
Sounds of Winchester (affiliate of Alear Records)
Source Records, Inc.
Source Unlimited Records
Southern Tracks Records
Star Record Co.

Starman Records
Stress Records
Studio Records Inc.
Studioeast Recording, Inc.
Sun Dance Records
Sundown Records
Sunset Records Inc.
Sureshot Records
Tabitha Records
3 G's Industries
Timeless Entertainment Corp.
Tomark Records
Tommy Boy Music, Inc.
Top Trax (charges to review)
Ugly Dog Records (not signing new artists)
Vicor Music Corp.
Virgin Boy Records
Watchesgro Music (affiliate of Interstate 40 Records)
Wedge Records
Westpark Music - Records, Production & Publishing
Wild Pitch Records Ltd.
Wilson's Music Co.; Maurice/NE Productions (charges to review)
Winchester Records (affiliate of Alear Records)
Wings Record Company

Record Producers

The independent producer can best be described as a creative coordinator. He's usually the one with the most creative control over the recording project and is ultimately responsible for the finished product. Although some larger record companies have their own in-house producers, it's more common for a record company today to contract out-of-house, independent producers for recording projects.

Producers can be valuable contacts for songwriters because they work so closely with the artists whose records they produce. They are usually creative and artistic people, typically with a lot more freedom than others in executive positions, and they are known for having a good ear for hit song potential. Many producers are songwriters, musicians and artists themselves. Since they have the most influence on a particular project, a good song in the hands of the producer at the right time stands a good chance of being cut. And even if the producer is not working on a specific project, they are well-acquainted with record company executives and artists, and they can often get material through doors not open to you.

Even so, it can be difficult to get your tapes to the right producer at the right time. Many producers write their own songs and even if they don't write, they might be involved in their own publishing companies so they have instant access to all the songs in their catalogs. It's important to understand the intricacies of the producer/publisher situation. If you pitch your song directly to a producer first, before another publishing company publishes the song, the producer may ask you for the publishing rights (or a percentage thereof) to your song. You must decide whether the producer is really an active publisher who will try to get the song recorded again and again, or whether he merely wants the publishing because it means extra income for him from the current recording project. You may be able to work out a co-publishing deal, where you and the producer split the publishing of the song. That means he will still receive his percentage of the publishing income, even if you secure a cover recording of the song by other artists in the future. But, even though you would be giving up a little bit initially, you may benefit in the future.

The listings that follow outline which aspects of the music industry each producer is involved in, what type of music he is looking for, what records and artists he's recently produced and what artists he produces on a regular basis. Study the listings carefully, noting the artists he works with, and consider if any of your songs might fit a particular artist's or producer's style.

A & R RECORDING SERVICES, 71906 Highway 111, Rancho Mirage CA 92270. (619)346-0075. Producer-Engineers: Wade Perluss and John Shipley. Record producer. Estab. 1978. Deals with artists. Fee derived from sales royalty when song or artist is recorded, outright fee from recording artist and outright fee from record company.

How to Contact: Submit demo tape by mail—unsolicited submissions are OK. Prefers cassette (or VHS videocassette if available) with 4 songs and lyric or lead sheets. SASE. Reports in 1 month.

Music: Mostly **pop, country** and **gospel;** also **rock.** Produced *It's In Your Hands,* written and recorded by Gloria Weigand on Accent Records; and "Nothing's Missing", written and recorded by John C. Shipley on S&R Records. Other artists include Steve Henderson, Cherie Hall and Jon Kodi.

"A" MAJOR SOUND CORPORATION, Suite 421, 49 Thorncliffe Park Dr., Toronto, Ontario M4H 1J6 **Canada.** (416)423-9046. Record Producer: Paul C. Milner. Record producer and recording engineer. Estab. 1985. Deals with artists and songwriters. Fee derived from sales royalty when song or artist is recorded, or outright fee from recording artist or record company.

How to Contact: Submit demo tape by mail—unsolicited submissions are OK. Prefers cassette (or DAT) with 3-4 songs and lyric sheet. Reports in 2 months.

Music: Mostly **rock, pop** and **metal;** also **R&B** and **gospel.** Produced *Assimilation* (by D. Mal/I. Ritchie), recorded by Paul Milner on Current/MCA Records; "Resurrection" (by A. Pricesmith) and *Heroes and Legends* (by K. Herdman/B. Boychick), both recorded by Paul Milner on INDI Records. Other artists include Hokus Pick Manouver, The Burns and Freshwater Drum.

Tips: "Strong pre-production is the key to developing a strong product."

A STREET MUSIC, Dept. SM, 445 W. 45th. St., New York NY 10036. (212)903-4773. A&R Director: K. Hall. Record producer, music publisher (A Street Music/ASCAP). Estab. 1986. Produces 6 LPs, 1 EP and 5 CDs/year. Deals with artists and songwriters. Fee derived from sales royalty or outright fee from recording artist or record company.

How to Contact: Submit demo tape—unsolicited submissions are OK. Prefers cassette or DAT with 3 songs. Lyric sheets optional. Reports in 1-2 months. Artists send pictures. *SASE only* will receive reply; include adequate postage for tape return if desired. Reports in 1-2 months.

Music: Mostly **rock, heavy metal, alternative rock** and **pop/rock;** will listen to **R&B, R&B/pop** and **dance.** Produced "Feeding Time At The Zoo" (by Nicarry/Strauss), recorded by Ripper Jack on A Street Records (heavy rock); "Zeudus" (by Weikle), recorded by Zeudus on A Street Records (heavy instrumental rock); and "Return To You" (by Brad Mason), recorded by Debbie O. on A Street Records (pop/blues). Other artists include The Mercuries, Parrish Blue, Rockamatic Street Kid and Donatello.

Tips: "Don't over-produce your demo; we want to hear the song. A good vocalist will help. Enclose an SASE."

ABERDEEN PRODUCTIONS, (A.K.A. Scott Turner Productions), 524 Doral Country Dr., Nashville TN 37221. (615)646-9750. President: Scott Turner. Record producer and music publisher (Buried Treasure/ASCAP, Captain Kidd/BMI). Estab. 1971. Deals with artists and songwriters. Works with 30 new songwriters/year. Produces 10 singles, 15-20 12″ singles, 8 LPs and 8 CDs/year. Fee derived from sales royalty and production fee.

How to Contact: Submit demo tape—unsolicited submissions OK. Prefers cassette with maximum 4 songs and lead sheet. SASE. Reports in 2 weeks.

Music: Mostly **country, MOR** and **rock;** also **top 40/pop.** Produced "I Will" (by S.C. Rose), recorded by Roy Clark, Mel Tillis and Bobby Bare on Hallmark Records (country); "Appalachian Blue" (by S.C. Rose), recorded by Roy Clark (country); and "Coming to My Senses" (by Audie Murphy, S. Turner, M. Jaden), recorded by Jim Cartwright (country). Other artists include Slim Whitman, Jonathan Edwards, Don Malena, Hal Goodson, Jimmy Clanton, Bobby Lewis and Del Reeves.

Tips: "Be unique. A great song doesn't care who sings it . . . but there is a vast difference between a good song and a great song."

*ACR PRODUCTIONS, P.O. Box 5236, Lubbock TX 79417-5236. (806)792-3804. Owner: Dwaine Thomas. Record producer, music publisher (Joranda Music/BMI) and record company (ACR Records). Estab. 1986. Deals with artists and songwriters. Produces 120 singles, 8-15 12″ singles, 25 LPs, 25 EPs and 25 CDs/year. Fee derived from sales royalty. "We charge for in-house recording only. Remainder is derived from royalties."

How to Contact: Submit demo tape by mail. Unsolicited submissions are OK. Prefers cassette (or VHS videocassette if available) with 5 songs and lyric sheet. Does not return unsolicited material. Reports in 6 weeks.

Music: Mostly **country swing, pop** and **rock**; also **R&B** and **gospel**. Produced *Shattered Dreams* and *Rodeo Cowboy* (by Dwaine Thomas); also *Break The Fall* (by Jerry Brownlon), all on ACR Records. Other artists include Rodeoactive (country band.)

ACTIVE SOUND PRODUCTIONS, Dept. SM, 64 W. Cedar St., Boston MA 02114. (617)269-0104. Owner: Larry Lessard. Record producer and recording studio. Estab. 1981. Deals with artists and songwriters. Produces 5 singles, 2 12″ singles, 3 LPs, 2 EPs and 2 CDs/year. Fee derived from sales royalty when song or artist is recorded. Charges for studio time.
How to Contact: Submit demo tape by mail—unsolicited submissions are OK. Prefers cassette (or 15 IPS reel-to-reel or DAT videocassette) with 3-5 songs and lyric sheet. SASE. Reports in 1 month.
Music: Mostly **pop** (A/C), **dance** and **rock**; also **R&B**. Produced *FTS* (by Nick Gerboth), recorded by FTS on Major Label Records (alternative). Other artists include Candy Machine.
Tips: "Concentrate on melody. Make the song honest. Know what market you're trying to go for. But most of all have fun and do music that satisfies you."

AKO PRODUCTION, Dept. SM, 20531 Plummer, Chatsworth CA 91311. (818)998-0443. President: A. Sullivan. Record producer and music publisher (Amiron). Deals with artists and songwriters. Produces 2-6 singles and 2-3 LPs/year. Fee derived from sales royalty.
How to Contact: Write first and obtain permission to submit. Prefers cassette (or Beta or VHS videocassette) and lyric sheet. SASE.
Music: **Pop/rock** and **modern country**. Produced *Lies in Disguise*, by Gang Back (pop); and *Touch of Fire* and "Try Me" (pop) by Sana Christian; all on AKO Records.

ALLEN-MARTIN PRODUCTIONS INC., Dept. SM, 9701 Taylorville Rd., Louisville KY 40299. (502)267-9658. Audio Engineer: Nick Stevens. Record producer and music publisher (Always Alive Music, Bridges Music/ASCAP, BMI). Estab. 1965. Deals with artists. Produces 10 singles, 5 12″ singles, 20 LPs, 5 EPs and 20 CDs/year. Fee derived from sales royalty when song or artist is recorded, outright fee from recording artist or outright fee from record company.
How to Contact: Submit demo tape by mail. Unsolicited submissions are OK. Prefers cassette (or ¾ or ½ videocassette) with several songs and lyric sheet. Artist photo is desirable. Does not return material. Reports in 2 months.
Music: Mostly **country, gospel** and **pop**; also **rock, R&B** and **rap**. Produced *Delta*, written and recorded by Duke Robillaro on Rovrene Records (R&B LP); *Exquisite Fashion*, written and recorded by Duke Robillaro on X Mode Records (rock LP); and *More Praise* (by Harold Moore), recorded by Duke Robillaro on X Mode Records (gospel LP). Other artists include J.P. Pennington, Larnelle Harris, Turley Richards, Shaking Family and Michael Jonathon.

*STUART J. ALLYN, Skylight Run, Irvington NY 10533. (212)486-0856. Associate: Jack Walker. Record producer. Estab. 1972. Deals with artists and songwriters. Produces 6 singles, 3-6 LPs and 3-6 CDs/year. Fee derived from sales royalty and outright fee from recording artist and record company.
How to Contact: Write first and obtain permission to submit. Prefers DAT, CD, cassette or 15 ips reel-to-reel (VHS videocassette) with 3 songs and lyric or lead sheets. Does not return unsolicited material. Reports in 12 months.
Music: Mostly **pop, rock, jazz** and **theatrical**; also **R&B** and **country**. Produced *Winter in Lisbon* w/ Dizzy Gillespie, *Mel Lewis & Jazz Orchestra*, on Atlantic Records (jazz); *Me & Him*, on Columbia Records (film score); and "Set Sail & Sea Fans," on Passage Home Records (video release); hundreds of commercials and industrials, all recorded by S. Allyn. Other artists include Billy Joel, Aerosmith, Carole Demas, Harry Stone, Bob Stewart, The Dixie Peppers, Nora York, Buddy Barnes and various video and film scores.

ALPHA MUSIC PRODUCTIONS, Box 14701, Lenexa KS 66285. (913)441-8618. President: Glenn Major. Record producer, music publisher (Alpha House Publishing/BMI) and record company (AMP Records). Estab. 1982. Deals with artists and songwriters. Produces 5 singles, 2 LPs and 1 CD/year. Fee derived from sales royalty when song or artist is recorded.
How to Contact: Submit demo tape by mail—unsolicited submissions are OK. Prefers cassette (or VHS videocassette if available) with 3-5 songs and lyric sheet. Include cover letter, bio and pictures. Does not return unsolicited material. Reports in 2 months.

The asterisk before a listing indicates that the listing is new in this edition. New markets are often the most receptive to unsolicited submissions.

Music: Mostly **country, rock** and **folk.** Produced *Repossesed My Heart* (by Jerry Dowell), recorded by 7 Thunders Band on Thunderhorse Records; *Scared Out of My Shoes* (by Chubby Smith), recorded by Chubby Smith Orchestra; and "Never Been to Nashville" (by Rick Hasley), recorded by Cowboy X, both on AMP Records. Other artists include the Jolly Rogers and Tall Tales.
Tips: "Be realistic in your expectations. Get lots of opinions from your peers."

BUZZ AMATO, 2310-D Marietta Blvd., Atlanta GA 30318. (404)355-0909. Producer: Buzz Amato. Record producer and record company (Ichiban, Gold Key, Curton, J&S). Estab. 1987. Deals with artists. Produces 8 singles, 4 12″ singles, 10 LPs and 4 CDs/year. Fee derived from sales royalty when song or artist is recorded.
How to Contact: Write first and obtain permission to submit. Prefers cassette with 3 songs and lyric or lead sheets. "List how material was cut—instruments, outboard, tape format, etc." SASE. Reports in 2 months.
Music: Mostly **R&B (urban), blues** and **pop;** also **jazz.** Produced *Love Dance,* written and recorded by Bob Thompson; "Headed Back to Hurtsville", written and recorded by Theodis Ealey; both on Ichiban Records; and *TSOP* (by Gambol/Hoff), recorded by Three Degrees on Sony Music. Other artists include The Impressions, Vernon Garrett, Ben E. King and Scott Topper.
Tips: "Pay attention to the artist and styles when sending demos. Too many times a writer will send material that has nothing to do with what that artist is about."

AMETHYST RECORDS, INC., Box 82158, Oklahoma City OK 73148. (405)794-2481. General Manager: Russell Canaday. Record company (Amethyst Records, Inc.). Estab. 1988. Deals with artists and songwriters. Produces 10 singles, 25 LPs, 3 EPs and 3 CDs/year. Recording cost derived from recording artist or Amethyst company. "If artist is unknown, we sometimes charge an outright fee. It depends on exposure and work."
How to Contact: Submit demo tape by mail—unsolicited submissions are OK. Prefers cassette with 3 songs and lyric or lead sheets. SASE. Reports in 3 months.
Music: Mostly **country, gospel, easy listening;** also **R&B.** Produced "Going on With My Jesus" recorded by Wanda Jackson; *Blues Man* (by Hank Williams, Jr.), recorded by Henson Cargi (country); and "Higher" (by Mark Bryan) recorded by Sherman Andrus (gospel), all on Amethyst Records. Other artists include Cissie Lynn, Wanda Jackson, Rita King and several Oklahoma Opry artists.
Tips: "Have one or two of your best songs professionally recorded so the prospective listener will understand more about the song and its production style."

*ANCIENT FUTURE MUSIC, P.O. Box 264, Kentfield CA 94914-0264. (415)459-1892. Producer: Matthew Montfort. Record producer. "Ancient Future is a world music group. Ancient Future Music publishes books on world music instruction." Estab. 1979. Deals with artists and songwriters. Produces 1 LP and 1 CD/year. Fee derived from sales royalty when song or artist is recorded, outright fee from recording artist or outright fee from record company.
How to Contact: Submit demo tape by mail. Unsolicited submissions are OK. Prefers cassette. "Recording quality not important, but musicianship and performance is." Does not return unsolicited material. Reports in 4 months.
Music: Mostly **world music, cross-cultural music** and **foreign language songs** *if* instrumentally excellent. Produced *Dusk Song of the Fishermen* (traditional), recorded by Zhao Hui on Narada Equinox Records; *El Gatillo of El Amadillo,* written and recorded by Ancient Future on Narada Collection Records; and *Amber,* written and recorded by Matthew Montfort, on Narada Lotus Records.
Tips: "Only submit material based on world music. High quality musicianship is important."

WARREN ANDERSON, Dept. SM, 2207 Halifax Cres NW, Calgary Alta. T2M 4E1 **Canada.** (403)282-2555. Producer/Manager: Warren Anderson. Record producer (Century City Music-SOCAN) and record company (Century City Records). Estab. 1983. Deals with artists and songwriters. Produces 1-6 singles, 1-2 LPs, 1-2 EPs and 1-2 CDs/year. Fee derived from sales royalty (typically 2%) and/or outright fee from record company.
How to Contact: Write first and obtain permission to submit. Prefers cassette (or VHS videocassette) with 4 songs and lyric or lead sheet. SASE. Reports in 4 weeks.
Music: Mostly **country rock, rock** and **folk rock;** also **alternative, jazz** and **C&W.** Produced "Angel" (by Warren Anderson), recorded by Fran Thieven on Bros. Records; "Hot from the Streets" (by Warren Anderson) recorded by Robert Bartlett on Century City Records; "1000 Miles Away" (by Damian Follett), recorded by Warren Anderson on Century City Records; all rock.
Tips: "Rockers moved over to C&W and took it places that the cowboy wouldn't recognize. I'm into Chris Isaak, Steve Earl, Blue Rodeo, k.d. lang, Roger McGuinn, John Cougar Mellencamp. I'm into pushing the envelope of country rock into the 21st century."

Listings of companies in countries other than the U.S. have the name of the country in boldface type.

ANDREW & FRANCIS, P.O. Box 882, Homewood IL 60430-0882. (708)258-3312. (708)755-1323. Contact: Brian Kalan. Record producer and management agency. Estab. 1984. Deals with artists and songwriters. Produces 4 LPs, 5 EPs and 1 CD/year.
How to Contact: Submit demo tape by mail—unsolicited submissions are OK. Prefers cassette (or VHS videocassette if available) with 1-3 songs and lyric sheet. "Don't be afraid to submit! We are here to help you by reviewing your material for possible representation or production." Does not return unsolicited material. Reports in 2 months.
Music: Mostly **rock (commercial)**, **hard rock** and **dance rock**; also **classical guitar, instrumental rock** and **solo guitar**. Produced "Let Me In," "You're the Good and Bad" and "Keri", all written by B.F. Clifford and recorded by Blake. Other artists include Pat O'Donnell (Irish folk), James Glowiak (disco/dance), Mike Martis (rock) and Johnny O.D. (rap).
Tips: "Song content is *very* important, whether it be a catchy hook/riff or a great story. If we can find a saleable element within your song, we will put our experience into bringing that element to the forefront. Focus on content, we will focus on displaying it."

ANGEL FILMS COMPANY, 967 Hwy 40, New Franklin MO 65247-9778. (314)698-3900. Vice President Production: Matthew Eastman. Record producer and record company (Angel One). Estab. 1980. Deals with artists and songwriters. Produces 5 LPs, 5 EPs and 5 CDs/year. Fee derived from sales royalty when song or artist is recorded.
How to Contact: Submit demo tape by mail—unsolicited submissions are OK. Prefers cassette (or VHS videocassette if available) with 3 songs. "Send only original material, not previously recorded, and include a bio sheet on artist." SASE. Reports in 1 month.
Music: Mostly **pop**, **rock** and **rockabilly**; also **jazz** and **R&B**. Produced *Faerie Ring*, written and recorded by Cat Arkin; *Mal Du Mare* (by James Bently), recorded by Kelly So; and *The Muny* (by Julian James), recorded by Linda Eastman, all on Angel One Records.
Tips: "Send us your best work. It doesn't need to be overworked. Just keep it simple, because expense to produce something doesn't make it better."

APON RECORD COMPANY, INC., P.O. Box 3082, Steinway Station, Long Island City NY 11103. (718)721-5599. Manager: Don Zemann. Record producer and music publisher (Apon Publishing). Estab. 1957. Deals with artists and songwriters. Produces 100 singles, 50 LPs and 50 CDs/year. Fee derived from sales royalty and outright fee from recording artist.
How to Contact: Write or call first and obtain permission to submit. Prefers cassette with 2-6 songs and lyric sheet. Does not return unsolicited material. Reports in 1-2 months.
Music: **Classical, folk, Spanish, Slavic, polka** and **Hungarian gypsy (international folk music)**. Produced *Czech Polkas* (by Slavko Kunst), recorded by Prague Singers on Apon Records; "Hungarian Gypsy" (by Deki Lakatos), recorded by Budapest on Apon Records; and "Polka - Dance With Me" (by Slavko Kunst), recorded by Prague on Apon Records.

*AROUND SOUNDS PUBLISHING (ASCAP), 4572 150th Ave. NE, Redmond WA 98052. (206)881-9322. Fax: (206)881-3645. Contact: Lary 'Larz' Nefzger. Estab. 1981. Deals with artists and songwriters. Produces 8 LPs and 8 CDs/year. Fee depends on negotiated agreement.
How to Contact: Write or call first and obtain permission to submit.

aUDIOFILE TAPES, 209-25 18th Ave., Bayside NY 11360. Sheriff, aT County: Carl Howard. Cassette-only label of alternative music. Estab. 1984. Deals with artists and songwriters. Produces about 25 cassettes/year. "Money is solely from sales. Some artists ask $1 per tape sold."
How to Contact: Submit demo tape by mail—unsolicited submissions are OK. Prefers cassette. "Relevant artist information is nice. Master copies accepted on metal cassette. SASE. Reports in 3-5 weeks.
Music: Mostly **psych/electronic rock**, **non-rock electronic music**, **progressive rock**; also **free jazz** and **world music**. Produced "Guilt Trip," recorded by Ron Anderson; "Magnavido," recorded by Screamin' Popeyes and "Live Bootleg from Switzerland," recorded by Ulterior Lux, all on audiofile Tapes. Other artists include Through Black Holes Band, Nomuzic, Alien Planetscapes, Doug Michael & The Outer Darkness, and Mental Anguish.
Tips: "Please, no industrial music, no deliberately shocking images of racism and sexual brutality. And no New Age sleeping pills. Unfortunately, we are not in a position to help the careers of aspirant pop idols. Only true devotees *really* need apply."

*AUGUST NIGHT MUSIC, P.O. Box 676 Station U, Etobicoke (Toronto), Ontario M8Z 5P7 **Canada**. (416)233-0547. Professional Manager/Producer: Denis D'Aoust. Record producer, record company (Whippet Records), music publisher, recording studio (MIDI Suite). Estab. 1988. Deals with artists and songwriters. Produces 6-10 singles and 1 LP/year. Fee derived from sales royalty when song or artist is recorded, or outright fee from recording artist. "Large projects require 50% deposit based on per song fee."

How to Contact: Submit demo tape by mail. Unsolicited submissions are OK. Prefers cassette (or VHS videocassette if available) with 3-4 songs and lyric sheet. "Be as professional as possible when dealing with professionals." SASE. Reports in 3 weeks.

Music: Mostly **pop/rock, ballads, country;** also **R&B, New Age.** Produced *Don't Let Your Heart Break* (by Dan Alksnis), recorded by Denny Doe (MOR); "Solitary Blue" (by Dan Hartland), recorded by Kathryn Eve (country); and *If We Could Start Again* (by D'Aoust/Courville), recorded by Denny Doe (light rock) all on Whippet Records. Other artists include Dan Hartland and Ric Marrero.

Tips: "Take a hint from Billboard charts, listen to as many songs as possible, in your style, and be willing to accept other peoples' opinions which would help turn your songs into hits."

AURORA PRODUCTIONS, 7415 Herrington N.E., Belmont MI 49306. Producer: Jack Conners. Record producer and engineer/technician. Big Rock Records and Ocean Records. Estab. 1984. Deals with artists and songwriters. Produces 2 singles, 2 LPs and 1 CD/year. Fee derived from outright fee from recording artist.

How to Contact: Write first and obtain permission to submit. Prefers cassette with 1 song. Does not return unsolicited material. Reports in 3 weeks.

Music: Mostly **classical, folk** and **jazz;** also **pop/rock** and **New Age.** Produced "Peace On Earth" (by John & Danny Murphy), recorded by The Murphy Brothers on Ocean Records (single); "Swimmer's Song," written and recorded by Steve Turner on Ocean Records (single); and *The Burdons*, written and recorded by The Burdons on Big Rock (LP).

*SUZAN BADER/D.S.M. PRODUCERS, 161 W. 54th St., New York NY 10019. (212)245-0006. Director of A&R: Ms. E.T. Toast. Contact: Associate Producer. Record producer, music publisher (ASCAP) and music library. Estab. 1979. Deals with artists and songwriters. Produces 3-5 12″ singles, 3 LPs and 20 CDs/year. Fee derived from sales royalty.

How to Contact: Write first and obtain permission to submit. Prefers cassette (or VHS videocassette) with 2 songs and lyric or lead sheets. SASE. Reports in 2-3 months.

Music: Mostly **dance, rock** and **pop;** also **country, jazz** and **instrumental.** Produced "You Don't Own Me," recorded by Aggie O and "Tell Your Mother" (by S. Aims/E. Rosa/L. Wagner), recorded by Aggie O, both on AACL Records; and "Little Bo Peep" (by S. Aims/E. Rosa/P. Mutzek), recorded by S. Aims/P. Mutzek. Other artists include Frank Lakewood (saxophone); Celeste (vocalist); Mark Cohen; Manny Garcia.

Tips: "Have your manager or lawyer contact us to produce you. If you are a new artist, follow the above procedure. It's getting more difficult for an artist who cannot present a master demo to a label. You're going to need financing in the future. Prepare."

BAL RECORDS, Box 369, LaCanada CA 91012-0369. (818)548-1116. President: Adrian Bal. Record producer and music publisher (Bal & Bal Music). Estab. 1965. Bal West estab. 1988. Deals with artists and songwriters. Produces 3-6 singles/year. Fee derived from sales royalty.

How to Contact: Submit demo tape by mail—unsolicited submissions are OK. Prefers cassette with 3 songs and lyric sheet. SASE. Reports in 6+ weeks.

Music: Mostly **MOR, country, jazz, R&B, rock** and **top 40/pop;** also **blues, church/religious, easy listening** and **soul.** Produced "Right To Know" and "Fragile" (by James Jackson), recorded by Kathy Simmons on BAL Records (rock); "Dance To The Beat of My Heart" (by Dan Gertz), recorded by Ace Baker on BAL Records (rock); and "You're A Part of Me," "Can't We Have Some Time Together," "You and Me," and "Circles of Time," written and recorded by Paul Richards on BAL Records (A/C).

Tips: "Write and compose what you believe to be commercial."

*BARTOW MUSIC, (formerly Homeboy/Ragtime Productions), 324 N. Bartow St., Cartersville GA 30120. (404)386-7243. Art Director: "Decky D" Maxwell. Record producer. Estab. 1988. Deals with artists and songwriters. Produces 3 singles, 1 12″ single and 1 LP/year. Fee derived from sales royalty.

How to Contact: Submit demo tape by mail. Unsolicited submissions are okay. Prefers cassette with 3 songs and lyric sheet. SASE. Reports in 1 month.

Music: Mostly **R&B, dance, rap, house** and **pop.** Produced "Rub It" and "Emerson Girl" (by Derrick Maxwell), recorded by D.G.I. Posse (rap); "Give You All My Love" and "Forever" (by Austin Hall), recorded by Daybreak (R&B), all recorded on Westview Records.

BAY FARM PRODUCTIONS, Box 2821, Duxbury MA 02364. (617)585-9470. Producer: Paul Caruso. Record producer and in-house 24-track recording facility. Estab. 1985. Deals with artists and songwriters. Produces 6 singles, 4 LPs, 2 EPs and 6 CDs/year. Fee derived from sales royalty when song or artist is recorded, outright fee from recording artist, or outright fee from record company.

How to Contact: Submit demo tape by mail—unsolicited submissions are OK. Prefers cassette or VHS videocassette with 3 songs and lyric sheet. "Please use a high quality cassette." SASE. Reports in 1-2 months.

Music: A/C, folk, pop, dance and R&B. Produced *Sweet Perfume*, recorded by Les Sampou (folk/blues); *Dancing in the Mystery*, recorded by Becky Williams (folk/pop/AC); and *Waiting For The Moon*, recorded by Kathy Hayden (folk/pop/AC). Other artists include Ali London, Fuego Latino and Tria.
Tips: "We specialize in producing individual solo artists in the new acoustic, folk, pop, A/C vein. Our clients benefit from intensive pre-production and outstanding studio musicians."

*THE BEAU-JIM AGENCY, INC., Box 2401, Sarasota FL 34230. President: Buddy Hooper. Record producer and music publisher (Beau-Jim Music, Inc.—ASCAP; Beau-Di Music, Inc.—BMI). Deals with artists and songwriters. Produces 4 singles and 1 LP/year.
How to Contact: Prefers cassette (or videocassette) with 3-5 songs and lyric sheet. SASE. Reports in 3 weeks.
Music: Mostly country.

BELL RECORDS INTERNATIONAL, Box 725, Daytona Beach FL 32115-0725. (904)252-4849. President: LeRoy Pritchett. Record producer, music publisher and record company (Bell Records International). Estab. 1985. Deals with artists and songwriters. Produces 12 singles, 12 LPs and 12 CDs/year. Fee derived from sales royalty when song or artist is recorded.
How to Contact: Write first and obtain permission to submit. Prefers cassette.
Music: Mostly R&B, gospel and rock; also country and pop. Produced *Hot In The Gulf* (R&B LP by Billy Brown) and *Hold To God's Hand* (gospel LP by James Martin), both recorded by Charles Vickers on Bell Records. Other artists include Bobby Blue Blane and Little Anthony.

HAL BERNARD ENTERPRISES, INC., P.O. Box 8385, Cincinnati OH 45208. (513)871-1500. Fax: (513)871-1510. President: Stan Hertzman. Record producer and music publisher (Sunnyslope Music Inc. and Bumpershoot Music Inc.). Deals with artists and songwriters. Produces 5 singles and 3-4 LPs/year. Fee derived from sales royalty.
How to Contact: Prefers cassette with 1-3 songs and lyric sheet. SASE. Reports in 1 month.
Music: Produced *Inner Revolution*, by Adrian Belew on Atlantic Records; *On The Grid*, recorded by psychodots on Strugglebaby Records; and *Young and Rejected*, recorded by Prizoner on Strugglebaby Records.

RICHARD BERNSTEIN, 2170 S. Parker Rd., Denver CO 80231. (303)755-2613. Contact: Richard Bernstein. Record producer, music publisher (M. Bernstein Music Publishing Co.) and record label. Deals with artists and songwriters. Produces 6 singles, 2 12″ singles, 6 LPs and 6 CDs/year. Fee derived from sales royalty, outright fee from songwriter/artist and/or outright fee from record company.
How to Contact: Prefers cassette and lyric or lead sheets. Does not return unsolicited material. Reports in 6-8 weeks.
Music: Rock, jazz and country.
Tips: "No telephone calls *please*."

BIG BEAR, Box 944, Birmingham, B16 8UT, **United Kingdom**. Phone: 44-21-454-7020. Managing Director: Jim Simpson. Record producer, music publisher (Bearsongs) and record company (Big Bear Records). Works with lyricists and composers; teams collaborators. Produces 10 LPs/year. Fee derived from sales royalty.
How to Contact: Write first about your interest, then submit demo tape and lyric sheet. Reports in 2 weeks.
Music: Blues and jazz.

BIG PICTURE RECORD CO., #7A, 101 E. 9th Ave., Anchorage AK 99501. (907)279-6900. Producer/Owner: Patric D'Eimon. Record producer and record company (Big Picture Records). Estab. 1983. Deals with artists and songwriters. Produces 5 LPs/year. Fee derived from outright fee from recording artist or record company.
How to Contact: Submit demo tape by mail. Unsolicited submissions are OK. Prefers cassette or VHS videocassette with 4 songs and lyric sheet. Does not return unsolicited material. Reports in 3 weeks.
Music: Mostly country, pop/rock, R&B; also folk, New Age, "in between styles." Produced "Quiet As A Mouse" written and recorded by Patric D'Eimon on Big Picture Records.
Tips: "Educate yourselves in the recording/production process."

BIG PRODUCTIONS AND PUBLISHING CO. INC., Suite 308, 37 E. 28th St., New York NY 10016. (212)447-6000. Fax: (212)447-6003. President: "Big" Paul Punzone. Record producer, music publisher (Humongous Music Publishing/ASCAP) and record company (Big Productions). Estab. 1989. Deals with artists and songwriters. Produces 12 12″ singles/year. Fee derived from sales royalty when song or artist is recorded, and outright fee from recording artist or record company. Charges upfront "only when hired for independent projects."

How to Contact: Write or call first to arrange personal interview. Prefers cassette with 3 songs and lyric sheet. "We are looking for artists and independent productions for release on Big Productions Records. Artists will be signed as a production deal to shop to other labels. We mainly release 12″ house tracks on Big Productions Records." SASE. Reports in 6 weeks.
Music: Mostly **house, hip-hop** and **pop/dance**. Produced "Big House" (by P. Punzone/H. Romero) and "Mission Accomplished" (by P. Punzone/B. Fisher/G. Sicard), both recorded by Big Baby; and "Loose Flutes" (by P.Punzone/B. Fisher/G. Sicard), recorded by Picture Perfect, all on Big Productions Records (all house 12″ singles). Also produced Charm, on Atlantic Records.
Tips: "Please submit only musical styles listed. We want finished masters of 12″ house material."

BLAZE PRODUCTIONS, 103 Pleasant Ave., Upper Saddle River NJ 07458. (201)825-1060. Record producer, music publisher (Botown Music) and management firm. Estab. 1978. Deals with artists and songwriters. Fee derived from sales royalty, outright fee from recording artist or record company.
How to Contact: Submit demo tape by mail—unsolicited submissions are OK. Prefers cassette (or VHS videocassette) with 1 or more songs and lyric sheet. Does not return unsolicited material. Reports in 3 weeks.
Music: **Pop, rock** and **dance**. Produced *Anything Can Happen*, by Voices; "Point of A Hulk" (by Peace/ Stevens), recorded by AK Peace; and "For Now," written and recorded by Blaze, all on Botown Records.

PETER L. BONTA, 2200 Airport Ave., Fredericksburg VA 22401. (703)373-6511. Studio Manager: Buffalo Bob. Record producer. Estab. 1980. Deals with artists and songwriters. Produces 8-12 singles, 5-8 LPs and 4-6 CDs/year. Fee derived from sales royalty, outright fee from recording artist or record company.
How to Contact: Write or call first and obtain permission to submit. Prefers cassette with 3-4 songs and lyric sheet. SASE. Reports in 6 weeks.
Music: Mostly **roots rock, country rock** and **blues**; also **country** and **bluegrass**. Produced *Call The Law*, written and recorded by Tom Principato, on Powerhouse Records; *It Ain't Me* (by Buffalo Bob), recorded by Buffalo Bob & The Heard on Greek Bros Records; and *Breakin' In a Brand New Heart* (by J. Kupersmith), recorded by Virginia Rose. Other artists include Billy Hancock, Lovesake, Tattoo Tribe, Little Ronnie & The Bluebeats, On Edge and Donnie Preston.

*BONY "E" PRODUCTIONS, INC., Joyce Avenue, Atlanta GA 30032. (404)286-1488. President: Edgar Anthony/Robin Jones. Record producer. Estab. 1980. Produces 15 singles/year. Fee derived from outright fee from recording artist or outright fee from record company.
How to Contact: Write or call first and obtain permission to submit or to arrange personal interview. Prefers cassette with 4-6 songs and lyric or lead sheet. Does not return unsolicited material. Reports in 4-6 weeks.
Music: Mostly **R&B, hip-hop** and **rap**; also **pop, rock** and **gospel**. Artists include Wendell Brown, Rodney James, Tab Money.
Tips: "Believe in what it is you're doing and hard work will definitely pay off."

BOOM PRODUCTIONS, INC., Dept. SM, 200 Regent Dr., Winston-Salem NC 27103. (919)768-1881. President: Dave Passerallo. Record producer, music publisher (DeDan Music/BMI) and record company (Boom/Power Play Records). Estab. 1989. Deals with artists and songwriters. Produces 2 singles, 2 LPs and 2 CDs/year. Fee derived from sales royalty.
How to Contact: Write first and obtain permission to submit. Prefers cassette (or VHS videocassette) with 2 songs and lead sheet. SASE. Reports in 2-3 weeks.
Music: Mostly **pop, rap** and **rock**. Produced "Ripped Jeans," by John Cody (pop); and "Guilty," by Paul Krege (rock/pop); both produced by Dave Passerallo on Boom Powerplay Records.
Tips: "Artist must be able to sign a production agreement."

ROBERT BOWDEN, Box 111, Sea Bright NJ 07760. President: Robert Bowden. Record producer, music publisher (Roots Music/BMI) and record company (Nucleus Records). Estab. 1979. Deals with artists and songwriters. Produces 3 singles and 1 LP/year. Fees derived from sales royalty.
How to Contact: Submit demo tape or write to arrange personal interview. Prefers cassette (or VHS videocassette if available) with 3 songs and lyric sheet. SASE. Reports in 1 month.
Music: Mostly **country**; also **pop**. Produced "Henrey C" and "Will You Miss Me Tonight" (by Bowden), recorded by Marco Sisison, all on Nucleus Records.

*BREADLINE PRODUCTIONS, Studio #3, 133 W. 14th St., New York NY 10011. (212)741-0165. Producer/Engineer: Gene Lavenue. Record producer. Estab. 1986. Deals with artists only. Produces 4 singles, 3 LPs and 3 CDs/year. Fee derived from sales royalty when song or artist is recorded, outright fee from recording artist or outright fee from record company.

How to Contact: Submit demo tape by mail. Unsolicited submissions are OK. Prefers cassette with 3 songs."Send the best quality tape. Portastudio recordings acceptable if they are of good quality." SASE. Reports in 3 weeks.

Music: Mostly **alternative** and **rock**. Produced debut records for Please and Me In A Box. Other artists include Indian Six, Brand New Fear, FIDO, Karen Ires.

Tips: "Send best quality tape and be original."

BRIEFCASE OF TALENT PRODUCTIONS, Suite 52, 1124 Rutland, Austin TX 78758. (512)832-1254. Owner: Kevin Howell. Record producer and live/recording engineer. Deals with artists. Produces 1 LP, 2 EPs and 1 CD/year. Fee derived from outright fee from recording artist or outright fee from record company.

How to Contact: Submit demo tape—unsolicited submissions OK. Prefers cassette (or VHS videocassette if available) with 4 songs and lyric sheet. Does not return unsolicited material. Reports in 2 months.

Music: Mostly **alternative progressive rock (classic)** and **heavy metal**; also **R&B**. Produced *Big Tim* and *Hell's Jazz*, written and recorded by Cold Six on Indus Records (jazz); and *Shut Her Mouth*, recorded by Blaze on Briefcase Records (rock).

Tips: "Eighty percent of the people listening to your submission are engineers of some sort, so a poor quality demo will not get past the first 30 seconds. Make it sound professional and as good as budget allows!"

RAFAEL BROM, Cosmotone Records, Suite 412, 3350 Highway 6, Houston TX 77478-4406. Producer: Rafael Brom. Record producer, music publisher (ASCAP), record company (Cosmotone Records). Estab. 1984. Deals with artists and songwriters. Produces 1 LP/year.

How to Contact: Write first to obtain permission to submit. Prefers cassette (or VHS videocassette if available) with several songs and lyric sheet. Does not return unsolicited material. "Will contact only if interested."

Music: All types. Produced "Padre Pio," "Sonnet XVIII," "The Sounds of Heaven," "Peace of Heart," "Dance For Padre Pio" and "The True Measure of Love", all written and recorded by Lord Hamilton on Cosmotone Records (Christian/rock pop). Other artists include Adrian Romero and Thomas Emmett Dufficy.

C.S.B. MIX INC., 50 Donna Court #11, Staten Island NY 10314. Contact: Carlton Batts. Record producer (The Bat Cave Recording Studio). Estab. 1989. Deals with artists and songwriters. Produces 15 singles, 4 12″ singles, 2 LPs and 1 EP/year. Fee derived from sales royalty when song or artist is recorded and outright fee from record company.

How to Contact: Submit demo tape by mail—unsolicited submissions are OK. Prefers cassette with 3 songs. "A picture and/or bio are a must!" Does not return unsolicited material. Reports in 2 weeks.

Music: Mostly **R&B, dance** and **hip-hop**; also **rap, jazz** and **pop**. Produced "Let It Flow" (by C. Batts), recorded by Troy Taylor on Motown Records (R&B/single); "Primetime" (by C. Batts), recorded by Jocelyn Brown on RCA Records (dance single); and "Thrills & Chills" (by C. Batts), recorded by Whitney Houston on Arista Records (R&B single). Other artists include Leslie Fine, The Boys Club, One on One and Alan Rules.

Tips: "Be ready to work your butt off."

*CAPITOL AD, MANAGEMENT & TALENT, 1300 Division St., Nashville TN 37203. (615)242-4722, (615)244-2440, (800)767-4984. Fax: (615)242-1177. Senior Producer: Robert Metzgar. Record producer, record company and music publisher (Aim High Music Co./ASCAP, Bobby & Billy Music Co./BMI, Aim High Records, Hot News Records, Platinum Plus Records, SHR Records). Estab. 1971. Deals with artists and songwriters. Produces 35 singles, 12-15 12″ singles, 20 LPs, 15 EPs and 35 CDs/year. Fee derived from sales royalty when song or artist is recorded, outright fee from recording artist, outright fee from record company, or from financial backer or investment group.

How to Contact: Submit demo tape by mail. Unsolicited submissions are OK. Prefers cassette (or videocassette) with 3-5 songs and lyric sheet. We are interested in hearing only from *serious* artist/songwriters. Does not return unsolicited material. Reports in 2 weeks to 1 month.

Music: Mostly **country music, gospel music** and **pop** and **R&B**; also **jazz, contemporary Christian** and **rock** and **pop-rock**. Produced *There's Another Man* (by Johnny Cash), recorded by Time/Warner Brothers; *Break Out The Good Stuff* (by Alan Jackson), recorded by Amherst Records/Inter; and *Half A Man* (by Willie Nelson), recorded by Time/Warner Brothers. Other artists include Carl Butler (CBS/Sony), Tommy Cash (Columbia), Mickey Jones (Capitol), Tommy Overstreet (MCA Records), Warner Mack (MCA Records), Bobby Enriquez (Sony/New York) and others.

Tips: "Every *hit artist* needs a *hit producer* to work with!"

PETER CARDINALI, Dept. SM, 12 Ecclesfield Dr., Scarborough, Ontario M1W 3J6 **Canada**. (416)494-2000. Record producer/arranger (Peter Cardinali Productions Inc./SOCAN) and music publisher (Cardster Music/BMI, SOCAN). Estab. 1975. Deals with artists and songwriters. Produces 6-8 singles, 4-5 12″ singles, 8-10 LPs and 8-10 CDs/year.
How to Contact: Write or call first and obtain permission to submit. Prefers cassette with 4-6 songs and lyric sheets. SASE. Reports within weeks.
Music: Mostly **pop, R&B, dance** and **funk/jazz.** Produced *Big Fat Soul*, written and recorded by John James on Attic/A&M Records (dance); "The Bear Walks" (by P. Cardinali/H. Marsh), recorded by Hugh Marsh on Duke St./WEA Records (R&B/jazz); and "Moments" (by J. Nessle), recorded by See on A&M Records (pop). Other artists include Rick James and Teena Marie.

CARLYLE PRODUCTIONS, 1217 16th Ave. South, Nashville TN 37212. (615)327-8129. President: Laura Fraser. Record producer, record company (Carlyle Records) and production company. Estab. 1986. Deals with artists and songwriters. Produces 6 singles and 6 LPs/CDs per year.
How to Contact: Submit demo tape by mail—unsolicited submissions are OK. Prefers cassette with 3 songs and lyric sheet. Does not return unsolicited material. Reports in 1 month.
Music: Mostly **rock, pop** and **country.** Produced "Orange Room" (by Michael Ake), recorded by The Grinning Plowman (pop/rock); *Sun* (by John Elliott), recorded by Dessau (dance); and *All Because of You*, written and recorded by Dorcha (rock), all on Carlyle Records.

CAROLINA PRIDE PRODUCTIONS, Dept. SM, Box 6, Rougemont NC 27572. (919)477-4077. Manager: Freddie Roberts. Record producer, music publisher (Freddie Roberts Music/BMI), record company, management firm and booking agency. Estab. 1967. Deals with artists, songwriters and session musicians. Produces 12 singles, 7 LPs, 2 EPs and 3 CDs/year. Fee derived from sales royalty.
How to Contact: Call or write first. Prefers 7½ ips reel-to-reel or cassette with 1-5 songs and lyric sheet. SASE. Reports in 5 weeks.
Music: Mostly **country, MOR** and **top 40/pop;** also **bluegrass, church/religious, gospel** and **country rock.** Produced "Restless Feeling," written and recorded by Rodney Hutchins (country/rock) on Catalina Records; "Empty" (by David Laws), recorded by Jerry Harrison (country) on Celebrity Circle Records; and "Redeemed" (by Jane Durham), recorded by The Roberts Family (Southern gospel) on Bull City Records. Other artists include Sleepy Creek, Lady Luck, Billy McKellar and C.J. Jackson.

EDDIE CARR, 900 10th Ave., Apt. 106, Nashville TN 37212-2125. (615)329-3991. President: Eddie Carr. Record producer, music publisher (Watchesgro Music) and record company (Interstate 40 Records). Estab. 1987. Deals with artists and songwriters. Produces 12 singles/year. Fee derived from sales royalty or outright fee from recording artist.
How to Contact: Submit demo tape by mail—unsolicited submissions are OK. Prefers cassette with 2 songs and lyric sheets. Does not return unsolicited submissions. Reports in 1 week.
Music: Mostly **country.** Produced "Bottom of a Mountain" (Soundwaves Records), "Fairy Tales" (Master Records), and "Cripple Cowboy" (Tracker #1 Records); all written and recorded by Don McKinnon. Movie and TV credits include "Young Guns of Texas," "The Story of Evil Knievel," "Alias Smith & Jones," *Cochise* and "Christopher Columbus Story." Other artists include Ripplin' Waters, Rosemary, Michael Angel, Chris Riley, Pete Tavarez, Sharon Hauge, Michael Jones, Marion Hammers; Frank Pilgrim and Chuck Carter.
Tips: "I want publishing on songs. Will try to place artist. It's costing more to break in new artists, so songs must be strong."

STEVE CARR, % Hit & Run Studios, 18704 Muncaster Rd., Rockville MD 20855. (301)948-6715. Owner/Producer: Steve Carr. Record producer (Hit & Run Studios). Estab. 1979. Deals with artists and songwriters. Produces 10 singles, 2 12″ singles, 8 LPs, 4 EPs and 10 CDs/year. Fee derived from outright fee from recording artist.
How to Contact: Write or call first and obtain permission to submit. Prefers cassette with 3 songs. "Do NOT send unsolicited material! Write name and phone number on cassette shell. Will call back if I can do anything with your material."
Music: Mostly **pop, rock** and **R&B;** also **country.** Produced/recorded *Billy Kemp* (by Billy Kemp), on Essential Records (LP); *Classic Rock*, written and recorded by various artists (oldies digital remaster) on Warner Bros. Records; "Frontier" (by R. Kelley), recorded by Frontier Theory on TOP Records (rock CD); *The Wolves* (by Band), on Top Records (LP); and "Bomb Squad" (by Lorenzo), on Their Own Records (single); all recorded by Hit & Run. Other artists include Beyond Words, Steve Nally/Deep End, Oho, Voodoo, Love Gods, Necrosis, Debra Brown and Universe. Produces and digitally remasters Time-Life Music's Rock n' Roll, Country Classics and R&B Series.

*CEDAR CREEK PRODUCTIONS, Suite 503, 44 Music Square E., Nashville TN 37203. (615)252-6916. Fax: (615)329-1071. President: Larry Duncan. Record producer, record company (Cedar Creek Records™), music publisher (Cedar Creek Music/BMI) and artist management. Estab. 1981. Deals with artists and songwriters. Produces 20 singles, 5 LPs and 5 CDs/year. Fee derived from outright fee from recording artist.

How to Contact: Submit demo tape by mail. Unsolicited submissions are OK. Prefers cassette (or VHS videocassette) with 4-6 songs and lyric sheet (typed). "Put return address and name on envelope. Put telephone number in packet." Does not return unsolicited material. Reports in 1 month.

Music: Mostly **country, country/pop** and **country/R&B**; also **pop, R&B** and **light rock**. Produced "Rough Road to Fame" and "Lifetime Affair," written and recorded by Larry Duncan, on Cedar Creek Records; and *One of the Good Ol' Boys* (by Debra McClure/Danny Neal/Tony Glenn Rast), recorded by Kym Wortham on ADD Records.

Tips: "Submit your best songs on a good fully produced demo or master."

JAN CELT, 4026 NE 12th Ave., Portland OR 97212. (503)287-8045. Owner: Jan Celt. Record producer, music publisher (Wiosna Nasza Music/BMI) and record company (Flying Heart Records). Estab. 1982. Deals with artists and songwriters. Produces 2 LPs, 1 EP and 2 CDs/year.

How to Contact: Submit demo tape by mail—unsolicited submissions are OK. Prefers cassette with 1-10 songs and lyric sheets. SASE. Reports in 4 months.

Music: Mostly **R&B, rock** and **blues**; also **jazz**. Produced "Voodoo Garden," written and recorded by Tom McFarland (blues); "Bong Hit" (by Chris Newman), recorded by Snow Bud & the Flower People (rock); and "She Moved Away" (by Chris Newman), recorded by Napalm Beach, all on Flying Heart Records. Other artists include The Esquires and Janice Scroggins.

Tips: "Be sure your lyrics are heartfelt; they are what makes a song your own. Abandon rigid stylistic concepts and go for total honesty of expression."

CHALLEDON PRODUCTIONS, 5th Floor, Pembroke One Bldg., Virginia Beach VA 23462. General Counsel: Richard Shapiro. Record producer and record company (Challedon Records). Estab. 1990. Deals with artists and songwriters. Fee derived from outright fee from record company.

How to Contact: Write first and obtain permission to submit. Prefers cassette (or VHS videocassette if available) with up to 3 songs and lyric sheet. Does not return unsolicited material. Reports in 1 month.

Music: Mostly **rock, pop** and **alternative/college rock**. Produced *Hired Gun* (by J. Sullivan), recorded by Challedon Productions at Master Sound on Challedon Records.

CHUCK CHAPMAN, Dept. SM, 228 W. 5th St., Kansas City MO 64105. (816)842-6854. Office Manager: Gary Sutton. Record producer and music publisher (Fifth Street Records/BMI). Estab. 1973. Deals with artists and songwriters. Fee derived from sales royalty when song or artist is recorded, outright fee from recording artist or outright fee from record company. "Charges upfront for recording only."

How to Contact: Write or call first and obtain permission to submit. Prefers cassette (or ½" or ¾" videocassette) with 3 songs and lyric sheet. Include SASE. Does not return material. Reports in 1 month.

Music: Mostly **country, gospel** and **rock**; also **rap, jazz** and **spoken word**. Produced "Rumor Has It" (by Sheli), recorded by Freddie Hunt on Fifth Street Records (country); and "Cold As Ashes" (by Lee Bruce), recorded by Montgomery Lee on Opal Records (country). Other artists include Conrad Morris and Eisel & The Haymakers.

CHROME DREAMS PRODUCTIONS, 5852 Sentinel St., San Jose CA 95120. (408)268-6066. Owner: Leonard Giacinto. Record producer. Estab. 1982. Deals with artists and songwriters. Produces 15 singles and 8 12″ singles/year. Fee derived from outright fee from recording artist.

How to Contact: Submit demo tape by mail—unsolicited submissions are OK. Write or call first to arrange personal interview. Prefers cassette (or ½" VHS videocassette if available). Does not return unsolicited material. Reports in 1 month.

Music: Mostly **rock, New Age, avant-garde** and **college radio**. Produced "Aluminum" (by G. Remick), recorded by Jump Start; "Deal Miester" (by W. Mailhot), recorded by The Krells; and "The Visitor," written and recorded by B. Lenny. Other artists include LMNOP, Meterz, and Wain Mailhot.

Tips: "Let's hear it!"

*COACHOUSE MUSIC, P.O. Box 1308, Barrington IL 60011. (312)822-0305. Fax: (312)464-0762. President: Michael Freeman. Record producer. Estab. 1984. Deals with artists and songwriters. Produces 4 LPs and 4 CDs/year. Fees vary with project.

How to Contact: Write first and obtain permission to submit. Prefers cassette (or VHS videocassette if available) with 3-5 songs and lyric sheet. Does not return material. Reports in 2 weeks.

Music: Mostly **pop, rock, blues**; also **alternative rock, progressive country**. Produced *Not Dead Yet* and *Squeezing The Puzzle* (by R. Covort), recorded by Bad Examples on Waterdog and *Crossover*, (by E. Harrington), recorded by Eddie Clearwater on Blind Pig Records. Other artists include Maybe/Definitely and Mick Freon.

Tips: "Be honest, be committed, strive for excellence."

COLLECTOR RECORDS, Box 2296, Rotterdam Holland 3000 CG **The Netherlands.** Phone: 1862-4266. Fax: 1862-4366. Research: Cees Klop. Record producer and music publisher (All Rock Music). Deals with artists and songwriters. Produces 8-10 singles and up to 30 LPs/year. Fee derived from sales royalty.
How to Contact: Submit demo tape—unsolicited submissions OK. Prefers cassette. SAE and IRC. Reports in 1 month.
Music: Mostly **50s rock, rockabilly** and **country rock;** also **piano boogie woogie.** Produced *Eager Boy* (by T. Johnson), recorded by Lonesome Orifier; *Tehm Saturday*, written and recorded by Malcolm Yelvington, both on Collector Records; and *All Night Rock*, written and recorded by Bobby Hicks on White Label Records (all 50s rock). Other artists include Teddy Redell, Gene Summers, Benny Joy and the Hank Pepping Band.

CONTINENTAL COMMUNICATIONS CORP., P.O. Box 565, Tappan NY 10983. President: Gene Schwartz. Record producer and music publisher (3 Seas Music/ASCAP and Northvale Music/BMI) and record company (3C Records and Laurie Records). Estab. 1985. Deals with artists and songwriters. Fee derived from sales royalty.
How to Contact: Submit demo tape by mail—unsolicited submissions are OK. Prefers cassette and lyric sheet. "Send only a few of your most commercial songs." SASE.
Music: Mostly **rock** and **pop;** also **dance-oriented** and **top 40/pop.** Produced "Stay With Me" (by James Denton), recorded by Maurice Williams; "Take Me" (by Peter Nechvatal), recorded by Maurice Williams; and "Someday Again," written and recorded by Bill Sunkel, all on Laurie Records.

COPPELIA, 21 rue de Pondichery, Paris 75015 **France.** Phone: (1)45673066. Fax: (1)43063026. Manager: Jean-Philippe Olivi. Record producer, music publisher (Coppelia/SACEM), record company (Olivi Records) and music print publisher. Deals with artists and songwriters. Produces 4 CDs/year. Fee derived from sales royalty or outright fee from recording artist or record company.
How to Contact: Prefers cassette. SAE and IRC. Reports in 1 month.
Music: Mostly **pop, rock** and **New Age;** also **background music** and **film/series music.** Produced "Voce Di Corsica" and "Corsica," recorded by Petru Guelfucci, both on Olivi Records. Other artists include Pino Lattuca, Christian Chevallier and Robert Quibel.

JOHNNY COPPIN/RED SKY RECORDS, Box 7, Stonehouse, Glos. GL10 3PQ **U.K.** Phone: 0453-826200. Record producer, music publisher (PRS) and record company (Red Sky Records). Estab. 1985. Deals with artists and songwriters. Produces 2 singles, 3 albums (CD & tape) per year. Fee derived from sales royalty when song or artist is recorded.
How to Contact: Submit demo tape by mail—unsolicited submissions are OK. Prefers cassette with 3 songs and lyric sheet. SASE. Reports in 6 months.
Music: Mostly **rock, modern folk** and **roots music.** Produced "West Country Christmas" and "Full Force of the River," written and recorded by Johnny Coppin; and "Dead Lively" by Paul Burgess, all on Red Sky Records. Other artists include Laurie Lee, David Goodland and Phil Beer.

*CORE PRODUCTIONS, Suite 254, 14417 Chase St., Van Nuys CA 91402. (818)909-0846. Fax: (818)780-4592. President: C. Marlo. Record producer and music publisher (Cocoloco Toons/ASCAP). Estab. 1986. Deals with artists and songwriters. Produces 2 LPs and 2 CDs/year. Fee derived from sales royalty when song or artist is recorded, outright fee from recording artist, outright fee from record company or publishing royalty.
How to Contact: Submit demo tape by mail. Unsolicited submissions are OK. Prefers cassette with 3-4 songs and lyric sheet. "If you are an artist please send a promo pack (pictures/tape/bio)." Does not return unsolicited material. Reports in 2 months.
Music: Mostly **pop, R&B** and **jazz;** also **rock** and **dance.** Produced *Speaking In Melodies*, written and recorded by Michael Ruff on Sheffield Lab Records; *The Last Protest Singer*, written and recorded by Harry Chapin on Dunhill Records; and *Antigua Blue* (by Russ Freeman), recorded by Kilauea on Brainchild Records. Artists include Pat Coil and Bill MacPherson.
Tips: "Don't try to follow trends—be who you are."

DANO CORWIN, 5839 Silvercreek Rd., Azle TX 76020. (817)560-3546. Record producer, music video and sound production company. Estab. 1986. Works with artists and songwriters. Produces 6 singles, 3 12″ singles, 5 EPs and 2 CDs/year. Fee usually derived from sales royalty, but negotiated on case-by-case basis.
How to Contact: Submit demo tape—unsolicited submissions are OK. Prefers cassette (or VHS videocassette if available) with 3 songs and lyric sheet. "Keep songs under 5 minutes. Only copyrighted material will be reviewed. Please do not send material without copyright notices." SASE, "but prefers to keep material on file." Reports in 6 weeks.

Music: Mostly **rock**; also **pop, New Age and dance.** Produced "BTB Wild" (by Kenny McClurg/Craig Cole), recorded by Sundog on MLM Records (rock); "New Tales" (by M. Howard), recorded by W-4's on Big D Records (rock); and "Maxzine" (by Gary Hall), recorded by Twice Four on Tootle Records. Other artists include Aria, W. Thomas Band and Complete.
Tips: "Keep songs simple and melodic. Write as many songs as possible. Out of a large quantity, a few quality songs may emerge."

DAVE COTTRELL, 1602 8th Ave. South, Fort Dodge IA 50501. Producer: Dave Cottrell. Record producer. Estab. 1984. Producer/composer of top 40 music, movie soundtracks and advertising jingles. Studio owner: Super Sound. Records and deals with songwriters, artists and producers. Produces 10 singles/yr and 5 LPs/yr. Publishing fees are not necessarily mandatory and are openly discussed per project.
How to Contact: Submit demo tape by mail—unsolicited submissions are OK. Prefers cassette. SASE. Reports in 1 week.
Music: Mostly **rock, pop** and **gospel**; also **country, R&B** and **disco.** Produced "Can You Rock Me?" and "Summertime," both written and recorded by Dave Cottrell; and "Change of Address," written and recorded by Donna Rogers. Credits include a lifetime listing in Marquis's Who's Who in Entertainment and work with Ray Manzerak of the Doors, Jan & Dean, Bobby Vee, The Beach Boys and their friends and family.
Tips: "Avoid clutter and multi-track overkill. Too many sounds and tracks ruin the sound. Write music that you enjoy. Be honest and creative. There is no room for the weak and inane in the music business."

*COUNTRY REEL ENTERPRISES, P.O. Box 99307, Stockton CA 95209. (209)473-8050. President: Mr. Dana C. Copenhaver. Record producer, music publisher (BMI) and record company (Country Reel Records). Estab. 1981. Deals with artists and songwriters. Fee derived from sales royalty or outright fee from recording artist or record company.
How to Contact: Write first and obtain permission to submit. Prefers cassette or VHS videocassette with lyric and lead sheets. "Send promo package (include copyrights)." SASE. Reports in 1 month.
Music: Traditional country and **country gospel.** Artists include Dana Clark, Jennifer Celeste and D.J. Birmingham.
Tips: "Write traditional type songs—country music is going back to traditional country sounds."

COUNTRY STAR PRODUCTIONS, Box 569, Franklin PA 16323. (814)432-4633. President: Norman Kelly. Record producer, music publisher (Country Star Music/ASCAP, Kelly Music/BMI and Process Music/BMI) and record company (Country Star, Process, Mersey and CSI Records). Estab. 1970. Deals with artists and songwriters. Produces 5-8 singles and 5-8 LPs/year. Works with 3-4 new songwriters/year. Works with composers and lyricists; teams collaborators. Fee derived from outright fee from recording artist or record company.
How to Contact: Submit demo tape—unsolicited submissions OK. Prefers cassette with 2-4 songs and lyric or lead sheet. SASE. Reports in 2 weeks.
Music: Mostly **country** (80%); also **rock** (5%), **MOR** (5%), **gospel** (5%) and **R&B** (5%). Produced "He Doesn't Love Here Anymore," written and recorded by Linn Roll; "Missing In Action" (by Len Marshall), recorded by Tom Booker; and "Whiskey Gone," written and recorded by Jeff Connors, all on Country Star Records. Other artists include Bob Stamper, Jeffrey Allan Connors and Mere Image.
Tips: "Submit only your best efforts."

*CREATIVE LIFE ENTERTAINMENT, INC., 196 Tuxedo Ave., Highland Park MI 48203. (313)537-0590. Producer: Juan Shannon. Record producer, record company and music publisher (CLE Production Complex, CLE Management Group/NY and CLE Filmworks). Estab. 1990. Deals with artists and songwriters. Produces 12 singles, 12 12" singles, 4 LPs, 2 EPs and 4 CDs/year."Fee varies depending on negotiation."
How to Contact: Write first and obtain permission to submit. Prefers cassette (or VHS videocassette) with 3-4 songs, lyric sheet and photo for groups/artist wanting to be signed. "Name, address and phone number on tape and cassette box." SASE. Reports in 3 weeks.
Music: Mostly **pop, rock** and **R&B**; also **hip hop (rap), alternative** and **gospel & country.** Produced "All Banged Up," written and recorded by EZ Bang; *Sex, Party, Rock & Roll*, written and recorded by EZ Bang and "If You Want A Man" (by Juan Shannon), recorded by Calvin May, all on CLE Records. Other artists include For Bad Girls Only.
Tips: "Send your best material first."

Refer to the Category Index (at the back of this book) to find exactly which companies are interested in the type of music you write.

CREATIVE MUSIC SERVICES, 838 Fountain St., Woodbridge CT 06525. Owner: Craig Calistro. Record producer (Ace Record Company). Estab. 1989. Deals with artists and songwriters. Produces 50 singles, 20 12″ singles, 15 LPs and 15 CDs/year. Fee derived from sales royalty when song or artist is recorded, outright fee from recording artist or record company.
How to Contact: Submit demo tape by mail—unsolicited submissions are OK. Prefers cassette (or VHS videocassette if available) and 1-3 songs and lyric and lead sheets. "Send photo if available." SASE. Reports in 3 weeks.
Music: Mostly **pop/top 40** and **dance;** also **jazz.** Produced "Tell Me" (by Craig Calistro), recorded by J. Lord (single); *Don't Throw This Love Away* (by Brenda Lee), recorded by Brenda Lee (LP); and *Pillow Talk* (by H.L. Reeves), recorded by Tanya (LP), all on Ace Records. Other artists include Mike Grella.

*CRYSTAL CLEAR PRODUCTIONS, Suite 114, 128 Grand Ave., Santa Fe NM 87501. (505)983-3245. Fax: (505)982-9168. Publisher/Producer: Susan Pond/David Anthony. Record producer and music publisher (Clear Pond Music/BMI). Estab. 1991. Deals with artists and songwriters. Produces 5-10 singles, 1 LP and 1 CD/year. Fee derived from sales royalty when song or artist is recorded or outright fee from record company.
How to Contact: Write first and obtain permission to submit. Prefers cassette with 1-3 songs and lyric sheet. Include cover letter stating your intentions. SASE. Reports in 1 month.
Music: Mostly **pop/rock, country (contemporary)** and A/C. Produced "Her Heart's On Fire," written and recorded by David Anthony on Paylode Records; "Runaway Heart," written and recorded by Michael Sierra on Comstock Records; and "There's Only You & Fallin' Star," written and recorded by David Anthony on Maxim Records. Other artists include J.D. Haring, Bennett Strahan, George Page and Erik Darling.
Tips: "Have backing, do your homework, know the business, read as much as possible regarding music, composition, lyric writing, etc."

WADE CURTISS, Box 1622, Hendersonville, TN 37077. A&R Director: Wade Curtiss. Record producer and record company (Terock Records). Estab. 1959. Deals with artists and songwriters. Produces 12-20 singles, 6 12″ singles, 12-20 LPs, 4 EPs and 6 CDs/year. Fee derived from outright fee from recording artist. Charges "artists for sessions."
How to Contact: Submit demo tape by mail—unsolicited submissions are OK. Prefers cassettes or "all kinds" of videocassettes (if available) with 4-10 songs and lyric sheets. SASE. Reports in 3-4 weeks.
Music: Interested in **"all kinds."** Produced "Hold Me" (by R. Derwald), on Terock Records; "That's It" (by Dixie Dee), on Rock-A-Billy Records; and *Baby, You're Gone* (by Don Rowlett), recorded by Susan Sterling on Toronto Records. Other artists include Greg Paul, Mickey Finn's Band, The Rappers, King Jackson and Rhythm Rockers.

*CYBORTRONIK RECORDING GROUP, 8927 Clayco Dr., Dallas TX 75243. (214)343-3266. Owner: David May. Record producer, record company (Sound Mind Productions Studio). Estab. 1990. Deals with artists and songwriters. Produces 4 12″ singles, 8 LPs, 4 EPs and 2 CDs/year. Fee derived from sales royalty when song or artist is recorded or outright fee from recording artist.
How to Contact: Submit demo tape by mail. Unsolicited submissions are OK. Prefers cassette or DAT (or VHS videocassette) with 4 songs. SASE. Reports in 3-4 weeks.
Music: Mostly **dance, techno** and **house;** also **hip-hop** and **industrial.** Produced "Thoratic/Glider Mix" (by Digital One), recorded by David May on Excel Records; "Traumatized" (by Liquid 25), recorded by David May on Cybortronik Records; and "Axioms" (by Axiomatic), recorded by E.J. on Cybortronik Records. Other artists include Proxima, Lift, Waveform, KBD, CWM, Sector 7 and Noise Matrix.
Tips: "Be patient and send decent recordings."

*D.B. PRODUCTIONS/PROMOTIONS, 2417 Hibiscus Rd., Ft. Myers FL 33905. (813)694-7763. Vice President: Dennis "D.B." Allen. Record producer and record company (Neal Hollander/Jerry Kravits Entertainment and Management). Deals with artists and songwriters. Produces 100 singles, 20 12″ singles, 4-6 LPs, 75 EPs and 75 CDs/year. Fee derived from sales royalty when song or artist is recorded, outright fee from recording artist or outright fee from record company.
How to Contact: Write or call first and obtain permission to submit. Prefers cassette (or videocassette) with 4 or more songs. Does not return unsolicited material.
Music: Mostly **rock and top 40, R&B and soul, dance** and **country;** also **gospel, jazz and blues** and **big time alternative.** Other artists include Huge Peter, Double Threat, Psycho Sativa, Nervous Milk Shake.
Tips: "Keep pluggin' away and eventually . . . "

S. KWAKU DADDY, Box 424794, San Francisco CA 94142-4794. (707)769-9479. President: S. Kwaku Daddy. Record producer and record company (African Heritage Records Co.). Deals with artists and songwriters. Produces 6 LPs/year.

How to Contact: Write first and obtain permission to submit. Prefers cassette. SASE. Reports in 2 weeks.
Music: Mostly **African pop, R&B** and **gospel.** Produced *Times of Change, Life's Rhythms* and *Heritage IV*, all by S. Kwaku Daddy, all on African Heritage Records.
Tips: "Place emphasis on rhythm."

DANNY DARROW, Suite 6-D, 150 West End Ave., New York NY 10023. (212)873-5968. Manager: Danny Darrow. Record producer, music publisher (BMI, ASCAP), record company (Mighty Records) and Colley Phonographics—Europe. Estab. 1958. Deals with songwriters only. Produces 1-2 singles, 1-2 12″ singles and 1-2 LPs/year. Fee derived from royalty.
How to Contact: Submit demo tape by mail—unsolicited submissions are OK. "No phone calls." Prefers cassette with 3 songs and lyric sheet. SASE. Reports in 1-2 weeks.
Music: Mostly **pop, country** and **dance**; also **jazz.** Produced "Wonderland of Dreams" (by Phil Zinn); "Telephones" (by R.L. Lowery/D. Darrow); and "Better Than You Know" (by M. Greer), all recorded by Danny Darrow on Mighty Records.
Tips: "Listen to the hits and write better songs from the heart!"

*DAVIS SOTO ORBAN PRODUCTIONS, #E3425, 601 Van Ness, San Francisco CA 94102. (415)775-9785. Fax: (415)775-3082. CEO: Glenn Davis. Record producer. Estab. 1984. Deals with artists and songwriters. Produces 3 LPs and 1 CD/year. Fee derived from sales royalty when song is recorded.
How to Contact: Submit demo tape by mail. Unsolicited submissions are OK. Prefers cassette (or VHS videocassette) with 4 songs and lyric sheet. Send full demo kit (bio, tape, tearsheets, pics, etc.) if possible. Does not return unsolicited material. Reports in 2 months.
Music: Mostly **world beat, infusion** and **modern**; also **rock, classical/poetry** and **pop.** Produced *Where Heaven Begins* (by Orban/Davis), *Transparent Empire* (by Orban) and *Summertime* (by Gershwin), all recorded by DSO on On The Wing Records.

MIKE DE LEON PRODUCTIONS, 14146 Woodstream, San Antonio TX 78231. (512)492-0613. Owner: Mike De Leon. Record producer, music publisher (BMI) and record company (Antonio Records). Member NARAS. Estab. 1983. Deals with artists and songwriters. Produces 15 singles and 5 LPs/year. Fee derived from sales royalty when song or artist is recorded and outright fee from record company.
How to Contact: Submit demo tape by mail—unsolicited submissions are OK. Prefers cassette (or VHS videocassette if available) with any number of songs and lyric or lead sheets. "Include contact number and any promo materials." Cannot return material.
Music: Mostly **pop/rock, R&B** and **Latin.** Produced *Marina's Momento*, recorded by Marina Chapa; *Elegante*, written and recorded by DeLeon Bros.; and *Debut*, written and recorded by Claudia.
Tips: "Feel free to submit material, but be patient. Need good pop and Latin material for existing artist clientele. All *good* material consistently suceeds. Se habla español."

*AL DE LORY AND MUSIC MAKERS, #11, 3000 Hillsboro Rd., Nashville TN 37215. (615)292-2140. Fax: (615)292-1634. President: Al DeLory. Record producer and career consultant (DeLory Music/ASCAP). Estab. 1987. Deals with artists and songwriters. Produces 10 singles, 5 12″ singles, 5 LPs, 5 EPs and 5 CDs/year. Fee derived from outright fee from record company, career consultant fees.
How to Contact: Call first and obtain permission to submit or to arrange personal interview. Prefers cassette (or VHS videocassette). Does not return unsolicited material.
Music: Mostly **pop, country** and **Latin.** "Two time Grammy winner for 'Gentle On My Mind' and 'By The Time I Get to Phoenix,' recorded by Glen Campbell on Capitol Records."
Tips: "Keep your dream alive, and continue to grow."

EDWARD DE MILES, 8th Floor, 4475 Allisonville Rd., Indianapolis IN 46205. (317)546-2912. President: Edward De Miles. Record producer, music publisher (Edward De Miles Music Co./BMI), record company (Sahara Records). Estab. 1981. Deals with artists and songwriters. Produces 15-20 singles, 15-20 12″ singles, 5-10 LPs and 5-10 CDs/year. Fee derived from sales royalty.
How to Contact: Submit demo tape—unsolicited submissions OK. Prefers cassette (or VHS or Beta ½″ videocassette if available) with 1-3 songs and lyric sheet. SASE. Reports in 1 month.
Music: Mostly **R&B/dance, top 40 pop/rock** and **contemporary jazz**; also **country, TV** and **film themes—songs** and **jingles.** Produced "Hooked on U," "Dance Wit Me" and "Moments," written and recorded by Steve Lynn (R&B), all on Sahara Records. Other artists include Lost in Wonder, D'von Edwards and Multiple Choice.
Tips: "Copyright all material before submitting. Equipment and showmanship a must."

DEMI MONDE RECORDS & PUBLISHING LTD., Foel Studio, Llanfair Caereinion, Powys, SY21 0RZ **Wales.** Phone: 0938-810758. Managing Director: Dave Anderson. Record producer, music publisher (PRS & MCPS) and record company (Demi Monde Records). Estab. 1982. Deals with artists and songwriters. Produces 5 singles, 15 12″ singles, 15 LPs and 10 CDs/year. Fee derived from combination of sales royalty, outright fee from recording artist, outright fee from record company and studio production time.

How to Contact: Submit demo tape by mail—unsolicited submissions are OK. Prefers cassette with 3 or 4 songs and lyric sheet. SASE. Reports in 1 month.

Music: Mostly **rock, pop** and **blues.** Produced *Average Man*, written and recorded by D. Carter (LP); *She*, written and recorded by D. Allen (LP/CD); and *Full Moon*, recorded by Full Moon (LP/CD), all on Demi Monde Records. Other artists include Gong, Amon Duul and Groonies.

WARREN DENNIS, 540 B. E. Todd Rd., Santa Rosa CA 95407. (707)585-1325. President/Owner: Warren Dennis Kahn. Record producer and independent producer. Estab. 1976. Deals with artists and songwriters. Produces 10 LPs and 10 CDs/year. Fee derived from sales royalty when song or artist is recorded, outright fee from recording artist, or outright fee from record company.

How to Contact: Write or call first and obtain permission to submit. Prefers cassette with 2-3 songs and lyric sheet. Reports in 1 month. Does not return unsolicited submissions.

Music: Mostly **New Age** or **world fusion,** also **pop, country, Christian** and **rock.** Produced *Music to Disappear in 2* (by Rafael), recorded by WDK on Hearts of Space Records (new age); *Dance Latitude* (by Tokewki) on Earthbeat Records (world); and *Queen of Mercy* (by M. Poirier) on Peartree Records (Christian). Engineer and Production Assist. for "Asian Fusion" by Ancient Future for Narada/MCA (World Fusion), and many others. Other artists include Cedella Marley Booker, Ladysmith Black Mambazo, Constance Demby, Georgia Kelly, Radhika Miller and UMA.

Tips: "I'm only interested in working with artists who have a clear sense of social and moral contribution to the planet. I'm looking for artists who compose and perform at an exceptional level and whose music has a well defined and original style."

DETROIT PRODUCTIONS, Box 265, N. Hollywood CA 91603-0265. (818)569-5653. President/Executive Producer: Randy De Troit. Vice President: Ciara Dortch. Co-Producer: Jade Young. Independent Television Producer of network TV shows, cable-TV series. Works with freelance producers/promoters for local and national broadcast on assignment basis only; gives unlimited assignments per year. Fee derived from sales royalty.

How to Contact: "Send edited version of work on VHS or broadcast quality tape. All categories of music plus surrealism, new concept, idealistic or abstract material by mail for consideration; provide resume/bio with photos (if available) for filing for possible future assignments." SASE. Reports within 2 weeks.

Music: Produces weekly Cable-TV series—"Inner-Tube Presents." Features actors, actresses, singers, bands, models, dancers, rappers and whole independent production companies for Chicago Access Network channels 19 and 21. Produces documentaries, industrials, commercials, musicals, talent showcases (new performers), news, plays, lectures, concerts, talk-show format with host, music-videos, contests. Uses all types of programming; formats are color Super-VHS, broadcast quality ¾" and 1" videotape, or film to video.

Tips: "An imaginative freelance producer is an invaluable asset to any production house, not only as a constant source of new and fresh ideas, but also for pre- and post-production supportive elements, contributing just as much as any staffer. Because of the nature of the business, we tend to be more open to outside sources, especially when it is to our benefit to keep new blood flowing. Indies tend to lean towards seeking unknowns, because their styles are usually, in our opinion, more unique."

JOEL DIAMOND ENTERTAINMENT, Dept. SM, 5370 Vanalden Ave., Tarzana CA 91356. (818)345-2558. Executive Vice President: Scott Gootman. Contact: Joel Diamond. Record producer and music publisher and manager. Deals with artists and songwriters. Fee derived from sales royalty.

How to Contact: Prefers cassette with 1-3 songs and lyric sheet. SASE.

Music: Dance, easy listening, country, R&B, rock, soul and **top 40/pop.** Produced "Do You Love Me," by David Hasselhoff on BMG Records; "Heaven In The Afternoon," by Lew Kyrton on Timeless; "I Am What I Am," by Gloria Gaynor; "Where the Boys Are," by Lorna; "One Night In Bangkok," by Robey; and "Love is the Reason" (by Cline/Wilson), recorded by E. Humperdinck and G. Gaynor on Critique Records (A/C).

*DINO M. PRODUCTION CO., #7, 2367 208th St., Torrance CA 90501. (310)782-0915. President: Dino Maddalone. Record producer. Estab. 1987. Deals with artists and songwriters. Produces 7 singles, 5 12" singles, 4 LPs, 2 EPs and 6 CDs/year. Fee derived from sales royalty when song or artist is recorded, outright fee from recording artist, outright fee from record company.

How to Contact: Submit demo tape by mail. Unsolicited submissions are OK. Prefers cassette (or videocassette if available) with 3 songs and lyric sheet. SASE. "Send photo and any press." Reports in 1 month.

Music: Mostly **rock, R&B, alternative;** also **pop, ballads.** Produced *All Great Things* (by Dennis Crupi) on Relativity Records (rock); *Leaning* (by P.K. Mitchell) on Patriot Records (rock); "Do-U-Wanna-B (by Jaci) (R&B).

Tips: "Believe in every note you write."

COL. BUSTER DOSS PRESENTS, Box 13, Estill Springs TN 37330. (615)649-2577. Producer: Col. Buster Doss. Record producer, record company (Stardust, Wizard) and music publisher (Buster Doss Music/BMI). Estab. 1959. Deals with artists and songwriters. Produces 100 singles, 10 12" singles, 20 LPs and 10 CDs/year.
How to Contact: Write first and obtain permission to submit. Prefers cassette with 2 songs and lyric sheet. SASE. Reports in 1 week.
Music: Pop, country and **gospel.** Produced "Fill 'er Up" (by Jess Demain), recorded by Tommy D on Doss Records; "Any Place In Texas" (by Buster Doss), recorded by Rooster Quantrell on Stardust Records; and "I'll Come Back" (by Buster Doss), recorded by Cliff Archer on Wizard Records. Other artists include Johnny Buck, Linda Wunder, Mick O'Reilly, Mike Montana and Benny Ray.

DUANE MUSIC, INC., 382 Clarence Ave., Sunnyvale CA 94086. (408)739-6133. President: Garrie Thompson. Record producer and music publisher. Deals with artists and songwriters. Fee derived from sales royalty.
How to Contact: Prefers cassette with 1-2 songs. SASE. Reports in 1 month.
Music: Blues, country, rock, soul and **top 40/pop.** Produced "Wichita," on Hush Records (country); and "Syndicate of Sound," on Buddah Records (rock).

*J.D. DUDICK, 6472 Seven Mile, South Lyon MI 48178. (313)486-0505. Producer: J.D. Dudick. Record producer (Ruffcut Productions). Estab. 1990. Deals with artists and songwriters. Produces 10 singles, 1 EP and 3 CDs/year. Fee derived from sales royalty when song or artist is recorded, outright fee from recording artist or outright fee from record company.
How to Contact: Submit demo tape by mail. Unsolicited submissions are OK. Prefers cassette (or VHS videocassette) with 3 songs and lyric sheet. SASE. Reports in 6 weeks.
Music: Mostly **modern rock, country rock** and **alternative;** also **funk/pop** and **country.** Produced "Passion's Fire" (by W. Bradley), recorded by Sassy on Fearless Records (country); *Hindsight* (by Doug Hopkins), recorded by Motherload on Ruffcut Records (modern rock); and "Breakin Down" (by Chris Pierce), recorded by Flavour Mouse on Rockit Records (rock). Other artists include Laya and Micheal Dean.
Tips: "Invest in your musical career. If you don't, how do you expect anyone else to!"

E P PRODUCTIONS, 7455 Lorge Cr., Huntington Beach CA 92647. (714)842-5524. Business Manager: Billy Purnell. Record producer and record company (Venue Records, Branden Records). Estab. 1987. Deals with artists and songwriters. Produces 5-10 singles, 1-2 12" singles, 2-5 LPs, 1-5 EPs and 1 CD/ year. Fee derived from sales royalty when song or artist is recorded, outright fee from recording artist and outright fee from record company. (All terms are negotiable.) "Some artists come to us for production work only—not on our label. For this we charge a flat fee. We *never* charge songwriters unless for demos only."
How to Contact: Submit demo tape by mail—unsolicited submissions are OK. Prefers cassette with 1-3 songs and lyric sheet. SASE. Reports in 2 months.
Music: Mostly **pop, R&B** and **contemporary Christian;** also **country** and **rock.** Produced *Surrounded By Angels,* written and recorded by Michelle Goodwin on Angelic Records; *Gift of Love,* written and recorded by Bob Hardy on Ocean Records; and *For An Evening* (by Bill and Kim Connors), recorded by The Look.
Tips: "Be professional—typed lyric sheets and cover letter are so much easier to work with along with a well-produced demo. Don't compromise on the quality of your songs or your package."

*E.S.R. PRODUCTIONS, 61 Burnthouse Lane, Exeter Devon EX2 6AZ U.K.. Phone: (0392)57880. Contact: John Greenslade. Record producer and record company (E.S.R.). Estab. 1965. Deals with artists and songwriters. Produces 4 singles and 10 LPs/year. Fee derived from outright fee from recording artist.
How to Contact: Submit demo tape by mail. Unsolicited submissions are OK. Prefers cassette with 4 songs and lyric sheet. SASE. Reports in 1 month.
Music: Mostly **country, pop** and **R&B.** Produced *There's You* (by J. Greenslade), recorded by Kaz Barron; *"Hey Lady"* (by J. Greenslade), recorded by Johnny Solo; and *It's For You* (by Mike Avis), recorded by Tony Royale, all on E.S.R. Records. Other artists include Sunset Haze, Tony Beard, and Barracuda.

*EARMARK AUDIO, P.O. Box 196, Vashon WA 98070. (206)567-4723. Owner: Jerry Hill. Record producer. Estab. 1991. Deals with artists and songwriters. Produces 2 LPs and 1 CD/year. Fee derived from outright fee from recording artist.

How to Contact: Submit demo tape by mail. Unsolicited submissions are OK. Prefers cassette (or VHS videocassette) with 1 song and lead sheet. Does not return unsolicited material. Reports in 2 months.

Music: Mostly **contemporary Christian, rock** and **country**. Produced *A New Day*, written and recorded by Randy Greco, on Angel Wing Records; *Gloria* (by P.D./Ron Feller), recorded by Ron & Marsha Feller on Art Factory Records; and *A Mighty Fortress* (by P.D.), recorded by Grace Church. Other artists include Smelter/Neves.

Tips: "Be willing to focus music on a specific target market."

LEO J. EIFFERT, JR., Box 5412, Buena Park CA 90620. (310)521-9511. Owner: Leo J. Eiffert, Jr. Record producer, music publisher (Eb-Tide Music/BMI, Young Country Music/BMI) and record company (Plain Country). Estab. 1967. Deals with artists and songwriters. Produces 15-20 singles and 5 LPs/year. Fee derived from sales royalty.

How to Contact: Submit demo tape by mail—unsolicited submissions are OK. Prefers cassette with 2-3 songs, lyric and lead sheet. SASE. Reports in 3-4 weeks.

Music: Mostly **country** and **gospel**. Produced "Like A Fool" by Pam Bellows on Plain Country Records and "Something About Your Love" by Chance Waite on Young Country Records. Other artists include Crawfish Band, Brandi Holland and David Busson.

Tips: "Just keep it real country."

8TH STREET MUSIC, 204 E. 8th St., Dixon IL 61021. Producer: Rob McInnis. Record producer. Estab. 1988. Deals with artists and songwriters. Fee derived from sales royalty when song or artist is recorded.

How to Contact: Submit demo tape by mail. Unsolicited submissions are OK. Prefers cassette with 3-6 songs and lyric sheet. "No phone calls please. Just submit material and we will contact if interested." SASE. Reports is 4-6 weeks.

Music: Mostly **top 40/pop, dance** and **new rock;** also **R&B, country** and **teen pop**. Produced "Black Roses," written and recorded by Michelle Goeking (alternative); and "Legend of Leo Mongorin," written and recorded by Jim Henkel (folk). Other artists include Jason Kermeen (country), Bob's Night Off (techno-dance), Jeff Widdicombe (country) and J&J (teen pop).

Tips: "Our current focus is on keyboard-oriented dance material, à la Information Society/Human League (male and/or female)."

*ELEMENT & SUPERSTAR PRODUCTION, Box 30260, Bakersfield CA 93385-1260. Producer: Jar the Superstar. Record producer, record company (Element Records, International Motion Pictures), music publisher (BMI).Estab. 1987. Deals with artists and songwriters. Produces 40 singles and 5 LPs/year. Fee derived from standard record sales.

How to Contact: Write first to arrange personal interview. Prefers cassette (or VHS videocassette if available) with 1 or more songs, lyric and lead sheet. Does not return material.

Music: Mostly **Christian/gospel, C/W** and **R&B;** also **pop, rap** and **rock**. Produced "Where You Are" (by Judge A. Robertson), recorded by Jar the Superstar (pop); "No One Wants to be Sad," written and recorded by Jar (R&B), both on Element Records; and "Brite & Morning Lite," written and recorded by Jar the Superstar (Christian).

GEOFFREY ENGLAND, 2810 McBain, Redondo Beach CA 90278. (213)371-5793. Contact: Geoffrey England. Record producer. Deals with artists and songwriters. Produces 10 singles/year. Fee derived from sales royalty and/or outright fee from record company.

How to Contact: Prefers cassette and lyric sheet. SASE. Reports in 2 weeks.

Music: Mainstream melodic rock. Produced "Steppenwolf Live" on Dunhill Records; and "If Licks Could Kill," by Virgin on Statue Records.

ESQUIRE INTERNATIONAL, Box 6032, Station B, Miami FL 33123. (305)547-1424. President: Jeb Stuart. Record producer, music publisher and management firm. Deals with artists and songwriters. Produces 6 singles and 2 LPs/year. Fee derived from sales royalty or independent leasing of masters and placing songs.

How to Contact: Submit demo tape—unsolicited submissions OK. Prefers cassette or disc with 2-4 songs and lead sheet. SASE. Reports in 1 month.

Music: Blues, church/religious, country, dance, gospel, jazz, rock, soul and **top 40/pop**. Produced "Hey Foxy Lady" (by J. Stuart), recorded by Shaka Zula A.R. (R&B); "All the Love I've Got" (by C. Jones), recorded by Jeb Stuart (jazz); and "Got To Be Crazy, Baby" (by J. Stuart), recorded by Jeb Stuart (R&B); all on Esquire Int'l Records. Other artists include Moments Notice, Cafidia and Night Live.

Tips: "When sending out material make sure it is well organized, put together as neatly as possible and it is of good sound quality."

*THE ETERNAL SONG AGENCY Suite 153, 6326 E. Livingston Ave., Columbus OH 43068. (614)868-9162. Executive Producer: Leopold Xavier Crawford. Record producer, record company and music publisher (Fragrance Records, Song of Solomon Records, Emerald Records, Lilly Records Ancient of Days Music, Anastacia Music). Estab. 1986. Deals with artists and songwriters. Produces 3 singles and 3 LPs/year. Fee derived from sales royalty when song or artist is recorded, outright fee from recording artist, outright fee from record company, an artist manager can agree to finance his client's demo or album.
How to Contact: Write first and obtain permission to submit. Prefers cassette (or videocassette) with 3 songs and lyric or lead sheet. "Send complete biography, pictures, tape. Type all printed material. Professionalism of presentation will get you an ear with us." Does not return unsolicited material. Reports in 4-6 weeks.
Music: Mostly **pop music/top 40, country** and **instrumental;** also **contemporary Christian, Christian inspirational** and **Southern gospel music.** Produced "Escape" (by L. Crawford), recorded by Robin Curenton on Fragrance Records (Christian); "Toll Free Love Line" (by L. Crawford), recorded by Doug Justice on Lilly Records (country); and "Starbright Sunshine," written and recorded by Greg Whightsel, on Emerald Records (jazz). Other artists include Yolanda Stewart, Streets of Gold.
Tips: "Develop people skills, be professional, be flexible, work hard, never stop learning."

*EXCELL PRODUCTIONS, Third Floor, 1900 S. Sepulveda Blvd., W. Los Angeles CA 90025. (310)477-1166. Fax: (310)479-5579. Production Coordinator: Ruth Maehara. Record producer, music publisher. Estab. 1990. Deals with artists and songwriters. Produces 12 CDs/year. Fee derived from sales royalty when song or artist is recorded.
How to Contact: Submit demo tape by mail. Unsolicited submissions are OK. Prefers cassette (or videocassette if available) and lyric sheet. SASE. Reports in 2 months.
Music: Mostly **pop, ballads, A/C.** Produced *Mom* (by Barry Fasman), and *All You Have To Do* (by Cami Ellen), both recorded by Tomoe Sawa on BMG Victor Records; *Lonely Mystery* (by Shun Suzuki), recorded by Shirley Kwan on Apollon Records. Other artists include Yumi Matsutoya, Nagabuchi, Takanaka, & Honda-Japan.

SHANE FABER, Dept. SM, #3, 501 78th St., North Bergen NJ 07047. (201)854-6266. Fax: (201)662-9017. Contact: Shane Faber. Record producer, music publisher (Now & Then Music/BMI) and record company (Now & Then Records). Estab. 1980. Deals with artists and songwriters. Produced 6 singles and 2 LPs/year. Fee derived from sales royalty or outright fee from recording artist or record company.
How to Contact: Submit demo tape by mail. Unsolicited submissions are OK. Prefers cassette with 4 songs and lyric sheet. SASE. Reports in 2 months.
Music: Mostly **pop, dance** and **R&B;** also **rap** and **New Age.** Produced "Partyline," recorded by 5th Platoon on SBK Records; "Turtle Power," recorded by Partners In Krime on SBK Records; and "U Shouldn't Wonder" (by Audrey Smith Bly). Other artists include Tenita Jordon (R&B), Blackhearts (rap) and T.T. (dance).

JIM FEMINO PRODUCTIONS, 429 South Lewis Rd., Royersford PA 19468. (215)948-8228. Fax: (215)948-4175. Branch: 1713 Beechwood Ave., Nashville TN 37212. (615)297-3171. President: Jim Femino. Music publisher (Fezsongs/ASCAP) record company (Road Records) and independent producer/engineer with own 24-track facility. Estab. 1970. Represents singer/songwriters; currently handles 2 acts.
How to Contact: Write or call first and obtain permission to submit. Prefers cassette with two songs only. SASE. Replies in 4-6 weeks.
Music: **Country** and **rock.** Works primarily with vocalists and songwriters. Currently working with Jim Femino (writer/artist).

DON FERGUSON PRODUCTIONS, Box 461892, Garland TX 75046. (214)271-8098. Producer: Don Ferguson. Record producer (Sultan Music/BMI and Illustrious Sultan/ASCAP), record company (Puzzle Records). Estab. 1972. Deals with artists and songwriters. Produces 10-15 singles, 4-5 cassettes and 2-3 CDs/year. "Fees are negotiated."
How to Contact: Submit demo tape by mail—unsolicited submissions are OK. Prefers cassette with 3 songs and lyric sheet. "Include bio." SASE. Reports in 2 weeks.
Music: **C&W, pop** and **MOR.** Produced "Knock on Wood" (by S. Cropper, E. Floyd), recorded by Diane Elliott (C&W); "The Woman on Your Mind" (by L. Schonfeld), recorded by Lonny Jay (pop); and "Eight Days a Week" (by Lennon, McCartney), recorded by Mary Craig (C&W); all on Puzzle Records. Other artists include Heartland (band), Flashpoint (band), Charlie Shearer, Derek Hartis, Phil Rodgers and Jimmy Massey.

FESTIVAL STUDIOS, Dept. SW, 3413 Florida Ave., Kenner LA 70065. (504)469-4403. Engineer/Producer: Rick Naiser/Michael Borrello. Record producer, music publisher (Homefront Music/BMI), record company (Homefront Records) and recording studio (Festival Studios). Estab. 1988. Deals with artists and songwriters. Produces 12 singles, 6 12″ singles, 15 LPs, 10 EPs and 5 CDs/year. Fee derived from sales royalty or outright fee from reocrding artist or record company.

How to Contact: Submit demo tape by mail. Unsolicited submissions are OK. Prefers cassette, DAT (or ½″ VHS or Beta videocassette) with 4 songs. "Send any pictures, press clips, reviews and any promo material available." Reports in 1 month.

Music: Mostly **rock, pop** and **New Age**; also **rap, R&B** and other. Produced *In It To Win It* (by Def Boyz), on Big T Records (rap); *EHG* (by EHG), on Intellectual Convulsion Records (sludge metal LP); and *Red Headed Step Children of Rock* (by Force of Habit), on Riffish Records (pop); all recorded by Festival. Other artists include Ice Mike, Ice Nine, RSBR, Common Knowledge and Mooncrikits.

Tips: "Concentrate on songwriting as a craft—don't spend time or money on embellishing demos. Raw demos leave room for the producer's creative input. Record demos quickly and move on to the next project."

FIRST TIME MANAGEMENT & PRODUCTION CO., Sovereign House, 12 Trewartha Rd., Praa Sands, Penzance, Cornwall TR20 9ST **England**. Phone: (0736)762826. Fax: (0736)763328. Managing Director: Roderick G. Jones. Record producer, music publisher (First Time Music Publishing U.K. Ltd. MCPS/PRS), record company (First Time, Mohock Records, Rainy Day Records and Pure Gold Records), licensed and subsidiary labels and management firm (First Time Management & Production Co.), commercial music library. Estab. 1986. Deals with artists and songwriters. Produces 5-10 singles and 5 LPs/year. EPs and CDs subject to requirements. Fee derived from sales royalty.

How to Contact: Prefers cassette with unlimited number of songs and lyric or lead sheets. SAE and IRC. Reports in 10 weeks.

Music: Mostly **country/folk, pop/top 40, country** with an Irish/Scottish crossover, **rock, soul, jazz funk, fusion, dance** and **reggae**. Produced "Yours Forever" (by Rod Jones/Colin Eade), recorded by Colin Eade on Panama Music Productions (instrumental); "Shades of Blue" (by Laurie Thompson), recorded by Laurie Thompson on Panama Music Productions (instrumental theme music); and "Baristoned" (by Simon Hipps), recorded by Simon Hipps on Panama Music Productions (jazz instrumental). Other artists include Rod Jones and Willow.

*FISHBOWL PRODUCTIONS, #3, 89 Clinton St., Everett MA 02149. (617)389-5816. President: Joe Miraglilo. Record producer. Estab. 1985. Deals with artists and songwriters. Produces 8 LPs/year. Fee derived from outright fee from recording artist.

How to Contact: Submit demo tape by mail. Unsolicited submissions are OK. Prefers cassette with 3-4 songs and lyric sheet. Does not return unsolicited material. Reports in 2-3 weeks.

Music: Mostly **electronic dance, funk/pop** and **pop/rap**; also **pop/rock, rock** and **jazz**. Produced "Snow" (by Cleopatra Jones), recorded by Joe Miraglilo, and "Dreamin' " (by Whirling Virtigo), recorded by Joe Miraglilo, both on Fishbowl Productions Records; and "Slip Away" (by Billy Ward), recorded by Joe Miraglilo on Hipshake Records. Other artists include Bill Hartzell, Mutiny, Minus One.

FOX FARM RECORDING, 2731 Saundersville Ferry Rd., Mt. Juliet TN 37122. (615)754-2444. President: Kent Fox. Record producer (Mercantile Productions) and music publisher (Mercantile Music/BMI and Blueford Music/ASCAP). Estab. 1970. Deals with artists and songwriters. Produces 20 singles/year. Fee derived from outright fee from recording artists. Charges in advance for studio time.

How to Contact: Submit demo tape by mail—unsolicited submissions are OK. Prefers cassette (or VHS videocassette if available). SASE. Reports in 3 months.

Music: **Country, bluegrass, gospel** and **contemporary Christian**.

BOB SCOTT FRICK, 404 Bluegrass Ave., Madison TN 37115. (615)865-6380. Contact: Bob Scott Frick. Record producer and music publisher (R.E.F.). Estab. 1958. Deals with artists and songwriters only. Produces 12 singles, 30 12″ singles and 30 LPs.

How to Contact: Submit demo tape by mail—unsolicited submissions are OK. Write first and obtain permission to submit.

Music: Produced "I Found Jesus in Nashville," recorded by Bob Scott Frick; "Love Divine," recorded by Backwoods; and "A Tribute," recorded by Visionheirs on R.E.F. (gospel). Other artists include Larry Ahlborn, Bob Myers Family, David Barton, The Mattingleys and Jim Pommert.

THE FRICON ENTERTAINMENT CO., INC., 1048 S. Ogden Dr., Los Angeles CA 90019. (213)931-7323. Attention: Publishing Department. Music publisher (Fricon Music Co./BMI, Fricon Music Co./ASCAP) and library material. Estab. 1981. Deals with songwriters only. Fee derived from sales royalty.

How to Contact: Write first and obtain permission to submit. Include SASE. Prefers cassette with 1 song and lyric and lead sheet. SASE. Reports in 8 weeks.

Music: Mostly **TV/film, R&B** and **rock**; also **pop, country** and **gospel**.

Tips: "Ask for permission, submit one song with typed lyrics and be patient."

G FINE, Box 180, Cooper Station, New York NY 10276. (212)995-1608. Vice President: Lyvio G. Record producer, music publisher (Rap Alliance, Inc.) and record company (G Fine). Estab. 1986. Fee derived from sales royalty.

How to Contact: Submit demo tape by mail. Unsolicited submissions are OK. Prefers high bias cassette or DAT with 3 or more songs. "Send photo, if possible." SASE. Reports in 2-3 months.

Music: "Undercore" **alternative rock, dance, rap** and **R&B.** Produced "Ring the Alarm" (by Fu-Schnickens/Lyvio G), recorded by Fu-Schnickens on Jive Records (rap/dance). Other artists include 8 Ball, Peter Righteous and 148th St. Black.

JACK GALE, Box 630755, Miami FL 33163. (305)935-4880. Contact: Jack Gale. Record producer, music publisher (Cowabonga Music/ASCAP) and record company (Playback Records). Estab. 1983. Deals with artists and songwriters. Produces 48 singles and 20 CDs/year. Fee derived from sales royalty.

How to Contact: Submit demo tape by mail. Unsolicited submissions are OK. Prefers cassette (or VHS videocassette if available) with 2 songs maximum and lyric sheets. Does not return unsolicited material. Reports in 2 weeks if interested.

Music: Mostly **contemporary country** and **country crossover.** Produced *The Old Violin*, written and recorded by Johnny Paycheck; *Any Lonely Women Here Tonight?* (by Charlie Daniels), and *Do You Know Where Your Man Is?* (by Chase/Gibson/Smith), recorded by Melba Montgomery, all on Playback Records (country). Other artists include Jimmy C. Newman, Sammi Smith, Sylvie, Tommy Cash, Jeannie C. Riley, Petrella, Robin Right and Del Reeves.

Tips: "Don't expect miracles—be patient!"

*THE GLAND PUPPIES, INC., 120 Highview, Yorkville IL 60560. (708)355-0161. President: Rikki Rockett. Record producer. Estab. 1989. Deals with artists and songwriters. Produces 7-10 singles and 2 LPs/year. Fee derived from sales royalty.

How to Contact: Submit demo tape by mail. Unsolicited submissions are OK. Prefers cassette with 4-8 songs and lyric sheet. "Send *your* favorite songs, not the songs your friends like, just because they sound like what's being played on the radio." SASE. Reports in 1 month.

Music: Mostly **New Age, pop/dance** and **folk** songs; also **comedy, gypsy/dance** and **thrash metal.** Produced *Gorgon 5* (by Bill Harris), recorded by Big Poo Generation on Spoo Disk Records; *Hyperzone* (by Dan Compton), recorded by Wacky Ball Kickers and "Nig-as-Kick-as" (by Mike Myers), recorded by Spongsters, both on Sick Dog Records. Other artists include The Martinis, Fag Newtons, Rockin' Retards, Walkie Talkies, Eschaton, Four Arm Mildew Freaks, Ice Cream, D.N.R and Turtle Future.

Tips: "Be crazy!"

*EZRA GOLD PRODUCTIONS, #15, 902 W. Franklin Ave. S., Minneapolis MN 55405. (612)871-2310. Producer: Ezra Gold. Deals with artists only. Produces 5 LPs, 3 EPs and 10 CDs/year. Fee derived from sales royalty when song or artist is recorded, outright fee from recording artist, outright fee from record company.

How to Contact: Submit demo tape by mail. Unsolicited submissions are OK. Prefers cassette, DAT with 3 songs and lyric sheet. Reports in 2 weeks.

Music: Mostly **alternative rock/pop, jazz, rock;** also **funk.** Produced *Raincan* (by Willie Wisely) and *Special K* (by S. Hurst) on Gark Records; and *Lullaby* (by J. Kimero) on Caroline Records, all recorded by E. Gold.

Tips: "I generally work with independent labels, including Gark, Twin Tone, Crackpot, Red Decibel plus Warner, Caroline . . . "

*GOODKNIGHT PRODUCTIONS, 25 W. New Haven Ave., Melbourne FL 32901. Coordinator: Robert John. Chief Producer: Greg Roberts. Record producer. Estab. 1992. Releases 2 cassettes, 2 LPs, 1 EP, 2 CDs/year. Works with musicians/artists on contract. Pays standard royalty to artists on contract; individually negotiated rate to publisher per song on record.

How to Contact: Submit demo tape by mail. "Unsolicited submissions are OK, but if you wish to call to find out current needs, by all means feel free." Prefers cassette (or VHS videocassette if available) with 6 songs and lyric sheet. SASE. Reports in 1 month.

Music: Mostly **pop** (clever lyric and strong melodies), **rock** (keep it entertaining!) and **film music** (keep it sensual and image-provoking.) Produced *Beloved* (by Greg Roberts), recorded by Lucifer Pope (progressive pop/rock); *Phantom Soul Thing*, recorded by Greg Roberts (pop/rock); *Won't You Be Mine Tonight* (by Kenneth Lee), recorded by Spectre (pop) all on GoodKnight Records. Other artists include Flip Dahlenburg, Fleshy Headed Mutants, Mucus.

Tips: "We're all in this for one main reason: to entertain! If you lose the feeling or substance that keeps it entertaining, take time to rework it. You can always get back to that initial inspiration if you give yourself time, or a different perspective. We want music that inspires, challenges and is high in romantic content."

*GRAFFITI PRODUCTIONS INC., Suite 205, 3341 Towerwood, Dallas TX 75234. (214)243-3735. Fax: (214)243-4477. Vice President: Dennis Lowe. Record producer, record company (Graffiti Records) and music publisher (Writing On The Wall Music Publishing) (Graffiti Recording Studios). Estab. 1989. Deals with artists and songwriters. Fee derived from outright fee from recording artist or record company.
How to Contact: Call first to arrange personal interview. Submit demo tape by mail. Unsolicited submissions are OK. Prefers cassette with 4 songs and lyric sheet. Also include bio and photos. Does not return unsolicited material. Reports in 2 weeks.
Music: Mostly **rock, industrial** and **R&B**; also **rap, country** and **New Age**. Produced *Time For Terror*, *Love You To Death* and *Call Me Devil* (by WWIII), recorded by Heaven on Graffiti Records (rock). Other artists include Bryan Robertson-Thin Lizzy, Yoko and Ralph The Dog.

GUESS WHO?? PRODUCTIONS, 140-23 Einstein Loop North, Bronx NY 10475-4973. (212)379-1831. Director: David Pellot. Record producer. Estab. 1988. Deals with artists and songwriters. Produces 10-15 singles/year. Fee derived from sales royalty or outright fee from recording artist or record company. "May charge in advance for services, depending on deal made with artist or songwriter."
How to Contact: Submit demo tape by mail—unsolicited submissions are OK. Prefers cassette and lyric sheet. SASE. Reports in 1-3 weeks.
Music: Mostly **dance/club, rap** and **R&B**; also **house/techno, ballads** and **top 40/pop**.

R.L. HAMMEL ASSOCIATES,INC., P.O. Box 531, Alexandria IN 46001-0531. Contact: Randal L. Hammel. Record producer, music publisher (Ladnar Music/ASCAP) and consultants. Estab. 1973. Deals with artists and songwriters. Produces 4 singles, 4 LPs, 2 EPs and 4 CDs/year. Fee derived from sales royalty, outright fee from artist/songwriter or record company, or negotiable fee per project.
How to Contact: Write first and obtain permission to submit, include brief resume (including experience, age, goal). Prefers cassette with 3 songs maximum. "Lyrics (preferably typed) *must* accompany tapes." SASE. Reports as soon as possible.
Music: **Blues, church/religious, country, easy listening, gospel, MOR, progressive, R&B, rock** (usually country), **soul** and **top 40/pop**.

*HANSEN PRODUCTIONS, 6531 S. Owensboro, West Jordan UT 84084. Producer: R. Mark Hansen. Estab. 1989 (as AMP). Deals with artists and songwriters. Produces 2-3 LPs and 1 EP/year. Fee derived from outright fee from songwriter/artist and/or outright fee from record company.
How to Contact: Prefers cassette with 3-4 songs and lyric sheet. Does not return unsolicited material.
Music: Any, especially **rock, country, rap, music in Spanish**. Produced *The Spirit of Christmas*, written and recorded by Celeste (Christmas); *Open Your Eyes*, written and recorded by Tormentor, (metal); *Urban Minstrels*, written and recorded by Narrow Escape (modern), all independent releases.
Tips: "I have a particular interest at this time in material with an anti-drug or anti-gang message."

HAPPY DAYS MUSIC/JEREMY MCCLAIN, Dept. SM, Box 852, Beverly Hills CA 90213. (818)769-2842. President: Jeremy McClain. Record producer and music publisher. Voting member of NARAS. Deals with artists and songwriters. Produces 12 singles, 1-2 12" singles and 3 LPs/year. Fee derived from sales royalty or outright fee from record company.
How to Contact: Submit demo tape—unsolicited submissions are OK. Prefers cassette (or VHS videocassette) and lyric or lead sheet. SASE. Reports in 4-6 weeks.
Music: Mostly **rock, top 40**, and **country**; also **contemporary gospel**. Produced "Devil With The Blue Dress," by Pratt & McClain/Warner Brothers Records (rock); and "The Way Things Used To Be," by Tom Gillan/Brother Love Records (country). "Worked with Michael Bolton. In addition, we have direct publishing access to Christopher Cross, Donna Summer, Debby Boone, Amy Grant and Michael Omartian."

HARD HAT PRODUCTIONS, 519 N. Halifax Ave., Daytona Beach FL 32118-4017. (904)252-0381. President/Producer: Bobby Lee Cude. Record producer, music publisher (Cude & Pickens Publishing) and record company (Hard Hat). Estab. 1978. Works with artists only. Produces 12 singles and 4 LPs/year.
How to Contact: Produces "only in-house material." Write first and obtain permission to submit. Prefers cassette with 4 songs and lyric sheet "from performing artists only."
Music: Mostly **pop, country** and **easy listening**; also **MOR, top 40/pop** and **Broadway show music**. Produced "Star of the Show," "Queenie" and "Tony the Tenor" (by Cude/Pickens), recorded by Fred Bogert.

STEPHEN A. HART/HART PRODUCTIONS, Dept. SM, 1690 Creekview Circle, Petaluma CA 94954. (707)762-2521. Executive Producer: Stephen A. Hart. Record producer. Estab. 1975. Deals with artists and songwriters. Produces 8 LPs and 8 CDs/year. Fee derived from outright fee from recording artist or record company.

How to Contact: Submit demo by mail—unsolicited submissions are OK. Prefers cassette with 3 songs and lyric sheet. SASE. Reports in 3 months.
Music: Mostly **pop, rock** and **instrumental**. Produced "10-9-91," written and recorded by Vasco Rossi (rock); and *Guernica* (by Vasco), recorded by Guernica (rock), both on FMI Records.
Tips: "Demo tape should have three songs maximum—big production not necessary."

HAWORTH PRODUCTIONS, Box 97, Climax Springs MO 65324. (314)374-1111. President/Producer: Dann E. Haworth. Record producer and music publisher (Southern Most Publishing/BMI). Estab. 1985. Deals with artists and songwriters. Produces 5 singles, 3 12″ singles, 10 LPs, 5 EPs and 10 CDs/year. Fee derived from sales royalty or outright fee from recording artist or record company.
How to Contact: Submit demo tape by mail—unsolicited submissions are OK. Prefers cassette or 7½ ips reel-to-reel with 3 songs and lyric or lead sheets. SASE. Reports in 6-8 weeks.
Music: Mostly **rock, country** and **gospel**; also **jazz, R&B** and **New Age**. Produced *Christmas Joy* (by Esther Kreak) on Serene Sounds Records (CD). Other artists include The Hollowmen, Jordan Border, Jim Wilson, Tracy Creech and Tony Glise.
Tips: "Keep it simple and from the heart."

*HEADING NORTH MUSIC, 107-895 Maple Ave., Burlington Ontario L7S 2H4 **Canada**. (416)632-5889. Producer: Ron Skinner. Record producer and recording engineer. Estab. 1989. Deals with artists and songwriters. Produces 1 LP, 1 EP and 1 CD/year.
How to Contact: Write or call first and obtain permission to submit. Prefers cassette or DAT with 3-5 songs and lyric sheet. "Presentation is everything." Does not return unsolicited material. Reports in 2 months. (This varies on material. If it's good will call right away.)
Music: **Pop-rock, heavy metal** and **A/C**; also **country, rap/dance** and **instrumental**. Produced *Dreamscape*, written and recorded by Gary Sykes; *What Is Life About*, recorded by Lesser Known; and *Avenue Road*, recorded by Small House Stories. Other artists include Valley Horses and I Spy.
Tips: "Presentation is everything. Quality package helps!"

HEARING EAR, Dept. SM, 730 S. Harvey, Oak Park IL 60304. (708)386-7355. Owner: Mal Davis. Record engineer and producer. Estab. 1970. Deals with artists and songwriters. Engineers and/or produces 6 LPs and 4 CDs/year. Fee derived from sales royalty when song or artist is recorded, outright fee from recording artist or outright fee from record company.
How to Contact: Write first and obtain permission to submit. Prefers cassette (or VHS videocassette) with up to 6 songs and lyric or lead sheets. Does not return material.
Music: Mostly **pop, gospel** and **rock**; also **R&B, rap** and **metal**. Engineered *Master & the Musician*, by Phil Keaggy; *Awaiting Your Reply*, by Resurrection Band; and *House of Peace*, recorded by Jim Croegaert (MOR/worship).

HEART CONSORT MUSIC, 410 1st St. W., Mt. Vernon IA 52314. (319)895-8557. Manager: Catherine Lawson. Record producer, record company, music publisher. "We are a single in-house operation." Estab. 1980. Deals with artists and songwriters. Produces 2-3 CDs/year. Fee derived from sales royalty or outright fee from recording artist or record company.
How to Contact: Submit demo tape by mail—unsolicited submissions are OK. Prefers cassette (or VHS videocassette if available) with 3 songs and 3 lyric sheets. SASE. Reports in 1-2 months.
Music: Mostly **jazz, New Age** and **contemporary**. Produced "Across the Borders," "Persia," (by James Kennedy), all recorded by James Kennedy on Heart Consort Music (jazz).
Tips: "Be original, don't copy someone else's style. We are interested in jazz/New Age artists with quality demos and original ideas. We aim for an international market."

*HEARTBEAT MUSIC, 282 Bruce Ct., Westerville OH 43081. (614)882-5919. Vice President: Stephen Bashaw. Record producer, record company and music publisher. Estab. 1987. Deals with artists and songwriters. Produces 3-5 LPs/year. Fee derived from sales royalty when song or artist is recorded, outright fee from recording artist, outright fee from record company.
How to Contact: Write or call first to arrange personal interview. Submit demo tape by mail. Unsolicited submissions are OK. Prefers cassette with 3-4 songs and lyric sheet. SASE. Reports in 3-4 weeks.
Music: Mostly **adult contemporary Christian, black gospel** and **inspirational**; also **Christian rock/pop**. Produced *The Word Is* and *Forgive Me* (by Matt Huesmann); and *Church, Do You Have It* (by James Mitchell), all recorded at Heartlight Studios on Pulse Records.

*HICKORY LANE PUBLISHING AND RECORDING, P.O. Box 2275, Vancouver, British Columbia V6B 3W5 **Canada**. (614)465-1408. President: Chris Michaels. A&R Manager: David Rogers. Record producer, record company, music publisher. Estab. 1988. Deals with artists and songwriters. Produces 3 singles, 3 LPs and 3 CDs/year. Fee derived from sales royalty when song or artist is recorded.

How to Contact: Submit demo tape by mail. Unsolicited submissions are OK. Prefers cassette (or VHS videocassette if available) with 1-5 songs and lyric sheet or lead sheet if available. "Be patient!" SASE. Reports in 4-6 weeks.
Music: Mostly **country, MOR, gospel**; also **soft rock, musical compositions, children's music.** Produced "Yesterdays Fool," "Country Drives Me Wild" and "Without You and Me," all written and recorded by Chris Michaels on Hickory Lane Records.
Tips: "Keep the vocals up front, have feeling in your songs with a strong melody, easy lyrics, be original."

HOBAR PRODUCTION, 27 Newton Pl., Irvington NJ 07111. (201)375-6633. President: Randall Burney. Record producer, record company (Independent). Estab. 1987. Deals with artists and songwriters. Produces 4 singles, 6 12″ singles and 2 LPs/year. Fee derived from royalty.
How to Contact: Submit demo tape by mail—unsolicited submissions are OK. Prefers cassette (or VHS videocassette if available) with 4 songs and lyric or lead sheets. SASE. Reports in 1 month.
Music: Mostly **R&B, pop** and **gospel**; also **country** and **rap.** Produced "Hold Me Tight" (by Bill Irving), recorded by Pam Robertson (R&B); "Watching You" (R&B) and "Get up Everybody" (by Robert Moss) (Hiphouse), both recorded by Inseperable, all on Atlantic East/West.

HOGAR MUSICAL PRODUCTIONS, 4225 Palm St., Baton Rouge LA 70808. (504)383-7885. President: Barrie Edgar. Record producer and music publisher (Silverfoot). Deals with artists and songwriters. Produces 0-5 singles and 0-2 LPs/year. Fee derived from outright fee from record company.
How to Contact: Submit demo tape—unsolicited submissions are OK. Prefers cassette with maximum 4 songs and lyric sheet. SASE. Reports in 1-6 months.
Music: Mostly **rock, blues ("not soul"), country** and **pop.** Produced "Louisiana's Basin Child," by Top Secret (rock single, Gulfstream Records).
Tips: "Don't give up—we've listened to five submissions over a four year period before we found something we liked by that writer."

HORIZON RECORDING STUDIO, Rte. 1, Box 306, Seguin TX 78155. (512)372-2923. Owner/Producer: H.M. Byron. Record producer, music publisher (Route One Music/BMI) and record company (Route One Records, Starmaker Records). Estab. 1988. Deals with artists and songwriters. Produces 25-30 singles and 5-7 LPs/year. Fee derived from sales royalty when song or artist is recorded or outright fee from recording artist.
How to Contact: Submit demo tape—unsolicited submissions are OK. Prefers cassette (or VHS videocassette if available) with a maximum of 5 songs and lyric sheet. SASE. Reports in 3 weeks.
Music: Mostly **country, gospel** and **pop.** Produced "The Last Song" (by B. Dees, R. Orbison), recorded by Mike Lord; "When We See Old Glory Fly," written and recorded by Stan Crawford (patriotic); and "Untitled," written and recorded by Brett Marshall (gospel), all on BSW Records. Other artists include Stan Crawford and Bobby O'Neal.
Tips: "Before spending megabucks to demo a song, submit it for appraisal. Piano or guitar and voice are all that is necessary."

HORRIGAN PRODUCTIONS, Box 41243, Los Angeles CA 90041. (213)256-0215. President/Owner: Tim Horrigan. Record producer and music publisher (Buck Young Music/BMI). Estab. 1982. Deals with artists and songwriters. Produces 5-10 singles, 3-5 LPs, 3-5 EPs and 3-5 CDs/year. Fee derived from sales royalty or outright fee from recording artist or record company. "We do some work on spec but the majority of the time we work on a work-for-hire basis."
How to Contact: Submit demo tape by mail. Unsolicited submissions are OK. Prefers cassette (or VHS videocassette if available) with 1-5 songs and lyric sheets. SASE. "Please do not call first; just let your music do the talking. Will reply if interested."
Music: Mostly **pop, rock** and **country.** Produced *Slap Your Catfish* (by Don Fenceton), recorded by The Nashville Cookin' Show Band on Country Heritage Records. Other artists include Mama Says (country) and Vicki Silver (alternative).
Tips: "Write from the heart with eyes on the charts."

How to Get the Most Out of Songwriter's Market (at the front of this book) contains comments and suggestions to help you understand and use the information in these listings.

I.Y.F. PRODUCTIONS, 4B, 500½ E. 84th St., New York NY 10028. (212)861-8745. A&R: Steven Bentzel. Record producer, music publisher (Mia Mind Music/ASCAP) and record company (Mindfield Records). Estab. 1990. Deals with artists and songwriters. Produced 30 singles, 8 12″ singles, 6 LPs and 8 CDs/year. Fee derived from outright fee from artist or record company.
How to Contact: Call first and obtain permission to submit, or to arrange personal interview. Reports in 6 weeks.
Music: Mostly **rap, house, hip hop**; also **dance, top 40** and **AOR.** Produced "Boyfriend," written and recorded by Baby Oil on Profile/CBS Records (rap, single); "I've Fallen," written and recorded by Baby Oil on Profile/CBS Records (house); and "Get Down" (by Bentzel), recorded by Madonna on Replay Records (hip house). Other artists include P.O.A., Electric Sun, Clark After Dark, Papa Haha, Q.O.S. and Datman.
Tips: "Submit demos on DAT cassettes for best sound quality."

*INNER SOUND PRODUCTIONS, 5205 44th Ave. S., Minneapolis MN 55417-2211. (612)729-5191. President/Owner: Sa'Id Q. 'Ubaydah. Record producer and project studio. Estab. 1989. Deals with artists and songwriters. Fee derived from outright fee from recording artist.
How to Contact: Submit demo tape by mail. Unsolicited submissions are OK. Prefers cassette with 3 songs and lyric sheet. Does not return unsolicited material. Reports in 1 month.
Music: Mostly **hip-hop, R&B** and **house/club**; also **dance hall.** Produced "Think About It," written and recorded by L. Turner; "Love Affair" (by B. Purcell/L. Turner), recorded by Qadir; and "Remember When?" (by B. Purcell/L. Turner), recorded by Rare Quality. Other artists include Asaad Abdul Rahman.
Tips: "It takes perseverance and a dedication to your art form."

INNERSOUNDS PRODUCTIONS, Dept. SM, 193 LaMartine St., Boston MA 02130. (617)524-3597. Writer/Producer: Jerry Smith, Jr. Record producer and commercial music firm. Estab. 1986. Deals with artists and songwriters. Produces 10-15 singles, 10 LP's and 1-2 CD's/year. Paid by outright fee from recording artist.
How to Contact: Write or call first and obtain permission to submit. Prefers cassette with 1-4 songs and lyric sheet. "Make sure tape is cued and labeled." SASE. Reports in 4-5 weeks.
Music: Mostly **pop, R&B** and **rock**; also **rap, country** and **New Age.** Produced "Hello Paradise" (by Cheryl Mason), recorded by Judy Collins for ABC's *One Life to Live*; *With Every Beat* (by Smith/ McManus), recorded by Oslo on Viking Records (CD); and "Different Tongues," written and recorded by Amy Beeton on Flammy Pie Records. Other artists include Fred Curry and Greg French.
Tips: "Be creative . . . I hear too many 'sound-alikes' today. MIDI is a very big market of the future. A computer is a necessary tool for today's writers."

INSPIRE PRODUCTIONS, INC., Suite 101, 302 E. Pettigrew St., Durham NC 27701. (919)688-8563. President: Willie Hill. Record producer (BMI) and record company (Joy Records). Estab. 1988. Deals with artists and songwriters. Produces 10 singles, 1 12″ single, 1 LP and 1 CD/year. Fee derived from sales royalty when song or artist is recorded.
How to Contact: Submit demo tape by mail—unsolicited submissions are OK. Prefers cassette with 4 songs and lyric sheet. Include bio and picture. Reports in 2 weeks.
Music: R&B, gospel, rap and pop. Produced "Step By Step" (by Walter Hill), recorded by Inspire on Joy Records (R&B).
Tips: "Do your homework."

*INTENSIFIED PRODUCTIONS, 6336 W. La Mirada Ave., Hollywood CA 90038. Fax: (213)469-5624. Proprietor: Danny Zelonky. Record producer. Estab. 1985. Deals with artists and songwriters. Produces 2 singles, 2 12″ singles, 1 LP and 1 CD/year. Fee derived from sales royalty when song or artist is recorded, outright fee from recording artist, outright fee from record company.
How to Contact: Submit demo tape by mail. Unsolicited submissions are OK. Prefers cassette with 2 songs and lyric sheet. Does not return unsolicited material.
Music: Mostly **dance (techno/house), rap** and **R&B**; also **rock, reggae** and **Japanese music.** Published "Rave It Up" (by Pappas/Zelonky), recorded by Javier on Rampart Records (dance); "Heaven 7" and *Fever Visions* (by Kogure/Zelonky), recorded by Casino Drive on Canyon Int'l Records (rock). Other artists include Theo Blackburn (reggae), Wayne Sangster (rap).
Tips: "We are far more interested in strong, individual character than in technique."

INTRIGUE PRODUCTION, Suite 206, 6245 Bristol Parkway, Culver CA 90230. (213)417-3084, ext. 206. Producer: Larry McGee. Record producer and record company (Intrigue Productions). Estab. 1986. Deals with artists and songwriters. Produces 6 singles, 3 12″ singles, 1 LP, 4 EPs and 2 CDs/year. Fee derived from sales royalty.

How to Contact: Submit demo tape by mail—unsolicited submissions are OK. Prefers cassette or reel-to-reel (or VHS videocassette if available) with 1-4 songs and lyric sheets. "Please put your strongest performance upfront. Select material based on other person's opinions." SASE. Reports in 2 months.
Music: Mostly **R&B, pop, rap** and **rock**; also **dance** and A/C. Produced *Starflower* (by Joe Caca Missa), recorded by Starflower (A/C); *Too Tough* (by Terrence Jones), recorded by En-Tux (pop); and *Got It Going On* (by Alan Walker), recorded by Executives (R&B), all on Mega Star Records.
Tips: "Make sure your song is commercial, crossover, and current as possible."

IVORY PRODUCTIONS, INC., Suite #3, 212 N. 12th St., Philadelphia PA 19107. (215)977-9777. Contact: Vincent Kershner, David Ivory. Record producer. Estab. 1986. Deals with artists, labels and managers/attorneys. Produces 5 CDs/year. Fee derived from "varying proportions of outright fee and royalties."
How to Contact: Submit demo tape—unsolicited submissions are OK. Prefers cassette with 3 songs. SASE. Reports in 6 weeks.
Music: Mostly **rock, pop** and **jazz**. Produced *Big Magic Blue*, written and recorded by Peter's Cathedral on 7 Records; *Reindeer Games* (written and recorded by Pat Godwin) and *It's A Tough Town*, written and recorded by The Cutaways!, both on Rage-N-Records. Other artists include The Spelvins, Chuck Treele, The Dream, Anthrophobia, Cryin' Out Loud, Kieran Kali, Tony Reyes, Don Himlin, Destroyer, Curiosity Shop, Jimmy Bruno, Inside Out, Mr. Mehta and Big Daddy Graham.

J.L. PRODUCTIONS, 4303 Teesdale Ave., Studio City CA 91604. Owner: Jeff Lorenzen. Record producer and engineer. Estab. 1988. Deals with artists only (no songwriters). Produces 5 singles, 5 12″ singles, 2 CDs/year.
How to Contact: Write first for permission to submit; solicited material only. Prefers cassette (or VHS videocassette if available) with 3 songs and lyric sheet. SASE. Reports in 6 weeks.
Music: Mostly **pop** and **R&B**; also **alternative pop** and **alternative rock**. Produced "Too Young To Love You," written and recorded by Timmy T. on Quality Records (pop). Mixed "Sweet November" (by Babyface), recorded by Troop on Atlantic Records (pop/R&B); and "Love Never Dies" (by Sami McKinney), recorded by Patti LaBelle on MCA Records (pop/R&B). Other artists include Go West, Curt Smith (from Tears for Fears), Paul Young, Fine Young Cannibals, Jody Watley, The Whispers, The Isley Bros., New Edition, The Jacksons, and many more.
Tips: "When writing songs, always start with a simple, memorable melody based on chords that capture a mood. Without that, nothing else in your song will matter, including the lyrics."

JAG STUDIO, LTD., 3801-C Western Blvd., Raleigh NC 27606. (919)821-2059. Record producer, music publisher (Electric Juice Tunes/BMI), record company (JAG Records) and recording studio. Estab. 1981. Deals with artists and songwriters. Produces 10 singles, 12 LPs and 6 CDs/year. Fee derived from outright fee from recording artist or record company.
How to Contact: Write first and obtain permission to submit. Does not return unsolicited material. Reports in 1-2 months.
Music: Mostly **pop/dance, rap** and **rock**; also **country** and **gospel**. Produced *Dream Train* (by the Accelerators), produced by Dick Hodgin for Profile Records (CD) and *Rockin with the Blues* (by Skeeter Brandon and Hwy. 61), recorded by Byron McCay for Bug You Records (CD). Other artists include Johnny Quest, Bad Checks, Hootie & the Blowfish, Annabel Lee, Ellen Harlow, Stacy Jackson, Doug Jervey, Katherine Kennedy, and Cry of Love.
Tips: "Be prepared. Learn something about the *BUSINESS* end of music first."

NEAL JAMES PRODUCTIONS, Box 121626, Nashville TN 37212. (615)726-3556. President: Neal James. Record producer, music publisher (Cottage Blue Music/BMI, Neal James Music/BMI) and record company (Hidden Cove Music/ASCAP), Estab. 1971. Produces 16 singles and 4 CDs and LPs/ year. Deals with artists and songwriters. Fee derived from sales royalty when song or artist is recorded, outright fee from recording artist and outright fee from record company.
How to Contact: Write or call first and obtain permission to submit. Prefers cassette (or VHS videocassette if available) with 2 songs and lyric sheet. SASE. Reports in 1 month.
Music: Mostly **country, pop/rock** and **R&B**; also **gospel**. Produced "Are You Sure" (by P.J. Hawk/ Neal James), recorded by P.J. Hawk; and "Don't Walk Down My Street," written and recorded by Judie Bell, both on Kottage Records. Other artists include Terry Barbay.

SUNNY JAMES, 1051 Saxonburg Blvd., Glenshaw PA 15116. (412)487-6565. Producer: Sunny James. Record producer, music publisher, record company (Golden Triangle). Estab. 1987. Deals with artists only. Produces 2 singles, 8 12″ singles, 18 LPs and 9 CDs/year. Fee derived from sales royalty or outright fee from record company.

How to Contact: Submit demo tape by mail—unsolicited submissions are OK. Prefers cassette, 15 ips reel-to-reel (or ½" VHS videocassette if available) with 3 songs and lyric or lead sheet. SASE. Reports in 2 months.

Music: Mostly **R&B, country, rock**; also A/C and **jazz**. Produced "Baby Blue," written and recorded by F. Johnson; "Dear Don't Wait For Me" (by F. Johnson), recorded by The Marcels; and "After You," written and recorded by F. Johnson; and "Blue Moon," "Most of All" and "10 Command-ments," all written by F. Johnson and recorded by The Marcels on Golden Trianble Records. Other artists include Joe DeSimone, Steve Grice (The Boxtops), The Original Marcels, Bingo Mundy, Corne-lius Harp, Fred Johnson, Richard Harris, Brian (Badfinger) McClain and City Heat.

ALEXANDER JANOULIS PRODUCTIONS, 1957 Kilburn Dr., Atlanta GA 30324. (404)662-6661. Presi-dent: Alex Janoulis. Record producer. Deals with artists and songwriters. Produces 6 singles and 2 CDs/year. Fee derived from sales royalty or outright fee from recording artist or record company.
How to Contact: Write first and obtain permission to submit. "Letters should be short, requesting submission permission." Prefers cassette with 1-3 songs. "Tapes will not be returned without SASE." Reports in 2 months.
Music: Mostly **top 40, rock, pop**; also **black** and **disco**. Produced "He's A Rebel" (by Gene Pitney), recorded by Secret Lover on HotTrax Records (pop single); *Stop!*, written and recorded by the Chester-field Kings on Mirror Records (rock LP); and *P is For Pig*, written and recorded by The Pigs on HotTrax Records (pop LP). Other artists include Night Shadows, Starfoxx, Splatter and Big Al Jano. "Album produced for Chesterfield Kings was reviewed in *Rolling Stone*."

JAY JAY PUBLISHING & RECORD CO., 35 NE 62nd St., Miami FL 33138. (305)758-0000. Owner: Walter Jagiello. Record producer, music publisher (BMI) and record company (Jay Jay Record, Tape and Video Co.). Estab. 1951. Deals with artists and songwriters. Produces 12 singles, 12 LPs and 12 CDs/year. Fee derived from sales royalty.
How to Contact: Submit demo tape—unsolicited submissions are OK. Prefers cassette (or VHS videocassette if available) with 6 songs and lyric and lead sheet. "Quality cassette or reel-to-reel, sheet music and lyrics." Does not return unsolicited material. Reports in 6 weeks.
Music: Mostly **ballads, love songs, country music** and **comedy**; also **polkas** and **waltzes**. Produced *No Beer in Heaven, God Bless Our Polish Pope*, and *Li'L Wally's Greatest Hits* (by Walter E. Jagiello), recorded by Li'L Wally, all on Jay Jay Records. Other artists include Eddie and the Slovenes, Polka Sizzlers, Americas Greatest Polka Band, Johnny Vadnal, Polka Bell Hops, Marion Lush, Captain Stubby and the Buccaneers and the Lucky Harmony Boys.
Tips: "We need songs with meaning and feeling—true to life. Submit simple ballads which are melodic with nice rhyming lyrics such as happy polkas, 40s, 50s and 60s and country music. Also big band with violins, saxes and muted trumpets."

*JAZMIN PRODUCTIONS, P.O. Box 6367, Long Beach CA 90806. (310)433-5546. Owner/Producer: Gregory D. Dendy. Record producer (C-Note Music Group). Estab. 1991. Deals with artists and songwriters. Produces 2-4 LPs/year. Fee derived from sales royalty when song or artist is recorded, outright fee from recording artist, outright fee from record company.
How to Contact: Submit demo tape by mail. Unsolicited submissions are OK. Prefers cassette with lyric sheet. SASE. Reports in 3-4 weeks.
Music: Mostly **gospel, R&B** and **hip-hop**. Artists include Pentecostal Community Choir and Sonya Griffin.
Tips: "A song is nothing but a bunch of words if no one ever hears it. Don't be afraid of selling your song!"

JAZZAND, 12 Micieli Pl., Brooklyn NY 11218. (718)972-1220. President: Rick Stone. Record producer, music publisher (BMI) and record company. Estab. 1984. Deals with artists only. Produces 1 LP/year. Fee derived from outright fee from recording artist or record company.
How to Contact: Write or call first and obtain permission to submit. Prefers cassette. Does not return unsolicited material. Reports in 2 weeks.
Music: Mostly **jazz (straight ahead), bebop** and **hard bop**. Produced *Blues for Nobody, Lullaby For Alex* and *Far East*, written and recorded by Rick Stone on Jazzand Records (jazz).
Tips: "We are only interested in acoustic, straight ahead jazz. Please do not send unsolicited demos. Call or write first!"

JERICHO SOUND LAB, Box 407, Jericho VT 05465. (802)899-3787. Owner: Bobby Hackney. Record producer, music publisher (Elect Music/BMI) and record company (LBI Records). Estab. 1988. Deals with artists and songwriters. Produces 5 singles, 2 12" singles and 3 LPs/year. Fee derived from sales royalty or outright fee from record company.

How to Contact: Submit demo tape—unsolicited submissions are OK. Prefers cassette or VHS videocassette with 3-4 songs and lyric sheet. SASE. Reports in 6 weeks.
Music: Mostly **reggae, R&B** and **pop**; also **New Age** and **rock**. Produced "Let's Go Flying" (by B. Hackney), recorded by Lambsbread (reggae); "This Love" (by B. Hackney), recorded by Hackneys; and "Like An Ocean," (by B. Hackney), recorded by Carrie Taylor, all on LBI Records.
Tips: "Make it clear what you want. We look for labels to distribute our songs, so we like finished product to present. We record it, or you record it, as long as it's a professional presentation."

*JET LASER PRODUCTIONS, 232 Madison Ave., Cresskill NJ 07626. (201)816-9144. Fax: (201)816-0782. Contact: Jeffrey Lesser. Record producer. Deals with artists and songwriters. Produces 5 singles, 6 LPs, 1 EP and 6 CDs/year. Fee derived from sales royalty when song or artist is recorded, outright fee from recording artist, or outright fee from record company.
How to Contact: Write or call first and obtain permission to submit. Prefers cassette with 3 songs and lyric sheet. Does not return material. Reports in 1 month.
Music: Mostly **rock, folk/rock** and **pop**; also **jazz** and **dance**. Recently produced *History*, written and recorded by Loudon Wainright III on Virgin Records; *What's Inside*, written and recorded by N.Y. Voices on GRP Records; and *Darden Smith*, written and recorded by Darden Smith on Sony Records. Other artists include Jeffrey Gaines.

JGM RECORDING STUDIO, (formerly Lito Manlucu), 4121 N. Laramie, Chicago IL 60641. Producer: Lito Manlucu. Record producer. Estab. 1991. Deals with artists and songwriters. Produces 1 single, 1 LP and 1 CD/year. Fee derived from sales royalty.
How to Contact: Submit demo tape—unsolicited submissions OK. Prefers cassette with 3 songs and lyric sheet. SASE. Reports in 1 month.
Music: Mostly **pop, R&B** and **rock**; also **foreign music, dance**. Produced "Blue Jean" (by Lito Manlucu), recorded by Jane Park on Independent Records (dance/pop).

RALPH D. JOHNSON, Dept. SM, 114 Catalpa Dr., Mt. Juliet TN 37122. (615)754-2950. President: Ralph D. Johnson. Record producer, music publisher (Big Wedge Music) and record company. Estab. 1960. Deals with artists and songwriters. Produces 10 singles/year. Fee derived from sales royalty and outright fee from record company.
How to Contact: Submit demo tape—unsolicited submissions are OK. Prefers cassette with maximum of 4 songs. SASE. Reports in 2 weeks.
Music: Mostly **country** and **novelty**. Recorded "Little Green Worm" (by Cal Veale), recorded by Dave Martin (novelty); "In the Middle of the Nighttime" (by Ralph D. Johnson), recorded by Joey Weltz (country); and "They Finally Got Around to You" (by T. J. Christian), recorded by T. J. Christian (country), all on Wedge Records.
Tips: "Be critical of your own material before submitting."

TYRONE JONES PRODUCTIONS, Tremont Ave., Orange NJ 07050. Owner: Tyrone Jones. Record producer. Estab. 1986. Deals with artists and songwriters. Produces 50 singles, 30 12″ singles, 40 LPs/year. Fee derived from outright fee from recording artist.
How to Contact: Submit demo tape—unsolicited submissions are OK. Prefers cassette (or VHS videocassette if available) and lyric sheet. "Include name, address, copyright notice." SASE. Reports in 2 weeks.
Music: Mostly **R&B, jazz** and **rap**. Produced "Let Me Bang U," written and recorded by MC Bang on Homeboy Records. Other artists include Linda Harris, Valentine.

JUMP PRODUCTIONS, 71 Langemunt, 9420 Aaigem **Belgium**. Phone: (053)62-73-77. General Manager: Eddy Van Mouffaert. Record producer and music publisher (Jump Music). Estab. 1976. Deals with artists and songwriters. Produces 25 singles, 2 LPs/year. Fee derived from sales royalty.
How to Contact: Prefers cassette. Does not return unsolicited material. Reports in 2 weeks.
Music: Mostly **ballads, up-tempo, easy listening, disco** and **light pop**; also **instrumentals**. Produced "Ach Eddy" (by Eddy Govert), recorded by Samantha and Eddy Govert on Carrere Records (light pop); "Al Wat Je Wilt" (by Eddy Viaene) recorded by Fransis on Scorpion Records (light pop); and "International" (by Eddy Govert), recorded by Le Grand Julot on B.M.P. (ambiance).

JUNE PRODUCTIONS LTD., "Toftrees," Church Rd., Woldingham, Surrey CR3 7JH **England**. Managing Director: David Mackay. Record producer, music producer (Sabre Music) and record company (Tamarin, PRT Records). Estab. 1970. Produces 6 singles, 3 LPs and 3 CDs/year. Deals with artists and songwriters. Fee derived from sales royalty.
How to Contact: Submit demo tape by mail—unsolicited submissions are OK. Prefers cassette with 1-2 songs and lyric sheet. SAE and IRC. Reports in 2 months.
Music: MOR, **rock** and **top 40/pop**. Produced *World In Motion* (by Pat Murphy), recorded by Up With People on UWP Records; *Already Gone* (by Roger Ronnie), recorded by Joe Fagin on Castle Records; and "Give Me Back," written and recorded by Simon Tauber on Tamarin Records.

*KAREN KANE PRODUCER/ENGINEER 17 Bodwin Ave., Toronto, Ontario M6P 1S4 **Canada**. (416)760-7896. Fax: (416)766-0453. Contact: Karen Kane. Record producer and recording engineer. Estab. 1978. Deals with artists and songwriters. Produces 5-10 singles and 5-10 CDs/year. Fee derived from outright fee from recording artist, outright fee from record company.
How to Contact: Submit demo tape by mail. Unsolicited submissions are OK. Prefers cassette (or VHS videocassette) with 5 songs and lyric or lead sheet—if possible. Does not return unsolicited material. Reports in 2 weeks.
Music: Mostly **acoustic** (i.e., **folk, New Age, bluegrass**), **country** and **rock**; also **reggae, R&B** and **jazz**. Produced *Outbound Plane* (by Tom Russell), recorded by Chad Mitchell on Silver City/Sony Records (country); *Love And Muscles* (by Jonathan Freeman), recorded by Twice Shy on Independent Records (R&B/rock); and *Planet Talk* (by Ana Perez), recorded by Ann Earthling & The Planets on Independent Records (reggae). Other artists include Kay Gardner, Alix Dobkin, Linda Worster.
Tips: "Quality songs with high-quality vocals is one important key for success."

*MATTHEW KATZ PRODUCTIONS, 29903 Harvester Rd., Malibu CA 90265. (213)457-4844. President: Matthew Katz. Record producer, music publisher (After You Publishing/BMI) and record company (San Francisco Sound, Malibu Records). Deals with artists and songwriters. Produces 6 singles, 6 12" singles, 2 LPs and 2 CDs/year. Fee derived from sales royalty when song or artist is recorded.
How to Contact: Submit demo tape by mail. Unsolicited submissions are OK. Prefers cassette (or 8mm videocassette) and lead sheet. Does not return unsolicited material.
Music: Mostly **rock** and **pop**. Produced Jefferson Airplane, Moby Grape, Tim Hardin, Fraternity of Man, Indian Puddin & Pipe, Tripsichord.

GENE KENNEDY ENTERPRISES, INC., 3950 N. Mt. Juliet Rd., Mt. Juliet TN 37122. (615)754-0417. President: Gene Kennedy. Vice President: Karen Jeglum Kennedy. Record producer, independent distribution and promotion firm and music publisher (Chip 'N' Dale Music Publishers, Inc./ASCAP, Door Knob Music Publishing, Inc./BMI and Lodestar Music/SESAC). Estab. 1975. Deals with artists and songwriters. Produces 40-50 singles and 3-5 LPs/year. Fee derived from sales royalty or outright fee from recording artist or record company.
How to Contact: Submit demo tape—unsolicited submissions are OK. Prefers 7½ ips reel-to-reel or cassette with up to 3 songs and lyric sheet. "Do not send in a way that has to be signed for." SASE. Reports in 1-2 weeks.
Music: Country and **gospel**. Produced "Lord Knows I'm Trying" (by Robert/Lonce), recorded by Bo Harrison (country); and "It Should Have Been Me" (by David Parr Preston), recorded by David Reed (gospel), both on Door Knob Records.

KINGSTON RECORDS AND TALENT, 15 Exeter Rd., Kingston NH 03848. (603)642-8493. Coordinator: Harry Mann. Record producer, music publisher (Strawberry Soda Publishing/ASCAP) and record company (Kingston Records). Estab. 1988. Deals with artists and songwriters. Produces 3-4 singles, 2-3 12" singles; 2-3 LPs and 1-2 CDs/year. Fee derived from sales royalty.
How to Contact: Submit demo tape—unsolicited submissions are OK. Prefers cassette with 1-2 songs and lyric sheet. SASE. Reports in 6-8 weeks.
Music: Mostly **rock, country** and **pop**; "no heavy metal." Produced *5¢ Strawberry Soda* (country rock LP) and "Message To You" (ballad rock single), written and recorded by Doug Mitchell; and *Songs Piped from the Moon*, written and recorded by S. Pappas (rock ballads, avante gard LP); all on Kingston Records. Other artists include Bob Moore, Candy Striper Death Orgy, Pocket Band, Jeff Walker, J. Evans, NTM and Miss Bliss.
Tips: "I believe electronic music is going a bit too far and there is an opportunity for a comeback of real as opposed to sequenced music."

KMA, Suite 900, 1650 Broadway, New York NY 10019-6833. (212)265-1570. A&R Director: Morris Levy. Record producer, music publisher (Block Party Music/ASCAP). Estab. 1987. Deals with artists and songwriters. Produces 2 12" singles, 3 LPs and 3 CDs/year. Fee derived from sales royalty or outright fee from recording artist or record company.
How to Contact: Submit demo tape by mail. Prefers cassette. SASE. Reports in 2 months.
Music: Mostly **R&B, dance** and **rap**; also **movie music**. Produced *In The Blood* (by Kissel/Halbreich), recorded by various artists on Ryko Records (African); *Let It Rain, Let It Pour* (by Kissel/Halbreich), recorded by Robin Clark and the David Bowie Band on HME/CBS Records; and *Steal This Disc* (by Kissel/Halbreich), recorded by Michael Case Kissel on Ryko Records.
Tips: "*Original* lyrics a huge plus."

The types of music each listing is interested in are printed in boldface.

GREG KNOWLES, Suite 216, 8306 Wilshire Blvd., Beverly Hills CA 91502. (818)352-9174. A&R: Dunia Abbushi. Record producer and record company (Helion Records). Estab. 1984. Deals with artists and songwriters. Produces 4 CDs/cassettes per year. Fee derived from outright fee from recording artist or record company. Charges for "production services for artists not signed to our company."
How to Contact: Call first and obtain permission to submit. Prefers cassette with 3-4 songs and lyric or lead sheet. "Mention in your cover letter if your demo is a production submission rather than for label consideration." SASE. Reports in 3 weeks.
Music: Produced *Angel*, written and recorded by Diana Blair (country); *Swingstreet* (by Miriam Cutler), recorded by Swingstreet (jazz); and "Car Phone," by Sheeler and Sheeler, all on Helion Records.
Tips: "The quality of demos has risen dramatically over the last couple years. Send in a high quality tape with a nice (promo) package. This way we hear and see you at your best."

KNOWN ARTIST PRODUCTIONS, 1219 Kerlin Ave., Brewton AL 36426. (205)867-2228. President: Roy Edwards. Record producer, music publisher (Cheavoria Music Co./BMI and Baitstring Music/ASCAP) and record company (Bolivia Records and Known Artist Records). Estab. 1972. Deals with artists and songwriters. Produces 10 singles and 3 LPs/year. Fee derived from sales royalty.
How to Contact: "Write first about your interest." Prefers cassette with 3 songs and lyric sheet. Reports in 1 month. "All tapes will be kept on file."
Music: Mostly **country, R&B** and **pop**; also **easy listening, MOR** and **soul**. Produced "Got To Let You Know," "You Are My Sunshine" and "You Make My Life So Wonderful," all written and recorded by Roy Edwards on Bolivia Records (R&B). Other artists include Jim Portwood, Bobbie Roberson and Brad Smiley.
Tips: "Write a good song that tells a good story."

FRANK E. KOEHL, Dept. SM, 6223 N. 51st Ave., Glendale AZ 85301. (602)435-0314. Owner: Frank E. Koehl. Record producer and music publisher (Auburn Records & Tapes, estab. 1962. Speedstar Music/BMI, estab. 1989). Deals with artists and songwriters. Produces 3-5 singles and 7 LPs/year. Fee derived from sales royalty.
How to Contact: Submit demo tape by mail. Unsolicited submissions are OK. Prefers cassette with 2-4 songs and lyric sheet. SASE. Reports in 3 weeks.
Music: Mostly **country, bluegrass** and **traditional music**. Produced "Mr. Woolworth" and "Burglar Man" (by Frank Koehl), recorded by Al Ferguson on Auburn Records (folk country); also "Shack Tree" written and recorded by Troy McCourt on Auburn Records (country). Other artists include Cherry River Boys.
Tips: "Keep it country. No rock. Looking for traditional country and bluegrass, mostly acoustic. Country is going back to the older traditional songs."

KREN MUSIC PRODUCTIONS, P.O. Box 5804, Hacienda Heights CA 91745. (818)855-1692. Co-owner: Kris Clark. Record producer, music publisher (BMI). Estab. 1985. Deals with artists and songwriters. Produces 10 singles and 4 LPs/year. Fee derived from sales royalty when song or artist is recorded.
How to Contact: Submit demo tape—unsolicited submissions are OK. Prefers cassette with 3 songs and lyric sheet. SASE. Reports in 4-6 weeks.
Music: Mostly **country, pop** and **rock**; also **gospel, R&B** and **New Age**. Produced *Twinkle, Twinkle Lucky Star* (country) and *Chill Factor* (country LP) both written and recorded by Merle Haggard on Epic/CBS Records; and "Where Fools Are Kings" (by Jeffrey Steele), recorded by Steve Wariner on CBS Records.
Tips: "The demo tape must show the best of the song you've got to offer."

L.A. ENTERTAINMENT, 29836 W. Rainbow Crest Dr., Agoura Hills CA 91301. (818)889-8578. Fax: (818)889-8578 Ext. 222. VP West Coast A&R: Glen D. Ducan. Record Producer (Jim Ervin Productions), record company (Blue Monkey Records) and music publisher (T&S Music Publishing/ASCAP). Estab. 1988. Deals with artists and songwriters. Fee derived from sales royalty when song or artist is recorded.
How to Contact: Submit demo tape—unsolicited submissions are OK. Prefers cassette (or videocassette if available) with 3 songs, lyric and lead sheets if available. "All written submitted materials (i.e. lyric sheets, letter, etc.) should be typed." SASE. Reports in 1 month.
Music: Mostly **R&B, New Age** and **alternative**; also **pop/rock, jazz** and **country**.
Tips: "A hit song is a hit song, whether it is recorded in a professional environment or at your home. Concentrate first on the writing of your material and then record it to the best of your ability. A professional sounding recording may help the presentation of a song, but it will not make or break a true hit."

LANDMARK AUDIO OF NASHVILLE, Box 148296, Nashville TN 37214-8296. Producers: Bill Anderson, Jr. and D.D. Morris. Record producer, music publisher (Newcreature Music/BMI) and TV/radio syndication. Deals with artists and songwriters. Produces 12 singles and 12 LPs/year. Works with 9 new songwriters/year. Works with composers and lyricists; teams collaborators. Fee derived from sales royalty.

How to Contact: Prefers 7½ ips reel-to-reel or cassette (or videocassette) with 4-10 songs and lyric sheet. SASE. Reports in 1 month.

Music: Mostly **country crossover**; also **blues, country, gospel, jazz, rock** and **top 40/pop.** Produced *Sincerely, Rhonda*, by Rhonda Ingle on Phonorama Records (MOR LP); and *The Traditional Continues*, by Vernon Oxford on Audiograph Records (country LP). Other artists include Pam Fenelon, Skeeter Davis, Teddy Nelson, JoAnne Cash Yates, Eveline, De Fox and Wayne Oldham.

LARI-JON PRODUCTIONS, 325 W. Walnut, Rising City NE 68658. (402)542-2336. Owner: Larry Good. Record producer, music publisher (Lari-Jon Publishing/BMI) and record company (Lari-Jon Records). Estab. 1967. Deals with artists and songwriters. Produces 10 singles and 5 LPs/year. "Producer's fees are added into session costs."

How to Contact: Submit demo tape by mail—unsolicited submissions are OK. "Must be a professional demo." SASE. Reports in 2 months.

Music: Country, gospel-Southern and **50s' rock.** Produced *Glory Bound Train*, written and recorded by Tom Campbell; *Hanging From the Bottom*, written and recorded by Johnny Nace; and "Pick Me Up On Your Way Down" (by Harlan Howard), recorded by Larry Good, all on Lari-Jon Records. Other artists include Kent Thompson.

Tips: "Be professional in all aspects of the music business."

LARK TALENT & ADVERTISING, Box 35726, Tulsa OK 74153. (918)749-1648. Owner: Jana Jae. Record producer, music publisher (Jana Jae Music/BMI) and record company (Lark Record Productions, Inc.). Estab. 1980. Deals with artists and songwriters. Fee derived from sales royalty when song or artist is recorded.

How to Contact: Submit demo tape—unsolicited submissions are OK. Prefers cassette or VHS videocassette with 3 songs and lead sheet. Does not return unsolicited material.

Music: Mostly **country, bluegrass** and **classical;** also **instrumentals.** Produced "Fiddlestix" (by Jana Jae); "Mayonnaise" (by Steve Upfold); and "Flyin' South" (by Cindy Walker); all country singles recorded by Jana Jae on Lark Records. Other artists include Sydni, Hotwire and Matt Greif.

JOHN LATIMER, Box 6541, Cleveland OH 44101. (216)467-0300. Producer: John Latimer. Record producer, record company (Play Records) and independent. Estab. 1985. Deals with artists and songwriters. Produces 1-2 LPs/year. Fee derived from sales royalty or outright fee from recording artist or record company.

How to Contact: Submit demo tape—unsolicited submissions are OK. Prefers cassette (or ¾" or VHS videocassette if available) with 5 songs and lyric or lead sheets. SASE. Reports in 6 weeks.

Music: Mostly **rock** and **alternative.** Produced *Exhibit A, Exhibit B* and *Exhibit C* (compilations) on Play Records. Other artists include The Bellows, I-TAL U.S.A., Serious Nature, Hipshot and Mike O'Brien.

JOHN LEAVELL, 2045 Anderson Snow, Spring Hill FL 34609. (904)799-6102. Producer: John Leavell. Record producer and recording studio. Estab. 1980. Deals with artists and songwriters. Produces 10-12 singles/year. Fee derived from outright fee from recording artist and record company. Charges artist upfront for demo production.

How to Contact: Submit demo tape—unsolicited submissions are OK. Prefers cassette (or VHS videocassette if available) with 4-5 songs and lyric sheet. SASE. Reports in 4 weeks.

Music: Mostly **Christian rock, Christian contemporary** and **gospel;** also **rock** and **country.** Produced "Sons of Thunder" (by Tom Butler), recorded by Sons of Thunder; *Mr. Hyde*, recorded by Mr. Hyde; and *Morning Star*, recorded by Morning Star, all on Leavell Records. Other artists include Greg Eadler, Jim Butler, Tom Martin, Final Stand and One Eyed Jack.

Tips: "Make the best first impression you can! Always keep writing new material."

LEE SOUND PRODUCTIONS, RON LEE, VALUE FOR MONEY, HOPPY PRODUCTIONS, Stewart House, Hill Bottom Road, Sands-Ind. Est., Highwycombe, Buckinghamshire HP12-4HJ **England.** Phone: (0630)647374. Fax: (0630)647612. Contact: Catherine Lee. Record producer. Estab. 1971. Deals with artists and songwriters. Fee derived from sales royalty.

How to Contact: Submit demo tape by mail—unsolicited submissions are OK. Prefers cassette (or VHS/PAL videocassette if available) with 3 songs and lyric sheet or lead sheets. SAE and IRC. Reports in 6 weeks.

Music: All types. Produced "Dona" (by M. Tyler), recorded by Mike Shereden; "Hot Stuff" and "Jukin' At the Joint" (by R.C. Bowman), recorded by Chromatics, all on Snoop Records. Other artists include Daniel Boone, Amazing Dark Horse and Orphan.

LEMON SQUARE PRODUCTIONS, Dept. SM, P.O. Box 671008, Dallas TX 75367. (214)750-0720. A&R: Mike Anthony. Producer: Bart Barton. Record producer, music publisher and record label. Deals with artists and songwriters. Produces 2 singles and 3 LPs/year. Fee derived from sales royalty. **How to Contact:** Write first and obtain permission to submit. Prefers cassette and lyric sheet or lead sheet. Does not return material. Reports in 2 months.
Music: Mostly **country** and **gospel.** Produced "Like Goin' Home" (by Allison Gilliam), recorded by Susie Calvin on Canyon Creek Records (country); "Still Fallin' " (by Dave Garner), recorded by Audie Henry on RCA/Canada Records (country); and "Lord If I Make It To Heaven" (by Dale Vest/T. Overstreet), recorded by Billy Parker on RCA/Canada Records (country). Other artists include Glen Baily, Susie Calvin and Bev Marie.

LEOPARD MUSIC, 23, Thrayle House, Stockwell Road, London, SW9 0XU **England.** Phone: (071)737-6681/081.672.6158. Fax: 071.737.7881. Executive Producer: Errol Jones. Record producer (F&J Music/PRS, BMI) and record company (Leopard Music, Jet Set International). Estab. 1978. Deals with artists and/or songwriters. Produces 6 singles, 6 12″ singles and 2 LPs/year. Fee derived from sales royalty.
How to Contact: Write first and obtain permission to submit. Prefers cassette (or VHS PAL videocassette) with 3 songs and lyric or lead sheets. "Include biography, resume and picture." SASE. Reports in 2 weeks.
Music: Mostly **dance music, soul** and **pop**; also **ballad, reggae** and **gospel.** Produced "Time After Time" (by Guy Spells), recorded by Rico J (single); "I Need You" (by E. Campbell and E. North Jr.), recorded by Big Africa (single); and *God is Beauty*, written and recorded by Evelyn Ladimeji (LP); all on Leopard Music. Other artists include Samantha Simone and The Sea.

*LETHAL AUDIO WORK("LAW"), 2610 Mackenzie St., Vancouver, B.C. V6K4A1 **Canada.** (604)738-0569. Producer: Mark Charpentier. Record producer, consulting. Estab. 1991. Deals with artists and songwriters. Produces 3 CDs/year. Fee depends on situation.
How to Contact: Submit demo tape by mail. Unsolicited submissions are OK. Prefers DAT or TDK SA-X cassette (or VHS/SVHS videocassette if available). "Include equipment used in demo." SASE. Reports in 2-4 weeks.
Music: **Video, film, scoring** and **post production.** NO rap, metal, def, pop stars.

LINEAR CYCLE PRODUCTIONS, Box 2608, Sepulveda CA 91393-2608. Producer: R. Borowy. Record producer. Estab. 1980. Deals with artists and songwriters. Produces 15-25 singles, 6-10 12″ singles, 15-20 LPs and 10 CDs/year. Fee derived from sales royalty.
How to Contact: Submit demo tape—unsolicited submissions are OK. Prefers cassette or 7⅜ ips reel-to-reel (or ½″ VHS or ¾″ videocassette if available). Does not return unsolicited material. Reports in 6 weeks to 6 months.
Music: Mostly **rock/pop, R&B/blues** and **country**; also **gospel** and **comedy.** Produced "The Rip" (by M. Pandanceski), recorded by Gush on Smashin' Records (AOR); "I Wanna Squee" (by E. Link), recorded by Tommy Squish on Froot Records (Dance); and "Fo' Mo' To' Yo' " (by PXL-32A76), recorded by Black Axs on Hip Hop Records (Rap). Other artists include M.C. Sheeee, Clem McClem, Wanna Meet a Rabbitte, De La Hoys featuring Taco Byter, Eugene Cornblatt, Captain Float and His Soggy Army and The Drinking Brothers.
Tips: "Send a high quality demo on high quality tapes."

LIVE PRODUCTIONS INC., Dept. SM, Box 448, Hanover VA 23069. (804)730-1765. Fax: (804)730-1838. President: Patrick D. Kelley. Record producer, music publisher (Studley Publishing), record company (Live Productions) and recording studio (The Fishing Hole). Estab. 1988. Deals with artists and songwriters. Produces 8 LPs/year. Fee derived from sales royalty. "We charge clients not on our label for studio time."
How to Contact: Submit demo tape—unsolicited submissions are OK. Prefers cassette (or VHS videocassette if available) with any number of songs and lyric sheet. "Be specific on what you are seeking (publishing, recording contract, etc.)." SASE. Reports in 1 month.
Music: **Country, gospel,** and **pop**; also **rock, folk** and **children's.** Produced *The Girl I Left Behind* (public domain), recorded by Southern Horizon (Civil War period music); *'Cause I'm on the Radio*, recorded by John Trimble, and *Magical Toy*, recorded by Andy and Cindy and Thensome.

*LOCO SOUNDS, 603 E. Broadway, Denver City TX 79323-3311. (806)592-8020. Fax: (806)592-9486. Producer/Owner: Jere' Lowe. Record producer, record company and music publisher (Fab 5 Records, Jere' Lowe Publishing/BMI). Estab. 1978. Deals with artists and songwriters. Produces 10 singles and 3+ CDs/year. Fee derived from sales royalty when song or artist is recorded, fee from recording artist, fee from record company.

How to Contact: Submit demo tape by mail. Unsolicited submissions are OK. Prefers cassette (or any videocassette) with 3 songs and lyric sheet. "Best songs only—better quality demos sell songs." Reports in 1 month.

Music: Mostly **new** or **young country, R&B, Spanish;** also **pop/top 40, children's, adult contemporary.** Produced "Prettiest Girl in Texas" (by Tony Vincent), recorded by Big Band Rodeo; "1956 Cadillac" (by Verda Luthi) and "Tell Me Who Are You" (by Richard Allen) both recorded by Clay Bohnam, all on Fab Five Records. Other artists include Kelli Weymouth.

Tips: "On demos please be very word strong—we need to hear your voice."

LOCONTO PRODUCTIONS, Box 16540, Plantation FL 33318. (305)741-7766. President: Frank X. Loconto. Record producer and music publisher. Estab. 1978. Deals with artists and songwriters. Produces 20 singles and 20 LPs/year. Fee derived from sales royalty, outright fee from songwriter/artist and/or outright fee from record company.

How to Contact: Write first and obtain permission to submit. Prefers cassette. SASE.

Music: Produced "Calypso Alive and Well," written and recorded by Obediah Colebrock (island music); "Standing on the Top" (by various artists), recorded by Mark Rone (C&W); and "Walking On Air" (by Ken Hatch), recorded by Frank Loconto (motivational); all on FXL Records. Other artists include Bruce Mullin, Bill Dillon and James Billie (folk music).

HAROLD LUICK & ASSOCIATES, Box B, Carlisle IA 50047. (515)989-3748. Record producer, music industry consultant and music publisher. Deals with artists and songwriters. Produces 20 singles and 6 LPs/year. Fee derived from sales royalty, outright fee from artist/songwriter or record company, and from consulting fees for information or services.

How to Contact: Call or write first. Prefers cassette with 3-5 songs and lyric sheet. SASE. Reports in 3 weeks.

Music: Traditional country, gospel, contemporary country and **MOR.** Produced Bob Everhart's LP *Everhart;* Don Laughlin's *Ballads of Deadwood S.D.* LP; Lee Mace's Ozark Opry albums; and Darrell Thomas' singles and LPs. "Over a 12-year period, Harold Luick has produced and recorded 412 singles and 478 albums, 7 of which charted and some of which have enjoyed independent sales in excess of 30,000 units."

Tips: "We are interested in helping the new artist/songwriter make it 'the independent way.' This is the wave of the future. As music industry consultants, our company sells ideas, information and results. Songwriters can increase their chances by understanding that recording and songwriting is a business. 80% of the people who travel to large recording/publishing areas of our nation arrive there totally unprepared as to what the industry wants or needs from them. Do yourself a favor. Prepare, investigate and only listen to people who are qualified to give you advice. Do not implement anything until you understand the rules and pitfalls."

M.R. PRODUCTIONS, 404 St-Henri, Montreal, Quebec H3C 2P5 **Canada.** (514)871-8481. Producer: Mario Rubnikowich. Record producer, record company (Nephelim Records, MGR). Estab. 1987. Deals with artists and songwriters. Produces 3 singles, 3 LPs and 4 CDs/year. Fee derived from outright fee from record company and sales.

How to Contact: Submit demo tape by mail—unsolicited submissions are OK. Prefers cassette, 15 ips reel-to-reel with 3 songs and lyric or lead sheets. Does not return unsolicited material. Reports in 5 weeks.

Music: Mostly **New Age, pop** and **rock.**

JIM McCOY PRODUCTIONS, Rt. 2, Box 114, Berkeley Springs WV 25411. President: Jim McCoy. Record producer and music publisher (Jim McCoy Music/BMI). Estab. 1964. Deals with artists and songwriters. Produces 12-15 singles and 6 LPs/year. Fee derived from sales royalty.

How to Contact: Submit demo tape—unsolicited submissions are OK. Prefers cassette or 7½ or 15 ips reel-to-reel (or Beta or VHS videocassette if available) with 6 songs and lyric or lead sheets. Does not return unsolicited material. Reports in 1 month.

Music: Mostly **country, rock** and **gospel;** also **country/rock** and **bluegrass.** Produced "Dyin' Rain" and "I'm Gettin Nowhere," both written and recorded by J.B. Miller on Hilton Records (country). Other artists include Mel McQuain, Red Steed, R. Lee Gray, John Aikens and Jim McCoy.

MAGIC APPLE RECORDS, Box 530547, Miami FL 33153-0547. (305)758-1903. Founders: Gregory W. Hill and Clancy T. Gaughan. A full service record, production and publishing company. Estab. 1990. Deals with artists and songwriters. Produces 3-5 singles and 3-5 12" singles/year. Fee derived from sales royalty when song or artist is recorded or advances from record company.

How to Contact: Submit demo tape—unsolicited submissions are OK. Prefers cassette (or VHS videocassette if available) with 1-3 songs. "Include pictures and bios if available." SASE. Reports in 2-3 weeks.

Music: Mostly **pop/dance,** and **R&B, dance** and **rap;** also **pop/rock.** Produced "Without Your Love" and "Don't Let Me Go," written and recorded by Nardy (dance); and "Hard Core Rebel" (by Rio & CAP) (rap); also "Jam On" (by Anonymous) all on Magic Apple Records.
Tips: "Know your field, and especially your business."

LEE MAGID PRODUCTIONS, Box 532, Malibu CA 90265. (213)463-5998. President: Lee Magid. Record producer and music publisher (Alexis Music, Inc./ASCAP, Marvelle Music Co./BMI, Gabal Music Co./SESAC), record company (Grass Roots Records and LMI Records) and management firm (Lee Magid Management). Estab. 1950. Deals with artists, songwriters and producers. Produces 4 singles, 4 12″ singles, 8 LPs and 8 CDs/year. Publishes 10-15 new songwriters/year. Works with artists and songwriters; teams collaborators. Fee derived from sales royalty and outright fee from recording artist.
How to Contact: "Send cassette giving address and phone number; include SASE." Prefers cassette (or VHS videocassette) with 3-6 songs and lyric sheet. "Please only one cassette, and photos if you are an artist/writer." Reports only if interested, "as soon as we can after listening."
Music: Mostly **R&B, rock, jazz** and **gospel;** also **pop, bluegrass, church/religious, easy listening, folk, blues, MOR, progressive, soul, instrumental** and **top 40.** Produced "What Shall I Do?" (by Quincy Fielding, Jr.); "I Got Joy" (by Quincy Fielding, Jr.) and "Whenever You Call" (by Calvin Rhone); all recorded by Tramaine Hawkins on Sparrow Records (gospel rock). Other artists include Julie Miller, Tramaine Hawkins and Perry "The Prince" Walker.
Tips: "Stick with your belief and a good melody and lyric."

MAJA MUSIC, 335 Lyceum Ave., Philadelphia PA 19128. (215)487-1359. Owners: Michael Aharon and John Anthony. Record producer. Estab. 1984. Deals with artists. Produces 3 LPs, 4 EPs and 3 CDs/year. Fee derived from outright fee from recording artist or record company. "Fee covers arrangement, production, pre-production and programming. For demos, fee also covers all recording costs."
How to Contact: Submit demo tape—unsolicited submissions are OK. Prefers cassette with 3-6 songs. Artists should include photo. Does not return unsolicited material. Reports in 3 weeks.
Music: Mostly **folk-rock** and **pop/urban contemporary;** also **New Age, world-beat** and **experimental.** Produced *I Will Stand Fast,* written and recorded by Fred Small on Flying Fish Records (folk/rock LP); *Out of the Darkness,* written and recorded by Tom Juravitch on Flying Fish Records (folk/rock LP); and *Jaguar,* written and recorded by Fred Small on Flying Fish Records (folk/rock LP). Other artists include Heather Mullen, Charlie Cooper Project and Julia Haines.
Tips: "Send material which exhibits your personal style and creativity, even if it is not 'commercial' material. Individuality is starting to matter again. Lyrics are starting to matter again. Singer-songwriters are on the radio again."

COOKIE MARENCO, Box 874, Belmont CA 94002. Record producer/engineer. Estab. 1981. Deals with artists and songwriters. Produces 10 CDs/year. Fee derived from sales royalty and outright fee from recording artist or record company.
How to Contact: Write first and obtain permission to submit. Prefers cassette with 8 songs and lyric sheet. Does not return unsolicited material. Reports in 8 months.
Music: Mostly **R&B, dance, alternative modern rock, instrumental, ethnic** and **avante-garde;** also **classical, pop** and **jazz.** Producer on *Winter Solstice II,* written and recorded by various artists; *Heresay* (by Paul McCandless); and *Turtle Island String Quartet* (by Turtle Island), all on Windham Hill Records (instrumental). Other artists include Modern Mandolin Quartet, Ladysmith Black Mambazo, Alex DeGrassi, Art Landem, Charlie Haden and Roy Hargrove.

PETE MARTIN/VAAM MUSIC PRODUCTIONS, Box 29688, Hollywood CA 90029-0688. (213)664-7765. President: Pete Martin. Record producer, music publisher (Vaam Music/BMI, Pete Martin Music/ASCAP) and record company (Blue Gem Records). Estab. 1982. Deals with artists and songwriters. Produces 12 singles and 5 LPs/year. Fee derived from sales royalty. (Send small packages only.)
How to Contact: Prefers cassette with 2 songs and lyric sheet. SASE. Reports in 1 month.
Music: Mostly **top 40/pop, country** and **R&B.** Producer of country acts: Sherry Weston, Frank Loren, Brian Smith & The Renegades. Pop acts: Victoria Limon, Cory Canyon.
Tips: "Study the market in the style that you write. Songs must be capable of reaching top five on charts."

*MASTERPIECE PRODUCTIONS & STUDIOS, 7002 O'Neil, Wichita KS 67212-3353. (316)943-1190. Owner/Producer: Tim M. Raymond. Record producer (Masterpiece Productions), studio owner (Masterpiece Studio), music publisher (ArtUnique Music/ASCAP). Estab. 1980. Deals with artists and songwriters. Produces 200 singles, 10 12″ singles, 25 LPs, 5 EPs and 20 CDs/year. Fee derived from sales royalty when song or artist is recorded, outright fee from recording artist, outright fee from record company.

How to Contact: Call first to arrange personal interview. Submit demo tape by mail. Unsolicited submissions are OK. Prefers cassette (or VHS videocassette) with 4-6 songs and lyric sheet. "Please send a complete promo pack (photos, tapes and bio). Prefers audio submissions on DAT tape, if available." SASE. Reports in 6 weeks.

Music: Mostly **gospel (Christian), pop (top 40), country**; also **R&B, vocal jazz** and **rap.** Produced *Layin' My Heart on the Line* (by A. Dixson), recorded by Ann Dixson on New Day Records; *Change Of Heart* (by A. Dixson), recorded by Kindred Spirits on Spirit Song Records; and "Help Me Thru The Rain" (by L. Dudeck), recorded by GiGi on DuSing Music Records. Other artists include Cat Paws in Motion, Homefire, Karen Carter, Sons Of Thunder, The Karr Sisters, Tyler Green, Earnest Alexander.

Tips: "We are always looking for a unique talent, whether it be an artist or songwriter—emphasize the quality which makes you unique!"

*DAVID MATHES PRODUCTIONS, P.O. Box 22653, Nashville TN 37202. (615)252-6912. President: David W. Mathes. AF-FM licensed. Record producer. Estab. 1962. Deals with artists and songwriters. Produces 6-10 singles, 4-16 12″ singles and 4-6 LPs/year.

How to Contact: Prefers 7½ or 15 ips reel-to-reel or cassette (or videocassette) with 2-4 songs and lyric sheet. "Enclose correctly stamped envelope for demo return." Reports as soon as possible.

Music: Mostly **country** and **gospel**; also **bluegrass, R&B** and **top 40/pop.** Produced "Hello Jesus Hello" (by Craig Anderson), recorded by DeAnna (country/gospel) on Heirborn Records; and "My Love for You" (by David Ideannia Mathes), recorded by Warner Mack (country) on Sapphire Records. Other artists include Johnny Newman, Nashville Sidemen and Singers, Silver Eagle Band and The Ballard's.

Tips: "We look for professional material and presentations. Don't expect miracles on the first song released. Try to be different in style."

PATRICK MELFI, 3365 W. Millerberg Way, W., Jordan UT 84084. (801)566-9542. Contact: Patrick Melfi. Record producer, music publisher (BMI) and record company (Alexas Records). Estab. 1984. Deals with artists and songwriters. Produces 6 singles, 2 LPs, 1 EP and 2 CDs/year. Fee derived from outright fee from recording artist or record company.

How to Contact: Submit demo tape—unsolicited submissions are OK. Prefers cassette (or VHS videocassette if available) with 1-6 songs and lyric or lead sheet. SASE. Reports in 2 months.

Music: Mostly **country** and **pop**; also **oldies** and **gospel.** Produced "She's On Her Own" (by P. Melfi/AJ Masters), recorded by AJ Masters; "Between Your Heart & Mine" (by Melfi) recorded by Prophesy on Atlantic Records (MOR); and "Child of God" (by Melfi/Kone), recorded by Sheri Sampson on Godley Music Records (gospel). Other artists include Crossfire and Hard Riders.

Tips: "Write from the heart! Write a good story and compliment it with a strong melody. Good production is a must. Always start with a great hook!"

*MIDWEST RECORDS, 3611 Cleveland Ave., Lincoln NE 68504-2452. (402)466-1446. Producer: Harold Dennis. Record producer, music publisher (Cornhusker/BMI) record company (Midwest Records) and Country Music Promotions. Estab. 1983. Deals with artists and songwriters. Produces 2 singles, 2 12″ singles and 2-3 LPs/year. Fee derived from outright fee from recording artist. "We do not charge songwriters; but we do charge artists."

How to Contact: Submit demo tape by mail. Unsolicited submissions are OK. Prefers cassette with 2 songs and lyric sheets. Does not return unsolicited material. Reports in 2 months.

Music: Mostly **country** and **crossover country.** Produced *Never Think for a Moment* and "Making a Life of Your Own," both written and recorded by Ricky Spains; and "Walk Me to the Door" (by Conway Twitty), recorded by Ron Royer, all on Midwest Records.

MR. WONDERFUL PRODUCTIONS, INC., 1730 Kennedy Rd., Louisville KY 40216. (502)774-1066. President: Ronald C. Lewis. Record producer, music publisher (Ron "Mister Wonderful" Music/BMI and 1730 Music/ASCAP) and record company (Wonderful Records and Ham Sem Records). Estab. 1984. Deals with artists and songwriters. Produces 2 singles and 3 12″ singles/year. Fee is derived from outright fee from recording artist or record company. "We also promote records of clients nationwide to radio stations for airplay."

How to Contact: Prefers cassette with 4 songs and lyric sheet. SASE. Reports in 2 weeks.

Music: Mostly **R&B, black gospel** and **rap.** Produced "Am I Good" (by Ron Lewis) and "Just Another In My Past" (by Pam Layne), both recorded by Amanda Orch (R&B); and "Just Do It," written and recorded by Boyz from the Ville (rap), all on Wonderful Records.

*A.V. MITTELSTEDT, 9717 Jensen Dr., Houston TX 77093. (713)695-3648. Producer: A.V. Mittelstedt. Record producer and music publisher (Sound Masters). Works with artists and songwriters. Produces 100 singles, 10 LPs and 20 CDs/year. Fee derived from sales royalty and outright fee from recording artist.

How to Contact: Prefers cassette. SASE. Reports in 3 weeks.
Music: Mostly **country, gospel, crossover;** also **MOR** and **rock.** Produced "Too Cold at Home" (by Bobby Harding), recorded by Mark Chestnutt on Cherry Records (country); "Two Will Be One," written and recorded by Kenny Dale on Axbar Records (country); and "Shake Your Hiney" (by Gradual Taylor), recorded by Roy Head on Cherry Records (crossover country). Other artists include Randy Corner, Bill Nash, Ron Shaw, Borderline, George Dearborne and Good, Bad and Ugly.

MJM PRODUCTIONS, Box 654, Southbury CT 06488. Owner: Michael McCartney. Record producer and music publisher (On The Button/BMI). Estab. 1988. Deals with artists and songwriters. Produces 5 singles/year. Fee derived from sales royalty or outright fee from recording artist.
How to Contact: Submit demo tape—unsolicited submissions are OK. Prefers cassette with 3-5 songs and lyric sheet. "Give details as to what your goals are: artist in search of deal or writer wishing to place songs." SASE. Reports in 1 month.
Music: Mostly **country/rock, pop rock** and **R&B.** Produced "Could've Been," "Movin' On" and "Separate Ways," all singles on Giant Records.

*MODERN MINSTREL MIXING, P.O. Box 19112, Minneapolis MN 55419. (612)824-4135. Fax: (612)332-6663. Contact: C.W. Frymire. Record producer. Estab. 1988. Deals with artists and songwriters. Fee derived from sales royalty when song or artist is recorded or outright fee from recording artist.
How to Contact: Submit demo tape by mail. Unsolicited submissions are OK. Prefers cassette (or videocassette) with 3 or more songs and lyric sheet. "Please include any press or previous airplay information along with photo and tour schedule." SASE.
Music: Mostly **acoustic, folk (contemporary), folk/rock;** also **ethnic/world, blues (acoustic).**

MOM AND POP PRODUCTIONS, INC., Box 96, El Cerrito CA 94530. Executive Vice President: James Bronson, Jr. Record producer, record company and music publisher (Toulouse Music/BMI). Deals with artists, songwriters and music publishers. Fee derived from sales royalty.
How to Contact: Prefers cassette with 2-4 songs and lyric sheet. SASE. Reports in 1 month.
Music: **Bluegrass, gospel, jazz, R&B** and **soul.** Artists include Les Oublies du Jazz Ensemble.

*MONTICANA PRODUCTIONS, P.O. Box 702, Snowdon Station, Montreal, Quebec H3X 3X8 Canada. Executive Producer: David Leonard. Record producer. Estab. 1963. Deals with artists, songwriters and artists' managers. Fee negotiable.
How to Contact: Submit demo tape by mail—unsolicited submissions are OK. Prefers cassette, phonograph record (or VHS videocassette) with maximum 10 songs and lyric sheet. "Demos should be as tightly produced as a master." Does not return unsolicited material.
Music: Mostly **top 40;** also **bluegrass, blues, country, dance-oriented, easy listening, folk, gospel, jazz, MOR, progressive, R&B, rock** and **soul.**

*MOON PRODUCTIONS AND RECORDING STUDIO, 1885 Pomeroy Rd., Arroyo Grande CA 93420. (805)489-8146. Producer/Owner: Thomas Gingell. Record producer, record company (Lunartic Records), recording studio, demo production/album production. Estab. 1989. Deals with artists and songwriters. Produces 2 singles, 4 LPs, 2-4 EPs and 1-2 CDs/year. Fee derived from outright fee from recording artist or album sales cassette/CD/studio rates.
How to Contact: Submit demo tape by mail. Unsolicited submissions are OK. Prefers cassette with 3-4 songs, lyric sheet or lead sheet. SASE. Reports in 6-8 weeks.
Music: Mostly **rock, country, Celtic;** also **folk rock, Christian, acoustic/New Age/jazz.** Produced *Under The Influence,* written and recorded by Jay Horn on Catch the Wind Records (Christian); *Save A Place,* written and recorded by Jill Knight (folk); and *Black Sheep* (by various), recorded by Moody Druids (Celtic). Other artists include Terry Lawless, Brian Gregory (Flatbed Band), Thomas E. Gingell, Sunny Country 102 FM and Jay Russell.
Tips: "If you love recording/songwriting/performing, then don't stop. If you want to just make money you probably won't."

GARY JOHN MRAZ, 1324 Cambridge Dr., Glendale CA 91205. (818)246-PLAY. Producer: Gary Mraz. Record producer. Estab. 1984. Deals with artists and songwriters. Produces 6-12 12″ singles and 2-6 LPs/year. Fee derived from sales royalty or outright fee from record company.
How to Contact: Submit demo tape—unsolicited submissions are OK. Prefers cassette (or VHS videocassette if available) with 3 songs and lyric sheets. "Does not return unsolicited material."
Music: Mostly **dance, pop** and **R&B.** Produced "Too Kind," recorded by Tara King on Radio Magic Records. Other artists include Bush Baby.
Tips: "Get your finished product to the untapped college radio market."

*MSH PRODUCTIONS, P.O. Box 121616, Nashville TN 37212. (615)269-9984. Producer: Mark Stephan Hughes. Record producer, record company, music publisher (Fresh Start Music Ministries, Baby Huey/Krimson Hues Music Publishing). Estab. 1969. Deals with artists and songwriters. Produces 4 LPs/year. Fee derived from sales royalty when song or artist is recorded.
How to Contact: Submit demo tape by mail. Unsolicited submissions are OK. Prefers cassette with 3 songs and lyric sheet. "Send only professional submissions." SASE. Reports in 3 months.
Music: Mostly **Christian, praise, worship**; also **scripture songs, most other Christian material**. Produced *Call Jesus*, written and recorded by Kathy Davis; *Worthy Alone*, written and recorded by Lanier Ferguson; and *You Are Exalted*, written and recorded by Mark Stephan Hughes, all on Fresh Start Records. Other artists include Fresh Start Ministries Worship Band.

*MUNICH RECORDS b.v., (formerly Munich Productions/Records B.V.), Vadaring 90, 6702 EB Wageningen, **The Netherlands**. 08370-21444. Fax: 22959. Producer/President: Job Zomer. Record producer, music publisher (Munich Music) and record company (Munich Records b.v.). Deals with artists and songwriters. 24-track studio. Produces 20 CD singles, 20 7" singles and 20 CDs/year.
How to Contact: Submit demo tape by mail—unsolicited submissions are OK. Prefers cassette (or Beta or VHS PAL videocassette if available). Does not return unsolicited material. Reports in 1 month.
Music: Mostly **jazz, reggae** and **blues**; also **new classical**. Artists include Toxedo Buck, Pia Bech, Bernard Berkhout, Charlestown Jazzband, The Rockmasters, Monti, Joe Guitar Huges, Evan Johns and Hans Zomer with Winterprism Schubert.

MUSIPLEX, 2091 Faulkner Road, N.E., Dept. SM, Atlanta GA 30324. (404)321-2701. Producer/Engineer: George Pappas. Record producer, engineer. Estab. 1967. Deals with artists and songwriters. Produces 5 singles, 5 12" singles, 3 LPs, 4 EPs and 5 CDs/year. Fee derived from outright fee from recording artist or record company.
How to Contact: Call first to arrange personal interview. Prefers cassette with 3-5 songs and lyric or lead sheets. "In order for any material to be returned a SASE must accompany any and all material submitted." Reports in 2 months.
Music: **Alternative rock, rap** and **R&B**; also **gospel, rock** and **pop**. Produced *Scarred But Smarter*, recorded by Drivin'n'Cryin' on Island Records; and *Stiff Kitty* on Drastic Measures Records and *Nihilist*, written and recorded by Nihilist on Metal Blade Records. Recently credited work: Bobby Brown/Big Daddy Kane; Lateasha (Motown); Kinetic Dissent (Road Racer); Michelle Shocked (Polygram); Georgia Satellites (Elektra).

*MUST ROCK PRODUCTIONZ WORLDWIDE, Suite 5C, 167 W. 81st St., New York NY 10024. (212)DOC-0310. President: Ivan Rodriguez. Record producer, recording engineer. Estab. 1980. Produces 5 singles, 5 12" singles, 2 LPs, 3 EPs and 2 CDs/year. Fee derived from fee and royalty.
How to Contact: Call first and obtain permission to submit. Prefers cassette (or VHS videocassette) and lyric sheet. Does not return unsolicited material. Reports in 2 weeks.
Music: Mostly **hip-hop, R&B, pop**; also **soul, ballads** and **soundtracks**. Produced "Poor Georgie" (by MC Lyte/DJ Doc), recorded by MC Lyte on Atlantic Records (rap); "Mama Said Knock You Out," recorded by LL Cool J on Def Jam (rap); and *Criminal Minded*, recorded by Boogie Down Productions on Jive/RCA (rap).

CHUCK MYMIT MUSIC PRODUCTIONS, 9840 64th Ave., Flushing NY 11374. Contacts: Chuck and Monte Mymit. Record producer and music publisher (Chuck Mymit Music Productions/BMI). Estab. 1978. Deals with artists and songwriters. Produces 8-10 singles, 2-4 12" singles, 3-5 LPs and 3-5 CDs/year. Fee derived from sales royalty.
How to Contact: Submit demo tape—unsolicited submissions are OK. Prefers cassette (or VHS videocassette if available) with 3-5 songs and lyric or lead sheet. SASE. Reports in 4-6 weeks.
Music: Mostly **pop, rock** and **R&B**. Produced *Wanna Love You* (by Monte Mymit), recorded by Laura Cabrera on SMC Records (rap/rock); "Easy Lovin'" (by C. Mymit-Donnell & Cody), recorded by Linda L. on RCA Records (pop); and *Give Me Your All* (by Monte Mymit), recorded by Gina Diamond on EDR Records (pop). Other artists include Rita Rose, Tony Spataro, and The Dellmonts.
Tips: "Keep writing—keep trying—you never know! We are also interested in female vocalists."

Market conditions are constantly changing! If you're still using this book and it is 1995 or later, buy the newest edition of Songwriter's Market at your favorite bookstore or order directly from Writer's Digest Books.

NARADA PRODUCTIONS, Dept. SM, 1845 North Farwell, Milwaukee WI 53202. (414)272-6700. A&R Coordinator: Michele Frane. Record producer, music publisher and record company (Narada Records). Estab. 1980. Deals with artists only. Produces 30 LPs and 30 CDs/year. Fee derived from sales royalty when song or artist is recorded.
How to contact: Submit demo tape by mail. Unsolicited submissions are OK. Prefers cassette (or VHS videocassette if available) with 5 songs. Does not return unsolicited material. Reports in 2 months.
Music: New Age, **instrumental** and **world beat**; also **film and television sound tracks.**
Tips: "We want instrumental music."

NASHVILLE COUNTRY PRODUCTIONS, 306 Millwood Dr., Nashville TN 37217. (615)366-9999. President/Producer: Colonel Jack Lynch. Record producer, music publisher (Jaclyn Music/BMI), record companies (Jalyn and Nashville Country Productions) and distributor (Nashville Music Sales). Estab. 1987. Works with artists and songwriters. Produces 1-12 LPs/year. Fee derived from sales royalty. "We do both contract and custom recording."
How to Contact: Submit demo tape, or write or call first and obtain permission to submit. Prefers cassette with 1-4 songs and lyric or lead sheet. SASE. Reports in 1 month.
Music: Mostly **country, bluegrass, MOR** and **gospel**; also **comedy.** "We produced Keith Whitley and Ricky Skaggs' first album." Produced *He Isn't You* (by Sara Hull), recorded by Elaine George on Jalyn Records; *I Want As Much Of You As I Can Get*, written and recorded by Lonnie Pierce on NCP-103 Records; *18 Wheels Rolling* (by Bill Parks), recorded by Doug Mounts on NQD-9526 Records.
Tips: "Prepare a good quality cassette demo, send to us along with a neat lyrics sheet for each song and a resume, picture and SASE."

NASHVILLE INTERNATIONAL ENTERTAINMENT GROUP, Box 121076, Nashville TN 37212-1076. (615)244-5357. President: Reggie M. Churchwell. Vice President: Mark Churchwell. General Manager, Music Group: Ben Haynes. Record producer, music publisher (Sir Winston Music/BMI and Four Seasons Music/ASCAP) and Reggie M. Churchwell Artist Management, Nashville International Talent and Nashville International Concerts. Labels include Phoenix Records and Nashville International Records. Deals with songwriters only. Produces 6 singles, 2 LPs and 2 CDs/year. Fee derived from sales royalty.
How to Contact: Write first about your interest. Prefers cassette with 1-4 songs and lyric sheet. Does not return unsolicited material "unless prior contact has been made and SASE included."
Music: **Country, MOR, pop** and **gospel (contemporary)**; also **R&B (crossover), rock (country, pop, power pop), soul (crossover)** and **top 40/pop.** Produced "Letter in Red," written and recorded by Kenny Durham (pop/gospel single); and *A Little Left of Center Line*, written and recorded by Howard Lips (LP), both on Phoenix Records; "Unluckiest Songwriter in Nashville," written and recorded by Sonny Shroger on Hazzard Records (single); and "Please," recorded by Howard Lips Christian Blues on Phoenix Records (single).

NEBO RECORD COMPANY, Box 194 or 457, New Hope AL 35760. Manager: Jim Lewis. Record producer, music publisher (Nebo Ridge Publishing/ASCAP) and record company (Nebo Record Company). Estab. 1985. Deals with artists and songwriters. Fee derived from sales royalty.
How to Contact: Submit demo cassette tape by mail—unsolicited submissions are OK. Prefers cassette tape or VHS videocassette with 1 song and lyric sheet. "It is OK to send a videocassette, but not a must. Songwriters should be sure to send a SASE. Send a neat professional package. Send only 1 song." Does not return unsolicited material. Reports "as soon as possible."
Music: Mostly **modern country, traditional country** and **gospel**; also **rock, R&B** and **pop.** Produced "Blue Again," written and recorded by Hal Jones (country); "Sweet Lovin'," written and recorded by Reba Harris (country); "Goin' Home," written and recorded by Ann Clark (gospel), all on Nebo Records. Other artists include Mary Stone, John Deal and others.
Tips: "We like to get to know songwriters and singers who contact us, so it would be a good idea for a songwriter or singer to send a personal bio and 1 or 2 full-length photos, when he or she contacts us. We also need several female singers for our Nebo Record label. Female singers should send a personal bio, 1 or 2 full-length photos, and 1 of their best songs on a cassette demo tape. We will be signing several—female singers—to our Nebo Record label, so female singers will need to contact us soon for a review."

BILL NELSON, 45 Perham St., W. Roxbury MA 02132. Contact: Bill Nelson. Record producer and music publisher (Henly Music/ASCAP). Estab. 1987. Deals with artists and songwriters. Produces 6 singles and 6 LPs/year. Fee derived from outright fee from recording artist.

How to Contact: Submit demo tape by mail—unsolicited submissions are OK. Prefers cassette with 3-4 songs and lyric sheet. SASE. Reports in 3-4 weeks.

Music: Mostly **country, pop** and **gospel.** Produced "Big Bad Bruce" (by J. Dean), recorded by B.N.O.; "Do You Believe in Miracles" (by B. Nelson), recorded by Part-Time Singers; and "Don't Hurry With Love" (by B. Bergeron), recorded by B.N.O.; all on Woodpecker Records.

*NEO SYNC LABS, 20 Colpitts Dr., Windsor NY 13865. (607)775-0200. Owner: Bob Damiano. Record producer, engineer/recording studio operator, solo artist, Exactly Opposite Music (BMI). Estab. 1987. Deals with artists and songwriters. Produces 2-3 LPs, 2-3 EPs, 1 CD. Fee derived from outright fee from recording artist.

How to Contact: Submit demo tape by mail. Unsolicited submissions are OK. Prefers DAT or cassette with 1-10 songs. Include SASE for response. Does not return unsolicited material. Reports in 2 weeks.

Music: Mostly **progressive rock, hard rock, country;** also **jazz** and **dance.** Produced *The Journey,* written and recorded by Joe Rose on Up Front Music (light rock); *Expect Love,* written and recorded by P.C. Mantree on Pure Water Records (light rock); *Media Burn* (by Ron Dokken), recorded by Simple Simon (progressive rock). Other artists include Angi Margaritis, Milk & Honey and Ice Water Mansion.

Tips: "Be original. Don't just jump on the 'grunge wagon.' Let us bring out strengths and downplay weaknesses."

THE NETWORK PRODUCTION GROUP, (formerly Com'tech Productions, Inc.), P.O. Box 28816, Philadelphia PA 19151. (215)473-5527. General Manager: Leroy Schuler. Record producer. Estab. 1990. Deals with artists and songwriters. Fee derived from royalty, outright fee from record company. Produces 6 singles, 25 12″ singles and 3 LPs/year.

How to Contact: Submit demo tape by mail. Unsolicited submissions are OK. Prefers cassette with 4 songs and lyric sheet. SASE. Reports in 3 weeks.

Music: Mostly **R&B, hip-hop** and **funk.** Produced "Secret Love Affair," recorded by Ken Chaney on Logic records; "Evil Stalks the Land," recorded by Savanna Gold featuring King; and "Once Upon A Time," recorded by Next Level.

*NEU ELECTRO PRODUCTIONS, P.O. Box 1582, Bridgeview IL 60455. (708)839-5978. Owner: Bob Neumann. Record producer, record company. Estab. 1984. Deals with artists and songwriters. Produces 16 singles, 16 12″ singles, 20 LPs, 4 CDs/year. Fee derived from outright fee from recording artist, outright fee from record company.

How to Contact: Submit demo tape by mail. Unsolicited submissions are OK. Prefers cassette (or VHS videocassette if available) with 3 songs and lyric sheet or lead sheet. "Accurate contact phone numbers and addresses, promo packages and photos." Does not return material. Reports in 2 weeks.

Music: Mostly **dance, house, techno, rap, rock;** also **experimental, New Age, top 40.** Produced "Juicy," written and recorded by Juicy Black on Dark Planet International Records (house); "Make Me Smile," written and recorded by Roz Baker (house); and *Take My Love* (by Bob Neumann), recorded by Beatbox-D on N.E.P. Records (dance).

Tips: "Quality of production will influence profitability."

NEW EXPERIENCE RECORDS, Box 683, Lima OH 45802 (219)424-5768 (Indiana); (419)228-8562 (Ohio). Music Publisher: James L. Milligan Jr. Vice President: Tonya Milligan. Record producer, music publisher and record company (New Experience Records, Grand-Slam Records, Rap Label). Estab. 1989. Deals with artists and songwriters. Produces 5 12″ singles, 2 LPs, 1 EP and 2 CDs/year. Fee derived from sales royalty when song or artist is recorded, outright fee from recording artist or outright fee from record company, "depending on services required."

How to Contact: Submit demo tape—unsolicited submissions are OK. Address material to A&R Dept. or Talent Coordinator (Carl Milligan). Prefers cassette with a minimum of 3 songs and lyric or lead sheets (if available). "If tapes are to be returned, proper postage should be enclosed and all tapes and letters should have SASE for faster reply." Reports in 1 month.

Music: Mostly **pop, R&B** and **rap;** also **gospel, contemporary gospel** and **rock.** Produced "All I Want," written and recorded by Lavel Jackson; "Putting My Heart on the Line" (by Peter Frampton), recorded by James Junior; and "Call on the Name of Jesus," written and recorded by Carl Milligan, all on New Experience Records. Other artists include Venesta Compton, Volume 10, Darryl Bacon.

Tips: "Believe in yourself. Work hard. Keep submitting songs and demos. Most of all, be patient; if there's interest you will be contacted."

NEW HORIZON RECORDS, 3398 Nahatan Way, Las Vegas NV 89109. (702)732-2576. President: Mike Corda. Record producer. Deals with singers preferably. Fee derived by sales royalty.
How to Contact: Call first and obtain permission to submit. Prefers cassette with 1-3 songs and lyric sheet. SASE.
Music: Blues, easy listening, jazz and **MOR.** Produced "Lover of the Simple Things," "Offa the Sauce" (by Corda & Wilson) and "Go Ahead and Laugh," all recorded by Mickey Rooney on Prestige Records (London). Artists include Bob Anderson, Jan Rooney, Joe Williams, Robert Goulet and Bill Haley and the Comets.
Tips: "Send good musical structures, melodic lines, and powerful lyrics or quality singing if you're a singer."

*NIGHTSTAR RECORDS INC., P.O. Box 602, Yarmouthport MA 02675 (508)362-3601. President: David M. Robbins. Record producer, music publisher (Dact Production/BMI) and record company (Nightstar Records Inc.). Estab. 1990. Deals with artists and songwriters. Produces 3-4 LPs and 3-4 CDs/year. Fee derived from sales royalty when song or artist is recorded. "May charge artists in advance. Monies could be used to cover studio time and pre-album costs. Nightstar covers all manufacturing and promotional costs."
How to Contact: Write first and obtain permission to submit. Prefers cassette (or VHS videocassette if available) with several songs. Include biography. SASE. Reports in 2-3 weeks.
Music: Mostly **movie soundtrack, New Age** and **acoustic.** Produced *Daydreams, By the Water's Edge* and *Dancing With the Moon,* all written and recorded by Deborah T. Robbins on Nightstar Records.
Tips: "Send us music from the heart, don't clutter the music. We primarily deal in instrumental music. The time is right for the reception of non-vocal music, both on the radio and at retail levels. There a growing market for relaxing music. New Age music as it is known is losing its appeal, because of some of the monotonous songs that artists create. Keep songs to 3-5 minutes, and let it flow."

DAVID NORMAN PRODUCTIONS, #1632, 639 Garden Walk Blvd., College Park GA 30349. (404)994-1770. Producer/Engineer: David Norman. Record producer. Estab. 1986. Deals with artists and songwriters. Produces 6 singles, 5 LPs, 5 EPs and 4 CDs/year. Fee derived from outright fee from recording artist or outright fee from record company.
How to Contact: Submit demo tape by mail—unsolicited submissions are OK. Prefers cassette with 5 songs. "Please send photo." SASE. Reports in 2 weeks.
Music: Mostly **funk** and **R&B;** also **techno-music.** Produced AC Black on Motown Records (dance/rock); "Derek Coile," recorded by Derek Coile on Macola Records (dance); and "Wages of Syn," recorded by Synical on Kudzu Records (techno). Engineer for Peabo Bryson—Sony Records.
Tips: "I see the music industry being overkilled by musical programming on computers. Hopefully, in the coming years, music will once again resort to real drummers and musicians actually playing the music themselves."

NOT RECORDS TAPES, Box 29161, Los Angeles CA 90029. President: Mike Alvarez. Record producer, record company and music publisher. Estab. 1984. Deals with artists and songwriters. Produces 2 singles, 2 12" singles, 2 LPs, 2 EPs and 2 CDs/year. Fee derived from sale of product.
How to Contact: Submit demo tape by mail—unsolicited submissions are OK. Prefers cassette with lyric sheet. Does not return unsolicited material. Reports in 1 month.
Music: Mostly **industrial, film** and **alternative.** Produced "Theme From the Magnificent 7 Elvis Impersonators" and "You Can Love Me Too," written and recorded by M. Alvarez on Not Records Tapes. Other artists include Roky Erickson, Woodshock and Ken Jones.
Tips: "Please submit final mixes. No preproductions please."

*RICK NOWELS PRODUCTIONS, INC., % Stuart A. Ditsky, CPA, PC, Suite 1900, 733 Third Ave., New York NY 10017. Contact: Business Management. Record producer, music publisher. Estab. 1983. Deals with artists and songwriters. Fee derived from sales royalty when song or artist is recorded, outright fee from recording artist or outright fee from record company.
How to Contact: Submit demo tape by mail. Unsolicited submissions are OK. Prefers cassette (or VHS videocassette) and lyric sheet or lead sheet. Does not return unsolicited material. Reports in 2 months.
Music: Mostly **rock, guitar, pop;** also **new wave, modern rock.** Produced *Heaven Is A Place On Earth* and *Leave a Light On,* recorded by Belinda Carlisle on Virgin Records; also *I Can't Wait,* recorded by Stevie Nicks on Modern/Atlantic Records.

NUCLEUS RECORDS, Box 111, Sea Bright NJ 07760. President: Robert Bowden. Record producer, music publisher (Roots Music/BMI) and record company (Nucleus Records). Estab. 1979. Deals with artists and songwriters. Produces 2 singles and 1 LP/year. Fee derived from sales royalty.

How to Contact: Submit demo tape—unsolicited submissions are OK. Prefers cassette with 3 songs and lyric sheets. SASE. Reports in 4 weeks.

Music: Mostly **country** and **gospel**; also **pop.** Produced "4 O'Clock Rock," "Henrey C," and "Will You Miss Me Tonight" (by Bowden), recorded by Marco Sision; all on Nucleus Records.

ORDER PRODUCTIONS, 6503 York Rd., Baltimore MD 21212. (410)377-2270. President: Jeff Order. Record producer and music publisher (Order Publishing/ASCAP and Orderlottsa Music/BMI). Estab. 1986. Deals with artists and songwriters. Fee derived from sales royalty and outright fee from recording artist and record company.

How to Contact: Submit demo tape—unsolicited submissions are OK. "Lyric sheets without recorded music are unacceptable." Prefers cassette with 3 songs and lyric sheet. SASE. Reports in 1 month.

Music: Works with **all types of music.** Produced "Won't You Dance With Me" (by Jeff Order), recorded by Tiny Tim (dance/single); *Sea of Tranquility, Isis Unveiled,* and *Keepers of the Light,* written and recorded by Jeff Order (New Age LPs). Other artists include Stephen Longfellow Fiske, Higher Octave and Rock Group Boulevard.

Tips: "We only work with songwriters and artists who are seriously committed to a career in music. Submissions must be professionally recorded. Learn as much about the business of music as possible. Don't expect someone to invest in your art if you haven't done it first!"

JOHN "BUCK" ORMSBY/ETIQUETTE PRODUCTIONS, Suite 273, 2442 N.W. Market, Seattle WA 98107. (206)524-1020. Fax: (206)524-1102. Publishing Director: John Ormsby. Record producer (Etiquette/Suspicious Records) and music publisher (Valet Publishing). Estab. 1980. Deals with artists and songwriters. Produces 1-2 singles, 3-5 LPs, and 3-5 CDs/year. Fee varies.

How to Contact: Submit demo tape by mail—unsolicited submissions are OK. Prefers cassette (or VHS videocassette if available) with lyric or lead sheet. SASE. Reports in 6-8 weeks.

Music: R&B, rock, pop and **country.** Produced *Snake Dance* (by Rogers), recorded by Kinetics on Etiquette Records (LP); *Hard to Rock Alone,* written and recorded by K. Morrill on Suspicious Records (LP); and *Crazy 'Bout You,* (by R. Rogers), recorded by Kinetics on Etiquette Records. Other artists include Don Walker and KJ Corye.

Tips: "Tape production must be top quality; lead or lyric sheet professional."

MICHAEL PANEPENTO/AIRWAVE PRODUCTION GROUP INC., 1916 28th Ave. South, Birmingham AL 35209. (205)870-3239. Producer: Michael Panepento. Record producer, music publisher (Panelips Music/BMI) and artist development company (ChapelLane Productions). Estab. 1985. Deals with artists and songwriters. Produces 5 singles, 2 12″ singles, 4 LPs, 5 EPs and 3 CDs/year.

How to Contact: Submit demo tape—unsolicited submissions are OK. Prefers cassette with 3 songs and lyric sheet. SASE. Reports in 10 weeks.

Music: Mostly **rock, R&B** and **pop;** also **jazz** and **country.** Produced *Home* (by Keith Hammrick), recorded by The Skeptics (modern rock); *Drivin Me Crazy* (by Larry Shaw) recorded by Radio Ranch (country); and *Diptones "Live"* (by various), recorded by The Diptones on Pandem Records (MOR). Other artists include Syntwister, Vallejo, Kelly Black and Elvis' Grave.

PANIO BROTHERS LABEL, Box 99, Montmartre, Saskatchewan S0G 3M0 **Canada.** Executive Director: John Panio, Jr. Record producer. Estab. 1977. Deals with artists and songwriters. Produces 1 single and 1 LP/year. Works with lyricists and composers and teams collaborators. Fee derived from sales royalty or outright fee from artist/songwriter or record company.

How to Contact: Submit demo tape—unsolicited submissions are OK. Prefers cassette with any number of songs and lyric sheet. SASE. Reports in 1 month.

Music: Country, dance, easy listening and **Ukrainian.** Produced *Ukranian Country,* written and recorded by Vlad Panio on PB Records.

PATTY PARKER, Suite 114, 10603 N. Hayden Rd., Scottsdale AZ 85260. (602)951-3115. Fax: (602)951-3074. Producer: Patty Parker. Record producer, record company (Comstock, Paylode), miscellaneous independent releases. Estab. 1978. Deals with artists and songwriters. Produces 18 singles, and 4-5 CDs/year. Fee derived from outright fee from recording artist or recording company. "We *never* charge to songwriters!! Artist's fee for studio production/session costs."

How to Contact: Submit demo tape—unsolicited submissions are OK. Prefers cassette (or VHS videocassette if available) with 4 songs and lyric sheet. Voice up front on demos. SASE. Reports in 2 weeks.

Music: Mostly **country—traditional** to **crossover, western** and some **A/C.** Produced "Sedona Serenade" (by Frank Fara), recorded by Jess Owen (country); "Denim Duster," written and recorded by Carl Freberg (country); and "When Mama Prayed" (by Will Yeats), recorded by Patti Mayo, all on Comstock Records. Other artists include Paul Gibson, Colin Clark, Claudia and The Roberts Sisters.

Tips: "Writers should strive to write medium to uptempo songs—there's an abundance of ballads. New artists should record medium to uptempo material as that can sometimes better catch the ear of radio programmers."

*CHRIS PATI PRODUCTIONS, INC., 289 Littleneck Rd., Centerport NY 11721. (516)754-6800. President: Chris Pati. Vice President: Glenn Deveau. Record producer, music publisher (Patitude Publishing), record company (Modern Voices Inc.) and recording studio (Modern Voices). Estab. 1984. Deals with artists and songwriters. Produces 10 singles, 10 12″ singles and 5 CDs/year. Fee derivation varies per situation. "Charges a studio fee (only)."
How to Contact: Write first to arrange personal interview. Prefers cassette (or VHS ½″ videocassette if available) with 4 songs and lyric sheet. Does not return unsolicited material. Reports in 1 month.
Music: Mostly **pop, dance/house** and **rock (metal,** etc.**)**; also **alternative, jazz** and **classical.** Produced "Sweat the Beat," by Iyong; "Move It," by Tony Mascolo; "I Want Love" by Tony Mascolo; and "I've Got a Notion" by Monaco.
Tips: "Make sure the song suits your voice. Strong vocal performance a must."

DAVE PATON, The Idea Bank, 16776 Lakeshore Dr., C-300, Lake Elsinore CA 92330. Contact: Dave Paton. Record producer and music publisher (Heaven Songs/BMI). Deals with artists and songwriters. Produces 20 singles and 3-5 LPs/year. Fee negotiable.
How to Contact: Submit demo tape—unsolicited submissions are OK. Prefers 7½ ips reel-to-reel or cassette with 3-6 songs and lyric sheet. SASE. Reports in 4 weeks.
Music: Country, dance, easy listening, jazz, MOR, progressive, R&B, rock, top 40/pop and comedy. Produced "Steal My Heart," "Heartache Highway" and "Love is a State of Mind," all written by A.J. Masters and recorded by Linda Rae on Hollyrock Records (country).

MARTIN PEARSON MUSIC, Seestrasse 91, Zurich, CH 8002 **Switzerland.** Phone: (01)202-4077. Contact: Martin Pearson. Record producer, music publisher and record company. Works with artists and songwriters. Produces 2 singles, 2 12″ singles, 1 LP and 1 CD/year. Fee derived from sales royalty or outright fee from record company or artist.
How to Contact: Submit demo tape—unsolicited submissions are OK. Prefers cassette (or PAL videocassette) with 6 songs and lyric sheet. Does not return unsolicited material. Reports in 2 months.
Music: Mostly **pop, rock** and **R&B;** also **disco/rock, disco** and **techno.** Produced *Wild, Wild Boy*, *I Really Don't Know* and *The Jailer*, all written by Sam/Pearson and recorded by Pearson on MPM Records. Other artists include Ashantis, Meanviles and Rick Braun.

PEGMATITE PRODUCTIONS, c/o The Outlook, Box 180, Star Route, Bethel ME 04217. (207)824-3246. Record producer. Deals with artists and songwriters. Produces 12 singles and 6 LPs/year. Fee derived from sales royalty and/or outright fee from record company.
How to Contact: Prefers cassette or 15 ips reel-to-reel (or VHS videocassette if available) with 1 song and lyric sheet. "Please include your name and phone number on the tape." Does not return unsolicited material. Reports in 4-6 weeks.
Music: Mostly **rock, pop** and **country;** also **new wave, heavy metal** and **avant-garde.** Produced *Frontierland*, written and recorded by Sky Frontier (rock); "Smell The Probe," written and recorded by Sonny Probe (rock humor); and *Private WA*, written and recorded by Willie Alexander (word) all on Tourmaline Records. Other artists include Julia Anderson, Peace Corpse.

*PERENNIAL PRODUCTIONS, 73 Hill Rd., Box 109, Redding CT 06875. (203)938-9392. Owner: Sean McNamara. Record producer. Estab. 1992. Deals with artists and songwriters. Fee derived from outright fee from recording artist.
How to Contact: Submit demo tape by mail. Unsolicited submissions are OK. Prefers cassette (or VHS videocassette) with 4-8 songs and lyric sheet or lead sheet. "Include a promo pack." Does not return unsolicited material. Reports in 3-5 weeks.
Music: Mostly **pop, contemporary jazz, alternative rock;** also **R&B, rock** and **adult contemporary.** Produced *Staten Island Rain* (by Urban Jazz Five).

*PERIDOT PRODUCTIONS, 17 Woodbine St., Cranston RI 02910. (401)785-2677. President: Amy Parravano. Record producer, record company, music publisher, performing artist. Estab. 1992. Deals with artists and songwriters. Produces 2 singles, 2 12″ singles and 1 LP/year. Fee derived from outright fee from recording artist.
How to Contact: Submit demo tape by mail. Unsolicited submissions are OK. Prefers cassette with 3-4 songs and lyric sheet. SASE. Reports in 1 month.
Music: Mostly **country, gospel, folk;** also **MOR, children's, novelty.** Produced "America" (by Stamm/Parravano), recorded by Amy Parravano (country); "His Light Shines Down on Me" on Peridot Records (country-gospel) and "Trust in Him" (gospel) both by Amy Parravano and recorded by Amy Beth.

Tips: "The acoustic sound is definitely back. Radio is playing singer-songwriters. Lyrics with good messages are getting listeners' attention."

PERSIA STUDIOS, 378 Bement Ave., Staten Island NY 10310. (718)816-6384. Studio Owner: Chris Vollor. Producer/engineer. Estab. 1982. Deals with artists and songwriters. Produces 5-10 singles, 10 LPs and 5 CDs/year. Fee derived from recording artist or record company. Charges for studio time—session players.
How to Contact: Submit demo tape—unsolicited submissions are OK. Prefers cassette/DAT (or VHS videocassette if available) with 3-4 songs. Does not return unsolicited material. Reports in 2 months.
Music: Mostly **rock, R&B, dance, ethnic, jazz** and **New Age.** Produced National Network PSA's for CARE; Two Gun Cupid, Test Infections, Jam-Mo'Stylen, Sleeper, Rhythm Method, many others.

PAUL PETERSON CREATIVE MANAGEMENT, 9005 Cynthia, #309, Los Angeles CA 90069. (310)273-7255. Contact: Paul Peterson. Record producer, music publisher and personal management firm. Estab. 1983. Deals with artists and songwriters. Produces 2 LPs and 2 CDs/year. Fee derived from sales royalty.
How to Contact: Submit demo tape—unsolicited submissions are OK. Prefers cassette and lyric sheet. SASE. Reports in 3 weeks.
Music: Mostly **rock, pop** and **jazz;** also **country.** Produced "Lost Cabin" (by Steve Cash), recorded by Ozark Mountain Daredevils on Legend Records (country/rock); "Country Pride" (by Paul Peterson and John Boylan), recorded by The Chipmunks on Epic Records (kids, novelty); "Shanghai" (by Brewer and Shipley) (country/pop); and *Everything's Alright,* written and recorded by Priscilla Bowman on Legend Records (blues/rock).

PHILLY BREAKDOWN, 216 W. Hortter St., Philadelphia PA 19119. (215)848-6725. President: Matthew Childs. Record producer, music publisher (Philly Breakdown/BMI) and record company (Philly Breakdown). Estab. 1974. Deals with artists and songwriters. Produces 3 singles and 2 LPs/year. Fee derived from sales royalty when song or artist is recorded.
How to Contact: Submit demo tape—unsolicited submissions are OK. Prefers cassette with 4 songs and lead sheet. SASE. Reports in 6 weeks to 2 months.
Music: Mostly **R&B, hip hop** and **pop;** also **jazz, gospel** and **ballads.** Produced "My Love For You" and "How Would You Feel," both written by Matt Childs and recorded by Gloria Clark on Philly Breakdown Records. Other artists include Leroy Christy, Mark Adam, Jerry Walker and Emmit King.
Tips: "Be original and creative and stay current. Be exposed to all types of music."

JIM PIERCE, 101 Hurts Ln., Hendersonville TN 37075. (615)824-5900. Fax: (615)824-8800. President: Jim Pierce. Record producer, music publisher (see Strawboss Music/BMI) and record company (Round Robin Records). Estab. 1974. Deals with artists and songwriters. Produces 50 singles, 5-6 EPs and 2-3 CDs/year. Fee derived from sales royalty or outright fee from recording artist. "Some artists pay me in advance for my services." Has had over 200 chart records to date.
How to Contact: Write first and obtain permission to submit or to arrange personal interview. Prefers cassette with any number of songs and lyric sheet. Does not return unsolicited material. Reports in 2-3 months.
Music: Mostly **country, contemporary, country/pop** and **traditional country.** Produced "Don't Call Us, We'll Call You," written and recorded by Harlen Helgeson; "You Can't Keep a Good Love Down" (by Jerry Fuller), recorded by Lenny Valenson and "If I Live To Be A Hundred" (by Mae Borden Axton), recorded by Arne Benoni all on Round Robin Records (country singles). Other artists include Bonnie Guitar, Jimmy C. Newman, Margo Smith, Bobby Helms, Sammi Smith, Blaine Dakota, Tim Gillis, Llowell McDowell, Roy Drusky and Harlan Craig.
Tips: "Don't let a 'no' stop you from trying."

PINE ISLAND MUSIC, #308, 9430 Live Oak Place, Ft. Lauderdale FL 37324. (305)472-7757. President: Jack P. Bluestein. Record producer and music publisher. Estab. 1973. Deals with artists and songwriters. Produces 5-10 singles/year. Fee derived from sales royalty.
How to Contact: Artist: query, submit demo tape. Songwriter: submit demo tape and lead sheet. Prefers cassette or 7½ ips reel-to-reel with 1-4 songs. SASE. Reports in 1-2 months.
Music: Mostly **blues, country, easy listening, folk, gospel, jazz, MOR, rock, soul** and **top 40/pop.** Produced "Drivin' Nails," written and recorded by Gary Oakes and *An Old Old Man* (by Beth Thliveris), recorded by Bernice Boyce, both on Quadrant Records. Other artists include Jeffrey Cash and Praise (gospel) and Paula Ma Yu-Fen.
Tips: "Write good saleable material and have an understandable demo made."

POKU PRODUCTIONS, 2090 St. Laurent Blvd., Ottawa, Ontario K1G 1A9 **Canada**. (613)731-0285. President: Jon E. Shakka. Record producer (SOCAN). Estab. 1988. Deals with artists and songwriters. Produces 1 single and 1 12″ single/year. Fee derived from sales royalty when song or artist is recorded, outright fee from recording artist or outright fee from record company.
How to Contact: Write or call first and obtain permission to submit. Prefers cassette (or VHS videocassette if available) with 4 songs and lyric sheet. SASE. Reports in 4 months.
Music: Mostly **funk, rap** and **house music**; also pop, ballads and funk-rock. Produced "Goodman" (by J. Poku/K. Poku), recorded by Jon E. Shakka on Poku Records (rap 12″ single); "Slap Attack" and "R-U Ready" (by J. Poku/K. Poku), recorded by August Skyy on Poku Records.
Tips: "Don't follow trends—set them. Be professional, and know the business. First, hold on to a piece of that publishing. All creativity comes from the God within."

POMGAR PRODUCTIONS, Box 707, Nashville TN 37076-0707. Manager: Don Pomgar. Record producer, music publisher (One Time Music/BMI, Two Time Music/ASCAP). Estab. 1989. Deals with artists and songwriters. Produces 1 12″ single, 1 EP and 4 CDs/year. Fee derived from sales royalty when song or artist is recorded, outright fee from record company.
How to Contact: Submit demo tape—unsolicited submissions are OK. Prefers cassette with 1 to 10 songs and lyric sheet. "If you're an artist send a picture and your best vocal songs. If you're a writer don't send a picture—just your best songs." SASE. Reports in 3 weeks.
Music: Mostly **country, pop** and **rock**. Produced *Leave It Alone* (by Tom Jenkins), recorded by Turmoil on Grit Records (rock) and *News to Me* (by Shannon/Jenkins), recorded by Sheila Shannon on CCR Records (country). Other artists include Danny Leader (country independent artist), Terry Bower (pop/rock) and Nina Byzantine.
Tips: "Here's what we're about. We try to find great songs to use with the artists we produce. Our artists are released on independent labels with the goal of shopping them to a major label for rerelease or distribution. We also pitch songs regularly to major artists through our publishing company. We're growing fast—we need songs."

*POPS NEON ENTERPRISES, P.O. Box 4125, West Hills CA 91308. Director: Steve Hobson. Record producer and music publisher (Auntie Argon Music/BMI). Estab. 1988. Deals with artists and songwriters. Produces 2 singles/year. Fee derived from sales royalty or outright fee from recording artist. Retainer required for production services.
How to Contact: Write first and obtain permission to submit. Prefers cassette with 1-3 songs and lyric sheets. Reports in 2 weeks. "Type lyric sheets. Don't overproduce demos. Piano/vocal or guitar/vocal are OK. Unsolicited tapes go straight in the trash, unopened and unheard."
Music: Mostly **mainstream, pop/top 40**. Produced "Goodness Will Come" and "In the Shadow of Your Wings," recorded by Jill Heller on Pops Neon Records.
Tips: "Submit songs that best represent your direction and best showcase your talents as an artist."

*PRAIRIE MUSIC LTD., P.O. Box 438, Walnut IA 51577. (712)366-1136. President: Robert Everhart. Record producer, music publisher (BMI) and record company (Prairie Music). Estab. 1964. Deals with artists and songwriters. Produces 2 singles and 2 LPs/year. Fee derived from outright fee from recording artist or record company.
How to Contact: Submit demo tape by mail. Unsolicited submissions are OK. Prefers cassette. SASE. Reports in 4 months.
Music: Mostly **traditional country, bluegrass** and **folk**. Produced "Time After Time," "Street Sleepers" and "Rock of Hollywood," all written and recorded by Bob Everhart on Folkways Records (traditional country). Other artists include Bonnie Sanford and Fiddlin' Grandad Kephart.

PREJIPPIE MUSIC GROUP, Box 2849, Trolley Station, Detroit MI 48231. President: Bruce Henderson. Record producer, music publisher (Prejippie Music Group/BMI) and record company (PMG Records). Estab. 1990. Deals with artists and songwriters. Produces 6-12 12″ singles, 2 LPs and 2 EPs/year. Negotiates between sales royalty and outright fee from artist or record company.
How to Contact: Submit demo tape—unsolicited submissions are OK. No phone calls please. Prefers cassette with 3-4 songs and lyric sheets. SASE. Reports in 6 weeks.
Music: Mostly **funk/rock** and **techno/house**; also **alternative rock, experimental music** (for possible jingle/scoring projects). Produced "Lolita" by Bourgeoisie Paper Jam and "Supermarket Obscene" by Prejippies; all by PMG Productions. Other artists include Urban Transit (house), Deep Six Honey (alternative/experimental) and Jezebel (house).
Tips: "We're looking for songwriters who have a good sense of arrangement, a fresh approach to a certain sound and a great melody/hook for each song."

THE PRESCRIPTION CO., 70 Murray Ave., Port Washington NY 10050. (516)767-1929. President: David F. Gasman. Vice President A&R: Kirk Nordstrom. Tour Coordinator/Shipping: Bill Fearn. Secretary: Debbie Fearn. Record producer and music publisher (Prescription Co./BMI). Deals with

artists and songwriters. Fee derived from sales royalty or outright fee from record company.
How to Contact: Write or call first about your interest then submit demo. Prefers cassette with any number of songs and lyric sheet. Does not return unsolicited material. Reports in 1 month. "Send all submissions with SASE or no returns."
Music: Mostly **bluegrass, blues, children's, country, dance, easy listening, jazz, MOR, progressive, R&B, rock, soul** and **top 40/pop.** Produced "You Came In" and "Rock 'n' Roll Blues," by Medicine Mike (pop singles, Prescription Records); and *Just What the Doctor Ordered,* by Medicine Mike (LP).
Tips: "We want quality—fads mean nothing to us. Familiarity with the artist's material helps too."

PROUD PORK PRODUCTIONS, 230 Montcalm St., San Francisco CA 94941. (415)648-9099. President: Scott Mathews. Record Producer and music publisher (Hang On to Your Publishing/BMI). Estab. 1975. Deals with artists and songwriters. Produces 6 singles, 6 CDs/year. Fee derived from sales royalty when song or artist is recorded, outright fee from recording artist on demo recordings.
How to Contact: Submit demo tape—unsolicited submissions are OK. Prefers cassette. SASE. Reports in 2 months.
Music: Mostly **rock/pop, country** and **R&B.** Produced *Right to Choose* (by J.W. Harding/S. Mathews), recorded by John Wesley Harding on Sire Records; *Slide of Hand,* written and recorded by Roy Rogers on Liberty Records; and *Volt* (by Various), recorded by Trip Shakespeare on A&M Records. Has produced Roy Orbison, John Hiatt, Rosanne Cash, Chuck Prophet, Jenni Muldaur and Dick Dale. Has recorded with everyone from Barbra Streisand to Sammy Hagar, including The Beach Boys, Keith Richards, John Lee Hooker, Van Morrison, Huey Lewis and Bonnie Raitt, to name but a few.

*RAINBOW RECORDING, 113 Shamrock Dr., Mankato MN 56001. (507)625-4027. Contact: Michael Totman. Record producer, recording studio. Estab. 1986. Deals with artists and songwriters. Produces 4 singles, 4 LPs and 1 EP/year. Fee derived from outright fee from recording artist or outright fee from record company.
How to Contact: Write or call first and obtain permission to submit or submit demo tape by mail. Unsolicited submissions are OK. Prefers cassette (or VHS videocassette) with 4 songs and lyric sheet or lead sheet. Does not return unsolicited material.
Music: Mostly **rock, country, top 40;** also **old time, punk-alternative** and **R&B.** Produced *Within* (by Counterpoint) (alternative); *Malicious Hooliganism* (by Libido Boyz) (alternative); "It's Not that I Don't Love You" (by Carol Gappa) (country), all recorded by Rainbow Recording.

RANDALL PRODUCTIONS, Box 265, N. Hollywood CA 91603-0265. (312)509-2945 and (818)569-5653. President: Ashley Brown. Record producer, video producer and musical services to artists/songwriters. Produces 5 singles, 2 LPs and 2 music videos/year. Fee derived from sales royalty.
How to Contact: Submit demo tape by mail—unsolicited submissions are OK. Prefers cassette (or VHS videocassette if available) with 3-5 songs and lyric sheet. "Clearly label each item you send. Include photo/bio if available." SASE. Does not return material without return postage. Reports in 1 month, "but be patient."
Music: Mostly **R&B, soul, funk, pop, blues, gospel;** also accepting finished masters of these and **rock (heavy, hard, metal,** some **acid)** for Grandville Rock Sampler album. Produced *Mama Was Right,* recorded by Mack Simmons on Grandville Records (blues/R&B LP); and *Mr. Joy,* recorded by The Jade (LP), with newest singles "Mr Joy/Sweet Love," "Thunderkeeper/The Poetry of You" released overseas and distributed by Timeless Records/London (R&B/pop).

*REEL ADVENTURES, 9 Peggy Lane, Salem NH 03079. (603)898-7097. Chief Engineer/Producer: Rick Asmega. Estab. 1972. Produces 45 singles, 1 12″ single, 20 LPs, 2 EPs and 6 CDs/year. Fee derived from outright fee from recording artist or outright fee from record company.
How to Contact: Submit demo tape by mail. Unsolicited submissions are OK. Prefers cassette (or VHS/8mm videocassette) and lyric sheet. Include photos and resume. SASE. Reports in 2-3 weeks.
Music: Mostly **pop, funk, country;** also **blues, reggae** and **rock.** Produced "New Crowd" (by Ned Claflin) on Touch Tone Records; *Hot-Hot-Hot* (by Jazz Hamilton) on Real Records; and "One Change" (by Buddy Sullivan) on Rock'n Records, all recorded by Reel Adventures. Other artists include Larry Sterling, Broken Men, Melvin Crockett, Fred Vigeant, Monster Mash, Carl Armand, Cool Blue Sky, Ransome, Backtrax, Too Cool for Humans and Burn Alley.

RIGEL MEDIASOUND, Box 678, Baird TX 79504. (915)893-2616. Producer/Engineer: Randy B. McCoy. Record producer. Estab. 1985. Deals with artists and songwriters. Produces 10 singles and 4 LPs/year. Fee derived from outright fee from artist or record company. Charges artist up front for "all phases of project from start to finish, including production, arrangements, presentation, etc."
How to Contact: Submit demo tape—unsolicited submissions are OK. Prefers cassette with 3-4 songs and lyric sheet. "Make sure vocals can be clearly heard, and keep the arrangments simple and basic." SASE. Reports in 3-4 weeks.

Music: Produced "Texas Gold," written and recorded by various on Code of the West Records (country); "Annex" (by various), recorded by Annex on Annex Records (rock); "2 Days Later" (by Stevens/Walker), recorded by 2 Days Later (contemporary Christian).
Tips: "Craft lyrics carefully, keep music production simple."

RIPSAW PRODUCTIONS, #805, 4545 Connecticut Ave. NW, Washington DC 20008. (202)362-2286. President: Jonathan Strong. Record producer, music publisher (Sugar Mama Music/BMI) and record company (Ripsaw Records). Deals with artists and songwriters. Produces 0-4 singles and 0-3 LPs/year.
How to Contact: Submit demo tape—unsolicited submissions are OK. Prefers cassette and lyric sheet. SASE. Reports "as quickly as time allows."
Music: Mostly **country, blues, rockabilly** and **roots rock.** Helped produce "It's Not the Presents Under My Tree," recorded by Narvel Fetts on Renegade Records (45) and "Oooh-Wow!" recorded by Uptown Rhythm Kings (LP & cassette); produced *Two Sides*, written and recorded by Bobby Smith (EP); and *Wanted: True R&R*, written and recorded by Billy Hancock (EP); last three recorded on Ripsaw Records.

ROCK & TROLL PRODUCTIONS, 19 Chase Park, Batavia NY 14020. (716)343-1722. Vice President: Guy E. Nichols. Record producer, music publisher and record company (Rock & Troll Records). Estab. 1981. Deals with artists and songwriters. Produces 25 singles and 2 LPs/year. Fee derived from sales royalty or outright fee from recording artist.
How to Contact: Submit demo tape—unsolicited submissions are OK. Prefers cassette with 4 songs and lyric sheet. SASE. Reports in 4 weeks.
Music: Mostly **rock, pop** and **R&B.** Produced *Heartbreaker*, written and recorded by Lost Angels; and *Little Trolls*, written and recorded by Little Trolls; both on R&T Records (rock).

ROCKIT RECORDS, INC., Suite 306, 35918 Union Lake Rd., Harrison Twp. MI 48045. (313)792-8452. Production Director: Joe Trupiano. Record Producer: J. D. Dudick. Record producer, music publisher, in-house studio (Ruffcut Recording Studio, Bad Grammar Music/BMI and Broadcast Music, Inc./BMI), record company (Rockit Records) and management company. Estab. 1985. Produces 10-20 singles and 4 CDs/year. Works with songwriters/artists on contract. Pays artists 10% royalty—statutory rate.
How to Contact: Prefers cassette (or videocassette if available) with 3-4 songs and lyric sheet. SASE. Unsolicited submissions are OK. Submit by mail. Reports in 6 weeks.
Music: Mostly **pop/rock, R&B/pop, mainstream rock, New Age** and **heavy metal;** also **alternative, industrial rock, new music, ballads, dance-oriented** and **MOR.** Produced "Choose Life," written and recorded by Laya Phelps (rock); "Main Emotion," written and recorded by Oscar Charles; and "Sin Alley" (by Bob Josey), recorded by Johnny Terry (pop); all on Rockit Records. Other artists include Laya Phelps, Joey Harlow and Carol Martini.
Tips: "We are presently open for producing outside projects *with self-supporting budgets.* This allows our clients the opportunity to shop their own master or sign it to Rockit Records *if* our A&R approves and also considering whether we have an open door policy at the time. Through this project several acts have been signed to major labels in the U.S., as well as indie labels in Europe. We have charted many of our acts on commercial radio in Europe as well as the U.S. We have now diversified into manufacturing all types of products: CDs, cassettes and cassette singles, vinyl EPs, etc. However, our manufacturing facilities offer a European presentation of the product for possible mechanical licensing in our European retail markets. So for artists who plan on manufacturing their own product, we offer an excellent outlet for mechanical retail licensing through our label. This is an avenue for raising extreme revenue so that artists may experience the luxury of producing future LP projects because their past release is raising revenue for them."

ROCKSTAR PRODUCTIONS, P.O. Box 131, Southeastern PA 19399. (215)3379556. Executive Vice President: Jeffrey Sacks. Director of Marketing: Roni Sacks. Record producer. Estab. 1988. Deals with artists and songwriters. Produces 5 singles/year. Fee derived from sales royalty.
How to Contact: Submit demo tape—unsolicited submissions are OK. Prefers cassette with 2 songs and lyric sheets. Does not return unsolicited material. Reports in 6 weeks.
Music: Mostly **rock** and **pop.** Produced "Caught on the Carpet," "Love Is A Luxury" and "Shakespeare Love Scene" written and recorded by Scot Sax on RKS Records (rock).
Tips: "Don't bore us, get to the chorus."

ROCKY MOUNTAIN HEARTLAND PRODUCTIONS, Box 6904, Denver CO 80206. (303)841-8208. Executive Producer: Steve Dyer. Record and video producer and advertising firm (full service—brochures, demo kits, promo packs, graphics, photography). Deals with artists and songwriters. Fee derived from sales royalty or outright fee from songwriter/artist or record company.

How to Contact: Submit demo tape—unsolicited submissions are OK. Prefers cassette (or videocassette if available) with 3-5 songs and lyric sheet or lead sheet. Does not return unsolicited material. Reports in 2-3 weeks.

Music: Mostly **gospel, top 40** and **rock;** also **jazz** and **country.** "Music open and not limited to these types." Produced *The Best Is Yet to Come*, by Kent Parry (big band and orchestra gospel LP); *From Here to Kingdom Come*, by Heart Song (mild gospel/top 40 LP); and *Going, Going, Gone*, by Heart Song (gospel rock LP); all on Record Harvest Records; and *From My Heart*, by Beth Chase. Also produced music for *Tom Slick* TV Show and a Best Western Hotel promotional video.

Tips: "Contact us for specific suggestions relating to your project."

*ROSE HILL GROUP, 1326 Midland Ave., Syracuse NY 13205. (315)475-2936. A&R Director: Vincent Taft. Record producer and music publisher (Katch Nazar Music/ASCAP, Bleecker Street Music/BMI). Produces 5 singles and 2 LPs/year. Fee derived from sales royalty or outright fee from artist/songwriter or record company.

How to Contact: Prefers cassette with 3 songs maximum. SASE. Reports in 2 weeks.

Music: Mostly **top 40/pop, rock, dance;** also **jazz** and **MOR.** Produced "Hot Button," by Prowlers (dance/R&B single); "Free World," by Z Team (dance/pop single); and "So What," by IO (dance/rock single).

MIKE ROSENMAN, 45-14 215 Pl., Bayside NY 11361. (718)229-4864. Producer: Mike Rosenman. Record producer and arranger. Estab. 1984. Deals with artists and songwriters. Produces 4-6 singles, 1 LP and 1 EP/year. Fee derived from sales royalty or outright fee from recording artist.

How to Contact: Submit demo tape—unsolicited submissions are OK. Prefers cassette (or VHS videocassette if available), with 2-4 songs and lyric sheet. Include address and phone number. Put phone number on cassette. Will not return any tapes without SASE. Reports in 2-3 months.

Music: Mostly **pop, R&B, dance/rap** and **rock.** Produced "Don't Bite the Hand That Feeds You" (by Ellen Parker), recorded by Dope Enough For Ya (rap/R&B); and "Child's Play," written and recorded by D.E.F. (rap/R&B), both on Homebase Records. Other artists include Michael Clark, Clilly and Ellen Parker.

Tips: "Send simple demos of good songs. Include SASE if you want your tape back."

RR & R MUSIC PRODUCTIONS INC., (formerly RR & R Productions), Suite 128, 3260 Keith Bridge Rd., Cumming GA 30131. (706)742-7408; also Suite 204, 23 Music Sq. East, Nashville TN 37203. (615)742-7408. Owner/President: Ron Dennis Wheeler. Record producer, music publisher (Super Rapp Publishing/BMI, Aicram Music Publishing/BMI and Do It Now Publishing/ASCAP) and record company (RR&R, Rapture, Ready Records and Yshua Records). Estab. 1964. Works with artists and songwriters. Produces 10-20 compilation CDs and 10-20 CDs/year.

How to Contact: Submit demo tape by mail—unsolicited submissions are OK. Prefers cassette (Type II) or 15 or 30 ips reel-to-reel (or VHS videocassette if available) with lyric chords and lead sheet. "Demo should have lead vocal and music and also a recording of music tracks without vocals." SASE. Reports only if interested—must be clearly produced.

Music: **All types** except **rap** or **New Age** and **satanic.** Produced "You, You, You" (by Richard McGibony), recorded by Ron Dennis Wheeler; "Two Shades of Blue" (by Richard McGibony/Ron Dennis Wheeler), recorded by Bill Scarbrough and Ron Dennis Wheeler; "Keeping Me Strong" (by Irene Gaskin's), recorded by Ron Dennis Wheeler; "Ain't It Just Like Him" and "If We Could See Our Brother" (by Louis Brown), recorded by Pam Jordan. Other artists include Tammie Bridge, "Heather," Voices of Joy, Patty Jones.

SAGITTAR RECORDS, 1311 Candlelight Ave., Dallas TX 75116. (214)298-9576. President: Paul Ketter. Record producer, record company and music publisher. Deals with artists and songwriters. Produces 12 singles and 3 LPs/year. Works with 3 new songwriters/year. Works with composers and lyricists; teams collaborators.

How to Contact: Submit demo tape by mail—unsolicited submissions OK. SASE. Reports in 3-6 weeks.

Music: Mostly **country;** also **folk, MOR (country)** and **progressive (country).** Produced "Stay Till I Don't Love You Anymore," "I Wanna Say 'I Do'" and "Lovin' Bound," by P.J. Kamel (country singles); "Theodore Csanta's Right-Hand-Man," by Dave Gregory (country single); *Only A Woman* by Bunnie Mills (country LP); and *Joe Johnson* by Joe Johnson (pop LP), all on Sagittar Records. Other artists include Jay Douglas, Jackie Rosser, Buddy Howard and Jodi Witt.

Remember: Don't "shotgun" your demo tapes. Submit only to companies interested in the type of music you write. For more submission hints, refer to Getting Started on page 7.

JOJO ST. MITCHELL, 273 Chippewa Dr., Columbia SC 29210-6508. Executive Producer and Manager: Jojo St. Mitchell. Record producer. Deals with artists and songwriters. Produces 10 singles and 4 LPs/ year. Fee derived from sales royalty, booking and licensing.
How to Contact: Prefers cassette (or VHS videocassette if available) with 3-7 songs; include any photos, biography. SASE. Reports in 3-6 weeks, if interested. Enclose return postage.
Music: Mostly **mainstream, pop** and **R&B**; also **rock, new music** and **jazz/rap.** Produced *Wheels of Steel* (by R. Clavon/J. Aiken), recorded by Unique Force (rap LP); *Can't Stop Thinking of You* (by L.S. Skinkle), recorded by Jr. Ellis (pop ballad, LP); "Complicated Love," recorded by True Identity; and *Miracle* (by K. Lyon/T. Lyon), recorded by Kat Lyon (pop LP). Other artists include Carnage, Synthetic Meat, Progress In April, Body Shop, Political Asylum, U.S. Steel, The Sages and Silhouette.

SAS CORPORATION/SPECIAL AUDIO SERVICES, Suite 520, 503 Broadway, New York NY 10012. (212)226-6271. Fax: (212)226-6357. Owner: Paul Special. Record producer. Estab. 1988. Deals with artists and songwriters. Produces 3 singles, 1 12″ single, 5 LPs, 1 EP and 5 CDs/year. Fee derived from sales royalty when song or artist is recorded, outright fee from recording artist or outright fee from record company.
How to Contact: Submit demo tape—unsolicited submissions are OK. Prefers cassette with 1-10 songs and lyric sheet. SASE. Reports in 2-3 weeks.
Music: Mostly **hard rock, funk rock** and **metal**; also **alternative, industrial** and **rap.** Produced "Color Of Darkness," written and recorded by Maria Excommunikata on Megaforce Records (alternative); "Love U/Duke," written and recorded by Heads Up! on Emergo Records (funk rock); "Hope/Emelda" (by Van Orden/Hoffman), recorded by The Ordinaires on Bar None Records (alternative); and *Embrace* (by Thompson), recorded by Wireless on Emergo Records. Other artists include Central Europe, Band Of Weeds, Peter Moffit and Kablama Chunk.
Tips: "Don't be afraid to bring up new and unusual ideas."

SEGAL'S PRODUCTIONS, 16 Grace Rd., Newton MA 02159. (617)969-6196. Contact: Charles Segal. Record producer, music publisher (Segal's Publications/BMI, Samro South Africa) and record company (Spin Records). Works with artists and songwriters. Produces 6 singles and 6 LPs/year. Fee derived from sales royalty.
How to Contact: Submit demo tape—unsolicited submissions are OK. Prefers cassette (or VCR videocassette) with 3 songs and lyric sheet or lead sheet of melody, words, chords. "Please record keyboard/voice or guitar/voice if you can't get a group." Does not return unsolicited material. Reports in 4 months.
Music: Mostly **rock, pop** and **country**; also **R&B** and **comedy.** Produced "Got No Place to Go" (by Segal), recorded by Rosemary Wills on Spin Records; "Only In Dreams" (by Michelle S.), recorded by Will Hauck on Hawk Records; and "One Step at a Time" (by C. Hays), recorded by Centre Group on Spin Records.
Tips: "I find that lots of artists are not ready for the big time when they've had their first hit record. So do your studying before that and listen to lots of artists/styles."

*SHADOWLAND PRODUCTIONS, 3 Lancet Court, Shawnee OK 74801. Music Editor: Russell Walker. Record producer, record company, music publisher (Calvary's Shadow Publications, Morning Dew Publications, Shadowland Records, Shadowland Productions). Estab. 1991. Deals with artists and songwriters. Produces 15-20 singles, 20-24 LPs/year. Fee derived from outright fee from recording artist or financial participation from writers.
How to Contact: Submit demo tape by mail. Unsolicited submissions are OK. Prefers cassette (or VHS videocassette) with 3 songs and lyric sheet or lead sheet. SASE. Reports in 6-8 weeks.
Music: Mostly **Southern gospel, MOR sacred, contemporary Christian**; also **choral anthems, children's songs** and **seasonal.** Produced *Lord, Lift Me Up*, written and recorded by Archer on Conarch Records (gospel); *The Power Line* (by Archer), recorded by Brashear on Courier Records (Southern gospel); *Love Beyond All Measure* (by Walker), recorded by Bethlehem Choir on Bethlehem Records (contemporary). Other artists include Great Gospels Guitars, Bethlehem Brass.
Tips: "Be willing to accept constructive criticism and rewriting. Be open to recording songs suggested by an arranger/producer. Communicate with audience."

SHARPE SOUND PRODUCTIONS, Box 140536, Nashville TN 37214. (615)391-0650. Producer/Engineer: Ed Sharpe. Record producer. Estab. 1990. Deals with artists and songwriters. Fee derived from sales royalty or outright fee from recording artist or record company.
How to Contact: Submit demo tape—unsolicited submissions are OK. Prefers cassette (or VHS videocassette if available) with 4 songs and lyric sheet. SASE. Reports in 2 months.
Music: Mostly **pop, R&B, rock, folk, country, contemporary Christian** and **storytelling.** Produced *The Flat Earth* (by dan gunn), recorded by Velocipede on Rare Finds Records; *Through the Door*, written and recorded by Ed Frisbee, and "Janie Rose," written and recorded by Susan Van Dyke, both on SSP Records. Other artists include Jason Tractenburg and "Dinky" Duncan.

Tips: "Look for a unique angle that sets your music apart."

*SHERWOOD PRODUCTIONS, #299, 2899 Agoura Rd., Westlake CA 91361. Owner: Bill Cobb. Record producer (Sherwood Studios). Estab. 1989. Deals with artists and songwriters. Produces 4-10 singles, 4-10 LPs and 4-10 CDs/year. Fee derived from sales royalty when song or artist is recorded, outright fee from recording artist or outright fee from record company.
How to Contact: Submit demo tape by mail. Unsolicited submissions are OK. Prefers cassette (or VHS videocassette) and lyric sheet. Does not return unsolicited material. Reports in 1-2 months.
Music: Mostly **rock, country, New Age.**

*SILENT PARTNER PRODUCTIONS, 14954 Tulipland Ave., Canyon Country CA 91351. (805)251-7509. Producer: Mark Evans. Record producer, Christopher Paris Productions (Instrumental Division), Canyon Studios (24 track audio studio). Estab. 1988. Deals with artists and songwriters. Produces 5-10 singles, 4-8 LPs, 5 EPs and 4-8 CDs/year. Fee derived from sales royalty when song or artist is recorded, outright fee from recording artist or outright fee from record company.
How to Contact: Submit demo tape by mail. Unsolicited submissions are OK. Prefers cassette (or VHS videocassette) with 3-5 songs and lyric sheet. Does not return unsolicited material.
Music: Mostly **R&B, country** and **New Age;** also **instrumental.** Produced "Freeks Anthem" (by M. Evans), recorded by Mark Free on Tommy Prods; *L.A. Girl*, written and recorded by Mark Richard on Private Music Records; *Butterflies*, written and recorded by Deborah Baxter on Aurel Arts Records. Other artists include Patti Principal.
Tips: "Never give up. Nothing is free. Love what you do."

*SILVER-LOOMAS PRODUCTIONS, Apt. D, 7205 Nashboro Blvd., Nashville TN 37217. (615)366-4975. Production Managers: Tommy Loomas and Alan Carter. Executive Director: Joe Silver. Record producer, music publisher (Lineage Publishing Co.) and record company (Capstan Records and Octagon Records). Deals with artists and songwriters. Produces 10 singles and 4 LPs/year. Fee derived from sales royalty, outright fee from songwriter/artist and/or outright fee from record company.
How to Contact: Write or call first and obtain permission to submit or to arrange personal interview. Prefers cassette (or VHS videocassette) with 4 songs and lyric or lead sheets. "Submissions must be professional." Reports in 6 weeks.
Music: Mostly **country, easy listening** and **bluegrass;** also **rock.** Produced "Angel," by Rock Candy on Capstan Records. Other artists include Fleming McWilliams and Skidrow Joe.

*SLAVESONG CORPORATION, INC., P.O. Box 41233, Dallas TX 75241-0233. (214)225-1903. Chief Executive Officer: Keith Hill. Record producer, music publisher. Estab. 1991. Deals with artists and songwriters. Produces 2 singles, 2 12" singles, 1 LP, 1 EP and 1 CD/year. Fee derived from sales royalty when song or artist is recorded or outright fee from recording artist.
How to Contact: Submit demo tape by mail. Unsolicited submissions are OK. Prefers cassette (or VHS videocassette) with 3-5 songs and lyric sheet. Send photo. SASE. Reports in 1 month.
Music: Mostly **R&B/dance, reggae** and **jazz;** also **world beat.** Produced "Oil Spill" and "Hi In My Hello" (by S.W./G.C.), recorded by George Clinton on WB Records (R&B); and "Why?" (by S.W./K.H./2 Pos.), recorded by Two Positive M.C. on Slavesong Records (rap). Other artists include X-Slave and Gold Tee.

*S'N'M RECORDING HIT RECORDS, 403 Halkirk, Santa Barbara CA 93310. (805)964-3035. Producers: Cory Orosco and Ernie Orosco. Record producer, record company (Night City Records, Warrior Records, Hit Records, Tell International Records), music publisher. Estab. 1984. Deals with artists and songwriters. Produces 4 singles, 2 12" singles, 4 LPs, 2 EPs and 2-4 CDs/year. Fee derived from outright fee from recording artist.
How to Contact: Call or write first and obtain permission to submit or arrange personal interview. Prefers VHS videocassette if available with 4 songs and lyric sheet. Does not return material. Reports in 1 month.
Music: Mostly **pop-rock, country, top 40;** also **top 40 funk, top 40 rock, top 40 country.** Produced *White Dove* (by Brian Faith) on Hit Records (pop), *From 50s-90s* (by Chan Romero) on Warrior Records (pop); *Partly in Montecito* (by Styling Bro²) on Hit Records (comedy/pop) all recorded by S'N'M. Other artists include New Vision, Jade, Ernie and the Emperors, Hollywood Heros, Cornelius Bumpus (Doobie Brothers), Tim Bogert (Vanilla Fudge, Jeff Beck), Floyd Sneed (3 Dog Night), Wayne Lewis, Peter Lewis (Moby Grape).
Tips: "Keep searching for the infectious chorus hook and don't give up."

SONGWRITERS' NETWORK, Box 190446, Dallas TX 75219. President: Phil Ayliffe. Record producer, music publisher (Songwriters' Network Music Publishing/ASCAP), and record company (Songwriters' Network Records). Estab. 1983. Deals with artists and songwriters. Produces 1 LP/year. Fee derived from sales royalty.

How to Contact: Submit demo tape—unsolicited submissions are OK. Prefers cassette (or videocassette if available) with 5 songs and lyric sheet. "Five songs should include an uptempo opener; an uptempo, positive song; a ballad; a hand-clapping rouser; and a dramatic, personal philosophy song as a closer. Vocal must be mixed up-front. Any straining to hear the lyric and the tape is immediately rejected." Does not return unsolicited material. Reports in 6 months.
Music: Mostly A/C, pop and MOR. Produced "Dark and Dirty Days," "Easter Basket Song" and "Bears," written and recorded by Phil Ayliffe on Songwriters' Network Records.
Tips: "We are most interested in working with the singer/songwriter/producer entrepreneur, so we would like the best produced material possible, though vocal and instrument demo is OK."

SOUND ARTS RECORDING STUDIO, 8377 Westview Dr., Houston TX 77055. (713)464-GOLD. President: Jeff Wells. Record producer and music publisher (Earthscream Music). Deals with artists and songwriters. Estab. 1974. Produces 12 singles and 3 LPs/year. Fee derived from outright fee from recording artist.
How to Contact: Submit demo tape—unsolicited submissions are OK. Prefers cassette with 2-5 songs and lyric sheet. SASE. Reports in 6 weeks.
Music: Mostly pop/rock and dance. Produced "Ride of a Lifetime" (by Greg New), recorded by Billy Rutherford on Earth Records (country); "Love Is" (by Gary Wade), recorded by Beat Temple (R&B/funk); "Life in the Jungle" (by Boss), recorded by 4-Deep (rap). Other artists include Perfect Strangers, Third Language and Pauline Knox.

SOUND COLUMN PRODUCTIONS, Division of Sound Column Companies, Country Manor, 812 S. 890 East, Orem UT 84058. (801)225-9975. President/General Manager: Ron Simpson. Record producer, media producer, music publisher (Ronarte Publications/ASCAP, Mountain Green Music/BMI) and record company (SCP Records). Estab. 1970. Looking for songs our artists can record. Produces singles as needed and 5 LPs/year. Fee derived from sales royalty or outright fee on media productions, demos and albums produced for outside labels.
How to Contact: Submit demo tape with lyric sheet—unsolicited submissions are OK. Three songs maximum with SASE. All styles OK except metal or rap (rap songs with melodic harmonized chorus OK)."We promise to listen to everything. We've had a big year in publishing, so we honestly do get behind. We cannot return materials or correspondence without SASE. No phone calls, please."
Music: All styles; needs vary according to artists we are working with. "We produce albums under contract for various labels, and demo packages for client artists." Produced "Goodbye I Love You" (by Kim Simpson and Emily Pearson) for Emily Pearson. Performed on Geraldo Show. Produced "Ballad of John Singer" (by Jim Cunningham). Featured on "60 Minutes." Produced "Breeze Among The Branches" (by Rob Honey) and "Grandma's Garden" (by Gary and Robin Earl), featured in "Tapestry: Weaving the Colors of Life" album and touring show for Russia, Baltic States, North Africa, and US locations.
Tips: "We respond to clean production and must have current-styled, well-crafted songs, targeted toward industry needs. Keep in mind that 'Norma Jean Riley,' a song from our Mountain Green Music catalog (by Rob Honey, Dan Truman and Monty Powell), went #1 last summer, as recorded by Diamond Rio on Arista Records, and also was honored as #1 on Radio and Records' list of the Top 92 Country Songs of 1992. It was the first cut ever for our writer, Rob Honey. Thanks, writers, for submitting some great songs last year—you helped make it our best year ever."

*SOUND SERVICES, Apt. 505, 39867 Fremont Blvd., Fremont CA 94538. (510)657-3079. Owner: Curtis Autin. Record producer, recording studio. Estab. 1986. Deals with artists and songwriters. Produces 1 single and 2 LPs/year. Fee derived from outright fee from recording artist.
How to Contact: Submit demo tape by mail. Unsolicited submissions are OK. Prefers cassette (or VHS videocassette) with 1 song and lyric sheet or lead sheet. SASE. Reports in 1 week.
Music: Mostly rock, R&B, pop; also jazz and country. Produced "People" (by Cardell Porter); "Lone Wolf" and *Night Ryder*, both by Dave Hamlett, all on Sound Services Records.

SOUNDS OF WINCHESTER, Rt. 2 Box 114, Berkley Springs WV 25411. Contact: Jim McCoy. Record producer, music publisher (New Edition Music, Jim McCoy Music and Sleepy Creek Music) and record company (Winchester, Faith and Master Records). Deals with artists and songwriters. Produces 20 singles and 10 LPs/year. Fee derived from sales royalty.
How to Contact: Submit demo tape—unsolicited submissions are OK. Prefers 7½ ips reel-to-reel or cassette with 4-10 songs and lead sheet. Does not return unsolicited material. Reports in 1 month.
Music: Mostly bluegrass, country, gospel and country/rock. Produced "Our Time" (Tommy Hill), recorded by J.B. Miller on Hilton Records; *Lover* (by Earl Howard), recorded by R. Lee Gray and *Mysteries of Life* (by various), recorded by Carroll County Ramblers, both on Winchester Records. Other artists include Red Steed, Kim Segler, Nitelifers and Jubilee Travelers.

SPHERE PRODUCTIONS, Box 991, Far Hills NJ 07931-0991. (908)781-1650. Fax: (908)781-1693. President: Tony Zarrella. Talent Manager: Louisa Pazienza. Record producer, artist development, management and placement of artists with major/independent labels. Produces 5-6 singles and 3 CDs/year. Estab. 1988. Deals with artists and songwriters. Fee derived from percentage royalty of deal, outright fee from record company.
How to Contact: Submit demo tape—unsolicited submissions are OK. Prefers cassette or CD (or VHS videocassette) with 3-5 songs and lyric sheets. Must include: photos, press, resume, goals and specifics of project submitted, etc." Does not return unsolicited material. Reports in 2 months.
Music: Specializes in **pop/rock (mainstream), progressive/rock, New Age** and **crossover country/pop.** Also film soundtracks. Produced *Take This Heart, It's Our Love* and *You and I (Are Dreamers)* (by T. Zarrella), recorded by 4 of Hearts (pop/rock) on Sphere Records. Also represents Oona Falcon, Sky-King and Forever More.
Tips: "Be able to take direction and have trust and faith in your producer or manager. Currently seeking artists/groups incorporating various styles into a focused mainstream product."

*SPUNK PRODUCTIONS, P.O. Box 1052, El Granada CA 94018. Producer: Bill Ford. Record producer (Spunk Media, We Like 'em Firm). Estab. 1982. Deals with artists and songwriters. Produces 15 singles, 5 LPs and 5 CDs/year. Fee derived from sales royalty when song or artist is recorded, outright fee from recording artist or outright fee from record company.
How to Contact: Submit demo tape by mail. Unsolicited submissions are OK. Prefers cassette. SASE. Reports in 1 month.
Music: Mostly **alternative rock, cutting edge pop** and **hard jazz/bop;** also **music beds** and **jingles.** Produced "Vatican Radio" (by Music Crowd), recorded by Refrigerators on Spunk Records; *Hey Open Up* (by Garzone) and *Drum Bobulation* (by Gillotti), both recorded by Fringe on ApGuGa Records.
Tips: "Interested in working with people interested in well-produced music—understandable lyrics."

JACK STANG, 753 Capitol Ave., Hartford CT 06106. (203)524-5656. Producer: Jack Stang. Record producer, music publisher (Stang Music/BMI) and record company (Nickel Records). Estab. 1970. Deals with artists and songwriters. Produces 5 singles and 5 12" singles/year. Fee derived from sales royalty.
How to Contact: Submit demo tape—unsolicited submissions are OK. Prefers cassette with 3 songs and lyric sheets. SASE. Reports in 3 weeks.
Music: Mostly **pop, rock** and **dance;** also **country.** Produced "For What We've Got," written and recorded by Ray Alaire (top 40); "Shortest Distance" (by Cléntel), recorded by Dagmar (top 40/dance); and "We Have It All," by Ray Alaire and Sky (A/C), all on Nickel Records (all singles).

STARK RECORDS AND TAPE CO., 628 S. South St., Mount Airy NC 27030. (919)786-2865. Contact: Paul E. Johnson. Record producer and music publisher (TomPaul Music Company/BMI). Estab. 1960. Deals with artists, songwriters, publishers and recording companies. Produces 8 singles and 3 LPs/year. Works with 80 new songwriters/year. Fee derived from sales royalty.
How to Contact: Submit demo tape—unsolicited submissions are OK. Prefers cassette with 4-6 songs and lyric sheet. SASE. "Return address should be on the SASE." Reports in 2 months.
Music: **Country, bluegrass, pop** and **gospel.** Produced "My Best Wishes Go With You" and "Memories of Pearl Harbor," written and recorded by Thurman Holden; and "Long Journey Home" (by Paul Edgar Johnson), recorded by Bobby Lee Atkins, all on Stark Records. Other artists include Carl Tolbert, Lee Martin, Early Upchurch, Clyde Johnson, Sanford Teague and Don Sawyers.

*STEPBRIDGE STUDIOS, P.O. Box 9202, Santa Fe NM 87504. (505)988-7051. Owner/Engineer: Tim Stroh. Recording studio. Estab. 1985. Deals with artists and songwriters. Fee derived from outright fee from recording artist or outright fee from record company.
How to Contact: Submit demo tape by mail. Unsolicited submissions are OK. Prefers cassette. SASE.
Music: All types.

*MIKE STEWART PRODUCTIONS, P.O. Box 2242, Austin TX 78768. (512)476-8067. A&R: Shannon Setcik. Record producer, music publisher and management company. Estab. 1985. Deals with artists and songwriters. Produces 10 singles, 6 LPs and 6 EPs/year. Fee derived from sales royalty when song or artist is recorded, outright fee from recording artist or outright fee from record company.

 The asterisk before a listing indicates that the listing is new in this edition. New markets are often the most receptive to unsolicited submissions.

How to Contact: Submit demo tape by mail. Unsolicited submissions are OK. Prefers cassette (or videocassette). Does not return unsolicited material. Reports in 2 weeks.
Music: All types. Produced "Run to Me," written and recorded by J. Tittle, and "I Woke Up" (by A. Tyler), recorded by Rockingbirds, both on Sony Records; and *Avalande Drive* (by B. Giddens), recorded by Illegal Artist on Avslavter Liebe Records. Other artists include Susan Voelz.

*STONE COLD PRODUCTIONS, P.O. Box 451423, Houston TX 77245-1423. Producer: Rodney Ballard. Record producer and music publisher (K. Benyard Music Co./BMI). Estab. 1990. Deals with artists and songwriters. Produces 4 singles, 4 12″ singles and 2 LPs/year. Fee derived from outright fee from recording artist or record company.
How to Contact: Write first and obtain permission to submit. Prefers cassette with 5-9 songs and lyric or lead sheet. Reports in 4 weeks.
Music: Mostly **R&B** and **R&B/rap**; also **dance.** Produced "Homeless Nation" (by K. Benyard); "Pretend The Love Away," "Saturday" and "I Can't Hide It" (by K. Benyard and Debra Watkins).
Tips: "Send your material only after permission is granted."

*STUART AUDIO SERVICES, 342 Main St., Gorham ME 04038. (207)839-3569. Producer/Owner: John A. Stuart. Record producer, music publisher, musical consultant/arranger. Estab. 1979. Deals with artists and songwriters. Produces 1-2 singles, 3 LPs and 3 CDs/year. Fee derived from sales royalty when song or artist is recorded, outright fee from recording artist, outright fee from record company or demo fees and consulting fees.
How to Contact: Write or call first and obtain permission to submit; write or call first to arrange a personal interview. Prefers cassette with 4 songs and lyric sheet. SASE. Reports in 3-4 weeks.
Music: Mostly **alternative folk-rock, rock** and **country**; also **contemporary Christian, children's** and **unusual.** Produced *Hungry Eyes*, written and recorded by Noel Paul Stookey on Gold Castle Records (new folk); *Winter to Summer* (by J.A. Stuart), recorded by John A. Stuart on C.T.W. Records (soundtrack); *Signs of Home* (by Romanow/Rowe), recorded by Schoonner Fare on OuterGreen Records (folk). Other artists include Bates Motel, Chris Heard, Al Mossberg, Bodyworks, Jim Newton, Rick Charette, music for Sesame Street (soundtrack work).

*STUDIO A, 87 Sherry Ave., Bristol RI 02809. (401)253-4183. Owners: Jim Wilson, Jr. and Jack Anderson. Recording studio, music production. Estab. 1988. Deals with artists and songwriters. Produces 2 singles, 4-6 LPs and 2-4 CDs/year. Fee derived from small fee from song/artist and standard royalties.
How to Contact: Write first and obtain permission to submit. Prefers cassette with 3 songs and lyric sheet or lead sheet. "Use good quality tape for demo." SASE. Reports in 1 month.
Music: Mostly **jazz, rock, fusion**; also **R&B** and **top 40.** Produced *Newburry St.* (by Zavoski/Michaels) on Dormitory Records (rock); "One More Chance" (by DeBurro/Wilson) on Make Mine Music Records; and *Viewpoints* (by Wilson/Anderson) on Studio A Records, all recorded by Studio A. Other artists include Yvonne Reis, Prestige and Steppin' Out.
Tips: "Be open to suggestions. *Copyright before sending!*"

STUDIO CITY PRODUCTIONS, 2810 McBain, Redondo Beach CA 90278. (213)371-5793. Staff Producer: Geoff England. Record producer. Estab. 1982. Deals with artists and songwriters. Produces 15 singles, 20 12″ singles, 10 LPs, 5 EPs and 35 CDs/year. Fee derived from sales royalty or outright fee from recording artist or record company.
How to Contact: Submit demo tape—unsolicited submissions are OK. Prefers cassette (or VHS videocassette if available) with 1-5 songs and lyric sheet. SASE. Reports in 2 weeks.
Music: Mostly **rock** and **pop.** Produced *Steppenwolf Live*, recorded by Steppenwolf on ABC Records (LP); *Ring Leader*, recorded by Ring Leader on Statue Records (LP); and *Rock City*, recorded by John Verla on Statue Records (LP).

SUCCESSFUL PRODUCTIONS, 1203 Biltmore Ave., High Point NC 27260. (919)882-9990. President: Doris Lindsay. Record producer, music publisher (Better Times Publishing/BMI) and record company (Fountain Records). Estab. 1979. Deals with artists and songwriters. Produces 3 singles and 2 LPs/year. Fee derived from sales royalty.
How to Contact: Submit demo tape—unsolicited submissions are OK. Prefers cassette with 2 songs and lyric sheet. "Send a professional demo." SASE. Reports in 2 months.
Music: Mostly **country, pop** and **contemporary gospel**; also **blues, children's** and **Southern gospel.** Produced "American Song" (by K. Roeder/M. Terry), recorded by Terry Michaels (country); "Back In Time," written and recorded by Mitch Snow (country) and "Crossroads of My Life" (by Larry Lavey/Dave Right) recorded by Larry La Vey (blues), all on Fountain Records. Other artists include Pat Repose.
Tips: "Use a professional demo service."

PRESTON SULLIVAN ENTERPRISES, Dept. SM, 1217 16th Ave. S., Nashville TN 37212. (615)327-8129. President: Preston Sullivan. Record producer. Deals with artists and songwriters. Produces 10 singles and 4 LPs/year.
How to Contact: Submit demo tape—unsolicited submissions are OK. Prefers cassette (or videocassette) and lyric sheet. Does not return unsolicited material. Reports in 3 weeks.
Music: Mostly **hard rock, alternative rock, pop** and **R&B.** Produced "The Grinning Plowman" (by Michael Ake), recorded by The Grinning Plowmen (pop/rock); "Dessau" (by John Elliott), recorded by Dessau (dance) and "Dorcha," recorded by Dorcha (rock), all on Carlyle Records.

SURPRIZE RECORDS, INC., P.O. Box 6562, Philadelphia PA 19138-6562. (215)276-8861. President: W. Lloyd Lucas. Record producer, music publisher (Delev Music Co./BMI, Sign of the Ram Music/ASCAP, Gemini Lady Music/SESAC) and management firm. Estab. 1981. Deals with artists, songwriters and publishers. Produces 3-6 singles, 2-3 12″ singles and 3-6 LPs/year. Fee derived from sales royalty.
How to Contact: Submit demo tape by mail—unsolicited submissions are OK. Prefers cassette with 1-3 songs and lyric or lead sheet. SASE. "We do not and will not accept certified mail." Reports in 1 month.
Music: Mostly **R&B, soul, top 40/pop, dance-oriented** and **MOR.** Recently released "Fat Girls," produced by Time-Nu Productions, written by B. Heston, E. Webb, L. Walker and J. Hudson, on Surprize Records. Other artists scheduled to be produced are Lamar and Jerry Dean. They will be shopped to the major labels for label and distribution deals on Surprize Records.
Tips: "We are impressed with very positive lyrics and great hooklines and near finished demo 'masters'. It does not matter if the artist has had extensive experience working in front of an audience, but it does matter if his or her attitude is in a positive posture. Determination and the ability to take constructive criticism is most important. We have no time for ego trippers."

SYNDICATE SOUND, INC., 475 5th St., Struthers OH 44471. (216)755-1331. President: Jeff Wormley. Audio and video production company and record and song promotion company. Estab. 1987. Deals with artists and songwriters. Produces 3-4 singles, 1-2 12″ singles, 15-20 LPs, 10-15 EPs and 4-5 CDs/year. Fee derived from combination of sales royalty when song or artist is recorded, outright fee from recording artist or record company hourly recording or producing fee and third party financing.
How to Contact: Submit demo tape—unsolicited submissions are OK. "Please send a promo package or biography (with pictures) of band, stating past and present concerts and records." SASE. Reports in 2 months.
Music: Mostly **rock, pop** and **Christian rock;** also **country, R&B** and **hardcore.** Produced *Spin* (by Brent Young), recorded by Februarys on Sad Face Records; *Meet Your Maker* (by Dion Pomponio) recorded by Tempo Tantrum on Chaotic Records; and *World's Fate* (by Toni Merlino), recorded by Prymordial on Syndicate Sound Records. Other artists include Tim Luman & the Lost Then Found, Count Down, Mathew Gold, Bangorillas, Strych-9, Nailz Maulner, Rambling Rock.

SYSTEM, Box 11301, Kansas City KS 66111. (913)287-3495. Executive Producer: Steve Vail. Record producer, management firm, booking agency and film company. Estab. 1978. Deals with artists and songwriters. Produces 1-3 CDs/year. Fee derived from outright fee from songwriter/artist or record company.
How to Contact: Submit demo tape by mail—unsolicited submissions are OK. Prefers cassette (or ½″ or ¾″ VHS or ½″ Beta videocassette if available) with 1-10 songs and lyric sheet. SASE. Reports in 2 months.
Music: Mostly **Classical rock, alternative** and **progressive** only. Produced *Echo Lake, Mother Earth Father Sky* and *The Path* (by Studna/Vail), recorded by Realm, all on System Records.
Tips: "We use non-commercial music."

GARY TANIN, 2139 N. 47th St., Milwaukee WI 53208. (414)444-2477. Producer: G. Tanin. Record producer. Estab. 1970. Deals with artists and songwriters. Produces 4 singles and 2 LPs/year. Fee derived from outright fee from recording artist or record company.
How to Contact: Write or call first and obtain permission to submit. Prefers cassette with 3 songs and lyric sheet. "On demos, piano line and vocals are OK. Prefer as complete a submission as possible." Does not return unsolicited material. Reports in 2 months.
Music: Mostly **rock, pop** and **New Age.** Produced "Can I Be Sure," written and recorded by G. Tanin; "Survive" (by B. Enos/J. Brantley), recorded by Junior Brantley; and "Just Say It's So" (by J. Brantley/G. Tanin), recorded by Junior Brantley, all on Softworks Records.

*TAVARES TELEPRODUCTIONS, 4351 Donlyn Court, Columbus OH 43232. (614)863-3421. Producer: Loren Moss. Record producer, full broadcast production facility (Soundscape Studios, Tamareco Artist Management, Danmo Publishing). Estab. 1988. Deals with artists and songwriters. Produces 6 singles, 2 LPs and 2 EPs/year. Fee derived from sales royalty when song or artist is recorded, outright fee from recording artist, outright fee from record company or fees from corporate clients commissioning creative works.

How to Contact: Submit demo tape by mail. Unsolicited submissions are OK. Prefers DAT or cassette (or ¾" videocassette) with 4 songs and lyric sheet. "Include pictures and biographical information." SASE. Reports in 2 weeks.

Music: Mostly **corporate/post scoring, reggae** and **hip hop/rap**; also **world beat, dance/house** and **R&B/top 40**. Produced "Long Stem Roses," by Clay B. Smith (country); "Get On The Bus" (by J.S. Sonic & A.J.), recorded by Teddy Bear (rap); "Friends In Leg Braces," written and recorded by Larry Ramey (country).

Tips: "Always present yourself in an organized, professional manner."

TEXAS MUSIC MASTERS/WRIGHT PRODUCTIONS, 11231 Hwy. 64 E., Tyler TX 75707. Record producer. 30 years in business. Fee derived from labels or producers.

How to Contact: Submit demo tape—unsolicited submissions are OK. Prefers cassette with 3 songs and lyric sheet. SASE. Reports in 3 weeks.

Music: Mostly **country, gospel** and **blues**. Produced "Room Full of Roses," recorded by Mickey Gilley; "The Road" (by Gene LeDoux), recorded by David Darst on Jukebox Records; and "Southern Ways," written and recorded by Craig Robbins on Quazar Records.

*THIRD FLOOR PRODUCTIONS, P.O. Box 40784, Nashville TN 37204. (615)331-1469. Producer: Steven Ray Pinkston. Record producer. Estab. 1982. Deals with artists and songwriters. Produces 3 singles, 10 LPs and 10 CDs/year. Fee derived from outright fee from recording artist and/or record company.

How to Contact: Submit demo tape by mail. Unsolicited submissions are OK. Prefers cassette (or VHS videocassette if available) or DAT with 2 songs. SASE. Reports in 2 months. Send to attention of Jim Chapman, A&R.

Music: Mostly **pop, rock, country** and **contemporary Christian**.

Tips: "Looking for artists now!"

STEVE THOMPSON PRODUCTIONS INC., P.O. Box 623, Centerport NY 11721. (516)754-5438. Business Manager: Andrew Kipnes (212-924-2929). Record producer, music publisher, production company (sign acts and place songs), Thompson & Barbiero Productions (ASCAP, NARAS). Estab. 1986. Deals with artists and songwriters. Fee derived from sales royalty when song or artist is recorded or outright fee from record company.

How to Contact: Submit demo tape by mail. Unsolicited submissions are OK. Prefers cassette (or VHS videocassette) with 4 songs and lyric sheet. SASE. Reports in 3 weeks to 1 month.

Music: Mostly **rock, alternative** and **pop**; also **R&B, dance** and **country**. Produced all Tesla LPs on Geffen Records; Expose on Arista Records and Snakeyedsue, on Giant/WB Records. Other artists include Guns 'n' Roses, Metallica and Soundgarden.

Tips: "Make your music stand out from the competition. Music must be contemporary and not corporate!!"

*TMC PRODUCTIONS, P.O. Box 12353, San Antonio TX 78212. (512)829-1909. Producer: Joe Scates. Record producer, music publisher (Axbar Productions/BMI, Scates & Blanton/BMI and Axe Handle Music/ASCAP), record company (Axbar, Trophy, Jato, Prince and Charro Records) and record distribution and promotion. Deals with artists and songwriters. Produces 12-15 singles, 3-4 LPs and 1-2 CDs/year. Fee derived from sales royalty or outright fee from recording artist or record company.

How to Contact: Call first and obtain permission to submit. Prefers cassette with 1-5 songs and lyric sheet. SASE. Reports "as soon as possible, but don't rush us."

Music: Mostly **traditional country**; also **blues, comedy** and **rock (soft)**. Produced *The Best of Billy D. Hunter*, written and recorded by Billy D. Hunter; "Country Girl Going to Town" (by Terrah Sloane), recorded by Denise Trapani; and "Sweet Judy Blue Eyes" (by Ron Knuth/Bert Mund), recorded by George Chambers, all on Axbar Records. Other artists include Kenny Dale, Juni Moon, Bubba Littrell, Rick Will, Don Nutt and Joe's Studio Band.

Tips: "Competition is very keen, so the average 'good' songs just don't make it anymore. Submit only your best efforts that have strong commercial possibilities. If we produce an artist, we prefer to use our own professional contract musicians but will consider recording a band intact if they are a quality group."

TOMSICK BROTHERS PRODUCTIONS, 21271 Chardon Rd., Dept. SM, Euclid OH 44117. (216)481-8380. President: Ken Tomsick. Record producer and record company. Estab. 1982. Deals with artists and songwriters. Produces 2-5 LPs/year. Also produces original music for TV, radio, video and ad jingles. Fee derived from outright fee from recording artist. Charges in advance for studio time.

How to Contact: Submit demo tape by mail—unsolicited submissions are OK. Prefers cassette. "We have arrangers to help produce your sound." Does not return unsolicited material. Reports in 6 months.

Music: Mostly **ethnic, polka** and **New Age/experimental**. Produced "A Brand New Beginning," written and recorded by David M. Lynch on T.B.P. Records; *Teacher's Pet* and *Sweet 16*, recorded by Nancy Hlad. Other artists include Matt Traum Trio (jazz trio) and The Polka-Poppers (polkas and waltzes).

*TORO'NA INT'L., P.O. Box 88022, Indianapolis IN 46208. Contact: Inga McDaniel. Professional record producer and musical arranger. A&R Director: Anthony Wiggins. Estab. 1987. Produces 3 singles and 1 12″ single/year. Fee derived from outright fee from record company.

How to Contact: Write first and obtain permission to submit. Prefers cassette with 3 songs. Does not return unsolicited material. Reports in 8 weeks.

Music: Mostly **top 40, R&B** and **gospel**; also **rap**. Produced "Somebody's Watching" (by Tony Clemmons), recorded by Royal Empire; "Do You Want Me" (by R.H. Duncan), recorded by Husbands to Be, both on Toro'na Records; and "Al Fredia," written and recorded by I. McDaniel on CD Review. Other artists include Ronea, One In A Million.

Tips: "Write first about your interests. Keep your ear to the trends of production."

TRAC RECORD CO., 170 N. Maple, Fresno CA 93702. (209)255-1717. Owner: Stan Anderson. Record producer, music publisher (Sellwood Publishing/BMI) and record company (Trac Records). Estab. 1972. Works with artists and songwriters. Produces 5 12″ singles, 5 LPs and 5 CDs/year. Fee derived from recording artist.

How to Contact: Submit demo tape—unsolicited submissions are OK. Prefers cassette with 3 songs and lyric sheet. "Studio quality." SASE. Reports in 3 weeks.

Music: Mostly **traditional country** and **country rock**. Produced "Whiskey Blues," "Dan" and "Night Time Places," all written and recorded by Jimmy Walker. Other artists include Jessica James and The Rackleys.

TURBO RECORDS (formerly Jay Gold-Turbo Records), Box 409, East Meadow NY 11554. (516)486-8699. President: Jay Gold. Record producer, music publisher (Jay Gold Music/BMI) and record company. Estab. 1981. Deals with artists and songwriters. Produces 5 singles and 2 12″ singles/year. Fee derived from sales royalty or outright fee from recording artist or record company.

How to Contact: Submit demo tape by mail—unsolicited submissions are OK. Prefers cassette with 3 songs and lyric sheet. Reports in 5 weeks.

Music: Mostly **pop** and **rock**. Produced "All the Wrong Reasons" (pop); "Better Love" (pop); and "Radio Riot" (rock); all written and recorded by Jay Gold on Turbo Records.

Tips: "Review your lyrics and be open to changes."

*12 METER PRODUCTIONS, (formerly TnT Productions), 7808 Green Lake Rd., Fayetteville NY 13066. (315)637-6656. Producers: Matt Tucker and Chris Horvath. Record producer. Estab. 1988. Deals with artists and songwriters. Produces 1-5 singles, 1-5 12″ singles 1-2 LPs and 1-2 CDs. Fee derived from sales royalty or outright fee from recording artist or record company.

How to Contact: Submit demo tape by mail. Unsolicited submissions are OK. Prefers cassette (or VHS videocassette if available) with 1-5 songs and lyric sheet. "Send photo, press kit or bio if available. No calls." SASE. Reports in 2-3 months.

Music: Mostly **top 40/pop, dance** and **rock**; also **rap** and **R&B**. Produced "How Can I Forget You," recorded by Jodi Bilotti and "Hello, America," recorded by Blue Steel, both on CCD Records; and "It Had All Just Been A Dream" (by Murray/Tucker), recorded by Love Is Blue, all written by Horvath/Tucker.

Tips: "Send what you feel is your best work. Don't restrict yourself to one type of music. We listen to everything. Be professional and be patient."

27TH DIMENSION INC., Box 1149, Okeechobee FL 34973-1149. (800)634-6091. President: John St. John. Record producer, music publisher (ASCAP, BMI) and music library. Estab. 1986. Deals with composers and songwriters. Produces 10 CDs/year.

How to Contact: Write first and obtain permission to submit. Prefers cassette. Does not return unsolicited submissions. Reports in 2 weeks.

Music: Mostly **industrial, pop jazz** and **industrial fusion**; also **pop, impressionism** and **descriptive**. "Instrumentals only!"

CHARLES VICKERS MUSIC ASSOCIATION, Box 725, Daytona Beach FL 32015-0725. (904)252-4849. President/Producer: Dr. Charles H. Vickers D.M. Record producer, music publisher (Pritchett Publication/BMI, Alison Music/ASCAP) and record company (King of Kings Records and L.A. International Records). Deals with artists and songwriters. Produces 3 singles and 6 LPs/year. Works with 1 new songwriter/year. Teams collaborators. Fee derived from sales royalty.

How to Contact: Write first and obtain permission to submit. Prefers 7½ ips reel-to-reel or cassette with 1-6 songs. SASE. Reports in 1 week.
Music: Mostly **church/religious, gospel** and **hymns**; also **bluegrass, blues, classical, country, easy listening, jazz, MOR, progressive, reggae (pop), R&B, rock, soul** and **top 40/pop.** Produced "Walking on the Water," "Let Us Pray," "Always Depend on Jesus," "The Lord is My Proctor" and "Everyday is a Holy Day," all written and recorded by C. Vickers on King of King Records.

VISUAL MUSIC, Box 86967, San Diego CA 92138-6967. (619)427-4290. Director of Production: Jay Henry. Record producer, record company and music publisher. Estab. 1977. Deals with artists and songwriters. Produces 6 singles, 2 12″ singles and 4 LPs/year. Fee derived from sales royalty, outright fee from recording artist, record company or investor.
How to Contact: Submit demo tape—unsolicited submissions are OK. Prefers cassette (or VHS videocassette if available) with 3-4 songs and lyric sheet. Does not return unsolicited material. Reports in 2-3 months.
Music: Mostly **R&B, rap** and **dance/pop;** also **progressive country, hip hop** and **disco** (70s style). Produced "Something New" (by J. Wittington), recorded by The Knaps on Vmeg Records; "Real Afrikan People" (by D. Colman), recorded by D.S.O.B. on N/A Records; and "Check Yourself" (by S. Adorno), recorded by Mumbles on Def-Soul Records.
Tips: "Have everything together before you contact a producer. If additional material or info is needed you can respond quickly."

WILLIAM F. WAGNER, Dept. SM, Suite 218, 14343 Addison St., Sherman Oaks CA 91423. (818)905-1033. Contact: Bill Wagner. Record producer. Estab. 1957. Deals with artists and songwriters. Produces 4-6 singles, 2-4 LPs and 2-4 CDs/year. Works with 25 new songwriters/year. Fee derived from sales royalty or outright fee from recording artist or record company.
How to Contact: Submit demo tape by mail—unsolicited submissions are OK. Prefers cassette with 1-5 songs and lead sheets. "No lyric sheets. Material should be copyrighted." SASE. Reports in 1 month.
Music: Mostly **top 40, pop, country** and **jazz;** also **blues, choral, gospel, easy listening, MOR, progressive, rock** and **soul.** Produced *Julie Is Her Name* (by Bobby Troup), recorded by H.A. Kratzsch on Four Freshmen Society Records; *What'll I Do* (by I. Berlin), recorded by Sandy Graham on Muse Records; and *All The Things You Are* (by Kern/Hammerstein), recorded by Page Cavanaugh on Starline Records.
Tips: "Either send a simple tune demo, or a finished record—but not both in the same track."

*CORNELL WARD, P.O. Box 57, LaGrange IL 60525. (708)378-1776. President: Cornell Ward. Producer, publisher (Gilcon Music/BMI) and arranger. Estab. 1983. Produces 8-16 singles and 2-3 CDs/year. Fee derived from sales royalty and outright fee from record company.
How to Contact: Submit demo tape by mail. Unsolicited submissions accepted. Prefers cassette (or VHS videocassette if available) with 3-5 songs and lyric sheet. "Absolutely no metal! or hard rock!!" *Absolutely no phone calls.* Does not return unsolicited material. Reports in 3-4 weeks.
Music: **Pop, top 40, R&B, easy listening, country/soft rock, gospel, rap** and **New Age vocals & instrumentals.** Produced *The Second Time,* recorded by The Dells on King-Japan, Veterans-USA Records (pop/R&B) and *Root Doctor,* recorded by Roy Hytower (blues), and the new Willie Clayton CD on Ichiban Records.
Tips: "Look for your best story and strongest hook. Musical production not as important as a 'great story.'"

*WATERBURY PRODUCTIONS, 6833 Murietta Ave., Van Nuys CA 91405. (818)909-9092. Owner: David. Record producer, record company (Ultimate of Cool Records). Estab. 1987. Deals with artists and songwriters. Produces 15 LPs and 3 CDs/year. Fee derived from royalty when song or artist is recorded, outright fee from recording artist or outright fee from record company.
How to Contact: Submit demo tape by mail. Unsolicited submissions are OK. Prefers cassette with 3-4 songs and lyric sheet. SASE. Reports in 3 weeks.
Music: Mostly **modern rock, dance** and **pop rock;** also **techno, alternative** and **blues rock.** Produced *Tales of Hollow* (by Johnny Rondo) on Night Hawk Records (folk-pop); *Bikini Beach Party* (by Dave Shavu) (dance) and *Calif. Coolest Vol. 3* (compilation by various bands) (rock, rap, hard) both on Ultimate of Cool Records. Other artists include WoodPeckers, Ultramatix, X-OT-X and Sonido.
Tips: "Be creative, unique."

*WAVE GROUP SOUND, P.O. Box 424, San Leandro CA 94577. (510)522-6463. Producer/Engineer: James Allen. Record producer. "Staff engineer for Skywalker Sound North, a division of Lucas Digital Services." Estab. 1981. Deals with artists and songwriters. Produces 2 singles, 4 LPs and 2 CDs/year. Fee derived from sales royalty when song or artist is recorded, outright fee from recording artists or record company.

How to Contact: Submit demo tape by mail. Unsolicited submissions are OK. Prefers cassette (or VHS videocassette if available) with 3 songs and lyric sheet or lead sheet. SASE. Reports in 2 months.
Music: Mostly **New Age, jazz, rock**; also **country, blues, R&B**. Co-produced *Half Moon Bay* and *Fantasy* (by William Aura), recorded by William Aura and James Allen on Higher Octave Records; and *Traveler* (by Paul Horn), recorded by Christopher Hedge and James Allen on CBS Records. Other artists include Pacific Heights, Bombay Heat and Dan Vicrey.
Tips: "Looking for very melodic material. Excellent hooks. Memorable. Visual. Impressionistic."

THE WEISMAN PRODUCTION GROUP, 449 N. Vista St., Los Angeles CA 90036. (213)653-0693. Contact: Ben Weisman. Record producer and music publisher (Audio Music Publishers). Estab. 1965. Deals with artists and songwriters. Produces 10 singles/year. Fee derived from sales royalty.
How to Contact: Prefers cassette with 3-10 songs and lyric sheet. SASE. "Mention *Songwriter's Market*. Please make return envelope the same size as the envelopes you send material in, otherwise we cannot send everything back. Just send tape." Reports in 1 month.
Music: Mostly **R&B, soul, dance, rap** and **top 40/pop**; also **all types of rock.**
Tips: "Work on hooks and chorus, not just verses. Too many songs are only verses."

*****WILBUR PRODUCTIONS,** #10, 159 W. 4th St., New York NY 10014. (212)727-3450. President: Will Schillinger. Record producer, recording engineer/studio owner, Wilbur Systems Inc. Estab. 1989. Deals with artists and songwriters. Produces 50 singles, 20 LPs and 20 CDs/year. Fee derived from sales royalty when song or artist is recorded or outright fee from record company.
How to Contact: Submit demo tape by mail. Unsolicited submissions are OK. Prefers cassette with 3-5 songs. Does not return unsolicited material. Reports in 2 weeks.
Music: Mostly **rock** and **country.** Produced "Something in Her Laughter," written and recorded by Marshall Crenshaw on WSL Records; *Walking On The Moon* (by Katie Moffit), recorded by Janet Burgan on WSL Records; and *5 Tunes*, written and recorded by Jon Herrington on Pioneer Records.

FRANK WILLSON, Box 2297, Universal City TX 78148. (512)653-3989. Producer: Frank Willson. Record producer (BMI) and record company (BSW Records). Deals with artists and songwriters. Estab. 1987. Produces 4 singles, 12-15 12″ singles, 10-12 LPs, 3 EPs and 5 CDs/year. Fee derived from sales royalty.
How to Contact: Submit demo tape—unsolicited submissions are OK. Prefers cassette with 3-4 songs and lyric sheets. SASE. Reports in 4 weeks.
Music: Mostly **country** and **rock.** Produced *Paradise Canyon* (by D. Fleming), recorded by Paradise Canyon; *Guessing Game*, written and recorded by C. Howard; and *On A Roll* (by Jess DeMaine), recorded by J. Demaine, all on BSW Records. Other artists include Mike Lord and Bobby Lloyd.

*****WILSHIRE ARTISTS,** Suite 870, 100 Wilshire Blvd., Santa Monica CA 90401. (310)576-1236. Producer: Daniel Leeway. Record producer, recording studios (The Leeway Studios, 32 Track Digital). Estab. 1991. Deals with artists and songwriters. Fee derived from outright fee from recording artist or record company, unless other arrangements have been made.
How to Contact: Write or call first to arrange personal interview, submit demo tape by mail. Unsolicited submissions are OK. Prefers cassette or CDs with 2+ songs and lyric sheet. SASE. Reports in 1 month minimum.
Music: Mostly **dance, pop, New Age.**
Tips: "We prefer to work with and develop new artists and talent. You are free to submit your work, but please be patient for a reply. Mail submissions only, please."

*****WIR (WORLD INTERNATIONAL RECORDS),** A-1090 Vienna, Servitengasse 24, **Austria.** Tel: 707-37-10. Fax: 707-84-22. Contact: Peter Jordan. Record producer, music publisher (Aquarius) and record company (WIR). Estab. 1986. Deals with artists and songwriters. Produces 5-10 singles and 5-8 LPs/year. Fee derived from outright fee from recording artist or record company.
How to Contact: Write or call first and obtain permission to submit. Prefers cassette. SASE. Reports in 2-4 weeks.
Music: Produced *Sexy Ole Lady* (by Pat Garrett), *We're In Love* (by Steve Haggard), *The Best Is Yet to Come* (by M. McLelland) and *Eight Eyes* (by Claudia Robot), all recorded by Aquarius on WIR Records. Other artists include Crossover, ABC Guitars, The Cones, Diana Blair, Doug McGinnis, Dale Davis and Harry Bonanza and Band.

WLM MUSIC/RECORDING, 2808 Cammie St., Durham NC 27705-2020. (919)471-3086. Owner: Watts Lee Mangum. Recording studio (small). Estab. 1980. Deals with artists and songwriters. Produces 6-8 singles/year. Fee derived from outright fee from recording artist. "In some cases—an advance payment requested for demo production."

How to Contact: Submit demo tape—unsolicited submissions are OK. Prefers cassette with 2-4 songs and lyric or lead sheets (if possible). SASE. Reports in 3 months.
Music: Mostly **country, country/rock** and **blues/rock;** also **pop, rock** and **R&B.** Produced "Ride 'Em Cowboy" (by Clayton/Hill) and "Wildflowers" (by Clayton Wrenn), both recorded by Clayton Wrenn on Crown Records. Other artists include Barry Hayes, Ron Davis, John Davis and Clint Clayton.
Tips: "Submit good demo tapes with artist's ideas, words, and music charted if possible."

*MARK WOLFSON PRODUCTIONS, Suite 134, 11684 Ventura Blvd., Studio City CA 91604. (818)506-5467. Fax: (818)980-9756. Producer/Engineer: Mark Wolfson. Record producer, engineer/music supervisor (The Tape Registry). Estab. 1972. Deals with artists and songwriters. Produces 12 singles, 2 12″ singles and 2 CDs/year. "Fee is negotiable."
How to Contact: Submit demo tape by mail. Unsolicited submissions are OK.

*RAY WOODS PRODUCTION, #110, 8855 SW Holly Lane, Wilsonville OR 97070. Record producer. Ray Woods is also a shareholder in Rainforest Records, Inc. (an independent record company) and Thorn-EMI. Estab. 1990. Deals with artists and songwriters. Produces 2 singles, 2 LPs and 2 CDs/year. Fee derived from sales royalty when song or artist is recorded, outright fee from recording artist or outright fee from record company.
How to Contact: Write first and obtain permission to submit. Prefers cassette with 4 songs and lyric sheet. SASE. Reports in 6-8 weeks.
Music: Mostly **alternative rock** and **hard rock/metal.** Produced "Marilyn Monroe" (by Brian Donnelly), recorded by The Refreshments; "I'm Flying," written and recorded by Roger Nusic; and "Rugburn" (by Wammo), recorded by W.O.R.M., all on Rainforest Records.
Tips: "The best collaborator in the world is a live audience."

STEVE WYTAS PRODUCTIONS, Dept. SM, 165 Linden St., New Britain CT 06051. (203)224-1811. Contact: Steven J. Wytas. Record producer. Estab. 1984. Deals with artists only. Produces 4-8 singles, 6 12″ singles, 3 LPs, 3 EPs and 2 CDs/year. Fee derived from outright fee from recording artist or record company. "Expenses, sub-contractor fees, etc."
How to Contact: Submit demo tape—unsolicited submissions are OK. Prefers cassette (or VHS-¾″ videocassette) with several songs and lyric or lead sheet. "Include live material if possible." Does not return unsolicited material. Reports in 2 months.
Music: Mostly **rock, metal, pop, top 40, country/acoustic;** also **R&B, soul** and **comedy.** Produced "Mental Gymnastics" on MGA records (single), *Free World* on TOTC Records (album disc) and "Indy Records" (single), written and recorded by Leigh Gregory. Other artists include Flying Nuns, Sons of Bob, MG's, Mud Solo, Stupe, Wayne and Garth, Savage Brothers and Those Melvins.

ZEKE PRODUCTIONS, INC., 345 E. 80th St., 15H, New York NY 10021. (212)744-2312. President: Chuck Dembrak. Record producer and music publisher (Cool One Music/ASCAP). Estab. 1978. Deals with artists and songwriters. Produces 3-6 12″ singles and 1-2 LPs/year. Fees derived from sales royalty and outright fee from record company. "Charges for consultation."
How to Contact: Submit demo tape by mail. Unsolicited submissions are OK. Call first to arrange personal interview. Prefers cassette (or VHS videocassette if available) with 3-4 songs and lyric sheets. SASE. Reports in 4 weeks.
Music: Mostly **R&B, pop** and **rock.** Produced *Surrender* (by J. Roach), recorded by Double Digit, and "Just A Touch" (by M. Ervin), recorded by Break-Uv-Dawn, both on Spy Records; and "Warmth" (by D. Oliver), recorded by Mesa on Esquire Records. Other artists include Larry Caldwell.

Record Producers/'93-'94 Changes

The following markets appeared in the 1993 edition of *Songwriter's Market* but are absent from the 1994 edition. Most of these companies failed to respond to our request for an update of their listing for a variety of reasons. For example, they may have gone out of business or they may have requested deletion from the 1994 edition because they are backlogged with material. If we know the specific reason, it appears within parentheses.

Accent Records
Affinity Private Music
Alstatt Enterprises
Bill Anderson Jr. (affiliate of
    Landmark Audio of Nash

ville)
April Recording Studios/Pro-
    ductions
Arcadia Productions, Inc.
Ted Barton (not accepting sub

missions)
Big City Music, Inc. (unable to
    contact)
Blade to the Rhythm Music
    Productions

Blue Baker Music (requested deletion)
Brooke Productions, Inc.
Broozbee Music, Inc. (requested deletion)
Don Casale Music, Inc.
The Club Studios
Coffee and Cream Productions
Cowboy Junction Flea Market and Publishing Co. (not accepting submissions)
Jerry Cupit Productions
Datura Productions
Dragon Records, Inc. (not accepting submissions)
Eric Elwell
English Valley Music
Executive Sound Productions
Factory Beat Records, Inc.
R.L. Feeney
Vito Fera Productions (requested deletion)
George D. Productions, Inc. (unable to contact)
Go Jo Production
Grapevine Studios
Grass Recording and Sound
Green Dream Productions
Mark Hannah Productions (requested deletion)
Neil Henderson Productions
Hit and Run Studios (same as Steve Carr)
Independent Audio Services
Jericho Sound Lab
Johnny Jet Records
Little Richie Johnson
Danny Jones Productions
Butch Kelly Production
Eddie Kilroy
Kingsport Creek Music
Robert R. Kovach
Lamon Records/Panhandel Records (unable to contact)
Scott Lea Productions (unable to contact)
Tommy Lewis, Jr. (requested deletion)
Ligosa Entertainment Corp.
Listen Productions
Jack Lynch/Nashville Country Productions (affiliate of

Nashville Country Productions)
Mac-Attack Productions, Inc. (unable to contact)
Butch McGhee, Tyra Management Group
Madison Station Productions
Makers Mark Music Productions
John Mars (requested deletion)
Metromedia Productions
Lena Michals Entertainment
Microstar Productions
Mighty Sounds and Filmworks (affiliate of Danny Darrow)
Robert E. Miles/King Eugene Productions
Jay Miller Productions
Mimac Productions
Mood Swing Productions
Mark J. Morette/Mark Manton (requested deletion)
Eric Morgeson
Mountain Therapy Music (requested deletion)
Ross Munro/Random Entertainment Inc.
Music Factory Enterprises, Inc.
New Dawn Productions/South Bound Productions
Nise Productions, Inc.
Not-2-Perfect Productions
Now + Then Music
Ogdenhouse Music Productions
Jeannine O'Neal Productions
Johnny Palazzotto/Pal Productions
Michael Panepento/Airwave Production Group Inc.
Paradise Alley Productions
John Penny
Phantom Productions, Inc.
Planet Dallas
Playtown Sound Productions
Pottemus Productions
Primal Productions, Inc.
Prince/SF Productions (not accepting submissions)
William Prines III
R.E.F. Records (affiliate of Bob Scott Frick)

Ray Mack Productions
Red Kastle Productions
Revolver FM Records Ltd.
Ridge Recording Studios
Rockland Music, Inc.
Adam Rodell/Rodell Records
Henry Rowe
Rushwin Productions
Rustron Music Productions
Saturn Productions
SCL Productions Inc.
Sierra West Music
Silicon Chip Recording Company (requested deletion)
Sir Garrett Productions
Mike Siskind (requested deletion)
Skylyne Records
Sneak Tip Records Inc./Hip Wreckin Records Ltd.
Sound Control Productions
Soundstage South
Southern Sound Productions
A. Stewart Productions
Sweet Inspiration Music (requested deletion)
Tabitha Productions
TCC Productions (not accepting submissions)
Terock Records (affiliate of Wade Curtiss)
Tough Guys Productions, Inc.
Trend Productions
Triplane Production
Turner Productions
Up All Night Enterprises
Lucien Vector
The Victory Label
Shane Wilder Productions
Tom Willett, Tommark Records
Wizards & Cecil B
Ray Woodbury/Woodbury/Lyman Management
Geoff Workman/Original Projects Unlimited
James Yarbrough
John Young
John Zapple
Zar Musik

Managers and Booking Agents

Managers and booking agents are part of the circle of music industry professionals closest to the artists themselves. Working for and with their clients, they are a vital part of an aspiring artist's career.

The artist manager is a valuable contact, both for the songwriter trying to get songs to a particular artist and for the songwriter/performer. Often the manager is the person closest to the artist, and he may have heavy influence in what type of material the performer uses. Don't expect managers of nationally-known acts to be the easiest people to approach, because they're not. Many songwriters are trying to get songs to these people, and in most cases they only accept material from music publishers or producers who they know personally or professionally.

You need not go further than your own hometown, however, to find artists hungry for good, fresh material. Managers of local acts often have more to say in the choice of material their clients perform and record than managers in major hubs, where the producer often makes the final decision on what songs are included in a particular project. Locally, it could be the manager who not only chooses songs for a recording project, but also selects the producer, the studio and the musicians.

If you are an artist or artist/songwriter seeking management, take care in selecting your representation. A manager needs to know about all aspects of the music industry. His handling of publicity, promotion and finances, plus his contacts within the industry will shape your career. Look for a manager or agency who will take an interest in your development. This can be worked into a management agreement to help insure management is working on your behalf. Above all don't be afraid to ask questions about any aspects of the relationship between you and a prospective manager. He should be willing to explain any confusing terminology or discuss plans with you before taking action. Remember: A manager works *for the artist*. His main function is advising and counseling his clients, not dictating to them.

Another function of the manager is to act as liaison between the artist and the booking agent. Some management firms may also handle booking. However, it may be in your interest to look for a separate booking agency. It will give you another member of the team working to get your work heard in live performance, and adds to the network necessary to make valuable contacts in the industry. Since their function is mainly to find performance venues for

INSIDER REPORT

When shopping for a manager, be very selective

Nashville-based Fat City Artists provides management and booking services for clients as diverse as Big Brother and the Holding Company, Chuck Berry, Tommy Tutone and the Dallas Cowboys Cheerleaders. "Today, our company has agreements with 117 artists that represent every genre of music," says Rusty Michael, president of Fat City. Michael also runs a publishing company and record company, and provides, among other things, consulting, investment and event management services for his clients.

Rusty Michael

With over 20 years in the music business, Michael is well aware of the important role a manager plays in an artist's career. "The primary responsibility of management," he says, "is to oversee the creative process and insure that all business related functions are handled in a professional manner. Management's objective should be career direction. Creative direction is the function of the artist, and management should be comfortable with that upon entering a management relationship. Before even considering a management agreement, however, the artist should educate himself on every aspect of the music business, including management, booking, publishing, etc."

When shopping for a manager, an artist should be extremely selective. "Management is like a marriage," Michael advises. "Don't rush it. Shop hard." An artist must ask specific questions and find out everything he can about a prospective manager. Some questions to consider, says Michael, are: "Does the prospective manager have a track record? Does management have a game plan specific to the individual artist? How knowledgable is management about the current climate in the industry? What other clients are being represented by management? Talk to previous and existing clients. What is management's reputation in the industry?"

Along with things to look for there are also some things an artist should avoid. "Avoid any potential management that seems to promise anything and everything," Michael advises, "or that insists on signing an agreement immediately without the opportunity to establish a basic relationship."

Artists aren't the only ones who should be selective; managers should also have requirements regarding the artists they decide to work with. What are the things Michael looks for in prospective clients? "Number one," he says, "is definitely professionalism. What is the artist's potential in today's market? And does the artist have the drive and determination to become successful?"

Perhaps the most important thing to remember when selecting a personal manager is the fact that you both must be able to work together. "No manager that I'm aware of is a miracle worker," Michael concludes. "It takes 110% from both artist and management."

their clients, booking agents represent many more acts than a management firm, and have less contact with the individual acts. A booking agent will charge a commission for his services, as will a management firm. Managers usually ask for a 15-20% commission on an act's earnings; booking agents charge less.

Talent, originality, credits, dedication, self-confidence and professionalism are qualities that will attract a manager to an artist—and a songwriter. Before submitting to a manager or booking agent, be sure he's searching for the type of music you offer. And, just as if you were contacting a music publisher or producer, always be as organized and professional as possible. *Billboard* also publishes a list of managers/booking agents in *Billboard's International Talent and Touring Directory*.

The firms listed in this section have provided information about the types of acts they currently work with and the type of music they're interested in (you will also want to refer to the Category Index at the back of the book). Each listing contains submission requirements and information about items to include in a press kit, and will also specify whether the company is a management firm, a booking agency or both.

*aaLN INTERNATIONAL, Pyckestraat 65 B-2018, B2500 Lier, Antwerp **Belgium**. Tel. and fax: (0)3 2384816. President: Luc Nuitten. Management firm, booking agency. Estab. 1991. Represents individual artists, groups, international touring acts and groups, regional artists (Flanders and Belgium), artists from anywhere; currently handles 6 acts. Receives 15% commission. Reviews material for acts.
How to Contact: Submit demo tape by mail. Unsolicited submissions are OK. Prefers cassette (or VHS videocassette) with 3 songs. If seeking management, press kit should include VHS video, CD or demo cassette, references, photos, bio, press book. "Always looking for new talent—please present a complete neat and self-explanatory promo kit." Does not return material. Reports in 1 month.
Music: Mostly **jazz, world music, contemporary**; also **blues** and **Latin**. Works primarily with concert tour bands and festival bands.

ABSOLUTE ENTERTAINMENT INC., 273 Richmond St. W, Toronto, Ontario M5V 1X1 **Canada**. Contact: Wayne Thompson. Management firm. Estab. 1973. Represents international individual artists and groups; currently handles 3 acts. Receives 20% commission. Reviews material for acts.
How to Contact: Submit demo tape by mail—unsolicited submissions are OK. Prefers cassette (or VHS videocasette if available) with 4 songs and lyric sheet. SASE. Reports in 2-3 weeks.
Music: Mostly **pop, rock** and **R&B**. Works primarily with vocalists, singer/songwriters. Current acts include The Nylons (a capella), Infidels (rock) and Scott Dibble (singer/songwriter).
Tips: "Be aggressive, be patient, be polite."

ACOUSTIWORKS, P.O. Box 120694, Nashville TN 37212. President: Tom Wilkerson. Management firm. Represents nationally known individual artists only; currently handles 4 acts. Receives 10-20% commission. Reviews material for acts.

The asterisk before a listing indicates that the listing is new in this edition. New markets are often the most receptive to unsolicited submissions.

How to Contact: Submit demo tape by mail—unsolicited submissions are OK. Prefers cassette with 3 songs. If seeking management, include photo, bio and letter stating goals. SASE. Reports in 2 weeks. **Music:** Mostly **country, gospel** and **contemporary Christian** and **pop.** Works primarily with vocalists. Current acts include Ed Bruce (singer/songwriter/actor), Billy Henson (singer/songwriter) and George Westermeyer (singer/songwriter).

AFTERSCHOOL PUBLISHING COMPANY, P.O. Box 14157, Detroit MI 48214. (313)571-0363. President: Herman Kelly. Management firm, booking agency, record company (Afterschool Co.) and music publisher (Afterschool Publishing Co.). Estab. 1978. Represents individual artists, songwriters, producers, arrangers and musicians. Currently handles 6 acts. Receives 5-50% commission. Reviews material for acts.
How to Contact: Submit demo tape by mail—unsolicited submissions are OK. Prefers cassette with 3 songs and lyric or lead sheet. If seeking management, include resume with demo tape and bio in press kit. SASE. Reports in 2 weeks to 1 month.
Music: Mostly **pop, jazz, rap, country** and **folk.** Works primarily with small bands and solo artists. Current acts include Herman Kelly, L. Curry and W. Stevenson.

*THE AGENCY, #200, 41 Britain St., Toronto, Ontario M4Y 1L6 **Canada.** (416)365-7833. Fax: (416)365-9692. Contact: A&R Department. Booking agency. Estab. 1977. Represents individual artists, groups, comedy artists (Kids in the Hall) from anywhere. Currently handles over 200 acts. Receives up to 15% commission. Reviews material for acts.
How to Contact: Submit demo tape by mail. Unsolicited submissions are OK. Prefers cassette (or VHS videocassette) with lyric sheet or lead sheet. Does not return material. Reports in 1-2 months.
Music: All types: **rock, pop, country;** also **tributes, alternative, top 40.** Current acts include Tom Cochrane, Barenaked Ladies, Rush, April Wine, Jeff Healey Band, 54:40 and Tragically Hip.

MARK ALAN AGENCY, P.O. Box 279, Hopkins MN 55343. (612)942-6119. President: Mark Alan. Management firm and booking agency. Represents individual artists, groups and songwriters; currently handles 8 acts. Receives 15-20% commission. Reviews material for acts.
How to Contact: Submit demo tape by mail—unsolicited submissions are OK. Prefers cassette (or VHS videocassette if available). If seeking management, include photo and bio in press kit. Does not return material. Reports in 2 months.
Music: Rock, pop, R&B and **alternative.** Works primarily with groups and solo artists. Current acts include Airkraft (rock band), Zwarté (rock band), Crash Alley (rock band), Lixx (rock band), the Stellectrics (alternative band) and Saturn Cats (rock band).
Tips: "We work with bands that tour nationally and regionally and record their original songs and release them on major or independent labels. We book clubs, colleges and concerts."

ALEXAS MUSIC PRODUCTIONS, (formerly Alexas Music Group), 3365 W. Millerberg Way, West Jordan UT 84084. (801)566-9542. President: Patrick Melfi. Management firm, booking agency (BMI) and record company (Alexas Records/ASCAP). Estab. 1976. Represents local, regional or international individual artists, groups and songwriters; currently handles 6 acts. Receives 15-20% commission. Reviews material for acts.
How to Contact: Write or call first and obtain permission to submit. Submit VHS videocassette only with 1-3 songs and lyric sheets. If seeking management, include bio, video and demo. SASE. Reports in 10 weeks.
Music: Mostly **country** and **pop;** also **New Age** and **gospel.** Represents well-established bands and vocalists. Current acts include A.J. Masters (singer/songwriter), Meisner, Rich & Swan, The Virgin River Band, The Drifters and The Crests.
Tips: "Be strong, be straight and be persistent/no drugs."

GREG ALIFERIS MANAGEMENT, P.O. Box 11841, Ft. Lauderdale FL 33339-1841. (305)561-4880. President: Greg Aliferis. Management firm, music publisher (Rumrunner Music/BMI) and record company (Rumrunner Records, Inc.). Estab. 1980. Represents local/southeast individual artists, groups and songwriters; currently handles 5 acts. Receives 20% commission. Reviews material for acts.
How to Contact: Submit demo tape by mail—unsolicited submissions are OK. Prefers cassette (or VHS videocassette) with 3 songs and lyric sheet. If seeking management, include 3- or 4-song demo cassette, photo, bio, video if available, and current address and phone number in press kit. SASE. Reports in 2-3 months.

Listings of companies in countries other than the U.S. have the name of the country in boldface type.

Music: Mostly **dance, rap** and **pop.** Works primarily with rap groups, dance groups and female vocalists. Current acts include Side F-X (rap), Mario (rap) and Don't Know Yet (dance).
Tips: "Think 'commercial.' "

ALL MUSICMATTERS!, (formerly Musicmatters), 9233 Gloxinia, San Antonio TX 78218. (512)651-6939. Manager: Jean Estes. Management firm. Represents local, regional and international individual artists, groups and songwriters; currently handles 2 acts. Receives 20% commission.
How to Contact: Write first and obtain permission to submit. Prefers cassette (or VHS videocassette if available) with 3 songs. SASE. Reports in 2 months.
Music: Mostly **jazz.** Current acts include Mike Brannon (jazz guitarist/songwriter) and True Diversity (jazz group).

*MICHAEL ALLEN ENTERTAINMENT DEVELOPMENT, P.O. Box 111510, Nashville TN 37222. (615)754-0059. Contact: Michael Allen. Management firm. Represents individual artists, groups and songwriters; currently handles 3 acts. Receives 15-25% commission. Reviews material for acts.
How to Contact: Submit demo tape by mail—unsolicited submissions are OK. Prefers cassette (or VHS videocassette) with 3 songs and lyric or lead sheets. Does not return unsolicited material. Reports in 3 months.
Music: Mostly **country, pop, R&B;** also **rock** and **gospel.** Works primarily with vocalists and bands. Currently doing public relations for Shotgun Red, Ricky Lynn Gregg and Sharon Walker.

ALOHA ENTERTAINMENT, P.O. Box 2204, 14 Sherman St., Auburn NY 13021. (315)252-1863. Publicist/Manager: Art Wenzel. Management and public relations firm. Estab. 1982. Represents local, Central New York, international and national touring acts and groups.
How to Contact: Submit demo tape by mail—unsolicited submissions are OK. Prefers CD or cassette. Does not return unsolicited material. If seeking management, include biography, photograph, clips, and CD or cassette.
Music: Mostly **rock, metal** and **blues;** also **jazz** and **R&B.** Current acts include Built For Comfort (blues), Paul Quinzi Project (pop), Bad Image (rock) and many more!
Tips: "Don't keep calling."

*AMAZING MAZE PRODUCTIONS, P.O. Box 282, Cranbury NJ 08512. (609)426-1277. Fax: (609)426-1217. Contact: Michael J. Mazur II. Management firm. Estab. 1987. Represents groups from anywhere. Currently handles 1 act.
How to Contact: Write or call first and obtain permission to submit. Prefers cassette (or VHS videocassette) with 2 songs. Does not return material. Current artists include Harmzway (rock).

*AMERICAN CONCERT, P.O. Box 24599, Nashville TN 37202. (615)244-2290. Booking agency. Estab. 1987. Represents individual artists and established recording stars; currently handles 6 acts. Receives 10% commission.
How to Contact: Does not review material, are a booking agency only.
Music: Mostly **country, adult contemporary** and **nostalgic rock.** Current acts include Dan Seals (country), Charly McClain (country), Wayne Massey (light rock), Avery Michaels (country), Joan Kennedy (country) and Johnny Rivers (nostalgic rock).

AMERICAN FAMILY ENTERTAINMENT, P.O. Box 605, Harrison AR 72602. (501)741-5250. Contact: Mike Bishop. Management firm. Estab. 1983. Represents regional individual artists and groups; currently handles 5 acts. Receives 10% commission. Reviews material for acts.
How to Contact: Submit demo tape by mail—unsolicited submissions are OK. Prefers cassette with 2-5 songs and lyric or lead sheets. If seeking management, include bio, photo, demo, etc. Does not return unsolicited material. Reports in 1 month.
Music: Mostly **country, pop** and **gospel;** also **bluegrass** and **patriotic.** Works primarily with vocalists/show bands. Current acts include Riverbend, Mike Bishop and Plainsmen.
Tips: "Send driving commercial country tunes for males. Send good love songs and gospel for females."

AMERICAN FAMILY TALENT, P.O. Box 87, Skidmore MO 64487. (816)928-3631. Personal Manager: Jonnie Kay. Management firm (Festival Family Ent. Ltd.), publisher (Max Stout Publishing/BMI) and record company (Max Stout Records). Estab. 1973. Currently handles 3 acts. Receives 10-15% commission. Reviews material for acts.
How to Contact: Submit demo tape by mail—unsolicited submissions are OK. Prefers cassette (or videocassette of performance) with 2 songs with lyric and lead sheets. Does not return unsolicited material. Reports in 4 months.
Music: Mostly **ballads, pop** and **country;** also **patriotic.** Works primarily with variety showbands and dance bands. Current acts include Britt Small and Festival (brass band/variety), Matt and Robyn Rolf (country show band) and Missouri Southern (country band).

Tips: "Be patient, we receive large amounts."

THE AMETHYST GROUP LTD., 273 Chippewa Dr., Columbia SC 29210-6508. (803)750-5391. Management and marketing firm. Represents individual artists, groups and songwriters; currently handles 24 acts. Receives 15-25% commission. "Signs original artists, producers, studios and composers."
How to Contact: Prefers cassette (or VHS videocassette if available) with 5-7 songs and lyric sheet. "Be creative, simple and to the point." SASE. Reports in 5 weeks if interested.
Music: Mostly **alternative, industrial, techno, dance, rock, metal** and **pop;** also **R&B** and **new music.** Current acts include Political Asylum, Bodyshop, Silhouette, The Sages, New Fire Ceremony, Progress In April, Carnage, and Ted Neiland.
Tips: "Be prepared to sign, if we're interested. We won't spend a lot of time convincing anyone what we can do for them. We are way too busy with current recording artists. We help organize radio and retail promotion for four record labels in the U.S. We develop recording artists and market them for further distribution, promotion. Our resources cover booking agencies, major and independent record companies, distributors, TV and radio stations, newspapers and trade publications, independent talent, record promoters and producers—all on national level. Most artists we represent *are not* in S.C. We are not just another small, local management firm. We also manufacture CDs, records, cassettes, photographs and other items to enhance an artist's career. Recently signed distribution and licensing with many territories in Europe."

*ANJOLI PRODUCTIONS, 24 Center Square Rd., Leola PA 17540. (717)656-8215. President: Terry Gehman. Management firm, booking agency and music publisher (Younger Bros. Music). Estab. 1984. Represents individual artists, groups and songwriters; currently handles 20 acts. Receives 15% commission. Reviews material for acts.
How to Contact: Prefers cassette or VHS videocassette (preferably a live show video, good quality. Segments of a variety of material with 15-minute maximum length) with 5 songs and lyric sheet. Does not return unsolicited material.
Music: **Country, pop** and **R&B.** Works primarily with vocalists and show groups. Current acts include Shucks (country show), Crossover (country shows), Marsha Miller (country show) and Anita Stapleton (country vocalist).

ARKLIGHT MANAGEMENT CO., (formerly Vic Arkilic), P.O. Box 261, Mt. Vernon VA 22121. (703)780-4726. Manager: Vic Arkilic. Management firm. Estab. 1986. Represents local individual artists and groups; currently handles 1 act. Receives 15% commission. Reviews material for acts.
How to Contact: Submit demo tape by mail—unsolicited submissions are OK. Prefers cassette (or VHS videocassette) with 4 songs and lyric sheet. If seeking management, include photo, bio, tape, video and lyric sheets. SASE. Reports in 3 months.
Music: Mostly **rock, pop** and **folk.** "We work with self-contained groups who are also songwriters."
Tips: "Please submit finished demos only!"

*ARTIST ALEXANDER/MIRACLE RECORDS, 8831 Sunset Blvd., Los Angeles CA 90069. (310)652-5050. Fax: (310)652-6421. Contact: Morey Alexander. Management firm, music publisher, record company, record producer. "30 years in business." Represents individual artists, groups, songwriters and producers from anywhere. Currently handles 15 acts. Receives 20% commission. Reviews material for acts.
How to Contact: Write or call first and obtain permission to submit. Prefers cassette. Press kit should contain "Anything the artist thinks is necessary to highlight their talents." Does not return unsolicited material. Reports in 6 weeks.
Music: **All types,** as long as it's a hit. Current acts include Timmy T, Kid Frost and Mellow Man Ace.

*ARTIST REPRESENTATION AND MANAGEMENT, 792 29th Ave. SE, Minneapolis MN 55414. (612)483-8754. Fax: (612)331-5091. Office Manager: Roger Anderson. Management firm, booking agency. Estab. 1983. Represents groups, artists from anywhere; currently handles 15 acts. Receives 15% commission.
How to Contact: Reviews material for acts. Call first and obtain permission to submit. Prefers cassette (or videocassette) with 3 songs and lyric sheet. If seeking management, press kit should include demo tape or videotape, preface, bio, etc. "Priority is placed on original artists with product who are willing to tour." Does not return material. Reports in 2 weeks.
Music: Mostly **rock, heavy metal** and **R&B;** also **Southern rock** and **pop.** Works primarily with bands. Current acts include Crow (R&B, rock), Freeman James (R&B, pop), Hericane Alice(metal).

ARTISTE RECORDS, (formerly Paul Levesque Management Inc.) 154 Grande Cote, Rosemere QC J7A 1H3 **Canada.** President/A&R Director: Paul Levesque. Record company, management firm and music publisher. Estab. 1987. Represents local, regional and international individual artists, groups and songwriters; currently handles 6 acts. Reviews material for acts.

How to Contact: Submit demo tape by mail—unsolicited submissions are OK. Prefers cassette (or VHS/Beta videocassette if available) with 3-6 songs and lyric sheet. "Send photos and bio if possible." SAE and IRC. Reports in 2 months.
Music: Mostly **rock/dance, pop** and **dance.** Current acts include Haze & Shuffle (rock band), Michael Dozier (pop/R&B singer) and Sonya Papp (pop singer/songwriter).

ARTISTIC DEVELOPMENTS INTERNATIONAL, INC. (A.D.I.), P.O. Box 6386, Glendale CA 91225. (818)501-2838. Management Director: Lisa Weinstein. Management firm. Estab. 1988. Represents local, regional and international individual artists, groups and songwriters. Reviews material for acts.
How to Contact: Call or write first and obtain permission to submit. Prefers cassette with unlimited number of songs and lyric sheet. SASE. Reports in 4-6 weeks.
Music: Mostly **cross-over artists, AC/pop** and **alternative/rock;** also **world beat/pop** and **R&B/dance.** Works primarily with singer/songwriters, bands and performance artists.
Tips: "A songwriter should have a professional quality tape that highlights his versatility and artistic vision. Lyric sheets should be included. An artist should submit a recent 8 × 10 photo that reflects his/ her musical vision. Name and phone number should be on everything! Both artist and songwriter should include a cover letter stating intent and artistic vision."

ASA PRODUCTIONS MANAGEMENT, P.O. Box 244, Yorba Linda CA 92686. (714)693-7629. President: Craig Seitz. Management firm. Estab. 1986. Represents local, regional and international individual artists and groups; currently handles 1 act. Receives 20% commission. Reviews material for acts.
How to Contact: Submit demo tape by mail—unsolicited submissions are OK. Prefers cassette (or VHS videocassette if available). SASE. Reports in 1 month.
Music: Mostly **country** and **bluegrass.** Works primarily with show/concert groups. Current acts include Sierrah Band.

ATCH RECORDS AND PRODUCTIONS, Suite 380, Fondren, Houston TX 77096-4502. (713)981-6540. President: Charles Atchison. Management firm, record company. Estab. 1989. Represents local, regional and international individual artists, groups and songwriters; currently handles 2 acts. Receives 20% commission. Reviews material for acts.
How to Contact: Submit demo tape—unsolicited submissions are OK. Prefers cassette with 2 songs and lyric sheet. Does not return unsolicited material. Reports in 3 weeks.
Music: Mostly **R&B, country** and **gospel;** also **pop, rap** and **rock.** Works primarily with vocalists and groups. Current acts include B.O.U. (rap) and Blakkk Media (rap).
Tips: "Be ready to work hard to obtain excellence."

***ATI MUSIC,** 75 Parkway Ave., Markham, Ontario L3P 2H1 **Canada.** (416)294-5538. President: Scoot Irwin. Management firm (ATI Music/SOCAN), music publisher, record company (ATI). Estab. 1983. Represents individual artists, groups from everywhere. Currently handles 14 acts. Reviews material for acts. Submit demo tape by mail.
How to Contact: Unsolicited submissions are OK. Prefers cassette (or VHS videocassette) with 2-3 songs and lyric sheet. If seeking management, press kit should include photo (2 different) bio and background. Does not return material. Reports in 1-2 weeks.
Music: Mostly **country, easy listening;** also **gospel.** Current acts include Dick Damron (country, singer/ writer award winner), The Fender Kings (country group/writers), Carmen Breckenridge (gospel singer/ writer).
Tips: "Material should be compatible with today's market."

BABY SUE, P.O. Box 1111, Decatur GA 30031-1111. (404)288-2073. President: Don W. Seven. Management firm, booking agency, record company (Baby Sue); "we also publish a magazine which reviews music." Estab. 1983. Represents local, regional or international individual artists, groups and songwriters; currently handles 3 acts. Receives 10% commission. Reviews material for acts.
How to Contact: Submit demo tape by mail—unsolicited submissions are OK. Prefers cassette (or VHS videocassette if available) with 4 songs and lyric sheets. Does not return unsolicited material. Reports in 2 weeks.
Music: Mostly **rock, pop** and **alternative;** also **country** and **religious.** Works primarily with multi-talented artists (those who play more than 1 instrument). Current acts include LMNOP (rock), Stephen Fievet (pop) and Bringbring (poetic music).

BACK PORCH BLUES, P.O. Box 14953, Portland OR 97214. (503)233-6827. General Manager: Jeffrey Dawkins. Management firm. Estab. 1988. Represents individual artists and groups from Pacific Northwest; currently handles 3 acts. Receives 20% commission. Reviews material for acts.
How to Contact: Write or call first and obtain permission to submit. Prefers cassette (or VHS videocassette if available) with 6 songs and lyric sheet. Does not return unsolicited material. Reports in 3 months.

Music: Mostly **traditional blues, R&B** and **country**; also **blues, gospel** and **solo piano.** Works primarily with blues bands, jazz singers and jazz groups. Current acts include Too Loose To Track, Back Porch (blues group) and Gordon Neal Herman.
Tips: "We want simple songs that tell a story. Good blues or country songs should touch the heart."

*BACKSTAGE PRODUCTIONS INTERNATIONAL, 1-3015 Kennedy Rd., Scarborough, Ontario M1V 1E7 **Canada.** (416)291-4913. President: Steve Thomson. Management firm, booking agency (Steve Thomson Agency), record company (Trilogy Records International), music publisher (Melmar Publishing/PROCAN and Star-Sattelite/CAPAC), and record producer. Represents individual artists, groups and songwriters. Currently handles 4 acts. Reviews material for acts.
How to Contact: Write first and obtain permission to submit. Prefers cassette (or VHS videocassette). SAE and IRC. Reports in 3 months.
Music: Mostly **rock, pop** and **country/crossover.** Works primarily with pop vocalists and rock bands; rock and country vocals. Current acts include Ronnie Hawkins and The Hawks (rockabilly), Patti Jannetta (pop), JK Gulley (country) and Manee (dance).

*BANDSTAND (INTERNATIONAL) ENTERTAINMENT AGENCY, P.O. Box 1010, Simcoe, Ontario N3Y 5B3 **Canada.** (519)426-0000. Fax: (519)426-3799. Florida Address: Unit 392, 1475 Flamingo Drive, Englewood FL 34224. President: Wayne Elliot. Management firm, booking agency. Estab. 1965. Represents individual artists and groups from anywhere. Currently handles 1 act. Receives 10-15% commission.
How to Contact: "Not interested at present time in material from songwriters." If seeking management, press kit should include promo, video and demo. Does not return material. Reports in 2 weeks.
Music: Mostly **rock, country**; also **novelty acts.** Works primarily with vocalists and bands. Current acts include Peggy Pratt.

BARNARD MANAGEMENT SERVICES (BMS), 2219 Main St., Santa Monica CA 90405. (213)396-1440. Agent: Russell Barnard. Management firm. Estab. 1979. Represents artists, groups and songwriters; currently handles 4 acts. Receives 10-20% commission. Reviews material for acts.
How to Contact: Write first and obtain permission to submit. Prefers cassette with 3-10 songs and lead sheet. Artists may submit VHS videocassette (15-30 minutes) by permission only. Does not return unsolicited material. Reports in 2 months.
Music: Mostly **country crossover**; also **blues, country, R&B, rock** and **soul.** Works primarily with country crossover singers/songwriters and show bands. Current acts include Helen Hudson (singer/songwriter), Mark Shipper (songwriter/author) and Mel Trotter (singer/songwriter).
Tips: "Semi-produced demos are of little value. Either save the time and money by submitting material 'in the raw,' or do a finished production version."

*BAUSE ASSOCIATES, Suite 3F, 1700 Pine St., Philadelphia PA 19103. (215)732-1053. Contact: Erik Bause. Management firm. Estab. 1992. Represents local individual artists and groups; currently handles 2 acts. Receives 10-20% commission.
How to Contact: Write or call first and obtain permission to submit. Prefers cassette. If seeking management, press kit should include cassette, photo, pertinent background information. SASE. Reports in 2-3 weeks.
Music: Mostly **heavy metal, hard rock.** Works primarily with groups, individual artists looking to join or form a group, original material—no cover bands. Current acts include Mind Shaker (hard rock band).

*BIG J PRODUCTIONS, 16-B Winnie Ct., Laplace LA 70068. (504)652-2645. Agent: Frankie Jay. Booking agency. Estab. 1968. Represents individual artists, groups and songwriters; currently handles over 50 acts. Receives 15-25% commission. Reviews material for acts.
How to Contact: Write or call first and obtain permission to submit. Prefers cassette (or VHS videocassette if available) with 3-6 songs and lyric or lead sheet. "It would be best for an artist to lip-sync to a prerecorded track. The object is for someone to see how an artist would perform more than simply assessing song content." Does not return unsolicited material. Reports in 2 weeks.
Music: Mostly **rock, pop** and **R&B.** Works primarily with groups with self-contained songwriters. Current acts include Zebra (original rock group), Lillian Axe (original rock group), Kyper (original dance) and Top Cats (original pop group).
Tips: "Have determination. Be ready to make a serious commitment to your craft because becoming successful in the music industry is generally not an 'overnight' process."

J. BIVINS' PRODUCTIONS, P.O. Box 966, Desoto TX 75123-0966. (214)709-7561. Management firm and record company (Avonna Records, Inc.). Estab. 1991. Represents individual artists, groups and songwriters from anywhere; currently handles 36 acts. Receives 25% commission. Reviews material for acts.

How to Contact: Submit demo tape by mail—unsolicited submissions are OK. Prefers cassette (or VHS videocassette if available) with 3 songs. Does not return unsolicited material. Reports in 2 weeks.
Music: Mostly **R&B, rock** and **gospel (top 40)**. Works primarily with vocalists and dance bands. Current acts include Sajo, Little Mike and TBA.

BLACK STALLION COUNTRY PRODUCTIONS, INC., P.O. Box 368, Tujunga CA 91043. (818)352-8142. President: Kenn E. Kingsbury, Jr.. Management firm, production company and music publisher (Black Stallion Country Publishing/BMI). Estab. 1979. Represents individual artists from anywhere; currently handles 5 acts. Receives 15-25% commission. Reviews material for acts.
How to Contact: Submit demo tape by mail—unsolicited submissions are OK. Prefers cassette with 3 songs and lyric sheet. SASE. Reports in 2 months.
Music: Mostly **country, R&B** and **A/C**. Works primarily with country acts, variety acts and film/TV pictures/actresses. Current acts include Lane Brody (singer country), Thom Bresh (musician), Gene Bear (TV host), Jenifer Green and Wayne Cornell, Australia (big band revue and act).
Tips: "Be professional in presentation. Make sure what you present is what we are looking for (i.e., don't send rock when we are looking for country)."

BLANK & BLANK, Suite 308, 1530 Chestnut St., Philadelphia PA 19102. (215)568-4310. Treasurer, Manager: E. Robert Blank. Management firm. Represents individual artists and groups. Reviews material for acts.
How to Contact: Submit demo tape by mail—unsolicited submissions are OK. Prefers videocassette. Does not return material.

*BOJO PRODUCTIONS INC., 3935 Cliftondale Pl., College Park GA 30349. (404)969-1913. Management firm and record company (Bojo Records). Estab. 1982. Represents local, regional or international individual artists, groups and songwriters; currently handles 5 acts. Receives 15% commission. Reviews material for acts.
How to Contact: Submit demo tape by mail. Unsolicited submissions are OK. Prefers cassette (or videocassette if available) with 3 songs and lyric or lead sheets. Does not return unsolicited material. Reports in 2 weeks.
Music: Mostly **R&B, gospel** and **country**; also **MOR**. Works primarily with vocalists and dance bands. Current acts include Ray Peterson (country), Jimmy Jordan (R&B) and George Smith (R&B/MOR).
Tips: "Send clean recording tape with leadsheets."

BOUQUET-ORCHID ENTERPRISES, 204 Crestview St., Minden LA 71055. President: Bill Bohannon. Management firm, booking agency, music publisher (Orchid Publishing/BMI) and record company (Bouquet Records). Represents individuals and groups; currently handles 4 acts. Receives 10-15% commission. Reviews material for acts.
How to Contact: Submit demo tape by mail—unsolicited submissions are OK. Prefers cassette (or videocassette if available) with 3-5 songs, song list and lyric sheet. Include brief resume. Press kits should include current photograph, 2-3 media clippings, description of act, and background information on act. SASE. Reports in 1 month.
Music: Mostly **country, rock** and **top 40/pop**; also **gospel** and **R&B**. Works primarily with vocalists and groups. Current acts include Susan Spencer, Jamey Wells, Adam Day and the Bandoleers.

*BILL BOYD PRODUCTIONS, Suite 245, 4219 W. Olive, Burbank CA 91505. (818)955-7570. Contact: Bill Boyd. Management firm and music publishers. Estab. 1984. Represents international individual artists, groups and songwriters; currently handles 2 acts. Receives 20% commission. Reviews material for acts.
How to Contact: Write or call first and obtain permission to submit. Prefers cassette with 3 songs and lyric sheet. Does not return unsolicited material. Reports in 2 weeks.
Music: Mostly **country**; also **blues**. Current acts include Maripat Davis (country singer) and Doo Wah Riders (country/rock band).

*BRIGHT SPARK SONGS PTY. LTD., P.O. Box 342, South Yarra, Victoria 3141 **Australia**. (613)827-6377. Fax: (613)827-5165. Director: John McDonald. Management firm, music publisher. Estab. 1991. Represents individual artists, groups and songwriters from anywhere; currently handles 25 acts. Reviews material for acts.
How to Contact: Submit demo tape by mail. Unsolicited submissions are OK. Prefers cassette (or VHS videocassette) with 2-4 songs and lyric sheet. SAE and IRC. Reports in 2-3 weeks.
Music: Mostly **rock, pop/dance** and **country**. Current acts include Danni'elle Gaha (singer/songwriter), Peter Crosbie (songwriter) and Lindsey Buckingham (singer/songwriter).

*BROADWEST MANAGEMENT, 17711 176th Ave. NE, Woodinville WA 98072. (206)885-9449. Fax: (206)485-8670. President: Luke L. Denn. Management firm. Estab. 1989. Represents individual artists, groups and songwriters from anywhere; currently handles 3 acts. Receives 15-20% commission. Reviews material for acts.
How to Contact: Submit demo tape by mail. Unsolicited submissions are OK. Prefers cassette (or VHS videocassette) with 4 songs and lyric sheet. If seeking management, press kit should include 1 cassette, 1 picture and 1-page bio. "Be sure to list what you are submitting tape for." SASE. Reports in 6 weeks.
Music: Mostly **alternative, dance-soul, R&B-rap;** also **songwriters** and **soundtracks.** Works primarily with vocalists, singer/songwriters and bands. Current acts include Jackie Young (pop-adult contemporary), Blackened Kill Symphony (alternative) and Jackie Young, Arthur Kohtz and Wayne Perkins (songwriters).
Tips: "Be short and direct to what you want. I'm looking for *national acts-writers* only."

DAVID BRODY PRODUCTIONS, 4086 Royal Crest, Memphis TN 38115. (901)362-1719. President: David or Gina Brody. Management firm and music publisher (Brody-Segerson Publishing/BMI). Estab. 1986. Represents international individual artists, groups and songwriters; currently handles 5 acts. Reviews material for acts.
How to Contact: Call first and obtain permission to submit. Prefers cassette (or VHS videocassette if available) with 3 songs and lyric sheet. If seeking management, include audio tape, bio and photos in press kit. SASE.
Music: Interested in **all music.** Works primarily with comedians, announcers, singers and actors. Current acts include Corinda Carford (country singer), Rick Landers (singer/songwriter) and Jimmy Segerson (R&B singer).

BROTHERS MANAGEMENT ASSOCIATES, 141 Dunbar Ave., Fords NJ 08863. (201)738-0880 or 738-0883. President: Allen A. Faucera. Management firm and booking agency. Estab. 1972. Represents artists, groups and songwriters; currently handles over 100 acts. Receives 15-20% commission. Reviews material for acts.
How to Contact: Submit demo tape by mail—unsolicited submissions are OK. Prefers cassette (or VHS videocassette if available) with 3-6 songs and lyric sheets. Include photographs and resume. If seeking management, include photo, bio, tape and return envelope in press kit. SASE. Reports in 2 months.
Music: Mostly **pop, rock, MOR** and **R&B.** Works primarily with vocalists and established groups. Current acts include Waterfront (R&B), Masquerade (dance) and 80 West (alternative).
Tips: "We need very commercial, chart-oriented material."

C & M PRODUCTIONS MANAGEMENT GROUP, 5114 Albert Dr., Brentwood TN 37027. (615)371-5098. Fax: (615)371-5317. Manager: Ronald W. Cotton. Management firm, booking agency and music publisher. Represents international individual artists; currently handles 3 acts on Polygram Records. Receives 15% commission.
How to Contact: Submit demo tape by mail—unsolicited submissions are OK. Prefers cassette (or VHS videocassette if available) with 3 songs and lead sheets. If seeking management, include picture, tape and bio in press kit. Does not return material. Reports in 2 weeks.
Music: Mostly **country, gospel** and **pop.** Current acts include Ronna Reeves (country) and Jeff Knight (country).

CAHN-MAN, Suite 201, 5273 College Ave., Oakland CA 94618. (510)652-1615. Contact: Elliot Cahn/Jeff Saltzman/David Hawkins. Management and law firm. Estab. 1986. Represents local, regional and international individual artists, groups and songwriters. Receives 20% commission; $175/hour as attorneys.
How to Contact: Submit demo tape by mail—unsolicited submissions are OK. Prefers cassette (or videocassette). If seeking management, include tape, photo, relevant press and bio in press kit. Does not return material. Artist should follow up with a call after 4-6 weeks.
Music: **All types,** with an emphasis on **alternative rock.** Current alternative acts include Primus (Interscope), Mudhoney (Warner Bros.), Hammerbox (A&M), Melvins (Atlantic) and The Muffs (Warner Bros.). Current singer/songwriters include Jesse Colin Young, Henry Gross, Kate Jacobs, Andy Milton and Neal Casal.
Tips: "As callous as it sounds, write great songs; but write songs for yourself, not for the industry."

CAM MUSIC, LTD., 6620 Swansdown Dr., Loves Pk IL 61111. (815)877-9678. Fax: (815)877-7430. CEO and General Manager: Chip Messiner. Management firm, booking agent, producer and publisher. Estab. 1983. Represents local and regional individual artists, groups and songwriters; currently handles 6 acts. Receives 15-25% commission. Reviews material for acts.

How to Contact: Write first and obtain permission to submit. Prefers cassette (or videocassette of performance, if available) with 3 songs, lyric sheets and SASE. If seeking management, include a cover letter, up to date info on writer or artist, photo (if looking to perform), bio, tape or CD. "Do not send full songs. 60-90 seconds is enough." Does not return unsolicited material. Reports in 2 months.
Music: Mostly **country, bluegrass** and **folk**; also **MOR, jazz** and **children's**. Works primarily with concert tour bands, show bands and festival bands. Current acts include Special Consensus (bluegrass), Southern Strut (country) and Sharon Polidan (children's).
Tips: "Don't expect to be an 'overnight success.' Take your time and do things right."

CAPITOL MANAGEMENT, 1300 Division St., Nashville TN 37203. (800)767-4984; (615)244-2440; (615)244-3377. Fax: (615)242-1177. Producer: Robert Metzgar. Management firm, booking agency, music publisher (Aim High Music Co., Bobby & Billy Music)) and record company (Stop Hunger Records International, Aim High Records, Hot News Records, Platinum Plus Records, SHR Records). Estab. 1971. Represents local, regional or international individual artists, groups and songwriters; currently handles 24 acts. Receives 15% commission. Reviews material for acts.
How to Contact: Submit demo tape by mail. Unsolicited submissions are OK. Prefers cassette (or videocassette of live performance, if available). If seeking management, include photo, bio, resume and demo tape. Does not return unsolicited material. Reports in 2 weeks.
Music: Mostly **traditional country, contemporary country** and **Southern gospel**; also **pop rock, rock-a-billy** and **R&B**. Works primarily with major label acts and new acts shopping for major labels. Current acts include Carl Butler (CBS records), Tommy Cash (CBS Records), Tommy Overstreet (CBS Records), Mark Allen Cash, Mickey Jones, The Glen Campbell Band (Warner Bros.) and Billy Walker (MCA Records).
Tips: "Call us on our toll-free line for advice before you sign with anyone else."

*CARAMBA ART, 3733 Hutchison, Montreal H2X 2H4 **Canada**. (514)844-7832. President: Bernardo Carrara. Management firm, booking agency, record company (Venus Landing), record producer. Estab. 1987. Represents individual artists, groups and songwriters from anywhere; currently handles 3 acts. Receives 10-20% commission. Reviews material for acts.
How to Contact: Call first and obtain permission to submit. Prefers cassette (or VHS videocassette) with 3-5 songs and lyric sheet. If seeking management, press kit should include photo, bio, tape, lyrics. Use strong padded envelope. SAE and IRC. Reports in 1 month.
Music: Mostly **pop-rock, pop** and **alternative**; also **blues, folk** and **New Age**. Works primarily with singer/songwriters/bands. Current acts include MollyBelle (pop-rock songwriter/performer/solo-artist) and Dax (pop rock/songwriter).

*CARMAN PRODUCTIONS, INC., 15456 Cabrito Rd., Van Nuys CA 91406. (213)873-7370. A&R: Tom Skeeter. Management firm, music publisher (Namrac/BMI, Souci/ASCAP) and record production company. Estab. 1969. Represents local, regional and international individual artists, groups, songwriters, producers and actors. Currently handles 5 acts. Receives 15-20% commission. Reviews material for acts.
How to Contact: Submit demo tape by mail—unsolicited submissions are OK. Prefers cassette with 5 songs and lyric sheets. Does not return unsolicited material. Reports in 6 weeks.
Music: Mostly **rock, dance, R&B, pop** and **country**. Current acts include Richard Carpenter, J.J. White, Ron Keel, Timothy Pantea and Jimmy DeMar.

CAT PRODUCTION AB, Rörstrandsgatan 21, Stockholm 11340 **Sweden**. Phone: (08)317-277. Managing Director: Christina Nilsson. Management firm and booking agency. Estab. 1972. Represents individual artists, groups and songwriters; currently handles 3 acts. Receives 15% commission. Reviews material for acts.
How to Contact: Submit demo tape by mail—unsolicited submissions are OK. Prefers cassette (or VHS videocassette if available) with 4-6 songs and lyric or lead sheet. If seeking management, include cassette tape or VHS videocassette, brief reviews, press clippings. Does not return material. Reports in 1 month.
Music: Mostly **R&B, rock** and **gospel**; also "texts for stand-up comedians." Works primarily with "concert bands like Janne Schaffer's Earmeal. Rock-blues-imitation shows." Current acts include Jan Schaffer (lead guitar, songwriter), Ted Ashton (singer, blues/rock guitar and harmonica player, stand up comedian) and Malou Berg (gospel singer).

How to Get the Most Out of Songwriter's Market (at the front of this book) contains comments and suggestions to help you understand and use the information in these listings.

CAVALRY PRODUCTIONS, P.O. Box 70, Brackettville TX 78832. (512)563-2759 and (512)563-2236 (studio). Contact: Rocco Fortunato. Management firm and record company. Estab. 1979. Represents regional (Southwest) individual artists and groups; currently handles 4 acts.
How to Contact: Submit demo tape—unsolicited submissions are OK. Prefers cassette with 3 songs and lyric sheet. SASE. Reports in 1 month.
Music: Mostly **country** and **Hispanic;** also **gospel** and **novelty.** Works primarily with single vocalists and various vocal groups "2 to 4 voices." Current acts include Bob Macon (country), Jose Lujan (Tejano), Blue Magic (Hispanic), Espuma (Hispanic).
Tips: "Material 'in the raw' is OK if you are willing to work with us to develop it."

*CEDAR CREEK PRODUCTIONS AND MANAGEMENT, Suite 503, 44 Music Square E., Nashville TN 37203. (615)252-6916. Fax: (615)329-1071. President: Larry Duncan. Management firm, music publisher (Cedar Creek Music/BMI), record company (Cedar Creek Records) and record producer. Estab. 1992. Represents individual artists, groups and songwriters from anywhere; currently handles one act. Receives 20% of gross. Reviews material for acts.
How to Contact: Submit demo tape by mail. Unsolicited submissions are OK. Prefers cassette (or VHS videocassette) with 4-6 songs and lyric sheet. If seeking management, press kit should include 8 × 12 color or b&w picture, bio, 4-6 songs on cassette tape, VHS video if available. Does not return material. Reports in 1 month.
Music: Mostly **country, country/pop** and **country/R&B;** also **pop, R&B** and **light rock.** Works primarily with vocalists, singer/songwriters and groups. "Looking for artists to represent now."
Tips: "Submit your best songs and a good full demo with vocal upfront with 5 instruments on tracks backing the singer; use a great demo singer."

*CFB PRODUCTIONS, INC., P.O. Box 357, Riverton CT 06065. (203)738-3801. Vice President: Wanda J. Rodgers. Management firm. Estab. 1980. Represents national, regional and international individual artists. Currently handles 5 acts. Reviews material for acts.
How to Contact: Submit demo tape by mail. Unsolicited submissions are OK. Prefer letter first. Prefers cassette (or VHS videocassette) with 3 songs and lyric sheet. Does not return material. Reports in 2 weeks to 1 month.
Music: Mostly **country, pop/top 40, dance.** Works primarily with established or touring artists.
Tips: "Send professional promo packages and demos including video."

PAUL CHRISTIE MANAGEMENT, Box 96, Avalon NSW 2107 **Australia.** Phone: (02)415-2722. Managing Director: Paul Christie. Management firm (Paul Christie Management/APRA). Estab. 1982. Represents local, regional and international individual artists, groups and songwriters; currently handles 5 acts. Receives 20% commission. Reviews material for acts.
How to Contact: Submit demo tape by mail—unsolicited submissions are OK. Prefers cassette or VHS videocassette with 4 songs and lyric or lead sheet. Does not return submitted material. Reports in 1 week.
Music: Mostly **rock, pop/rock** and **pop/R&B.** Works primarily with rock acts, singer/writers, all composers. Current acts include Party Boys (2-guitar power rock) and Zillian and the Zig Zag Men (surf punk/thrash).
Tips: "Divorce yourself from all the rock music industry mythology and all the emotional issues, and assess yourself in terms of 'what really is'."

CIRCUIT RIDER TALENT & MANAGEMENT CO., 123 Walton Ferry Rd., 2nd Floor, Hendersonville TN 37075. (615)824-1947. Fax: (615)264-0462. President: Linda S. Dotson. Management firm, booking agency and music publisher (Channel Music, Cordial Music). Represents individual artists, songwriters and actors. Currently handles 6 acts (for management) but works with a large number of recording artists, songwriters, actors, producers. (Includes multi Grammy winning producer/writer Skip Scarborough). Receives 15% commission. Reviews material for acts.
How to Contact: Write or call first and obtain permission to submit. Prefers cassette (or videocassette) with 3 songs and lyric sheet. Videocassettes required of artist's submissions. SASE. Reports in 6 weeks. If seeking management, press kit should include bio, photo, and tape with 3 songs.
Music: Mostly **pop, country** and **gospel;** also **R&B** and **comedy.** Works primarily with vocalists, special concerts, movies and TV. Current acts include Sheb Wooley (country & comedy), Buck Trent (country & comedy), Shauna D (R&B), Willie John Ellison (blues), Frank White (blues) and Alton McClain (gospel).
Tips: "Artists have your act together. Have a full press kit, videos and be professional. Attitudes are a big factor in my agreeing to work with you (no egotists). This is a business and your career we will be building."

CLASS ACT PRODUCTIONS/MANAGEMENT, P.O. Box 55252, Sherman Oaks CA 91413. (818)980-1039. President: Peter Kimmel. Management firm, music publisher, production company. Estab. 1985. Represents local, regional or international individual artists, groups, songwriters, actors and screenwriters. Receives 20% commission. Reviews material for acts.
How to Contact: Submit demo tape by mail—unsolicited submissions are OK. Include pictures, bio, lyric sheets (essential), and cassette tape or CD in press kit. SASE. Reports in 1 month.
Music: Mostly **rock, pop** and **country rock**; also **dance, R&B** and **country**.

*CLE MANAGEMENT GROUP/NY, P.O. Box 43723, Detroit MI 48243. (313)537-0590. Contact: A&R Department. Management firm, music publisher, record company (Creative Life Entertainment/ BMI), record producer. Estab. 1993. Represents individual artists, groups and songwriters from anywhere; currently handles 6 acts. Receives 15% commission. Reviews material for acts.
How to Contact: Write first and obtain permission to submit. Prefers cassette (or VHS videocassette) with 3-4 songs and lyric sheet and photo for groups or artists that want to be signed. If seeking management, press kit should include press clippings, endorsement letters, list of accomplishments and goals. "Be professional." SASE. Reports in 3 weeks.
Music: Mostly **pop, rock, R&B**; also **hip hop (rap), alternative** and **gospel** and **country**. Works primarily with singer/songwriters and bands. Current acts include EZ Bang (commercial rock), Calvin May (R&B-pop) and Brigade (rap).
Tips: "Be willing to listen and hear. Be flexible and professional."

CLOCKWORK ENTERTAINMENT MANAGEMENT AGENCY, 227 Concord St., Haverhill MA 01831. (508)373-5677. President: Bill Macek. Management firm and booking agency. Represents groups and songwriters throughout New England; currently handles 2 acts. Receives 15% commission. Reviews material for acts.
How to Contact: Query or submit demo tape. Prefers cassette with 3-12 songs. "Also submit promotion and cover letter with interesting facts about yourself." Does not return unsolicited material unless accompanied by SASE. Reports in 1 month.
Music: **Rock (all types)** and **top 40/pop**. Works primarily with bar bands and original acts.

*THE NEIL CLUGSTON ORGANIZATION PTY. LTD., P.O. Box 387 Glebe, Sydney, N.S.W. 2037 **Australia**. (02)5523277. Fax: (02)5523713. Managing Director: Neil Clugston. Management firm. Estab. 1989. Represents individual artists, groups and actors from anywhere; currently handles 4 acts. Reviews material for acts.
How to Contact: Submit demo tape by mail. Unsolicited submissions are OK. Prefers cassette (or PAL VHS videocassette) with 2 songs and lyric sheet. If seeking management, press kit should include bio, photo, cassette. SAE and IRC. Reports in 1 month.
Music: Mostly **rock, pop, dance**; also **A/C**. Current acts include Craig McLachlan (rock singer/songwriter), Girl Overboard (rock group/songwriters), Alyssa-Jane Cook (rock/pop singer).
Tips: "Only send your best material."

RAYMOND COFFER MANAGEMENT, 26 Park Road, Bushey Herts WD2 3EQ UK. Phone: (081)420-4430. Fax: (081)950-7617. Contact: Raymond Coffer. Branch: 15201 Sutton St., Sherman Oaks, CA 91403. Phone (818)783-0011. Fax: (818)783-0375. Contact: Andy Gershon. Management firm. Estab. 1984. Represents local, regional and international individual artists and groups; currently handles 7 acts. Receives 20% commission.
How to Contact: Submit demo tape by mail—unsolicited submissions are OK. Prefers cassette (or PAL or VHS videocassette if available) with 3 songs and lyric sheet. Does not return unsolicited material.
Music: Mostly **rock** and **pop**. Works primarily with bands. Current acts include Love & Rockets, Daniel Ash, David J, Cocteau Twins, Swell, Ian McCulloch, Smashing Pumpkins, Curve, and The Sundays.

*COLWELL ARTS MANAGEMENT, RR#1, New Hamburg, Ontario N0B 2G0 **Canada**. (519)662-3499. Fax: (519)662-2777. Director: Jane Colwell. Management firm, booking agency. Estab. 1985. Represents individual artists, groups from anywhere. Currently handles 17 acts. Receives 10-20% commission.
How to Contact: Submit demo tape by mail. Unsolicited submissions are OK. Prefers cassette (or VHS videocassette) with 4 songs and lyric sheet. If seeking management, press kit should include tape, photo, resume, reviews, 2 letters of recommendation. Does not return material. Reports in 3 weeks.
Music: Mostly **classical, cross-over, choral**. Works primarily with singers.
Tips: "Be prepared. Be honest. Have something special to offer."

CONCEPT 2000 INC., 2447 W. Mound St., Columbus OH 43204. President: Brian Wallace. Management firm and booking agency (Concept 2000 Music/ASCAP). Estab. 1981. Represents international individual artists, groups and songwriters; currently handles 5 acts. Receives 10-20% commission. Reviews material for acts.
How to Contact: Submit demo tape by mail—unsolicited submissions are OK. Prefers cassette with 4 songs. If seeking management, include photo and bio. Does not return unsolicited material. Reports in 2 weeks.
Music: Mostly **country, gospel** and **pop**; also **jazz, R&B** and **soul.** Current acts include Kelli Reisen (gospel), Bryan Hitch (gospel), The Breeze (country), Marilyn Cordial (pop) and Gene Walker (jazz).
Tips: "Send quality songs with lyric sheets. Production quality is not necessary."

*CONCERT EVENT, #410, 1949 Stemmons Freeway, Dallas TX 75207. (214)504-8831. Fax: (214)742-9411. President: Mike Itashiki. Director of Bookings: Jim Gasewicz. Booking agency. Estab. 1988. Represents groups from anywhere. Currently handles 7 groups. Receives 15-20% commission. Reviews material.
How to Contact: Submit demo tape by mail. Unsolicited submissions are OK. Prefers cassette. Does not return material. Reports in 2 weeks.
Music: Mostly **world beat, strings, New Age**; also **death metal.** Current acts include Okutara, Okinawan Folk Act, North East Terms Symphony (classical), Crucifix (death metal).
Tips: "Provide description and materials the average non-musical person on the street could understand."

*CORVALAN-CONDLIFFE MANAGEMENT, Suite 5, 1010 Fourth St., Santa Monica CA 90403. (213)393-6507. Manager: Brian Condliffe. Management firm. Estab. 1982. Represents local and international individual artists, groups and songwriters; currently handles 3 acts. Receives 15% commission.
How to Contact: Call first and obtain permission to submit. Prefers cassette with 4-6 songs. If seeking management, include bio, professional photo and demo. Does not return unsolicited material. Reports in 1 month.
Music: Mostly **R&B, pop** and **rock**; also **Latin** and **dance.** Works primarily with jazz/instrumental ensembles and pop/rock/world beat club bands. Current acts include The Wild Cards (R&B-Latin-pop), T-Square (jazz, NAC) and Big Daddy (pop/nostalgia).
Tips: "Submit as professional a package or presentation as possible."

COUNTDOWN ENTERTAINMENT, 109 Earle Ave., Lynbrook NY 11563. (516)599-4157. President: James Citkovic. Management firm, consultants. Estab. 1983. Represents local, regional and international individual artists, groups, songwriters and producers; currently handles 2 acts. Receives 20-30% commission. Reviews material for acts, and for music publishing.
How to Contact: Submit demo tape by mail—unsolicited submissions are OK. Prefers cassette (or VHS, SP speed videocassette) if available with songs and lyric sheet. If seeking management, include cassette tape of best songs, 8 × 10 pictures, VHS video, lyrics, press and radio playlists in press kit. SASE. Reports in 6 weeks.
Music: Mostly **pop/rock, nu-music** and **alternative/dance**; also **R&B, pop/dance** and **hard rock.** Deals with all styles of artists/songwriters/producers. Current acts include: Deke Rivers (honky tonk), World Bang (euro-dance). Also producers: Bob Buontempo, John Ward Piser, Ken Kushner, Drew Miles and Hal Gold.
Tips: "Send hit songs, only hit songs, nothing but hit songs."

COUNTRY MUSIC SHOWCASE INTERNATIONAL, INC., P.O. Box 368, Carlisle IA 50047. (515)989-3676 or (515)989-3748. President: Harold L. Luick. Vice President: Barbara A. Lancaster. Management firm and booking agency "for acts and entertainers that are members of our organization." Estab. 1984. Represents individual artists, groups and songwriters; currently handles 8 acts. Receives 10-20% commission.
How to Contact: Write first and obtain permission to submit. Prefers cassette with 3 songs and lyric sheet (or VHS videocassette showing artist on the job, 3 different venues). If seeking management, include 8 × 10 pictures, resume, past performance, audio tape and video tape of act in press kit. SASE. Reports in 3 weeks. "Must be paid member of Country Music Showcase International, Inc., to receive review of work."
Music: Mostly **contemporary, hard core country** and **traditional country**; also **bluegrass, western swing** and **comedy.** Works primarily with "one person single acts, one person single tape background acts and show bands." Current acts include Mr. Elmer Bird (banjo virtuoso), Country Classics USA (12-piece stage show), Joe Harris Country Music Show, The Dena Kaye Show and Britt Small.
Tips: "We want artists who are willing to work hard to achieve success and songwriters who are skilled in their craft. Through educational and informative seminars and showcases we have helped many artist and songwriter members achieve a degree of success in a very tough business. For information

on how to become a member of our organization, send SASE to the above address. Memberships cost $40.00 per year for artist or songwriter."

COUNTRY STAR ATTRACTIONS, 439 Wiley Ave., Franklin PA 16323. (814)432-4633. Contact: Norman Kelly. Management firm, booking agency, music publisher (Country Star Music/ASCAP) and record company (Country Star, Process, Mersey and CSI Records). Estab. 1970. Represents artists and musical groups; currently handles 6 acts. Receives 10% commission. Reviews material for acts.
How to Contact: Submit demo tape—unsolicited submissions are OK. Prefers cassette with 2-4 songs and lyric or lead sheet; include photo. SASE. Reports in 2 weeks.
Music: Mostly **country** (85%); **rock** (5%), **gospel** (5%) and **R&B** (5%). Works primarily with vocalists. Current acts include Junie Lou, Ron Lauer and Jeffrey Alan Connors, all country singers.
Tips: "Send only your very best efforts."

*COUNTRYWIDE PRODUCERS, 2466 Wildon Dr., York PA 17403. (717)741-2658. President: Bob Englar. Booking agency. Represents individuals and groups; currently handles 8 acts. Receives 10-15% commission. Reviews material for acts.
How to Contact: Query or submit demo with videocassette of performance, if available. Include photo. SASE. Reports in 1 week.
Music: Bluegrass, blues, classical, country, disco, folk, gospel, jazz, polka, rock (light), soul and **top 40/pop.** Works primarily with show bands. Current acts include Carroll County Ramblers (bluegrass), Ken Lightner (country), Rhythm Kings (country), Junction (variety), the Bruce Van Dyke Show (variety) and Big Wheeley & the White Walls (country rock).

COURTRIGHT MANAGEMENT INC., 201 E. 87th St., New York NY 10128. (212)410-9055. Contacts: Hernando or Doreen Courtright. Management firm. Estab. 1984. Represents local, regional and international individual artists, groups, songwriters and producers. Currently handles 1 act. Receives 20% commission. Reviews material for acts.
How to Contact: Write or call first and obtain permission to submit. Prefers cassette (or VHS videocassette if available) with 3 or 4 songs and lyric sheet. If seeking management, include photos, bio, video, tape and press in press kit. SASE. Reports in 1 month.
Music: Mostly **rock** and **metal**; also **pop** and **blues.** Current acts include Deena Miller (alternative) and various producers.

CRASH PRODUCTIONS, P.O. Box 40, Bangor ME 04402-0040. (207)794-6686. Manager: Jim Moreau. Booking agency. Estab. 1967. Represents individuals and groups; currently handles 9 acts. Receives 10-25% commission.
How to Contact: Submit demo tape by mail—unsolicited submissions are OK. Prefers cassette (or VHS videocassette if available) with 4-8 songs. "To all artists who submit a video: We will keep it on file for presentation to prospective buyers of talent in our area—no longer than 15 minutes please. The quality should be the kind you would want to show a prospective buyer of your act." Include resume and photos. "We prefer to hear groups at an actual performance." If seeking management, include 8×10 b&w photos, resume, cassette, press clips and a video cassette in press kit. Does not return unsolicited material. Reports in 3 weeks.
Music: Mostly **50s-60s** and **country rock, top 40**; also **rock** and **Polish.** Works primarily with groups who perform at night clubs (with an average of 150-200 patrons) and outdoor events (festivals and fairs). Current acts include Coyote (country rock), Dakota (rock) and Airfare (top 40).
Tips: "My main business is booking acts to entertainment buyers. To sell them I must have material that tells these potential buyers you are great and they need you. A photocopy press kit doesn't do it."

CREATIONS, LTD., 308 Hampstead N., Antioch TN 37013. (615)367-0988. Owners: Carmen Robinson and Jewell Frazier. Management firm. Estab. 1991. Represents individual Southern artists, groups, songwriters and dancers; currently handles 1 act. Receives 15% commission. Reviews material for acts.
How to Contact: Write first and obtain permission to submit. Prefers cassette with 2 songs and lyric sheet. SASE. If seeking management, include photo, bio, promotional material (if available) and lyric sheet. Reports in 1 month.
Music: Mostly **R&B, pop** and **gospel**; also **dance.** Works primarily with vocalists and dance bands. Current acts include Menáge (songwriter/performers), Prime Time (dance) and "D" (singer).
Tips: "Believe that with God, all things are possible."

*CREATIVE STAR MANAGEMENT, 1331 E. Washington Blvd., Ft. Wayne IN 46803. (219)424-5766. Department of Creative Services: James Milligan. Management firm, booking agency, music publisher (Party House Publishing/BMI), record company (New Experience Records/Grand Slam Records).

Estab. 1989. Represents individual artists, groups, songwriters from anywhere. Currently handles 10 acts. Receives 15% commission. Reviews material for acts.
How to Contact: Write first and obtain permission to submit. Prefers cassette (or VHS videocassette) with 3-5 songs and lyric sheet. If seeking management, press kit should include press clippings, bios, resume, 8×10 glossy photo, any information that will support material and artist. Does not return unsolicited material. Reports in 1 month.
Music: Mostly **R&B, pop, country;** also **rap, contemporary gospel, soul/funk.** Current acts include T.M.C. (R&B/group), Lavel (solo artist) and Volume Ten (rapper).
Tips: "Develop your own musical style. Believe in yourself—keep submitting updates and most of all be patient. If there's interest you will be contacted."

BOBBY LEE CUDE'S GOOD AMERICAN MUSIC/TALENT/CASTING AGENCY, 519 N. Halifax Ave., Daytona Beach FL 32118-4017. Fax: (904)252-0381. CEO: Bobby Lee Cude. Music publisher (BMI) and record company (Hard Hat). Estab. 1978. Represents international individual artists. Receives 15% commission. Reviews material for acts.
How to Contact: Write first and obtain permission to submit. Prefers cassette (or videocassette) with 2 songs, lyrics and lead sheets. "No unsolicited material reviewed."
Music: Mostly **pop** and **country.** Current acts include Fred Bogert and "Pic" Pickens.
Tips: "Read music books for the trade."

*CURLY MAPLE MEDIA, P.O. Box 543, Santa Monica CA 90406. (310)396-1664. Fax: (310)396-1884. President: Matt Kramer. Management firm. Estab. 1973. Represents individual artists, groups and songwriters from anywhere; currently handles 2 acts. Receives 15-20% commission. Reviews material for acts.
How to Contact: Submit demo tape by mail. Unsolicited submissions are OK. Prefers cassette (or VHS videocassette) with 4 songs and lead sheet. If seeking management, press kit should include bio. SASE. Reports in 2-4 weeks.
Music: Mostly **pop, R&B, world beat;** also **folk, folk rock, Latin.** Current acts include Richard Elliot (R&B, pop saxophonist) and Lauren Wood (performer/songwriter).
Tips: "Be patient, relaxed and realistic. Maintain artistic integrity and don't take it personally if many in the industry don't respond."

*D & M ENTERTAINMENT AGENCY, P.O. Box 19242, Johnston RI 02919. (401)944-6823. President and Manager: Ray DiMillio. Management firm and booking agency. Estab. 1968. Represents local groups; currently handles 28 acts. Receives 15% commission. Reviews material for acts.
How to Contact: Write first and obtain permission to submit or call to arrange personal interview. Prefers cassette (or VHS videocassette) with 3 songs and lyric or lead sheet. Does not return unsolicited material. Reports in 2 weeks.
Music: Mostly **R&B** and **pop;** also **rock.** Current acts include XPO, Sunshyne and Rykoche.

D & R ENTERTAINMENT, 308 N. Park, Broken Bow OK 74728. (405)584-9429. President: Don Walton. Management firm. Estab. 1987. Represents international individual artists and groups; currently handles 2 acts. Receives 15-20% commission. Reviews material for acts.
How to Contact: Submit demo tape by mail—unsolicited submissions are OK. Prefers cassette with any number of songs and lyric or lead sheet. Does not return unsolicited material. "I would like to know publishing company of any material sent." Reports in 3 months "if interested."
Music: Country and **pop country.** Current acts include Rick Thompson (country) and Rachel Garrett (country).
Tips: "Make sure everything submitted is copyrighted! If it isn't, I won't consider it."

D&D TALENT ASSOCIATES, P.O. Box 308, Burkeville VA 23922. (804)767-4150. Owner: J.W. Dooley, Jr. Booking agency. Estab. 1976. Currently handles 2 acts. Receives 10% commission. "Reviews songs for individuals in the jazz and 40s-50s field only."
How to Contact: Submit demo tape by mail—unsolicited submissions are OK. Prefers cassette (or videocassette) with 1-6 songs and lead sheet. SASE. Reports in 2 weeks.
Music: Mostly **jazz** and **40s-50s music.** Works primarily with vocalists, comics. Current acts include Johnny Pursley (humorist) and David Allyn (vocalist).
Tips: "Just send the best songs possible—although I am doing no booking now, for practical reasons, I will try to give free advice if possible. Since I am not in a metro area, possible contacts are probably out at this time. Don't contact me to produce miracles. I can be a sounding board for the music only—someone to at least listen and hopefully, make suggestions."

Refer to the Category Index (at the back of this book) to find exactly which companies are interested in the type of music you write.

BRIAN de COURCY MANAGEMENT, Box 96, South Yarra, Melbourne, Victoria 3141 **Australia**. Phone: (03)836-9621. Fax: (03)888-5662. C.E.O.: Brian de Courcy. Management firm. Estab. 1974. Represents local, regional or international individual artists, groups, songwriters, DJ's, music journalists and TV performers; currently handles 10 acts. Receives 15-25% commission. Reviews material for acts.
How to Contact: Write or call first and obtain permission to submit. Prefers cassette, CD (any videocassete if available) with lyric and lead sheet. SAE and IRC. Reports in 2 weeks.
Music: Mostly **rock** and **pop**. Works primarily with rock/pop acts and movie/stage music.

THE EDWARD DE MILES COMPANY, 8th Floor, Vantage Point Towers, 4475 N. Allisonville Rd., Indianapolis, IN 46205. (317)546-2912. President & CEO: Edward De Miles. Management firm, booking agency, entertainment/sports promoter and TV/radio broadcast producer. Estab. 1984. Represents film, television, radio and musical artists; currently handles 15 acts. Receives 10-20% commission. Reviews material for acts. Regional operations in Chicago, Dallas, Houston and Nashville through marketing representatives. Licensed A.F. of M. booking agent.
How to Contact: Write first and obtain permission to submit or write to arrange personal interview. Prefers cassette with 3-5 songs, 8x10 black and white photo and lyric sheet. "Copyright all material before submitting." If seeking management, include demo cassette with 3-5 songs, 8 × 10 black & white photo and lyric sheet in press kit. SASE. Reports in 1 month.
Music: Mostly **country, dance, R&B/soul, rock, top 40/pop** and **urban contemporary**; also looking for material for television, radio and film productions. Works primarily with dance bands and vocalists. Current acts include Lost in Wonder (progressive rock), Steve Lynn (R&B/dance) and Multiple Choice (rap).
Tips: "Performers need to be well prepared with their presentations (equipment, showmanship a must)."

DEBBIE DEAN AND ASSOC., P.O. Box 687, Ashland City TN 37015. (615)746-2758. Fax: (615)746-2758. Contact: Debbie Dean. Overseas booking agency, record promotion and public relations firm. Estab. 1988. Represents local, regional and international individual artists; currently handles 7 acts. Receives 15% commission. Reviews material for acts.
How to Contact: Submit demo tape by mail—unsolicited submissions are OK. Prefers cassette with 3 songs and lyric sheet. If seeking management, include good quality black & white photo, good one page bio and released or soon to be released 45, CD, album or cassette in press kit. SASE. Reports in 2 weeks.
Music: Mostly **country traditional** and **MOR country**. Works primarily with artists who can also play a guitar or some instrument. Current acts include Ed Parker, Terresa Jhene, Don Acuff, Steve Haggard, Ann Holland, Charlie Fields and Barry McCloud.

*DEMORE MANAGEMENT, P.O. Box 36152, Oklahoma City OK 73136. (405)424-8612. President: Kerwin James. Management firm (Wink Two Music/BMI), record company (Ganvo Records). Estab. 1988. Represents individual artists from anywhere. Currently handles 5 acts. Receives 20% commission. Reviews material for acts.
How to Contact: Submit demo tape by mail. Unsolicited submissions are OK. Prefers cassette with 3-5songsand lyric sheet. If seeking management, press kit should include bio, publicity print. Does not return material. Reports in 4-6 weeks.
Music: Mostly **soul/R&B, hip hop, gospel**; also **soft rock, contemporary jazz**. Works primarily with soul/R&B vocalists, singer/songwriters. Current acts include Tune N 2 (hip hop), Ava Gardner Soul (R&B), Church of Triumphant (gospel).
Tips: "Have your mind made up that this is really what you want to do; don't start if you're not serious."

*DIETROLEQUINTE ART COMPANY, Via Orti 24, Milano 20122 **Italy**. (+39)2-55184004. Fax: (+39)2-59902676. Managing Director: Francesco Fontana. Management firm, booking agency. Represents individual artists and groups from anywhere; currently handles 5-7 acts. Receives 20% commission. Reviews material for acts.
How to Contact: Submit demo tape by mail. Unsolicited submissions are OK. Prefers cassette (or PAL videocassette) with 3 songs. If seeking management, press kit should include 2 b&w photos and tape. Does not return material. Reports in 2 months.
Music: Mostly **world music, Latin rock, new projects**. Works primarily with bands. Current acts include Les Pires (gypsy music), Cheb Kader (räi music) and Les Vrp (cabaret rock).
Tips: "Be original, friendly, ready to travel a lot."

ANDREW DINWOODIE MANAGEMENT, Box 1936, Southport, QLD **Australia** 4215. Phone: (075)376222. Manager: Andrew Dinwoodie. Management firm, booking agency. Estab. 1983. Represents regional (Australian) individual artists, groups and songwriters; currently handles 3 acts. Receives 10-20% commission. Reviews material for acts.

How to Contact: Submit demo tape by mail—unsolicited submissions are OK. Prefers cassette (VHS PAL if available) with lyric sheet. SAE and IRC. Reports in 6 weeks.
Music: Mostly **country, R&B** and **rock/pop**; also **bluegrass, swing** and **folk**. Current acts include Bullamakanka, Donna Heke and the Moderation Band.
Tips: "Be imaginative and stay your own individual; don't try to conform to the norm if you are different."

*DIRECT BOX MUSIC, P.O. Box 19410, New Orleans LA 70179. (504)895-3246. Fax: (504)895-7069. Vice President of A&R: Kent E. Birkle. Management firm, record company (Fireproof Records), record producer. Estab. 1982. Represents individual artists, groups, songwriters from anywhere. Currently handles 4 acts. Receives 15-20% commission. Reviews material for acts.
How to Contact: Write first and obtain permission to submit or arrange personal interview. Prefers cassette (or VHS videocassette) with 3 songs and lyric sheet or lead sheet. If seeking management, press kit should include photo, song list, bio, tape, press. Does not return material. Reports in 2 weeks.
Music: Mostly **R&B, rock, alternative**; also **zydeco, cajun, second line**. Current acts include Dreams in Action, (R&B/hip hop), Quiere Woods (R&B/top 40) and Harum Scarum (rock).
Tips: "Have yourself totally prepared musically, professionally, and know the music business."

MICHAEL DIXON MANAGEMENT, 119 Pebblecreek R., Franklin TN 37064. (615)791-7731. Management firm. Estab. 1982. Represents major label rock artists, individual artists, groups and songwriters; currently handles 4 acts. Receives 20% commission.
How to Contact: Submit demo tape by mail—unsolicited submissions are OK. Prefers cassette (or VHS videocassette if available) with 3-4 songs and lyric sheet. Does not return unsolicited submissions.
Music: Mostly **rock, pop** and **alternative**; also **gospel** and **R&B**. Works primarily with rock bands with mostly self written material with an occasional outside song(s). Current acts include Thurn & Taxis (progressive rock), Rosemarys (alternative/pop) and Chris Carmichael (pop/rock).
Tips: "All it takes is a unique, one of a kind, said in a new and different way, song that is stunning. One great song will open the door. 2-3 good songs will get you on our list of developing songwriters with potential."

DMR AGENCY, Suite 250, Galleries of Syracuse, Syracuse NY 13202-2416. (315)475-2500. Contact: David M. Rezak. Booking agency. Represents individuals and groups; currently handles 50 acts. Receives 15% commission.
How to Contact: Submit demo tape by mail—unsolicited submissions are OK. Submit cassette (or videocassette) with 1-4 songs and press kit. Does not return material.
Music: Mostly **rock (all styles), pop** and **blues**. Works primarily with dance, bar and concert bands; all kinds of rock for schools, clubs, concerts, etc. Current acts include Tryx (rock), Windsong (dance/pop) and Jeff Gordon (rock).
Tips: "We strictly do booking and have no involvement in artist repertoire. We prefer regionally-based bands with a high percentage of cover material."

COL. BUSTER DOSS PRESENTS, Drawer 40, Estill Springs TN 37330. (615)649-2577. Producer: Col. Buster Doss. Management firm, booking agency, record company (Stardust Records) and music publisher (Buster Doss Music/BMI). Estab. 1959. Represents individual artists, groups, songwriters and shows; currently handles 12 acts. Receives 15% commission. Reviews material for acts.
How to Contact: Write first and obtain permission to submit. Prefers cassette with 2-4 songs and lyric sheet. SASE. Reports in 1 week.
Music: **Country, gospel** and **progressive**. Works primarily with show and dance bands, single acts and package shows. Current acts include Mick O'Reilly, Mike Montana, "Bronco" Buck Cody.
Tips: "Write good songs—send only your best."

*DRIVEN RAIN MANAGEMENT, Suite 607, 330 Washington Blvd., Marina Del Rey CA 90292. (310)823-3106. Fax: (310)574-1866. President: Gail Gellman. Management firm. Estab. 1989. Represents individual artists and songwriters from anywhere. Currently handles 4 acts. Receives 20% commission.
How to Contact: Submit demo tape by mail. Unsolicited submissions are OK. Prefers cassette (or VHS videocassette) with 1 song and lyric sheet. If seeking management, press kit should include photo, bio and tape. Reports in 1 month.
Music: Mostly **country, folk, blues**. Works primarily with singer/songwriters. Current acts include Blakey St. John, country artist and Doug Forrest, country artist.
Tips: "Be professional, submit a well designed kit for our review."

ECI, INC., 1646 Bonnie Dr., Memphis TN 38116. (901)346-1483. Vice President: Bernice Turner. Management firm, booking agency, music publisher and record company (Star Trek). Estab. 1989. Represents local, regional and international individual artists and groups; currently handles 3 acts. Receives 25% commission. Reviews material for acts.

How to Contact: Submit demo tape by mail—unsolicited submissions are OK. Prefers cassette with 2 songs. If seeking management, include good demo tape, background of recorded materials, and any promo materials on writer in press kit. SASE. Reports in 5 weeks.
Music: Mostly **R&B** and **country**. Works primarily with show groups. Current acts include Kool and The Gang, Robby Turner and Ashley Allison.

EL GATO AZUL AGENCY, 64 Mill St., Chico CA 95928. (916)345-6615. Owner/Agent: Karen Kindig. Management firm and booking agency. Estab. 1989. Represents local/regional individual artists, groups and songwriters; currently handles 3 acts. Receives 10-15% commission. Reviews material for acts.
How to Contact: Submit demo tape by mail—unsolicited submissions are OK. Prefers cassette (or VHS videocassette if available) with 3 songs and lyric and lead sheet. If seeking management, include bio, discography, photo, demo tape and press clippings in press kit. SASE. Reports in 2 weeks.
Music: Mostly **jazz/pop**, **"ethno-pop"** and **pop-rock**. Works primarily with jazz artists, pop artists/ groups (especially "rock en español"), vocalists, ethnic musicians. Current acts include Alejandro Santos (composer/flutist), Dino Saluzzi (composer/bandoneonist) and Andy Cardel (singer/song-writer).
Tips: "Have faith in your abilities and be patient and persistent."

*EMARCO MANAGEMENT, P.O. Box 867, Woodland Hills CA 91365. President: Mark Robert. (818)225-0061. Fax: (818)225-0069. Management firm and publishing company. Estab 1982. Represents local, regional or individual artists, groups and songwriters and professional baseball players. Currently handles 8 acts. Receives 15% commission. Reviews material for acts.
How to Contact: Call first and obtain permission to submit. Prefers cassette with 3 songs or less and lyric sheets. Returns with SASE. Reports in 6 weeks.
Music: Mostly **pop** and **rock**. Current acts include Robbie Rist, Gabriela Rozzi, and Wonderboy (rock).
Tips: "Don't send material in until it is ready to be heard. We generally give an act *one* best shot to pitch us."

*EME INTERNATIONAL, 935 The Queensway #340, Toronto, Ontario M8Z 5P7 **Canada.** (416)255-5166. Managing Director: A.O. Darmstadt Ph.D., C.S.T. Management firm. Estab. 1981. Represents individual artists and songwriters from anywhere; currently handles 3 acts. Receives 10-25% commission. Reviews material for acts. Write first and obtain permission to submit or arrange personal interview. Prefers cassette (or VHS videocassette) with 3 songs and lyric sheet. If seeking management, press kit should include 8×10 glossy photo, bio and references of engagements, song list. Does not return material.
Music: Mostly **rock**, **country rock** and **rockin' blues**. Works primarily with vocalists and singer/song-writers. Current acts include Sab, Bitchin and Pulsations.

ENCORE TALENT, INC., 2137 Zercher Rd., San Antonio TX 78209. (512)822-2655. President: Ronnie Spillman. Management firm and booking agency. Estab. 1978. Represents regional individual artists and groups from Texas. Currently handles 6 acts. Receives 15% commission. Reviews material for acts.
How to Contact: Submit demo tape by mail—unsolicited submissions are OK. Prefers cassette with 4 songs. SASE. Reports in 2 weeks.
Music: Mostly **country**. Works primarily with bands. Current acts include Jay Eric (writer/country singer), The Nashville Sounds (country band) and Jody Jenkins (country singer/writer).

*ENTERTAINMENT PRODUCTIONS CO., P.O. Box 387, South Bethlehem NY 12161. (518)767-2744. CEO: Jim Staats. Management firm. Estab. 1978. Represents individual artists and songwriters from anywhere. Currently handles 2 acts. Reviews material for acts.
How to Contact: Write first and obtain permission to submit. Prefers cassette with 2-3 songs and lyric sheet. SASE. Reports in 1 month.
Music: Mostly **contemporary country, traditional country, blues**; also **country rock**. Works primarily with vocalists. Current acts include Mirinda James and Alex Craig, both contemporary country.
Tips: "Send us songs that are 'commercial' with grit and soul, blue collar vein."

ENTERTAINMENT UNLIMITED ARTIST INC., 64 Division Ave., Levittown NY 11956. (516)735-5550. Senior Agent: George I. Magdaleno. Management firm and booking agency. Estab. 1960. Represents local, regional and international individual artists, groups and songwriters; currently handles 30-40 acts. Receives 15% commission. Reviews material for acts.
How to Contact: Call first and obtain permission to submit or write first to arrange personal interview. Prefers cassette (or VHS videocassette if available) with 4 songs and lyric and lead sheet. If seeking management, include tape, bio and photos in press kit. SASE. Reports in 3-5 weeks.

Music: Mostly **rock, pop** and **R&B**; also **country** and **jazz.** Current acts include Blood, Sweat and Tears (rock), Richie Havens (folk) and Judy Collias.
Tips: "Follow up!"

*ETERNAL TALENT/SQUIGMONSTER MANAGEMENT, 1598 E. Shore Dr., St. Paul MN 55106-1121. (612)771-0107. Fax: (612)774-8319. President/Owner: Robert (Squiggy) Yezek. Management firm, booking agency, record company (PMS Records). Estab. 1983. Represents groups from anywhere. Handles 17 acts. Receives 10% commission. Reviews material for acts.
How to Contact: Submit demo tape by mail—unsolicited submissions are OK. Prefers CD (if available) with songs (no limit) and lead sheet. If seeking management, press kit should include CD or tape, bio, promo package and any press. SASE. Reports in 2-8 weeks.
Music: Mostly **alternative rock, heavy metal, hard rock;** also **comedy, new pop.** Works primarily with alternative hard rock and heavy metal acts for nationwide concert and showcase nite clubs. Current acts include No Man's Land (alternative metal), Drop Hammer (metal) and Fat Tuesday (rock).
Tips: "You must be willing to work hard and be dedicated to your goal of success."

EVENTS UNLIMITED, P.O. Box 6541, Cleveland OH 44101. (216)467-0300. President: John Latimer. Management firm, booking agency, record company (Play Records) and TV show ("Alternate Beat"). Estab. 1985. Represents local, regional and international individual artists, groups and songwriters. Currently handles 18 acts. Receives 25% commission. Reviews material for acts.
How to Contact: Submit demo tape by mail—unsolicited submissions are OK. Prefers cassette with 5 songs. SASE. Reports in 6 weeks.
Music: Mostly **rock** and **alternative.** Current acts include I-Tal (reggae club band), The Bellows (rock concert acts) and Serious Nature (rock concert act).
Tips: "Be professional, persistent, and patient. Correspond by mail only."

FAT CITY ARTISTS, Suite #2, 1226 17th Ave. South, Nashville TN 37212. (615)320-7678. Fax: (615)321-5382. President: Rusty Michael. Management firm, booking agency, lecture bureau and event management consultants. Estab. 1972. Represents international individual artists, groups, songwriters and authors; currently handles over 100 acts. Receives 20% commission. Reviews material for acts.
How to Contact: Submit demo tape and any other promotional material by mail—unsolicited submissions are OK. Prefers cassette, CD or video with 4-6 songs. Does not return unsolicited material. Reports in 2 weeks.
Music: Mostly **rock, top 40, country** and **blues;** also **rockabilly, alternative** and **jazz.** "We represent all types of artists." Current acts include Big Brother & The Holding Co., Tommy Tutone (rock), Doug Clark & The Hot Nuts, Poo Nanny & The Stormers (top 40), Lucky & The Hot Dice, The Belmont Playboys (rockabilly), Michael Dillon & Guns (country rock), Jimmy Markham & The Jukes (blues) and Ten Zen Men (alternative).
Tips: "Send all available information including audio, video, photo and print. Creative Communications Workshop, our advertising/promotion division, specializes in developing effective artist promotional packages, including demos, videos, photography and copy. We will evaluate your present promotional material at no cost."

*S.L. FELDMAN & ASSOCIATES, 10520 River Dr., Richmond, British Columbia V6X 1Z4 **Canada.** (604)734-5945. Fax: (604)732-0922. Contact: Janet York. Management firm, booking agency. Estab. 1970. Represents individual artists and groups from anywhere; currently handles numerous acts. Reviews material for acts.
How to Contact: Submit demo tape by mail. Unsolicited submissions are OK. Prefers cassette and lyric sheet.
Music: Current acts include Barenaked Ladies, Grapes of Wrath and Bryan Adams.

FRED T. FENCHEL ENTERTAINMENT AGENCY, 2104 S. Jefferson Avenue, Mason City IA 50401. (515)423-4177. General Manager: Fred T. Fenchel. Booking agency. Estab. 1964. Represents local and international individual artists and groups. Receives 15% commission. Reviews material for acts.
How to Contact: Submit demo tape by mail (videocassette if available). Unsolicited submissions are OK. Does not return unsolicited material.
Music: Mostly **country, pop** and some **gospel.** Works primarily with dance bands, show groups; "artists we can use on club dates, fairs, etc." Current acts include The Memories, D.C. Drifters, Convertibles and Cadillac. "We deal primarily with established name acts with recording contracts, or those with a label and starting into popularity."
Tips: "Submit good material with universal appeal and be informative on artist's background."

FIRST TIME MANAGEMENT, Sovereign House, 12 Trewartha Rd., Praa Sands-Penzance, Cornwall TR20 9ST **England.** Phone: (0736)762826. Fax: (0736)763328. Managing Director: Roderick G. Jones. Management firm. Estab. 1986. Represents local, regional and international individual aritsts, groups and songwriters. Receives 20% commission. Reviews material for acts.

How to Contact: Submit demo tape by mail—unsolicited submissions are OK. Prefers cassette or 15 ips reel-to-reel (or VHS videocassette) with 3 songs and lyric sheets. SAE and IRC. Reports in 4-8 weeks.

Music: Mostly **dance, top 40, rap, country, gospel** and **pop**; also **all styles**. Works primarily with songwriters, composers, vocalists, groups and choirs. Current acts include Pete Arnold (folk) and Willow.

Tips: "Become a member of the Guild of International Songwriters and Composers. Keep everything as professional as possible. Be patient and dedicated to your aims and objectives."

FLASH ATTRACTIONS AGENCY, 38 Prospect St., Warrensburg NY 12885. (518)623-9313. Agent: Wally Chester. Management firm and booking agency. Estab. 1952. Represents artists and groups; currently handles 10 exclusive and 96 non-exclusive acts. Receives 15-20% commission. Reviews material for acts. "We are celebrating 40 years in business, and are fully licensed by the American Federation of Musicians and the State of New York."

How to Contact: Submit demo tape by mail—unsolicited submissions are OK. Prefers cassette for singers, VHS videocassette for acts, with 1-6 songs with lead and lyric sheets. Songwriters and artists may submit "professionally done" videocassettes. If seeking management, entertainers should include professionally-done videotape or cassette, 8×10 photo, resume, song list and history of the act in press kit. Songwriters should include professionally-done cassette, lead sheet, lyrics and music. SASE. Reports in 1 month.

Music: Mostly **country, calypso, Hawaiian** and **MOR**; also **blues, dance, easy listening, jazz, top 40, country rock** and **Latin**, plus **American Indian Shows**. Works primarily with vocalists, dance bands, lounge acts, floor show groups and ethnic shows. Current acts include Prince Pablo's Caribbean Extravaganza (steel drum band and floor show), The Ronnie Prophet Country Music Show (Canada's #1 recording and TV star), Robin Right (country).

Tips: "Submit songs that have public appeal, good story line and simplicity."

*FLEMING ARTISTS MANAGEMENT, 5975 Park Ave., Montreal, Quebec H2V 4H4 **Canada**. (514)276-5605. Contact: Director. Management firm, booking agency, record producer. Estab. 1986. Represents local and regional individual artists, groups and songwriters. Currently handles 10 acts. Receives 15-20% commission.

How to Contact: Call first and obtain permission to submit. Prefers CD. Does not return material unless accompanied by SAE and IRC. Replies only if interested.

Music: Mostly **jazz, folk, ethnic**; also **blues, gospel, country**. Works primarily with jazz and folk artists. Current artists include Lorraine Desmarais (jazz), Penny Lang (folk/blues), Orealis (Celtic) and Trio François Bourassa (jazz).

FREADE SOUNDS ENTERTAINMENT & RECORDING STUDIO, N. 37311 Valley Rd., Chattaroy WA 99003. (509)292-2201. Fax: (509)292-2205. Agent/Engineer: Tom Lapsansky. Agent: Tim Deleo. Booking agency and recording studio. Estab. 1967. Represents groups; currently handles 10-13 acts. Receives 10% commission. Reviews material for acts.

How to Contact: Query by mail or submit demo. Prefers cassette (or videocassette, "please pick best vocal song, best instrumental and best song performer likes to perform") with 4-6 songs and pictures/song list. SASE. Reports in 2 weeks.

Music: Mostly **top 40/rock**; also **R&B** and **production rock**. Works primarily with dance/concert groups and bar bands. Current acts include Lynx, Boss Dagan, Crying Out Loud, Partners in Crime, Unlimited Demand, Nobody Famous, Rockaholics, Crazy Legs, Mr. E. and Uncle Nasty.

*PETER FREEDMAN ENTERTAINMENT, 7th Floor, 1775 Broadway, New York NY 10019. (212)265-1776. Fax: (212)265-3678. President: Peter Freedman. Management firm. Estab. 1986. Represents individual artists, groups and songwriters from anywhere. Currently handles 4 acts. Receives 15-20% commission. Reviews material for acts.

How to Contact: Write or call first and obtain permission to submit. Prefers cassette (or VHS videocassette) with 1-2 songs. If seeking management, press kit should include 3-4 song demo/ short bio and picture. Does not return material. Reports in 2 weeks.

Music: Mostly **alternative/pop, dance**, and **R&B/pop**. Works primarily with bands, singer/songwriters. Current acts include +Live+ (alternative/pop), The Ocean Blue (alternative/pop) and The Spelvins (alternative/pop).

Tips: "Write, write and write some more."

BOB SCOTT FRICK ENTERPRISES, 404 Bluegrass Ave., Madison TN 37115. (615)865-6380. President: Bob Frick. Booking agency, music publisher (Frick Music Publishing Co./BMI and Sugarbaker Music Publishing/ASCAP) and record company (R.E.F. Recording Co). Represents individual artists and songwriters; currently handles 5 acts. Reviews material for acts.

How to Contact: Submit demo tape by mail, or write or call first to arrange personal interview. Prefers cassette with 3 songs and lyric sheet. SASE. Reports in 1 month.

Music: Mostly **gospel, country** and **R&B.** Works primarily with vocalists. Current acts include Bob Scott Frick (guitarist, singer), Larry Ahlborn (singer), Bob Myers (singer), Teresa Ford, Eddie Isaacs, Scott Frick, Jim and Ruby Mattingly and David Barton.

*KEN FRITZ MANAGEMENT, 648 N. Robertson Blvd., Los Angeles CA 90069. (310)854-6488. Fax: (310)854-1015. Associate Managers: Michon C. Stanco, Pamela Byers, Martha Hertzberg. Management firm. Estab. 25+ years. Represents individual artists and groups from anywhere. Currently handles 5 acts. Receives 15% commission. Reviews material for acts.

How to Contact: Write first and obtain permission to submit. Prefers cassette (or VHS cassette) with 2-3 songs and lyric sheet. "Submissions should be short and to the point." SASE. Reports in 1-3 months.

Music: Mostly **alternative, rock, pop;** also **jazz** and **kids.** Current acts include Naked Soul (alternative), George Benson (jazz guitar/vocalist) and Peter, Paul & Mary (folk singer/songwriters).

FULL TILT MANAGEMENT, P.O. Box 1578, Sioux Falls SD 57106. (605)332-0078. President: Chris Van Buren. Management firm, booking agency and record company (Top Shelf Records). Estab. 1972. Represents regional Mid-West groups; currently handles 20 acts. Receives 15-20% commission. Reviews material for acts.

How to Contact: Submit demo tape by mail—unsolicited submissions are OK. Prefers cassette with 3 songs and lyric sheet. SASE. Reports in 6 weeks.

Music: Mostly **rock;** also **pop** and **country.** Works primarily with rock, dance and country bands. Current acts include Desert Rain (country), Ransom (rock) and Street Legal (rock/pop).

Tips: "Submit things that will sell."

FUTURE STAR ENTERTAINMENT, 315 South Beverly Dr., Beverly Hills CA 90212. (310)553-0990. President: Paul Shenker. Management firm. Estab. 1982. Represents local, regional or international individual artists and groups; currently handles 6 acts. Receives 20% commission. Reviews material for acts.

How to Contact: Call first and obtain permission to submit. Prefers cassette (or VCR optional) with 3-5 songs and lyric sheet. Does not return unsolicited material. Reports in 4-6 weeks.

Music: Mostly **rock, pop** and **R&B.** Works primarily with rock bands. Current acts include Pigmy Lovecircus (band), Tom Batoy (solo pop artist), Crowbar (band) and Seed (band).

*GANGLAND ARTISTS, 707-810 W. Broadway, Vancouver, British Columbia V5Z 1J8 **Canada.** (604)872-0052. Contact: Allen Moy. Management firm, production house and music publisher. Estab. 1985. Represents artists and songwriters; currently handles 3 acts. Reviews material for acts.

How to Contact: Write first and obtain permission to submit. Prefers cassette (or VHS videocassette if available) and lyric sheet. "Videos are not entirely necessary for our company. It is certainly a nice touch. If you feel your audio cassette is strong—send the video upon later request. Something wildly creative and individual will grab our attention." SAE and IRC.

Music: **Rock, pop** and **R&B.** Works primarily with "original rock/left of center" show bands. Current acts include 54-40 (rock/pop), Sons of Freedom (hard/rock) and Mae Moore (pop).

*GAYLE ENTERPRISES, INC., 51 Music Sq. E., Nashville TN 37203. (615)327-2651. Fax: (615)327-2657. Contact: Jay Lee Webb. Individual artists. Currently handles 1 act. Reviews material for acts.

How to Contact: Submit demo tape by mail. Unsolicited submissions are OK. Prefers cassette (with no more than 3 songs) and lyric sheet. SASE.

Music: Mostly **country, gospel/Christian.** Works primarily with vocalists. Current acts include Crystal Gayle.

GLOBAL ASSAULT MANAGEMENT, Suite 1632, 639 Gardenwalk Blvd., College Park GA 30349. (404)994-1770. Contact: David Norman. Management firm and booking agency. Represents groups and production teams. Currently handles 5 acts. Receives 15-20% commission. Reviews material for acts or available on consultant basis.

How to Contact: Submit demo tape by mail—unsolicited submissions are OK. Send photo, bio, 8 × 10 photos, VHS videocassette, audio cassette, songlist. SASE. Reports in 2 weeks.

Music: Mostly self-contained **R&B** and **alternative** groups. Current acts include Fonzo-S, Shyrod, About Face, AC Black, Frontrunner, and Tempest.

Tips: "If you are a group that is highly polished and professional and think internationally about your music, you should definitely contact us. We are presently also booking groups in Asia and Europe."

GOLDEN BULL PRODUCTIONS, P.O. Box 81153, Chicago IL 60681-0153. (312)509-2914. Manager: Jesse Dearing. Management firm. Estab. 1984. Represents local and regional (Midwest) individual artists, groups and songwriters; currently handles 4 acts. Receives 12-30% commission. Reviews material for acts.
How to Contact: Write first and obtain permission to submit. Prefers cassette (or VHS videocassette) with 4-5 songs and lyric or lead sheet. If seeking management, include demo tape, bio and 8 × 10 black and white photo in press kit. Does not return unsolicited material. Reports in 2 months.
Music: Mostly **R&B**, **pop** and **rock**; also **gospel, jazz** and **blues**. Works primarily with vocalists, bands. Current acts include Lost and Found (R&B band), Keith Stewart (songwriter) and A. Lock (singer).

*GOLDEN GURU ENTERTAINMENT, 301 Bainbridge St., Philadelphia PA 19147. (215)574-2900. Fax: (215)440-7367. Co-Owner: Eric J. Cohen, Esq.. Management firm, music publisher, record company (presently being set up; label will be for "singer-songwriters who tour"). Estab. 1988. Represents individual artists, groups and songwriters from anywhere; currently handles 2 acts. Reviews material for acts.
How to Contact: Submit demo tape by mail. Unsolicited submissions are OK. Prefers cassette (or VHS videocassette) with 3-6 songs. If seeking management, press kit should include photo, etc. Does not return material. Reports in 2-4 weeks.
Music: Mostly **rock, singer/songwriters, urban, pop**; "anything that is excellent!" Current acts include Jeffrey Gaines and Susan Werner (both singer/songwriters with "rock-folk vibe").
Tips: "Be patient for a response. Our firm also renders legal and business affairs services. We also do bookings for the *Tin Angel*, the premier acoustic venue (200 capacity) in Philadelphia."

*GREAT SOUTH ARTISTS/GSA MUSIC MANAGEMENT, 1435 Lakeridge Dr., Baton Rouge LA 70802. (504)383-7605. Owner: Mr. Lynn Ourso. Management firm, booking agency, music publisher (Great South Artists Songs/BMI), record producer, record company (GSA Records). Estab. 1969. Represents individual artists/writers, groups, songwriters from anywhere; currently handles 2 recording acts and 10 booking. Receives 10-15% commission. Reviews material for acts.
How to Contact: Submit demo tape by mail. Unsolicited submissions are OK. Prefers cassette (or VHS videocasette) with 3 songs. SASE. Reports in 3 weeks.
Music: Mostly **rock, country, R&B**; also **blues** and **pop hits**. Works primarily with bands/writers. Current acts include Fantasy (rock dance) and Louisiana Boys (country rock).
Tips: "Send 3 best songs in 'good' demo form."

CHRIS GREELEY ENTERTAINMENT, P.O. Box 593, Bangor ME 04402-0593. (207)827-4382. General Manager: Christian D. Greeley. Management firm and booking agency. Estab. 1986. Represents local, regional and international individual artists, groups, songwriters and disc-jockeys; currently handles 6 acts. Receives 10-15% commission. Reviews material for acts.
How to Contact: Submit demo tape by mail—unsolicited submissions are OK. Prefers cassette (or VHS videocassette if available) with 1-4 songs. SASE. Reports in 2 weeks.
Music: Mostly **rock, country** and **pop**. "I'm open to anything marketable." Wide range of musical styles. Current acts include Hey Mister (acoustic duo) and Soundtrac (regional top 40 dance band).
Tips: "Don't be afraid to work hard and do what it takes to make it."

*HALE ENTERPRISES, Rt. 1, Box 49, Worthington IN 47471. (812)875-3664. Contact: Rodger Hale. Management firm, booking agency and record company (Projection Unlimited). Estab. 1976. Represents artists, groups, songwriters and studio musicians; currently handles 15 acts. Receives 10-15% commission. Reviews material for acts.
How to Contact: Query by mail or call to arrange personal interview. Prefers cassette (or videocassette) with 2-10 songs and lyric sheet. "Include personal and business bio, photo and references." Does not return unsolicited material. Reports in 2 weeks.
Music: Mostly **country** and **top 40**; also **MOR, progressive, rock** and **pop**. Works primarily with show bands, dance bands and bar bands. Current acts include Indiana (country show band); Seventh Heaven (top 40 show) and Cotton (show band).

*HAWKEYE ATTRACTIONS, 102 Geiger St., Huntingburg IN 47542. (812)683-3657. President: David Mounts. Booking agency. Estab. 1982. Represents individual artists and groups. Currently handles 1 act. Receives 10% commission. Reviews material for acts.
How to Contact: Submit demo tape by mail—unsolicited submissions are OK. Prefers cassette with 4 songs and lyric sheet. SASE. Reports in 9 weeks.
Music: Mostly **country** and **western swing**. Works primarily with show bands, Grand Ole Opry style form of artist and music. Current acts include Bill Mounts (singer/songwriter) and Midwest Cowboys (country/western swing).
Tips: "Don't copy anybody, just be yourself. If you have talent it will show through."

*PAUL H. HAWKINS MANAGEMENT ASSOCIATES, 222 Stratford Ave., Pittsburgh PA 15206. (412)362-0310. President: Paul H. Hawkins. Management firm. Estab. 1992. Represents local and mid-Atlantic states individual artists and groups. Currently handles 2 acts. Commission varies. Reviews material for acts.
How to Contact: Write first and obtain permission to submit or arrange personal interview. If seeking management, press kit should include a clear description of group/artist background, philosophy and goals. "We respond to written inquiry only and will provide submission instructions at that time." Does not return material. Reports in 1-2 weeks.
Music: Mostly **R&B, pop,** and **hip hop.** Works primarily with young adult vocalists/groups with strong visual/audio appeal.
Tips: "In the coming year, we will be looking for one or two solo/group artists with strong values and an unbridled commitment to success at the national/international level. Unlike most management companies which handle a large number of acts, we are looking for only a choice few to which we can make a strong mutual commitment of time and energy."

HEAVYWEIGHT PRODUCTIONS & UP FRONT MANAGEMENT, 2734 E. 7th St., Oakland CA 94601. (415)436-5532. Vice President: Charles M. Coke. Management firm, music publisher and record company (Man Records). Estab. 1988. Represents local, regional and international individual artists, groups, songwriters and producers; currently handles 8 acts. Receives 20% commission. Reviews material for acts.
How to Contact: Submit demo tape by mail—unsolicited submissions are OK. Prefers cassette with 4 songs and lyric or lead sheet (optional). If seeking management, include good bio and pictures, good 4-song tape and phone number to reach sender in press kit. SASE. Reports within 3-4 weeks.
Music: Mostly **R&B, rock** and **country;** also **pop, Latin** and **jazz.** Works primarily with vocalists. Current acts include John Payne (R&B), Bedroom Cowboys and Christy McCod.
Tips: "Never quit."

*HENDERSON GROUP MUSIC, 125 Powell Mill Rd., Spartanburg SC 29301. (803)576-0226. President: Dr. Barry Henderson. Management firm, music publisher, HPL Communications/BMI. Estab. 1990. Represents individual artists, groups and songwriters from anywhere. Currently handles 5 acts. Receives 15-25% commission. Reviews material for acts.
How to Contact: Submit demo tape by mail. Unsolicited submissions are OK. Prefers cassette (or VHS videocassette) with 3 songs. If seeking management, press kit should include info about artist/group; original material; photo; goals. Does not return material. Reports in 2-3 months.
Music: Mostly **country, pop, rock.** Current acts include Joe Bennett (songwriter), Jeff Stone (singer-songwriter), Randy Powell (singer-songwriter).
Tips: "Must be polished and professional with commercial songs. Must have desire to work hard and travel."

*HIGH TIDE MANAGEMENT, 5015 Wind River Dr., McKees Rock PA 15136. (412)331-5275. Contact: A&R. Management firm. Estab. 1992. Represents songwriters from anywhere; currently handles 3 acts. Commission rate varies.
How to Contact: Submit demo tape by mail. Unsolicited submissions are OK. Prefers cassette with 1-3 songs and lyric sheet. Copyrighted material only. "No calls please." SASE. Reports in 3-5 weeks.
Music: Mostly **country, country-pop, MOR;** also **pop/rock.** Current acts include John Lo Bello (singer/writer-country), Shoogy Harem (singer/writer-pop/rock) and Blue Highway (pop/rock band).
Tips: "Write every day. Be patient and *do not get discouraged*. Also send neat packages."

HOLIDAY PRODUCTIONS, 1786 State Line Road, Lagrange GA 30240. (404)884-5369. President: Phyllis Imhoff. Management firm and music publisher (Silverstreak Music/ASCAP). Estab. 1983. Represents local, regional and international individual artists and songwriters; currently handles 2 acts. Receives 20% commission. Reviews material for acts.
How to Contact: Submit demo tape by mail—unsolicited submissions are OK. Prefers cassette or VHS videocassette and lyric sheet. SASE. Reports in 2 weeks.
Music: Mostly **country** and **pop.** Works primarily with dance bands and show bands with strong lead vocalists. Current acts include Scooter Lee (country singer) and Dealer's Choice (country band).

Market conditions are constantly changing! If you're still using this book and it is 1995 or later, buy the newest edition of Songwriter's Market at your favorite bookstore or order directly from Writer's Digest Books.

DOC HOLIDAY PRODUCTIONS, 5405 Echo Pines Circle W., Fort Pierce FL 34951. (804)827-8733 or (407)595-1441. Vice President: Judith Guthro. Management firm, booking agent, music publisher (BMI, ASCAP, SESAC) and record company (Tug Boat Records). Estab. 1985. Represents international individual artists, groups and songwriters; currently handles 104 acts. Receives 15-25% commission. Reviews material for acts.
How to Contact: Submit demo tape by mail. Unsolicited submissions are okay. Prefers cassette with 1 song and lyric sheet. If seeking management, include 8 × 10 photo, press clippings, and demo tape in press kit. Does not return unsolicited material. Reports in 2 weeks.
Music: Mostly **country, pop** and **rock**. Works primarily with vocalist dance bands. Current acts include Doug "The Ragin Cajun" Kenshaw (cajun), Big Al Downing (country), Doc Holiday (country rock), Wyndi Renee (country), John Lockhart (bluegrass), James Clayton (country rock), Narvel Felts (country), Fats Domino (rock & roll), Side Winder (metal) and King-B-and the New Jack Crew (rap).

HORIZON MANAGEMENT INC., 659 Westview Station, Binghamton NY 13905. (607)772-0857. Contact: New Talent Department. Management firm and booking agency. Estab. 1968. Represents local, regional or international individual artists, groups and songwriters; currently handles 1,500 acts. Receives 20% commission. Reviews material for acts.
How to Contact: Call first and obtain permission to submit. Prefers cassette (or VHS videocassette if available) with 1-4 songs and 1 lyric or lead sheet. If seeking management, include photo, bio, song list, equipment list, audio and/or video, press clippings, reviews, etc. Does not return unsolicited material. Reports in 1 week.
Music: Mostly **top 40 lounge** and **show, top 40 country** and **top 40 rock**; also **classic rock, oldies** and **original**. Works primarily with bands (all styles). Current acts include Beatlemania (Broadway show), The Boxtops (60s recording act) and Joey Dee & Starlighters (50s recording artist).

*HULEN ENTERPRISES, Suite 2-2447 Falcon Ave., Ottawa, Ontario K1V 8C8 **Canada**. (613)738-2373. Fax: (613)526-3481. President, General Manager: Helen Lenthall. Management firm, record producer. Represents individual artists, groups, songwriters from anywhere. Commission negotiable. Reviews material for acts.
How to Contact: Write first and obtain permission to submit, then submit demo tape by mail. Unsolicited submissions are OK. Prefers cassette (or VHS videocassette with 3-8 songs maximum and lyric sheet or lead sheet. If seeking management, press kit should include bio, media package, photos, reviews, tracking if available. SAE and IRC. Reports in 3 weeks to 2 months.
Music: Mostly **soul, pop/rock, country**; also **hip hop, rap, gospel**. Primarily works with bands, vocalists.

*ILLUMINATI GROUP, 37 Bennett Village Terrace, Buffalo NY 14214-2201. (716)832-5894. Partners: Ron Weekes/Donnell Mueller. Public relations and marketing communications for the entertainment industry. Represents solo artists, groups, TV, film and variety artists; currently handles 4 acts. Retainer and/or fee-per-project basis.
How to Contact: Submit demo tape by mail or send brief, one paragraph description on you and your goals and career needs. Unsolicited submissions are OK. "Do not call." Prefers professional quality cassette (VHS ¾" videocassette if available) with 4 songs and lyric sheet. SASE. Reports "as soon as humanly possible. Like to see headshots and any print publicity."
Music: Mostly **top 40/pop** and **R&B**; also **alternative, urban contemporary** and some **MOR**. Works primarily with vocalists/instrumentalists but open to other promising actors, etc.
Tips: "Words and images are important to us. Know how to construct a sentence, spell, communicate in professional manner. Know what publicists do. Read Sherry Eaker's *Back Stage Handbook for Performing Artists*. Artists with no prior contract should have funding for promotion. It's not enough to only invest time and money in your demo. Make all aspects of your career a priority – including promotion. High degree of professionalism and winning attitude vital. Read about visualization in Claude Bristol's book *The Magic of Believing*. We're interested in long-term relationships, not a flash in the pan. Prefer to deal through accredited personal managers but will consider artists with knowledge of the business."

*IMANI ENTERTAINMENT INC., P.O. Box 139, Brooklyn NY 11215. (718)622-2132. Director: Guy Anglade. Management firm, music publisher (Imani Hits/BMI). Estab. 1991. Represents individual artists, groups, songwriters, producers and remixers from anywhere; currently handles 3 acts. Receives 10-20% commission. Reviews material for acts.
How to Contact: Submit demo tape by mail. Unsolicited submissions are OK. Prefers cassette (or VHS videocassette) with 3 songs and lyric sheet. If seeking management, press kit should include a bio, photograph, demo tape and any press received. SASE. Reports in 1 month.
Music: Mostly **pop/dance, R&B, hip-hop**; also **alternative rock, country, New Age**. Works primarily with vocalists, singer/songwriters. Current acts include Robyn Celia (pop/rock singer), Wonda Lenee (R&B vocalist) and Tucka (rapper).
Tips: "Be specific and to the point."

INTERMOUNTAIN TALENT, P.O. Box 942, Rapid City SD 57709. (605)348-7777. Owner: Ron Kohn. Management firm, booking agency and music publisher (Big BL Music). Estab. 1978. Represents individual artists, groups and songwriters; currently handles 30 acts. Receives 10-20% commission. Reviews material for acts.

How to Contact: Submit demo tape by mail—unsolicited submissions are OK. Prefers cassette with 3 songs and lyric sheet. Artist may submit videocassette. If seeking management, include tape, video and photo in press kit. SASE. Reports in 1 month.

Music: Mostly **rock**; also **country/rock**. Works with solo acts, show bands, dance bands and bar bands. Current acts include Dial 911 (rock), Roadhouse (blues) and Moment's Notice (country).

INTERNATIONAL TALENT NETWORK, 17580 Frazho, Roseville MI 48066. Executive Vice President of A&R: Ron Geddish. Booking agency. Estab. 1980. Represents Midwest groups; currently handles 3 acts. Receives 25% commission. Reviews material for acts.

How to Contact: Submit demo tape by mail—unsolicited submissions are OK. Prefers cassette (or VHS videocassette of performance if available) with 3-5 songs and lyric sheet. Does not return unsolicited material. Reports in 1 month.

Music: Works primarily with **rock, pop** and **alternative-college acts**. Current acts include His Name Is Alive (group/alternative), Elvis Hitler (rock group) and The Look (A&M/Canada rock group).

Tips: "If we hear a hit tune—rock, pop, alternative college—we are interested."

*IRON JOHN MANAGEMENT, #5, 360 N. Sycamore Ave., Los Angeles CA 90036. (213)931-7945. President: John Axelrod. Management firm, music publisher (Ivy League Music/BMI). Estab. 1991. Represents individual artists, groups, songwriters and producers from anywhere. Currently handles 3 acts. Receives 20% commission. Reviews material for acts.

How to Contact: Submit demo tape by mail—unsolicited submissions are OK. Prefers cassette (or VHS videocassette) with 3 songs. If seeking management, press kit should include photo, bio, press, tape, video. " 'Good news travels fast' policy on response." Does not return material.

Music: Mostly **pop, jazz, rock/dance**; also **industrial, grunge, country**. Works primarily with instrumentalists, groups, vocalists. Current acts include Warren Hill (contemporary jazz) and Breathe (pop).

Tips: "Four ingredients we look for: 1. talent, 2. charisma, 3. vision, 4. resilience."

ISSACHAR MANAGEMENT, Suite 10F, 111 Third Ave., New York NY 10003. (212)477-7063. Fax: (212)477-1469. President: Jack Flanagan. Management firm specializing in tour consulting. Represents international individual artists, groups, studio engineers and musicians; currently handles 3 acts.

How to Contact: Submit demo tape by mail—unsolicited submissions are OK. If seeking management, include tape, lyrics, photo, bio and press clips in press kit. Reports in 3 weeks.

Music: Mostly **rock, R&B** and **reggae**; also **pop** and **funk**. Current acts include Chuck Valle, Todd Youth, Murphy's Law (rock), David Simeon (reggae) and Shinin' Time (rock).

ITS HAPPENING PRESENT ENTERTAINMENT, P.O. Box 222, Pittsburg CA 94565. (510)427-1314. President: Bobellii Johnson. Management firm, booking agency and record company (Black Diamond Records and D. City Records—affiliate). Estab. 1989. Represents local, regional or international individual artists and songwriters; currently handles 8 acts. Receives 15% commission. Reviews material for acts.

How to Contact: Submit demo tape by mail—unsolicited submissions are OK. If seeking management, include bio and 8×10 b&w photo. Prefers cassette with 2 songs and lyric sheet. Does not return unsolicited material. Reports in 3 weeks to 2 months.

Music: Mostly **pop, R&B** and **jazz**; also **rap, country** and **classical**. Works primarily with vocalist songwriters, rap groups, bands, instrumentalists. Current acts include Jerry "J." (vocalist jazz/R&B) and Deanna Dixon (urban/contemporary).

Tips: "Please, copyright all your material as soon as possible. Don't let anyone else hear it until that's done first. You have to be swift about hearing, slow about speaking and slow about giving. Be true to the game or your art or craft."

J & V MANAGEMENT, 143 W. Elmwood, Caro MI 48723. (517)673-2889. Management: John Timko. Management firm and booking agency. Represents local, regional or international individual artists, groups and songwriters. Currently handles 2 acts. Receives 20% commission. Reviews material for acts.

How to Contact: Submit demo tape by mail—unsolicited submissions are OK. Prefers cassette with 3 songs maximum and lyric sheet. If seeking management, include cassette or video tape, lyric sheet, photo and short reference bio in press kit. SASE. Reports in 3 weeks.

Music: Mostly **country**. Works primarily with vocalists and dance bands. Current acts include John Patrick (country singer/songwriter) and John Patrick Timko (songwriter).

JACKSON ARTISTS CORP., (Publishing Central), Suite 200, 7251 Lowell Dr., Shawnee Mission KS 66204. (913)384-6688. President: Dave Jackson. Management firm, booking agency (Drake/Jackson Productions), music publisher (All Told Music/BMI, Zang/Jac Publishing/ASCAP and Very Cherry/ ASCAP), record company and record producer. Represents artists, groups and songwriters; currently handles 12 acts. Receives 15-20% commission from individual artists and groups; 10% from songwriters. Reviews material for acts.

How to Contact: Call first and obtain permission to submit or submit demo tape by mail. Prefers cassette (or VHS videocassette of performance if available) with 2-4 songs and lead sheet. "List names of tunes on cassettes. May send up to 4 tapes. Although it's not necessary, we prefer lead sheets with the tapes—send 2 or 3 that you are proud of. Also note what 'name' artist you'd like to see do the song. We do most of our business by phone. We prefer good enough quality to judge a performance, however, we do not require that the video or cassettes be of professional nature." Will return material if requested with SASE. Reports in 3 months.

Music: Mostly **gospel, country** and **rock**; also **bluegrass, blues, easy listening, disco, MOR, progressive, soul** and **top 40/pop**. Works with acts that work grandstand shows for fairs as well as bar bands that want to record original material. Current acts include Dixie Cadillacs (country/rock), Impressions (50's and 60's), The Booher Family (bluegrass/pop/country), Paul & Paula, Bill Haley's Comets, Max Groove (jazz) and The Dutton Family (classical to pop).

Tips: "Be able to work on the road, either as a player or as a group. Invest your earnings from these efforts in demos of your originals that have been tried out on an audience. And keep submitting to the industry."

JACKSON/JONES MANAGEMENT, 5917 West Blvd., Los Angeles CA 90043. (213)296-8742. Manager: E.J. Jackson. Management firm. Estab. 1984. Represents local, regional and international individual artists and groups; currently handles 4 acts. Receives 25% commission. Reviews material for acts.

How to Contact: Submit demo tape by mail—unsolicited submissions OK. Prefers cassette (or VHS videocassette if available) with 3 songs and lyric sheet. If seeking management, include bio, photo and demo tape in press kit. SASE. Reports in 4 weeks.

Music: Mostly **R&B, pop** and **top 40**. Works primarily with vocalists, producers and dance bands. Current acts include Vesta (R&B/pop singer), Glamour (R&B female trio) and Karel (dance/urban).

***JAM PRESENTS**, Box 6588, San Antonio TX 78209. (210)828-1319. Fax: (210)828-5221. Production: Sammy Allen. Management firm. Estab. 1970. Represents individual artists and group from anywhere. Currently handles 2 acts. Receives 15% commission. Reviews material for acts.

How to Contact: Submit demo tape by mail. Unsolicited submissions are OK. Prefers cassette with 3-10 songs and lyric sheet. If seeking management, press kit should include picture, tape, lyrics, bio, SASE. Does not return material. Reports within days.

Music: Mostly **rock, country**; also **children's stories, children's songs**. Current acts include Scudder (songwriter); Rio Trouble (rock band).

Tips: "Be true to yourself."

ROGER JAMES MANAGEMENT, 10A Margaret Rd., Barnet, Herts EN4 9NP **England**. Phone: (01)440-9788. Professional Manager: Laura Skuce. Management firm and music publisher (R.J. Music/ PRS). Estab. 1977. Represents songwriters. Receives 50% commission (but negotiable!). Reviews material for acts.

How to Contact: Submit demo tape by mail—unsolicited submissions are OK. Prefers cassette with 3 songs and lyric sheet. Does not return unsolicited material.

Music: Mostly **pop, country** and *"any good song."*

***JAMPOP LTD.**, 27 Parkington Plaza, Kingston 10 W.I. **Jamaica**. Phone: (809)968-9235. Fax: (809)968-2199. President: Ken Nelson. Management firm and booking agency. Estab. 1990. Represents local, regional and international individual artists, groups and songwriters; currently handles 30 acts. Receives 10% commission. Reviews material for acts.

How to Contact: Submit demo tape by mail. Unsolicited submissions are OK. Prefers cassette with lyric sheets. SAE and IRC. Reports in 4 weeks.

Music: Mostly **R&B** and **pop**; also **gospel**. Works primarily with vocalists. Current artists include Chalice, Telford Nelson, Sophia George and Calypso Rose.

***JANA JAE ENTERPRISES**, #520, 4815 S. Harvard, Tulsa OK 74135. (918)749-1647. Vice President: Diana Robey. Booking agency, music publisher (Jana Jae Publishing/BMI) and record company (Lark Record Productions, Inc.). Estab. 1979. Represents individual artists and songwriters; currently handles 12 acts. Receives 15% commission. Reviews material for acts.

How to Contact: Prefers cassette (or videocassette of performance if available). SASE. Reports in 1 month.
Music: Mostly interested in **country, classical** and **jazz instrumentals**; also **pop**. Works with vocalists, show and concert bands, solo instrumentalists. Represents Jana Jae (country singer/fiddle player), Matt Greif (classical guitarist), Sydni (solo singer) and Hotwire (country show band).

C. JUNQUERA PRODUCTIONS, P.O. Box 393, Lomita CA 90717. (213)325-2881. Co-owner: C. Junquera. Management consulting firm and record company (NH Records). Estab. 1987. Represents local, regional and international individual artists and songwriters; currently handles 1 act. Receives a flat fee, depending on project costs. Reviews material for acts.
How to Contact: Write first and obtain permission to submit. Prefers cassette with 1-3 songs and lyric sheet. If seeking management, include 8×10 photo, business card, bio, photocopies of news articles and sample of product. SASE. Reports in 1-2 months.
Music: Mostly **traditional country** and **country pop**; also **easy listening**. Works primarily with vocalists. Current recording acts include Nikki Hornsby (singer/songwriter), N. Kelel (songwriter) and Tom Wayne (singer/songwriter).
Tips: "Set goal to obtain as artist or songwriter—submit sample of product and *don't* give up! Obtain financial support for your productions."

*SHELDON KAGAN PRODUCTIONS, 1020-5th Ave., Dorval, Quebec H9S 1J2 **Canada.** (514)631-2160. Fax: (514)631-4430. President: Sheldon Kagan. Booking agency. Estab. 1965. Represents local individual artists and groups. Currently handles 4 acts. Reviews materials for acts.
How to Contact: Submit demo tape by mail. Unsolicited submissions are OK. Prefers cassette (or VHS videocassette) with 6 songs. If seeking management, press kit should include picture and bio. SASE. Reports in 2 weeks.
Music: Mostly **top 40**. Works primarily with vocalists and bands.

R.J. KALTENBACH PERSONAL MANAGEMENT, P.O. Box 510, Dundee IL 60118-0510. (708)428-4777. President: R.J. Kaltenbach. Management firm. Estab. 1980. Represents national touring acts only (individual artists and groups); currently handles 3 acts. Receives 15-20% commission. Reviews material for acts.
How to Contact: Submit demo tape by mail—unsolicited submissions are OK. Prefers cassette (or VHS ½" videocassette) with 3 songs and lyric sheet. Does not return unsolicited material. Reports in 1 month "if we are interested in material."
Music: **Country** and **rock/pop**. Works primarily with "national acts with recording contracts or deals pending." Current acts include T.G. Sheppard (national recording artist), Mike Redmond and Magazine (Chicago-based rock act) and Joe K (NY based rock act/alternative).
Tips: "We deal only with professionals who are dedicated to their craft and show lots of promise."

KAUFMAN HILL MANAGEMENT, Suite 613, 410 S. Michigan Ave., Chicago IL 60605. (312)427-3241. Contact: Don Kaufman or Shawn Hill. Management firm (also Mozart Midnight Productions, Inc.). Estab. 1982. Represents individual artists, groups and songwriters; currently handles 4 acts. Receives 20% commission. Reviews material for acts.
How to Contact: Submit demo tape by mail—unsolicited submissions are OK. Prefers cassette (VHS videocassette if available) with 2-6 songs and photo. If seeking management, include photo, cassette, note as to why submitting in press kit. Does not return any material. Reports back only if interested.
Music: **Rock, smooth jazz, pop** and **rap**. Works primarily with singer/songwriters, bands, groups and vocalists. Current acts include Kevin Irving (lead singer of Club Nouveau, R&B), Jeannie Withrow (pop/rock singer/songwriter), Darcsyde (rap) and Psycho Circus (hard rock group).
Tips: "Submit by mail. If you have what we need, we will be in touch."

JEFF KIRK, 7108 Grammar Rd. S.W., Fairview TN 37062. (615)799-8674. Owner/President: Jeff Kirk. Management firm and booking agency. Estab. 1981. Represents regional (mid-South) individual artists; currently handles 3 acts. Commission varies. Reviews material for acts.
How to Contact: Submit demo tape by mail—unsolicited submissions are OK. Prefers cassette (or VHS videocassette if available) with 1-3 songs and lyric or lead sheet. If seeking management, include bio, recent performance, recent recordings and picture (optional). Does not return unsolicited material. Reports in 1 month.
Music: Mostly **jazz, pop** and **rock**. Works primarily with jazz groups (4-6 members), instrumental and vocal. Current acts include Jeff Kirk Quartet (mainstream jazz) and New Vintage (jazz fusion).
Tips: "Please submit brief demos with as high audio quality as possible."

BOB KNIGHT AGENCY, 185 Clinton Ave., Staten Island NY 10301. (718)448-8420. President: Bob Knight. Management firm, booking agency, music publishing and royalty collection firm. Estab. 1971. Represents artists, groups and songwriters; currently handles 7 acts. Receives 10-25% commission.

Reviews material for acts and for submission to record companies and producers.
How to Contact: Submit demo tape by mail—unsolicited submissions are OK. Prefers cassette (or videocassette) with 5 songs and lead sheet "with bio and references. Send photos of artists and groups." If seeking management, include bios, video cassette and audio cassette in press kit. SASE. Reports in 1 month.
Music: Mostly **top 40/pop**; also **easy listening, MOR, R&B, soul** and **rock (nostalgia 50s and 60s)**. Works primarily with recording and name groups and artists—50s, 60s and 70s acts, high energy dance, and show groups. Current acts include The Elegants (oldie show); Gengo & Gregorio (top 40); and The AD-LIBS (oldie show).

*KOOCH MANAGEMENT, INC., P.O. Box 21185, Los Angeles CA 90021. (213)622-2511. Fax: (213)614-8633. President: Greg Kooch. Management firm. Estab. 1987. Represents individual artists and groups from anywhere. Receives 15-20% commission. Reviews material for acts.
How to Contact: Write or call first and obtain permission to submit. Prefers cassette or CD (or VHS videocassette) with 3 songs and lyric sheet. If seeking management, press kit should include tape, photo and bio. "Send only 'A' material." Does not return unsolicited material. Reports in 1 month.
Music: Mostly **heavy alternative, everything atypical**; also **unique hybrids, no generic pop rock**. Call for current roster.
Tips: "Be amazing or stay home."

*KUPER-LAM MANAGEMENT, P.O. Box 66274, Houston TX 77266. (713)520-5791. Fax: (713)780-7227. President: Ivan Kuper. Management firm, music publisher (Kuper-Lam Music/BMI). Estab. 1988. Represents individual artists, groups and songwriters from anywhere. Currently handles 1 act. Receives 20% managerial commission. Reviews material for acts.
How to Contact: Accepts unsolicited submissions. Prefers cassette. If seeking management, press kit should include photo, bio, cassette, press clippings (reviews etc.). Does not return material. Reports in 1 month.
Music: Mostly **rap, urban contemporary, alternative college rock**. Works primarily with rap groups (self contained and self produced). Current acts include rap group Def Squad, Mr. Henry (Ichiban Records).
Tips: "Create a market value for yourself, produce your own master tapes, create a cost-effective situation."

*L.D.F. PRODUCTIONS, P.O. Box 406, Old Chelsea Station, New York NY 10011. (212)925-8925. President: Mr. Dowell. Management firm and booking agency. Estab. 1982. Represents artists and choirs in the New York area. Currently handles 2 acts. Receives 20% commission.
How to Contact: Submit demo tape by mail. Prefers cassette (or videocassette of performance—well-lighted, maximum 10 minutes) with 2-8 songs and lyric sheet. SASE. Reports in 1 month. "Do not phone expecting a return call unless requested by L.D.F. Productions. Videos should be imaginatively presented with clear sound and bright colors."
Music: Mostly **gospel, popular, rock** and **jazz**. Works primarily with inspirational and contemporary pop artists. Current acts include L.D. Frazier (gospel artist/lecturer) and Jonathan Mayo (bassist/composer).
Tips: "Those interested in working with us must be original, enthusiastic, persistent and sincere."

LANDSLIDE MANAGEMENT, 928 Broadway, New York NY 10010. (212)505-7300. Principals: Ted Lehrman and Libby Bush. Management firm and music publisher (Kozkeeozko Music). Estab. 1978. Represents singers, singer/songwriters and actor/singers; currently handles 3 acts. Receives 15% commission. Reviews material for acts.
How to Contact: Write first to obtain permission to submit."Potential hit singles only." SASE. "Include picture, resume and (if available) ½″ videocassette if you're submitting yourself as an act." Reports in 2-3 weeks.
Music: Dance-oriented, MOR, rock (soft pop), soul, top 40/pop and **country/pop**. Current acts include Deborah Dotson (soul/pop/jazz), Sara Carlson (pop/rock) and Tedd Lawson (songwriter).

LARI-JON PROMOTIONS, 325 W. Walnut, P.O. Box 216, Rising City NE 68658. (402)542-2336. Owner: Larry Good. Music publisher (Lari-Jon Publishing Co./BMI) and record company (Lari-Jon Records). "We also promote package shows." Represents individual artists, groups and songwriters; currently handles 5 acts. Receives 15% commission. Reviews material for acts.
How to Contact: Submit demo tape by mail—unsolicited submissions are OK. Prefers cassette with 5 songs and lyric sheet. If seeking management, include 8×10 photos, cassette and bio sheet in press kit. SASE. Reports in 2 months.
Music: Mostly **country, gospel** and **50s rock**. Works primarily with dance bands and show bands. Represents Kent Thompson (singer), Nebraskaland 'Opry (family type country show) and Brenda Allen (singer/comedienne).

Tips: "Be professional in all aspects of the business."

THE LET US ENTERTAIN YOU CO., Suite 204, 900 19th Ave. S., Nashville TN 37212-2125. (615)321-3100. Administrative Assistant: T.R. Management firm, booking agency and music publisher (ASCAP/SESAC/BMI). Estab. 1968. Represents groups and songwriters; currently handles 100+ acts. Receives 15-20% commission. Reviews material for acts.
How to Contact: Submit demo tape by mail—unsolicited submissions are OK. Prefers cassette or videocassette and lyric sheet. Does not return unsolicited material. Reports only if interested.
Music: Mostly **country, pop, R&B**; also **rock** and **new music**. Works with all types of artists/groups/songwriters. Current acts include Country Song (group); Southern Accent (show group); and Trader Price (group/songwriters).

LEVINSON ENTERTAINMENT VENTURES INTERNATIONAL, INC., Suite 650, 1440 Veteran Avenue, Los Angeles CA 90024. (213)460-4545. President: Bob Levinson. Management firm. Estab. 1978. Represents national individual artists, groups and songwriters; currently handles 6 acts. Receives 15-20% commission. Reviews material for acts.
How to Contact: Write first and obtain permission to submit or to arrange personal interview. Prefers cassette (or VHS videocassette) with 6 songs and lead sheet. "Inquire first. Don't expect tape to be returned unless SASE included with submission and specific request is made." Reports in 2-3 weeks.
Music: Rock, MOR, R&B and **country**. Works primarily with rock bands and vocalists.
Tips: "Should be a working band, self-contained and, preferably, performing original material."

RICK LEVY MGT, 1602 Shenandoah Ct., Allentown PA 18104. (215)398-2686. President: Rick Levy. Management firm, booking agency, music publisher (Flying Governor Music/BMI) and record company (Luxury Records). Estab. 1985. Represents local, regional or international individual artists and groups; currently handles 3 acts. Receives 10-20% commission. Reviews material for acts.
How to Contact: Submit demo tape by mail—unsolicited submissions are OK. Prefers cassette (or VHS videocassette if available) with 3 songs and lyric sheet. If seeking management, include tape, VHS video, photo and press. SASE. Reports in 1 month.
Music: Mostly **R&B** (no rap), **pop** and **country**. Current acts include Jay & Techniques (60s hit group), Rock Roots (variety-classic rock, rockabilly) and Levy/Stocker (songwriters).
Tips: "In this business, seek out people better and more successful than you. Learn, pick their brains, be positive, take criticism and keep pluggin' no matter what."

LINE-UP PROMOTIONS, INC., 9A, Tankerville Place, Newcastle-Upon-Tyne NE2 3AT **United Kingdom.** Phone: (091)2816449. Fax: (091)212-0913. Director: C.A. Murtagh. Management firm, promotion company, record company (On-Line Records), music publisher (On Line Records & Publishing) and record producer. Represents individual artists, groups and songwriters; currently handles 6-8 acts. Receives 15% commission.
How to Contact: Submit demo tape—unsolicited submissions are OK. Prefers audio cassette (and videocassette if available) and lyric sheet. "Send full press kit, commitments and objective." Does not return unsolicited material. Reports in 1 month. "We're looking for professional acts who can entertain in city centers and unusual situations; e.g., tea dances, supermarkets, metro stations and traditional venues."
Music: Mostly **acoustic pop, rock, new world, Afro** and **reggae**; also **country, Celtic** and **English**. Works primarily with original groups (not MOR). Current acts include Swimming Pool (fine art rock), Royal Family (post punk exploitative), APU (Andean music), Big Life (country/folk/pop), The Tommy Chase Quartet (swing jazz) and Hank Wangford (country).

LMP MANAGEMENT FIRM, Suite 206, 6245 Bristol Pkwy., Culver City CA 90230. Contact: Larry McGee. Management firm, music publisher (Operation Perfection, Inc.) and record company (Boogie Band Records Corp.). Represents individual artists, groups and songwriters; currently handles 40 acts. Receives 15% commission. Reviews material for acts.
How to Contact: Submit demo tape—unsolicited submissions are OK. Prefers cassette (or videocassette of performance) with 1-4 songs and lead sheet. "Try to perform one or more of your songs on a local TV show. Then obtain a copy of your performance. Please only send professional quality material. Keep it simple and basic." If seeking management, include audio cassette, videocassette, photo and any additional promotional materials in press kit. SASE. Reports in 2 months.
Music: Mostly **pop-oriented R&B**; also **rock** and **MOR/adult contemporary**. Works primarily with professionally choreographed show bands. "Current acts include Love-Child (vocal group), The Executives (vocal group), Alan Walker (producer).
Tips: "Present material that reflects the current market place."

*LOCONTO PRODUCTIONS, 10244 NW 47 St., Sunrise FL 33351. (305)741-7766. Contact: Phyllis Finney Loconto. Management firm. Estab. 1978. Represents 3 clients. Receives 5% commission. Reviews material for acts.
How to Contact: "Not presently soliciting material."
Music: All types, including **dance music, Latin** and **country**; also **bluegrass, children's, church/religious, easy listening, folk, gospel, MOR** and **top 40/pop**. Works primarily with country vocalists, country bands, MOR vocalists and bluegrass artists. Current acts include Bill Dillon, Rob Mellor, Jennifer Geiget, The Lane Brothers and Frank X. Loconto.
Tips: "Material must be 'top shelf.'"

LOWELL AGENCY, 4043 Brookside Ct., Norton OH 44203. (216)825-7813. Contact: Leon Seiter. Booking agency. Estab. 1985. Represents regional (Midwest and Southeast) individual artists; currently handles 3 acts. Receives 10% commission. Reviews material for acts.
How to Contact: Submit demo tape by mail—unsolicited submissions are OK. Prefers cassette with 4 songs and lyric sheet. If seeking management, include demo cassette tape in press kit. SASE. Reports in 2 months.
Music: Mostly **country**. Works primarily with country vocalists. Current acts include Leon Seiter (country singer/entertainer/songwriter), Ford Nix (bluegrass singer and 5 string banjo picker) and Tom Durden (country singer, co-writer of "Heartbreak Hotel").

LUSTIG TALENT ENTERPRISES, INC., P.O. Box 32005, W. Palm Beach FL 33420-2005. (407)832-1232. President: Richard Lustig. Booking agency. Estab. 1986. Represents local, regional and international individual artists and groups. Reviews material for acts.
How to Contact: Call first and obtain permission to submit. Prefers cassette or VHS videocassette. If seeking management, include pictures, resume, song list, audio cassette demo tape, and video demo tape in press kit. Does not return unsolicited material.
Music: All types. Works primarily with dance bands and disc jockeys. Current acts include Nightfall (band), Tony Mitchell (magician) and Richard Lustig (disc jockey).
Tips: "Have good promo kit. Be easy to work with. Do a professional job for the client."

RICHARD LUTZ ENTERTAINMENT AGENCY, 5625 0 St., Lincoln NE 68510. (402)483-2241. General Manager: Cherie Worley. Management firm and booking agency. Estab. 1964. Represents individuals and groups; currently handles 200 acts. Receives 15-20% minimum commission.
How to Contact: Submit demo tape by mail—unsolicited submissions are OK. Prefers cassette (or videocassette) with 5-10 songs "to show style and versatility" and lead sheet. "Send photo, resume, tape, partial song list and include references. Add comedy, conversation, etc., to your videocassette. Do not play songs in full—short versions preferred." If seeking management, include audio cassette and photo in press kit. SASE. Reports in 1 week.
Music: Mostly **top 40** and **country**; also **dance-oriented** and **MOR**. Works primarily with bar and dance bands for lounge circuit. "Acts must be uniformed." Current acts include The Partners (variety), Badd Habit (country) and Imposters (nostalgia).

*M & M TALENT AGENCY INC., 146 Round Pond Lane, Rochester NY 14662. (716)723-0514. Contact: Carl Labate. Management firm, booking agency and record producer. Represents artists and groups; currently handles 3 acts. Receives 20-25% commission.
How to Contact: Submit demo tape by mail—unsolicited submissions are OK. Prefers cassette (or VHS or Beta videocassette) with minimum 3 songs and lyric sheet. May send video if available; "a still photo would be good enough to see the type of performance; if you are a performer, it would be advantageous to show yourself or the group performing live. Theme videos are not helpful." If seeking management, include photos, bio, markets established, tape and/or videos. SASE. Reports in 3 weeks.
Music: Blues, rock and **R&B**. Works primarily with touring bands, dance bands and barbands; also vocalists, and recording artists. Current acts include The Coupe DeVilles (blues, recording artists, national touring band); The Bonedippers (Reggae, recording artists, college touring band) and The Chesterfield Kings (alternative rock, international touring band).
Tips: "My main interest is with groups or performers that also write their own material. If all you do is write songs, you are better off pursuing publishing companies or music producers."

MĆ LAVENE & ASSOCIATES, P.O. Box 26852, Oklahoma OK 73126. President: Suzette McCurtis. Management firm, booking agency, music publisher (C.A.B. Independent Publishing Company/BMI) and record company (MśQue Records). Estab. 1988. Represents local, regional and international individual artists, groups and songwriters; currently handles 18 acts. Receives 10-20% commission. Reviews material for acts.
How to Contact: Write first and obtain permission to submit. Prefers cassette (or VHS videocassette if available) with 3 songs and lead sheet. If seeking management, include professional demo with 3 of your best songs, photo if possible and more background information in press kit. SASE. Reports in 2 months.

Music: Mostly jazz, pop and R&B; also rock. Works primarily with dance bands and vocalists. Current acts include Magnolia (rock group), Heart (jazz) and Liesure (jazz).
Tips: "Sing and write about what you know and feel."

THE McDONNELL GROUP, 27 Pickwick Lane, Newtown Square PA 19073. (215)353-8554. Contact: Frank McDonnell. Management firm. Estab. 1985. Represents local, regional or international individual artists, groups and songwriters; currently handles 5 acts. Receives 20-25% commission. Reviews material for acts.
How to Contact: Submit demo tape by mail—unsolicited submissions are OK. Prefers cassette (or VHS videocassette if available) with 4 songs and lyric sheet. If seeking management, include press, tape or video, recent photos, bio. SASE. Reports in 1 month.
Music: Mostly rock, pop and R&B; also country. Current acts include Johnny Bronco (rock group), Mike Forte (producer/songwriter) and Jim Salamone (producer/songwriter/arranger).

*ANDREW MCMANUS MANAGEMENT, 191 Darlinghurst Rd., Kings Cross NSW 2011 **Australia**. Phone: (02)361-4644. Fax: (02)361-5009. Manager: Andrew McManus. Management firm. Estab. 1986. Represents local, regional and international individual artists, groups, songwriters and producers; currently handles 4 acts. Receives 15-20% commission. Reviews material for acts.
How to Contact: Write or call first to arrange personal interview or submit demo tape. Prefers cassette (or VHS videocassette if available) with several songs. SAE and IRC. Reports in 2-3 weeks.
Music: Mostly rock, pop and dance. Works primarily with rock bands and dance artists. Current acts include Divinyls (rock), Candy Harlots (rock), Living Daylights (pop/rock) and Lost Angels (rock).

MAGIANˢᵐ (a div. of Universal World Unlimited, Inc.), 6733 Rhode Island Dr., E., Jacksonville FL 32209. (904)766-1181 or (904)764-3685. Founder & President: Morris King, Jr.. Management firm. Estab. 1985. Represents local, regional and national individual artists, groups, songwriters and producers; currently handles 6 acts. Receives negotiable commission. Reviews material for acts.
How to Contact: Submit demo tape by mail—unsolicited submissions are OK. Prefers cassette (or VHS videocassette if available) with 3-5 songs and lyric sheet. If seeking management, include bio, press, photos. SASE. Reports in 2 weeks.
Music: Mostly pop, R&B and jazz; also rock, gospel and country. Works primarily with vocalists, message rappers, top 40 bands. Current acts include Vedia (vocalist/songwriter), Just Twoˢᵐ (vocal duo) and Mike Hughes (vocalist/musician/songwriter).
Tips: "Do not approach MAGIANˢᵐ if you are not dedicated, patient, and if you are looking for a miracle."

MAGIC MANAGEMENT AND PRODUCTIONS, 196-39 Dunton Ave., Jamaica NY 11423. (718)464-6560. President: Bryan Sanders. General Manager: Marjolie Sanders. Management firm, booking agency and concert productions firm. Estab. 1987. Represents regional (New York tri-state) individual artists, groups and disc-jockeys; currently handles 6 acts. Receives 20-25% commission. Reviews material for acts.
How to Contact: Submit demo tape by mail—unsolicited submissions are OK. Prefers cassette (or VHS videocassette if available) with minimum of 2 songs and lyric sheet. "Be natural and relaxed. Tape of a song should be no more than 5-6 minutes in length. Performance length (VHS) no longer than 20 minutes and 4 songs." Does not return unsolicited material. Reports in 1-2 months.
Music: Mostly R&B, crossover club music and rap; also club DJ mixes, gospel and jazz. Works primarily with dance bands, vocalists and disc-jockeys. Current acts include K-Nice (rapper), The Wonder Ones (rappers) and S.W.A.T. (rappers and dance group).
Tips: "Keep in mind that it's not necessarily the size of the company but what that company can do for you that makes the difference."

MAGNUM MUSIC CORPORATION LTD., 8607-128 Ave., Edmonton Alberta **Canada** T5E 0G3. (403)476-8230. Fax: (403)472-2584 Manager: Bill Maxim. Booking agency, music publisher (Ramblin' Man Music Publishing/PRO, High River Music Publishing/ASCAP) and record company (Magnum Records). Estab. 1984. Represents international individual artists, groups and songwriters; currently handles 4 acts. Reviews material for acts.
How to Contact: Write first and obtain permission to submit. Prefers cassette with 3-4 songs. If seeking management, include photo and bio in press kit. SAE and IRC. Reports in 1 month.
Music: Mostly country and gospel. Works primarily with "artists or groups who are also songwriters." Current acts include Catheryne Greenly (country), Thea Anderson (country) and Nolan Murray (country). "Prefers finished demos."

MANAGEMENT ASSOCIATES, INC., 10620 Marquis Lane, Dallas TX 75229. (214)350-4650. Fax: (214)350-4652. President: Dan Hexter. Management firm and booking agency. Estab. 1975. Represents national and international individual artists and groups; currently handles 4 attractions. Receives 10-25% commission. Reviews material for artists.

How to Contact: Write first and obtain permission to submit. Prefers cassette (or VHS videocassette if available) with 3 songs and lyric sheets. Does not return unsolicited material. Reports in 2 months.
Music: Mostly **country**, with St. Paul, Minnesota office for **pop** and **urban** music. Current acts include Charley Pride (RCA Records), Neal McCoy (Atlantic Records) and The Commodores (SBR Records).
Tips: "Be patient. Review your own material and take time prior to submitting. Do not submit the first three songs you have written."

*MARDI GRAS MUSIC FEST, INC., Suite 1102, 147 Carondelet St., New Orleans LA 70130. (504)552-9777 or (504)581-0300. Executive Producer: Virgil Sorina, Jr.. Management firm and booking agency. Estab. 1985. Represents individual artists, groups, songwriters from anywhere; currently handles 20+ non-exclusive acts. Receives 10-20% commission. Reviews material for acts.
How to Contact: Submit demo tape by mail. Unsolicited submissions are OK. Prefers cassette (or VHS videocassette) with 3-7 songs and lyric sheet or lead sheet. If seeking management, press kit should include photo, bio, demo, etc. SASE. Reports in 6-8 weeks.
Music: Mostly **rock/R&B**, **pop/soul** and **ethnic**; also **New Age**, **contemporary jazz** and **60s retro**. Works primarily with all types of acts (musical), voice-over talent, songwriters, studio musicians—promo tours for major labels a specialty.
Tips: "Send *complete* promo kit (with influences), stress versatility, (prolific songwriting a big plus)."

*MARK ONE-THE AGENCY, P.O. Box 62, Eastwood 5063 **South Australia**. (08)340-1661. Fax: (08)364-1206. Owner: Mark Draper. Management firm, booking agency, music publisher. Estab. 1981. Represents individual artists, groups, songwriters from anywhere; currently handles 20 acts. Receives 10-20% commission. Reviews material for acts.
How to Contact: Submit demo tape by mail. Unsolicited submissions are OK. Prefers cassette (or VHS videocassette) with 3 songs and lyric sheet. If seeking management, press kit should include photograph, 1 page bio, comprehensive contact list. SAE and IRC. Reports in 1 month.
Music: Mostly **rock, pop, dance**. Works primarily with bands. Current acts include B.N.I. (pop band) and Jungle Alley (rock band).
Tips: "Be honest, reliable and available."

RICK MARTIN PRODUCTIONS, 125 Fieldpoint Road, Greenwich CT 06830. (203)661-1615. President: Rick Martin. Personal manager and independent producer. Holds the Office of Secretary of the National Conference of Personal Managers. Represents groups, artists/songwriters, actresses/vocalists. Currently handles 5 acts. Receives 15-25% commission. "Occasionally, we are hired as consultants, production assistants or producers of recording projects." Reviews material for acts.
How to Contact: Submit demo tape by mail—unsolicited submissions are OK. "Enclose an SASE if you want tape back. Do not write for permission—will not reply, just send material." Prefers cassette (or VHS videocassette) with 2-4 songs. "Don't worry about an expensive presentation to personal managers or producers; they'll make it professional if they get involved." Artists should enclose a photo. "We prefer serious individuals who will give it all they have for a music career." Reports in 2 weeks.
Music: Mostly **top 40, rock** and **dance**; also **easy listening** and **pop**. Produces dance groups, female vocalists and songwriters. Current acts include Babe, Marisa Mercedes (vocalist/pianist/songwriter), Robert and Steven Capellan (songwriters/vocalists), the Gonzalez Family (vocal group) and McKenna's Breed (dance group).
Tips: "The tape does not have to be professionally produced—it's really not important what you've done—it's what you can do now that counts."

MASTER ENTERTAINMENT, (formerly Master Talent), 245 Maple Ave. W., Vienna VA 22180. (703)281-2800. Owner/Agent: Steve Forssell. Booking agency. Estab. 1989. Represents local and regional (mid-Atlantic) individual artists and groups. Receives 10-20% commission.
How to Contact: Submit demo tape—unsolicited submissions are OK. Prefers cassette (or VHS/

The types of music each listing is interested in are printed in boldface.

Beta videocassette) with 4+ songs and lyric or lead sheet. SASE. Reports in 1 month.
Music: Mostly **hard rock/metal, progressive/alternative** and **R&B/dance**; also **variety/covers**. Works primarily with hard rock groups. Current acts include The Excentrics (rock), Silence (thrash metal), Danny Blitz (power pop), Blues Saraceno (guitar rock), Asante (African), Carl Filipiak (jazz) and Randy Coven (bass instrumental rock).
Tips: "Submit only best work when it's *ready*. We're looking for professionally managed groups/artists with good publicist/promotion. Product in market is a plus."

PHIL MAYO & COMPANY, P.O. Box 304, Bomoseen VT 05732. (802)468-5011. President: Phil Mayo. Management firm and record company (Thrust Records). Estab. 1981. Represents international individual artists, groups and songwriters. Receives 15-20% commission.
How to Contact: Submit demo tape by mail—unsolicited submissions are OK. Prefers cassette (or VHS videocassette) with 3 songs and lyric or lead sheet. If seeking management, include bio, photo and lyric sheet in press kit. Does not return unsolicited material. Reports in 1-2 months.
Music: Mostly **rock, pop** and **R&B**; also **gospel**. Works primarily with dance bands, vocalists, rock acts. Current acts include The Drive (R&B act) and Blind Date.

MCI MUSIC GROUP, P.O. Box 8442, Universal City CA 91608. (818)506-0488. Fax: (818)505-0420. Director: Max Diamond. Management firm, music publisher (Kellijai and Pollyann Music/ASCAP, Janikki Songs, and Branmar Songs/BMI and Lonnvaness Music/SESAC) and record company (PPL, Bouvier, Credence Records). Estab. 1979. Represents local, regional and international individual artists, groups and songwriters. Currently handles 15 acts. Receives 25% commission. Reviews material for acts.
How to Contact: Write first and obtain permission to submit. Prefers cassette (or videocassette of performance) with no more than 4 songs and lyric or lead sheets. Does not return unsolicited material. Reports in 6 weeks.
Music: Mostly **R&B, pop** and **dance**. Current acts include I.B. Phyne, Lejenz, D.M. Groove, Phuntaine, The Band AKA, Katrina Gibson and Yvette Craddock.

*MEDIA PROMOTION ENTERPRISES, 423 6th Ave., Huntington WV 25701. (304)697-4222. Management firm and booking agency. Represents individual artists, groups and songwriters; currently handles 3 acts. Receives 15-20% commission. Reviews material for acts.
How to Contact: Submit demo tape by mail (prefers live videocassette), "the simpler, the better." Does not return unsolicited material. "Wait for us to contact you." Reports in 1-6 months.
Music: Mostly **MOR, country, pop** and **R&B**. Works primarily with name entertainers, show groups, dance bands, and variety shows. Current acts include Allen Stotler (pianist/composer), Phillip Swann (songwriter/singer/keyboardist) and Michelle Rowe (songwriter/singer).
Tips: "Submit your tunes to major labels while working dates for us."

ALEX MELLON MANAGEMENT, P.O. Box 614, New Kensington PA 15068. (412)335-5152. President: Alex Mellon. Estab. 1978. Represents individual artists, groups and songwriters; currently handles 3 acts. Receives 20% commission. Reviews material for acts.
How to Contact: Submit demo tape by mail—unsolicited submissions are OK. Prefers cassette or videocassette with 3-4 songs. "Video is almost a must. Everyone I deal with wants to 'see' the act." Does not return unsolicited material. If seeking management, include all press clippings, a photo, brief bio and a good quality demo in press kit. Reports in 1 month.
Music: Mostly **pop, rock** and **country**. Works primarily with pop acts and songwriters. Current acts include Stan Xidas (producer/songwriter), The Poni-Tails (oldies) and Shelly Rae (singer/songwriter).

*GREG MENZA & ASSOCIATES, P.O. Box 7558, Marietta GA 30062-7558. (404)427-5335. Fax: (404)590-ROCK. Director: Greg Menza. Management firm, booking agency and concert producers. Represents artists, groups and songwriters; currently handles 7 acts. Receives 20% commission. Reviews material for acts.
How to Contact: Write first and obtain permission to submit. Prefers cassette (or VHS videocassette) with 3-6 songs. "Professional quality only." If seeking management, include bio, photo, references and demo. Reports in 2 months. "Include SASE if you wish material returned. Send only high quality finished demos."
Music: Gospel, **rock** and **country,** "**contemporary Christian** rock bands and clean cut positive secular acts." Works primarily with contemporary Christian rock artists. Current acts include Jerome Olds, Jacob's Trouble, Randy Matthews, E.T.W., hoi Polloi, The Brothers, and Chuckie Perez.
Tips: "Don't send anything with apologies."

MERRI-WEBB PRODUCTIONS, P.O. Box 5474, Stockton CA 95205. (209)948-8186. President: Nancy L. Merrihew. Management firm, music publisher (Kaupp's & Robert Publishing Co./BMI), record company (Kaupp Records). Represents regional (California) individual artists, groups and songwriters; currently handles 10 acts. Receives 10-15% commission. Reviews material for acts.
How to Contact: Write or call first and obtain permission to submit. Prefers cassette (or VHS videocassette if available) with 3 songs maximum and lyric sheet. SASE. Reports in 1 month.
Music: Mostly **country, A/C rock, R&B**; also **pop, rock** and **gospel**. Works primarily with vocalists, dance bands and songwriters. Current acts include Rick Webb (singer/songwriter), Dan Alice (rock/songwriter) and Stephen Bruce (singer/songwriter).
Tips: "Know what you want, set a goal, focus in on your goals, be open to constructive criticism, polish tunes and keep polishing."

JOSEPH C. MESSINA, CARTOON RECORDS, INC., 424 Mamaroneck Ave., Mamaroneck NY 10543. (914)381-2565. Attorney/Manager. Represents artists, groups, songwriters, movie directors and screen writers; currently handles 3 acts. Receives negotiable commission.
How to Contact: Prefers cassette with 1-2 songs and lead sheet. Does not return unsolicited material.
Music: Works primarily with male and female **vocal/dance.** Current acts include Andrea (top 40 dance).

METROPOLITAN TALENT AUTHORITY, 109 Earle Ave., Lynbrook NY 11563. (516)599-4157. President: J.C. Management firm and consultants. Estab. 1985. Represents local and international individual artists, groups and songwriters; currently handles 4 acts. Receives 20-30% commission. Reviews material for acts.
How to Contact: Submit demo tape by mail—unsolicited submissions are OK. Prefers cassette and lyric sheet. If seeking management, include cassette tape of best songs, 8× 10 pictures, bio, press, radio play lists and VHS video in press kit. SASE. Reports in 4-5 weeks.
Music: Mostly **rock, nu-music** and **pop/rock/dance;** also **R&B, rap** and **hard rock.** Works primarily with bands, songwriters, producers. Current acts include Pleasure Chamber, Fighter Town, Oh Boy, and Fatal Attraction.
Tips: "Have people in the business tell you that you're ready before you think you are."

M-5 MANAGEMENT, INC., Suite 306, 1128 Harmon Place, Minneapolis MN 55403. (612)339-5117. Fax: (612)339-5140. President: Micah McFarlane. Management firm. Estab. 1988. Represents Midwest groups; currently handles 3 acts. Receives 15% commission. Reviews material for acts.
How to Contact: Write or call first and obtain permission to submit. Prefers cassette or VHS videocassette with 3 songs and lyric sheet. If seeking management, include lyric sheet, glossy photo and bio in press kit. Does not return unsolicited material. Reports in 1 month.
Music: Mostly **pop, reggae** and **rock;** also **R&B** and **gospel.** Works primarily with pop and reggae groups. Current acts include Ipso Facto (rock/reggae), Julitta McFarlane (R&B/reggae) and Kalaharé (acoustic/soul/pop).
Tips: "Make sure songs are complete in structure."

MIDCOAST, INC., 1002 Jones Rd., Hendersonville TN 37075. (615)264-3896. Managing Director: Bruce Andrew Bossert. Management firm and music publisher (MidCoast, Inc./BMI). Estab. 1984. Represents individual artists, groups and songwriters; currently handles 3 acts. Reviews material for acts.
How to Contact: Submit demo tape—unsolicited submissions are OK. Prefers cassette (or VHS videocassette) or DAT with 2-4 songs and lyric sheet. If seeking management, include "short" bio, tape, photo and announcements of any performances in Nashville area in press kit. SASE. Reports in 6 weeks if interested.
Music: Mostly **rock, pop** and **country.** Works primarily with original rock and country bands and artists. Current acts include Ghost Money (rock), Cinema (rock) and Lee Owens (singer/songwriter).
Tips: "We need good songs and good voices."

*MIGHTY MANAGEMENT, 21 Castle St., Randwick, Sydney 2031 **Australia.** (02)3983200. Fax: (02)3988216. Manager: Mick Mazzone. Management firm. Represents local individual artists and groups; currently handles 4 acts. Receives 15-20% commission. Reviews material for acts.
How to Contact: Submit demo tape by mail. Unsolicited submissions are OK. Prefers cassette with 3 songs and lyric sheet. If seeking management, press kit should include tape, photo and bio. SASE. Reports in 2 weeks.
Music: Mostly **rock, pop, blues;** also **MOR, A.O.R.** Works primarily with singer/songwriters and bands. Current acts include Ian Moss (rock pop/singer songwriter), Radiators (rock), Wrecking Crew (hard rock).
Tips: "Label all material and work towards quality not quantity."

*MILESTONE MEDIA, P.O. Box 869, Venice CA 90291. (310)396-1234. Fax: (310)392-3205. Co-President: Mr. Sverdlin. Management firm. Estab. 1985. Represents individual artists, groups and songwriters from anywhere. Currently handles 3 acts. Receives 20% commission. Reviews material for acts.
How to Contact: Submit demo tape by mail. Unsolicited submissions are OK. Prefers cassette (or videocassette) with 3 songs. Does not return material.
Music: Moslty **rap, rock, dance;** also **country, house, movie.** Works primarily with singers, producer and composers. Current acts include Ruben Hall (singer), Ray Rae (producer) and Ausie Menace (alternative rock).

*THOMAS J. MILLER & COMPANY, 1802 Laurel Canyon Blvd., Los Angeles CA 90046. (213)656-7212. Fax: (213)656-7757. Artist Relations: Karen Deming. Management firm, music publisher, record company (Wilshire Park Records). Estab. 1975. Represents individual artists, groups and songwriters from anywhere; currently handles 12 acts. Reviews material for acts.
How to Contact: Submit demo tape by mail. Unsolicited submissions are OK. Prefers cassette (or NTSC videocassette) and lyric sheet. If seeking management, press kit should include photos, bio, video. Does not return material. Reports in 2-3 weeks.
Music: Mostly **pop, rock, jazz;** also **stage** and **country.** Current acts include Manowar, Gipsy Kings and Champaign.

MOORE ENTERTAINMENT GROUP, 11 Possum Trail, Saddle River NJ 07458. (201)327-3698. President: Barbara Moore. Estab. 1984. Represents individual artists and groups; currently handles 8 acts. Receives 10% commission. Reviews material for acts.
How to Contact: Submit demo tape by mail—unsolicited submissions are OK. Prefers cassette (or videocassette if available) and lyric sheet. "Include photo and bio." If seeking management, include tape, photo and bio in press kit. SASE. Reports in 3 weeks.
Music: Mostly **dance, rock, R&B** and **pop.** Works primarily with vocalists. Current acts include Mike Giorgio (rock/pop), Lou Taylor (dance/rock), Mike Tyler (R&B), Paradise (dance/R&B), Jeni England (pop), Katani (R&B), Sue Oriavong (dance/pop) and Susan Moss (country/crossover).
Tips: "Have dedication and drive to accomplish what you want out of your career."

*MT. HIGH ENTERTAINMENT, 9356 La Mesa Dr., Alta Loma CA 91701. (909)980-3571. Fax: (909)944-5018. Owner: Michael Scafuto. Estab. 1984. Individual artists, groups and songwriters from anywhere. Currently handles 22 acts. Receives 10-15% commission. Reviews material for acts.
How to Contact: Submit demo tape by mail. Unsolicited submissions are OK. Prefers cassette (or videocassette) with lyric sheet or lead sheet. Does not return material. Reports in 2-3 weeks.
Music: Mostly **all types.**
Tips: "Write about what you know."

*MUSIC CITY CO-OP, INC., (formerly Tommy Loomas), Suite 323, 107 Music City Circle, Nashville TN 37214. (615)885-1333. President: Joe Silver. Artist Development Company. Estab. 1992. "We provide the following services for new recording artists: Audio production, CD and cassette manufacturing, video production, radio promotion, national publicity, image consultation, photography, make-up, stage presentation, choreography, song search, showcases, booking and management."
How to Contact: Write or phone for permission to submit. Does not return unsolicited material. If seeking management, include tape, bio and press information. Reports in 3 weeks.
Music: Mostly **country** and **cross-over acts.** Current acts include The Breeze, Jim Purdy and Pat Tucker.
Tips: "Move to Nashville and start writing with Nashville staff writers. Co-writing is very important in Nashville."

MUSIC MATTERS, P.O. Box 3773, San Rafael CA 94912-3773. (415)457-0700. Management firm. Estab. 1990. Represents local, regional or international individual artists, groups and songwriters; currently handles 3 acts. Receives 15% commission. Reviews material for acts.
How to Contact: Submit demo tape by mail—unsolicited submissions are OK. Prefers cassette (or VHS videocassette if available) with lyric sheet. If seeking management, include history, bio and reviews. Does not return unsolicited material.
Music: Mostly **rock, blues** and **pop;** also **jazz** and **R&B.** Works primarily with songwriting performers/bands (rock). Current acts include Canned Heat (rock/blues group), Olivia Rosestone (singer/songwriter) and Sam Andrew (singer/songwriter from Big Brother and The Holding Company).
Tips: "Write great *radio-friendly* songs."

MUSKRAT PRODUCTIONS, INC., 1 Paulding St., Elmsford NY 10523. (914)592-3144. Contact: Bruce McNichols. Estab. 1970. Represents individuals and groups; currently represents 15 acts. Deals with artists in the New York City area. Reviews material for acts.

How to Contact: Write first. Prefers cassette (or short videocassette of performance) with 3 songs minimum. Does not return unsolicited material. Reports "only if interested."
Music: "We specialize in **old-time jazz, dixieland** and **banjo music**," also **old time, nostalgia, country** and **jazz**. Works primarily with dixieland, banjo/sing-along groups to play parties, Mexican mariachi bands and specialty acts for theme parties, dances, shows and conventions. Current acts include Smith Street Society Jazz Band (dixieland jazz), Las Antillas Mexican Mariachis (authentic Mexican) and Harry Hepcat and the Boogie Woogie Band (50s rock revival).

FRANK NANOIA PRODUCTIONS AND MANAGEMENT, 1999 N. Sycamore Ave., Los Angeles CA 90068. (213)874-8725. President: Frank Nanoia. Management and production firm. Represents artists, groups and songwriters. Produces TV specials and concerts. Currently handles 15 acts. Receives 15-25% commission. Reviews material for acts.
How to Contact: Submit demo tape by mail—unsolicited submissions are OK. Prefers 7½, 15 ips reel-to-reel or cassette (or videocassette of live performance, if available) with 3-5 songs and lyric lead sheets. "Professional quality please. Check sound quality as well." If seeking management, include photo, bio, clippings and resume. Does not return unsolicited material. Reports "only if material is above average. No phone calls please."
Music: Mostly **R&B** and **dance**; also **top 40/pop, jazz fusion, country, easy listening, MOR, gospel** and **soul**. Works primarily with soloists, Latin jazz and R&B groups. Current acts include Marc Allen Trujillo (vocalist/songwriter); Paramour (R&B show group), and Gilberto Duron (recording artist). Current productions include The Golden Eagle Awards, The Caribbean Musical Festival and The Joffrey Ballet/CSU Awards.
Tips: "No phone calls!"

NASH ANGELES INC., P.O. Box 363, Hendersonville TN 37077. (615)824-8845. Manager: Wilson Frazier. Management firm and music publisher (BMI). Represents individual artists, groups and songwriters; currently handles 1 act. Receives 25% commission. Reviews material for acts.
How to Contact: Prefers cassette (or videocassette) with lyric sheet. If seeking management, include photo, bio, all press, audio and videotape. Does not return unsolicited material. Reports in 1 month.
Music: Mostly **country-pop, AOR, country** and **pop**; also **rock**. Works primarily with vocalists. Current act is Eddie Reasoner (singer/songwriter).

*NASON ENTERPRISES, INC., 2219 Polk St. NE, Minneapolis MN 55418-3713. (612)781-8353. Fax: (612)781-8355. President: Christopher Nason. Management firm, record label, video production, music publisher/ASCAP. Estab. 1989. Represents individual artists, groups and songwriters from anywhere; currently handles 5 acts. Commission rate varies. Reviews material for acts.
How to Contact: Submit demo tape by mail. Unsolicited submissions are OK. Prefers cassette (or VHS videocassette) with 1-3 songs and lyric sheet. If seeking management, press kit should include photo, bio, cassette and/or CD, clubs and regions performed. "Label everything." SASE. Reports in 2 weeks to 2 months.
Music: Mostly **commercial radio, rock/heavy metal, crossover/pop**; also **country**. Current acts include Cymon DelGrail (singer/songwriter), Billy Gramer (singer/songwriter), Wendy T. (country/solo artist), The Stud Brothers (R&B) and Adrian (rock/funk).

NATIONAL ENTERTAINMENT, INC., Suite 6, 5366 N. Northwest Hwy., Chicago IL 60630. (312)545-8222. Fax: (312)545-3714. President/General Manager: Roger Connelly. Management firm and booking agency. Estab. 1989. Represents local, regional and international individual artists, groups and songwriters; currently handles 100 acts. Receives 15% commission. Reviews material for acts.
How to Contact: Submit demo tape by mail—unsolicited submissions are OK. Prefers cassette (or VHS videocassette if available) with 1 song and lyric sheet. If seeking management, include cassette audio or videotape (VHS) for each song and lyric sheets in press kit. SASE. Reports in 2 weeks.
Music: Mostly **pop, rock, country** and **blues**. Works primarily with dance bands, singers and singer/songwriters. Current acts include Dave Pisciotto (guitarist/songwriter), Dynasty (8 piece dance band) and Chip Messiner (singer/songwriter).
Tips: "Your promotional package is our only representation of your talent. Be prepared to take the necessary steps to organize your materials into a professional presentation."

JACK NELSON & ASSOCIATES, 5800 Valley Oak Dr., Los Angeles CA 90068. (213)465-9905. Assistant: Shawn Brogan. Management firm. Estab. 1981. Represents local, regional or international individual artists, groups and songwriters; currently handles 6 acts. Receives 15% commission. Reviews material for acts.
How to Contact: Call first and obtain permission to submit. Prefers cassette (or videocassette if available) with 2-4 songs and lyric sheets. If seeking management, include quality demo, lyric sheet and bio in press kit. SASE. Reports in 1 month.
Music: Currents acts include Jeffrey Osborne, Kathy Sledge and Joey Diggs.

*NELSON ROAD MANAGEMENT, 832 Montague St., Albert Park, Victoria 3206 **Australia.** (61-3)6991000. Fax: (61-3)6709983. Managing Director: Dr. Nathan Brenner. Management firm. Estab. 1979. Represents local individual artists, groups and songwriters; currently handles 5 acts. Receives 20% commission. Reviews material for acts.
How to Contact: Submit demo tape by mail. Unsolicited submissions are OK. Prefers cassette (or PAL videocassette) with 3 excellent songs (1 pop commercial radio, 1 different tempo friendly, 1 own choice highlighting individuality) and lyric sheet or lead sheet. "Be yourself and kindly persistent." Does not return material. Reports in 3 weeks (add 2 weeks from o/s).
Music: All types except classical, operatic, instrumental. Works with all types of acts. Current acts include F.O.F.C. Band (dance/pop), Julie Anne Evans (singer/writer).
Tips: "Be the best you can be. Push yourself to the limits of your abilities, then go beyond. Listen to all types of music. Good ideas both melodic and lyric can be found and assimilated, if desired. Love what you do and suffer for it—feel it."

*NETWORK ENTERTAINMENT SERVICE INC., Suite 245, 1280 Winchester Pkwy., Atlanta GA 30080. (404)319-8822. President: Mike Hooks. Management firm, booking agency. Estab. 1985. Represents local and regional individual artists and groups. Currently handles 10 acts. Receives 10-20% commission. Reviews material for acts.
How to Contact: Call first and obtain permission to submit. Prefers cassette. If seeking management, press kit should include whatever is available. SASE. Reports in 1 week.
Music: Mostly **rock, country**. Works primarily with bands. Current acts include Wet Willie, Kelly Hogan, Normaltown Flyers and Metal Rose.
Tips: "If you are truly talented and your songs are as strong as you hear on the radio, then you have a great chance of being successful."

*NEW ARTIST'S PRODUCTIONS, 131 Connecticut Ave., N. Bay Shore NY 11706. Professional Department: Jeannie G. Walker. Management firm, record company and music publisher. Estab. 1984. Represents individual artists, groups and songwriters; currently handles 45-60 acts. Receives 20% commission. Reviews material for acts.
How to Contact: Submit demo tape by mail—unsolicited submissions are OK. Prefers cassette (or professionally prepared videocassette) and lyric sheet; prefers professional videos. SASE. Reports in 3 months.
Music: Mostly **pop, country** and **easy listening**; also **rock, gospel** and **blues**. Works primarily with vocalists and dance bands. Current acts include Cherokee (vocalist & dance band), Anjel (vocalist) and Ronnie D. Russell (vocalist).
Tips: "Put together a professional cassette recording and don't submit inexpensive tapes."

*NIC OF TYME PRODUCTIONS, INC., P.O. Box 2114, Valparaiso IN 46384. (219)477-2083. Fax: (219)477-4075. President: Tony Nicoletto. Management firm, record promoter. Estab. 1990. Represents individual artists, groups and songwriters from anywhere. Receives 20-25% commission. Reviews material for acts.
How to Contact: Submit demo tape by mail. Unsolicited submissions are OK. Prefers cassette (or videocassette) with 3 songs and lyric sheet. If seeking management, press kit should include picture, demo tape, words and autobiography on the artist. "Must be original and copyright material." Does not return material. Reports in 1 month.
Music: Mostly **country, R&B, pop**; also **rock, jazz, contemporary**. Works primarily with singers, bands and songwriters. Current acts include Bobby Lewis (R&B singer/songwriter), John Kontol (pop singer/songwriter), Pepper Thom (pop/country singer/songwriter) and Dawn O'Day (country singer/songwriter).
Tips: "Review your material for clean-cut vocals. Keep trying hard and don't give up. We work primarily as a record promoter for the artist in mind. We pre-solicit labels that are interested in your style of music."

NORTHSTAR MANAGEMENT INC., 33532 Five Mile Rd., Livonia MI 48154. (313)427-6010. President: Angel Gomez. Management firm. Estab. 1979. Represents local/international individual artists, groups and songwriters; currently handles 6 acts. Receives 10-25% commission. Reviews material for acts.
How to Contact: Write first and obtain permission to submit. Prefers cassette (or videocassette of performance) with 3-5 songs. If seeking management, include photo, tape, bio and schedule. Does not return unsolicited material. Reports in 4-6 weeks.
Music: Mostly **rock, pop** and **top 40**; also **metal**. Works primarily with individual artists, groups (bar bands) and songwriters. Current artists include Craig Elliott (new music), Slyboy (rock), RH Factor (rock), Hunter Brucks (rock), Reckless Youth (rock) and Planet Of Fun (rock).
Tips: "Have at least a general knowledge of the music business."

*NOVEAU TALENT, 1006 S. Marshall, Midland TX 79701. Also: Suite 501, 3000 W. Kansas Ave., Midland TX 79701. (915)689-8058. Producer/Manager: Amelio Hinojos. Artist development and an independent songwriter/producer. Represents local, regional and international individual artists, groups, songwriters and musicians. Currently handles 3 acts. Receives 10% commission. Reviews material for acts.
How to Contact: Submit demo tape by mail. Unsolicited submissions are OK. Prefers cassette with 2-4 songs and lyric or lead sheets (if possible). SASE. Reports in 1 month.
Music: Mostly **pop, R&B, Spanish** and **soul**; also **new styles**. Works primarily with vocalists and bands. Current artists include Nostalgia (Spanish pop); Brillo II (Spanish Te Jand); Sonic (pop/ballad).
Tips: "Never quit. Success is defined 'persistence!' "

CRAIG NOWAG'S NATIONAL ATTRACTIONS, 6037 Haddington Drive, Memphis TN 38119-7423. (901)767-1990. Owner/President: Craig Nowag. Booking agency. Estab. 1958. Represents local, regional and international individual artists and groups; currently handles 22 acts. Receives 15-25% commission.
How to Contact: Submit demo tape by mail—unsolicited submissions are OK. Prefers cassette (or VHS videocassette if available) with 3-5 songs. Does not return unsolicited material. Reports in 5 weeks.
Music: Mostly **R&B, pop** and **blues**; also **pop/rock, crossover country** and **re-makes**. Works primarily with oldies record acts, dance bands, blues bands, rock groups, R&B dance bands and nostalgia groups. Current acts include Famous Unknowns, Dianne Price, and The Coasters.
Tips: "If the buying public won't buy your song, live act or record you have no saleability, and no agent or manager can do anything for you."

OAK STREET MUSIC, 1067 Sherwin Rd., Winnipeg, Manitoba R3H 0T8 **Canada**. Phone: (204)694-3101. Fax: (204)697-0903. CEO: Gilles Paquin. Record label and music publisher. Estab. 1987. Roster includes performers, songwriters and musicians; currently handles 13 acts. Sister company, PEG Music, a division of Oak Street Music, is a record label for AC/Country/Roots artists.
How to Contact: Submit demo tape by mail—unsolicited submissions are OK. Prefers cassette (or VHS videocassette if available) with maximum 4 songs and lyric or lead sheet. "Something which shows the artist's capabilities—doesn't need to be fancy. Be *factual*." SAE and IRC. Reports in 3 months.
Music: Primarily a **family entertainment** label, with interest also in the **AC/Country/Roots** genre. Current acts include Fred Penner (children's entertainer), Al Simmons (singer/actor/comic) and Valdy.

OB-1 ENTERTAINMENT, P.O. Box 22552, Nashville TN 37202. (615)672-0307. Partners: Jim O'Baid and Karen Hillebrand. Management firm, artist development and songplugging. Estab. 1990. Represents local, regional and international individual artists, groups and songwriters; currently handles 3 acts. Receives 10% commission. Reviews material for acts.
How to Contact: Submit demo tape by mail—unsolicited submissions are OK. Prefers cassette (or VHS videocassette if available) with 3 songs. If seeking management, include cassette with 3 songs, 8×10 photo, bio and video cassette (if possible) in press kit. Does not return unsolicited material. SASE must accompany all other submissions. Reports in 2 months.
Music: Primarily **country**, but **pop** and **rock** also. Current acts include Jeannie Cruz, Tom Stanko and Rosilee.
Tips: "Make sure your ideas are as strong as possible before making a submission. You've got about about 15 seconds to make an impression."

*THE OFFICE, INC., Suite 44G, 322 W 57th, New York NY 10019. President: John Luongo. Management firm, music publisher (ASCAP/BMI) and production company. Estab. 1983. Represents local, regional and international individual artists, groups, songwriters and producer/engineers. Currently handles 6 acts. Receives 25% commission. Reviews material for acts.
How to Contact: Write or call first and obtain permission to submit. Prefers cassette (or VHS videocassette if available) with 2 songs and lyric sheets. Does not return unsolicited material. Reports in 4 weeks.
Music: Mostly **hard rock/pop, R&B** and **CHR/top 40**; also **dance**. Works primarily with groups—female vocalists; solo R&B, male or female. Current acts include Joy Winter (female/dance), Traci Blue (female rock) and Oliver Who? (R&B male vocalist on Zoo/BMG).
Tips: "Do your homework before you submit."

ON THE LEVEL MUSIC!, 807 S. Xanthus Place, Tulsa OK 74104-3620. President: Fred Gage. Management firm and booking agency. Estab. 1971. Represents individual artists, groups and songwriters; currently handles 12 acts. Receives 25% commission. Reviews material for acts.

How to Contact: Submit demo tape by mail—unsolicited submissions are OK. Prefers cassette (or VHS videocassette if available) with 4 songs and lyric or lead sheets. For video: "Full length not needed, short clips only." If seeking management, include picture, 4-song demo (video if possible) and short bio in press kit. Does not return unsolicited material. Reports in 1 month.
Music: Mostly **rock**, **pop** and **gospel**. Works primarily with rock groups. Current acts include Second Chapter of Acts, Chase, and Rick Cua.
Tips: "Be great not just good and be hungry to make it."

ONTARIO BLUEGRASS INC., 64 Market St., Brockport NY 14420. (716)637-2040. President: Paul Pickard. Booking agency. Estab. 1984. Represents local and regional groups; currently handles 1 group. Receives 20% commission. Reviews material for acts.
How to Contact: Write or call first and obtain permission to submit. Prefers cassette with 6 songs. Does not return unsolicited material.
Music: Strictly **gospel**. Current acts include Pickard Brothers.

OPERATION MUSIC ENTERPRISES, 1400 E. Court St., Ottumwa IA 52501. (515)682-8283. President: Nada C. Jones. Management firm and booking agency. Represents artists, groups and songwriters; currently handles 4 acts. Receives 15% commission. Reviews material for acts.
How to Contact: Submit demo tape—unsolicited submissions are OK. Prefers cassette (or VHS videocassette if available) and lyric sheet. "Keep material simple. Groups—use *only group* members—don't add extras. Artists should include references." Does not return unsolicited material. Reports in 4-6 weeks.
Music: Mostly **country**; also **blues**. Works primarily with vocalists and show and dance groups. Current acts include Reesa Kay Jones (country vocalist and recording artist), John Richards Show and White River Country (country/bluegrass).

OREGON MUSICAL ARTISTS, P.O. Box 122, Yamhill OR 97148. (503)662-3309. Contact: Michael D. LeClair. Management firm and production agency. Estab. 1982. Represents artists, groups and songwriters; currently handles 4 acts. Receives 10-25% commission. Reviews material for acts.
How to Contact: Submit demo tape by mail—unsolicited submissions are OK. Prefers cassette with 3-10 songs and lyric sheet (or videocassette if available). Does not return unsolicited material.
Music: Mostly **top 40/pop** and **R&B**; also **blues, church/religious, country, dance, easy listening, gospel, jazz, MOR, progressive, hard** and **mellow rock** and **soul**. Works primarily with writers and bar bands "with excellent vocalists." Current acts include The Hoyt Brothers (easy country ballads), Lee Garrett (songwriter) and Boomer Band (50's bar band).

*PACIFIC RIM PRODUCTIONS, P.O. Box 635 Wynnum, Brisbane 4178 Queensland, **Australia**. (07)32962861. Fax: (07)362992. Managing Director: Jon Campbell. Management firm. Estab. 1988. Represents individual artists. Reviews material for acts.
How to Contact: Submit demo tape by mail. Unsolicited submissions are OK. Prefers cassette with lyric sheet. SAE and IRC. Reports in 6 weeks.
Music: Mostly **folk, MOR** and **adult contemporary**; also **country ballads** and **classical**. Current acts include Suzanne Clachair (singer/songwriter, recording artist).

DAVE PATON MANAGEMENT, Suite C-300, 16776 Lakeshore Dr., Lake Elsinore CA 92530. (714)699-9339. Contact: Dave Paton. Management firm and record company (Hollyrock Records). Estab. 1973. Represents local, regional or international individual artists; currently handles 2 acts. Receives 20-25% commission. Reviews material for acts. "Associated with 'Artist Viability Research' placing acts with major labels."
How to Contact: Submit demo tape by mail—unsolicited submissions are OK. Prefers cassette (or VHS videocassette if available) with 4 songs and lyric sheet. SASE. Reports in 1 month.
Music: Mostly **country, country/rock** and **rock**; also **pop**. Works primarily with vocalists. Current acts include Linda Rae (country artist) and Breakheart Pass (country group).

JACKIE PAUL MANAGEMENT AND CONSULTANT FIRM, 559 Wanamaker Rd., Jenkintown PA 19046. (215)884-3308. Fax: (215)884-1083. President: Jackie Paul. Management firm (Terrance Moore Music, Inc./BMI). Estab. 1985. Represents local and national artists, groups, producers and musicians. Currently handles 2 acts. Receives 15-35% commission. Reviews material for acts.

Remember: Don't "shotgun" your demo tapes. Submit only to companies interested in the type of music you write. For more submission hints, refer to Getting Started on page 7.

How to Contact: Write or call first and obtain permission to submit. Prefers cassette (or VHS videocassette if available) with 1-3 songs and lyric or lead sheets. "It's not mandatory but if possible, I would prefer a videocassette. A video simply helps get the song across visually. Do the best to help portray the image you represent, with whatever resources possible." If seeking management, include no more than 3 copyrighted songs, photo, bio (short and to the point), video (if possible), contact name, telephone number and address in press kit. SASE.
Music: Mostly **rap, pop** and **R&B/dance**. Works primarily with vocalists (all original acts). Current acts include Blue Eagle (pop/AC singer/songwriter, producer/musician) and Terrance T'Luv (R&B-dance singer/songwriter/producer).

THE PERCEPTION WORKS INC., Suite F-2, 3390 W. 86th St., Indianapolis IN 46268. (317)876-5776. President: Lawrence Klein. Management firm. Estab. 1986. Deals with local, regional or international individual artists and groups; currently handles 4 acts. Receives 10% commission. Reviews material for acts.
How to Contact: Submit demo tape by mail—unsolicited submissions are OK. Prefers cassette (or VHS videocassette if available) with 4 songs and lyric sheet. If seeking management, include bio and press clippings. Does not return unsolicited material. Reports in 2 months.
Music: Mostly **rock, R&B** and **pop**; also **country** and **blues**. Works primarily with rock bands, R&B bands, blues bands, jazz bands, pop bands. Current acts include Under Fire (classic rock), JUS 4 U (rock), Michael Brown Group (jazz) and The Bitter Ends (alternative).

*RONNIE PERKINS PRODUCTION AND MANAGEMENT INC., Suite A-1, 1986 Dallas Dr., Baton Rouge LA 70806. (504)924-5922. Fax: (504)927-1638. Contact: Ronnie Perkins. Management firm, music publisher (RonPerk/BMI), record company and record producer. Estab. 1982. Represents individual artists and groups from anywhere; currently handles 6 acts. Receives 20% commission. Reviews material for acts.
How to Contact: Submit demo tape by mail. Unsolicited submissions are OK. Prefers cassette with lyric sheet. If seeking management, press kit should include presentation letter of interest with cassette and picture if available. SASE. Reports in 2 weeks.
Music: Mostly **dance music, R&B** and **rap**; also **gospel**. Acts include Gregory D. and DJ Mannie Fresh, Warren Mayes, La'Paris, Sin-Muzic, Ronnie "Rude Boy," Egyptian Lover and Johnny O.
Tips: "Make sure everything is in proper order."

*PERSONAL MANAGEMENT, INC., P.O. Box 88225, Los Angeles CA 90009. (310)677-4415. CEO: Debbie DeStafano. Management firm (BMI and ASCAP affiliated). Estab. 1981. Represents individual artists, bands, songwriters, producers, recording studio musicians. Currently handles 8-12 individual artists and groups. Reviews material for acts, artist direction and consultation, music supervision, album project coordination and production, publishing management.
How to Contact: Submit demo tape by mail. Unsolicited submissions are OK. Prefers cassette (or VHS videocassette) with 2-3 songs and lyric sheet or lead sheet. If seeking management, press kit should include bio, cassette demo tape, photos, videotape. "Not necessary to write or phone first!!" Does not return material. Reports in less than 30 days.
Music: Mostly **rock, pop, folk**; also **country cross-over, alternative, blues/soul**. Works primarily with vocalists, singer/songwriters, bands.
Tips: "Great writing/extraordinary material—Be sure the songs and the voice are there."

GREGORY PITZER ARTIST MANAGEMENT, P.O. Box 460527, Houston TX 77056. (713)223-4806. President: Gregory Pitzer. Estab. 1987. Represents local, regional or national individual artists, groups and songwriters; currently handles 6 acts. Receives 20-30% commission. Reviews material for acts.
How to Contact: Submit demo tape by mail—unsolicited submissions are OK. Prefers cassette (or VHS videocassette if available) with 3-5 songs and lyric or lead sheets. If seeking management, include photo, tape, bio, VHS video. Does not return unsolicited material. Reports in 3 weeks.
Music: Mostly **rock, pop** and **alternative**; also **country**. Works primarily with bands/vocalists. Current acts include Rapture Mine (alternative/hard rock), Ashley (alternative/pop), Tony Vila (folk-rock), Twenty Mondays (pop/alternative), Under The Sun (pop/rock) and Hayden Minor (pop singer/songwriter).

PLACER PUBLISHING, P.O. Box 11301, Kansas City KS 66111. (913)287-3495. Owner: Steve Vail. Management firm, booking agency, music publisher (ASCAP) and record company (System Records). Estab. 1980. Represents local, regional and international individual artists, groups and songwriters; currently handles 3 acts. Receives 20% commission. Reviews material for acts.
How to Contact: Submit demo tape by mail—unsolicited submissions are OK. Prefers cassette (or VHS or Beta videocassette) with lyric sheets. Does not return unsolicited material. Reports in 2 months.

Music: Mostly New Age and **progressive.** Works primarily with esoteric or avant-garde groups or individuals. Current acts include Realm (progressive rock group), Darrel Studna and Lake Furney.
Tips: "Be creative. Please no mainstream tunes."

PLATINUM EARS LTD., 285 Chestnut St., West Hempstead NY 11552. (516)489-0738. Fax: (516)565-9425. President: Mike Siskind. Vice President: Rick O'Larsch. Management firm, music publisher (Siskatune Music Publishing Co./BMI). Estab. 1988. Represents national and international individual artists, groups and songwriters; currently handles 3 acts. Receives 20% commission.
How to Contact: Write first and obtain permission to submit. "No calls!" Prefers cassette with 1-3 songs and lyric sheet. If seeking management, include tape, photo, bio and tearsheets in press kit. SASE only. Reports in 3 months.
Music: Rock, pop and **R&B.** Current acts include Georgi Smith (rock), In Fear Of Roses (rock) and Michael Ellis (songwriter).
Tips: "If a deal seems too good to be true, many times it is."

PLATINUM GOLD MUSIC, Suite 1220, 9200 Sunset Blvd., Los Angeles CA 90069. Managers: Steve Cohen/David Cook. Management firm, production company and music publisher. ASCAP. Estab. 1978. Represents local or regional (East or West coasts) individual artists, groups and songwriters; currently handles 4 acts. Receives 20% commission. Reviews material for acts.
How to Contact: Write or call first and obtain permission to submit. Prefers cassette (or VHS videocassette if available) with 3 songs and lyric sheets. If seeking management, include photo, cassette or videocassette, bio and press clip if available in press kit. Does not return unsolicited material. Reports in 1-2 months.
Music: Mostly **contemporary R&B, dance/pop, hip hop/rap;** also **pop rock, hard rock** and **pop.** Works most often with vocalists. Current acts include Troop (R&B vocal group), Def Jef (rap/hip hop), Ku De Tah (alternative rock), Tairrie B. (pop/rap), Brigette McWilliams (R&B), Kill Big Brother (hard rock).
Tips: "No ballads. We do not look for potential; be prepared and professional before coming to us— and ready to relocate to West Coast if necessary."

POWER STAR MANAGEMENT, #618, 6981 N. Park Dr., Pennsauken NJ 08109. (609)486-1480. President: Brian Kushner. Management firm. Estab. 1981. Represents international individual artists and groups; currently handles 7 acts. Receives 20% commission. Reviews material for acts.
How to Contact: Submit demo tape by mail—unsolicited submissions are OK. Prefers cassette with 4 songs and lyric sheet. SASE. Reports in 3 weeks.
Music: Mostly **pop/dance, rock** and **R&B.** Current acts include Britny Fox, Linear, Tuff, Andrea Mychaels, Divine Judgement, Stuttering John and After Alice.
Tips: "Send me smash hits!"

PRO TALENT CONSULTANTS, P.O. Box 1192, Clearlake Oak CA 95423. (707)998-3587. Coordinator: John Eckert. Assistant General Manager: Bryan Hyland. Management firm and booking agency. Estab. 1979. Represents individual artists and groups; currently handles 9 acts. Receives 9% commission. Reviews material for acts.
How to Contact: Submit demo tape—unsolicited submissions are OK. Prefers cassette (or VHS videocassette if available) with at least 4 songs and lyric sheet. "We prefer audio cassette (4 songs). Submit videocassette with live performance only." If seeking management, include an 8×10 photo, a cassette of at least 4-6 songs, a bio on group/artist and business card or a phone number with address to contact in press kit. Does not return unsolicited material. Reports in 3 weeks.
Music: Mostly **country, country/pop** and **rock.** Works primarily with vocalists, show bands, dance bands and bar bands. Current acts include John Richards (country singer), Glenn Elliott Band (country group) and Just Us (country).
Tips: "Keep working hard and place yourself with as many contacts as you can—you will succeed with strong determination!"

*GARY RABIN MANAGEMENT, 42 Spencer Rd., Cremorne NSW 2090 **Australia.** (02)908-3192. Fax: (02)908-3697. Director: Gary Rabin. Management firm. Represents individual artists, groups, songwriters, producers/engineers etc. from anywhere; currently handles 5 acts. Receives 15-20% commission. Reviews material for acts.
How to Contact: Submit demo tape by mail. Unsolicited submissions are OK. Prefers cassette with lyric sheet. If seeking management, press kit should include photos, bio, reviews and copies of press. Does not return material. Reports in 2-3 months.
Music: Mostly **rock, heavy rock** and **contemporary pop;** also **pop rock, indie** and **country.** Works primarily with singer/songwriters and bands. Current acts include Ross Wilson (singer/songwriter), The Poor Boys (heavy rock band) and The Angels (rock band).

RAINBOW COLLECTION LTD., 4501 Spring Creek Rd., Bonita Springs FL 33923. (813)947-6978. Executive Producer: Richard (Dick) O'Bitts. Management firm, record company (Happy Man Records) and music publisher (Rocker Music and Happy Man Music). Represents individual artists, groups, songwriters and producers; currently handles 7 acts. Receives 10-20% commission. Reviews material for acts.
How to Contact: Submit demo tape by mail—unsolicited submissions are OK. Prefers cassette (or VHS videocassette of live performance, if available) with 4 songs and lyric sheet. If seeking management, include photos, bio and tapes in press kit. SASE. Reports in 1 month.
Music: Mostly **country, pop** and **rock**. Works primarily with writer/artists and groups of all kinds. Current acts include Holly Ronick, Colt Gipson (traditional country), Overdue (rock), Flo Carter and the Bengter Sisters (gospel), Scott Emerick (traditional country) and The Challengers (country pop).

*RANA INTERNATIONAL MUSIC GROUP, INC., P.O. Box 106, Valhalla NY 10595. (914)741-2576. President: Raffaele A. Nudo. Vice President: Wesley C. Kranitz. Management firm, music publisher, record company (CHRISMARIE Records). Estab. 1990. Represents individual artists, groups and songwriters from anywhere; currently represents 13 acts. Receives 20% commission. Reviews material for acts.
How to Contact: Submit demo tape by mail. Unsolicited submissions are OK. Prefers cassette (or VHS videocassette) with 3-4 songs and lyric sheet. If seeking management, press kit should include bio and photos. Include SASE. Does not return unsolicited material. Reports in 6 weeks.
Music: Mostly **pop, rock** and **ballads**; also **country, R&B** and **new music**. Primarily works with singer/songwriters, bands and performance artists. Current acts include Niko (singer/songwriter), DECLARATION (rock) and Tom Hughes (singer/songwriter).
Tips: "We are currently working both in the USA and Europe. Our European office in Milan, Italy, has featured our clients on regional/national radio and television. So if you are serious about this business and want to pursue your dream, send in the material as we've requested, stay positive and have faith in your talent. All submissions must include name, phone number, etc. on all items. Ciao!"

*RON RANKE & ASSOCIATES, LTD., P.O. Box 852, Barrington IL 60011. Managing Director: Ron Ranke. Management firm, music publisher, record company (Hallmark). Represents "name" and international individual artists and groups. Currently handles 6 acts. Receives varied commission.
How to Contact: Write first and obtain permission to submit. "Please no calls!" Prefers cassette (or VHS videocassette) and lyric sheet. If seeking management, press kit should include whatever materials best describe your overall capabilities. Does not return material. Reports in 1 month.
Music: Mostly **country, pop, cross-over**; also **patriotic, international**. Works primarily with vocalists. Current acts include Roy Clark, Pia Zadora, Krystof (Eastern Europe's number one recording artist).
Tips: "Patience!"

*RAW ENTERTAINMENT, 1230 Hill St., Santa Monica CA 90405-4708. (310)452-7004. President: Robert Anderson. Management firm. Estab. 1990. Represents individual artists, groups, songwriters from anywhere. Currently handles 5 acts. Receives 15-20% commission. Reviews material for acts.
How to Contact: Submit demo tape by mail. Unsolicited submissions are OK. Prefers cassette (or DAT) with up to 5 songs. If seeking management, include tape, photo and brief bio. SASE. Reports in 1 month.
Music: Mostly **rock, pop, R&B**; also **country, rap**. Works primarily with vocalists, pop/rock bands, and rap. Current acts include Tony Kishman (pop/rock-writer), Paul Sabu (rock songwriter, producer), Only Child (band).
Tips: "Don't hesitate to forward your songs to us."

RED GIANT RECORDS AND PUBLISHING, 3155 South., 764 East., Salt Lake City UT 84106. (801)486-4210. President: Anthony Perry. Music publisher (Red Giant Records) and record company (Red Giant). Estab. 1982. Represents local, regional and international individual artists, groups and songwriters. Curently represents 6 artists and groups. Receives 12% commission. Reviews material for acts.
How to Contact: Submit demo tape by mail—unsolicited submissions are OK. Prefers cassette (or ½ VHS videocassette if available) with 3-4 songs and lyric or lead sheets. If seeking management, include tape or CD, press kit and cover letter. Does not return unsolicited material. Reports in 1-3 months.
Music: Mostly **jazz, avant rock, country/R&B** and **R&B**. Works primarily with instrumentalists, vocalists and bands. Current acts include John Herron (songwriter), Spaces (vocal group), House of Cards (blues/rock), Armed & Dangerous (R&B), Zion Tribe (reggae/rock) and Alan Roger Nichols (jazz/New Age songwriter).

REED SOUND RECORDS, INC., 120 Mikel Dr., Summerville SC 29485. (803)873-3324. Contact: Haden Reed. Management firm. Represents artists and groups; currently handles 2 acts. Receives 5% commission. Reviews material for acts.

How to Contact: Write first to arrange personal interview. Prefers cassette with 1-4 songs. Does not return unsolicited material.
Music: Mostly **country**; also **church/religious, easy listening** and **gospel**. Current acts include Haden Reed (country songwriter), Vocalettes (gospel) and Happy Jack Band (country).

REM MANAGEMENT, 9112 Fireside Dr., Indianapolis IN 46250. President: Bob McCutcheon. Management firm. Estab. 1987. Represents local, regional and international individual artists and groups; currently handles 1 act. Receives 20% commission. Reviews material for acts.
How to Contact: Write first and obtain permission to submit. Prefers cassette with 3 songs. SASE. Reports in 6 weeks.
Music: Mostly **hard rock** and **R&B**. Current acts include Beautiful Authentic Zoo Gods (alternative) and Signal (Capitol Records).
Tips: "I don't take on an artist for management unless I get a record deal."

***RENAISSANCE ENTERTAINMENT GROUP**, Suite 3A, 21 Mohawk Ave., Middlesex NJ 08846. (908)627-0651. Fax: (908)633-7863. Directors: Kevin A. Joy and Anthony Tucker. Management firm, booking agency, record company (Suburan Records); record producer (Onyx Music, Bo^{2}Legg Productions). Estab. 1992. Represents local and regional individual artists, groups, songwriters. Currently handles 5 acts. Receives 20% commission. Reviews material for acts.
How to Contact: Submit demo tape by mail. Unsolicited submissions are OK. Prefers cassette with 3 songs and lyric sheet or lead sheet. If seeking management, press kit should include pictures and bio. SASE. Reports in 5 weeks.
Music: Mostly **R&B, rap, club**. Works primarily with R&B groups, rap and vocalists. Current acts include Lori Stephens (singer/writer), Damon Washington (singer/writer), Truth & Honesty (rap).
Tips: "Hard work doesn't guarantee success, but without it you don't have a chance."

***REVEL MANAGEMENT**, #106, 9015 Owensmouth, Canoga Park CA 91304. (818)341-0454. V.P. of Development: Mary Revel. Management firm, booking agency, music publisher (Jongleur Music/ASCAP, BMI) record company (Top's Records) and Revel Pictures (develops motion pictures). Estab. 1980. Represents local, regional and international individual artists, groups, songwriters and screenplay writers; currently handles 23 acts. Reviews material for acts.
How to Contact: Write first and obtain permission to submit or call (900)990-7729 for information. Prefers cassette (or VHS videocassette if available). Does not return unsolicited material.
Music: Deals with **all genres** of entertainment. Current acts include Todd Taylor (banjo man/artist), Mor-Amor (pop/rock group), Big Deal (heavy rock), JB Holloway (songwriter, screenplay writer, actor), Willie Hutch (songwriter, recording artist, producer), Curtise Revel (recording artist, songwriter), Rebecca Revel (recording artist) and Dale Tuttle (country-MOR recording artist).

RIOHCAT MUSIC, P.O. Box 764, Hendersonville TN 37077-0764. (615)824-1435. Contact: Robert Kayne. Management firm, booking agency, record company (Avita Records) and music publisher (Riohcat Music/BMI). Estab. 1975. Represents individual artists and groups; currently handles 4 acts. Receives 20% commission. Reviews material for acts.
How to Contact: Submit demo tape by mail—unsolicited submissions are OK. Prefers cassette and lead sheet. If seeking management, include resume, previous experience, tape, photo and press clippings in press kit. Does not return unsolicited material. Reports in 2 weeks.
Music: Mostly **contemporary jazz** and **fusion**. Works primarily with jazz ensembles. Current acts include Jerry Tachoir Quartet, Marlene Tachoir and Jerry Tachoir/Van Manakas Duo.
Tips: "Be organized, neat and professional."

A.F. RISAVY, INC., 1312 Vandalia, Collinsville IL 62234. (618)345-6700. Divisions include Artco Enterprises, Golden Eagle Records, Swing City Music and Swing City Sound. Contact: Art Risavy. Management firm and booking agency. Estab. 1960. Represents artists, groups and songwriters; currently handles 75 acts. Receives 10% commission. Reviews material for acts.
How to Contact: Submit demo tape by mail—unsolicited submissions are OK. Prefers 7½ ips reel-to-reel or cassette (or VHS videocassette if available) with 2-6 songs and lyric sheet. If seeking management, include pictures, bio and VHS videocassette in press kit. SASE. Reports in 2 weeks.

 The asterisk before a listing indicates that the listing is new in this edition. New markets are often the most receptive to unsolicited submissions.

Music: Mostly **rock, country, MOR** and **top 40.** Current acts include Sammy and the Snow Monkeys, The Blast, Bedrock, Billy-Peek, Jules Blatner, Seen, Catch, Inside Out, Cruz'n, Fallback, Lang & McClain, Jim & Dave and the Chapman Brothers.
Tips: Artists should be "well-dressed, polished and ambitious. VHS videotapes are very helpful."

*PETER RIX MANAGEMENT P/L, P.O. Box 144 Milsons Point, NSW 2061 **Australia.** (612)922-6077. Fax: (612)922-6603. M.D.: Peter Rix. Assistant to M.D.: Diana Freeman. Management firm, music publisher, record company. Estab. 1970. Represents local individual artists; currently handles 3 acts. Reviews material for acts.
How to Contact: Submit demo tape by mail. Unsolicited submissions are OK. Prefers cassette (PAL videocassette) with lyric sheet. SAE and IRC. Reports in 4-5 weeks.
Music: Mostly **rock/pop, R&B** and **dance.** Primarily works with vocalists. Current acts include Deni Hines, Marcia Hines and Jon English (all singer/songwriter/actors).
Tips: "All artists require quality lyric content."

RNJ PRODUCTIONS, INC., 11514 Calvert St., North Hollywood CA 91606. (818)762-6105. President: Rein Neggo, Jr. Management firm. Estab. 1974. Represents individual artists; currently handles 10 acts. Receives 10-25% commission. Reviews material for acts.
How to Contact: Submit demo tape by mail—unsolicited submissions are OK. Prefers cassette with 3 songs and lead sheet. Does not return unsolicited material. Reports in 1 month.
Music: Mostly **A/C, country, pop** and **folk.** Works primarily with vocalists and concert artists. Current acts include Glenn Yarbrough, Arizona Smoke Review, Limeliters, Bill Zorn, Jon Benns, The Kingston Trio and The New Christy Minstrels.

ROCK-A-BILLY ARTIST AGENCY, P.O. Box 1622, Hendersonville TN 37077. (615)822-1044. A&R Director: S.D. Neal. Management firm, booking agency and record company. Estab. 1974. Represents artists and groups; currently handles 20-30 acts. Receives 20% commission. Reviews material for acts.
How to Contact: Submit demo tape—unsolicited submissions are OK. Prefers cassette (or VHS videocassette if available) with 2-6 songs and lyric sheet. SASE. Reports in 3 weeks.
Music: Mostly **rock** and **country**; also all other types including **rockabilly.** Works primarily with vocalists and bands. Current acts include Dixie Dee, Rhythm Rockers, Rufus Thomas, Richie Derwald, Mickey Finn Band and Greg Paul, Susan Sterling, Buddy Knox, and C.W.S. Wrestling.

ROGUE MANAGEMENT, 109 Earle Ave., Lynbrook NY 11563. (516)599-4157. President: James Citkovic. Partner: Ralph Beauchamp. Management firm. Estab. 1986. Represents local, regional or international individual artists, groups, songwriters and producers; currently handles 4 acts. Receives 10-30% commission. Reviews material for acts.
How to Contact: Submit demo tape by mail—unsolicited submissions are OK. Prefers cassette (or VHS videocassette if available), 8 × 10 pictures, press, bio, tape with 4 songs and lyric sheet. SASE. Reports in 4-5 weeks.
Music: Mostly **alternative, rock** and **pop/dance;** also **industrial, rave** and **techno.** Current acts include The Fiction Scene (major label music), Jeff Gordon (folk), Spiritual Loveaffair and The Eye Camera (music/art/film).

*JAY B. ROSS ENTERTAINMENT, 838 W. Grand Ave., Chicago IL 60622. (312)633-9000. Fax: (312)633-9090. President: Jay B. Ross. Estab. 1968. Represents individual artists and groups from anywhere. Currently handles 3 acts. Receives 15-20% commission. Reviews material for acts.
How to Contact: Write first and obtain permission to submit. Prefers cassette (or VHS videocassette) with 3 songs, "unless you want a publishing deal—then send more." If seeking managment, press kit should include photo. SASE. Reports in 2-4 weeks.
Music: Mostly **dance** and **rap, rock metal alternative, blues gospel;** also **jazz, pop, country.** Works primarily with vocalists, singer/songwriters and bands. Current acts include IDF (techno dance), Goodfellows (rap), Spike Dapper (rap).

*CHARLES R. ROTHSCHILD PRODUCTIONS INC., 330 E. 48th Street, New York NY 10017. (212)421-0592. President: Charles R. Rothschild. Booking agency. Estab. 1971. Represents local, regional and international individual artists, groups and songwriters; currently handles 10 acts. Receives 15-25% commission. Reviews material for acts.
How to Contact: Write or call first and obtain permission to submit. Prefers cassette or CD (or VHS videocassette if available) with 1 song and lyric and lead sheet. If seeking management, include photo, bio and reviews. SASE. Reports in 3 months.
Music: Mostly **rock, pop** and **folk;** also **country** and **jazz.** Current acts include Judy Collins (pop singer/songwriter), Leo Kottke (guitarist/composer) and Emmylou Harris (country songwriter).

*ROUND ROBIN, 101 Hurt Rd., Hendersonville TN 37075. (615)824-5900. Fax: (615)824-8800. Contact: Jim Pierce. Management firm, music publisher (Strawboss Music/BMI) and record company (Round Robin Records). Handles 3 acts. Receives 20% commission. Reviews material for acts.
How to Contact: Write or call first to arrange personal interview. Prefers cassette and lyric sheets. Does not return unsolicited material. Reports in 2 months.
Music: All types of **country**. Works primarily with single acts. Current acts include Arne Benoni (country), Lenny Valens (country/pop) and Blaine Dakota (country).

*RUSCH ENTERTAINMENT AGENCY, 3588 N. Thomas Rd., Freeland MI 48623. (517)781-1553. President: Dean A. Rusch. Booking agency. Estab. 1970. Represents groups in Michigan; currently handles 250-300 acts. Receives 10-15% commission. Reviews material for acts. Is a member of the International Talent Artists Association.
How to Contact: Write first and obtain permission to submit. Prefers cassette (or VHS videocassette if available) with 3-10 songs and lyric sheet. SASE. Reports in 2 weeks.
Music: Mostly **top 40/pop;** also **country, dance-oriented, MOR, easy listening** and **rock**. Works primarily with dance bands. Current acts include Ceyx, Dedication, Harmony, Loose Change, Evergreen, Infinity (all dance bands), Nights Society Orchestra and the Uptown Review (dance band/10 piece orchestra), Skyline (band, horn) and Ovation (dance band).

RUSTRON MUSIC PRODUCTIONS, Send all artist song submissions to: 1156 Park Lane, West Palm Beach FL 33417-5957. (407)686-1354. Main Office: 33 Whittier, Hartsdale, NY 10530. ("Main office does not review new material—only South Florida Branch office does.") Artists' Consultants: Rusty Gordon and Davilyn Whims. Composition Management: Ron Caruso. Management firm, booking agency, music publisher (Rustron Music Publishers/BMI and Whimsong Publishing/ASCAP) and record producer (Rustron Music Productions). Estab. 1970. Represents individuals, groups and songwriters; currently handles 25 acts. Receives 10-25% commission for management and/or booking only. Reviews material for acts.
How to Contact: Write or call first to discuss submittals. Prefers cassette with 3-6 songs and lyric or lead sheet. "SASE required for all correspondence." Reports in 2-4 months.
Music: **Blues** (country folk/urban, Southern), **country** (rock, blues, progressive), **easy listening** (ballads), **women's music, R&B, folk/rock, New Age instrumentals** and **New Age folk fusion**. Current acts include Relative Viewpoint (socio/environmental folk), Flash Silvermoon (blues and New Age) and Boomslang (contemporary folk and humorous songs).
Tips: "Send cover letter, typed lyric sheets for all songs. Carefully mix demo, don't drown the vocals, 3-6 songs in a submission. Send photo if artist is seeking marketing and/or production assistance. Very strong hooks, definitive melody, evolved concepts, unique and unpredictable themes."

*S.T.A.R.S. PRODUCTIONS, 2nd Floor, 1 Professional Quadrangle, Sparta NJ 07871. (201)729-7242. Fax: (201)729-2979. President: Steve Tarkanish. Booking agency. Estab. 1983. Represents individual artists, groups, songwriters from anywhere; currently handles 35 acts. Receives 15-20% commission. Reviews material for acts.
How to Contact: Submit demo tape by mail. Unsolicited submissions are OK. Prefers cassette with lyric sheet or lead sheet. If seeking management, press kit should include biography, photo, cassette, list of clubs played and upcoming dates. Does not return material. Reports in 6-8 weeks.
Music: Mostly **rock, alternative** and **country;** also **singles/duos** and **folk**. Primarily works with bands. Current acts include The Nerds (rock band, songwriters), Voices (rock band, songwriters) The Jox, Bums in the Park, Stuttering John (of the Howard Stern Show), Who Brought the Dog and Koz McDawgz. Bookings include the Spin Doctors, Air Supply and Kansas.

*BRANDON SAUL MANAGEMENT, 1/19 Eastbank Ave., Sydney 2097 **Australia**. (612)971-6953. Fax: (612)971-0368. Manager: Brandon Saul. Management firm. Estab. 1988. Represents individual artists, groups and songwriters from anywhere; currently handles several acts. Receives 15-20% commission. Reviews material for acts.
How to Contact: Submit demo tape by mail. Unsolicited submissions are OK. Prefers cassette (or VHS videocassette). If seeking management, press kit should include photo. Does not return material. Reports in 2 weeks.
Music: Mostly **rock, reggae** and **blues;** also **retro, acoustic** and **world**.

LONNY SCHONFELD AND ASSOCIATES, P.O. Box 460086, Garland TX 75046. (214)497-1616. President: Lonny Schonfeld. Management firm (G-Town Entertainment-promotions), promotions, public relations and music publisher (Lonny Tunes/BMI). Estab. 1988. Represents local, regional or international individual artists, groups and songwriters; currently handles 3 acts. Receives 15% commission. Reviews material for acts.

How to Contact: Submit demo tape—unsolicited submissions are OK. Prefers cassette with 3-5 songs and lyric sheet. If seeking management, include 8×10 head shot, bio, studio demo, live demo. Does not return unsolicited material. Reports in 2 weeks.
Music: Mostly **country, pop,** and **rock.** Works primarily with vocal groups and comedians. Current acts include Paul Phillips (comedian), Owl Creek Band (pop) and Doug Richardson (comedian).
Tips: "Make sure your songs are commercial. Listen to the current 'hits' to see how your song stacks up, because that's what you're competing with."

*DEBBIE SCHWARTZ MANAGEMENT, 7 E, 211 W. 56th St., New York NY 10019. (212)586-1514. Fax: (212)586-0139. President: Debbie Schwartz. Management firm. Estab. 1980. Represents individual artists, groups and songwriters from anywhere; currently handles 4 acts. Receives 15-20% commission. Reviews material for acts.
How to Contact: Call first and obtain permission to submit. Prefers cassette with 4 songs and lyric sheet. If seeking management, press kit should include demo tape and picture with bio and/or press. Does not return material. Reports in 3 weeks "with artist making the follow-up call."
Music: Mostly **rock, alternative/folk** and **pop.** Primarily works with singer/songwriters and bands with main songwriter lead vocalist. Current acts include Doug James (singer/songwriter, wrote "How Am I Supposed to Live Without You" with Michael Bolton), Robert Hazard (writer, wrote "Girls Just Wanna Have Fun") and Billy Robertson (recording artist).
Tips: "Submit demo tape by mail with follow-up 3-4 weeks after submission. Keep package simple."

*DICK SCOTT ENTERTAINMENT, 29th Floor, 888 7th Ave., New York NY 10019. (212)581-2500. Fax: (212)581-3596. President: Dick Scott. Management firm and record company. Estab. 1975. Represents individual artists and groups from anywhere; currently handles 7 acts. Reviews material for acts.
How to Contact: Call first and obtain permission to submit or submit demo tape by mail. Unsolicited submissions are OK. Prefers cassette. If seeking management, press kit should include tape, photo and bio. Does not return material.
Music: Mostly **pop, R&B** and **rap.** Current acts include Marky Mark, Teddy Riley and New Kids on the Block.

*WILLIAM SEIP MANAGEMENT, INC., 1615 Highland Rd., Kitchener, Ontario N2G 3W5 **Canada.** (519)741-1252. Fax: (519)742-3398. Manager: William Seip. Management firm. Estab. 1978. Represents individual artists, groups, songwriters from anywhere. Currently handles 2 acts. Receives 15% commission. Reviews material for acts.
How to Contact: Submit demo tape by mail. Unsolicited submissions are OK. Prefers cassette and lyric sheet. If seeking management, press kit should include tape and photo. Does not return material. Reports in 1 month.
Music: Mostly **rock** and **country.**
Tips: "Send in good material."

770 MUSIC INC., Box 773 Bondi Junction, New South Wales 2022 **Australia.** Phone: (612)302770. Fax: (612)365-7361. A&R Representative: Mr. Nun. Management firm, booking agency, music publisher (770 Music), record company (770 Music) and record producer (770 Productions). Estab. 1980. Represents individual artists, groups and songwriters; currently handles 44 acts. Receives 25% commission. Reviews material for acts.
How to Contact: Submit demo tape—unsolicited submissions are OK. Prefers CD (or VHS or Beta videocassette) with 10 songs and lyric or lead sheets. Does not return unsolicited material. Reports in 3 months.
Music: Mostly **triple crossover—country, rock** and **pop.** Works primarily with dance bands, showbands and individual artists and songwriters. Current acts include Andy and Kouros (soft rock), Little Sharky and the White Pointer Sisters (heavy metal), Havoc in the Ballroom (jazz/blues) and Stratosphere (top 100).

*SHEILS/CAMPBELL AND ASSOCIATES, 9772 Pavia, Burbank CA 91504. (818)767-6272. Vice President: Doug Campbell. Management firm. Estab. 1988. Represents individual artists and groups from anywhere. Currently handles 4 acts. Receives 15% commission. Reviews material for acts.
How to Contact: Submit demo tape by mail. Unsolicited submissions are OK. Prefers cassette. If seeking management, press kit should include cassette, concert dates. Does not return material. Reports in 2 weeks.
Music: Mostly **alternative, rock.** Works primarily with bands. Current acts include April's Motel Room (tribal alternative), Bungee Chords (funk alternative), Shane Thornton (twang rock).

MICKEY SHERMAN ARTIST MANAGEMENT & DEVELOPMENT, P.O. Box 20814, Oklahoma City OK 73156. (405)755-0315. President: Mickey Sherman. Management firm. Estab. 1974. Represents individual artists and songwriters; currently handles 6 acts. Receives 10-15% commission. Reviews material for acts.

How to Contact: Submit demo tape—unsolicited submissions are OK. Prefers cassette (or VHS videocassette of live performance, if available) with 3 songs and lyric sheet or lead sheet. If seeking management, include thumbnail biography/picture/press clippings and resume in press kit. "Keep videos simple. Use good lighting." Does not return unsolicited material. Reports in 3 months.
Music: Mostly **blues, pop** and **country**; also **R&B, rock** and **easy listening**. Works primarily with vocalists and showbands. Current acts include Janjo (singer/harmonica), Benny Kubiak (fiddler), Charley Shaw (vocalist) and Dale Langley (gospel/country singer).

*SHOE STRING BOOKING AGENCY, 696 The Queensway, Toronto Ontario M8Y 1K9 **Canada.** (416)255-5166. Contact: Armin Darmstadt. Management firm and booking agency. Represents local artists; currently handles 10-15 acts. Receives 15% commission. Reviews material for acts.
How to Contact: Write first and obtain permission to submit. Prefers cassette (or VHS videocassette if available) with 2-4 songs and lyric sheet. If seeking management, include 8×10 glossy, bio and personal letter outlining motivation. Does not return unsolicited material. Reports in 3 weeks.
Music: Mostly **dance, rock, R&B/pop** and **country/rock.** Works primarily with vocalists, bar bands and dance bands. Current acts include SAB (rock), Pulsations (dance) and Bitchin' (female top 40).

*SILVER CREEK PARTNERSHIP, P.O. Box 33, Pope Valley CA 94567. (707)965-2277. Managing Partner: Carla L. Forrest. Management firm and music publisher (Ohana Music Productions/ASCAP). Estab. 1988. Represents local and regional (Northern California) artists, groups and songwriters; currently handles 3 acts. Receives 10-12% commission.
How to Contact: Submit demo tape by mail. Unsolicited submissions are OK. Prefers cassette with 3-4 songs and lyric and lead sheet. SASE. Reports in 1 month.
Music: Mostly **country** and **country rock.** Works primarily with vocalists/musicians. Current acts include Wild Blue (country), Silver Creek (country) and Kimo Forrest (singer/songwriter).
Tips: "Demos should be uncluttered with vocals upfront. Strong melody and 'hook.' "

*BRAD SIMON ORGANIZATION, INC., 122 E. 57th St., New York NY 10022. (212)980-5920. Fax: (212)980-3193. President: Brad Simon. Represents individual artists and musical groups; currently handles 30 acts. Receives 20% commission.
How to Contact: Prefers cassette (or VHS videocassette if available) with minimum 3 songs. SASE. Reports in 2 months.
Music: **R&B/pop, children's music, jazz, progressive** and **top 40/pop (new A/C).** Works with artists and groups in contemporary rock, pop, jazz with strong commercial appeal and crossover potential, vocal and instrumental artists with strong performing and writing skills. Current acts include Tom Grant (pop/jazz), Nelson Rangell (jazz), Bob McGrath (children's), Frank Cappelli (children's), Sam Wright (children's) and Rory (children's).

THE RON SIMPSON MUSIC OFFICE, (formerly Music Management Associates), A Sound Column Company, Country Manor, 812 S. 890 East, Orem UT 84058. President: Ron Simpson. Estab. 1991. Management company. Represents individual artists, bands and songwriters. "Our specialty is helping our clients take the 'significant next step,' i.e. market focus, material selection, demo recordings, image/photos, contacting industry on artist's behalf, etc." Various fee structures include commission, project bid, hourly rate. Currently handles 2 acts. Receives 10-20% commission. Reviews material for acts.
How to Contact: Submit demo tape by mail—unsolicited submissions are OK. Should include cassette, VHS video (optional), photos. No returned materials or correspondence without SASE and sufficient postage. "No phone calls, please." Reports in 3 months.
Music: **Country, pop.** Current artists include Rob Honey, whose song "Norma Jean Riley" went #1 in 1992 as recorded by Diamond Rio on Arista, singer/songwriters Kim Simpson and Gary Voorhees.
Tips: "We're looking for one or two artists or writers. We'll know it when we hear it."

SINGERMANAGEMENT, INC., Suite 1403, 161 W. 54th St., New York NY 10019. (212)757-1217. President: Robert Singerman. Management consulting firm. Estab. 1982. Represents local, regional or international individual artists and groups; currently handles 8 acts. Receives hourly fee, plus 5% commission. Reviews material for acts.
How to Contact: Submit demo tape by mail—unsolicited submissions are OK. Prefers cassette (or VHS videocassette if available). Does not return unsolicited submissions. If seeking management consultation, include tape, lyric sheet and bio in press kit. Reports in 2 weeks.
Music: Current acts include Jamie Block (grunge folk), Black Rain (cyber punk) and John McDowell (world rock).

T. SKORMAN PRODUCTIONS, INC., Suite 250, 3660 Maguire Blvd., Orlando FL 32803. (407)895-3000. Fax: (407)895-1422. President: Ted Skorman. Management firm and booking agency. Estab. 1983. Represents groups; currently handles 40 acts. Receives 10-25% commission. Reviews material for acts.

How to Contact: "Phone for permission to send tape." Prefers cassette with 3 songs (or videocassette of no more than 15 minutes). "Live performance—no trick shots or editing tricks. We want to be able to view act as if we were there for a live show." SASE. Reports in 6 weeks.

Music: Top 40, techno, dance, MOR and pop. Works primarily with high-energy dance acts, recording acts, and top 40 bands. Current acts include Ravyn and The End (funk and roll), Tim Mikus (rock), Gibralter (R&B) and Closer to Rhythm (rave).

Tips: "We have many pop recording acts, and are looking for commercial material for their next albums."

SKYLINE MUSIC CORP., P.O. Box 31, Lancaster NH 03584. (608)586-7171. Fax: (603)586-7078. President: Bruce Houghton. Management firm (Skyline Management), booking agency (Skyline Music Agency), record company (Adventure Records) and music publisher (Campfire Music and Skyline Music). Estab. 1984. Currently handles 20 acts. Receives 10-20% commission. Reviews material for acts.

How to Contact: Submit demo tape by mail—unsolicited submissions are OK. Prefers cassette (or videocassette if available) with 3 songs. "Keep it short and sweet." If seeking management, include photo, bio and reviews. Does not return unsolicited material. Reports in 2 months.

Music: Mostly rock and folk; also pop. Works primarily with concert rock and folk attractions. Current acts include Foghat (rock), The Outlaws (rock), Rick Danko, New Riders of the Purple Sage, Leslie West (rock), Billy Davis (singer/songwriter) and the Boneheads (rock).

SKYSCRAPER ENTERTAINMENT, 113 S. 21st St., Philadelphia PA 19103. (215)851-0400. Contact: Alan Rubens. Management and consulting firm and music publisher (BMI/ASCAP). Estab. 1989. Represents local, regional or international individual artists, groups and songwriters; currently handles 6 acts. Receives 15-20% commission. Reviews material for acts.

How to Contact: Write or call first and obtain permission to submit. Prefers cassette with 2 or 3 songs and lyric sheet. If seeking management, include tape, picture and bio. SASE. Reports in 2-3 weeks.

Music: Mostly pop and dance, R&B and hip-hop. Works primarily with vocalists (solo or group). Current acts include Barrio Boyzz, Kwame, Pretty Poison and New Born.

SOPRO, INC., P.O. Box 227, Chicago Ridge IL 60415. (312)425-0174. Contact: Bud Monaco or Red Rose. Management firm and artist development firm. Represents artists and groups in the local region; currently handles 5 acts. Receives maximum 15-20% commission. Reviews material for acts.

How to Contact: Write first and obtain permission to submit. Prefers cassette with 2-3 songs and lead sheet. SASE. Reports in 1 month.

Music: Mostly rock, blues and top 40; also R&B, MOR and progressive rock. Works primarily with concert rock, blues and dance-oriented bands. Current acts include Don Griffin and The Griff Band (rock/blues), The Midwest Expedition (rock), Jody Noa & The Sho'Nuff Blues Band (blues), Joe Jammer & The Kissing Bandits (rock) and Tommy Biondo (rock).

SOUND '86 TALENT MANAGEMENT, P.O. Box 222, Black Hawk SD 57718. (605)343-1412. Management firm. Estab. 1974. Represents 5-10 artists and groups. Receives 20% commission. Reviews material for acts.

How to Contact: Submit demo tape by mail—unsolicited submissions are OK. Prefers cassette (or VHS videocassette-professional) with 3-8 songs and lyric sheet. SASE. Reports in 1 month.

Music: Rock (all types); also bluegrass, country, dance, easy listening and top 40/pop. Works primarily with single artists. Current artists include Danny Wayne (songwriter), Bold Lightning (band), Buckskin Lancaster (songwriter), Dr. K. and the Shantays (band) and Black Hills Country Band.

*SOUTHERN NIGHTS INC., 2707 No. Andrews Ave., Ft. Lauderdale FL 33311. (305)563-4000. President: Dick Barten. Management firm and booking agency. Estab. 1976. Represents local and regional individual artists and groups; currently handles 25 acts. Receives 15-20% commission. Reviews material for acts.

How to Contact: Call first and obtain permission to submit. Prefers cassette (or VHS videocassette if available) with minimum of 4 songs and lyric or lead sheets. If seeking management, include audio cassette or VHS (min. of 4 songs) and any additional promo available. "Keep videos simple—we are not interested in special effects on original material." Does not return unsolicited material. Reports in 3-4 weeks.

Music: Mostly top 40/pop and rock. Works primarily with current top 40, high energy show and dance groups. Current acts include F/X (top 40 rock show), US#1 (touring top 40/dance act), Donna Allen (soul), Flashpoint (top 40/rock) and Hotline (R&B/pop).

Tips: "Be prepared; send complete package of promo material and be ready to audition."

SP TALENT ASSOCIATES, P.O. Box 475184, Garland TX 75047. Talent Coordinator: Richard Park. Management firm and booking agency. Represents individual artists and groups; currently handles 7 acts. Receives negotiable commission. Reviews material for acts.
How to Contact: Prefers VHS videocassette with several songs. Also, send photo and bio with material submitted. SASE. Reports back as soon as possible.
Music: Mostly **rock, nostalgia rock, country**; also **specialty acts** and **folk/blues**. Works primarily with vocalists and self-contained groups. Current acts include Joe Hardin Brown (C&W), Rock It! (nostalgia) and Renewal (rock group).
Tips: "Appearance and professionalism are *musts!*"

SPIDER ENTERTAINMENT CO., Forever Endeavor Music, Inc., 5 Portsmouth Towne, Southfield MI 48075. (313)559-8230. President: Arnie Tencer. Vice President: Joel Zuckerman. Management firm. Estab. 1977. Represents artists, groups and songwriters; currently handles 1 act. Receives minimum 20% commission. Reviews material for acts.
How to Contact: Submit demo tape by mail—unsolicited submissions are OK. Prefers cassette (or videocassette if available) with 3 songs. If seeking management, include picture, songs and bio in press kit. SASE. Reports in 3 weeks.
Music: Mostly **rock and roll, contemporary pop**; also **top/40 pop**. Works primarily with "rock bands with good songs and great live shows." Current acts include Legal Tender (rock band) and The Romantics catalog.
Tips: Artists "must have commercially viable material."

SQUAD 16, P.O. Box 65, Wilbraham MA 01095. (413)599-1456. President: Tom Najemy. Booking agency. Estab. 1990. Represents Northeast individual artists, groups and songwriters; currently handles 7 acts. Receives 15-20% commission. Reviews material for acts.
How to Contact: Submit demo tape by mail—unsolicited submissions are OK. Prefers cassette with 4 songs. Does not return unsolicited material. Reports in 1 month.
Music: Mostly **contemporary, funk/hiphop** and **rock**; also **reggae, world beat** and **jazz & blues**; also **contemporary rock, funk**, or **dance bands** and **acoustic performers**. Current acts include Chuck (funk, hiphop, rap), Letters to Cleo (progressive rock band) and The Equalites (reggae).
Tips: "Do as much on your own so as to impress and put a buzz in the ears of those who can help you go further in the business."

*STATE OF THE ART ENTERTAINMENT, 50½ E. 64th St., New York NY 10021. (212)421-0221. Fax: (212)421-0225. Managing Director: Adam Schatz. Management firm. Estab. 1991. Represents individual artists, groups and songwriters from anywhere; currently handles 3 acts. Receives 15-20% commission. Reviews materials for acts.
How to Contact: Submit demo tape by mail. Unsolicited submissions are OK. Prefers cassette with 4 songs and lyric sheet. If seeking management, press kit should include demo tape, lyric sheets, bio, picture, letter describing ambitions and styles. Reports in 1-2 months.
Music: Mostly **rock, rap** and **pop**; also **reggae/dancehall**. Works primarily with songwriter/performers. Current acts include TOMER (pop songwriter), Glorified Chicken (rock ensemble) and David Mendelsohn (songwriter).
Tips: "Send us your best material; we are always interested in new talent. But please, don't harass us with phone calls to see if we received your demo. We will contact you."

STEELE MANAGEMENT, 7002 124th Terrace N., Largo FL 34643. (813)530-9291. President: Brett R. Steele. Management firm. Estab. 1987. Represents local, regional or international individual artists, groups and songwriters; currently handles 1 act. Receives 20% commission. Reviews material for acts.
How to Contact: Submit demo tape by mail—unsolicited submissions are OK. Prefers cassette (or VHS videocassette if available) with 5 songs and lyric sheet. If seeking management, include bio and photo. SASE. Reports in 1 month.
Music: Mostly **rock and pop**; also **dance pop** and **R&B**. Works primarily with rock bands, songwriters. Current acts include Roxx Gang (glam rock) and Kevin Steele (songwriter).
Tips: "Send only your best songs, make a *quality* recording and include a lyric sheet."

STEELE PRODUCTION, 400 E. Main St., Centerport NY 11787. (516)261-1859. President: Bob Wieser. Management firm and booking agency. Estab. 1982. Represents local, regional or international individual artists, groups and songwriters; currently handles 3 acts. Receives negotiable commission. Reviews material for acts.
How to Contact: Submit demo tape by mail—unsolicited submissions are OK. Prefers cassette (or VHS videocassette if available) with 2-5 songs and lyric sheet. Does not return unsolicited material. Reports in 2-3 weeks.

Music: Pop, rock and **R&B;** also **metal** and **thrash.** "Open to all types of music." Current acts include Diane O'Neill (songwriter), Dymyn (pop group) and Vision (metal band).
Tips: "Plan to work really hard and be ready to do what needs to be done."

BILL STEIN ASSOCIATES INC., P.O. Box 1516, Champaign IL 61824. Artists Manager: Bill Stein. Management firm and booking agency. Estab. 1983. Represents artists and groups; currently handles 6 acts. Receives 10-15% commission. Reviews material for acts.
How to Contact: Submit demo tape by mail—unsolicited submissions are OK. Prefers cassette (or Beta videocassette of live performance, if available) with 3-6 songs and promotional material. "Send complete promo package including video and audio tapes, pictures, references, song and equipment lists." SASE. Reports in 1 month.
Music: Mostly **pop rock, country** and **nostalgia;** also **dance, R&B, progressive** and **soul.** Works primarily with local, regional and national acts. Current acts include Gator Alley (country), Kick in the Pants (nostalgia), High Sierra (country rock), Greater Decatur R&B Revue (nostalgia), Pink Flamingoes (nostalgia), Keith Harden Band (blues rock), Griz England Band (country) and Ken Carlyle Band (country).

AL STRATEN ENTERPRISES, 10303 Hickory Valley, Ft. Wayne IN 46835. President: Allan Straten. Management firm, music publisher (Hickory Valley Music/ASCAP and Straten's Songs/BMI) and record company (Yellow Jacket Records). Represents individual artists and songwriters; currently handles 5 acts. Receives 10-20% commission. Reviews material for acts.
How to Contact: Submit demo tape by mail—unsolicited submissions are OK. Prefers cassette with a maximum of 4 songs and lyric sheet. If seeking management, include photos, video if possible, tape/CD and bio. SASE. Reports in 1 month.
Music: Mostly **traditional** and **contemporary country**—no rock. Works primarily with vocalists and writers. Current acts include April (country vocalist), Mike Vernaglia (country/MOR/singer/songwriter) and Sylvia Grogg (writer).

STRICTLEY BIZINESS MUSIC MANAGEMENT, 691½ N. 13th St., Philadelphia PA 19123. (215)765-1382. CEO: Justus. President: Corey Hicks. Management firm and booking agency. Estab. 1989. Represents local, regional and international individual artists, groups, songwriters and producers; currently handles 10 acts. Receives 20-25% commission. Reviews material for acts.
How to Contact: Submit demo tape by mail—unsolicited submissions are OK. Prefers cassette or VHS videocassette with 3-5 songs, lyric sheet and photo. Does not return unsolicited material. Reports in 1 month.
Music: Mostly **R&B, pop, rock** and **rap;** also **gospel.** Current acts include Ron Ali (vocalist) and Rich Tucker (producer/writer).

SUMMIT PRODUCTIONS/STELLAR PRODUCTIONS, Suite 301, 1115 N. 5th St., Reading PA 19601. (215)376-0577. Fax: (215)929-2436. President: Michael Gryctko. Management firm, booking agency and record company (Arctic Records). Estab. 1982. Represents local, regional and international individual artists and groups; currently handles 5 acts. Receives 15-20% commission. Reviews material for acts.
How to Contact: Submit demo tape by mail—unsolicited submissions are OK. Prefers cassette (or VHS videocassette if available) with 3 songs and lyric sheet. SASE. Reports in 1 month.
Music: Mostly **rock, pop/top 40** and **R&B.** Current acts include Bashful (rock), Ripper Jack (rock), Bast Rachet (modern rock), Savage Bliss (rock) and Chambermaids (touted as "the next big thing out of New Jersey" by *Live Wire Magazine*).
Tips: "Be persistent, devoted and believe in yourself."

*SUNRIZE BAND, P.O. Box 3322, Darwin, N.T. 0801 **Australia.** (61)89819561. Fax: (089)795931. Manager: Denise Officer Brewster. Management firm, ABC/Aust. Estab. 1990. Represents local and regional individual artists; currently handles 1 act.
How to Contact: Write or call first and obtain permission to submit. Prefers cassette (or VHS/PAL converted videocassette) with 2-3 songs and lyric sheet. SASE. Reports in 2 months.
Music: Mostly **rock, heavy rock** and **blues;** also **traditional.** Works primarily with singer/songwriters and bands. Current acts include Ben Pascoe.

Refer to the Category Index (at the back of this book) to find exactly which companies are interested in the type of music you write.

THE T.S.J. PRODUCTIONS INC., 422 Pierce St. NE, Minneapolis MN 55413-2514. (612)331-8580. Vice President/Artist Manager: Katherine J. Lange. Management firm and booking agency. Estab. 1974. Represents artists, groups and songwriters; currently handles 1 international act. Receives 20% commission. Reviews material for acts.
How to Contact: Submit demo tape by mail—unsolicited submissions are OK. Prefers "cassette tapes only for music audio (inquire before sending video), with 2-6 songs and lyric sheet." SASE. Reports in 3 weeks.
Music: Mostly **country rock, symphonic rock, easy listening** and **MOR;** also **blues, country, folk, jazz, progressive, R&B** and **top 40/pop.** Currently represents Thomas St. James (songwriter/vocalist).
Tips: "We will view anyone that fits into our areas of music. However, keep in mind we work only with national and international markets. We handle those starting out as well as professionals, but all must be marketed on a professional level, if we work with you."

TALENT ASSOCIATES OF WISCONSIN, INC., P.O. Box 588, Brookfield WI 53008. (414)786-8500. President: John A. Mangold. Booking agency. Estab. 1971. Represents local groups; currently handles 20 acts. Receives 15-20% commission. Reviews material for acts.
How to Contact: Submit demo tape by mail—unsolicited submissions are OK. Prefers cassette (or VHS videocassette if available) with 3 songs. Does not return unsolicited material. Reports in 1 month.
Music: Mostly **variety shows, rock/pop** and **dance;** also **R&B** and **jazz.** Works primarily with variety, rock and dance bands. Current acts include Mirage (top 40 dance band), Catch A Wave (Beach Boys show & more), Backbeat X, (alternative-pop-rock) and Hat Trick (Tex-Mex, zydeco, cajun).
Tips: "We're always looking for bands with high energy and a good stage presence, who enjoy what they're doing and radiate that through the audience, leaving all parties involved with a good feeling."

TAS MUSIC CO./DAVE TASSE ENTERTAINMENT, Route 2 Knollwood, Lake Geneva WI 53147-9731. Contact: David Tasse. Booking agency, record company and music publisher. Represents artists, groups and songwriters; currently handles 20 acts. Receives 10-20% commission. Reviews material for acts.
How to Contact: Submit demo tape by mail—unsolicited submissions are OK. Prefers cassette (or videocassette if available) with 2-4 songs and lyric sheet. Include performance videocassette if available. Does not return unsolicited material. Reports in 2 weeks.
Music: Mostly **pop** and **jazz;** also **dance, MOR, rock, soul** and **top 40.** Works primarily with show and dance bands. Current acts include Geneva Band (pop), Highlights (country) and Major Hamberlin (jazz).

TEXAS MUSIC MASTERS, 11231 State Hwy. 64 E., Tyler TX 75707-9587. (903)566-5653. Fax: (903)566-5750. Vice President: Lonnie Wright. Management firm, music publisher and record company (TMM, Juke Box, Quazar). Estab. 1970. Represents international individual artists, groups and songwriters; currently handles 3 acts. Reviews material for acts.
How to Contact: Prefers cassette with 3 songs. If seeking management, include short bio and photo with press kit. SASE. Reports in 3 weeks.
Music: Mostly **country, gospel** and **blues.** Works primarily with vocalists, writers and dance bands. Current acts include Aubrey T. Heird (singer), Ronny Redd (singer), Craig Robbins (singer), Ty Black (singer), Jim Needham and David Darst.

THEATER ARTS NETWORK/STEPHEN PRODUCTIONS, 15 Pleasant Dr., Lancaster PA 17602. (717)394-0970. Promotions: Stephanie Lynn Brubaker. Management firm and booking agency. Estab. 1977. Represents East Coast individual artists and groups; currently handles 5 acts. Receives 10-20% commission. Reviews material for acts.
How to Contact: Submit demo tape by mail—unsolicited submissions are OK. Prefers cassette (or VHS videocassette if available). Does not return unsolicited material. Reports in 2 weeks if interested.
Music: Mostly **comedy/music, Christian contemporary** and **rock.** Current acts include Stephen and Other Dummies (comedy/music/ventriloquism), Bryan Wilder (comedy) and The Following (Christian contemporary).
Tips: "Looking for coffee house acts only."

*TERRI TILTON MANAGEMENT, Suite 601, 7135 Hollywood, Los Angeles CA 90046. (213)851-8552. Fax: (213)850-1467. Personal Manager: Terri Tilton Stewart. Management firm. Estab. 1984. Represents individual artists and groups, from anywhere; currently handles 2 acts. Receives 20% commission. Reviews material for acts.
How to Contact: Write first and obtain permission to submit. Prefers cassette. SASE. Reports in 1-2 months.
Music: Mostly **jazz, pop** and **R&B.** Current acts include Jimmy Stewart (jazz) and Erik Essix (jazz).

A TOTAL ACTING EXPERIENCE, Suite 206, Dept. Rhymes-1, 14621 Titus St., Panorama City CA 91402. Agent: Dan A. Bellacicco. Talent agency. Estab. 1984. Represents vocalists, lyricists, composers and groups; currently handles 27-30 acts. Receives 10% commission. Reviews material for acts. Agency License: TA-0698.
How to Contact: Submit demo tape by mail—unsolicited submissions are OK. Prefers cassette (or VHS videocassette if available) with 3-5 songs and lyric or lead sheets. Please include a revealing "self talk" at the end of your tape. "Singers or groups who write their own material must submit a VHS videocassette with photo and resume." If seeking management, include VHS videotape, 5 8 × 10 photos, cover letter, professional typeset resume and business card in press kit. SASE. Reports in 3 months only if interested.
Music: Mostly **top 40/pop, jazz, blues, country, R&B, dance** and MOR; also "theme songs for new films, TV shows and special projects."
Tips: "No calls please. We will respond via your SASE. Your business skills must be strong. Please use a new tape and keep vocals up front. We welcome young, sincere talent who can give total commitment, and most important, *loyalty*, for a long-term relationship. We are seeking female vocalists (a la Streisand or Whitney Houston) who can write their own material, for a major label recording contract. Your song's story line must be as refreshing as the words you skillfully employ in preparing to build your well-balanced, orchestrated, climactic last note! Try to eliminate old, worn-out, dull, trite rhymes. A new way to write/compose or sing an old song/tune will qualify your originality and professional standing."

*TRANSATLANTIC MANAGEMENT, P.O. Box 2831, Tucson AZ 85702. (602)881-5880. Owner: English Cathy. Management firm. Estab. 1979. Represents individual artists, groups and songwriters from anywhere; currently handles 19 acts. Receives 15-20% commission. Reviews material for acts.
How to Contact: Write or call first and obtain permission to submit. Prefers cassette (or VHS videocassette) with 3-4 songs and lyric sheet. If seeking management, press kit should include tape/CD/bio. Does not return material. Reports in 3 weeks.
Music: Mostly **all types** from **New Age to country to hard rock.** Current acts include Vince Black (dance), Sunyata (worldbeat) and Big Bang Rodeo (pop).
Tips: "Call or write just to see if we are compatible."

*TRIAGE INTERNATIONAL, 1A, 418½ E. 9th St., New York NY 10009. (212)353-2002. Contact: Bob or Marc. Management firm. Estab. 1990. Represents individual artists, groups and labels from anywhere; currently handles 5 acts. Receives various % commission. Reviews material for acts.
How to Contact: Submit demo tape by mail. Unsolicited submissions are OK. "Don't call." Prefers cassette. If seeking management, press kit should include just music. "If you want your material returned, include SASE." Reports in 2 weeks.
Music: Mostly **alternative-progressive** and **indie rock.** Works primarily with alternative bands. Current acts include Thumper (indie rock), Funeral Party (dark pop) and Earwig (esoteric pop).

THE TRINITY STUDIO, P.O. Box 1417, Corpus Christi TX 78403. (512)880-9268. Owner: Jim Wilken. Management firm, booking agency, record company (TC Records) and recording studio. Estab. 1988. Represents individual artists, songwriters and dancers from Texas; currently handles 4 acts. Receives 5-15% commission. Reviews material for acts.
How to Contact: Submit demo tape by mail—unsolicited submissions are OK. Prefers cassette (or VHS videocassette if available). SASE. Reports in 2 weeks.
Music: Mostly **Christian, country** and A/C; also **pop, gospel** and **rock.** Works primarily with vocalists, dancers and songwriters. Current acts include Leah (singer), Merrill Lane (singer/songwriter) and Lofton Kline (singer/songwriter).
Tips: "You must maintain a positive attitude about your career. Have faith in your work and don't get discouraged—keep at it."

*TRYCLOPS LTD., 115 New Barn Lane, Cheltenham, Glouchestershire GL52 3LQ **England**. Phone: 0242-234045. Director: Ian Beard. Booking agency and concert promotional company. "We do not manage acts." Estab. 1971. Represents individual artists and groups; currently handles 25 acts on a non-exclusive basis. Receives 10-15% commission.
How to Contact: Write or call first and obtain permission to submit. Prefers cassette (or VHS videocassette of live performance). Does not return unsolicited material. Reports in 1-2 months if interested.
Music: Mostly **rock, contemporary folk, pop;** also **R&B** and **jazz.** Works with very wide range of artists/acts from singer/songwriters to trios and jazz bands. No artists solely represented. Current acts include singer/songwriters Johnny Coppin, Steve Ashley and Dave Cartwright.

TSMB PRODUCTIONS, P.O. Box 1388, Dover DE 19903. (302)734-2511. Chief Executive Officer: Terry Tombosi. Management firm, booking agent, music publisher (BMI) and record company (TSMB Records). Estab. 1983. Represents local, regional or international individual artists, groups and song-

writers; currently handles 20 acts. Receives 10-15% commission. Reviews material for acts.
How to Contact: Submit demo tape by mail—unsolicited submissions are OK. Prefers cassette (or VHS videocassette if available) with 3 songs and lyric or lead sheets. SASE. Reports in 6 weeks.
Music: Mostly **rock, blues** and **country**; also **Xmas songs**. Works primarily with show bands and bands with 3 year longevity. Current acts include The Hubcaps, The Admirals and The Cutters (all show groups).
Tips: "Follow directions. Be completely prepared. The standard things like demos, pictures, set lists, bios need to be ready but often they aren't."

UMBRELLA ARTISTS MANAGEMENT, INC., P.O. Box 8385, 2612 Erie Ave., Cincinnati OH 45208. (513)871-1500. Fax: (513)871-1510. President: Stan Hertzman. Management firm. Represents artists, groups and songwriters; currently handles 7 acts.
How to Contact: Submit demo tape by mail—unsolicited submissions are OK. Prefers cassette with 3 songs and lyric sheet. SASE. If seeking management, press kit should include a short bio, reviews, photo and cassette. Reports in 2 months.
Music: **Progressive, rock** and **top 40/pop.** Works with contemporary/progressive pop/rock artists and writers. Current acts include psychodots (modern band), Prizoner (rock band), America Smith (modern band), The Groovy Cools (modern band), Hawkins Brothers (modern band), Jeffrey Lee Powers (country) and Adrian Belew (artist/producer/songwriter/arranger whose credits include Frank Zappa, David Bowie, Talking Heads, Tom Tom Club, King Crimson, Cyndi Lauper, Laurie Anderson, Paul Simon, The Bears and Mike Oldfield).

*UNIVERSAL MUSIC MARKETING, P.O. Box 2297, Universal City TX 78148. (210)653-3989. Contact: Frank Willson. Management firm, booking agency, music publisher, record producer. Estab. 1987. Represents individual artists, groups from anywhere. Currently handles 13 acts. Receives 15% commission. Reviews material for acts.
How to Contact: Submit demo tape by mail—unsolicited submissions are OK. Prefers cassette (or ¾" videocassette) with 3 songs and lyric sheet. If seeking management, include tape, bio, photo, background. SASE. Reports in 3 weeks.
Music: Mostly **country, light rock**; also **blues.** Works primarily with vocalists, singer/songwriters and bands. Current acts include Paradise Canyon, Candee Land and Bobby Lloyd.

*VALEX TALENT AGENCY, and Pyramid Sound Records, P.O. Box 241, Ithaca NY 14851. (607)273-3931. Publishing President: John Perialas. Booking Agent: Fred Johnson. Management firm, booking agency and music publisher. Estab. 1959. Represents artists, groups and songwriters in Northeast US; currently handles 5-10 acts. Receives 15% commission. Reviews material for acts.
How to Contact: Submit demo tape by mail—unsolicited submissions are OK. Prefers 7½ ips reel-to-reel or cassette with 3-6 songs and lead sheet. SASE. Reports in 1 month. "Songwriters please send cassettes or 7½ ips reel-to-reel in care of John Perialas, Copper John Music. After sending material allow appropriate time for material to be reviewed (3-4 weeks); then follow with call."
Music: Mostly **top 40, rock** and **new wave**; also **country pop, dance, easy listening, MOR, R&B, rock,** and **pop.** Works with vocalists, show, dance and bar bands. Current acts include Atlas (contemporary funk/rock), Backtalk (top 40/pop), Bernie Milton (soul/R&B), and Kinetics (new wave).
Tips: "Be sincere, package your materials professionally."

HANS VAN POL MANAGEMENT, P.O. Box 9010, Amsterdam HOL 1006AA **Netherlands.** Phone: (31)20610-8281. Fax: (31)20610-6941. Managing Director: Hans Van Pol. Management firm and booking agency. Estab. 1984. Represents regional (Holland/Belgium) individual artists and groups; currently handles 6 acts. Receives 20-30% commission. Reviews material for acts.
How to Contact: Submit demo tape by mail—unsolicited submissions are OK. Prefers cassette or VHS videocassette with 3 songs and lyric sheets. If seeking management, include demo, possible video (VHS/PAL), bio, photo, release information. SASE. Reports in 1 month.
Music: Mostly **dance: rap/swing beat/hip house/R&B/soul/c.a.r.** Current acts include Tony Scott (dance/rap), Zhype (swingbeat singer), and Twenty 4 Seven (house).

*RICHARD VARRASSO MANAGEMENT, P.O. Box 387, Fremont CA 94537. (510)792-8910. Fax: (510)792-0891. President: Richard Varrasso. Management firm. Estab. 1976. Represents individual artists, groups and songwriters from anywhere; currently handles 12 acts. Receives 20% commission. Reviews material for acts.
How to Contact: Submit demo tape by mail. Unsolicited submissions are OK. Prefers cassette. Does not return material. Reports in 3 months.
Music: Mostly **rock.** Works primarily with concert headliners and singers. Current acts include Greg Kihn, Jimmy Lyon, Chaz Ross, Rattleshake and Susan Steele.

*VELVETT RECORDING COMPANY, 517 W. 57th St., Los Angeles CA 90037. (213)753-7893. Manager: Aaron Johnson. Management firm and record company. Represents artists, groups and songwriters; currently handles 5 acts. Reviews material for acts.
How to Contact: Prefers cassette with 2-3 songs and lead sheet. SASE.
Music: Mostly **blues** and **gospel**; also **church/religious, R&B, rock, soul** and **top 40/pop**. Works primarily with show and dance bands and vocalists. Current acts include Arlene Bell (soul/top 40/pop artist) and Chick Willis (blues artist).

VICTORY ARTISTS, 1054 Conifer Ln., Petaluma CA 94954. (707)762-4858. Contact: Gary Daniel. Management firm, music publisher (ASCAP) and record company (Victory Label/Bay City). Estab. 1985. Represents Northern California individual artists and groups; currently handles 2 acts. Receives 15% commission. Reviews material for acts.
How to Contact: Write first and obtain permission to submit. Prefers cassette (or VHS videocassette if available) with 3 songs and lyric sheets. If seeking management, include photo, tape (video preferred), cover letter. Does not return unsolicited material. Reports in 2 months.
Music: Mostly **rock, pop** and **country**. Works primarily with female front with band. Current acts include Ciroe (rock/alternative), Shelly T (rock singer), and Mark Allan (songwriter).
Tips: "Don't hype us. Just give us your best examples."

*VISION MANAGEMENT, 7958 Beverly Blvd., Los Angeles CA 90048. (213)658-8744. Owner/Artist Manager: Shelly Heber. Management firm. Represents local, regional or international individual artists and groups; currently handles 4 acts.
How to Contact: Write or call first and obtain permission to submit. Prefers cassette with 3 songs maximum. If seeking management, include music, press and bio. SASE. Reports in 6 weeks.
Music: Current acts include Dave Koz (sax), Jeff Lorber (keyboardist), Dave Alvin (guitarist/songwriter/vocalist) and Marilyn Scott (vocalist/songwriter).
Tips: "Present no more than three songs in as professional manner as possible."

VOKES BOOKING AGENCY, P.O. Box 12, New Kensington PA 15068-0012. (412)335-2775. President: Howard Vokes. Represents individual traditional country and bluegrass artists. Books name acts in on special occasions. For special occasions books nationally known acts from Grand Ole Op'ry, Jamboree U.S.A., Appalachian Jubliee, etc. Receives 10-20% commission.
How to Contact: New artists send 45 rpm record, cassette, LP or CD. Reports back within a week.
Music: Traditional **country, bluegrass, old time** and **gospel**; definitely no rock or country rock. Current acts include Howard Vokes & His Country Boys (country) and Mel Anderson.
Tips: "We work mostly with traditional country bands and bluegrass groups that play various bars, hotels, clubs, high schools, malls, fairs, lounges, or fundraising projects. We work at times with other booking agencies in bringing acts in for special occasions. Also we work directly with well-known and newer country, bluegrass and country gospel acts not only to possibly get them bookings in our area, but in other states as well. We also help 'certain artists' get bookings in the overseas market-place."

*WARREN PRO-MOTIONS, P.O. Box 120, Pinehurst TX 77362. (713)955-1282. Fax: (713)351-8415. President: Bill Warren. Management firm and booking agency. Estab. 1989. Represents local and regional (South) individual artists and groups; currently handles 3 acts. Receives 10-15% commission. Reviews material for acts.
How to Contact: Submit demo tape by mail. Unsolicited submissions are OK. Prefers cassette (or VHS videocassette) with 5 songs and lyric sheet. If seeking management, press kit should include short bio, photo. SASE. Reports in 1 month.
Music: Mostly **rock, alternative rock** and **R&B**; also **country**. Works primarily with vocalists and bands. Current acts include Aesthesia (rock) and Johnny Reverb Band (R&B).
Tips: "Be professional; take the time to make it right."

*WAVE DIGITAL/GRIF MUSIK/PRODUCER ERIC "GRIFFY" GREIF-SOLVBJERG, (formerly Edge Entertainment, Inc./Producer Eric "Griffy" Greif), 4262 Grand Ave., Gurnee IL 60031. (708)336-7702, (708)336-7754. Fax: (708)336-8477. Owners: Michael Witte, Alan Pangelman, Eric Greif-Solvbjerg. Management firm, 24-track digital recording studio, record producer and music publisher (Griffy Guy Music/BMI). Estab. 1987. Represents local, regional (Midwest) and international individual artists and groups. "Will work with management as recording producer and creative direction. Have state-of-the-art recording facilities." Commission negotiable.
How to Contact: Submit demo tape by mail. Unsolicited submissions are OK. Prefers cassette (or VHS videocassette if available) with 3-5 songs and lyric sheet. Does not return unsolicited material. Reports in 2 months only if interested.
Music: Mostly **heavy metal, commercial rock** and **alternative new music**; also **thrash metal, death metal** and **speed metal**. "We mostly work with groups, but will produce demos of individual performers."

Tips: "We will consider working with talented acts with great material, either as representation, or if they are seeking a producer to channel their energy and abilities. We specialize in competitive, cutting edge demo production as well as representation of the finished product to independent and major labels if requested. Remember that it is the songs that perk the interest—if they aren't happening, you're not happening as an artist."

WESTWOOD ENTERTAINMENT GROUP, 167 Main St., Metuchen NJ 08840. (908)548-6700. Fax: (908)548-6748. President: Victor Kaplij. VP of Artist Development/A&R: Kevin McCabe. Artist management agency (Westunes Music/ASCAP). Estab. 1985. Represents regional artists and groups; currently handles 3 acts. Receives 15% commission. Reviews material for acts.
How to Contact: Write first and obtain permission to submit. Prefers cassette with 3 songs, lyric sheet, bio and photo. SASE. Reports in 6 weeks.
Music: Mostly **rock**; also **pop**. Works primarily with singer/songwriters, show bands and rock groups. Current acts include Kevin McCabe (rock), Ground Zero (rock) and Tradia (rock).
Tips: "Present a professional promotional/press package with 3 song limit."

SHANE WILDER ARTISTS' MANAGEMENT, P.O. Box 3503, Hollywood CA 90078. (818)508-1433. President: Shane Wilder. Management firm, music publisher (Shane Wilder Music/BMI) and record producer (Shane Wilder Productions). Represents artists and groups; currently handles 10-12 acts. Receives 15% commission. Reviews material for acts.
How to Contact: Submit demo tape by mail—unsolicited submissions are OK. Prefers cassette (or videocassette of performance if available) with 4-10 songs and lyric sheet. If seeking management, include good 8 × 10 glossy prints, resume and press releases in press kit. SASE. Reports in 1 month.
Music: **Country**. Works primarily with single artists and groups. Current acts include Inez Polizzi, Billy O'Hara and Melanie Ray (songwriters).
Tips: "Make sure your work is highly commercial. We are looking for strong female country songs for major artists. Material should be available for publishing with Shane Wilder Music/BMI. We do not accept any songs for publishing with a reversion clause."

RICHARD WOOD ARTIST MANAGEMENT, 69 N. Randall Ave., Staten Island NY 10301. (718)981-0641. Contact: Richard Wood. Management firm. Estab. 1974. Represents musical groups; currently handles 3 acts. Receives 20% commission. Reviews material for acts.
How to Contact: Submit demo tape—unsolicited submissions are OK. Prefers cassette and lead sheet. SASE. Reports in 1 month.
Music: Mostly **dance, R&B** and **top 40/pop**; also **MOR**. Works primarily with "high energy" show bands, bar bands and dance bands. Current acts include Positive Vibe (R&B) and Anonymous (R&B band).
Tips: "Try to be on the cutting edge of whatever style you are writing in. Be original and commercial. It can be done."

WORLD WIDE MANAGEMENT, P.O. Box 599, Yorktown Heights NY 10598. (914)245-1156. Director: Steve Rosenfeld. Management firm and music publisher (Neighborhood Music/ASCAP). Estab. 1971. Represents artists, groups, songwriters and actors; currently handles 4 acts. Receives 20% commission. Reviews material for acts.
How to Contact: Write or call first and obtain permission to submit or to arrange personal interview. Prefers cassette (or videocassette of performance) with 3-4 songs. SASE. Reports in 2 months.
Music: Mostly **contemporary pop, folk, folk/rock** and **New Age**; also **A/C, rock, jazz, bluegrass, blues, country** and **R&B**. Works primarily with self-contained bands and vocalists. Current acts include Bill Popp & The Tapes, M,M,M&S, Syncope, and Small Things Big.

*WOW MANAGEMENT P/L, P.O. Box 61, Darlinghurst NSW **Australia** 2010. (02)332-3522. Fax:(02)332-3424. Director: Neil Wiles. Management firm. Estab. 1988. Represents local individual artists, groups, songwriters and producers; currently handles 3 acts. Reviews material for acts.
How to Contact: Submit demo tape by mail. Unsolicited submissions are OK. Prefers cassette (or VHS videocassette) with 4 songs and lyric sheet. If seeking management, press kit should include photo/bio/tape/video/press clippings. "Young acts preferred unless established." Does not return material. Reports in 1 month.
Music: Mostly **rock, rock/R&B** and **pop/dance**; also **ballads**. Works primarily with vocalists, singer/songwriters, bands. Current acts include Boom Crash Opera (multi-platinum rock band), The Sharp (pop/rock/funk), sub rosa (70s meets 90s rock n' roll) and Richard Pleasance (singer/songwriter/producer).
Tips: "Be prolific and work hard. The 90s are about survival."

WYATT MANAGEMENT WORLDWIDE, INC., 10797 Onyx Circle, Fountain Valley CA 92708. (714)839-7700; Fax: (714)775-4300. President: Warren Wyatt. Management firm. Estab. 1976. Represents regional and international individual artists, groups and songwriters; currently handles 3 acts. Receives 10-20% commission. Reviews material for acts.
How to Contact: Submit demo tape by mail—unsolicited submissions are OK. Prefers cassette (or ½" VHS videocassette) with 2-10 songs and lyric sheet. If seeking management, include band biography, photos, video, members' history, press and demo reviews in press kit. Does not return unsolicited material. Reports in 4 weeks.
Music: Mostly **rock, pop** and **R&B**; also **heavy metal, hard rock** and **top 40**. Works primarily with pop/rock groups. Current acts include Crimson Glory (hard rock), Saigon Kick (alternative/hard rock), and Zerop (pop rock).
Tips: "Always submit new songs/material, even if you have sent material that was previously rejected; the music biz is always changing."

Y-NOT PRODUCTIONS, P.O. Box 902, Mill Valley CA 94942. (415)898-0027. Administrative Asst.: Lane Lombardo. Management firm and music publisher (Lindy Lane Music/BMI). Estab. 1989. Represents West Coast-USA individual artists, groups and songwriters; currently handles 6 acts. Receives 10-20% commission. Reviews material for acts.
How to Contact: Submit demo tape by mail—unsolicited submissions are OK. Prefers cassette (or VHS videocassette if available) with 3 songs. SASE. Reports in 1 month.
Music: Mostly **contemporary jazz, pop** and **R&B/rock**. Works primarily with instrumental groups/vocalists. Current acts include Tony Saunders (bassist/songwriter), Paradize (contemporary jazz) and Jennifer Youngdahl (pop songwriter).

ZOOM EXPRESS, (formerly Bob Hinkle Management), Suite 1104, 568 Broadway, New York NY 10021. (212)274-0200; Fax: (212)274-9776. President: Bob Hinkle. Management firm. Founded in May 1992, Zoom Express is a co-venture of BMG Kidz, a division of the Bertelsmann Music Group (BMG). Zoom Express develops, produces and markets musical artists, video, events, projects and product lines for children and families. Currently handles 7+ artists.
How to Contact: Call for permission prior to submitting material. Once approved, send an audio cassette with 2-4 songs and lyric sheet. Videocassette should accompany audio where possible.
Music: Children's. Current roster includes: Mary-Kate & Ashley Olsen (The Olsen Twins), Jim Henson Records, Where In The World Is Carmen Sandiego?, Glenn Bennett, Karan and the Musical Medicine Show, Lois LaFond and the Rockadiles, and Fred Miller.

Managers and Booking Agents/'93-'94 Changes

The following markets appeared in the 1993 edition of *Songwriter's Market* but are absent from the 1994 edition. Most of these companies failed to respond to our request for an update of their listing for a variety of reasons. For example, they may have gone out of business or they may have requested deletion from the 1994 edition because they are backlogged with material. If we know the specific reason, it appears within parentheses.

A•C•E Talent Management
Academy Award Entertainment
Adams & Green Entertainment
Adelaide Rock Exchange
AKO Productions
All Star Talent & Promotions
All Star Talent Agency
American Artist, Inc.
David Anthony Promotions
Aristomedia (requested deletion)
The Artist Group
Back Door Management
Big House Management Pty Ltd.
T.J. Booker Ltd.
BSC Productions, Inc. (affiliate of Black Stallion Country

Productions, Inc.)
Dott Burns Talent Agency
Ernie Cash Enterprises
Centerfield Productions
Class Acts
Cliffside Music Inc.
Cocos Island Records, Inc.
Cole Classic Management
Common Sense Management, Ltd.
Mike Constantia Entertainment
Cover Agency
Crawfish Productions
Criss-Cross Industries
The Current Entertainment Corporation
Current Records/Management
D.A.G. Promotions Ltd.
D Management Company

D.S.M. Producers Inc.
Darkhorse Entertainment
DAS Communications, Ltd.
Bill Detko Management
DSI Theatrical Productions
Earth Tracks Artists Agency
Steve Eck Entertainment
Ellipse Personal Management
Entertainment Management Enterprises
Entertainment Works
Evans-Schulman Productions, Inc.
Far West Entertainment, Inc.
Fireball Management
Five Star Entertainment
The Flying Dutchman
Folsom Management
William Ford Personal Management Inc.

Franklyn Agency (charges to
   review)
Freefall Talent Group
Glo Gem Productions, Inc.
Michael Godin Management,
   Inc.
Golden City International
Geoffrey Hansen Enterprises,
   Ltd.
Hitch-A-Ride Management
   (requested deletion)
Kathy Howard Management
Impresario Limited
Inerje Productions, Records,
   Management
Java Management
Johns & Associates
(KAM) Executive Records
Key Artist Management & En-
   tertainment Consultants
Howard King Agency, Inc.
S.V. Kyles & Associates
Landmark Direction Company,
   Inc.
David Lefkowitz Management
   (no longer handling song-
   writers)
Lemon Square Music
Long Distance Entertainment
   Productions Inc.
Loose Leaf Records
Ron Luciano Music Co.
   (charges to review)
McFadden Artist Corporation
   (requested deletion)
Majestic Productions
MC Promotions & Public Rela-
   tions
Meier Talent Agency
M-80 Management Co.
Mid-East Entertainment Inc.
The Gilbert Miller Agency, Inc.

MKM Music Productions Ltd.
   (not accepting submissions)
Morse Entertainment Group,
   Inc.
Mozart Midnight Productions
   (affiliate of Kaufman Hill
   Management)
Music, Marketing & Promo-
   tions, Inc.
N&M Entertainment Agency
Neko Entertainment & Music
   Management Co.
Nelson Management
Next Millennium, Ltd.
N2D
On Tour Productions
Onstage Management Group
Dee O'Reilly Management,
   Ltd.
Original Projects Unlimited,
   Inc.
Overland Productions
Richard A. Painter & Associ-
   ates
Paquin Entertainment Group
Performers of the World
Personified Management
Paul Peterson Creative Man-
   agement
Phil's Entertainment Agency
   Limited
Premier Artists
Premier Artists Services, Inc.
Process Talent Management
   (affiliate of Country Star
   Attractions)
R.V.O. (Robert Verkaik Orga-
   nization)
The Rainbow Collection, Ltd.
Raw Ltd.
Richard Reiter Productions
Reneri International Produc

tions
Joey Ricca, Jr.'s Entertainment
   Agency
Rich + Famous Management
   Inc.
Sa'mall Management (affiliate
   of MCI Music Group)
Samuel Roggers & Assoc.
Jeffrey Ross Music
Sandcastle Productions
Select Artists Associates
Shapiro & Company, C.P.A.
Phill Shute Management Pty.
   Ltd. (charges to review)
Sidartha Enterprises, Ltd.
Simmons Management Co.
Dan Smith Agency
Southern Concerts
Spirit Sound Co.
Star Artist Management Inc.
Starcrest Productions, Inc.
The Starsound Entertainment
   Group
Starstruck Productions
Ronald Stein Productions
Successful Productions
Tabitha Music
3L Productions
Timeless Productions
Trend Records
Triangle Talent, Inc.
United Entertainment
Van Dyke Enterprises
Ben Wages Agency
Walker Management
Wise Artist Management
Wise Entertainment, Inc.
Zane Management, Inc.
Zar Management
Zee Talent Agency

Advertising, AV and Commercial Music Firms

The music used in commercial and audiovisual presentations is secondary to the picture (for TV, film or video) or the message being conveyed. Commercial music must enhance the product. It must get the consumer's attention, move him in some way and, finally, motivate him—all without overpowering the message or product it accompanies. Songwriters in this area are usually strong composers, arrangers and, sometimes, producers.

More than any other market listed in this book, the commercial music market expects a composer to have made an investment in his material before beginning to submit. When dealing with commercial music firms, especially audiovisual firms and music libraries, high quality production is very important. Your demo may be kept on file at one of these companies and used or sold as you sent it. Also, a list of your credits should be part of your submission to give the company an idea of your experience in this field. In general, it's important to be as professional as you can in your submissions to these markets. Fully-produced demo tapes and complete press kits will get your product recognized and heard.

Commercial music and jingle writing can be a lucrative field for the composer/songwriter who is energetic, has a gift for strong hook melodies, and is able to write in many different styles. The problem is, there are many writers and few jobs—it's a very competitive field.

Advertising agencies

Ad agencies work on assignment as their clients' needs arise. They work closely with their clients on radio and TV broadcast campaigns. Through consultation and input from the creative staff, ad agencies seek jingles and music to stimulate the consumer to identify with a product or service.

When contacting ad agencies, keep in mind they are searching for music that can capture and then hold an audience's attention. Most jingles are quick, with a strong, memorable hook that the listener will easily identify with. Remember, though, that when an agency is listening to a demo, they are not necessarily looking for a finished product so much as for an indication of creativity and diversity. Most composers put together a reel of excerpts of work from previous projects, or short pieces of music which show they can write in a variety of styles.

Audiovisual firms

Audiovisual firms create a variety of products. Their services may range from creating film and video shows for sales meetings (and other corporate gatherings) and educational markets, to making motion pictures and TV shows. With the increase of home video use, how-to videos are a big market now for audiovisual firms, as are spoken word educational videos.

Like advertising firms, AV firms look for versatile, well-rounded songwriters. The key to submitting demos to these firms is to demonstrate your versatility in writing specialized background music and themes. Listings for companies will tell what facet(s) of the audiovisual field they are involved in and what types of clients they serve.

Commercial music houses and music libraries

Commercial music houses are companies which are contracted (either by an advertising agency or the advertiser himself) to compose custom jingles. Since they are neither an ad agency or an audiovisual firm, their main concern is music. And they use a lot of it—some composed by inhouse songwriters and some contributed by outside writers.

Music libraries are a bit different in that their music is not custom composed for a specific client. They provide a collection of instrumental music in many different styles that, for an annual fee or on a per use basis, the customer can use however he chooses (most often in audiovisual and multi-media applications).

When searching for a commercial music house or music library, they will be indicated in the listings as such by **bold** typeface.

The commercial music market is similar to most other businesses in one aspect, experience is important. Keep in mind that until you develop a list of credits, pay for your work may not be high. Also, don't pass up work opportunities if the job is non- or low paying. Remember, these assignments will help make contacts, add to your experience and improve your marketability.

Most of the companies listed in this section pay by the job, but there may be some situations where the company asks you to sign a contract that will specify royalty payments. If this happens, be sure you research the contract thoroughly, and that you know exactly what is expected of you and how much you'll be paid.

Sometimes, depending upon the particular job and the company, a composer/songwriter will be asked to sell one-time rights or all rights. One time rights entail using your material for one presentation only. All rights means that the buyer can use your work any way he chooses for as long as he likes. Again, be sure you know exactly what you're giving up, and how the company may use your music in the future.

Commercial firms look for high quality demos

For a songwriter interested in writing music for the commercial market, it's important to remember that the quality of the production is as important as the quality of the compositions. "As I review demos," says Jonathan L. Barkan, executive producer at Communications for Learning, "my major concerns are a distinctive, 'non-commercial' style, excellent musicianship and the highest technical recording quality." Communications for Learning, an Arlington, Massachusetts based audiovisual firm, works with clients from multi-national corporations, large and small nonprofits and the government.

Jonathan L. Barkan

photo by Brian Smith

Barkan is open to receiving unsolicited submissions and emphasizes that first impressions are important. "A few seconds of playback are all that's needed for an initial judgment," he says. "I'm specifically attracted to colorful, visual, emotional pieces." In the past few years, Barkan has found several successful works that were sent to him by *Songwriter's Market* readers. "I can cite at least seven major productions that have incorporated music discovered through *Songwriter's Market*," he says. "Music that we'd never have found if not for the service. Quite a few of our soundtracks include theme or background music discovered on these unsolicited submissions."

Barkan's advice to commercial music writers on sending submissions is quite specific. "Send hi-bias cassette recordings or CDs usable for mastering as is, and include a log with the tape sleeve itself rather than a separate sheet," he advises. "Follow-up recordings are welcomed. Budget flexibility is always attractive. One musician with whom we work frequently describes our fees as 'free money'—he loves our calls because it's cash in his pocket for existing music."

'Existing music' is just what commercial music firms are looking for. Your material must be able to stand on its own, since most companies aren't interested in redoing your work—they want to use it as is. "We're less likely to commission original music than we are to negotiate use rights for existing music," Barkan explains.

As in any other segment of the industry, the writer must continually educate himself about the workings of the business. "Listen—observe—criticize," says Barkan. "Watch TV documentaries, review commercial libraries. Feature film scores are of themselves an education. Don't be afraid to volunteer for experience and exposure. Be persistent—and be absolutely certain of the quality of your submissions."

Dedication and love of your work are vital to success in the commercial music market. "Creative services are among the most difficult services to sell," Barkan concludes. "You've got to love what you're doing and be driven beyond any doubts."

For additional names and addresses of advertising agencies who may use jingles and/or commercial music, refer to the *Standard Directory of Advertising Agencies* (National Register Publishing Co.). For a list of audiovisual firms, check out the latest edition of *Audiovisual Marketplace* (published by R.R. Bowker).

THE AD AGENCY, Box 2316, Sausalito CA 94965. Creative Director: Michael Carden. Advertising agency and **jingle/commercial music production house**. Clients include business, industry and retail. Estab. 1971. Uses the services of music houses, independent songwriter/composers and lyricists for jingles for public relations/promotions/publicity and commercials for radio and TV. Commissions 20 composers and 15 lyricists/year. Pays by the job.
How to Contact: Query with resume of credits. Prefers cassette with 5-8 songs and lyric sheet. SASE, but prefers to keep materials on file. Reports in 2 weeks.
Music: Uses variety of musical styles for commercials, promotion, TV, video presentations.
Tips: "Our clients and our needs change frequently."

THE AD TEAM, 15251 NE 18th Ave., N. Miami Beach FL 33162. (305)949-8326. Vice President: Zevin Auerbach. Advertising agency. Clients include automobile dealerships, radio stations, TV stations, retail. Seeking background music for commercials and jingles. Uses the services of independent songwriters for jingles for commercials. Commissions 4-6 songwriters. Pays by the job.
How to Contact: Submit demo tape of previously aired work. Prefers cassette. SASE.
Music: Uses all styles of music for all kinds of assignments. Most assignments include writing jingles for radio and television campaigns.

ADVANCE ADVERTISING AGENCY, 606 E. Belmont, Fresno CA 93701. (209)445-0383. Manager: Martin Nissen. Advertising agency. Clients include manufacturers, retailers, marketers, financial institutions. Estab. 1950. Uses the services of music houses and lyricists for commercials for radio and TV. Pays "by prior agreement." Buys all rights.
How to Contact: Submit demo tape. Prefers cassette with any number of songs. SASE, but prefers to keep materials on file. Include business card. Reports in 2 weeks.
Music: Uses easy listening, up-tempo, Dixieland and C&W for commercials.
Tips: "Listen carefully to the assignment. Don't be too sophisticated or abstract. Stay simple and translatable. Aim toward individual listener."

ALEXIS MUSIC INC. (ASCAP), MARVELLE MUSIC CO. (BMI), Box 532, Malibu CA 90265. (213)463-5998. President: Lee Magid. Music publishing and production. Clients include all types—record companies and advertising agencies. Estab. 1960. Uses the services of independent songwriters and composers for jingles, for commercials, for radio and TV and manufacturers, events, conventions, etc. Commissions 5 composers and 5 lyricists/year. Pays by the job or by royalty. Buys all rights.
How to Contact: Submit demo tape of previous work or tape demonstrating composition skills or query with resume of credits. Prefers cassette (or VHS videocassette) with 3 pieces and lyric sheets. "If interested, we will contact you." Does not return material. Include phone number and address on tape. Reports in 6 weeks.
Music: Uses R&B, gospel, jazz, Latin, Afro-Cuban, country; anything of substance.
Tips: "Stay with it and keep your ears to the melody."

*ALLEGRO MUSIC, 6500-4 Vanalden Ave., Reseda CA 91316. (818)708-1917. Owner: Daniel O'Brien. Scoring service, **jingle/commercial music production house**. Clients include film-makers, advertisers, network promotions and aerobics. Estab. 1991. Uses the services of independent songwriters/composers for scoring of feature films and commercials for radio and TV. Commissions 3 composers and 1 lyricist/year. Pays $500-1,500/job; or 50% royalty (composers). Buys publishing rights (50%).
How to Contact: Query with resume of credits, write first to arrange personal interview, or submit demo tape of previous work. Prefers cassette and lyric sheet. Does not return material. Reports in 3-6 weeks (if interested). Please, no phone calls.
Music: Varied: Contemporary pop to orchestral for educational jingles.
Tips: "Strive for a fresh approach. Be persistent."

Listings of companies within this section which are either commercial music production houses or music libraries will have that information printed in boldface type.

*PAUL ANAND MUSIC, Suite E. #200, 474 Adelaide St., Toronto, Ontario M5A 1N6 **Canada.** (416)203-2649. Fax: (416)203-2650. President: Paul Anand. **Jingle/commercial music production house.** Clients include corporate production companies. Estab. 1989. Uses the services of vocalists/ musicians for background music for video and commercials for radio. Commissions 3-4 composers/ year. Pays ACTRA/Union scale. Buys all rights.
How to Contact: Query with resume of credits. Prefers cassette. Keeps submitted material on file. Reports in 2 weeks.
Music: All styles for corporate audio production.

ANDERSON COMMUNICATIONS, Dept. SM, 2245 Godbyrd, Atlanta GA 30349. (404)766-8000. President: Al Anderson. Producer: Vanessa Vaughn. Advertising agency and syndication operation. Estab. 1971. Clients include major corporations, institutions and media. Uses the services of music houses for scoring and jingles for TV and radio commercials and background music for TV and radio programs. Commissions 5-6 songwriters or composers and 6-7 lyricists/year. Pays by the job. Buys all rights.
How to Contact: Call first and obtain permission to submit. Prefers cassette. SASE, but prefers to keep material on file. Reports in 2 weeks or "when we have projects requiring their services."
Music: Uses a variety of music for music beds for commercials and jingles for nationally syndicated radio programs and commercials targeted at the black consumer market.
Tips: "Be sure that the composition plays well in a 60 second format."

ANGEL FILMS COMPANY, 967 Hwy. 40, New Franklin MO 65274-9778. Phone/Fax: (314)698-3900. President: Arlene Hulse. Motion picture and record production company (Angel One Records). Estab. 1980. Uses the services of independent songwriters/composers and lyricists for scoring and background music for feature films, music videos, cartoons, television productions and records. Commissions 12-20 composers and 12-20 lyricists/year. Payment depends upon budget; each project has a different pay scale. Buys all rights.
How to Contact: Submit demo tape of previous work or tape demonstrating composition skills; submit manuscript showing music scoring skills; query with resume of credits. Prefers cassette (or VHS videocassette) with 3 pieces and lyric and lead sheet. "Do not send originals." SASE, but prefers to keep material on file. Reports in 3 weeks to 1 month.
Music: Uses basically MOR, but will use anything (except C&W and religious) for record production, film, television and cartoon scores.
Tips: "We prefer middle of the road music, but are open to all types. We use a lot of background music in our work, plus we have our own record label, Angel One, that is looking for music to record. Don't copy other work. Just be yourself and do the best that you can. That is all that we can ask."

ANGLE FILMS, Suite 240, 1341 Ocean Ave., Santa Monica CA 90401. President: John Engel. Motion picture production company and freelance producer. Estab. 1985. Clients include advertising agencies and motion picture production/distribution companies. Uses the services of music houses and independent songwriters/composers for scoring of films and commercials for TV. Pays by the job. Buys all rights.
How to Contact: Submit demo tape of previous work. Prefers cassette with 5 pieces and lyric sheet. Does not return material; prefers to keep on file. Reports only if interested.
Music: Uses all genres for short drama and feature films.
Tips: "Present varied composition talents. Orchestration important."

APON PUBLISHING COMPANY, INC., Dept. SM, Box 3082 Steinway Station, Long Island City NY 11103. (718)721-5599. Manager: Don Zeemann. **Jingle/commercial music production house, classical music library, music sound effect library** and **background music.** Clients include background music companies, motion picture companies and advertising agencies. Estab. 1957. Uses the services of music houses for background music, jingles for advertising agencies and commercials for radio and TV. Payment is negotiated. Buys all rights.
How to Contact: Query with resume of credits, or call first to arrange personal interview. Send demo cassette with background music, no voices. Prefers cassette with 2-5 pieces. Does not return unsolicited material. Reports in 2 months. No certified or registered mail accepted.
Music: Uses only background music, no synthesizer life instruments.

The asterisk before a listing indicates that the listing is new in this edition. New markets are often the most receptive to unsolicited submissions.

ATLANTIC FILM AND VIDEO, Dept. SM, 171 Park Lane, Massapequa NY 11758. (516)798-4106. Sound Designer: Michael Canzoneri. Motion picture production company. Clients include industrial/ commercial. Estab. 1986. Uses the services of independent songwriters/composers and lyricists for background music for movies and commercials for TV. Commissions 1 composer and 1 lyricist/year. Pays $250/job. Buys one-time rights.
How to Contact: Submit demo tape of previous work. Prefers cassette or 7½ ips reel-to-reel. "Please specify what role you had in creating the music: composer, performer, etc." SASE, but prefers to keep material on file. Reports in 2 months.
Music: Uses jazz—modern, classical for films.
Tips: "Have patience and good songs."

BALL COMMUNICATIONS, INC., 1101 N. Fulton Ave., Evansville IN 47710. (812)428-2300. President/ Creative Director: Martin A. Ball. Audiovisual and television production and meeting production firm. Clients include Fortune 500 firms. Estab. 1960. Uses the services of lyricists and independent songwriters/composers for jingles, background music and theme songs. Commissions 4 songwriters and 4 lyricists/year. Pays $1,500-2,500/job. Buys all rights.
How to Contact: Prefers cassette or ½" videocassette. Does not return material; prefers to keep on file. Responds by letter or telephone. SASE. Reports in 2 months.
Music: All types. Uses theme songs/jingles.

B&C PRODUCTIONS, Box 1012, Trenton, Ontario K8V 6E6 **Canada**. (613)392-5144. Fax: (613)392-6296. Director of Publishing Division: Eric Baragar. **Jingle/commercial music production**, songwriting and publishing company. Clients include national and regional Canadian clients. Estab. 1981. Uses the services of independent songwriters/composers and lyricists for jingles and commercials for radio and TV. Commissions 5 composers and 5 lyrcists/year. Pays $500/job. Buys all rights.
How to Contact: Submit demo tape of previous work. Prefers cassette and lyric sheet. Does not return material; prefers to keep on file. Reports in 4-6 weeks.
Music: Uses diverse music styles, "30 second hits" mostly for jingles, some film and corporate presentations.
Tips: "We are currently working with creative people who can present a finished musical work usually a standard MIDI file. Listen to the music on radio and TV commercials and write something similar but fresh and exciting."

TED BARKUS COMPANY, INC., 1512 Spruce St., Philadelphia PA 19102. (215)545-0616. President: Allen E. Barkus. Advertising agency. Uses the services of independent songwriters and music houses for jingles and background music for commercials. Commissions 1-3 songwriters/year. Pays by the job. Buys all rights.
How to Contact: Call to arrange personal interview or write to obtain permission to submit. Prefers cassette (or VHS videocassette) with 3-5 pieces. SASE, but prefers to keep material on file "when the style matches our objectives."
Music: Uses various styles of music depending upon client needs for "positioning concepts with musical beds, doughnut for inserted copy."
Tips: "Learn as much as possible about the product and who the consumer will be before starting a project. Understand that the commercial also has to work with the print and television media in terms of everything else the client is doing."

AUGUSTUS BARNETT ADVERTISING/DESIGN, Dept. SM, 632 St. Helens Ave., Tacoma WA 98402. (206)627-8508. President/Creative Director: Augustus Barnett. Advertising agency/design firm. Clients include food and service, business to business and retail advertisers. Estab. 1981. Uses the services of independent songwriters/composers for scoring of and background music for corporate video work, and commercials for radio. Commissions 1-2 composers and 0-1 lyricist/year. Buys all rights, one-time rights or for multiple use.
How to Contact: Query with resume of credits; write first to arrange personal interview. Prefers cassette. Does not return unsolicited material; prefers to keep on file. Reports in 4 months.
Music: Uses up-tempo, pop and jazz for educational films and slide presentations.

BASSET & BECKER ADVERTISING, Box 2825, Columbus GA 31902. (706)327-0763. Partner: Bill Becker. Advertising agency. Clients include medical/healthcare, banking, auto dealers, industrial, family recreation/sporting goods, business to business advertisers. Estab. 1972. Uses the services of music houses and independent songwriters/composers for scoring of and background music for TV spots and AV presentations, jingles for TV spots, AV presentations, and commercials for radio and TV. Commissions 2 composers/year. "Prefers to work with engineer/producer, not directly with composer." Pays by the job. Buys all rights.
How to Contact: Submit demo tape of previous work. Prefers cassette, 7.5/15 ips reel-to-reel, or ¾ or VHS videocassette. Does not return unsolicited material; prefers to keep on file.

RON BERNS & ASSOCIATES, 520 N. Michigan Ave., Chicago IL 60611. (312)527-2800. President: Ron Berns. Advertising agency. Uses services of independent songwriters for jingles. Pays by the job. Buys all rights.
How to Contact: Submit demo tape of previous work. Prefers cassette. Prefers studio produced demo. Does not return unsolicited material; prefers to keep on file. Reports when needed.

THE BLACKWOOD AGENCY, INC., 2125 University Park Dr., Okemos MI 48864. (517)349-6770. Production Manager: Steven Gaffe. Advertising agency. Estab. 1979. Clients include financial and package goods firms. Uses services of music houses for scoring of commercials and training films, background music for slide productions, jingles for clients and commercials for radio and TV. Commissions 3 composers/year. Pays by the job. Buys all rights.
How to Contact: Submit demo tape of previous work. Prefers cassette (or ¾" videocassette) with 6-10 songs. SASE, but prefers to keep material on file.
Tips: "Give us good demo work."

BLATTNER/BRUNNER INC., 814 Penn Ave., Pittsburgh PA 15222. (412)263-2979. Broadcast Production Coordinator: Nan Quatchak. Clients include retail/consumer, service, high-tech/industrial/medical. Estab. 1975. Uses the services of music houses and independent songwriters/composers for background music for TV/radio spots, jingles for TV and spots and commercials for radio, TV. Commissions 2-3 composers/year. Pays by the job. Buys all rights or one-time rights, depending on the job.
How to Contact: Submit demo tape of previous work demonstrating composition skills or query with resume of credits. Prefers clearly labeled cassette (or VHS or ¾" videocassette) with 5-10 songs. Does not return material. Reports in 1-2 months.
Music: Uses up-beat, "unique-sounding music that stands out" for commercials and industrial videos.
Tips: "Rate cards would by *very* helpful when accompanied by demos."

BRAUNCO VIDEO, INC., Dept. SM, Box 236, Warren IN 46792. (219)375-3148. Producer: Magley Tocsin. Video production company. Estab. 1988. Clients include industrial manufacturing, service companies, factories, United Way agencies, entertainers, songwriters, etc. Uses the services of independent songwriters/composers and house studio bands for jingles and background music for corporate video presentations. Commissions composers. Pays by the job. Buys all rights.
How to Contact: Submit demo tape of previous work or write to arrange personal interview. Prefers cassette or 15 ips reel-to-reel (or ¾" videocassette) with many pieces. "We have no use for lyric or vocals." Does not return unsolicited material.
Music: Uses up-tempo, heavy metal, R&B with a bit of jazz influence and soft music for promotional corporate demos.
Tips: "Believe in yourself."

BUTWIN & ASSOCIATES, INC., Suite 120, 7515 Wayzata Blvd., Minneapolis MN 55426. (612)546-0203. President: Ron Butwin. Clients include corporate and retail. Estab. 1977. Uses the services of music houses, lyricists and independent songwriters/composers for scoring, background music, jingles and commercials for radio, TV. Commissions 3-5 composers and 1-3 lyricists/year. Pays varying amount/job. Buys all rights and one-time rights.
How to Contact: Submit demo tape of previous work. Write first to arrange personal interview. Prefers cassette, ¼" videocassette. "We are only interested in high-quality professional work." SASE, but prefers to keep material on file.
Music: Uses easy listening, up-tempo, pop and jazz for slide presentations and commercials.

CALDWELL VANRIPER, 1314 N. Meridian, Indianapolis IN 46202. (317)632-6501. Vice President/Executive Producer: Sherry Boyle. Advertising agency and public relations firm. Clients include industrial, financial and consumer/trade firms. Uses the services of music houses for jingles and background music for commercials. Commissions 25 pieces/year.
How to Contact: Submit demo tape of previously aired work. Prefers standard audio cassette. Does not return material. Prefers to keep materials on file. "Sender should follow up on submission. Periodic inquiry or reel update is fine."
Tips: "Show range of work on reel, keep it short."

THE CAMPBELL GROUP, 326 N. Charles St., Baltimore MD 21201. (410)547-0600. Associate Creative Director: Randi Abse. Advertising agency. Clients include hotels, restaurants, destinations, automobile dealerships, publications. Estab. 1986. Uses the services of music houses and independent songwriters/composers for scoring of video sales presentations, background music for radio and TV, jingles for radio and TV and commercials for radio and TV. Commissions 10 composers/year. Pays $3,000-6,000/job. Buys all rights or one-time rights.

How to Contact: Submit demo tape of previous work. Prefers cassette (or ½″ VHS or ¾″ cassette) with 5-10 songs. Does not return unsolicited material; prefers to keep on file. Reports in 2-3 weeks.
Music: Uses up-tempo, pop, jazz and classical for commercials.
Tips: "Send demo of work, rates, brochure if available."

CANARY PRODUCTIONS, Box 202, Bryn Mawr PA 19010. (215)825-1254. President: Andy Mark. **Music library.** Estab. 1984. Uses the services of music houses and independent songwriters for background music for AV use, jingles for all purposes, and commercials for radio and TV. Commissions 10 composers/year. Pays $100 per job. Buys all rights. "No songs, please!"
How to Contact: Submit demo tape of previous work. Prefers cassette with 5-10 pieces. Does not return material. Reports in 1 month.
Music: All styles, but concentrates on industrial. "We pay cash for produced tracks of all styles and lengths. Production value is imperative. No scratch tracks accepted."
Tips: "Be persistent and considerate of people's time."

CANTRAX RECORDERS, Dept. SM, 2119 Fidler Ave., Long Beach CA 90815. (310)498-6492. Owner: Richard Cannata. Recording studio. Clients include anyone needing recording services (i.e. industrial, radio, commercial). Estab. 1980. Uses the services of independent songwriters/composers and lyricists for scoring of jingles, soundtracks, background music for slide shows and films, jingles for radio and TV. Commissions 10 composers/year. Pays by the job. Buys all rights.
How to Contact: Query with resume of credits. Submit demo tape of previous work. Prefers cassette or 7½/15 ips reel-to-reel (or VHS videocassette) with lyric sheets. "Indicate noise reduction if used. We prefer reel to reel." SASE, but prefers to keep material on file. Reports in 3 weeks.
Music: Uses jazz, New Age, rock, easy listening and classical for slide shows, jingles and soundtracks.
Tips: "Send a 7½ or 15 ips reel for us to audition; you must have a serious, professional attitude."

CAPITOL-OGM PRODUCTION MUSIC, (formerly Capitol Production Music), Suite 718, 6922 Hollywood Blvd., Hollywood CA 90028. (213)461-2701. Managing Director: Ole Georg. Scoring service, **jingle/commercial music production house, music sound effect library.** Clients include broadcast, corporate/industrial, theatrical, production/post-production houses. Uses the services of independent songwriters/composers for 35-70 minutes of music beds for CD library. Commissions 6 composers/year. Pays by the job. Buys all rights.
How to Contact: Submit resume of credits and compositional styles. No tapes please. All resumes kept on file for future consideration. "No report unless we have interest." No calls please. Reports in 4-6 months.
Music: Uses hot pop, "big acoustic," corporate industrial, atmospheric.
Tips: "Material most likely to be considered is that with heavy dynamics and strong edit-points."

CARLETON PRODUCTIONS INC., 1500 Merivale Rd., Ottawa K2E 6Z5 Ontario **Canada.** (613)224-1313. Fax: (613)224-9074. Producer: Bill Graham/Mark Ross/Randi Hansen. Audiovisual firm and TV & video production. Clients include Canadian and American TV networks, government, corporate and producers. Estab. 1973. Uses the services of music houses, independent songwriters/composers and lyricists for scoring of music beds, stings, bridges, openings, background music for corporate and sales plus drama, jingles for sales presentations and commercials for TV. Commissions 25-50 composers and 1-3 lyricists/year. Pays by the job or by royalty. Buys one-time rights "determined by project."
How to Contact: Submit demo tape of previous work. Prefers cassette. "Include past credits." Does not return unsolicited material; prefers to keep on file.
Music: Uses all types for mainly corporate video, sales video and TV beds.

CASANOVA-PENDRILL PUBLICIDAD, 3333 Michelson, Irvine CA 92715. (714)474-5001. Production: Kevan Wilkinson. Advertising agency. Clients include consumer and corporate advertising—Hispanic markets. Estab. 1985. Uses the services of music houses, independent songwriters/composers and lyricists for radio, TV and promotions. Pays by the job or per hour. Buys all rights or one-time rights.
How to Contact: Submit demo tape of previous work, tape demonstrating composition skills and manuscript showing showing music scoring skills. Prefers cassette (or ¾ videocassette). "Include a log indicating spot(s) titles." Does not return unsolicited material; prefers to keep on file.
Music: All types of Hispanic music (salsa, merengue, flamenca, etc.) for television/radio advertising.

CHAPMAN RECORDING STUDIOS, 228 W. 5th, Kansas City MO 64105. (816)842-6854. Contact: Chuck Chapman. Custom music and production. Clients include video producers, music producers, musicians and corporations. Estab. 1973. Uses the services of independent songwriters/composers and arrangers for background music for video productions; jingles for radio, TV, corporations; and commercials for radio and TV. Commissions 4 composers and 4 lyricists/year. Buys all rights.

How to Contact: Call to arrange submission of tape demo. Prefers cassette. SASE, but prefers to keep material on file. Reports in 2 months.
Music: Uses all styles, all types for record releases, video productions, and TV and radio productions; and up-tempo and pop for educational films, slide presentations and commercials.

CINEVUE, Box 428, Bostwick FL 32007. (904)325-5254. Director/Producer: Steve Postal. Motion picture production company. Estab. 1955. Serves all types of film distributors. Use the services of independent songwriters and lyricists for scoring of and background music for movies and commercials. Commissions 10 composers and 5 lyricists/year. Pays by the job. Buys all rights or one-time rights.
How to Contact: Query with resume of credits or submit demo tape of previous work. Prefers cassette with 10 pieces and lyric or lead sheet. SASE, but prefers to keep material on file. "Send good audiocassette, then call me in a week." Reports in 1 week.
Music: Uses all styles of music for features (educational films and slide presentations). "Need horror film music on traditional instruments—no electronic music."
Tips: "Be flexible, fast—do first job free to ingratiate yourself and demonstrate your style."

CLEARVUE/eav INC., Dept. SM, 6465 N. Avondale, Chicago IL 60631. (312)775-9433. Chairman of the Board: William T. Ryan. President: Mark Ventling. Audiovisual firm. Serves the educational market. Estab. 1969. "We only produce core curriculum and enrichment videos for pre-primary through high school students." Uses the services of music houses and independent songwriters. Commissions 3 songwriters or composers/year. Pays by the job.
Music: Query with resume of credits, then submit demo tape of previous work. "We are seeking original video proposal and finished product focusing on the teaching of music skills." SASE. Reports in 2 weeks.
Tips: "Submit a resume and demo tape. Follow up with a phone call in 3 weeks. Be sure to send SASE for a reply."

COAKLEY HEAGERTY, 1155 N. 1st St., San Jose CA 95112. (408)275-9400. Creative Director: Susann Rivera. Advertising agency. Clients include consumer, business to business and high tech firms. Estab. 1966. Uses the services of music houses for jingles for commercials. Commissions 15-20 songwriters/year. Pays by the job. Buys all rights.
How to Contact: Submit demo tape of previously aired work. Prefers cassette or 7½ ips reel-to-reel with 8-10 pieces. Does not return material; prefers to keep on file. Reports in 6 months.
Music: All kinds of music for jingles and music beds.
Tips: "Don't be pushy and call. I'll call when I find something I want. I'm turned off by aggressive behavior from vendors."

COMMUNICATIONS CONCEPTS INC., Box 661, Cape Canaveral FL 32920. (407)783-5320. Manager: Jim Lewis. Audiovisual firm. Clients include resorts, developments, medical and high tech industries. Uses the services of music houses, independent songwriters, lyricists and music libraries and services for scoring of TV shows and AV presentations, background music for AV programs and marketing presentations, jingles for commercials and AV programs, and commercials for radio and TV. Commissions 2-3 composers/year and 1-2 lyricists/year. Buys all rights or one-time rights.
How to Contact: Submit demo tape of previous work. Prefers cassette. Does not return material; prefers to keep on file.
Music: Corporate, contemporary and commercial.

COMMUNICATIONS FOR LEARNING, 395 Massachusetts Ave., Arlington MA 02174. (617)641-2350. Executive Producer/Director: Jonathan L. Barkan. Audiovisual and design firm. Clients include multinationals, industry, government, institutions, local, national and international nonprofits. Uses services of music houses and independent songwriters/composers for scoring and background music for TV, audiovisual and video soundtracks. Commissions 1-2 composers/year. Pays $2,000-3,000/job. Buys one-time rights of "library" music.
How to Contact: Submit demo tape of previous work or tape demonstrating composition skills. Prefers cassette or 7½ or 15 ips reel-to-reel (or ½" or ¾" videocassette). Does not return material; prefers to keep on file. "For each job we consider our entire collection." Reports "depending on needs."
Music: Uses all styles of music for all sorts of assignments.
Tips: "Please don't call. Just send good material and when we're interested, we'll be in touch."

CONTINENTAL PRODUCTIONS, Box 1219, Great Falls MT 59405. (406)761-5536. Production Sales/Marketing: Ken Kathy. Video production house. Clients include advertising agencies, business, industry and government. Uses the services of independent songwriters/composers for TV commercials and non broadcast programs and jingles for TV commercials. Commissions 1-6 composers/year. Pays $85-500/job. Buys all rights or one-time rights.

How to Contact: Write or call first and obtain permission to submit. Prefers cassette (or ½" VHS videocassette). SASE, but prefers to keep on file. Reports in 2 weeks.
Music: Uses contemporary music beds and custom jingles for TV and non-broadcast video.
Tips: "Songwriters need to build a working relationship by providing quality product in short order at a good price."

CORPORATE COMMUNICATIONS INC., Main St., Box 854, N. Conway NH 03860. (603)356-7011. President: Kimberly Beals. Advertising agency. Estab. 1983. Uses the services of music houses, independent songwriters/composers for background music, jingles and commercials for radio and TV. Commissions 2 or more composers/year. Pays by the job. Buys all rights or one-time rights.
How to Contact: Submit demo tape of previous work demonstrating composition skills. Prefers cassette (or ½" videocassette) with 5 songs. Does not return material; prefers to keep on file.
Music: Uses varying styles of music for varying assignments.

CREATIVE ASSOCIATES, Dept. SM, 44 Park Ave., Madison NJ 07940. (201)377-4440. Production Coordinator: Susan Graham. Audiovisual/multimedia firm. Clients include commercial, industrial firms. Estab. 1975. Uses the services of music houses and independent songwriters/composers for scoring of video programs, background music for press tours and jingles for new products. Pays $300-5,000+/job. Buys all or one-time rights.
How to Contact: Submit demo tape of previous work demonstrating composition skills or query with resume of credits. Prefers cassette or ½" or ¾" VHS videocassette. Prefers to keep material on file.
Music: Uses all styles for many different assignments.

CREATIVE AUDIO PRODUCTIONS, 326 Santa Isabel Blvd., Laguna Vista, Port Isabel TX 78578. (210)943-6278. Owner: Ben McCampbell. **Jingle/commercial music production house.** Serves ad agencies, broadcast stations (TV and radio), video/film production houses and advertisers. Uses the services of independent songwriters/composers and lyricists for jingles for commercials for radio and TV. Commissions 1 composer and 2 lyricists/year. Fees negotiable. Buys one-time or all rights.
How to Contact: Submit demo tape of previous work. Prefers cassette with 3-5 songs. Does not return material; prefers to keep on file. Reports in 1 month.
Music: Uses pop, up-tempo, country, rock and reggae for commercials.

CREATIVE HOUSE ADVERTISING, INC., Suite 301, 30777 Northwestern Hwy., Farmington Hills MI 48334. (313)737-7077. Senior Vice President/Executive Creative Director: Robert G. Washburn. Advertising agency and graphics studio. Serves commercial, retail, consumer, industrial, medical and financial clients. Uses the services of songwriters and lyricists for jingles, background music for radio and TV commercials and corporate sales meeting films and videos. Commissions 3-4 songwriters/year. Pays $1,500-5,000/job depending on job involvement. Buys all rights.
How to Contact: Query with resume of credits or submit tape demo showing jingle/composition skills. Submit cassette (or ¾" videocassette) with 6-12 songs. SASE, but would prefer to keep material on file. "When an appropriate job comes up associated with the talents/ability of the songwriters/musicians, then they will be contacted."
Music: "The type of music we need depends on clients. The range is multi: contemporary, disco, rock, MOR and traditional."
Tips: "Be fresh, innovative and creative. Provide good service and costs."

*THE CREATIVE IMAGE GROUP, 780 Charcot Ave., San Jose CA 95131. (408)434-0490. Fax: (408)434-0284. CEO: Ed Mongievi. Clients include video game developers/publishers, corporations, retail outlets. Estab. 1988. Uses the services of music houses, independent songwriters/composers for background music for commercials for radio, TV and video games. Commission 10+ composers and less than 10 lyricists/year. Pays per job. Buys all rights or one-time rights, depends on project.
How to Contact: Submit letter and demo tape. Include cassette (or VHS or Beta SP videocassette) with 3+ songs. Prefers to keep submitted material on file.
Music: Uses hard rock, classical rock, pop, hip hop, rap, up-tempo, modern/alternative rock, any new/trendy sound for video games.

CREATIVE SUPPORT SERVICES, 1950 Riverside Dr., Los Angeles CA 90039. (213)666-7968. Contact: Michael M. Fuller. **Music/sound effects library.** Clients include audiovisual production houses. Estab. 1978. Uses the services of independent songwriters and musicians for background music for commercials for TV. Commissions 3-5 songwriters and 1-2 lyricists/year. Buys all rights.
How to Contact: Submit demo tape of previous work. Prefers cassette ("chrome or metal only") or 7½ ips reel-to-reel with 3 or more pieces. Does not return material; prefers to keep on file. "Will call if interested."
Music: Uses "industrial music predominantly, but all other kinds or types to a lesser degree."
Tips: "Don't assume the reviewer can extrapolate beyond what is actually on the demo."

dbF A MEDIA COMPANY, Box 2458, Waldorf MD 20604. (301)843-7110. President: Randy Runyon. Advertising agency, audiovisual firm and audio and video production company. Clients include business and industry. Estab. 1981. Uses the services of music houses, independent songwriters/composers and lyricists for background music for industrial videos, jingles for radio and TV and commercials for radio and TV. Commissions 5-12 composers and 5-12 lyricists/year. Pays by the job. Buys all rights.
How to Contact: Submit demo tape of previous work. Prefers cassette or 7½ IPS reel-to-reel (or VHS videocassette) with 5-8 songs and lead sheet. SASE, but prefers to keep material on file. Reports in 1 month.
Music: Uses up-tempo contemporary for industrial videos, slide presentations and commercials.
Tips: "We're looking for commercial music, primarily adult contemporary."

DELTA DESIGN GROUP, INC., Dept. SM, 409 Washington Ave., Greenville MS 38701. (601)335-6148. President: Noel Workman. Advertising agency. Serves industrial, health care, agricultural and retail commercial clients. Uses the services of music houses for jingles and for commercials for radio and TV. Commissions 3-6 pieces/year. Pays by the job. Buys "rights which vary geographically according to client. Some are all rights; others are rights for a specified market only. Buy out only. No annual licensing."
How to Contact: Submit demo tape showing jingle/composition skills. Prefers 7½ ips reel-to-reel with 3-6 songs. "Include typed sequence of cuts on tape on the outside of the reel box." Does not return material. Reports in 2 weeks.
Music: Needs "30- and 60-second jingles for agricultural, health care, gambling casinos, vacation destinations, auto dealers and chambers of commerce."

DISK PRODUCTIONS, 1100 Perkins Rd., Baton Rouge LA 70802. (504)343-5438. Director: Joey Decker. **Jingle/production house.** Clients include advertising agencies, slide production houses and film companies. Estab. 1982. Uses independent songwriters/composers and lyricists for scoring of TV spots and films and jingles for radio and TV. Commissions 7 songwriters/composers and 7 lyricists/year. Pays by the job. Buys all rights.
How to Contact: Submit demo tape of previous work. Prefers cassette or 7½ ips reel-to-reel (or ½" videocassette) and lead sheet. Does not return material. Reports "immediately if material looks promising."
Music: Needs all types of music for jingles, music beds or background music for TV and radio, etc.
Tips: "Advertising techniques change with time. Don't be locked in a certain style of writing. Give me music that I can't get from pay needle-drop."

DSM PRODUCERS INC., Suite 803, 161 W. 54th St., New York NY 10019. (212)245-0006. Vice President, National Sales Director: Doris Kaufman. Scoring service, **jingle/commercial music production house** and original stock library called "All American Composers Library," record producers. Clients include networks, corporate, advertising firms, film and video, book publishers (music only). Estab. 1979. Uses the services of independent songwriters/composers and "all signed composers who we represent" for scoring of film, industrial films, major films—all categories; background music for film, audio cassettes, instore video—all categories; jingles for advertising agencies and commercials for radio and TV. Pays 100% of writer royalty from performance affiliation. Publishes 25 new composers annually.
How to Contact: Write or call first to arrange to submit 1-2 available tunes for publishing. Prefers cassette (or VHS videocassette) with 2 songs and lyric or lead sheet. "Use a large enough return envelope to put in a standard business reply letter." Reports in 3 months.
Music: Uses dance, New Age, country and rock for adventure films and sports programs.
Tips: "Keep the vocals up in the mix. Most artists and TV shows want to hear the master version. Invest in yourself and it will make a better presentation."

ROY EATON MUSIC INC., 595 Main St., Roosevelt Island NY 10044. (212)980-9046. President: Roy Eaton. **Jingle/commercial music production house.** Clients include advertising agencies, TV and radio stations and film producers. Estab. 1982. Uses the services of independent songwriters/composers and lyricists for scoring of TV commercials and films; background music for TV programs; jingles for advertising agencies and commercials for radio and TV. Commissions 10 composers and 1 lyricist/year. Pays $50-3,000/job. Buys all rights.
How to Contact: Submit demo tape of previous work. Prefers cassette with 3-5 pieces. Does not return unsolicited material; prefers to keep on file. Reports in 6 months.
Music: Uses jazz fusion, New Age and rock/pop for commercials and films.

ELITE VIDEO PRODUCTIONS, 1612 E. 14th St., Brooklyn NY 11229. (718)627-0499. President: Kalman Zeines. Video production company. Clients include educational and industrial. Estab. 1978. Uses the services of music houses, lyricists and independent songwriters/composers for background music for narration and commercials for TV. Commissions 2 lyricists and 5 composers/year. Pays $35-1,800/job. Buys all rights.

How to Contact: Submit demo tape of previous work. Prefers cassette. "Call first." Does not return material; prefers to keep on file. Reports back in 2 weeks. Assignments include work on educational films.

EMERY ADVERTISING, 1519 Montana, El Paso TX 79902. (915)532-3636. Producer: Steve Osborn. Advertising agency. Clients include automotive dealerships, banks, hospitals. Estab. 1977. Uses the services of music houses, independent songwriters/composers and lyricists for jingles and commercials for television and radio. Commissions 6 composers and 4 lyricists/year. Pays $250-1,000/job. Buys all rights and one-time rights.

How to Contact: Submit demo tape of previous work. Prefers cassette. Does not return unsolicited material; prefers to keep on file. Reports in 2 weeks.

Music: Uses up-tempo and pop for commercials.

ENSEMBLE PRODUCTIONS, Box 2332, Auburn AL 36831. (205)826-3045. Owner: Barry J. McConatha. Audiovisual firm and video production/post production. Clients include corporate, governmental and educational. Estab. 1984. Uses services of music houses and independent songwriters/composers for scoring of documentary productions, background music for corporate public relations and training videos, jingles for public service announcements, and for montage effects with AV and video. Commissions 0-5 composers/year. Pays $50-250/job depending upon project. Buys all rights.

How to Contact: Submit demo tape of previous work demonstrating composition skills. "Needs are sporadic, write first if submission to be returned." Prefers cassette or 7½ or 15 ips reel-to-reel (or VHS videocassette) with 3-5 songs. "Most needs are up-beat industrial sound but occasional mood setting music also. Inquire for details." Does not return material; prefers to keep on file. Reports in 3 months if interested."

Music: Uses up-beat, industrial, New Age, and mood for training film. PR, education and multimedia.

Tips: "Do not overly synthesize music."

ENTERTAINMENT PRODUCTIONS, INC., #744, 2210 Wilshire Blvd., Santa Monica CA 90403. (310)456-3143. President: Edward Coe. Motion picture and television production company. Clients include motion picture and TV distributors. Estab. 1972. Uses the services of music houses and songwriters for scores, production numbers, background and theme music for films and TV and jingles for promotion of films. Commissions/year vary. Pays by the job or by royalty. Buys all rights.

How to Contact: Query with resume of credits. Demo should show flexibility of composition skills. "Demo records/tapes sent at own risk—returned if SASE included." Reports by letter in 1 month, "but only if SASE is included."

Tips: "Have resume on file. Develop self-contained capability."

*ALAN ETT MUSIC, Suite 1470, 3500 W. Olive Ave., Burbank CA 91505. (818)248-7105. Fax: (818)955-7067. Vice President: Scott Liggett. Scoring service and **jingle/commercial music production house** for TV/advertising/corporate. Estab. 1990. Uses the services independent songwriters/composers and lyricists for scoring of background music for jingles for commercials for radio and TV. Commissions 6 composers/year. "Pays negotiable amount." Buys all or one-time rights.

How to Contact: Query with resume of credits. "Write first . . . no unsolicited submissions accepted." Does not return material.

*ETV, P.O. Box 31, FDR Station, New York NY 10150. (212)755-7322. Contact: J. Edwards. Motion picture production company. Estab. 1960. Uses the services of music houses and lyricists for scoring and background music.

How to Contact: Submit demo tape of previous work, tape demonstrating composition skills or manuscript showing music scoring skills. Prefers cassette with lyric and lead sheets. Does not return material. Reports in 6 months.

Music: Uses jazz and pop rock for educational films, slide presentations, commercials, etc.

F.C.B., INC., (formerly F.C.B. Lewis, Gilman & Kynette, Inc.), Dept. SM, 200 S. Broad St., Philadelphia PA 19102. (215)790-4100. Broadcast Business Manager: Valencia Tursi. Advertising agency. Serves industrial and consumer clients. Uses music houses for jingles and background music in commercials. Pays creative fee asked by music houses.

How to Contact: Submit demo tape of previously aired work. "You must send in previously published work. We do not use original material." Prefers cassette. Will return with SASE if requested, but prefers to keep on file.

Music: All types.

*FILM CLASSIC EXCHANGE, 143 Hickory Hill Circle, Osterville MA 02655. (508)428-7198. Vice President: Elsie Aikman. Motion picture production company. Clients include motion picture industry/ TV networks and affiliates. Estab. 1916. Uses the services of music houses, independent songwriters/ composers and lyricists for scoring, background music, jingles and commercials for motion pictures, TV movies, TV shows and specials. Commissions 10-20 composers and 10-20 lyricists/year. Pays by the job. Buys all rights.
How to Contact: Submit demo tape of previous work. Prefers cassette (or VHS videocassette). SASE, but prefers to keep material on file. Reports in 3 weeks to 2 months.
Music: Uses pop and up-tempo for theatrical films/TV movies.
Tips: "Be persistent."

FINE ART PRODUCTIONS, 67 Maple St., Newburgh NY 12550. (914)561-5866. Producer/Researcher: Richard Suraci. Advertising agency, audiovisual firm, scoring service, **jingle/commercial music production house**, motion picture production company and **music sound effect library**. Clients include corporate, industrial, motion picture, broadcast firms. Estab. 1987. Uses services of music houses, independent songwriters/composers and lyricists for scoring, background music and jingles for various projects and commercials for radio and TV. Commissions 1-10 songwriters or composers and 1-10 lyricists/ year. Pays by the job, by royalty or by the hour. Buys all rights or one-time rights.
How to Contact: Submit demo tape of previous work or tape demonstrating composition skills or query with resume of credits. Prefers cassette (or ½", ¾", or 1" videocassette) with as many songs as possible and lyric or lead sheets. SASE, but prefers to keep material on file. Reports in 3-6 months.
Music: Uses all types of music for all types of assignments.

GARY FITZGERALD MUSIC PRODUCTIONS, Suite B29, 37-75 63rd St., Woodside NY 11377. (718)446-3857. Producer: Gary Fitzgerald. Scoring service, **commercial music production house and music/sound effects library**. "We service the advertising community." Estab. 1987. Uses the services of music houses, independent songwriters, vocalists, lyricists and voice-over talent for scoring of TV, radio and industrials; background music for movies; jingles for TV, radio and industrials; and commercials for radio and TV. Commissions 4-5 composers and 2 lyricists/year. Pays per project. Rights purchased depends on project.
How to Contact: Call first to obtain permissions to submit demo tape of previous work. Prefers cassette. Does not return material; prefers to keep on file. "A follow-up call must follow submission."
Music: Uses all styles of music.
Tips: "Complete knowledge of how the advertising business works is essential."

FREDRICK, LEE & LLOYD, 235 Elizabeth St., Landisville PA 17538. (717)898-6092. Vice President: Dusty Rees. **Jingle/commercial music production house**. Clients include advertising agencies. Estab. 1976. Uses the services of independent songwriters/composers and staff writers for jingles. Commissions 2 composers/year. Pays $650/job. Buys all rights.
How to Contact: Submit tape demonstrating composition skills. Prefers cassette or 7½ ips reel-to-reel with 5 jingles. "Submissions may be samples of published work or original material." SASE. Reports in 3 weeks.
Music: Uses pop, rock, country and MOR.
Tips: "The more completely orchestrated the demos are, the better."

FREED & ASSOCIATES, Suite 220, 3600 Clipper Mill Rd., Dept. SM, Baltimore MD 21211. (410)243-1421. Senior Writer/Broadcast Producer: Bob Canale. Advertising agency. Clients include a variety of retail and non-retail businesses. Estab. 1960. Uses the services of music houses and independent songwriters/composers for background music for television commercials, jingles for TV/radio commercials and commercials for radio and TV. Commissions 4-5 composers and 2-4 lyricists/year. Pays $2,000-10,000/job. Buys all rights or one-time rights, depending on the project.
How to Contact: Submit demo tape of previous work. Prefers cassette (or ½" or ¾" videocassette). Does not return unsolicited material; prefers to keep on file. Reports in 1 month.
Music: Uses varying styles for commercials and corporate videos.

PAUL FRENCH AND PARTNERS, 503 Gabbettville Rd., LaGrange GA 30240. (706)882-5581. Contact: Charles Hall. Audiovisual firm. Uses the services of music houses and songwriters for musical scores in films and original songs for themes; lyricists for writing lyrics for themes. Commissions 20 composers and 20 lyricists/year. Pays minimum $500/job. Buys all rights.
How to Contact: Submit demo tape of previous work. Prefers reel-to-reel with 3-8 songs. SASE. Reports in 2 weeks.

FRONTLINE VIDEO & FILM, 243 12th St., Del Mar CA 92014. (619)481-5566. Production Manager: Bonnie Kristell. Television and video production company. Clients include sports programming in jetskiing, surfing, yachting, skiing, skateboarding, boardsailing; medical patient education; and various

industrial clients. Estab. 1983. Uses the services of independent songwriters/composers for background music for sports programming and industrial clients; intros, extros. Commissions 5 composers/year. Pays by the composition $35-150 per cut. Buys all rights.
How to Contact: Submit demo tape of previous work. Prefers cassette. Does not return material; prefers to keep on file. "We contact artists on an 'as needed' basis when we're ready to use one of their pieces or styles."
Music: Uses up-tempo, jazzy, rock. "We buy works that come to us for national and international TV programming."
Tips: "Be patient, because when we need a 'sound' yours may be the 'one.' "

BOB GERARDI MUSIC PRODUCTIONS, 160 W. 73rd St., New York NY 10023. (212)874-6436. President: Bob Gerardi. Scoring service and **jingle/commercial music production house.** Clients include feature film producers, television producers, advertising agencies. Estab. 1975. Uses the services of independent songwriters/composers, lyricists and sound designers for scoring for film and television; background music for industrials, commercials for radio and TV. Commissions 2 composers and 2 lyricists/year. Pays by the job. Buys all rights.
How to Contact: Write or call first to arrange personal interview. Prefers cassette with 3 songs. "Keep demo short." Does not return unsolicited material; prefers to keep on file.
Music: Uses pop, easy listening and jazz for commercials, education film, feature and TV.

GK & A ADVERTISING, INC., Suite 510, 8200 Brookriver Dr., Dallas TX 75247. (214)634-9486. Advertising agency. Clients include retail. Estab. 1982. Uses the services of music houses, independent songwriters/composers and lyricists for jingles for commercials for radio and TV. Commissions 1 composer and 1 lyricist/year. Buys all rights.
How to Contact: Submit demo tape of previous work. Prefers cassette (or VHS videocassette). Does not return material; prefers to keep on file. Reports in 2 weeks.
Music: Uses all types for commercials.

*GOODRUM LEONARD & ASSOC. INC., (formerly Madden & Goodrum), 4301 Hillsboro Rd., Nashville TN 37215. (615)292-4431. President, Creative Director: Mil Leonard. Advertising agency. Estab. 1970. Serves retail, service businesses and manufacturers. Uses independent songwriters and music houses for jingles and background music for commercials. Commissions 4-6 composers and 4-6 lyricists/year. Pays by the job. Buys all rights or one-time rights.
How to Contact: "Send a demo; send address and phone number." SASE. Reports "when we need them."
Music: Needs vary.

GREINKE, EIERS AND ASSOCIATES, Suite 332, 2448 N. Lake Dr., Milwaukee WI 53211-4345. (414)962-9810. Fax: (414)964-7479. Staff: Arthur Greinke, Patrick Eiers, Lora Nigro. Advertising agency and public relations/music artist management and media relations. Clients include small business, original music groups, special events. Estab. 1984. Uses the services of independent songwriters/composers, lyricists and music groups, original rock bands and artists for scoring of video news releases, other video projects, jingles for small firms and special events and commercials for radio and TV. Commissions 4-6 composers and 4-6 lyricists/year. Paid by a personal contract.
How to Contact: Query with resume of credits. Prefers compact disc or cassette (or DAT tape or VHS videocassette) with any number of songs and lyric sheet. "We will contact only when job is open — but will keep submissions on file." Does not return material.
Music: Uses original rock, pop, heavy rock for recording groups, commercials, video projects.
Tips: "Try to give as complete a work as possible without allowing us to fill in the holes. High energy, be creative, strong hooks!"

GRS, INC., 13300 Broad St., Pataskala OH 43062. (614)927-9566. Manager: S.S. Andrews. Teleproduction facility. Estab. 1969. Varied clients. Uses the services of music houses and independent songwriters/composers for jingles and background music. Pays by the job. Buys all rights.
How to Contact: Submit demo tape of previous work. Prefers cassette. Does not return material; prefers to keep on file.
Music: All styles for commercials.
Tips: "Follow our instructions exactly."

HEPWORTH ADVERTISING CO., 3403 McKinney Ave., Dallas TX 75204. (214)526-7785. President: S.W. Hepworth. Advertising agency. Clients include financial, industrial and food firms. Estab. 1952. Uses services of songwriters for jingles. Pays by the job. Buys all rights.
How to Contact: Write first to arrange personal interview. Prefers cassette. Does not return material. Reports as need arises.

HEYWOOD FORMATICS & SYNDICATION, 1103 Colonial Blvd., Canton OH 44714. (216)456-2592. Owner: Max Heywood. Advertising agency and consultant. Clients include radio, television, restaurants/lounges. Uses the services of independent songwriters/composers for jingles and commercials for radio and TV. Payment varies per project. Buys all rights.
How to Contact: Submit demo tape of previous work. Prefers cassette or 7½ or 15 ips reel-to-reel (or VHS/Beta videocassette). Does not return material.
Music: Uses pop, easy listening and CHR for educational films, slide presentations and commercials.

HILLMANN & CARR INC., 2121 Wisconsin Ave. NW, Washington DC 20007. (202)342-0001. President: Alfred Hillmann. Vice President/Treasurer: Ms. Michal Carr. Audiovisual firm and motion picture production company. Estab. 1975. Clients include corporate, government, associations and museums. Uses the services of music houses and independent songwriters/composers for scoring of films, video productions and PSA's for radio and TV. Commissions 2-3 composers/year. Payment negotiable.
How to Contact: Query with resume of credits, or submit demo tape of previous work or tape demonstrating composition skills, or write to arrange personal interview. Prefers cassette (or ¾" VHS or Beta videocassette) with 5-10 pieces. Does not return material; prefers to keep on file only when interested. Reports in 1 month. SASE.
Music: Uses contemporary, classical, up-tempo and thematic music for documentary film and video productions, multi-media exposition productions, public service announcements.

THE HITCHINS COMPANY, 22756 Hartland St., Canoga Park CA 91307. (818)715-0510. President: W.E. Hitchins. Advertising agency. Estab. 1985. Uses the services of independent songwriters/composers for jingles and commercials for radio and TV. Commissions 1-2 composers and 1-2 lyricists/year. Will negotiate pay.
How to Contact: Query with resume of credits or write or call first to arrange personal interview. Prefers cassette or VHS videocassette. "Check first to see if we have a job." Does not return material; prefers to keep on file.
Music: Uses variety of musical styles for commercials.

HODGES ASSOCIATES, INC., P.O. Box 53805, 912 Hay St., Fayetteville NC 28305. (919)483-8489. President/Production Manager: Chuck Smith. Advertising agency. Clients include industrial, retail and consumer ("We handle a full array of clientele."). Estab. 1974. Uses the services of music houses and independent songwriters/composers for background music for industrial films and slide presentations, and commercials for radio and TV. Commissions 1-2 composers/year. Pays by the job. Buys all rights.
How to Contact: Submit demo tape of previous work. Prefers cassette. Does not return unsolicited material; prefers to keep on file. Reports in 2-3 months.
Music: Uses all styles for industrial videos, slide presentations and TV commercials.

HOME, INC., 731 Harrison Ave., Boston MA 02118. (617)266-1386. Director: Alan Michel. Audiovisual firm and video production company. Clients include cable television, nonprofit organizations, pilot programs, entertainment companies and industrial. Uses the services of independent songwriters/composers for background music for videos and TV commercials. Commissions 2-5 songwriters/year. Pays up to $1,000/job. Buys all rights or one-time rights.
How to Contact: Query with resume of credits. Prefers cassette with 6 pieces. Does not return material; prefers to keep on file. Reports as projects require.
Music: Mostly synthesizer. Uses all styles of music for educational videos.
Tips: "Have a variety of products available and be willing to match your skills to the project and the budget."

IZEN ENTERPRISES, INC., Dept. SM, 26 Abby Dr., E. Northport NY 11731. (516)368-0615. President: Ray Izen. Video services. Clients are various. Estab. 1980. Uses the services of music houses and independent songwriters/composers for background music. Commissions 2 composers and 2 lyricists/year. Pay is open. Buys all rights.
How to Contact: Submit demo tape of previous work. Prefers cassette or VHS videocassette. Does not return material, prefers to keep on file.

THE JAYME ORGANIZATION, 25825 Science Park Dr., Cleveland OH 44122. (216)831-0110. Sr. Art Director: Debbie Klonk. Advertising agency. Uses the services of songwriters and lyricists for jingles and background music. Pays by the job. Buys all rights.
How to Contact: Query first; submit demo tape of previous work. Prefers cassette with 4-8 songs. SASE. Responds by phone as needs arise.
Music: Jingles.

K&R'S RECORDING STUDIOS, 28533 Greenfield, Southfield MI 48076. (313)557-8276. Contact: Ken Glaza. Scoring service and **jingle/commercial music production house.** Clients include commercial, industrial firms. Services include sound for pictures (music, dialogue). Uses the services of independent songwriters/composers for scoring, background music, jingles and commercials for radio and TV, etc. Commissions 1 composer/month. Pays by the job, royalty or hour. Buys all rights.
How to Contact: Write or call first to arrange personal interview. Prefers cassette (or ¾" or VHS videocassette) with 5-7 pieces minimum. "Show me what you can do in 5 to 7 minutes." SASE. Reports in 2 weeks.
Music: "Be able to compose with the producer present."

KAUFMANN ADVERTISING ASSOCIATES, INC., Dept. SM, 1626 Frederica Rd., St. Simons Island GA 31522. (912)638-8678. President: Harry Kaufmann. Advertising agency. Clients include resorts. Estab. 1964. Uses the services of independent songwriters/composers and lyricists for scoring of videos, background music for videos, radio, TV, jingles for radio and commercials for radio and TV. Commissions 0-2 composers and 0-2 lyricists/year. Pays by the job.

KEATING MAGEE LONG ADVERTISING, 2223 Magazine, New Orleans LA 70130. (504)523-2121. President: Thomas J. Long. Advertising agency. Clients include retail, consumer products and services, business-to-business. Estab. 1981. Uses the services of music houses and independent songwriters/composers for commercials for radio and TV. Commissions 4 composers/year. Pays by the job. Buys all rights.
How to Contact: Submit demo tape of previous work. Prefers cassette (or VHS videocassette). Does not return material; prefers to keep on file.
Music: Uses all for commercials, presentations.

KEN-DEL PRODUCTIONS INC., First State Production Center, 1500 First State Blvd., Wilmington DE 19804-3596. (302)999-1164. Fax: (302)999-1656. Estab. 1950. A&R Director: Shirley Kay. General Manager: Edwin Kennedy. Clients include publishers, industrial firms and advertising agencies. Uses services of songwriters for slides, film scores and title music. Pays by the job. Buys all rights.
How to Contact: Submit demo of previous work. Will accept audio or video tapes. SASE, but prefers to keep material on file. Reports in 2 weeks.

SID KLEINER MUSIC ENTERPRISES, 10188 Winter View Dr., Naples FL 33942. (813)566-7701 and (813)566-7702. Managing Director: Sid Kleiner. Audiovisual firm. Serves the music industry and various small industries. Uses the services of music houses, songwriters and inhouse writers for background music; lyricists for special material. Commissions 5-10 composers and 2-3 lyricists/year. Pays $25 minimum/job. Buys all rights.
How to Contact: Query with resume of credits or submit demo tape of previously aired work. Prefers cassette with 1-4 songs. SASE. Reports in 5 weeks.
Music: "We generally need soft background music, with some special lyrics to fit a particular project. Uses catchy, contemporary, special assignments for commercial/industrial accounts. We also assign country, pop, mystical and metaphysical. Submit samples—give us your very best demos, your best prices and we'll try our best to use your services."

KTVU RETAIL SERVICES, Box 22222, Oakland CA 94623. (510)874-0228. TV station and retail Marketing Director: Richard Hartwig. Retail TV commercial production firm. Estab. 1974. Clients include local, regional and national retailers. Uses the services of music houses and independent songwriters/composers for commercials, background music and jingles for radio and TV. Commissions 50 composers and 4 lyricists/year. Pays by the job. Buys all rights.
How to Contact: Submit demo tape of previous work. Prefers cassette or 7½ ips reel-to-reel with 6 pieces. Does not return material. Reports in 1 week.
Music: All styles for TV and radio commercials.

LANGE PRODUCTIONS, 7661 Curson Terrace, Hollywood CA 90046. (213)874-4730. Production Coordinator: Victoria Joyce. Medical video production company. Clients include doctors, hospitals, corporations. Estab. 1987. Uses services of music houses and independent songwriters/composers for background music for medical videos. Commissions 6 composers/year. Pays by the job, $300-700. Buys all rights.

Listings of companies within this section which are either commercial music production houses or music libraries will have that information printed in boldface type.

How to Contact: Submit demo tape of previous work. Does not return material; prefers to keep on file. Reports in 1 month.

LAPRIORE VIDEOGRAPHY, 86 Allston Ave., Worcester MA 01604. (508)755-9010. Owner: Peter Lapriore. Video production company. Clients include business, educational and sports. Estab. 1985. Uses the services of music houses, independent songwriters/composers and lyricists for scoring, jingles and music for industrial productions and commercials for TV. "We also own a music library." Commissions 2 composers/year. Pays $150-1,000/job. Buys all rights, one-time rights and limited use rights.
How to Contact: Submit demo tape of previous work demonstrating composition skills. Prefers cassette or VHS videocassette with 5 songs and lyric sheet. Does not return material; prefers to keep on file. Reports in 3 weeks.
Music: Uses medium, up-tempo, jazz and classical for marketing, educational films and commercials.

*LEISURE-FOR-PLEASURE, 5 Burcot Avenue, Wolverhampton West Midlands WV 12SB **England**. Phone: (0902) 52194. Chairman: John B. Thomas. Advertising agency, audiovisual firm and scoring service. Estab. 1980. Uses the services of music houses, independent songwriters/composers and lyricists for background music, jingles and commercials for radio and TV. Commissions 2 composers and 2 lyricists/year. Pays by the job. Buys all rights or one-time rights.
How to Contact: Submit tape demonstrating composition skills or manuscript showing music scoring skills, or write or call to arrange personal interview. Prefers cassette (or videocassette) with 2 songs and lyric or lead sheet. SAE and IRC. Does not return unsolicited material; prefers to keep on file. Reports in 1 month.
Music: Uses easy listening music for educational films.

WALTER P. LUEDKE & ASSOCIATES, INC., 5633 E. State St., Rockford IL 61108. (815)398-4207. Secretary: Joan Luedke. Advertising agency. Estab. 1959. Uses the services of independent songwriters/composers and lyricists for background music for clients, jingles for clients and commercials for radio and TV. Commissions 1-2 composers and 1-2 lyricists/year. Pays by the job. Buys all rights.
How to Contact: Submit demo tape of previous work demonstrating composition skills, or write first to arrange personal interview. Prefers cassette. "Our need is infrequent, best just let us know who you are." SASE, but prefers to keep material on file. Reports in 1 month.
Music: Uses various styles.

LUNA TECH, INC., Dept. SM, 148 Moon Dr., Owens Cross Roads AL 35763. (205)725-4224. Chief Designer: Ken Coburn. Fireworks company. Clients include theme parks, municipalities and industrial show producers. Estab. 1969. Uses music houses, independent songwriters and client music departments for scoring of music for fireworks displays. Commissions 1-2 composers/year. Pays $500-3,000/job. Buys all rights or one-time rights.
How to Contact: Query with resume of credits or submit demo tape of previous work. Prefers cassette (or VHS videocassette) with 1-5 pieces. Does not return unsolicited material; prefers to keep on file. Reports in 1 month; will call if interested.
Music: "Music for fireworks choreography: dynamic, jubilant, heraldic, bombastic, original."
Tips: "Send us a demo tape showing your composition skills and tailored as much as possible toward our needs."

LYONS PRESENTATIONS, 715 Orange St., Wilmington DE 19801. (302)654-6146. Audio Producer: Gary Hill. Audiovisual firm. Clients include mostly large corporations: Dupont, ICI, Alco Standard. Estab. 1954. Uses the services of independent songwriters/composers and lyricists for scoring of multi-image, film and video. Commissions 8-12 composers/year. Pays by the job. Buys all rights.
How to Contact: Submit demo tape of previous work. Prefers cassette, 15 IPS reel-to-reel, (or VHS or ¾" videocassette) with 3-4 songs. "No phone calls please, unless composers are in local area." SASE, but prefers to keep submitted materials on file.
Music: Usually uses up-tempo motivational pieces for multi-image, video or film for corporate use.
Tips: "Pays close attention to the type of music that is used for current TV spots."

MCCAFFREY AND MCCALL ADVERTISING, 8888 Keystone Crossing, Indianapolis IN 46240. (317)574-3900. V.P./Associate Creative Director: William Mick. Advertising agency. Serves consumer electronics, technical ecucation, retail and commercial developers. Estab. 1984. Uses the services of music houses for scoring, background music and jingles for radio and TV commercials. Commissions 3 composers/year; 1 lyricist/year. Pays $3,000-5,000/job. Buys all rights.
How to Contact: Submit demo tape of previous work and write to arrange personal interview. Prefers cassette (or ¾" videocassette) with 6 songs. SASE, but prefers to keep submitted materials on file.
Music: High-energy pop, sound-alikes and electronic for commercials.
Tips: "Keep in touch, but don't be a pest about it."

McCANN-ERICKSON WORLDWIDE, Dept. SM, Suite 1900, 1360 Post Oak Blvd., Houston TX 77056. (713)965-0303. Creative Director: Jesse Caesar. Advertising agency. Serves all types of clients. Uses services of songwriters for jingles and background music in commercials. Commissions 10 songwriters/year. Pays production cost and registrated creative fee. Arrangement fee and creative fee depend on size of client and size of market. "If song is for a big market, a big fee is paid; if for a small market, a small fee is paid." Buys all rights.
How to Contact: Submit demo tape of previously aired work. Prefers 7½ ips reel-to-reel. "There is no minimum or maximum length for tapes. Tapes may be of a variety of work or a specialization. We are very open on tape content; agency does own lyrics." SASE, but prefers to keep material on file. Responds by phone when need arises.
Music: All types.

MARK CUSTOM RECORDING SERVICE, INC., 10815 Bodine Rd., Clarence NY 14031-0406. (716)759-2600. Vice President: Mark T. Morette. **Jingle/commercial music production house**. Clients include ad agencies. Estab. 1962. Uses the services of independent songwriters/composers for commercials for radio and TV. Commissions 2 composers/year. Pays $25/hour.
How to Contact: Write. Prefers cassette with 3 songs. Does not return material; prefers to keep on file.
Music: Uses pop and jazz for radio commercials.

MASTER MANAGEMENT MUSIC, #242, 1626 W. Wilcox St., Los Angeles CA 90028. (213)871-8054, ext. 516. President/CEO: George Van Heel. Advertising agency, **jingle/commercial music production house,** promotion/production company and music publishing company (BMI). Estab. 1987. Uses the services of independent songwriters/composers for scoring, background music and jingles for campaigns and commercials for radio/TV. Commissions 1 composer and 1 lyricist/year. Pays 100% royalty. Buys all rights.
How to Contact: Query with resume of credits or submit demo tape or previous work. "No personal deliveries; by appointment only!" Prefers cassette or VHS videocassette with 3 songs and lyric and lead sheets. "All songs must be patriotic." Does not return material; prefers to keep materials on file. Reports in 2 months.
Music: Pop/rock style for campaigns, educational and music videos.
Tips: "Work hard, be patient and follow up by a letter for recommended materials submitted."

MAXWELL ADVERTISING INC., Dept. SM, 444 W. Michigan, Kalamazoo MI 49007. (616)382-4060. Creative Director: Jess Maxwell. Advertising agency. Uses the services of lyricists and music houses for jingles and background music for commercials. Commissions 2-4 lyricists/year. Pays by the job. Buys all rights or one-time rights.
How to Contact: Submit demo tape of previously aired work or tape demonstrating composition skills. Prefers cassette (or VHS videocassette). Does not return material; prefers to keep on file. Reports in 1-2 months.
Music: Uses various styles of music for jingles and music beds.

*MEDIA ASSOCIATES ADVERTISING, 3808 W. Dorian St., Boise ID 83705. (208)384-9278. President: Danny Jensen. Advertising agency. Clients include radio-TV commercial accounts, corporate and industrial video production. Uses the services of independent songwriters/composers for jingles and commercials for radio and TV. Commissions 2-5 composers and 2-5 lyricists/year. "Pay is negotiable." Buys all rights.
How to Contact: Submit demo tape of previous work. Prefers cassette and lyric sheet. Prefers to keep submitted material on file. Reports in 1-2 months.
Music: Uses up-tempo, adult contemporary, contemporary hits for radio and TV commercials, jingles.
Tips: "A good demo says it all."

MEDIA CONSULTANTS, Box 130, Sikeston MO 63801. (314)472-1116. Owner: Richard Wrather. Advertising agency. Clients are varied. Estab. 1979. Uses the services of music houses, independent songwriters/composers and lyricists for background music for jingles, industrial video and commercials for radio and TV. Commissions 10-15 composers and 10-15 lyricists/year. Pays varying amount/job. Buys all rights.

The asterisk before a listing indicates that the listing is new in this edition. New markets are often the most receptive to unsolicited submissions.

How to Contact: Submit a demo tape of previous work demonstrating composition skills. Prefers cassette (or ½" or ¾" videocassette). Does not return material; prefers to keep on file.
Music: Uses all styles of music for varied assignments.

MID-OCEAN RECORDING STUDIO, 1578 Erin St., Winnepeg Namitoba R3E 2T1 **Canada.** (204)774-3715. Producer/Engineer: Dave Zeglinski. **Jingle/commercial music production house.** Clients include retail/corporate. Estab. 1980. Uses the services of independent songwriters/composers and producers for jingles for commercials for radio and TV. Commissions 3-5 composers/year. Pays $300-500/job. Buys all rights.
How to Contact: Submit demo tape of previous work. Prefers cassette with 1 or 2 songs. Does not return unsolicited material; prefers to keep submitted material on file. Reports in 1 month.
Music: Uses easy listening, up-tempo, pop for commercials.

JON MILLER PRODUCTION STUDIOS, 7249 Airport Rd., Bath PA 18014. (215)837-7550. Executive Producer: Jon Miller. Audiovisual firm, **jingle/commercial music production house** and video production company. Clients include industrial, commercial, institutional and special interest. Estab. 1970. Uses the services of independent songwriters/composers and lyricists for scoring of themes, background music for audio and video production and live presentations and commercials for radio and TV. Commissions 5-15 composers and 2-5 lyricists/year. Buys all rights or one-time rights.
How to Contact: Query with resume of credits and references. Prefers cassette with 7 songs and lyric or lead sheets. SASE. Reports in 2-3 weeks.
Music: Uses up-tempo and title music, introduction music for industrial marketing and training videos.
Tips: "Provide professional product on time and within budget."

MITCHELL & ASSOCIATES, Dept. SM, 7830 Old Georgetown Rd., Bethesda MD 20814. (301)986-1772. President: Ronald Mitchell. Advertising agency. Serves food, high-tech, transportation, financial, real estate, professional services automotive and retail clients. Uses independent songwriters, lyricists and music houses for background music for commercials, jingles and post-TV scores for commercials. Commissions 3-5 songwriters and 3-5 lyricists/year. Pays by the job. Buys all rights.
How to Contact: Submit demo tape of previously aired work. Prefers cassette or 7½ ips reel-to-reel. Does not return material; prefers to keep on file.
Music: "Depends upon client, audience, etc."

MONTEREY BAY PRODUCTION GROUP, INC., 561 Arthur Rd., Watsonville CA 95076. (408)722-3132. Fax: (408)728-2709. President: Larry W. Eells. Audio/video production services. Clients include industrial business and broadcast. Estab. 1985. Uses the services of independent songwriters/composers for scoring of promotional, educational and commercial videos. Commissions 3-10 composers/year. Pays negotiable royalty.
How to Contact: Submit demo tape of previous work. Query with resume of credits. Prefers cassette (or VHS videocassette) with 5 songs. SASE, but prefers to keep material on file. Reports in 1 month.
Music: Uses all types for promotional, training and commercial.

MORRIS MEDIA, Dept. SM, #105, 2730 Monterey, Torrance CA 90503. (310)533-4800. Acquisitions Manager: Roger Casas. TV/video production company. Estab. 1984. Uses the services of music houses, independent songwriters/composers and lyricists for jingles for radio and TV commercials. Commissions 5 composers and 2 lyricists/year. Pays by the job or by the hour. Buys all rights.
How to Contact: Query with resume of credits. "Write first with short sample of work." Does not return unsolicited material; prefers to keep submitted material on file. Reports in 2 weeks.
Music: Uses classical, pop, rock and jazz for music video/TV.
Tips: "Persist with good material, as we are very busy!"

MOTIVATION MEDIA, INC., 1245 Milwaukee Ave., Glenview IL 60025. (708)297-4740. Production Manager: Glen Peterson. Audiovisual firm, video, motion picture production company and business meeting planner. Clients include business and industry. Estab. 1969. Uses the services of music houses, songwriters and composers "mostly for business meetings and multi-image production"; lyricists for writing lyrics for business meeting themes, audience motivation songs and promotional music for new product introduction. Commissions 3-5 composers/year. Payment varies. Buys one-time rights.
How to Contact: Submit demo tape of previous work. Prefers cassette with 5-7 songs. Does not return material. Responds in 3-4 weeks.
Music: Uses "up-beat contemporary music that motivates an audience of sales people."
Tips: "Be contemporary."

ERIC MOWER & ASSOCIATES, Dept. SM, 96 College Ave., Rochester NY 14607. (716)473-0440. President/Chief Creative Officer: Bill Murtha. Advertising agency. Member of AFTRA, SAG, ASCAP. Serves consumer and business-to-business clients. Uses independent songwriters, lyricists and

music houses for jingles. Commissions 12 songwriters and 4 lyricists/year. Pays $5,000-40,000/job.
How to Contact: Query. Prefers cassette with 3-5 songs. SASE.
Music: "We're seriously interested in hearing from good production sources. We have some of the world's best lyricists and songwriters working for us, but we're always ready to listen to fresh, new ideas."

MULTI IMAGE PRODUCTIONS, Dept. SM, 8849 Complex Dr., San Diego CA 92123. (619)560-8383. Sound Editor/Engineer: Jim Lawrence. Audiovisual firm and motion picture production company. Serves business, corporate, industrial, commercial, military and cultural clients. Uses music houses, independent songwriters/composers/arrangers and lyricists for scoring of industrials, corporate films and videos; background music for AV, film, video and live shows; and jingles and commercials for radio and TV. Commissions 2-10 composers and 2-5 lyricists/year. Pays $500+/job. Buys all rights.
How to Contact: Query with resume of credits or write to obtain permission to submit. Prefers 7½ or 15 ips reel-to-reel with 2-5 pieces. Does not return unsolicited material; prefers to keep on file. Reports in 6 weeks.
Music: Uses "contemporary, pop, specialty, regional, ethnic, national and international styles of music for background scores written against script describing locales, action, etc. We try to stay clear of stereotypical 'canned' music and prefer a more commercial and dramatic (film-like) approach."
Tips: "We have established an ongoing relationship with a local music production/scoring house with whom songwriters would be in competition for every project; but an ability to score clean, full, broad, contemporary commercial and often 'film score' type music, in a variety of styles would be a benefit."

MUSIC LANE PRODUCTIONS, Dept. SM, Box 3829, Austin TX 78764. (512)476-1567. Owner: Wayne Gathright. Music recording, production and **jingle/commercial music production house.** Estab. 1980. Serves bands, songwriters and commercial clients. Uses the services of music houses and independent songwriters/composers for jingles and commercials for radio and TV. Pays by the job. Buys one-time rights.
How to Contact: Submit demo tape of previous work or tape demonstrating composition skills; or query with resume of credits. Prefers cassette. Does not return unsolicited material; prefers to keep on file. Reports in 6 weeks.
Music: Uses all styles.

MUSIC MASTERS, 2322 Marconi Ave., St. Louis MO 63110. (314)773-1480. Producer: Greg Trampe. **Commercial music production house** and **music/sound effect library.** Clients include multi-image and film producers, advertising agencies and large corporations. Estab. 1976. Uses the services of independent songwriters/composers and lyricists for background music for multi-image and film, jingles and commercials for radio and TV. Commissions 6 composers and 2 lyricists/year. Pays by the job. Buys all rights.
How to Contact: Query with resume of credits or submit demo tape of previous work. Prefers cassette or 7½ or 15 ips reel-to-reel (or Beta or VHS videocassette) with 3-6 pieces. SASE, but prefers to keep material on file. Reports in 2 months.
Music: "We use all types of music for slide presentations (sales & motivational)."
Tips: "Resume should have at least 3 or 4 major credits of works completed within the past year. A good quality demo is a must."

MYERS & ASSOCIATES, Dept. SM, Suite 203, 3727 SE Ocean Blvd., Stuart FL 34996. (407)287-1990. Senior Vice President: Doris McLaughlin. Advertising agency. Estab. 1973. Serves financial, real estate, consumer products and hotel clients. Uses music houses for background music for commercials and jingles. Commissions 2-3 songwriters/year and 2-3 lyricists/year. Pays by the job. Buys all rights.
How to Contact: Submit demo tape of previously aired work. Prefers cassette. Does not return unsolicited material; prefers to keep on file.
Music: Uses "various styles of music for jingles, music beds and complete packages depending on clients' needs."

FRANK C. NAHSER, INC., Dept. SM, 18th Floor, 10 S. Riverside Plaza, Chicago IL 60606. (312)845-5000. Contact: Bob Fugate. Advertising agency. Serves insurance, telecommunications, toys, bicycles, hotels, and other clients. Uses the services of independent songwriters/composers, lyricists and music houses for scoring of television commercials, background music for commercials for radio and TV and music for industrial/sales presentations and meetings. Commissions 6-10 songwriters and 4 lyricists/year. Pays $5,000-15,000 for finished production or varying royalty. Buys one-time rights.
How to Contact: Submit demo tape of previous work. Prefers cassette. Does not return unsolicited material; prefers to keep on file. "No phone calls, please. When a cassette is submitted we listen to it for reference when a project comes up. We ignore most cassettes that lack sensitivity toward string and woodwind arrangements unless we know it's from a lyricist."

Music: "We mostly use scores for commercials, not jingles. The age of the full sing jingle in national TV spots is quickly coming to an end. Young songwriters should be aware of the difference and have the expertise to score, not just write songs."
Tips: "The writing speaks for itself. If you know composition, theory and arrangement it is quickly evident. Electronic instruments are great tools; however, they are no substitute for total musicianship. Learn to read, write, arrange and produce music and, with this book's help, market your music. Be flexible enough to work along with an agency. We like to write and produce as much as you do."

NEW & UNIQUE VIDEOS, 2336 Sumac Dr., San Diego CA 92105. (619)282-6126. Contact: Pat Mooney. Production and worldwide distribution of special interest videotapes to varied markets. Estab. 1981. Uses the services of independent songwriters for background music in videos. Commissions 2-3 composers/year. Pays by the job. Buys all rights.
How to Contact: Query with resume of credits or submit demo tape of previous work. Prefers cassette. SASE. Reports in 1-2 months.
Music: Uses up-tempo, easy listening and jazz for educational film and action/adventure, nature and love stories.
Tips: "We are seeking upbeat, versatile music, especially for fast action sports videos (among others)."

NOBLE ARNOLD & ASSOCIATES, Dept. SM, Suite 740, 1515 Woodfield Rd., Schaumburg IL 60173. (708)605-8808. Creative Director: John Perkins. Advertising agency. Clients include communication and health care firms. Estab. 1970. Uses the services of independent songwriters/composers for jingles. Commissions 1 composer and 1 lyricist/year. Pays by the job. Buys all rights.
How to Contact: Submit demo tape of previous work. Prefers cassette. Does not return unsolicited material. Reports in 4 weeks.

NORTHLICH STOLLEY LAWARRE, INC., 200 W. Fourth St., Cincinnati OH 45202. (513)421-8840. Broadcast Producer: Judy Merz. Advertising agency. Clients include banks, hospitals, P&G, Cintas, ChoiceCare, 5/3 Bank, Mead Paper. Estab. 1949. Uses the services of independent songwriters and music houses for jingles and background music for commercials. Commissions 3-5 composers/year. Pays by the job. Rights purchased varies.
How to Contact: Submit demo tape of previous work demonstrating composition skills. Prefers cassette. SASE, but prefers to keep material on file.
Music: Uses all kinds for commercials.

NORTON RUBBLE & MERTZ, INC. ADVERTISING, Suite 206, 156 N. Jefferson, Chicago IL 60661. (312)441-9500. President: Sue Gehrke. Advertising agency. Clients include consumer products, retail, business to business. Estab. 1987. Uses the services of music houses and independent songwriters/composers for jingles and background music for radio/TV commercials. Commissions 2 composers/year. Pays by the job.
How to Contact: Submit tape of previous work; query with resume of credits. Prefers cassette. Does not return materials; prefers to keep on file.
Music: Uses up-tempo and pop for commercials.

OMNI COMMUNICATIONS, Dept. SM, 655 W. Carmel Dr., Carmel IN 46032-2669. (317)844-6664. President: W. H. Long. Television production and audiovisual firm. Estab. 1978. Serves industrial, commercial and educational clients. Uses the services of music houses and songwriters for scoring of films and television productions; background music for voice overs; lyricists for original music and themes. Pays by the job. Buys all rights.
How to Contact: Query with resume of credits. Prefers reel-to-reel, cassette (or videocassette). Does not return material. Reports in 2 weeks.
Music: Varies with each and every project; from classical, contemporary to commercial industrial.
Tips: "Submit a good demo with examples of your range to grab the attention of our producers."

ON-Q PRODUCTIONS, INC., 618 Gutierrez St., Santa Barbara CA 93103. (805)963-1331. President: Vincent Quaranta. Audiovisual firm. Clients include corporate accounts/sales conventions. Uses the services of music houses, independent songwriters/composers and lyricists for scoring of and background music and jingles for AV shows. Commissions 1-5 composers and 1-5 lyricists/year. Buys all or one-time rights.
How to Contact: Query with resume of credits. Prefers cassette or 15 ips reel-to-reel (or VHS videocassette). SASE, but prefers to keep material on file. Reports in 1 month.
Music: Uses up-tempo music for slide and video presentations.

OWENS & ANNA MENDIVIL ASSOCIATES, (formerly Owens Pollick and Associates), Suite 1500, 2800 N. Central, Phoenix AZ 85004. (602)230-7557. Broadcast Producer: Anna Mendivil. Advertising agency. Clients include health care, automotive aftermarket and newspapers. Estab. 1986. Uses the

services of music houses for scoring of background music and jingles for commercials for radio/TV. Commissions 4-10 composers/year; 4-10 lyricists/year. Pays $2,000/job. Buys all rights.
How to Contact: Submit demo tape of previous work. Prefers cassette or ¾" videocassette. Does not return material; prefers to keep on file. Reports in 6-8 weeks.
Music: Up-tempo, jazz and classical for commercials.

PAISANO PUBLICATIONS/EASYRIDERS HOME VIDEO, Box 3000, Agoura Hills CA 91364. (818)889-8740. Producer: Kit Maira. Home video and TV productions. Clients include consumer/motorcycle enthusiasts. Estab. 1971. Uses the services of music houses, independent songwriters/composers and pre-recorded bands for scoring of video and TV, background music for video and TV. Commissions 2-3 composers/year. Pays $100/minute of usage. Buys all rights.
How to Contact: Write first to arrange personal interview. Prefers cassette. SASE, but prefers to keep material on file. Reports in 1-2 months.
Music: Uses rock/country/contemporary.
Tips: "Harley riders a plus."

*PDS COMMUNICATIONS, INC., P.O. Box 412477, Kansas City MO 64141-2477. (800)473-7550. Vice President/General Manager: Derrick Shivers. **Jingle/commercial music production house.** Clients include ad agencies, radio, TV, film and broadcast companies. Estab. 1990. Uses the services of music houses, independent songwriters/composers, lyricists and voice talent for scoring of motion picture sound tracks, background music for industrial films, jingles and commercials for radio and TV and voice-overs. Commissions 4-5 composers and 10-12 lyricists/year. Pays union scale + percentage of royalty. Buys all rights.
How to Contact: Query with resume of credits. Prefers cassette (or VHS videocassette) with 2-3 songs and lyric sheet. "Follow directions and be patient." Does not return material. Reports in 2-3 months.
Music: Uses pop, R&B, jazz, classical, dance/house for jingles, commercials, soundtracks, voice-overs.
Tips: "Quality not quantity will get you through."

PHD VIDEO, 143 Hickory Hill Cir., Osterville MA 02655. (508)428-7198. Acquisitions: Violet Atkins. Motion picture production company. Clients include business and industry, production and post-production video houses and ad agencies. Estab. 1985. Uses the services of music houses, independent songwriters/composers and lyricists for scoring and background music for commercials, home video and motion pictures and jingles for TV commercials. Commissions 10-12 composers and 10-12 lyricists/year. Pay is negotiable. Buys all rights.
How to Contact: Submit demo tape of previous work. Prefers cassette (or VHS videocassette). SASE but prefers to keep material on file. Reports in 1-2 months.
Music: Uses up-tempo and pop for commercials, motion pictures and TV shows.
Tips: "Be persistent. Constantly send updates of new work. Update files 1-2 times per year if possible. We hire approximately 25% new composers per year. Prefer to use composers/lyricists with 2-3 years track record."

PHILADELPHIA MUSIC WORKS, INC., Box 947, Bryn Mawr PA 19010. (215)825-5656. President: Andy Mark. **Jingle producers/music library producers.** Uses independent composers and music houses for background music for commercials and jingles. Commissions 20 songwriters/year. Pays $100-300/job. Buys all rights.
How to Contact: Submit demo tape of previous work. Prefers cassette. "We are looking for quality jingle tracks already produced, as well as instrumental pieces between 2 and 3 minutes in length for use in AV music library." Does not return material; prefers to keep on file. Reports in 4 weeks.
Music: All types.
Tips: "Send your best and put your strongest work at the front of yiour demo tape."

PHOTO COMMUNICATION SERVICES, INC., Box 508, Acme MI 49610. (616)922-3050. President: M'Lynn Hartwell Jackson. Audiovisual firm and motion picture production company. Serves commercial, industrial and nonprofit clients. Uses services of music houses, independent songwriters, and lyricists for jingles and scoring of and background music for multi-image, film and video. Negotiates pay. Buys all rights or one-time rights.
How to Contact: Submit demo tape of previous work, tape demonstrating composition skills or query with resume of credits. Prefers cassette or 15 ips reel-to-reel (or VHS videocassette). Does not return material; prefers to keep on file. Reports in 6 weeks.
Music: Uses mostly industrial/commercial themes.

*PLAYERS MUSIC INC., 216 Carlton St., Toronto, Ontario M5A 2L1 **Canada.** (416)961-5290. Fax: (416)961-7754. Operations Manager: Jennifer Ward. Scoring service, **jingle/commercial music production house, production music library,** post audio production. Clients include advertising industry.

Estab. 1980. Uses the services of lyricists for scoring of background music, jingles and commercials for radio and TV. Commissions 5 lyricists/year. Payment negotiable. Buys all rights
How to Contact: Submit demo tape of previous work. Prefers cassette (or VHS videocassette). Does not return material; prefers to keep on file. Reports in 1 month.
Music: Uses all types for jingles.
Tips: "Have a talent at songwriting, not just programming."

PPI (PETER PAN INDUSTRIES), PARADE VIDEO, CURRENT RECORDS, COMPOSE RECORDS, 88 St. Frances St., Newark NJ 07105. (201)344-4214. Product Manager: Marianne Eggleston. Video, record label, publishing. Clients include songwriters, music and video. Estab. 1928. Uses the services of music houses, independent songwriters/composers, for scoring, background music, jingles and commercials for radio and TV. Commissions hundreds of composers and lyricists/year. Pays by the job, royalty and per agreement. Rights negotiable.
How to Contact: Submit demo tape and manuscript showing previous work, composition and scoring skills, or write to arrange personal interview. Prefers cassette (or ½ or ¾ videocassette) with 6 songs and lyric sheet. Also include a picture and bio of the artist. SASE. Prefers to keep material on file "if we like it for possible reference when we're looking for new materials. Completed projects preferred!" Reports in 3 weeks to 3 months (if we like it, immediately!)
Music: Uses all musical styles, including children's and health and fitness.
Tips: "Make your presentation as professional as possible and include your name, address and phone number on the tape/cassette in case it gets separated from the package."

PREMIER VIDEO, FILM AND RECORDING CORP., Dept. SM, 3033 Locust St., St. Louis MO 63103. (314)531-3555. President: Wilson Dalzell. Audiovisual firm, album producer and motion picture production company. Estab. 1931. Uses the services of songwriters for jingles and scoring and original background music and lyrics to reinforce scripts. Commissions 6-10 pieces and 5-10 lyricists/year. Pays by the job or by royalty. Buys all rights and "occasionally one-time rights with composer retaining title."
How to Contact: Query with resume of credits. Prefers 7½ or 15 ips reel-to-reel or cassette with any number of songs. SASE. Reports "as soon as possible with a short note using self-addressed envelope enclosed with submitted work informing talent they are on file for future reference."
Music: "As we serve every area of human development, all musical art forms are occasionally used."
Tips: "A limited need for music makes freelance writers a necessity. Be flexible. Have a simple, precise portfolio. Be sure your resume is direct, to-the-point and includes an honest review of past efforts. Be patient."

PRICE WEBER MARKETING COMMUNICATIONS, INC., Dept. SM, Box 99337, Louisville KY 40223. (502)499-9220. Producer/Director: Kelly McKnight. Advertising agency and audiovisual firm. Estab. 1968. Clients include Fortune 500, consumer durables, light/heavy industrials and package goods. Uses services of music houses, and independent songwriters/composer for scoring, background music and jingles for industrial and corporate image films and commercials for radio and TV. Commissions 6-8 composers/year. Pays by the job ($500-2,000). Buys all rights or one-time rights.
How to Contact: Submit demo tape of previous work demonstrating composition skills. Prefers cassette with 10 pieces. "Enclose data sheet on budgets per selection on demo tape." Does not return unsolicited material; prefers to keep on file. "We report back only if we use it."
Music: Uses easy listening, up-tempo, pop, jazz, rock and classical for corporate image industrials and commercials.
Tips: "Keep us updated on new works or special accomplishments. Work with tight budgets of $500-2,000. Show me what you're best at—show me costs."

PULLIN PRODUCTIONS LTD., 822 5th Ave. SW, Calgary, Alberta T2P 0N3 **Canada**. (403)234-7885. President: Chris Pullin. Clients include business and industry. Uses the services of music houses, songwriters and lyricists for "original songs and themes for multi-image, motion picture and multimedia." Commissions 4 composers and 2 lyricists/year. Pays minimum $500/job. Buys all rights.
How to Contact: Submit demo tape (or videocassette) of previous work. Prefers reel-to-reel with 4-10 songs but "any format is OK." Does not return unsolicited material. "Contact is made only if interested."

Market conditions are constantly changing! If you're still using this book and it is 1995 or later, buy the newest edition of Songwriter's Market at your favorite bookstore or order directly from Writer's Digest Books.

Music: Looking for "strong themes for any number of instruments/vocals (single instrument to full orchestra). Requirements for each job are very carefully specified."

QUALLY & COMPANY INC., #3, 2238 Central St., Evanston IL 60201-1457. (708)864-6316. Creative Director: Robert Qually. Advertising agency. Uses the services of music houses, independent songwriters/composers and lyricists for scoring, background music and jingles for radio and TV commercials. Commissions 2-4 composers and 2-4 lyricists/year. Pays by the job, by royalty sometimes. Buys various rights depending on deal.
How to Contact: Submit demo tape of previous work or query with resume of credits. Prefers cassette (or ¾″ Beta videocassette). SASE, but prefers to keep material on file. Reports in 2 weeks.
Music: Uses all kinds of music for commercials.

BILL QUINN PRODUCTIONS, 710 Cookman Ave., Asbury Park NJ 07712. (908)775-0500. Production Manager: Pat McManus. Audiovisual firm and motion picture production company. Estab. 1983. Clients include corporate, advertisers on cable and network TV and production companies. Uses the services of independent songwriters/composers and music houses for scoring of original productions and industrial films, background music for client accounts, commercials for radio and TV and video/film production. Commissions 15-20 composers/year. Pays by the job or approximately $25/hour. Buys one-time rights or all rights.
How to Contact: Submit demo tape of previous work or query with resume of credits. Call first to arrange personal interview. Prefers cassette. Will return unsolicited material accompanied by an SASE, but prefers to keep on file. "We respond by phone whenever we find music that fits a particular need."
Music: "We don't use one type of music more than another because our client list is rather lengthy and extremely varied. We use rock, pop, MOR, C&W, etc. Most often we commission music for TV and radio commercials. Interested in doing business with people in the New York and New Jersey area."
Tips: "Be flexible, able to work quickly and possess a working knowledge of all types of music."

RAMPION VISUAL PRODUCTIONS, 316 Stuart St., Boston MA 02116. (617)574-9601. Director/Camera: Steven V. Tringali. Motion picture production company. Clients include educational, independent producers, corporate clients and TV producers. Estab. 1982. Uses the services of independent songwriters/composers for jingles, background music and scoring to longer form programming. Commissions 4-6 composers/year. Pays by the job. Buys all rights.
How to Contact: Submit demo tape of previous work or query with resume of credits. Prefers cassette with variety of pieces. Does not return material; prefers to keep on file.
Music: Uses all styles for corporate, educational and original programming.
Tips: "Submit a varied demo reel showing style and client base."

RED HOTS ENTERTAINMENT, (formerly Winmill Entertainment), 813 N. Cordova St., Burbank CA 91505-2924. (818)954-0065. Director/Music Videos: Chip Miller. Motion picture and music video production company. Clients include record labels, network/cable TV, MTV and motion picture studios. Estab. 1987. Uses the services of music houses, lyricists and independent songwriters/composers for scoring of motion pictures, background music for motion pictures, and music videos for special accounts (i.e. fashion, etc.). Commissions 3-12 composers and 1-3 lyricists/year. Pay commensurate with film budget allocation. Rights bought depends on project.
How to Contact: Query with resume of credits. SASE. Report back depends on project deadline and needs.
Music: Music depends upon the project.

REED PRODUCTIONS, INC., Box 977, Warsaw IN 46580. (219)267-4199. President: Howard Reed. Audiovisual firm and motion picture production company. Serves medical-industrial clients. Uses the services of music houses, independent songwriters/composers and lyricists for background music for audiovisual and video and commercials for TV. Commissions 1 composer and 1 lyricist/year. Pays $100-500/job. Buys all rights or one-time rights.
How to Contact: Submit demo tape of previous work. Prefers cassette (or VHS videocassette). SASE. Reports in 3 weeks.
Music: Uses traditional music for industrial, medical, audiovisual and video projects.

RESPONSE GRAPHICS, P.O. Box 130666, Tyler TX 75713. (903)595-4701. President: Bill Bell. Advertising agency, audiovisual firm and **music sound effect library.** Clients include full service, banks, retail, industrial and music industry. Estab. 1954. Uses the services of music houses for background music for commercials, audiovisual presentations and jingles for commercials for radio and TV. Commissions 4-5 composers/year. Pays $250-2,000/job. Buys shared rights.

How to Contact: Submit demo tape of previous work. Prefers cassette or 7½ or 15 ips reel-to-reel with 3-4 songs and lyric sheet. SASE, but prefers to keep material on file. Reports in 3 weeks.
Music: Uses modern contemporary and C&W for films, commercials and audiovisual.
Tips: "Be cost effective."

RIGHT TRACKS PRODUCTIONS LTD., Dept. SM, 226 B. Portage Ave., Saskatoon, Sasketchewan S7J 4C6 **Canada.** (306)933-4949. Producer/Studio Manager: Lyndon Smith. Scoring service and **jingle/ commercial music production house.** Clients include ad agencies, corporations, film and video producers. Estab. 1986. Uses the services of independent songwriters/composers, lyricists, singers, session players, programmers, and arrangers for scoring of film and broadcast television, jingles for radio and TV, commercials for radio and TV and AV soundtracks. Commissions 5 composers and 5 lyricists/ year. Pays by the job, by royalty, or per hour. Buys all rights.
How to Contact: Submit demo tape of previous work; query with resume of credits. Prefers cassette or 7½/15 ips reel-to-reel. Does not return material; prefers to keep on file.
Music: "Depends on job/target market."

*RS MUSIC, 378 Brooke Ave., Toronto, Ontario M5M 2L6 **Canada.** (416)787-1510. President: Richard Samuels. Scoring service, **jingle/commercial music production house.** Clients include songwriters (private sector), ad agencies, direct retailers, communications companies. Estab. 1989. Uses the services of independent songwriters/composers and lyricists for jingles for commercials for radio and TV. Commissions 2-3 composers and 4-6 lyricists/year. Pays per job or pre-determined royalty. Buys one time rights.
How to Contact: Write or call first to arrange personal interview or submit demo tape of previous work. Prefers cassette (or VHS videocassette) with 4 songs and lyric sheet. Prefers to keep submitted material on file. Reports in 1 month.
Music: Uses up-tempo and pop for jingles, corporate video underscore.
Tips: "Be professional in the presentation package."

RTG PUBLISHING, INC., 130 E. 6th St., Cincinnati OH 45202. President: John Henry. Music Publisher. Clients include network TV (US), foreign TV and syndicated television producers. Uses services of MIDI composers to supply background and feature music. Currently seeking produced, unpublished, original songs for placement on TV programs. Writers paid performance royalties through BMI/ ASCAP.
How to Contact: Composers should submit resume and demo cassette of appropriate material (i.e. examples of TV background scoring only). Songwriters should send no more than three songs on one cassette. SASE. Do not call. Reports in 4-6 weeks.
Music: Song should be pop or A/C. No country, heavy metal, or rap.
Tips: "Listen to what the marketplace is using. Study TV music before submitting material."

RUFFCUT RECORDING, 6472 Seven Mile, Dept. SM, South Lyon MI 48178. (313)486-0505. Production Manager: J.D. Dudick. **Jingle/commercial production house.** Clients include advertising agencies and industrial accounts. Estab. 1990. Uses the services of independent songwriters/composers for background music for industrial films, jingles for local and national accounts and commercials for radio and TV. Commissions 4-5 composers and 1-2 lyricists/year. Pays by the job ($100-2,500) or by royalty (10-20%). Buys one-time rights.
How to Contact: Submit tape demonstrating composition skills. Prefers cassette with 3-5 songs and lyric sheets. Does not return unsolicited material; keeps material on file. Reports in 2-4 weeks.
Music: "All styles that are creative and unique" for commercials/radio, film presentations.
Tips: "Don't worry about the production; keep it catchy with a melody you will hum to."

CHARLES RYAN ASSOCIATES, Dept. SM, Box 2464, Charleston WV 25329. (304)342-0161. Vice President/Account Services: Tad Walden. Advertising agency. Clients in a variety of areas. Uses the services of music houses for scoring, background music, jingles and commercials for radio and TV. Commissions 2-3 songwriters/composers/year. Pays by the job. Buys all rights.
How to Contact: Submit demo tape of previous work or tape demonstrating composition skills; query with resume of credits; or write to arrange personal interview. Prefers cassette with 15-20 songs. SASE, but prefers to keep on file.
Music: Uses easy listening, pop, jazz, classical for educational films, slide presentations and commercials.
Tips: "The first 2 songs/samples on demo tape better be good or we'll listen no further."

S.A. PRODUCTIONS, INC., Dept. SM, 330 W. 58th St., New York NY 10019. (212)765-2669. President: Stan Applebaum. Scoring service, **commercial music production house.** Clients include motion picture production companies and advertising agencies, Broadway, music publishing and industrials. Estab. 1968. Uses the services of lyricists for jingles for national radio and TV commercials and industrials.

Pays by the job. Buys all rights, one-time rights or negotiates rights purchased.
How to Contact: Query with resume of credits, or submit demo tape of previous work demonstrating skills, or write to arrange personal interview. Prefers cassette or 15 or 7½ ips reel-to-reel with 5-10 pieces. SASE, but prefers to keep material on file. Reports in 1 month.

SCHEMBRI VISION, Dept. SM, 2156 Story Ave., Bronx NY 10473. (212)863-2986. Manager: Sal Schembri, Jr. **Jingle/commercial music production house.** Advertising agency. Serves retail and industrial clients. Uses the services of independent songwriters/composers for background music and jingles for TV commercials. Pays $250/job. Buys one-time rights.
How to Contact: Submit demo tape of previous work. SASE. Reports in 3 weeks.
Music: Uses easy listening and rap music for commercials.

CARL SCHURTZ MUSIC, #1437, 3000 Olympic Blvd., Santa Monica CA 90404-5041. Contact: Carl Schurtz. **Jingle/commercial music production house.** Corporate clients, TV, cable, film, radio, recorded books and museum tours. Uses the services of independent songwriters/composers for scoring of film and TV. Commissions 1 composer/year. Pays by the job. Buys all rights.
How to Contact: Query with resume of credits. Prefers cassette. Does not return material; prefers to keep on file. Reports in 2 months.
Music: Pop to classical, copy cats or pop tunes for industrials, multi image, videos (corporate) and jingles.

SHAFFER SHAFFER SHAFFER, INC., Dept. SM, 1070 Hanna Bldg., Cleveland OH 44115. (216)566-1188. President: Harry Gard Shaffer, Jr. Advertising agency. Clients include consumer and retail. Uses services of songwriters, lyricists and music houses for jingles and background music. Commissions 6 songwriters/year. Pays $2,000-15,000/job. Buys all rights.
How to Contact: Query with resume of credits. Prefers cassette with 6-12 songs. Prefers to keep material on file. Responds as needs arise.

SINGER ADVERTISING & MARKETING, INC., 1035 Delaware Ave., Buffalo NY 14209. (716)884-8885. Senior Vice President: Marilyn Singer. Advertising agency. Clients include health care, professional football, travel service and industrial. Estab. 1969. Uses the services of music houses, independent songwriters/composers and lyricists for background music for slide presentations, industrial videos, jingles for health care and professional football and commercials for radio and TV. Commissions 1-2 composers and 1-2 lyricists/year. Pay varies. Buys all rights.
How to Contact: Submit demo tape of previous work. Prefers cassette or 15 ips reel-to-reel (or ½" videocassette). SASE. "We will hold some material if we think there may be an appropriate upcoming opportunity."
Music: Uses up-tempo pop and New Age jazz for commercial jingles and slide presentations.
Tips: "Study our client list and their current work and then submit."

ROBERT SOLOMON AND ASSOCIATES ADVERTISING, Dept. SM, Suite 1000, 505 N. Woodward, Bloomfield Hills MI 48304. (313)540-0660. Creative Director: Neil Master. Advertising agency. Clients include "food service accounts, convenience stores, retail accounts and small service businesses." Uses independent songwriters, lyricists and music houses for jingles and special presentations. Commissions 1-10 songwriters and 1-10 lyricists/year. Pays by the job. Buys all rights.
How to Contact: Submit demo tape of previously aired work. Prefers cassette or 7½ ips reel-to-reel with 1-5 pieces and lyric or lead sheets. "Submissions must be up-to-date and up to industry standards." Does not return unsolicited material; prefers to keep on file.
Music: "MOR, pop or rock jingles describing specific products or services."
Tips: "Please make sure all information presented is CURRENT!"

SORIN PRODUCTIONS, INC., Freehold Executive Center, 4400 Route 9 S., Freehold NJ 07728. (908)462-1785. President: David Sorin. Audiovisual firm. Serves corporate and industrial clients. Uses services of music houses and independent songwriters/composers for background music for industrials. Commissions 1-3 composers and 1-3 lyricists/year. Pays by the job. Buys all rights.
How to Contact: Query with resume of credits. "No submissions with initial contact." Does not return unsolicited material; prefers to keep solicited materials on file. Reports in 1 month.
Music: Uses up-tempo and pop for audio, video and slides.

SOTER ASSOCIATES INC., 209 North 400 W., Provo UT 84601. (801)375-6200. President: N. Gregory Soter. Advertising agency. Clients include financial, health care, municipal, computer hardware and software. Estab. 1970. Uses services of music houses, independent songwriters/composers and lyricists for background music for audiovisual presentations and jingles for radio and TV commercials. Commissions 1 composer, 1 lyricist/year. Pays by the job. Buys all rights.

How to Contact: Submit tape demonstrating previous work and composition skills. Prefers cassette or VHS videocassette. Does not return unsolicited submissions; prefers to keep material on file.

SOUND IDEAS, Suite #4 105 W. Beaver Creek Rd., Richmond Hill, Ontario L4B 1C6 **Canada**. (416)886-5000. Fax: (416)866-6800. President: Brian Nimens. **Music/sound effect library**. Clients include broadcast, post-production and recording studios. Estab. 1978. Uses the services of music houses. Commissions 5-10 composers/year. Pays by the job. Buys all rights.
How to Contact: Submit demo tape of previous work. Prefers cassette with 5-10 songs. Does not return material; prefers to keep on file. Reports in 1 month.
Music: Uses full range for all kinds of assignments.

SOUND WRITERS PUBLICATIONS, INC., Dept. SM, 223-225 Washington St., Newark NJ 07102. (201)642-5132. Producer/Engineer: Kevin Ferd. Advertising agency, audiovisual firm and **jingle/commercial music production house**. Clients include major labels and large corporations. Estab. 1980. Uses the services of independent songwriters/composers and lyricists for scoring of jingles and TV commercials. Most writing, producing and engineering done in-house. Buys all rights and one-time rights.
How to Contact: Submit demo tape of previous work. Prefers cassette or ¾" videocassette. "We have a no return policy on all material." Prefers to keep material on file. Reports back in 4 weeks.
Music: Uses all types of music for commercials, training tapes and music videos.
Tips: "We don't like big egos."

SPIVACK ADVERTISING, INC., 90-K Painter Mill Rd., Owings Mills MD 21117. (410)585-3636. President: Irvin Spivack. Advertising agency. Clients include retail, financial, banking, medical and business-to-business. Estab. 1979. Uses the services of music houses for jingles for commercials for radio. Pay is negotiable.
How to Contact: Submit demo tape of previous work. Prefers cassette. SASE, but prefers to keep material on file.
Music: Generally up-tempo, but it really depends on clients.

STATION BREAK PRODUCTIONS, Dept. SM, Suite 1, 40 Glen St., Glen Cove NY 11542. (516)759-7005. Producer: Stephen Meyers. Advertising agency and **jingle/commercial music production house**. Clients include ad agencies, retail businesses, hotels, restaurants, corporate and special projects. Estab. 1985. Uses the services of independent songwriters/composers and singers, and MIDI composers with performer voice overs for commercials for radio and TV. Commissions 2 composers and 1 lyricist/year. Pays by the job. Buys all rights.
How to Contact: Submit demo tape of previous work or write to arrange personal interview. Prefers cassette with 4 pieces. Does not return unsolicited material; prefers to keep material on file. Reports in 1 month.
Music: Uses pop, classical and dance for industrial and commercials.
Tips: "Send your best work to date. Start with your strongest style."

STRATEGIC PROMOTIONS, INC., Dept. SM, Suite 250, 2602 McKinney, Dallas TX 75204. (214)871-1016. President: Grahame Hopkins. Promotional marketing agency. Clients include fast food, retail food, food service, beverage, beer. Estab. 1978. Uses the services of independent songwriters/composers and lyricists for scoring of music tracks for TV commercials and background music for TV & radio commercials. Commissions 2-3 composers/year. Pays by the job. Buys all rights.
How to Contact: Submit demo tape of previous work. Prefers cassette (or ¾" videocassette) with 4-5 songs. "No phone calls please." Does not return material; prefers to keep on file. Reports in 6 weeks.
Music: Uses all types of music for industrial videos, slide presentations and commercials.
Tips: "Be flexible, creative and open to input."

STRAUCHEN ASSOCIATES, INC., Dept. SM, 3388 Erie Ave., Cincinnati OH 45208. (513)871-5353. Fax: (513)871-5498. President: Stephen H. Strauchen. Advertising agency. Clients include financial, food, business-to-business and insurance. Estab. 1981. Uses the services of music houses and independent songwriters/composers for scoring of commercial jingles and sales films and background music for radio, TV and audiovisual presentations. Commissions 3-4 composers/year; 1 lyricist/year. Pays $500-1,000/job or $35-40/hour. Buys all rights.

Listings of companies within this section which are either commercial music production houses or music libraries will have that information printed in boldface type.

How to Contact: Submit demo tape of previous work. Prefers cassette, 7½ ips reel-to-reel or VHS videocassette. SASE, but prefers to keep materials on file.
Music: Easy listening, up-tempo, pop and jazz.
Tips: "Be specific regarding rates, use rights, etc."

SULLIVAN & FINDSEN ADVERTISING, Dept. SM, 2165 Gilbert Ave., Cincinnati OH 45206. (513)281-2700. Director of Broadcast Production: Kirby Sullivan. Advertising agency. Clients include consumer and business-to-business firms. Uses the services of music houses for jingles and commercials for radio and TV. Commissions 3 composers and 3 lyricists/year. Pays by the job. Buys all rights.
How to Contact: Submit demo tape of previous work. Prefers cassette. Does not return material; prefers to keep on file. "We report back when we need some work."
Music: Uses all styles for commercials.
Tips: "Don't call!"

TEEMAN/SLEPPIN ENTERPRISES INC., Dept. SM, 147 W. 26 St., New York NY 10001. (212)243-7836. President: Bob Teeman. Vice President: Stu Sleppin. Management, motion picture and music video production company. Clients include artists, film companies, TV stations and corporate sponsors. Uses the services of independent songwriters/composers and lyricists for scoring of TV shows and films and original songs. Commissions 3 composers and 3 lyricists/year. Pays by the job. Rights negotiable.
How to Contact: Submit demo tape of previous work or write to arrange personal interview. Prefers cassette (or VHS or ¾" videocassette). SASE, but prefers to keep material on file. Reports in 2 months.
Music: Uses pop and dance for original songs tied into a film or campaign.

TELECINE SERVICES & PRODUCTION LTD., 23 Seapoint Ave., Blackrock, Co. Dublin **Ireland**. Phone: 353 1 2808744. Fax: 353 1 808679. Director: Keith Nolan. Audiovisual firm and video production house. Estab. 1977. Clients include advertising and commercial business. Uses the services of songwriters and music houses for scoring of audiovisual programs. Commissions 5 songwriters/composers and 3 lyricists for 20 pieces/year. Pays $10,000/job. Buys all rights or rights within one country.
How to Contact: Submit tape demonstrating composition skills. Prefers 15 ips reel-to-reel/DAT cassette with 3-10 songs. Does not return material. Reports in 1 month.
Tips: "Understand our marketing needs; know the difference between European and U.S. tastes."

TEXAS AFFILIATED PUBLISHING COMPANY, "STREETPEOPLES WEEKLY NEWS," Box 270942, Dallas TX 75227-0942. (214)941-7796. Contact: Editor. Advertising agency and newspaper publisher. Clients are corporate and retail. Estab. 1977. Uses the services of independent songwriters/composers, lyricists and music houses for jingles and commercials for radio and TV. Pays negotiable amount. Buys all rights and one-time rights.
How to Contact: Submit demo tape of previous work or query with resume of credits. "No phone calls please. Send *no* originals, include SASE for returns. Our current project is about the problems of the 'homeless.' Persons writing songs about this may want to send for a copy of 'Streetpeoples Weekly News' to get an idea of what's involved. Send $2 to cover handling/postage." SASE, but prefers to keep materials on file. Reports in 1 week.
Music: Uses easy listening, up-tempo for commercials. "We're interested in many types/styles according to job need of our clients. Also need music production for intros on radio talk shows."
Tips: "NOTE: Since most inquiries do *not* contain SASE's, policy now dictates that $3 be sent for job's package. Simple queries requesting response without either of the above will *not* be handled."

*TPS VIDEO SVC., Box 1233, Edison NJ 08818. (201)287-3626. President: R.S. Burkt. Audiovisual firm, motion picture production company and **music/sound effects library**. Clients include AT&T, IBM and Xerox (industrial firms). Uses the services of independent composers and arrangers for scoring of industrials, background music and jingles for radio and TV commercials. Does not buy songs. Commissions 20-100 composers/year. Pays by the job. Buys all rights or one-time rights.
How to Contact: Submit demo tape of previous work demonstrating composition skills. Prefers cassette. SASE for response. Reports in 3 weeks.
Music: Considers all types of music for advertising.

*TRANSWORLD WEST MUSIC GROUP, Suite #83, 1102 N. Brand Blvd., Glendale CA 91202. (818)543-7538. Fax: (818)241-2494. Managing Director: Timothy M. Burleson. Scoring service, **jingle/commercial music production house,** music marketing consultants and music publisher. Clients include the "advertising, broadcasting, film and cable/television industries." Estab. 1991. Uses the services of music production libraries, independent songwriters/composers, lyricists, producers and other music publishers for special projects. Commissions 10-15 composers or songwriters/year. "Fee is negotiable." Buys all rights or one-time rights.

How to Contact: "No initial phone calls." Submit demo tape of original work. Unsolicited submissions OK. Prefers cassette, ½" VHS videocassette, or 7½ ips reel to reel with 8 songs/instrumentals and lyric or lead sheet. Does not return unsolicited material; prefers to keep on file. Reports in 1 month.
Music: All styles for custom soundtracks, jingles, underscores for the advertising, broadcasting, film cable/television industries worldwide.
Tips: "Send well produced quality demos that represent your best material. Innovative and progressive individuals will get top priority and consideration! We only handle the alternative markets listed above, so please stay focused on current market trends. And most important, KEEP THE FAITH! The world will always need good music, and the special people who create it."

TRF PRODUCTION MUSIC LIBRARIES, Dept. SM, 747 Chestnut Ridge Rd., Chestnut Ridge NY 10977. (800)899-6874. President: Michael Nurko. **Music/sound effect libraries.** Estab. 1931. Uses services of independent composers for jingles, background and theme music for all media including films, slide presentations, radio and television commercials. Pays 50% royalty.
How to Contact: Submit demo tape of new compositions. Prefers cassette with 3-7 pieces.
Music: Primarily interested in instrumental music for assignments in all media.

TRI VIDEO TELEPRODUCTION, Box 8822, Incline Village NV 89452-8822. (702)323-6868. Director: Jon Paul Davidson. Documentary and corporate television production firm. Clients include corporate accounts, primarily in health care and environment. Estab. 1978. Uses the services of music houses and independent songwriters/composers for background music for transitions and presentations. Commissions 0-1 composers/year. Pays $500-2,000/job. Buys all rights and/or one-time rights.
How to Contact: Query with resume of credits. Prefers cassette with 1-3 pieces. Does not return material; prefers to keep on file. "We do not report back. We will use on-file tapes to demo to clients when making selection. If your work is what client likes and is appropriate, we will contact you."
Music: Uses easy, up-tempo and classical for educational and corporate clients.
Tips: "The corporate market is quite varied. Needs are of every type. Just keep in touch. We do mostly custom work rather than volume, so number of projects is small each year."

TULLYVISION STUDIOS INC., Dept. SM, 914 Forest Grove Rd., Furlong PA 18725-1360. Producer: Michelle A. Powell. Audiovisual firm. Clients include corporate/industrial. Estab. 1983. Uses the services of independent songwriters/composers for marketing, training and corporate image videotapes. Commissions 3 composers/year. Pays $500/job. Buys all rights.
How to Contact: Submit demo tape of previous work. Prefers cassette (or ¾" VHS videocassette) with 3 songs. Does not return material; prefers to keep on file.
Music: Uses up-tempo and pop for educational films and slide presentations.

*24 CARAT PRODUCTIONS–LITTLE GEMSTONE MUSIC, P.O. Box 1703, Fort Lee NJ 07024. (201)488-8562. Owner: Kevin Noel. **Jingle/commercial music production house**, motion picture soundtracks company, corporate theme songs. Clients include commercial and independent clients. Estab. 1983. Uses the services of independent songwriters/composers (in-house) for scoring of background music for jingles for commercials for radio and TV. Commissions 15 composers and 12 lyricists/year. Pays flat-rate or percentage royalty.
How to Contact: Query with resume of credits, write first to arrange personal interview or submit demo tape of previous work. Prefers cassette. Prefers to keep submitted material on file. Reports in 2 weeks.
Music: Uses contemporary rock, pop, R&B, New Age music for commercial and private sources.

27TH DIMENSION INC., Box 1149, Okeechobee FL 34973-1149. (800)634-0091. President: John St. John. Scoring service, **jingle/commercial music production house** and **music sound effect library.** Clients include audiovisual producers, video houses, recording studios and radio and TV stations. Estab. 1986. Uses the services of independent songwriters/composers for scoring of library material and commercials for radio and TV. Commissions 10 composers/year. Pays $100-1,000/job; publishing (performance fees). "We buy the right to use in our library exclusively." Buys all rights except writer's publishing. Writer gets all performance fees (ASCAP or BMI).
How to Contact: Submit tape demonstrating composition skills or call. Prefers cassette. "Call before sending." SASE, but prefers to keep on file. Reports in 1 month.
Music: Uses industrial, pop jazz, sports, contemporary and New Age for music library.
Tips: "Follow style instructions carefully."

UNITED ENTERTAINMENT PRODUCTIONS, 3947 State Line, Kansas City MO 64111. (816)756-0288. Operations Manager: Dave Maygers. Recording studio, artist management, publishing company and record company. Serves musical groups, songwriters and ad clients. Estab. 1972. Uses the services of independent songwriters, lyricists and self-contained groups for scoring of album projects, background

music for ads and industrial films, jingles and commercials for radio and TV. Pays negotiable royalty. Buys all rights or one-time rights.
How to Contact: Submit demo tape of previous work demonstrating composition skills. "Send cassette of material and lyric sheet when applicable." Does not return unsolicited material; prefers to keep material on file.
Music: "Rock, pop, R&B, jazz, country to be used in music projects."

*VIDEO ARTS, Box 433, Manasquan NJ 08736. (908)223-5999. Producer: Nicholas G. Kuntz. **Music sound effect library.** Clients include professional video production companies and cable TV industry. Estab. 1987. Uses the services of independent songwriters/composers for background music for video productions and advertising and commercials for TV. Pays by the job. Buys all rights.
How to Contact: Submit demo tape of previous work. Prefers cassette with 3-5 songs. "All work must be composed and recorded via MIDI and, if selected, MIDI files must be provided. The library to be marketed will be entirely in MIDI format. All styles will be considered." Does not return material; prefers to keep on file. "Reports back on submissions only if selected."
Music: Uses all styles (must be written using MIDI) for background music for video production and cable advertisements.
Tips: "Know MIDI and be able to work in the format."

VINEBERG COMMUNICATIONS, Dept. SM, Suite B-408, 61-20 Grand Central Pkwy., Forest Hills NY 11375. (718)760-0333. President: Neil Vineberg. **Jingle/commercial music production house.** Clients include TV/film producers. Estab. 1986. Uses the services of independent songwriters/composers and lyricists for background music for TV/film, corporate videos/film and commercials for radio and TV. Commissions 5 composers and 2 lyricists/year. Pays by the job. Buys all rights and one-time rights.
How to Contact: Submit demo tape of previous work. Submit tape demonstrating composition skills. Query with resume of credits. Write first to arrange personal interview. Prefers cassette or VHS videocassette with 4 songs and lead sheet (if possible). "No calls. Write only." SASE, but prefers to keep material on file. Reports in 1 month.
Music: Uses all types except classical.

VIP VIDEO, Film House, 143 Hickory Hill Cir., Osterville MA 02655. (508)428-7198. President: Jeffrey H. Aikman. Audiovisual firm. Clients include business, industry and TV stations. Estab. 1983. Uses the services of music houses, independent songwriters/composers and lyricists for scoring of multi-image productions, background music for videotapes and motion pictures and jingles for TV commercials. Commissions 15-20 composers and 15-20 lyricists/year. Pays by the job, amounts vary depending on the length and complexity of each project. Buys all rights, but can handle one-time rights for special projects.
How to Contact: Submit demo tape of previous work. Prefers cassette with 1-2 songs. SASE, but prefers to keep material on file unless specifically stated. Reports in 6-8 weeks.
Music: Uses easy listening, pop and up-tempo for feature films, TV series, TV pilots and background for videotapes. Currently working on scoring series of 26 feature length silent films. If project is successful, this series will be added to at the rate of 13 per year.
Tips: "Constantly update your files. We like to hear from songwriters, lyricists and composers at least 3-4 times/year."

*VISION STUDIOS, 3765 Marwick Ave., Long Beach CA 90808. (310)429-1042. Proprietor: Arlan H. Boll. Audiovisual firm, scoring service, **jingle/commercial music production house, music sound effect library.** Clients include ad agencies, film and video directors, producers, etc. Estab. 1989. Uses the services of independent songwriters/composers and lyricists for scoring of background music for all media: film, radio and TV. Commissions 2-4 composers and 2-4 lyricists/year. "Payment is negotiable." Buys all rights or one-time rights.
How to Contact: Write first to arrange personal interview. Does not return material.
Music: Uses all types of music for all types of assignments.

WEBER, COHN & RILEY, 444 N. Michigan Ave., Chicago IL 60611. (312)527-4260. Executive Creative Director: C. Welch. Advertising agency. Serves real estate, business, financial and food clients. Estab. 1960. Uses music houses for jingles and background music for commercials. Commissions 2 songwriters and 2 lyricists/year. Pays $500 minimum/job. Buys all rights or one-time rights, "open to negotiation."
How to Contact: Write a letter of introduction to creative director. SASE. "We listen to and keep a file of all submissions, but generally do not reply unless we have a specific job in mind." Songwriters may follow up with a phone call for response.
Music: "We use music for a variety of products and services. We expect highly original, tight arrangements that contribute to the overall concept of the commercial. We do not work with songwriters who have little or no previous experience scoring and recording commercials."

Tips: "Don't aim too high to start. Establish credentials and get experience on small local work, then go after bigger accounts. Don't oversell when making contacts or claim the ability to produce any kind of 'sound.' Producers only believe what they hear on sample reels. Produce a sample reel that's professional and responsive to today's needs. Present a work that is creative and meets our strategies and budget requirements."

WEST COAST PROJECTIONS, #100, 11245 W. Bernardo Ct., San Diego CA 92127. (619)452-0041. Producer: David Gibbs. Video production. Estab. 1980. Uses the services of independent songwriters/composers for scoring and background music. Commissions 3 composers/year. Pays by the job. Buys one-time rights.
How to Contact: Submit demo tape of previous work. Prefers cassette (or any videocassette). Does not return material; prefers to keep on file. Reports only if interested.
Music: Uses up tempo pop for rock videos and corporate image presentations.

WESTON WOODS STUDIOS, 389 Newtown Turnpike, Weston CT 06883. Production Manager: Paul R. Gagne. Audiovisual firm, motion picture production company. "We produce films and audio visual products based on children's picture books." Clients include educational/institutional market and home market video. Estab. 1955. Uses services of independent composers and copyists for scoring of short films and filmstrip soundtracks. Commissions 3-5 composers/year. Pays $600-3500/job. Buys all rights.
How to Contact: Submit demo tape of previous work, tape demonstrating composition scores or query with resume of credits. Prefers cassette. "Write only; we cannot accept telephone queries." SASE, but prefers to keep material on file. Reports in 6-12 months.
Music: "Uses serious non-commercial scoring for acoustic instruments (synthesizer OK) in classical, folk, or ethnic styles for educational films and filmstrips of children's stories; no driving rhythm tracks; no songs, please—especially 'kiddie songs.' "

WHITE PRODUCTION ARCHIVES, INC., Dept. SM, 5525 W. 159th St., Oak Forest IL 60452. (708)535-1540. President: Matthew White. Motion picture production company. Produces home video entertainment programs. Estab. 1987. Uses the services of independent songwriters/composers for scoring of offbeat documentaries; videogame tapes. Commissions 5 composers/year. Pays by the job. Buys all rights.
How to Contact: Submit demo tape of previous work. Prefers cassette. Does not return unsolicited material. Prefers to keep submitted materials on file.
Music: Uses material for home videos.

EVANS WYATT ADVERTISING, 346 Mediterranean Dr., Corpus Christi TX 78418. (512)854-1661. Owner: E. Wyatt. Advertising agency. Clients are general/all types. Estab. 1975. Uses the services of music houses and independent songwriters/composers for background music for soundtracks, jingles for advertising and commercials for radio and TV. Commissions 10-12 composers/year. Pays by the job. Buys all rights.
How to Contact: Submit demo tape of previous work demonstrating composition skills, query with resume of credits or write first to arrange personal interview. Prefers cassette. SASE, but prefers to keep material on file. Reports in 2 months.
Music: Uses all types for commercials plus videos mostly.
Tips: "Make it *easy* to judge your work! Be sure you've got the talent you claim and present it clearly. If we don't like your presentation immediately, chances are we won't like your work."

GREG YOUNGMAN MUSIC, Box 381, Santa Ynez CA 93460. (805)688-1136. Advertising agency/audio production. Serves all types of clients. Local, regional and national levels. Uses the services of music houses and independent composers/copywriters for commercials, jingles and audiovisual projects. Commissions 12-20 composers/year. Pays $500-10,000/project. Buys all or one-time rights.
How to Contact: Submit demo tape of previously aired work. Prefers cassette, R-DAT or reel-to-reel. Does not return material; prefers to keep on file. Reports in 1 month.
Music: Uses all types for radio commercials, film cues.
Tips: "Keeps demos to 10 minutes."

Advertising, AV and Commercial Music Firms/'93-'94 Changes

The following markets appeared in the 1993 edition of *Songwriter's Market* but are absent from the 1994 edition. Most of these companies failed to respond to our request for an update of their listing for a variety of reasons. For example, they may have gone out of business or they may have requested deletion from the 1994 edition because they are backlogged with material. If we know the specific reason, it appears within parentheses.

American Media Concepts, Inc.
Authentic Marketing
Avid Productions (overstocked)
Baxter, Gurian & Mazzei, Inc. (requested deletion)
Bell & Roberts
Bradley Communications (not accepting submissions)
Broach and Co. (not accepting submissions)
Broadcast Video, Inc. (requested deletion)
Calf Audio
Channell One Video (not accepting submissions)
Channel One Video Tape Inc.
Channel 3 Video
Chase/Ehrenberg & Rosene, Inc.
Checkmark Communications Multi-Media (not accepting submissions)
Chiat/Day/Mojo Advertising (minimal music needs)
T. Cooke Productions, Inc.
Creswell, Munsell, Fultz & Zirbel
R.J. Dale Advertising Inc.
The Dennis Group, Inc.
Donchrist Visual Communications
DRGM
Richard R. Falk Assoc.
Film America, Inc. (no longer in music business)
Foremost Films and Video, Inc.
French & Rogers, Inc.
Furman Films, Inc. (no longer in music business)

Jan Gardner and Associates
Geer DuBois Advertising Inc.(unable to contact)
Gillespie Advertising, Inc. (requested deletion)
Glazen Advertising
Gold Coast Advertising Association Inc.
Hodges Media Group
Hoffman/Lewis
Intermedia (overstocked)
International Media Services, Inc.
Katsin/Loeb and Partners
Kelliher/Samets
La Bov and Beyond Music Production
Lane Audio Productions, Inc.
Ledford Productions, Inc.
S.R. Leon Company, Inc.
Lott Walker Advertising (minimal music needs)
McDonald Davis & Assoc.
Lee Magid Inc. (affiliate of Alexis Music Inc./ASCAP, Marvelle Music Co./BMI)
Mann Advertising (not accepting submissions)
The Marketing Connection
Media Productions
MTC Production Center (unable to contact)
Overcash & Moore, Inc. (overstocked)
Photo Communications Corp. (in different business)
Pop International Corporation (unable to contact)
Prestige Productions (requested deletion)
Pro Video Sales Company (in

different business)
Professional Media Services
Publicis, Inc.
Pyramid Productions
Chuck Ruhr Advertising
Patrick William Salvo
Seaside Productions
Signature Music, Inc. (requested deletion)
Silver Burdett & Ginn (overstocked)
Sonic Images Productions, Inc. (requested deletion)
Sopersound Music Library (not accepting submissions)
Sound*Light Productions (minimal music needs)
Spectrum Sound Studios, Inc.
Starwest Productions, Inc. (minimal music needs)
Studio M Productions Unltd.
Talco Productions (not accepting submissions)
Top of the Mountain Publishing/Powell Productions (requested deletion)
Tully-Menard, Inc. (requested deletion)
Umbrella Media
Video I-D, Inc.
Vision Film Group, Inc.
Voices/Living Library (minimal music needs)
Ben Wages Agency
Western Publishing Company, Inc. (overstocked)
Yardis Corporation
ZM Squared (minimal music needs)
Z-Note Music (unable to contact)

Play Producers
and Publishers

Writing music for the stage is a considerable challenge in the theater of the 1990s. Conventional wisdom says that if a composer or playwright doesn't have a production to his credit, he will have a difficult time establishing himself. Play producers in the major markets, especially Broadway, won't often take a chance on unproven talent when productions routinely cost millions of dollars and a show must run for several years to break even. It's a classic "Catch-22"; the aspiring playwright needs experience to get his work produced, but can't get that experience without production.

Fortunately, the conventional wisdom about musical theater may not be accurate. Many venues for new musical works exist; this section lists them. Contained within are listings of theater companies, producers, dinner theaters, and publishers of musical theater works. We've separated this section into two subsections: one for publishers and one for producers. All these markets are interested in and actively seeking new musical theater works of all types for their stages or publications.

Many of these listings are small theaters run on a nonprofit basis. Their budgets for production and rehearsal time will of necessity be limited. Keep this in mind when preparing to submit your work. When submitting, ask about other opportunities available for your work. Some companies or theaters may like your work, but may wish to present it in revue form. Others may be looking for incidental music for a spoken word play. Do research and ask questions to help increase your chances of consideration.

Use research and further education to help you enrich your personal experience and therefore your work. As a composer for the stage, you need to know as much as possible about the theater and how it works, its history and the different roles played by the people involved in it. Flexibility is a key to successful productions, and having a knowledge of how the theater works will only aid you in cooperating and collaborating with the work's director, producer, technical people and actors.

Read the following listings carefully for information on each market, the type of work being sought, and their submission procedures. Research further the markets that you believe will be interested in your work. And when you've decided on the best markets for your work, follow submission procedures meticulously.

INSIDER REPORT

Regional theater nurtures new playwrights

While Broadway may be the place most people think of when they hear the words "musical theater," regional theater is where most new playwrights get their start. Regional theater companies actively seek new material from aspiring writers; rather than focusing on producing one big show, they are more interested in helping writers develop their careers. Regional theater can provide a supportive and nurturing environment for a writer just starting out in the field.

"The regional theater scene is alive and crying for new material," says Allan Chambers, artistic coordinator of New Tuners Theatre/Workshop in Chicago. "Not every musical needs to be a 30 character and chorus 'Broadway Musical.' Art should not be judged by the size of the canvas."

Allan Chambers

New Tuners Theatre is a not-for-profit theater company dedicated to the development of new composers, lyricists and writers and the production of their works. Chambers, in his role as artistic coordinator, looks for certain elements in the submissions he receives from writers. "I usually focus on the dramatic structure of a new musical. We're looking for new musical voices, with fresh points of view as seen through the organic development of characters. And we need to challenge the audience, not alienate them."

For a writer just breaking into musical theater, it's important to be aware of the collaborative effort that goes into the production of a musical. "I wish," says Chambers, "that more authors of new musicals would get involved in the production of new works other than their own to understand the complete scope of collaboration." The best way to do this is to get involved in any aspect of the theater you can. "Professional internships are available for artists all across the country," Chambers adds. "Find a store-front theater that will let you hang out and get involved with the day to day building of a new show."

Chambers advises playwrights to always keep in mind one very important element—the audience. "Enlighten and embrace the audience," he says. "Don't confuse. Music has been and will continue to be associated with individual emotion and random states of feeling. When coupled with a specific lyric or image this music will evoke controlled response. Explore this coupling to your advantage."

Since musical theater is such a competitive field, it's important for the aspiring writer to stay objective and be persistent. "We've all had flops and will continue to have projects that don't find an audience," says Chambers. "Be prepared for rejection but don't be discouraged. Listen to the audience. Cultivate artistic relationships and create."

Play Producers

*A.D. PLAYERS, 2710 W. Alabama, Houston TX 77098. (713)526-2721. Dramaturg: Martha Doolittle. Play producer. Estab. 1967. Produces 4-5 full-length, 4 children's and approximately 20 1 acts in repertory and 1-2 musicals/year. General public tend to be conservative—main stage shows, children/ families—children's shows; churches schools, business—repertory shows. Payment varies.
How to Contact: Query with synopsis, character breakdown and set description. Reports in 6-12 months.
Musical Theater: "We prefer musicals for family and/or children, comedy or drama, full-length, original or classic adaptations with stories that reflect God's relevence and importance in our lives. Any style. Maximum 10 actors. No fly space required. Minimum wing space required. No New Age; anything contradictory to a Christian perspective; operatic; avant garde cabaret. Music should be simple, easy to learn and perform, we utilize a broad range of musical ability; will consider musical revue to musical comedy, play with music."
Productions: *Narnia*, by Jules Tasca (children, family, fantasy, musical); *Smoke on the Mountain*, by Connie Ray and Alan Bailey (family gospel, hymn heritage); *Galley Proof*, by Jeanette Cliff George (musical comedy, biblical characters, and storyline).
Tips: "Learn the craft, structure and format of scriptwriting before submitting. Then be flexible and open to learning from any producing theater which takes an interest in your work."

THE ACTING COMPANY, Dept. SM, Box 898, Times Square Station, New York NY 10108. (212)564-3510. Play producer. Estab. 1972. Produces 2-3 plays/year. "Have done musicals in the past. We are a national touring company playing universities and booking houses." Pays by royalty or negotiated fee/commission.
How to Contact: Submit through agent only. SASE. Reports in 12 weeks.
Musical Theater: "We would consider a wide variety of styles—although we remain a young, classical ensemble. Most of our classical plays make use of a lot of incidental music. Our company consists of 17 actors. All productions must be able to tour easily. We have no resident musicians. Taped sound is essential. Actors tend to remain active touring members for 2-3 seasons. Turnover is considerable. Musical ability of the company tends to vary widely from season to season. We would avoid shows which require sophisticated musical abilities and/or training."

ALLEGHENY HIGHLANDS REGIONAL THEATRE, 526 W. Ogle St., Ebensburg PA 15931. (814)472-4333. Managing Director: Noel Feeley. Play producer. Estab. 1974. Produces 4 plays and 2 musicals (1 new musical every third year). "Rural audience, many elderly, many families; we play in a 200 seat arena." Pays $50-125/performance.
How to Contact: Query with synopsis, character breakdown and set description. Does not return unsolicited material. Reports in 6 months.
Musical Theater: "Small cast, full-length musicals, preferably orchestrated for no more than 6 musicians. Anything set in Pennsylvania about Pennsylvanians is of particular interest. Especially interested in musicals for children, up to 60 minutes in length. Roles for children are a plus. We have difficulty finding men to audition. Few men's roles are a plus. No more than 19-20 including chorus, no more than 2-3 settings. We had original music scored for scene changes and intermission music for *She Stoops To Conquer*. Perhaps some underscoring for a mystery would be fun."
Productions: *Oklahoma!*, by Rodgers & Hammerstein; *Cabaret*, by Kander & Ebb; *Quilters*, by Newman and Damashek; *Robber Bridegroom*, by Robert Waldman; *Anything Goes*, by Cole Porter; *Oliver!*, by Lionel Bart.

AMAS MUSICAL THEATRE INC., Suite 2J, 450 W. 43rd St., New York NY 10036. (212)563-2565. Executive Director: William Michael Maher. Founder/Artistic Director: Rosetta Lenoire. Produces 1 or 2 original musicals/year—readings/workshops only. Presents 1 children's theater production. "AMAS is a multi-racial theater, dedicated to bring all people—regardless of race, creed, color or religion—together through the performing arts." Does not pay for manuscripts but "provides a top quality New York showcase with a good record of commercial pick-ups."
How to Contact: Query first with SASE. Please do not send script and tapes.
Musical Theater: Musicals only. "All works to be performed by multi-racial casts. Musical biographies especially welcome. Cast size should be under 10 if possible, including doubling. Because of physical space, set requirements should be relatively simple. We do not want to see material with explicit sex

The asterisk before a listing indicates that the listing is new in this edition. New markets are often the most receptive to unsolicited submissions.

or violence or very strong language. Prefer themes of love, joy and togetherness."
Productions: *Gunmetal Blues*, by Marion Adler, Craig Bohmler and Scott Wentworth; and *Junkyard*, by Mandel and Sahl.
Tips: "Write economically: cast, sets, theme, etc."

*AMERICAN LIVING, History Theater, Box 2677, Hollywood CA 90078. (213)876-2202. President and Artistic Director: Dorene Ludwig. Play producer. Estab. 1975. Produces 1-2 plays/year. All over U.S., but mostly Southern California—conventions, schools, museums, universities, libraries, etc. Pays by royalty.
How to Contact: Query first. SASE. Reports in 6 months.
Musical Theater: "We use only primary source, historically accurate material: in music—*Songs of the Civil War* or *Songs of the Labor Movement*, etc.—presented as a program rather than play would be the only use I could foresee. We need music historians more than composers."
Tips: "Do not send fictionalized historical material. We use primary source material only."

AMERICAN STAGE FESTIVAL, Dept. SM, Box 225, Milford NH 03055. (603)673-4005. Producing Director: Matthew Parent. Play producer. Estab. 1975. Produces 5 mainstage plays, 10 children's and 1-2 musicals/year. Plays are produced in 496 seat proscenium stage for a general audience.
How to Contact: Submit query letter with synopsis. Reports in 6 months.
Musical Theater: "We seek stories about interesting people in compelling situations. Besides our adult audience we have an active children's theater. We will not do a large chorus musical if cast size is over 18. We use original music in plays on a regular basis, as incidental music, pre-show and between acts, or as moments in and of themselves."
Productions: *Little Shop of Horrors*, by Howard Ashman and Alan Menken; *Crimes of the Heart*, by Beth Henley; *Love Letters*, by A.R. Gurney; *The Country Girl*, by Clifford Odets and *Lost in Yonkers*, by Neil Simon. The American Stage Festival has produced many new musicals in the past five years including Ken Ludwig's *Gilbert and Sullivan*, the Tony Award-nominated *Starmites* and the musical version of the classic comedy *Peg O' My Heart*.
Tips: "Write about characters. Understand the reasons why characters break into song. Submit legible script and listenable cassette. And please keep writing!"

*ARDEN THEATRE COMPANY, P.O. Box 801, Philadelphia PA 19105. (215)829-8900. Fax: (215)829-1735. Producing Artistic Director: Terrence J. Nolen. Play producer. Estab. 1988. Produces 5 plays and 1-2 musicals/year. Adult audience—diverse. 150-175 seats, flexible. Pays 5% royalty.
How to Contact: Submit complete ms, score and tape of songs. SASE. Reports in 6 months.
Musical Theater: Full length plays and musicals. Intimate theater space, maximum cast approximately 15, minimum can be smaller. Not interested in children's music. Will consider original music for use in developing or pre-existing play. Composers should send samples of music on cassette.
Productions: *Sweeney Todd*, by Sondheim/Wheeler (musical thriller); *Change Partners & Dance*, by Dennis Raymond Smeal (new play—romantic comedy); *The Tempest*, by Shakespeare (classic).
Tips: "Send cassette."

ARIZONA THEATRE COMPANY, P.O. Box 1631, Tucson AZ 85702. (602)884-8210. Artistic Director: David Goldstein. Professional regional theater company. Members are professionals. Performs 6 productions/year, including 1 new work. Audience is middle and upper-middle class, well-educated, aged 35-64. "We are a two-city operation based in Tucson, where we perform in a 603-seat newly renovated, historic building, which also has a 100-seat flexible seating cabaret space. Our facility in Phoenix, the Herberger Theater Center, is a 712-seat, proscenium stage." Pays 4-10% royalty.
How to Contact: Query first. Reports in 5 months.
Musical Theater: Musicals or musical theater pieces. 15-16 performers maximum including chorus. Instrumental scores should not involve full orchestra. No classical or operatic.
Productions: Barbara Damashek's *Quilters* (musical theater piece); Sondheim/Bernstein's *Candide* (musical); and Anita Ruth/American composer's *Dreamers of the Day* (musical theater piece).
Tips: "As a regional theater, we cannot afford to produce extravagant works. Plot line and suitability of music to further the plot is an essential consideration."

ARKANSAS REPERTORY THEATRE, 601 Main, P.O. Box 110, Little Rock AR 72203. (501)378-0445. Contact: Brad Mooy. Play producer. Estab. 1976. Produces 7 plays and 4 musicals (1 new musical)/year. "We perform in a 354-seat house and also have a 99 seat blackbox." Pays 5-10% royalty or $75-150 per performance.
How to Contact: Query with cover letter, 10-page synopsis and cassette. SASE. Reports in 6 months.
Musical Theater: "Small casts are preferred, comedy or drama and prefer shows to run 1:45 to 2 hours maximum. Simple is better; small is better, but we do produce complex shows. We aren't interested in children's pieces, puppet shows or mime. We always like to receive a tape of the music with the book."

Productions: *Into the Woods*, by Sondheim/Lapine (Grimm's Fairy Tales compilation); *Oil City Symphony*, by Hardwick Craver, Monk, Murfitt (American small town spoof); *Nunsense*, by Dan Goggin (Catholicism revue, nuns tap dancing).
Tips: "Include a *good* cassette of your music, *sung well*, with the script."

ASHLAWN-HIGHLAND SUMMER FESTIVAL, Box 37, Route 6, Charlottesville VA 22902. (804)293-4500. General Manager: Judith H. Walker. Play producer. Estab. 1977. Produces 1 musical and 2 operas/year. "Our operas and musicals are performed in a casual setting. The audience is composed of people from the Charlottesville area."
How to Contact: Query first. SASE. "We try to return items after review but depending on the time of year response time may vary."
Musical Theater: "We are very open to new ideas and young artists. Included in our season is a summer Saturday program designed for children. We enjoy puppet shows, story tellers and children-related plays. We are a small company with a limited budget. Our cast is usually 12 performers and a volunteer local chorus. Minimal scenery is done. Our audience is composed of families with children and retired adults. Material should suit their tastes." Would consider original music for use in a play being developed.
Productions: Rodgers and Hammerstein's *Carousel*; Mozart's *Don Giovanni* and Donizetti's *Don Pasquale*.

ASOLO THEATRE COMPANY, (formerly Asolo Center for the Performing Arts), Dept. SM, 5555 N. Tamiami Trail, Sarasota FL 34243. (813)351-9010. Contact: Literary Manager. Play producer. Produces 7-8 plays (1 musical)/year. Plays are performed at the Asolo Mainstage (500-seat proscenium house). Pays 5% minimum royalty.
How to Contact: Query with synopsis, character breakdown, set description and one page of dialogue. SASE. Reports in 3 months.
Musical Theater: "We want small to mid-size non-chorus musicals only. They should be full-length, any subject. There are no restrictions on production demands; however, musicals with excessive scenic requirements or very large casts may be difficult to consider."
Productions: Julie Boyd's *Sweet and Hot*; Boyd, Wildhorn and Bettis' *Svengali* and Ebb, Martin and Kander's *70, Girls, 70*.

BAILIWICK REPERTORY, Dept. SM, 1225 West Belmont, Chicago IL 60657. (312)883-1091. Executive Director: David Zak. Play producer. Estab. 1982. Produces 5 mainstage, 5 one-act plays and 1-2 new musicals/year. "We do Chicago productions of new works on adaptations that are politically or thematically intriguing and relevent. We also do an annual director's festival which produces 50-75 new short works each year." Pays 5-8% royalty.
How to Contact: "Send SASE (business size) first to receive manuscript submission guidelines. Material returned if appropriate SASE attached."
Musical Theater: "We want innovative, dangerous, exciting and issue-oriented material."
Productions: *Wild Honey*, by Chekha/Frayn; *Animal Farm*, by Orwell/Hall/Peaslee/Mitchell (musical); *Nebraska*, by Logan; *Blues in the Night* (musical); and *Songs of the Season* (musical).
Tips: "Be creative. Be patient. Be persistent. Make me believe in your dream."

BERKSHIRE PUBLIC THEATRE, P.O. Box 860, 30 Union St., Pittsfield MA 01202. (413)445-4631. Artistic Director: Frank Bessell. Play producer. Estab. 1976. Produces 9 plays (2 musicals)/year. "Plays are performed in a 285-seat proscenium thrust theatre for a general audience of all ages with wide-ranging tastes." Pays negotiable royalty or amount per performance.
How to Contact: Unsolicited submissions OK; send tapes when available. SASE. Reports in 3 months.
Musical Theater: Seeking musicals with "no more than 3 acts (2½ hours). We look for fresh musicals with something to say. Our company has a flexible vocal range. Cast size must be 2-50, with a small orchestra." Would also consider original music "for a play being developed and possibly for existing works."
Productions: *Jesus Christ Superstar*, by Rice/Lloyd-Webber (gospel/life of Christ); *Rhapsody*, by George Gershwin (revue of Gershwin music); *Company*, by Sondheim/Furth (modern relationships).
Tips: "We are a small company. Patience is a must. Be yourself—open, honest. Experience is not necessary but is helpful. We don't have a lot of money but we are long on nurturing artists! We are developing shows with commercial prospects to go beyond the Berkshires, i.e., a series of rock music revues is now in its fifth year."

BRISTOL RIVERSIDE THEATRE, Dept. SM, Box 1250, Bristol PA 19007. (215)785-6664. Artistic Director: Susan D. Atkinson. Play producer. Estab. 1986. Produces 5 plays, 2 musicals/year (1 new musical every 2 years). "New 302-seat proscenium Equity theater with audience of all ages from small towns and metropolitan area." Pays by royalty 6-8%.

How to Contact: Submit complete ms, score and tape of songs. SASE. Reports in 6 months.
Musical Theater: "No strictly children's musicals. All other types with small to medium casts and within reasonable artistic tastes. Prefer one-set; limited funds restrict. Does not wish to see anything catering to prurient interests."
Productions: *The Robber Bridegroom*, by Alfred Uhry/R. Waldman (E. Welty novella - 1790s Mississippi delta); *A Day in Hollywood/A Night*, by Frank Lazarus/D. Vosburgh (1930s Hollywood); *Sally Blane, World's Greatest Girl Detective*, by David Levy/Leslie Eberhard (spoof of teen detective genre); *Moby Dick*, by Mark St. Germain, music by Doug Katsarous; and *Alive and Well*, by Larry Gatlin.
Tips: "He or she should be willing to work with small staff, open to artistic suggestion, and aware of the limitations of newly developing theaters."

*WILLIAM CAREY COLLEGE DINNER THEATRE, William Carey College, Hattiesburg MS 39401. (601)582-6218. Managing Director: O.L. Quave. Play producer. Produces 2 plays (2 musicals)/year. "Our dinner theater operates only in summer and plays to family audiences." Payment negotiable.
How to Contact: Submit complete manuscript and score. SASE. Reports as soon as possible.
Musical Theater: "Plays should be simply-staged, have small casts (8-10 maximum), and be suitable for family viewing; two hours maximum length. Score should require piano only, or piano, synthesizer."
Productions: *Ernest in Love*; *Rodgers and Hart: A Musical Celebration*; and *Side by Side by Sondheim*.

*CENTENARY COLLEGE, THEATRE DEPARTMENT, Shreveport LA 71134-1188. (318)869-5011. Chairman: Robert R. Buseick. Play producer. Produces 6 plays (1-2 new musicals)/year. Plays are presented in a 350-seat playhouse to college and community audiences.
How to Contact: Submit manuscript and score. SASE. Reports in 1 month.
Productions: *Man of La Mancha*; *Nunsense*; *Chicago*; *Broadway Bound*; *Into the Woods*; *Little Shop of Horrors*; and *Jerry's Girls*, by Todd Sweeney.

CIRCA' 21 DINNER PLAYHOUSE, Dept. SM, Box 3784, Rock Island IL 61204-3784. (309)786-2667. Producer: Dennis Hitchcock. Play producer. Estab. 1977. Produces 1-2 plays, 4-5 musicals (1 new musical)/year. Plays produced for a general audience. Two children's works/year, concurrent with major productions. Pays by royalty.
How to Contact: Query with synopsis, character breakdown and set description or submit complete manuscript, score and tape of songs. SASE. Reports in 8 weeks.
Musical Theater: "We produce both full length and one act children's musicals. Folk or fairy tale themes. Works that do not condescend to a young audience yet are appropriate for entire family. We're also seeking full-length, small cast musicals suitable for a broad audience." Would also consider original music for use in a play being developed.
Productions: *Singin' in the Rain*, by Betty Comden and Adolph Green; *Phantom*, by Kopit/Yestin; *Pump Boys and Dinettes*; *Me and My Girl*; and *Snow White Goes West*, by Jim Eiler.
Tips: "Small, upbeat, tourable musicals (like *Pump Boys*) and bright musically-sharp children's productions (like those produced by Prince Street Players) work best. Keep an open mind. Stretch to encompass a musical variety—different keys, rhythms, musical ideas and textures."

CIRCLE IN THE SQUARE THEATRE, Dept. SM, 1633 Broadway, New York NY 10019. (212)307-2700. Literary Advisor: Nancy Bosco. Play producer. Estab. 1951. Produces 3 plays/year; occasionally produces a musical. Pays by royalty.
How to Contact: Query with a letter, 1-page synopsis and script sample (10 pages). Reports in 6 months.
Musical Theater: "We are looking for original material with small cast and orchestra requirements. We're not interested in traditional musical comedies." Will consider original music for use in a play being developed or in a pre-existing play at the option of the director.
Productions: *Pal Joey*, *Sweeney Todd* and *Anna Karenina*.

CITY THEATRE COMPANY, INC., 57 S. 13th St., Pittsburgh PA 15203. (412)431-4400. General Manager: Adrienne Keriotis. Play producer. Estab. 1974. Produces 5 plays/year. "Plays are performed in an intimate 225 seat thrust-stage or proscenium configuration theatre to an adventurous subscriber base."
How to Contact: Query with synopsis, character breakdown and set description. "We select plays through Play Showcases (Louisville, Denver and Rochester), Summer Workshop Programs (Shenandoah, New Harmony and Carnegie Mellon University) and local playwright centers and organizations from new dramatists in New York, Chriog Dramatists Workshop and Southeast Playwrights project. Also various scriptshare and play catalog newsletters."
Musical Theater: "We want sophisticated plays with music. We prefer a small cast with no more than 10 (including musicians) and single set because we have small stage capabilities only. We don't want traditional, large cast musical comedies."

Productions: *Painting It Red*, by Steven Dietz (modern romance); *Lovers and Keepers*, by Irene Fornes (failed romance); *Maybe I'm Doing It Wrong*, by Randy Newman (musical review); *Evelyn and the Polka King*, by John Olive (light comedy); and *Cabaret Verboten*, by Jeremy Lawrence (historical political cabaret).

COCKPIT IN COURT SUMMER THEATRE, 7201 Rossville Blvd., Baltimore MD 21237. (410)786-6534. Managing Director: F. Scott Black. Play producer. Estab. 1973. Produces 6-8 plays and 5-7 musicals/ year. "Audiences range from mature to senior citizens. Plays are produced at 3 locations: Mainstage (proscenium theater), Courtyard (outdoor theater) and Cabaret (theater-in-the-round)."
How to Contact: Query first. SASE. Reports in 1 month.
Musical Theater: "Seeking musical comedy and children's shows. We have the capacity to produce large musicals with up to 76 cast members."
Productions: *I Remember Mama*, by Richard Rodgers; *Chicago*, by Kander and Ebb; *Carnival*, by Merrill and Stewart and *Heidi*, by Johanna Spyri.
Tips: "We look for material that is perhaps different but still appeals to a community theater audience."

THE COTERIE, 2450 Grand Ave., Kansas City MO 64108. (816)474-6785. Artistic Director: Jeff Church. Play producer. Estab. 1979. Produces 7-8 plays/year. Plays produced at Hallmark's Crown Center in downtown Kansas City in The Coterie's resident theater (capacity 240). A typical performance run is one month in length. "We retain some rights on commissioned plays. Writers are paid a royalty for their work per performance or flat fee."
How to Contact: Query with synopsis and character breakdown. Submit complete manuscript and score "if established writer in theater for young audiences. We will consider musicals with smaller orchestration needs (3-5 pieces), or a taped score." SASE. Reports in 6 months.
Musical Theater: "Types of plays we produce: pieces which are universal in appeal; plays for all ages. They may be original or adaptations of classic or contemporary literature. Limitations: Typically not more than 12 in a cast—prefer 5-9 in size. No fly space or wing space. No couch plays. Prefer plays by seasoned writers who have established reputations. Groundbreaking and exciting scripts from the youth theater field welcome. It's perfectly fine if your musical is a little off center."
Productions: *Animal Farm*, by Sir Peter Hall; *The Wind in the Willows* (adapted), by Doug Post; and *The Ugly Duckling*, by Pamela Sterling, music by Chris Limber.
Tips: "Make certain your submitted musical is very theatrical and not cinematic. Writers need to see how far the field of youth and family theater has come—the interesting new areas we're doing—before sending us your query or manuscript. We LIKE young protagonists in our plays, but make sure they're not romanticized or stereotyped good-and-bad like the children's theater playwrights of yesterday would have them."

CREATIVE PRODUCTIONS, INC., 2 Beaver Pl., Aberdeen NJ 07747. (908)566-6985. Director: Walter L. Born. Play producer. Estab. 1970. Produces 3 musicals (1-2 new musicals)/year. "Our audience is the general community with emphasis on elderly and folks with disabilities. We use local public school theater facilities." Pays by royalty or per performance, as required by broadway rental houses.
How to Contact: Query with synopsis, character breakdown, tape of music and set description. SASE. Reports in 1 month or less.
Musical Theater: "We want family type material (i.e. *Brigadoon*, *Charlie Brown*) with light rock to classical music and a maximum running time of two hours. The subject matter should deal with older folks or folks with disabilities. We have no flying capability in facility; cast size is a maximum 10-12; the sets are mostly on small wagons, props aren't anything exotic; the orchestra is chamber size with standard instruments. We don't want pornographic material or children's shows. We want nothing trite and condescending in either the material or the treatment. We like the unusual treatment well-structured and thought out, with minimal sets and changes. We can't handle unusual vocal requirements. We prefer an integrated piece with music a structural part from the beginning."
Productions: *Gift of Magi*, by O. Henry (unselfish love); *Wind in Willows*, by Jane Iredale; and *Reluctant Dragon*, by Rone/Anderson.
Tips: "Prepare/send representative script and music based on above criteria and follow up with phone call after our response."

CREATIVE THEATRE, 102 Witherspoon St., Princeton NJ 08540. (609)924-3489. Artistic Director: Eloise Bruce. Play producer. Estab. 1969. Produces 5 plays, all with music (1 new musical)/year. "Plays are performed for young audiences grades K-6. The plays are always audience participation and done in schools (45 minute format)." Pays a fee for writing and production and royalty for two seasons. Then per performance royalty fee.

How to Contact: Query with synopsis, character breakdown and set description. SASE. Reports in 1 month.

Musical Theater: "Audience participation plays, 45 minutes in length, 4-6 performers, usually presentational style. Topics can range from original plots to adaptations of folk and fairytales. Staging is usually in the round with audience of no more than 300/seating on the floor. No lighting and usually piano accompaniment. Actor is focus with strong but very lean set and costume design." Does not wish to see plays without audience participation. "We are not doing as many 'heavy musicals,' but are looking for light plays with less music."

Productions: *The Bremen Town Musicians*, by Joan Prall (original fairy tale); *Where Snow Falls Up*, by Mark Schaeffer (original holiday show); and *The Island of Yaki Yim Bamboo*, by Fred Rohan Vargas.

Tips: "Develop child centered work which encourages the imaginations of the audience and is centered in child play."

CREEDE REPERTORY THEATRE, P.O. Box 269, Creede CO 81130. (719)658-2541. Producing/Artistic Director: Richard Baxter. Play producer. Estab. 1966. Produces 6 plays and 1 musical/year. Performs in 243-seat proscenium theatre; audience is ½ local support and ½ tourist base from Texas, Oklahoma, New Mexico and Colorado. Pays 7% royalty.

How to Contact: Query first. SASE. Reports in 1 year.

Musical Theater: "We prefer historical Western material with cast no larger than 11. Staging must be flexible as space is limited."

Productions: *Baby Doe Tabor*, by Kenton Kersting (Colorado history); *A Frog in His Throat*, by Feydeau, adapted by Eric Conger, (French farce); and *Tommyknockers*, by Eric Engdahl, Mark Houston and Chris Thompson (mining).

Tips: "Songwriter must have the ability to accept criticism and must be flexible."

THE DEPOT THEATRE, Box 414, Westport NY 12993. (518)962-4449. Associate Director: Keith Levenson. Play producer. Estab. 1979. Produces 3-5 plays/year; produces 2-3 musicals (1 new musical)/year. "Plays are performed in a renovated 19th century train depot with 136 seats and proscenium stage. Audience is regional/tourist from north of Albany to Montreal." Pays by commission.

How to Contact: Submit manuscript and score through agent only. SASE. Reports in 1 month.

Musical Theater: "We have no restrictions on the type of musical, though we prefer full-length. We are currently interested in cast sizes that do not exceed 13 people—preferably smaller! Our theater has no fly or wing space to speak of and designs tend to be limited to unit or 'conceptual' sets. Our orchestra is limited to acoustic piano and synthesizers. We do not wish to see previously produced scripts unless there have been radical changes to the material or previous presentation was in workshop form. The purpose of the Depot Theatre's New American Musicals Project is to nurture the development of new musicals by emerging songwriters/composers. Our intent is to give the musical a full production so that the writers can see what they have and so the piece can have a life beyond our stage. We look for writers willing to listen to directors, work with them toward a common goal of the best production possible and be able to maintain a sense of humor and an understanding of our limited resources." Would consider original music for use in a play being developed.

Productions: *Winchell*, by Martin Charnin and Keith Levenson (Walter Winchell); *Willpower*, by Danny Troob and Jamie Donnelly (reverse Pygmalion theme, contemporary); and *Galileo*, by Jeanine Levenson, Alexa Junge and Keith Levenson.

Tips: "We enjoy working with people who view the process as a collaborative adventure, can be flexible, accept constructive criticism and keep smiling."

EL TEATRO CAMPESINO, P.O. Box 1240, San Juan Bautista CA 95045. (408)623-2444. Theater company. Members are professionals and amateurs. Performs 2 concerts/year including 2 new works. Commissions 0-1 composer or new work/year. "Our audiences are varied—non-traditional and multicultural. We perform in our own theater as well as area theaters and other performing arts spaces (indoor and outdoor)." Pays $50-750 for outright purchase.

How to Contact: Query first. SASE. Reports in 1 month.

Music: "We are interested in cultural and multi-cultural music in all styles and lengths. We are especially interested in blends of cultural/contemporary and indigenous music."

Productions: *La Vizgen Del Tepeyac* (cultural); *The Rose of the Rancho* (Old California); and *Zoot-Suit* (1940s).

THE EMPTY SPACE THEATRE, P.O. Box 1748, Seattle WA 98111-1748. (206)587-3737. Artistic Director: Eddie Levi Lee. Play producer. Estab. 1970. Produces 5 plays and varying number of new musicals/year. "We have a subscription audience, mainly composed of professionals. We produce in our own theater." Pays by royalty.

How to Contact: Query with synopsis, character breakdown and set description. SASE. Reports in 4 months.

Musical Theater: "We want broadly comic, satirical or political pieces and all musical idioms, from classical to whatever is the current end of the musical spectrum. We have no limitations, though we rarely produce more than one large cast show per year. We don't want old-fashioned show biz yawners, or yuppie angst. We regularly employ composers/sound designers."

Productions: *Smokey Joe's Cafe*, by Burke Walker (song revue).

Tips: "Avoid musical-comedy formulas."

*GEOF ENGLISH, PRODUCER, Saddleback College, 28000 Marguerite Pkwy., Mission Viejo CA 92692. (714)582-4763. Performing Arts Director: Geofrey English. Play producer for musical theater. Produces 4 musicals/year. Community audience of mostly senior citizens. Pays by royalty and performance.

How to Contact: Submit complete ms, score and tape of songs. Does not return unsolicited material. Reports in 2-3 months.

Musical Theater: Looking for mainly family musicals. No limitations, open to options. It is important that music must be sent along with scripts. Best not to call. Just send materials.

Productions: More than 50 musicals produced since company formed in 1978. 1993 season included *Oklahoma*, *Nunsense* and *Sweeney Todd*.

Tips: "Submit materials in a timely manner—usually at least one year in advance."

FOOLS COMPANY, INC., 358 W. 44th St., New York NY 10036. (212)307-6000. Artistic Director: Martin Russell. Play producer. Estab. 1970. Produces 4-6 plays/year; produces 1-2 musicals (1-2 new musicals)/year. "Audience is comprised of general public and teens, ages 16-20. Plays are performed at various Manhattan venues."

How to Contact: Submit complete manuscript, score and tape of songs. SASE. Reports in 2 weeks.

Musical Theater: "We seek new and unusual, contemporary and experimental material. We would like small, easy-to-tour productions. Nothing classical, folkloric or previously produced." Would also consider original music for use in a play being developed.

Productions: *She Closed Her Eyes to the Sun*, by Jill Russell and Lewis Flinn (fantasies and realities of relationships).

Tips: "Be open to suggestions; be able to work within a group."

*THE FOOTHILL THEATRE COMPANY, P.O. Box 1812, Nevada City CA 95959. (916)265-9320. Artistic Director: Philip Charles Sneed. Play producer. Estab. 1977. Produces 6-10 plays and 1-2 musicals/year. Rural audience, with some urban visitors to the area. 250-seat historic proscenium house; built in 1865 (oldest in CA). "We haven't yet produced a new play, but will seriously consider it within the next 2 years; payment will be decided later."

How to Contact: Query with synopsis, character breakdown and set description. SASE. Reports in 3-6 months.

Musical Theater: "We're particularly interested in works which deal with the region's history or with issues relevant to the area today. We are also interested in one-act musicals and children's musicals. We have limited space backstage, especially in the wings. We also have very limited fly space. We're interested in original ideas, nothing derivative (except in an adaptation, of course). A good rock musical would be nice. Will consider original music for use in a play being developed, or for use in a pre-existing play. The use will depend upon the play: could be preshow, or underscoring, or scene change, or any combination."

Productions: *Two Rooms*, by Lee Blessing (hostage drama); *Betrayal*, by Harold Pinter (love triangle); and *Rumors*, by Neil Simon (comedy).

Tips: "Know something about our region and its history."

THE WILL GEER THEATRICUM BOTANICUM, P.O. Box 1222, Topanga CA 90290. (213)455-2322. Artistic Director: Ellen Geer. Play producer. Produces 4 plays, 1-2 new musicals/year. Plays are performed in "large outdoor amphitheater with 60'x 25' wooden stage. Rustic setting." Pays per performance.

How to Contact: Query with synopsis, tape, character breakdown and set description. SASE. Submit scripts from September through November.

Musical Theater: Seeking social or biographical works, children's works, full length musicals with cast of up to 10 equity actors (the rest non-equity). Requires "low budget set and costumes. We emphasize paying performers." Would also consider original music for use in a play being developed. Does not wish to see "anything promoting avarice, greed, violence or apathy."

Productions: *Worker's U.S.A.*, a compilation work (labor unions).

Tips: "Reach us with idea and show enthusiasm for theater."

GEORGE STREET PLAYHOUSE, 9 Livingston Ave., New Brunswick NJ 08901. (908)846-2895. Associate Artistic Director: Wendy Liscow. Producing Director: Gregory Hurst. Produces 7 plays, including 1 new musical/year. "We are a 367-seat thrust theater working under a LORT C-contract with a 5,500 subscriber base." Fees vary. "Each situation is handled individually."
How to Contact: "Professional recommendation only." SASE. Reports in 4-6 months.
Musical Theater: Seeking musical adaptations. "We are interested in a variety of themes and formats. We aren't seeking to limit the things we read."
Productions: *Johnny Pye and the Fool Killer*, by Mark St. Germain and Randy Courts (Americana); *Jekyll and Hyde*, by Lee Thuna, Herman Sachs and Mel Mandel; and *Fields of Ambrosia*, by Joel Higgins and Martin Silvestri.

GREAT AMERICAN CHILDREN'S THEATRE COMPANY, Dept. SM, 304 E. Florida, Milwaukee WI 53204. (414)276-4230. Managing Director: Annie Jurczyk. Producer: Teri Mitze. Play producer. Estab. 1976. Produces 1 or 2 plays/musical/year. Has done new musicals in the past. Audience is school age children. Pays a negotiable royalty.
How to Contact: Query with synopsis, character breakdown and set description. Does not return unsolicited material. Reports as quickly as possible, "depending on our workload."
Musical Theater: Children's musicals. Average cast size is 13. No adult productions. "We have used original music as background for our plays."
Productions: *Charlie & the Chocolate Factory*, by Roald Dahl (children's story); *Charlotte's Web*, by Joseph Robinette (children's story); and *Cinderella*, by Moses Goldberg (children's story).
Tips: "Persevere! Although we don't use a lot of musicals, we will consider one that is of excellent quality."

*GREAT AMERICAN HISTORY THEATRE, 30 E. 10th St., St. Paul MN 55101. (612)292-4323. Play producer. Estab. 1978. Produces 5-6 plays, 1 or 2 musicals (1 or 2 new musicals)/year. 597-seat thrust. Royalty varies.
How to Contact: Query first (after March 1994) with synopsis, character breakdown and set description. SASE. Reports in 6-8 months.
Musical Theater: "Plays based on people, events, ideas in history. Preferrably Midwestern or American history. However, must be *real* plays, we *do not* teach history. *No* pageants. No larger than cast of 10. Technical considerations must be simple. We like non-realism."
Productions: *The Meeting*, by Jeff Stetson (Martin Luther King meets Malcolm X); *The Great Gatsby*, by F. Scott Fitzgerald (adapted by J. Carlisle, the novel of love and murder); and *Days of Rondo*, by Greg Williams (a black neighborhood in St. Paul destroyed in the 1950s).

*GREEN MOUNTAIN GUILD, Box 659, Pittsfield VT 05762. (802)746-8320. Managing Director: Marjorie O'Neill-Butler. Play producer. Estab. 1971. Produces 10 plays (6 musicals)/year. Produces plays for a summer theater audience in Killington, Vermont. Pays 5% royalty.
How to Contact: Submit complete ms, score and tape of songs. SASE. Reports in 3 months.
Musical Theater: "We are looking for musicals with a small cast, a good story line, well-developed characters, songs and music that come naturally out of the story and music that works with piano and drums only." No frivolous material. Prefers one-set shows.
Productions: *Jenny Lind*, by David Harvey (an original play); *Sweeney Todd*, by Stephen Sondheim; *Student Prince*, by Sigmund Romberg; and *Yours Anne*, by Enid Fetterman/Michael Cohen.

*THE GROWING STAGE THEATRE, P.O. Box 132, Chester NJ 07930. (908)879-4946. Fax: (908)879-6893. Executive Director: Stephen L. Fredericks. Play producer. Estab. 1981. Produces 5 plays and 3-4 musicals (2 new musicals)/year. A theater for young audiences and their families. Pays for outright purchase or commissioned for specific work.
How to Contact: Submit complete ms, score and tape of songs. SASE. Reports in 2 months.
Musical Theater: "While main focus is theater for young audiences, appeal should be there for adults and older siblings. Production usually limited to 5 to 10 characters. Just because our theater is for young audiences, don't be cute; give the audience the same respect you would want for your work."
Performances: *Alice In Wonderland*; *Jack And The Beanstalk*; *Pippi Longstocking*.
Tips: "Include quality cassette, and developed script breakdowns."

HIP POCKET THEATRE, 1627 Fairmount Ave., Ft. Worth TX 76104-4237. (817)927-2833. Producer: Diane Simons. Play producer. Produces 7 plays/year (including new musicals). Estab. 1977. "Our audience is an eclectic mix of Ft. Worth/Dallas area residents with varying levels of incomes and backgrounds. Payment varies according to type of script, reputation of playwright, etc."
How to Contact: Query with synopsis, character breakdown and set description; "please include tape if possible." SASE. Reports in 2 months.
Musical Theater: "We are not interested in cabaret revues, but rather in full-length pieces that can be for adults and/or children. We tend to produce more fanciful, whimsical musicals (something not likely to be found anywhere else), but would also consider political pieces. Basically, we're open for

anything fresh and well-written. We require no more than 15 in a cast, and a staging would have to adapt to an outdoor environmental thrust stage." Would also consider original music for use in a play being developed.

Productions: *Huzzytown*, by Johnny Simons (premiere); *The Tempest*, by William Shakespeare, with original music by Joe Rogers; *Saint Joan of the Stockyards*, by Bertolt Brecht, with original music by Little Jack Melody and his Young Turks; *Scarfish Vibrato*, by Johnny Simons (premiere); and *Everyman*, (anonymous author).

Tips: "Think creative, complex thoughts and musical visions that can be transformed into reality by creative, visionary musicians in theaters that rarely have the huge Broadway dollar. Cast size must be kept to a minimum (no more than 15)."

*THE HONOLULU IMPROVISATIONAL THEATRE CO., 3585 Pinao St., Honolulu HI 96822. (808)988-4859. Director: Rod Martin. Estab. 1989. Produces 3 plays and 3 musicals (3 new musicals)/year. Performs at community theaters and on public access TV. Pay negotiable.

How to Contact: Query with synopsis, character breakdown and set description. Reports in 7 weeks.

Musical Theater: "Prefer comedy and children's shows. A videotape of a production is helpful (VHS). A cassette tape should accompany musicals. We will consider original music for entrance/exit music."

Productions: *Running Away to Broadway*, by Alex Gril (children's musical); *Star Pieces*, by Rod Martin (science fiction musical); and *Love Hurts but Murder Kills*, by Rod Martin (musical farce).

Tips: "Read your play aloud to friends first and make improvements. Be willing to collaborate and make changes."

HORIZON THEATRE CO., P.O. Box 5376, Station E, Atlanta GA 30307. (404)584-7450 or (404)523-1477. Artistic Co-Director: Lisa Adler. Play producer. Estab. 1983. Produces 3 plays and 1 musical/year. "Our audience is comprised mostly of young professionals looking for contemporary comedy with a little social commentary. Our theater features a 160-200 seat facility with flexible stage." Pays 6-8% royalty.

How to Contact: Query with synopsis, character breakdown, set description and resume. SASE. Reports in 1-2 years.

Musical Theater: "We prefer musicals that have a significant book and a lot of wit (particularly satire). Our casts are restricted to 10 actors. We prefer plays with equal number of male and female roles, or more female than male roles. We have a limited number of musicians available. No musical revues and no dinner theater fluff. One type of play we are currently seeking is a country musical with women's themes. We generally contract with a musician or sound designer to provide sound for each play we produce. If interested send resume, references, tape with music or sound design samples."

Productions: *Angry Housewives*, by A.M. Collins and Chad Henry.

Tips: "Have patience and use subtle persistence. Work with other theater artists to get a good grasp of the form."

*INVISIBLE THEATRE, 1400 N. First Ave., Tucson AZ 85719. (602)882-9721. Associate Producer: Deborah Dickey. Play producer. Estab. 1971. Produces 10-12 plays and 1-2 musicals/year. Royalty negotiated.

How to Contact: Query with synopsis, character breakdown and set description. "We do not accept unsolicited material." Reports in 3-6 months.

Musical Theater: "We are looking for all contemporary topics and trends. Small company reviews under 8 characters. Simple sets and small combo scores. 78 set house."

Productions: *Accomplice*, by Rupert Holmes (mystery/thriller); *Driving Miss Daisy*, by Alfred Uhry (comedy/aging); and *Shirley Valentine*, by Willy Russell (one-character comedy).

Tips: "Think small, simple with subjects from the provocative to outrageous."

JEWISH REPERTORY THEATRE, 1395 Lexington Ave., New York NY 10128. Director: Ran Avni. Artistic Director: Edward M. Cohen. Play producer. Estab. 1974. Produces 4 plays and 1-2 new musicals/year. Pays 6% royalty.

How to Contact: Submit complete manuscript, score and tape of songs. SASE. Reports in 4 weeks.

Musical Theater: Seeking "musicals in English relating to the Jewish experience. No more than 8 characters. We do commission background scores for straight plays."

Productions: *The Special* (musical comedy); *Theda Bara and the Frontier Rabbi* (musical comedy); and *The Shop on Main Street* (musical drama).

THE LAMB'S THEATRE CO., Dept. SM, 130 W. 44th St., New York NY 10036. (212)997-0210. Literary Manager: James Masters. Play producer. Estab. 1984. Produces 2-3 plays, 1 musical (1 new musical)/year. Plays are performed for "the off-Broadway theater audience, also group sales including school programs from New York public high schools and colleges in the area." Pays by royalty.

How to Contact: Query with synopsis, character breakdowns and set description. SASE. Reports in 6 months.

Musical Theater: "We are looking for full length musicals that are entertaining, but moving, and deal with serious issues as well as comic situations. No one-act plays. Large-cast epics are out. Both our spaces are intimate theaters, one an 160-seat black box space and one a 349-seat proscenium. Material with explicit sex and nudity and plays which require large amounts of obscene language are not appropriate for this theater. We require a small orchestra in a musical."

Productions: *Johnny Pye & The Foolkiller*, by R. Courts/M. St. Germain (original musical based on Stephen V. Benet short story); *The Gifts of the Magi*, by R. Courts/M. St. Germain (original musical based on O. Henry short stories).

LOS ANGELES DESIGNERS' THEATRE, P.O. Box 1883, Studio City CA 91614-0883. (818)769-9000, (213)650-9600 or (310)247-9800. Fax: (818)985-9200. Artistic Director: Richard Niederberg. Play producer. Estab. 1970. Produces 20-25 plays, 8-10 new musicals/year. Plays are produced at several locations, primarily Studio City, California. Pays by royalty.

How to Contact: Submit complete manuscript, score and tape of songs, character breakdown and set descriptions. Video tape submissions are also accepted. Does not return materials. Reports in 4+ months but faster if cassette of show is included with script.

Musical Theater: "We seek out controversial material. Street language OK, nudity is fine, religious themes, social themes, political themes are encouraged. Our audience is very 'jaded' as it consists of TV, motion picture and music publishing executives who have 'seen it all.' " Does not wish to see bland, "safe" material. "We like first productions. In the cover letter state in great detail the proposed involvement of the songwriter, other than as a writer (i.e. director, actor, singer, publicist, designer, etc.). Also, state if there are any liens on the material or if anything has been promised."

Productions: *Offenbach in the Underworld*, by Frederick Grab (biography with can-can); *Is Nudity Required*, by Stephen Oakley (comedy); and *Wonderful World of Waiver?* (backstage musical). Also *Vine Street*, by H.D. Parkin III (street musical with film/video elements); *All Coked Out* by S. Oakley and M Guestello (musical tragedy on drug use); *Rainbows' End* by Margaret Keifer (songwriters struggle/musical); *Hostages* (political musical) and *Love Song of Ned Wells* (poetry set to music; urban unrequited love story).

Tips: "Make it very 'commercial' and inexpensive to produce. Allow for non-traditional casting. Be prepared with ideas as to how to transform your work to film or videotaped entertainment."

MAGNIFICENT MOORPARK MELODRAMA AND VAUDEVILLE CO., 45 E. High St., Moorpark CA 93021. (805)529-1212. Producer: Linda Bredemann. Play producer. Estab. 1982. Produces 7 new musicals/year. "Our audience is family and church groups, ages 2 to 90." Pays by royalty, outright purchase or per performance.

How to Contact: Submit complete manuscript, score and tape of songs. SASE. Reports in 12 months.

Musical Theater: "We want plays set in any era, but must have a villain to boo—hero to cheer—heroine to ahh. Each act should run no more than 1 hour with a 2 act maximum. We want family-oriented comedies only. Cast should be no more than 20. We have a small stage (30×30). We don't want obscene, vulgar or off-color material. We want up beat music—can be popular songs or old time."

Productions: *Aladdin and His Magical Lamp*, by Tim Kelly (fairy tale); *Newscast Murder*, by William Gleason (murder spoof); and *Road to Paradise*, by Scott Martin (40s South Sea war spoof).

Tips: "Have fun. Make the characters memorable, lovable and believable. Make the music tuneful and something to hum later."

MANHATTAN THEATRE CLUB, Dept. SM, 453 W. 16th St., New York NY 10011. (212)645-5590. Director of Musical Theater Program: Clifford Lee Johnson III. Artistic Associate: Michael Bush. Play producer. Estab. 1971. Produces 8 plays and sometimes 1 musical/year. Plays are performed at the Manhattan Theatre Club before varied audiences. Pays negotiated fee.

How to Contact: Query with synopsis, "5-10 page libretto and lyric sample and tape of three songs." SASE. Reports in 6 months.

Musical Theater: "Small cast, original work."

Productions: *Urban Blight*, by Richard Maltby, Jr., David Shire and others; *1-2-3-4-5*, by Maury Yeston and Larry Gelbart; and *Putting It Together*, by Stephen Sondheim.

MILWAUKEE REPERTORY THEATER, Dept. SM, 108 E. Wells St., Milwaukee WI 53202. (414)224-1761. Cabaret Director: Fred Weiss. Play producer. Estab. 1954. Produces 17 plays and 5 cabaret shows/year. "The space is a 106 seat cabaret with a very small playing area (8×28)." Pay is negotiable.

How to Contact: Submit complete ms, score and tape of songs. SASE. Reports in 3-4 months.

Musical Theater: "Cast size must be limited to 3 singers/performers with minimum movement. Suitable for cabaret. Must appeal to a broad adult audience and should not run longer than 1 hour. We also seek to explore a multi-cultural diversity of material."

Productions: *Irish Reunion*, by Ed Morgan (Irish music); *Duke's Place*, by Isaiah Sheffer (Duke Ellington Review); and *Hula Hoop Sha-Boop*, by John Lercht and Larry Deckel (50s musical revue).

MIXED BLOOD THEATRE CO., 1501 S. 4th St., Minneapolis MN 55454. (612)338-0937. Script Czar: David Kunz. Play producer. Estab. 1976. Produces 4-5 plays a year and perhaps 1 new musical every 2 years. "We have a 200-seat theater in a converted firehouse. The audience spans the socio-economic spectrum." Pays 7-10% royalty.
How to Contact: Query first, then submit complete manuscript, score and tape of songs. SASE. Reports in 6 weeks.
Musical Theater: "We want full-length, non-children works with a message. Always query first. Never send unsolicited script or tape."
Productions: *Black Belts*, in house production (great African-American singers).
Tips: "Always query first. Be professional. Surprise us."

*MOORHEAD STATE UNIVERSITY, Moorhead MN 56563. (218)236-4613. Director of Theatre: David Grapes. Play producer. Produces 16-20 plays and 5 musicals (1 new musical)/year. Educated, community/university audience. Pays $50-300/performance.
How to Contact: Submit complete ms, score and tape of songs. SASE. Reports in 6 months.
Musical Theater: "We look for outstanding works in all categories."
Productions: *Good News*, by DeSylva; *Grapes of Wrath*; and *Seekers of the Light*, by Zinober.

MUSICAL THEATRE WORKS, INC., Dept. SM, 440 Lafayette St., New York NY 10003. (212)677-0040. General Manager: Marilyn Stimac. Artistic Director: Anthony J. Stimac. Develops new musicals exclusively in stage readings and workshop productions. Estab. 1983. Fourteen productions have transferred to Broadway, off-Broadway and regional theater. Produces 3-4 workshop productions and 12-16 readings each season. Workshops and readings are held at 440 Lafayette St. in a flexible 80-seat rehearsal space. No payment for productions.
How to Contact: Submit complete script, cassette tape of songs and SASE. Reply in 2-4 months.
Musical Theater: "We are seeking musicals which have never been produced. Fourteen cast maximum. Full, but modest. Only completed drafts will be considered for development."
Productions: *Whatnot*, by Howard Crabtee and Mark Waldrop (won 1990 Richard Rodgers Award); *Love in Two Countries*, by Sheldon Harnick and Tom Shepard (operetta); *Collette Collage*, by Tom Jones and Harvey Schmidt (on the life of French writer Collette); *Ruthless!*, by Marvin Laird and Joel Paley; *Starmites*, by Barry Keating and Stuart Ross (nominated for 4 Tony awards, including Best Musical); and *The No Frills Revue*, developed by Masrtin Charnin.

MUSIC-THEATRE GROUP INC., 29 Bethune St., New York NY 10014. (212)924-3108. Director: Diane Wondisford. Music-theater production company. Produces 6 music-theater pieces/year. General works are performed "off-Broadway in New York City; year round in Stockbridge, MA."
How to Contact: Query with synopsis and tape of music. SASE. Reports in 3 months maximum.
Musical Theater: "We don't seek developed properties, but examples of people's work as an indication of their talent in the event that we might want to suggest them for a future collaboration. The music must be a driving element in the work. We generally work with no more than 10-12 in cast and a small band of 4-5."
Productions: *Cinderella/Cendrillon*, based on the opera by Jules Massenet; *The Garden of Earthly Delights*, by Martha Clarke; and *Juan Darien*, by Julie Taymor and Elliot Goldenthal.
Tips: "Don't try to imitate a formula or style—write from your own impulses."

NATIONAL MUSIC THEATER CONFERENCE, O'Neill Theater Center, #901, 234 W. 44th St., New York NY 10036. (212)382-2790. Artistic Director: Paulette Haupt. "The Conference develops new music theater works." Estab. 1978. Develops 3-4 musicals each August. 8-10 professional songwriters/musicians participate in each event. Participants include songwriters, composers, opera/musical theater and lyricists/librettists. "The O'Neill Theater Center is in Waterford, Connecticut. The audiences for the staged readings of works-in-progress are a combination of local residents, New York and regional theater professionals. Participants are selected by artistic director and selection panel of professionals." Pays a stipend, room and board, and all costs of the workshops are covered.
How to Contact: Query first. SASE. Response within 2-3 months. Entry fee $20.
Musical Theater: "The Conference is interested in all forms of music theater. Staged readings are presented with script in hand, minimal props, piano only. There are no cast limitations. We don't accept works which have been previously produced by a professional company."
Productions: *Avenue X*, by John Jiler and Ray Leslee; *Christina Alberta's Father*, by Polly Pen; and *The Wild Swans*, by Adele Ahronheim and Ben Schaechter.

THE NEW CONSERVATORY CHILDREN'S THEATRE COMPANY & SCHOOL, Dept. SM, 25 Van Ness, San Francisco CA 94102. (415)861-4914. Executive Director: Ed Decker. Play producer. Estab. 1981. Produces about 5 plays and 1 or 2 musicals (1 new musical)/year. Audience includes families and community groups; children ages 14-19. "Performance spaces are 50-150 seat theater, but we also tour some shows. Pays $25-35 per performance. If we commission, playwright receives a commission for the initial run and royalties thereafter; otherwise playwright just gets royalties."
How to Contact: Query with synopsis, character breakdown and set description. SASE. Reports in 3 months.
Musical Theater: "We seek innovative and preferably socially relevant musicals for children and families, with relatively small cast (stage is small), in which all roles can be played by children. We have a small stage, thus cannot accommodate plays casting more than 10 or 12 people, and prefer relatively simple set requirements. Children cast are in the 9-19 age range. We do not want mushy, cute material. Fantasy is fine, as is something like Sendak & King's *Really Rosie*, but nothing gooey. We are very interested in using original music for new or existing plays. Songwriters should submit a resume and perhaps a tape to let us know what they do."
Productions: *Runaways*, by Elizabeth Swados; *Free to be a Family*, by Marlo Thomas; and *Don't Count Your Chickens*, by Carol Lynn Pearson.
Tips: "Be flexible, able to revise and open to suggestions!"

NEW TUNERS THEATRE, Theatre Building, 1225 Belmont, Chicago IL 60657. (312)929-7287. Artistic Coordinator: Allan Chambers. Play producer. Estab. 1968. Produces 3 musicals (3 new musicals)/year. "We play to mixed urban and suburban audiences. We produce in a 148-seat theater in the Theatre Building." Pays negotiable royalty.
How to Contact: Query with synopsis and character breakdown. Does not return unsolicited material. Reports in 3 months.
Musical Theater: "We look at all types of musical theater, traditional as well as more innovative forms. Fifteen is the maximum cast size we can consider and less is decidedly better. We work with a younger (35 and under) company of actors.
Productions: *Trask & Fenn*, by Ken Stone and Jan Powell (Victorian love triangle); *Stocking Stuffers '92*, by various workshop authors (10-minute musical-holiday); and *Chicago Stories*, by various workshop authors (10-minute musical-urban jungle).
Tips: "Write the musical that speaks and sings to you. Write the musical that you would be willing to invest your own money toward."

NEW WORKS PRODUCTIONS, (formerly Music Theatre of Arizona), P.O. Box 9722, Scottsdale AZ 85252-3722. (602)946-9200. Artistic Director: Ron Newcomer. Music theater production company specializing in new works for the stage. Members are professionals and amateurs. Performs 2-4 productions/year using a variety of theaters, plus local and regional tours. Pays by royalty (varies). Very full schedule, please submit a letter of inquiry before sending script/score.
Music: Any style, from country to jazz, pop to traditional Broadway. Small casts preferred. Looking for creative ideas that are well structured, with strong character moods. Creators must be willing to workshop material.
Productions: *The Incredible Adventures of Doktor Thrill* (musical); *The All-American Dream* (musical); *How to Buy the Brooklyn Bridge* (comedy w/music).

NEW YORK STATE THEATRE INSTITUTE, 155 River St., Troy NY 12181. (518)274-3200. Producing Director: Patricia B. Snyder. Play producer. Produces approximately 5 plays (1 new musical)/year. Plays performed for student audiences grades K-12, family audiences and adult audiences. Theater seats 900 with full stage. Pay negotiable.
How to Contact: Submit complete ms and tape of songs. SASE. Response in 3-4 months.
Musical Theater: Looking for "intelligent and well-written book with substance, a score that enhances and supplements the book and is musically well-crafted and theatrical. Length: up to 2 hours. Could be play with music, musical comedy, musical drama. Excellence and substance in material is essential. Cast could be up to 12; orchestra size up to 8."
Productions: *Pied Piper*, by Adrian Mitchell/Dominic Muldowney (musical adaptation of the classic tale); *The Snow Queen*, by Adrian Mitchell/Richard Peaslee (musical adaptation of the Andersen fairy tale).
Tips: "There is a great need for musicals that are well-written with intelligence and substance which are suitable for family audiences."

NEW YORK THEATRE WORKSHOP, 18th Floor, 220 W. 42 St., New York NY 10036. (212)302-7737. Artistic Director: James C. Nicola. Play producer. Produces 4 mainstage plays and approximately 50 readings/year. "Plays are performed in our theater on East 4th St. Audiences include: subscription/ single ticket buyers from New York area, theater professionals, and special interest groups." Pays by negotiable royalty.

How to Contact: Query with synopsis, character breakdown and set description. SASE. Reports in 5 months.

Musical Theater: "As with our non-musicals, we seek musicals of intelligence and social consciousness that challenge our perceptions of the world and the events which shape our lives. We favor plays that possess a strong voice, distinctive and innovative use of language and visual imagery. Integration of text and music is particularly of interest. Musicals which require full orchestrations would generally be too big for us. We prefer 'musical theater pieces' rather than straightforward 'musicals' per-se. We often use original music for straight plays that we produce. This music may be employed as pre-show, post-show or interlude music. If the existing piece lends itself, music may also be incorporated within the play itself. Large casts (12 or more) are generally prohibitive and require soliciting of additional funds. Design elements for our productions are of the highest quality possible with our limited funds—approximately budgets of $10,000 are allotted for our productions."

Productions: *The Waves*, adopted from Virginia Woolf's novel, music and lyrics by David Bucknam and text and direction by Lisa Peterson; *My Children! My Africa*, by Athol Fugard; and *Mad Forest*, by Caryl Churchill.

Tips: "Submit a synopsis which captures the heart of your piece; inject your piece with a strong voice and intent and try to surprise and excite us."

NEXT ACT THEATRE, Dept. SM, Box 394, Milwaukee WI 53201. (414)278-7780. Fax: (414)278-5930. Producing Director: David Cecsarini. Estab. 1984. Three productions/year, of which 1 is a musical. Playwrights paid by royalty (5-8%). "Performances seat 200. We have 800 season subscribers and single ticket buyers of every age range and walk of life." Pays $30-50 per performance.

How to Contact: Submit complete ms, score and tape of songs with at least one professional letter of recommendation. SASE.

Musical Theater: "We produce Broadway and off-Broadway style material, preferring slightly controversial or cutting edge material (i.e., *March of the Falsettos*). We have never produced a work that has not been successful in some other theatrical center. We are very limited financially and rarely stage shows with more than 6 in the cast. Props, sets and costumes should be minimal. We have no interest in children's theater, mime shows, puppet shows, etc. We have never yet used original music for our plays. We may consider it, but there would be little if any money available for this purpose."

Productions: *Billy Bishop Goes to War*, by John Gray/Eric Peterson (World War I flying ace); *A . . . My Name is Alice*, by various writers (women's themes); and *Damn Tango*, by Helena Dynerman (European translation of 17 tangos with cast of 17 singer/dancers).

NORTHSIDE THEATRE COMPANY OF SAN JOSE, 848 E. William St., San Jose CA 95116. (408)288-7820. Artistic Director: Richard T. Orlando. Play producer. Estab. 1979. Produces 5 plays, a touring show and an occasional musical/year. "Family entertainment, plays are performed at the Olinder Theatre." Pays by royalty.

How to Contact: Query with synopsis, character breakdown and set description. SASE. Reports in 6 weeks.

Musical Theater: "Classic family plays (with a twist or different concept)." Cast size: 6-15. Sets: Unit in concept with simple additions. Staging: proscenium with thrust. Small 90 seat theater fully equipped. "We are interested in new ideas and approaches. Production should have social relevancy." Will consider using original music for already existing plays. "Example: the underscoring of a Shakespeare piece."

Productions: *A Christmas Carol*, by Charles Dickens (seasonal); *After the Rain*, by John Bowen (future civilization); and *Voices from the High School*, by Peter Dee (youth and their lives).

Tips: "Be aggressive, sell your idea and be able to work within the budget and limitations that the artistic director is confined to."

ODYSSEY THEATRE ENSEMBLE, Dept. SM, 2055 S. Sepulveda Blvd., Los Angeles CA 90025. (310)477-2055. Literary Manager: Jan Lewis. Play producer. Estab. 1969. Produces 9 plays, 1 musical and 1-2 new musicals/year. "Our audience is predominantly over 35, upper middle-class audience interested in eclectic brand of theater which is challenging and experimental." Pays by royalty (percentage to be negotiated).

How to Contact: Query with synopsis, character breakdown and set description. Query should include resume(s) of artist(s) and tape of music. SASE. "Unsolicited material is not read or screened at all." Reports on query in 2 weeks; manuscript in 6 months.

Musical Theater: "We want nontraditional forms and provocative, unusual, challenging subject matter. We are not looking for Broadway-style musicals. Comedies should be highly stylized or highly farcical. Works should be full-length only and not requiring a complete orchestra (small band preferred.) Political material and satire are great for us. We're seeking interesting musical concepts and approaches. The more traditional Broadway-style musicals will generally not be done by the Odyssey. If we have a work in development that needs music, original music will often be used. In such a case, the writer and composer would work together during the development phase. In the case of a pre-existing play, the concept would originate with the director who would select the composer."

Productions: *Symmes' Hole*, by Randolph Dreyfuss (search for the center of the earth); *Spring Awakening*, by Frank Wedekind (sexual awakening in youth); *McCarthy*, by Jeff Goldsmith (Senator Joe McCarthy); *Struggling Truths* (the Chinese invasion of Tibet); and *It's A Girl* (a capella musical for 5 pregnant women).

Tips: "Stretch your work beyond the ordinary. Look for compelling themes or the enduring questions of human existence. If it's a comedy, go for broke, go all the way, be as inventive as you can be."

OLD GLOBE THEATRE, P.O. Box 2171, San Diego CA 92112. (619)231-1941. Literary Manager: Raul Moncado. Artistic Director: Jack O'Brien. Produces 12 or 13 plays/year, of which a varying number are musicals. "This is a regional theater with three spaces: 600-seat proscenium, 225-seat arena and large outdoor summer stage. We serve a national audience base of over 260,000."

How to Contact: Query with synopsis and letter of introduction, or submit through agent or professional affiliation. No unsolicited material please. SASE. Reports in 4-8 months.

Musical Theater: "We look for skill first, subject matter second. No prescribed limitations, though creators should appreciate the virtues of economy as well as the uses of extravagance. Musicals have been produced on all three of our stages."

Productions: *Pastorela '91*, by Raul Moncada (traditional Latin-American Christmas); *Lady Day at Emerson's Bar and Grill*, by Lanie Robertson (Billie Holiday); *Forever Plaid*, by Stuart Ross (50/60s male quartet).

Tips: "Fall in love with a great book and a great writer."

OMAHA MAGIC THEATRE, 1417 Farnam St., Omaha NE 68102. (402)346-1227. Artistic Director: Jo Ann Schmidman. Play producer. Estab. 1968. Produces 8 performance events with music/year. "Plays are produced in our Omaha facility and on tour throughout the nation. Our audience is a cross-section of the community." Pays standard royalty, outright purchase ($500-1,500), per performance $20-25.

How to Contact: Query with synopsis, character breakdown and set description. SASE. Reports in 6 months.

Musical Theater: "We want the most avant of the avant garde—plays that never get written, or if written are buried deep in a chest because the writer feels there are not production possibilities in this nation's theaters. Plays must push form and/or content to new dimensions. The clarity of the playwright's voice must be strong and fresh. We do not produce standard naturalistic or realistic musicals. At the Omaha Magic Theatre original music is considered as sound structure and for lyrics."

Productions: *Body Leaks*, by Megan Terry, Jo Ann Schmidman and Sora Kimberlain (self-censorship); *Sound Fields/Are We Here*, by Megan Terry, Jo Ann Schmidman and Sora Kimberlain (a new multi-dimensional performance event about acute listening); and *Belches on Couches*, by Megan Terry, Jo Ann Schmidman and Sora Kimberlain.

THE OPEN EYE: NEW STAGINGS, Dept. SM, 270 W. 89th St., New York NY 10024. (212)769-4143. Artistic Director: Amie Brockway. Play producer. Estab. 1972. Produces 9 one-acts, 3 full length or new stagings for youth; varying number of new musicals. "Plays are performed in a well-designed and pleasant theater seating 115 people." Pays on a fee basis or by commission.

How to Contact: "We are pleased to accept unsolicited play manuscripts under the following conditions: 1) The script must be clean (no pencil marks, magic markers, paste overs, etc.); 2) It must be bound; 3) A self-addressed stamped envelope must be enclosed for each manuscript's return. Also keep in mind: the best time for submission is from April through July. We receive many scripts, and reading takes time. Please allow 6 months for a response. Please do not send synopses of your plays. Instead, please consider carefully whether you think your play is something New Stagings should read, and if it is, send the complete script."

Musical Theater: "New Stagings is committed to innovative collaboration and excellence in performance of both classic and new material, presenting the finest of professional talents—established artists and relative newcomers alike. We produce plays which invite us as artists and audience to take a fresh look at ourselves and the world of which we are a part. We seek to involve the performers and the audience in the live theater experience. And we are making a concerted effort to reach new audiences, young and old, and of all ethnic backgrounds. New Stagings for Youth is a not-for-profit professional theater company whose aim is to develop new theater audiences by producing plays for children and young people. New Stagings Lab offers opportunities to performing artists (directors, playwrights, actors, dancers, musicians) to develop new theater pieces through a program of rehearsed readings and workshops. Our stage is roughly 20' x 25' which limits the size of the set, cast and other related details and also, we do not have the height for a fly system. We seldom do political or propaganda related plays. We frequently use music to enhance a script, as well as performing plays with music in them, and also musicals. We believe in using various forms of art (music, movement) in most of our productions."

Productions: *The Odyssey*, adapted by Amie Brockway, music by Elliot Sakolov; *The Wise Men of Chelin*, by Sandra Fenichel Asher; and *Freedom is My Middle Name*, by Lee Hunkins.
Tips: "Come see our work before submitting."

PAPER MILL PLAYHOUSE, Brookside Dr., Milburn NJ 07041. (201)379-3636. Contact: Angelo Del Rossi. Executive producer. Equity Theater producing 2 plays and 4 musicals/year. "Audience based on 42,000 subscribers; plays performed in 1,192-seat proscenium theater."
Musical Theater: "Paper Mill runs a Musical Theatre Lab Project which develops 4-6 readings/season, 3 of which went on to fully staged productions. The theater runs an open submission policy, and is especially interested in large scale shows, however, due to funding cuts, this program has been suspended for the '93-'94 season and we are unable to accept scripts at this time."
Productions: *The Wizard of Oz, Sweeney Todd, Don't Dress for Dinner, Lost in Yonkers, My Fair Lady* and Kopit Yeston's *Phantom*.

PENNSYLVANIA STAGE COMPANY, 837 Linden St., Allentown PA 18101. (215)434-6110. Artistic Director: Charles Richter. Play producer. Estab. 1979. Produces 7 plays (1 new musical)/season "when feasible. We are a LORT D theatre with a subscriber base of approximately 6,000 people. Plays are performed at the Pennsylvania Stage Company in the J.I. Rodale Theatre." Playwrights paid by 5% royalty (per Dramatist's Guild contract).
How to Contact: Query with synopsis, character breakdown, set description and a tape of the music. "Please do not send script first." SASE. Reports in 2 months.
Musical Theater: "We are interested in full-length musicals which reflect the social, historical and political fabric of America. We have no special requirements for format, structure or musical involvement. We ask that once submission of a musical has been requested, that it be bound, legibly typed and include SASE. Cast limit of 10, but we prefer cast limit of 8. One set or unit set. Ours is a 274 seat house, there is no fly area, and a 23-foot proscenium opening."
Productions: *Just So*, by Mark St. Germain (based on Rudyard Kipling's *Just So Stories*); *Smilin' Through*, by Ivan Menchell (British Music Hall circa WWII); *Song of Myself*, by Gayle Stahlhuth, Gregory Hurst and Arthur Harris.
Tips: "Avoid duplication of someone else's style just because it's been successful in the past. I see far too many composers aping Stephen Sondheim's songwriting, for example, without nearly as much success. Despite all the commercial constraints, stick to your guns and write something original, unique."

PLAYHOUSE ON THE SQUARE, 51 S. Cooper, Memphis TN 38104. (901)725-0776. Executive Producer: Jackie Nichols. Play producer. Produces 12 plays (4 musicals)/year. Plays are produced in a 260-seat proscenium resident theater. Pays $500 for outright purchase.
How to Contact: Submit complete ms and score. Unsolicited submissions OK. SASE. Reports in 4 months.
Musical Theater: Seeking "any subject matter—adult and children's material. Small cast preferred. Stage is 26' deep by 43' wide with no fly system." Would also consider original music for use in a play being developed.
Productions: *Gypsy*, by Stein and Laurents; *The Spider Web*, by Agatha Christie (mystery); and *A Midsummer Night's Dream*, by William Shakespeare.

PLAYWRIGHTS HORIZONS, 416 W. 42nd St., New York NY 10036. (212)564-1235. Artistic Director: Don Scardino. Assistant Artistic Director: Nicholas Martin. Literary Manager: Tom Sanford. Musical Theater Co-ordinator: Dana Williams. Play producer. Estab. 1971. Produces about 6 plays and 2 new musicals/year. "A general New York City audience." Pays by fee/royalty.
How to Contact: Send script and tape (not necessarily complete). SASE. Reports in 6 months.
Musical Theater: American writers. "No revivals or children's shows; otherwise we're flexible. We can't do a Broadway-size show. We generally develop work from scratch; we're open to proposals for shows, and ideas from bookwriters or songwriters. We have frequently commissioned underscoring and incidental music."
Productions: *Once on This Island*, by Lynn Ahrens/Stephen Flaherty (musical comedy) and *Later Life*, by A.R. Gurney.

How to Get the Most Out of Songwriter's Market (at the front of this book) contains comments and suggestions to help you understand and use the information in these listings.

PUERTO RICAN TRAVELING THEATRE, Dept. SM, 141 W. 94th St., New York, NY 10025. (212)354-1293. Producer: Miriam Colon Valle. Play Producer. Estab. 1967. Produces 4 plays and 1 new musical/year. Primarily an Hispanic audience. Playwrights are paid by stipend.
How to Contact: Submit complete ms and tape of songs. SASE. Reports in 6 months.
Musical Theater: "Small cast musicals that will appeal to Hispanic audience. Musicals are bilingual; we work in Spanish and English. We need simple sets and props and a cast of about 8, no more. Musicals are generally performed outdoors and last for an hour to an hour and 15 minutes."
Productions: *Chinese Charades*, by Manuel Perralras, Sergio Garcia and Saul Spangenberg (domestic musical); *El Jardin*, by Carlos Morton, Sergio Garcia (Biblical musical); and *Lady With A View*, by Eduardo Ivan Lopez and Fernando Rivas (Statue of Liberty musical).
Tips: "Deal with some aspect of the contemporary Hispanic experience in this country."

THE REPERTORY THEATRE OF ST. LOUIS, P.O. Box 191730, St. Louis MO 63119. (314)968-7340. Associate Artistic Director: Susan Gregg. Play producer. Estab. 1966. Produces 9 plays and 1 or 2 musicals/year. "Conservative regional theater audience. We produce all our work at the Loretto Hilton Theatre." Pays by royalty.
How to Contact: Query with synopsis, character breakdown and set description. Does not return unsolicited material. Reports in 1 year.
Musical Theater: "We want plays with a small cast and simple setting. No children's shows or foul language. After a letter of inquiry we would prefer script and demo tape."
Productions: *1940's Radio Hour*, by Walt Jones; *Almost September*, by David Schechter; *The Merry Wives of Windsor, Texas*, by John Haber.

*SAN JOSE REPERTORY THEATRE, P.O. Box 2399, San Jose CA 95109. (408)291-2266. Fax: (408)995-0737. Literary Manager: J.R. Orlando. Play producer. Estab. 1980. Produces 6 plays and 2 musicals/year. 500-seat, proscenium stage. Pays various royalty.
How to Contact: Query with synopsis, character breakdown and set description. SASE. Reports in 6-8 months.
Musical Theater: "We seek light-hearted, small-cast musicals for our Christmas and summer shows. Musical Reviews are considered if they have an interesting format. Cast and musicians required should equal no more than 10."
Productions: *Cole!*, by Alan Strachan and Benny Green (Cole Porter review); *1940s' Radio Hour*, by Walton Jones (Christmas show); and *Fire in the Rain*, by Holly Near (autobiographical).
Tips: "Send 5-10 pages of sample dialogue with your synopsis."

SEATTLE GROUP THEATRE, 305 Harrison St., Seattle WA 98109. (206)441-9480. Producing Director: Paul O'Connell. Artistic Director: Tim Bond. Estab. 1978. Produces 6 plays and 1 possible musical/year. 200 seat intimate theater; 10' ceiling limit; 35' wide modified thrust; 3 piece band.
How to Contact: Query with synopsis, sample pages of dialogue, a cassette of music and a SASE large enough to accommodate return of cassette. Address all submissions to Nancy Griffiths, Dramaturg/Literary Manager.
Musical Theater: "Multicultural themes; relevant social, cultural and political issues relevant to the contemporary world (race relations, cultural differences, war, poverty, women's issues, homosexuality, physically challenged, developmentally disabled). Address the issues that our mission focuses on." Past musicals include *Rap Master Ronnie, Jacques Brel is Alive, Stealing, Voices of Christmas*. Cast size of 10 maximum.
Productions: *Dear Miss Elena*, by Ludmilla Pasumovskaya; *The Snowflake Avalanche*, by Y. York; *Tod, the Boy, Tod*, by Talvin Hills; *Kind Ness*, by Ping Chong; and *A . . . My Name Is Still Alice*, by Julianne Boyd and Joan Micklin-Silver.

SECOND STAGE THEATRE, P.O. Box 1807, Ansonia Station, New York NY 10023. (212)787-8302. Dramaturg/Literary Manager: Erin Sanders. Play producer. Estab. 1979. Produces 4 plays and 1 musical (1 new musical)/year. Plays are performed in a small, 108 seat off-Broadway House." Pays variable royalty.
How to Contact: Query with synopsis, character breakdown and set description. No unsolicited manuscripts. SASE. Reports in 4 months.
Musical Theater: "We are looking for innovative, unconventional musicals that deal with sociopolitical themes."
Productions: *In a Pig's Valise*, by Eric Overmyer and Kid Creole (spoof on 40's film noir); *Boho Days*, by Jonathan Larson (New York angst); and *The Good Times Are Killing Me*, by Lynda Barry (a play with music).
Tips: "Query with synopsis, character break-down and set description. Invite to concert readings in New York area."

*SHENANDOAH PLAYWRIGHTS RETREAT (A PROJECT OF SHENAN ARTS, INC.), Rt. 5, Box 167-F, Staunton VA 24401. (703)248-1868. Director of Playwriting and Screenwriting Programs: Robert Graham Small. Play producer. Estab. 1976. Develops 12-15 plays/year. Pays fellowships.
How to Contact: Query first. SASE. Replies annually on June 10.
Productions: *The Wall*, by Roger Waters (rock musical adaptation); *Gods Trombones*, by James Weldon Johnson (gospel musical adaptation); and *American Yarn*, by Robert Graham Small (tall tales).
Tips: "Submit materials January-March 1 for Shenandoah Playwrights Retreat. Submit synopsis and demo tape to Paul Hildebrand for touring and full production."

SOUTH WESTERN COLLEGE, 900 Otay Lakes Rd., Chula Vista CA 92010. (619)421-6700. Artistic Director: W. Virchis. Play, mime and performance art work producer. Estab. 1964. Produces 6 plays and 2 musicals (1 new musical)/year.
How to Contact: Query with synopsis, character breakdown and set description. SASE. Reports in 6 weeks.
Productions: Lawrence Myers' *Matador* (world college premiere); and *My Life Is A Dream* (jazz opera based on Calderon de la Vida Es Sueno—world premiere).

STAGE ONE, 425 W. Market St., Louisville KY 40202. (502)589-5946. Producing Director: Moses Goldberg. Play producer. Estab. 1946. Produces 8-10 plays and 0-2 musicals (0-2 new musicals)/year. "Audience is mainly young people ages 5-18." Pays 3-6% royalty, $1,500-3,000 fee or $25-75 per performance.
How to Contact: Submit complete manuscript and score. SASE. Reports in 4 months.
Musical Theater: "We seek stageworthy and respectful dramatizations of the classic tales of childhood, both ancient and modern. Ideally, the plays are relevant to young people and their families, as well as related to school curriculum. Cast is rarely more than 12."
Productions: *Bridge to Terabitha*, by Paterson/Toland/Leibman (contemporary novel); *Little Red Riding Hood*, by Goldberg/Cornett (fairytale); and *Tale of Two Cities*, by Kesselmann (French Revolution).
Tips: "Stage One accepts unsolicited manuscripts that meet our artistic objectives. Please do not send plot summaries or reviews. Include author's resume, if desired. In the case of musicals, a cassette tape is preferred. Cast size is not a factor, although, in practice, Stage One rarely employs casts of over 12. Scripts will be returned in approximately 3-4 months, if SASE is included. No materials can be returned without the inclusion of a SASE. Due to the volume of plays received, it is not possible to provide written evaluations."

*TACOMA ACTORS GUILD, 901 Broadway Plaza, Tacoma WA 98402. (206)272-3107. Fax: (206)272-3358. Company/Literary Manager: Nancy Hoadley. Play producer. Estab. 1978. Produces 6-7 plays and 1-2 musicals/year. "Payment is negotiable."
How to Contact: Query with synopsis, character breakdown and set description; submit complete ms, score and tape of songs (upon request). SASE. Reports in 6-12 months.
Musical Theater: Side stream, mainstream, adaptions, standard, non-standard fare, revue, full-length, family, cutting edge. 10-12 cast/minimal set changes preferred. No extensive orchestration. No puppet, mime or children's pieces.
Productions: *Virtus*, by Gregg Loughridge (Men's movement); *Guys and Dolls*, by Abe Burrows/Loesser; *Beehive*, by Larry Gallagher (60s girl groups).

TADA!, 120 W. 28th St., New York NY 10001. (212)627-1732. Artistic Director: Janine Nina Trevens. Play producer. Estab. 1984. Produces 4 staged readings and 2-4 new musicals/year. "TADA! is a company producing works performed by children ages 6-17 for family audiences in New York City. Performances run approximately 30-45 performances. Pays 5% royalty."
How to Contact: Query with synopsis and character breakdown or submit complete ms, score and tape of songs. SASE. Reports in 2-3 months.
Musical Theater: "We do not produce plays as full productions. At this point, we do staged readings of plays. We produce original commissioned musicals written specifically for the company."
Productions: *B.O.T.C.H.*, by Daniel Feigelson and Jon Agee (the action takes place in the subway system where children, finding their way out run into fun); and *Everything About Camp (Almost)*, (a new musical review about fun times, first times and freaky times at camp). Scenes by Michael Slade. Music and lyrics by various artists including Robby Merkin, Jamie Vernstein, Faye Greenberg, David Lawrence, David Evans, James Beloff, Mary Ehlinger and others.
Tips: "When writing for children don't condescend. The subject matter should be appropriate but the music/treatment can still be complex and interesting."

*THE TEN-MINUTE MUSICALS PROJECT, Box 461194, West Hollywood CA 90046. (213)656-8751. Producer: Michael Koppy. Play producer. Estab. 1987. All pieces are new musicals. Pays equal share of 6-7% royalty, $250 award upon selection.
How to Contact: Submit complete manuscript, score and tape of songs. SASE. Reports in 2 months after annual deadline.
Musical Theater: Seeks complete short stage musicals of between 8 and 15 minutes in length. Maximum cast: 9. "No parodies—original music only."
Productions: *The Furnished Room*, by Saragail Katzman (the O. Henry story); *An Open Window*, by Enid Futterman and Sara Ackerman (the Saki story); *Pulp*, by David Spencer and Bruce Peyton (an original detective mystery), many others.
Tips: "Start with a *solid* story—either an adaptation or an original idea—but with a solid beginning, middle and end (probably with a plot twist at the climax)."

TENNESSEE REPERTORY THEATRE, 427 Chestnut St., Nashville TN 37203. (615)244-4878. Associate Artistic Director: Don Jones. Play producer. Estab. 1985. Produces 5-6 plays/year; produces 3-4 musicals (1-2 new musicals)/year. "A diverse audience of theater goers including people from Nashville's music business. Performances in a 1000-seat state-of-the-art proscenium stage."
How to Contact: Query with synopsis, character breakdown and set description, 10-page dialogue sample and cassette. If material is to be returned, send SASE. Reports in 6-8 months.
Musical Theater: "We are interested in all types of new musicals, with a leaning toward musicals that are indigenous or related to the Southern experience. We also prefer musicals with social merit. For our workshop productions there is minimal use of most elements because work on the piece is primary. For a mainstage production there are no particular limits. We budget accordingly."
Productions: *Some Sweet Day*, by D. Jones, M. Pirkle and L. Sikelu (overcoming racism to form a union); *Ain't Got Long to Stay Here*, by Barry Scott (Martin Luther King); and *A House Divided*, by M. Pirkle and Mike Reid (Civil War).
Tips: "You should submit your work with an open mind toward developing it to the fullest. Tennessee Rep can be integral to that."

*THEATRE WEST, 3333 Cahuenga Blvd. W., Los Angeles CA 90068. (213)851-4839. Contact: Writer's Workshop Moderator. Play producer. Estab. 1962. Produces 6 plays and 0-4 musicals, 0-4 new musicals/year. Audience is mainly young urban professionals—25 to 50. Plays are performed in a 180 seat proscenium theater. Pays $25/performance.
How to Contact: Query first. SASE. Reports in 2 months.
Musical Theater: "Sets are minimalistic. Writer must ask for membership in our company. Would consider original music for use as background or pre-show music."
Productions: *Sermon*, by James Dickey (women's sexuality); *Survival of the Heart*, by Dayton Callie (sitcom-relationships); *The Routine*, by David Abbott (magician's life).
Tips: "Theatre West is a dues-paying membership company. Only members can submit plays for production. So, consequently, you must seek membership in our workshop company."

THEATRE WEST VIRGINIA, Box 1205, Beckley WV 25802. (800)666-9142. Play producer. Estab. 1955. Produces 7-9 plays and 2-3 musicals/year. "Audience varies from mainstream summer stock to educational tours to dinner theater." Pays 5% royalty or $25/performance.
How to Contact: Query with synopsis, character breakdown and set description; should include cassette tape. SASE. Reports in 2 months.
Musical Theater: "Theatre West Virginia is a year-round performing arts organization that presents a variety of productions including community performances such as dinner theater, *The Nutcracker* and statewide educational programs on primary, elementary and secondary levels. This is in addition to our summer, outdoor dramas of *Hatfields & McCoys* and *Honey in the Rock*, now in their 29th year." Anything suitable for secondary school tours and/or dinner theater type shows. No more than 7 in cast. Play should be able to be accompanied by piano/synthesizer.
Productions: *Thomas Jefferson Still Survives*, by Nancy Moss (historical); *Frogsong*, by Jean Battlo (literary/historical); *Guys & Dolls*, by Frank Loesser; *Grease*, by Jim Jacobs and Warren Casey; and *Murder at the Howard Johnsons*, by Ron Clark/Sam Bobrick (comedy).

THEATREVIRGINIA, 2800 Grove Ave., Richmond VA 23221-2466. (804)367-0840. Artistic Director: George Black. Play producer. Estab. 1955. Produces 5-9 plays (2-5 musicals)/year. "Plays are performed in a 500-seat LORT-C house for the Richmond-area community." Payment negotiable.
How to Contact: "Please submit synopsis, sample of dialogue and sample of music (on cassette) along with a self-addressed, stamped letter-size envelope. If material seems to be of interest to us, we will reply with a solicitation for a complete manuscript and cassette. Response time for synopses is 4 weeks; response time for scripts once solicited is 5 months."

Musical Theater: "We do not deal in one-acts or in children's material. We would like to see full length, adult musicals. There are no official limitations. We would be unlikely to use original music as incidental/underscoring for existing plays, but there is potential for adapting existing plays into musicals."

Productions: *West Memphis Mojo*, by Martin Jones; *Sweeney Todd*, by Stephen Sondheim; and *South Pacific*, by Rodgers and Hammerstein.

Tips: "Read plays. Study structure. Study character. Learn how to concisely articulate the nature of your work. A beginning musical playwright, wishing to work for our company should begin by writing a wonderful, theatrically viable piece of musical theatre. Then he should send us the material requested in our listing, and wait patiently."

THEATREWORKS, 1305 Middlefield Rd., Palo Alto CA 94301. (415)323-8311. Literary Manager: Jeannie Barroga. Play producer. Estab. 1970. Produces 7 plays and 5 musicals (2 new musicals)/year. Theatrically-educated suburban area bordering Stanford University 30 miles from San Francisco and San Jose—3 mainstages and 2 second stage performance spaces. Pays per contract.

How to Contact: Submit complete ms, score or sample songs and tape of songs; synopses and character breakdowns helpful. SASE. Reports in 3-5 months.

Musical Theater: "We use original songs and music in many of our classics productions, for instance specially composed music was used in our production of the *The Tempest* for Ariel's song, the pageant song, the storm and the music of the isles. We are looking both for full-scale large musicals and smaller chamber pieces. We also use original music and songs in non-musical plays. No ancient Roman, ancient Greek or biblical settings please!"

Productions: 1993-1994 productions include: *La Bete*, *The Heidi Chronicles*, *Josephine*, *The Skin of Our Teeth*, *Marvin's Room*, *The World Goes 'Round*, *Honor Song for Crazy Horse*, *Almost September*, *The Music of Stephen Swartz*, *Tiny Tim is Dead*, *Scotland Road* and *Small Delegation*.

Tips: "Write a great musical. We wish there were more specific 'formula,' but that's about it. If it's really terrific, we're interested."

THEATREWORKS/USA, 890 Broadway, New York NY 10003. (212)677-5959. Literary Manager: Barbara Pasternack. Play producer. Produces 10-13 plays, all are musicals (3-4 new musicals)/year. Audience consists of children and families. Pays 6% royalty and aggregate of $1500 commission-advance against future royalties.

How to Contact: Query with synopsis, character breakdown and sample scene and song. SASE. Reports in 6 months.

Musical Theater: "One hour long, 5-6 adult actors, highly portable, good musical theater structure; adaptations of children's literature, historical or biographical musicals, issues, fairy tales—all must have something to say. We demand a certain level of literary sophistication. No kiddy shows, no camp, no fractured fables, no shows written for school or camp groups to perform. Approach your material, not as a writer writing for kids, but as a writer addressing any universal audience. You have one hour to entertain, say something, make them care—don't preach, condescend. Don't forget an antagonist. Don't waste the audience's time. We always use original music—but most of the time a project team comes complete with a composer in tow."

Productions: *Jekyll and Hyde*, book and lyrics by David Crane and Marta Kaufmann, music by Michael Sklopf; *Columbus*, by Jonathan Bolt, music by Doug Cohen, lyrics by Thomas Toce; *Class Clown*, book by Thomas West, music by Kim Oles, lyrics by Alison Hubbard; and *Freaky Friday*, music by Mary Rodgers, book and lyrics by John Forster.

Tips: "Write a good show! Make sure the topic is something we can market! Come see our work to find out our style."

13TH STREET REPERTORY COMPANY, 50 W. 13th St., New York NY 10011. (212)675-6677. Dramaturg: Ken Terrell. Play producer. Estab. 1974. Produces 6 plays/year including 2 new musicals. Audience comes from New York and surrounding area. Children's theater performs at 50 W. 13th in NYC. "We do not pay. We are an off off Broadway company and provide a stepping stone for writers, directors, actors."

How to Contact: Query with synopsis, character breakdown and set description. SASE. Reports in 2 months.

Musical Theater: Children's musicals and original musical shows. Small cast with limited musicians. Stagings are struck after each performance. Would consider original music for "pre-show music or incidental music."

Productions: *Journeys*, a collaborative effort about actors' work in New York City; and *The Smart Set*, by Enrico Garzilli.

*DON TONER, 311 Nueces, Austin TX 78701. Fax: (512)472-7199. Literary Manager: Amparo Garcia. Play producer. Produces 8 plays and 2-3 musicals (1 new musical)/year. "Audience is mixed—we are a large university town so we attract a variety of people. Family oriented." 280 seat proscenium. "We follow Samuel French or other publisher's agreement."

How to Contact: Query with synopsis, character breakdown and set description. SASE. Reports in 3-6 months.

Musical Theater: "Musicals with widest appeal. We reserve the experimental genres to development/ readings—musicals are biggest \$ draw so we choose more established work. We appreciate all great writing; however, an original musical has a chance of production if it is a finalist in our new play awards."

Productions: *Nine*, by Authur Kopit/Maury Yeston (based on Fellini's *8½*); *Dancing at Lughnasa*, by Brian Friel (family portrait); and *Fiddler on the Roof*, by J. Stein, J. Buck and Sheldon Hamick.

UNIVERSITY OF ALABAMA NEW PLAYWRIGHTS' PROGRAM, P.O. Box 870239, Tuscaloosa AL 35487-0239. (205)348-5283. Director/Dramaturg: Dr. Paul Castagno. Play producer. Estab. 1982. Produces 8-10 plays and 1 musical/year; 1 new musical every other year. University audience. Pays by arrangement. Stipend is competitive. Also expenses and travel.

How to Contact: Submit complete manuscript, score and tape of songs. SASE. Reports in 2 months.

Musical Theater: Any style or subject (but no children's or puppet plays). No limitations—just solid lyrics and melodic line. Drama with music, musical theater workshops, and chamber musicals. "We would love to produce a small-scale musical."

Productions: *Gospel According to Esther*, by John Erlanger.

Tips: "Take your demos seriously. We really want to do something small scale, for actors, often without the greatest singing ability. Use fresh sounds not derivative of the latest fare. While not ironclad by any means, musicals with Southern themes might stand a better chance."

THE UNUSUAL CABARET, 14½ Mt. Desert St., Bar Harbor ME 04609. (207)288-3306. Artistic Director: Gina Kaufmann. Play producer. Estab. 1990. Produces 4 plays and 4 new musicals/year. Educated adult audiences. 50 seat cabaret. "A casual, festive atmosphere." Pays by royalty (12% of Box).

How to Contact: Submit complete ms, score and tape of songs. SASE. Reports in 1 month.

Musical Theater: "We produce both musical and non-musical scripts—45 minutes to 1¼ hours in length. Stylistically or topically unique scripts are encouraged. We strive for as diverse a season as possible within our technical limitations. Our maximum cast size is 8, but cast sizes of 4 or fewer are necessary for some of our productions. Our technical capabilities are minimal. Audience participation and non-traditional staging are possible because of the cabaret setting. We encourage musical *plays* as well as more traditional musicals. Piano is usually the only instrument. We consider adaptations if the written material is being used in an original way in conjunction with the music."

Productions: *Hamlet: the Anti-Musical*, by Mark Milbauer and David Becker; *Dead Poets*, by Jeff Goode and John Gay (Emily Dickinson, Walt Whitman and Edgar Allen Poe); *The Beggar's Opera* (adaptation), by John Gay/adaptation: Gina Kaufmann (economic and social structure of society).

Tips: "We come from the Brecht/Weill tradition of challenging ourselves and our audiences stylistically and intellectually."

WALNUT STREET THEATRE COMPANY, 825 Walnut St., Philadelphia PA 19107. (215)574-3584. Literary Manager: Alexa Kelly. Play producer. Estab. 1982. Produces 8 plays and 2 musicals (1 new musical)/ year. Plays produced on a mainstage with seating for 1,052 to a family audience; and in studio theaters with seating for 79-99 to adult audiences. Pays by royalty or outright purchase.

How to Contact: Query with synopsis, character breakdown, set description, and ten pages. SASE. Reports in 6 months.

Musical Theater: "Adult Musicals. Plays are for a subscription audience that comes to the theatre to be entertained. We seek musicals with lyrical non-operatic scores and a solid book. We are looking for a small musical for springtime and one for a family audience at Christmas time. We would like to remain open on structure and subject matter and would expect a tape with the script. Cast size: around 20 equity members (10 for smaller musical); preferably one set with variations." Would consider original music for incidental music and/or underscore. This would be at each director's discretion.

Productions: *Jesus Christ Superstar*, by Rice/Lloyd-Webber; *Into the Woods*, by Sondheim; and *Another Kind of Hero*, by Steele/Alexander.

Tips: "Invest in sending the best quality musical tape that you can—don't leave us to imagine the orchestration and good singing."

*WAREHOUSE THEATRE, P.O. Box 454, Greenville SC 29602. (803)235-6948. Fax: (803)235-6729. Artistic Director: Jack Young. Play producer. Estab. 1974. Produces 1 musical/year. 105-seat loft space. Pays 5-10% royalty. Submit complete ms, score and tape of songs. SASE. Reports in 6 months.

Musical Theater: "Contemporary, *small* cast and sets because of our limited facility. No 'kiddie' puppet shows."
Productions: *Closer Than Ever*, by Maltby and Saire; *Speed of Darkness*, by Steve Tesich; and *Crossing Delancey*.
Tips: "As new Artistic Director at the Warehouse, I'm interested in shows that comment on life *now* — would love to see things with American Southern point of view, as well."

WATERLOO COMMUNITY PLAYHOUSE, Box 433, Waterloo IA 50704. (319)235-0367. Managing Director: Charles Stilwill. Play producer. Estab. 1917. Produces 12 plays (1-2 musicals)/year. "Our audience prefers solid, wholesome entertainment, nothing risque or with strong language. We perform in Hope Martin Theatre, a 368-seat house." Pays $15-150/performance.
How to Contact: Submit complete manuscript, score and cassette tape of songs. SASE.
Musical Theater: "Casts may vary from as few as 6 people to 54. We are producing children's theater as well. We're *especially* interested in new adaptations of classic children stories."
Productions: *Music Man*, by Meredith Wilson (traditional); *Nunsense*, by Dan Goggin; *Oklahoma*, by Rodgers & Hammerstein (traditional).
Tips: "Looking for new adaptations of classical children's stories or a good Christmas show."

WEST COAST ENSEMBLE, Box 38728, Los Angeles CA 90038. (213)871-8673. Artistic Director: Les Hanson. Play producer. Estab. 1982. Produces 6-9 plays and 1 new musical/year. "Our audience is a wide variety of Southern Californians. Plays will be produced in one of our two theaters on Hollywood Boulevard." Pays $35-50 per performance.
How to Contact: Submit complete manuscript, score and tape of songs. SASE. Reports in 6 months.
Musical Theater: "There are no limitations on subject matter or style. Cast size should be no more than 12 and sets should be simple. If music is required we would commission a composer, music would be used as a bridge between scenes or to underscore certain scenes in the play."
Productions: *Gorey Stories*, by Stephen Currens (review based on material of Edward Gorey) and *The Much Ado Musical*, by Tony Tanner (adaptation of Shakespeare).
Tips: "Submit work in good form and be patient. We look for musicals with a strong book and an engaging score with a variety of styles."

WILMA THEATER, 2030 Sansom St., Philadelphia PA 19103. (215)963-0249. Artistic Producing Director: Jiri Zizka; Artistic Producing Director: Blanka Zizka. Play producer. Produces 4-5 plays (1-2 musicals)/year. Plays are performed for a "sophisticated, adventurous, off-beat and demanding audience," in a 100-seat theater. Pays 6-8% of gross income.
How to Contact: Submit synopsis, score and tape of songs. SASE. Reports in 2 months.
Musical Theater: Seeks "innovative staging, universal issues, political implications and inventive, witty approach to subject. We emphasize ensemble style, group choreography, actors and musicians overlapping, with new, inventive approach to staging. Do not exceed 4-5 musicians, cast of 12, (ideally under 8), or stage space of 30x20." Also interested in plays with music and songs.
Productions: *Hairy Ape*, by O'Neill (search for self-identity); *The Mystery of Irma Vep* by Charles Ludlum; *Incommunicado*, by Tom Dulak; *Marat/Sade* (basic questions of human existence); *Three Guys Naked From the Waist Down* (worship of success); and *Oedipus The King*, by Sophocles (with original music).
Tips: "Don't think what will sell. Find your own voice. Be original, tune to your ideas. characters and yourself."

WOMEN'S PROJECT AND PRODUCTIONS, JULIA MILES, ARTISTIC DIRECTOR, 7 W. 63rd St., New York NY 10023. (212)873-3040. Literary Manager: Susan Bougetz. Estab. 1978. Produces 3 plays/year. Pays by outright purchase.
How to Contact: Submit synopsis, 10 sample pages of dialogue and sample tape. SASE. Reports in 3 months. "Adult audience. Plays by women only."
Musical Theater: "We usually prefer a small to medium cast of 3-6. We produce few musicals and produce *only* women playwrights."
Productions: *A . . . My Name is Alice*, conceived by Joan Micklin Silver and Julianne Boyd (satire of women's issues); *Ladies*, by Eve Ensler (homelessness); *O Pioneers!*, by Darrah Cloud (adapted) from Willa Cather's novel; and *Skirting the Issues* (musical cabaret).
Tips: "Resist sending early drafts of work."

WOOLLY MAMMOTH THEATRE CO., Dept. SM, 1401 Church St. NW, Washington DC 20005. (202)234-6130. Literary Manager: Jim Byrnes. Play producer. Estab. 1980. Produces 4 plays/year.
How to Contact: Submit letter of inquiry or full package (i.e., complete manuscript and score and tape of songs). SASE.
Musical Theater: "We do unusual works. We have done one musical, the *Rocky Horror Show* (very successful). 8-10 in cast. We do not wish to see one-acts. Be professional in presentation."
Productions: '92-'93 season was devoted exclusively to world premieres: *Billy Nobody, Free Will and Wanton Lust, The Cockburn Rituals* and *Strindberg in Hollywood.*
Tips: "Just keep writing! Too many people expect to make it writing one or two plays."

Play Publishers

AMELIA MAGAZINE, 329 "E" St., Bakersfield CA 93304. (805)323-4064. Editor: Frederick A. Raborg, Jr. Play publisher. Estab. 1983. Publishes 1 play/year. General audience; one-act plays published in *Amelia Magazine.* Best play submitted is the winner of the annual Frank McClure One-Act Play Award.
How to Contact: Submit complete manuscript and score per contest rules by postmark deadline of May 15. SASE. Reports in 6-8 weeks. "We would consider publishing musical scores if submitted in clean, camera-ready copy—also single songs. Best bet is with single songs complete with clear, camera-ready scoresheets, for regular submissions. We use only first North American serial rights. All performance and recording rights remain with songwriter. Payment same as for poetry—$25 plus copies."
Tips: "Be polished, professional, and submit clear, clean copy."

ARAN PRESS, 1320 S. Third St., Louisville KY 40208. (502)636-0115. Editor/Publisher: Tom Eagan. Play publisher. Estab. 1983. Publishes 40-50 plays, 1-2 musicals and 1-2 new musicals/year. Professional, college/university, community, summer stock and dinner theater audience. Pays 50% production royalty or 10% book royalty.
How to Contact: Submit ms, score and tape of songs. SASE. Reports in 1-2 weeks.
Musical Theater: "The musical should include a small cast, simple set for professional, community, college, university, summer stock and dinner theater production."
Publications: *Comedy of History*, by Dick W. Zylstra (musical history); *The Big Dollar*, by Herschel Steinhardt (real estate business); and *Caribbean Blue*, by Jonathan Lowe (tropical island revolution).

ART CRAFT PUBLISHING CO., (formerly C. Emmett McMullen), Box 1058, Cedar Rapids IA 52406. (319)364-6311. Editor: C. Emmett McMullen. Play publisher. Estab. 1928. Publishes 10-15 plays/year. "We publish plays and musicals for the amateur market including middle schools, junior and smaller senior high schools and church groups."
How to Contact: Submit complete manuscript and score. SASE. Reports in 2 months.
Musical Theater: "Seeking material for high school productions. All writing within the scope of high school groups. No works with X-rated material or questionable taboos. Simplified staging and props. Currently seeking material with larger casts, preferably with more women than male roles."
Publications: *Robin Hood*, by Dan Neidermyer; *Invisible Boy*, by Robert Frankel; and *Murder At Coppersmith Inn*, by Dan Neidermyer.
Tips: "We are interested in working with new writers. Writers need to consider that many plays are presented in small, often not well-established stages."

BAKER'S PLAYS, 100 Chauncy St., Boston MA 02111. (617)482-1280. Editor: John B. Welch. Play publisher. Estab. 1845. Publishes 15-22 plays and 3-5 new musicals/year. Plays are used by children's theaters, junior and senior high schools, colleges and community theaters. Pays 50% royalty or 10% book royalty.
How to Contact: Submit complete manuscript, score and cassette tape of songs. SASE. Reports in 2-6 months.
Musical Theater: "Seeking musicals for teen production and children's theater production. We prefer large cast, contemporary musicals which are easy to stage and produce. Plot your shows strongly, keep your scenery and staging simple, your musical numbers and choreography easily explained and blocked out. Originality and style are up to the author. We want innovative and tuneful shows but no X-rated material. We are very interested in the new writer and believe that, with revision and editorial help, he can achieve success in writing original musicals for the non-professional market." Would consider original music for use in a play being developed or in a pre-existing play.
Publications: *The High School That Dripped Gooseflesh*, by Tim Kelly, Ole Kittleson and Arne Christianson (rock 'n roll high school horror spoof); *Just Friends*, by Scanlan/Cangiano (high school friendships); and *Silent Bells*, by Jane O'Neill, Charles Apple (Christmas fable).
Tips: "As we publish musicals that can be produced by high school theater departments with high school talent, the writer should know if their play can be done on the high school stage. I recommend that the writer go to performances of original musicals whenever possible."

CONTEMPORARY DRAMA SERVICE, 885 Elkton Dr., Colorado Springs CO 80907. (719)594-4422. Executive Editor: Arthur Zapel. Assistant Editor: Rhonda Wray. Play publisher. Estab. 1979. Publishes 40-50 plays and 4-6 new musicals/year. "We publish for young children and teens in mainstream Christian churches and for teens and college level in the secular market. Our musicals are performed in churches, schools and colleges." Pays 10% royalty (for music books), 50% royalty for performance and "sometimes we pay royalty up to buy-out fee for minor works."

How to Contact: Submit complete ms, score and tape of songs. SASE. Reports in 6 weeks.

Musical Theater: "For churches we publish musical programs for children and teens to perform at Easter, Christmas or some special occasion. Our school musicals are for teens to perform as class plays or special entertainments. Cast size may vary from 5-25 depending on use. We prefer more parts for girls than boys. Music must be written in the vocal range of teens. Staging should be relatively simple but may vary as needed. We are not interested in elementary school material. Elementary level is OK for church music but not public school elementary. Music must have full piano accompaniment and be professionally scored for camera-ready publication."

Publications: *Christmas on the Brink*, by Jim Thompson/Larry Nestor (Christmas from a 60s perspective); *Medan, the Stable Mouse* by Karen Gazzillo/Peter Candela (Christmas musical); and *Beauty and the Beast*, by Lee Ahlin and Philip Hall (the classic love story set to music).

Tips: "Familiarize yourself with the type of musicals we publish. Note general categories, then give us something that would fit, yet differs from what we've already published."

THE DRAMATIC PUBLISHING COMPANY, 311 Washington St., Woodstock IL 60098. (815)338-7170. Music Editor: Dana Wolworth. Play publisher. Publishes 35 plays (3-5 musicals)/year. Estab. 1885. Plays used by community theaters, high schools, colleges, stock and professional theaters, churches and camps. Pays standard royalty.

How to Contact: Submit complete manuscript, score and tape of songs. SASE. Reports in 10-12 weeks.

Musical Theater: Seeking "children's musicals not over 1¼ hours, and adult musicals with 2 act format. No adaptations for which the rights to use the original work have not been cleared. If directed toward high school market, large casts with many female roles are preferred. For professional, stock and community theater small casts are better. Cost of producing a play is always a factor to consider in regard to costumes, scenery and special effects." Would also consider original music for use in a pre-existing play "if we or the composer hold the rights to the non-musical work."

Publications: *The Phantom of the Opera*, book by Joseph Robinette and music by Robert Chauls (new musical based on the original book by Gaston Leroux); *Narnia*, book by Jules Tasca, lyrics by Ted Drachman and music by Thomas Tierney (musical based on C.S. Lewis' *The Lion, The Witch, and The Wardrobe*); *Sail Away*, book and music by Noel Coward; *Shakespeare and the Indians*, book and lyrics by Dale Wasserman, music by Allan Jay Friedman (from the author of *Man of La Mancha* comes this new musical).

Tips: "We are looking for new innovative works with small ensembles. The knowledge of synthesizers is an asset for today's market. Children's musicals are our main interest."

ELDRIDGE PUBLISHING CO., INC., P.O. Drawer 216, Franklin OH 45005. (513)746-6531. Editor: Nancy S. Vorhis. Play publisher. Estab. 1906. Publishes 20 plays and 2-3 musicals/year. Seeking "large cast musicals which appeal to students. We like variety and originality in the music, easy staging and costuming. We serve the school and church market, 6th grade through 12th; also Christmas and Easter musicals for churches." Would also consider original music for use in a play being developed; "music that could make an ordinary play extraordinary." Pays 50% royalty and 10% copy sales in school market.

How to Contact: Submit tape with manuscript if at all possible. Unsolicited submissions OK. SASE. Reports in 2 months.

Publications: *Phantom of the Soap Opera*, by Sodaro; *I am A Star!*, by Billie St. John and Wendell Jimerson (high schoolers vying for movie roles); *Triple Play*, by Hal Kesler and Larry Nestor (1920s baseball game).

Tips: "We're always looking for talented composers but not through individual songs. We're only interested in complete school or church musicals. Lead sheets, cassette tape and script are best way to submit. Let us see your work!"

ENCORE PERFORMANCE PUBLISHING, P.O. Box 692, Orem UT 84057. (801)225-0605. Editor: Michael C. Perry. Play publisher. Estab. 1979. Publishes 10-20 plays (including musicals)/year. "We are interested in plays which emphasize strong family values and play to all ages of audience." Pays by royalty; 50% performance, 10% book.

How to Contact: Query with synopsis, character breakdown and set description, then submit complete manuscript, score and tape of songs. SASE. Reports in 4 weeks to 6 months.
Musical Theater: Musicals of all types for all audiences. Can be original or adapted. "We tend to favor shows with at least an equal male/female cast. Do not wish to see works that can be termed offensive or vulgar. However, experimental theater forms are also of interest."
Publications: *Nine Candles for David* and *Aesop! Aesop!*, by Barbara Schapp; and *Turn the Gas Back On!*, by Max Golightly, C. Michael Perry and Neil Newell.
Tips: "Always write with an audience in mind."

THE FREELANCE PRESS, Box 548, Dover MA 02030. (508)785-1260. Managing Editor: Narcissa Campion. Play publisher. Estab. 1979. Publishes 20 plays/year; 19 musicals (3 new musicals/year.) "Pieces are primarily for elementary to high school children; large casts (approximately 30); plays are produced by schools and children's theaters." Pays 10% of purchase price of script or score, 50% of collected royalty.
How to Contact: Query first. SASE. Reports in 6 months.
Musical Theater: "We publish previously produced musicals and plays for children in the primary grades through high school. Plays are for large casts (approximately 30 actors and speaking parts) and run between 45 minutes to 1 hour and 15 minutes. Subject matter should be contemporary issues (sibling rivalry, friendship, etc.) or adaptations of classic literature for children (*Alice in Wonderland*, *Treasure Island*, etc.). We do not accept any plays written for adults to perform for children."
Publications: *Monopoly*, by T. Dewey/Megan (3 high school students live out the board game); *No Zone*, by T. Dewey/Campion (environmental fantasy about effects of global warming); *The Pied Piper*, P. Houghton/Hutchins (adaptation of Browning poem).
Tips: "We enjoy receiving material that does not condescend to children. They are capable of understanding many current issues, playing complex characters, acting imaginative and unconventional material, and singing difficult music."

SAMUEL FRENCH, INC., 45 W. 25th St., New York NY 10010. (212)206-8990. Editor: Lawrence Harbison. Play publisher. Estab. 1830. Publishes 90-100 plays and 5-6 new musicals/year. Amateur and professional theaters. Pays 80% of amateur royalties; 90% of professional royalties.
How to Contact: Query first, then submit complete manuscript and tape of songs. SASE. Reports in 6 weeks to 8 months.
Musical Theater: "We publish primarily successful musicals from the NYC stage." Don't submit large-cast, big "Broadway" musicals which haven't been done on Broadway.
Publications: *Starmites*, by Keating and Ross; *Me and My Girl*, by various; and *Chess*, by Nelson/Rice/Ulvaeus/Andersson.

HEUER PUBLISHING CO., (formerly Heuer Publishing Co./Art Craft Publishing Co.), Box 248, Cedar Rapids IA 52406. (319)364-6311. Publisher: C. Emmett McMullen. Musical play publisher. Estab. 1928. Publishes plays and musicals for the amateur market including middle schools, junior and senior high schools and church groups.
How to Contact: Submit complete ms and score or query with synopsis, character breakdown and set description. SASE. Reports in 2 months.
Musical Theater: "We prefer two or three act comedies or mystery-comedies with a large number of characters.

LILLENAS DRAMA RESOURCES, P.O. Box 419527, Kansas City MO 64141. (816)931-1900. Editor/Consultant: Paul M. Miller. Play publisher. Estab. 1912. Publishes 10 collections (2 full-length) and 4 program collections, 3 musicals (3 new musicals)/year. "Our plays and musicals are performed by churches, Christian schools, and independent theater organizations that perform 'religious' plays." Pays 10% royalty, by outright purchase ($5 per page for program material only), or $10-25/performance (selected).
How to Contact: Submit complete ms and score or, preferably, submit complete ms, score and tape of songs. SASE. Reports in 3 months.
Publications: *Characters*; *Drama 'Til You Drop*; *Childhood is a Stage*; and *Worship, Drama Library Volumes 1-5*.
Tips: "Remember that religious theater comes in all genres: do not become historically biblical; take truth and couch in terms that are understandable to contemporary audiences in and out of the church. Keep 'simplicity' as a key word in your writing; cast sizes, number of scenes/acts, costume and set requirements will affect the acceptance of your work by the publisher and the market."

MERIWETHER PUBLISHING, LTD. (CONTEMPORARY DRAMA SERVICE), 885 Elkton Dr., Colorado Springs CO 80907. (719)594-4422. Executive Editor: Arthur Zapel. Play publisher. Estab. 1968. Publishes 40 plays and 5-10 musicals (5 new musicals)/year. "We publish musicals for church school, elementary, middle grade and teens. We also publish musicals for high school secular use. Our musicals are performed in churches or high schools." Pays 10% royalty or by negotiated sale from royalties. "Sometimes we pay a royalty to a limited maximum."

How to Contact: Query with synopsis, character breakdown and set description or submit script with cassette tape of songs. SASE. Reports in 1 month.

Musical Theater: "We are always looking for good church/school musicals for children. We prefer a length of 15-20 minutes, though occasionally we will publish a 3-act musical adaptation of a classic with large casts and sets. We like informal styles, with a touch of humor, that allow many children and/or adults to participate. We like musicals that imitate Broadway shows or have some name appeal based on the Classics. Box office appeal is more critical than message—at least for teenage and adult level fare. Musical scripts with piano accompaniments only. We especially welcome short, simple musicals for elementary and teenage, church use during the holidays of Christmas and Easter. We would like to know of arrangers and copyists."

Publications: *Beauty and the Beast*, by Lee Ahlin and Philip Hall (classic love story); *Pinnochio*, by Larry Nestor and Miriam Schuman (children's story); and *Steamboat*, by Charles Boyd and Yvonne Boyd.

Tips: "Tell us clearly the intended market for the work and provide as much information as possible about its viability."

PIONEER DRAMA SERVICE, P.O. Box 22555, Denver CO 80222. (303)759-4297. Play publisher. Estab. 1963. "Plays are performed by junior high and high school drama departments, church youth groups, college and university theaters, semi-professional and professional children's theaters, parks and recreation departments." Playwrights paid by royalty (10% sales) $250-500 or by outright purchase and 50% performance royalty.

How to Contact: Query with synopsis, character breakdown and set description. SASE. Reports in 2 months.

Musical Theater: "We seek full length children's musicals, high school musicals and one act children's musicals to be performed by children, secondary school students, and/or adults. As always, we are seeking musicals easy to perform, simple sets, many female roles and very few solos. Must be appropriate for educational market. Developing a new area, we are actively seeking musicals to be produced by elementary schools—20 to 30 minutes in length, with 2 to 3 songs and large choruses. We are not interested in profanity, themes with exclusively adult interest, sex, drinking, smoking, etc. Several of our full-length plays are being converted to musicals. We edit them, decide where to insert music and then contact with someone to write the music and lyrics."

Publications: *You Ain't Nothin But A Werewolf*, by Tim Kelly/Bill Francoeur (spoof of '50s "B" horror films); *The Frog Prince*, by D.J. Leonard/David Reiser (tale by Bros. Grimm); and *Bedside Manor*, by Tim Kelly/G.V.Castle/M.C. Vigilant (hospital farce).

Tips: "Learn what our markets are and what those markets' needs are."

PLAYERS PRESS, INC., Box 1132, Studio City CA 91614. (818)789-4980. Associate Editor: Marjorie Clapper. Vice President: Robert W. Gordon. Play publisher. Estab. 1965. Publishes 10-20 plays and 1-3 new musicals/year. Plays are used primarily by general audience and children. Pays 10% royalty or 25% of performance.

How to Contact: Query first or submit complete manuscript, score and tape of songs. SASE. Reports in 1 year.

Musical Theater: "We will consider all submitted works. Presently musicals for adults and high schools are in demand. When cast size can be flexible (describe how it can be done in your work) it sells better."

Publications: *The Deerstalker*, by Doug Flack (Sherlock Holmes-musical); *Rapunzel N the Witch*, by William-Alan Landes (children's musical); and *Sunnyside Junior High*, by Rick Woyiwoda (teen musical).

Tips: "When submitting, it is best to send a clean, clear sounding tape with music. We do not publish a play or musical which has not been produced."

Play Producers and Publishers/'93-'94 Changes

The following markets appeared in the 1993 edition of *Songwriter's Market* but are absent from the 1994 edition. Most of these companies failed to respond to our request for an update of their listing for a variety of reasons. For example, they may have gone out of business or they may have requested deletion from the 1994 edition because they are backlogged with material. If we know the specific reason, it appears within parentheses.

Arkansas State University-Beebe Campus
Arrow Rock Lyceum Theatre
California Music Theatre (unable to contact)
Center Theater
Citiarts Theatre
The Cleveland Play House
Cleveland Public Theatre (not accepting submissions)
Department of Theatre, Michigan State University
Steve Dobbins Productions
East West Players (EWP)

Ensemble Theatre of Cincinnati
The Firehouse Theatre
Heritage Artists at the Music Hall
Laguna Playhouse
John B. Lynch, Jr.
Merry-Go-Round Playhouse
National Music Theater Network, Inc.
New Theatre
New Vic Supper Theatre
Off Center Theatre
Ozark Actors Theatre

Salome: A Journal for the Performing Arts (requested deletion)
Theatre for Young America (unable to contact)
Theatre Off Park
Washington Jewish Theatre (no longer producing shows)
Jenny Wiley Theatre
Wisdom Bridge Theatre
Worcester Foothills Theatre Co.

Fine Arts

For the aspiring composer it is vital to have his work performed for interested listeners. A resume of performances aids in identifying a composer within the concert music community. One excellent, exciting performance may lead to others by different groups or commissions for new works.

All of the groups listed in this section are interested in hearing new music. From chamber groups to symphony orchestras, they are open to new talent and feel their audiences are progressive and interested enough to support new music.

Bear in mind the financial and artistic concerns as you submit material. Fine arts groups have extremely high standards. Don't hurt your chances by sending anything but your best compositions. Always follow their submission instructions diligently. Be professional when you contact the music directors, and keep in mind the typical fine arts audience they are selecting music for. Chamber musicians and their audiences, for instance, are a good source for performance opportunities. Their repertoire is limited and most groups are enthusiastic about finding or commissioning new works. Furthermore, the chamber music audience is smaller and likewise enthusiastic enough to enjoy contemporary music.

Don't be disappointed if the payment offered by these groups seems small. Most fine arts music organizations are struggling economically and can't pay large fees to even the most established composers. Inquire into other opportunities to submit your work; many of these groups also offer periodic competitions for new works. Also, most of these ensembles belong to a blanket organization representing that genre. See the Organizations and Contests and Awards sections for more information and possibilities.

AFTER DINNER OPERA CO., INC., 23 Stuyvesant St., New York NY 10003. (212)477-6212. Executive Director: Dr. Richard Flusser. Opera Company. Estab. 1949. Members are professionals. Performs 30 concerts/year, including 4 new works. Concert hall "varies from 200 to 900 seats." Pays $0-500/performance.
How to Contact: "Send SASE with postage, or materials cannot be returned. Do not send your only copy. Mail to: Dr. Richard Flusser (H140), After Dinner Opera Co., Inc., Queensborough Community College, 222-05 56th Ave., Bayside, NY 11364-1497. We report to all submissions in May of every year."
Music: "Seeks piano vocal scores with indications of instruments from 2-17, chamber size operas from 10 minutes long to 2 hours; no more than 10 singers. Especially interested in 3 character operas under one hour in length. Also interested in operas for children. No gospel or heavy metal rock."
Performances: H.H. Beach's *Cabildo* (one act opera), William Grant Still's *Troubled Island* (opera), Seymour Barab's *Fair Means or Foul* (children's opera), and Duke Ellington's *Queeny Pie*.
Tips: "Start with an interesting, singable libretto. Make sure that you have the rights to the libretto."

THE AKRON CITY FAMILY MASS CHOIR, 429 Homestead St., Akron OH 44306. (216)773-8529. President: Walter E.L. Scrutchings. Vocal ensemble. Estab. 1984. Members are professionals. Performs 5-7 concerts/year; performs 30-35 new works/year. Commissions 10-15 composers or new works/

year. Audience mostly interested in new original black gospel music. Performs in various venues. Composers paid 50% royalty.

How to Contact: Submit complete score and tapes of piece(s). Does not return material. Reports in 2 months.

Music: Seeks "traditional music for SATB black gospel; also light contemporary. No rap or non-spiritual themes."

Performances: R.W. Hinton's *I Can't Stop Praising God*; W. Scrutchings' *A Better Place*; and Rev. A. Wright's *Christ In Your Life*.

THE AMERICAN BOYCHOIR, Lambert Dr., Princeton NJ 08540. (609)924-5858. Music Director: James H. Litton. Professional boychoir. Estab. 1937. Members are highly skilled children. Performs 225 concerts/year, including 15-25 new works. Commissions 1-2 composers or new works/year. Performs community concerts and for local concert associations, church concert series and other bookings. Pays by commission.

How to Contact: Query first. SASE. Reports in 6 months.

Music: "Dramatic works for boys voices (age 10-14); 15 to 20 minutes short opera to be staged and performed throughout the US." Choral pieces, either in unison, SSA, SA or SSAA division; unaccompanied and with piano or organ; occasional chamber orchestra accompaniment. Pieces are usually sung by 26 to 50 boys. Composers must know boychoir sonority.

Performances: Ned Rorem's *Who Has Seen The Wind* (song cycle for boys' voices); Daniel Pinkham's *Angels are Everywhere* (song cycle for boys' voices); Milton Babbitt's *Glosses* (motet for boys' voices); David Diamond's *This Sacred Ground*; and Daniel Gawthrop's *Mary Speaks*.

*AMHERST SAXOPHONE QUARTET, 137 Eagle St., Williamsville NY 14221-5721. (716)632-2445. Director: Steve Rosenthal. Chamber music ensemble. Estab. 1978. Performs 80-100 concerts/year including 10-20 new works. Commissions 2-4 composers or new works/year. "We are a touring ensemble." Payment varies.

How to Contact: Query first. SASE. Reports in 1 month.

Music: "Music for soprano, alto, tenor and baritone (low A) saxophone. We are interested in great music of many styles. Level of difficulty is commensurate with full-time touring ensembles."

Performances: Lukas Foss's *Saxophone Quartet*; David Stock's *Sax Appeal*; and Chan Ka Nin's *Saxophone Quartet*, all chamber music.

Tips: "Professionally copied parts help! Write what you truly want to write."

*ARCADY MUSIC SOCIETY, P.O. Box 780, Bar Harbor ME 04809. (207)288-3151. Artistic Director: Masanobu Ikemiga. Nonprofit presenter. Estab. 1980. Members are volunteers; performers are professionals. Performs 50 concerts/year including 1-5 new works. Commissions 0-1 new composer or new work/year. "Perform mainly in churches."

How to Contact: Query first. SASE.

Music: "Chamber music, from 5-15 minutes in length. No symphonic work. Not interested in popular songs."

Performances: Several études by Robert Dick (flute); Radrilovich (orchestral) and Mayazumi (piano concerto).

ASHEVILLE SYMPHONY ORCHESTRA, P.O. Box 2852, Asheville NC 28802. (704)254-7046. Music Director: Robert Hart Baker. Symphony orchestra, chamber ensemble, and youth orchestra. Performs 20 concerts/year, including 2 new works. Members are professionals. Commissions 1 composer or new work/year. Concerts performed in Thomas Wolfe Auditorium, which seats 2,400. Subscription audience size is approximately 1,900. Pays by outright purchase (up to $1,000 when commissioning) or via ASCAP or BMI.

How to Contact: Submit complete score and tape of pieces. SASE. Reports in 10 weeks.

Music: Seeks "classical, pops orchestrations, full modern orchestral works, concertos and chamber music. Winds in triplicate maximum; not too many extreme high ranges or exotic time signatures/notation. Do not send unaccompanied choral works or songs for voice and piano only."

Performances: Douglas Ovens' *Play Us A Tune* (cycle for mezzo and orchestra); Howard Hanger's *For Barbara* (for jazz ensemble and orchestra); and Robert Hart Baker's *Fantasie* (arrangement of Chopin work for orchestra).

The asterisk before a listing indicates that the listing is new in this edition. New markets are often the most receptive to unsolicited submissions.

*ASHLAND SYMPHONY ORCHESTRA, P.O. Box 13, Ashland OH 44805. (419)289-5115. General Manager: James E. Thomas. Symphony orchestra. Estab. 1970. Members are professionals and amateurs. Performs 5 concerts/year. "We usually perform in a hall which seats 729. For larger events there is another which seats 1,100. Audience comes from local university-oriented community and surrounding area."
How to Contact: Submit complete score. Does not return material. Reports in 6 months.
Music: "For full symphony orchestra all styles, with caution for extremely contemporary orchestration and arrangements."

AUREUS QUARTET, 22 Lois Ave., Demarest NJ 07627-2220. (201)767-8704. Artistic Director: James J. Seiler. Vocal ensemble (a cappella). Estab. 1979. Members are professionals. Performs 40-50 concerts/year, including 3 to 10 new works. Pays for outright purchase.
How to Contact: Query first. SASE. Reports in 2 months.
Music: "We perform anything from pop to classic—mixed repertoire so anything goes. Some pieces can be scored for orchestras as we do pops concerts. Up to now, we've only worked with a quartet. Could be expanded if the right piece came along. Level of difficulty—no piece has ever been too hard." Does not wish to see electronic or sacred pieces. "Electronic pieces would be hard to program. Sacred pieces not performed much. Classical/jazz arrangements of old standards are great!"
Tips: "We perform for a very diverse audience—luscious, four part writing that can showcase well-trained voices is a must. Also, clever arrangements of old hits from '20s through '50s are sure bets. (Some pieces could take optional accompaniment.)"

BALTIMORE OPERA COMPANY, INC., 101 W. Read St., Baltimore MD 21201. (301)727-0592. Artistic Administrator: James Harp. Opera company. Estab. 1950. Members are professionals. Performs 16 concerts/year. "The opera audience is becoming increasingly diverse. Our performances are given in the 3,000-seat Lyric Opera House." Pays by outright purchase.
How to Contact: Submit complete score and tapes of piece(s). SASE. Reports in 1-2 months.
Music: "Our General Director, Mr. Michael Harrison, is very much interested in presenting new works. These works would be anything from Grand Opera with a large cast to chamber works suitable for school and concert performances. We would be interested in perusing all music written for an operatic audience."
Performances: Verdi's *Don Carlo*; Donizetti's *La Fille Du Régiment*; and Mozart's *Die Zauberflöte*.
Tips: "Opera is the most expensive art form to produce. Given the current economic outlook, opera companies cannot be too avant garde in their selection of repertoire. The modern operatic composer must give evidence of a fertile and illuminating imagination, while also keeping in mind that opera companies have to sell tickets."

*THE GARY BEARD CHORALE, 40 E. Parkway S., Memphis TN 38104. (901)458-1652. Fax: (901)458-0145. Director: Gary Beard. Vocal ensemble. Estab. 1987. Members are professionals and amateurs. Performs 25 concerts/year including 1-5 new works. "Audience consists of musically educated people with eclectic tastes, like variety in each concert. Concerts are performed in a church sanctuary, excellent acoustics, seats 1,200."
How to Contact: Submit complete score and tape of piece(s). Does not return material. Reports in 2 months.
Music: "Choral, with orchestrations if possible, no longer than 45 minutes, include vocal solos in composition, nothing overly 'avant.' Most performers read music, including atonal, yet compositions should have 'likeable' qualities to the average audience member's ear. Level of difficulty is open for interpretation. Must submit clean scores, orderly, be very well organized, utilize choral and solo on ensemble passages."
Performances: Poulenc's *Gloria* (concert setting of Gloria); various *Broadway Cabaret* (concert of Broadway music); Barber's *Sure On This Shining Night* (art song).
Tips: "Be well organized, thorough, submit clean scores, not overly atonal compositions, supply English translations of foreign languages as well as transliterations."

BILLINGS SYMPHONY, Suite 530, Box 7055, 401 N. 31st St., Billings MT 59103. (406)252-3610. Music Director: Dr. Uri Barnea. Symphony orchestra, orchestra and chorale. Estab. 1950. Members are professionals and amateurs. Performs 12-15 concerts/year, including 3-7 new works. Audience: general public. Hall: Alberta Bair Theater (capacity 1,418).
How to Contact: Query first. SASE. Reports in 1-6 months.
Music: Any style. Traditional notation preferred.
Performances: Tania Leon's *Batá* (orchestra); David Ott's *Concerto for Two Cellos*; and William Wallace's *Introduction & Bessacaglia* (orchestra).
Tips: "Write good music. Make parts and score easily legible. Try to get a recorded rehearsal if possible."

*BIZARRE ARTE ENSEMBLE, 320 Milledge Terrace, Athens GA 30606-4940. (706)354-4445. Musical Director: David Boardman. Chamber music ensemble. Estab. 1975. Members are professionals. Performs 2-3 concerts/year including 4-6 new works. Commissions 1-2 composers or new works/year. Audience consists mainly of the university community. Pays various for outright purchase, performance tape provided.

How to Contact: Submit complete score and tape of pieces (if available; not necessary.) SASE.

Music: "Ensemble consists of four percussionists. Addition of other instrumentalists/performers okay. Style left up to discretion of composer. Serious pieces okay. Comic pieces okay. Experimental/improvisational pieces okay."

Performances: David Boardman's *Sferics* and *Sally's Wedding Piece* (percussion); and Robert Sheppard's *Without You* (percussion w/vocal).

Tips: "Sense of humor a must."

THE BOSTON MUSICA VIVA, Suite 612, 295 Huntington Ave., Boston MA 02116-5713. Manager: Hilary Field. Chamber music ensemble. Estab. 1969. Members are professionals. Performs 5-12 concerts/year, including 6-10 new works. Commissions 3-5 composers or new works/year. "We perform our subscription series in a hall that seats 300, and our audience comes from Boston, Cambridge and surrounding areas. Frequent tours have taken the ensemble across the U.S. and the world." Pays by commission.

How to Contact: Submit complete score and tapes of piece(s). Does not return unsolicited material. Reports in months.

Music: "We are looking for works for: flute, clarinet, percussion, piano, violin, viola and cello plus vocalist (or any combination thereof). Made for no more than 10 performers. We're looking for exciting avant garde music. We don't particularly want to see anything on the pop side."

BRECKENRIDGE MUSIC INSTITUTE, P.O. Box 1254, Breckenridge CO 80424. (303)453-9142. Executive Director: Pamela G. Miller. Chamber orchestra with ensembles: brass and woodwind quintets and a vocal quartet. Estab. 1980. Members are professionals. Performs more than 30 concerts/year, including several new works. "We perform our main festival season in the new Riverwalk Center, a performing arts amphitheater—we are in a resort area, so our audiences are a mix of local citizens and visitors." Chamber orchestra concerts: 800 people; chamber ensemble recitals: 125-250 people; choral/orchestra concert: 450 people. "Our concerts include remarks, notes and commissioned work."

How to Contact: Query first. Does not return material. Usually reports in several months, but depends on the time of year the work is submitted.

Music: "Typically, we try to premiere an orchestral piece each year and highlight the composer's other work during a 4-5 day composer-in-residence program. We need *chamber* orchestra or ensemble music only—nothing for more instrumentation." Doesn't want to see "pops."

Performances: Dan Welcher's *Bridges, Songs on e.e. cummings* and *High Tech Etudes;* and William Schmidt's *Miniatures for Chamber Orchestra* (world premiere).

BREMERTON SYMPHONY ASSOCIATION INC., 535B 6th St., P.O. Box 996, Bremerton WA 98310. (206)373-1722. Contact: Music Director. Symphony orchestra. Estab. 1942. Members are amateurs. Performs 7-8 concerts/year, including a varying number of new works. The audience is half seniors, half adult. 1,200-seat hall in Bremerton High School; excellent acoustics.

How to Contact: Submit complete score and tape of piece(s). SASE. Reports in 1 month. Full season is planned each spring.

Music: Submit works for full orchestra, chorus and soloists. "Should be good for competent community orchestras." Do not wish to see "pop" music charts.

Performances: Rick Vale's *Symphony #1 "Christmas"* (orchestra/chorus/soloists).

BREVARD SYMPHONY ORCHESTRA, INC., P.O. Box 361965, Melbourne FL 32936-1965. (407)242-2024. Chairman: Craig Suman. Symphony orchestra. Estab. 1954. Members are professionals and amateurs. Performs 15-20 concerts/year. "King Center for the Performing Arts, Melbourne, FL: 1,842 seats; Fine Arts Auditorium, Cocoa, FL: 599 seats; Astronaut High School Auditorium, Titusville, FL: 399 seats." Pay negotiable "(VERY limited funding)."

How to Contact: Submit complete score and tapes of piece(s). SASE. Reports in 2 months.

Music: "Submit orchestral works with and without soloists, full symphonic orchestration, 5-45 minutes in length, contemporary and popular styles as well as serious compositions." "No non-orchestral materials. Our community is fairly conservative and inexperienced in contemporary music, so a subtle, gradual introduction would be appropriate."

Performances: 1993-94 season includes: Weber's *Der Freischutz Overture;* Hayden's Trumpet Concerto and Brahms' *Symphony #1.*

Tips: "Remember the audience that we are trying to introduce and educate."

*BRONX ARTS ENSEMBLE, % Golf House, Van Cortlandt Park, Bronx NY 10471. (212)601-7399. Artistic Director: William Scribner. Symphony orchestra and chamber music ensemble. Estab. 1972. Members are professionals. Performs 90 concerts/year including 12 new works. Commissions 3 new works/year. "Performs concerts at colleges and various historic sites in the Bronx; also in halls in Manhattan." Pays per performance.
How to Contact: Query first. Does not return unsolicited material.
Music: Seeks "primarily chamber music or orchestral. No pops or jazz."
Performances: Meyer Kupferman's *Images of Chagall*; David Chesky's *Trumpet Concerto*; and Roberto Sierra's *El Mensajero de la Plata*.

*BUFFALO GUITAR QUARTET, 402 Bird Ave., Buffalo NY 14213. (716)883-8429. Fax: (716)673-3397. Executive Director: James Piorkoswki. Chamber music ensemble, classical guitar quartet. Estab. 1976. Members are professionals. Performs 35 concerts/year including 2 new works. Commissions 1 composer or new work/2 years. Pays by outright purchase.
How to Contact: Query first. SASE. Reports in 1 month.
Music: "Any style or length. 4 classical guitarists, high level of difficulty."
Performances: Leslie Bassett's *Narratives* (5 short movements); S. Funk Pearson's *Mummychogs (le Monde)* (prepared guitars); Leo Brouwer's *Cuban Landscape with Rumba* (minimalist).
Tips: "Learn what the guitar does well, stay away from what it does poorly."

CANADIAN CHILDREN'S OPERA CHORUS, #215, 227 Front St. E., Toronto, Ontario M5A 1E8 **Canada.** (416)366-0467. Manager: Suzanne Bradshaw. Children's vocal ensemble. Estab. 1968. Members are amateurs. Performs 40 operas and concerts/year. Performs choral Christmas concert, spring opera production often at Harbourfront, Toronto. Pays by outright purchase; "CCOC applies to Ontario Arts Council or the Canada Council for commission fees."
How to Contact: Query first. SAE and IRC. Reports in 2 months.
Music: "Operas of approximately 1 hour in length representing quality composers. In addition, the portability of a production is important; minimal sets and accompaniment. CCOC prefers to engage Canadian composers whose standards are known to be high. Being a nonprofit organization with funding difficulties, we prefer piano accompaniments or just a few instruments."
Performances: W.A. Mozart's *Bastien & Bastienne*; Poulenc's *Petites Voix*; and John Rutter's *Dancing Day*.

*CANADIAN OPERA COMPANY, 227 Front St. E., Toronto, Ontario M5A 1E8 **Canada.** (416)363-6671. Scheduling Manager: Sandra J. Gavinchuk. Opera company. Estab. 1950. Members are professionals. 70 performances, including a minimum of 1 new work/year. "New works are done in the Texaco Opera Theatre, which seats approximately 400." Pays by contract.
How to Contact: Query first, then submit complete score and tapes of piece(s).
Music: Vocal works, preferably operatic in nature. 12 singers maximum, 1½ hour in duration and 18 orchestral players. "Do not submit works which are not for voice. Ask for requirements for the Composers In Residence program."
Performances: Randolph Peters's *Nosferatu*; Bartok's *Bluebeard's Castle*; and Schöenberg's *Erwartung*.
Tips: "We have a Composers-in-Residence program which is open to Canadian composers or landed immigrants."

CANTATA ACADEMY, 2441 Pinecrest Dr., Ferndale MI 48220. (313)546-0420. Music Director: Frederick Bellinger. Vocal ensemble. Estab. 1961. Members are professionals. Performs 10-12 concerts/year including 5 to 7 new works. Commissions 1-2 composers or new works/year. "We perform in churches and small auditoriums throughout the Metro Detroit area for audiences of about 500 people." Pays $100-500 for outright purchase.
How to Contact: Submit complete score. SASE. Reports in 1-3 months.
Music: Four-part a cappella and keyboard accompanied works, two and three-part works for men's or women's voices. Some small instrumental ensemble accompaniments also acceptable. Work must be suitable for forty voice choir. No works requiring orchestra or large ensemble accompaniment. No pop.
Performances: Charles S. Brown's *Five Spirituals* (concert spiritual); Kirke Mechem's *John Brown Cantata*; and Libby Larsen's *Ringeltanze* (Christmas choral with handbells & keyboard).
Tips: "Be patient. Would prefer to look at several different samples of work at one time."

Listings of companies in countries other than the U.S. have the name of the country in boldface type.

Marimolin offers a unique opportunity for classical composers

Marimolin is a classical duo consisting of Sharan Leventhal and Nancy Zeltsman, who combine violin and marimba to create a truly original and innovative sound. The pair provides a unique opportunity to aspiring composers through their annual composition contest, which they began in 1987.

"When we started Marimolin," they explain, "there was virtually no repertoire for violin and marimba. One of our goals was to create a body of literature for this unusual combination. With limited sources for grants to commission new works and a limit to the number of composer-friends whose arms we could twist to donate pieces, the composition contest was a means of reaching out to more composers."

Each year, Marimolin receives more and more submissions from new composers. "It has grown to be truly international," they say. "The winners have ranged from distinguished professors to undergraduate students. We feel especially pleased to provide an avenue for composers in the early stages of their careers."

In the dozens of submissions they receive each year, Zeltsman and Leventhal are searching for one specific element. "What we're looking for is simple: quality. Aside from being 'well-constructed,' the winning works have always had a clearly conceived sound-world. As the judges, we choose works we have a desire to learn, will enjoy performing and will feel proud of.

"During the judging process, we look carefully at each score and read it at least twice. On one occasion the winning piece was extremely challenging and clearly needed many hours of work to learn, but the substance of the piece was immediately apparent. Somehow by the end of the judging, the winner always stands out."

In the highly competitive world of contemporary classical music, Zeltsman and Leventhal feel that the best way for a composer to get his work heard is to work with the performers they're writing for. "It is of utmost importance for a composer to work directly with performers," they explain. "In this way, the performer(s) may gain a personal investment in the work. When performers have a true understanding and enjoyment of a piece, they are better able to convey it—and inspire the same in—an audience. Furthermore, such performers become the composer's best advocates, which may ultimately lead to more opportunities for him or her.

"It can also be advantageous to write for groups who perform together on an ongoing basis. The pieces we've performed regularly are most likely the most frequently played works by those composers. In addition, those pieces are being heard by other performers who often ask about getting a score."

Also important for the classical composer to realize is the limited financial resources available for new works. "There are a number of grants and fellowship opportunities available, but it's important not to turn your back on working for free with equally dedicated musicians. In the beginning, our most fruitful collaborations were undertaken simply for love of art."

For Marimolin, love of art is imperative. "Follow the muse," they advise. "It's important to remember when entering any contest that the judges may not share your aesthetic, but it's not worth trying to please others. Write what's in your heart!"

(For more information on the Marimolin composition contest, see their listing in the Contests and Awards section.)

photo by Susan Wilson

Marimolin: Nancy Zeltsman (left) and Sharan Leventhal.

❝It is of utmost importance for a composer to work directly with performers. When performers have a true understanding and enjoyment of a piece, they are better able to convey it—and inspire the same in—an audience.❞

—Leventhal and Zeltsman

CAPITAL UNIVERSITY CONSERVATORY OF MUSIC OPERA/MUSICAL THEATRE, 2199 E. Main St., Columbus OH 43209-2394. (614)236-6122. Director, Opera/Musical Theatre: William Florescu. College opera/musical theater program. Estab. 1970. Members are students. Performs 2 concerts/year, including 1-2 new works. Commissions 1 composer or new work/year. "The audience is basically a community arts audience and family and friends of performers. Mees Hall Auditorium (cap. 946) is where we perform big, standard works. The Huntington Recital Hall (cap. 255) is where we perform chamber and experimental works." Pays by royalty or $50-150 per performance.
How to Contact: Submit complete score and tapes of piece(s). SASE. Reports in 2 weeks.
Music: "I am seeking music theater pieces, particularly of a 'chamber' nature. I am open to a wide variety of musical styles, although the music should be singable for undergraduates; piano or small ensemble accompaniment. Ideally, pieces should be for 4-6 performers, most of whom will be able to tackle a wide variety of musical styles. Ideal length for works should be 15 minutes to 45 minutes. I am not particularly interested in 'rock' pieces, although if they work theatrically, I would certainly consider them."
Performances: Aaron Copland's *The Tender Land*; Libby Larsen's *The Silver Fox*; and Milton Granger's *The Proposal* (chamber opera).
Tips: "If a composer is interested in writing for the situation we have here at Capital, I would suggest he or she either write or call me to *specifically* discuss a project. This will help both sides bring the performance about."

CARSON CITY CHAMBER ORCHESTRA, P.O. Box 2001, Carson City NV 89702-2001 or 191 Heidi Circle, Carson City NV 89701-6532. (702)883-4154. Conductor: David C. Bugli. Amateur community orchestra. Estab. 1984. Members are amateurs. Performs 5 concerts, including 1 new work/year. "Most concerts are performed in the Carson City Community Center Auditorium, which seats 840. We have no provisions for paying composers at this time but may later."
How to Contact: Submit complete score. Does not return material. Reports in 2 months.
Music: "We want classical, pop orchestrations, orchestrations of early music for modern orchestras, concertos for violin or piano, holiday music for chorus and orchestra (children's choirs and handbell ensemble available), music by women, music for brass choir. Most performers are amateurs, but there are a few professionals who perform with us. Available winds and percussion: 2 flutes and flute/piccolo, 2 oboes (E.H. double), 2 clarinets, 1 bass clarinet, 2 bassoons, 3 or 4 horns, 3 trumpets, 3 trombones, 1 tuba, timpani, and some percussion. Harp and piano. Strings: 8-10-3-5-2. Avoid rhythmic complexity (except in pops); and music that lacks melodic appeal. Composers should contact us first. Each concert has a different emphasis. Note: Associated choral group, Carson Chamber Singers, performs several times a year with the orchestra and independently."
Performances: Ernest Martinez' *Torbellino*; David Bugli's *State of Metamorphosis*, *Variations on "My Dancing Day"*; Kenneth Linoner's *Sonata for Trumpet*; and Ronald R. Williams' *Noah: Suite After Andre Obey*. Premieres also include arrangements of Christmas and popular tunes.
Tips: "It is better to write several short movements well than to write long, unimaginative pieces, especially when starting out. Be willing to revise after submitting the work, even if it was premiered elsewhere."

CASCADE SYMPHONY ORCHESTRA, 9630 214th Place SW, Edmonds WA 98020. (206)778-6934. Director/Conductor: Roupan Shakarian. Manager: Ed Aliverti. Symphony orchestra. Estab. 1962. Members are professionals and amateurs. Performs 4-5 concerts/year, including 2-3 new works. "Audience is knowledgeable with a variety of backgrounds and interests—excellent cross-section. Perform in a rather old auditorium seating 950."
How to Contact: Submit complete score and tapes of pieces. SASE. Reports in 6 weeks.
Music: "Music should be suitable for symphony orchestra. Nothing over 20 minutes."
Performances: Paul Creston's *Dance Overture* (various dance rhythms); and Daniel Barry's *Sound Scapes* (premiere based on ostenatos).

*CENTER FOR CONTEMPORARY OPERA, Box 1350, Gracie Station, New York NY 10028-0100. (212)308-6728. Director: Richard Marshall. Opera. Estab. 1982. Members are professionals. Performs 3 operas/year; all are modern works. 600-seat theater. Pays royalties.
How to Contact: Query first. SASE.
Music: "Looking for full-length operas. Limited orchestras and choruses. Orchestra—not over 25."
Performances: Sullivan's *Dream Play* (opera); Britten's *The Prodigal Son* (opera); Beeson's *My Heart is in the Highlands* (stage premiere, opera); and Kelmanoff's *Insect Comedy* (premiere).
Tips: "Make work practical to perform. Have an excellent libretto. Have contacts to raise money."

CHAMBER MUSIC IN YELLOW SPRINGS, INC., P.O. Box 448, Yellow Springs OH 45387. (513)767-1458. President: Ruth Bent. Chamber music presenting organization. Estab. 1983. "Members are volunteer staff. Performs 5 concerts/year including 4-7 new works. The audience is very enthusiastic and quite knowledgeable in chamber music. The hall is a church, seating 280 with excellent acoustics." Pays $5,000 for outright purchase.

How to Contact: Query first. Does not return material.

Music: "We are interested in innovative chamber music; however the composer should approach us with an ensemble identified. We are a chamber music presenting organization. We rarely present groups with more than 6 performers." Does not wish to see popular music.

Performances: Rick Sowash's *Anecdotes and Reflections* (instrumental, chamber work, violin, cello, piano, clarinet).

Tips: "We book primarily on the quality of ensemble. A composer should make an arrangement with a top-notch group and approach us through the ensemble's agent."

*CHEYENNE SYMPHONY ORCHESTRA, P.O. Box 851, Cheyenne WY 82003. (307)778-8561. CSO Music Director: Mark Russell Smith. Symphony orchestra. Estab. 1955. Members are professionals. Performs 6 concerts/year including sometimes 1 new work. "Orchestra performs for a conservative, mid-to-upper income audience at a 1,496 seat civic center." Pay negotiable.

How to Contact: Query first. Does not return material.

Performances: Bill Hill's *Seven Abstract Miniatures* (orchestral).

CHORUS OF WESTERLY, 16 High St., Westerly RI 02891. (401)596-8663. Music Director: George Kent. Community chorus. Estab. 1959. Members are professionals and amateurs. Performs 12 major and new works/year. "4 'major works' concerts/year and 2 'pops' concerts/year. Summer pops reaches audiences of 28,000." Pays by outright purchase.

How to Contact: Submit complete score and tapes of pieces. Reports in 3 weeks.

Music: "We normally employ a full orchestra from Boston. Major works desired – although 'good' pops charts considered."

Performances: Brahms' *Requiem*, Holst's *Choral Symphony*, Honegter's *King David* and W. Walton's *Belshazzar's Feast.*

COLORADO CHILDREN'S CHORALE, Suite 1020, 910 15th St., Denver CO 80202. (303)892-5600. Artistic Director: Duain Wolfe. Vocal ensemble and highly trained children's chorus. Estab. 1974. Members are professionals and amateurs. Performs 100-110 concerts/year, including 3-5 new works. Commissions 1-3 composers or new works/year. "Our audiences' ages range from 5-80. We give school performances and tour (national, international). We give subscription concerts and sing with orchestras (symphonic and chamber). Halls: schools to symphony halls to arenas to outdoor theaters." Pays $100-500 outright purchase (more for extended works).

How to Contact: Submit complete score and tapes of piece(s). Does not return unsolicited material. Reports in 2 months.

Music: "We want short pieces (3-5 minutes): novelty, folk arrangement, serious; longer works 5-20: serious; staged operas/musicals 30-45 minutes: piano accompaniment or small ensemble; or possible full orchestration if work is suitable for symphony concert. We are most interested in SA, SSA, SSAA. We look for a variety of difficulty ranges and encourage very challenging music for SSA-SSAA choruses (32 singer, unchanged voices). We don't want rock, charts without written accompaniments or texts that are inappropriate for children. We are accessible to all audiences. We like some of our repertoire to reflect a sense of humor, others to have a message. We're very interested in well crafted music that has a special mark of distinction."

Performances: Henry Milliconi's *The Midnight Ride of Paul Revere* (contemporary); Randall Thompson's *The Place of the Blest* (sacred, medieval text); Sherman and Sherman's *Tom Sawyer*; and Lee Hoiby's *The Nations Echo 'Round.*

Tips: "Submit score and tape with good cover letter, resume and record of performance. Wait at least 3 weeks before a follow-up call or letter."

COMMUNITY MUSIC PROJECT, 116 E. 3rd St., Jamestown NY 14701-5402. (716)664-2227. General Manager/Artistic Director: Philip Morris/Lee Spear. Vocal ensemble and community chorus. Estab. 1978. Members are both professionals and amateurs. Performs 12-15 concerts/year including 4-6 new works. "Performs in various venues: Civic center (1300 seat) and local churches (200-500 seat). Jamestown is a small city in Western NY state with a moderately sophisticated audience."

How to Contact: Query first. SASE. Reports in 6 months.

Music: 3-10 minute choral work, SATB, in English, with or without accompaniment. "Emphasis on sensitive English language prosody."

Performances: Gerald M. Shapiro's *Prayer for the Great Family*; Lee Kesselman's *Buzzings*; and Stefania de Kenesseay's *Jumping Jacks.*

CONCORDIA: A CHAMBER SYMPHONY, 21st Floor, 330 Seventh Ave., New York NY 10001. (212)967-1290. Executive Director: Leslie Stifelman. Symphony orchestra. Estab. 1984. Members are professionals. Performs 5 concerts/year, including 5-6 new works. Commissions 2-3 composers or new

works/year. "Lincoln Center, Alice Tully Hall. Audiences between 28 and 50 years, mostly." Pays contest winner's prize and copying.
How to Contact: Query first. SASE. Reports in 4 months.
Music: 11 minutes, 2,2,2,2/2,2,1,0/strings percussion; piano.
Performances: Jon Deak's *The Legend of Spuyten Duyvil*; Laura Karpman's *Switching Stations* (jazz fusion); Michael Daugherty's *Snap*; and Jeffrey Hass's *City Life* (jazz scored for chamber orchestra).
Tips: In 1992 Concordia introduced The Concordia American Composer's Award sponsored by American Express Company. Call for information.

CONNECTICUT CHORAL ARTISTS/CONCORA, 90 Main St., New Britain CT 06051. (203)224-7500. Artistic Director: Richard Coffey. Professional concert choir. Estab. 1974. Members are professionals. Performs 10-15 concerts/year, including 2-3 new works. "Mixed audience in terms of age and background; performs in various halls and churches in the region." Payment "depends upon underwriting we can obtain for the project."
How to Contact: Call and obtain permission to submit. "No unsolicited submissions accepted." SASE. Reports in 6 months.
Music: Seeking "works for mixed chorus of 36 singers; unaccompanied or with keyboard and/or small instrumental ensemble; text sacred or secular/any langauge; prefers suites or cyclical works, total time not exceeding 15 minutes. Performance spaces and budgets prohibit large instrumental ensembles. Works suited for 750-seat halls are preferable. Substantial organ or piano parts acceptable. Scores should be very legible in every way."
Performances: Bernstein's *Missa Brevis* (1988 regional premiere; based upon his *The Lark*); Frank Martin's *Mass for Double Chorus* (regional premiere); Villa-Lobos' *Magdalena* (performed 1987 revival at Lincoln Center and recorded for CBS).
Tips: "Use conventional notation and be sure manuscript is legible in every way. Recognize and respect the vocal range of each vocal part. Work should have an identifiable *rhythmic* structure."

CYPRESS "POPS" ORCHESTRA, P.O. Box 2623, Cypress CA 90630-1323. (714)527-0964. Music Director: John E. Hall III. Symphony orchestra. Estab. 1989. Members are professionals. Performs 10-12 concerts/year including 15-20 new works. Commissions 2 composers or new works/year. Average family size 4—popular entertainment for all age levels. Pays by outright purchase $200-500.
How to Contact: Submit complete score and tapes of piece(s). SASE. Reports in 1-2 months.
Music: Strictly popular light classical selections, 5-12 minute duration for full orchestra. #1 level of proficiency—very high. Contemporary films, TV themes/songs of 70s to present.
Performances: Friedman's *Gershwin Showcase* and *Salute to the Big Bands*.
Tips: "1990s composers need to be conscious of audiences listening capabilities. Should compose or arrange material in popular styled selections."

DENVER CHAMBER ORCHESTRA, #1360, 1616 Glenarm Pl., Denver CO 80202. (303)825-4911. Executive Director: Lynn Case. 35 piece chamber orchestra. Estab. 1968. Members are professionals. Performs 25 concerts/year, including 1 new work. Commissions 1 composer or new work/year. "Performs in a 500-seat auditorium in an arts complex and at Historic Trinity Church in Denver which seats 1,100. Usually pays the composer's air fare and room and board for the performance; sometimes an additional small stipend."
How to Contact: Query first. SASE. Reports in 2 months.
Music: Seeks "10-12 minute pieces orchestrated for 35-40 instruments. No pop, symphonic."
Performances: Edward Smaldone and Otto Luening's *Dialogue*; and Steven Heitzig's *Flower of the Earth: Homage to Georgia O'Keefe*.
Tips: "Submit a query, which we will submit to our music director."

DESERT CHORALE, P.O. Box 2813, Santa Fe NM 87504-2813. (505)988-2282. Fax: (505)988-7522. Music Director: Lawrence Bandfield. Vocal ensemble. Members are professionals. Performs 50 concerts/year including 2 new works. Commissions 1 new composer or new work/year. "Highly sophisticated, musically literate audiences. We sing most concerts in a 220-year-old adobe church which seats 250." Pays by royalty and/or additional commission.
How to Contact: Query first. Submit complete score and tape *after* query. Does not return unsolicited material. Reports in 8 months.
Music: "Challenging chamber choir works 6 to 20 minutes in length. Accompanied works are limited by space—normally no more than 5 or 6 players. No more than 24 singers, but they are all highly skilled musicians. No short church anthem-type pieces."
Performances: Dominick Argento's *al Toccata of Galuppi's* (mixed choir, strigrtet, harpsichord); Lawrence Cave's *The Seasons of Meng-Hao-Jan* (unaccompanied mixed choir); and Steven Sametz's *O Llama de Amor Viva* (unaccompanied mixed choir).

*DÚO CLÁSICO, 31-R Fayette St., Cambridge MA 02139-1111. (617)864-8524. Fax: (617)491-4696. Contact: David Witten. Chamber music ensemble. Estab. 1986. Members are professionals. Performs 8 concerts/year including 10 new works. Commissions 2 composers or new works/year. Performs in small recital halls.
How to Contact: Query first. SASE. Reports in 5 weeks.
Music: "We welcome scores for flute solo, piano solo or duo. Particular interest in Latin American composers."
Performances: Lee Brouwer's (Cuban) *La Region Más Transparente* (flute/piano duo); and Aaron Copland's (US) *Duo for Flute & Piano* (flute/piano duo).
Tips: "Extended techniques, or with tape, are fine!"

*EAKEN PIANO TRIO, Dickinson College, Carlisle PA 17013-2896. (717)245-1433. Fax: (717)245-1899. Director: Nancy Baun. Chamber music ensemble. Estab. 1986. Members are professionals. Performs 35-40 concerts/year including 4-6 new works. Commissions 1-2 composers or new works/year. Audience is fairly unsophisticated, enjoy melodic, romantic works. Concerts are performed on standard concert stage.
How to Contact: Submit complete score and tape of piece(s). SASE. Reports in 3-6 months.
Music: "Romantic style—mood, energy are important elements. Piano trio (violin, cello, piano) only. Prefer standard notation. We encourage composers to visit with group prior to a commission to discuss mutual goals. Must be available for residencies."
Performances: George Rochberg's *Piano Trio*; Margaret Garwood's *Homage Suite*; and Timothy Greatbatch's *Tarantella*, both piano trios.
Tips: "Recognize that we, the performers, need to be moved by the work so we can move others."

EASTERN NEW MEXICO UNIVERSITY, Station 16, Portales NM 88130. (505)562-2736. Director of Orchestral Activities: Robert Radmer. Symphony orchestra, small college-level orchestra with possible choral collaboration. Estab. 1934. Members are students (with some faculty). Performs 8 concerts/year. "Our audiences are members of a college community and small town. We perform in a beautiful, acoustically fine 240-seat hall with a pipe organ."
How to Contact: Query first, submit complete score and tapes of piece(s), submit complete score. SASE. Reports in 3 weeks.
Music: "Pieces should be 12-15 minutes; winds by 2, full brass. Work shouldn't be technically difficult. Organ, harpsicord, piano(s) are available. We are a small college orchestra; normal instrumentation is represented but technical level uneven throughout orchestra. We have faculty available to do special solo work. We like to see choral-orchestral combinations and writing at different technical levels within each family, i.e., 1st clarinet might be significantly more difficult than 2nd clarinet."
Performances: David Uber's *Gettysburg* (brass choir).
Tips: "I would like to see a choral/orchestral score in modern idiom for vocal solo(s), a chamber choir and large chorus used in concertino/ripieno fashion, with full brass and percussion, featuring first chair players."

EUROPEAN COMMUNITY CHAMBER ORCHESTRA, Fermain House, Dolphin St., Colyton EX13 6LU United Kingdom. Phone: (44)297 552272. General Manager: Ambrose Miller. Chamber orchestra. Members are professionals. Performs 70 concerts/year, including 5 new works. Commissions 2 composers or new works/year. Performs regular tours of Europe, Americas and Asia, including major venues.
How to Contact: Query first. SAE and IRC.
Music: Seeking compositions for strings, 2 oboes and 2 horns with a duration of about 10 minutes.
Performances: John McCabe's *Red Leaves* (strings, 2 oboes, 2 horns); Poul Ruders' *Trapeze*; and Alfred Schnitke's *Moz-art à la Haydn*.
Tips: "European Community Chamber Orchestra works without conductor, so simplicity is paramount."

*FINE ARTS STRINGS, 14507 Trading Post Dr., Sun City West AZ 85375. (602)584-6989. Musical Director & Conductor: Walter F. Moeck. String orchestra (27 members). Members are professionals and amateurs. Performs 4-6 concerts/year including 2 new works/year. "Concert Hall at the Scottsdale Jr. College. Other various halls in and around Phoenix and Scottsdale, Arizona."
How to Contact: Query first explaining type of composition. SASE. Reports in 4-5 weeks.
Music: "The 'Fine Arts' Orchestra is a string orchestra. We perform Mozart, Bach, Corelli and modern music for string orchestra. We have 27 performers in the orchestra. We perform rather difficult music. Example—Poulencs' *Organ Concerto*. We look for good musical substance for strings. Good rhythmic and melodic qualities."
Performances: Diamond's *Elegy*; Barber's *Adagio for Strings*; and Jaio's *Choreagraphy*.
Tips: "Write practical for the instruments and know their limitations and in a manner that shows off the instruments' best qualities."

FLORIDA SPACE COAST PHILHARMONIC, INC., P.O. Box 3344, Cocoa FL 32924 or 2150 Lake Dr., Cocoa FL 32926. (407)632-7445. General Manager: Alyce Christ. Artistic Director and Conductor: Maria Tunicka. Philharmonic orchestra and chamber music ensemble. Estab. 1986. Members are professionals. Performs 7-14 concerts/year. Concerts are performed for "average audience—they like familiar works and pops. Concert halls range from 600 to 2,000 seats." Pays 10% royalty (rental); outright purchase of $2,000; $50-600/performance; or by private arrangement.
How to Contact: Query first; submit complete score and tape of piece(s). SASE. Reports 1-3 months. "Our conductor tours frequently; we have to keep material until she has a chance to see and hear it."
Music: Seeks "pops and serious music for full symphony orchestra, but not an overly large orchestra with unusual instrumentation. We use about 60 musicians because of hall limitations. Works should be medium difficulty—not too easy and not too difficult—and not more than 10 minutes long." Does not wish to see avante-garde music.
Performances: Marta Ptaszynska's *Marimba Concerto* (marimba solo); Dr. Elaine Stone's *Christopher Columbus Suite for Symphony Orchestra* (world premiere).
Tips: "If we would commission a work it would be to feature the space theme in our area."

FONTANA CONCERT SOCIETY, 821 W. South St., Kalamazoo MI 49007. (616)382-0826. Artistic Director: Paul Nitsch. Chamber music ensemble presenter. Estab. 1980. Members are professionals. Performs 20 concerts/year including 1-3 new works. commissions 1-2 composers or new works/year. Audience consists of well-educated people who expect to be challenged but like the traditional as well. Summer—180 seat hall; Fall/winter—various venues, from churches to libraries to 500-seat theaters.
How to Contact: Submit complete score and tapes of piece(s). SASE. Reports in 1 month.
Music: "Good chamber music—any combination of strings, winds, piano." No "pop" music, new age type. "We like to see enough interest for the composer to come for a premiere and talk to the audience."
Performances: Ramon Zupko's *Folksody* (piano trio-premiere); Sebastian Currier's *Vocalissimus* (soprano, 4 percussion, strings, winds, piano-premiere); and Mark Schulte's *Work for Horn & Piano* (premiere).
Tips: "Provide a resume and clearly marked tape of a piece played by live performers."

*THE GLORIAN DUO, 176 Logan Rd., New Canaan CT 06840. (203)966-7616. Contact: Wendy Kerner. Chamber music ensemble. Estab. 1986. Members are professionals. Performs 30 concerts/year including 3-5 new works. Commissions 1-2 new works/year. Pay various. "We receive many works free of charge."
How to Contact: Submit complete score and tape of piece(s). Reports in 2-3 months.
Music: "We are particularly interested in flute and harp works that are openers, jazz-element work and other flute and harp or flute, harp and other instrument works. We are a duo—flute and harp but often work with other instruments—flute, harp and cello, 2 flutes and harp, flute, harp and voice, flute, harp and orchestra etc."
Performances: David Diamond's *Concert Piece* (concert work—15 minutes), Vaclav Nelhybel's *Concertante*; and Yoon-Hee Kim-Hwang's *dharma-Dharma* (concert work based on Korean themes and Zen Buddhist poetry).
Tips: "Make the work interesting and compelling."

GREAT FALLS SYMPHONY ASSOCIATION, Box 1078, Great Falls MT 59403. (406)453-4102. Music Director and Conductor: Gordon J. Johnson. Symphony orchestra. Estab. 1959. Members are professionals and amateurs. Performs 7 concerts (2 youth concerts)/year, including 2-3 new works. "Our audience is conservative. Newer music is welcome; however, it might be more successful if it were programatic." Plays in Civic Center Auditorium seating 1,850. Negotiable payment.
How to Contact: Submit complete score and tapes of pieces. SASE.
Music: "Compositions should be for full orchestra. Should be composed ideomatically for instruments avoiding extended techniques. Duration 10-20 minutes. Avoid diverse instruments such as alto flute, saxophones, etc. Our orchestra carries 65 members, most of whom are talented amateurs. We have a resident string quartet and woodwind quintet that serve as principals. Would enjoy seeing a piece for quartet or quintet solo and orchestra. Send letter with clean score and tape (optional). We will reply within a few weeks."
Peformances: Bernstein's *Chichester Psalms* (choral and orchestra); Hodkinson's *Boogie, Tango and Grand Tarantella* (bass solo); and Stokes' *Native Dancer*.
Tips: "Music for orchestra and chorus is welcome. Cross cues will be helpful in places. Work should not require an undue amount of rehearsal time (remember that a concerto and symphony are probably on the program as well)."

*GREELEY PHILHARMONIC ORCHESTRA, P.O. Box 1535, Greeley CO 80632. (303)353-1384. Secretary/Bookkeeper: Beverley Skinner. Symphony orchestra. Estab. 1911. Members are professionals and some amateurs. Performs 12 concerts/year. "We give 6 regular subscription concerts (mixed audience)

and 2 nights of opera and 4 other special concerts. We have a wonderful 5 year old hall seating 1,664."
How to Contact: Query first. SASE. Reports in 1 month.
Music: "We want high quality popular programming for pops, park and youth concerts; 5-15 minutes in length utilizing full orchestra. We don't want electric instruments. We like nostalgia, pops or light classical arrangement."
Performances: Peck's *Glory, The Grandeur* (orchestra with percussion ensemble) and *Thrill of the Orchestra* (children's concert); and Harbeson's *Remembering Gatsby* (orchestra).

THE GRINNELL ORCHESTRA, Dept. of Music, Grinnell College, Grinnell IA 50112. (515)269-3064. Assistant Professor of Music: Jonathan Knight. Chamber orchestra. Members are amateurs and college students. Performs 4-5 concerts/year. "Our audience includes students, faculty and staff of the college, members of the community of Grinnell and nearby towns; performances in Herrick Chapel, seating capacity about 700." Composers are not paid.
How to Contact: Submit complete score and tapes of piece(s). SASE. Reports in 2-3 months.
Music: "We can perform scores for chamber-size orchestras: about 20 strings, pairs of woodwinds and brass, harp and keyboard instruments. Please avoid exotic percussion. I would consider any length or style, as long as the difficulty of the work did not exceed the ability of the group, which may be characterized as a fairly good undergraduate ensemble, but not as capable as a conservatory orchestra. No 'pops' music."
Performances: Schubert's *Symphony No. 6*; Lou Harrison's *Seven Pastorales*; and Charles Ives's *The Gong on the Hook and Ladder*.
Tips: "Composers may submit completed works to me, with or without tapes, for consideration. As the relative strengths of my orchestra change from year to year due to normal student turnover, it is difficult to give specific tips other than those above regarding size and difficulty of scores."

HASTINGS SYMPHONY ORCHESTRA, Fuhr Hall, 9th & Ash, Hastings NE 68901. (402)463-2402. Conductor/Music Director: Dr. James Johnson. Symphony orchestra. Estab. 1926. Members are professionals and amateurs. Performs 6-8 concerts/year, including 1 new work. "Audience consists of conservative residents of mid-Nebraska who haven't heard most of the classics." Concert Hall: Masonic Temple Auditorium (950). Pays commission or rental.
How to Contact: Submit complete score and tapes of piece(s). Does not return unsolicited material. Reports in 2 months.
Music: "We are looking for all types of music within the range of an accomplished community orchestra. Write first and follow with a phone call."
Performances: Bernstein's *Candide Overture*; Richard Wilson's *Silhouette (1988)*; Menotti's *Double-bass Concerto (1983)*; and James Oliverio's *Pilgrimage Concerto for Brass and Orchestra* (1992).
Tips: "Think about the size, ability and budgetary limits. Confer with our music director about audience taste. Think of music with special ties to locality."

*THE HELIOS STRING QUARTET, 1305 Fruit Ave. NW, Albuquerque NM 87104. (505)764-9851. Cellist: Adam Gonzalez. Chamber music ensemble. Estab. 1987. Members are professionals. Performs 25 concerts/year. Commissions 1 composer or new work each 3-4 years. "Audiences range from 175-400 depending on venue. Students to adults—serious chamber music lovers." Performs in churches, concert halls at universities. Pays $1,000 for outright purchase.
How to Contact: Query first. SASE. Reports in 1 month.
Music: "Standard quartet length is 15-20 minutes. 3-4 movements. A one movement work 8-10 minutes is also very good. We specialize in music from Latin America. Look for dance rhythms, great melodies—can even be based on pop tunes, folk tunes, but treated in classical style. Trio, Quartet, Quintet, any combination using strings and one instrument. No electronics—up to high degree of difficulty."
Performances: Juan Orrego-Salas' *Quartet #1* (string quartet); Seven Block's *Quartet #2* (Quartet); and Michael Iatauro's *Westward Movements* (Quintet).
Tips: "Call us. Send parts and scores. Work on finding funding from your side to pay for the commission of the work. Most groups *do not* have a large enough budget to commission works on their own. They can play it, but they can't usually pay it."

THE PAUL HILL CHORALE (AND) THE WASHINGTON SINGERS, 5630 Connecticut Ave. NW, Washington DC 20015. (202)364-4321. Music Director: Paul Hill. Vocal ensemble. Estab. 1967. Members are professionals and amateurs. Performs 8-10 concerts/year, including 4 new works. Commissions one new composer or work every 3-4 years. "Audience covers a wide range of ages and economic levels drawn from the greater Washington DC metropolitan area. Kennedy Center Concert Hall seats 2,700." Pays by outright purchase.

How to Contact: Submit complete score and tapes of pieces. SASE. Reports in 2 months.
Music: Seeks new works for: 1)large chorus with or without symphony orchestras; 2)chamber choir; and 3)small ensemble.
Performances: Gregg Smith's *Holy, Holy Holy*; Ned Rorem's *We Are the Music-Makers*; William Bolcom's *The Mask*; and David Maslanka's *Litany for Courage and the Seasons* (all choral).
Tips: "We are always looking for music that is high quality and accessible to Washington audiences."

HOUSTON YOUTH SYMPHONY & BALLET, P.O. Box 56104, Houston TX 77256. (713)621-2411. Orchestra Operations Manager: Jesse P. Johnson. Symphony orchestra. Estab. 1947. Members are students. Performs 6 concerts/year. "Performs in Alice Pratt Brown Hall, Rice University, 800-seat concert hall for general audiences."
How to Contact: Query first. SASE.
Music: Uses string orchestra music suitable for players age 7-14. "Full orchestra music suitable for players 14-23."
Performances: Dzubay's *Ascension* (brass/percussion); and Turner's *Opening Night* (symphony).

I CANTORI DI NEW YORK, P.O. Box 4165, New York NY 10185-0035. (212)439-4758. Artistic Director: Mark Shapiro. Vocal ensemble. Estab. 1984. Members are professionals and amateurs. Performs 5 concerts/year. "Performs in Merkin Hall, St. Peter's Church and comparable spaces."
How to Contact: Submit complete score. Tape optional. Material returned with SASE. Reports in 3 months.
Music: "Seeks a cappella music or works with up to 7 instruments, performable by nonprofessional singers in terms of vocal and musical difficulties. We will consider various styles and lengths. I Cantori has 24 voices. Divisi should not exceed 8 parts. No pop or sacred music of inferior quality. We are especially interested in a dramatic work lasting 30 minutes or so with extensive use of the chorus, and no more than three or four difficult solo roles."
Performances: Ronald Roseman's *Psalm 42* (cantata); Samuel Adler's *5 Choral Pictures* (a cappella set); John Harbison's *Songs of Experience*; and shorter works.
Tips: "Composers should write well (idiomatically) for voices. Choose a classy text: avoid vocalises (laborious to rehearse)."

IDAHO STATE—CIVIC SYMPHONY, P.O. Box 8099, Pocatello ID 83209. (208)236-3479. Music Director/Conductor: Dr. Thom Ritter George. Symphony orchestra. Estab. 1934. Members are professionals and amateurs. Performs 12 concerts/year, including 4 new works. "Audience varied, ranges from highly musically educated to little background in music; in general, prefer music with which they have some familiarity. The symphony performs in Goranson Hall, on the campus of Idaho State University—seats 444, good acoustics." Pays by outright purchase or per performance.
How to Contact: Query first. SASE. Reports in 1 month.
Music: "We consider works by composers scoring for full orchestra. The majority of our activities are oriented to the classical music audience." Does not wish "any kind of 'popular music'; music by living composers written in historic styles (e.g. Baroque; chamber music; opera)."
Performances: Prokofiev's *Romeo and Juliet*, Haydn's *The Creation*; and Peter Schmalz's *The Swans of Apollo* (tone poem, Idaho premiere).
Tips: "Write a work which is structurally sound and scored idiomatically for the symphony orchestra."

INTER SCHOOL ORCHESTRAS OF NEW YORK, 207 E. 85th St., New York NY 10028. (212)288-0763. Music Director: Jonathan Strasser. Youth orchestras. Estab. 1972. Members are young musicians aged 6-19 making up 5 youth orchestras on three levels. Perform 20-25 concerts/year. "Varied churches to major halls like Carnegie or Alice Tully. Varied audiences."
How to Contact: Query first. Does not return material.
Music: Advanced orchestra of 70: 30 strings, full winds and brass; intermediate orchestra of 70; 3 beginner orchestras with 30-40 each. "Composers should realize that players are 19 and younger so works should not be outrageously complicated or difficult."
Performances: Peter Schickele's *A View from the Roof*; G.C. Menotti's *Piano Concerto*; and L. Bernstein's *West Side Story*.
Tips: "Remember that we are an educational, music making organization seeking to give the youngsters in our orchestras the best learning and performing experiences possible. We wish to stretch their experience but not present them with impossibilities."

KENNETT SYMPHONY ORCHESTRA, Box 72, Kennett Square PA 19348. (215)444-6363. Music Director: Mary Woodmansee Green. Symphony orchestra. Estab. 1941. Members are professionals. Performs 6-7 concerts/year including 1-2 new works. "Performs at Kennett High School Auditorium (750), and in summer, Longwood Garden Open Air Theatre (2,000) for a predominantly white middle class (35+) audience. Pays per performance through publisher.

How to Contact: Submit complete score and tape pieces. Does not return material.

Music: Piece which can attract minority concert goers, children's concert, narrated pieces and program music (no more than 20-30). Limited stage area and budget. Nothing including extensive electronic instruments or huge percussion. No piano concertos (don't have concert instrument). We have 2-3 rehearsals for each concert—must work (with reset of concert rep) in that amount of time.

Performances: Ron Nelson's *Five Pieces After Paintings by Andrew Wyeth* (full orchestra program); Ann Wyeth McCoy's *In Memoriam* (piano transcription); and Peter Schickele's *The Chenoo Who Stayed to Dinner* (narrated children's fable).

Tips: "Have clean, easy-to-read parts, keep in mind unsophisticated audience."

KENTUCKY OPERA, 631 S. Fifth St., Louisville KY 40202-2201. (502)584-4500. Opera. Estab. 1952. Members are professionals. Performs 22 times/year. Performs at Whitney Hall, The Kentucky Center for the Arts, seating is 2,400; Bomhard Theater, The Kentucky Center for the Arts, 620; Macauley Theater, 1,400. Pays by royalty, outright purchase or per performance.

How to Contact: Submit complete score and tapes of piece(s). SASE. Reports in 6 months.

Music: Seeks opera—1 to 3 acts with orchestrations. No limitations.

Performances: 4/year. *La Boheme, H.M.S. Pinafore, The Phantom of the Opera* and *Rigoletto*.

KITCHENER-WATERLOO CHAMBER ORCHESTRA, Box 937, Waterloo, Ontario N2J 4C3 **Canada**. (519)744-3828. Music Director: Graham Coles. Chamber Orchestra. Estab. 1985. Members are professionals and amateurs. Performs 6 concerts/year, including some new works. "We perform mainly baroque and classical repertoire, so that any contemporary works must not be too dissonant, long or far fetched." Pays per performance.

How to Contact: "It's best to query first so that we can outline what not to send. Include: complete CV—list of works, performances, sample reviews." Reports in 4 weeks.

Music: "Musical style must be accessible to our audience and players (3 rehearsals). Length should be under 20 minutes. Maximum orchestration 2/2/2/2 2/2/0/0 Timp/1 Percussion Harpsichord/organ String 5/5/3/3/1. We have limited rehearsal time, so keep technique close to that of Bach-Beethoven. We also play chamber ensemble works—octets, etc. We do not want choral or solo works."

Performances: John Weinzweig's *Divertimento I* (flute and strings); Peter Jona Korn's *4 Pieces for Strings* (string orch.); and Graham Coles *Variations on a Mozart Rondo* (string orch.).

Tips: "If you want a first-rate performance, keep the technical difficulties minimal."

KNOX-GALESBURG SYMPHONY, Box 31 Knox College, Galesburg IL 61401. (309)343-0112, ext. 208. Music Director: Bruce Polay. Symphony orchestra. Estab. 1951. Members are professionals and amateurs. Performs 7 concerts/year including 1 new work. Middle age audience; excellent, recently renovated historical theater. Pays by performance.

How to Contact: Submit complete score and tapes of piece(s). SASE. Reports in 3-6 weeks.

Music: Moderate difficulty 3222/4331/T piano, harpsichord, celesta and full strings. No country.

Performances: Polay's *Perspectives for Tape & Orchestra* (1989 world premiere); and *Tranquil Cycle for Tenor & Orchestra (1992); Finko's 2nd Symphony* (US premiere); and Sisson's *October Light*.

L.A. SOLO REPERTORY ORCHESTRA, 7242 Louise Ave., Van Nuys CA 91406. (818)342-8400. Music Director: James Swift. Symphony orchestra. Estab. 1968. Members are professionals and amateurs. Performs 5 symphonic and 5 chamber music concerts/year including 5-10 new works. Commissions 1 composer or new work/year. "General audience. Hall of Liberty: 1,400 seats, Van Nuys Jr. High School auditorium: 800 seats and major houses for chamber music." Pay is negotiated.

How to Contact: Submit complete score and tapes of pieces. SASE. Reports in 2 months.

Music: "20th century symphonic, particularly with solo instruments and chamber music. Many composers extend development to point of boredom, so we reserve right to cut or perform single movements. Use of odd instruments or greatly extended sections tends to inhibit performance. No hard rock—even when intended for large orchestra."

Performances: Stephen Chandler's *Symphony No. 2*; Richard Nanes' *Concerto Grosso for 3 Brasses*; and Richard Fisk's *A Psalm of Praise (Psalm 33)* (cantata).

Tips: "Tapes are nice, but a good score is essential. Edit the work! Keep the moderately sophisticated audience in mind. Compose for audience enjoyment if you want your work repeated. Do not bore your audience. Think like Mozart, not like Mahler."

*LA STELLA FOUNDATION, 14323-64th Ave. W., Edmonds WA 98026. (206)743-5010. Managing Director: Thomas F. Chambers. Opera company. Estab. 1990. Members are professionals. Performs 1-2 concerts/year. Produces operatic performances exclusively for recordings, video and television markets. Payment individually negotiated.

How to Contact: Query first. SASE. Reports in 6 months.
Music: Music must have strong melodic value (Puccini-ish) with good harmonic chord structures and regular solid rhythms. Smaller casts with no chorus parts and smaller orchestras will get first consideration. Do not submit contemporary "a-tonal," non-harmonic, non-melodic, rhythmically weird garbage!!! Looking for pieces with romantic flavor like Puccini and dramatic movement like Verdi, written to showcase heavy lyric voices (i.e. soprano, tenor, baritone).
Performances: Mozart's *Bastien & Bastienne* and *Impresario* (contemporary libretto and script written in English); and Bizet's *Djamileh* (condensed version in English written with new contemporary translation).
Tips: "We are looking for hit arias and duets which fit above listed criteria with emphasis on repertoire for heavy lyric tenor/soprano voices."

LEHIGH VALLEY CHAMBER ORCHESTRA, Box 20641, Lehigh Valley PA 18002-0641. (215)770-9666. Music Director: Donald Spieth. Symphony orchestra. Estab. 1979. Performs 35 concerts/year, including 1-2 new works. Members are professionals. Commissions 1-2 composers or new works/year. Orchestra has "over 1,000 subscribers for Friday/Saturday pairs of concerts. Also offers youth programs, pops, etc." Pays by outright purchase for commissioned work.
How to Contact: Submit complete score and tape of pieces. Reports in 2 months.
Music: "Original compositions for chamber orchestra instrumentation: 2/2/2/2-2/2/1/0 percussion, strings (7/6/4/4/2); amateur of no interest. A composer should not write specifically for us without an agreement."
Performances: Libby Larsen's *Cold, Silent Snow* (flute and harp concerto); James Brown's *Symphony for Chamber Orchestra* (symphony in 3 movements); and Larry Lipkis' *Capprizio* (15 minute, one movement work).
Tips: "Send a sample type and score of a work(s) written for the requested medium."

LITHOPOLIS AREA FINE ARTS ASSOCIATION, 3825 Cedar Hill Rd., Canal Winchester OH 43110-9507. (614)837-8925. Series Director: Virginia E. Heffner. Performing Arts Series. Estab. 1973. Members are professionals and amateurs. Performs 5-6 concerts/year, including 1 or 2 new works. "Our audience consists of couples and families 35-85 in age. Our hall is acoustically excellent and seats 400. It was designed as a lecture-recital hall in 1925." Composers "may apply for Ohio Arts Council Grant under the New Works category."
How to Contact: Query first. Does not return material.
Music: "We prefer that a composer is also the performer and works in conjunction with another artist, so that they could be one of the performers on our series. Piece should be musically pleasant and not too dissonant. It should be scored for small vocal or instrumental ensemble. Dance ensembles have difficulty with 15' high 15' deep and 27' wide stage. We do not want avant-garde or obscene dance routines. No ballet (space problem). We're interested in something historical—national or Ohio emphasis would be nice. Small ensembles or solo format is fine."
Tips: "Call me to see what our series is consisting of that year."

*LIVINGSTON SYMPHONY ORCHESTRA, P.O. Box 253, Livingston NJ 07039. (201)731-2841. Music Director/Conductor: Antonia Joy Wilson. Symphony orchestra. Estab. 1957. Members are professionals and amateurs. Performs 4 concerts/year including 1 or less new works. Commissions 1 or less composers or new works/year. Concerts are performed in a 900 seat high school auditorium. Pays $1,000-2,000 for outright purchase. Query first. SASE. Reports in 2-8 months.
Music: "We are looking for symphonic overtures, fanfares, concerti, etc.—not complete symphonic. Also music 10-15 minutes suitable for children's concerts. Orchestra has approximately 60-65 members, many of whom are amateur. New work should not be beyond the ability of orchestra to perform well after 7-9 rehearsals. We do not want extremely dissonant, 'far out' music. This is a fairly conservative audience."
Performances: Mona Lyn Reese's *Electron Wind* (teaching piece for young audience); Howard Blake's *The Snowman* (narrated story); Schubert's *Wanderer Fantasy* (concerto for piano).
Tips: "Submit a query, be prepared to submit score and/or tape."

LONG BEACH COMMUNITY BAND, 6422 Keynote St., Long Beach CA 90808. (714)527-0964. Music Director: John E. Hall III. Community band. Estab. 1947. Members are professionals and amateurs. Performs 15 concerts/year including 6-8 new works. Average age level of audiences: 40's-50's. Performs mostly in outdoor venues such as parks. Pays by outright purchase.
How to Contact: Query first. SASE. Reports in 1-2 months.
Music: 3-10 minute pieces for concert band of medium difficulty. Looking for arrangements of film and TV music, songs of '70s to present.
Performances: Dan Friedman's *Millenium* (concert band overture).
Tips: "Compose music that is easy for audiences' ears."

*LONGAR EBONY ENSEMBLE LTD., P.O. Box 1208, New York NY 10025. (212)663-8819. Secretary: Roberta L. Long. Symphony orchestra and chamber music ensemble. Estab. 1982. Members are professionals. Performs 6 concerts/year including 3 new works. Commissions 2 composers or new works/year. "Audience is mainly classical music oriented and multicultural."

How to Contact: Submit complete score and tape of piece(s). SASE. Reports in 1 month.

Music: "Longar Ebony Ensemble, Ltd. wishes classical music to be premiered at New York's major concert halls. String quartets, quintets, chamber orchestra music with choral or vocal solos is highly desirable."

Performances: Stephen Beck, George Broderick and Leslie Adams' *Songs of Passion* (chamber music).

THE LOUISVILLE ORCHESTRA, 611 W. Main St., Louisville KY 40202. (502)587-8681. Contact: James Palermo. Symphony orchestra. Estab. 1937. Members are professionals. Performs 100 concerts/year, including 6 new works. Commissions 2 composers or new works/year. MasterWorks classical subscription concerts are performed in the 2,400-seat Whitney Hall of the Kentucky Center for the Arts. "Our audience varies in age from University students to seniors and comes from the areas surrounding Louisville in Kentucky and Indiana." Pays by commission.

How to Contact: Submit complete score and tapes of piece(s). Does not return unsolicited material. Reports in months. Planning done year in advance of performance.

Music: "All styles appropriate to symphony orchestras. No chamber works, pop music or lead sheets." Orchestration for standard symphony orchestra. No pop music/pop vocal/New Age. Enclose a tape of performance or keyboard realization.

Tips: "For information on New Music Competition in conjunction with Indiana State University, contact Pat Jenkins. For score submission, contact James Palermo."

*LYRIC OPERA OF CHICAGO, 20 N. Wacker Dr., Chicago IL 60606. (312)332-2244. Fax: (312)419-8345. Music Administrator: Philip Morehead. Opera company. Estab. 1953. Members are professionals. Performs 75 concerts/year including 1 new work in some years. Commissions 1 composer or new work every 3 or 4 years. "Performances are held in a 3,563 seat house, for a sophisticated opera audience, predominantly 30+ years old." Pays by contract (to be negotiated)—royalty or fee.

How to Contact: Query first. Does not return unsolicited material. Reports in 2 months or longer.

Music: "Full-length opera suitable for a large house with full orchestra. No musical comedy or Broadway musical style. We rarely perform one-act operas. We are only interested in works by composers and librettists with extensive theatrical experience. We have few openings for new works, so candidates must be of the highest quality. Do not send score or other materials without a prior contact."

Performances: William Bolcom's *McTeague*; Carlysle Floyd's *Susannah*; and Serge Prokofief's *The Gambler* (all operas).

Tips: "Have extensive credentials. We are not the right place for a novice opera composer."

MANITOBA CHAMBER ORCHESTRA, 202-1317A Portage Ave., Winnipeg, Manitoba R3G OV3 **Canada.** (204)783-7377. General Manager: Rita Manzies. Chamber orchestra. Estab. 1972. Members are professionals. Performs 9 concerts/year, including 2 new works. "Audiences are generally professionals—also many young people. We perform at Westminster Church (seats 1,000)." Pays by commission.

How to Contact: Query first. SAE and IRC.

Music: Seeks "music for string orchestra and one solo instrument. Limitations: 22 strings; no pop music."

Performances: Gary Kulesha's *Concerto for Recorder and Small Orchestra* (Canada Council Commission world premiere); and Andrew McDonald's *Violin Concerto op. 22* (world premiere).

MEASURED BREATHS THEATRE COMPANY, #3R, 193 Spring St., New York NY 10012. (212)334-8402. Artistic Director: Robert Press. Nonprofit music-theater producing organization. Estab. 1989. Members are professionals. Performs 2 concerts/year. "Performances in small (less than 100 seats) halls in downtown Manhattan; strongly interested in highly theatrical/political vocal works for avant-garde audiences." Pays $500 for outright purchase.

How to Contact: Query first. SASE. Reports in 1 month.

Music: "Traditionally, we have produced revivals of baroque or modern vocal works. We are interested in soliciting new works by theatrically adept composers. Typical orchestration should be 7 pieces or less. Would prefer full-length works." Chamber-size, full-length operas preferred. At most 10 performers. Difficult works encouraged.

Performances: Lully's *Amadis* (opera, French; 1684); Monteverdi's *The Madrigals of Love & War* (opera, Italian; 1638); Handel's *Tamerlano* (opera, English; 1724). All works performed in English translation.

*MIAMI CHAMBER SYMPHONY, 5690 N. Kendall Dr., Miami FL 33133. (305)858-3500. Music Director: Burton Dines. 33 player chamber orchestra. Estab. 1981. Members are professionals. Performs 5 concerts/year. Performs for a typical mature audience of local residents, most of whom attended concerts in large northern communities. Performances are held in a 600 seat hall at the U. of Miami. Best acoustics in South Florida. "We have no budget for new music. We will cooperate in obtaining grants for new music."
How to Contact: Query first. Send resume—describe piece. Submit complete score and tape of piece(s). Does not return material. Reports in 6 months.
Music: "We prefer highly accessible pieces of important artistic quality, especially Latin with nationalistic characteristics. Mostly works which a well known soloist is prepared to perform. Length from 5 to 20 mintutes. Chamber orchestra: 2222-2200-Timp. + 19 strings. We will add two more horns and trombones on occasion. The orchestra is very highly professional but we have, at the most, 7½ hours rehearsal. We are interested only in highly professional work of composers with some real background."
Performances: Jose Serebrier's *Winter* (violin and orchestra); Morton Gould's *Tap Dance Concerto* (tap dancer and orchestra); and Jorge Martinez's *Escenas Paraguayas* (nationalistic piece based on popular songs for Paraguyan Harp and Orchestra).
Tips: "Write an accessible work that a well known artist will perform or premiere with us."

*MILWAUKEE YOUTH SYMPHONY ORCHESTRA, 929 N. Water St., Milwaukee WI 53202. (414)272-8540. Executive Director: Frances Richman. Youth orchestra. "We also have a Junior Wind Ensemble." Estab. 1956. Members are students. Performs 12-15 concerts/year, including 1-2 new works. "Our groups perform in Uihlein Hall at the Performing Arts Center in Milwaukee plus area sites. The audiences usually consist of parents, music teachers and other interested community members. We usually are reviewed in either the Milwaukee Journal or Sentinel."
How to Contact: Query first. Does not return material.
Performances: Ruggeri's *Symphonia for Strings*.
Tips: "Be sure you realize you are working with students and not professional musicians. The music needs to be technically on a level students can handle. Our students are 8-18 years of age, in 5 different orchestras."

THE MIRECOURT TRIO, #11M, 3832 Quail Place, Waterloo IA 50701. (319)232-2388. Fax: (319)232-1238. Contact: Terry King. Chamber music ensemble; violin, cello, piano. Estab. 1973. Members are professionals. Performs 25 concerts/year, including 6 new works. Commissions 2 composers or new works/year. Concerts are performed for a "general chamber music audience of 100-1,500."
How to Contact: Query first. SASE. Reports in 6 months.
Music: Seeks "music of short to moderate duration (5-20 minutes) that entertains, yet is not derivative or cliched. Orchestration should be basically piano, violin, cello, occasionally adding soprano and/or clarinet. We do not wish to see academic or experimental works."
Performances: Lou Harrison's *Trio*; Otto Leuning's *Fantasia No. 2*; and Henry Conello's *Scenario*.
Tips: "Submit works that will engage the audience or relate to them; works that will reward the players as well."

MISSOURI SYMPHONY SOCIETY, P.O. Box 1121, Columbia MO 65205. (314)875-0600. Artistic Director and Conductor: Hugo Vianello. Symphony orchestra, chamber music ensemble, youth orchestra and pops orchestra. Estab. 1970. Members are professionals. Performs 22 concerts/year. Commissions one composer or new work/year. "Our home base is a 1,200-seat renovated 1928 movie palace and vaudeville stage. Our home audience is well-educated, including professionals from Columbia's five hospitals and three institutions of higher education. Our touring program reaches a broad audience, including rural Missourians and prison inmates." Pays through ASCAP and BMI.
How to Contact: Query first. SASE.
Music: "We want good orchestral (chamber) music of any length—2222/2200/timp/strings/piano. There are no limitations on difficulty."
Performances: Ibert's *Divertissement*; Copland's *Music For Movies*; Daniel's *Deep Forest Op. 34 #1*.

MOHAWK TRAIL CONCERTS, P.O. Box 75, Shelburne Falls MA 01370. (413)625-9511. Managing Director: Bob Stowe. Artistic Director: Arnold Black. Chamber music presenter. Estab. 1970. Members are professionals. Performs approximately 10 concerts/year, including 2-3 new works. "Audience ranges from farmers to professors, children to elders. Concerts are performed in churches and town halls around rural Franklin County, Massachusetts." Pays by performance.
How to Contact: Query first. Does not return unsolicited material. Reports in months.
Music: "We want chamber music, generally not longer than 30 minutes. We are open to a variety of styles and orchestrations for a maximum of 8 performers. We don't want popular, rock or theater music."

Performances: Michael Cohen's *Fantasia for Flute, Piano and Strings* (chamber); William Bolcom's *Nes Songs* (piano/voice duo); and Arnold Black's *Laments & Dances* (string quartet and guitar duo).
Tips: "We are looking for artistic excellence, a committment to quality performances of new music, and music that is accessible to a fairly conservative (musically) audience."

*MOZART FESTIVAL ORCHESTRA, INC., 33 Greenwich Ave., New York NY 10014. (212)675-9127. Conductor: Baird Hastings. Symphony orchestra. Estab. 1960. Members are professionals. Performs 1-4 concerts/year, including 2 new works. Audience members are Greenwich Village professionals of all ages. Performances are held at the 1st Presbyterian Church, Fifth Ave. and 12th St., wonderful acoustics. Pay varies.
How to Contact: Query first. SASE. Reports in 2 weeks.
Music: "We are an established chamber orchestra interested in *unusual* music of all periods, but not experimental. Orchestra size usually under 20 performers."

THE NEW YORK CONCERT SINGERS, Dept. SM, 401 E. 80th St., New York NY 10021. (212)879-4412. Music Director/Conductor: Judith Clurman. Chorus. Estab. 1988. Performs 4-5 concerts/year, including new works. Commissions 1 composer or new work/year. "Audience is mixture of young and old classical music 'lovers.' Chorus performs primarily at Menkin Concert Hall and Lincoln Center, NYC." Pays per performance.
How to Contact: Send score and tape with biographical data. SASE.
Music: Seeks music "for small professional ensemble, with or without solo parts, a cappella or small instrumental ensemble. Not for large orchestra and chorus (at this stage in the group's development). Looking for pieces ranging from 7-20 minutes."
Performances: William Bolcom's *Alleluia* (a cappella); Arvo Part's *Summa and Magnificent* (a cappella); and Milhaud's *Service Sacre* (chorus and ensemble).
Tips: "When choosing a piece for a program I study both the text and music. Both are equally important."

NORFOLK CHAMBER MUSIC FESTIVAL/YALE SUMMER SCHOOL OF MUSIC, 96 Wall St., New Haven CT 06520. (203)432-1966. Summer music festival. Estab. 1941. Members are international faculty/artists plus fellows who are young professionals. Performs 12 concerts, 14 recitals/year, including 3-6 new works. Commissions 1 composer or new work/year. "The 1,100-seat Music Shed (built in 1906 by architect Eric K. Rossiter) is lined with California redwood, with a peaked cathedral, which creates wonderful acoustics." Pays a commission fee (set fee). Also offers a Composition & Contemporary Music Seminar: "This is a workshop designed for composers as well as instrumentalists. With respected composers and performers serving as mentors, fellows will be exposed to a broad range of topics ranging from compositional techniques to performance practice. Entry fee is $290."
How to Contact: Submit complete score and tapes of piece(s). SASE. Reports in 1 month.
Music: "Chamber music of combinations, particularly for strings, woodwinds, brass and piano. There are 1-2 chamber orchestra concerts per season which include the students and feature the festival artists. Other than this, orchestra is not a featured medium, rather, chamber ensembles are the focus."
Performances: Scott Lindroth (new work for brass quintet); Joan Tower (new elegy for trombone and string quartet); and Ronald Roseman's *Double Quintet for Woodwinds & Brass*.

NORTH ARKANSAS SYMPHONY ORCHESTRA, P.O. Box 1243, Fayetteville AR 72702. (501)521-4166. Music Director: Carlton Woods. Symphony orchestra, chamber music ensemble, youth orchestra and community chorus. Estab. 1954. Members are professionals and amateurs. Performs 20 concerts/year, including 1-2 new works. "General audiences—performs in Walton Arts Center (capacity 1,200)." Pays $500 or more/performance.
How to Contact: Query first. SASE.
Music: Seeks "audience pleasers—rather short (10-15 minutes); and full orchestra pieces for subscription (classical) concerts. Orchestra is 60-70 members."
Performances: Mahler's *Symphony #1* and Beethoven's *9th Symphony*.

*OPERA MEMPHIS, MSU South Campus #47, Memphis TN 38152. (901)678-2706. (901)678-3506. Artistic Director: Michael Ching. Opera company. Estab. 1965. Members are professionals. Performs 12 concerts/year including 1 new work. Commissions 1 composer or new work/year. Audience consists

of older, wealthier patrons, along with many students and young professionals. Pay negotiable.
How to Contact: Query first. Does not return material. Reports in 1 year.
Music: Accessible practical pieces for educational or main stage programs. Educational pieces should not exceed 90 minutes or 4-6 performers. We encourage songwriters to contact us with proposals or work samples for theatrical works. We are very interested in crossover work.
Performances: David Olney's *Light in August* (folk opera); and John Baur's *The Violin of John Brown* (opera).
Tips: "Spend many hours thinking about the synopsis (plot outline)."

OPERA ON THE GO, 184-61 Radnor Rd., Jamaica Estates NY 11432. (718)380-0665. Artistic Director: Jodi Rose. American opera chamber ensemble. Estab. 1985. Members are professionals. Performs about 30 operas/year; all new works. "We perform primarily in schools and community theaters. We perform only American contemporary opera. It must be lyrical in sound and quality as we perform for children as well as adults. We prefer pieces written for children based on fairy tales needing 4 to 6 singers." Pays $20 per performance.
How to Contact: Submit complete score and tapes of piece(s). SASE. Reports ASAP if submissions are requested; if unsolicited, about 2-3 months.
Music: Need works in all age groups including adults. For older ages the pieces can be up to 60 minutes. Rarely use orchestra. "Keep the music as short as possible since we do a prelude (spoken) and postlude involving the children's active participation and performance. If it is totally atonal it will never work in the schools we perform in."
Performances: Edith Hemenway's *Goldilocks and the 3 Bears* (opera for N-3 grade); Mark Bucci's *Sweet Betsy From Pike* (opera for 6 grade-adult); and Seymour Barab's *Little Red Riding Hood* (children's opera).
Tips: "Be flexible. Through working with children we know what works best with different ages. If this means editing music to guarantee its performance, don't get offended or stubborn. All operas must have audience participatory sections."

PERRY COUNTY COUNCIL OF THE ARTS, P.O. Box 354, Newport PA 17074. (717)567-7023. Executive Director: Carol O. Vracarich. Arts organization presenting various programs. Estab. 1978. Members are professionals and amateurs and anyone who pays membership dues. Performs 5-7 concerts/year. "Performances are presented outdoors at a local state park or in a 500-seat high school auditorium. Outdoor area seats up to 5,000." Pays $50-2,000 per performance.
How to Contact: Submit complete tapes (or videocassette if available) and background info on composer/performer. Does not return unsolicited material.
Music: "We present a wide variety of programs, hence we are open to all types of music (folk, rock, classical, blues, jazz, ethnic). Most programs are 1-2 hours in length and must be suitable as family entertainment."

*PFL MANAGEMENT, 2424 W. Sepulveda Blvd., Torrance CA 90501. (213)325-8708. Personal Manager: Priscilla LaMarca. Vocal ensemble (all American, Broadway, jazz, light rock, pop, variety, suitable for ages 12-18 group and 20-40 year old group). Soloists available to demo pop, rock, blues (R&B), country music. They also need songs for shows and record demos. Estab. 1978. Members are professionals and amateurs. Performs 10 concerts/year, including 10 new works. No commission or budget. Will accept music to showcase. "We perform at private parties, conventions, amusement parks, clubs—indoors and out."
How to Contact: Submit complete score and tapes of piece(s). Background desired without soloist if selected. Include this on side B. SASE. Reports in 2 weeks.
Music: "We want up-beat tempos, strong rhythms with variety between sections, 3-minute songs, theme medleys—5-10 minutes. We don't want sex, drugs, profanity. Young love is OK. Songs about dreams, aspirations, gratitude, farewells, positive thoughts desired. Country tunes may have heartache, but up-beat preferred. Stage show format, short introductions, sharp endings, variety in sections and instrumentations that motivate interesting choreography appeal to us."
Performances: Priscilla LaMarea's *Children of the Earth* (pop/rock); Greg Scelsa's *The World Is A Rainbow* (ballad); and Mark Brymer's *Surfin' USA Medley)* (pop/rock).

*PHILADELPHIA COLLEGE OF BIBLE, 200 Manor Ave., Langhorne PA 19047-2992. (215)752-5800. Associate Professor: Dale Donovan Shepfer. Symphony orchestra and symphonic band. Estab. 1980. Members are professionals and amateurs. Performs 6 concerts/year, including 4 new works which must be privately funded. "Our audience is composed of 30-ish classical and sacred music lovers." Hall seats 700. Acoustics are moderately good. Small stipend only.
How to Contact: Query first. Submit complete score and tape of piece(s). SASE. Reports in 6 weeks.
Music: "We want non-avante garde, tonal, accessible, challenging and beautiful music in a 6-hour rehearsal format over a four-week span. Some meaningful religious or spiritual perspective. Orchestral or with chorus or soloists."

Performances: Ronald Alan Matthews' *Antiphonal Fanfare* (6 trumpets and orchestra); Kyle Smith's *Sing a Joyful Song* (cantata/orchestra); David Long's *In Remembrance*; Paul Jones' *Welsh Suite* (with male chorus); Paul Hofreiter's *Liturgical Symphony* (with male chorus); Daniel Nightingale's *Canticles* and many others.

Tips: "We want something breathtakingly thrilling, uplifting, neo-romantic, spotlighting sections, superb principals and including some grand tutti climaxes. Help us find funding, as this is a priority. Showcase the full color of an orchestra, at least on occasion. Provide a spiritual base for the piece."

PICCOLO OPERA COMPANY, 24 Del Rio Blvd., Boca Raton FL 33432-4737. (800)282-3161. Executive Director: Marjorie Gordon. Opera company. Estab. 1962. Members are professionals. Commissions 1 composer or new work/year. Concerts are performed for a mixed audience of children and adults. Pays by royalty or outright purchase.
How to Contact: Query first. SASE.
Music: "Musical theater pieces, lasting about one hour, for adults to perform for adults and/or youngsters. Performers are mature singers with experience. The cast should have few performers (up to 10), no chorus or ballet, accompanied by piano or orchestra. Skeletal scenery. All in English."
Performances: *Cosi Fan Tutte* (opera); *The Telephone* (opera); *The Old Maid & The Thief* (opera).

PLYMOUTH MUSIC SERIES OF MINNESOTA, 1900 Nicollet Ave., Minneapolis MN 55403. (612)870-0943. General Manager: Frank Stubbs. Choral orchestral performing society. Estab. 1969. Members are professionals and amateurs. Performs 6-8 concerts. Audience is generally all ages from late 20s. Comes from entire Twin Cities metro area. "We perform in Ordway Music Theatre, Orchestra Hall, cathedrals in both Minneapolis and St. Paul." Pays commission fee.
How to Contact: Query first. SASE.
Music: All styles appropriate to a choral/orchestral society except pop or rock. "Text used is of special concern. If the work is over ½ hour, the use of soloists is preferred."
Performances: Conrad Susa's *Carols & Lullabies* and Paul McCartney's *Liverpool Oratorio*.
Tips: "Be patient. We have a very small staff and are constantly behind in reviewing scores. Tapes are very helpful."

*PRISM SAXOPHONE QUARTET, 257 Harvey St., Philadelphia PA 19144. (215)438-5282. Vice President, New Sounds Music Inc. Prism Quartet: Matthew Levy. Chamber music ensemble. Estab. 1984. Members are professionals. Performs 80 concerts/year including 15 new works. Commissions 7 composers or new works/year. "Performances are primarily held in concert halls for chamber music concert audiences." Pays royalty per performance from BMI or ASCAP or commission range from $100 to $5,000.
How to Contact: Submit complete score (with parts) and tape of piece(s). Does not return material.
Music: "Orchestration—sax quartet SATB or AATB, Lengths—5-60 minutes. Styles—contemporary classical, jazz, crossover, ethnic, gospel, avant-garde. No limitations on level of difficulty. No more than 4 performers (SATB or AATB sax quartet). No arrangements or transcriptions. The Prism Quartet places special emphasis on crossover works which integrate a variety of musical styles."
Performances: Michael Rusczzynski's *Fantasy Quartet* (neo-romantic); Franch Amsallem's *The Farewell* (jazz); *Tooka-Ood Zasch* (ethnic-world music).

*QUEENS OPERA, 313 Bay 14th St., Brooklyn NY 11214. (718)256-6045. General Director: Joe Messina. Opera company. Estab. 1961. Members are professionals. Performs 9 concerts/year, including 1 new work.
How to Contact: SASE. Reports in 1 month.
Music: "Operatic scores and songs, small orchestra."
Performances: Rossini's *Il Barbiere di Siviglia*; Verdi's *Il Trovatore* and *La Traviata*; and Owen's *Tom Sawyer*.

*RENO POPS ORCHESTRA, P.O. Box 9838, Reno NV 89507. (702)673-2276. Conductor, Musical Director: Joyce Williams. Symphony orchestra. Estab. 1983. Members are professionals and amateurs. Performs 6 concerts/year usually including 1 new work. Performances are held in 600-1,400 seat theaters and off site locations, i.e. schools, community centers for a mixed audience. Pay negotiable.
How to Contact: Query first. SASE. Reports in 1 month.
Music: 15-20 minutes with strong rhythm, lyrical melodies of joyous, optimistic matter. Nothing for large orchestras.
Tips: "Write a playable piece that would work for college or community ensembles."

RIVER CITY BRASS BAND, P.O. Box 6436, Pittsburgh PA 15212. (412)322-7222. Music Director: Robert Bernat. Professional brass band. Estab. 1980. Members are professionals. Performs 85-95 concerts/year including 10-20 new works. Commissions 3-6 composers or new works/year. Older audience (50-70), affluent, professionals and homemakers. Self-produced concert series (56 performances) in Carnegie Music Hall, (1,800 seats) university and high school auditoriums. Contracted performances (30-40 per year) in wide variety of venues. Pays $1,000-3,000 for outright purchase and normal publishing and performance royalties of work selected for publication by inhouse publishing firm, begun late 1993.

How to Contact: Query first. SASE.

Music: Seeks "Accessible, tonal works of 3-20 minutes duration for either American-style, 28-piece, brass band or 12-piece brass ensemble (4 cornets/trumpets, horn, baritone, euphonium, tenor trombone, bass trombone, tuba, 2 percussion). Must be performable with 2-3 hours of rehearsal by highly accomplished professional musicians. No post-Weber, academic avant garde, educational pieces or popular/commercial songs."

Performances: Philip Sparke's *Royal Salute* (concert march); George Lloyd's *Royal Parks* (3 movement suite); and Gordon Langford's *Fanfare and Ceremonial Prelude* (overture).

Tips: "Have a good command of writing for brass band. Be able to use tonal materials imaginatively. Write with players' and audience's enjoyment in mind."

*ST. LOUIS CHAMBER CHORUS, P.O. Box 11558, Clayton MO 63105. (314)458-4343. Music Director: Philip Barnes. Vocal ensemble, chamber music ensemble. Estab. 1956. Members are professionals and amateurs. Performs 5/6 concerts/year including approx. 5 new works. Performances take place at various auditoria noted for their excellent acoustics—churches, synagogues, schools and university halls. Pays by arrangement.

How to Contact: Query first. SASE. Reports in 1 to 2 months.

Music: "Only *a cappella* writing; no contemporary 'popular' works; historical editions welcomed. No improvisatory works. Our programs are tailored for specific acoustics—composers should indicate their preference."

Performances: John Harbison's *Ave Maria* (motet); Henry Gorecki's *Totus Tuus* (motet); Andrew Carter's *Ack Varmeland* (folksong).

Tips: "Show awareness of the unique qualities of the voice."

SALT LAKE SYMPHONIC CHOIR, Box 45, Salt Lake City UT 84110. (801)466-8701. Manager: Richard M. Taggart. Professional touring choir. Estab. 1949. Members are professionals and amateurs. Performs 4-15 concerts/year, including 1-3 new works. Commissions 1-3 new works or composers/year. "We tour throughout U.S. and Canada for community concert series, colleges and universities." Pay is negotiable.

How to Contact: Query first. Does not return unsolicited material. Reports in 3 months.

Music: Seeking "4- to 8-part choral pieces for a 100-voice choir—from Bach to rock."

*SASKATOON SYMPHONY ORCHESTRA, Box 1361, Saskatoon, Sasketchewan S7K 3N9 **Canada.** (306)665-6414. Fax: (306)652-3364. General Manager: Shirley Spafford. Symphony orchestra. Members are professionals and amateurs. Performs 7 full orchestra concerts/year.

How to Contact: Query first. Does not return material.

Music: "We are a semi-professional orchestra with a full time core of ten artists-in-residence. Our season runs from September to April with 7 classical concerts, pops series, chamber series, children's series and baroque series."

Performances: David Scott's *Nazca Lines* (symphonic) and *Epigrams* (reed trio); and Elizabeth Raum's *Concerto for Bass* (string quartet).

SEAWAY CHORALE AND ORCHESTRA, INC., 2450 Middlefield Rd., Trenton MI 48183. (313)676-2400. Conductor, Executive Director: David M. Ward. Auditioned chorus and orchestra. Estab. 1975. Members are professionals and amateurs. Performs 5 major concerts/year, including 4 new works/year. Commissions 0-2 composers or new works/year. "We perform in halls, some church settings and high school auditoriums—large stage with orchestra pit. Our audience is ecumenically, financially, racially, socially, musically, multi-generation and a cross section of our area." Pays by negotiation.

How to Contact: Submit score and tape of piece(s). SASE. Reports in 3 months.

Music: "We want 3-minute ballads for orchestra and chorus (for subscription concerts); sacred music, either accompanied or a cappella; Christmas music for chorus and orchestra. We have three performing groups: Voices of the Young—4th through 8th grades (40 members); Youth Sings—9th through 12th grades (a show choir, 24 members); Chorale—adults (70 members). Charismatic Christian music is not high on our priority list. Country music runs a close second. Our major concerts which draw large audiences utilize light selections such as show music, popular songs and music from movies. We present two concerts each year which we call Choral Masterpieces. These concerts include music from master composers of the past as well as contemporary. Our choral masterpieces concerts require Biblical or secular thoughts that are well-conceived musically."

Tips: "Don't settle for one musical avenue. Be as creatively prolific as possible. You may discover a lot about your own abilities and avoid redundancies as a result."

*SINGERS FORUM, 39 W. 19th St., New York NY 10011. (212)366-0541. Fax: (212)366-0546. Administrator: Denise Galon. Vocal school and presenting organization. Estab. 1978. Members are professionals and amateurs. Performs more than 50 concerts/year, including 4 new works. Commissions 2 composers or new works/year. 75 seat performance space with varied audience. Pay through donations from patrons.
How to Contact: Query first. SASE. Reports in 2 months.
Music: "All popular music, art songs, full musicals, small operas with minimal orchestration. No rock. I'm always looking for works to fit our current voices. Mainly new operas and musicals."
Performances: Maria Kildegaard and Valerie Osterwalder's *Angels Part I* (new music); mixed *Women of a Certain Age Carrying On* (collection of women's music); mixed *Big Girls Don't Cry* (contemporary mixed cabaret).
Tips: "Think of the voice."

SINGING BOYS OF PENNSYLVANIA, P.O. Box 206, Wind Gap PA 18091. (215)759-6002. Director: K. Bernard Schade, Ed. D. Vocal ensemble. Estab. 1970. Members are professional children. Performs 120 concerts/year, including 7-12 new works. Commissions 1-2 composers or new works/year. "We attract general audiences: family, senior citizens, churches, concert associations, university concert series and schools." Pays by outright purchase.
How to Contact: Query first. SASE. Reports in 3 months.
Music: "We want music for commercials, music for voices in the SSA or SSAA ranges, sacred works or arrangements of American folk music with accompaniment. Our range of voices are from G below middle C to A (13th above middle C). Reading ability of choir is good but works which require a lot of work with little possibility of more than one performance are of little value. We sing very few popular songs except for special events. We perform music by composers who are well-known and works by living composers who are writing in traditional choral forms. Works of music which have a full orchestral score are of interest. The orchestration should be fairly light, so as not to cover the voices. Works for Christmas have more value than some other, since we perform with orchestras on an annual basis."
Performances: Don Locklair's *The Columbus Madrigals* (opera).
Tips: "It must be appropriate music and words for children."

SUSQUEHANNA SYMPHONY ORCHESTRA, P.O. Box 485, Forest Hill MD 21050. (410)838-6465. Music Director: Sheldon Bair. Symphony orchestra. Estab. 1978. Members are amateurs. Performs 4 subscription concerts/year, plus 2 outdoor concerts in June, including 2 new works. "We perform in 2 halls. One is more intimate, 600 seats; the other is larger, 999 seats; both with fine acoustics. Our audience encompasses all ages." Composers are normally not commissioned, just ASCAP or BMI royalties.
How to Contact: Query first. SASE. Reports in 6+ months.
Music: "We desire works for large orchestra any length, in a 'conservative 20th century' style. Seek fine, tonal music for chamber or large orchestra (large orchestra is preferable). We are a community orchestra, so the music must be within our grasp. Violin I to 7th position by step only; Violin II—stay within 3rd position, English horn and harp are OK. We don't want avant-garde music. Full orchestra pieces preferred."
Performances: Unger's *Variations for Orchestra* (tonal variations); Finke's *Piano Concerto "Moses"*; and Yaruminn's *Chorale-Prelude*.

TORONTO MENDELSSOHN CHOIR, 60 Simcoe St., Toronto, Ontario M5J 2H5 **Canada**. Phone: (416)598-0422. Manager: Michael Ridout. Vocal ensemble. Members are professionals and amateurs. Performs 25 concerts/year including 1-3 new works. "Most performances take place in Roy Thomson Hall. The audience is reasonably sophisticated, musically knowledgeable but with moderately conservative tastes." Pays by commission and ASCAP/SOCAN.
How to Contact: Query first or submit complete score and tapes of pieces. SASE. Reports in 6 months.
Music: All works must suit a large choir (180 voices) and standard orchestral forces or with some other not-too-exotic accompaniment. Length should be restricted to no longer than ½ of a nocturnal concert. The choir sings at a very professional level and can sight-read almost anything. "Works should fit naturally with the repertoire of a large choir which performs the standard choral orchestral repertoire."
Performances: Holman's *Jezebel* (world premiere); Orff's *Catulli Carmina*; and Lambert's *Rio Grande*.

*TRIO OF THE AMERICAS, 16823 Liggett St., Sepulveda CA 91343. (818)892-8737. Director: Dr. Janice Foy. Chamber music ensemble. Estab. 1993. Members are professionals. Performs 4 concerts/year including 2 new works. "Focus of repertoire is music of the Americas. We perform on a concert stage; sometimes private residences or university halls."

How to Contact: Submit complete score and tape of piece(s). SASE. Reports in a few weeks.
Music: "Contemporary chamber music, which could include the addition of voice and/or other instruments. 'Trio of the Americas' consists of clarinet, cello and piano. Preferable length is from 8-15 minutes. Try not to write for more than 5 performers. Could write for anything less than that, including duets and solos. Difficulty does not matter since the performers are among L.A.'s finest. Not interested in computer music. Very interested in the incorporation of jazz and the use of folk material. Prefer melodic/rhythmic interest in the music. All styles are acceptable. (No Steve Reich approaches please.)"
Performances: Zita Carno, *Extrapolations I* and *Intermezzo* for clarinet and cello (world premiere), Alberto Ginastera's *Sonata for Cello and Piano* (West Coast premiere) and John Naples' *Phantasmagoria* (world premiere).
Tips: "Please be open to criticism/suggestions about your music and try to appeal to mixed audiences."

UNIVERSITY OF HOUSTON OPERA THEATRE, School of Music, Houston TX 77204-4893. (713)749-4370 or 749-1116. Director of Opera: Buck Ross. Opera/music theater program. Members are professionals, amateurs and students. Performs 8-10 concerts/year, including 1 new work. Performs in a proscenium theater which seats 1,100. Pit seats approximately 40 players. Audience covers wide spectrum, from first time opera-goers to very sophisticated." Pays by royalty.
How to Contact: Submit complete score and tapes of piece(s). SASE. Reports in 3 months.
Music: "We seek music that is feasible for high graduate level student singers. Chamber orchestras are very useful. No more than 2½ hours. We don't want serial pieces, aleatoric or children's operas."
Performances: Carlisle Floyd's *Bilby's Doll* (opera); Mary Carol Warwick's *Twins* (opera); and Robert Nelson's *Tickets, Please* (opera).

VANCOUVER CHAMBER CHOIR, 1254 W. 7th Ave., Vancouver, British Columbia V6H 1B6 **Canada**. Artistic Director: Jon Washburn. Vocal ensemble. Members are professionals. Performs 40 concerts/year; performs 5-8 new works/year. Commissions 3-4 composers or new works/year. Pays statutory SOCAN royalty.
How to Contact: Submit complete score and tapes of piece(s). Does not return material. Reports in 6 months.
Music: Seeks "choral works of all types for small chorus, with or without accompaniment, soloists. 'Serious' concert music only. Choir made up of 20 singers. Large or unusual instrumental accompaniments are less likely to be appropriate. No pop music."
Performances: Alice Parker's *That Sturdy Vine* (cantata for chorus, soloists and orchestra); R. Murray Schafer's *Magic Songs* (SATB a capella); and Jon Washburn's *A Stephen Foster Medley* (SSAATTBB/piano).
Tips: "We are looking for music that is performable yet innovative and choral music which has the potential to become 'standard repertoire.' Although we perform much new music it is only a small portion of the scores which are submitted."

*VENTUS MUSICUS, P.O. Box 141, Redlands CA 92373. (909)793-0513. Trumpet Player: Larry Johansen. Chamber music ensemble (organ/trumpet duo). Estab. 1978. Members are professionals. Performs 3-10 concerts/year including 1-4 new works (as available). Most performances done in churches ("we need a pipe organ . . . .")
How to Contact: Query first. SASE. Reports in 2 months.
Music: "Most organ/trumpet material is church oriented (hymns, chants, stained glass, etc.); this is useful, but not mandatory—we play for college and A.G.O. Groups as well as church recital series. We are open to pretty much anything, except improvised jazz. We are interested in the composer's ideas, not ours. Go for it! And we'll try it."
Performances: Donald Grantham's *Ceremony* (sonata); Daniel Pinkham's *Psalms* (sonata); Hermann Schroeder's *Impromptu* (fanfare).
Tips: "Unfortunately, we have no commission money, but we do play at conferences around the country, and we can offer some exposure."

WARMINSTER SYMPHONY ORCHESTRA, 524 W. Pine St., Trevose PA 19053. (215)355-7421. Music Director/Principal Conductor: Gil Guglielmi, D.M.A. Community symphony orchestra. Estab. 1966. 12 "pros" and amateurs. Performs 4 concerts/year, including perhaps 1 new work. "We *try* to commission one composer or new work/year." Audience is blue collar and upper middle-class. The concert

The asterisk before a listing indicates that the listing is new in this edition. New markets are often the most receptive to unsolicited submissions.

hall is a local junior high school with a seating capacity of 710. "We operate on a small budget. Composers are not paid, or paid very little (negotiable)."

How to Contact: Composer should contact Dr. Guglielmi. Does not return material.

Music: Romantic style. Length: 10 minutes to a full symphony. Orchestration: full orchestra with no sound effects, synthesizers, computers, etc. "We play from Mozart to Tchaikovsky. Performers: we have a maximum of about 60 players. Level of difficulty: medium advanced—one grade above a good high school orchestra. We rehearse 2 hours a week so that anything written should take about 20 minutes a week rehearsal time to allow rehearsal time for the remaining selections. Our musicians and our audiences are middle-of-the-road. The composer should write in *his* style and not try to contrive a piece for us. The orchestra has a full string section, 4 horns, 3 clarinets, 3 flutes, 2 bassons, 3 trumpets, 2 oboe, 1 English horn, 3 trombones, 1 tuba, 1 harp and a full percussion section."

Performances: Al Maene's *Perla Bella* (mini symphony); and David Finke's *The Wailing Wall* (tone poem).

Tips: "Do not expect the Philadelphia Orchestra. My musicians are primarily lay-people who are dedicated to the performance of good music. What they lack in expertise they more than make up or in practice, work and dedication."

WAUKEGAN SYMPHONY ORCHESTRA, 39 Jack Benny Dr., Waukegan IL 60087. (708)360-4742. Director: Dr. Richard Hynson. Symphony orchestra. Estab. 1972. Members are professionals and amateurs. Performs 4 concerts/year including 1 new work. "We have a middle-aged and older audience, basically conservative. We perform in a 1,800 seat house." Paid through BMI and ASCAP.

How to Contact: Query first. SASE. Reports in 3 months.

Music: "We want conservative music, especially regarding rhythmic complexities, four to ten minutes in length, orchestrated for wind pairs, standard brass, strings, etc., up to 4 percussionists plus timpani. The number of performers basically limited to 75 member orchestra, difficulty level should be moderate to moderately difficult, more difficulty in winds and brass than strings. We don't want aleatoric 'chance' music, pointillistic—to a large extent non-melodic music. We are always looking for beautiful music that speaks to the heart as well as the mind, music with a discernable structure is more attractive."

Performances: Howard Hanson's *Symphony No. 2 "Romantic"* and Roy Harn's *Symphony No. 3*.

Tips: "Write beautiful, listenable music. Make the composition an exercise in understanding the orchestral medium, not an academic exercise in rehearsal problems."

WAYNE CHAMBER ORCHESTRA, 300 Pompton Rd., Wayne NJ 07470. (201)595-2694. Managing Director: Sheri Newberger. Chamber orchestra. Estab. 1986. Members are professionals. Performs 4 concerts/year including 1 new work. Regional audience from North Jersey area. Attractive and modern concert hall seating 960 patrons.

How to Contact: Query with bio first. SASE. Reports in 2 months.

Music: "We are looking for new American music for a 40-piece orchestra. Our only method of funding would be by grant so music may have to tie in with a theme. Although we have not yet performed new works, we hope to in the future."

Performances: Louise Talma's *Toccatta* (orchestra); Benny Golson's *Solo for Double Bass & Orchestra* (jazz inspired); and George Walker's *Lyric for Strings* (orchestral).

WHEATON SYMPHONY ORCHESTRA, 1600 E. Roosevelt, Wheaton IL 60187. (708)668-8585. Manager: Donald C. Mattison. Symphony orchestra. Estab. 1959. Members are professionals and amateurs. Performs 3 concerts/year, including 1 new work. Composers are paid $100/performance.

How to Contact: Submit complete score and tape of piece(s). SASE. Reports in 2 months.

Music: "This is a *good* amateur orchestra that wants pieces in a traditional idiom. Large scale works for orchestra. No avant garde, 12-tone or atonal material. Pieces should be 20 minutes or less and must be prepared in 3 rehearsals. Instrumentation is woodwinds in 3s, full brass 4-3-3-1, percussion, etc."

Performances: Jerry Bilik's *Aspects of Man* (4-section suite); Walton's *Variations on a Theme of Hindemith's*; and Augusta Read Thomas' *A Crystal Planet*.

*THE WILLIAMSBURG SYMPHONIA, Box 400, Williamsburg VA 23187. (804)229-9857. Artistic Director: M.E. Andersen. Chamber orchestra. Estab. 1984. Members are professionals. Performs 8 concerts/year. "Our audience is made up of members of Williamsburg and surrounding communities and Virginia Peninsula—Norfolk to Richmond. We use the public library auditorium, Colonial Williamsburg facilities, or the Phi Beta Kappa Hall at the College of William and Mary."

How to Contact: Query first. SASE.

Music: "We want traditional music for chamber orchestrations."

WOMEN'S PHILHARMONIC, Suite 218, 330 Townsend St., San Francisco CA 94107. (415)543-2297. Philharmonic orchestra. Estab. 1980. Members are professionals. Performs 15 concerts/year; performs 6 new works/year. Commissions 3 composers or new works/year. "Audience median age is 39; urban professional. Performance space is downtown hall in prime retail district with 1,100 reserved seating." Pays by commission.
How to Contact: Query first. SASE.
Music: Seeks symphonic/orchestral music with or without soloist by women composers, for performance and/or inclusion in National Women Composers Resource Center database.
Performances: Hilary Tann's *Open Field*; Chen Yi's *Duo Ye #2*; and Joan Tower's *Piano Concerto* (all orchestral).

*YOUTH ORCHESTRA OF GREATER FORT WORTH, 4401 Trail Lake Dr., Fort Worth TX 76109. (817)923-3121. General Manager: Freda Wise. Youth orchestra. Estab. 1965. Members are amateurs. Performs 12-16 concerts/year, including a few new works. "Audiences are adults and children." Orchestra hall has 385 seats; Ed Landrteh Auditorium has 1200 seats (2 levels). Pays by outright purchase.
How to Contact: Query first. SASE.
Music: Seeks "challenging, but possible, for advanced teen-aged musicians. 8-10 (possibly longer) minutes in length—full orchestra winds in threes; four trumpets; four trombones; tuba, six percussion, keyboard. No chamber pop."
Performances: Bill Hofelot's *Chaconne* (intermediate level).
Tips: "Look for exposure, very little money! Our budget for commissions is $0."

Fine Arts/'93-'94 Changes

The following markets appeared in the 1993 edition of *Songwriter's Market* but are absent from the 1994 edition. Most of these companies failed to respond to our request for an update of their listing for a variety of reasons. For example, they may have gone out of business or they may have requested deletion from the 1994 edition because they are backlogged with material. If we know the specific reason, it appears within parentheses.

Adrian Symphony Orchestra
Artea Chamber Orchestra
Arts Council of Greater Kingsport
Augsburg Choir (Augsburg College)
Central Kentucky Youth Orchestra
Cinnabar Opera Theater
Commonwealth Opera Inc.
Dallas Chamber Orchestra
Diablo Valley Philharmonic
The Florida Orchestra
Grand Teton Music Festival
High Desert Symphony Orchestra
Huntsville Youth Orchestra

Jackson Symphony Orchestra (requested deletion)
Johnson City Symphony Orchestra
Lakeside Summer Symphony
Lexington Philharmonic Society
Lincoln Youth Symphony Orchestra
Lindenwood Concerts (same as Gary Beard Chorale)
L.A. Jazz Choir
The Lyric Opera of Dallas
Mid-America Singers and Children's Choirs
Moravian Philharmonic Olomouc

Music Programs: Los Angeles County Museum of Art
Nashville Opera Association
National Association of Composers/USA
Nebraska Chamber Orchestra
Nebraska Jazz Orchestra Inc. (requested deletion)
Old Stoughton Musical Society
Oregon Symphony
Paragon Ragtime Orchestra
Pro Arte Chamber Orchestra of Boston
Sacramento Master Singers
Vancouver Youth Symphony Orchestra Society
Zion Chamber Orchestra

Resources

Organizations

The vast majority of songwriter organizations are nonprofit groups with membership open to anyone interested in songwriting. Whether local, statewide or national in scope, such organizations can provide helpful information and much-needed encouragement to amateur and professional songwriters alike.

Songwriting organizations can provide you with an abundance of different opportunities. They're great places to meet collaborators, if you're searching for a co-writer but don't know where to find one. Songwriting organizations can provide excellent forums for having your work heard and critiqued in a constructive way by other songwriters and industry professionals, helping to improve your craft. They can help keep you abreast of the latest music industry news as it relates to songwriters, and can provide tips on publishers, artists and record companies looking for new material. And, perhaps most importantly, these organizations give you the opportunity to expand your network of friends and contacts in the music industry, which is vital to any songwriter wanting success in the music business.

Most organizations offer regular meetings of their general membership and occasional special events such as seminars and workshops to which music industry people are invited—to share their experiences and perhaps listen to and critique demo tapes. There are songwriting organizations all over the United States. If you can't find one within an easy distance from your home, you may want to consider joining one of the national groups. These groups, based in New York, Los Angeles and Nashville, welcome members from across the country and keep them involved and informed through newsletters and magazines, regular meetings and large yearly get-togethers. They are an excellent way for writers who feel "stranded" somewhere in the middle of the country to keep up contacts and get their music heard in the major music centers.

The type of organization you choose to join depends on what you want to get out of it. Local groups can give you the friendly, supportive encouragement you need to continue in your career. Larger, national organizations can give you access to music business executives and other songwriters across the country. In each of the following listings, organizations describe what they have to offer. Write to any that interest you for further information.

ACADEMY OF COUNTRY MUSIC, #923, 6255 Sunset Blvd., Hollywood CA 90028. (213)462-2351. Membership: David Young. Estab. 1964. Serves producers, artists, songwriters, talent buyers and others involved with the country music industry. Eligibility for professional members is limited to those individuals who derive some portion of their income directly from country music. Each member is classified by one of the following categories: artist/entertainer, club operator/employee, musician/trend leader, DJ, manager/booking agent, composer, music publisher, promotion, publications, radio, TV/motion picture, record company or affiliated (general). The purpose of ACM is to promote and enhance the image of country music. "The Academy is involved year round in activities important to the country music community. Some of these activities include charity fund raisers, participation in country music seminars, talent contests, artist showcases, assistance to producers in placing country music on television and in motion pictures and backing legislation that benefits the interests of the country music community. The ACM is governed by directors and run by officers elected annually." Also offers a newsletter. Applications are accepted throughout the year. Membership is $40/year.

AMERICAN MUSIC CENTER, INC., Suite 1001, 30 W. 26th St., New York NY 10010-2011. (212)366-5260. Executive Director: Nancy Clarke. Estab. 1939. For composers and performers. Members are American composers, performers, critics, publishers and others interested in contemporary concert music and jazz. Offers circulating library of contemporary music scores and advice on opportunities for composers and new music performers; disseminates information on American music. Purpose is to encourage the recognition and performance of contemporary American music. Members receive professional monthly "Opportunity Updates," eligibility for group health insurance and the right to vote in AMC elections.

AMERICAN MUSICIANS UNION INC., 8 Tobin Ct., Dumont NJ 07628. (201)384-5378. President and Treasurer: Ben Intorre. Estab. 1948. Serves musicians and vocalists of all age groups, all ethnic groups, music from gay 90's to contemporary, ballroom music, banquets, weddings, rock, disco, western, Latin, standards, etc. "We assist musicians in their efforts to perform and serve the public. We offer membership in a union, life insurance, meetings and a union publication. Applicant must be a musician, vocalist or manager. Disc-jockeys are not eligible." Offers newsletter and performance opportunities. Applications accepted year-round. Annual dues $27; $10 initiation. Services include life insurance ($2,000 to age 65, reduced insurance to age 70) and advertisements in *Quarternote* are usually free to members. "We have locals in the U.S., in New Jersey, Minnesota, Michigan, etc."

AMERICAN ORFF-SCHULWERK ASSOCIATION INC., P.O. Box 391089, Cleveland OH 44139-8089. (216)543-5366. Fax: (216)543-4057. Executive Secretary: Cindi Wobig. Estab. 1969. Serves musicians and music educators; preschool, kindergarten and classroom teachers; music therapists; church musicians; college students and retired music educators. Offers workshops, annual conference and a quarterly publication. Chapters located in most states.

AMERICAN SOCIETY OF COMPOSERS, AUTHORS AND PUBLISHERS (ASCAP), 1 Lincoln Plaza, New York NY 10023. (212)621-6000. Contacts: Lisa K. Schmidt, Michael Kerker (Musical Theatre), Ivan Alvarez (Latin Music) in New York office; or the following branch offices: Todd Brabec, Suite 300, 7920 Sunset Blvd., Los Angeles, CA 90046; Debra Cain, 2nd Floor, 3500 W. Hubbard St., Chicago, IL 60610; Connie Bradley, 2 Music Square W., Nashville, TN 37203; James Fisher, 52 Haymarket, London SW1Y 4RP **England.** Members are songwriters, composers, lyricists and music publishers. Applicants must "have at least one song copyrighted for associate membership; have at least one song commercially available as sheet music, available on rental, commercially recorded, or performed in media licensed by the Society (e.g., performed in a nightclub or radio station) for full membership. ASCAP is a membership-owned, performing right licensing organization that licenses its members' nondramatic musical compositions for public performance and distributes the fees collected from such licensing to its members based on a scientific random sample survey of performances." Primary value is "as a clearinghouse, giving users a practical and economical bulk licensing system and its members a vehicle through which the many thousands of users can be licensed and the members paid royalties for the use of their material. All monies collected are distributed after deducting only the Society's cost of doing business."
Tips: "The Society sponsors a series of writers' workshops in Los Angeles, Nashville and New York open to members and nonmembers. Grants to composers available to members and nonmembers."

*AMERICAN WOMEN COMPOSERS, INC., Suite 409, 1690 36th St. NW, Washington DC 20007. (202)342-8179. President: Judith Shatin. Estab. 1976. Serves songwriters and musicians. Members are women and men who wish to further compositions written by American women including composers, performers and musicologists. We have a national membership with large concentrations in New York,

California, Massachusetts, Illinois and Washington DC metropolitan areas. Eligibility requirements are to pay dues and complete application form. Since we are a support organization, we do not limit ourselves to just professionals. We promote compositions by American women through our concerts and publications and circulating library. The primary value in this organization for a songwriter is free publicity. If songs are performed we mention in our newsletters; music placed in our library is circulated; newsletters provide information on competitions, grants and opportunities for composers in all musical media. Offers library, newsletter, performance opportunities and contact with others interested in women's music. Applications accepted year-round. Annual dues: composer/songwriter, $30; other professionals, $30; senior citizens/students, $15; institutions $40.

ARKANSAS SONGWRITERS, 6817 Gingerbread, Little Rock AR 72204. (501)569-8889. President: Peggy Vining. Estab. 1979. Serves songwriters, musicians and lovers of music. Any interested may join. To promote and encourage the art of songwriting. Offers competitions, instruction, lectures, newsletter, performance opportunities, social outings and workshops. Applications accepted year-round. Membership fee is $15/year.
Tips: "We also contribute time, money and our energies to promoting our craft in other functions. Meetings are held on the first Tuesday of each month at 6:45 p.m."

*ASSOCIATED MALE CHORUSES OF AMERICA, Box 106, RR1, Dunsford, Ontario K0M 1L0 **Canada**. Executive Secretary: William J. Bates. Estab. 1924. Serves musicians and male choruses of US and Canada. "Our members are people from all walks of life. Many of our directors and accompanists are professional musicians. Age ranges from high school students to members in their 70's and 80's. Potential members must be supportive of Male Chorus Singing. They do not have to belong to a chorus to join. We have both Associate and Affiliate memberships. Our purpose is to further the power of music, not only to entertain and instruct, but to uplift the spirit, arouse the finest instincts, and develop the soul of man. With so little male chorus music being written, we as a 2,000 member organization provide a vehicle for songwriters, so that the music can be performed." Offers competitions, instruction, lectures, library, newsletter, performance opportunities, social outings and workshops. Applications accepted year-round. Membership fees are Regular Members: $4; Associate and Affiliate Members: $7.50; Student Members: $2; Life Members: $100 (one time fee).

*ATLANTIC CANADIAN COMPOSERS ASSOCIATION, 214 Jones St., Moncton, New Brunswick E1C 6K3 **Canada**. (506)388-4224. Member at Large: Richard Gibson. Estab. 1980. "Our membership consists of people who write 'serious' (as opposed to commercial, pop, jazz, industrial) music. An applicant must be resident in one of the four Atlantic Canadian provinces and must be able to demonstrate a fluency with a variety of genres of notated music. An applicant must be prepared to submit five completed scores. The main purpose of this organization is the promotion of the music of our membership." Offers performance opportunities. Applications accepted year-round. Membership fee is thirty-five Canadian dollars.

*BRITISH LIBRARY NATIONAL SOUND ARCHIVE, 29 Exhibition Rd., London SW7 2AS **England**. (071)589-6603. Fax: (071)823-8970. Serves songwriters, musicians and anyone interested in recorded sound. Estab. 1955. "We answer the needs of researchers interested in all aspects of recorded sound. The primary value of our organization is the availability to listeners of recordings of all kinds (900,000 discs, 125,000 tapes, etc.)." Offers lectures, library and listening facilities. "The National Sound Archive is a unique resource center for the study of all kinds of music, recorded speech and theater, and wildlife sounds; it is a prime source for broadcasters, filmmakers, theater companies, advertising agencies, the record industry and the general public. The Archive holds copies of almost all United Kingdom current commercial records (including compact discs), as well as a vast catalogue of recordings from as early as the 1890s. The Archive houses a wide range of broadcast materials, including duplicates of BBC Sound Archives recordings. There are also thousands of hours of unique unpublished recordings and a growing collection of videos. The National Sound Archive is one of the most extensive sources of information about recording in the world. It is up to our users to exploit this resource in whatever way suits their needs. Access can also be arranged at the Archive to over 90,000 musical scores. Use of the library and information service are free."

BROADCAST MUSIC, INC. (BMI), 320 W. 57th St., New York NY 10019. (212)586-2000; 8730 Sunset Blvd., Los Angeles CA 90069, (310)659-9109; and 10 Music Square E., Nashville TN 37203, (615)291-6700. President and CEO: Frances W. Preston. Senior Vice President, Performing Rights: Del R. Bryant. Vice President, California: Rick Riccobono. Vice President, Nashville: Roger Sovine. BMI is a performing rights organization representing over 140,000 songwriters, composers and music publishers in all genres of music, including pop, rock, country, R&B, rap, jazz, Latin, gospel and contemporary classical. "Applicants must have written a musical composition, alone or in collaboration with other writers, which is commercially published, recorded or otherwise likely to be performed. Purpose: BMI acts on behalf of its songwriters, composers and music publishers by insuring payment for performance of their works through the collection of licensing fees from radio stations, broadcast and cable TV stations, hotels, nightclubs, aerobics centers and other users of music. This income is distributed to the writers and publishers in the form of royalty payments, based on how the music is used. BMI also undertakes intensive lobbying efforts in Washington D.C. on behalf of its affiliates, seeking to protect their performing rights through the enactment of new legislation and enforcement of current copyright law. In addition, BMI helps aspiring songwriters develop their skills through various workshops, seminars and competitions it sponsors throughout the country." Applications accepted year-round. There is no membership fee for songwriters; a one-time fee of $50 is required to affiliate a publishing company.

CALIFORNIA COUNTRY MUSIC ASSOCIATION, Box 5037, Anaheim CA 92814-1037. (714)991-7311. Executive Director: Tom Potts. Serves songwriters, musicians and country music fans and business. "Our members are of all ages, from the very young to the very old. They come from a wide variety of vocations, talents and professions. Their common interest is country music. A preferred geographic location would be the state of California, although a member may live out of state. All musicians, artists, and songwriters are eligible to compete in our chapter and statewide award shows, as long they have not charted on a major chart list in the last two years. The main purpose of this organization is to support, sponsor, organize, inform, and promote all facets of country music and entertainment. Our organization works together with the aspiring artist. We recognize, support and award their talents throughout the state and within our chapters. This organization cooperates with and supports country music radio stations, country music publications, charitable organizations, and the country music industry. We are a non-profit organization and our motto is 'God, country and country music.' Country music people are our number one concern." Offers competitions, instruction, lectures, newsletter, performance opportunities, social outings, workshops, showcases and award shows. Applications accepted year-round. Membership fee is $20/year.

CANADA COUNCIL/CONSEIL DES ARTS DU CANADA, P.O. Box 1047, Ottawa, Ontario K1P 5V8 **Canada**. (613)598-4365. Information Officer: Lise Rochon. Estab. 1957. The Council provides a wide range of grants and services to professional Canadian musicians and music organizations. To apply for grants, artists must be Canadian citizens or permanent residents of Canada. Professional songwriters and musicians may apply to the *Grants to Artists Program* to pursue their own personal and creative development. There are specific deadline dates for the various fields of music. Call or write for more details.

CANADIAN ACADEMY OF RECORDING ARTS & SCIENCES (CARAS), 3rd Floor, 124 Merton St., Toronto, Ontario M4S 2Z2 **Canada**. (416)485-3135. Fax: (416)485-4978. Executive Director: Daisy C. Falle. Serves songwriters and musicians. Membership is open to all employees (including support staff) in broadcasting and record companies, as well as producers, personal managers, recording artists, recording engineers, arrangers, composers, music publishers, album designers, promoters, talent and booking agents, record retailers, rack jobbers, distributors, recording studios and other music industry related professions (on approval). Applicants must be affiliated with the Canadian recording industry. Offers newsletter, performance opportunities, Canadian artist record discount program, nomination and voting privileges for Juno Awards and discount tickets to Juno awards show. Also discount on trade magazines and complimentary Juno Awards CD. "CARAS strives to foster the development of the Canadian music and recording industries and to contribute toward higher artistic standards." Applications accepted year-round. Membership fee is $45/year. Applications accepted from individuals only, not from companies or organizations.

*CANADIAN AMATEUR MUSICIANS/MUSICIENS AMATEURS DU CANADA (CAMMAC), #8224, 1751 Richardson, Montreal, Quebec H3K 1G6 **Canada**. (514)932-8755. Fax: (514)932-9811. Administrative Assistant: Joy-Anne Murphy. Estab. 1953. Serves amateur musicians of all ages and skill levels. "CAMMAC is a nonprofit organization that provides opportunities for amateur musicians of all ages and levels to develop their skills in a supportive and non-competitive environment, and to enjoy making music together. We provide contact with musicians of varying levels and interests—the perfect testing ground for any number of styles and challenges. We also offer composition workshops at our summer camp at Lake McDonald (Arundel, Québec)." Offers performance opportunities, library, instruction, newsletter, workshops and summer camp (families and individuals). Applications accepted year-round. Membership fee is Adult: $35, Family: $50, Student and Senior: $20, Group $50 plus $2/ member for library borrowing privileges.

CANADIAN COUNTRY MUSIC ASSOCIATION (CCMA), Suite 127, 3800 Steeles Ave. W., Woodbridge, Ontario L4L 4G9 **Canada**. (416)739-5014. Executive Director: Sheila Hamilton. Estab. 1976. Members are songwriters, musicians, producers, radio station personnel, managers, booking agents and others. Offers newsletter, workshops, performance opportunities and annual awards. "Through our newsletters and conventions we offer a means of meeting and associating with artists and others in the industry. During our workshops or seminars (Country Music Week), we include a songwriters' seminar. The CCMA is a federally chartered, nonprofit organization, dedicated to the promotion and development of Canadian country music throughout Canada and the world and to providing a unity of purpose for the Canadian country music industry." Send for application.

CANADIAN MUSICAL REPRODUCTION RIGHTS AGENCY LIMITED (CMRRA), Suite 320, 56 Wellesley St. W., Toronto, Ontario M5S 2S3 **Canada**. (416)926-1966. Fax: (416)926-7521. President: David A. Basskin. Estab. 1975. Serves songwriters and copyright owners or administrators of musical compositions (composers, authors and music publishers). "Eligibility requirements a songwriter/musician must meet for membership: must own the copyright or have administration rights in one or more musical compositions for the territory of Canada. The organization's main purpose is to license the reproduction rights of copyrighted musical works and to collect and distribute the royalties collected to the rights owners on the basis of the licenses. The primary value in this organization for a songwriter is the administration and protection of their copyrights and the collection of royalties due to them." Applications accepted year-round. "There are no membership fees or annual dues. For administering the copyright owner's work, CMRRA retains a 5% commission on revenues collected for mechanical rights and 10% for synchronization rights. Where money is received from a foreign society, CMRRA distributes it to its member clients at a 3% charge. CMRRA is the principal mechanical rights agency in Canada. It was primarily responsible for securing passage of amendments to Canada's *Copyright Act* abolishing the compulsory license and statutory rate for songs used by record companies. This action permitted the royalty rate for recorded songs to rise for the first time in over 64 years."

CONNECTICUT SONGWRITERS ASSOCIATION, Box 1292, Glastonbury CT 06033. (203)659-8992. Executive Director: Don Donegan. "We are an educational, nonprofit organization dedicated to improving the art and craft of original music. Founded in 1979 by Don Donegan, CSA has grown to become one of the best known songwriter's associations in the country. Membership in the CSA admits you to 16-24 seminars/workshops/song critique sessions per year at 5 locations throughout Connecticut. Out of state members may mail in songs for critique at our meetings. Noted professionals deal with all aspects of the craft and business of music including lyric writing, music theory, music technology, arrangement and production, legal and business aspects, performance techniques, song analysis and recording techniques. CSA also offers showcases and concerts which are open to the public and designed to give artists a venue for performing their original material for an attentive, listening audience. CSA benefits have helped United Cerebral Palsy, Muscular Dystrophy, group homes, hospice, world hunger, libraries, nature centers, community centers and more. CSA shows encompass ballads to bluegrass and Bach to rock. Our monthly newsletter, *Connecticut Songsmith*, offers free classified advertising for members, and has been edited and published by Bill Pere since 1980. Annual dues are $40; senior citizen and full time students $20; Organizations $80. Memberships are fully tax deductible as business expenses or as charitable contributions to the extent allowed by law."

COUNTRY MUSIC SHOWCASE INTERNATIONAL, INC., Box 368, Carlisle IA 50047. (515)989-3676 or 989-3748. President: Harold L. Luick. Vice President: Barbara A. Lancaster. "We are a nonprofit, educational performing arts organization for songwriters, recording artists and entertainers. The organization showcases songwriters at different seminars and workshops held at the request of its members in many different states across the nation. It also showcases recording artists/entertainer members at many Fair Association showcases held across the United States. When a person becomes a member they receive a membership card, newsletters, an educational information packet (about songwriting/ entertainment business), a question and answer service by mail or phone, a song evaluation and critique service, info on who's looking for song material, songwriters who are willing to collaborate, and songwriting contests. Members can submit 1 song per month for a critique. We offer good constructive criticism and honest opinions. We maintain that a songwriter, recording artist or entertainer should associate himself with professional people and educators that know more about the business of music than they do; otherwise, they cannot reach their musical goals." Supporting Songwriter membership donation and Supporting Recording Artist/Entertainer membership donation is $40/year; Supporting Band, Group or music related business membership donation is $60/year. For free information, brochure or membership application send SASE to the above address.

DALLAS SONGWRITERS ASSOCIATION, 2932 Dyer St., Dallas TX 75205. (214)750-0916. President: Barbara McMillen. Estab. 1988. Serves songwriters and lyricists of Dallas/Ft. Worth metroplex. Members are adults ages 18-65, Dallas/Ft. Worth area songwriters/lyricists who are 18 years and older who are or aspire to be professionals. Purpose is to provide songwriters an opportunity to meet other songwriters, share information, find co-writers and support each other through group discussions at monthly meetings; to have their songs heard and critiqued by peers and professionals by playing cassettes and providing an open mike at monthly meetings and by offering contests judged by publishers; to meet other music business professionals by inviting guest speakers to monthly meetings and the Dallas Songwriters Seminar which is held annually each April; to learn more about the craft of songwriting and the business of music by presenting mini-workshops at each monthly meeting. "We offer a chance for the songwriter to learn from peers and industry professionals and an opportunity to belong to a supportive group environment to encourage the individual to continue his/her songwriting endeavors." Offers competitions, field trips, instruction, lectures, newsletter, performance opportunities, social outings, workshops and seminars. "Our members are eligible to join the Southwest Community Credit Union and for discounts at several local music stores and seminars." Applications accepted year-round. Membership fee is $35 US, $45 Foreign. When inquiring by phone, please leave complete mailing address and phone number where you can be reached day and night.

THE DRAMATISTS GUILD, INC., 234 W. 44th St., New York NY 10036. (212)398-9366. Executive Director: Andrew B. Farber. The Dramatists Guild is the professional association of playwrights, composers and lyricists, with more than 7,000 members across the country. All theater writers, whether produced or not, are eligible for Associate membership ($65 a year); those who are engaged in a drama-related field but are not a playwright are eligible for Subscribing membership ($65 a year); students enrolled in writing degree programs at colleges or universities are eligible for Student membership ($25 a year); writers who have been produced on Broadway, Off-Broadway or on the main stage of a resident theater are eligible for Active membership ($100 a year). The Guild offers its members the following activities and services: use of the Guild's contracts (including the Approved Production Contract for Broadway, the Off-Broadway contract, the LORT contract, the collaboration agreements for both musicals and drama, the 99 Seat Theatre Plan contract, the Small Theatre contract and the Underlying Agreements contract; advice on all theatrical contracts including Broadway, Off-Broadway, regional, showcase, Equity-waiver, dinner theater and collaboration contracts); a nationwide toll-free number for all members with business or contract questions or problems; advice and information on a wide spectrum of issues affecting writers; free and/or discounted ticket service; symposia led by experienced professionals in major cities nationwide; access to two health insurance programs and a group term life insurance plan; a reference library; a spacious and elegant meeting room which can accommodate up to 50 people for readings and auditions on a rental basis to members; and a Committee for Women. The Guild's publications are: *The Dramatists Guild Quarterly*, a journal which contains articles on all aspects of the theater and, in the spring and summer editions, an annual marketing directory with up-to-date information on agents, grants, producers, playwriting contests, conferences and workshops; and *The Dramatists Guild Newsletter*, issued 8 times a year, with announcements of all Guild activities and more immediate information of interest to dramatists.

*FEDERATION INTERNATIONAL DES ORGANISATIONS DE FESTIVALS (F.I.D.O.F.), #105, 4230 Stansbury Ave., Sherman Oaks CA 91423. (818)789-7569. Fax: (818)784-9141. Secretary General: Prof. Armando Moreno. Estab. 1967. Serves songwriters, musicians, festival and events managers and organizers. Members are of all ages, from 62 countries around the world. "We coordinate dates of festivals, and coordinate the interests of all involved with festivals and cultural events (artists, songwriters, record, TV, video, publishing and other companies from around the world, as well as the press)." Offers competitions, field trips, instruction, lectures, library, newsletter, performance opportunities, social outings, workshops, annual meetings on international and national levels, exhibition opportunities and free world-wide promotion through F.I.D.O.F.'s Monthly Bulletins. Applications accepted year-round. Annual membership fee is $200.

THE FOLK ALLIANCE, P.O. Box 5010, Chapel Hill NC 27514. (919)542-3957. Contact: Art Menius. Estab. 1989. Serves songwriters, musicians and folk music and dance organizations. Members are organizations and individuals involved in traditional and contemporary folk music and dance in the US and Canada. Members must be active in the field of folk music (singers/songwriters in any genre — blues, bluegrass, Celtic, Latino, old-time, etc.). The Folk Alliance serves members through education, advocacy, field development, professional development, networking and showcases. Offers newsletter, performance opportunities, social outings, workshops and "database of members, organizations, presenters, folk radio, etc." Applications accepted year-round. Membership fee is $35/year/individual (voting); $75-350/year for organizational.
Tips: The Folk Alliance hosts its annual conference in late February at different locations in the US and Canada. 1994 site: Boston, MA; 1995: Portland, OR; 1996: Washington, DC. "We *do not* offer songwriting contests."

FORT BEND SONGWRITERS ASSOCIATION, P.O. Box 1273, Richmond TX 77406-1273. (713)665-4676. Info line: 713-CONCERT (Access Code FBSA). Contact: Membership Director. Estab. 1991. Serves "any person, amateur or professional, interested in songwriting or music. Our members write pop, rock, country, rockabilly, gospel, R&B, children's music and musical plays." Open to all, regardless of geographic location or professional status. The FBSA provides its membership with help to perfect their songwriting crafts by conducting workshops, seminars, publishing a monthly newsletter and holding songwriting and vocal performance competitions and showcases. The FBSA provides instruction for beginning writers and publishing and artist tips for the more accomplished writer."

Offers competitions, field trips, instruction, lectures, newsletter, performance opportunities, workshops, mail-in critiques and collaboration opportunities. Applications accepted year-round. Membership fees are: Regular: $35; Renewals; $25; Family or Band: $45; Renewals: $35; Associate: $20; Business: $150; and Lifetime: $250. For more information send SASE.

GOSPEL MUSIC ASSOCIATION, 7 Music Circle North, Nashville TN 37203. (615)242-0303. Membership Coordinator: Martha Stoughton. Estab. 1964. Serves songwriters, musicians and anyone directly involved in or who supports gospel music. Professional members include advertising agencies, musicians, agents/managers, composers, retailers, music publishers, print media, broadcast media, and other members of the recording industry. Associate members include supporters of gospel music and those whose involvement in the industry does not provide them with income. The primary purpose of the GMA is to promote the industry of gospel and Christian music, and provide professional development series for industry members. Offers library, newsletter, performance opportunities and workshops. Applications accepted year-round. Membership fee is $50/year (professional); and $25/year (associate).

THE GUILD OF INTERNATIONAL SONGWRITERS & COMPOSERS, Sovereign House, 12 Trewartha Rd., Praa Sands, Penzance, Cornwall TR20 9ST **England**. Phone: (0736)762826. Fax: (0736)763328. Secretary: C.A. Jones. Serves songwriters, musicians, record companies, music publishers, etc. "Our members are amateur and professional songwriters and composers, musicians, publishers, independent record publishers, studio owners and producers. Membership is open to all persons throughout the world of any age and ability, from amateur to professional. The Guild gives advice and services relating to the music industry. A free magazine is available upon request with an SAE or 3x IRC's. We provide contact information for artists, record companies, music publishers, industry organizations; free copyright service; *Songwriting & Composing Magazine*; and many additional free services." Applications accepted year-round. Annual dues are £20 in the U.K.; £25 in E.E.C. countries; £25 overseas. (Subscriptions in pounds sterling only).

HAWAIIAN ISLANDS COUNTRY MUSIC, P.O. Box 75148, Honolulu HI 96836. Owner: Maitai. Estab. 1977. Serves songwriters, musicians and entertainers. Members are anyone who loves music. Main purpose is to promote the emerging aspiring artist. Offers competitions, lectures, performance opportunities, workshops and promotion/management. Applications are accepted year-round. Membership fee is $20.

IDAHO SONGWRITERS ASSOCIATION, P.O. Box 382, Firth ID 83236-0382. President: Harry Nash. Secretary/Treasurer: Kenny Williams. Estab. 1991. "A nonprofit organization designed to promote Idaho songwriters by showing the world that Idaho has more than great potatoes, we have great talent too." Offers workshops, seminars, contests and showcases. ISA publishes a monthly newsletter and sponsors several songwriting contests a year. We are working to establish a network of connections in the music business to help members market their material. We offer a Partners Finder service for writers needing collaborators and a critique/review service for members' songs. Annual membership fees: Full membership $30, Limited membership $15 (Student and military full memberships $5 off). Trial membership $8 for 3 months. For more information send large SASE to the listed address.

*INDEPENDENT MUSICIANS CO-OP, P.O. Box 571205, Murray UT 84157. (801)268-0174. President: Mark McLelland. Estab. 1992. "Our members range from young to old, from interested listener to accomplished songwriter/performer. Prospective members must be living in the United States, have a love for new music and be willing to help promote the independent music market. The IMC is a network sales organization dedicated to selling and promoting independent music product. Our members help to promote and sell member tapes and CDs to friends, family and associates. Our goal is to create a mid level market for the independent artist/songwriter. Songwriters will have new chances at release, as our independent artists finally have a market to sell their product. We are creating a 'middle class' in the music industry. More releases will translate into more songwriters being paid. Call or write for free information." Offers performance opportunities, newsletter and product distribution. Applications accepted year-round. Membership fee is $40 1st year, $30 year renewal.

INTERNATIONAL COMPUTER MUSIC ASSOCIATION, 2040 Polk, San Francisco CA 94109. (817)566-2235. President: Larry Austin. Estab. 1978. Serves songwriters, musicians and computer music specialists. Membership includes a broad spectrum of composers, scientists, educators and hobbyists. The function of this organization is "to serve the interests of computer music practitioners and sponsor annual computer music conferences." Primary value in this organization is "music technology information." Offers lectures, performance opportunities, workshops and newsletters to members. Applications are accepted throughout the year. Membership fee is $50/year (individual); $15/year (student); $150/year (nonprofit organization); and $100/year (sustaining).

INTERNATIONAL LEAGUE OF WOMEN COMPOSERS, Box 670, Southshore Rd., Pt. Peninsula, Three Mile Bay NY 13693. (315)649-5086. Chairperson: Elizabeth Hayden Pizer. Estab. 1975. Serves women composers of serious concert music. "Members are women composers and professional musicians, music libraries, institutions and organizations. Full composer membership is open to any woman composer whose seriousness of intent has been demonstrated in one or more of the following ways: (1) by any single degree in composition (if the degree is not recent, some evidence of recent activity should be offered); (2) by holding a current teaching position at the college level, (3) by having had a serious work published; (4) by having had a work performed at a recognized symposium or by professional musicans; or (5) by submitting two compositions to the Executive Board for review, exhibiting competence in scoring for chamber ensemble. Admission is governed neither by stylistic nor regional bias; however, primarily educational music is not considered sufficient. The ILWC is devoted to creating and expanding opportunties for, and documenting information about, women composers of serious music. This organization will help composers stay informed of various career/performance opportunties plus allow them to participate in projects spear-headed by ILWC." Offers competitions, newsletter and performance opportunities. Applications accepted year-round. Annual dues are $25 for individuals; $15 for students/senior citizens; $35 for institutions/organizations.

INTERNATIONAL SONGWRITERS ASSOCIATION LTD., 37b New Cavendish St., London WI **England**. (071)486 5353. Membership Department: Anna M. Sinden. Serves songwriters and music publishers. "The ISA headquarters is in Limerick City, Ireland, and from there it provides its members with assessment services, copyright services, legal and other advisory services and an investigations service, plus a magazine for one yearly fee. Our members are songwriters in more than 50 countries worldwide, of all ages. There are no qualifications, but applicants under 18 are not accepted. We provide information and assistance to professional or semi-professional songwriters. Our publication, *Songwriter*, which was founded in 1967, features detailed exclusive interviews with songwriters and music publishers, as well as directory information of value to writers." Offers competitions, instruction, library and newsletter. Applications accepted year-round. Membership fee for European writers is £19.95; for non-European writers, it is US $30.

KERRVILLE MUSIC FOUNDATION INC., P.O. Box 1466, Kerrville TX 78029-1466. (210)257-3600. Executive Director: Rod Kennedy. The Kerrville Music Foundation was "founded in 1975 for the recognition and promotion of original music and has awarded more than $25,000 to musicians over the last 21 years through open competitions designed to encourage excellence in songwriting. Annually, 40 new folk finalists are selected to sing their two songs entered and six new folk Award Winners are invited to share 20 minutes of their songs at the Kerrville Folk Festival with one or more selected to perform on the main stage the next year." Opportunities include: The New Folk Concerts for Emerging Songwriters at the Kerrville Folk Festival.

KEYBOARD TEACHERS ASSOCIATION INTERNATIONAL, INC., 361 Pin Oak Lane, Westbury NY 11590-1941. (516)333-3236. President: Dr. Albert DeVito. Estab. 1963. Serves musicians and music dealers/keyboards. "Our members are music teachers, music dealers and music publishers, especially keyboard/piano/organ. Active members must be teachers. We also have Friend Members who are not teachers. The main purpose of this organization is to keep keyboard teachers informed of what is happening in their field, student evaluation, teacher certification, etc. The primary value in this organization for a songwriter is being in contact with keyboard players, publishers and dealers." Offers evaluations of students, instruction, newsletter and workshops. Applications accepted year-round. Membership fee is $25.
Tips: "Each student in auditions receives a certificate according to grade level. It is a great experience for them with the encouragement given."

*KNOXVILLE SONGWRITERS ASSOCIATION, P.O. Box 603, Knoxville TN 37901. (615)933-4488. Coordinator: Sara Williams. Estab. 1982. Serves songwriters of all ages. "Members must be interested in learning the craft of songwriting. Not only a learning organization but a support group of songwriters who want to learn what to do with their song after it has been written. We open doors for aspiring writers. The primary benefit of membership is to supply information to the writer on how to write a song (eight members have received major cuts.)" Offers competitions, instruction, lectures, library, newsletter, performance opportunities, evaluation services and workshops. Applications accepted year-round. Memberships fee is $30 per year.

THE LAS VEGAS SONGWRITERS ASSOCIATION, P.O. Box 42683, Las Vegas NV 89116-0683. (702)459-9107. President: Betty Kay Miller. Estab. 1980. "We are an educational, nonprofit organization dedicated to improving the art and craft of the songwriter. We offer quarterly newsletters, monthly general information meetings, workshops three times a month and seminars held quarterly with professionals in the music business." Dues are $20 per year. Members must be at least 18 years of age.

THE LOS ANGELES SONGWRITERS SHOWCASE (LASS), Box 93759, Hollywood CA 90093. (213)467-7823. Fax: (213)467-0531. Showcase Hotline: (213)467-0533. Co-Directors: Len H. Chandler, Jr. and John Braheny. General Manager: Stephanie Perom. Membership Director: Josh Bernard. "The Los Angeles Songwriters Showcase (LASS) is a nonprofit service organization for songwriters, founded in 1971 and sponsored by Broadcast Music, Inc. (BMI). LASS also provides counseling and conducts classes and seminars. At our weekly Showcase, we feature Cassette Roulette™, in which a different publisher every week critiques songs submitted on cassette that night; and Pitch-A-Thon™, in which a different producer or record company executive every week screens songs for his/her current recording projects and/or acts for their labels. The Showcase takes place every Tuesday night in front of an audience of songwriters and the music industry guests; there is no prescreening necessary. LASS also produces an annual Songwriters Expo in October." General membership: $120/year. Professional membership: $150/year. Included in both "general" and "professional" membership benefits are: priorities to have tapes listened to first at Pitch-A-Thon™ sessions; discounts on numerous items such as blank tapes, books, demo production services, tapes of Songwriters Expo sessions and other seminars; discounts on admission to the weekly showcase; career counseling (in person or by phone) and a subscription to the LASS 'Songwriters Musepaper," a magazine for songwriters (also available to non-members for $19 bulk rate/$29 first class). Professional membership is available to general members by invitation or audition only and features special private pitch-a-thon sessions and referrals.
Tips: "Members may submit tapes to the weekly Cassette Roulette™ and Pitch-A-Thon™ sessions from anywhere in the world and be sent the recorded comments of the industry guests for that week. Most of the record companies, publishers and producers will not accept unsolicited material, so our Tuesday night showcase is the best way to get material heard by these music industry professionals."

LOUISIANA SONGWRITERS ASSOCIATION, P.O. Box 80425, Baton Rouge LA 70898-0425. (504)924-0804. President: Janice Calvert. Vice Presidents, Membership: Robin H. Tanner/Patricia Allemand. Serves songwriters. "LSA has been organized to educate songwriters in all areas of their trade, and promote the art of songwriting in Louisiana. We are of course honored to have a growing number of songwriters from other states join LSA and fellowship with us. LSA membership is open to people interested in songwriting, regardless of age, musical ability, musical preference, ethnic background, etc. One of our goals is to work together as a group to establish a line of communication with industry professionals in order to develop a music center in our area of the country. LSA offers competitions, lectures, library, newsletter, directory, marketing, performance opportunities, workshops, discounts on various music related books and magazines, discounts on studio time, and we are developing a service manual that will contain information on music related topics, such as copyrighting, licensing, etc." General membership dues are $25/year.

LOUISVILLE AREA SONGWRITERS' COOPERATIVE, P.O. Box 16, Pewee Valley KY 40056. President: Paul M. Moffett. Estab. 1986. Serves songwriters and musicians of all ages, races and musical genres. "The Louisville Area Songwriters' Cooperative is a nonprofit corporation dedicated to the development and promotion of songwriting. Membership is open to any person in the Louisville area (and beyond) who is interested in songwriting. We offer a songwriter showcase 4 times/year, a series of tapes of songs by members of the cooperative, meetings, speakers, the LASC newsletter, a songwriting contest, referral for collaboration, promotion and song plugging to local, regional and national recording artists and occasional bookings for performing members." Applications accepted year-round. Dues are $25/year.

MEMPHIS SONGWRITERS' ASSOCIATION, 1857 Capri St., Memphis TN 38117. (901)763-1957. President: Juanita Tullos. Estab. 1973. Serves songwriters, musicians and singers. Age limit: 18 years and up. No specific location requirement. Must be interested in music and have the desire to learn the basics of commercial songwriting. "We instruct potential songwriters on how to structure their songs and correctly use lyrics, commercially. We critique their material. We help them obtain copyrights and give them a chance to expose their material to the right people, such as publishers and A&R people. We hold monthly workshops, instructing members in the Commercial Music Techniques of songwriting. We have an annual Songwriters Showcase where their material is performed live for people in the publishing and recording professions and the general public. We have an annual Shindig, for bands and musicians and an annual seminar." Offers competitions, instruction, lectures, newsletter, performance opportunities and workshops. Applications accepted year-round. Annual dues: $25.
Tips: "Our association was founded in 1973. We have a charter, by laws and a board of directors (8). All directors are professionals in the music field. We are a nonprofit organization. No salaries are paid. Our directors donate their services to our association. We have a president, vice president, secretary, treasurer, music instructor and consultant, production manager, assistant production manager and executive director."

*MICHIGAN SONGWRITERS ASSOCIATION, 28935 Flanders Dr., Warren MI 48093. (313)771-8145. President: Terri Senecal. Estab. 1990. Serves songwriters, musicians, artists and beginners. "Members are from NY, IL, MI, OH, etc. with interests in country, pop, rock and gospel. The main purpose of this organization is to educate songwriters, artists and musicians in the business of music." MSA offers performance opportunities, evaluation services, instruction, newsletter and workshops. Applications accepted year-round. Membership fee is $35 a year, $50 for people who have cut a record!
Tips: "To be educated in this field is the most important thing in your career; without any knowledge you can bet you will be used."

MIDWESTERN SONGWRITERS ASSOCIATION, 91 N. Terrace Ave., Columbus OH 43204. (614)274-2169. President: Al VanHoose. Estab. 1978. Serves songwriters. All interested songwriters are eligible—either amateur or professional residing in the midwestern region of US. Main purpose is the education of songwriters in the basics of their craft. Offers competitions, instruction, lectures, library, newsletter, weekly tip sheet, social outings and workshops. Applications accepted year-round. Membership fee is $20 per year, pro-rated at $5 per calendar quarter (March, June, September, December). "We are offering membership to band members at $30 per year."
Tips: "We do not refer songwriters to publishers or artists—we are strictly an educational organization."

MISSOURI SONGWRITERS ASSOCIATION, INC., 693 Green Forest Dr., Fenton MO 63026. (314)343-6661. President: John G. Nolan, Jr. Serves songwriters and musicians. No eligibility requirements. "The MSA (a non-profit organization founded in 1979) is a tremendously valuable resource for songwriting and music business information outside of the major music capitals. Only with the emphasis on education can the understanding of craft and the utilization of skill be fully realized and in turn become the foundation for the ultimate success of MSA members. Songwriters gain support from their fellow members when they join the MSA, and the organization provides 'strength in numbers' when approaching music industry professionals." As a means toward its goals the organization offers: (1) an extremely informative newsletter; (2) Annual Songwriting Contest; prizes include: CD and/or cassette release of winners, publishing contract, free musical merchandise and equipment, free recording studio time, plaque or certificate; (3) Annual St. Louis Original Music Celebration featuring live performances, recognition, showcase, radio simulcast, videotape for later broadcast and awards presentation; (4) seminars on such diverse topics as creativity, copyright law, brainstorming, publishing, recording the demo, craft and technique, songwriting business, collaborating, etc.; (5) workshops including song evaluation, establishing a relationship with publishers, hit song evaluations, the writer versus the writer/artist, the marriage of collaborators, the business side of songwriting, lyric craft, etc; (6) services such as collaborators referral, publisher contacts, consultation, recording discounts, musicians referral, library, etc. "The Missouri Songwriters Association belongs to its members and what a member puts into the organization is returned dynamically in terms of information, education, recognition, support, camaraderie, contacts, tips, confidence, career development, friendships and professional growth." Applications accepted year-round. Tax deductible dues are $50/year.

MUSIC MILL/SOURCE, (formerly Music Mill), P.O. Box 1341, Lowell MA 01853. (508)686-5791. Chairman: Peter Keyes Burwen. Estab. 1985. Serves songwriters, musicians, producers and engineers. Members are active in New England's music industry 18 and over. Purpose is to "act as a 'networking clearing house' for the regional music/entertainment industry and to provide economic opportunities and promotion for artists and songwriters." Publishes the *Music Mill Source* magazine. Membership is free. Contact for membership information. "The Music Mill is New England's only central communication link within the regional industry."

NASHVILLE SONGWRITERS ASSOCIATION INTERNATIONAL (NSAI), 15 Music Square W., Nashville TN 37203. (615)256-3354. Executive Director: Pat Rogers. Purpose: a not-for-profit service organization for both aspiring and professional songwriters in all fields of music. Membership: Spans the United States and several foreign countries. Songwriters may apply in one of four annual categories: Active ($55—for songwriters who have at least one song contractually signed to a publisher affiliated with ASCAP, BMI or SESAC); Associate ($55—for songwriters who are not yet published or for anyone wishing to support songwriters); Student ($25—for full-time college students or for students of an accredited senior high school); Professional ($100—for songwriters who derive their primary source of income from songwriting or who are generally recognized as such by the professional songwriting community). Membership benefits: music industry information and advice, song evaluations by mail, quarterly newsletter, access to industry professionals through weekly Nashville workshop and several annual events, regional workshops, use of office facilities, discounts on books and blank audio cassettes, discounts on NSAI's three annual instructional/awards events. There are also "branch" workshops of NSAI. Workshops must meet certain standards and are accountable to NSAI. Interested coordinators may apply to NSAI.

NATIONAL ACADEMY OF POPULAR MUSIC—SONGWRITERS' HALL OF FAME, 26th Floor, 885 Second Ave., New York NY 10017-2201. (212)319-1444. Projects Director: Bob Leone. Estab. 1969. The main purpose of the organization is to honor great songwriters and support a Hall of Fame museum. Activities include: songwriting workshops, music industry panels and songwriter showcases. Offers newsletter. "Nowhere else on the East Coast can a writer learn more about the craft of songwriting, the business of songwriting and the world of songwriting, in general. And nowhere are there more opportunities to meet with all types of music industry professionals. Our activities are available to all of our members, so networking is inevitable." Membership is open to everyone, but consists primarily of songwriters, publishers and other music industry professionals who are eligible to vote in annual inductee election. Annual awards dinner. Applications accepted year-round. Membership fee is $25/ year.

NATIONAL ACADEMY OF SONGWRITERS (NAS), Suite 780, 6381 Hollywood Blvd., Hollywood CA 90028. (213)463-7178. Executive Director: Dan Kirkpatrick. A nonprofit organization dedicated to the education and protection of songwriters. Estab. 1973. Offers group legal discount; toll free hotline; *SongTalk* newspaper with songwriter interviews, collaborators network and tipsheet; plus Los Angeles based *SongTalk* seminar series featuring top names in songwriting, song evaluation workshops, song screening sessions, open mics and more. "We offer services to all songwriter members from street-level to superstar: substantial discount on books and tapes, song evaluation through the mail, health insurance program and mail in publisher pitches for members. Our services provide education in the craft and opportunities to market songs. The Academy is also active in addressing political issues affecting the profession. We produce the TV show *Salute to the American Songwriter*." Memberships: General—$75; Professional—$125; Gold—$200.

*NATIONAL ASSOCIATION FOR CAMPUS ACTIVITIES (NACA), 13 Harbison Way, Columbia SC 29212-3401. (803)732-6222. Director of Convention and Member Services: Louis A. Ross. Estab. 1960. Serves songwriters, musicians and all types of talent, school and university activities programs. "Our members are 1185 colleges and universities across the U.S. and Canada and more than 550 firms in entertainment or related services for the campus activities market. Songwriters/musicians must join NACA to participate in our conventions, conferences, listings, mailing lists, etc. or be handled by an agency that is a member of NACA. NACA provides assitance for member institutions to establish and produce quality campus activities programming by providing education, information and resources for students and staff to facilitate cooperative consumer efficiency and marketplace effectiveness. The primary value in this organization for a songwriter is: access to the college market for performance or personal appearance exposure; graphics assistance for one-stop shopping approach to posters, brochures, album design; advertising opportunities; outlet to agencies dealing with college market." Offers instruction, lectures, library, newsletter, performance opportunities, workshops, magazine, directory, conferences and conventions. Applications accepted May 1-April 30. National membership—$420 (annual); Regional membership—$210 (annual).

NATIONAL ASSOCIATION OF COLLEGE BROADCASTERS (NACB), 2nd Floor, 71 George St., Providence RI 02912-1824. (401)863-2225. Executive Director: Glenn Gutmacher. Estab. 1988. Serves musicians, college radio and TV stations, broadcast/communications departments and others interested in the college media market. Members also include students, faculty members, record companies and manufacturers who want to tap into the college media market. Any songwriter/musician may join under Professional Member status. The primary benefits of membership in NACB are the music reviews in every issue of our magazine (which features major label, independent and unsigned acts in equal proportion). It reaches the stations most likely to play new music (audio and video). Offers conferences, instruction, lectures, newsletter, performance opportunities, workshops, magazine subscription, satellite network, station handbook, consulting hotline, legal advice and more. On-line computer bulletin board lets you communicate with college stations and music industry pros across the country instantly. Applications accepted year-round. Membership fee is $30/year. "Low-cost advertising in our magazine and newsletter lets you expose your music to all 2,000 U.S. college radio and TV stations—more than other publications. Our mailing list of all 2,000 college stations (even more comprehensive than what the major labels use) is available for purchase at low cost, letting you target new music stations with releases, tour dates, etc."

*NATIONAL ASSOCIATION OF SCHOOLS OF MUSIC, Suite 21, 11250 Roger Bacon Dr., Reston VA 22090. (703)437-0700. Executive Director: Samuel Hope. Associate Director: Karen P. Moynahan. Estab. 1924. Serves songwriters, musicians and anyone interested in music in higher education. Individual Membership in NASM is open to everyone. The major responsibilities of the National Association of Schools of Music are the accreditation of post-secondary educational programs in music. In addition, NASM publishes books and reports, holds an annual meeting and other forums and provides information to the general public about educational programs in music. Offers a newsletter. Applications accepted year-round.

NATIONAL BAND AND CHORAL DIRECTORS HALL OF FAME, 519 N. Halifax Ave., Daytona Beach FL 32118. (904)252-0381. Director: Dr. Watie Riley Pickens. Estab. 1985. Serves band and choral directors. Members are "high school, college band and choral directors and other nationally recognized choral directors. The main purpose of our organization is to recognize, honor and promote the profession of Band and Choral Directors." Offers competitions; clearing house for band and choral directors. Applications are accepted by invitation only. There are no annual fees or dues.

*NATIONAL FEDERATION OF MUSIC CLUBS, 1336 N. Delaware St., Indianapolis IN 46202. (317)638-4003. Executive Secretary: Patricia Midgley. Estab. 1898. Serves songwriters and musicians. "All ages—in 3 categories: junior, student, senior (also affiliate groups). Must become a member in the state where you live. Opportunities to membership in local clubs in many areas. We promote good music in all areas, American music and American composers." Competitions and performances leading to awards in many categories, including composition, piano, instrumentalist, orchestra, conducting, vocal and handicapped. Offers competitions, lectures, newsletter, performance opportunities, social outings, workshops board meetings and conventions. Applications accepted year-round.

NATIONAL HIGH SCHOOL BAND INSTITUTE, 519 N. Halifax Ave., Daytona Beach FL 32118. (904)252-0381. Director: Dr. Watie Riley Pickens. Serves musicians. Members are high school band directors. "Professional high school band directors who have had national recognition are invited to submit their candidacy for nomination to the N.H.S.B.D. Hall of Fame. The main purpose of our organization is to recognize, honor and promote the profession of marching band directors." Offers competitions, instruction, lectures, library, newsletter, performance opportunities and National High School Band Directors Hall of Fame. Applications are accepted by invitation only. There are no annual fees or dues.

NATIONAL JAZZ SERVICE ORGANIZATION, P.O. Box 50152, Washington DC 20004-0152. (202)347-2604. Contact: John Murph, Willard Jenkins or Sara Warner. Estab. 1985. Serves songwriters, musicians, jazz educators and programs. Members include jazz musicians, enthusiasts, related organizations, schools, jazz media and state arts agencies. The NJSO is a not-for-profit public benefit corporation founded in 1985. The purpose of NJSO is to nuture the growth of and enhancement of jazz music as an American art form. The NJSO functions as a consultant and referral service for the jazz community. NJSO provides help through their Technical Assistance program. The songwriter would have untold access of resources available through our Technical Resource Program. His or her membership would further enhance the status of jazz as an art in the United States. Offers instruction, newsletter and Technical Assistance Program and subscription discounts to *Down Beat*, *The Wire*, *Insights on Jazz*, *Jazziz* and *Jazz Times*. Membership fee $30-500. "We have a comprehensive jazz database of presenters, radio stations, record companies, managers/booking, press contacts, NJSO members and musicians."

NATIONAL TRADITIONAL MUSIC ASSOCIATION, INC., P.O. 438, Walnut IA 51577. (712)784-3001. President: Robert Everhart. Estab. 1976. Serves songwriters and musicians. "Crosses all boundaries. They should be interested in traditional acoustic music." To preserve, perform and promote traditional acoustic music. Offers competitions, field trips, instruction, lectures, newsletter, performance opportunities, social outings and workshops. Applications accepted year-round. Membership fee is $12/year. **Tips:** Members also receive *Tradition* magazine 6 times a year.

*NETWORK OF LYRICISTS & SONGWRITERS, INC., P.O. Box 890425, Houston TX 77289-0425. (713)264-4330. President: Sybrina Durant. Estab. 1991. "NLS is made up of every age group and every skill level. Members are interested in every genre of music including but not limited to country, pop, rock, rap, gospel, symphonic, musical plays, alternative, techno and children's. Members do not need to know how to read or write music or play a musical instrument. Some of our most active volunteers are simply music lovers. Our membership is open to anyone in the world. We welcome amateurs and professional songwriters and performers as well as managers, attorneys, public relations pros, etc. The main purpose of the Network of Lyricists & Songwriters, Inc. is to educate, protect and promote lyricists, songwriters, producers and performers of original music. We are a nonprofit organization. We provide opportunities for songwriters to learn about all aspects of the music industry through our publication, *SONGNET* and through workshops and seminars. They also have plenty of opportunities to showcase their songs and themselves via performance showcases, open mikes, song contests and song pitch sessions." NLS offers competitions, lectures, performance opportunities, field trips, library, evaluation services, instruction, newsletter, workshops, song pitch sessions, locator service, collaborator list, vocal registry, song tips, music expo. Applications accepted year-round. "The regular yearly membership fee is $30. Senior citizens and students receive a discount of $10 off the regular fee. Cross memberships are strongly encouraged by offering members of any other arts related organization a yearly fee of $20. Proof of membership is required. Bands and families may join for $40. Business memberships are $120. Business members receive 12 reduced rate business card ads in *SONGNET*.

This is a savings of $60 off the regular rate. We conduct an annual songwriting competition. The grand prize is $500. The deadline for entry is November of each year. Last year, we received over 700 entries. Our aim is to help songwriters avoid 'song sharks' and other mistakes by teaching them how to better educate themselves about this very complex business."

NEW ENGLAND SONGWRITERS/MUSICIANS ASSOCIATION, 87 Lafayette Rd., Hampton Falls NH 03844. (800)448-3621 or (603)929-1128. Director: Peter C. Knickles. "Our organization serves all ages and all types of music. We focus primarily on the business of songwriting and overall, the music business. We have done various co-promotions of seminars with BMI in the past and may continue to do so in the future. Membership is free. Call to be on our mailing list and receive our free quarterly newsletter."

*THE NEW YORK SINGING TEACHERS' ASSOCIATION (NYSTA), Apt. 3B, 317 W. 93rd St., New York NY 10025. (212)662-9338. Register: Lawrence Chelsi. Estab. 1906. Serves vocalists. Voice teachers of all ages and backgrounds (Actives). Voice coaches, composers, conductors, language coaches, speech teachers and others who support singers, professional singers (all above—Associates). Arts education relating to singing. Conducts monthly meetings, awards prizes in three competitions; two for classical singers, one for music theater singers, gives awards to opera professionals for career excellence, holds public symposia on important musical/vocal topics annually. NYSTA provides experts in all fields of voice, allowing for colleagues to exchange information and ideas also offers lectures, performance opportunitites (limited), social outings and workshops meetings on specific topics. Applications accepted October through May. $30/year for active members, payable upon application. $25/year for associate members payable upon application. Must be US citizens, residing within 100 miles of New York City. The organization is the oldest and largest independent group of voice teachers in the United States (and maybe in the world).

*NORTH FLORIDA CHRISTIAN MUSIC WRITERS ASSOCIATION, P.O. Box 10394, Jacksonville FL 32247. (904)786-2372. President: Jackie Hand. Estab. 1974. "People from all walks of life who promote Christian music. Not just composers. Not just performers. But anyone who wants to share today's message in song with the world. NO age limit. Anyone interested in promoting Christian music is invited to join. If you are talented in several areas you might be asked to conduct a training session or workshop. Your expertise is wanted and needed by our group. The group's purpose is to serve God by using our God given talents and abilities and to assist our fellow songwriter, getting their music in the best possible form to be ready for whatever door God chooses to open for them concerning their music. Members works are included in songbooks published by our organization—also biographies." Offers competitions, performance opportunities, field trips, instruction, newletter, workshops and critique. Applications accepted year-round. Membership fee is $15 per year. $20 for husband/wife team.
Tips: "If you are serious about your craft, you need to fellowship with others who feel the same. A Christian songwriting organization is where you belong if you write Christian songs."

NORTHERN CALIFORNIA SONGWRITERS ASSOCIATION, Suite 211, 855 Oak Grove Ave., Menlo Park CA 94025. (415)327-8296. Fax: (415)327-0301, or (800)FORSONG (California and Nashville only). Executive Director: Ian Crombie. Serves songwriters and musicians. Estab. 1979. "Our 1,200 members are lyricists and composers from ages 16-80, from beginners to professional songwriters. No eligibility requirements. Our purpose is to provide the education and opportunities that will support our writers in creating and marketing outstanding songs. NCSA provides support and direction through local networking and input from Los Angeles and Nashville music industry leaders, as well as valuable marketing opportunities. Most songwriters need some form of collaboration, and by being a member they are exposed to other writers, ideas, critiquing, etc." Offers annual Northern California Songwriting Conference, "the largest event in northern California. This 2-day event held in September features 16 seminars, 50 screening sessions (over 1,200 songs listened to by industry professionals) and a sunset concert with hit songwriters performing their songs." Also offers monthly visits from major publishers, songwriting classes, seminars conducted by hit songwriters ("we sell audio tapes of our seminars—list of tapes available on request"), a monthly newsletter, monthly performance opportunities and workshops. Applications accepted year-round. Dues: $60/year; $30 extra for industry tipsheet (sent out on a quarterly basis).
Tips: "NCSA's functions draw local talent and nationally recognized names together. This is of a tremendous value to writers outside a major music center. We are developing a strong songwriting community in Northern California. We serve the San Jose, Monterey Bay, East Bay and San Francisco area and we have the support of some outstanding writers and publishers from both Los Angeles and Nashville. They provide us with invaluable direction and inspiration."

OHIO SONGWRITERS ASSOCIATION, 3682 W. 136th St., Cleveland OH 44111. (216)941-0461. (216)731-SONG. President: Jim Wunderle. Serves songwriters, musicians and related craftspeople (lyricists, arrangers, sound engineers, producers, vocalists, etc.). "Members of the OSA encompass young adults to senior citizens, at all ranges of musical and theoretical advancement, from professionals to amateurs who have written their first song and don't know what to do next. Prospective members are required to submit cassette tape with samples of their material, up to 3 pieces." Purpose is "to preserve and promote the creation of original music through education and opportunity." Services include marketing and copyright assistance, recording time, professional arrangement, lead sheets, career consultation, independent record production, music lessons, printing/artwork/logo designs, legal counsel with staff music attorneys, secretarial services, copyist, engineering/studio musicians/vocalists, practice space rental, collaboration pool, musicians referral service, competitions, lectures, library, newsletter, performance opportunities, educational/video tape rental library, numerous books on songwriting and the music industry at 15% discount to members; educational/audio cassettes on songwriting in the music industry. OSA has classes in songwriting and seminars on the art and craft of songwriting in the music business. Professional members may open an account with OSA and make monthly payments, interest-free, on their recording projects. Members are eligible for substantial discounts on studio time at Sessions, Inc., 16-track state of the art recording studio offering digital mixdowns." Applications accepted year-round. Annual membership fee is $40.

Tips: "The main goal of OSA is to help songwriters get their 'creative ideas' to the market place. OSA seminars have included nationally known songwriters, representatives of ASCAP and BMI, professional studio engineers, music industry professionals with proven track records, presenting invaluable information to amateur and professional songwriters. OSA has its own independent label, Hall of Fame of Records, Tapes and Compact Discs, and their own publishing company, Tower City Publishing."

OPERA AMERICA, Suite 520, 777 14th St. NW, Washington DC 20005. (202)347-9262. Estab. 1970. Members are composers, musicians and opera/music theater producers. "OPERA America maintains an extensive library of reference books and domestic and foreign music periodicals, and the most comprehensive operatic archive in the United States. OPERA America draws on these unique resources to supply information to its members." Offers conferences. Publishes directories of opera/music theater companies in the US and Canada. Publishes directory of opera and musical performances world-wide and US. Applications accepted year-round. Membership fee is on a sliding scale. Please contact for more information.

PACIFIC NORTHWEST SONGWRITERS ASSOCIATION, Box 98564, Seattle WA 98198. (206)824-1568. "We're a nonprofit association, and have served the songwriters of the Puget Sound area since 1977. Our focus is on professional songwriting for today's commercial markets. We hold monthly workshops and publish a quarterly newsletter. Our workshops are a great place to meet other writers, find collaborators, critique each other's songs and share news and encouragement. Our members get immediate contact with hundreds of the biggest national artists, producers, publishers and record companies. Members also get free legal advice from our staff attorney. All this for only $35 per year. We welcome new members. If you have any questions, just give us a call."

PENNSYLVANIA ASSOCIATION OF SONGWRITERS, COMPOSERS, P.O. Box 4311, Allentown PA 18105. (215)433-6788. President: John Havassy. Secretary: Charlene Havassy. Estab. 1979. Serves songwriters and musicians. "Teens to 50s, mostly contemporary, pop, country and gospel. We are dedicated to helping the songwriter further develop and perfect his craft. We act as an information center, offering up-to-date information through the use of our complete music library and industry consultants; this includes legal information and copyright materials. Some of our services include sponsoring music seminars, songwriter workshops, yearly songwriting contests, and venues for original music performance, while keeping you in touch with the pulse of the industry nationwide." Applications accepted year-round. Dues are $15 yearly. "Any performing songwriters should send tape and bio and other promotional materials for consideration for bookings. We maintain a library of business and educational publications and copywright information."

PITTSBURGH SONGWRITERS ASSOCIATION, 408 Greenside Ave., Canonsburg PA 15317. (412)745-9497. President: Frank J. DeGennaro. Estab. 1983. Serves songwriters. "Any age group is welcome. Current members are from mid-20s to mid-50s. All musical styles and interests are welcome. Country and pop predominate the current group; some instrumental, dance, rock and R&B also. Composers and lyricists in group. Our organization wants to serve as a source of quality material for publishers and other industry professionals. We assist members in developing their songs and getting their works published. Also, we provide a support group for area songwriters, network of contacts and collaboration opportunities. We offer field trips, instruction, lectures, library and social outings. Annual dues are $25. We have no initiation fee." Interested parties please contact membership coordinator: Roger Horne, 175 Melody Lane, Washington PA 15301.

PORTLAND SONGWRITERS ASSOCIATION, P.O. Box 5323, Aloha OR 97007. (503)642-4738. "The P.S.A. is a non-profit organization dedicted to offering songwriters education, opportunities and growth. All songwriters, lyricists, and musicians are welcome. The association offers monthly workshops, a Songwriters Showcase, and seminars to all members and non-members. If you want to *do* something about your songwriting career, we want to hear from you. Dues are $35 per year. For more information please call us."

RECORDING INDUSTRY ASSOCIATION OF AMERICA, Suite 200, 1020 19th St. NW, Washington DC 20036. President: Jason S. Berman. Estab. 1952. Serves recording companies. RIAA membership is corporate. Members include US-based manufacturers of sound recordings. "Membership in RIAA is not open to individuals. RIAA has extensive programs on behalf of our industry in the areas of government relations, public relations and anti-piracy enforcement. RIAA also addresses challenges facing the U.S. industry in the international market place. RIAA also coordinates industry market research and is the certifying body for gold and platinum records. We will provide, upon request, samples of RIAA publications, including our industry sourcebook, newsletter and annual statistical overview. Dues are corporate, and computed in confidence by an outside auditing firm."

*RED RIVER SONGWRITERS ASSOCIATION, P.O. Box 412, Ft. Towson OK 74735. (405)326-9453. President: Dan Dee Beal. Estab. 1991. Members range from beginners to accomplished writers of all ages. Primarily country music. "The main purpose of this organization is to help songwriters get record cuts and to obtain information and continually learn more about songwriting." Offers lectures, performance opportunities, library, evaluation services, instruction, newsletter and workshops. Applications accepted year-round. Membership fee is $10/year; $2/month dues.

*ROCKY MOUNTAIN MUSIC ASSOCIATION, Suite 210, Union Station, 1701 Wynkoop, Denver CO 80222. (303)623-6910. Director of Membership: Andrea Ferguson. Estab. 1987. "We are open to all ages but the largest concentration ages of our current members is 28-45. They are original musical performers and songwriters mostly and range in skills from amateur to professional. Membership is open to anyone interested in the music industry. The only requirement is submiting an application with appropriate amount of membership dues. The main purpose of the Rocky Mountain Music Assoc. is to encourage and support the development and performance of original music by providing educational programs broadening public appreciation, facilitating national access and exposure to regional talent and acting as central database for the regional community. The primary benefit of membership is to help in exposing talent and honing skills." Offers competitions, lectures, performance opportunities, evaluation services, newsletter and workshops. Applications accepted year-round. Membership fee is $35 Individual, $50 Band, $25 Student, $100 Business, $250 Patron, $500 Sponsor, $1,000 Benefactor.

SAN FRANCISCO FOLK MUSIC CLUB, 885 Clayton, San Francisco CA 94117. (415)661-2217. Serves songwriters, musicians and anyone who enjoys folk music. "Our members range from age 2 to 80. The only requirement is that members enjoy, appreciate and be interested in sharing folk music. As a focal point for the San Francisco Bay Area folk music community, the SFFMC provides opportunities for people to get together to share folk music, and the newsletter *The Folknik* disseminates information. We publish 2 songs an issue (6 times a year) in our newsletter, our meetings provide an opportunity to share new songs, and at our camp-outs there are almost always songwriter workshops." Offers library, newsletter, informal performance opportunities, annual free folk festival, social outings and workshops. Applications accepted year-round. Membership fee is $5/year.

SANTA BARBARA SONGWRITERS' GUILD, Box 22, Goleta CA 93116. (805)967-8864. President: Gary Heuer. Estab. 1981. "The Guild helps to open doors to music industry professionals which otherwise would be closed to them. We are a nonprofit organization for aspiring songwriters, performers, those interested in the music industry, and anyone interested in original music. Our members are able to meet other songwriters, to learn more about the craft of songwriting, to get their songs heard, and to network. The Guild sponsors monthly cassette tape presentations to L.A. publishers called Songsearches. We also sponsor workshops, classes and lectures on music, record production, song marketing, music composition, lyric writing and vocal techniques. Discounts available to members include the following: books that deal with a wide range of pertinent music industry information, studio time at local recording studios, equipment and supplies at local music stores." Membership is $35/year.

*SCARBOROUGH ARTS COUNCIL, 1859 Kingston Rd., Scarborough, Ontario M1N 1T3 **Canada**. (416)698-7322. Fax: (416)698-7972. Executive Director: Myrna Miller-Tait. Estab. 1979. Membership is open to anyone interested in the visual, literary and performing arts. All ages. Skill level not applicable. The main purpose of this organization is "to promote and develop the visual, literary and performing arts for the benefit of the artists and the community at large. Although membership is open to all, our annual songwriters' competition is for Canadian citizens only. Information and entry form sent on request." Offers competitions, performance opportunities and workshops. Applications accepted year-round. Membership fee is Adults—$20, Senior Citizens/students—$10

SESAC INC., 421 W. 54th St., New York NY 10019. (212)586-3450; 55 Music Square E., Nashville TN 37203. (615)320-0055 President and Chief Operating Officer: Vincent Candilora. Vice President: Dianne Petty, Nashville. Serves writers and publishers in all types of music who have their works performed by radio, television, nightclubs, cable TV, etc. Purpose of organization is to collect and distribute performance royalties to all active affiliates. "Prospective affiliates are requested to present a demo tape of their works which is reviewed by our Screening Committee." For possible affiliation, call Nashville or New York for appointment.

*SNOWBELT SONGWRITERS' GUILD, #15, 329 Maple St., Oswego NY 13126. (315)343-8693. President and Founder: Carolyn A. Gunther. Estab. 1985. Serves songwriters, musicians, and "anyone interested in the creative and business aspects of songwriting. We have members from many counties in New York State. Individual members are from 14 to 68 years of age and write easy listening, MOR, rock, R&B, bluegrass, C&W, folk, gospel and others that defy categorization. We come from all walks of life but share a love for songwriting. We serve beginning, intermediate and advanced writers. Types of memberships available: Active Membership: open to persons who have been or are presently involved with the actual composition of music and/or lyrics. An active member may hold office, vote and be on the board of directors. Dues are $25 per year. Associate Membership: open to persons interested in learning the craft of songwriting and/or assisting in guild activities. Friend/Patron dues are $10/year. Patron/Friend Membership: open to persons interested in contributing their resources to Guild Development. Among the requirements are an interest in songwriting as a serious art form, and the desire to become involved in it through the sharing of songs and ideas with peers and the community. We support the individual songwriter in his endeavors to have songs published, recorded and performed. We provide technical assistance with copywriting, locating publishers and songwriter advocacy. The primary benefits of membership for the songwriter are: 1) education through meetings, workshops and seminars; 2) the opportunity to share material and receive feedback from peers; 3) collaboration opportunities; 4) technical assistance in the business aspects of the craft; and 5) contact with other songwriting associations, professional organizations, and music industry professionals. Each of us individually pursues our craft and career dictated by choice. The sharing of information and fellowship is our nucleus, backbone and strength. In our unique odyssey, we are not alone. There are others going with us. We are called 'Songwriters'!"

SOCIETY FOR THE PRESERVATION AND ENCOURAGEMENT OF BARBER SHOP QUARTET SINGING IN AMERICA, INC. (S.P.E.B.S.Q.S.A., INC.), 6315 Third Ave., Kenosha WI 53143-5199. (414)653-8440. Membership Development Coordinator: Patrick Tucker-Kelly. Estab. 1938. Serves songwriters, musicians and world's largest all male singing organization. "Members are from pre-teen to elderly. All are interested in vocal harmony (4 singing, barbershop style). The main purpose of this organization is to perpetuate and preserve the musical art form known as Barbershop Harmony. We are always looking for new songs that will adapt to barbershop harmonization and style." Offers competitions, instruction, lectures, library, newsletter, performance opportunities, social outings and workshops. "A week-long 'Harmony College' is presented each year, open to over 700 men. Instruction in all areas of music: vocal techniques, arranging, songwriting, show production, chorus directing, etc. A Youth Outreach program featuring Harmony Explosion Student A Cappella Clubs and an annual Collegiate Quartet Competition, is offered, especially designed to appeal to high school and college age young men. Approved by MENC and ACDA. Our publishing program, which at present offers over 650 songs, is arranged in the barbershop style. The Society offers the opportunity for songwriters to have their music arranged and published. We maintain a library of over 750,000 pieces of sheet music—most of which is turn of the century to the mid-late 20s." Applications accepted year-round. Membership is usually in local chapters with dues about $70 annually. A chapter-at-large membership, The Frank H. Thorne Chapter, is available at $70 annually.

SOCIETY OF COMPOSERS, AUTHORS AND MUSIC PUBISHERS OF CANADA (SOCAN), Head Office: 41 Valleybrook Dr., Don Mills, Ontario M3B 2S6 **Canada.** (416)445-8700. Fax: (416)445-7108. General Manager: Michael Rock. (415)445-8700. In March, 1990, CAPAC and PROCAN merged to form a single, new Canadian performing rights society. The purpose of the society is to collect music user license fees and distribute performance royalties to composers, authors and music publishers. The SOCAN catalogue is licensed by ASCAP and BMI in the United States.

*SODRAC INC., 54 Le Royer W., Montreal, Quebec H2Y 1W7 **Canada.** (514)845-3268. Fax: (514)845-3401. Membership Department: Robert Hurtubise. Estab. 1985. Serves those with an interest in songwriting and music publishing no matter what their age or skill level is. "Members must have written or published at least one musical work that has been reproduced on an audio (CD, cassette, LP) or audio-visual support (TV, video . . .) The main purpose of this organization is to administer the reproduction rights of its members: authors/composers and publishers. The new member will benefit of a society working to secure his reproduction rights (mechanicals)." Applications accepted year-round. "There is no membership fee or annual dues. SODRAC retains a commission currently set at

10% for amounts collected in Canada and 5% for amounts collected abroad."

SONGWRITERS & LYRICISTS CLUB, %Robert Makinson, Box 023304, Brooklyn NY 11202-0066. Director: Robert Makinson. Estab. 1984. Serves songwriters and lyricists. Gives information regarding songwriting: creation of songs, reality of market, collaboration, disc jockeys and other contacts. Only requirement is ability to write lyrics or melodies. Beginners are welcome. The primary benefits of membership for the songwriter are opportunities to collaborate and assistance with creative aspects and marketing of songs through publications and advice. Offers newsletter and assistance with lead sheets and demos. Applications accepted year-round. Dues are $30/year, remit to Robert Makinson. Write with SASE for more information. "Plan and achieve realistic goals. If you have a great song, we'll make every effort to help promote it."

*SONGWRITERS AND POET'S CRITIQUE, 11599 Coontz Rd., Orient OH 43146. (614)877-1727. (614)488-8308. Contact: Ellis Cordle or Don Baker. "We have over 100 members from over 16 states at several levels of ability from novice to advanced, and try to help and support each other with the craft and business of songs and poetry. We have published writers and recorded artists. We share information about how to pitch, send and package a demo, and who to send it to. Musicians and singers welcome even if you don't write." Applications accepted year-round. Annual dues are $20.

SONGWRITERS ASSOCIATION OF WASHINGTON, Suite 632, 1377 K St. NW, Washington DC 20005. (301)654-8434. President: Meg Dinger. Estab. 1979. "S.A.W. is a nonprofit organization committed to providing its members with the means to improve their songwriting skills, learn more about the music business and gain exposure in the industry. S.A.W. sponsors various events to achieve this goal, such as workshops, song swaps, seminars, meetings, showcases and the Mid-Atlantic song contest. S.A.W. publishes *S.A.W. Notes*, a quarterly newsletter containing information on the music business, upcoming events around the country, and provides free classifieds to its members. For more information regarding membership write or call.

THE SONGWRITERS GUILD OF AMERICA, Suite 306, 276 Fifth Ave., New York NY 10001. (212)686-6820. West Coast: Suite 317, 6430 Sunset Blvd., Hollywood CA 90028. (213)462-1108. Nashville: United Artists Tower, 50 Music Square W., Nashville TN 37203. (615)329-1782. Founded as the Songwriters' Protective Association in 1931, name changed to American Guild of Authors and Composers in 1958, and expanded to AGAC/The Songwriters Guild in 1982. Effective 1985, the organizational name is The Songwriters Guild of America. "The Songwriters Guild of America is the nation's largest, oldest, most respected and most experienced songwriters' association devoted exclusively to providing songwriters with the services, activities and protection they need to succeed in the business of music." President: George David Weiss. Executive Director: Lewis M. Bachman. National Projects Director: George Wurzbach. West Coast Regional Director: Aaron Meza. Nashville Regional Director: Kathy Hyland. "A full member must be a published songwriter. An associate member is any unpublished songwriter with a desire to learn more about the business and craft of songwriting. The third class of membership comprises estates of deceased writers. The Guild contract is conceded to be the best available in the industry, having the greatest number of built-in protections for the songwriter. The Guild's Royalty Collection Plan makes certain that prompt and accurate payments are made to writers. The ongoing Audit Program makes periodic checks of publishers' books. For the self-publisher, the Catalogue Administration Program (CAP) relieves a writer of the paperwork of publishing for a fee lower than the prevailing industry rates. The Copyright Renewal Service informs members a year in advance of a song's renewal date. Other services include workshops in New York and Los Angeles, free Ask-A-Pro rap sessions with industry pros (see Workshops), critique sessions, collaborator service and newsletters. In addition, the Guild reviews your songwriter contract on request (Guild or otherwise); fights to strengthen songwriters' rights and to increase writers' royalties by supporting legislation which directly affects copyright; offers a group medical and life insurance plan; issues news bulletins with essential information for songwriters; provides a songwriter collaboration service for younger writers; financially evaluates catalogues of copyrights in connection with possible sale and estate planning; operates an estates administration service; and maintains a nonprofit educational foundation (The Songwriters Guild Foundation)."

SONGWRITERS OF OKLAHOMA, 211 W. Waterloo Rd., Edmond OK 73034. (405)348-6534. President: Harvey Derrick. Estab. 1983. Serves songwriters and musicians, professional writers, amateur writers, college and university faculty, musicians, poets and others from labor force as well as retired individuals. Age range is from 18 to 90. "Must be interested in writing and composing and have a desire to help others in any way possible. We have members from coast to coast. We offer workshops, critique sessions, contests, civic benefits, education of members on copyright, contracts, publishers, demos, record companys, etc., as well as a sounding board of peers, education, camaraderie and sharing of knowledge." Offers competitions, field trips, instruction, lectures, library, newsletter, performance opportunities, social outings and workshops. Applications accepted year-round. Membership fee is $15/year.

SONGWRITERS OF WISCONSIN, P.O. Box 874, Neenah WI 54957-0874. (414)725-1609. Director: Tony Ansems. Estab. 1983. Serves songwriters. "Membership is open to songwriters writing all styles of music. Residency in Wisconsin is recommended but not required. Members are encouraged to bring tapes and lyric sheets of their songs to the meetings, but it is not required. We are striving to improve the craft of songwriting in Wisconsin. Living in Wisconsin, a songwriter would be close to any of the workshops and showcases offered each month at different towns. The primary value of membership for a songwriter is in sharing ideas with other songwriters, being critiqued and helping other songwriters." Offers competitions, field trips, instruction, lectures, newsletter, performance opportunities, social outings, workshops and critique sessions. Applications accepted year-round. $10 subscription fee for newsletter.

*SOUTHWEST VIRGINIA SONGWRITERS ASSOCIATION, P.O. Box 698, Salem VA 24153. (703)389-1525. President: Sidney V. Crosswhite. Estab. 1981. 80 members—all ages—all levels—mainly country and gospel and rock but other musical interest too. "Prospective members are subject to approval by SVSA Board of Directors. The purpose of SVSA is to increase, broaden and expand the knowledge of each member and to support, better and further the progress and success of each member in songwriting and related fields of endeavor." Offers performance opportunities, evaluation services, instruction, newsletter, workshops, monthly meetings, monthly newsletter. Application accepted year-round. Membership fee is $15 one time fee (initiation); $12/year—due in January.

TULSA SONGWRITERS ASSOCIATION, INC., P.O. Box 254, Tulsa OK 74101-0254. (918)437-SONG. President: Joyce Ur. Estab. 1983. Serves songwriters and musicians. Members are age 18-65 and have interests in all types of music. Main purpose of the organization is "to create a forum to educate, develop, improve, discover and encourage songwriting in the Tulsa area." Offers competitions, lectures, performance opportunities, field trips, social outings, instruction, newsletter and workshops. Applications accepted year-round. Dues are $30/year.
Tips: "We hold a monthly 'Writer's Night' open to the public for performance of original songs to expose the many talented writers in Tulsa."

UTAH SONGWRITERS ASSOCIATION (USA), P.O. Box 71325, Salt Lake City UT 84107. (801)596-3058 or (801)451-2831. Secretary/Treasurer: Marie Vosgerau. Vice President: Cori Connors. Estab. 1984. Serves ages 19-70. Beginning songwriters; advanced; any songwriters. Lyric writers; melodies or both lyrics and melodies. Musicians are also welcome. All types of music. "Anyone who is interested in songwriting may join. Primarily we want to promote the craft of songwriting. USA is a support group for songwriters. We distribute information; teach workshops on how to write better songs; showcase members original material; give other instruction and news. Provides song critiques, contest opportunities; meeting professional music business people. The newsletter, *The Melody Line*, gives valuable information on contests, publishers looking for material, tips, etc. Workshops and showcases build confidence. Annual seminar with publishers, etc." Offers competitions, performance opportunities, evaluation services, instruction, newsletter, workshops. Contribute talents and other items to worthy benefit causes. Applications accepted year-round. Membership fee is $25 per member per year or $30 for a family membership per year.
Tips: "The USA exchanges newsletters with many songwriting associations across the United States. We welcome any exchange of ideas with other songwriting associations."

VERMONT SONGWRITERS ASSOCIATION, RD 2 Box 277, Underhill VT 05489. (802)899-3787. President: Bobby Hackney. Estab. 1991. "Membership open to anyone desiring a career in songwriting, or anyone who seeks a supportive group to encourage co-writing, meeting other songwriters, or to continue their songwriting endeavors." Purpose is to give songwriters an opportunity to meet industry professionals at monthly meetings and seminars, to have their works critiqued by peers and to help songwriters learn more about the craft and the complete business of songwriting. Offers competitions, instruction, lectures, library, newsletter, performance opportunities, workshops. Applications accepted year-round. Membership fee is $30/year.
Tips: "We are a nonprofit association dedicated to creating opportunities for songwriters. Even though our office address in in Underhill, Vermont, our primary place of business is in Burlington, Vermont, where monthly meetings and seminars are held."

VICTORY MUSIC, P.O. Box 7515, Bonney Lake WA 98390. (206)863-6617. Estab. 1969. Serves songwriters, audiences and specifically local acoustic musicians of all music styles. Victory Music provides places to play, showcases, opportunities to read about the business and other songwriters, referrals and seminars. Produced 5 albums of NW songwriters. Offers library, 32 pg. magazine, newsletter, performance opportunities and business workshops. Applications accepted year-round. Membership fee is $20/year single; $50/year business; $28/year couple; $175 lifetime.

*THE VIRGINIA ORGANIZATION OF COMPOSERS AND LYRICISTS, P.O. Box 34606, Richmond VA 23234. (804)733-5908. Membership Director: Colin Campbell. Estab. 1986. Songwriters of all ages, all styles, all skill levels. "Applicants must have an interest in songwriting, or recording or musical production or original material. The main purpose of this organization is educational—to teach songwriters about the business of songwriting, song structure and musical and lyrical composition. We offer a wealth of information from many sources—other songwriters groups, newsletters and publications. Offers competitions, lectures, performance opportunities, field trips, evaluation services (free) and newsletter. Applications accepted year-round. Membership fee as of March 31, 1993—$20 annually.

VOLUNTEER LAWYERS FOR THE ARTS, 6th Floor, 1 E. 53rd St., New York NY 10022. (212)319-2787. Estab. 1969. Serves songwriters, musicians and all performing, visual, literary and fine arts artists and groups. Offers legal assistance and representation to eligible individual artists and arts organizations who cannot afford private counsel. Also sells publications on arts-related issues. In addition, there are affiliates nationwide who assist local arts organizations and artists. Offers conferences, lectures, seminars and workshops. Call for membership information.

*WEST COAST AMATEUR MUSICIANS SOCIETY, 943 Clements Ave., North Vancouver, B.C. V7R 2K8 **Canada.** (604)980-5341. Secretary: Mrs. Ruth Downs. Estab. 1981. Serves all ages and levels of ability—ages 6 to seniors with an interest in music-making and listening to music. "Both amateur and professional musicians belong. The main purpose of this organization is to provide activities for amateur musicians at a resonable cost." The primary benefit of membership would be to "improve skills, meet other amateur musicians, and study computer music at our summer music camp." Offers performance opportunities, library, instruction, newsletter, workshops. Shawnigan Lake Music Holiday: July 18-25 and/or July 25-August 1 a summer music camp for adults and families. Membership fee Individual $25/year; Senior $13/year; Student $12/year; Family $35/year. Group rate without library privileges $35; Group rate with library priv. $35 for leader (+$1.50 per member), max. $100.

WESTERN NORTH CAROLINA SONGWRITER'S ASSOC. INC., P.O. Box 72, Alexander NC 28701. (704)683-9105. President: Henry C. Tench. Estab. 1991. Serves songwriters and musicians. Persons 18 years or older who want to write lyrics, songs and musicians both professional and amateur. Members are welcome from all states who are trying to learn or better the craft of songwriting in general. "Endeavors to assist those interested in becoming great songwriters through a series of meetings, critiques, workshops and other educational means available. We are serious but still have fun. Association with other songwriters, locally as well as a national organization. Serious songwriters need to study their craft as well as have them critiqued in a constructive way and make contacts in songwriting profession from other parts of the country. We take this to be serious business on our part and will handle it in a professional manner." Offers competitions, field trips, instruction, lectures, library, newsletter, performance opportunities, social outings and workshops. Applications accepted year-round. One time initiation fee of $20, then $24/year.
Tips: "Application must be approved by board. If you are serious about learning the craft of songwriting, come on and participate and support your local as well national songwriting organizations. We at WNCSA, Inc. will assist all who are sincere in their endeavor to excel in the songwriter's profession."

WHITEWATER VALLEY SONGWRITERS AND MUSICIANS ASSOC., Box 112, RR #4, Liberty IN 47353. (317)458-6152. Founder: Ann Hofer. Serves songwriters and musicians. Estab. 1981. "Our members are songwriters of all ages. We have artists, musicians, lyricists and melody writers. Our purpose is to assist our members with finding co-writers, keep them informed on publishers accepting material, help them make demo contacts, provide list of record companies, and to educate them on the ever-changing music and songwriting business. We are available to assist the songwriter in any way we can; we are dedicated to his/her needs. We want to encourage songwriters to believe in themselves." Offers competitions, instruction, lectures, library, performance opportunities, social outings and song critique sessions. For more information call Ann at (317)458-6152 or send SASE.

WICHITA SONGWRITERS GROUP, 2450 Somerset, Wichita KS 64204. (316)838-6079. Contact: David Kinion. Estab. 1988. Serves songwriters. Members include teenagers to retired people from the community. Members must live close enough to be present at meetings. Main purpose is to provide a sense of community for songwriters while helping them write better songs. Wichita Songwriters Group provides instruction, common support and a songwriter's network for placement of songs. Offers field trips, instruction, lectures, library, performance opportunities and workshops. Applications accepted year-round. Fee of $1 per meeting.
Tips: WSG meets on the first Monday of each month (except holidays) at 7:30 pm at Miller Music, 4235 West Central, Wichita KS.

Workshops

Evaluation, suggestions, feedback and motivation. All are important to the aspiring songwriter. A songwriting organization may provide these, but to gain an idea of how your music stacks up in the larger world of music, alternatives are needed. Conferences and workshops provide a means for songwriters to have songs evaluated, hear suggestions for further improvement and receive feedback and motivation from industry experts in a broader context. They are also an excellent place to make valuable industry contacts.

Usually these workshops take place in the music hubs: New York, Los Angeles and Nashville. In the past few years, major regional conferences have gained a lot of attention. Also, organizations exist that offer traveling workshops on just about every songwriting topic imaginable — from lyric writing and marketing strategy to contract negotiation. More small and mid-size cities with strong songwriter organizations are running their own workshops, drawing on resources from within their own group or bringing in professionals from the music centers.

A workshop exists to address every type of music. There are programs for songwriters, performers of all styles, musical playwrights and much more. Many also include instruction and suggestions on related business topics. The following list includes national and local workshops with a brief description of what each offers. For more information, write to the sponsoring organization.

ANNUAL NATIONAL CONFERENCE OF COLLEGE BROADCASTERS & REGIONAL CONFERENCES OF COLLEGE BROADCASTERS, 71 George St., 2nd Floor, Providence RI 02912-1824. (401)863-2225. Association Director: JoAnn Forgit. Estab. 1988. "The purpose of these conferences is to bring top media leaders together with students from college broadcasting to learn and share ideas. Several sessions on music licensing, record company relations and alternative/new music programming trends are typically included. We conduct the National College Radio Awards and National TV Programming Awards (not open to songwriters). We also have a comprehensive awards/competitions listing every month in *College Broadcaster* magazine, many of which relate to musicians. The Annual Conference (November) and Regional Conferences (Spring) last 1-3 days at various host college campuses around the U.S. Participants include artists, producers, TV/radio program directors, amateur and professional songwriters, bands, composers and record label reps. The National Conference Trade Show typically includes numerous record labels and programming syndicators. Participants are selected through submission of demo tapes and leads from college broadcasting stations. For information about dates and participation, call JoAnn Forgit at (401)863-2225. Closing date for application is September/October for the National Conference and one month prior to each regional conference. There is a $70 registration fee at National Conference, $30 at Regional Conferences. Music showcases, receptions and refreshments throughout the day are included. A discount hotel package is available to attendees."

APPEL FARM ARTS AND MUSIC FESTIVAL, Box 888, Elmer NJ 08318. (609)358-2472. Artistic Director: Sean Timmons. Estab. Festival: 1989; Series: 1970. "Our annual open air festival is the highlight of our year-round Performing Arts Series which was established to bring high quality arts programs to the people of South Jersey. Festival includes acoustic and folk music, blues, etc." Programs for songwriters and musicians include performance opportunities as part of Festival and Performing Arts Series. Programs for musical playwrights also include performance opportunities as part of Performing

Arts Series. Festival is a one-day event held in June, and Performing Arts Series is held year-round. Both are held at the Appel Farm Arts and Music Center, a 176-acre farm in Southern New Jersey. Up to 20 songwriters/musicians participate in each event. Participants are songwriters, individual vocalists, bands, ensembles, vocal groups, composers, individual instrumentalists and dance/mime/ movement. Participants are selected by demo tape submissions. Applicants should send a press packet, demonstration tape and biographical information. Application materials accepted year round. Faculty opportunities are available as part of residential Summer Arts Program for children, July/August.

APPLE HILL SUMMER CHAMBER MUSIC FESTIVAL, Apple Hill Center for Chamber Music, Box 217, E. Sullivan NH 03445. (603)847-3371. "Apple Hill welcomes 45-50 students of all ages and abilities to each of 5 summer music sessions for coaching by the Apple Hill Chamber Players and distinguished guest faculty artists and opportunities to perform chamber music of all periods. Musicians may choose from 5 short sessions (10 days each), in which participants are assigned to 2 or 3 ensembles coached daily for up to 1½ hours. Programs are offered June-August. 55 musicians participate in each workshop. Participants are amateur and professional individual instrumentalists, singers and ensembles. Participants are selected by demo tape submissions. Send for application. Suggested application deadline: May 1st. There is an application fee. Total cost for the short sessions: $835-870. Programs take place on a 70-acre New England farm. Includes the Louise Shonk Kelly Concert Barn, home of countless rehearsals, student performances and festival concerts; general meeting place and dining hall/bathroom facilities; rehearsal barn; faculty and student cabins; tennis courts, hiking trails, nearby ponds for swimming."

ASH LAWN-HIGHLAND SUMMER FESTIVAL, Rt. 6, Box 37, Charlottesville VA 22901. (804)293-4500. General Manager: Judy Walker. Estab. 1978. 4 Music At Twilight programs—classical or contemporary concerts. Opera series in repertoire with orchestra. Summer only. June, July and August. 12 songwriters/musicians participate in each festival. Participants are amateur and professional individual vocalists, ensembles, individual instrumentalists and orchestras. Participants are chosen by audition. Auditions are held in February in New York and Washington D.C. Send for application. Closing date: January 15.

*ASPEN MUSIC FESTIVAL, #10E, 250 W. 54th St., New York NY 10019-5585. (22)581-2196. Fax: (212)582-2757. Estab. 1949. "Promotes classical music." Offers programs for composers. Offers other programs in the summer from June to August in Aspen CO. About 925 participate in workshop. Participants are amateur and professional composers, individual instrumentalists and ensembles. Participants are selected by audition in person or submit demonstration tape. Send for application. Charges $2,000 for 9 weeks, $1,350 for 4½ weeks.

BMI-LEHMAN ENGEL MUSICAL THEATRE WORKSHOP, 320 W. 57th St., New York NY 10019. (212)830-2515. Director of Musical Theatre: Norma Grossman. Estab. 1961. "BMI is a music licensing company, which collects royalties for affiliated writers. We have departments to help writers in jazz, concert, Latin, pop and musical theater writing." Offers programs "to musical theater composers and lyricists. The BMI-Lehman Engel Musical Theatre Workshops were formed in an effort to refresh and stimulate professional writers, as well as to encourage and develop new creative talent for the musical theater." Each workshop meets one afternoon a week for two hours at BMI, New York. Participants are professional songwriters, composers and playwrights. "BMI-Lehman Engel Musical Theatre Workshop Showcase presents the best of the workshop to producers, agents, record and publishing company execs, press, directors for possible option and production." Call for application. Tape and lyrics of 3 compositions required with application.

BROADWAY TOMORROW PREVIEWS, % Broadway Tomorrow Musical Theatre, Suite 53, 191 Claremont Ave., New York NY 10027. Artistic Director: Elyse Curtis. Estab. 1983. Purpose is the enrichment of American theater by nurturing *new musicals*. Offers series in which composers living in New York City area present scores of their new musicals in concert. 2-3 composers/librettists/lyricists of same musical and 1 musical director/pianist participate. Participants are professional singers, composers and opera/musical theater writers. Submission by recommendation of past participants only. Submission is by audio cassette of music, script if completed, synopsis, cast breakdown, resume, reviews, if any, acknowledgement postcard and SASE. Participants selected by screening of submissions. Programs are presented in fall and spring with possibility of full production of works presented in concert. No entry fee.

*CALGARY INTERNATIONAL ORGAN FESTIVAL, P.O. Box 1200, Station "M", Calgary, Alberta T2P 4P9 **Canada**. Phone: (403)294-7401. President: D.M. Lauchlan. Estab. 1988. Promotes the Carthy Organ and organ music in general. Workshops and master classes are included in the festival. Offers competition for organists 32 years or younger, winners of major competitions or organists recommended by teachers on an invitation basis. Every four years beginning October 13-19, 1990. Festival lasts one week and takes place in Calgary, Alberta, Canada. Participants are amateur and professional instrumentalists. Performers selected by invitation only. A number of hotels are centrally available around the Centre. The large portion of the event centers around the Jack Singer Concert Hall, in the Calgary Centre for Performing Arts. A new work is commissioned for the Festival for organ and orchestra. This work is part of the repertoire for competitors at the Final Round in Calgary and a cash prize is given to the winner.

*CONTEMPORARY RECORD SOCIETY (CRS), 724 Winchester, Broomall PA 19008. (215)544-5920. Fax: (215)544-5921. Administrative Assistant: Caroline Hunt. Estab. 1990. Offers programs for songwriters, composers and performers. Sponsors the Contemporary Music Festival and the CRS National Festival for the Performing Arts Competition held in the Philadelphia vicinity. 200 songwriters/musicians participate in each workshop. Participants are professional songwriters, composers, individual vocalists, individual instrumentalists, bands and ensembles. Participants are selected by demo tape audition. Send for application. Deadline: July 19th. Fee $35.

C-SC OPERA WORKSHOP, Culver-Stockton College, Division of Fine Arts, Canton MO 63435. (314)288-5221. Director of Opera Workshop: Dr. Carol Fisher Mathieson. "C-SC Opera Workshop provides students with experience in chamber opera through study and performance. We do one-act, small-cast chamber operas which require no chorus." Workshops offered annually, lasting 1 month (usually in February or March) with 1-4 performances. Performers are usually college students (3-8 per workshop) and occasional guests. "The new Mabee Theatre at Culver-Stockton College seats 150-200. It can be used as a thrust or arena stage. There is no curtain nor is there fly space. Lighting is state of the art. We will present the works of composers of chamber opera which are within the ability range of our students (undergraduate) and require a small cast with no chorus. Keyboard or small wind ensemble accompaniment is necessary. Ours is a small workshop which aims at introducing students to the art of chamber opera. Our students are undergraduates; Culver-Stockton College is a liberal arts college. If a work is useful to our workshop, it will also be marketable to other small colleges, undergraduate workshops at universities and some civic groups. We are a church-related school, affiliated with the Christian church (Disciples of Christ), and would provide a testing ground for works marketable to church dramatic groups, too."

*CYMC, P.O. Box 3056, Courtenay, British Columbia V9N 5N3 **Canada**. (604)338-7463. Fax: (604)338-7480. General Manager: Lucille Parsons. Estab. 1967. Promotes jazz and classical; performance in small or large groups with few solos. Offers programs for performers. "CYMC is a summer music school where an open admissions policy and quality faculty combine to bring together musicians of all ages and abilities. The summer music festival is a natural spin-off of this talent. A concerto competition is held each year. Players rehearse a concerto 'movement' and the winner of the competition plays with the festival orchestra on final night of school." Offers other programs summer only. Workshops take place July to August. 300+ amateur and professional musicians. Participants are individual vocalists, individual instrumentalists, bands and ensembles. Participants are selected by open admissions. Send for application. Entry fee varies dependent on course taken. Dormitory style accomodations available at school; many local campgrounds, hotels, motels, bed and breakfasts.
Tips: "We are both a summer music school (CYMC) and a professional concert festival. Students pay fees that range from $600-1,100 dependent on course. Our programs offer a wide range of options from jazz to Canada's only full orchestral training program. Our aim is to provide a musical environment that nurtures and identifies the stars of tomorrow, but also the teacher, amateur and audience."

*THE ELORA FESTIVAL, P.O. Box 990, 33 Henderson, Elora, Ontario N1E 4P5 **Canada**. (519)846-0331. Fax: (519)846-5947. General Manager: Michael Grit. Estab. 1979. "The Festival presents a program of classical and contemporary music. We generally focus on contemporary Canadian music and artists." Offers programs for performers. "The program is the Young Performer Series for instrumental and voice students from the ages of 11 to 20 inclusive. Auditions are held three months before the festival. Winners are invited to perform as part of the festival, plus they receive a cash award and a certificate of performance. Commissions at least one new Canadian work each festival." Workshops take place July to August in "a variety of different venues from churches to former limestone quarries to sand barns." 200 songwriters/musicians participate in each workshop. Participants are amateur and professional composers, individual vocalists, individual instrumentalists, bands and ensembles. Participants are selected by audition in person and performers selected by invitation. Auditions are held "within the Village of Elora. Location is determined by the number of individuals who take part in the process." Send for application.

*FIREFLY FESTIVAL FOR THE PERFORMING ARTS, Suite 845, 202 S. Michigan, South Bend IN 46601. (219)288-3472. Executive Director: Carol Weiss Rosenberg. Estab. 1980. "We are a performing arts presenter and all types of music are presented." Offers programs for songwriters, composers, musical playwrights and performers. "We offer workshops, both theatrical and musical, dealing with the technical and creative sides of the arts." Summer only. Workshops take place June to August at Robert J. Fischgrund Center for the Performing Arts, St. Patrick's County Park, Southbend IN. 10 performances/numerous performers. Participants are professional songwriters, composers, individual vocalists, individual instrumentalists, bands and ensembles. Participants are selected by demo tape audition. Send promo material and tape. Deadline: December 1993 for 1994 season. "Festival is held at an outdoor performing arts amphitheater with state of the art sound and lighting equipment."

FOLK ALLIANCE ANNUAL CONFERENCE, Box 5010, Chapel Hill NC 27514. (919)542-3997. Contact: Art Menius. Estab. 1989. Conference/workshop topics change each year. Subjects covered at 1991 conference include "Survival on the Road," "Career Management" and "Grants for Folk Artists." Conference takes place mid-February and lasts 4 days at a different location each year. 150 amateur and professional musicians participate. "Offers songwriter critique sessions." Artist showcase participants are songwriters, individual vocalists, bands, ensembles, vocal groups and individual instrumentalists. Participants are selected by demo tape submission. Applicants should write for application form. Closing date for application is July 1. Charges $50 on acceptance. Additional costs vary from year to year. For 1993 the cost was $95 in advance, which covered 3 meals, a dance, workshops and our showcase. Performers' housing is separate for the event, which is usually held in Convention hotel. 1994: Boston MA; 1995: Portland OR; 1996: Washington DC.

*INTERNATIONAL CHORAL KATHAUMIXW, Powell River Academy of Music, Box 334, Powell River, British Columbia, V8A 5C2 **Canada.** (604)483-3346. Administrator: Terry Sabine. Estab. 1984. Purpose is "to present a children's, youth and adult choral festival and competition; to provide a musical and educational experience for the participants; to encourage understanding and goodwill by bringing together choirs from various parts of the world; to create a forum for choral conductors and singers; and to exhange information, musical expertise, repertoire and techniques. Programs include the Kathaumixw International Conducting Course. Six participants rehearse and perform, attend symposia and concerts in conjunction with the Kathaumixw Festival. Prizes are given for various competitions, including: children's choirs, youth choirs, adult choirs, chamber ensembles, contemporary choral music, junior, youth and adult solos. The festival is held biennially in July for a duration of 5 days in Powell River, British Columbia Canada. 1200 musicians participate in the festival. Participants are amateur vocalists, ensembles and vocal groups. Participants are selected by demo tape submissions. Send for application. Closing date is November. An entry fee of $75 is assessed. Festival is held in the Powell River Complex. Concerts and competitions are held in the Theatre and Great Hall (arena). Overseas visitors are billeted; North American choirs stay in hotels and dorms."

KERRVILLE FOLK FESTIVAL, Kerrville Festivals, Inc., P.O. Box 1466, Kerrville TX 78029. (210)257-3600. Founder/President: Rod Kennedy. Estab. 1972. Hosts 3-day songwriters school and new folk concert competition sponsored by the Kerrville Music Foundation. Programs held in late spring and late summer. Spring festival lasts 18 days and is held outdoors at Quiet Valley Ranch. Around 110 acts participate. Performers are professional instrumentalists, songwriters and bands. "Now hosting an annual 'house concert' seminar to encourage the establishment and promotion of monthly house concerts for traveling singer/songwriters to provide additional dates and income for touring." Participants selected by submitting demo tape, by invitation only. Send cassette, promotional material and list of upcoming appearances. "Songwriter schools are $100 and include breakfast, experienced professional instructors, camping on ranch and concerts. Rustic facilities—no electrical hookups. Food available at reasonable cost. Also sponsor a 4-day American Indian songwriters festival (estab. 1991) featuring a dozen prominent native contemporary and traditional performers in eight two-hour concerts. Festival of the Eagle is succeeding in undoing the typical stereotype cartoon and movie Indian image while also providing a rare opportunity for Indian songwriters. Audition tapes accepted at P.O. Box 1466, Kerrville, TX 78029."

*LAKE OSWEGO FESTIVAL OF THE ARTS, P.O. Box 368, Lake Oswego OR 97034. (503)636-3634. Director: Joan Sappington. Estab. 1963. Purpose is to bring a variety of work in the visual and performing arts to the Portland Metropolitan area. A 3-day event with 3 or 4 performances of jazz, ensemble and classical instrument soloists. Offered annually in late June. Festival lasts 3 days. Festival performances presented in 200 seat theater or in outdoor park (3-4,000). "Offer local area artists opportunity to perform in a casual setting in the large visual arts tent pavillion. It is a venue that works best for single or duo performances as the audience wanders through the art exhibit. Entry Fee $2 (under 18 free)."

THE LEHMAN ENGEL MUSICAL THEATRE WORKSHOP, 6425 Hollywood Blvd., Hollywood CA 90028. (213)465-8818. Fax: (213)465-0162. Co-Director: John Sparks. Estab. 1968. Musical theater (plays with music, opera, etc.). Offers programs for songwriters, composers and musical playwrights. Programs include 1 year curriculum writing songs and scenes for playwrights, composers and lyricists. Intermediate and advanced workshop forum offers writers a peer review of works-in-progress following the curriculum year. All writers are offered funds (as available) for staged readings and skeletal productions of worthy material. Offers other programs year-round. Workshops take place September through June, annually, at ACMT (American Center for Musical Theatre), 6425 Hollywood Boulevard, Hollywood, CA 90028. 25-75 songwriters/musicians participate in each workshop. Participants are amateur and professional songwriters, composers and musical playwrights. Participants are selected by demo tape, lyrics or scene and personal interview. Send for application. Deadline: August 1. Fee: $200 for 1 year's participation. Offers office, rehearsal studios and meeting room.

*MANCHESTER MUSIC FESTIVAL, P.O. Box 735, Manchester VT 05254. (802)362-1956. Director: Michael Rudiakov. Estab. 1974. "Music students from 16 years and up take part in instruction on their instrument, chamber music and chamber orchestra. We give scholarships to those who need and deserve them." Festival features 5 faculty concerts and 5 student concerts and takes place in Manchester VT from July 5-August 15. Participants are professional ensembles and individuals. Participants are selected by auditions. Contact by mail or phone. Tuition $1,200. Registration fee $40.

MUSIC BUSINESS FILE, P.O. Box 841, Gloucester MA 01930. (617)639-1971. Instructor: Peter W. Spellman. Estab. 1990. Purpose is "to empower independent songwriters and musicians with strategic business and industry information towards accelerating their careers. Applicable to all types of popular music." Offers instruction in "writing and implementing business plans. Targets marketing plans. Offers national and international media contact lists and 'Tip Sheets for the Working Musician' covering practical music business matters." Offers programs year round. Workshops last anywhere from 5-15 hours. Workshops held at area colleges and universities. 15-20 amateur and professional songwriters, composers, individual vocalists and instrumentalists, bands, ensembles and vocal groups participate in each event. "Open to all. Telephone consultations also available. Send for free brochure describing our services. Specify music style(s) you work in. Prices vary according to length of workshop. We also offer management and promotion of world music acts including reggae, worldbeat, New Age and contemporary jazz."

MUSIC BUSINESS SEMINARS, LTD., 87 Lafayette Rd., Hampton Falls NH 03844. (800)448-3621 and (603)929-1128. Director: Peter C. Knickles. "Now in its eighth year MBS, Ltd., presents 'Doing Music & Nothing Else: The Music Business Seminar.' The program is a two-day long, classroom style, multimedia educational experience that is presented in 24 major cities each year. Seminar is for all ages, all styles of music, bands and soloists, who are pursuing a career in original music songwriting, recording and performing. Learn how to establish goals, attract a songwriting or recording contract, book profitable gigs, raise capital and much, much more. Aftercare opportunities include toll free counseling with the instructor, A&R Tip Sheet/Showcase program and 2 free directories (A&R and T-100). Seminar is also available on 12 audio tapes with workbook. This is the only music seminar in US with a money back guarantee. Call for 2-year complimentary quarterly journal subscription and seminar brochure."

NATIONAL ACADEMY OF SONGWRITERS (NAS), Suite 780, 6381 Hollywood Blvd., Hollywood CA 90028. (213)463-7178. Staff Members: Dan Kirkpatrick and Steve Schalchlin. Estab. 1972. "Offers programs for songwriters including Publishers' Evaluation Workshops and SONGTALK seminar series, featuring top names in songwriting, lyric writing, demo production and more." Attendance: up to 30/workshop. Participants are amateur and professional songwriters, singers, bands and composers. Length: 2-4 hours/workshop. Membership is $75/year, professionals $125/year; Gold membership $200/year. Call hotline for application: 1-800-826-7287. "NAS is a nonprofit membership organization dedicated to the protection and education of songwriters. NAS also provides a bimonthly newsletter containing tipsheet (*Open Ears*) and collaborators' network."

NATIONAL MUSIC THEATER CONFERENCE, 234 W. 44th St., New York NY 10036. (212)382-2790. Artistic Director: Paulette Haupt. Estab. 1978. Sponsored by the Eugene O'Neill Theater Center. 8-10 songwriters/musicians participate in each event. Participants are professional composers, opera/musical theater writers, lyricists, playwrights in collaboration with composers. "The Conference offers composers, lyricists and book writers the opportunity to develop new music theater works of all forms during a 2-4 week residency at the O'Neill Theater Center in Waterford, CT. Some works are given publicly staged readings; others are developed in private readings during the conference with artistic staff and dramaturgs. All works selected are developed over at least a 2-3 month period. A professional company of approximately 20 singer/actors provides the writers with daily musical and dramatic readings during the Conference period. Staged works are read with script in hand, with minimal lighting and no physical properties, to allow flexibility for day-to-day rewrites. The Conference is held in August of each year. Participants are selected by Artistic Director and a panel of theater professionals. Composers and writers selected receive room, board and a stipend." Send SASE for application after Sept. 15.

NW ARKANSAS SONGWRITERS' WORKSHOP, P.O. Box 224, Bentonville AR 72712. (501)273-2698. Coordinator: Connie Sue Hunt. Estab. 1990. Promotes country, gospel, Christian, folk and Western music. Offers programs for songwriters, composers and performers, including songwriter showcase events. Song contest yearly with recording time and merchandise prizes. Contest deadline is January 31 yearly at Bentonville AR and surrounding area. Up to 150 amateur songwriters, composers, bands and individual vocalists participate. Submit demonstration tape for consideration. Charges entry fee of $5 for return of tape, postage and clerical. "Our songwriters group is sponsored by the Branson Star Review—Jane Frost sets up showcases for us in Branson MO and surrounding areas. We also have been featured at the Ozark Festival in Eureka Springs AR."

SONGCRAFT SEMINARS, 441 E. 20th St., New York NY 10010-7515. (212)674-1143. Estab. 1986. Year-round classes for composers and lyricists conducted by teacher/consultant Sheila Davis, author of *The Craft of Lyric Writing*, *Successful Lyric Writing* and *The Songwriter's Idea Book*. The teaching method, grounded in fundamental principles, incorporates whole-brain writing techniques. The objective: To express your unique voice. All courses emphasize craftsmanship and teach principles that apply to every musical idiom—pop, theater, or cabaret. For details on starting dates, fees and location of classes, write or call for current listing.
Successful Lyric Writing: A 3-Saturday course. Three 6-hour classes on the fundamental principles of writing words for and to music. Required text: *Successful Lyric Writing*. Held 3 times a year at The New School. Limited to 12.
Beyond the Basics: An 8-week workshop open to all "grads" of the *Successful Lyric Writing* Basics Course. It features weekly assignments and in-depth criticism to help writers turn first drafts into "music-ready" lyrics. Held four times a year at The Songwriters Guild of America (SGA).
Song by Song by Sondheim: A one-day seminar focused on the elements of fine craftsmanship exemplified in the words and music of Stephen Sondheim, America's pre-eminent theater writer. Significant songs are played and analyzed from the standpoint of form, meter, rhyme, literary devices and thematic development. Attendees are helped to apply these elements to their own writing. Held in April and November at The New School.
Whole-Brain Creativity: A five-week workshop that puts you in touch with your thinking/writing style through an understanding of split-hemispheric specialization. While having fun doing exercises to access each quadrant of the brain, you'll acquire new tools for increased creativity and successful songwriting.
Successful Lyric Writing Consultation Course: This course, an outgrowth of the instructor's book, covers the same theory and assignments as The Basics Course. Participants receive critiques of their work by the book's author via 1-hour phone sessions.

*SONGWRITER SEMINARS AND WORKSHOPS, 928 Broadway, New York NY 10010. (212)505-7332. President: Ted Lehrman. Vice President: Libby Bush. Estab. 1975. Offers programs for songwriters: introduction to pop songwriting; advanced workshop; and at-home songwriter workshop. Cycles begin in September and February. Approximately 10 in each songwriter workshop; participants are songwriters/composers, singers and bands. Each cycle lasts 8 weeks. "Our programs stress the craft and business realities of *today's* pop music industry. We guide our members in the writing of the hit single song (both lyrics and music) for those recording artists who are open to outside material. We also share with them our considerable experience and expertise in the marketing of commercial pop music product. Our instructors, Ted Lehrman and Libby Bush, both members of ASCAP, have had between them more than 80 songs recorded and commercially released here and abroad. They continue to be highly active in writing and placing pop songs for publication. Industry guests (record producers, record company, A&R people, publishers) frequently attend workshop sessions." Workshops: Pop Songwriting—Preparing for the Marketplace; Advanced Songwriter Seminar and Workshop—Ready for the Marketplace. Cost of 8 week workshops: $175-185. Cost of at-home songwriter workshop: $25/lyric; $35/song. Private song and career consultation sessions: $50/hour. Top 40 single stressed. Collaboration opportunities available. No housing provided. Interviews/auditions held for songwriters and singer/songwriters to determine which workshop would be most helpful. Call for free brochure and/or to set up interview. "No group sessions planned until February 1995. At present, private song and career consultation sessions only."

THE SONGWRITERS ADVOCATE (TSA), 47 Maplehurst Rd., Rochester NY 14617. (716)266-0679. Director: Jerry Englerth. "TSA is a nonprofit educational organization that is striving to fulfill the needs of the songwriter. We offer opportunities for songwriters which include song evaluation workshops to help songwriters receive an objective critique of their craft. TSA evaluates tapes and lyric sheets via the mail. We do not measure success on a monetary scale, ever. It is the craft of songwriting that is the primary objective. If a songwriter can arm himself with knowledge about the craft and the business, it will increase his confidence and effectiveness in all his dealings. However, we feel that the songwriter should be willing to pay for professional help that will ultimately improve his craft and attitude." Membership dues are $10/year. Must be member to receive discounts or services provided.

THE SONGWRITERS GUILD FOUNDATION, Suite 1002, 6430 Sunset Blvd., Hollywood CA 90028. (213)462-1108. West Coast Director: B. Aaron Meza. Estab. 1931.
Ask-a-Pro/Song Critique: SGA members are given the opportunity to present their songs and receive constructive feedback from industry professionals. A great chance to meet industry people, make contacts, ask questions and get your song heard! Free to SGA members. Reservations required. Call for schedule. Members outside regional area send tape with lyric and SASE for tape return.
Jack Segal's Songshop: This very successful 9-week workshop focuses on working a song through to perfection, including title, idea, rewrites and pitching your songs. Please call for more information regarding this very informative workshop. Dates to be announced. Fee.
Broadway on Sunset: The only west coast musical theater program promoting craft, business and development of new shows. Whether you have completed a show or dreamed of writing one, this program will give you the tools you need to write a successful stage musical. For further information contact SGA or Broadway On Sunset at (818)508-9270. Fee.
Special Seminars and Workshops: Held through the year. Past workshops included Sheila Davis on lyrics, tax workshops for songwriters, MIDI workshops, etc. Call for schedule.

THE SONGWRITERS GUILD OF AMERICA, 276 Fifth Ave., New York NY 10001. (212)686-6820. National Projects Director: George Wurzbach. Estab. 1931.
Ask-a-Pro: "2-hour bi-weekly music business forum to which all writers are welcome. It features industry professionals—publishers, producers, A&R people, record company executives, entertainment lawyers, artists—fielding questions from new songwriters." Offered year-round, except during summer. Charge: free to members, $2 for nonmembers.
Song Critique: "New York's oldest ongoing song critique. Guild songwriters are invited to either perform their song live or present a cassette demo for feedback. A Guild moderator is on hand to direct comments. Nonmembers may attend and offer comments. Free to members, $2 charge for nonmembers.
The Practical Songwriter: This is a 4-week nuts and bolts seminar dealing with industry networking, song marketing, contracts and publishing. Sessions are highlighted by visits from industry professionals. Instructor is songwriter/musician George Wurzbach. Fee: $130 for SGA members, $175 for nonmembers.
Pro-Shop: For each of 6 sessions an active publisher, producer or A&R person is invited to personally screen material from professional Guild writers. Participation is limited to 10 writers. Audition of material is required. Coordinator is producer/musician/award winning singer, Ann Johns Ruckert. Fee; $75 (SGA members only).
Writing for the Nashville Market: An important 4 session workshop for any writer considering writing for the expanding market of country/pop music. Developed to give writers a realistic approach to breaking into this market. Instructor is hit songwriter, author of *How To Pitch and Promote Your Songs* (Writer's Digest Books), Fred Koller. Fee; $60 for SGA members, $80 for non-members.

*SUMMER LIGHTS FESTIVAL, %Greater Nashville Arts Foundation, 201 Church St. Centre, Nashville TN 37219. (615)726-1875. Program Coordinator: Erika Wollam. Estab. 1981. Goal is to present the arts of Nashville to the world. Featured music is the music of Nashville: jazz, bluegrass, country, rock and gospel. Nashville Songwriters Association International always has a featured segment of the festival. Offers programs year-round. GNAF presents music programs all year; festival lasts 4 days. Approximately 2,000 songwriters/musicians participate in festival. Participants are amateur and professional individual vocalists, bands, ensembles, vocal groups, composers, individual instrumentalists, orchestras and opera/musical theater writers. Performers selected by invitation only. Take name and number and present before Programming Committee, which issues invites. Performers work outside on stages and in the street of the city; those from out of town stay in hotels and motels.

THE SWANNANOA GATHERING—CONTEMPORARY FOLK WEEK, (formerly Great Smokies Song Chase & Performing Artists Workshops), Warren Wilson College, 701 Warren Wilson Rd., Swannanoa NC 28778. (704)298-5099. Director: Jim Magill. "For anyone who ever wanted to make music for an audience, we offer a comprehensive week in artist development, divided into four major subject areas: Songwriting, Performance, Sound & Recording and Vocal Coaching, along with daily panel discussions of other business matters such as promotion, agents and managers, logistics of touring, etc. 1993 staff includes Fred Koller, Tim O'Brien, Bob Franke, Freyda Epstein, Kristina Olsen and Eric Garrison. For a brochure or other info contact Jim Magill, Director, The Swannanoa Gathering, at the phone number/address above. Tuition: $235. Housing (including all meals): $155. Annual program of The Swannanoa Gathering Folk Arts Workshops."

*THE TEN-MINUTE MUSICALS PROJECT, Box 461194, West Hollywood CA 90046. (213)656-8751. Producer: Michael Koppy. Estab. 1986. Promotes short complete stage musicals. Offers programs for songwriters, composers and musical playwrights. "Works selected are generally included in full-length 'anthology musical'—11 of the first 16 selected works are now in the show 'Stories,' for instance."

Awards a $250 royalty advance annually. Rounds end annually on August 31st. Various songwriters/ musicians participate in each workshop. Participants are amateur and professional songwriters, composers and musical playwrights. Participants are selected by demonstration tape, script, lead sheets. Send for application. Deadline: August 31st annually.

*WATERLOO FESTIVAL AND SCHOOL OF MUSIC, Village of Waterloo, Stanhope NJ 07874. (201)347-0900. Fax: (201)347-3573. Administrative Director: Carole Delaire. Estab. 1978. "Waterloo has programmed important 20th century works by such little-played composers as Malcolm Arnold, Boris Blacher, Carlos Chavez, Albert Roussel, Hans Pfitzer and William Walton. Central to Waterloo is the music of Bach. Waterloo features a program of study and performance for students who are beginning their professional careers. The faculty is chosen from major American Universities and Conservatories, Orchestras and Symphonies and they perform in collaboration with the students in weekly Orchestral Concerts that feature major artists. The renowned faculty perform weekly Chamber Concerts and weekly Student Chamber Concerts are open to the public. Students are chosen on the basis of juried auditions by the Waterloo faculty and by tapes submitted for adjudication. Students are informed of The Waterloo School of Music through their universities and conservatories and their principal teachers. We advertise in trade papers and send over 1,650 announcements." Offers other programs summer only and annually. Workshops take place July 20 to August 1. "The students and faculty reside at Princeton University, NJ and rehearse there during the week. The Chamber Concerts are performed Friday evenings at Princeton, and Orchestra Concerts are at the Village of Waterloo on six Saturday evenings while the school is in session." 130 songwriters/musicians participate in each workshop. Participants are amateur and professional individual instrumentalists. Participants are selected by in-person audition. Auditions are held in New York; Los Angeles; Indianapolis, IN; Princeton, NJ; Seattle, WA and Vancouver, British Columbia, Canada. Send for application. Deadline: March 15. Fee: $40 "for application processing. Concerts are performed in a Concert Tent. Chamber Concerts are performed at Richardson Auditorium, Princeton University. Both concerts are performed under professional conditions. The tent seats 2,700 people and Richardson seats 800. Composer David Diamond has participated at rehearsals of his compositions to be performed. He has also been honored at concerts. Waterloo celebrates its 18th season of giving performances of beautiful music and training qualified students for their professional careers."

Contests and Awards

A songwriter should approach a contest, award or grant just as he would a music publisher or record company: with care, thorough research and professionalism. Treat your contest submission as you would any other; appropriate marketing techniques shouldn't be disregarded. Remember, you're still selling yourself and your work—and you always want both presented in the best light possible.

Participation in contests is a great way to gain exposure for your music. Winners receive cash prizes, musical merchandise, studio time and perhaps a recording deal. It can lead to performances of the work for musical theater and concert music composers. Even if you don't win, valuable contacts can be made. Some contests are judged by music publishers and other music industry professionals, so your music may reach the ears of important people. The bottom line is there is a chance that a beneficial relationship could result from entering.

Be sure to do proper research to ensure that you're not wasting your time and money on less-than-legitimate contests. We have confidence in the contests listed in this edition of *Songwriter's Market*. But, before entering any contest, be aware of several things. After obtaining the entry forms and contest rules, be sure you understand the contest stipulations BEFORE signing your name or sending an entrance fee. If a publishing contract is involved as a prize, don't give away your publishing rights. If you do, you're endangering possible future royalties from the song. This is clearly not in your best interest. In evaluating any contest, you must weigh what you will gain against what you will give up. Be particularly wary of exorbitant entry fees. And if you must give up any of your publishing rights or copyright, it's almost always a good idea to stay away.

Contests listed in this section encompass all types of music and all levels of competition. Read each listing carefully and contact the sponsoring organization if the contest interests you. Remember: When you receive the contest information, read the rules carefully and be sure you understand them before entering.

ALEA III INTERNATIONAL COMPOSITION PRIZE, 855 Commonwealth Ave., Boston MA 02215. (617)353-3340. Executive Administrator: Synneve Carlino. For composers. Annual award.
Purpose: To promote and encourage young composers in the composition of new music.
Requirements: Composers 40 years of age and younger may apply; one score per composer. Works may be for solo voice or instrument or for chamber ensemble up to 15 members lasting between 6 and 15 minutes. All works must be unpublished. Deadline: March 15. Send for application. Samples of work required with application. "Real name should not appear on score; a nome de plume should be

signed instead. Sealed envelope with entry form should be attached to each score."
Awards: ALEA III International Composition Prize: $2,500. Awarded once annually. Between 8-10 finalists are chosen and their works are performed in a competition concert by the ALEA III contemporary music ensemble. One grand prize winner is selected by a panel of judges.
Tips: "Emphasis placed on works written in 20th century compositional idioms."

*AMERICAN SONGWRITER LYRIC CONTEST, 42 Music Square W., Nashville TN 37203-3206. (615)244-6065. Fax: (615)244-4314. Editor: Vernell Hackett. Estab. 1987. For songwriters. Award for each bimonthly issue of magazine, plus grand prize at year-end.
Purpose: To promote the art of songwriting and to allow readers the opportunity to be actively involved.
Requirements: Lyrics must be typed and check for $10 must be enclosed. Deadlines: February 1, April 1, June 1, August 1, October 1, December 1. Samples are not required.
Awards: A guitar, with different sponsors each year. Good for 3 months. Lyrics judged by 5-6 industry people—songwriters, publishers, journalists.

*ARTISTS' FELLOWSHIPS, New York Foundation for the Arts, 14th Floor, 155 Avenue of Americas, New York NY 10013. (212)366-6900. Fax: (212)366-1778. Director, Artists' Programs and Services: Penelope Dannenberg. For composers. Annual award. Estab. 1984.
Purpose: "Artists' Fellowships are $7,000 grants awarded by the New York Foundation for the Arts to individual originating artists living in New York State. The Foundation is committed to supporting artists from all over New York State at all stages of their professional careers. Fellows may use the grant according to their own needs; it should not be confused with project support."
Requirements: Must be 18 years of age or older; resident in New York State for 2 years prior to application; and cannot be enrolled in any graduate or undergraduate degree program. Deadline: Fall (call for dates). Samples of work are required with application. 1 or 2 original compositions on separate audiotapes and at least 2 copies of corresponding scores or fully harmonized lead sheets.
Awards: All Artists' Fellowships awards are for $7,000. Payment of $6,500 upon verification of NY State residency, and remainder upon completion of a mutually agreed upon public service activity. Nonrenewable. "Fellowships are awarded on the basis of the quality of work submitted and the evolving professional accomplishments of the applicant. Applications are reviewed by a panel of 5 composers representing the aesthetic, ethnic, sexual and geographic diversity within New York State. The panelists change each year and review all allowable material submitted."

ASCAP FOUNDATION GRANTS TO YOUNG COMPOSERS, ASCAP Bldg., 1 Lincoln Plaza, New York NY 10023. (212)621-6327. Contact: Frances Richard.
Purpose: To provide grants to young composers to encourage the development of talented young American composers.
Requirements: Applicants must be citizens or permanent residents of the United States of America who have not reached their 30th birthday by March 15. Original music of any style will be considered. However, works which have earned awards or prizes in any other national competition or grant giving program are ineligible. Arrangements are ineligible. Each applicant must submit a completed application form; one reproduction of a manuscript or score; biographical information listing prior music studies, background and experience; a list of compositions to date; and one professional recommendation to be mailed by the referee directly to ASCAP under separate cover. A cassette tape of the composition submitted for the competition may be included if it is marked with the composer's name, the title of the work and the names of the performers. Tapes of electronic music must also be accompanied by written information concerning source material and electronic equipment used. A composition that involves a text must be accompanied by information about the source of the text with evidence that it is in the public domain or by written permission from the copyright proprietor. Deadline: All materials must be postmarked no later than March 15.
Awards: ASCAP Foundation awards total $20,000 and grants range from $500-2,500. Length: 1 year. Applications judged by screening-panel of composers.

*CHRIS AUSTIN SONGWRITING CONTEST AT THE MERLE WATSON FESTIVAL, P.O. Box 120, Wilkesboro NC 28697. (919)651-8691. Fax: (919)651-8749. Festival Coordinator: Brenda Shepherd. Contest established in 1993, festival established in 1988. For songwriters. Annual award.
Purpose: "Open to individuals who consider themselves amateur songwriters."
Requirements: One song per category: country, bluegrass, gospel, general. Each song must be on a separate cassette, labeled with category, song title, name of songwriter, phone. Each song must be accompanied by a typed lyric sheet. Deadline: March 31. Write for information and enclose SASE. 1st place winners will perform winning song on the Cabin Main Stage at the Festival. Submissions will be judged by a panel of selected songwriters and music publishers from the Nashville music industry.

BALTIMORE OPERA COMPETITION FOR AMERICAN OPERATIC ARTISTS, 101 W. Read St., Baltimore MD 21201. (410)727-0592. Competition Coordinator: James Harp. For performing artists. Annual award.

Purpose: "Prizes are awarded to talented operatic artists in order to further their development in the study of languages, voice and acting."

Requirements: Singers must be between the ages of 20 and 35, inclusive, and must be citizens of the United States. They must present two letters of recommendation from recognized musical authorities." Deadline: May 15. Send for application. Singers must audition in person.

Awards: 1st Prize: $10,000; 2nd Prize $8,000; 3rd Prize $5,000; Steber Award $2,500; Puccini Award $2,000; Janowski Award $1,000; Collinge Memorial Award $1,000; $150 stipends to all semifinalists. Prize may be renewed upon audition. Singers are judged by a panel of internationally recognized judges eminent in the field of opera.

Tips: "The purpose of the competition is to encourage young operatic talent on the verge of a career. Singers must demonstrate potential in singing, fluency in languages and histrionic capability."

*BUSH ARTIST FELLOWSHIPS, E-900 First National Bank Bldg., 332 Minnesota St., St. Paul MN 55101. (612)227-5222. Director, Bush Artist Fellowships: Sally Dixon. Estab. 1976. For composers, playwrights, screenwriters, visual artists, writers and choreographers. Annual award. Applications in music composition, scriptwriting (including playwriting & screenwriting), film, video, multi-media, performance art and choreography are accepted in alternate years.

Purpose: "To provide uninterrupted time (6-18 months) for artists to pursue their creative development – do their own work."

Requirements: Applicant must be a Minnesota, North Dakota, South Dakota or western Wisconsin resident for 12 of preceeding 36 months, 25 years or older, not a student. Deadline: October-November. Send for application. Samples of work on cassette required with application. "Music composition applications will not be taken again until the fall of 1994. Applications will be taken in the fall of 1993 in the following areas: fiction, creative non-fiction, poetry, choreography, film, video, multimedia, performance art, painting, photography, drawing, printmaking, artists books and sculpture."

Awards: Bush Artist Fellowships: $26,000 stipend and $7,000 additional for production and travel. Award is good for 6-18 months. "5 years after completion of preceeding fellowship, one may apply again." Applications are judged by peer review panels.

CINTAS FELLOWSHIP, I.I.E 809 UN Plaza, New York NY 10017. (212)984-5370. Program Officer: Vanessa Palmer. For composers and musical playwrights. Annual award. Estab. 1964.

Requirements: "Fellowships awarded to persons of Cuban citizenship or lineage for achievement in music composition (architecture, painting, sculpture, printmaking, photography and literature); students wishing to pursue academic programs are not eligible, nor are performing artists. Applicants must be creative artists of Cuban descent who have completed their academic and technical training." Deadline: March 1. Send for application. Samples of work required with application. "Send complete score and a cassette tape. Compositions submitted must be serious contemporary works. Popular songs and ballads will not be accepted."

Awards: Cintas Fellowship: $10,000 per grantee. Fellowship is good for 12 months. Applicant may receive an award no more than twice. Selection committee reviews applications.

COLUMBIA ENTERTAINMENT COMPANY'S JACKIE WHITE MEMORIAL PLAYWRITING CONTEST, 309 Parkade Blvd., Columbia MO 65202. (314)874-5628. Chairperson, CEC Contest: Betsy Phillips. For musical playwrights. Annual award.

Purpose: "We are looking for top-notch scripts for theater school use, to challenge and expand the talents of our students, ages 10-15. We want good plays with large casts (20-30 characters) suitable for use with our theater school students. Full production of the winning script will be done by the students. A portion of travel expenses, room and board offered to winner for production of show."

Requirements: "Must be large cast plays, original story lines and cannot have been previously published. Please write for complete rules." Deadline: June 30. Send for application; then send scripts to address above. Full-length play, neatly typed. No name on title page, but name, address and name of play on a 3×5 index card. Cassette tape of musical numbers required. $10 entry fee. SASE for entry form."

Awards: $250 first prize and partial travel expenses to see play produced. Second place winner gets no prize money but receives production of the play by the theater school plus partial travel expenses. This is a one-time cash award, given after any revisions required are completed. "The judging committee is taken from members of Columbia Entertainment Company's Executive and Advisory boards. At least eight members, with at least three readings of all entries, and winning entries being read by entire committee. We are looking for plays that will work with our theater school students."

Tips: "Remember the play we are looking for will be performed by 10-15 year old students with normal talents – difficult vocal ranges, a lot of expert dancing and so forth will eliminate the play. We especially like plays that deal with current day problems and concerns. However, if the play is good enough, any suitable subject matter is fine. It should be fun for the audience to watch."

CONCOURS OSM COMPETITION, 85 St. Catherine St. W., Montreal Quebec H2X 3P4 **Canada**. (514)842-3402. For performing artists. Annual award alternates between winds and strings, and voice and piano.
Requirements: Contestants must be Canadian citizens or landed immigrants. Age requirements: Piano and Strings, Class A: 18-25; Piano and Strings, Class B: 17 and under; Winds: 16-25; Voice: 18-30. Send or phone for application.
Awards: Grand total of prizes of $15,000 (Canadian) given in various categories. First prize winners perform as soloists with l'Orchestre Symphonique de Montréal in concert. Total of 10 prizes. Judged by jury during three eliminations.

CRS NATIONAL COMPOSERS COMPETITION, 724 Winchester Rd., Broomall PA 19008. (215)544-5920. Administrative Assistant: Caroline Hunt. For songwriters, composers and performing artists. Annual award.
Requirements: Send for application. Samples of work required with application. Audio or video recording of composition.
Awards: 1st Prize: Commercial recording grant. Applications are judged by panel of judges including: Yo-Yo Ma, Lydia Walton Ignacio, William Smith, George Crumb and John Russo.

*DELTA OMICRON TRIENNIAL COMPOSITION COMPETITION, 2297 Tennessee Place, Lakewood CO 80228. National Competition Chairperson: Mrs. Fred Eidson. For composers of college age or over. Every three years.
Purpose: "To encourage composers, to give their work public performances and to further the cause of contemporary music.
Requirements: "The composition shall not have been published or publicly performed. An entry fee of $10 for each manuscript." Send for application.
Awards: "There is one award for $500 and the composition is performed at the Delta Omicron Triennial Conference. The next one is 1996. There are three National judges selected by the fraternity Board of Directors. Each a national/internationally known composer."
Tips: "Our next composition competition will not begin until September of 1993. At that time a new classification will be determined and the competition will run for two years."

EAST & WEST ARTISTS INTERNATIONAL AUDITIONS, #313, 310 Riverside Dr., New York NY 10025. Phone/Fax: (212)222-2433. Executive Director/Founder: Miss Adolovni Acosta. For performing artists. Annual award.
Requirements: "Open to all classical instrumentalists, singers and ensembles (up to 4 members) of any nationality who have not given a New York recital debut." There is no age limit. Deadline: February 1, 1994. Send SASE for information and application forms.
Awards: "A fully subsidized solo debut at Weill Recital Hall at Carnegie Hall; performing opportunities in New York City; cash awards."

ECKHARDT-GRAMATTÉ NATIONAL MUSIC COMPETITION FOR THE PERFORMANCE OF CANADIAN MUSIC, Queen Elizabeth II Music Bldg., Brandon University, Brandon, Manitoba R7A 6A9 **Canada**. (204)728-8212. Administrative Officer: Mrs. Lynne Bailey. For performing artists. Annual competition alternating each year between voice, piano and strings.
Purpose: To encourage young musicians to perform the works of modern (especially but not exclusively Canadian) composers.
Requirements: Must be citizens of Canada or resident in Canada for 2 years, must be 18 years of age as of January 1 of competition year and must be under 30 years of age for piano and strings, and under 35 for voice. Deadline: October. Send for application. Samples are not required.
Awards: 1st Prize: $5,000 and national recital tour. 2nd Prize: $3,000. 3rd Prize: $2,000. Best performance of imposed piece: $700. Preliminaries: Tape recordings are forwarded to jurors to mark. The tapes are numbered, not named. Semi-finalists: Attend competition in May where 4 jurors listen and compare. Finalists: Same as semi-finals.

*FAMILY ONE-ACT PLAY FESTIVAL, P.O. Box 22551, Nashville TN 37202. (615)780-3777. Fax: (615)758-3399. Executive Director: Don Breedwell. Estab. 1992. For musical playwrights. Annual award.
Purpose: "Promoting family oriented entertainment via theater musicals or non-musicals. Comedies always welcome."
Requirements: "Non-published, 1-act plays, running time 45 minutes or less with small casts." Deadline February 1st each year. Samples of work are required with application. Submit plays—one-acts, less than 45 min. in length. 1st Place $250, 2nd Place $150, 3rd Place $100. One time award. Previous

winners can win each year. Applications are judged "By a team of judges selected each year from New York, Los Angeles, Nashville and other major cities."
Tips: "Material must be of a family nature. Wholesome, entertaining and with some kind of message. Musicals must be accompanied by cassette tape. Scored music not required for judging, but must be available for production if selected as winner."

*FORT BEND SONGWRITER'S ASSOCIATION ANNUAL SONG & LYRIC CONTEST, P.O. Box 1273, Richmond TX 77406-1273. Chairman: Dave Davidson. For songwriters. Annual award.
Purpose: To promote song and lyric writing all the way from the first attempt to becoming a recorded composer.
Requirements: Any songwriter who wishes to enter may do so. It is our belief that songwriters must learn to compete with the best in order to reach their goals. Deadline: April 13. Send for application. Samples of work are required with application. Send one song per entry on a cassette with plainly written or typed label and lyric sheet. Lyric sheet only for lyric contest.
Awards: Each year the prizes are based on the number of entries; we give back at least half of the entry money after expenses plus merchandise and studio time donated by our supporters.
Tips: "Read all books on lyric writing, practice to become a better musician because your melodies will only be as good as your playing ability most of the time. If you only play 3 chords, you may not write any melodies that go beyond that. Write every day even if it's just a line or a hook or a different way of saying the same thing. Learn the art of collaboration, most hits listed in *Billboard* have two or more names as writers. Learn to accept rejection, if your song is passed over by someone it doesn't mean it was a bad song, just not what that individual was listening for on that particular day."

FULBRIGHT SCHOLAR PROGRAM, COUNCIL FOR INTERNATIONAL EXCHANGE OF SCHOLARS, Suite 5M, 3007 Tilden St. NW, Washington DC 20008-3009. (202)686-7877. Estab. 1946. For songwriters, composers, performing artists, musical playwrights and scholars/artists in all disciplines. Annual award.
Purpose: "Awards for university lecturing and advanced research abroad are offered annually in virtually all academic disciplines including musical composition."
Requirements: "U.S. citizenship at time of application; M.F.A., Ph.D. or equivalent professional qualifications; for lecturing awards, university teaching experience." Application materials for the competition become available in March each year, for grants to be taken up 1½ years later. Application deadlines: August 1, all world areas. Write or call for application. Samples of work are required with application. Applicant should refer to checklist in application packet.
Awards: "Benefits vary by country, but generally include round-trip travel for the grantee and for most full academic-year awards, one dependent; stipend in U.S. dollars and/or local currency; in many countries, tuition allowance for school age children; and book and baggage allowance. Grant duration ranges from 2 months-1 academic year. Applications undergo a two-stage peer review by CIES advisory committees; first by subject matter specialists and then by an interdisciplinary group of geographic area specialists. After nomination, applications are sent to the J. William Fulbright Scholarship Board and the host countries for final review."
Tips: "Suggestions on preparing a competitive application, as well as in-depth information about the review committee structure, etc., are contained in the Application Booklet."

GILMAN & GONZALEZ-FALLA THEATRE FOUNDATION MUSICAL THEATER AWARDS, 109 E. 64th St., New York NY 10021. (212)734-8001. Contact: Miss C. Kempler. For composers, musical playwrights any composer/lyricist/creative team with a produced musical to his/her/their credit. Annual award.
Requirements: Send for application.
Awards: $25,000.

HENRICO THEATRE COMPANY ONE-ACT PLAYWRITING COMPETITION, Box 27032, Richmond VA 23273. (804)672-5100. Cultural Arts Coordinator: J. Larkin Brown. For musical playwrights. Annual award.
Purpose: Original one-act musicals for a community theater organization.
Requirements: "Only one-act plays or musicals will be considered. The manuscript should be a one-act original (not an adaptation), unpublished, and unproduced, free of royalty and copyright restrictions. Scripts with smaller casts and simpler sets may be given preference. Controversial themes should be avoided. Standard play script form should be used. All plays will be judged anonymously, therefore, there should be two title pages; the first must contain the play's title and the author's complete address and telephone number. The second title page must contain only the play's title. The playwright must submit two excellent quality copies. Receipt of all scripts will be acknowledged by mail. Scripts will be returned if SASE is included. No scripts will be returned after the winner is announced. The HTC does not assume responsibility for loss, damage or return of scripts. All reasonable care will be taken." Deadline: September 1st. Send for application first.

Awards: 1st prize $250. 2nd prize $125. 3rd prize $125.

INTERMOUNTAIN SONGWRITING COMPETITION, Box 71325, Salt Lake City UT 84107. (801)596-3058. Estab. 1987. For songwriters. Annual award by Utah Songwriters Association.
Requirements: Call (801)596-3058 for information or send SASE for entry forms. All amateur songwriters may enter. Deadline: January 31. One song per tape. Contest runs from October 15 to January 31 each year. Entry must be postmarked by January 31. Entry fee: $10 for first song, $5 each additional song.
Awards: First place winner receives $500 cash or trip to the Los Angeles Songwriters Expo.
Tips: "Submit a well-written song with a good vocal and instruments well in tune. Have the vocals out front and the words clear. Remember, this is a competition so make your song competitive by having a good recording. Type lyric sheets neatly and *please* have your lyrics match the words on your recording. We look for songs that say something important and have a good hook."

INTERNATIONAL NEW MUSIC COMPETITION, 5215 Webster St., Omaha NE 68132. Chairman 1993 Competition: Mrs. Ann L. McGill. For composers. Annual award.
Requirements: Send for application.
Awards: International New Music Competition: $2,000. Premiere performance by Omaha Symphony Chamber Orchestra.

*INTINET RESOURCE CENTER POLY-POSITIVE MUSIC AWARD, P.O. Box 150474-X, San Rafael CA 94915. (415)507-1739. Contact: Dr. Deborah Anapol. Estab. 1993. For songwriters and performing artists. One time award.
Purpose: "The objective of the award is to promote the creation and performance of songs that positively portray ethical and responsible multipartner intimate relationships."
Requirements: Original music of any style will be considered, as will performances of traditional pieces. There are no restrictions on previous awards or performances. Deadline: June 1, 1994. Send for application. Samples of work required with application. "Submit one or more songs on cassette with lyric sheet, plus completed application form. Enclose SASE for acknowledgement of entry. Entries will be judged on musical quality, poly-positive message, and impact. Evidence of impact could include published reviews of performances or recordings, lists of bookings, and/or letters of recomendation from music industry figures. Judges will be drawn from members of IRC and the music industry."
Awards: 1st prize: $1,000. Grant is nonrenewable.

*KATE NEAL KINLEY MEMORIAL FELLOWSHIP, #110, 608 E. Lorado Taft Dr., Champaign IL 61820. (217)333-1661. Secretary: Ruth Wilcoxon. Estab. 1931. For students of architecture, art or music. Annual award.
Purpose: The advancement of study in the Fine Arts.
Requirements: "The Fellowship will be awarded upon the basis of unusual promise in the Fine Arts." Deadline: February 15. Send for application or call. Samples of work are required with application.
Awards: "Two or three major Fellowships which yield the sum of $7,000 each which is to be used by the recipients toward defraying the expenses of advanced study of the Fine Arts in America or abroad." Good for 1 year. Grant is nonrenewable.

*LEE KORF PLAYWRITING AWARD, Cerritos College, Dept. of Theatre, 11110 Alondra Blvd., Norwalk CA 90650. (310)924-2100. Fax: (310)860-9680. Theatre Production: Gloria Manriquez. For musical playwrights and playwrights. Annual award.
Purpose: "We look for promising playwrights who have something exciting to say with a fresh innovative way of saying it."
Requirements: "Submit two firmly bound manuscripts with SASE for return." Deadline: January 1 postmark. Send for guidelines. Samples are not required.
Awards: Lee Korf Playwriting Award: $750 plus full scale production. Award is one time only. Award is nonrenewable. "Submissions are read by faculty. Recommended scripts are discussed by directors."
Tips: "Include any production history of submitted piece."

*L.A. DESIGNERS' THEATRE–MUSIC AWARDS, P.O. Box 1883, Studio City CA 91614-0883. (818)769-9000, (213)650-9600, (310)247-9800. Fax: (818)985-9200. Artistic Director: Richard Niederberg. For songwriters, composers, performing artists, arrangers, lyricists, performance rights owners, musical playwrights, artists and rights holders of music.

Purpose: To produce new musicals, operettas, opera-boufes and plays with music, as well as new dance pieces with new music scores.

Requirements: None—submit a cassette, tape, CD or other medium. Acceptance: continuous. Submit nonreturnable materials with cover letter. Samples of work are required with application.

Awards: Music is commissioned for a particular project. Amounts are negotiable. Award/grant good upon receipt. Award is renewable. Applications judged by our artistic staff.

Tips: "Make the material 'classic,' yet commercial' and easy to record/re-record. Make sure rights are totally free of all 'strings,' 'understandings,' 'promises,' etc. ASCAP/BMI registration is OK, as long as 'grand' or 'performing rights' are understood."

McCLAREN MEMORIAL COMEDY PLAYWRITING COMPETITION, 2000 W. Wadley, Midland TX 79705. (915)682-2544. Chair: Mary Lou Cassidy. For musical playwrights. Annual award.

Purpose: "Awards a comedy script with presentation in reader's theater at a community theater in Texas in memorium to Mike McClaren, a very funny guy." Deadline: January 31, 1993. Entry Fee: $5. "Send script, only returned if SASE included."

Awards: $400 plus plane fare to Midland, TX for rehearsal period and production of reader's theater production of the play. Awarded in April. Reader's theater production of play in June or July of the same year.

Tips: *Must be funny.* No limit to number of scenes, scenery, number of characters."

MARIMOLIN COMPOSITION CONTEST, % Nancy Zeltsman, 475 Lake Dr., Princeton NJ 08540. (609)252-1262. For composers. Annual award.

Purpose: To encourage the creation of works for the combination of marimba and violin.

Requirements: Open to all composers. Deadline: July 1. Send for application. A completed new work for violin and marimba. 2 scores, or 1 score and parts. Winners announced by August 1.

Awards: "Up to 3 winners will be selected. A total of $600 will be awarded at the judges' discretion. The winning work(s) will be premiered during the following season."

MAXIM MAZUMDAR NEW PLAY COMPETITION, One Curtain Up Alley, Buffalo NY 14202-1911. (716)852-2266. Dramaturg: Joyce Stilson. For musical playwrights. Annual award.

Purpose: Alleyway Theatre is dedicated to the development and production of new works. Winners of the competition will receive production and royalties.

Requirements: Unproduced full-length work not less than 90 minutes long with cast limit of 10 and unit or simple set, or unproduced one-act work less than 60 minutes long with cast limit of 6 and simple set; prefers work with unconventional setting that explores the boundaries of theatricality; limit of submission in each category; guidelines available, no entry form. $5 playwright entry fee, script, resume, SASE optional. Cassette preferred, but not mandatory.

Awards: $400, production with royalty and travel and housing to attend rehearsals for full-length play or musical; $100 and production for one-act play or musical.

Tips: Entries may be of any style, but preference will be given to those scripts which take place in unconventional settings and explore the boundaries of theatricality. No more than ten performers is a definite, unchangeable requirement.

MID-SOUTH PLAYWRIGHTS CONTEST, 51 S. Cooper, Memphis TN 38104. (901)725-0776. Executive Director: Jackie Nichols. For musical playwrights. Annual award. Estab. 1983.

Requirements: Send script, tape, SASE. "Playwrights from the South will be given preference." Open to full-length, unproduced plays. Musicals must be fully arranged for the piano when received. Deadline: April 1.

Awards: Grants may be renewed. Applications judged by 3 readers.

MIXED BLOOD VERSUS AMERICA PLAYWRITING CONTEST, 1501 S. 4th St., Minneapolis MN 55454. (612)338-0937. Script Czar: Dave Kunz. For musical playwrights. Annual award. Estab. 1983.

Purpose: To encourage emerging playwrights (musical playwrights).

Requirements: "Send previously unproduced play (musical), resume, cover letter stipulating contest entry." Deadline March 15. Send SASE for copy of contest guidelines. Samples are not required.

Awards: Winner: $2,000 and full production of winning play/musical.

Tips: "Professionalism is always a plus. Surprise us. All subject matter accepted. Political satires and shows involving sports (baseball, golf etc.) always of interest."

MUSEUM IN THE COMMUNITY COMPOSER'S AWARD, Box 251, Scott Depot WV 25560. (304)562-0484. Contest Administrator: Trish Fisher. For composers. Biennial.

Purpose: The Composer's Competition is to promote the writing of new works for string quartet—two violins, viola and cello.

Requirements: Work must not have won any previous awards nor have been published, publicly performed or used commercially. Requires 3 copies of the original score, clearly legible and bound. Title to appear at the top of each composition, but the composer's name must not appear. Entry forms must be filled out and a SASE of the proper size enclosed for return of entry. Enclose $25 entry fee (non-refundable). Send for application.

Awards: Museum in the Community Composer's Award First place: $2,500. "Up to 3 honorable mentions will be awarded at the discretion of the judges." Jurors will be 3 nationally known musicologists. Winning composer will be awarded $2,500 prize and a premiere concert of the composition by the Montani String Quartet, the resident string quartet of the West Virginia Symphony. Transportation to the premiere from anywhere in the continental United States will be provided by the Museum.

Tips: "Read *and* follow rules listed in Prospectus. Neatness still counts!"

NACUSA YOUNG COMPOSERS' COMPETITION, NACUSA, Box 49652 Barrington Station, Los Angeles CA 90049. (213)541-8213. President, NACUSA: Marshall Bialosky. For NACUSA members 18-30 years of age. Annual award.

Purpose: Goal is "to encourage the writing and performance of new American concert hall music."

Requirements: Must have NACUSA membership and meet age restrictions. Samples are not required. Write for information.

Awards: Judged by a committee of composers.

NETWORK OF LYRICISTS & SONGWRITERS SONGWRITING & LYRIC WRITING CONTEST, (formerly Songwriters Network of Houston Songwriting and Lyric Writing Contest). P.O. Box 890425, Houston TX 77289-0425. (713)264-4330. Contact: Sybrina Durant. For songwriters and lyricists. Annual award.

Purpose: Objective is to promote the growth of songwriting by providing an arena of competition for amateur writers and lyricists and to recognize works of more accomplished writers.

Requirements: Applicants in the amateur division must be of amateur status, must not have ever received royalties from ASCAP, BMI or SESAC, and must not have ever been or currently be signed to a *national* record label. Deadline: November 30. Samples of work required with application. "One song on a cassette with 2 neatly printed or typed copies of the lyrics. Label lyric sheet and tape with name of song, songwriter, address and phone number. Cue tape before sending. Entry forms may be ordered after July 30th by sending 2 29¢ stamps to the above address."

Awards: Songwriting category: Grand prize is $500 plus recording time and/or merchandise from sponsor as made available. Judged by impartial personnel from the music industry.

Tips: "Our judges have made the following comments about past entries in our contests. Use word economy but make each word count. Have a 'pay off' in your song, i.e. an unexpected or surprise ending. 'Marry' your lyrics to your music by not 'shoving' words together within the bars of music. Pick topics that will appeal to the majority of your audience. Use idioms and word play to make your lyrics more interesting. Maintain a consistent time progression, i.e. morning, noon, night or past to present. Don't 'jump around' in time. Select a point of view, first person, second person, etc. and stick with it throughout the song. Limit the length of your song to 3 minutes or less."

NEW FOLK CONCERTS FOR EMERGING SONGWRITERS, Box 1466, Kerrville TX 78029. (210)257-3600. Attn: New Folk. For songwriters and composers. Annual award.

Purpose: "Our objective is to provide an opportunity for unknown songwriters to be heard and rewarded for excellence."

Requirements: Songwriter enters 2 previously unpublished songs on same side of cassette tape—$8 entry fee; no more than one tape may be entered; 6-8 minutes total for 2 songs. No written application necessary; no lyric sheets or press material needed. Deadline: April 15th. Call for detailed information.

Awards: New Folk Award Winner. Forty finalists invited to sing the 2 songs entered during The Kerrville Folk Festival. Six writers are chosen as award winners. Each of the 6 receives a cash award of $150 and performs at a winner's concert during the Kerrville Folk Festival. Initial round of entries judged by the Festival Producer. Forty finalists judged by panel of 3 performer/songwriters.

Tips: "Make certain cassette is rewound and ready to play. Do not allow instrumental accompaniment to drown out lyric content. Don't enter without complete copy of the rules. Former winners include Lyle Lovett, Nanci Griffith, Hal Ketchum, John Gorka, David Wilcox, Lucinda Williams and Robert Earl Keen."

*OPERA-MUSICAL THEATER PROGRAM, National Endowment for the Arts, 1100 Pennsylvania Ave. NW, Washington DC 20506. (202)682-5447. Estab. 1979. Contact: Program Director or Assistant Director, Opera-Musical Theater Program. For composers, performing artists and/or musical playwrights working with producing organizations, or who are themselves producers.

Purpose: "The Opera-Musical Theater Program assists all forms of music theater generally involving voice, from experimental musical theater to operetta, from ethnic musical theater to classic musical comedy, from grand opera to still-developing forms. Grants are awarded to support professional opera-musical theater organizations that produce works of high artistic quality and of national or regional significance; regional touring; the creation, development, rehearsal, and production of new American works and/or the support of seldom-produced works; independent producers, artist-producers, artist fellowships; and national and regional service organizations."

Requirements: "Eligibility requirements and deadline dates vary from category to category. Applicants should send or call for application guidelines. Samples of work are required with application. The grant is good up to one-year, then applicants/grantees must reapply. Upon receipt of the Opera-Musical Theater Program Guidelines, applicants must carefully review the sections labeled 'We Fund' and 'We Do Not Fund.' Applicants must then consult the general instructions for application procedures for their category. These instructions list what supporting material is required with the application. Applicants are advised not to send supporting materials separately from the applications. If an applicant has any questions or needs help in completing the application forms or other required materials, they should contact the Opera-Musical Theater Program staff. Late applications are rejected. Incomplete applications are not likely to be funded. After the Opera-Musical Theater Program staff has checked the application for completeness, the appropriate Opera-Musical Theater Program Advisory Panel, a rotating committee of experts in the field, reviews them. Following panel review, the National Council on the Arts makes recommendations to the Chairman of the Arts Endowment for final decision."

Awards: Grants are awarded in 5 categories and may range from $5,000-500,000 for organizations; $5,000-120,000 for individuals.

Tips: "Call and talk to a program specialist after carefully reading the Guidelines to determine eligibility."

*PERFORMERS OF CONNECTICUT YOUNG ARTISTS COMPETITION, 17 Morningside Dr. S., Westport CT 06880. (203)227-8998. Fax: (203)792-9210. Contact: Dr. Courtnay V. Caublé. Estab. 1972. For performing artists. Annual award.

Purpose: "To provide opportunities and support to outstanding young professional, classical musicians."

Requirements: Voice—Between 19-33 years of age on 12/4/93; Strings—Between 18-30 years of age on 12/4/93. No professional management. Deadline: October 11. Send or call for application. Samples of work required with application.

Awards: Prizes in each category (voice and strings) are $2,000 and $1,000. Applicants are judged by a panel of distinguished musicians at each level of the competition.

*PRO MUSICIS INTERNATIONAL AWARD, 140 W. 79th St., New York NY 10024. (212)787-0993. Fax: (212)362-0352. Executive Director: John Haag. For performing artists. Annual award.

Purpose: "Artistic inspiration is the purest gift offered by God to humanity. To enable this gift to express itself, and to share it with the widest possible audience in both concert halls and institutions, is the unique and precious mission of Pro Musicis. The Award fosters the international exchange of artists by providing a concert tour through major cities. With every promotional concert, the artist performs two community service concerts."

Requirements: "To be a Pro Musicis International Award winner, one must be an emerging artist of world-class potential, a recitalist with exceptional technical ability, a lover of both music and people and an artist committed to sharing one's talent with both concert and underserved audience." Deadline March 1, 1994. Send for application. Samples of work are required with application. Two cassette copies of an unedited recording of one's most recent (within one year) live public recital. "The award winner receives a concert tour through major US cities, and to the extent possible, Paris and Rome. In addition to receiving a fee, the soloists benefit from professional promotion, the exposure of critical review, and the opportunity to perform community service concerts for underserved audience. The members of Music committee undertake preliminary evaluations to identify whether an applicant is outstanding, acceptable or below standard. The committee then meets to listen to the outstanding and acceptable candidates and further narrow the list for the semi-finals. From this number, the committee selects the finalists for audition."

Tips: "A high quality recorded cassette will certainly improve your chances. In addition, there is no age limit. Eligible solo categories rotate on a 2-year cycle. 1993 and odd years—harp, harpsichord, winds, voice. 1994 and even years—guitar, piano, strings."

PULITZER PRIZE IN MUSIC, 702 Journalism, Columbia University, New York NY 10027. (212)854-3841. For composers and musical playwrights. Annual award.

Requirements: "The piece must have its American premiere between March 15 and March 1 of the one-year period in which it is submitted for consideration." Deadline: March 1. Samples of work are required with application and $20 entry fee. "Send tape and score."

Awards: "1 award: $3,000. Applications are judged first by a nominating jury, then by the Pulitzer Prize Board."

THE QUINTO MAGANINI AWARD IN COMPOSITION, 37 Valley View Rd., Norwalk CT 06851. Contest Coordinator: Russell Cooper. For composers.
Requirements: The competition is open to all American composers. Entries should be submitted anonymously, with Social Security Number as identification and appropriate return envelope and return postage. In an accompanying sealed envelope, composer should give name, address, social security number, and brief resume. The composition is to be scored for standard symphonic orchestra, and should not exceed 15 minutes in length; no soloists or concerti. Write for more information. Deadline January 31.
Awards: The recipient will receive a cash award ($2,500) and will have the composition performed in world premiere by the Norwalk Symphony Orchestra under the direction of Jesse Levine, Musical Director, during the 1993-94 season.

*RICHARD RODGERS PRODUCTION AWARD, American Academy of Arts and Letters, 633 W. 155th St., New York NY 10032. (212)368-5900. Assistant to the Executive Director: Betsey Feeley. Estab. 1978. "The Richard Rodgers Production Award subsidizes a production by a nonprofit theater group in New York City of a work by composers and writers who are not already established in the field of musical theater. Development grants for staged readings or workshop productions may be given in lieu of the Production Award or in addition to it. The award is only for musicals—songs by themselves are not eligible. The authors must be citizens or permanent residents of the United States." (Guidelines for this award may be obtained by sending a SASE to above address.)

ROME PRIZE FELLOWSHIP, 41 E. 65th St., New York NY 10021. (212)517-4200. Contact: Fellowships Coordinator. For composers. Annual award.
Purpose: "A center for artistic creation and for independent study and advanced research in the humanities, the academy provides living and working space for artists and scholars at the Academy's ten-building, eleven-acre campus in Rome."
Requirements: "U.S. citizens only may apply. B.A. required in field of musical composition." Deadline: Nov. 15. Send or call for application. Samples of work are required with application. Tapes and scores.
Awards: "Rome Prize Fellowships—2 available in musical composition: $7,000 stipend, $500 European travel, $800 travel allowance, room, board, studio. One year in Rome. Judged by independent juries of professionals in the field."
Tips: "Write a good proposal explaining why a year in Rome would be invaluable to your development as a composer. Explain what you would do in Rome."

LOIS AND RICHARD ROSENTHAL NEW PLAY PRIZE, % Cincinnati Playhouse, P.O. Box 6537, Cincinnati OH 45206. (513)345-2242. Contact: Artistic Associate. For musical playwrights, songwriters and composers. Annual award.
Purpose: The Lois and Richard Rosenthal New Play Prize was established in 1987 to encourage the development of new plays that are original, theatrical, strong in character and dialogue and that are a significant contribution to the literature of American Theatre. Lois Rosenthal is the author of books in the consumer information field and is the editor of "Story" magazine, the classic literary quarterly. Richard Rosenthal operates F&W Publications, a family company founded in 1910, which publishes books and magazines for writers and artists. Residents of Cincinnati, the Rosenthals are committed to supporting arts organizations and social agencies that are innovative and that foster social change.
Requirements: "The play must be full-length and can be of any style: comedy, drama, musical, etc. Individual one-acts are not acceptable. Collaborations are welcome, in which case the prize benefits are shared. The play must not have received a full-scale, professional production, and it must be unpublished prior to submission. A play that has had a workshop, reading or non-professional production is eligible. Playwrights with past production experience are especially encouraged to submit new work. Any play previously submitted for the Rosenthal Prize is ineligible. Only one submission per playwright. Submit a 2-page maximum abstract of the play including title, playwright, character breakdown, story synopsis, a short bio of the playwright and any other information you wish to provide. Also send up to five pages of sample dialogue. All abstracts will be read. From these, selected manuscripts will be solicited. Do not send a manuscript with or instead of the abstract. All unsolicited manuscripts will be returned unread. The Rosenthal Prize is open for submission from October 15th to February 1st."
Awards: The Rosenthal Prize play is produced at the Cincinnati Playhouse in the Park as part of the theater's annual season, and it is given regional and national promotion. The playwright receives a $2,000 advance on royalties, a $3,000 stipend, travel expenses and residency in Cincinnati during production. In addition, appropriate royalties are paid for a full-scale, professional production of the play. In addition to the prize winning play, a number of plays are selected to be given a workshop at the Playhouse with a professional director and actors. Playwrights are provided travel expenses and residency in Cincinnati for these workshops. It is possible for a play that has been given a workshop to be chosen as the Rosenthal Prize recipient for the following season with complete prize benefits.

SONGWRITERS ASSOCIATION OF WASHINGTON MID-ATLANTIC SONG CONTEST, Suite 632, 1377 K St. NW, Washington DC 20005. (301)654-8434. Contact: Director. Estab. 1982. Gives awards to songwriters and/or composers annually.

Purpose: "Contest is designed to afford *amateurs* the opportunity of receiving awards/exposure/feedback of critical nature in an environment of peer competition. Applicants must send for application; rules and regulations explained—amateur status is most important requirement. Samples of work are required with application: cassette, entry form and 3 copies of lyrics."

Awards: "Awards usually include free recording time, merchandise and cash. Awards vary from year to year. Awards must be used within one calendar year."

Requirements: "Applications are judged by a panel of 3 judges per category, for 3 levels, to determine top winners in each category and to arrive at the grand prize winner. Reduced entry fees are offered for SAW members. Membership also entitles one to a newsletter and reduced rates for special events/seminars."

Tips: "Please check to see that you have followed *all* the rules, cue song to beginning—make lyric sheets legible and neat, no long introductions."

SORANTIN YOUNG ARTIST AWARD, (formerly Hemphill-Wells Sorantin Young Artist Award), Box 5922, San Angelo TX 76902. (915)658-5877. For performing artists. Annual award. Estab. 1959.

Purpose: "There are 3 divisions of competition: Vocal, Instrumental and Piano. All candidates will be judged by the highest artistic standards, in regard to technical proficiency, musicianship, rhythm, selection of repertoire and stage presence. Objective: to further the career of the young artist."

Requirements: Piano/instrumental: not reached their 28th birthday by competition. Vocal: not reached their 31st birthday by competition. All contestants will perform all repertoire from memory. Deadline: October 25. Send for application. Judged on performance contest weekend.

Awards: A winner and runner-up will be declared in each division. The division winner will receive a cash award of $500; the runner-up will receive $250. An overall winner will be selected to appear with the San Angelo Symphony Orchestra, and will receive an additional $1,500 cash award. $500 to be paid at time of selection and $1,000. Title held as winner of that year. Printed on all future information. Contest held every year. Can only win once. No limit on number of times you may enter. This is a competition for the young artist; highest priority will be placed on artistry, communication and stage presence.

STANLEY DRAMA AWARD, Wagner College, Dept. of Humanities, Howard Ave. and Campus Rd., Staten Island NY 10301. For musical playwrights and playwrights. Annual award.

Purpose: "The Stanley Drama Award offers a $2,000 prize for an original full-length play or musical which has not been professionally produced or received tradebook publication."

Requirements: "Plays must be recommended by a teacher of drama or creative writing, a critic, an agent, a director or another playwright or composer. The person recommending must have read or seen the play in question and address the recommendation to that specific play." Deadline: September 1. Send for application. Samples of work are required with application. "All scripts must be accompanied by a completed application, a professional recommendation (no self-recommendations, please) and a stamped, self-addressed return envelope large enough to accomodate the script(s). Include a self-addressed post card if you wish to be advised that we have received your script. Writers of musicals are urged to submit music on cassette tapes (not reel-to-reel) as well as book and lyrics."

Awards: Stanley Drama Award — $2,000. Grant nonrenewable.

THE JULIUS STULBERG INTERNATIONAL STRING COMPETITION, (formerly The Julius Stulberg Auditions, Inc.), Box 50107, Kalamazoo MI 49005. (616)375-2808. Business Manager: Mrs. Zoe Forsleff. For performing artists. Annual award.

Purpose: "To encourage continued excellence in musical education and accomplishment for young string players studying violin, viola, cello and double bass."

Requirements: Must be 19 years of age or younger. There is a $30 application fee. Send for application. Prefers cassette tape, not to exceed 20 minutes in length. "Music on tape must be from standard repertoire, and accompanied."

Awards: 1st place: $3,000 solo performance with Kalamazoo Junior Symphony; 2nd place: $1,500 and recital performance with Fontana Concert Society; 3rd place: $1,000.

Tips: The cassette tapes are screened by a local panel of judges, from which 12 finalists are selected to compete in live competition. An outstanding panel of three judges is engaged to choose the winners. The 1990 judges were Sir Yehudi Menuhin, Maestro Catherine Comet and internationally-known violist, Csaba Erdelyi. The 1994 live competition will be February 26, 1994.

TALENT SEARCH AMERICA, 273 Chippewa Dr., Columbia SC 29210-6508. For songwriters, composers, poets and lyricists. Awards given quarterly.

Purpose: "To discover and award new songwriters and lyricists."

Requirements: Deadlines are February 1, May 2, August 3, and November 4. Send SASE for entry forms and information. Samples of work on cassette and lyric sheet are required for entry *with entry form.* "All inquiries must be by mail. No phone calls, please. Many entrants have gained contracts and other interests with many music and creative writing companies. Winners' lists are sent to winners only. Talent Search America is co-sponsored by selected companies in the music and creative writing businesses. Talent Search America is a national nonprofit contest partnership. Entrant information will not be returned or disclosed without written permission from winning entrants. Proper postage must be sent to gain entry forms. Entrants from around the world are welcome. All inquiries must include *first class postage for each entry form* desired. Non-published/unpublished lyrics and music accepted."

Awards: 6 awards given every quarter: 3 for songwriters, 3 for lyricists (cash awards and award certificates). Entries are judged on creativity, commercial appeal and originality.

MARVIN TAYLOR PLAYWRITING AWARD, Box 3030, Sonora CA 95370. (209)532-3120. Estab. 1980. For musical playwrights.

Purpose: To encourage new voices in American theater.

Requirements: Mail script with SASE. "We accept phone calls or written inquiry." No application form or fee. Submissions must be full-length, typewritten. SASE if manuscript is to be returned. Prefers cassette to written score with original submissions. No more than 2 prior productions of script. Deadline: August 31.

Awards: Marvin Taylor Playwriting Award: $500 and possible full staging. Applications are judged by a committee of the theater's artistic staff.

V.O.C.A.L. SONGWRITER'S CONTEST, P.O. Box 34606, Richmond VA 23234. President: Gary Shaver (804)796-1444. Song Contest Director: Robert (Cham) Laughlin (804)733-5908. For songwriters and composers. Annual award with up to 14 categories.

Purpose: "To recognize good songs and lyrics as well as the writers of same."

Requirements: "Original songs/lyrics/compositions only." Postal deadline: March 31 of the contest year. Send for entry forms and information. Song entries must be on cassette tape. Lyric entries should be typed or neatly printed on white paper." Contest entries and inquiries should be sent to V.O.C.A.L. Song Contest, P.O. Box 2438, Petersburg VA 23804.

Awards: Prizes for first, second, third places overall, most appropriate production, and first, second and third places in each category plus honorable mention. Prizes include: Cash, merchandise, T-shirts, certificates and more.

Tips: "Be sure to use a clean, fresh tape to record your entry. Listen to the entry to be sure it's not distorted or too low in volume. A decent sounding tape stands a much better chance. The judges can only grade based on what they hear. Don't over produce your entry. That will take away from the song itself. Fill out the entry form completely and follow all rules of the contest. The contest begins January 1st and entries must be postmarked no later than March 31 of that contest year. Mail your entry early."

ELIZABETH HARPER VAUGHN CONCERTO COMPETITION, Kingsport Symphony Orchestra, Room 311, 1200 E. Center St., Kingsport TN 37660. (615)392-8423. General Manager: Barbara S. Gerwe. For performing artists. Annual award.

Purpose: To further the careers of young professional musicians.

Requirements: Call or send for application. Deadline: Dec. 31. Samples of work are required with application. Cassette tape of concerto or musical composition to be performed.

Awards: Honorarium of $1,000 and opportunity to perform with Kingsport Symphony Orchestra the following season. Judged by jury of peers—accredited professors of music in college.

WEST COAST ENSEMBLE—MUSICAL STAIRS, Box 38728, Los Angeles CA 90038. (213)871-8673. Artistic Director: Les Hanson. For composers and musical playwrights. Annual award.

Purpose: To provide an arena and encouragement for the development of new musicals for the theater.

Requirements: Send a copy of the script and a cassette of the score. Send script and score to West Coast Ensemble at above address.

Awards: The West Coast Ensemble Musical Stairs Competition Award includes a production of the selected musical and $500 prize. The selected musical will be part of the 1994 season. Panel of judges read script and listen to cassette. Final selection is made by Artistic Director.

Tips: "Submit libretto in standard playscript format along with professional sounding cassette of songs."

YOUNG ARTIST COMPETITION, Fort Collins Symphony, Box 1963, Fort Collins CO 80522. (303)482-4823. Office Manager: Merrilee Pouliot. For performing artists. Annual award.
Purpose: To encourage young people to pursue excellence in the study and mastery of orchestral instruments.
Requirements: Deadline: January 20. Send for application.
Awards: Senior Division: First Place, The Adeline Rosenberg Memorial Prize $2,000. Second Place: $1,000. Third Place: $500. Junior Division: Piano First Place: $250. Second Place: $50. Instrumental First Place: $250. Second Place: $50. Senior Division: Panel of judges listen to tapes in Round I, select semi-finalists to play before judges for Round II, who select 3 finalists to perform with symphony and be judged in Round III. Junior Division: Panel of judges listen to all applicants in a recital-type environment. Winners selected the same day.
Tips: "The first round is judged on the strength of your tape. The tape and your performance must be with accompaniment."

*YWCA STUDIO CLUB COMPETITION, 610 Lexington Ave., New York NY 10022. (212)735-9763. Auditions Coordinator: Ms. Cora Etta Brown Caldwell. For young opera singers age 18-35. Annual award.
Purpose: First prize $2,500; second prize $2,000, third prize $1,500, fourth prize $1,000, awarded to the winners from the final competition.
Requirements: "Call Ms. Cora Etta Caldwell at (212)735-9763 for an application. All applications should be sent back as soon as you receive them (we do get booked up fast.) For Opera singers. One of the selections should be in English, the other in original foreign language. One art song, one aria."

ANNA ZORNIO MEMORIAL CHILDREN'S THEATRE PLAYWRITING AWARD, Dept. of Theatre and Dance, Univ. of NH, Durham NH 03824-3538. Attn: Peggy Rae Johnson. Annual award.
Purpose: Playwriting contest for new plays and musicals, with an award of up to $250 to a winning playwright(s), and a guaranteed production by the UNH Theatre In Education Program. The award will be administered by the Directors of the UNH Theatre Resources For Youth Program. This faculty will reserve the right to withhold the award if, in their opinion, no plays merit the award. Production of the prize-winning script will be scheduled by the UNH Theatre In Education Program during the 1994-95 academic year.
Requirements: The contest is open to all playwrights in the United States and Canada. The contest is for new plays, with a maximum length of 60 minutes, suitable for elementary through middle school audiences. Plays submitted must not have been: previously published; previously produced by a professional Equity company; a previously produced winner of an award or prize in another playwriting contest; and must not be under contract for publication before UNH's announcement of the award winner. Playwrights may submit more than one play, but not more than three. Deadline: April 15, 1994. Send for rules of entry for a complete list of requirements.
Awards: Anna Zornio Award: $250 and production of the play/musicals.

Publications of Interest

Knowledge about the music industry is essential for both creative and business success. Staying informed requires keeping up with constantly changing information. Updates on the changing trends in the music business are available to you in the form of music magazines, music trade papers and books. There is a publication aimed at almost every type of musician, songwriter and music fan, from the most technical knowledge of amplification systems to the gossip about your favorite singer. These publications can enlighten and inspire you and provide information vital in helping you become a more well-rounded, educated and, ultimately, successful musical artist.

This section lists all types of magazines and books that you may find interesting. From home-grown fanzines and glossy music magazines to tip sheets and how-to books, there should be something listed here that you'll enjoy and benefit from.

Periodicals

*ACOUSTIC GUITAR, published by String Letter Press. P.O. Box 767, San Anselmo CA 94979. (415)485-6946. Fax: (415)485-0831. Contact: Circulation Dept. Bimonthly magazine; 104 pages. Subscription price: $19.95/year. Estab. 1990. "We cover all sorts of music that involves acoustic guitar, with performer interviews, instructional articles and reviews of recordings and equipment. Each issue features a number of guitar solos or songs to play, and the Song Craft department profiles a notable singer-songwriter guitarist in each issue, along with a transcription of one of his or her songs."

*AMERICAN SONGWRITER MAGAZINE, 42 Music Square W., Nashville TN 37203. (615)244-6065. Contact: Circulation Department. Bi-monthly magazine; 48-56 pages. Subscription price: $15.95/year. Estab. 1984. "A magazine for and about songwriters, the craft of songwriting and the songwriting industry. We cover all genres: pop, rock, gospel, country and R&B. *American Songwriter* provides articles and interviews with professional songwriters, publishers and producers. It also includes several columns which discuss the writing of lyrics and music, as well as columns by professional songwriters. Additionally, there is a column containing the latest news from publishing communities, including Los Angeles, New York and Nashville."

ASCAP IN ACTION, published by ASCAP—American Society of Composers, Authors & Publishers, One Lincoln Plaza, New York NY 10023. Editor: Murdoch McBride. Quarterly (semi-annual) magazine; 44 pages. Free to ASCAP members and music industry, this has been ASCAP's membership magazine for several years. *ASCAP In Action* is ASCAP's premiere publication. The magazine features news about ASCAP members, events sponsored by the Society (ASCAP Pop Awards, Film and Television Awards, showcases and workshops) and a variety of articles on leading songwriters. Topics of interest to composers, lyricists and publishers are also covered at length along with summaries on ASCAP legislative efforts. ASCAP members can have their career updates published in the *Steppin' Out* section of the magazine: Send notices to *Steppin' Out*, % Editor, *ASCAP In Action*, One Lincoln Plaza, New York, New York 10023. *Steppin' Out* notices must come directly from the ASCAP member and should be written in the style used in that section of the magazine. Space limitations preclude more than one listing per member in each issue.

ASCAP PLAYBACK, published by ASCAP-American Society of Composers, Authors and Publishers, One Lincoln Plaza, New York NY 10023. Editor: Murdoch McBride. A semi-annual supplement to *ASCAP in Action, ASCAP PlayBack* features photo coverage of numerous ASCAP events, member news and related music industry activities. 8-12 pages.

AWC NEWS/FORUM, American Women Composers, Inc., Suite 409, 1690 36th St. NW, Washington, DC 20007. (202)342-8179. Annual; 20 pages. Subscription price: $15. Estab. 1976. "*AWC News/Forum* is an annual publication which is mailed free of charge to members and is subscribed to by numerous colleges and universities throughout the US. It contains articles of interest to women, about women, notices of performances of women composers, information about composition competitions, etc. The News/Forum is supplemented bi-annually with the AWC News-Update."

*BABYLON, P.O. Box 691365, Los Angeles CA 90069. (818)760-3699. Editor: Bambi LaRue. Bi-monthly magazine; 24 pages. Subscription price: $6. Estab. 1989. "A tabloid covering all forms of entertainment and dedicated to fun."

*BACTERIA OF DECAY, 63 Lennox Ave., Buffalo NY 14226. Subscriptions: Curt. Bimonthly magazine; 40 pgs. Subscription price: $10/year. Estab. 1988. "We are a 'do it yourself' free thinking magazine that centralizes on punk, hardcore and thrash music, but we are always open to different forms. We try to help smaller bands get noticed via interviews and reviews and do what they want, not what some major label or producer wants them to do."

*BIG SHOUT MAGAZINE, published by Red Ink, Inc., 3207 Miller Rd., Wilmington DE 19802. (302)762-2724. Fax: (302)762-2070. Contact: Office Circulation. Monthly magazine; 36 pages. Subscription price: $18/year. Estab. 1988. "Monthly music magazine, regionally covering Philadelphia and Delaware market. Major musician markets, most major labels have subscriptions to *Big Shout*, we review records locally and nationally."

*B-SIDE MAGAZINE, edited by Carol Schutzbank, senior editor. P.O. Box 1830, Burlington NJ 08016. Contact: Sandra A. Garcia, Managing Editor. Bi-monthly magazine; pages vary. Estab. 1986. "*B-Side* provides a bridge between home-grown fanzines and the commercial magazines. We cover a myriad of styles, artists and genres. . . we are both informative and entertaining."

*CALIFORNIA COUNTRY MUSIC NEWS, published by Ray Nelson Productions. P.O. Box 9602, San Jose CA 95157-0602. (408)370-7005. Fax: (408)379-1063. Contact: Louise Nelson, Editor. Monthly newspaper; 24 pages. Subscription price: $30. Estab. 1990. "The only statewide publication focusing on country music."

CANADIAN MUSICIAN, #7, 23 Hannover Dr. St., Catharines, Ontario L2W 1A3 **Canada.** (416)641-3471. Special Projects Coordinator: Penny Campbell. Published 6 times/year; 70 pages; $21/year. Estab. 1979. "We provide musicians and music makers with in-depth information that they can put to use in furthering their musical endeavors. Through regular columns on many aspects of playing and performing, we keep readers up-to-date and in touch with the Canadian music scene. Feature articles on successful Canadian songwriters provide young musicians with valuable information and insight. Columns on songwriting, arranging and publishing, usually written by musicians, producers or music publishers, offer pointers and advice on the music-making process and the business of songwriting."

*CMJ NEW MUSIC REPORT, published by Robert K. Haber, 3rd Floor, 245 Great Neck Rd., Great Neck NY 11021. (516)466-6000. Fax: (516)466-7159. Sales & Marketing: Diane Snyder. Music Editor: Megan McLaughlin. Weekly magazine; 75 pages. Subscription price: $295/year. Estab. 1979. College radio and alternative music tip sheet.

*COUNTRY MUSIC LIFE (CML), (formerly *Country Music Lives*), published by A.R. Arnone, P.O. Box 558, Lake Mohegan NY 10547-0558. (914)528-0919. Editor: A.R. Arnone. Monthly magazine; 8-16 pages. Subscription price: $15. Sample issue: $2. Estab. 1989. "Totally dedicated to promote country music. We now support 'Indies' in our new 'Indie' section. We are currently subscribed to by readers nationwide, European and Canada."

*COUNTRY MUSIC SCENE, INC., P.O. Box 493, Clifton NJ 07015. (201)478-0435. Editor: Donald N. Bender. Publishes 10 issues/year; 64-72 pages. Subscription price: $7.50. Estab. 1974. "We'll tell you 'Where It's At' in Country Music in the Northeastern U.S."

COUNTRY SONG ROUNDUP, 63 Grand Ave., River Edge NJ 07661. (201)487-6124. Contact: Editorial Dept.—Celeste Gomes, Editor. Published monthly; 64 pages. Subscription Price: $25/(12 issues). Estab. 1947. "In-depth stories and interviews with country music artists and songwriters plus the lyrics to more than 30 top songs."

*COUNTRY WESTERN CORNER, published by Entertainment News, P.O. Box 40, Santa Fe TX 77517. (409)925-4539. President: Edward H. King. Monthly magazine; 30 pages. Subscription price: $15/year US—$25/year elsewhere. Estab. 1985. "Helping to bring songwriters, publishers, entertainers and DJs together. Both indie and major recording industry."

*COVER MAGAZINE, published by Jeffrey C. Wright, P.O. Box 1213 Cooper Station, New York, NY 10276. (212)673-1152. Monthly magazine; 40 pages. Subscription price: $10/year, $15/2 years. Estab. 1987. "*Cover Magazine* is the only publication devoted exclusively to covering all the arts, from rock, jazz, hip hop and orchestral to painting, sculpture, film, theater, books, poetry, dance and performers."

DIRTY LINEN, Dirty Linen, Ltd., P.O. Box 66600, Baltimore MD 21239. (410)583-7973. Contact: Susan Hartman. Magazine published 6 times/year; 80 pages. Subscription price: $20/year U.S., $24 (overseas, surface), $30 (overseas, airmail). Estab. 1983. "Dirty Linen is the magazine of folk, electric folk, traditional and world music. Each issue contains articles or interviews on major performers in a variety of styles. Also, news, new releases listings, extensive reviews of recordings, videos, books, etc. Comprehensive tour schedule listing."

*THE DRAMATISTS GUILD QUARTERLY, 234 W. 44th St., New York NY 10036. Published quarterly for members of The Dramatists Guild; 64 pages. Estab. 1964. "The magazine is an intercom for the authors of stage musicals."

*FILE 13, P.O. Box 175, Concord MA 01742. Editor: Mark Lo. Magazine published 3 times/year; 48 pages. Subscription price: $6/year. Estab. 1988. "*File 13* focuses on new and/or obscure artists in rock, punk, industrial/experimental, dance and rap. We also review demo tapes and self-produced releases."

*FLAGPOLE MAGAZINE, published by Cat Holmes/Dennis Greenia, P.O. Box 1027, Athens GA 30603. (706)549-9523. Fax: (706)548-8981. Promotions Director: Shannon Diadeggo. Weekly magazine; 20-30 pages. Subscription price: $20/6 months, $38/year. Estab. 1987. "Alternative arts and entertainment source for Athens, GA. The source for the Athens scene."

GAJOOB MAGAZINE, P.O. Box 3201, Salt Lake City UT 84110. (801)355-8946. Fax: (801)355-5552. Editor: Bryan Baker. Triannually; 80 pages. Subscription price: $12/4 issues; Sample Issue $3.50. Estab. 1988. "*Gajoob Magazine* has the unique distinction of focusing exclusively on DIY audio and video recording and distribution. Each issue reviews over 200 independently produced releases, along with articles and interviews by and about the people behind these works. *Gajoob* effectively offers its pages as an international forum for independent recording artists."

HEARTSONG REVIEW RESOURCE GUIDE, Wahaba Heartsun, P.O. Box 1084, Cottage Grove OR 97424. Biannual; 56 pages. Subscription price: $8/year, $15 for 2 years. Estab. 1986. "As a consumer's resource guide for socially and spiritually conscious music, we review New Age music of many styles; including vocal and instrumental, children's, chanting, folk, world/fusion, electronic/space and quiet relaxation. Our goal is to encourage consciousness expansion through music. Free music samplers accompany each issue to all subscribers. We publish a list of radio stations requesting play copies. We write descriptive reviews of little known, independently published albums which would have a hard time getting attention elsewhere."

HIT PARADER, Hit Parader Publications, Inc., 40 Violet Ave., Poughkeepsie NY 12601. (914)454-7420. Monthly magazine; 96 pages. Subscription price: $29.50. Contains articles and interviews on rock music personalities, information about trends in the music industry and rock music in particular. Also rock song lyrics, record and book reviews, new product reviews and reader mail. "We don't print song lyrics by unsigned bands."

*HOT WIRE, The Journal of Women's Music and Culture, published by Empty Closet Enterprises, 5210 N. Wayne, Chicago IL 60640. (312)769-9009. Fax: (312)728-7002. Editor: Toni Armstrong Jr. Published 3 times/year; 64 pages. Subscription price: $17. Estab. 1984. "The only publication devoted to the woman—identified women's music and culture scene. We also publish *Women's Music Plus*, a directory of resources of women's music."

*ILLINOIS ENTERTAINER, published by Roberts Publishing, Inc., Suite 150, 2250 E. Devon, Des Plaines IL 60018. (708)298-9333. Fax: (208)298-7973. Editor: Michael C. Harris. Monthly magazine; 80 pages. Subscription price: $19 3rd class; $29 1st class. Estab. 1974. "We are a Chicago-based music/entertainment mag focused on local, national and international alternative music. We do lots of record reviews, and the majority of our copy is freelance generated."

THE INSIDER, T.O.G.™, P.O. Box 4542, Arlington VA 22204. (703)685-0199. Publisher: T.O.G. Every other month; 1 page newsletter. Subscription price: $5 for 6 issues. Estab. 1989. "We highlight live local music and review almost all cassettes received."

*JAZZ TIMES, published by Jazz Times Inc., #303, 7961 Eastern Ave., Silver Spring MD 20910. (301)588-4114. Fax: (301)588-5531. Circulation Manager: Wayne Kline. Magazine published 10 times/year; 92 pages. Subscription price: $21.95. Estab. 1970. "Jazz magazine filled with profiles, features news and reviews of jazz artists and products. Also provides valuable directories of record labels, festivals, nightclubs and education programs."

*LA JAZZ SCENE NEWSPAPER, #254, 12439 Magnolia Blvd., N. Hollywood CA 91607. (818)504-2115. Editor: Myrna Daniels. Monthly magazine; 24 pages. $20. Estab. 1987. "Tabloid sized newspaper with emphasis on jazz community in Southern California; CD reviews, profiles, calendars, club/concert reviews, events, promotion of all aspects of jazz, contemporary music, blues, etc."

*THE LEDGE, P.O. Box 9441, Cincinnati OH 45209. (513)561-5814. Editor/Publisher: Cindy Laufenberg. Magazine published 4 times/year; 10-12 pages. Subscription price: $5/6 issues. Sample issue: $1. Estab. 1987. "*The Ledge* covers the local alternative music scene in Cincinnati and beyond, with interviews, feature stories, record and concert reviews, etc."

LOUISVILLE MUSIC NEWS, 7400 Cross Creek Blvd., Louisville KY 40228. (502)231-5559. Editor: Jean Metcalfe. Monthly; 24-28 pages. Subscription price: $10, bulk mail; $15, first class. Estab. 1989. "*Louisville Music News* is dedicated to promoting music and musicians, songwriters, etc. in Louisville and surrounding areas. It publishes concert, record, book and recording studio reviews, as well as features on local musicians, groups and people connected with the music business. National acts are also covered when they appear in the area. Contains the newsletter of the Louisville Area Songwriters' Cooperative."

*LUCILLE'S BLUESLETTER, P.O. Box 483, Williamsburg MA 01096. (413)268-3821. Editor: Lisa Danforth. Bimonthly magazine; 16 pages. Subscription price: $15. Estab. 1992. "*Lucille's Bluesletter* is an independently-produced national newsletter of blue thought and all that concerns the world of blues today. Each issue features commentary, interviews, record and video reviews and classifieds."

*METAL EDGE, published by Sterling/Macfadden, 355 Lexington Ave., New York NY 10017. (212)973-3200. Fax: (212)986-5926. Contact: Sterling/Macfadden, 35 Wilbur St., Wynbrook NY 11563. Monthly magazine; 108 pages. Subscription price: $24/year. Estab. 1985. "Pictures, interviews and features about hard rock/heavy metal bands, geared for the 12-25 market."

MUSIC BUSINESS DIRECTORY, Ray McGinnis. P.O. Box 120675, Nashville TN 37212. (615)255-1068. Published every 6 months, May and November; 96 pages. Subscription price: $14.95. Estab. 1983. "The only directory you'll ever need, with listings of song publishers, booking agents, artist managers, record companies, recording studios, etc. All with names, phone numbers and addresses. A great source of information for new writers and singers."

MUSIC CONNECTION MAGAZINE, 6640 Sunset Blvd., Hollywood CA 90028. (213)462-5772. Contact: Subscription Dept. Biweekly magazine; 56-100 pages. Estab. 1977. "*Music Connection Magazine* is a musicians'/songwriters' trade publication. Departments include a gig guide connecting musicians and songwriters with agents, producers, publishers and club owners; a free classified section; music personal ads; interviews with music industry executives and major artists; and articles on songwriting, publishing and the music business. We cover current news, stories and interviews with up-and-coming music business people as well as established industry executives and major artists. *Music Connection Magazine* connects musicians, songwriters, producers and other music business personnel with each other. Our 'cutting edge' cover stories have included Poison, Guns N' Roses and the Bangles prior to their great successes. A must read publication for anyone in the music business. Every issue of *Music Connection* contains a 2-page editorial spread which includes: Songworks—current activities of music publishers, songwriters and record company signings; and Publisher Profile—an in-depth spotlight on a music publisher." Subscription rate is $40 for one year/25 issues; $65 for two years/50 issues.

MUSIC MAKERS, The Sunday School Board of the Southern Baptist Convention, 127 9th Ave. N, Nashville TN 37234. (615)251-2000. Contact: Church Music Dept. Music Editor: Sheryl Davis Tallant. Quarterly magazine; 32 pages. Cost is 93¢. Estab. 1970. Publishes music for use by 1st, 2nd and 3rd graders in choir at church. Includes 12 pages of spiritual concept, musical concept and fun songs, 20 pages of stories, activities, musical games, art activities and puzzles. "*Music Makers* magazine is an example of quality music education for children in the church choir setting. We provide opportunity for publication of spiritual concept songs, as well as fun/activity songs; there is an accompanying cassette which contains some of the printed songs plus movement, instrumental and listening activities."

MUSIC MONTHLY—A MARYLAND MUSICIAN PUBLICATION, (formerly *Maryland Musician Magazine*), Maryland Musician Magazine Inc., 7510 Harford Rd., Baltimore MD 21234. (410)444-3776. Fax: (410)444-1807. President: Susan E. Mudd. Monthly; 56 pages. Subscription price: $20. Estab. 1984. "A monthly publication which covers all genres of music: rock, blues, country, jazz, classical, metal.

We also review local and national releases as well as rock and metal demos."

*THE MUSIC PAPER, published by Sound Resources, P.O. Box 304, Manhasset NY 11050. (516)883-8898. Editor-in-Chief: Karen Cavill. Monthly magazine; 60 pages. Subscription price: $12/year. Estab. 1979. "Artist profiles, technical and instruction columns, industry news, product news and updates."

*THE MUSIC REVIEW, 46 Robin Rd., Poughkeepsie NY 12601. General Manager: Rick Carbone. Published bi-monthly; 10-30 pages. $15/year. *"The Music Review* reviews country, pop and gospel singles by independent artists and their labels and gives the addresses of where our readers can purchase the records, or write to the independent labels who usually are very willing to listen to and publish a lot of new songwriters. We also provide a monthly chart of the top 40 independent country records and the top 30 independent gospel records based on reviews, promotional campaigns of the label, and airplay reported to us by over 200 radio stations. Also have the top 25 independent adult contemporary chart and the top 25 club dance chart. For sample copy send SASE with 58¢ postage."

MUSIC ROW MAGAZINE, Published by Music Row Publications, Inc. 1231 17th Ave. S., Nashville TN 37212. (615)321-3617. Fax: (615)329-0852. Magazine published 23 times a year; 32 pages. Price: $50/year. Estab. 1981. *"Music Row Magazine* is Nashville's music industry publication. We supply information about producers and publishers, and interviews with key players and writers. Subscription includes *In Charge: Music Row's Decision Makers,* a book updated yearly. Book includes photos, phone, fax and mini-bios on over 400 Nashville music executives, producers, publishers and more."

THE MUSICAL QUARTERLY, Oxford University Press, 200 Madison Ave., New York NY 10016. Manager, Customer Service: Gloria Bruno. Quarterly magazine; 180 pages. Subscription price: $34 US – £23 UK and $48 rest of the world. Estab. 1915. *"The Musical Quarterly* is a journal written for professional musicians as well as dedicated amateurs. Articles feature all types of music, from the most ancient to the most recent, and cover a range of topics as diverse as the musical world it has chronicled for 75 years. Articles include analysis of musical scores providing an insight as to how our greatest composers and musicians created and performed music."

*MUSICWORKS, Music Gallery, 1087 Queen St. West, Toronto, Ontario M6J 1H3 **Canada**. Phone: (416)533-0192. Fax: (416)536-1849. Business Manager: Nadene Thèriault. Editor: Gayle Young. Managing Editor: Lauren Pratt. Triannual; 64 pages, published with 60 minute cassette. Subscription price: $20 paper only, $36 with cassette, $42 with CD. Estab. 1978. "Articles by composers and musicians about their own work. Tend to focus on avant-garde experimental and non-mainstream music – everything from Cree drumming to Maryanne Amacher."

*THE NARROW GATE, (formerly *Screaming Rock*), Shauna Sky, 6334 S. Long, Chicago IL 60638. (312)735-1584. Editor/Publisher: Shauna Sky. Monthly; 18 pages. Subscription price: $12 (12 issues), $6 (6 issues), and $1 single issue. Estab. 1992. *"The Narrow Gate* is a zine that covers all forms of Christian music: thrash, industrial, rap, alternative, etc. *T.N.G.* includes articles, interviews, poetry and classifieds. Free to prisoners or those who cannot afford to pay."

*NIGHTFLYING, published and edited by Peter Read, P.O. Box 250276, Little Rock AR 72225. (501)664-5099. Associate Editor: Sondra Goode. Monthly magazine; 52 pages. Subscription price: $25/year. Estab. 1980. *"Nightflying* is one of the only totally targeted publications in the country for the working, independent musician. Our work guide/club listing extends into 5 states (Arkansas, Texas, Oklahoma, Tennessee and Missouri), and includes calendars, open dates, booking information and contacts, phone numbers and addresses for 6-8 weeks at a time. We are the only publication of its kind in this part of the country. Record reviews of independent products are most important, as well as the support of the working artist in general."

THE NOISE, T Max, 74 Jamaica St., Jamaica Plain MA 02130. (617)524-4735. Publisher/Editor: T Max. Monthly (except Aug.); 24 pages. Subscription price: $12; sample issue $1.50. Estab. 1981. *"The Noise* covers the underground music scene in the greater Boston area (New England) with feature stories, record reviews, live reviews, tape reviews, gossip column, pictorials and cartoons."

Market conditions are constantly changing! If you're still using this book and it is 1995 or later, buy the newest edition of Songwriter's Market at your favorite bookstore or order directly from Writer's Digest Books.

PROBE AND CANADIAN COMPOSER, Society of Composers, Authors and Music Publishers of Canada (SOCAN), 41 Valleybrook Dr., Don Mills, Ontario M3B 2S6 **Canada**. (416)445-8700. Editor: Rick MacMillan. Published through the SOCAN public relations department: Nancy Gyokeres, Director. PROBE is a monthly 8-page newsletter. It is incorporated in Canadian Composer (24 pages), the quarterly magazine of SOCAN. Estab. 1990. Advertising is not accepted. "The publications are published by SOCAN to publicize the activities of composer, author and publisher members and to keep them informed of music-industry activities, both foreign and domestic." Cost: $10 annually to cover postage and handling.

*PROGRESSIVE SONGWRITER, 1826 Broadmoor Ave., Livermore CA 94550. Editor: T.L. Wallis. Monthly magazine; 16 pages. Subscription price: $19.95/year. "A newsletter dedicated to the serious songwriter."

*PUBLIC NEWS, published by Bert Woodall, 1540 W. Alabama, Houston TX 77006. (713)520-1520. Fax: (713)520-9390. Office Manager: Melissa Cherry. Weekly magazine; 30 pages. Subscription price: $60. Estab. 1980. "Covers alternative music, art, theater and journalism."

*RADIO & RECORDS, 1930 Century Park W., Los Angeles CA 90067. (310)553-4330. Circulation Services: Kelley Schieffelin. Estab. 1974. R&R is a weekly newspaper; 100 pages, $275/year (51 weeks); $75/quarter. This trade publication is the leading information source for the radio and record industries.

*RAP SHEET, published by Jeffrey Stern, Box B4, 2270 Centinela Ave., Santa Monica CA 90064. Contributing Editor: Darryl James. Monthly magazine. Subscription price: $12.95. Estab. 1992. "*Rap Sheet* is the magazine of hip hop straight up. It reports from the perspective of the rap community, covering what artists, industry folks and core fans want to read about."

*RIP, published by LFP Inc., #300, 9171 Wilshire Blvd., Beverly Hills CA 90210. (310)858-7100. Fax: (310)275-3857. Contact: Subscription Dept.. Monthly magazine; 96 pages. Subscription price: $24.95. Estab. 1986. "A heavy metal/hard rock monthly publication catering to the fan and artist."

*SECONDS, published and edited by Steven Blush, Suite 405, 24 5th Ave., New York NY 10011. Contact: Subscription Dept.. Magazine published 6 times/year; 64 pages. Subscription price: $18. "Features interviews with both established and up-and-coming musicians, as well as literary and film characters with music/pop culture interest. Covering black & white music, art and entertainment. Note: do not send paperwork unaccompanied by recordings!!"

SING OUT! THE FOLK SONG MAGAZINE, Box 5253, Bethlehem PA 18015-0253. Contact: Subscription Department. Published quarterly; 120 pages. $18/year (US). Estab. 1950. "*Sing Out!* is a folk music magazine for musicans or music lovers dedicated to bringing its readers a diverse and entertaining selection of songs and information about traditional and contemporary folk music. We print about 20 songs and tunes in each issue. Some are traditional, some are newly written; most are solicited, some are not. We print songs in lead sheet format: first verse and chorus with chords and complete lyrics. We publish many new songwriters. Best form of song submission is on cassette with lyric and lead sheet."

SONG PLACEMENT GUIDE, 4376 Stewart Ave., Los Angeles CA 90066-6134. Publisher: M. Singer. Marketing Director: C. Dickson (216)294-2492. Monthly newsletter; 2 pages; $6 introductory, $65/year. Estab. 1980. "A 13-year-old endorsed Los Angeles tipsheet for music publishers/songwriters. The Song Placement Guide is designed to educate songwriters about craft and business. Editorial is not the thrust however, it's the "tips" on who's looking for songs for recording. Includes monthly list of artists and producers looking for hit songs. In addition to inside information on who's looking for what material and where to submit, we provide an InnerView with an industry pro, or write a column to educate and inspire readers. Also small classified and news flash section."

*SONGNET, published by The Network of Lyricists & Songwriters, P.O. Box 890425, Houston TX 77289-0425. (713)264-4330. Editor: Sybrina Durant. Monthly magazine; 16 pages. Subscription price: $15. Estab. 1991. "*Songnet* is a publication of The Network of Lyricists & Songwriters, Inc., a nonprofit organization dedicated to educating, protecting and promoting lyricists, songwriters, producers and performers of original music. *Songnet* is full of educational articles as well as interviews with famous and up and coming songwriters. It also features a collaborator list, fresh song tips and information on current songwriting competitions."

*SONGPUBLISHER, P.O. Box 645, Jericho NY 11753-0645. (516)486-8699. Fax: (516)564-1217. Editor: Jay Gold. Monthly newsletter: 4-8 pages. Subscription price: $99/year. Estab. 1993. "*Songpublisher* is a monthly professional tip-sheet for songwriters who want to get their songs heard by aggressive music companies and industry pros who are actually looking for new songs for catalog acquisition, exploitation and record production. A tip sheet is only as good as the people behind it. Jay Gold is an 18-year music industry veteran formerly on the professional staff of Warner Bros. Music and April/ Blackwood Music CBS. *Songpublisher* provides the songwriter with the hot leads needed to pitch their own tunes. Listings include company/contact names and addresses, type of material needed and submission requirements. Subscribers are also entitled to free songwriter services including review and critique of songs that will help songwriter select only the most commercially viable songs for submission to *Songpublisher* listings."

SONGWRITER MAGAZINE, International Songwriters Association Ltd., P.O. Box 46 Limerick City, Ireland. Phone: (061)28837. Subscription Manager: Anna Sinden. Annual yearbook, monthly newsletter, number of pages varies. "A publication for songwriters and music publishers, featuring exclusive interviews with top American and European writers and publishers and recording artists. Readers can avail of unlimited free advice, song assessment, song copyright and other services. Readers in 61 countries worldwide. Correspondence in English, French, Spanish and Italian." UK office: 37b Cavendish Street, London W1, UK. Phone: (071) 486 5353.

*SONGWRITER PRODUCTS, IDEAS AND NECESSITIES, NSP Music Publishing, 345 Sprucewood Rd., Lake Mary FL 32746-5917. (407)321-3702. Fax: (407)321-2361. Semi-annual catalog. Free. "Songwriting tips, tools, accessories, stationery materials, critique forms, sample letters, music contracts, books, publications, guide to song associations, short-cuts, how-to information, bio and photographic services, songwriter small quantity cassette duplication and presentation packages for music publishers and record labels. This complete guide for those "hard-to-find" songwriter necessities is free and available to songwriters, composers, musicians, publishers and record companies. This pocket size catalog will save you tons of valuable time. We've done all the research for you!"

SONGWRITING AND COMPOSING MAGAZINE, The Guild of International Songwriters & Composers, Sovereign House 12 Trewartha Rd., Praa Sands, Penzance Cornwall TR20 9ST **United Kingdom.** Phone: (0736)762826. Fax: (0736)763328. Subscription Secretary: Carole A. Jones. Quarterly; 20 pages. Estab. 1986. Membership subscriptions: £18-United Kingdom; £20 E.E.C. countries; £25 overseas non-E.E.C. countries. Free to all members of the Guild of International Songwriters and Composers. "An international magazine for songwriters, composers, music publishers, record companies and the music industry. *Songwriting and Composing* features interviews and biographies of artists, publishers, songwriters, record companies and other music industry personnel and organizations. Lists details of artists, publishers, producers, record companies looking for songs. Lists publishers and other music industry contacts. Readers have access to unlimited free advice, free copyright service, free collaboration service, free song assessment service, and numerous other services on an international basis. Readers worldwide. A free news magazine is available upon request with an SAE or 2× IRCs."

THE STAR MAGAZINE, published by Jellee Works, Inc., P.O. Box 16572, Kansas City MO 64133. (800)283-SONG. Editor: James E. Lee. Monthly magazine; 28-32 pages. Subscription price: $24/year. Write or call for a free sample issue. Purpose is "to educate the aspiring songwriter about the industry. Includes 'how to' articles every month on the craft, business and legal issues an aspiring songwriter must face and deal with. Features stories on grassroots to successful songwriters. Also offers more contests for songwriters than any other publication, giving out over $10,000 per year in prizes and merchandise. Provides more publisher and record company tips on who's looking for material than any other publication."

SYNTHESIS, Jason Marcewicz, 219 Napfle St., Philadelphia PA 19111. (215)725-1686. Managing Editor: Jason Marcewicz. Quarterly; 12 pages. Subscription price: $10/year. Estab. 1989. "*SYNTHESIS* exists as a 'forum for musicians and fans of electronic music (EM)' . . . i.e., music that is predominantly synthesizer, keyboard, or computer based. New releases on cassette, album and CD are listed, if not reviewed, artists are interviewed, and various articles and editorials are written. Through interviews and reviews of their music, we grant musicians exposure and give feedback about their current releases. Addresses of the artists, for fan correspondence, are *always* printed."

TEXAS BEAT MAGAZINE, Keith Allen Ayres, P.O. Box 4429, Austin TX 78765-4429. (512)441-2242. Publisher/Editor: Keith Ayres. Monthly; 32 pages. Subscription price: $20/13 issues. Estab. 1989. "Arts and entertainment monthly with primary thrust on Texas music. Includes artist features, interviews, live reviews (local and national acts), record reviews (local and national acts). Monthly studio activity report from Dallas, Austin, Houston and San Antonio. Quarterly Texas Music Industry Guide gives comprehensive industry contacts."

*TEXAS MUSIC INDUSTRY DIRECTORY, Texas Music Office—Office of the Governor, P.O. Box 13246, Austin TX 78711. (512)463-6666. Fax: (512)463-4114. Program Director: Casey Monahan. Editor: Deb Freeman. Annual directory; 250 pages. Subscription price: $16.50. Estab. 1990. "*TMID* is the annotated business 'white pages' of the Texas music industry. More than 4,100 businesses are listed in 82 categories."

*TORONTO PROGRAMMER'S ASSOCIATION (TOPA) NEWSLETTER, Toronto Programmer's Association (TOPA), 209 Pineway Blvd. North York, Ontario M2H 1B4 **Canada**. Phone: (416)512-0652. Fax: (416)512-0652. Director: Randy Brill. Bi-weekly; 2 pages. Subscription price $30. Estab. 1981. "Our newsletter pertains to the Toronto and surrounding area club dance music scene. In the past, songwriters have been introduced to producers of dance music material due to the TOPA Newsletter. Emphasis is on dance music records and club playlists. However, there is a 'Streetalk' section which reports on any dance music news including the songwriting aspect."

TRUSTY INTERNATIONAL NEWSLETTER, 8771 Rose Creed Rd., Nebo KY 42441. (502)249-3194. Publisher: Elsie Childers. Monthly; 1 page. Subscription price: $39.95/year (12 issues). "Overseas orders add $6.50/year." Estab. 1974. "Names and addresses of artists and producers and publishers needing new songs for recording sessions. Items of subscribers' song placements given. Also gives readers where and when to send songs for possible recordings. Send 25¢ for current issue of tip sheet plus 29¢ SAE."

*URBAN NETWORK, published by The Network Group, #207, 120 N. Victory Blvd., Burbank CA 91502. (818)843-5800. Fax: (818)843-4800. Office Manager: Dusean Dawson. Weekly magazine; 50 pages. Subscription price: $280. Estab. 1988. "Weekly industry-only trade that promotes the best music at black radio and retail on a weekly basis."

URBAN SPELUNKER, (formerly *Wire Magazine*), Tansy Publishing/Denis W. Toomey, 2319 N. 45th, No. 143, Seattle WA 98103. (206)932-3027. Subscription price: $18/year, $22 international. Sample copy $2. "*Urban Spelunker* explores the alternative viewpoint for music/arts/lifestyle for the Seattle area. The scope is local to national with music/video reviews from tape to major releases. All types of music are considered for review and articles. 20,000 copies in and around Seattle each month."

WASHINGTON INTERNATIONAL ARTS LETTER, Allied Business Consultants, Inc., P.O. Box 12010, Des Moines IA 50312. (515)255-5577. Fax: (515)255-5577. Founder: Daniel Millsaps, III. Publisher: Nancy A. Fandel. Magazine published 10 times/year; 6-8 pages. Institutional rate $124/year. Special Individual Rate $55/year. "WIAL concentrates on discovering sources of funding for the arts and keeping up with policy changes in funding by governments, private foundations, and businesses which give out grants to institutions and individual creative and performing artists. In addition, we publish the Arts Patronage Series, which are directories where all information is under one cover and updated periodically. We are the major source of information about funding for the arts in the US. Songwriters and composers can get grants for their work through our information and keep informed about congressional actions which affect their lives. Areas covered include problems of taxation, etc., as well as how to get money for projects."

YOUNG MUSICIANS, The Sunday School Board of the Southern Baptist Convention, 127 9th Ave. N., Nashville TN 37234. (615)251-2000. Contact: Church Music Dept. Music Editor: Sheryl Davis Tallant. Quarterly magazine; 52 pages. Cost: $1.36. Publishes music for use by 4th, 5th and 6th graders in church choirs. Includes spiritual and musical concept songs, activities, games, hymn studies and author/composer studies; plus 15-page music insert containing four or five anthems. There is also an accompanying Young Musicians Cassette containing music in the 15-page insert and other appropriate recorded material, such as movement, instrumental and listening activities. "This is an excellent publication to which songwriters whose interests and skills lie in the area of composing for children may submit their original manuscripts."

Books

ATTENTION: A&R, 2nd edition, by Teri Muench and Susan Pomerantz, Published by Alfred Publishing Co., Inc., Box 10003, Van Nuys CA 91410-0003. (818)891-5999. "Order from a music dealer or bookstore. If it cannot be located write to Alison Jordan, Customer Service Dept." Revised 1990. 116 pages. Price: $16.95; paperback. "This invaluable book by Teri Muench (former A&R Director for Contemporary Music – RCA Records) and Susan Pomerantz (hit songwriter and publisher) provides a step-by-step guide for approaching record industry executives who can help bring you closer to breaking into the music business. Includes the do's and don'ts of submitting your tape; recording, distributing and publishing deals; a listing of prominent management companies and colleges with music business courses, plus much more!"

GET YOUR WORK INTO THE RIGHT BUYERS' HANDS!

You work hard... and your hard work deserves to be seen by the right buyers. But with the constant changes in the industry, it's not always easy to know who those buyers are. That's why you'll want to keep up-to-date and on top with the most current edition of this indispensable market guide.

Totally Updated Each Year

SONGWRITER'S MARKET

Where & how to market your songs
2,500 listings of music publishers, record companies/producers, AV firms, managers, classical groups, theater companies!

Keep ahead of the changes by ordering *1995 Songwriter's Market* today. You'll save the frustration of getting your songs returned in the mail, stamped MOVED: ADDRESS UNKNOWN. And of NOT submitting your work to new listings because you don't know they exist. All you have to do to order the upcoming 1995 edition is complete the attached post card and return it with your payment or charge card information. Order now, and there's one thing that won't change from your *1994 Songwriter's Market* - the price! That's right, we'll send you the 1995 edition for just $19.95. *1995 Songwriter's Market* will be published and ready for shipment in September 1994.

Don't let another opportunity slip by...get a jump on the industry with the help of *1995 Songwriter's Market* . Order today! You deserve it!

550 New Markets! **80%** Newly Updated!

(See other side for more books to help you write and sell your songs)

To order, drop this postpaid card in the mail.

☐ **Yes!** I want the most current edition of *Songwriter's Market*. Please send me the 1995 edition at the 1994 price - $19.95.* (NOTE: *1995 Songwriter's Market* will be ready for shipment in September 1994.) #10386

Also send me these books to help me write and sell my songs:

_____ (#10320) The Songwriters Idea Book ~~$17.95~~ $15.25* (available NOW)
_____ (#10287) 88 Songwriting Wrongs & How to Right Them ~~$17.95~~ $15.25* (available NOW)
_____ (#10195) Music Publishing: A Songwriter's Guide ~~$18.95~~ $16.10 * (available NOW)
_____ (#10365) Networking in the Music Business ~~$17.95~~ $15.25* (available NOW)

*Plus postage and handling: $3.00 for one book, $1.00 for each additional book. Ohio residents add 5½% sales tax.

Credit card orders call toll-free 1-800-289-0963

☐ Payment enclosed (Slip this card and your payment into an envelope)
☐ Please charge my: ☐ Visa ☐ MasterCard

Account #_____ Exp. Date_____
Signature _____ Phone (   )_____
Name_____
Address_____
City _____ State _____ Zip _____
(This offer expires May 1, 1995)

| 30-Day Money Back Guarantee |

Writer's Digest Books
1507 Dana Avenue
Cincinnati, OH 45207   6399

Save Up To $2.85 On These Great Titles!

The Songwriters Idea Book
Sheila Davis, noted songwriter/teacher and best selling music author, shows you 40 proven songwriting strategies - guaranteed to spark your imagination and keep your creative flame burning. 240 pages/~~$17.95~~ $15.25/hardcover

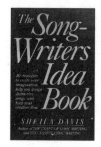

88 Songwriting Wrongs & How To Right Them
Your song's just not right…but you can't identify what's wrong. That's where this book comes in! Pat & Pete Luboff help you figure out the problem and show you how to fix it - resulting in songs strong in emotion, musically beautiful and very salable. 144 pages/~~$17.95~~ $15.25/paperback

ASCAP-Deems Taylor Award Winner!
Music Publishing: A Songwriter's Guide
Don't venture into the competitive field of music publishing alone! This indispensable guide points you in the right direction with practical advice on royalties, sub-publishing, copyrights, songwriter options in publishing, plus much more.
144 pages/~~$18.95~~ $16.10/paperback

NEW! Networking in the Music Business
A guide to making the necessary contacts to succeed in the music business. Once you have the "what you know" nailed down, this book helps you improve your odds with "who you know" and "who know you." 128 pages/~~$17.95~~ $15.25/paperback

Use coupon on other side to order today!

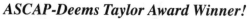

BEGINNING SONGWRITER'S ANSWER BOOK, by Paul Zollo. Published by Writer's Digest Books, 1507 Dana Ave., Cincinnati OH 45207. (800)289-0963. Attention: Book Order. Revised 1993; 120 pages. Price: $16.95; paperback. Zollo has collected and answered 218 questions most often asked by songwriters calling the National Academy of Songwriters telephone hotline. "You'll find terms and techniques explained with plenty of helpful illustrations, and you'll gain insight into the working methods of successful songwriters and musicians."

*CMJ DIRECTORY, Editor-in-Chief: Diane Turofsky. Publisher: Robert K. Haber. 3rd Floor, 245 Great Neck Rd., Great Neck NY 11021. (516)466-6000. Fax: (516)466-7519. Sales and Marketing: Diane Snyder. Published annually. $60 plus shipping. Lists radio, retail, video, artist management, agency and press as well as a market-by-market breakdown.

THE CRAFT AND BUSINESS OF SONGWRITING, by John Braheny. Published by Writer's Digest Books, 1507 Dana Ave., Cincinnati OH 45207. (800)289-0963. Attention: Book Order. Published 1988; 322 pages. Price: $19.95; hardcover. A powerful, information-packed—and the most up-to-date—book about the songwriting industry that thoroughly covers all the creative and business aspects songwriters need to know to maximize their chances of success.

THE CRAFT OF LYRIC WRITING, by Sheila Davis. Published by Writer's Digest Books, 1507 Dana Ave., Cincinnati OH 45207. (800)289-0963. Attention: Book Order. Published: 1985. 350 pages. Price: $19.95; hardcover. Davis, a gold-record lyricist, identifies and illustrates the elements that shape successful popular songs. The book contains the complete lyrics to the great standards by such writers as Larry Hart, Ira Gershwin, Oscar Hammerstein, Johnny Mercer, Lennon & McCartney, Paul Simon, Harry Chapin, Joni Mitchell, Jim Webb and Sting, along with Davis' analysis of those qualities of craftsmanship that produce Grammy, Tony and Oscar winners. A highly-praised reference work that defines and illustrates over 100 literary terms and devices. ASCAP calls it "Required reading for anyone who aspires to a career in songwriting."

*DEAN'S COUNTRY RADIO LIST, by Dean Enterprises Music Group, P.O. Box 620, Redwood Estates CA 95044. (408)353-1006. Executive Director: Ron Dean Tomich. Price: $59. "List (not labels) provides addresses of country music radio stations for US/Canada and many foreign countries. $59 for 2,200+ listings. A necessity for record companies, record producers, managers, booking agents and country artists." Allow 2-3 weeks for delivery. Mail check or money order (no cash), to above address; made payable to Dean Enterprises Group.

*DEMO SERVICE COMPANY DIRECTORY, by Sybrina Dubrant, P.O. Box 1342, Friendswood TX 77548. President: Sybrina Dubrant. Published annually. 24 pages. Listing of demo companies and the services they offer. Updated annually.

GETTING NOTICED: A Musician's Guide to Publicity & Self-Promotion, by James Gibson. Published by Writer's Digest Books, 1507 Dana Ave., Cincinnati OH 45207. (800)289-0963. Attention: Book Order. Published 1987; 240 pages. Price: $12.95; paperback. "Gibson shows musicians how, with just a few simple secrets and very little cash, to create attention-getting publicity materials, then use them to make more money with their music. Includes a wealth of business information on press releases, letter writing, and handling unpaid bills and broken contracts."

HOW TO OPEN DOORS IN THE MUSIC INDUSTRY—THE INDEPENDENT WAY, by Frank Fara/Patty Parker. Published by Autumn Gold Publishing; distributed by Starfield Press, Suite 114, 10603 N. Hayden Rd., Scottsdale AZ 85260. (602)951-3115. Fax: (602)951-3074. Published: 1987. 110 pages. List price: $8.95; $10 mail order. Book written from the "viewpoint of an unpublished writer or writer/artist needing to know the ground rules for succeeding in today's marketplace. Topics covered include song pitching, record promotion, international music markets, importance of a studio producer, independent record labels and how they can promote artist masters, and how to find the right publisher or record label. Also, where to work from: home or a music center, and the most frequently asked questions and answers on royalties, production, record sales and publishing. Popular music myths dispelled."

HOW TO PITCH AND PROMOTE YOUR SONGS, by Fred Koller. Published by Writer's Digest Books, 1507 Dana Ave., Cincinnati OH 45207. (800)289-0963. Attention: Book Order. Published 1988; 114 pages. Price: $12.95; paperback. This book shows how to make a living as a full-time songwriter—exactly what it's like to be self-employed in the music industry and how to set up a step-by-step business plan to achieve your goals, including getting started: sources of motivation, how to expose your work through professional associations, seminars and support groups; running a business: basic supplies, expenses and accounts, legalities and financial considerations; planning to succeed: creation, protection and exploitation of new songs as well as older material, where the money comes from, how often and from whom; publishing: the difference between writing for a major publisher and self-publishing, advantages/disadvantages of co-publishing.

*JINGLES: HOW TO WRITE, PRODUCE AND SELL COMMERCIAL MUSIC, by Al Stone. Published by Writer's Digest Books, 1507 Dana Ave., Cincinnati OH 45207. (800)289-0963. Attention: Book Order. Published 1990; 144 pages. Price: $18.95; paperback. Stone takes you through the entire process of becoming successful as a jingle writer: from contacting potential clients, to composing and polishing the jingle and marketing it successfully.

*MAKING MONEY MAKING MUSIC, *Revised Edition* by James Dearing. Published by Writer's Digest Books, 1507 Dana Ave., Cincinnati OH 45207. (800)289-0963. Attention: Book Order. Published 1990; 192 pages. Price: $18.95; paperback. Dearing gives you strategies and practical advice on finding success and fulfillment as a musician in your own hometown.

THE MUSIC BUSINESS HANDBOOK, by Jojo St. Mitchell. Published by Amethyst Press, 273 Chippewa Dr., Columbia SC 29210-6508. Published 1987. Price: $16.95; paperback. "A brief overview of the music business for the newcomer with over 100 contacts in the music business, all in plain English for the inexperienced. A motivational tool to read over and over. Helps to give confidence, direction and a better understanding of how to view the music business. Discusses investors, booking, video, promotion and more. Easy to understand and affordable."

MUSIC DIRECTORY CANADA SIXTH EDITION, Edited by Shauna Kennedy. Published by CM Books, #7, 23 Hannover Dr., St. Catherine's, Ontario L2W 1A3 **Canada.** (416)641-2612. Fax: (416)641-1648. Published 1993; approx. 700 pages. Price: $29.95. "The most comprehensive and complete resource guide to the Canadian music industry available anywhere. The new sixth edition of the directory compiles over 6,000 entries in 60 categories. Contacts for record companies, management companies, music publishers and more are at your fingertips, keeping you up-to-date on the dynamic and ever-changing Canadian music scene."

MUSIC PUBLISHING: A SONGWRITER'S GUIDE, by Randy Poe. Published by Writer's Digest Books, 1507 Dana Ave., Cincinnati OH 45207. (800)289-0963. Attention: Book Order. Published 1990; 144 pages. Price: $18.95; paperback. Poe describes the modern world of music publishing in depth, and gives advice on getting the best publishing deals for your songs. Winner of the 1991 ASCAP Deems-Taylor Award.

PLAYING FOR PAY: HOW TO BE A WORKING MUSICIAN, by James Gibson. Published by Writer's Digest Books, 1507 Dana Ave., Cincinnati OH 45207. (800)289-0963. Attention: Book Order. Published 1990; 160 pages. Price: $17.95; paperback. Gibson shows you how to develop a well-organized and strategic "Personal Music Marketing System" that will help you make money with your music.

SOME STRAIGHT TALK ABOUT THE MUSIC BUSINESS, 2nd edition, by Mona Coxson. #7, 23 Hannover Dr., St. Catharine's, Ontario L2W 1A3 **Canada.** (416)641-2612. Fax: (416)641-1648. Published 1989; 207 pages. Price: $19.95. "The book's sixteen chapters show the musician how to make the right career choices, how to get started and progress, and how to reach goals and avoid pitfalls. The book discusses all facets of the music business including music publishing and song demos. Coxson, a freelance consultant, writer and college music teacher, has taken nothing for granted and has outlined each step of the way so that every musician can avoid unnecessary mistakes." The book is especially valuable to those interested in the growing Canadian market. Published by CM Books.

SONGWRITERS CREATIVE MATRIX, by Carl E. Bolte, Jr. Published by Holly Productions, 800 Greenway Terrace, Kansas City MO 64113. (816)444-8884. Published 1975. 25-page workbook. Price: $11.50. A unique matrix/guideline for composers/lyricists including examples, instructions and 25 blank forms. "This unique guideline is 'a musical road map,' as well as a checklist regarding the composer's song form, chords, words, rhyme schemes, range, key signature and more. It makes one promise: to help songwriters compose better songs more easily."

THE SONGWRITER'S DEMO MANUAL AND SUCCESS GUIDE, by George Williams. Music Business Books. Box 935, Dayton NV 89403. (800)487-6610. Revised 1992. 200 pages. Price: $12.95. "A practical guide to selling songs and landing a record contract. Teaches how to work in the studio to prepare songs for professional presentation. Tells who the important people are and how to contact them. The author is a recording studio owner, jingle writer and producer with twenty years experience in the Los Angeles music business."

THE SONGWRITER'S GUIDE TO CHORDS AND PROGRESSIONS, by Joseph R. Lilore. Box 1272, Dept. WD, Clifton NJ 07012. Published: 1982. 48-page method/instruction book and 90 minute cassette. Price: $14.95 plus $1.50 postage. "Gives songwriters ideas for new and commercially proven chords and progressions. There are 58 individual song outlines with complete directions for creating thousands of songs in any style. The accompanying cassette allows songwriters to hear each new idea as it is introduced and helps them compose anywhere, anytime." Available through Lionhead Publishing at the above address or at your local music store. "Special offer to Writer's Digest Books' readers—get **both** the *Songwriter's Guide to Melodies* and to *Chords and Progressions* for only $20.00 plus $2.50 postage and handling."

THE SONGWRITER'S GUIDE TO COLLABORATION, by Walter Carter. Published by Writer's Digest Books, 1507 Dana Ave., Cincinnati OH 45207. (800)289-0963. Attention: Book Order. Published 1988; 198 pages. Price: $12.95; paperback. Devoted entirely to the subject of co-writing, this guide covers everything from finding a partner and sharing writing responsibilities to splitting the costs and royalties. As an added feature, top-name songwriters tell how they worked together to write their songs and get them recorded. Songwriters will learn: the mechanics of a writing relationship—how to complement lyric- or melody-writing strength, increase exposure and advance reputation by working with a better-known writer; the legal aspects of collaboration; how to deal with publishers, co-produce demos and plan pitching strategy; where to give credit when credit is due, and tips on sharing the glory (or rejection).

*SONGWRITER'S GUIDE TO MELODIES, by Joseph R. Lilore, Published by Lionhead Publishing, Box 1272, Dept. WD, Clifton NJ 07012. Published 1989; 80 pages. Price: $10.95 + $1.50 postage. "A systematic study of how to create melodies, starting with simple 'phrases' and developing them into complete songs in any style of music. Helps you grow musically, no matter what your level. Special offer to Writer's Digest Books' readers—get *both* the *Songwriter's Guide to Melodies* and to *Chords and Progressions* for only $20 plus $2.50 postage and handling."

*SUBMISSION GUIDELINES FOR NEW MUSICAL PROJECTS AT MEMBER COMPANIES, published by National Alliance for Musical Theatre, Lobby B, 330 W. 45th St., New York NY 10036-3854. (212)265-5376. Fax: (212)582-8730. Associate Director: Joseph McConnell. Published 1992 (updated and re-published each September); 10 pages. Price: $5 (includes postage and handling). "*NAMT* is a service organization for 80 professional theater companies specializing in production of stage musicals. The published *Submission Guidelines* is a directory of those NAMT members who are interested in producing and/or developing original musicals: contacts, submission procedures, etc. Copies of the directory may be acquired by written request through the mail *only*. Note: NAMT is not a producing entity; do *not* send unsolicited materials to this office."

SUCCESSFUL LYRIC WRITING, A STEP-BY-STEP COURSE AND WORKBOOK, by Sheila Davis. Published by Writer's Digest Books, 1507 Dana Ave., Cincinnati OH 45207. (800)289-0963. Attention: Book Order. Published: 1988. 292 pages. Price $19.95; paperback. Modelled after the author's noted classes at The Songwriters Guild of America, this companion to *The Craft of Lyric Writing* presents the first complete textbook on writing professional lyrics for every genre—from country to cabaret. Davis guides the reader in taking each vital step in the lyric writing process—with a series of 45 warmup exercises and 10 graduated assignments that develop writing skill as they reinforce theory. Features include: diagrams of music forms, lyric time frames and viewpoint; an illustrated ten-point guideline for figurative language; a primer on right-brain/left-brain writing; and a blueprint for conducting songwriting critique sessions.

SUCCESSFUL SONGWRITING, by Carl E. Bolte, Jr. Published by Holly Productions, 800 Greenway Terrace, Kansas City MO 64113. Published 1988; 206 pages. Price: $11.50 paperback. "In 34 chapters, from inspiration through publication, *Successful Songwriting* will guide your musical creative ability, whether you are a full-time professional or a fun-time hobbyist. Contains guidelines, statistics and how other songwriters found success. Learn about song topics, titles, lyric quantity, song forms, melody composition, key signatures, rhythm and time values, songwriter organizations. Explains why songs don't get published. This how-to book is fun and easy to read, with clear directions for making a song a hit song."

Glossary

A&R Director. Record company executive in charge of the Artists and Repertoire Department who is responsible for finding and developing new artists and matching songs with artists.

A/C. Adult contemporary music.

ACM. Academy of Country Music.

Advance. Money paid to the songwriter or recording artist before regular royalty payment begins. Sometimes called "up front" money, advances are deducted from royalties.

AFM. American Federation of Musicians. A union for musicians and arrangers.

AFTRA. American Federation of Television and Radio Artists. A union for performers.

AIMP. Association of Independent Music Publishers.

Air play. The radio broadcast of a recording.

AOR. Album-Oriented Rock. A radio format which primarily plays selections from rock albums as opposed to hit singles.

Arrangement. An adaptation of a composition for a performance or recording, with consideration for the melody, harmony, instrumentation, tempo, style, etc.

ASCAP. American Society of Composers, Authors and Publishers. A performing rights organization.

A-side. The side of a single which is considered to have "hit" potential and is promoted as such by the record company.

Assignment. Transfer of rights of a song from writer to publisher.

Audiovisual. Refers to presentations which use audio backup for visual material.

Bed. Prerecorded music used as background material in commercials.

Beta. ½″ videocassette format. The Beta System uses a smaller cassette than that used with the VHS system.

BMA. Black Music Association.

BMI. Broadcast Music, Inc. A performing rights organization.

B-side. The flip side of a single promoted by a record company. Sometimes the B-side contains the same song as the A-side so there will be no confusion as to which song should receive airplay.

Booking agent. Person who solicits work and schedules performances for entertainers.

Business manager. Person who handles the financial aspects of artistic careers.

b/w. Backed with. Usually refers to the B-side of a single.

C&W. Country and western.

CARAS. Canadian Academy of Recording Arts and Sciences. An association of individuals involved in the Canadian music and recording industry.

Catalog. The collected songs of one writer, or all songs handled by one publisher.

CD. Compact Disc (see below).

Chart. The written arrangement of a song.

Charts. The trade magazines' lists of the best selling records.

CHR. Comtemporary Hit Radio. Top 40 pop music.

CIRPA. Canadian Independent Record Producers Association.

CMA. Country Music Association.

CMPA. Church Music Publishers Association.

CMRRA. Canadian Musical Reproduction Rights Association. A mechanical rights agency.

Collaborator. Person who works with another in a creative endeavor.

Compact disc. A small disc (about 4.7 inches in diameter) holding digitally encoded music that is read by a laser beam in a CD player.

Co-publish. Two or more parties own publishing rights to the same song.

Copyright. The exclusive legal right giving the creator of a work the power to control the publishing, reproduction and selling of the work.

Cover record. A new version of a previously recorded song.

CRIA. Canadian Recording Industry Association.

Crossover. A song that becomes popular in two or more musical categories (e.g., country and pop).

Cut. Any finished recording; a selection from an LP. Also to record.

DAT. Digital Audio Tape. A professional and consumer audio cassette format for recording and playing back digitally-encoded material. DAT cassettes are approximately one-third smaller than conventional audio cassettes.

DCC. Digital Compact Cassette. A consumer audio cassette format for recording and playing back digitally-encoded tape. DCC tapes are the same size as analog cassettes.

Demo. A recording of a song submitted as a demonstration of writer's or artist's skills.

Distributor. Marketing agent responsible for getting records from manufacturers to retailers.

Donut. A jingle with singing at the beginning and end and instrumental background in the middle. Ad copy is recorded over the middle section.

Engineer. A specially trained individual who operates all recording studio equipment.

EP. Extended play record (usually 12″) containing more selections than a standard single, but fewer than a standard LP.

Exploit. To seek legitimate uses of a song for income.

Folio. A softcover collection of printed music prepared for sale.

GMA. Gospel Music Association.

Harry Fox Agency. Organization that collects mechanical royalties.

Hip-hop. A dance oriented musical style derived from a combination of disco, rap and R&B.

Hit. A song or record that achieves top 40 status.

Hook. A memorable "catch" phrase or melody line which is repeated in a song.

House. Dance music created by DJ's remixing samples from other songs. Also called freestyle or techno.

IMU. International Musicians Union.

Indie. An independent record label, music publisher or producer.

ips. Inches per second; a speed designation for tape recording.

IRC. International reply coupon, necessary for the return of materials sent out of the country. Available at most post offices.

Jingle. Usually a short verse set to music designed as a commercial message.

Label. Record company, or the "brand" name of the records it produces.

LASS. Los Angeles Songwriters Showcase.

Lead sheet. Written version (melody, chord symbols and lyric) of a song.

Leader. Plastic (non-recordable) tape at the beginning and between songs for ease in selection.

LP. Designation for long-playing record played at 33⅓ rpm.

Lyric sheet. A typed or written copy of a song's lyrics.

Market. A potential song or music buyer; also a demographic division of the record-buying public.

Master. Edited and mixed tape used in the production of records; a very high-quality recording; the best or original copy of a recording from which copies are made.

Maxi-single. The cassette equivalent of a 12″ single. Also called Maxi-cassettes or Maxi-plays. (See 12″ Single.)

MD. MiniDisc. A 3.5 inch disk for recording and playing back digitally-encoded music.

Mechanical right. The right to profit from the physical reproduction of a song.

Mechanical royalty. Money earned from record, tape and CD sales.

MIDI. Musical instrument digital interface. Universal standard interface which allows musical instruments to communicate with each other and computers.

Mix. To blend a multi-track recording into the desired balance of sound.

MOR. Middle of the road. Easy-listening popular music.

Ms. Manuscript.

Music jobber. A wholesale distributor of printed music.

Music publisher. A company that evaluates songs for commercial potential, finds artists to record them, finds other uses (such as TV or film) for the songs, collects income generated by the songs and protects copyrights from infringement.

NAIRD. National Association of Independent Record Distributors.

NARAS. National Academy of Recording Arts and Sciences.

NARM. National Association of Record Merchandisers.

NAS. National Academy of Songwriters, formerly Songwriters Resources and Services (SRS).

Needle-drop. Use of a prerecorded cut from a stock music house in an audiovisual soundtrack.

NMPA. National Music Publishers Association.

NSAI. Nashville Songwriters Association International.

One-off. A deal between songwriter and publisher which includes only one song or project at a time. No future involvement is implicated. Many times a single song contract accompanies a one-off deal.

One-stop. A wholesale distributor of records (and sometimes videocasettes, blank tapes and record accessories), representing several manufacturers to record stores, retailers and jukebox operators.

Overdub. To record an additional part (vocal or instrumental) onto a basic multi-track recording. To sweeten.

Payola. Dishonest payment to broadcasters in exchange for airplay.

Performing rights. A specific right granted by US copyright law that protects a composition from being publicly performed without the owner's permission.

Performing rights organization. An organization that collects income from the public performance of songs written by its members and then proportionally distributes this income to the individual copyright holder based on the number of performances of each song.

Personal manager. A person who represents artists, in numerous and varying ways, to develop and enhance their careers. Personal managers may negotiate contracts, hire and dismiss other agencies and personnel relating to the artist's career, review possible material, help with artist promotions and perform many services.

Piracy. The unauthorized reproduction and selling of printed or recorded music.

Pitch. To attempt to sell a song by audition; the sales talk.

Playlist. List of songs that a radio station will play.

Plug. A favorable mention, broadcast or performance of a song; to pitch a song.

Points. A negotiable percentage paid to producers and artists for records sold.

Producer. Person who supervises every aspect of recording a song or album.

Product. Records, CDs and tapes available for sale.

Production company. Company that specializes in producing jingle packages for advertising agencies. May also refer to companies that specialize in audiovisual programs.

Professional manager. Member of a music publisher's staff who screens submitted material and tries to get the company's catalog of songs recorded.

Program director. Radio station employee who screens records and develops a playlist of songs that station will broadcast.

PRS. Performing Rights Society of England.

PSA. Public Service Announcement: a free broadcast "advertisement" for a nonprofit service organization.

Public domain. Any composition with an expired, lapsed or invalid copyright.

Publish. To reproduce music in a saleable form and distribute to the public by sale or other transfer of ownership (rent, lease or lending).

Purchase license. Fee paid for music used from a stock music library.

Query. A letter of inquiry to a potential song buyer soliciting his interest.

R&B. Rhythm and blues.

Rack jobber. A wholesaler of records, tapes and accessories to retailers and mass-merchandisers not primarily in the record business (e.g., department stores).

Rate. The percentage of royalty as specified by contract.

Release. Any record issued by a record company.

Residuals. In advertising or television, payments to singers and musicians for subsequent use of a performance.

RIAA. Recording Industry Associations of America.

Royalty. Percentage of money earned from the sale of records or use of a song.

RPM. Revolutions per minute. Refers to phonograph turntable speed.

SAE. Self-addressed envelope (with no postage attached).

SASE. Self-addressed stamped envelope.

Self-contained. A band or recording act that writes all their own material.

SESAC. A performing rights organization.

SFX. Sound effects.

Shop. To pitch songs to a number of companies or publishers.

Single. 45 rpm record with only one song per side. A 12" single refers to a long version of one song on a 12" disc, usually used for dance music.

SOCAN. Society of Composers, Authors and Music Publishers of Canada. A performing rights organization formed in 1990 by the merger of CAPAC and PROCAN.

Solicited. Songs or materials that have been requested.

Song plugger. A songwriter representative whose main responsibility is promoting uncut songs to music publishers, record companies, artists and producers.

Song shark. Person who deals with songwriters deceptively for his own profit.

The Songwriters Guild of America. Organization for songwriters, formerly called AGAC.

Soundtrack. The audio, including music and narration, of a film, videotape or audiovisual program.

Split publishing. To divide publishing rights between two or more publishers.

Standard. A song popular year after year.

Statutory royalty rate. The maximum payment for mechanical rights guaranteed by law that a record company may pay the songwriter and his publisher for each record or tape sold.

Subpublishing. Certain rights granted by a US publisher to a foreign publisher in exchange for promoting the US catalog in his territory.

Synchronization. Technique of timing a musical soundtrack to action on film or video.

Synchronization rights. Rights to use a composition in film or video.

Take. Either an attempt to record a vocal or instrumental part, or an acceptable recording of a performance.

Top 40. The first forty songs on the pop music charts at any given time. Also refers to a style of music which emulates that heard on the current top 40.

Track. Divisions of a recording tape (e.g., 24-track tape) that can be individually recorded in the studio, then mixed into a finished master.

Trades. Publications that cover the music industry.

12" Single. A twelve inch record containing one or more remixes of a song, originally intended for dance club play.

U/C. Urban contemporary music.

Unsolicited. Songs or materials that were not requested and are not expected.

VHS. ½" videocassette format. The VHS system uses a larger cassette than that used with the Beta system.

Work. To pitch or shop a song.

Category Index

This list of 18 general music categories includes companies from the Music and Music Print Publishers, Record Companies and Producers and Managers and Booking Agents sections. If you write country songs, check the Country section. There you will find a list of interested companies. Once you locate those listings, read their Music subheadings *carefully* to determine which are most interested in the *type* of country music you write.

Some markets in the book are not in the Category Index because they don't indicate a preference; most are interested in "all types" of music. Listings that are very specific, or whose music doesn't quite fit into these categories, also do not appear.

Adult Contemporary

Aberdeen Productions
a Hi-Tek Publishing Co.
Alleged Iguana Music
Allegheny Music Works
Amalgamated Tulip Corp.
American Concert
Amethyst Records, Inc.
Amicos II Music, Ltd.
Amiron Music
Amiron Music/Aztec Prod.
Another Approach Music Publishing Company
Another Approach Recording Company
Antelope Publishing Inc.
Antelope Records Inc.
Apon Publishing Co.
Artistic Developments International, Inc. (A.D.I.)
Associated Artists Int.
ATI Music
Atlantic Recording Corp.
Axbar Productions
Bad Grammar Music
Bal & Bal Music Publishing
Bal Records
Balance Of Power Music
Bay Farm Productions
Bethlehem Music
Black Stallion Country Prod.
Blue Hill Music/Tutch Music
Boam
Bok Music
Bolivia Records
Boogie Band Records
Brothers Management
Buried Treasure Music
California Country Music
Cam Music, Ltd.
Camex Music
Capstan Record Production
Carmel Records
Carolina Pride Productions
Cimirron/Rainbird Records
Clear Pond Music
Clugston Organization

Comstock Records Ltd.
Connell Publishing Co.
Country Star Music
Country Star Productions
Courier Records
Crystal Clear Productions
Cude & Pickens Publishing
Dale Productions, Alan
Dean Enterprises
Denny Music Group
Diamond Entertainment
Duane Music, Inc.
Dupuy
Earth Dance Music
Element Movie and Music
Excell Productions
Fame and Fortune
Ferguson Productions, Don
Flash Attractions Agency
Gary Music, Alan
Goldband Records
Golden Triangle Records
Greenlee Records
Gubala Music, Frank
Hale Enterprises
Hammel Associates, Inc.
Hard Hat Productions
Heading North Music
Heaven Songs
Heavy Jamin' Music
Hickory Lane
Hickory Valley Music
High Desert Music Co.
High-Minded Moma
Hitsburgh Music Co.
Hollyrock Records
Holy Spirit Music
Holyrood Productions
Intrigue Production
Jackson Artists Corp.
Jaclyn Music
James, Sunny
Ja/Nein Musikverlag GmbH
Jellee Works Music
Jump Music
Jump Productions
Jump Records & Music

June Productions Ltd.
Junquera Productions, C.
Just a Note
Kansa Records Corporation
Kaupp Records
Kaupp's & Robert Pub.
Kingsport Creek Music Pub.
Knight Agency, Bob
Known Artist Productions
Kommunication Koncepts
Kozkeeozko Music
Lackey Publishing Co.
Landslide Management
LBJ Productions
Le Matt Music Ltd.
Lineage Publishing Co.
Little Pond Productions
LMP Management Firm
Loco Sounds
Loconto Productions
Lowe Publishing, Jere
Lowery Group, The
Lucifer Records, Inc.
Luick & Associates, Harold
Magid Productions, Lee
Martin Productions, Rick
Media Promotion Ent.
Merri-Webb Productions
Merry Marilyn Music Pub.
Mittelstedt, A.V.
Monticana Productions
Monticana Records
Montina Music
Music in the Right Keys
Music Sales Corporation
Nanoia Productions
Nashville International Entertainment Group
Nebo Ridge Publishing Co.
New Artist's Productions
New Horizon Records
New Rap Jam Publishing, A
Nicoletti Music Co.
Oak Street Music
Okisher Music
Oldham Music Publishing
Operation Perfection

Oregon Musical Artists
Otto Publishing Co.
Pacific Rim Productions
Pajer Records
Panio Brothers Label
Parc Records Inc.
Parker, Patty
Parravano Music
Paton, Dave
Pegasus Music
Perennial Productions
Peridot Productions
Peridot Records
Pine Island Music
PPI/Peter Pan Industries
Prescription Co., The
Prescription Company
Pustaka Muzik EMI
R. J. Music
Reed Sound Records, Inc.
Risavy, Inc., A.F.
RNJ Productions, Inc.
Roberts Music, Freddie
Rob-Lee Music
Rockford Music Co.
Rockit Records, Inc.
Roots Music
Rose Hill Group
Rosemark Publishing
Rusch Entertainment Agency
Rustron Music Productions
Seeds Records
Segal's Publications
Sha-La Music, Inc.
Sherman Artist Management &
    Development
Siegel Music Companies
Silicon Music Publishing
Silver-Loomas Productions
Simon Organization, Inc.
Skorman Productions, Inc.
Songfinder Music
Songrite Creations Prod.
Songwriters' Network
Songwriters' Network Music
    Publishing
Sopro, Inc.
Sound Column Publications
Sound '86 Talent Mgmt.
Studio B Records
Sugarfoot Productions
Sultan Music Publishing
Surprize Records, Inc.
Susan Records
T.S.J. Productions Inc., The
Tas Music Co./Dave Tasse
Tedesco Music Co., Dale
Ten Squared, Inc.
Terock Records
Tompaul Music Co.
Treasure Coast Records
Trend Records
Trinity Studio, The
Trusty Records
Tuffin Music Enterprises
UBM
Valex Talent Agency
Vickers Music Association
Wagner, William F.

Ward, Cornell
Wes Music, Bobe
Whitewing Music
Wind Haven Publishing
Wingate Records
Woodrich Publishing Co.
World Wide Management
Your Best Songs Publishing

Alternative

A Street Music
Agency, The
Alan Agency, Mark
Alcazar Records
Alternative Records
Amethyst Group Ltd., The
Amethyst Group Ltd./Antithe-
    sis Records, The
Anderson, Warren
Angry Neighbor Records
Another Amethyst Song
Artistic Developments Int.
Astron Music Publishing
Atlantic Recording Corp.
Aztlan Records
Baby Raquel Music
Baby Sue
Balance Of Power Music
Beyond Records Corp.
Black & Blue
Breadline Productions
Briefcase of Talent Prod.
Broadwest Management
Caffeine Disk
Cahn-Man
Camex Music
Caramba Art
Caroline Records, Inc.
Cat's Voice Productions
Century City Music Pub.
Challedon Productions
Challedon Records
Chrome Dreams Prod.
CLE Management Group
Coachouse Music
Community 3
Countdown Entertainment
Creative Life Ent.
Cumberland Music Group
D.B. Productions/Promo.
Davis Soto Orban Prod.
Detroit Municipal Rec.
Dino M. Production Co.
Direct Box Music
Direct Management Group
Dixon Management
Dudick, J.D.
Earache Records/Earache
Eternal Talent/Squigmonster
Eudaemonic Music
Events Unlimited
Fat City Artists
Fat City Publishing
Forefront Records
Freedman Entertainment
Fritz Management, Ken
Fullmoon Entertainment/
    Moonstone Records
G Fine

G Fine Records/Prod.
G Fine Sounds
Generic Records, Inc.
Global Assault Man.
Gold Productions, Ezra
Halogram
Homestead Records
Humongous Music Pub.
Ichiban Records
Illuminati Group
Imani Entertainment Inc.
International Talent Network
Iron John Management
J.L. Productions
Jedo Inc.
Josena Music
Kenning Productions
Kooch Management, Inc.
Kuper-Lam Management
L.A. Entertainment
Lansdowne and Winston
Latimer, John
Le Grande Fromage/Cheddar
    Cheese Music
Let Us Entertain You Co.
Limited Potential Records
Lucrecia Music
March Records
Marenco, Cookie
Master Entertainment
Merkin Records Inc.
MFE Records
Mirror Records, Inc.
Modern Voices Productions
Morgan Creek Music Grp.
Music Factory Enterprises
Musiplex
Nashville Music Group
Nettwerk Productions
No Mas Music
Not Records Tapes
Now & Then Records
Nowels Productions, Inc.
Old School Records
Pati Productions, Inc., Chris
Penguin Records, Inc.
Perennial Productions
Personal Management, Inc.
Pitzer Artist Management
Placer Publishing
Planet Dallas
Play Records
PMG Records
Prejippie Music Group
Presto Records
Publishing Central
Rabin Management, Gary
Rainbow Recording
Rainforest Records
Rana International
Raving Cleric
Righteous Records
Rock Dog Records
Rockit Records, Inc.
Rogue Management
RooArt Records
Ross Entertainment, Jay B.
Ruffcut Records
S.T.A.R.S. Productions

Balance of Power Music
Bandit Records
Bandstand
Barking Foe The Master's Bone
Barnard Management Services
Beacon Records
Beau-Jim Agency, Inc., The
Beau-Jim Records Inc.
Beecher Publishing, Earl
Bell Records International
Belmont Records
Bernstein, Richard
Best Buddies, Inc.
Better Times Publishing
Betty Jane/Josie Jane Music Publishers
Beyond Records Corp.
BGM Records
Big Picture Record Co.
Black & Blue
Black Diamond Records
Black Stallion Country Productions, Inc.
Black Stallion Country Pub.
Blenheim Music
Blue Gem Records
Blue Hill Music/Tutch Music
Blue Spur Music Group
Boam
BoDe Music
Bogart Records
Bojo Productions Inc.
Bolivia Records
Bonnfire Publishing
Bonta, Peter L.
Bouquet Records
Bouquet-Orchid Enterprises
Bovine Int. Record Co.
Bowden, Robert
Boyd Productions, Bill
Brentwood Music, Inc.
Briarhill Records
Bright Spark Songs Pty. Ltd.
BSW Records
Bull City Records
Buried Treasure Music
Butler Music, Bill
C & M Productions
California Country Music
Calinoh Music Group
Cam Music, Ltd.
Capitol Ad
Capitol Management
Capstan Record Production
Caravell Main Sail Music
Carlyle Productions
Carman Productions, Inc.
Carolina Pride Productions
Carousel Records, Inc.
Carr, Eddie
Carr, Steve
Casaro Records
Cash Music, Inc., Ernie
Castle Music Corp.
Cat's Voice Productions
Cavalry Productions
Cedar Creek Music
Cedar Creek Productions

Cedar Creek
Cedar Creek Records™
Cellar Records
Century City Music Pub.
CFB Productions, Inc.
Cha Cha Records
Chapie Music
Chapman, Chuck
Cheavoria Music Co.
Cherry Records
Cherry Street Records
Chestler Publishing Co.
Christopher Publishing
Cimirron Music
Cimirron/Rainbird Records
Circle "M" Records
Circuit Rider
Cisum
CITA Communications Inc.
Class Act Productions/Man.
CLE Management Group
Clear Pond Music (BMI)
Clearwind Publishing
Clevère Musikverlag, R.D.
Clientele Music
Cling Music Publishing
Coachouse Music
Cod Oil Productions Ltd.
Coffee and Cream Pub. Co.
Collector Records
Comma Records & Tapes
Comstock Records Ltd.
Concept 2000 Inc.
Connell Publishing Co.
Continental Records
Cornelius Companies, The
Cosgroove Music Inc.
Cottage Blue Music
Cottrell, Dave
Country Breeze Music
Country Breeze Records
Country Music Showcase International, Inc.
Country Reel Enterprises
Country Showcase America
Country Star Attractions
Country Star International
Country Star Music
Country Star Productions
Countrywide Producers
Cowboy Junction Flea Market and Publishing Co.
Craig Music, Loman
Crash Productions
Creative Life Ent., Inc.
Creative Star Management
Creekside Music
Crown Music Company
Crystal Clear Productions
CSB Kaminsky GMBH
Cude & Pickens Publishing
Cude's Good American Music
Cumberland Music Group
Cupit Music
Cymbal Records
D & R Entertainment
D.B. Productions/Prom.
D.S.M. Producers Inc.
Dale Productions, Alan

Dan the Man Music
Darbonne Publishing Co.
Darrow, Danny
De Lory And Music Makers
De Miles Co., The Edward
De Miles, Edward
De Miles Music Company
Dean and Assoc., Debbie
Dean Enterprises
Delev Music Company
Dell Music, Frank
Delpha's Music Publishers
Dennis, Warren
Denny Music Group
Diamond Entertainment
Diamond Wind Music
Diamond Wind Records
Dinwoodie Management
Doc Publishing
Domino Records, Ltd.
Don Del Music
Doss Music, Buster
Doss Presents, Col. Buster
Driven Rain Management
Duane Music, Inc.
Dudick, J.D.
E P Productions
E.S.R. Productions
E.S.R. Records
Earitating Music Publishing
Earmark Audio
Earthscream Music Pub. Co.
Eccentrax Music Co.
ECI Inc.
Eiffert, Jr., Leo J.
8th Street Music
Elect Music Publishing Co.
Element & Superstar Prod.
Element Movie and Music
EME International
Emperor of Emperors
Empty Sky Music Company
Empty Sky Records
Emzee Music
Emzee Records
Encore Talent, Inc.
Entertainment Productions
Entertainment Services Music Group
Entertainment Unlimited Artist Inc.
Ertis Music Company
ESB Records
Esquire International
Eternal Song Agency, The
Etiquette/Suspicious Records
Excursion Music Group
Excursion Records
Eye Kill Music
Eye Kill Records
Faiella Publishing, Doug
Fame and Fortune
Farr Records
Fat City Artists
Fat City Publishing
Fearless Records
Fenchel Entertainment
Ferguson Productions, Don
Fezsongs

Menza & Associates, Greg
Merri-Webb Productions
Merry Marilyn Music Pub.
Metro Records
Midcoast, Inc.
Midwest Records
Mighty Records
Miles Ahead Records
Milestone Media
Miller & Company, Thomas
Miracle Mile Music
Missile Records
Mittelstedt, A.V.
MJM Productions
Modern Music Ventures
Mom and Pop Productions
Monticana Productions
Monticana Records
Montina Music
Moon June Music
Moon Productions
Morgan Creek Music Group
Mountain Railroad Records
Mud Cat Music
Mule Kick Records
Music City Co-Op, Inc.
Music in the Right Keys
Music Sales Corporation
Music Service Management
Musica Arroz Publishing
Muskrat Productions, Inc.
Myko Music
Nanoia Productions and Management, Frank
Nash Angeles Inc.
Nashville Country Prod.
Nashville International
Nashville Music Group
Nashville Sound Music Pub.
Nason Enterprises, Inc.
National Entertainment
National Talent
Nautical Music Co.
Nebo Record Company
Nebo Ridge Publishing
Nelson, Bill
Neo Sync Labs
Nervous Publishing
Network Entertainment Service Inc.
New Artist's Productions
New Experience Rec/Grand Slam Records
New Rap Jam Publishing, A
Newcreature Music
NIC Of Tyme Productions
Nicoletti Music Co.
Nightflite Records Inc.
Non-Stop Music Publishing
North Star Records
Nowag's National Attractions, Craig
Nucleus Records
Oak Street Music
OB-1 Entertainment
Oh My Gosh Music
Okisher Music
Old Slowpoke Music
Oldham Music Publishing

O'Lyric Music
One for the Money
One Hot Note Music Inc.
Operation Music Enterprises
Orbit Records
Orchid Publishing
Oregon Musical Artists
Ormsby/Etiquette Productions, John "Buck"
Otto Publishing Co.
Outstanding & Morrhythm Records
Pacific Artists Records
Pacific Rim Productions
Pajer Records
Palmetto Productions
Pancho's Music Co.
Panepento/Airwave
Panio Brothers Label
Paragold Records & Tapes
Parchment Harbor Music
Parker, Patty
Parravano Music
Paton, Dave
Paton Management, Dave
Pecos Valley Music
Pegasus Music
Pegmatite Productions
Perception Works Inc., The
Perfection Music Pub.
Peridot Productions
Peridot Records
Personal Management, Inc.
Peters Music, Justin
Peterson Creative Man.
Phoenix Records, Inc.
Pierce, Jim
Pilot Records and Tape Co.
Pine Island Music
Pitzer Artist Management
Playback Records
Pleasure Records
Pomgar Productions
Pop Record Research
Portage Music
Prairie Music Ltd.
Prairie Music Records Ltd.
Pravda Records
Prescription Co., The
Prescription Company
Price Music Publisher
Pritchett Publication
Pro Talent Consultants
Prodisc (Prodisc Limitada)
Proud Pork Productions
Publishing Central
Purple Haze Music
Pustaka Muzik EMI
Puzzle Records
Quan-Yaa Records
R.E.F. Records
R. J. Music
Rabin Management, Gary
Rahsaan Publishing
Rainbow Collection Ltd.
Rainbow Recording
RANA International
Ranke & Associates, Ltd.
Raving Cleric Music Pub.

Raw Entertainment
Razor & Tie Music
Reca Music Production
Red Boots Tunes
Red Giant Records and Pub.
Reed Sound Records, Inc.
Reel Adventures
Reveal
Ridge Music Corp.
Ripsaw Productions
Ripsaw Record Co.
Risavy, Inc., A.F.
RNJ Productions, Inc.
Roach Records Co.
Road Records
Robbins Records, Inc.
Roberts Music, Freddie
Rock-A-Billy Artist Agency
Rocker Music
Rockford Music Co.
Rocky Mountain Heartland
RooArt Records
Roots Music
Rose Hill Group
Rosemark Publishing
Rosie Records
Ross Entertainment, Jay B.
Rothschild Productions
Roto-Noto Music
Round Robin
Royal Flair Publishing
RR&R Records
Ruffcut Records
Rusch Entertainment
Rustron Music Productions
S.T.A.R.S. Productions
Sabteca Music Co.
Sabteca Record Co.
Saddlestone Publishing
Saddlestone Records
Sagittar Records
Samuel Three Productions
San-Sue Recording Studio
Sariser Music
Scene Productions
Schonfeld and Associates
Scott Music Group, Tim
Seaside Records
Seeds Records
Segal's Productions
Segal's Publications
Seip Management, Inc.
Sellwood Publishing
770 Music Inc.
Sharpe Sound Productions
Sherman Artist Management
Sherwood Productions
Shoe String Booking Agency
Shore Records
Siegel Music Companies
Silent Partner Productions
Silicon Music Publishing
Silver Thunder Music Group
Silverfoot Publishing
Silver-Loomas Productions
Simply Grand Music, Inc.
Simpson Music Office, Ron
Singing Roadie Music Grp.
Siskatune Music Publishing

F&J Music
First Time Management
First Time Management & Production Co.
First Time Records
Fishbowl Productions
Flash Attractions Agency
Freedman Entertainment
Fricon Entertainment Co.
Fullmoon Entertainment
G Fine
G Fine Records/Prod.
G Fine Sounds
Gary Music, Alan
Genetic Music Publishing
Gland Puppies, Inc., The
Greenlee Records
Grooveland Music
Gubala Music, Frank
Guess Who?? Productions
Halogram
Hammer Musik GmbH
Hamstein Publishing Co.
Heading North Music
Heaven Songs
Hicky's Music
Hit & Run Music Pub.
Hitsource Publishing
Holyrood Productions
Humongous Music Pub.
I.Y.F. Productions
Imani Entertainment Inc.
Inner Sound Productions
Intensified Productions
International Music Network
Intrigue Production
Jackson Artists Corp.
Jag Studio, Ltd.
Janoulis Productions
Jet Laser Productions
JGM Recording Studio
Joey Boy Records Inc.
Joey Boy Publishing Co.
Jump Music
Jump Productions
Jump Records & Music
Keep Calm Music Limited
KMA
Koke, Moke & Noke Music
Kommunication Koncepts
Kozkeeozko Music
Landslide Management
Le Matt Music Ltd.
Lennon Music Ltd., John
Leopard Music
Loading Bay Records
Loconto Productions
Lucifer Records, Inc.
Lutz Entertainment Agency
McManus Management
Magic Apple Records
Magic Management and Productions
Majestic Control Music
Majestic Control Records
Manapro
Marenco, Cookie
Mark One-The Agency
Martin Productions, Rick

Master Entertainment
MCI Music Group
Mega Records APS.
Mega-Star Music
Metropolitan Talent Auth.
Mighty Records
Milestone Media
Mindfield Records
Modern Voices Productions
Moneytime Publishing Co.
Moneytime Records
Monticana Productions
Monticana Records
Montina Music
Moore Entertainment Group
Mraz, Gary John
MUSICA Schallplatten Vertrieb GES.M.B.H.
Myko Music
Nanoia Productions
Neo Sync Labs
Nep-Tune Records, Inc.
Nettwerk Productions
Network Sound Music Pub.
Neu Electro Productions
No Mas Music
Now & Then Records
Office, Inc., The
O'Lyric Music
On Top Records
One Hot Note Music Inc.
Oregon Musical Artists
Panio Brothers Label
Parc Records Inc.
Pati Productions, Inc., Chris
Paton, Dave
Paul Management and Consultant Firm, Jackie
Pearson Music, Martin
Penguin Records, Inc.
Perkins Production and Mgmt.
Persia Studios
Platinum Gold Music
PMG Records
Poku Productions
Polygram Records
Power Star Management
Prejippie Music Group
Prescription Co., The
Prescription Company
Red Dot/Puzzle Records
Renaissance Entertainment
Rix Management P/L, Peter
Rob-Lee Music
Rockford Music Co.
Rockit Records, Inc.
Rogue Management
Rose Hill Group
Rosenman, Mike
Ross Entertainment, Jay B.
Rusch Entertainment Agency
Sha-La Music, Inc.
Shankman De Blasio Melina
Shoe String Booking Agency
Shore Records
Siegel Music Companies
Single Minded Music
Sirr Rodd Record & Pub.
Siskatune Music Publishing

Skorman Productions, Inc.
Skylyne Records
Skyscraper Entertainment
Slak Records
Slavesong Corporation, Inc.
Sneak Tip Music
Soul Street Music Pub.
Sound Arts Recording Studio
Squad 16
Stang, Jack
Stargard Records
Steele Management
Stein Associates Inc., Bill
Stone Cold Productions
Stuart Music Co., Jeb
Sugarfoot Productions
Sunsongs Music
Surprize Records, Inc.
Susan Records
Talent Associates of WI
Tas Music Co.
Tavares Teleproductions
Tedesco Music Co., Dale
This Beats Workin' Music
Thompson Productions
T-Jaye Record Company
TKO Music, Inc.
Top Records
Total Acting Experience, A
Transition Music Corp.
Tropical Beat Records/Polygram
Trusty Publications
Trusty Records
12 Meter Productions
Valet Publishing Co.
Valex Talent Agency
Van Pol Management
Vibe Records Inc.
Victory Music
Visual Music
Waldoch Publishing, Inc.
Waterbury Productions
Weisman Production Group
Wes Music, Bobe
West Broadway Music
Wilshire Artists
Winston & Hoffman House
Wood Artist Management
Wow Management P/L
Yorgo Music
Young Bob Publishing Co.
Young Star Productions
Zauber Music Publishing

Folk
Adobe Records
Afterschool Publishing
Alcazar Records
Alear Records
Alexis
Alpha Music Productions
Amiron Music/Aztec Prod.
Anderson, Warren
Apon Publishing Co.
Apon Record Company
ArkLight Management Co.
Auburn Records and Tapes
Aurora Productions

Autogram Records
Bay Farm Productions
Beacon Records
Big Picture Record Co.
Black Dog Records
Boam
Cam Music, Ltd.
Caramba Art
Carmel Records
Century City Music Pub.
Cha Cha Records
Cimirron Music
Clevère Musikverlag, R.D.
Coppin/Red Sky Records
Countrywide Producers
Cumberland Music Group
Curly Maple Media
Dean Enterprises
Dinwoodie Management
Don Del Music
Driven Rain Management
Earitating Music Publishing
Emperor of Emperors
Eudaemonic Music
First Time Music
First Time Records
Fleming Artists Man.
Gland Puppies, Inc., The
Goldband Records
Green Dog Productions
Green Meadows Publishing
Halo International
Heaven Songs
Heavy Jamin' Music
Heupferd Musik Verlag
Hollyrock Records
Ivory Palaces Music
Jet Laser Productions
Kane Producer/Engineer
Kicking Mule Records, Inc.
Lackey Publishing Co.
Live Productions Inc.
Loconto Productions
Magid Productions, Lee
Maja Music
Mirror Records, Inc.
Modern Minstrel Mixing
Monarch Recordings
Monticana Productions
Monticana Records
Montina Music
Moon Productions
Mountain Railroad Records
Nettwerk Productions
North Star Records
Nucleus Records
OBH Musikverlag Otto B. Hartmann
Pacific Rim Productions
Parravano Music
Peridot Productions
Peridot Records
Personal Management, Inc.
Pilot Records and Tape
Pine Island Music
Platinum Productions Pub.
Prairie Music Ltd.
Prairie Music Records Ltd.
Prescription Company

Raspberry Records
Reca Music Production
Red Sky Records
Righteous Records
RNJ Productions, Inc.
Robbins Records, Inc.
Rockford Music Co.
Roots Music
Rothschild Productions
Royal Flair Publishing
Rustron Music Productions
S.T.A.R.S. Productions
Sagittar Records
Schwartz Management
Sharpe Sound Productions
Skyline Music Corp.
SP Talent Associates
Stuart Audio Services
Sunfrost Music
Susan Records
T.S.J. Productions Inc., The
Terock Records
Tompaul Music Co.
Trusty Records
Tryclops Ltd.
Universal Stars Music, Inc.
Wizmak Productions
Woodrich Publishing Co.
World Wide Management

Jazz

aaLN International
Adobe Records
Afterschool Publishing
Airwave Production Group
Alexis
Aljoni Music Co.
All Musicmatters!
Allyn, Stuart J.
Aloha Entertainment
Amato, Buzz
Americatone International
Americatone Records International USA
Amethyst Group Ltd./Antithesis Records, The
Amiron Music/Aztec Prod.
Anderson, Warren
Angel Films Company
Another Approach Music Publishing Company
Another Approach Recording Company
Antelope Publishing Inc.
Antelope Records Inc.
Artifex Records
Atlantic Recording Corp.
aUDIOFILE Tapes
Aurora Productions
B. Sharp Music
Bader/D.S.M. Producers
Bal & Bal Music Publishing
Bal Records
Bearsongs
Benyard Music Co.
Bernstein, Richard
Big Bear
Black Diamond Records
Bovine Int. Record Co.

Brentwood Music, Inc.
C.A.B. Independent Pub.
C.S.B. Mix Inc.
Cam Music, Ltd.
Capitol Ad
Cardinali, Peter
Casaro Records
Celt, Jan
Chapie Music
Chapman, Chuck
Cherry Street Records
CITA Communications Inc.
Cling Music Publishing
Community 3
Concept 2000 Inc.
Connell Publishing Co.
Core Productions
Countrywide Producers
Creative Music Services
Cumberland Music Group
Cunningham Music
Cymbal Records
D.B. Productions/Promo.
D.S.M. Producers Inc.
Dale Productions, Alan
D&D Talent Associates
Darrow, Danny
De Miles, Edward
DeMore Management
Duke Street Records
Dupuy Records
E.A.R.S. Inc.
El Gato Azul Agency
Element Movie and Music
Emperor of Emperors
Entertainment Unlimited
Esquire International
Fat City Artists
Fat City Publishing
Fifth Street Records
First Time Management
Fishbowl Productions
Flash Attractions Agency
Fleming Artists Man.
Flying Heart Records
Fresh Entertainment
Fritz Management, Ken
Ganvo Records
Genetic Music Publishing
Giftness Enterprise
Global Pacific Records
GlobeArt Publishing
Gold Productions, Ezra
Golden Bull Productions
Golden Triangle Records
Gordon Music Co. Inc.
Grass Roots Record & Tape
Greenlee Records
Hallway International Records
Hammer Musik GmbH
Happy Hour Music
Haworth Productions
Heart Consort Music
Heaven Songs
Heavy Jamin' Music
Heavyweight Productions
Heupferd Musik Verlag
Hibi Dei Hipp Records
Hollyrock Records

Holy Grail Publishing
Horizon Recording Studio
Hot Records
Hottrax Records
Iron John Management
Its Happening Present Ent.
Ivory Productions, Inc.
James, Sunny
Jana Jae Enterprises
J&J Musical Enterprises
Jazzand
Jet Laser Productions
Joey Boy Records Inc.
Joey Boy Publishing Co.
Jones Productions, Tyrone
Kane Producer/Engineer
Kaufman Hill Management
Kenning Productions
Kirk, Jeff
L.A. Entertainment
L.D.F. Productions
Landmark Audio of Nashville
Landmark Communications
Lansdowne and Winston
Le Grande Fromage
Mé LaVene & Associates
MAGIAN^{sm}
Magic Management
Magid Productions, Lee
Mardi Gras Music Fest, Inc.
Marenco, Cookie
Masterpiece Productions
Metro Records
Mighty Records
Miller & Company, Thomas
Modern Music Ventures
Mom and Pop Productions
Monticana Productions
Monticana Records
Montina Music
Moon Productions
Ms'Que Records Inc.
Mule Kick Records
Munich Records b.v.
Music Matters
Musica Arroz Publishing
Muskrat Productions, Inc.
Nadine Music
Nanoia Productions
Neo Sync Labs
New Horizon Records
Newcreature Music
NIC of Tyme Productions
Non-Stop Music Publishing
OBH Musikverlag
Okisher Music
Old Slowpoke Music
O'Lyric Music
On Top Records
One Hot Note Music Inc.
Oregon Musical Artists
Orinda Records
Outstanding & Morrhythm
Pacific Artists Records
Panepento/Airwave Production
  Group, Michael
Parc Records Inc.
Pati Productions, Inc., Chris
Paton, Dave

Perennial Productions
Persia Studios
Peterson Creative Man.
Philippopolis Music
Philly Breakdown
Pine Island Music
Play Records
PPI/Peter Pan Industries
Prescription Co., The
Prescription Company
Prodisc (Prodisc Limitada)
Pustaka Muzik EMI
Puzzle Records
Rage-N-Records
Red Giant Records and Pub.
Ridge Music Corp.
Righteous Records
Riohcat Music
Rising Star Music Pub.
Rising Star Records Inc.
Roach Records Co.
Rock Dog Records
Rockford Music Co.
Rocky Mountain Heartland
RooArt Records
Rose Hill Group
Ross Entertainment, Jay B.
Rothschild Productions Inc.
Roto-Noto Music
Sahara Records
St. Mitchell, Jojo
Saulsby Music Company
Seeds Records
Simon Organization, Inc.
Sirr Rodd Record & Pub.
Slavesong Corporation, Inc.
Sound Services
Sphemusations
Spunk Productions
Squad 16
Stuart Music Co., Jeb
Studio A
Sugarfoot Productions
Susan Records
T.S.J. Productions Inc., The
Talent Associates of WI
Tas Music Co.
Tedesco Music Co., Dale
Ten of Diamonds Music Pub.
Terock Records
Tilton Management, Terri
Total Acting Experience, A
Touche Records
Toulouse Music Publishing
Trend Records
Tryclops Ltd.
27th Dimension Inc.
UBM
Vickers Music Association
Wagner, William F.
Warner/Chappell Music
Wave Group Sound
Wazuri Music
Weedhopper Music
Windham Hill Productions
Winston & Hoffman House
Woodrich Publishing Co.
Woodrich Records
World Wide Management

Y-Not Productions
Young Star Productions

Latin
aaLN International
Alexis
Americatone International
Americatone Records Interna-
  tional USA
Amicos II Music, Ltd.
Apon Record Company
Cavalry Productions
Corvalan-Condliffe Man.
Curly Maple Media
De Leon Productions, Mike
De Lory And Music Makers
Dietrolequinte Art Co.
D'Nico International
Element Movie and Music
Galaxia Musical
Grass Roots Record & Tape
Hansen Productions
Heavy Jamin' Music
Heavyweight Productions
Johnson Music, Little Richie
Josena Music
Latin American Music Co.
Loco Sounds
Loconto Productions
Lowe Publishing
Manben Music
Modern Music Ventures
Musica Arroz Publishing
Noveau Talent
Padrino Music Publishing
Pancho's Music Co.
Pleasure Records
Prodisc (Prodisc Limitada)
Quan-Yaa Records
Societe D'Editions Musicales
Sounds-Vision Music
Sueño Publishing Co.
Sugarfoot Productions
Supreme Enterprises Int'l
Terock Records
Wes Music, Bobe

Metal
"A" Major Sound Corp.
Aarson Records
Aloha Entertainment
Amethyst Group Ltd., The
Amethyst Group Ltd./Antithe-
  sis Records, The
Artist Representation and
  Management
Astron Music Publishing
Avc Entertainment Inc.
AVC Music
Azra International
Bause Associates
Big Snow Music
Black & Blue
Briefcase of Talent Prod.
Cellar Records
Concert Event
Cosgroove Music Inc.
Courtright Management
Earache Records

Emperor of Emperors
Eternal Talent/Squigmonster
    Management
Forefront Records
Gland Puppies, Inc., The
Gopaco Limited
Heading North Music
Keno Publishing
King Klassic Records
Kommunication Koncepts
Master Entertainment
Nason Enterprises, Inc.
Nephelim Record
Nep-Tune Records, Inc.
Northstar Management Inc.
Pati Productions, Inc., Chris
Pegmatite Productions
Pravda Records
Randall Productions
Rockit Records, Inc.
Ross Entertainment, Jay B.
SAS Corporation
Shaky Records
Shore Records
Sound Cellar Music
Steele Production
Victory Music
Waldoch Publishing, Inc.
Wave Digital
Woods Production, Ray
Wyatt Management
Wytas Productions, Steve
Yorgo Music
Your Best Songs Publishing
Zanzibar Records

New Age
Alexas Music Productions
Aliso Creek Productions
Apon Publishing Co.
Arion Records
Astrodisque Publishing
August Night Music
Aurora Productions
Beacon Records
Big Picture Record Co.
Black Dog Records
Bogart Records
C.A.B. Independent Pub.
Cactus Records
Caramba Art
Cat's Voice Productions
Chapie Music
Chrome Dreams Prod.
Concert Event
Coppelia
Corwin, Dano
Dale Productions, Alan
Dat Beat Records, Inc.
Dennis, Warren
Dingo Music
Elect Music Publishing
Emperor of Emperors
Faber, Shane
Festival Studios
Flaming Star West
Four Newton Publishing
Foxworthy Music Inc.
Gland Puppies, Inc., The

Global Pacific Records
GlobeArt Publishing
Go Star Music
Gorr Custom Music, Jon
Graffiti Productions Inc.
Halogram
Hartel Musikverlag, Johann
Haworth Productions
Heart Consort Music
Imani Entertainment Inc.
Innersounds Productions
Jericho Sound Lab
Kane Producer/Engineer
Kren Music Productions
Kren Music Publishing
L.A. Entertainment
Little Pond Productions
M.R. Productions
Maja Music
Manapro
Mardi Gras Music Fest, Inc.
MFE Records
Moon Productions
Music Factory Enterprises
Narada Productions
Nephelim Record (Studio
    Works)
Neu Electro Productions
Nightflite Records Inc.
Nightstar Records Inc.
Non-Stop Music Publishing
Pacific Artists Records
Paradigm Distribution
Persia Studios
Placer Publishing
PMG Records
Powercoat Records
Presence Records
Prodisc (Prodisc Limitada)
QUARK, Inc.
Rahsaan Publishing
Rising Star Music Pub.
Rising Star Records Inc.
Rock Dog Records
Rock In Records
Rockit Records, Inc.
Rustron Music Productions
Sherwood Productions
Silent Partner Productions
Sinus Musik Produktion
Sound Resources
Southern Most Publishing
Sphere Productions
Tanin, Gary
Tiki Enterprises, Inc.
Tomsick Brothers Prod.
Ward, Cornell
Wave Group Sound
Wilshire Artists
World Wide Management

Novelty
Auntie Argon Music
Azra International
Bandstand
Better Times Publishing
Briarhill Records
Cavalry Productions
Cisum

Dean Enterprises
Doré Records
Gland Puppies, Inc., The
Green Dog Productions
Johnson, Ralph D.
Luick & Associates, Harold
MOR Records
Nasetan Publishing
Parravano Music
Peridot Productions
Peridot Records
Rosie Records
Songrite Creations Prod.
TMC Productions
Treasure Coast Records
Tuffin Music Enterprises

Pop
A & R Recording Services
"A" Major Sound Corp.
A Street Music
Aberdeen Productions
Abiding Love Music Pub.
Absolute Entertainment
Accent Publishing Co.
AcoustiWorks
ACR Productions
Active Sound Productions
Afterschool Publishing
Agency, The
Air Central Recordings
Airwave Production Group
AKO Production
Alan Agency, Mark
Alcazar Records
Alexas Music Productions
Alexis
Aliferis Management, Greg
Aliso Creek Productions
Allagash Country Records
Alleged Iguana Music
Allegheny Music Works
Allen Entertainment
Allen-Martin Productions
Allyn, Stuart J.
Alphabeat
Alternative Direction Music
    Publishers
Alternative Records
Alyssa Records
Amalgamated Tulip Corp.
Amato, Buzz
American Family Ent.
American Family Talent
Amethyst Group Ltd./Antithe-
    sis Records, The
Amethyst Group Ltd.
AMI Records
Amicos II Music, Ltd.
Amiron Music
Amiron Music/Aztec Prod.
Angel Films Company
Angelsong Publishing Co.
Anjoli Productions
Another Amethyst Song
ArkLight Management Co.
Art Audio Pub. Co./Tight Hi-Fi
    Soul Music
Art of Concept Music

Artist Representation and Management
Artiste Records
Artistic Developments Int.
Associated Artists Int.
Associated Artists Music
Astron Music Publishing
Atch Records and Prod.
Atlantic Recording Corp.
Attack Records
August Night Music
Auntie Argon Music
Aurora Productions
Avc Entertainment Inc.
AVC Music
Baby Raquel Music
Baby Sue
Backstage Productions Int.
Bad Grammar Music
Bader/D.S.M. Producers
Bal & Bal Music Publishing
Bal Records
Balance Of Power Music
Barking Foe The Master's Bone
Bartow Music
Bay Farm Productions
Beecher Publishing, Earl
Bell Records International
Berandol Music
Bernard Enterprises, Inc.
Best Buddies, Inc.
Better Times Publishing
Beyond Records Corp.
Big J Productions
Big Picture Record Co.
Big Productions and Pub.
Big Productions Records
Big Rock Pty. Ltd.
Big Snow Music
Black Dog Records
Blaze Productions
Blenheim Music
Blue Gem Records
Blue Hill Music/Tutch Music
Bogart Records
Bok Music
Bolivia Records
Bonaire Management Inc.
Bony "E" Productions, Inc.
Boogie Band Records
Boom Productions, Inc.
Bouquet-Orchid Enterprises
Bovine Int. Record Co.
Bowden, Robert
Bright Spark Songs Pty. Ltd.
Broken Records Int.
Bronx Flash Music, Inc.
Brothers Management
Bull City Records
Buried Treasure Music
C.A.B. Independent Pub.
C & M Productions
C.S.B. Mix Inc.
Cactus Records
California Country Music
Calinoh Music Group
Camex Music
Capitol Ad, Management

Capitol Management
Caramba Art
Caravell Main Sail Music
Cardinali, Peter
Carlyle Productions
Carman Productions, Inc.
Carolina Pride Productions
Carr, Steve
Casaro Records
Cash Music, Inc., Ernie
Castle Music Corp.
Catharine Courage Music
Cedar Creek Music
Cedar Creek Productions
Cedar Creek Productions and Management
Cedar Creek Records™
Cellar Records
CFB Productions, Inc.
Challedon Productions
Challedon Records
Chapie Music
Cheavoria Music Co.
Cherry Records
Christie Management, Paul
Cimirron/Rainbird Records
Circuit Rider Talent
Cisum
City Publishing Co.
Class Act Productions/Man.
CLE Management Group
Clear Pond Music
Clearwind Publishing
Clevère Musikverlag, R.D.
Clientele Music
Clockwork Entertainment
Clotille Publishing
Clugston Organization Pty.
Coachouse Music
Coffee and Cream Pub.
Coffer Management
Comma Records & Tapes
Concept 2000 Inc.
Continental Comm.
Coppelia
Core Productions
Cornelius Companies, The
Corvalan-Condliffe Man.
Corwin, Dano
Cosgroove Music Inc.
Cottage Blue Music
Cottrell, Dave
Countdown Entertainment
Countrywide Producers
Courtright Management
Craig Music, Loman
Creations, Ltd.
Creative Life Ent.
Creative Music Services
Creative Star Management
Creole Music Ltd.
Crown Music Company
Crystal Clear Productions
CSB Kaminsky GMBH
Cude & Pickens Publishing
Cude's Good American Music
Cumberland Music Group
Cunningham Music
Curly Maple Media

Cymbal Records
D & M Entertainment
Dagene Music
Dagene Records
Dan the Man Music
Darrow, Danny
Dat Beat Records, Inc.
Davis Soto Orban Prod.
de Courcy Management
De Dan Music
De Leon Productions, Mike
De Lory And Music Makers
De Miles Company
De Miles, Edward
De Miles Music Company
Dean Enterprises
Delev Music Company
Dell Music, Frank
Delpha's Music Publishers
Demi Monde Records & Pub.
Dennis, Warren
Diamond Entertainment
Diamond Wind Music
Diamond Wind Records
Dingo Music
Dino M. Production Co.
Direct Management Group
Discovering Music Ltd.
Dixon Management
DMR Agency
D'Nico International
Doss Presents, Col. Buster
Dream Sequence Music
Duane Music, Inc.
Dudick, J.D.
Duke Street Records
Dupuy Records
E P Productions
E.S.R. Productions
Earthscream Music Pub.
Eccentrax Music Co.
Edition Musica
8th Street Music
El Gato Azul Agency
Element & Superstar Prod.
Element Movie and Music
Emarco Management
Emperor of Emperors
Empty Sky Music Company
Empty Sky Records
Emzee Music
Emzee Records
Entertainment Services
Entertainment Unlimited
Esquire International
Eternal Song Agency, The
Eternal Talent
Etiquette/Suspicious Records
Ever-Open-Eye Music
Excell Productions
Exclusive Recording Co.
Excursion Music Group
Excursion Records
Faber, Shane
Fame and Fortune
Famous Music Publishing
F&J Music
Farr Records
Fat City Artists

Hulen Enterprise
I.Y.F. Productions
Imani Entertainment Inc.
Inner Sound Productions
Innersounds Productions
Inspire Productions, Inc.
Intensified Productions
Intrigue Production
Its Happening Present Ent.
Jag Studio, Ltd.
Jasper Stone Music
Jazmin Productions
Joey Boy Records Inc.
Joey Boy Publishing Co.
JOF-Dave Music
Jones Productions, Tyrone
Jungle Boy Music
Kaufman Hill Management
Keno Publishing
KMA
Koke, Moke & Noke Music
Kuper-Lam Management
Lamar Music Group
Landslide Records
Lennon Music Ltd., John
Lin's Lines
Magic Apple Records
Magic Management
Majestic Control Music
Majestic Control Records
Makers Mark Gold
Manben Music
Masterpiece Productions
Metropolitan Talent Auth.
Milestone Media
Mindfield Records
Missile Records
Mr. Wonderful Prod.
Modern Music Ventures
Monarch Recordings
Moneytime Publishing Co.
Moneytime Records
Musica Arroz Publishing
Musiplex
Must Rock Productionz
Nep-Tune Records, Inc.
Nettwerk Productions
Network Production Group
Neu Electro Productions
New Experience Rec/Grand
  Slam Records
New Experience Records
New Rap Jam Publishing, A
Nickle Plate Records
Now & Then Records
N-The Water Publishing
Ocean Records Inc.
On Top Records
One Hot Note Music Inc.
Operation Perfection
Outstanding & Morrhythm
Pandisc Records
Paul Management
PDS Music Publishing
Penguin Records, Inc.
Perkins Production
Philly Breakdown
Platinum Productions Pub.
Poku Productions

Quan-Yaa Records
Rainforest Records
Rap-A-Lot Records, Inc.
Raving Cleric Music Pub./Euro
  Export Ent.
Raw Entertainment
Renaissance Entertainment
Rosenman, Mike
Ross Entertainment, Jay B.
St. Mitchell, Jojo
SAS Corporation
Saulsby Music Company
Scott Entertainment, Dick
Scott Music Group, Tim
Shu'Baby Montez Music
Sirr Rodd Record & Pub.
Skylyne Records
Skyscraper Entertainment
Sneak Tip Music
Soul Street Music Pub.
Sound Cellar Music
Squad 16
Stargard Records
State of the Art Ent.
Stellar Music Industries
Stone Cold Productions
Strictley Biziness Music Mgmt.
Stuart Music Co., Jeb
Sweet Glenn Music (BMI)
Tandem Records
Tavares Teleproductions
Tawas Records
This Beats Workin' Music
Toro'na Int'l.
Toro'na Music
Trusty Publications
12 Meter Productions
Van Pol Management
Vibe Records Inc.
Visual Music
Ward, Cornell
Warner/Chappell Music
Weisman Production Grp.
Winston & Hoffman House
Zanzibar Records

R&B
A Company Called W
"A" Major Sound Corp.
A Street Music
A Street Music
Abiding Love Music Pub.
Absolute Entertainment
Accent Publishing Co.
ACR Productions
Active Sound Productions
Air Central Recordings
Airwave Production Group
Alan Agency, Mark
Alcazar Records
Alexis
Alhart Music Publishing
Aljoni Music Co.
Allagash Country Records
Allegheny Music Works
Allen Entertainment
Allen-Martin Productions
Allyn, Stuart J.
Aloha Entertainment

Alphabeat
Alternative Direction
Alyssa Records
Amalgamated Tulip Corp.
Amato, Buzz
Amethyst Group Ltd., The
Amethyst Records, Inc.
Amicos II Music, Ltd.
Amiron Music
Angel Films Company
Anjoli Productions
Another Amethyst Song
Another Approach Music
Another Approach Recording
  Company
Art Audio Pub. Co.
Artist Representation
Artistic Developments Int.
Astrodisque Publishing
Atch Records and Prod.
Atlantic Recording Corp.
Attack Records
Audio Music Publishers
August Night Music
Avc Entertainment Inc.
AVC Music
Back Porch Blues
Bal & Bal Music Publishing
Bal Records
Balance Of Power Music
Barking Foe The Master's
  Bone
Barnard Management
Bartow Music
Bay Farm Productions
Bell Records International
Benyard Music Co.
Bernard Enterprises, Inc.
Best Buddies, Inc.
Beth-Ridge Music Pub.
Betty Jane/Josie Jane
Big J Productions
Big Picture Record Co.
Big Productions Records
Big Rock Pty. Ltd.
Bivins' Productions, J.
Black Diamond Records
Black Dog Records
Black Stallion Country
Black Stallion Country Pub.
Blue Gem Records
Blue Wave
Boam
Bogart Records
Bojo Productions Inc.
Bok Music
Bolivia Records
Bony "E" Productions, Inc.
Boogie Band Records
Bouquet-Orchid Enterprises
Bovine International
Briefcase of Talent Prod.
Broadwest Management
Bronx Flash Music, Inc.
Brothers Management
Butler Music, Bill
C.A.B. Independent Pub.
C.S.B. Mix Inc.
California Country Music

Capitol Ad
Capitol Management
Cardinali, Peter
Carman Productions, Inc.
Carr, Steve
Casaro Records
Cash Music, Inc., Ernie
Cat Production AB
Catharine Courage Music
Cat's Voice Productions
Cedar Creek Music
Cedar Creek Productions
Cedar Creek Productions and
    Management
Cedar Creek Records™
Cellar Records
Celt, Jan
Chapie Music
Cheavoria Music Co.
Christie Management, Paul
Circle "M" Records
Circuit Rider Talent
Cisum
Class Act Productions/Man.
CLE Management Group
Clearwind Publishing
Clevère Musikverlag, R.D.
Clientele Music
Clotille Publishing
Coffee and Cream Pub.
Comma Records & Tapes
Concept 2000 Inc.
Core Productions
Corvalan-Condliffe Man.
Cosgroove Music Inc.
Cottage Blue Music
Cottrell, Dave
Countdown Entertainment
Country Star Attractions
Country Star Music
Country Star Productions
Countrywide Producers
Creations, Ltd.
Creative Life Entertainment
Creative Star Management
Cunningham Music
Curly Maple Media
D & M Entertainment
D.B. Productions/Promo.
D.S.M. Producers Inc.
Daddy, S. Kwaku
Dagene Music
Dagene Records
Dat Beat Records, Inc.
De Leon Productions, Mike
De Miles Company
De Miles, Edward
De Miles Music Company
Dean Enterprises
Delev Music Company
Demi Monde Records & Pub.
DeMore Management
Diamond Entertainment
Diamond Wind Music
Diamond Wind Records
Dingo Music
Dino M. Production Co.
Dinwoodie Management
Direct Box Music

Discovering Music Ltd.
Disc-tinct Music, Inc.
Dixon Management
D'Nico International
Domino Records, Ltd.
Don Del Music
Dream Sequence Music, Ltd.
Duane Music, Inc.
Dupuy Records/Productions
E P Productions
E.S.R. Productions
Eccentrax Music Co.
ECI Inc.
8th Street Music
Elect Music Publishing
Element & Superstar Prod.
Element Movie and Music
Emperor of Emperors
Emzee Music
Emzee Records
Entertainment Unlimited
Esquire International
Etiquette/Suspicious Records
Ever-Open-Eye Music
Excursion Music Group
Excursion Records
Faber, Shane
Famous Music Publishing
F&J Music
Farr Records
Fearless Records
Festival Studios
Fifth Street Records
Fink-Pinewood Records
First Million Music, Inc.
First Time Management
First Time Music (Publishing)
    U.K. Ltd.
First Time Records
Five Roses Music Group
Flaming Star West
Flying Heart Records
Four Newton Publishing
Foxworthy Music Inc.
Freade Sounds
Freedman Entertainment
Fresh Entertainment
Fresh Start Music Ministries
Frick Enterprises, Bob
Fricon Entertainment Co.
Frog and Moose Music
Frontline Music Group
Frozen Inca Music
Fullmoon Entertainment
Future Star Entertainment
G Fine
G Fine Records/Prod.
G Fine Sounds
Gangland Artists
Ganvo Records
Gary Music, Alan
General Jones Music
Genetic Music Publishing
Giftness Enterprise
Global Assault Man.
Global Pacific Records
GlobeArt Publishing
Go Star Music
Gold City Records, Inc.

Goldband Records
Golden Bull Productions
Golden Triangle Records
Goldwax Record Co., Inc.
GO-ROC-CO-POP Records
Gowell Music, Richard E.
Graffiti Productions Inc.
Grass Roots Record & Tape
Great South Artists
Green Meadows Publishing
Greenlee Records
Grooveland Music
Guess Who?? Productions
Hallway International
Halogram
Hammel Associates, Inc.
Hamstein Publishing Co.
Harmony Street Music
Harmony Street Records
Hawkins Management
Hawk's Bill Music
Haworth Productions
Hearing Ear
Heath & Associates
Heaven Songs
Heavy Jamin' Music
Heavyweight Productions
Helion Records
Hibi Dei Hipp Records
Hicky's Music
High Desert Music Co.
Hit & Run Music Pub.
Hitsource Publishing
Hobar Production
Homebased Entertainment
Horizon Recording Studio
Hot Records
Hulen Enterprises
Humongous Music Pub.
Ichiban Records
Illuminati Group
Imani Entertainment Inc.
Inner Sound Productions
Innersounds Productions
Inspire Productions, Inc.
Intensified Productions
International Music Network
Interplanetary Music
Intrigue Production
Issachar Management
Its Happening Present Ent.
J.L. Productions
Jackson Artists Corp.
Jackson/Jones Management
Jaelius Enterprises
James Productions, Neal
James, Sunny
Jampop Ltd.
Janoulis Productions
Jasper Stone Music
Jazmin Productions
Jedo Inc.
Jericho Sound Lab
JGM Recording Studio
Joey Boy Publishing Co.
JOF-Dave Music
Jones Productions, Tyrone
Jungle Boy Music
Just a Note

Kane Producer/Engineer
Kaupp Records
Kaupp's & Robert Pub.
Keep Calm Music Limited
Keno Publishing
Keystone Music Group Inc.
Kicking Mule Records, Inc.
Kingsport Creek Music Pub.
KMA
Knight Agency, Bob
Known Artist Productions
Koke, Moke & Noke Music
Kommunication Koncepts
Kottage Records
Kozkeeozko Music
Kren Music Productions
L.A. Entertainment
Lackey Publishing Co.
Lamar Music Group
Landmark Communications
Landslide Management
Landslide Records
Lanor Records
Lansdowne and Winston
LBJ Productions
Le Grande Fromage
Le Matt Music Ltd.
Lennon Music Ltd., John
Leopard Music
Let Us Entertain You Co.
Levinson Entertainment
Levy Mgt, Rick
Lighthouse Music Co.
Linear Cycle Productions
Lin's Lines
Lion Hunter Music
LMP Management Firm
Loco Sounds
Loveforce International
Lowe Publishing
Lucifer Records, Inc.
Lucrecia Music
M & M Talent Agency Inc.
Mé LaVene & Associates
McDonnell Group, The
Macman Music, Inc.
MAGIAN℠
Magic Apple Records
Magic Management
Magid Productions, Lee
Majestic Control Music
Makers Mark Gold
Manapro
Mardi Gras Music Fest, Inc.
Marenco, Cookie
Martin/Vaam Music Prod.
Marvel Music, Andy
Master Entertainment
Masterpiece Productions
Master-Trak Enterprises
Mathes Productions, David
Mayo & Company, Phil
MCI Music Group
Media Productions
Media Promotion
Mega-Star Music
Merri-Webb Productions
Metropolitan Talent Auth.
M-5 Management, Inc.

Miles Ahead Records
Miracle Mile Music
Missile Records
Mr. Wonderful Prod.
MJM Productions
Modern Blues Recordings
Modern Voices Productions
Mom and Pop Productions
Monarch Recordings
Moneytime Publishing Co.
Moneytime Records
Monticana Productions
Monticana Records
Montina Music
Moore Entertainment Group
Morgan Creek Music Group
Mountain Railroad Records
Mraz, Gary John
Ms'Que Records Inc.
Music In the Right Keys Pub.
Music Matters
Music Room Publishing
Music Sales Corporation
Musiplex
Must Rock Productionz World-
wide
Myko Music
Mymit Music Productions
Nadine Music
Namax Music Publishing
Nanoia Productions
Nashville International
Nebo Record Company
Nephelim Record
Nep-Tune Records, Inc.
Nervous Publishing
Network Production Group
Network Sound Music Pub.
New Experience Records
New Rap Jam Publishing, A
Newcreature Music
NIC Of Tyme Productions
Nickel Records
Nickle Plate Records
Nicoletti Music Co.
No Mas Music
Non-Stop Music Publishing
Norman Productions, David
North Star Records
Noveau Talent
Now & Then Records
Nowag's National Attractions,
Craig
N-The Water Publishing
OBH Musikverlag Otto B. Har-
tmann
Ocean Records Inc.
Office, Inc., The
Okisher Music
Old School Records
Old Slowpoke Music
Oldham Music Publishing
O'Lyric Music
One for the Money Music
Operation Perfection
Orbit Records
Oregon Musical Artists
Ormsby/Etiquette Productions,
John "Buck"

Outstanding & Morrhythm Re-
cords
P.I.R.A.T.E. Records/H.E.G.
Music Publishing
Pajer Records
Pandisc Records
Panepento/Airwave Production
Group, Michael
Parc Records Inc.
Paton, Dave
Paul Management and Consul-
tant Firm, Jackie
PDS Music Publishing
Pearson Music, Martin
PeerMusic
Penguin Records, Inc.
Perception Works Inc., The
Perennial Productions
Perkins Production and Mgmt.
Persia Studios
Personal Management, Inc.
Peters Music, Justin
Philly Breakdown
Pine Island Music
Platinum Ears Ltd.
Platinum Gold Music
Platinum Productions Pub.
Play Records
Pleasure Records
Polygram Records
Pop Record Research
Power Star Management
PPI/Peter Pan Industries
Prescription Co., The
Prescription Company
Prodisc (Prodisc Limitada)
Proud Pork Productions
Purple Haze Music
Quan-Yaa Records
Rage-N-Records
Rahsaan Publishing
Rainbow Recording
RANA International Music
Group, Inc.
Randall Productions
Rap-A-Lot Records, Inc.
Raving Cleric Music Pub./Euro
Export Ent.
Raw Entertainment
Razor & Tie Music
Red Boots Tunes
Red Giant Records and Pub.
Red-Eye Records
Rem Management
Ren Maur Music Corp.
Renaissance Entertainment
Roach Records Co.
Rob-Lee Music
Rock & Troll Productions
Rock Dog Records
Rock In Records
Rockit Records, Inc.
Rosemark Publishing
Rosenman, Mike
Roto-Noto Music
RR&R Records
Rustron Music Productions
Sabteca Music Co.
Sabteca Record Co.

Religious

Cat Production AB
Cavalry Productions
Cha Cha Records
Chapie Music
Chapman, Chuck
Charis Music
Chestler Publishing Co.
Cimirron Music
Circle "M" Records
Circuit Rider
Cisum
CITA Communications Inc.
City Publishing Co.
CLE Management Group
Clearwind Publishing
Clientele Music
Coffee and Cream Pub.
Comstock Records Ltd.
Concept 2000 Inc.
Connell Publishing Co.
Continental Records
Cottage Blue Music
Cottrell, Dave
Country Breeze Music
Country Reel Enterprises
Country Star Attractions
Country Star Music
Country Star Productions
Countrywide Producers
Courier Records
Cowboy Junction
Craig Music, Loman
Creations, Ltd.
Creative Life Ent.
Creative Star Management
Creekside Music
Cude & Pickens Publishing
Cunningham Music
Cupit Music
D.B. Productions/Promo.
Daddy, S. Kwaku
Dagene Records
Dale Productions, Alan
Darbonne Publishing Co.
Dell Music, Frank
Delpha's Music Publishers
DeMore Management
Dennis, Warren
Denny Music Group
Dingo Music
Dixon Management
Doss Presents, Col. Buster
E P Productions
Earitating Music Publishing
Earmark Audio
Eiffert, Jr., Leo J.
Element & Superstar Prod.
Element Movie and Music
Emandell Tunes
Emperor of Emperors
Empty Sky Music Company
Empty Sky Records
Emzee Records
Esquire International
Eternal Song Agency, The
Ever-Open-Eye Music
Excursion Music Group
Excursion Records
Faiella Publishing, Doug

F&J Music
Fenchel Entertainment
Fink-Pinewood Records
First Time Management
First Time Music (Publishing)
   U.K. Ltd.
First Time Records
Five Roses Music Group
Flaming Star West
Fleming Artists Man.
Focal Point Music Pub.
Foster Music Company
Fountain Records
Four Newton Publishing
Fox Farm Recording
Fresh Entertainment
Fresh Start Music Ministries
Fretboard Publishing
Frick Enterprises, Bob
Frick Music Publishing Co.
Fricon Entertainment Co.
Frog and Moose Music
Frontline Music Group
Frozen Inca Music
Ganvo Records
Gayle Enterprises, Inc.
Gift Of Grace Music
Giftness Enterprise
GlobeArt Publishing
Go Star Music
Gold City Records, Inc.
Golden Bull Productions
Goldwax Record Co., Inc.
GO-ROC-CO-POP Records
Grass Roots Record & Tape
Green Meadows Publishing
Hammel Associates, Inc.
Hamstein Publishing Co.
Happy Days Music
Harmony Street Music
Harmony Street Records
Haworth Productions
Hearing Ear
Heartbeat Music
Heath & Associates
Heavy Jamin' Music
Henly Music Associates
Hickory Lane
Hicky's Music
High Desert Music Co.
History Publishing Co.
Hobar Production
Holy Grail Publishing
Holy Spirit Music
Homebased Entertainment
Horizon Recording Studio
Hot Records
Inspire Productions, Inc.
Ivory Palaces Music
Jackson Artists Corp.
Jaclyn Music
Jaelius Enterprises
Jag Studio, Ltd.
Jalyn Recording Co.
James Productions, Neal
Jampop Ltd.
Jazmin Productions
Jellee Works Music
Jennaco-Alexas Publishing

Jerjoy Music
Josena Music
Just a Note
Kansa Records Corporation
Kaupp Records
Kaupp's & Robert Pub.
Kaylee Music Group, Karen
Kennedy Enterprises, Inc.
King of Kings Record Co.
Kingsport Creek Music Pub.
Kommunication Koncepts
Kottage Records
Kren Music Productions
Kren Music Publishing
L.D.F. Productions
Lackey Publishing Co.
Landmark Audio of Nashville
Landmark Communications
Landslide Records
Lari-Jon Records
Lari-Jon Productions
Lari-Jon Promotions
Lari-Jon Publishing
LBJ Productions
LCS Music Group, Inc.
Leavell, John
Legs Records
Lemon Square Productions
Lennon Music Ltd., John
Leopard Music
Lindsay Publishing, Doris
Linear Cycle Productions
Lin's Lines
Lion Hill Music Publishing
Lithics Group
Little Pond Productions
Live Productions Inc.
Lorenz Corporation, The
Loveforce International
Lowery Group, The
Luick & Associates, Harold
M.R.E. Recording Prod.
McCoy Productions, Jim
McCoy Music, Jim
Mack Music, Danny
MAGIAN^{sm}
Magic Management and Pro-
   ductions
Magid Productions, Lee
Magnum Music Corp.
Marco Music Group Inc.
Masterpiece
Mathes Company, The
Mathes Productions, David
Mayo & Company, Phil
Media Productions
Melfi, Patrick
Menza & Associates, Greg
Merri-Webb Productions
M-5 Management, Inc.
Miles Ahead Records
Missile Records
Mr. Wonderful Productions
Mittelstedt, A.V.
Mom and Pop Productions
Monticana Productions
Monticana Records
Montina Music
Moon Productions

Mymit Music Productions
Nash Angeles Inc.
Nashville International
Nashville Music Group
Nason Enterprises, Inc.
National Entertainment
Nebo Record Company
Nebo Ridge Publishing
Neo Sync Labs
Nephelim Record
Nep-Tune Records, Inc.
Nervous Publishing
Nettwerk Productions
Network Entertainment
Network Sound Music Pub.
Neu Electro Productions
New Artist's Productions
New Experience Records
New Rap Jam Publishing, A
Newcreature Music
NIC Of Tyme Productions
Nickel Records
Nickle Plate Records
Nicoletti Music Co.
Nightflite Records Inc.
North Star Records
Northstar Management Inc.
Nowag's National Attractions, Craig
Nowels Productions, Inc.
Nucleus Records
OB-1 Entertainment
OBH Musikverlag Otto B. Hartmann
Office, Inc., The
Old School Records
Old Slowpoke Music
Oldham Music Publishing
O'Lyric Music
On The Level Music!
One for the Money Music
One Hot Note Music Inc.
Operation Perfection
Orbit Records
Oregon Musical Artists
Ormsby
Outstanding & Morrhythm
Pancho's Music Co.
Panepento/Airwave
Parc Records Inc.
Parchment Harbor Music
Pati Productions, Inc., Chris
Paton, Dave
Paton Management, Dave
Pearson Music, Martin
Pecos Valley Music
PeerMusic
Pegmatite Productions
Penguin Records, Inc.
Perception Works Inc., The
Perennial Productions
Persia Studios
Personal Management, Inc.
Peterson Creative Man.
Phoenix Records, Inc.
Pilot Records and Tape
Pine Island Music
Pitzer Artist Management
Planet Dallas Recording

Platinum Ears Ltd.
Platinum Gold Music
Platinum Productions Pub.
Play Records
Pleasure Records
PMG Records
Poku Productions
Polygram Records
Pomgar Productions
Portage Music
Power Star Management
Pravda Records
Prejippie Music Group
Prescription Co., The
Prescription Company
Presence Records
Pritchett Publication
Pro Talent Consultants
Prodisc (Prodisc Limitada)
Proud Pork Productions
Publishing Central
Pustaka Muzik EMI
Puzzle Records
R.E.F. Records
R.J. Music
Rabin Management, Gary
Rage-N-Records
Rahsaan Publishing
Rainbow Collection Ltd.
Rainbow Recording
RANA International Music Group, Inc.
Randall Productions
Raw Entertainment
Razor & Tie Music
Red Boots Tunes
Red Dot/Puzzle Records
Red Giant Records and Pub.
Red Sky Records
Red-Eye Records
Reel Adventures
Rem Management
Ren Maur Music Corp.
Reveal
Ridge Music Corp.
Ripsaw Productions
Ripsaw Record Co.
Risavy, Inc., A.F.
Rix Management P/L, Peter
Roach Records Co.
Roberts Music, Freddie
Rob-Lee Music
Rock & Troll Productions
Rock In Records
Rock-A-Billy Artist Agency
Rocker Music
Rockford Music Co.
Rockit Records, Inc.
Rock'n'Roll Records
Rockstar Productions
Rocky Mountain Heartland
Rogue Management
RooArt Records
Roots Music
Rose Hill Group
Rosenman, Mike
Rothschild Productions Inc.
Roto-Noto Music
RR&R Records

Ruffcut Records
Rusch Entertainment Agency
Rustron Music Productions
S.T.A.R.S. Productions
Saddlestone Publishing
Saddlestone Records
St. Mitchell, Jojo
Sariser Music
SAS Corporation
Saul Management, Brandon
Scene Productions
Schonfeld and Associates
Schwartz Management
Sci-Fi Music
Scott Music Group, Tim
Seaside Records
Segal's Productions
Segal's Publications
Seip Management, Inc.
Seip Music Incorporated
770 Music Inc.
Shaky Records
Sha-La Music, Inc.
Shankman De Blasio Melina
Shaolin Film & Records
Shaolin Music
Sharpe Sound Productions
Sheils/Campbell and Assoc.
Sherman Artist Management
Sherwood Productions
Shoe String Booking Agency
Shore Records
Silicon Music Publishing
Silverfoot Publishing
Silver-Loomas Productions
Simply Grand Music, Inc.
Single Minded Music
Sinus Musik Produktion
Siskatune Music Publishing
Skyline Music Corp.
S'N'M Recording Hit
Songfinder Music
Sopro, Inc.
Sound Arts Recording Studio
Sound Cellar Music
Sound '86 Talent Man.
Sound Masters
Sound Resources
Sound Services
Sounds of Winchester
Southern Most Publishing
Southern Nights Inc.
SP Talent Associates
Sphere Productions
Spider Entertainment Co.
Spinwilly Music Publishing
Squad 16
Stang, Jack
Stang Music Inc.
Stardust
State of the Art Ent.
Statue Records
Steele Management
Steele Production
Stein Associates Inc., Bill
Stellar Music Industries
Strictley Biziness Music Mgmt.
Stuart Audio Services
Stuart Music Co., Jeb

General Index

OTHER BOOKS TO HELP YOU MAKE
MONEY AND THE MOST OF
YOUR MUSIC TALENT

Songwriter "Do's" and "Don'ts"

Do:

1. Read contracts carefully and have them reviewed by a music industry attorney.

2. Research before signing contracts with companies asking for payment in advance.

3. Ask companies for supporting material or samples of successful work.

4. Read song contest rules and procedures carefully.

5. Ask questions if you don't understand!